GREEK

AN
INTENSIVE
COURSE

GREEK

AN INTENSIVE COURSE

Hardy Hansen *and* Gerald M. Quinn

NEW YORK
FORDHAM UNIVERSITY PRESS

© Copyright 1978, 1979, by Hardy Hansen & Gerald M. Quinn
© Copyright 1980, 1982, 1985, 1987, 1992 by Fordham University Press
All rights reserved.
LC 91–37223
ISBN 0–8232–1664–0 (hardcover)
ISBN 0–8232–1663–2 (paperback)
Preliminary edition 1980
Revised edition 1987
Second revised edition 1992
Second printing 1992
Third printing 1995
Fourth printing 1996
Library of Congress Cataloging-in-Publication Data

Hansen, Hardy.
Greek, an intensive course / Hardy Hansen and Gerald M. Quinn.
p. cm.
Includes index.
ISBN 0–8232–1351–X: ISBN 0–8232–1663–2 (pbk.)
1. Greek language—Grammar—1950–   I. Quinn, Gerald M.
II. Title.
PA258.H34 1992
488.2′421—dc20   91–37223   CIP

Manufactured in the United States of America

TO

S. D.

ΑΝΤΙΔΩΡΟΝ

ABBREVIATIONS

Parts of Speech

adv. (adverb)
conj. (conjunction)
prep. (preposition)

Case

nom. (nominative)
gen. (genitive)
dat. (dative)
acc. (accusative)
voc. (vocative)

Gender

M (masculine)
F (feminine)
N (neuter)

Number

S *or* sing. (singular)
D (dual)
P *or* pl. (plural)

Symbols

* (hypothetical form)
> (becomes)
< (comes from)
/ (when used with Greek forms: alternative forms)
‖ precedes Appendix pages in Index

Mood

ind. (indicative)
subj. (subjunctive)
opt. (optative)
imper. (imperative)

Voice

act. (active)
mid. (middle)
pass. (passive)

Syllables

a (antepenult)
p (penult)
u (ultima)

Tense

pres. (present)
imperf. (imperfect)
fut. (future)
aor. (aorist)
perf. (perfect)
plup. (pluperfect)

Other

trans. (transitive)
intrans. (intransitive)
infin. (infinitive)
part. (participle)
pers. (person)

ACKNOWLEDGMENTS

Ten years after we began work on this text, and seven years (and four printings) since the publication of the preliminary edition, we have the welcome but daunting task of thanking all those whose suggestions, comments, criticisms, and corrections have helped us so much along the way. We owe a special debt to Floyd L. Moreland and Rita M. Fleischer, whose *LATIN: An Intensive Course* provided the original inspiration for this book, developed for use in the Greek Institute of the City University of New York. During the winter of 1977/78, Floyd, Rita, and Stephanie Russell read successive drafts of this text and criticized acutely our oral presentation of each of the lessons. Over the nine summers of the Greek Institute other members of the staff have also given us invaluable help; we would like to mention particularly Seth Benardete, David Brafman, John F. Collins, Dennis Curry, Dennis Looney, and David Sider. We are greatly indebted, also, to Brooklyn College and to the Graduate Center of the City University for their continuing support of the Latin/Greek Institute, and especially to Ethyle R. Wolfe, Provost of Brooklyn College, without whose support and encouragement the program might never have begun.

We cannot thank by name all those who have used the earlier versions of this text with classes elsewhere and who have kindly sent us their comments, but we must mention in particular Anthony C. Sirignano and James Clauss. Thanks also to Jerry Clack, George Goold, Fred Schreiber, Leslie Threatte, Stephen V. Tracy, and David C. Young for their help and support, and to Peg Kershenbaum, Michael O'Neill, and George Shea for their comments on the proofs of the present edition.

The last group of friends and helpers is the largest. They are also the most critical, the most demanding, the most lynx-eyed, the most indefatigable: the 350 students of the Greek Institute during the past nine years. They have taken great pleasure in pointing out every misplaced accent and missing macron, and every slightly odd turn of phrase they could find, and they have greatly improved this book thereby. And the students of Summer 1986 merit special praise: using as their text the bound page proofs of this edition, they were a formidable phalanx of proofreaders.

For the errors and inaccuracies which must, we fear, remain, we are of course solely responsible. Users of this text are invited, once again, to send us their corrections, comments, and suggestions.

HARDY HANSEN   GERALD M. QUINN

Brooklyn College and   *Fordham University*

The Graduate Center

The City University of New York

October 1986

Thanks to the never-ending vigilance of users of this text, especially the students of CUNY's Greek Institute, we have been able in this new edition to make a few corrections and improvements. To all who gave us suggestions we offer our thanks and again solicit from users of this text their comments.

October 1991   H.H. & G.M.Q.

The second edition was at the printer when the terrible news arrived that Gerald M. Quinn had died in an automobile accident. All those who knew him mourn the loss of such a generous, caring, and committed teacher, colleague, and friend. Gerry's enthusiasm and humor, his real personal concern for every individual, his unflagging dedication to the highest standards—all were evident in everything he did, most recently as Dean since 1989 of Fordham University's College at Lincoln Center and as a member of the 1991 Greek Institute. Every word of this book bears his imprint. He was unique, and irreplaceable.

November 21, 1991   Hardy Hansen

ON THE USE OF THIS TEXT

Users of the preliminary edition of this text will be pleased, we trust, by some major improvements: continuous pagination, an index, and a now complete English–Greek vocabulary. We would also like to draw attention to some minor changes: the second aorist has been moved to Unit 7 from Unit 8, and the imperative to Unit 11 from Unit 17. The comparative is now introduced in Unit 17, and additional material has been incorporated into Unit 20. Certain rules are highlighted in SMALL CAPITALS, and new terms are given in **boldface**.

Although this text was written for use in the intensive summer Greek Institute of the City University of New York, the experience of the last decade has shown that it can be used successfully in a wide variety of regularly paced courses.

We present the grammar in such a way as to enable students to grasp whole morphological and syntactical systems as soon as possible: all principal parts of all verbs are learned as soon as the verb is encountered, and by Unit 8 the student has acquired the complete conjugation of the thematic verb, except for the imperative mood. It is especially important that the subjunctive and optative are introduced early, in Unit 3.

In the Greek Institute each unit is presented in a two-hour afternoon session during which the students practice the material they are learning by doing some of the drills of the unit. These drills focus on the points of morphology and syntax which are new, but, except where necessary, they do not employ any of the new vocabulary of the unit. *Thus students can immediately practice new morphology and syntax with familiar words.* We strongly urge instructors of regularly paced courses to use these drills orally as the new material is being presented, before the students go home to master it. We indicate in the text of the first ten units where the drills can appropriately be done. In the Greek Institute these drills add liveliness to the grammar presentations and give the students self-confidence.

The exercises in each unit employ the new vocabulary; there are enough of them so that not all need be assigned. In the two-hour morning sessions of the Greek Institute, the students are expected to translate the assigned sentences and to do others at sight. They are always responsible for identifying every form fully and for accounting for it syntactically. Most of the morning session is spent in ringing changes upon the sentences: e.g., changing from singular to plural, active to passive, or an aorist to a future.

The result of this process is that when the students read real, unedited Greek they hold themselves to the same standards of explication. It is hard work, but they get a real grasp on their first substantial text, Plato's *Ion*, which they begin in their seventh week.

Starting with a number of fragments of Menander in Unit 4, unaltered selections from ancient authors are presented at the end of each unit; by Unit 16 students are capable of starting a passage of Plato's *Gorgias* which continues through Unit 20. Glosses at the bottom of the page give standard vocabulary listings for each word which the students do not yet know. Not every unit needs a full two hours for the presentation of new material, and, time allowing, some of these passages from ancient authors are read at sight in the afternoon sessions; others are used in optional sight readings during the lunch breaks. These sight readings serve two functions: first, it is very important that students learn how to handle unseen Greek systematically and without fear; second, although the concentrated practice necessary for mastering the morphology and syntax of ancient Greek cannot be provided by unedited ancient texts, students want and need the reward of reading real Greek. Thus, the readings are something of a treat, but they also show the students the linguistic strengths they are building through doing the drills and exercises.

During the summer, each unit requires about four hours for the presentation of the material and the doing of the exercises. In adapting the book to a regularly paced class, teachers may want to assign some of the drills as homework while the student masters the vocabulary and the first half of the grammar of the unit. Some teachers may also want to spend more than four hours on certain units, e.g., Unit 5 or Unit 8.

The pronunciation suggested in the text is that used most frequently in the United States. Others may want to use the pronunciation reconstructed by modern philology; they need only explain their system to their students when they present the alphabet and the accents.

When the grammar is presented at the Greek Institute, students are given one- or two-page handouts for each Unit which serve as summaries of the material to be learned. Copies of these for reproduction will be sent to those instructors requesting them from the publisher on their letterhead:

> Fordham University Press
> University Box L
> Bronx, New York 10458–5172

CONTENTS

Greek: An Intensive Course is divided into a Text, with twenty Units, and an Appendix. Each Unit is divided into Sections which are numbered continuously (1–153). At the end of each Unit there are Vocabulary, Vocabulary Notes, Drills, Exercises, and, beginning with Unit 4, Readings of original Greek texts. The Appendix contains additional grammar (Sections 154–168); a summary, for reference, of morphology and syntax; Greek–English and English–Greek vocabularies; and an Index of the Text and Appendix. The Appendix has a separate table of contents.

UNIT 15

UNIT 16

UNIT 17

PASSAGES FROM GREEK AUTHORS

INTRODUCTION

1. THE GREEK LANGUAGE

Ancient Greek belongs to a large family of languages which includes English, Russian, Latin and the Romance languages, Persian, and Sanskrit, whose common characteristics show that they are descended from a single ancestral language, called Indo-European.

The history of Greek extends back from modern times to the second millennium B.C., and the language, as written in different locales and in different ages, varies. At any one time there are various dialects, differing somewhat in pronunciation, vocabulary, and grammar, but mutually comprehensible. Over the centuries also, the language has steadily changed.

This book presents Attic Greek, the dialect of Athens, as it appears in prose authors of the fifth and fourth centuries B.C.—the Greek of Plato, Lysias, Xenophon, Demosthenes, Thucydides. Attic prose lays the foundation for reading the poetry of Attic tragedy and comedy, the closely related Ionic dialect of the historian Herodotus, and the archaic Ionic poetry of Homer. Also, there developed out of Attic Greek the later Koine or "common dialect" in which the New Testament is written.

1

2. THE GREEK ALPHABET

LETTER		NAME	PRONOUNCED LIKE THE **boldface** LETTER(S)	EXAMPLE
A	α	alpha	(*long*: ā) f**a**ther (*short*: a) dram**a**	δρᾱματικός
B	β	beta	**b**it	βιβλίον
Γ	γ	gamma	**g**et	λόγος
Δ	δ	delta	**d**en	δημοκρατίᾱ
E	ε	epsilon	(*always short*) g**e**t	σκεπτικός
Z	ζ	zeta	a**dds**, ga**dz**ooks (= dz)	βαπτίζω
H	η	eta	(*always long*) w**ai**t, b**ai**t	Δημοσθένης
Θ	θ	theta	**th**ought	θέᾱτρον
I	ι	iota	(*long*: ī) m**ee**t (*short*: ι) b**i**t	κῑνητικός
K	κ	kappa	**k**it	κῶμα
Λ	λ	lambda	**l**it	λωτός
M	μ	mu	**m**eet	μέτρον
N	ν	nu	**n**eat	νέκταρ
Ξ	ξ	xi	coa**x**, e**x**cept, ta**x**i (= ks)	Ξέρξης
O	o	omicron	(*always short*) th**ou**ght, b**ou**ght	χορός
Π	π	pi	**p**en	περίμετρον
P	ρ	rho	d**r**ama (*slightly rolled*)	βάρβαρος
Σ	σ ς	sigma	**s**et (ς *replaces* σ *at* *the ends of words*)	σύνθεσις
T	τ	tau	**t**en	πεντάγωνον
Y	υ	upsilon	(*long*: ū) b**oo**t (*short*: υ) p**u**t	ψῡχή γυμναστική
Φ	φ	phi	**f**it	φιλοσοφίᾱ
X	χ	chi	bac**kh**and, lun**kh**ead (*or German* la**ch**en)	χαρακτήρ
Ψ	ψ	psi	fla**ps**, u**ps**et (= ps)	Κύκλωψ
Ω	ω	omega	(*always long*) t**o**tal	Σωκράτης

3. ROUGH AND SMOOTH BREATHING

Greek also has an *h*-sound, which occurs only at the beginning of certain words (cf. English **h**and, **h**is). This sound is indicated not by a separate letter but by a **rough breathing** (῾) placed above the initial vowel of a word and pronounced before the vowel sound.

ἑξάγωνον   hexagon

When a word is capitalized, the rough breathing is written before the initial vowel.

Ἑλένη   **H**elen

In words beginning with a vowel and lacking an *h*-sound, the absence of this sound is indicated by a **smooth breathing** (᾽) placed in the same manner as a rough breathing.

ὀλιγαρχίᾱ   oligarchy
Ἠλέκτρᾱ   Elektra

All words beginning with a vowel **must** have either a smooth breathing or a rough breathing. All words beginning with upsilon have a rough breathing.

ὑπόθεσις   hypothesis

Likewise, all words beginning with rho have a rough breathing; this is not pronounced. Note the name of the letter: rho. Rho is the only consonant which takes a breathing.

ῥητορική   rhetoric

4. LONG AND SHORT VOWELS

Greek vowels can be classified into five **long vowels** and five corresponding **short vowels**. Long vowels took approximately twice as long to pronounce as short vowels.

The vowels alpha, iota, and upsilon are either long or short. Greek did not mark the length of these vowels, but in this text a **long mark** or **macron** (‾) will be placed above these vowels when they are long, as in the chart below. Short vowels and those vowels which are *always* long (eta, omega) will not be marked.

LONG VOWELS	SHORT VOWELS
ᾱ	α
η	ε
ῑ	ι
ω	ο
ῡ	υ

Pronunciation Drill I, page 11, may now be done.

5. DIPHTHONGS

Certain pairs of vowels, called **diphthongs**, are pronounced together to produce one continuous sound. Words beginning with diphthongs, like words beginning with vowels, require a rough or smooth breathing; this breathing is placed over the *second* letter of the diphthong, as in the examples below.

All diphthongs are counted as *long*.

DIPHTHONG	PRONOUNCED LIKE THE **boldface** LETTER(S)	EXAMPLE
αι	de**fy**, f**i**ne	αἰθήρ
ει	w**ai**t, b**ai**t	εἰρήνη
οι	b**oy**	οἶνος
υι	w**i**t	Εἰλείθυια
αυ	sc**ow**, pl**ow**	αὐτόνομος
ευ	(ε + υ)	᾿Οδυσσεύς
ηυ	(η + υ)	ηὕρηκα
ου	b**oo**t	Οὐρανός

Note that the diphthong ει and the long vowel η are pronounced alike. Likewise, the diphthong ου and the long vowel ῡ are pronounced alike.

A Greek word has as many syllables as it has vowels or diphthongs.

αὐ-τό-νο-μος
᾿Ο-δυσ-σεύς
οἶ-νος
Εἰ-λεί-θυι-α
φι-λο-σο-φί-ᾱ

6. IOTA SUBSCRIPT AND ADSCRIPT

When the long vowels ᾱ, η, and ω are combined with short iota, the iota is written *beneath* the long vowels as an **iota subscript** and is *not pronounced*.

ᾳ   η   ῳ

If the long vowel is capitalized, the iota is written *after* the long vowel as an **iota adscript** and is *not pronounced*. A rough or smooth breathing is written *before* the long vowel.

ᾠδή   (iota subscript)
᾿Ωιδή   (iota adscript)

Contrast the placement of the breathing over the second vowel of a diphthong.

Εἰλείθυια

Pronunciation Drill II, page 11, may now be done.

7. GAMMA COMBINED WITH CERTAIN CONSONANTS

The consonant gamma, when combined with a palatal ($κ$, $γ$, $χ$, or $ξ$; see Section 8) has the sound of *ng* in such English words as "baking."

COMBINATION	*SOUND*	*EXAMPLE*
$γγ$	anger	ἄγγελος
$γκ$	banker, anchor	ἄγκῡρα
$γξ$	larynx, Sphinx	λάρυγξ, Σφίγξ
$γχ$	(*ng* in baking + $χ$) lunkhead	Ὀξύρρυγχος

Pronunciation Drill III, page 11, may now be done.

8. CLASSIFICATION OF CONSONANTS

Certain consonants are classified according to the part of the mouth in which they are formed.

Labials	$π$	$β$	$φ$
Dentals	$τ$	$δ$	$θ$
Palatals	$κ$	$γ$	$χ$

The lips are used in forming labials, the teeth in forming dentals, the palate in forming palatals.

The consonants $ζ$ (= dz), $ξ$ (= ks), and $ψ$ (= ps) are **double consonants.**

The combination of any labial with $σ$ produces the double consonant $ψ$.

$$\left.\begin{array}{l} πσ \\ βσ \\ φσ \end{array}\right\} \quad ψ$$

The combination of any palatal with $σ$ produces the double consonant $ξ$.

$$\left.\begin{array}{l} κσ \\ γσ \\ χσ \end{array}\right\} \quad ξ$$

The consonants $φ$, $θ$, and $χ$ were originally **aspirated**: they indicated a labial, dental, or palatal accompanied by a puff of air. (Cf. English "**p**ea," "**t**ea," "**k**ey.") Thus certain unaspirated consonants, when followed by a word beginning with a rough breathing (= *h*), are written as aspirates.

$$π + {}^{\text{‘}} = φ$$
$$τ + {}^{\text{‘}} = θ$$
$$κ + {}^{\text{‘}} = χ$$

This text adopts the standard pronunciation of unaspirated Greek π, τ, and κ as English *p*, *t*, and *k* (sometimes aspirated, sometimes not: contrast "**p**in," "s**p**ot") and the standard pronunciation of aspirated Greek φ, θ, and χ as the **fricatives** *f* (as in "**f**it"), *th* (as in "**th**ought") and *ch* (as in German "la**ch**en").

9. PUNCTUATION AND CAPITALIZATION

Greek employs the same comma and period as does English.

A single mark serves as both colon and semicolon. This is a dot written above the line.

> *Ἕλληνες · Σοφοκλῆς, Περικλῆς, Δημοσθένης.*
> Greeks: Sophokles, Perikles, Demosthenes.

The question mark is the same as the English semicolon.

> *Σοφοκλῆς; Περικλῆς; Δημοσθένης;*
> Sophokles? Perikles? Demosthenes?

Proper names are capitalized, as are the first words of paragraphs and of quotations. But the first word of a sentence is *not* normally capitalized.

Greek did not employ quotation marks, but in some texts quotation marks are occasionally employed.

Pronunciation Drill IV, page 12, may now be done.

10. ACCENT

Most Greek words had one syllable whose musical pitch varied slightly from that of the other syllables of the word. Such a syllable is said to be **accented**, and this difference of pitch is called the word's **accent**. In English, accent is shown by an increased stress on the accented syllable (e.g., **re**lative, re**li**gious, recon**struct**) rather than by a difference in musical pitch.

Unlike written English, written Greek marks accents wherever they occur.

THE ACCENT OF A GREEK WORD MUST BE LEARNED AS AN INTEGRAL PART OF ITS SPELLING.

Greek indicates accent in the following ways:

´	**Acute accent**	Marked a raising of the musical pitch.
`	**Grave accent**	Marked a lowering of pitch or substitution of a steady for a raised pitch.
˜	**Circumflex accent**	Marked a raising and lowering of pitch in the same syllable.

Since native speakers of English are used to a stress accent, it is customary to pronounce all accented syllables of Greek words, whichever of the three accents they have, with a slight stress as in English.

The range of possible accentuation of Greek words is strictly limited by the following rules:

General rule for Greek accents: No matter how many syllables a word may have, the accent can appear only over one of the last three syllables.

The final syllable is called the **ultima** (from the Latin for "last") and is abbreviated "u." The next-to-last syllable is called the **penult** (from the Latin for "almost last") and is abbreviated "p." The third syllable from the end is called the **antepenult** (from the Latin for "before the next-to-last") and is abbreviated "a."

Rules for ACUTE accent: appears over the ultima, the penult, and the antepenult.

appears over short vowels or long vowels or diphthongs.

Restrictions:

CAN appear over the ultima ONLY when a pause follows, i.e., at the end of a sentence or before a comma or semicolon.

CANNOT appear over the penult when it is accented and contains a long vowel or diphthong and the ultima contains a short vowel.

CAN appear over the antepenult ONLY when the ultima contains a short vowel.

Rules for GRAVE accent: appears ONLY over the ultima.

appears over short vowels or long vowels or diphthongs.

Restrictions:

MUST replace an acute accent over the ultima when another word follows directly without a pause.

CANNOT appear otherwise.

Rules for CIRCUMFLEX accent: appears ONLY over the ultima and the penult.

appears ONLY over long vowels or diphthongs.

Restrictions:

MUST appear over the penult when the penult is accented and contains a long vowel or diphthong and the ultima contains a short vowel.

CANNOT appear over the penult when the ultima contains a long vowel or diphthong.

Accents are placed directly over vowels, and over the second letter of diphthongs.

Ἑλένη, Εἰλείθυια, δρᾶμα, ψεῦδος

When an acute or grave accent and a breathing appear over the same syllable, the breathing is written first.

ἄνθρωπος, ὕμνος, ὅν

When a circumflex accent and a breathing appear over the same syllable, the breathing is written under the circumflex.

ἦτα

Accents, like breathings, are written before capitalized vowels, including vowels followed by iota adscript, but over the second letter of diphthongs whose first letter is capitalized.

Ὅμηρος, Ἦτα, Αἵρεσις, Ἅιδης

Since the circumflex accent is written only over long vowels or diphthongs, the macron is not written over long alpha, iota, or upsilon when these letters have circumflex accents over them. Contrast δρᾶμα and δημοκρατίᾱ; both the circumflex accent and the macron indicate that the alpha over which they appear is long.

POSSIBILITIES OF ACCENT

(1) -a-p-ú + pause
(2) -a-p-ù + word without a pause
(3) -a-p̂-u BUT NOT -a-p̂-ŭ
(4) -á-p-ŭ
(5) -a-p-ū̂
(6) -a-p̂-ŭ MUST, if -p̄- is accented BUT never -p̂-, if -ū

∪ = short vowel
– = long vowel or diphthong
Not marked = short vowel, long vowel, or diphthong

11. RECESSIVE ACCENT

The accent of a word is said to be **recessive** when it goes back from the end of the word as far as allowed by the rules for the possibilities of accent. Most verb forms have recessive accent.

Consider the accent on the following forms of the verb which means "stop."

    (1) ἔπαυσα

The ultima contains a short vowel and thus permits the accent to go back as far as the antepenult.

    (2) ἐπαύσω

The ultima contains a long vowel and thus prevents the accent from going beyond the penult. The length of the ultima also prevents the accent on the penult from being a circumflex.

    (3) παῦσον

The accent has to be on the penult. It contains a diphthong, and the ultima has a short vowel. The accent must be a circumflex on the penult.

    (4) παύσῃ

The accent has to be on the penult. Although the penult contains a diphthong, the ultima contains a long vowel, which prevents the accent from being a circumflex; it must be an acute.

Thus, to accent a word of three or more syllables which has recessive accent, check the ultima. If it contains a short vowel, the word has an acute accent on the antepenult. If the ultima contains a long vowel or a diphthong, the accent will be an acute on the penult. Contrast the verb forms παίδευε and παιδεύει.

In a two-syllable word which has recessive accent, the accent must be on the penult and is an acute or a circumflex depending on the length of the vowels in both the penult and the ultima. To accent such a word, check the penult first. If it contains a short vowel, the accent must be an acute, since the circumflex cannot appear over a short vowel: μένε. If the penult contains a long vowel or a diphthong, check the length of the vowel in the ultima. If the ultima contains a short vowel, the accent is a circumflex; if the ultima contains a long vowel or a diphthong, the accent is an acute: μεῖνον, μείνῃς.

Accent Drill I, page 12, may now be done.

12. PERSISTENT ACCENT

The accent of a word is said to be **persistent** when it tries to stay the same accent, over the same vowel or diphthong, in all the forms of the word unless forced by the rules for the possibilities of accent to change in nature (e.g., from circumflex to acute) or position (e.g., from antepenult to penult). Persistent accents change in nature, exhausting all possibilities for remaining on the same syllable, before changing in position. The accent on most noun forms is persistent and is learned as part of the vocabulary.

Observe carefully the accents on the following set of words, the original accent of which is given by the first form.

(1) βιβλίον, βιβλίου

The accent is given by the first form. (The rules for the possibilities of accent would have allowed the word also to be pronounced with the accent on the antepenult or the ultima, but we know from the manuscript tradition that the word was accented on the penult.) In βιβλίου, even though the ultima now contains a diphthong, no change of accent is necessary; the accent stays the same as in the first form.

(2) ἄνθρωπος, ἀνθρώπου

The accent can appear on the antepenult of ἄνθρωπος because the ultima contains a short vowel. In ἀνθρώπου the ultima contains a diphthong, and so the acute accent cannot remain over the α of the antepenult; it is forced to move to the ω of the penult.

(3) νῆσος, νήσου

The accent of νῆσος is on the penult, which contains a long vowel, and the ultima has a short vowel; the accent *must* be a circumflex. In νήσου the ultima contains a diphthong, and so the accent cannot remain a circumflex over the η; it changes to an acute.

(4) δρᾶμα, δράματος, δραμάτων

The accent of δρᾶμα would like to stay over the initial α. In δρᾶμα the initial α is in the penult, which contains a long vowel while the ultima has a short vowel; the accent *must* be a circumflex. In δράματος the initial α is now in the antepenult; the accent *cannot* remain a circumflex but changes to an acute. In δραμάτων the ultima now contains a long vowel; the accent cannot remain on the antepenult but moves to the penult.

Accent Drill II, pages 12–13, may now be done.

PRONUNCIATION DRILLS

For these Pronunciation Drills, pronounce any syllable with an accent mark
(´, `, ῀) with a slight stress.

I.
1. ἄνθρωπος
2. Ἀγαμέμνων
3. δράματα
4. βιβλίον
5. βάρβαρος
6. γραφική
7. Δημοσθένης
8. ἐπιστολή
9. Ἕκτωρ
10. ἑξάγωνον
11. Ἑλένη
12. ζωή
13. Ἠλέκτρᾱ
14. ἥλιος
15. Ἡρακλῆς
16. θέατρον
17. θεός
18. ἱστορίᾱ

19. Ἱπποκράτης
20. κίνημα
21. κῑνητικός
22. Κύκλωψ
23. λόγος
24. λωτός
25. μέτρον
26. μῑμητικός
27. νέκταρ
28. νεκρός
29. Νέστωρ
30. Ξέρξης
31. Ξενοφῶν
32. ἀξίωμα
33. ὀλιγαρχίᾱ
34. Ὅμηρος
35. ὀρχήστρᾱ
36. πεντάγωνον

37. Περικλῆς
38. περίμετρον
39. ῥητορική
40. ῥυθμός
41. σκεπτικός
42. Σοφοκλῆς
43. σύνθεσις
44. τέρμα
45. Τῑτᾶνες
46. τρίμετρον
47. ὕμνος
48. ὑπερβολή
49. φιλοσοφίᾱ
50. χορός
51. Χρῑστός
52. Χάρυβδις
53. ψῡχή
54. Ὠκεανός

II.
1. αἰθήρ
2. Αἰθιοπίᾱ
3. εἰρήνη
4. Λύκειον
5. Οἰδίπους
6. οἶνος
7. Εἰλείθυια

8. αὐτόνομος
9. Ζεύς
10. Εὐρῑπίδης
11. Ὀδυσσεύς
12. ψεῦδος
13. ηὕρηκα
14. ναυτικός

15. Οὐρανός
16. ᾅδης
17. Ἄϊδης
18. ζῷον
19. ᾠδή
20. Ὠιδή

III.
1. σπόγγος
2. λύγξ
3. ἄγχι
4. ὄγκος

5. ἐγκυκλοπαιδείᾱ
6. ἔγχελυς
7. ἐγκέφαλος
8. φόρμιγξ

9. φόρμιγγι
10. φόρμιγξιν

IV. *Read aloud the following oracular pronouncement*:

Σοφὸς Σοφοκλῆς, σοφώτερος δὲ Εὐρῑπίδης,
ἀνδρῶν δὲ πάντων Σωκράτης σοφώτατος.

ACCENT DRILLS

I. *The accent on the following words is* **recessive**. *Put the proper accent on the words and be able to account for the accent according to the rules of accent.*

1. λῦω, λῦομεν, λῦετε, λῦετω, λῦσον

2. παιδευω, ἐπαιδευον, παιδευσεις, παιδευσον, παιδευσαι

3. διδασκει, διδασκε, διδαξον, διδαξω

4. ταττειν, ταττομεν, ταττοντων, ταττῃς, ταττε

5. βλαψῃς, βλαψομεν, ἐβλαβην

6. ἐπεισα, ἐπεισατε, πεισωμεν, ἐπεισθην

7. δουλευεις, ἐδουλευον, ἐδουλευετε

8. κλεπτω, κλεψεις, ἐκλεπτον, ἐκλεπτετε

9. ἀγγελλω, ἠγγελλον, ἠγγελλετε

10. ἐλθῃς, ἠλθον, ἠλθετε

II. *The accent on the following words is* **persistent** *and is given by the first of the forms in the following series. Put the proper accent on the other words in the series and be able to account for the accent according to the rules of accent.*

1. Σωκράτης, Σωκρατους, Σωκρατει, Σωκρατη

2. ἄγγελος, ἀγγελου, ἀγγελῳ, ἀγγελον, ἀγγελους

3. φιλίᾱ, φιλιᾱν, φιλιαι, φιλιαις, φιλιᾱς

4. φίλος, φιλου, φιλῳ, φιλοι, φιλους

5. λῦμα, λῦματος, λῦματι, λῦματων, λῦματα

6. πόλεμος, πολεμου, πολεμῳ, πολεμον, πολεμων, πολεμοις

7. ξένος, ξενου, ξενῳ, ξενον, ξενοι, ξενους

8. ἆθλον, ἀθλου, ἀθλα, ἀθλων, ἀθλοις

9. ζῷον, ζῳου, ζῳῳ, ζῳα, ζῳοις

10. ἀρετή, ἀρετην, ἀρεται, ἀρετᾱς

11. δημοκρατίᾱ, δημοκρατιᾳ, δημοκρατιᾶν, δημοκρατιαις

12. εἰρήνη, εἰρηνης, εἰρηνην, εἰρηναις

13. ἄδικος, ἀδικου, ἀδικον, ἀδικων, ἀδικα

14. στέφανος, στεφανου, στεφανον, στεφανοις

15. ἀνάξιος, ἀναξιου, ἀναξιων, ἀναξια, ἀναξιε

16. δῆμος, δημου, δημῳ, δημον, δημους

17. γέφῡρα, γεφῡρᾱς, γεφῡραν, γεφῡραις

18. μοῖρα, μοιρᾱς, μοιρᾳ, μοιραν, μοιραις

19. βουλή, βουλην, βουλαι, βουλᾱς

20. θάλαττα, θαλαττης, θαλατταν, θαλατταις

ACCENT EXERCISES

I. *The accent on the following words is* **recessive**. *Put the proper accent on the words and be able to account for the accent according to the rules of accent.*

1. ἦρξαν, ἠρξατε, ἀρξῃς, ἀρξετε, ἀρξητε, ἀρξατω

2. ἔβαλον, ἐβαλομεν, βαλω, βαλε, ἐβαλε, ἐβαλετε

3. ἐδυνατο, ἐδυναμεθα, ἐδυνασθε, ἐδυνω

4. ἀγγελλεις, ἀγγελλετε, ἠγγειλα, ἠγγελθην, ἠγγειλατε

5. ἐδεχετο, ἐδεχομεθα, ἐδεχου, ἐδεχεσθε

6. ἐκρῖνα, ἐκρῖνατε, κρῖνε, κρῖνατε, κρῖνον, κρῖνω

7. γιγνομεθα, ἐγιγνετο, γιγνεσθω, ἐγιγνοντο

8. ἑλωσιν, ἑλῃς, εἱλον, εἱλετε

9. ἐδοξα, ἐδοξατε, ἐδοξαμεν, δοξῃς, δοξητε

10. ἠκουσα, ἠκουσας, ἠκουσαμεν, ἠκουσατε

11. ἐλαυνω, ἐλαυνε, ἐλαυνετε, ἠλαυνον, ἠλαυνετε

12. ἀπωλεσα, ἀπωλεσατε, ἀπωλεσαν, ἀπολεσῃς

13. ἐδιδαξα, ἐδιδαξατε, διδαξω, διδαξεις, διδαξετε

14. βουλῃ, βουλεσθω, βουλεσθε, ἐβουλου

15. ἑσπομην, ἑσπου, ἑσπετο, ἑπομεθα

16. εὑρω, ηὑρον, εὑρομεν, ηὑρετε

17. ἐθαψα, ἐθαψατε, ἐθαψαν, θαψητε, θαψατω

18. θύω, θῦε, θύετε, θυέτω, θῦσον, θύσατε, θυσάτω

19. ἔδειξα, ἐδείξατε, ἔδειξαν, δείξω, δείξωσιν

20. γέγραφα, γεγράφατε, ἐγέγραφη, ἐγεγράφετε

II. *The accent on the following forms is* **persistent** *and is given by the first of the forms in the following series. Put the proper accent on the other words of the series and be able to account for the accent according to the rules of accent.*

1. δίκη, δικης, δικην, δικαι

2. ἡμέτερος, ἡμετερα, ἡμετερα, ἡμετερων

3. ἀθάνατος, ἀθανατον, ἀθανατοις, ἀθανατον

4. ζωγράφος, ζωγραφου, ζωγραφοι, ζωγραφων

5. τράπεζα, τραπεζης, τραπεζη, τραπεζαν, τραπεζᾱς

6. νῆσος, νησῳ, νησον, νησους

7. δοῦλος, δουλῳ, δουλον, δουλοις

8. δαίμων, δαιμονος, δαιμονι, δαιμονων, δαιμονας, δαιμον

9. κῆρυξ, κηρυκος, κηρυκι, κηρυκων, κηρυξιν

10. ἀδελφός, ἀδελφον, ἀδελφοι, ἀδελφους

11. ἐλεύθερος, ἐλευθερον, ἐλευθερα, ἐλευθερᾱ

12. πρᾶγμα, πρᾱγματος, πρᾱγματων, πρᾱγμασι

13. ἥττων, ἧττον, ἥττω, ἥττοσιν

14. δῆλος, δηλη, δηλαις, δηλα

15. θυσίᾱ, θυσιᾱν, θυσιαι, θυσιαις

16. ἀγών, ἀγωνος, ἀγωνι, ἀγωνων, ἀγωσι

17. κρείττων, κρειττον, κρειττονος, κρειττονων

18. τάχιστος, ταχιστην, ταχιστους, ταχιστα

19. αἴξ, αἰγας, αἰγες, αἰγα

20. δόξα, δοξης, δοξαν, δοξαι

21. σωτήρ, σωτηρος, σωτηρι, σωτηρων

22. ἔμπειρος, ἐμπειρῳ, ἐμπειροις, ἐμπειρα

23. γῆ, γης, γῃ, γην

24. τέχνη, τεχνης, τεχναι, τεχνᾱς

25. Ἀθηναῖος, Ἀθηναιᾱς, Ἀθηναια, Ἀθηναιαις

26. σώφρων, σωφρον, σωφρονα, σωφρονων

27. ψῡχή, ψῡχην, ψῡχαι, ψῡχᾱς

28. ὕστερος, ὕστερου, ὕστερα, ὑστερῳ

29. χώρᾱ, χωρᾱς, χωρᾱν, χωραις

30. χρόνος, χρονου, χρονῳ, χρονον

31. αἰτίᾱ, αἰτιᾳ, αἰτιαι, αἰτιαις

32. φάλαγξ, φαλαγγος, φαλαγγων, φαλαγξιν

33. ψεῦδος, ψευδους, ψευδει, ψευδεσιν

34. δουλείᾱ, δουλειᾱς, δουλειᾳ, δουλειᾱν

35. χείρων, χειρον, χειρονος, χειρονων

36. θέᾱτρον, θεᾱτρου, θεᾱτρα, θεᾱτροις

37. ἀλήθεια, ἀληθειᾱς, ἀληθειαν

38. φόβος, φοβου, φοβῳ, φοβοι

39. χορός, χοροι, χορον, χορους, χορε

40. Λακεδαιμόνιος, Λακεδαιμονιᾳ, Λακεδαιμονια

41. χρῆμα, χρηματος, χρηματων, χρημασι

PRONUNCIATION EXERCISE

(a) Practice reading aloud the following passage (the final paragraph of Plato's Republic, adapted).

(b) Copy out the passage.

    Καὶ οὕτως, ὦ Γλαύκων, μῦθος ἐσώθη καὶ ἡμᾶς ἂν σώσειεν,
    ἂν πειθώμεθα αὐτῷ, καὶ τὸν τῆς Λήθης ποταμὸν εὖ
    διαβησόμεθα καὶ τὴν ψῡχὴν οὐδαμῶς μιανθησόμεθα.
    ἀλλὰ ἂν ἐμοὶ πειθώμεθα, νομίζοντες ἀθάνατον ψῡχὴν
5   καὶ δυνατὴν πάντα μὲν κακὰ φέρειν, πάντα δὲ ἀγαθά,
    τῆς ἄνω ὁδοῦ ἀεὶ ἑξόμεθα καὶ δικαιοσύνην παντὶ τρόπῳ
    ἐπιτηδεύσομεν, ἵνα καὶ ἡμῖν αὐτοῖς φίλοι ὦμεν καὶ
    τοῖς θεοῖς, αὐτοῦ μένοντες ἐνθάδε καὶ ἐπειδὰν τὰ ἆθλα
    αὐτῆς κομιζώμεθα, νῑκηφόροι περιιόντες, καὶ ἐνθάδε
10   καὶ τῇ χῑλιέτει πορείᾳ, ἣν διεληλύθαμεν, εὖ πρᾱ́ττωμεν.

UNIT
1

13. NOUNS: OVERVIEW

Greek nouns have **gender, number,** and **case.**

1. GENDER

All Greek nouns are considered to be of **masculine, feminine,** or **neuter** gender. Gender in Greek is a grammatical category and is not identical with sex. Usually, however, words that refer to living beings of the male sex are of masculine gender, and those which refer to living beings of the female sex are of feminine gender. Nouns which in English are neuter, i.e., those referring to non-living things without sex, are in Greek of the masculine, feminine, or neuter (grammatical) gender. Thus, λόγος, "word," is of masculine gender; τέχνη, "art," is of feminine gender; and ἔργον, "work," is of neuter gender. In memorizing the vocabulary, the gender of each word must be learned separately; it cannot be guessed. Gender will be indicated in the vocabulary lists by the appropriate form of the definite article "the": ὁ for masculine nouns, ἡ for feminine nouns, and τό for neuter nouns.

2. NUMBER

By number is meant whether a noun is **singular** (one) or **plural** (more than one). In addition to the singular and the plural, Greek has another number, the **dual,** for things thought of as pairs. (The dual is relatively rare; its forms will be found in the Appendix.)

3. CASE

The case of a Greek noun indicates its grammatical relation to the rest of the sentence, e.g., subject, direct object. Each Greek noun can be divided into two

17

parts: a **stem**, which shows the dictionary meaning of the word, and an **ending**, which shows the noun's number and case. The various relations a noun can have to the other words of a sentence are shown by changes in the endings. Changing the ending of a word to convey different information is called **inflection**, and a language which uses this device is said to be **inflected**. The inflection of a noun is called its **declension**, and nouns are said to be **declined**. The inflection of a verb is called its **conjugation**, and verbs are said to be **conjugated**.

Modern English shows grammatical relations by word order or by the use of prepositions. For example, the subject usually comes before the verb and the direct object after it; the indirect object can be indicated by word order or by a preposition.

> The girl gives the boy the rose.
> The girl gives the rose to the boy.

In these two sentences, *girl* is the subject, *rose* is the direct object, and *boy* or *to the boy* is the indirect object.

English has only a few traces of inflection left, e.g., *man/man's*, where the *-'s* is used to show possession; *he/his/him*, where *he* can only be the subject of a verb, *his* shows possession, and *him* can only be the object of a verb or preposition. In English, however, even where inflection is still used, word order is still usually essential to show the relations among the words. In Greek, inflection alone can show the relation among the words of a sentence.

Greek nouns have five cases: **nominative, genitive, dative, accusative,** and **vocative**; each case puts the noun in one of a possible number of relations to the rest of the words in the sentence.

4. THE GREEK CASE SYSTEM

In Indo-European, the language from which both Greek and English developed, there were eight cases, each noun having various endings in the singular or plural to show different relations to the rest of the sentence. The Greek noun lost three of the eight original Indo-European cases and redistributed the functions of the three lost cases among the remaining five. Thus, some of the Greek cases have more than one basic function.

The Greek cases and their functions are as follows:

(1) NOMINATIVE CASE: used as the subject of a sentence and as the predicate nominative with linking verbs like "am," and when one wishes to state the name of a thing.

(2) GENITIVE CASE: (a) used to make one noun limit or depend upon another. The relation between the two nouns can usually be shown by the English preposition *of* when it is used as it is in the phrases "a man of courage," "a building of glass and steel," or "the father of the boy." (Note that *of* when it equals *about* as in "Let us speak of cabbages and kings" is NOT the equivalent of a Greek genitive.)

(b) also used to indicate motion away from or separation, the idea expressed by such English prepositions as *away from* or *out of*.

Thus, the genitive case has two separate basic functions.

(3) DATIVE CASE: (a) used to show someone or something other than the subject or the direct object of the sentence affected by or interested in an action or a state of being. The relation of this kind of dative to the rest of the sentence can usually be shown by the English prepositions *to* or *for* as they are used in the sentences "The boy gives the rose to the girl" or "This is good for the man." (Note that the English preposition *to* when indicating motion to is NOT the equivalent of a Greek dative.)

(b) also used to show instrumentality, i.e., the means by which one does something, or accompaniment, the ideas conveyed by the English prepositions *by* and *with* when they are used as they are in the phrases "hit by a bat," "written with a pen," or "together with my brother."

(c) also used to show place where or time when, the idea conveyed by the English prepositions *at* or *in*.

Thus, the dative case has three separate basic functions.

(4) ACCUSATIVE CASE: used as the direct object of verbs, or to convey the idea of motion toward or length of space or of time.

(5) VOCATIVE CASE: used to show that the noun is being addressed directly, e.g., "*John*, I like Mary."

SUMMARY OF GREEK CASES

> (1) NOMINATIVE: subject, predicate nominative, naming things
> (2) GENITIVE: *of*; *away from/out of*
> (3) DATIVE: *to/for*; *by/with*; *in/at*
> (4) ACCUSATIVE: direct object, motion toward, or length of space or time
> (5) VOCATIVE: shows that a noun is being addressed directly

At times, the case alone can express the relation of the noun to the rest of the sentence, e.g., when the dative shows instrumentality (*by/with*), no preposition is used in Greek. At other times, a preposition is used with the case, e.g., the dative showing place where usually needs the preposition ἐν, "in."

The following diagram shows the relation between the nominative, accusative, and dative cases in a simple sentence with a transitive verb:

```
┌NOMINATIVE──────verb──────→ ACCUSATIVE┐   DATIVE
│Subject                     Direct Object │   Interested Party
└                                       ┘
     The girl        gives      the rose         to  the  boy.
     The boy         does       this             for his father.
```

In both these English sentences, the relation of each of the nouns to the rest of the sentence is shown by word order and prepositions. In Greek all of these relations would be shown by the endings. The same grammatical relations could be expressed by the endings with the words in different order and the different word order would show different emphasis.

The accusative, genitive, and dative cases can indicate movement or lack of movement in space and time. The accusative shows motion toward a place; the genitive, motion away from a place; and the dative, the absence of motion, i.e., location in a place. Since there can be various types of motion away from or toward a place, or of location (e.g., "away from the inside of" in contrast to "away from the outside of"), prepositions are often used to specify the general notions of these cases. The following diagram represents the relations among these cases:

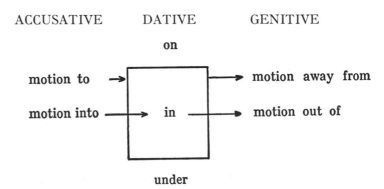

5. DECLENSIONS OF NOUNS

The vocabulary entry for each noun consists of its nominative and genitive forms, an article which indicates the noun's gender, and the English meaning of the word. Thus the vocabulary entry "τέχνη, τέχνης, ἡ . . . art, skill, craft" consists of the following four items:

(1) τέχνη = nominative singular
(2) τέχνης = genitive singular
(3) ἡ = nominative feminine singular of the article, which shows that the gender of the noun is feminine
(4) the English meaning(s) of the word.

TO DECLINE ANY NOUN, TAKE THE GENITIVE SINGULAR, REMOVE THE GENITIVE SINGULAR ENDING TO GET THE STEM, AND THEN ADD THE PROPER SET OF ENDINGS TO THE STEM.

There are three different patterns of endings for Greek nouns, each of which is called a declension. Each noun belongs to only one declension and can have only the endings that belong to that particular declension. Those nouns most of whose endings use the vowels -η- or -ā- belong to the **first declension**. Those nouns most of whose endings use the vowel -o- belong to the **second declension**. The remaining nouns form the **third declension**.

14. FIRST-DECLENSION NOUNS (Nominative in -η or -ā)

Most of the nouns of the first declension end in -η or -ā in the nominative singular; -ā will be found only in nouns whose stems end in ε, ι, or ϱ. All first-declension nouns ending in -η or -ā are feminine. The first-declension -η and -ā endings are:

NOMINATIVE SINGULAR	-η	-ā
GENITIVE	-ης	-ᾱς
DATIVE	-ῃ	-ᾳ
ACCUSATIVE	-ην	-ᾱν
VOCATIVE	-η	-ā
NOMINATIVE PLURAL	-αι	-αι
GENITIVE	-ῶν	-ῶν
DATIVE	-αις	-αις
ACCUSATIVE	-ᾱς	-ᾱς
VOCATIVE	-αι	-αι

Thus, to decline τέχνη, τέχνης, ἡ, "art," take the genitive singular τέχνης, remove the genitive singular ending -ης to get the stem τεχν-, and add the appropriate endings to the stem. (A model inflection of a noun or a verb, such as that of τέχνη given below, is called a **paradigm.**)

NOMINATIVE SINGULAR	τέχνη	(an) art as subject, predicate nominative
GENITIVE	τέχνης	of (an) art; from (an) art (with the preposition ἐκ, "from")
DATIVE	τέχνῃ	to/for (an) art; by/with (an) art; in (an) art (with the preposition ἐν, "in")
ACCUSATIVE	τέχνην	(an) art as direct object, object of certain prepositions
VOCATIVE	τέχνη	art being addressed directly
NOMINATIVE PLURAL	τέχναι	arts as subject, predicate nominative
GENITIVE	τεχνῶν	of arts; from arts (with the preposition ἐκ, "from")
DATIVE	τέχναις	to/for arts; by/with arts; in arts (with the preposition ἐν, "in")
ACCUSATIVE	τέχνᾱς	arts as direct object, object of certain prepositions
VOCATIVE	τέχναι	arts being addressed directly

Observations: (1) Greek does not have an indefinite article like the English "a, an." Such an indefinite article must occasionally be supplied in an English translation.

(2) THE ACCENT OF NOUNS IS AS A RULE PERSISTENT. Thus, the accent of τέχνη is given by the nominative singular and stays on the -ε- of the penult except in the genitive plural, which is an exception to the rule. THE GENITIVE PLURAL OF ALL FIRST-DECLENSION NOUNS IS -ῶν WITH A CIRCUMFLEX ACCENT ON THE ULTIMA. Whenever the accent on an ending violates the rules for persistent or recessive accent, the accent will be indicated on the ending when it is first given (cf. -ῶν on page 21).

Compare the declension of τέχνη with that of χώρᾱ, χώρᾱς, ἡ, "land." Note the use of abbreviations for the names of the cases and for singular and plural. Note also that when the vocative is the same as the nominative it will be given

with the nominative. THE VOCATIVE IS THE SAME AS THE NOMINATIVE IN THE
PLURAL OF ALL NOUNS.

Nom./Voc. S	τέχνη	χώρᾱ
Gen.	τέχνης	χώρᾱς
Dat.	τέχνῃ	χώρᾳ
Acc.	τέχνην	χώρᾱν
Nom./Voc. P	τέχναι	χῶραι
Gen.	τεχνῶν	χωρῶν
Dat.	τέχναις	χώραις
Acc.	τέχνᾱς	χώρᾱς

Observations: (1) There is no difference in meaning between first-declension
nouns ending in -η and those in -ᾱ. Originally, all such nouns
ended in -ᾱ. In Attic Greek, this -ᾱ changed to -η except
after ε, ι, or ρ.

(2) Note that the form χώρᾱς can be either genitive singular or
accusative plural. Context usually allows one to distinguish
the two cases.

(3) First-declension nouns differ only in the singular. ALL
FIRST-DECLENSION NOUNS FOLLOW THE SAME PATTERN IN
THE PLURAL.

(4) THE DIPHTHONG -αι WHEN FINAL (AT THE END OF A WORD)
COUNTS AS A SHORT VOWEL FOR PURPOSES OF ACCENTUA-
TION. Hence in the nominative plural χῶραι the accent
changes from an acute to a circumflex, since the penult is
accented and contains a long vowel, and the diphthong of
the ultima counts as short for purposes of accentuation.

(5) Once again, note that, as with all first-declension nouns,
the genitive plural ending is -ῶν with a *circumflex accent on
the ultima.*

WHEN A FIRST-DECLENSION NOUN HAS AN ACUTE ACCENT ON THE ULTIMA
IN THE NOMINATIVE, THE ACCENT IS CHANGED TO A CIRCUMFLEX IN THE GENITIVE
AND DATIVE, IN BOTH THE SINGULAR AND THE PLURAL. Compare the declension
of ψῡχή, ψῡχῆς, ἡ, "soul," and ἀγορά, ἀγορᾶς, ἡ, "market place," with those of
the words learned thus far.

Nom./Voc. S	τέχνη	ψῡχή	χώρᾱ	ἀγορά
Gen.	τέχνης	ψῡχῆς	χώρᾱς	ἀγορᾶς
Dat.	τέχνῃ	ψῡχῇ	χώρᾳ	ἀγορᾷ
Acc.	τέχνην	ψῡχήν	χώρᾱν	ἀγοράν
Nom./Voc. P	τέχναι	ψῡχαί	χῶραι	ἀγοραί
Gen.	τεχνῶν	ψῡχῶν	χωρῶν	ἀγορῶν
Dat.	τέχναις	ψῡχαῖς	χώραις	ἀγοραῖς
Acc.	τέχνᾱς	ψῡχᾱς	χώρᾱς	ἀγορᾱς

Drill I.1–10, page 34, may now be done.

15. SECOND-DECLENSION NOUNS

Nouns of the second declension have either the nominative singular ending -ος for masculine and (more rarely) feminine nouns, or -ον for the neuter. The endings for the second declension are:

	Masculine/Feminine	Neuter
Nom. S	-ος	-ον
Gen.	-ου	-ου
Dat.	-ῳ	-ῳ
Acc.	-ον	-ον
Voc.	-ε	-ον
Nom./Voc. P	-οι	-α
Gen.	-ων	-ων
Dat.	-οις	-οις
Acc.	-ους	-α

Thus, to decline λόγος, λόγου, ὁ, "word," take the genitive singular λόγου, remove the genitive singular ending -ου to get the stem λογ-, and add the masculine/feminine declension endings to get:

Nom. S	λόγος	(a) word as subject, predicate nominative
Gen.	λόγου	of (a) word; from a word (with the preposition ἐκ, "from")
Dat.	λόγῳ	to/for (a) word; by/with (a) word; in (a) word (with the preposition ἐν, "in")
Acc.	λόγον	(a) word as direct object, object of certain prepositions
Voc.	λόγε	word being addressed directly
Nom./Voc. P	λόγοι	words as subject, predicate nominative, or being addressed directly
Gen.	λόγων	of words; from words (with the preposition ἐκ, "from")
Dat.	λόγοις	to/for words; by/with words; in words (with the preposition ἐν, "in")
Acc.	λόγους	words as direct object, object of certain prepositions

Observations: (1) The vocative singular has a form different from that of the nominative singular. In the plural, as in all nouns, the nominative and the vocative are the same.

(2) Note that the accent in the genitive plural does NOT shift to a circumflex on the ultima as in the first declension.

To decline the neuter noun ἔργον, ἔργου, τό, "work," take the genitive singular ἔργου, drop the genitive singular ending -ου to get the stem ἐργ-, and add the neuter declension endings to the stem to get:

Nom./Voc. S	ἔργον	(a) work as subject, predicate nominative, or being addressed directly
Gen.	ἔργου	of (a) work; from (a) work (with the preposition ἐκ, "from")
Dat.	ἔργῳ	to/for (a) work; by/with (a) work; in (a) work (with the preposition ἐν, "in")
Acc.	ἔργον	(a) work as direct object, object of certain prepositions
Nom./Voc. P	ἔργα	works as subject, predicate nominative, or being addressed directly
Gen.	ἔργων	of works; from works (with the preposition ἐκ, "from")
Dat.	ἔργοις	to/for works; by/with works; in works (with the preposition ἐν, "in")
Acc.	ἔργα	works as direct object, object of certain prepositions

Observations: (1) IN ALL NEUTER NOUNS, THE ACCUSATIVE AND THE VOCATIVE
ARE THE SAME AS THE NOMINATIVE, BOTH IN THE SINGULAR
AND IN THE PLURAL.

(2) THE NOMINATIVE/VOCATIVE AND ACCUSATIVE PLURAL
ENDING OF ALL NEUTER NOUNS IS -α.

The paradigms of the second-declension nouns given above are uncomplicated
by questions of accentuation. To see how inflection can affect accent, compare
the declension of λόγος with that of the following second-declension nouns:

ἄνθρωπος, ἀνθρώπου, ὁ   man
ἀδελφός, ἀδελφοῦ, ὁ   brother
νῆσος, νήσου, ἡ   island
δῶρον, δώρου, τό   gift

Nom. S	λόγος	ἄνθρωπος	ἀδελφός	νῆσος	δῶρον
Gen.	λόγου	ἀνθρώπου	ἀδελφοῦ	νήσου	δώρου
Dat.	λόγῳ	ἀνθρώπῳ	ἀδελφῷ	νήσῳ	δώρῳ
Acc.	λόγον	ἄνθρωπον	ἀδελφόν	νῆσον	δῶρον
Voc.	λόγε	ἄνθρωπε	ἄδελφε	νῆσε	δῶρον
Nom./Voc. P	λόγοι	ἄνθρωποι	ἀδελφοί	νῆσοι	δῶρα
Gen.	λόγων	ἀνθρώπων	ἀδελφῶν	νήσων	δώρων
Dat.	λόγοις	ἀνθρώποις	ἀδελφοῖς	νήσοις	δώροις
Acc.	λόγους	ἀνθρώπους	ἀδελφούς	νήσους	δῶρα

Observations: (1) The accent of nouns is by rule persistent and is given by the
nominative singular. Thus, in ἄνθρωπον, the accusative
singular of ἄνθρωπος, the accent is the same as that on the
nominative, since the ending -ον contains a short vowel
which allows the accent to remain on the antepenult. In
those endings which contain a long vowel or diphthong, the
accent cannot remain on the antepenult but must move to
the penult.

(2) Just as the diphthong -αι when final counts as a short vowel
for purposes of accentuation (cf. the first-declension nominative plural χῶραι), so too THE DIPHTHONG -οι WHEN FINAL
ALSO COUNTS AS SHORT FOR PURPOSES OF ACCENTUATION.
This allows the accent to remain an acute on the antepenult
in the nominative plural ἄνθρωποι.

(3) As in the first declension, WHEN A SECOND-DECLENSION NOUN HAS AN ACUTE ACCENT ON THE ULTIMA IN THE NOMINATIVE SINGULAR, THE ACCENT IS CHANGED TO A CIRCUMFLEX IN THE GENITIVE AND THE DATIVE, BOTH IN THE SINGULAR AND IN THE PLURAL. The change in accent from ἀδελφός to ἀδελφοῦ is similar to the change in accent from ψῡχή to ψῡχῆς in the first declension.

(4) The accent on the vocative singular ἄδελφε is an exception which must be learned separately. Other words, however, of the second declension which accent the ultima of the nominative do keep the accent on the ultima in the vocative (cf. ὁδέ, the vocative singular of ὁδός, ὁδοῦ, ἡ, "road, way").

(5) The changing accents on νῆσος and δῶρον are governed by the rules for circumflex accent. In the nominative singular of both nouns, the penult is accented and contains a long vowel while the ultima contains a short vowel; the circumflex accent is thus required. Whenever the ending contains a long vowel or a diphthong, the accent cannot remain a circumflex on the penult, but must change to an acute (e.g., νήσου, νήσῳ, δώροις). Remember that the diphthong -οι when final counts as short for purposes of accentuation; hence the circumflex accent on the nominative/vocative plural νῆσοι.

Drills I.11–25 and II, pages 34–35, may now be done.

16. THE ARTICLE

1. DECLENSION

Greek has an article which is roughly equivalent to the English article "the." The Greek article has different endings for the different genders, numbers, and cases. (In the paradigm which follows note the abbreviations M, F, and N for masculine, feminine, and neuter.)

	M	F	N
Nom. S	ὁ	ἡ	τό
Gen.	τοῦ	τῆς	τοῦ
Dat.	τῷ	τῇ	τῷ
Acc.	τόν	τήν	τό
Nom. P	οἱ	αἱ	τά
Gen.	τῶν	τῶν	τῶν
Dat.	τοῖς	ταῖς	τοῖς
Acc.	τούς	τάς	τά

Observations: (1) The similarity of the endings of the article to those of the nouns of the first and second declensions should be obvious. Note, however, the absence of the final -ς in the masculine singular nominative and the absence of final -ν in the neuter singular nominative and accusative.

(2) The masculine and feminine nominative, both singular and plural, have neither the initial τ- which appears in the rest of the forms nor an accent. Such words without accents, which are pronounced closely with the following word, are called **proclitics**.

(3) Note the change in accent from an acute to a circumflex in the genitive and dative, both singular and plural.

2. AGREEMENT OF ARTICLE AND NOUN

The article agrees with the noun it modifies in gender, number, and case. This **agreement** is grammatical; any external identity of ending is merely coincidental. Thus in the phrase τοὺς ἀνθρώπους the article and the noun have the same gender (masculine), number (plural), and case (accusative) and have endings that look identical. Yet in the phrase τὰς νήσους the article and the noun also agree in gender (feminine), number (plural), and case (accusative), although the endings do not look identical.

Drill III, page 35, may now be done.

3. ATTRIBUTIVE POSITION

Any words which limit or depend upon a noun (e.g., genitives, prepositional phrases, and adjectives) and which are preceded by an article which agrees in gender, number, and case with that noun are said to be in the **attributive position**. There are three varieties of attributive position.

(1) Words in the attributive position can appear between the article and the noun with which it agrees:

      (a) *οἱ τοῦ ἀδελφοῦ λόγοι*   the words of the brother

      (b) *οἱ ἐν τῇ χώρᾳ ἀδελφοί*   the brothers in the country

(2) Sometimes the article is repeated after the noun and the words in the attributive position follow the repeated article:

      (c) *οἱ λόγοι οἱ τοῦ ἀδελφοῦ*   the words of the brother

      (d) *οἱ ἀδελφοὶ οἱ ἐν τῇ χώρᾳ*   the brothers in the country

When the article is repeated and the words in the attributive position follow it, greater emphasis is placed on the noun, and the words in the attributive position seem to come as an afterthought. To translate the last example given above as "the brothers, [I mean] the ones in the country," would be to exaggerate the effect, but it gives some idea of the difference between examples (b) and (d).

(3) Sometimes even, the article does not appear before the noun, but only after it:

      (e) *λόγοι οἱ τοῦ ἀδελφοῦ*   words, the ones of the brother

      (f) *ἀδελφοὶ οἱ ἐν τῇ χώρᾳ*   brothers, the ones in the country

In the last two examples the words in the attributive position are even more of an afterthought.

The genitive showing possession usually appears in the attributive position but may appear outside of it.

4. USE OF THE ARTICLE

(1) The article is used in Greek to point out **particular** individuals:

    ὁ ἀδελφός   the brother

    τοῖς ἀνθρώποις   for the men (particular men)

(2) The article is also used with **generic** classes:

    τοῖς ἀνθρώποις   for men (all men)

Context will usually make clear whether the article is particular or generic.

(3) The article is used with abstract nouns:

    ἡ ἀρετή   virtue
                 (The article with abstract nouns is sometimes omitted in Greek as it always is in English.)

(4) The article can be used with names of persons famous or previously mentioned:

> ὁ Ὅμηρος   Homer

(5) Where the context makes it clear, the article can be used where English uses the possessive pronoun:

> ὁ Ὅμηρος παιδεύει τὸν ἀδελφόν.
> Homer educates *his* brother.

> ὁ Ὅμηρος δῶρα τῷ ἀδελφῷ πέμπει.
> Homer sends gifts to *his* brother.

(6) The article is often not used in Greek with words that refer to something unique and well known:

> ἐν ἀγορᾷ   in the market place   (There was only one main market place in Athens.)

Note: in the two sentences given above in (5), there are two verb forms which will be used to make sentences in the Drills and Exercises of this Unit: παιδεύει, "educates," and πέμπει, "sends." These verb forms will be fully explained in Unit 2.

17. WORD ORDER

The basic grammatical relations of subject, verb, and direct object are shown in Greek by the inflection of nouns and verbs. Word order is free to express emphasis, contrast, balance, and variety. Much of this can be seen only in the context of whole paragraphs. Consider, however, the following variations on the idea "Homer educates his brother."

> (a) ὁ Ὅμηρος τὸν ἀδελφὸν παιδεύει.
> (b) παιδεύει ὁ Ὅμηρος τὸν ἀδελφόν.
> (c) τὸν ἀδελφὸν ὁ Ὅμηρος παιδεύει.

The first example can be considered neutral word order. The subject more often than not does precede the verb, as does the direct object. The second example puts greater emphasis on the verb; it would be a good answer to the question, "What does Homer do?" "Homer *educates* his brother." The third example puts emphasis on the direct object; it would be a good answer to the question, "Whom does Homer educate?" "Homer educates *his brother*." "*It is his brother* Homer educates."

Drill IV, pages 35–36, may now be done.

VOCABULARY

ἀγορά, ἀγορᾶς, ἡ	market place
ἀδελφός, ἀδελφοῦ, ὁ (voc. ἄδελφε)	brother
ἄνθρωπος, ἀνθρώπου, ὁ	man, human being
βιβλίον, βιβλίου, τό	book
δῶρον, δώρου, τό	gift; bribe (especially in pl.)
εἰς (prep.) + acc.	into, to; for (purpose)
ἐκ, ἐξ (prep.) + gen.	from, out of
ἐν (prep.) + dat.	in
ἔργον, ἔργου, τό	work, deed
θεός, θεοῦ, ὁ or ἡ	god, goddess
καί (conj. or adv.)	(conj.) and
	(adv.) even, also
καί . . . καί (conjs.)	both . . . and
λόγος, λόγου, ὁ	word, speech, story
μάχη, μάχης, ἡ	battle
νῆσος, νήσου, ἡ	island
ὁ, ἡ, τό	the; often shows possession
ὁδός, ὁδοῦ, ἡ	road
οἰκία, οἰκίας, ἡ	house
Ὅμηρος, Ὁμήρου, ὁ	Homer (epic poet)
παιδεύει	educates, teaches
πέμπει	sends
τέχνη, τέχνης, ἡ	art, skill, craft
χώρα, χώρας, ἡ	land, country
ψῡχή, ψῡχῆς, ἡ	soul
ὦ (interjection)	used with vocative

VOCABULARY NOTES

The word ἀγορά, ἀγορᾶς, ἡ designated a good deal more than just a "market place"; it was a combination of shopping center, civic center, and cultural center.

In ἀδελφός, ἀδελφοῦ, ὁ, "brother," note the shift in accent in the vocative singular: ἄδελφε.

ἄνθρωπος, ἀνθρώπου, ὁ generally means "man" as opposed to a god or an animal; hence the second meaning given, "human being."

Not all δῶρα (nom./acc./voc. plural of δῶρον, δώρου, τό, "gift") were, of course, bribes; but in a political or legal context, this is a frequent meaning of the word.

The prepositions εἰς, ἐκ, and ἐν are **proclitics**, as are the forms ὁ, ἡ, οἱ and αἱ of the definite article. These three prepositions fit the diagram on page 20 which illustrates the relations among the cases when they indicate movement or lack of movement:

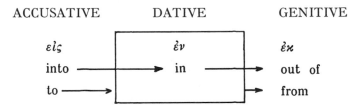

Before words beginning with a consonant, ἐκ is used; ἐξ is used before words beginning with a vowel or diphthong: ἐκ τῆς οἰκίας but ἐξ ἀγορᾶς.

When used with νῆσος, νήσου, ἡ, "island," ἐν means "on": ἐν τῇ νήσῳ, "on the island."

In addition to indicating motion toward a place, εἰς can indicate purpose, "for": "They put on their armor **εἰς** μάχην (**for** battle)."

The word θεός, θεοῦ, ὁ or ἡ can be either masculine or feminine, "god" or "goddess." Assume that the word is masculine unless feminine gender is indicated by a word that agrees with it, e.g., τῆς θεοῦ, "of the goddess."

When καί connects two words, phrases, clauses, or sentences, it is a conjunction and means "and": Ὅμηρος **καὶ** ὁ ἀδελφός, "Homer **and** his brother." When καί is used with only one item, it is an adverb and means "even" or "also": **καὶ** Ὅμηρος, "**even/also** Homer." In καί . . . καί, the first καί is translated as "both" and the second by "and": **καὶ** Ὅμηρος **καὶ** ὁ ἀδελφός, "**both** Homer **and** his brother."

Of the many possible English translations of λόγος, λόγου, ὁ, only a few are given here. The word is a verbal noun related to the verb for "say" and can mean "anything one says" from an individual word (actually a fairly rare meaning of the word) to a whole speech or story. Among other additional meanings are "account" (both in the sense of "narrative" and "accounting") and "reason" (both as "explanation or justification" and as "the faculty with which one decides something").

Note the feminine gender of νῆσος, νήσου, ἡ, "island," and ὁδός, ὁδοῦ, ἡ, "road"; most second-declension nouns are masculine.

The forms of the article ὁ, ἡ, οἱ and αἱ are proclitics; for the use of the article, see Section 16.4, pages 29–30.

The verb παιδεύει is a **denominative**, i.e., it is formed from a noun stem by the addition of a suffix. The noun in question is the noun for "child," and παιδεύει means doing what one does to a child, "educates, teaches."

τέχνη, τέχνης, ἡ ranges from the "skill, craft" of a plumber to the "art" of a Michelangelo; it is essentially the "knowing how to do something."

χώρā, χώρāς, ἡ can mean anything from "space" or "spot" to "land, country." As "country," the word has the sense of "country" as nation or "country" as opposed to city.

ψῡχή, ψῡχῆς, ἡ means "soul" as vital principle (= life) or as personality.

The interjection ὦ is the normally polite way of attracting the attention of someone addressed in the vocative case; it should not be translated. When it is absent in Greek prose, "o" should be supplied in English.

COGNATES AND DERIVATIVES

English has many words which are related to Greek words. Those words which developed in both languages from a common ancestor (e.g., "father," πατήρ) are called **cognates**. Those words that English borrowed from Greek either directly, or through Latin, or by using Greek roots to make a new English word are called **derivatives**. Knowing cognates and derivatives can aid one in memorizing Greek vocabulary. Cognates will be listed in italics.

In the list of words which follows, note how the Greek letters have been adapted to English.

ἀγορά	agoraphobia (fear of public places)
ἀδελφός	Philadelphia (the Quaker city of **brotherly** love, although the name in antiquity commemorated the incestuous love of Ptolemy Philadelphos for his sister)
ἄνθρωπος	anthropology
βιβλίον	bibliophile
δῶρον	Dorothy, Theodore (**gift** of a god)
εἰς	Istanbul (**to** the city)
ἐκ, ἐξ	ecstatic (standing **out** of oneself), Exodus

ἐν	*in*; energy
ἔργον	*work*; energy
θεός	theology, Dorothy, Theodore
καί	triskaidekaphobia (fear of three-**and**-ten =thirteen)
λόγος	logic, anthropology, theology
μάχη	theomachy, tauromachy (bull**fight**)
νῆσος	Polynesia (land of many **islands**)
ὁδός	Exodus, odometer (note the absence of "h" in English)
οἰκίᾱ	economics (managing **household** finances)
παιδεύει	propaedeutic (what must be done before **teaching** a subject)
τέχνη	technology
ψῡχή	psychology

DRILLS

I. (a) *Identify the following forms, giving gender, number, and case. If the form is nominative or accusative, translate and say how the form could be used in a sentence, e.g.,* **λόγον**: *masculine, singular, accusative, "word" possibly used as the direct object of a verb; if the form is not nominative or accusative, simply translate, e.g.,* **λόγων**: *masculine, plural, genitive, "of words."*

(b) *Change the number, from singular to plural or from plural to singular.*

1. τέχναι (2 possibilities)
2. ψῡχήν
3. τεχνῶν
4. ἀγορᾱς
5. ἀγορᾱς
6. ψῡχαῖς
7. τέχνῃ
8. χώρᾱ (2)
9. ἀγορᾷ
10. τέχνᾱς
11. λόγων
12. ἀνθρώποις
13. ἄνθρωπον
14. λόγῳ
15. ἔργα   (3)
16. ἀδελφοῦ
17. λόγον
18. δῶρον   (3)
19. ἀδελφοί (2)
20. ἔργων
21. χώρᾱς   (2)
22. δώροις
23. ἄνθρωπε
24. ἀδελφοῖς
25. δῶρα   (3)

II. *Below are given the accented nominative form and two other forms of a series of nouns. Put the accent on the unaccented forms and account for the accent you have given.*

1. Ὅμηρος	Ὁμηρῳ	Ὁμηρον
2. θεός	θεῳ	θεοι
3. νῆσος	νησῳ	νησοι
4. βιβλίον	βιβλιων	βιβλια
5. τέχνη	τεχνων	τεχναις
6. χώρᾱ	χωραι	χωρων
7. ἀγορά	ἀγοραις	ἀγορᾱς, ἀγορᾱς
8. ἀδελφός	ἀδελφων	ἀδελφους
9. δῶρον	δωρον	δωρα
10. ψῡχή	ψῡχαι	ψῡχαις

III. (a) *Decline the following words or phrases in the usual order.*

(b) *Keeping the usual order of the cases, give both the singular and the plural for each case and name the case.*

Example: (a) λόγος, λόγου, λόγῳ, λόγον, λόγε, λόγοι, etc.

(b) λόγος, λόγοι, nominative; λόγου, λόγων, genitive; etc.

1. ἀδελφός
2. ψῡχή
3. ἡ χώρᾱ
4. τὸ δῶρον
5. ὁ ἄνθρωπος
6. ἡ ὁδός

IV. *Translate the following.*

1. τοὺς ἀδελφούς
2. ἐν τῇ νήσῳ
3. ἐν νήσοις
4. τέχναι
5. εἰς ἀγορᾱν
6. ἀδελφῶν
7. τὴν τοῦ ἀδελφοῦ ψῡχήν
8. τὴν ψῡχὴν τοῦ Ὁμήρου
9. ἔργῳ

10. τὰ τῶν ἀδελφῶν δῶρα

11. τὰ δῶρα τὰ τῶν ἀδελφῶν

12. τὰ τοῖς ἀδελφοῖς δῶρα

13. δῶρα τοῖς ἀδελφοῖς

14. τὰ τῶν ἀδελφῶν δῶρα τὰ τοῖς ἀνθρώποις

15. τὰ τοῖς θεοῖς δῶρα τὰ τῶν ἀνθρώπων

16. τὰ τοῖς ἀδελφοῖς δῶρα τὰ ἐν ἀγορᾷ

17. τὸν ἀδελφὸν ὁ Ὅμηρος παιδεύει.

18. ὁ ἀδελφὸς τὰ δῶρα εἰς τὰς νήσους πέμπει.

UNIT 1 EXERCISES

I. 1. ὁ Ὅμηρος τὸν ἄνθρωπον παιδεύει.

2. ὁ Ὁμήρου ἀδελφὸς παιδεύει τὸν ἄνθρωπον.

3. τὸν Ὅμηρον παιδεύει ὁ ἄνθρωπος.

4. Ὅμηρος τοὺς ἀνθρώπους παιδεύει.

5. Ὅμηρος τοὺς ἀνθρώπους ἐν τῇ ἀγορᾷ παιδεύει.

6. ὁ ἀδελφὸς τοῦ Ὁμήρου παιδεύει τοὺς ἀνθρώπους τοὺς ἐν τῇ ἀγορᾷ.

7. ἐν ταῖς ἀγοραῖς τὰς τῶν ἀνθρώπων ψυχὰς ὁ Ὅμηρος τοῖς βιβλίοις παιδεύει.

8. ὁ θεὸς δῶρον τῷ Ὁμήρου ἀδελφῷ πέμπει εἰς τὴν χώραν.

9. ὦ Ὅμηρε, ἡ θεὸς τοῖς ἐν τῇ χώρᾳ ἀνθρώποις δῶρα πέμπει.

10. τὰ τῶν θεῶν δῶρα πέμπει ὁ τοῦ ἀνθρώπου ἀδελφὸς ἐκ τῆς οἰκίας εἰς τὰς νήσους.

11. ὁ ἐν τῇ νήσῳ ἄνθρωπος τοὺς ἀδελφοὺς εἰς μάχην πέμπει.

12. ὁ ἀδελφὸς ὁ Ὁμήρου βιβλίον ἐκ τῆς ἀγορᾶς εἰς τὴν νῆσον πέμπει.

13. ὁ ἀδελφὸς δῶρα, τὰ βιβλία τὰ τοῦ Ὁμήρου, πέμπει εἰς τὰς τῶν ἀνθρώπων οἰκίας.

14. ἐν τῇ οἰκίᾳ ὁ ἄνθρωπος τὸν ἀδελφὸν λόγῳ καὶ ἔργῳ παιδεύει.

15. ὁ ἄνθρωπος τοὺς ἀδελφοὺς καὶ λόγῳ καὶ ἔργῳ παιδεύει.

16. ὦ ἄδελφε, καὶ ἐν μάχῃ ὁ θεὸς τοὺς ἀνθρώπους, τοὺς τοῦ Ὁμήρου ἀδελφούς, παιδεύει.

17. ὦ θεοί, τοῖς λόγοις παιδεύει ὁ Ὅμηρος τοὺς ἀνθρώπους τοὺς ἐν ταῖς ὁδοῖς.

18. τῇ ὁδῷ τῇ ἐξ ἀγορᾶς εἰς τὴν χώραν πέμπει Ὅμηρος τὰ τοῖς ἀνθρώποις δῶρα.

19. τέχνῃ καὶ τὸν ἀδελφὸν παιδεύει ὁ Ὅμηρος.

20. ἐν τῇ τέχνῃ τὸν ἀδελφὸν βιβλίῳ παιδεύει ὁ Ὅμηρος.

21. ὁ Ὅμηρος βιβλίοις παιδεύει τὸν ἀδελφὸν τὴν τέχνην.

22. ὁ θεὸς λόγους εἰς τὰς τῶν ἀνθρώπων ψῡχὰς πέμπει.

II. 1. The god educates the men.

2. The man sends Homer's brother to the market place.

3. Man, Homer's brother sends to the gods a gift from the island.

4. With his stories Homer educates his brothers on the islands.

UNIT
2

18. VERBS: OVERVIEW

The Greek verb, like the Greek noun, is **inflected**: just as nouns add endings to a stem in order to produce different case forms, so do verbs add endings to various stems in order to produce the various possible forms. A noun has a **declension** and is **declined**; a verb has a **conjugation** and is **conjugated**.

Most verb forms have:

(1) PERSON
(2) NUMBER
(3) TENSE (which can show *TIME* and *ASPECT*)
(4) MOOD
(5) VOICE

1. PERSON

A verb is in the **first person** if the subject is "I" or "we," the **second person** if the subject is "you," and the **third person** if the subject is "he," "she," "it," "they," "the man," "the men," etc.

2. NUMBER

Verbs which have person are either **singular**, when the subject is a single person or thing ("I," "you," "he," "she," "it," "Homer," etc.), or **plural**, when the subject is more than one person or thing ("we," "you," "they," "the men," etc.).

Originally Greek verbs, like Greek nouns, had another number, the **dual**, which indicated a pair of subjects. The dual is rare in Attic Greek; its forms are given in the Appendix.

3. TENSE

Tense ALWAYS conveys information about *aspect* and SOMETIMES conveys information about *aspect and time*.

(1) *TIME*

Time is **present, past,** or **future**. Cf. the English sentences "I fall," "I fell," "I shall fall."

(2) *ASPECT*

Aspect indicates how the occurrence of the action is viewed: whether the action simply occurs, is in progress, is repeated, or is already completed. The following English sentences will illustrate this.

> (1) We fell.
> (2) We were falling.
> (3) We used to fall.
> (4) We had fallen.

These verbal expressions are the same in person (first), number (plural), and time (past). *They differ only in aspect.*

The verb in sentence (1) presents the action plainly and simply and has **simple aspect**; the verb in sentence (2) presents the action as being in progress and has **progressive aspect**; the verb in sentence (3) presents the action as repeated or habitual and has **repeated aspect**; the verb in sentence (4) presents the action as already completed and has **completed aspect**.

Greek verbs express both progressive and repeated aspect by a single form. Thus Greek verbs have the following three aspects:

> **simple aspect**
> **progressive/repeated aspect**
> **completed aspect**

Verb forms having progressive/repeated aspect must be translated, according to context, either as having progressive aspect or as having repeated aspect.

In the indicative mood (the mood of factual statements and questions: see Section 18. 4[1] below) the tense of a Greek verb expresses a certain combination of time and aspect.

Greek has *seven tenses* in the indicative mood:

(1) The **present tense** describes an action in *present time* with *progressive/repeated aspect* ("I am falling"; "I fall [habitually]").

(2) The **future tense** describes an action in *future time* and can have either *simple aspect* ("I shall fall") or *progressive/repeated aspect* ("I shall be falling"; "I shall fall [habitually]").

(3) The **perfect tense,** whose name comes from the Latin word for "completed," describes an action in *present time* and always has *completed aspect* ("I have fallen").

(4) The **pluperfect tense,** whose name comes from the Latin expression for "more than completed," and which is also called the **past perfect tense,** describes an action in *past time* and always has *completed aspect* ("I had fallen").

> The difference in time between the perfect tense and the pluperfect tense is emphasized by the adverbs in the following examples:
> "I have **now** fallen" (present time).
> "I had **then** fallen" (past time).

(5) The **future perfect tense** describes an action in *future time* and always has *completed aspect* ("I shall have fallen"). This tense is rare in Greek and is not given in this text.

(6) The **imperfect tense,** whose name comes from the Latin word for "un-completed," describes an action in *past time* and always has *progressive/repeated aspect* ("I was falling"; "I used to fall," "I fell [habitually]").

(7) The **aorist tense** describes an action in *past time* and always has *simple aspect* ("I fell"). It describes an event which happens once and for all.

The chart below shows how these tenses express the possible combinations of time and aspect. The meanings of the tenses are given by the English verb "fall."

	SIMPLE ASPECT	*PROGRESSIVE / REPEATED ASPECT*	*COMPLETED ASPECT*
PRESENT TIME		PRESENT TENSE I am falling I fall (habitually)	PERFECT TENSE I have fallen
PAST TIME	AORIST TENSE I fell	IMPERFECT TENSE I was falling I used to fall I fell (habitually)	PLUPERFECT TENSE I had fallen
FUTURE TIME	FUTURE TENSE I shall fall	FUTURE TENSE I shall be falling I shall fall (habitually)	FUTURE PER-FECT TENSE I shall have fallen

Note that the future tense can express both simple aspect and progressive/repeated aspect. The context will help to determine the appropriate translation.

Note also that in English the translation of Greek verbs with simple aspect and repeated aspect can be the same: "I fell," for example, can mean that I fell on one occasion (simple aspect) or that I fell habitually (repeated aspect). Contrast the sentences "I fell at 2:15 P.M. yesterday" and "I fell every time I walked on the ice": Greek requires an aorist for the verb of the first, an imperfect for the verb of the second. By itself the English "I fell" is ambiguous, but the Greek forms are not. One must take special care when translating such English expressions into Greek.

Those tenses which, in the indicative mood, describe actions in *present time* or *future time* are called **primary tenses**. These are the present, future, perfect, and future perfect tenses (the top and bottom lines of the chart).

Those tenses which, in the indicative mood, describe actions in *past time* are called **secondary tenses**. These are the aorist, imperfect, and pluperfect tenses (the middle line of the chart).

In the indicative mood, the secondary tenses of the verb, those which express past time, receive the **past indicative augment**. This consists of the vowel $\acute{\varepsilon}$- prefixed to the appropriate stem where that stem begins with a consonant. The past indicative augment is the sign of a factual statement or question in past time.

Drill I, page 58, may now be done.

4. MOOD

Mood indicates the type of statement which one is making: factual, hypothetical, wishful, commanding, and so forth. The Greek verb has four moods: *indicative*, *subjunctive*, *optative*, and *imperative*.

(1) *THE INDICATIVE MOOD*

The **indicative mood** is the mood of factual statements and factual questions. The verb forms encountered so far are in the indicative mood.

(2) *THE SUBJUNCTIVE MOOD*

Unlike verbs in the indicative mood, verbs in the **subjunctive mood** cannot be translated according to any fixed formula. Their meaning varies considerably with the type of clause or sentence in which they appear.

The following English expressions will give an idea of the range of meanings which Greek verbs in the subjunctive mood can have.

> If we see . . .
> . . . in order that we may see . . .
> Let us see !

The subjunctive mood will be introduced in Section 31.

(3) *THE OPTATIVE MOOD*

Like verbs in the subjunctive mood, verbs in the **optative mood** cannot be translated according to any fixed formula.

The following English expressions will give an idea of the range of meanings which Greek verbs in the optative mood can have.

> If we should see . . .
> We might see . . .
> May we always see the truth!

The optative mood will be introduced in Section 31.

(4) *THE IMPERATIVE MOOD*

Verbs in the **imperative mood** give a command.

> Look! See!

The imperative mood will be introduced in Section 89.

5. VOICE

Voice defines the way in which the subject of the verb is involved in the action of the verb. The subject can be performing the action (**active voice**), receiving the action from some outside agency (**passive voice**), or (in Greek) performing the action with a special personal involvement (**middle voice**).

(1) *THE ACTIVE VOICE*

When a verb is in the **active voice** the subject *performs* the action indicated.

> The man walks down the street.

When no direct object of the action is specified, a verb in the active voice is **intransitive**.

> Homer educates.

When a direct object is specified, a verb in the active voice is **transitive**.

> Homer educates his brother.

(2) *THE PASSIVE VOICE*

When a verb is in the **passive voice** the subject *receives* the action indicated.

> Homer is educated by his brother.

The passive voice will be introduced in Section 43.

(3) *THE MIDDLE VOICE*

Greek also has a **middle voice.** Like the active voice, the middle voice indicates that the subject *performs* the action. But the subject has a special interest in the action; the action somehow returns to the subject.

The nuance added by the middle voice varies from verb to verb and cannot be translated by any fixed formula. Greek would employ the middle voice, for example, to indicate that Homer, instead of merely performing the act of educating his brother (active voice), was doing so for an ulterior motive of his own, or that Homer, instead of personally educating his brother, was having someone else educate him.

The middle voice will be introduced in Section 57.

19. PRINCIPAL PARTS

The minimum number of forms which one must know in order to generate all possible forms of a verb are called the **principal parts** of that verb. In English there are three principal parts: e.g., sing, sang, sung; do, did, done; bake, baked, baked.

The Greek verb has *six* principal parts. ALL must be learned whenever a new verb is encountered. Although the principal parts of a given verb often resemble each other, no principal part can be derived from any other principal part.

From these six forms, according to rules which will be presented below and in later sections, various **tense stems** are derived. To these tense stems various sets of **endings** are added in order to produce all the possible forms of a verb.

Here are the principal parts of one Greek verb:

I.	Form:	παιδεύω
	Translation:	I am educating, I educate
	Identification:	*first person singular,*
		present indicative active
II.	Form:	παιδεύσω
	Translation:	I shall educate, I shall be educating
	Identification:	*first person singular,*
		future indicative active
III.	Form:	ἐπαίδευσα
	Translation:	I educated
	Identification:	*first person singular,*
		aorist indicative active
IV.	Form:	πεπαίδευκα
	Translation:	I have educated
	Identification:	*first person singular,*
		perfect indicative active

V.   Form: πεπαίδευμαι
     Translation: I have been educated
     Identification: *first person singular,*
                         perfect indicative passive

VI. Form: ἐπαιδεύθην
     Translation: I was educated
     Identification: *first person singular,*
                         aorist indicative passive

All Greek verbs are named by Principal Part I. Thus the forms given above are the principal parts of the verb παιδεύω.

All verb forms are to be identified as in the list above: *person, number, tense, mood, voice.*

The rules for deriving tense stems from principal parts are the same for most verbs, as are the sets of endings which must be added to these tense stems.

Thus the verb παιδεύω will serve as a **paradigm** or example of the conjugation of many Greek verbs.

20. PRESENT INDICATIVE ACTIVE

To form the present indicative active, obtain the **present tense stem** by dropping the ending -ω from Principal Part I. To this stem add the following endings, which indicate person and number:

		SINGULAR (S)	PLURAL (P)
FIRST PERSON	(1)	-ω	-ομεν
SECOND PERSON	(2)	-εις	-ετε
THIRD PERSON	(3)	-ει	-ουσι or -ουσιν

Note: the letter **ν**, called **nu-movable**, may be added to certain endings of nouns and verbs when the following word begins with a vowel, or at the end of a sentence. Henceforth in paradigms this letter, which may be added to the third person plural ending above, will be indicated in parentheses thus: -ουσι(ν).

Thus the present tense stem of παιδεύω is παιδευ-, and the forms of the present indicative active are as follows:

	S	
1	παιδεύω	I am educating I educate
2	παιδεύεις	you are educating you educate
3	παιδεύει	he/she/it is educating he/she/it educates

	P	
1	παιδεύομεν	we are educating we educate
2	παιδεύετε	you are educating you educate
3	παιδεύουσι(ν)	they are educating they educate

While most nouns have a persistent accent, which stays over the same vowel unless the rules of the possibilities for accent force it to change its position or its nature, most verb forms have a *recessive accent*, which falls as far away from the end of the word as the rules of accentuation allow.

The accent on the verb forms above is recessive: παιδεύει, for example, has a long ultima and accents the penult; παιδεύομεν has a short ultima and accents the antepenult.

Note: Greek, unlike English, has separate forms for the second person singular and plural. It does not use the plural as a polite form of the singular.

21. IMPERFECT INDICATIVE ACTIVE

To form the imperfect indicative active, prefix the *past indicative augment ἐ-* to the present tense stem. To the **augmented present tense stem** add the following endings:

	S	P
1	-ον	-ομεν
2	-ες	-ετε
3	-ε(ν)	-ον

Thus the augmented present tense stem of παιδεύω is ἐπαιδευ-, and the forms of the imperfect indicative active are as follows:

S

1   ἐπαίδευον   I was educating
                                 I used to educate
                                 I educated (habitually)

2   ἐπαίδευες   you were educating
                                 you used to educate
                                 you educated (habitually)

3   ἐπαίδευε(ν)   he/she/it was educating
                                 he/she/it used to educate
                                 he/she/it educated (habitually)

    P

1   ἐπαιδεύομεν   we were educating
                                 we used to educate
                                 we educated (habitually)

2   ἐπαιδεύετε   you were educating
                                 you used to educate
                                 you educated (habitually)

3   ἐπαίδευον   they were educating
                                 they used to educate
                                 they educated (habitually)

Observations: (1) The imperfect tense, which is built upon the present tense stem, is distinguished from the present tense both by the past indicative augment and by its different set of endings. In the first and second persons plural, however, the endings are the same in both tenses.

(2) The first person singular and third person plural of the imperfect indicative active are identical in form. Context will make the meaning clear.

(3) The third person singular ending has a nu-movable. Note that the nu of the first person singular and third person plural endings is NOT a nu-movable.

(4) Many of the endings seen so far consist of two parts: the vowel ε or o, called a **thematic vowel** (o before μ and ν, ε before other consonants), and a **person marker** (e.g., $-\mu\varepsilon\nu$ for the first person plural, $-\tau\varepsilon$ for the second person plural). WHEN MEMORIZING THE SETS OF ENDINGS, MEMORIZE THE THEMATIC VOWEL AND THE PERSON MARKER TOGETHER AS A UNIT.

22. FUTURE INDICATIVE ACTIVE

To form the future indicative active, obtain the **future tense stem** by dropping
the ending -ω from Principal Part II. To this stem add the same endings as
those employed in forming the present indicative active.

Thus, the future tense stem of παιδεύω is παιδευσ-, and the forms of the future
indicative active are as follows:

	S	
1	παιδεύσ**ω**	I shall educate
		I shall be educating
2	παιδεύσ**εις**	you will educate
		you will be educating
3	παιδεύσ**ει**	he/she/it will educate
		he/she/it will be educating
	P	
1	παιδεύσ**ομεν**	we shall educate
		we shall be educating
2	παιδεύσ**ετε**	you will educate
		you will be educating
3	παιδεύσ**ουσι(ν)**	they will educate
		they will be educating

Observations: (1) Only the tense stem distinguishes the future indicative
active from the present indicative active: cf. **παιδεύ**ομεν
(first person plural, present indicative active) and
παιδεύσομεν (first person plural, future indicative active).

(2) The future tense can have either simple aspect or progressive/
repeated aspect. Thus, for example, παιδεύσομεν can mean
either "we shall educate (once)" or "we shall be educating"
or "we shall educate (often)."

23. AORIST INDICATIVE ACTIVE

To form the aorist indicative active, drop the ending -α from Principal Part
III. There remains the **aorist tense stem** together with the prefixed past
indicative augment. To this **augmented aorist tense stem** add the following
endings:

	S	P
1	-α	-αμεν
2	-ας	-ατε
3	-ε(ν)	-αν

Thus the augmented aorist tense stem of παιδεύω is ἐπαιδευσ-, and the forms of the aorist indicative active are as follows:

S
1 ἐπαίδευσα   I educated
2 ἐπαίδευσας   you educated
3 ἐπαίδευσε(ν)   he/she/it educated

P
1 ἐπαιδεύσαμεν   we educated
2 ἐπαιδεύσατε   you educated
3 ἐπαίδευσαν   they educated

Observations: (1) The aorist tense has simple aspect.

(2) Compare the endings of the aorist indicative active with those of the present and imperfect indicative active. Note that, except for the third person singular, all of the aorist indicative active endings begin with the **tense vowel α** instead of the thematic vowel ε/o. All of the sets of endings seen so far use the person markers $-\varsigma$ for the second person singular, $-\mu\varepsilon\nu$ for the first person plural, and $-\tau\varepsilon$ for the second person plural.

Drill II, pages 58–59, may now be done.

24. AGREEMENT OF SUBJECT AND VERB

Unlike most English verb forms, each of the Greek verb forms presented above can, without the addition of any noun or pronoun, express a complete subject and predicate: contrast the one Greek word παιδεύομεν with the two English words "we educate."

When a noun or pronoun in the nominative case accompanies the verb in order to specify more clearly or emphatically the subject, that noun or pronoun becomes the only subject and overrides the less definite information conveyed by the verb form itself.

παιδεύει.
He/She/It is educating.
He/She/It educates.

ὁ ἄνθρωπος παιδεύει.
The man is educating.
The man educates.

A SINGULAR NOUN OR PRONOUN REQUIRES A SINGULAR VERB, AND A PLURAL NOUN OR PRONOUN REQUIRES A PLURAL VERB. This is called the **agreement** of subject and verb.

BUT NEUTER PLURAL NOUNS TAKE SINGULAR VERBS.

οἱ ἄνθρωποι τοὺς ἀδελφοὺς **παιδεύουσιν.**
The men are educating their brothers.
The men educate their brothers.

τὰ τῶν θεῶν **ἔργα** τοὺς ἀνθρώπους **παιδεύει.**
The deeds of the gods are educating men.
The deeds of the gods educate men.

25. QUESTIONS

In Greek, questions are sometimes indicated only by a question mark, and sometimes also by the introductory word **ἆρα**, which is not separately translated.

In the English translation, the auxiliary verb "does" ("did," etc.) must often be employed.

ὁ ἄνθρωπος παιδεύει;
Is the man educating?
Does the man educate?

ἆρα ὁ ἄνθρωπος παιδεύει;
Is the man educating?
Does the man educate?

26. INFINITIVES AND THEIR USE

Verb forms having person and number are **finite**: they "limit" the meaning of the verb to a definite person and number. All verb forms introduced so far are finite.

The Greek verb also has **non-finite** forms which *do not specify person or number.*

One such form is the **infinitive,** which usually can be translated by the English infinitive (e.g., "to educate"). The infinitive lacks person, number, and mood, and has *only tense and voice.* Its function is to name a verbal action.

1. PRESENT INFINITIVE ACTIVE

To form the present infinitive active, add to the present tense stem the ending -**ειν**.

Thus the present infinitive active of παιδεύω is

> παιδεύειν
> to be educating
> to educate (habitually)

This infinitive is in the active voice (cf. the infinitive passive "to be educated") and it is in the present tense. But in the infinitive the present tense does NOT indicate time; it indicates *aspect only*; its aspect is always *progressive/repeated.*

2. AORIST INFINITIVE ACTIVE

To form the aorist infinitive active, obtain the **unaugmented aorist tense stem** by dropping from Principal Part III both the ending -α and the past indicative augment ἐ-. To this stem add the ending -**αι**.

THE AORIST INFINITIVE ACTIVE IS ALWAYS ACCENTED ON THE PENULT. The accent on this verbal form is NOT recessive. Note that the final diphthong -αι, as usual, counts as short for purposes of accentuation.

Thus, the unaugmented aorist tense stem of παιδεύω is παιδευσ-, and the aorist infinitive active is

> παιδεῦσαι
> to educate

In the aorist infinitive active, as in the present infinitive active, tense does NOT indicate time; it indicates *aspect only.*

The aorist infinitive active has *simple aspect*: "to educate (once and for all)."

The present infinitive active, by contrast, has progressive/repeated aspect: "to be educating," "to educate (habitually)."

Note that the English infinitive "to educate" can, depending on context, be equivalent either to a Greek present infinitive active or to a Greek aorist infinitive active.

3. USE OF THE INFINITIVE

Greek employs the infinitive just as English does with certain verbs of ordering or commanding. One such Greek verb is κελεύω, "order, command."

The Greek infinitive, like the English infinitive, can where appropriate take a direct or indirect object.

τὸν Ὅμηρον κελεύετε τὸν ἀδελφὸν παιδεύειν.
You command Homer to be educating his brother.
You command Homer to educate his brother (habitually).

τὸν Ὅμηρον κελεύετε τὸν ἀδελφὸν παιδεῦσαι.
You command Homer to educate his brother (once and for all).

Other uses of the infinitive will be introduced later.

Drill III, page 59, may now be done.

27. SYNOPSIS

To give a synopsis of a verb, write all six of its principal parts, all of the finite forms of the verb *in one person and number*, e.g., third person plural, and all the non-finite forms of the verb. Below is given a synopsis of παιδεύω in the first person plural. As new verb forms are learned, the synopsis will be expanded. A synopsis is given in each of the self-correcting examinations, the first set of which follows Unit 3.

PRINCIPAL PARTS: παιδεύω, παιδεύσω, ἐπαίδευσα, πεπαίδευκα, πεπαίδευμαι, ἐπαιδεύθην

Present Indicative Active	παιδεύομεν
Imperfect Indicative Active	ἐπαιδεύομεν
Future Indicative Active	παιδεύσομεν
Aorist Indicative Active	ἐπαιδεύσαμεν
Present Infinitive Active	παιδεύειν
Aorist Infinitive Active	παιδεῦσαι

VOCABULARY

ἄγγελος, ἀγγέλου, ὁ	messenger
ἀπό (prep.) + gen.	from, away from
ἆρα (particle)	*introduces a question*
γάρ (postpositive conj.)	for (*explanatory*)
δέ (postpositive conj.)	but
ἕξ (indeclinable numeral)	six
εὖ (adv.)	well
ζῷον, ζῴου, τό	animal
ἤ (conj.)	or
ἤ . . . ἤ (conjs.)	either . . . or
κελεύω, κελεύσω, ἐκέλευσα,	order, command
κεκέλευκα, κεκέλευσμαι, ἐκελεύσθην	
λύω, λύσω, ἔλῡσα,	unbind, free, release; dissolve;
λέλυκα, λέλυμαι, ἐλύθην	destroy
μέν . . . δέ (postpositive conjs.)	on the one hand . . .
	on the other hand
νῦν (adv.)	now
ξένος, ξένου, ὁ	guest-friend, host, stranger,
	foreigner
οὐ, οὐκ, οὐχ (adv.)	not
παιδεύω, παιδεύσω, ἐπαίδευσα,	educate, teach
πεπαίδευκα, πεπαίδευμαι, ἐπαιδεύθην	
παρά (prep.) + gen.	from (the side of)
+ dat.	at (the side of), at the house of
+ acc.	to (the side of), beside;
	contrary to
πέμπω, πέμψω, ἔπεμψα,	send
πέπομφα, πέπεμμαι, ἐπέμφθην	
πέντε (indeclinable numeral)	five
πόλεμος, πολέμου, ὁ	war
πρό (prep.) + gen.	before; in front of
στέφανος, στεφάνου, ὁ	crown, wreath
φίλος, φίλου, ὁ	friend
φιλίᾱ, φιλίᾱς, ἡ	friendship
χρῡσός, χρῡσοῦ, ὁ	gold

VOCABULARY NOTES

The preposition ἀπό + gen., "from, away from," since it has an accent, is not a proclitic as are the prepositions εἰς, ἐκ, and ἐν. It differs from the preposition ἐκ in that its primary meaning indicates motion which begins at the boundary of something and moves away, rather than motion which begins within something and moves outside.

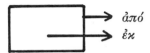

The meanings of these two prepositions can, however, overlap.

The particle ἆρα stands first in its clause and shows, along with the question mark (;), that a question is being asked; this particle is not separately translated. One can also ask a question without using ἆρα, in which case the question mark alone shows the question. Unlike English, Greek does not change the word order to mark a question (e.g., She is singing./Is she singing?).

The conjunction γάρ, "for," is **postpositive** (literally, "put after"). It never stands first in its clause but comes after one word or after a whole phrase. It links the entire clause to what preceded. Do not confuse the meaning of γάρ with the meaning "for" of the dative case.

I like Homer. **For** Homer is teaching men.

὿Ομηρος **γὰρ** παιδεύει τοὺς ἀνθρώπους.
ὁ **γὰρ** ὿Ομηρος παιδεύει τοὺς ἀνθρώπους.
ὁ ὿Ομηρος **γὰρ** παιδεύει τοὺς ἀνθρώπους.

Note that γάρ can come between an article and a noun.

Unlike English, Greek uses such connectives in almost every sentence.

The postpositive conjunction δέ, "but," takes the same positions as the postpositive conjunction γάρ. In a series of clauses or sentences, sometimes each is connected with the one before by δέ, and this conjunction then has a meaning closer to "and" than "but." For the use of δέ together with the postpositive conjunction μέν, see below.

The indeclinable numeral ἕξ, "six," must not be confused with the preposition ἐκ, ἐξ which is a proclitic and has a smooth breathing. The numeral ἕξ is not inflected:

οἱ **ἕξ** ἄνθρωποι   the **six** men
τῶν **ἕξ** ἀνθρώπων   of the **six** men

Adverbs such as εὖ, "well," are not inflected:

"Ομηρος τὸν ἀδελφὸν **εὖ** παιδεύει.
Homer educates his brother **well**.

When the conjunction ἤ, "or," is repeated, the first ἤ means "either" and the second ἤ means "or."

"Ομηρος **ἢ** ὁ ἀδελφός   Homer **or** his brother
ἢ "Ομηρος **ἢ** ὁ ἀδελφός   **either** Homer **or** his brother

Here, for comparison, are the Principal Parts of the four verbs presented in this Unit. Each is discussed in its place below.

I	II	III	IV	V	VI
κελεύω	κελεύσω	ἐκέλευσα	κεκέλευκα	κεκέλευσμαι	ἐκελεύσθην
λύω	λύσω	ἔλῡσα	λέλυκα	λέλυμαι	ἐλύθην
παιδεύω	παιδεύσω	ἐπαίδευσα	πεπαίδευκα	πεπαίδευμαι	ἐπαιδεύθην
πέμπω	πέμψω	ἔπεμψα	πέπομφα	πέπεμμαι	ἐπέμφθην

Principal Parts II and III often, but not always, have a stem ending in -σ-. Principal Parts IV and V often show **reduplication**: the initial consonant is doubled, and -ε- is inserted between the two consonants: compare κελεύω with κεκέλευκα. Principal Part VI often has a stem ending in -θ-. Principal Parts III and VI prefix the past indicative augment. REMEMBER THAT ALL PRINCIPAL PARTS OF ALL VERBS MUST BE LEARNED SEPARATELY !

The verb κελεύω, κελεύσω, ἐκέλευσα, κεκέλευκα, κεκέλευσμαι, ἐκελεύσθην, "order, command," takes a direct object, in the accusative case, of the person commanded and an infinitive of the action commanded. Cf. Section 26.

The verb λύω, λύσω, ἔλῡσα, λέλυκα, λέλυμαι, ἐλύθην has the basic meaning "unbind, dissolve" and is cognate with English "loose"; cf. the derivatives "analysis," "dialysis," which involve the mental or physical breaking apart of something. In some contexts λύω means "destroy (by taking apart)": e.g., to destroy a bridge, to destroy a democracy. Note the change from ῡ to υ in Principal Parts IV, V, and VI.

The postpositive conjunction μέν, "on the one hand," usually indicates the first of a pair of contrasting items, the second of which is picked up in the following clause by δέ, which here means "on the other hand."

ὁ **μὲν** "Ομηρος παιδεύει, ὁ **δὲ** ἀδελφὸς δῶρα πέμπει.
Homer, **on the one hand**, educates; his brother,
    on the other hand, sends gifts.

English would tend to say simply "Homer educates, but his brother sends gifts" or even "Homer educates; his brother sends gifts." But Greek strongly prefers that each clause have its own connective in order to show clearly the structure of the entire statement.

For the Greeks the relationship between guest and host was sacred and carried substantial obligations. Both parties to this relationship were called ξένος. Thus the various meanings of this word.

The adverb οὐ, οὐκ, οὐχ, "not," is a proclitic and expresses negation. It normally precedes the word which it negates. The form οὐ appears before words beginning with a consonant; the form οὐκ, before words beginning with a vowel or diphthong with a smooth breathing; and the form οὐχ, before words beginning with a rough breathing (cf. Section 8).

οὐ παιδεύεις.	οὐκ ἀδελφός	οὐχ Ὅμηρος
You do not educate.	not a brother	not Homer

When it ends a sentence, this adverb has the form οὔ, taking an acute accent:

παιδεύεις, ἢ οὔ;

Do you educate, or not?

In the verb παιδεύω, παιδεύσω, ἐπαίδευσα, πεπαίδευκα, πεπαίδευμαι, ἐπαιδεύθην, "educate, teach," note how Principal Parts I–IV are similar to those of κελεύω, and note the differences in Principal Parts V and VI:

κεκέλευσμαι	ἐκελεύσθην
πεπαίδευμαι	ἐπαιδεύθην

All Principal Parts of all verbs must be learned separately!

The preposition παρά refers to relationships involving "the side of . . . ." Its basic meanings with the genitive, dative, and accusative cases bring out the force of those cases. This preposition is used most often of people.

παρὰ τοῦ Ὁμήρου	from (the side of) Homer
παρὰ τῷ Ὁμήρῳ	by (the side of) Homer; at Homer's house
παρὰ τὸν Ὅμηρον	to (the side of) Homer

The genitive shows motion away from; the dative shows place where; the accusative shows motion toward (cf. Section 13.4). In addition, παρά with the accusative can show place where or can mean "beyond" or "contrary to" (cf. the English phrase "beyond the law").

In the verb πέμπω, πέμψω, ἔπεμψα, πέπομφα, πέπεμμαι, ἐπέμφθην, "send," note in Principal Part IV the change in vowel from ε to ο. This is the same type of vowel change that produced, e.g., English "sing, sang, sung." Such changes tend to form patterns which will become apparent as more verbs are encountered.

Note also that in Principal Parts IV and VI φ replaces π: an aspirated consonant replaces a non-aspirated consonant (cf. Section 8).

In Principal Part V note the absence of a labial before the -μαι of πέπεμμαι. The form was originally *πέπεμπμαι, which was simplified to πέπεμμαι. (An * in front of a form means that it is not attested but has been reconstructed.)

The preposition πρό + genitive indicates that something is ahead of something else either spatially or in time:

πρὸ τῆς οἰκίας   in front of (before) the house

πρὸ τοῦ πολέμου   before the war

The noun φιλία, φιλίας, ἡ, "friendship," is formed from the noun φίλος, φίλου, ὁ, "friend," and denotes the state of being a φίλος. Many such **abstract nouns** have a nominative singular in -ιᾱ.

When one vocabulary word is thus derived from another, it will be listed after the word from which it is derived, and the entry will be indented, as in the vocabulary above.

COGNATES AND DERIVATIVES

ἄγγελος	angel (a **messenger** of God)
ἀπό	apogee (farthest point **from** the earth)
ἕξ	*six*; hexagon
εὖ	eugenics (science of **well**-produced babies)
ζῷον	zoology (the study of **animals**)
λύω	*loose*
νῦν	*now*
ξένος	xenophobia (fear of **strangers** or **foreigners**)
οὐ	utopia (**no**-place, an imaginary society)
παρά	parallel (describes lines **beside** each other); paradox (what is true **contrary** to opinion)
πέμπω	pomp
πέντε	*five*; pentagon
πόλεμος	polemic (a **war**like pronouncement)
πρό	prologue (something spoken **before**)
στέφανος	Stephen
φίλος	Philadelphia; philosophy (**love** of wisdom)
χρῡσός	chrysanthemum (**gold**en flower)

DRILLS

I. (a) *In each of the English sentences below, identify the time and the aspect of the verb.*

   (b) *Name the tense of the Greek verb which conveys this combination of time + aspect.*

                                        time + aspect = Greek tense

Example: I **am sending** the letter.   *present   progressive   PRESENT TENSE*

1. We **were sending** the letter.
2. We **shall send** the letter.
3. We **sent** the letter.
4. We **have sent** the letter.
5. We **used to send** letters.
6. We **send** letters.
7. We **shall be sending** the letter.
8. We **had sent** the letters.
9. We **shall send** letters.
10. We **are sending** the letter.

II. (a) *Translate the verbs below, identifying the past indicative augment (if any), the tense stem, and the ending.*

   (b) *Change singular forms to plural, and plural forms to singular.*

1. παιδεύσεις	15. ἔπεμπον (2)
2. ἐπαίδευσας	16. παιδεύσω
3. παιδεύεις	17. ἐπαιδεύσαμεν
4. ἔλῦον (2)	18. παιδεύετε
5. πέμψομεν	19. ἐπαιδεύετε
6. ἔπεμψαν	20. παιδεύσετε
7. λύει	21. ἐπαιδεύσατε
8. πέμψουσιν	22. λύσομεν
9. πέμπουσι	23. ἐλύσαμεν
10. ἔλῦεν	24. λύομεν
11. ἐπαίδευον (2)	25. ἐλύομεν
12. πέμπομεν	26. οὐ πέμψεις
13. ἔπεμψεν	27. οὐκ ἔπεμψας
14. ἔπεμπεν	28. οὐκ ἔπεμπες

29. παιδεύουσι   33. λύουσιν
30. παιδεύσουσιν   34. ἐλύσατε
31. λύσει   35. λύεις
32. ἔπεμπες   36. ἔλῦες

III. Translate, identifying all verb forms.

1. ὦ Ὅμηρε, τοὺς ἀνθρώπους ἐπαίδευες.
2. τὸν Ὅμηρον εἰς τὴν ἀγορὰν πέμψω.
3. τὸν ἀδελφὸν εἰς τὰς νήσους ἐπέμψατε.
4. οἱ θεοὶ λόγοις τὸν Ὅμηρον ἐπαίδευσαν.
5. λύσομεν τὸν ἀδελφόν.
6. τοὺς ἐν τῇ οἰκίᾳ ἀνθρώπους ἐλύομεν.
7. τὸν Ὁμήρου ἀδελφὸν παιδεύει.
8. ὁ Ὅμηρος τοὺς ἀδελφοὺς ἐπαίδευεν.
9. τὰ τῶν θεῶν ἔργα τοὺς ἀνθρώπους παιδεύει.
10. ἡ θεὸς λόγους εἰς τὴν Ὁμήρου ψῡχὴν ἔπεμπεν.
11. λύσουσιν οἱ θεοὶ τοὺς ἀνθρώπους τοὺς ἐν τῇ νήσῳ.
12. τὸν ἀδελφὸν τέχνῃ ἐπαίδευον.
13. ὁ θεὸς τὸν Ὅμηρον λύειν τοὺς ἀνθρώπους ἐκέλευσεν.
14. ὁ θεὸς τὸν Ὅμηρον λῦσαι τοὺς ἀνθρώπους ἐκέλευσεν.
15. τὸν ἀδελφὸν εἰς ἀγορὰν ἔπεμπες.
16. τὰ Ὁμήρου βιβλία ἐπαίδευε τοὺς ἀνθρώπους.
17. τοὺς ἀδελφοὺς λύομεν.
18. καὶ λόγοις καὶ ἔργοις ἐπαίδευσας τὸν ἀδελφόν.
19. τὸν ἀδελφὸν ἐκ τῆς χώρᾱς πέμψουσιν.
20. τὸν Ὅμηρον ἐκελεύομεν βιβλία εἰς τὴν νῆσον πέμψαι.

EXERCISES

I.   1. οἱ θεοὶ δῶρα ἔπεμπον εἰς τὴν χώρᾱν.
2. πέντε βιβλία τοῖς ξένοις ἔπεμψεν ὁ Ὅμηρος.
3. πρὸ τοῦ πολέμου οἱ ἐν τῇ νήσῳ ἄνθρωποι πέμψουσι παρὰ τοὺς
   φίλους ἓξ ἀγγέλους.
4. ἆρα λύσετε καὶ τὴν τῆς θεοῦ φιλίᾱν;
5. τοὺς πολέμους ἢ λόγοις ἢ ἔργοις ἐλύομεν.
6. τοὺς παρὰ τῷ Ὁμήρῳ φίλους λόγων τέχνην ἐπαίδευσας.
7. τοῖς μὲν ξένοις στεφάνους πέμψομεν, τοῖς δὲ φίλοις βιβλία.

8. οὐκ ἔλῡσαν οἱ ξένοι τὸν ἐν τῇ οἰκίᾳ φίλον;

9. ἔργῳ, οὐ λόγῳ, τοὺς φίλους ἔλῡον.

10. πρὸ τῆς μάχης ἐκελεύσατε τοὺς φίλους δῶρα τῷ θεῷ πέμψαι ἐκ τῆς οἰκίας εἰς τὴν νῆσον.

11. οὐ λύσεις, ὦ ξένε, τὸν ἐν τῇ οἰκίᾳ φίλον;

12. τὰ βιβλία τὰ παρὰ τῶν ξένων ἐπαίδευε τοὺς ἐν τῇ ἀγορᾷ ἀνθρώπους, τοὺς Ὁμήρου φίλους.

13. οἱ ἓξ ἀδελφοὶ χρῡσοῦ στέφανον ἐκ τῆς χώρᾱς ἔπεμπον παρὰ τὸν Ὅμηρον καὶ τὸν Ὁμήρου ἀδελφόν.

14. ὁ μὲν Ὅμηρος τοὺς ἐν τῇ οἰκίᾳ φίλους λόγοις εὖ παιδεύσει, οἱ δὲ ἀδελφοὶ ἔργοις.

15. τὸν παρὰ τῶν ξένων ἄγγελον ἀπὸ τῆς ἀγορᾶς εἰς τὴν νῆσον ἐπέμψαμεν. ἐκελεύομεν γὰρ τοὺς ἐν τῇ νήσῳ ἀνθρώπους τὸν πόλεμον λῦσαι.

16. ὦ ἄδελφε, ζῷα πέμπεις εἰς ἀγορὰν ἢ οὔ;

17. καὶ νῦν παιδεύει ὁ Ὅμηρος τὰς ξένων ψῡχάς. θεοὶ γὰρ ἐπαίδευον τὸν Ὅμηρον τὴν τέχνην.

18. οἱ θεοὶ τὸν Ὅμηρον κελεύσουσι τοῖς μὲν φίλοις χρῡσὸν πέμπειν, τοῖς δὲ ξένοις τοῖς ἐν τῇ χώρᾳ στεφάνους.

19. τὰ τῶν ἐν τῇ χώρᾳ θεῶν ἔργα τοὺς ἀνθρώπους εὖ παιδεύσει.

20. ἆρα εἰς μάχην τοὺς ἀδελφοὺς πέμψεις;

21. Ὅμηρον ἐκέλευες βιβλία εἰς τὰς νήσους πέμψαι. τοὺς γὰρ ἐν ταῖς νήσοις ἀνθρώπους ἐπαίδευες.

22. οἱ μὲν θεοὶ πολέμους λύουσιν, οἱ δὲ ἄνθρωποι τοὺς φίλους εἰς μάχᾱς πέμπουσιν.

23. ἡ θεὸς τοὺς ἐν τῇ χώρᾳ ἀνθρώπους κελεύσει χρῡσὸν ἢ στέφανον τοῖς φίλοις πέμπειν.

II. In translating from English to Greek use the singular of the second person unless the plural is indicated by the context or in parentheses.

1. You used to send gifts from the market place to the gods of the island.
2. Did you (pl.) order Homer to free the five men in the house or not?
3. They will educate their brothers by words and deeds.
4. The goddess is now ordering the six brothers to send gold to their friends on the island.
5. The gifts of their brothers freed the six men.

UNIT
3

28. PERFECT INDICATIVE ACTIVE

To form the perfect indicative active, obtain the **perfect active tense stem** by dropping the ending -α from Principal Part IV. To this stem, add the following endings:

	S	P
1	-α	-αμεν
2	-ας	-ατε
3	-ε(ν)	-ᾱσι(ν)

Thus, the perfect active tense stem of παιδεύω is πεπαιδευκ-, and the forms of the perfect indicative active are as follows:

	S	
1	πεπαίδευκα	I have educated
2	πεπαίδευκας	you have educated
3	πεπαίδευκε(ν)	he/she/it has educated
	P	
1	πεπαιδεύκαμεν	we have educated
2	πεπαιδεύκατε	you have educated
3	πεπαιδεύκᾱσι(ν)	they have educated

Observations: (1) The perfect indicative active indicates an action complete from the point of view of present time, e.g., πεπαίδευκα, "I have (now) educated." The time of the tense is present; the aspect, completed. Cf. Section 18.3.

(2) The endings of the perfect indicative active are identical with those of the aorist indicative active EXCEPT in the third person plural. Compare the perfect πεπαιδεύκᾱσι(ν) with the aorist ἐπαίδευσαν.

(3) Many perfect tense stems are formed with a reduplication of the initial consonant of the present tense stem with the letter -ε- inserted between the two consonants, e.g., πεπαίδευκα (παιδεύω), λέλυκα (λύω). There are patterns for the formation of the perfect tense stem, but they are not predictable; hence the need for memorizing the perfect indicative as one of the principal parts.

29. PLUPERFECT INDICATIVE ACTIVE

To form the pluperfect indicative active, prefix the *past indicative augment ἐ-* to the perfect active tense stem. To the **augmented perfect active tense stem** add the following endings:

	S	P
1	-η	-εμεν
2	-ης	-ετε
3	-ει(ν)	-εσαν

Thus, the augmented perfect active tense stem of παιδεύω is ἐπεπαιδευκ-, and the forms of the pluperfect indicative active are as follows:

	S	
1	ἐπεπαιδεύκη	I had educated
2	ἐπεπαιδεύκης	you had educated
3	ἐπεπαιδεύκει(ν)	he/she/it had educated
	P	
1	ἐπεπαιδεύκεμεν	we had educated
2	ἐπεπαιδεύκετε	you had educated
3	ἐπεπαιδεύκεσαν	they had educated

Observations: (1) The pluperfect indicative active indicates an action complete from the point of view of the past: e.g., ἐπεπαιδεύκη, "I had (by then) educated." The time of the tense is past; the aspect, completed. Both the perfect and the pluperfect indicative active have completed aspect; they differ only in time. Like the other past tenses of the indicative, the pluperfect indicative active prefixes the past indicative augment.

(2) With the exception of the -ει of the third person singular, the tense vowel of the pluperfect indicative active shows an alternation between -η- in the singular and -ε- in the plural.

(3) Note that the third person singular, pluperfect indicative active can take a nu-movable.

30. PERFECT INFINITIVE ACTIVE

To form the perfect infinitive active, add to the perfect active tense stem the ending -έναι.

Thus, the perfect infinitive active of παιδεύω is

>   πεπαιδευκέναι
>   to have educated

The perfect infinitive active is always accented on the penult.

Like the other infinitives learned so far, the tense of the perfect infinitive shows *aspect only*, not time. Compare:

παιδεύειν	to be educating/to educate (progressive/repeated aspect)
παιδεῦσαι	to educate (simple aspect)
πεπαιδευκέναι	to have educated (completed aspect)

31. SUBJUNCTIVE AND OPTATIVE MOODS
PRESENT SUBJUNCTIVE ACTIVE

The subjunctive and the optative, in contrast to the indicative, show that the speaker views the action as non-factual, i.e., non-indicative. The translation of subjunctives or optatives varies considerably, depending upon the type of clause they appear in. Therefore, no translation of a subjunctive or an optative appears in the paradigms. The first type of clause in which the subjunctive and optative appear is the purpose clause. See Section 36.

The tense of a subjunctive or an optative, like that of an infinitive, does not indicate factual time but only aspect: the present tense shows progressive/ repeated aspect; the aorist tense, simple aspect; and the perfect tense, completed aspect. Of these three, the perfect tense is rarely used, and is given only in the Appendix.

To form the present subjunctive active, add the following endings to the *present tense stem* (the formula for finding the present tense stem is given in Section 20; for a chart of all the tense stems and the tenses built on them, see Section 60, pages 172–73):

	S	P
1	-ω	-ωμεν
2	-ης	-ητε
3	-η	-ωσι(ν)

Thus, the forms of the present subjunctive active of παιδεύω are as follows:

	S	P
1	παιδεύω	παιδεύωμεν
2	παιδεύης	παιδεύητε
3	παιδεύη	παιδεύωσι(ν)

Observations: (1) Since the translation of a subjunctive varies according to the kind of clause in which it is used, no one translation of a subjunctive is given in the paradigm.

(2) The endings of the subjunctive active are the same as those of the present indicative active except that, where possible, the thematic vowel of the ending has been lengthened. Compare the subjunctive παιδεύωμεν with the indicative παιδεύομεν. In the second and third person singular endings, when the -ε- of the -ει- is lengthened to -η-, the -ι- becomes an iota subscript. Note that when the -ε- of the second person plural ending -ετε is lengthened to -η-, there is no iota subscript.

(3) The first person singular of the present subjunctive active has the same form as the first person singular of the present indicative active. Context usually allows one to distinguish between the two.

(4) The tense of the present subjunctive indicates *progressive/repeated aspect*; it does not show present time.

32. AORIST SUBJUNCTIVE ACTIVE

To form the aorist subjunctive active, add to the *UNAUGMENTED aorist tense stem* the same endings as in the present subjunctive active.

Thus, the forms of the aorist subjunctive active of παιδεύω are as follows:

	S	P
1	παιδεύσω	παιδεύσωμεν
2	παιδεύσης	παιδεύσητε
3	παιδεύση	παιδεύσωσι(ν)

Observations: (1) The aorist subjunctive active uses the same endings as the present subjunctive active. The two tenses are distinguished by the different *tense stems*.

(2) The past *indicative* augment is not used in the aorist subjunctive.

(3) The first person singular of the aorist subjunctive active often has the same form as the first person singular of the future indicative active, as in παιδεύσω. Context usually allows one to distinguish the two. Remember that there is NO FUTURE SUBJUNCTIVE.

(4) Like the aorist infinitive, the aorist subjunctive indicates only *simple aspect*; it does not indicate past time.

33. PRESENT OPTATIVE ACTIVE

To form the present optative active, add the following endings to the *present tense stem*:

	S	P
1	-οιμι	-οιμεν
2	-οις	-οιτε
3	-οι	-οιεν

Thus, the forms of the present optative active of παιδεύω are as follows:

	S	P
1	παιδεύοιμι	παιδεύοιμεν
2	παιδεύοις	παιδεύοιτε
3	παιδεύοι	παιδεύοιεν

Observations: (1) Since the translation of an optative varies considerably according to the kind of clause in which it is used, no one translation of the optative is given in the paradigm.

(2) Note that all the endings of the present optative active begin with the diphthong -οι- (thematic vowel -ο- and suffix -ι-). Compare the following first person plural forms :

present indicative active   παιδεύομεν

present subjunctive active   παιδεύωμεν

present optative active   παιδεύοιμεν

(3) Unlike the final -οι of the nominative plural of the second-declension masculine and feminine nouns, THE FINAL DIPHTHONG -OΙ IN THE THIRD PERSON SINGULAR OF THE PRESENT OPTATIVE ACTIVE COUNTS AS LONG FOR PURPOSES OF ACCENTUATION. Compare νῆσοι (where, since the penult is accented and contains a long vowel while the ultima contains a diphthong that counts as short, the penult has a circumflex accent) with παιδεύοι (where the diphthong in the ultima is counted as long and prevents the accent from going back beyond the penult, which receives the acute).

(4) Like the present infinitive and the present subjunctive, the present optative indicates only *progressive/repeated aspect*, not present time.

34. AORIST OPTATIVE ACTIVE

To form the aorist optative active, add the following endings to the *UN-AUGMENTED aorist tense stem*:

	S	P
1	-αιμι	-αιμεν
2	-αις/-ειας	-αιτε
3	-αι/-ειε(ν)	-αιεν/-ειαν

Thus, the forms of the aorist optative active of παιδεύω are as follows:

	S	P
1	παιδεύσαιμι	παιδεύσαιμεν
2	παιδεύσαις/ παιδεύσειας	παιδεύσαιτε
3	παιδεύσαι/ παιδεύσειε(ν)	παιδεύσαιεν/ παιδεύσειαν

Observations: (1) The past *indicative* augment is not used in the aorist optative.

(2) Note that, with the exception of the alternative forms, all the endings of the aorist optative active begin with the diphthong -αι- (the aorist tense vowel -α- and the optative suffix -ι-). Compare the following first person plural forms:

aorist indicative active	ἐπαιδεύσαμεν
aorist subjunctive active	παιδεύσωμεν
aorist optative active	παιδεύσαιμεν
present optative active	παιδεύοιμεν

(3) Like the final -οι of the third person singular of the present optative active, THE FINAL DIPHTHONG -αι OF THE THIRD PERSON SINGULAR OF THE AORIST OPTATIVE ACTIVE COUNTS AS LONG FOR PURPOSES OF ACCENTUATION. Everywhere else the diphthong -αι when final counts as short for purposes of accentuation. Distinguish the optative παιδεύσαι (in which the diphthong of the ending is long and prevents the accent from going back beyond the penult and from being a circumflex) from the aorist infinitive active παιδεῦσαι (in which the accent is fixed on the penult and the diphthong counts as short for purposes of accentuation).

(4) In the aorist optative active, the second person singular, the third person singular, and the third person plural all have alternative forms with no distinction of meaning. Since both are used, both must be learned.

(5) Like the aorist infinitive and the aorist subjunctive, the aorist optative indicates only *simple aspect*, not past time.

Drill I, page 74, may now be done.

For a synopsis using all moods and tenses presented so far, see pages 78 and 82.

35. SEQUENCE OF MOODS

As seen in Section 18.3, the tenses of the indicative are divided into two categories, primary and secondary. The **PRIMARY tenses** are those which refer to PRESENT and FUTURE time: the *present, future, perfect,* and *future perfect tenses.* The **SECONDARY tenses** of the indicative are those which refer to PAST time: the *imperfect, aorist,* and *pluperfect tenses.* The secondary tenses of the indicative all have the past indicative augment.

Sequence of moods means that in complex sentences certain kinds of dependent clauses will have a verb in either the subjunctive or the optative mood, depending on whether the main verb of the sentence is either a primary or a secondary tense of the indicative. A primary tense of the indicative governs a subjunctive in the dependent clause; this is called **primary sequence.** A secondary tense of the indicative governs an optative in the dependent clause; this is called **secondary sequence.**

Both the present subjunctive and the aorist subjunctive are governed by primary tenses of the indicative. As in the infinitive, TENSE IN THE SUBJUNCTIVE INDICATES ASPECT, NOT TIME: the present subjunctive shows progressive/repeated aspect; the aorist subjunctive shows simple aspect.

Both the present optative and the aorist optative are governed by secondary tenses of the indicative. TENSE IN THE OPTATIVE ALSO INDICATES ASPECT, NOT TIME: the present optative shows progressive/repeated aspect; the aorist optative shows simple aspect.

The following chart summarizes the sequence of moods:

MAIN VERB   *DEPENDENT VERB*

PRIMARY SEQUENCE

Present Indicative ⎫
Future Indicative ⎬   Subjunctive Mood
Perfect Indicative ⎭   *(Tense shows aspect.)*

───

SECONDARY SEQUENCE

Imperfect Indicative ⎫
Aorist Indicative   ⎬   Optative Mood
Pluperfect Indicative ⎭   *(Tense shows aspect.)*

36. PURPOSE CLAUSES

The idea of purpose can be expressed in English in many ways, e.g., by an infinitive: "I am coming **to see my friend**"; by a clause: "I am coming **in order that I may see my friend**." To express purpose, Greek does not normally use an infinitive but rather a clause introduced by the conjunctions **ἵνα, ὡς**, or **ὅπως**, all of which mean "in order that." A negative purpose clause is introduced by **ἵνα μή, ὡς μή**, or **ὅπως μή**, which mean "in order that . . . not, lest."

A purpose clause has a verb in the subjunctive or the optative according to the rules for the sequence of moods: a primary main verb calls for the subjunctive; a secondary, for the optative. The tense of the subjunctive or the optative shows aspect.

(1) *πέμπομεν δῶρα* ⎧ *ἵνα* ⎫ *λύητε τοὺς ἀδελφούς.*
                    ⎨ *ὡς* ⎬
                    ⎩ *ὅπως* ⎭

We ⎧ are sending ⎫ gifts in order that you ⎧ may be releasing ⎫ the
   ⎩ send   ⎭   ⎩ may release   ⎭ brothers.

Observation: The main verb is in the present tense, which is a primary tense. The verb in the purpose clause must therefore be in the subjunctive mood (primary sequence). The tense of the subjunctive is present, which indicates either progressive aspect ("that you may be releasing") or repeated aspect ("that you may [habitually] release").

(2) πέμπομεν δῶρα $\left\{ \begin{array}{l} \text{ἵνα} \\ \text{ὡς} \\ \text{ὅπως} \end{array} \right\}$ λύσητε τοὺς ἀδελφούς.

We $\left\{ \begin{array}{l} \text{are sending} \\ \text{send} \end{array} \right\}$ gifts in order that you may release the brothers.

Observation: The aorist tense of the subjunctive (still primary sequence after a main verb in the present indicative) indicates simple aspect, "that you may release (once and for all)."

(3) ἐπέμπομεν δῶρα $\left\{ \begin{array}{l} \text{ἵνα} \\ \text{ὡς} \\ \text{ὅπως} \end{array} \right\}$ λύοιτε τοὺς ἀδελφούς.

We $\left\{ \begin{array}{l} \text{were sending} \\ \text{used to send} \end{array} \right\}$ gifts in order that you $\left\{ \begin{array}{l} \text{might be releasing} \\ \text{might release} \end{array} \right\}$ the brothers.

Observations: (1) The main verb is in the imperfect tense, which is a secondary tense. The verb in the purpose clause in secondary sequence is an optative. The present tense of the optative indicates progressive aspect ("that you might be releasing") or repeated aspect ("that you might [habitually] release").

(2) IN TRANSLATING PURPOSE CLAUSES INTO ENGLISH, "MAY" SHOULD ALWAYS BE USED WHEN TRANSLATING PRIMARY SEQUENCE AND "MIGHT" WHEN TRANSLATING SECONDARY SEQUENCE.

(4) ἐπέμπομεν δῶρα $\left\{ \begin{array}{l} \text{ἵνα} \\ \text{ὡς} \\ \text{ὅπως} \end{array} \right\}$ λύσαιτε τοὺς ἀδελφούς.

We $\left\{ \begin{array}{l} \text{were sending} \\ \text{used to send} \end{array} \right\}$ gifts in order that you might release the brothers.

Observation: The aorist tense of the optative (still secondary sequence after an imperfect main verb) indicates simple aspect: "that you might release the brothers (once and for all)."

(5) τὸν ῞Ομηρον εἰς τὴν νῆσον ἐπέμψαμεν $\left\{\begin{array}{l} ἵνα\ μὴ \\ ὡς\ μὴ \\ ὅπως\ μὴ \end{array}\right\}$ παιδεύσειε τὸν ἀδελφόν.

We sent Homer to the island in order that he might not educate his brother.

To give the **syntax** of a verb one must identify both the mood and the tense and account for both mood and tense. For example, the syntax of λύοιτε in sentence (3) is *present optative*: *optative* in a purpose clause in secondary sequence after the imperfect main verb ἐπέμπομεν; *present tense* to show progressive/repeated aspect.

To give the syntax of a noun, one must identify the case and give the reason for it. For example, the syntax of ῞Ομηρον in sentence (5) is *accusative*: direct object of the verb ἐπέμψαμεν.

Drill II, pages 74–75, may now be done.

VOCABULARY

ἆθλον, ἄθλου, τό		prize
ἀλλά (conj.)		but
ἀντί (prep.)	+ gen.	instead of
ἀρετή, ἀρετῆς, ἡ		excellence, virtue
βουλή, βουλῆς, ἡ		will; council
γράφω, γράψω, ἔγραψα, γέγραφα,		write, draw
γέγραμμαι, ἐγράφην		
δή (postpositive particle)		in fact, of course
δῆμος, δήμου, ὁ		the people
δημοκρατίᾱ, δημοκρατίᾱς, ἡ		democracy
διά (prep.)	+ gen.	through
	+ acc.	on account of
εἰρήνη, εἰρήνης, ἡ		peace
ἐκκλησίᾱ, ἐκκλησίᾱς, ἡ		assembly
ἐπεί (conj.)		after, when, since
ἐπειδή (conj.)		after, when, since
θύω, θύσω, ἔθῡσα, τέθυκα,		sacrifice
τέθυμαι, ἐτύθην		
θυσίᾱ, θυσίᾱς, ἡ		sacrifice
ἵνα (conj.)		in order that
μή (adv.)		not
νίκη, νίκης, ἡ		victory
ὅπως (conj.)		in order that
ὀφθαλμός, ὀφθαλμοῦ, ὁ		eye
παύω, παύσω, ἔπαυσα, πέπαυκα,		make stop, stop
πέπαυμαι, ἐπαύθην		
περί (prep.)	+ gen.	concerning, about
	+ dat.	around
	+ acc.	around, concerning
φυλάττω, φυλάξω, ἐφύλαξα,		guard
πεφύλαχα, πεφύλαγμαι, ἐφυλάχθην		
ὡς (conj.)		in order that

VOCABULARY NOTES

The conjunction ἀλλά, "but," stands at the beginning of its clause and introduces a stronger contrast than the conjunction δέ, "but."

The noun ἀρετή, ἀρετῆς, ἡ, "excellence, virtue," originally referred to "excellence" in general, whether of warriors in battle, animals such as horses, or things such as land. Later its meaning was sometimes narrowed to "moral excellence" or "virtue."

The noun βουλή, βουλῆς, ἡ means either "will" (the faculty of the soul) or "council" (in the Athenian democracy a deliberative body of 500 citizens).

The verb γράφω, γράψω, ἔγραψα, γέγραφα, γέγραμμαι, ἐγράφην, "write, draw," originally meant "scratch" or "graze" (as with a pointed object). Then the verb came to refer to the making of marks of various sorts. Note that Principal Part VI, ἐγράφην, lacks the -θ- seen in the verbs presented thus far.

The particle δή can be translated as "in fact" or "of course"; it indicates that what is said is really true.

In the Athenian democracy, all citizens (adult males) had a right to take part in the ἐκκλησία, ἐκκλησίας, ἡ, "assembly," literally a "calling out" of the people.

The conjunctions ἐπεί and ἐπειδή mean "after, when, since," and both introduce **temporal** and **causal clauses**. ἐπειδή consists of the conjunction ἐπεί + the particle δή; but there is no great distinction in meaning between the two conjunctions, although ἐπειδή is used more frequently in temporal clauses than in causal clauses. Both conjunctions govern a past tense of the indicative when referring to a definite event in the past:

ἐπειδὴ τὸν ἀδελφὸν ἔλῡσαν, δῶρα ἔπεμψα.
After/since they freed my brother, I sent gifts.

The noun θυσία, θυσίας, ἡ is a **verbal noun** related to θύω, θύσω, ἔθῡσα, τέθυκα, τέθυμαι, ἐτύθην, "sacrifice." Note the long vowel in the first three principal parts and the short vowel in the last three (as in λύω); the vowel of the stem of the noun is also short.

Note that the reduplication in Principal Parts IV and V of θύω shows τ- and not θ-. The forms had originally been *θέθυκα and *θέθυμαι. When Greek had two syllables each beginning with an aspirate (see Section 8), the first of the aspirates usually lost its aspiration; this is called the **dissimilation of aspirates**. Principal Part VI was originally *ἐθύθην, which became ἐτύθην.

The conjunctions ἵνα, ὡς, and ὅπως all introduce purpose clauses with no difference in meaning.

The adverb μή, "not," is NOT interchangeable with οὐ, οὐκ, οὐχ, "not." μή *must* be used to negate purpose clauses; οὐ, οὐκ, οὐχ *must* be used to negate factual statements and questions with verbs in the indicative mood. Note that, unlike οὐ, μή is not a proclitic.

The preposition περί basically indicates the idea of "around"; cf. *perimeter*. The dative is used of wearing clothes, weapons, etc. "around" the body: In "They wear golden necklaces around their necks" the preposition περί + the dative would be used. The accusative is used with verbs of motion: In "They send ships around the island" the preposition περί + the accusative would be used. περί with both the genitive and the accusative means "concerning." The genitive is used with words of speaking or thinking: "I speak about . . ." would be περί + genitive. "We fight about . . ." would be περί + accusative. This distinction, however, is not always maintained.

In Principal Part IV of φυλάττω, φυλάξω, ἐφύλαξα, πεφύλαχα, πεφύλαγμαι, ἐφυλάχθην, "guard," the stem ends in an aspirated consonant, -χ-; cf. πέπομφα from πέμπω. Such perfects are called **aspirated perfects**. Note also the dissimilation of aspirates in πεφύλαχα and πεφύλαγμαι.

COGNATES AND DERIVATIVES

ἆθλον	athlete
ἀντί	antipope
γράφω	*carve, crab*; telegraph, graphic
δῆμος	democracy, demagogue
διά	diagonal, diameter
εἰρήνη	Irene
ἐκκλησίᾱ	ecclesiastical (the church is the **assembly** of God)
νίκη	Nike missile or running shoes (bring **victory**)
ὀφθαλμός	ophthalmologist
παύω	pause (a **stop** in the action)
περί	perimeter
φυλάττω	prophylactic, phylactery

DRILLS

I. (a) *Translate indicatives and infinitives; identify subjunctives and optatives.*
    (b) *Change from singular to plural and from plural to singular where possible.*

    1. πεπόμφαμεν
    2. ἐπεπόμφεσαν
    3. ἔπεμπες
    4. πέπομφεν
    5. ἔπεμψα
    6. ἐπεπόμφειν
    7. πεπομφέναι
    8. πέμψει
    9. πέμπῃ
    10. πέμψῃς
    11. πέμψεις
    12. πέμπωμεν
    13. πέμψουσιν
    14. πέμψωσι
    15. πέμψω (2)
    16. πέμποιμι
    17. πέμψειεν
    18. πέμψαι (2)
    19. πέμποιεν
    20. πέμπειν
    21. ἐπεπόμφη

II. *Translate the following sentences, accounting for the mood and tense of sub-*
    junctives and optatives.

    1. πέμπεις χρῦσὸν ἵνα πέμπωμεν βιβλία.
    2. πέμπεις χρῦσὸν ἵνα πέμψωμεν βιβλία.
    3. πέμψεις χρῦσὸν ἵνα πέμψωμεν βιβλία.
    4. ἔπεμψας χρῦσὸν ἵνα πέμψαιμεν βιβλία.
    5. λελύκατε τοὺς ἀδελφοὺς ὡς πέμψῃ δῶρα.
    6. ἐλελύκετε τοὺς ἀδελφοὺς ὡς πέμψειε δῶρα.
    7. ἐλύετε τοὺς ἀδελφοὺς ὡς πέμψαι δῶρα.

8. ἐπαίδευε τοὺς ἀδελφοὺς ὅπως χρῡσὸν πέμψειας.

9. ἐπαίδευσε τοὺς ἀδελφοὺς ὅπως χρῡσὸν πέμψαις.

10. ὅπως χρῡσὸν πέμπῃς παιδεύσει τοὺς ἀδελφούς.

11. οὐ πέμψομεν χρῡσὸν ἵνα μὴ ζῷα πέμψωσιν.

12. οὐκ ἐπέμπομεν χρῡσὸν ἵνα ζῷα μὴ πέμποιεν.

EXERCISES

I. 1. ὁ δῆμος ἐν ταῖς ὁδοῖς τοῖς θεοῖς θύσει ἵνα τὸν πόλεμον παύσωσιν.

2. ὡς τὸν πόλεμον παύωσιν ὁ δῆμος ταῖς θεοῖς θύει.

3. ἀγγέλους ἔπεμψαν ἐξ ἀγορᾶς οἱ ξένοι ὅπως λύσαιεν τὴν εἰρήνην.

4. ἀγγέλους ἔπεμπον περὶ τὴν νῆσον ὅπως μὴ λύοιτε τὴν εἰρήνην.

5. ἵνα λύσωμεν τὸν Ὅμηρον δῶρα πεπόμφᾱσιν.

6. βιβλίον δὴ περὶ πολέμου γράψαι κελεύετε Ὅμηρον ὅπως εὖ παιδεύητε τοὺς ἀδελφούς. φυλάξουσι γὰρ τὴν χώρᾱν.

7. καὶ τῇ ἐκκλησίᾳ καὶ τῇ βουλῇ χρῡσὸν ἔπεμψεν ἵνα μὴ λύσειαν τὴν φιλίᾱν.

8. τοὺς μὲν ὀφθαλμοὺς Ὁμήρου οὐκ ἐφύλαξαν οἱ θεοί· τὰ δὲ βιβλία τὰ περὶ τῆς τῶν ἀνθρώπων ἀρετῆς εὖ πεφυλάχᾱσιν.

9. λόγῳ μὲν τὴν εἰρήνην ἐλελύκεσαν, ἔργῳ δὲ οὔ.

10. ἆρα γράψεις πέντε βιβλία περὶ τῶν τοῖς θεοῖς θυσιῶν ἵνα δῶρα παρὰ τοὺς θεοὺς πέμπωμεν;

11. διὰ τὴν τῶν θεῶν βουλὴν ἐπεπαύκεμεν τὸν πόλεμον, ἀλλὰ στεφάνους εἰς ἀγορὰν οὐκ ἐπέμψαμεν.

12. ἐπειδὴ τοὺς παρὰ τῶν ξένων ἀγγέλους ἐφυλάξαμεν, τὴν δημοκρατίᾱν οὐκ ἔλῡσαν.

13. ἆρα ὁ Ὅμηρος τοὺς ἀδελφοὺς τῇ περὶ τοὺς λόγους τέχνῃ πεπαίδευκεν ὡς τὴν ἀρετὴν ἐν ταῖς μάχαις εὖ φυλάττωσιν;

14. διὰ τὰς ἀρετὰς τοῖς φίλοις στεφάνους, ἆθλα νίκης, ἐπεπόμφεμεν.

15. ἐπεὶ οὐκ ἐθύσαμεν πρὸ τοῦ πολέμου τῇ θεῷ, νῦν καὶ ἐν τῇ νήσῳ καὶ ἐν τῇ ἀγορᾷ τεθύκαμεν ἵνα ἀρετὴν εἰς τὰς ψῡχὰς πέμψῃ.

16. ἐκ τῆς χώρᾱς εἰς τὴν νῆσον ἔπεμψεν ὁ δῆμος καὶ τὸν ξένον ἵνα τὴν εἰρήνην μὴ λύσειεν. ἓξ γὰρ βιβλία περὶ πολέμου ἐγεγράφειν.

17. ὦ Ὅμηρε, τῷ μὲν ἀδελφῷ βιβλίον ἀντὶ χρυσοῦ πέμπεις, τῷ δὲ
θεῷ στέφανον ἀντὶ ζῴου.

18. ἔθυες τοῖς θεοῖς ἵνα παιδεύοιεν τοὺς ξένους τοὺς ἐν τῇ νήσῳ
περὶ τῆς ἀρετῆς.

19. τοὺς ἀδελφοὺς ἐκέλευσε τὸν πόλεμον παῦσαι πρὸ τῆς νίκης.

20. ἢ τῇ βουλῇ ἢ τῇ ἐκκλησίᾳ δῶρα πέμψουσιν οἱ ξένοι ἵνα μὴ
λύσητε τὴν φιλίαν.

21. τὰ τοῦ Ὁμήρου βιβλία τοὺς ξένους πεπαίδευκεν.

22. ἀπὸ τῆς ἀγορᾶς
παρὰ τῷ τοῦ Ὁμήρου ἀδελφῷ
διὰ τῆς οἰκίας
παρὰ τὸν Ὅμηρον
διὰ τῆς νήσου
τεθυκέναι
πεπαυκέναι

II. 1. We have freed the brothers in order that you may not destroy the peace.

2. But you had sent prizes to Homer in order that he might educate your
brother.

3. He had written a book about peace in order that we might stop wars.

REVIEW: UNITS ONE TO THREE

I. *Translate.*

1. χρῡσὸν δὴ πέμψουσιν ἢ τῇ βουλῇ ἢ τῇ ἐκκλησίᾳ ἵνα παύσῃ ὁ δῆμος
   τὸν πόλεμον.
   (dative of indirect object; purpose clause in primary sequence; accusatives of direct object)

2. ὁ μὲν Ὅμηρος τὰς ἀνθρώπων ψῡχὰς τέχνῃ, δώρῳ τῶν θεῶν,
   πεπαίδευκεν, ὁ δὲ ἀδελφὸς ἔργοις.
   (instrumental datives; apposition; ellipsis of verb)

3. ἆρα πρὸ τῆς νίκης ἐκελεύσατε τοὺς φίλους ταῖς θεοῖς θῦσαι ὅπως εὖ
   φυλάττοιεν τὴν χώρᾱν;
   (question introduced by ἆρα; direct object and infinitive with κελεύω;
   indirect object of the infinitive θῦσαι; purpose clause in secondary
   sequence)

4. εἰς ἀγορᾱν, διὰ τῆς χώρᾱς, ἐκ τῶν οἰκιῶν,
   ἀντὶ χρῡσοῦ, ἀπὸ τῆς νήσου, ἐξ ἀγορᾶς,
   διὰ τὴν ἀρετήν, ἐν τῇ ἀγορᾷ, ἐν τῇ νήσῳ,
   περὶ λόγους, περὶ τῇ οἰκίᾳ, περὶ πολέμου,
   παρὰ Ὁμήρου, παρὰ Ὁμήρῳ, παρὰ Ὅμηρον,
   πρὸ τῆς μάχης, ἐξ ἀγγέλων

5. ὡς μὴ βιβλία ξένοις γράψειεν, στέφανον παρὰ τὸν Ὁμήρου φίλον
   ἐπεπόμφετε.
   (purpose clause in secondary sequence)

6. τὰ δῶρα τὰ παρὰ θεῶν ἀνθρώπους ἐπαίδευεν. θεοῖς γὰρ ἔθῡον.
   (neuter plural subject agreeing with singular verb; sentence connection)

7. ὦ ἄνθρωπε, τὸν ἀδελφὸν τὴν τέχνην οὐ παιδεύεις;
   (vocative; question; double accusative with παιδεύω)

8. τὸν φίλον κελεύσεις δῶρα καὶ θεοῖς καὶ ἀνθρώποις πέμπειν.
   (direct object and infinitive with κελεύω; direct and indirect objects
   of the infinitive πέμπειν)

II. *Translate into Greek.*

We have ordered the men from the island to send both gold and wreaths in
order that by means of words we may teach our brothers the art of war.

SELF-CORRECTING EXAMINATION 1A

I. *Place the accent on the following words and account for the accent.*

1. χωρων
2. δωρα
3. κελευσαι (infinitive)
4. φυλαττετε
5. θεοις

II. *Change from singular to plural or from plural to singular.*

1. τὰς νήσους
2. ταῖς θεοῖς
3. τῆς ἐκκλησίας
4. τὸν στέφανον
5. αἱ νῖκαι

6. παύῃ
7. ἐλύσατε
8. ἐπαίδευεν
9. θύσαι
10. κελεύσουσιν

III. *Give a synopsis of γράφω in the second person plural.*

PRINCIPAL PARTS: _____
_____

Present Indicative Active _____
Imperfect Indicative Active _____
Future Indicative Active _____
Aorist Indicative Active _____
Perfect Indicative Active _____
Pluperfect Indicative Active _____
Present Subjunctive Active _____
Aorist Subjunctive Active _____
Present Optative Active _____
Aorist Optative Active _____
Present Infinitive Active _____
Aorist Infinitive Active _____
Perfect Infinitive Active _____

IV. *Translate each of the following sentences into English and then follow the specific instructions after each sentence, if there are any.*

1. ἆρα πρὸ τῆς μάχης τὸν ἄγγελον τὸν παρὰ τῶν ξένων πέμψουσιν ἐξ ἀγορᾶς διὰ τῆς χώρας παρὰ τοὺς ἐν τῇ οἰκίᾳ ἀνθρώπους;

2. ὡς τὴν εἰρήνην μὴ λύσειαν Ὅμηρον ἐκελεύομεν τοὺς ἀπὸ τῆς νήσου ἀνθρώπους βιβλίοις παιδεῦσαι.
   (a) *Give the alternative form of* λύσειαν.
   (b) *Change* ἐκελεύομεν *to the perfect and make any other necessary changes.*
   (c) *Give the syntax of* βιβλίοις.

3. βιβλίον περὶ τῆς τοῖς θεοῖς θυσίας γέγραφας ἵνα καὶ ζῷα καὶ στεφάνους, δῶρα τῇ θεῷ, εἰς τὴν νῆσον πέμψωμεν.
   (a) *Change* γέγραφας *to the future and make any other necessary changes.*
   (b) *Give the syntax of* δῶρα.
   (c) *Give the syntax of* πέμψωμεν.

4. λόγῳ μὲν τὸν ἐν τῇ χώρᾳ πόλεμον ἐπαύετε, ἔργῳ δὲ τοὺς ἀδελφοὺς εἰς μάχην ἐπέμπετε.

5. ὁ μὲν Ὅμηρος τὸν φίλον ἐπεπαιδεύκειν ὅπως τοῖς θεοῖς θύοιεν, ὁ δὲ ἀδελφὸς οὔ.
   (a) *Give the syntax of* τοῖς θεοῖς.
   (b) *Give the syntax of* θύοιεν.

V. *Translate into Greek.*

We shall not order Homer to write books about battles. For books do not stop wars.

I. 1. χωρῶν: the accent on all first-declension nouns in the genitive plural is a circumflex on the ultima.

 2. δῶρα: the word is a noun with a persistent accent on the first syllable. Thus, the penult is accented and contains a long vowel, and the ultima has a short vowel. The accent must be a circumflex.

 3. κελεῦσαι (infinitive): the accent on the aorist infinitive active is always on the penult. Since the penult contains a diphthong, and final -αι counts as short for purposes of accentuation, the accent must be a circumflex.

 4. φυλάττετε: verb form, recessive accent, short ultima.

 5. θεοῖς: second-declension nouns with an acute on the ultima in the nominative take a circumflex on the ultima in the dative.

II. 1. τὴν νῆσον   6. παύωσι(ν)
 2. τῇ θεῷ   7. ἔλῦσας
 3. τῶν ἐκκλησιῶν   8. ἐπαίδευον
 4. τοὺς στεφάνους   9. θύσαιεν/θύσειαν
 5. ἡ νίκη   10. κελεύσει

III. PRINCIPAL PARTS: γράφω, γράψω, ἔγραψα, γέγραφα, γέγραμμαι, ἐγράφην

Present Indicative Active	γράφετε
Imperfect Indicative Active	ἐγράφετε
Future Indicative Active	γράψετε
Aorist Indicative Active	ἐγράψατε
Perfect Indicative Active	γεγράφατε
Pluperfect Indicative Active	ἐγεγράφετε
Present Subjunctive Active	γράφητε
Aorist Subjunctive Active	γράψητε
Present Optative Active	γράφοιτε
Aorist Optative Active	γράψαιτε
Present Infinitive Active	γράφειν
Aorist Infinitive Active	γράψαι
Perfect Infinitive Active	γεγραφέναι

IV. 1. Before the battle will they send/be sending the messenger from the strangers from the market place through the country to the men in the house?

2. In order that they might not destroy the peace we were ordering/used to order/ordered (habitually) Homer to educate the men from the island by means of books.

(a) λύσαιεν

(b) κεκελεύκαμεν; change λύσειαν to λύσωσιν.

(c) βιβλίοις is an instrumental dative.

3. You have written a book about (the) sacrifice to the gods in order that we may send both animals and crowns, gifts for the goddess, to the island.

(a) γράψεις; no other change necessary.

(b) δῶρα is accusative, in apposition to ζῷα and στεφάνους, the direct objects of πέμψωμεν.

(c) πέμψωμεν is aorist subjunctive: subjunctive in a purpose clause in primary sequence introduced by a perfect indicative; aorist to show simple aspect.

4. By word, on the one hand, you were stopping/used to stop/stopped (habitually) the war in the country; by deed, on the other hand, you were sending/used to send/sent (habitually) your brothers into battle.

5. Homer, on the one hand, had educated his friend in order that they might be sacrificing/sacrifice (habitually) to the gods; his brother, on the other hand, had not.

(a) τοῖς θεοῖς is a dative of indirect object.

(b) θύοιεν is present optative: optative in a purpose clause in secondary sequence introduced by a pluperfect indicative; present to show progressive/repeated aspect.

V. τὸν Ὅμηρον οὐ κελεύσομεν βιβλία περὶ μαχῶν γράφειν/γράψαι. (τὰ) βιβλία γὰρ οὐ παύει (τοὺς) πολέμους.

SELF-CORRECTING EXAMINATION 1B

I. *Place the accent on the following words and account for the accent.*

1. ὁδοις
2. γραφομεν
3. δημοι
4. παιδευσαι (optative)
5. οἰκιων

II. *Change from singular to plural or from plural to singular.*

1. τῆς φιλίας
2. τῷ βιβλίῳ
3. πολέμους
4. ἡ νῆσος
5. ὦ ἀδελφοί

6. θύσειεν
7. ἐπαιδεύομεν
8. φυλάξωσιν
9. κελεύσετε
10. ἔλῡσα

III. *Give a synopsis of παύω in the third person singular.*

PRINCIPAL PARTS: _____

_____

Present Indicative Active	_____
Imperfect Indicative Active	_____
Future Indicative Active	_____
Aorist Indicative Active	_____
Perfect Indicative Active	_____
Pluperfect Indicative Active	_____
Present Subjunctive Active	_____
Aorist Subjunctive Active	_____
Present Optative Active	_____
Aorist Optative Active	_____
Present Infinitive Active	_____
Aorist Infinitive Active	_____
Perfect Infinitive Active	_____

IV. *Translate each of the following sentences into English and follow the specific instructions after each sentence, if there are any.*

1. ἆρα τὴν τῆς δημοκρατίας ψῡχὴν λύσετε ἵνα τὸν πόλεμον παύσωσιν οἱ ἄνθρωποι;

   (a) *Give the syntax of* παύσωσιν.

2. τοὺς ἐξ ξένους τοὺς ἐν τῇ νήσῳ εἰς ἀγορὰν πεπόμφᾱσιν ὅπως τὸν δῆμον τὴν ἐκκλησίᾱν λῦσαι κελεύσωσιν.

   (a) *Change* πεπόμφᾱσιν *to the future and make any other necessary changes.*

   (b) *Give the syntax of* ἐκκλησίᾱν.

3. περὶ τοῦ πολέμου ἔγραψα ὡς τὴν εἰρήνην ἀρετῇ φυλάξειαν.

   (a) *Give the syntax of* φυλάξειαν.

   (b) *Give the syntax of* ἀρετῇ.

4. ἐπειδὴ τὴν νῆσον ἔργῳ ἐφύλαττεν ἡ θεὸς ἵνα θυσίᾱς θύοιεν, ἐκελεύσαμεν τοὺς ἀνθρώπους θύειν.

5. εἰς τὴν Ὁμήρου οἰκίᾱν βιβλία ἐπεπόμφειν ὅπως καὶ τὴν βουλὴν τὴν τῆς νήσου παιδεύσαι.

V. *Translate into Greek.*

He will write about the battle in the road in order that they may educate the people both by word and by deed.

I.   1. ὁδοῖς: second-declension nouns with an acute on the ultima in the nominative take a circumflex on the ultima in the dative.
2. γράφομεν: verb form, recessive accent, short ultima.
3. δῆμοι: the word is a noun with a persistent accent on the first syllable. Thus, the penult is accented and contains a long vowel, and the ultima ends in the diphthong -οι, counted as short for purposes of accentuation. The accent must be a circumflex.
4. παιδεῦσαι (optative): this is a verb form whose ultima contains a diphthong counted as long for purposes of accentuation. The accent cannot recede beyond the penult and must be an acute.
5. οἰκιῶν: the accent on all first-declension nouns in the genitive plural is a circumflex on the ultima.

II. 1. τῶν φιλιῶν   6. θύσειαν/θύσαιεν
2. τοῖς βιβλίοις   7. ἐπαίδευον
3. πόλεμον   8. φυλάξῃ
4. αἱ νῆσοι   9. κελεύσεις
5. ὦ ἄδελφε   10. ἐλύσαμεν

III. PRINCIPAL PARTS: παύω, παύσω, ἔπαυσα, πέπαυκα, πέπαυμαι, ἐπαύθην

Present Indicative Active	παύει
Imperfect Indicative Active	ἔπαυε(ν)
Future Indicative Active	παύσει
Aorist Indicative Active	ἔπαυσε(ν)
Perfect Indicative Active	πέπαυκε(ν)
Pluperfect Indicative Active	ἐπεπαύκει(ν)
Present Subjunctive Active	παύῃ
Aorist Subjunctive Active	παύσῃ
Present Optative Active	παύοι
Aorist Optative Active	παύσαι/παύσειε(ν)
Present Infinitive Active	παύειν
Aorist Infinitive Active	παῦσαι
Perfect Infinitive Active	πεπαυκέναι

84

IV. 1. Will you destroy/be destroying the soul of the democracy in order that the men may stop the war?

    (a) παύσωσιν is aorist subjunctive: subjunctive in a purpose clause in primary sequence introduced by a future indicative; aorist to show simple aspect.

  2. They have sent the six strangers on the island to the market place in order that they may command the people to dissolve the assembly.

    (a) πέμψουσιν; no other change necessary.

    (b) ἐκκλησίαν is accusative, the direct object of the infinitive λῦσαι.

  3. I wrote about (the) war in order that they might guard (the) peace by means of virtue.

    (a) φυλάξειαν is aorist optative: optative in a purpose clause in secondary sequence introduced by an aorist indicative; aorist to show simple aspect.

    (b) ἀρετῇ is an instrumental dative.

  4. Since the goddess was guarding/used to guard/guarded (habitually) the island by deed in order that they might be sacrificing/sacrifice (habitually) sacrifices, we ordered the men to be sacrificing/sacrifice (habitually).

  5. He/she had sent books into the house of Homer in order that he might educate also the council of the island.

V. περὶ τῆς ἐν τῇ ὁδῷ μάχης/τῆς μάχης τῆς ἐν τῇ ὁδῷ γράψει ἵνα/ὡς/ ὅπως τὸν δῆμον καὶ λόγῳ καὶ ἔργῳ παιδεύωσιν/παιδεύσωσιν.

UNIT

4

37. FIRST-DECLENSION NOUNS: CONCLUDED

1. FEMININE NOUNS WITH NOMINATIVE SINGULAR IN SHORT -α

In addition to first-declension nouns whose nominative singular ends in
-η or -ᾱ, there are others, also feminine, whose nominative singular ends
in short -α. Their declension is different only in having short -α in the
nominative/vocative and accusative singular. In the genitive and dative
singular and in all of the cases of the plural, the endings are identical with
those of the first-declension nouns already learned. Their endings are:

	S		P
Nominative/Vocative	-α	-α	-αι
Genitive	-ης	-ᾱς	-ῶν
Dative	-ῃ	-ᾳ	-αις
Accusative	-αν	-αν	-ᾱς

The following nouns will serve as examples:

> θάλαττα, θαλάττης, ἡ sea
> μοῦσα, μούσης, ἡ muse
> γέφυρα, γεφύρᾱς, ἡ bridge
> μοῖρα, μοίρᾱς, ἡ fate

Nom./Voc. S	θάλαττα	μοῦσα	γέφυρα	μοῖρα
Gen.	θαλάττης	μούσης	γεφύρᾱς	μοίρᾱς
Dat.	θαλάττῃ	μούσῃ	γεφύρᾳ	μοίρᾳ
Acc.	θάλατταν	μοῦσαν	γέφυραν	μοῖραν

87

Nom./Voc. P	θάλατται	μοῦσαι	γέφυραι	μοῖραι
Gen.	θαλαττῶν	μουσῶν	γεφυρῶν	μοιρῶν
Dat.	θαλάτταις	μούσαις	γεφύραις	μοίραις
Acc.	θαλάττᾱς	μούσᾱς	γεφύρᾱς	μοίρᾱς

Observations: (1) In nouns whose stem ends in ε, ι, or ρ, the endings of the genitive and dative singular have ᾱ instead of η.

(2) The accent, as in all nouns, is persistent. Note, however, the changes in accent necessitated by the rules for the possibilities of accent as the length of the ultima changes. As in all first-declension nouns, the genitive plural receives a circumflex on the ultima.

2. MASCULINE NOUNS WITH NOMINATIVE SINGULAR IN -ης OR -ᾱς

Some first-declension nouns are *masculine* and have a nominative singular ending in -ης or, when the stem of the noun ends in ε, ι, or ρ, a nominative singular ending in -ᾱς. The endings of these nouns differ from those of feminine first-declension nouns only in the nominative, genitive, and (sometimes) vocative singular. In the dative and accusative singular, and in all forms of the plural, these masculine nouns have the same endings as feminine first-declension nouns. Their endings are:

	S		P
Nom.	**-ης**	**-ᾱς**	-αι
Gen.	**-ου**	**-ου**	-ῶν
Dat.	-ῃ	-ᾱͅ	-αις
Acc.	-ην	-ᾱν	-ᾱς
Voc.	**-α, -η**	**-ᾱ**	-αι

The following nouns will serve as examples:

πολίτης, πολίτου, ὁ citizen
ποιητής, ποιητοῦ, ὁ poet
νεᾱνίᾱς, νεᾱνίου, ὁ young man

Nom. S	πολίτης	ποιητής	νεᾱνίᾱς
Gen.	πολίτου	ποιητοῦ	νεᾱνίου
Dat.	πολίτῃ	ποιητῇ	νεᾱνίᾱͅ
Acc.	πολίτην	ποιητήν	νεᾱνίᾱν
Voc.	πολῖτα	ποιητά	νεᾱνίᾱ

Nom./Voc. P	πολῖται	ποιηταί	νεανίαι
Gen.	πολῑτῶν	ποιητῶν	νεανιῶν
Dat.	πολίταις	ποιηταῖς	νεανίαις
Acc.	πολίτᾱς	ποιητάς	νεανίᾱς

Observations:

(1) The -ς of the nominative singular ending was borrowed from the nominative singular ending of masculine second-declension nouns (e.g., ἄνθρωπος).

(2) The genitive singular ending is the same as that of masculine second-declension nouns (cf. ἀνθρώπου, πολίτου).

(3) Accent is persistent, but as in ALL first-declension nouns, the genitive plural receives a circumflex on the ultima.

(4) As in all other nouns of the first and second declensions, masculine first-declension nouns accented on the ultima receive a circumflex rather than an acute accent in the genitive and dative, singular and plural (e.g., ποιητής, ποιητοῦ).

(5) In nouns whose stem ends in ε, ι, or ρ, the endings of the nominative, dative, and accusative singular have ᾱ instead of η. In the vocative singular of these nouns long ᾱ appears instead of short α (νεανίᾱ). Note that the accusative plural of these nouns is identical with the nominative singular; context will determine meaning.

(6) Some nouns with nominatives in -ης employ the vocative singular ending -η (instead of -α). These nouns will be noted as they occur.

Drill I, page 105, may now be done.

38. ADJECTIVES OF THE FIRST AND SECOND DECLENSIONS

Just as all forms of the article and the noun have *gender*, *number*, and *case*, so do all forms of the adjective. Like the article, the adjective must agree in gender, number, and case with the noun which it modifies. This grammatical agreement does not require that the endings of adjective and noun always be identical in form: compare the examples which follow the paradigms below.

The adjectives presented in this Section have endings either of the first and second declensions or of the second declension alone. They fall into two groups: **three-ending adjectives** with separate sets of endings for each of the three genders, and **two-ending adjectives** with one set of endings for both masculine and feminine and another set of endings for the neuter.

Adjectives will be listed as vocabulary items by giving all possible forms of the nominative singular, as in the examples below.

1. THREE-ENDING ADJECTIVES OF THE FIRST AND SECOND DECLENSIONS

ἀγαθός, ἀγαθή, ἀγαθόν, good

	M	F	N
Nom. S	ἀγαθός	ἀγαθή	ἀγαθόν
Gen.	ἀγαθοῦ	ἀγαθῆς	ἀγαθοῦ
Dat.	ἀγαθῷ	ἀγαθῇ	ἀγαθῷ
Acc.	ἀγαθόν	ἀγαθήν	ἀγαθόν
Voc.	ἀγαθέ	ἀγαθή	ἀγαθόν
Nom./Voc. P	ἀγαθοί	ἀγαθαί	ἀγαθά
Gen.	ἀγαθῶν	ἀγαθῶν	ἀγαθῶν
Dat.	ἀγαθοῖς	ἀγαθαῖς	ἀγαθοῖς
Acc.	ἀγαθούς	ἀγαθάς	ἀγαθά

Observations: (1) Except for the accent of the vocative singular, the masculine endings are the same as those of ἀδελφός (Section 15); the feminine endings are the same as those of ψῡχή (Section 14); the neuter endings are the same as those of ἔργον (Section 15), although the accent of ἀγαθόν falls on the ultima.

(2) Like that of nouns, THE ACCENT OF ADJECTIVES IS PERSISTENT AND IS GIVEN BY THE NEUTER NOMINATIVE SINGULAR. ADJECTIVES OF THE FIRST AND SECOND DECLENSIONS, WHEN ACCENTED ON THE ULTIMA, TAKE A CIRCUMFLEX IN THE GENITIVE AND DATIVE, SINGULAR AND PLURAL.

ἄξιος, ἀξίᾱ, ἄξιον, worthy

	M	F	N
Nom. S	ἄξιος	ἀξίᾱ	ἄξιον
Gen.	ἀξίου	ἀξίᾱς	ἀξίου
Dat.	ἀξίῳ	ἀξίᾳ	ἀξίῳ
Acc.	ἄξιον	ἀξίᾱν	ἄξιον
Voc.	ἄξιε	ἀξίᾱ	ἄξιον

Nom./Voc. P	ἄξιοι	ἄξιαι	ἄξια
Gen.	ἀξίων	ἀξίων	ἀξίων
Dat.	ἀξίοις	ἀξίαις	ἀξίοις
Acc.	ἀξίους	ἀξίᾱς	ἄξια

Observations: (1) When the stem of a first- and second-declension adjective ends in ε, ι, or ρ, the feminine singular endings have ᾱ instead of η.

(2) Final -οι and -αι in the masculine and feminine nominative/vocative plural (as everywhere except in the third person singular optative active endings) count as short for purposes of accentuation: thus ἄξιοι, ἄξιαι.

(3) THE ACCENT IN THE FEMININE GENITIVE PLURAL, UNLIKE THAT OF FIRST-DECLENSION NOUNS, DOES NOT SHIFT TO THE ULTIMA. Instead, it follows the regular rules of accent.

2. TWO-ENDING ADJECTIVES OF THE SECOND DECLENSION

Some adjectives have only two sets of endings, one for both masculine and feminine, the other for the neuter.

ἄδικος, ἄδικον, unjust

	M/F	N
Nom. S	ἄδικος	ἄδικον
Gen.	ἀδίκου	ἀδίκου
Dat.	ἀδίκῳ	ἀδίκῳ
Acc.	ἄδικον	ἄδικον
Voc.	ἄδικε	ἄδικον
Nom./Voc. P	ἄδικοι	ἄδικα
Gen.	ἀδίκων	ἀδίκων
Dat.	ἀδίκοις	ἀδίκοις
Acc.	ἀδίκους	ἄδικα

Observation: Accent is persistent.

39. AGREEMENT OF ADJECTIVE AND NOUN

Just as the definite article agrees in gender, number, and case with the noun which it modifies, but does not necessarily have an identical ending, so too adjectives agree in *gender*, *number* and *case* with the nouns which they modify regardless of any external difference in the form of the endings.

Each of the following phrases shows agreement.

> τοῖς ἀνθρώποις   (masculine dative plural)
> to the men
>
> ταῖς νήσοις   (feminine dative plural)
> to the islands
>
> ἀγαθὴ ψῡχή   (feminine nominative singular)
> a good soul
>
> ἀξίᾱ ψῡχή   (feminine nominative singular)
> a worthy soul
>
> ἄδικος ψῡχή   (feminine nominative singular)
> an unjust soul

40. POSITION OF THE ADJECTIVE

1. ATTRIBUTIVE POSITION

An adjective which modifies a noun and is preceded by an article agreeing with the noun is in the **attributive position.** The three varieties of attributive position are presented in Section 16.3.

An adjective in the attributive position, together with the noun which it modifies, forms a *phrase* but NOT a complete sentence.

> ὁ ἀγαθὸς ἄνθρωπος   the good man
> ὁ ἄνθρωπος ὁ ἀγαθός   the good man (the man, the good one)
> ἄνθρωπος ὁ ἀγαθός   the good man (a man, the good one)

The phrases above differ not in meaning but in emphasis only; the translations in parentheses exaggerate the emphasis of the Greek.

2. PREDICATE POSITION

An adjective which agrees with a noun accompanied by the article, but which itself is not preceded by the article, is in the **predicate position**.

The phrase consisting of noun and article becomes the subject, and the adjective the **predicate adjective**, of a complete sentence.

In order to translate such a sentence into English the linking verb "is" or "are" must be supplied, but such sentences, called **nominal sentences**, are complete as they stand in Greek. The article, noun, and adjective, standing in the nominative case, provide all the necessary information.

> ὁ ἄνθρωπος ἀγαθός.
> The man is good.

> ἀγαθὸς ὁ ἄνθρωπος.
> The man is good.
> The man is *good*.

> οἱ ἄνθρωποι ἀγαθοί.
> The men are good.   (*specific use of the article*)
> Men are good.   (*generic use of the article*)

Carefully distinguish these nominal sentences, where the adjective is not preceded by the article, from the phrases where the adjective is preceded by the article.

A nominal sentence can also consist of two nouns, one used as a subject, the other as a **predicate noun**. The subject usually has the article, but the predicate noun does not.

> τὸ βιβλίον δῶρον.
> The book is a gift.

> δῶρον τὸ βιβλίον.
> The book is a gift.
> The book is a *gift*.

Drills II and III, pages 105–106, may now be done.

41. CONDITIONAL SENTENCES

A **conditional sentence** consists of two statements. One makes an assumption ("If A ... "); the other states a conclusion which follows from that assumption ("... then B"). The assumption is called the **protasis**; the conclusion, the **apodosis**. The negative of the protasis is μή, that of the apodosis οὐ. The protasis can be stated either before or after the apodosis.

> If it rains (*protasis*), they will stay home (*apodosis*).
> They will stay home (*apodosis*) if it rains (*protasis*).

Six types of conditional sentence are presented below. For each, a formula for the protasis, a formula for the apodosis, and a translation formula will be given. In the translation formula the English verb "do" will stand for any English verb.

NO VERB IN A CONDITIONAL SENTENCE CAN BE TRANSLATED UNTIL THE TYPE OF CONDITIONAL SENTENCE IS IDENTIFIED.

These six conditional sentences are summarized at the end of this Section.

1. FUTURE MORE VIVID CONDITIONAL SENTENCE

Protasis: ἐάν ("if") + subjunctive
Apodosis: future indicative
Translation formula: does/will do

$$ἐὰν\ ἄγγελον\ \begin{Bmatrix} πέμπῃ \\ πέμψῃ \end{Bmatrix},\ τὴν\ μάχην\ παύσουσιν.$$

If he sends a messenger, they will stop the battle.

The protasis of the future more vivid conditional sentence makes an assumption about the future; the apodosis draws a conclusion based on that assumption.

In the protasis the choice between present subjunctive and aorist subjunctive depends on the aspect which one wishes to express: progressive/repeated aspect (present subjunctive) or simple aspect (aorist subjunctive).

2. FUTURE LESS VIVID CONDITIONAL SENTENCE

Protasis: εἰ ("if") + optative
Apodosis: optative + ἄν
Translation formula: should do/would do

$$εἰ\ ἄγγελον\ \begin{Bmatrix} πέμποι \\ πέμψαι/ \\ πέμψειεν \end{Bmatrix},\ τὴν\ μάχην\ \begin{Bmatrix} παύοιεν \\ παύσαιεν/ \\ παύσειαν \end{Bmatrix}\ ἄν.$$

If he should send a messenger, they would stop the battle.

The protasis of a future less vivid conditional sentence, like that of a future more vivid conditional sentence, makes an assumption about the future, but the assumption is viewed as less likely to come true; the apodosis draws a conclusion based on this less likely assumption.

In both protasis and apodosis the choice between present optative and aorist optative depends on the aspect which one wishes to express.

The particle ἄν is necessary to complete the meaning of the apodosis, but it is NOT separately translated. Its position is flexible, but it cannot begin a clause or sentence. The apodosis of the sentence above could be written:

$$\ldots \tau \grave{\eta} \nu \; \mu \acute{\alpha} \chi \eta \nu \; \ddot{\alpha} \nu \; \left\{ \begin{array}{c} \pi \alpha \acute{\upsilon} o \iota \varepsilon \nu \\ \pi \alpha \acute{\upsilon} \sigma \alpha \iota \varepsilon \nu / \\ \pi \alpha \acute{\upsilon} \sigma \varepsilon \iota \alpha \nu \end{array} \right\}.$$

There is no difference in meaning.

The introductory particles ἐάν and εἰ both mean "if," but they are NOT interchangeable: each belongs ONLY to certain types of conditional sentence.

3. PRESENT GENERAL CONDITIONAL SENTENCE

Protasis: ἐάν + subjunctive
Apodosis: present indicative
Translation formula: does/does

$$\dot{\varepsilon} \grave{\alpha} \nu \; \ddot{\alpha} \gamma \gamma \varepsilon \lambda o \nu \; \left\{ \begin{array}{c} \pi \acute{\varepsilon} \mu \pi \eta \\ \pi \acute{\varepsilon} \mu \psi \eta \end{array} \right\}, \; \tau \grave{\eta} \nu \; \mu \acute{\alpha} \chi \eta \nu \; \pi \alpha \acute{\upsilon} o \upsilon \sigma \iota \nu.$$

If he sends a messenger, they stop the battle.
If he (ever) sends a messenger, they (always) stop the battle.

The protasis of a present general conditional sentence makes an assumption in present time; the apodosis states a conclusion which follows as a general rule. The adverbs "ever" and "always" in the second translation above emphasize this.

The protasis of a present general conditional sentence is the same as the protasis of a future more vivid conditional sentence, but its meaning is substantially different. ONE CANNOT TRANSLATE THE VERBS IN EITHER PART OF ANY CONDITIONAL SENTENCE WITHOUT FIRST IDENTIFYING BOTH PROTASIS AND APODOSIS.

In the protasis, the choice between present subjunctive and aorist subjunctive depends on the aspect which one wishes to express.

4. PAST GENERAL CONDITIONAL SENTENCE

Protasis: εἰ + optative
Apodosis: imperfect indicative
Translation formula: did/did

$$εἰ \ ἄγγελον \begin{Bmatrix} πέμποι \\ πέμψαι/ \\ πέμψειεν \end{Bmatrix}, \ τὴν \ μάχην \ ἔπαυον.$$

If he sent a messenger, they stopped the battle.
If he (ever) sent a messenger, they (always) stopped the battle.

The protasis of a past general conditional sentence makes an assumption in past time; the apodosis states a conclusion which follows as a general rule in past time. The adverbs "ever" and "always" in the second translation above emphasize this.

The protasis of a past general conditional sentence is the same as the protasis of a future less vivid conditional sentence, but its meaning is substantially different.

Identify both protasis and apodosis of all conditional sentences before translating.

In the protasis, the choice between present optative and aorist optative depends on the aspect which one wishes to express.

5. PRESENT CONTRAFACTUAL CONDITIONAL SENTENCE

Protasis: εἰ + imperfect indicative
Apodosis: imperfect indicative + ἄν
Translation formula: were doing/would be doing

εἰ ἄγγελον ἔπεμπεν, τὴν μάχην ἔπαυον ἄν.

If he were sending a messenger, they would be stopping the battle.
If he were sending a messenger (but he is not), they would be stopping the
 battle (but they are not).

The present contrafactual conditional sentence assumes in its protasis something which the speaker knows is untrue at the present time. (Compare the English protasis "If I had a million dollars now . . . .") The apodosis draws a conclusion based on this unreal assumption.

In this type of conditional sentence the indicative mood describes an *unreal* action or state of being. The particle ἄν in the apodosis, not separately translated, distinguishes the apodosis of a present contrafactual conditional sentence from that of a past general conditional sentence. *Identify both protasis and apodosis of all conditional sentences before translating.*

6. PAST CONTRAFACTUAL CONDITIONAL SENTENCE

Protasis: εἰ + aorist indicative
Apodosis: aorist indicative + ἄν
Translation formula: had done/would have done

εἰ ἄγγελον ἔπεμψεν, τὴν μάχην ἔπαυσαν ἄν.

If he had sent a messenger, they would have stopped the battle.
If he had sent a messenger (but he did not), they would have stopped the battle (but they did not).

The past contrafactual conditional sentence assumes in its protasis something which the speaker knows was untrue in the past. (Compare the English protasis "If I had had a million dollars yesterday. . . .") The apodosis draws a conclusion based on this unreal assumption.

Note the difference between the imperfect indicative of the present contrafactual conditional sentence and the aorist indicative of the past contrafactual conditional sentence.

7. SUMMARY OF CONDITIONAL SENTENCES

NAME	PROTASIS	APODOSIS
FUTURE MORE VIVID	ἐάν + subjunctive *does*	future indicative *will do*
FUTURE LESS VIVID	εἰ + optative *should do*	optative + ἄν *would do*
PRESENT GENERAL	ἐάν + subjunctive *does*	present indicative *does*
PAST GENERAL	εἰ + optative *did*	imperfect indicative *did*
PRESENT CONTRA- FACTUAL	εἰ + imperf. indic. *were doing*	imperfect indicative + ἄν *would be doing*
PAST CONTRA- FACTUAL	εἰ + aorist indic. *had done*	aorist indicative + ἄν *would have done*

8. FURTHER NOTE ON CONDITIONAL SENTENCES

Attic Greek has other types of conditional sentences which need not be learned now; these are explained in the Appendix.

Sometimes the protasis of one type of conditional sentence is combined with the apodosis of another type. Such **mixed conditional sentences** will be introduced in the Exercises of later Units. Examples are given in the Appendix.

Drills IV and V, page 106, may now be done.

42. ELISION

When a word ends with a short vowel and the following word begins with a vowel or a diphthong, the vowel at the end of the first word is sometimes dropped or **elided**. This is called **elision**. An apostrophe (') marks the missing vowel.

Here are some examples of elision. Elision is never mandatory in writing Greek.

πέμπετε ἀγγέλους.	(unelided)
πέμπετ᾽ ἀγγέλους.	(elided)
ἔπεμψα ἀγγέλους.	(unelided)
ἔπεμψ᾽ ἀγγέλους.	(elided)
οἱ δὲ ἄνθρωποι	(unelided)
οἱ δ᾽ ἄνθρωποι	(elided)
ἐπαιδεύσατε Ὅμηρον;	(unelided)
ἐπαιδεύσαθ᾽ Ὅμηρον;	(elided)

In the last example above, note the change from the *unaspirated* consonant τ to the *aspirated* consonant θ because of the rough breathing (= h) which follows immediately in elision. Cf. Section 8.

The addition of a nu-movable, where possible, avoids elision:

ἔπεμψεν ἀγγέλους.

In the English-to-Greek sentences all words are to be written out in full.

VOCABULARY

ἀγαθός, ἀγαθή, ἀγαθόν	good
ἄν (particle)	used in some conditional sentences
ἄξιος, ἀξίā, ἄξιον	worthy, worth (+ gen.)
ἀνάξιος, ἀνάξιον	unworthy (+ gen.)
ἀρχή, ἀρχῆς, ἡ	beginning; rule, empire
γέφῡρα, γεφύρᾱς, ἡ	bridge
διδάσκω, διδάξω, ἐδίδαξα, δεδίδαχα,	teach
δεδίδαγμαι, ἐδιδάχθην	
δίκη, δίκης, ἡ	justice; lawsuit
ἄδικος, ἄδικον	unjust
δίκαιος, δικαίā, δίκαιον	just
ἐθέλω, ἐθελήσω, ἠθέλησα, ἠθέληκα,	be willing, wish
——, ——	
εἰ (particle)	if
ἐάν (particle)	if
ἡμέρᾱ, ἡμέρᾱς, ἡ	day
θάλαττα, θαλάττης, ἡ	sea
θάπτω, θάψω, ἔθαψα, ——,	bury
τέθαμμαι, ἐτάφην	
καίτοι (particle)	and further, and yet
κακός, κακή, κακόν	bad, evil
καλός, καλή, καλόν	beautiful, noble, good
μετά (prep.) + gen.	with
+ acc.	after
μοῖρα, μοίρᾱς, ἡ	fate
μοῦσα, μούσης, ἡ	muse
νεᾱνίᾱς, νεᾱνίου, ὁ	young man
ὅπλον, ὅπλου, τό	tool; (pl.) weapons
ὁπλίτης, ὁπλίτου, ὁ	hoplite, heavy-armed foot-soldier
πάλαι (adv.)	long ago
ποιητής, ποιητοῦ, ὁ	poet, author
πολίτης, πολίτου, ὁ	citizen
στρατιώτης, στρατιώτου, ὁ	soldier

σύν (prep.)   + dat.   with
τάττω, τάξω, ἔταξα, τέταχα,   draw up in order, station, appoint
    τέταγμαι, ἐτάχθην
φίλος, φίλη, φίλον   dear, beloved, one's own

VOCABULARY NOTES

The particle ἄν is employed in the apodoses of future less vivid, present contra-factual, and past contrafactual conditional sentences. It is NOT translated separately but is essential in identifying these conditional sentences: it cannot be omitted. It is placed most frequently after a verb, or after the negative adverb οὐ, οὐκ, οὐχ, but its position is flexible. It cannot, however, stand first in its clause.

The adjective ἄξιος, ἀξίᾱ, ἄξιον, "worthy, worth," is often accompanied by a noun in the genitive case to indicate that *of which* someone or something is worthy. This usage is called the **genitive of value**.

> ἄνθρωπος **ἄθλου** ἄξιος
> a man worthy **of a prize**

The adjective ἄξιος can also be accompanied by an infinitive to indicate an activity that someone or something is worthy of performing or receiving. This is called an **epexegetical infinitive** or "explaining" infinitive.

> ἄνθρωπος **παιδεύειν** ἄξιος
> a man worthy **to educate** (i.e., to educate others)
> = a man who deserves to educate

Also, the adjective ἄξιος can be accompanied by a noun in the dative case to indicate the person(s) from whose point of view someone or something is worthy (**dative of reference**).

> ἄνθρωπος **τοῖς πολίταις** ἄθλον ἄξιος
> a man **to the citizens** worthy of a prize
> = a man, **in the citizens' eyes**, worthy of a prize

The adjective ἀνάξιος, ἀνάξιον, "unworthy," takes the same constructions as the adjective ἄξιος. It is a **compound adjective** consisting of the adjective ἄξιος + the prefix ἀν-, which expresses negation. This negative prefix has two forms: ἀν- when followed by a vowel or diphthong, and ἀ- when followed by a consonant. The alpha of this prefix is called **alpha privative**. Both forms derive from a prefix consisting of the consonant *ν* alone; they are cognate with the English negative prefixes "in-" and "un-."

All compound adjectives such as ἀνάξιος, ἀνάξιον have only two sets of endings (masculine/feminine and neuter) rather than three.

The noun ἀρχή, ἀρχῆς, ἡ, "beginning; rule, empire," conveys the notion of being first, in the sense either of a beginning or of rule and authority over others.

The verb διδάσκω, διδάξω, ἐδίδαξα, δεδίδαχα, δεδίδαγμαι, ἐδιδάχθην, "teach," has a narrower meaning than παιδεύω, "educate, teach," and takes the same constructions.

The noun δίκη, δίκης, ἡ, "justice; lawsuit," has a wide range of meanings. It can refer to traditional custom or practice, to judgments based on traditional usage, to lawsuits or trials or penalties exacted, or to the principle of justice.

The adjective ἄδικος, ἄδικον, "unjust," consists of the stem of the noun δίκη + alpha privative. As a compound adjective, it has only two sets of endings.

The verb ἐθέλω, ἐθελήσω, ἠθέλησα, ἠθέληκα, ——, ——, "be willing, wish," lacks Principal Parts V and VI. The absence of one or more Principal Parts will be indicated by dashes, as above. Note that the *ἐ-* of Principal Parts I and II *belongs to the stem* and is NOT the past indicative augment. Note also that Principal Part III begins with *ἠ-* rather than with the past indicative augment *ἐ-*. The unaugmented aorist tense stem of this verb is ἐθελησ-. IN VERBS WHERE THE STEM BEGINS WITH A VOWEL, THE PAST INDICATIVE AUGMENT IS SHOWN NOT BY THE PREFIX *ἐ-* BUT BY A LENGTHENING OF THE INITIAL VOWEL OF THE STEM.

The various initial vowels and diphthongs are usually augmented as in the chart below. Exceptions will be pointed out in the Vocabulary Notes. Note that short *α* is lengthened to *η*, NOT to *ᾱ*.

UNAUGMENTED	*AUGMENTED*
α	η
ε	η
ι	ῑ
ο	ω
υ	ῡ
αι	ῃ
αυ	ηυ
ει	ῃ
ευ	ηυ
οι	ῳ

Initial ου is not augmented. Also, the diphthongs listed above are sometimes left unaugmented. Initial long vowels remain the same, except that ᾱ changes to η.

The rules above are to be learned as new vowels are encountered.

Thus, the imperfect indicative active of ἐθέλω is conjugated ἤθελον, ἤθελες, etc. Note also that in Principal Part IV of ἐθέλω initial ἠ- is part of the tense stem; in the pluperfect it remains unchanged.

The verb ἐθέλω takes an infinitive to indicate the action which one wishes to perform. This infinitive, like the infinitive with κελεύω, is called an **object infinitive** because it serves as the direct object of the main verb. The infinitive, in turn, can take a direct and/or indirect object of its own.

> ἐθέλω τὸν ἀδελφὸν παιδεῦσαι.
> I wish to educate my brother.

The negative οὐκ ἐθέλω can often be translated "refuse."

The particles εἰ and ἐάν both mean "if"; each introduces the protasis of certain types of conditional sentence (cf. Section 41). The particle εἰ is proclitic; the particle ἐάν consists of εἰ + ἄν. They are NOT interchangeable.

The accent of the particle καίτοι, "and further, and yet," is an exception to the rules for the possibilities of accent.

The adjective καλός, καλή, καλόν, "beautiful, noble, good," combines the idea of physical beauty with that of moral goodness. The adjective ἀγαθός, ἀγαθή, ἀγαθόν, "good," combines the ideas of moral goodness and serviceability.

The preposition μετά can take either the genitive or the accusative case. With the genitive it expresses accompaniment and means "with" as in the English sentence "He went *with* me to the store." Distinguish this use from the instrumental meaning "with" of the dative case (e.g., "He persuaded me *with* words"). When it takes the accusative case, μετά means "after" either in space or in time.

μετὰ τῶν φίλων	with the friends
μετὰ τὴν μάχην	after the battle
μετὰ τὸν Ὅμηρον	after Homer

The noun μοῖρα, μοίρας, ἡ, "fate," has the basic meaning "portion" or "allotment." What is allotted to man constitutes his destiny.

The noun μοῦσα, μούσης, ἡ, "muse," denotes the goddesses invoked by poets such as Homer.

The noun νεᾱνίᾱς, νεᾱνίου, ὁ, "young man," contains the root νε-, which is cognate with English *new*.

The noun ὁπλίτης, ὁπλίτου, ὁ, "hoplite, heavy-armed foot-soldier," is formed from the stem of the noun ὅπλον, ὅπλου, τό, "tool; (*pl.*) weapons" + the suffix -ῑτης. Many nouns denoting those who perform a certain function have this suffix. The noun ὅπλον, in a specialized usage, designated the large shield which hoplites carried. Cf. the noun πολίτης, πολίτου, ὁ, which denotes a "citizen" of a city and is formed from the noun for "city." Cf. also the nouns ποιητής, ποιητοῦ, ὁ, "poet," and στρατιώτης, στρατιώτου, ὁ, "soldier," which have a similar suffix, -της. The noun ποιητής means literally "he who makes"; the noun στρατιώτης comes from the word for "army" and means literally "army man."

The adverb πάλαι, "long ago," can be used in the attributive position with nouns, as can the adverb νῦν, "now."

οἱ **πάλαι** ἄνθρωποι
men **long ago**
= men of old

οἱ **νῦν** ἄνθρωποι
men **now**
= men of the present day

The preposition σύν + dat., "with," indicates accompaniment or manner. To indicate that one person accompanies another, the preposition μετά + gen. is usually employed in Attic prose, but σύν appears in certain traditional phrases, and also where the notion of joint effort is important.

σὺν θεοῖς   (accompaniment)
with (the help of the) gods

σὺν ὅπλοις   (accompaniment)
with weapons

σὺν δίκῃ   (manner)
with justice

The prepositional phrase σὺν ὅπλοις means that people have weapons with them, but the dative ὅπλοις standing alone shows instrumentality: e.g., "The soldiers are standing at attention *with* (σύν) their weapons"; "the soldiers killed the enemy *with* their weapons" (dative case without a preposition).

The adjective φίλος, φίλη, φίλον, "dear, beloved, one's own," is identical in the masculine with the noun φίλος, φίλου, ὁ, "friend." Compare ὁ φίλος, "the friend," with ὁ φίλος ποιητής, "the beloved poet."

COGNATES AND DERIVATIVES

ἀγαθός	Agatha
ἄξιος	axiom (an assumption whose **worth** is self-evident), axiology (the study of **values**)
ἀρχή	anarchy (the absence of **rule**), archaic
διδάσκω	didactic
δίκη	theodicy (a vindication of divine **justice**)
ἡμέρᾱ	ephemeral (lasting only for a **day**)
θάλαττα	thalassocracy (rule over the **sea**; derived from the dialect form θάλασσα)
θάπτω	epitaph (inscribed where someone is **buried**)
κακός	cacophony
καλός	calisthenics
μετά	*middle*; metaphysics (the study of things **beyond** the physical; literally, "**after** physics")
μοῖρα	merit (the **portion** which one deserves, from the Latin cognate *mereō*)
μοῦσα	music (one of the arts which the **Muses** superintend)
ὅπλον	panoply (a full array of **weapons**)
πάλαι	Palaeolithic (the **Old** Stone Age)
ποιητής	poet
πολίτης	political
στρατιώτης	strategy (the science of leading **soldiers**)
σύν	synchronize (to time one thing together **with** another)
τάττω	tactics (a science involving the **stationing** of troops)
σύν + τάττω	syntax (the way in which words are **drawn up in order with** other words to form grammatical structures)

DRILLS

I. *For each of the words below:*

    (a) *supply the proper form of the article, or* ὦ;

    (b) *translate;*

    (c) *change plurals to singulars and singulars to plurals.*

1. θαλάτταις
2. θάλατταν
3. γεφύρᾱς (2)
4. θάλαττα (2)
5. πολίτης
6. πολῖτα
7. νεᾱνίᾱν
8. πολίτου
9. ποιητῇ
10. νεᾱνίαις
11. πολῖται (2)
12. νεᾱνίου
13. ποιητάς
14. νεᾱνίαι (2)
15. νεᾱνίᾱ

II. *Translate; change singulars to plurals and plurals to singulars.*

1. οἱ κακοὶ ἀδελφοί
2. οἱ κακοὶ πολῖται
3. ταῖς κακαῖς ψῡχαῖς
4. ταῖς ἀδίκοις ψῡχαῖς
5. τοὺς ποιητὰς τοὺς κακούς
6. ψῡχὴ ἡ ἀξίᾱ
7. τῷ ἀδίκῳ πολίτῃ
8. τῶν ἀξίων ψῡχῶν
9. τὰ ἔργα τὰ κακά
10. τῷ ἀδίκῳ νεᾱνίᾳ
11. τὴν ἀξίᾱν θάλατταν
12. ἡ γέφῡρα ἡ κακή

III. *Translate; place a period at the end of each nominal sentence.*

1. ὁ κακὸς ἀδελφός
2. ὁ ἀδελφὸς ὁ κακός
3. κακὸς ὁ ἀδελφός
4. ὁ ἀδελφὸς κακός
5. ἀδελφὸς ὁ κακός

6. ἡ τοῦ ἀδελφοῦ ψῡχὴ ἡ ἄδικος
7. ἡ τοῦ ἀδελφοῦ ψῡχὴ ἄδικος
8. ἄδικος ἡ τοῦ ἀδελφοῦ ψῡχή
9. ἡ ψῡχὴ ἀξίᾱ
10. ἀξίᾱ ἡ ψῡχή
11. ἔργα τὰ ἄδικα
12. τὰ ἔργα ἄδικα

IV. *Here are some conditional sentences in English. In each:*

   (a) *identify the protasis and the apodosis;*
   (b) *name the equivalent Greek conditional sentence;*
   (c) *give the formula for the protasis and the apodosis of the Greek conditional sentence.*

1. If she wins, she will celebrate.
2. If he should win, he would celebrate.
3. If she wins, she celebrates.
4. If he won, he celebrated.
5. If he were winning, he would be celebrating.
6. If she had won, she would have celebrated.
7. He loses an hour's pay if he is late.
8. If a letter was wrongly addressed, I returned it.
9. You will be sorry if you do that.
10. If you were having fun, you would not be so anxious to leave.
11. I would have gotten a bonus if I had finished on time.
12. If it should snow tomorrow, what would you do?

V. *Identify the conditional sentences; translate.*

1. ἐὰν τοῖς θεοῖς θύσῃς, δῶρα πέμψουσιν.
2. εἰ τοῖς θεοῖς θύσαιτε, δῶρα πέμψαιεν ἄν.
3. εἰ τοῖς θεοῖς θύσαιτε, δῶρα ἔπεμπον.
4. ἐὰν τοῖς θεοῖς θύσῃς, δῶρα πέμπουσιν.
5. εἰ τοῖς θεοῖς ἐθύσατε, δῶρα ἔπεμψαν ἄν.
6. εἰ τοῖς θεοῖς ἐθύετε, δῶρα ἔπεμπον ἄν.
7. ἐὰν τοὺς ἀδελφοὺς μὴ φυλάττω, λύσουσι τὴν δημοκρατίᾱν.
8. εἰ τοὺς ἀδελφοὺς ἐφύλαττον, οὐκ ἂν ἔλῡον τὴν δημοκρατίᾱν.
9. λύουσι τὴν δημοκρατίᾱν, ἐὰν τοὺς ἀδελφοὺς μὴ φυλάττω.
10. εἰ τοὺς ἀδελφοὺς μὴ ἐφύλαξα, ἔλῡσαν ἂν τὴν δημοκρατίᾱν.
11. εἰ τοὺς ἀδελφοὺς μὴ φυλάττοιμι, λύοιεν ἂν τὴν δημοκρατίᾱν.
12. εἰ τοὺς ἀδελφοὺς μὴ φυλάττοιμι, ἔλῡον τὴν δημοκρατίᾱν.

EXERCISES

I. 1. ἐὰν αἱ μοῦσαι τὸν ἀγαθὸν ποιητὴν εὖ διδάξωσιν, γράψει καλὸν
       βιβλίον περὶ τῶν ἐν ἀγορᾷ θυσιῶν.

    2. ἡ μὲν μάχη στρατιώταις κακή, ἀγαθὴ δὲ ἡ νίκη.

    3. ὦ φίλε στρατιῶτα, εἰ τὴν χώρᾱν μετὰ τῶν δικαίων ἀνθρώπων
       ἐφύλαττες, οἱ νεᾱνίαι οἱ ἀπὸ τῆς νήσου οὐκ ἂν ἔλῡον τὴν
       εἰρήνην.

    4. ἆρα τοὺς καλοὺς καὶ ἀγαθοὺς ὁπλίτᾱς παρὰ τῇ γεφύρᾳ τέταχας ἵνα
       μετὰ τὴν μάχην φυλάττωσι τὴν χώρᾱν;

    5. εἰ οἱ ποιηταὶ βιβλία περὶ δίκης γράψειαν, ταῖς μούσαις, ταῖς
       ποιητῶν θεοῖς, ἔθῡον. δίκαιοι γὰρ οἱ ποιηταί.

    6. εἰ τὴν δημοκρατίᾱν λύοιτε, ὦ κακοὶ πολῖται, λύοιτ᾽ ἂν καὶ τὴν ἐν
       ταῖς καλαῖς νήσοις εἰρήνην.

    7. εἰ τοὺς στρατιώτᾱς εἰς τὴν μάχην σὺν ὅπλοις ἔπεμψας, τοὺς νεᾱνίᾱς
       ἐν τῇ ἀγορᾷ ἐτάξαμεν ἂν ὡς τὰς οἰκίᾱς φυλάττοιεν.

    8. ἡ μὲν τοῦ νεᾱνίου ψῡχὴ δικαίᾱ, ἡ δὲ τοῦ στρατιώτου ψῡχὴ ἄδικος.

    9. θύω τῇ καλῇ θεῷ, ἐὰν ἀγαθὸν ζῷον πέμψῃς.

   10. ἐὰν κακοὺς ἀνθρώπους εἰς πόλεμον πέμψωμεν, ἀγαθοὺς ἀνθρώπους
       θάψομεν.

   11. ἄξιοι ἀρχῆς οἱ πολῖται οἱ ἀγαθοὶ καὶ δίκαιοι. ἐθέλουσι γὰρ παῦσαι
       τὸν κακὸν πόλεμον.

   12. μοῖρα στρατιώτου ἡ μάχη.

   13. ὅπως ἀγαθὸν βιβλίον γράψειεν, ὁ ποιητὴς ὁ δίκαιος τοῖς θεοῖς ζῷα
       καλὰ ἔθῡεν.

   14. εἰ ὁ φίλος Ὅμηρος τῇ θεῷ θύειν μὴ ἠθέλησεν, ἀγαθὸν βιβλίον περὶ
       ἀνθρώπων ἀρετῆς οὐκ ἂν ἔγραψεν.

   15. ὦ φίλοι, ἐὰν διὰ τὴν τοῦ θεοῦ βουλὴν λύσωμεν τὴν δημοκρατίᾱν,
       πέμψομεν τοὺς πολίτᾱς τοὺς ἀρχῆς ἀναξίους ἐκ τῆς χώρᾱς
       παρὰ τοὺς ἐν τῇ νήσῳ ξένους.

   16. ἀγαθὴ δὴ τοῖς ἀνθρώποις ἡ νίκης ἡμέρᾱ.

   17. εἰ τὰ τῶν θεῶν ἔργα παιδεύσαι τὸν νεᾱνίᾱν τὸν ἐν τῇ οἰκίᾳ, οὐκ
       ἂν ἐθέλοι ὅπλα πέμπειν παρὰ τοὺς στρατιώτᾱς τοὺς ἀδίκους.

18. εἰ ὁ θεὸς τὸν φίλον ποιητὴν κελεύοι τοὺς νεανίας διδάσκειν, τῇ
μούσῃ ἔθυεν.

19. ἐπειδὴ οἱ ἓξ ἄγγελοι οἱ παρὰ τῶν ξένων δῶρ᾽ ἔπεμψαν καὶ τῇ
βουλῇ καὶ τῇ ἐκκλησίᾳ, ὁ δῆμος οὐκ ἐθέλει τοὺς ἀγαθοὺς
ὁπλίτᾱς τάξαι εἰς μάχην.

20. εἰ χρῡσὸν ἢ στέφανον τοῖς ἄθλου ἀξίοις ὁπλίταις ἔπεμπες, ὦ νεᾱνίᾱ,
οὐκ ἂν ἔλῡον τὴν εἰρήνην.

21. ἐὰν τὴν μάχην μὴ παύσητε, καλοὺς ὁπλίτᾱς διὰ τῆς χώρᾱς παρὰ
τὴν θάλατταν πέμψομεν ἵνα λύσωσι τοὺς δικαίους φίλους τοὺς
ἐν τῇ οἰκίᾳ.

22. οἱ ἀγαθοὶ πολῖται δῶρα πέμπουσιν ἐὰν οἱ ποιηταὶ οἱ χρῡσοῦ
ἄξιοι βιβλία γράψωσι περὶ δίκης.

23. πάλαι τοὺς ἀδίκους πολίτᾱς παρὰ τῇ θαλάττῃ ἐθάπτετε, ἀλλὰ νῦν
τοὺς ἀνθρώπους τοὺς κακοὺς καὶ ἀδίκους καὶ ἀναξίους πέμπετ᾽
εἰς τὴν νῆσον τὴν οὐ καλήν.

24. ἄθλου ἀνάξιος ἡ τοῦ κακοῦ πολίτου ψῡχή. καίτοι δῶρα κακοῖς
πολίταις πέμπειν ἐθέλετε.

25. ἐὰν χρῡσὸν μὴ πέμπητε, τοὺς ἀγαθοὺς νεᾱνίᾱς τὴν τέχνην διδάσκειν
οὐκ ἐθέλω.

26. πρὸ τῆς μάχης   27. νεᾱνίαι οἱ ἀγαθοί
    μετὰ τῶν στρατιωτῶν   ἀγαθοὶ οἱ νεᾱνίαι
    μετὰ τὸν πόλεμον   ἡ καλὴ γέφῡρα
    περὶ λόγους   ἡ γέφῡρα καλή
    περὶ ταῖς οἰκίαις   φίλος ὁ ποιητής
    σὺν τοῖς θεοῖς
    διδάξαι
    τεταχέναι

28. ὁ ποιητὴς ὁ ἀγαθὸς ἄξιος τοῖς πολίταις διδάσκειν τοὺς νεᾱνίᾱς.

II. 1. If the poet writes a good book about battle, the young men will dissolve
       the peace.

   2. If you (pl.) should sacrifice animals to the gods, we would stop the war.

   3. If I had guarded the island, you would have guarded the bridge.

   4. The citizens refused to send animals in order that the soldiers on the
      island might sacrifice to the gods.

   5. The soul of the unjust man is not worthy of the prize.

READINGS

A. Menander, *Γνῶμαι μονόστιχοι*

Excerpts from a collection of one-line quotations from the plays of Menander.

293. κακὸν φέρουσι καρπὸν οἱ κακοὶ φίλοι.

303. καλὸν φέρουσι καρπὸν οἱ σεμνοὶ τρόποι.

316. λῦπαι γὰρ ἀνθρώποισι[1] τίκτουσιν νόσον.

  56. ἄλυπον ἄξεις τὸν βίον χωρὶς γάμου.

217. ἡ γὰρ παράκαιρος ἡδονὴ τίκτει βλάβην.

ἄγω, ἄξω, ἤγαγον, ἦχα, ἦγμαι, ἤχθην   lead

ἄλυπος, ἄλυπον   without pain

βίος, βίου, ὁ   life, means of living

βλάβη, βλάβης, ἡ   harm

γάμος, γάμου, ὁ   wedding, marriage

γνώμη, γνώμης, ἡ   opinion, judgment

ἡδονή, ἡδονῆς, ἡ   pleasure

κακός, κακή, κακόν   bad

καλός, καλή, καλόν   beautiful, noble, good

καρπός, καρποῦ, ὁ   fruit

λύπη, λύπης, ἡ   pain, grief

μονόστιχος, μονόστιχον   consisting of one line

νόσος, νόσου, ἡ   sickness

παράκαιρος, παράκαιρον   ill-timed

σεμνός, σεμνή, σεμνόν   august, majestic, honorable

τίκτω, τέξομαι, ἔτεκον, τέτοκα, ——, ——   bear, give birth to

τρόπος, τρόπου, ὁ   way, manner; character

φέρω, οἴσω, ἤνεγκα/ἤνεγκον, ἐνήνοχα, ἐνήνεγμαι, ἠνέχθην   bring, bear, carry;
    (*mid.*) win

χωρίς (*prep.* + *gen.*)   without

1. ἀνθρώποισι = ἀνθρώποις

B. *The Gospel According to John*, Chapter 1

Ἐν ἀρχῇ ἦν ὁ λόγος, καὶ ὁ λόγος ἦν πρὸς τὸν θεόν, καὶ θεὸς ἦν ὁ λόγος.
οὗτος ἦν ἐν ἀρχῇ πρὸς τὸν θεόν.

ἀρχή, ἀρχῆς, ἡ   beginning; rule, empire

ἦν (*third person sing., imperf. indic. active of the verb "to be"*)
   he/she/it was, there was

οὗτος, αὕτη, τοῦτο (*demonstrative adjective/pronoun*) this, that

πρός (*prep.*) (+ *gen.*) in the eyes of, in the name of; (+ *dat.*) near; in addition to; (+ *acc.*) toward, with, in the presence of

UNIT
5

43. PASSIVE VOICE

All verb forms seen thus far have been in the **active voice**, in which the
subject performs the action: John loves Mary. In the **passive voice**, the
subject of the verb receives the action of the verb: John is loved by Mary.

Drills I and II, p. 133, may now be done.

1. PRESENT INDICATIVE PASSIVE

To form the present indicative passive, add the following endings to the present
tense stem:

	S	P
1	-ομαι	-ομεθα
2	-η/-ει	-εσθε
3	-εται	-ονται

Thus, the forms of the present indicative passive of παιδεύω are as follows:

	S	
1	παιδεύομαι	I am being educated I am educated (habitually)
2	παιδεύη/παιδεύει	you are being educated you are educated (habitually)
3	παιδεύεται	he/she/it is being educated he/she/it is educated (habitually)

111

	P	
1	παιδευόμεθα	we are being educated we are educated (habitually)
2	παιδεύεσθε	you are being educated you are educated (habitually)
3	παιδεύονται	they are being educated they are educated (habitually)

Observations: (1) The endings of the present indicative passive consist of the thematic vowel -ε/o- and the **primary passive person markers** -μαι, -σαι, -ται, -μεθα, -σθε, -νται. In the second person singular, the original form of the ending was *-εσαι. The **intervocalic -σ-** (one occurring between two vowels) dropped out, and the remaining vowel and diphthong combined to give the alternative endings -η and -ει, *with no difference in meaning.*

(2) The alternative ending -ει of the second person singular, present indicative passive is the same as that of the third person singular, present indicative active. Thus, without any context, there are two possible sets of translations for the form παιδεύει: "you are being educated/are educated (habitually)" and "he/she/it is educating/educates (habitually)." Context usually allows one to identify the person and voice of the form.

(3) The alternative ending -η of the second person singular, present indicative passive is the same as that of the third person singular, present subjunctive active. Context usually allows one to distinguish between the indicative παιδεύη ("you are being educated/are educated [habitually]") and the subjunctive (e.g., in a purpose clause, "in order that he/she/it may be educating/may educate [habitually]").

2. IMPERFECT INDICATIVE PASSIVE

To form the imperfect indicative passive, prefix the past indicative augment to the present tense stem. To the augmented present tense stem add the following endings:

	S	P
1	-ομην	-ομεθα
2	-ου	-εσθε
3	-ετο	-οντο

Thus, the forms of the imperfect indicative passive of παιδεύω are as follows:

S

1	ἐπαιδευόμην	I was being educated
		I used to be educated
2	ἐπαιδεύου	you were being educated
		you used to be educated
3	ἐπαιδεύετο	he/she/it was being educated
		he/she/it used to be educated

P

1	ἐπαιδευόμεθα	we were being educated
		we used to be educated
2	ἐπαιδεύεσθε	you were being educated
		you used to be educated
3	ἐπαιδεύοντο	they were being educated
		they used to be educated

Observation: The endings of the imperfect indicative passive consist of the thematic vowel -ε/ο- and the **secondary passive person markers** -μην, -σο, -το, -μεθα, -σθε, -ντο. In the second person singular, the original form of the ending was *-εσο. The intervocalic -σ- dropped out, and the two vowels combined to give the ending -ου.

3. PRESENT SUBJUNCTIVE PASSIVE

To form the present subjunctive passive, add the following endings to the present tense stem:

	S	P
1	-ωμαι	-ωμεθα
2	-ῃ	-ησθε
3	-ηται	-ωνται

Thus, the forms of the present subjunctive passive of παιδεύω are as follows:

	S	P
1	παιδεύωμαι	παιδευώμεθα
2	παιδεύῃ	παιδεύησθε
3	παιδεύηται	παιδεύωνται

Observations: (1) No translation of any subjunctive is ever given in the paradigms. A present subjunctive passive differs from a present
subjunctive active in voice alone and will be used in the same
kinds of clauses as the present subjunctive active.

(2) As do the endings of the subjunctive active, the endings of
the subjunctive passive show a lengthening of the thematic
vowel of the ending. Compare, e.g., the first person plurals of
the

present indicative active   παιδεύομεν
present subjunctive active   παιδεύωμεν
present indicative passive   παιδευόμεθα
present subjunctive passive   παιδευώμεθα.

(3) Note that the present subjunctive passive uses the primary
person markers -μαι, -σαι, -ται, -μεθα, -σθε, -νται.

(4) The original form of the second person singular, present
subjunctive passive was *-ησαι. The intervocalic -σ- dropped
out, and the remaining vowel and diphthong combined to
give the ending -ῃ. Since this ending has two other uses,
the form παιδεύῃ can be one of three different things:

third person singular, present subjunctive active
second person singular, present indicative passive
second person singular, present subjunctive passive.

Context usually allows one to determine the meaning.

4. PRESENT OPTATIVE PASSIVE

To form the present optative passive, add the following endings to the present
tense stem:

	S	P
1	-οιμην	-οιμεθα
2	-οιο	-οισθε
3	-οιτο	-οιντο

Thus, the forms of the present optative passive of παιδεύω are as follows:

	S	P
1	παιδευοίμην	παιδευοίμεθα
2	παιδεύοιο	παιδεύοισθε
3	παιδεύοιτο	παιδεύοιντο

Observations: (1) No translation of any optative is ever given in the paradigms. A present optative passive differs from a present optative active in voice alone and is used in the same kinds of clauses as the present optative active.

(2) As in the endings of the present optative active, all the endings of the present optative passive begin with the initial diphthong -οι- (thematic vowel -ο- and optative suffix -ι-). Compare, e.g., the first person plural forms of the

present indicative active	παιδεύομεν
present subjunctive active	παιδεύωμεν
present optative active	παιδεύοιμεν
present indicative passive	παιδευόμεθα
present subjunctive passive	παιδευώμεθα
present optative passive	παιδευοίμεθα

(3) Note that the present optative passive uses the secondary passive person markers -μην, -σο, -το, -μεθα, -σθε, -ντο.

(4) The ending of the second person singular, present optative passive was *-οισο. The intervocalic -σ- dropped out to give the ending -οιο.

5. PRESENT INFINITIVE PASSIVE

To form the present infinitive passive, add to the present tense stem the ending -εσθαι.

Thus, the present infinitive passive of παιδεύω is

παιδεύεσθαι
to be being educated
to be educated

As in the present infinitive active, tense in the present infinitive passive shows progressive/repeated aspect, not time.

6. AORIST INDICATIVE PASSIVE

Unlike the present passive, which is formed from the same tense stem as the present active and which shows its passive voice by the use of passive endings, the aorist passive uses a different tense stem derived from Principal Part VI. The aorist passive endings use *active* person markers; voice is shown by the tense stem itself.

To form the aorist indicative passive, drop the ending -ην from Principal Part VI. There remain the past indicative augment ἐ- and the aorist passive tense stem. To the **augmented aorist passive tense stem** add the following endings:

	S	P
1	-ην	-ημεν
2	-ης	-ητε
3	-η	-ησαν

Thus, the augmented aorist passive tense stem of παιδεύω is ἐπαιδευθ-, and the forms of the aorist indicative passive are as follows:

	S	
1	ἐπαιδεύθην	I was educated
2	ἐπαιδεύθης	you were educated
3	ἐπαιδεύθη	he/she/it was educated

	P	
1	ἐπαιδεύθημεν	we were educated
2	ἐπαιδεύθητε	you were educated
3	ἐπαιδεύθησαν	they were educated

Observation: The aorist passive endings consist of the tense vowel -η- and a set of active person markers: -ν, -ς, —, -μεν, -τε, -σαν (cf., e.g., the imperfect ἐπαίδευον, ἐπαίδευες, ἐπαίδευε-, ἐπαιδεύομεν, ἐπαιδεύετε, and the third person plural, aorist indicative active ἐπαίδευσαν [where, of course, the -σ- is part of the tense stem]). Thus, in the aorist indicative passive, voice is shown not by the person marker but by the aorist passive tense stem alone.

7. AORIST SUBJUNCTIVE PASSIVE

To form the aorist subjunctive passive, add the subjunctive active endings to the **unaugmented aorist passive tense stem**, which is obtained by dropping the past indicative augment and the ending -ην from Principal Part VI.

Thus, the unaugmented aorist passive tense stem of παιδεύω is παιδευθ-, and the forms of the aorist subjunctive passive of παιδεύω are as follows:

	S	P
1	παιδευθῶ	παιδευθῶμεν
2	παιδευθῇς	παιδευθῆτε
3	παιδευθῇ	παιδευθῶσι(ν)

Observations: (1) As in the aorist indicative passive, voice in the aorist sub-junctive passive is shown by the tense stem alone, and not by the person markers of the endings.

(2) The accent on the aorist subjunctive passive in all its forms is a circumflex on the initial vowel of the ending. The original form was παιδευθέω, with -ε-, a short-vowel grade of the tense vowel -η- of the indicative, and the usual subjunctive active endings. The two vowels contracted to give -ῶ, etc.

8. AORIST OPTATIVE PASSIVE

To form the aorist optative passive, add the following endings to the un-augmented aorist passive tense stem:

	S	P
1	-ειην	-εῖμεν/-ειημεν
2	-ειης	-εῖτε/-ειητε
3	-ειη	-εῖεν/-ειησαν

Thus, the forms of the aorist optative passive of παιδεύω are as follows:

	S	P
1	παιδευθείην	παιδευθεῖμεν/παιδευθείημεν
2	παιδευθείης	παιδευθεῖτε/παιδευθείητε
3	παιδευθείη	παιδευθεῖεν/παιδευθείησαν

Observations: (1) The optative passive ending -ειην can be analyzed as con-sisting of the tense vowel -ε- (short-vowel grade of the -η- of ἐπαιδεύθην; cf. παιδευθῶ < *παιδευθέω) + -ιη- (optative suffix) + -ν (first person singular person marker; cf. the imperfect indicative active ἐπαίδευον and the aorist indica-tive passive ἐπαιδεύθην). In the plural, the optative suffix was either -ι- or -ιη-, both of which combined with the tense vowel -ε- to form the diphthong -ει-.

Note that in the third person plural the ending with the optative suffix -ι- uses the person marker -εν; the alternative ending with the optative suffix -ιη- uses the person marker -σαν. There is no difference in meaning between the alternative forms.

(2) As in the aorist indicative and subjunctive passive, voice is shown by the tense stem alone, not by the person markers of the endings.

(3) NOTE THAT THE ACCENT IN THE AORIST OPTATIVE PASSIVE NEVER GOES BACK BEYOND THE -ι- OF THE ENDING. It is acute or circumflex as the rules for the possibilities of accent dictate.

9. AORIST INFINITIVE PASSIVE

To form the aorist infinitive passive, add to the unaugmented aorist passive tense stem the ending **-ῆναι**.

Thus, the aorist infinitive passive of παιδεύω is

> παιδευθῆναι
> to be educated

Like all the other infinitives, the aorist infinitive passive shows aspect only. Compare:

present infinitive passive	παιδεύεσθαι	to be being educated
		to be educated (habitually)
aorist infinitive passive	παιδευθῆναι	to be educated (once and for all)

Observation: IN AN INFINITIVE, THE SYLLABLE PRECEDING THE ENDING -ναι IS ALWAYS ACCENTED.

10. FUTURE INDICATIVE PASSIVE

The future indicative passive is formed on a stem different from that of the future indicative active. In this respect, it is similar to the aorist indicative passive, which is also formed on a stem different from that of the aorist indicative active.

To form the future indicative passive, to the *unaugmented aorist passive tense stem* add the suffix -ησ- to form the **future passive tense stem.** To the future passive tense stem add the same endings as those used in the present indicative passive.

Thus, the unaugmented aorist passive tense stem of παιδεύω is παιδευθ-, and the future passive tense stem is παιδευθησ-. The forms of the future indicative passive of παιδεύω are as follows:

S

1	παιδευθήσομαι	I shall be educated I shall be being educated
2	παιδευθήσει/ παιδευθήσῃ	you will be educated you will be being educated
3	παιδευθήσεται	he/she/it will be educated he/she/it will be being educated

P

1	παιδευθησόμεθα	we shall be educated we shall be being educated
2	παιδευθήσεσθε	you will be educated you will be being educated
3	παιδευθήσονται	they will be educated they will be being educated

Observations: (1) The passive voice is shown in the future indicative passive by the future *passive tense stem* and by the *passive endings*.

(2) The -σ- of the future passive tense stem is similar to the -σ- which appears so frequently in the future indicative active. Cf. παιδεύσω.

(3) Like the future indicative active, the future indicative passive can express either simple or progressive/repeated aspect.

11. PERFECT INDICATIVE PASSIVE

To form the perfect indicative passive, obtain the **perfect passive tense stem** by dropping the ending -μαι from Principal Part V. To the perfect passive tense stem add the following endings:

	S	P
1	-μαι	-μεθα
2	-σαι	-σθε
3	-ται	-νται

Thus, the perfect passive tense stem of παιδεύω is πεπαιδευ-, and the forms of the perfect indicative passive are as follows:

	S	
1	πεπαίδευμαι	I have been educated
2	πεπαίδευσαι	you have been educated
3	πεπαίδευται	he/she/it has been educated
	P	
1	πεπαιδεύμεθα	we have been educated
2	πεπαίδευσθε	you have been educated
3	πεπαίδευνται	they have been educated

Observations: (1) The endings of the perfect indicative passive are simply the person markers of the primary passive endings without the thematic vowel. Compare the first person singular, perfect indicative passive πεπαίδευμαι with the first person singular, present indicative passive παιδεύομαι.

(2) Note that the second person singular, perfect indicative passive ending retains the -σ- that had dropped out of the other second person singular forms; cf., e.g., παιδεύῃ < *παιδεύεσαι.

(3) Like the perfect indicative active, the perfect indicative passive shows completed aspect in present time.

12. PLUPERFECT INDICATIVE PASSIVE

To form the pluperfect indicative passive, prefix the past indicative augment to the perfect passive tense stem. To the **augmented perfect passive tense stem** add the following endings:

	S	P
1	-μην	-μεθα
2	-σο	-σθε
3	-το	-ντο

Thus, the augmented perfect passive tense stem of παιδεύω is ἐπεπαιδευ-, and the forms of the pluperfect indicative passive are as follows:

	S	
1	ἐπεπαιδεύμην	I had been educated
2	ἐπεπαίδευσο	you had been educated
3	ἐπεπαίδευτο	he/she/it had been educated

P

1	ἐπεπαιδεύμεθα	we had been educated
2	ἐπεπαίδευσθε	you had been educated
3	ἐπεπαίδευντο	they had been educated

Observations: (1) The endings of the pluperfect indicative passive are simply the person markers of the secondary passive endings without the thematic vowel. Compare the first person singular, pluperfect indicative passive ἐπεπαιδεύμην with the first person singular, imperfect indicative passive ἐπαιδευόμην.

(2) Note that the second person singular of the pluperfect indicative passive retains the -σ- that had dropped out of other second person singular forms; cf., e.g., ἐπαιδεύου > *ἐπαιδεύεσο.

(3) Like the pluperfect indicative active, the pluperfect indicative passive indicates action complete from the point of view of past time.

13. PERFECT INFINITIVE PASSIVE

To form the perfect infinitive passive, add to the perfect passive tense stem the ending -σθαι.

Thus, the perfect infinitive passive of παιδεύω is

πεπαιδεῦσθαι
to have been educated

The perfect infinitive passive shows completed aspect only.

Observations: (1) The ending of the perfect infinitive passive is the same as that of the present infinitive passive except that it lacks the thematic vowel. Compare the present infinitive passive παιδεύεσθαι with the perfect infinitive passive πεπαιδεῦσθαι.

(2) THE PERFECT INFINITIVE PASSIVE DOES NOT HAVE RECESSIVE ACCENT; IT IS ALWAYS ACCENTED ON THE PENULT. Final -αι, as usual, counts as short for purposes of accentuation.

Drill III.1–15, page 133, may now be done.

14. CONSONANT STEMS

When the perfect passive tense stem ends in a vowel or a diphthong, as in
λέλυμαι or πεπαίδευμαι, adding the endings of the perfect passive or the pluperfect passive presents no problem. But when the perfect passive tense stem
ends in a consonant, adding the endings produced awkward clusters of consonants at the juncture between stem and ending. Greek altered many such consonant clusters in order to make them easier to pronounce, and Principal Part V
often has the final consonant of the stem in an altered form. For example, in
the verb γράφω, the original first person singular, perfect indicative passive had
been *γέγραφμαι, but the final -φ- of the stem was changed to -μ- before
the -μ- of the ending -μαι. Thus, one cannot simply drop the ending -μαι from
Principal Part V and use γεγραμ- as a tense stem. Instead, one must add the
endings to the *original* consonant of the tense stem and make any changes
necessary.

Whatever the original final consonant of the stem may have been, in the verbs
learned thus far the various combinations of final consonant and -μαι give only
three possible results in Principal Part V:

  -μμαι (where the original consonant was a labial [π, β, φ]):
    e.g., γέγρα**μμ**αι, τέθα**μμ**αι, πέπε**μμ**αι

  -γμαι (where the original consonant was a palatal [κ, γ, χ]):
    e.g., δεδίδα**γμ**αι, πεφύλα**γμ**αι, τέτα**γμ**αι

  -σμαι (where the original consonant usually was a dental [τ, δ, θ] or
    σ): e.g., κεκέλευ**σμ**αι

Changes must be made in the final consonants of the stems of these verbs in
accordance with the patterns given below. The perfect passive of verbs not
following these patterns will be given in the vocabulary notes as these verbs are
introduced.

1. PERFECT INDICATIVE PASSIVE OF CONSONANT STEMS

  -μμαι

S 1 γέγρα**μμ**αι (*γέγραφμαι)   πέπε**μμ**αι (*πέπεμπμαι)

  2 γέγρα**ψ**αι (*γέγραφσαι)   πέπε**μψ**αι (*πέπεμπσαι)

  3 γέγρα**πτ**αι (*γέγραφται)   πέπε**μπτ**αι (πέπεμπται)

P	1	γεγράμμεθα (*γεγράφμεθα)	πεπέμμεθα (*πεπέμπμεθα)
	2	γέγραφθε (*γέγραφσθε)	πέπεμφθε (*πέπεμπσθε)
	3	*** (*γεγράφνται)	*** (*πεπέμπνται)

Observations: (1) Most verbs with a Principal Part V ending in -μμαι will be conjugated like γέγραμμαι; those that are not will be pointed out in the vocabulary notes. Note that any labial (π, β, φ) gives ψ in the second person singular, π in the third person singular, and μ in the first person plural. In the second person plural, the σ of -σθε is dropped and the final labial of the stem becomes the aspirate φ. In the third person plural, the original form *γεγράφνται was replaced by a compound form which is given in the Appendix.

(2) In πέπεμμαι the stem is πεπεμπ-, to which -μαι was added. The resulting form *πέπεμπμαι was simplified to πέπεμμαι; the same simplification also appears in the first person plural πεπέμμεθα. Elsewhere, both the nasal and the labial of the tense stem πεπεμπ- appear, with the labial the same as that in γέγραμμαι: πέπεμψαι, πέπεμπται, πέπεμφθε.

		-γμαι		-σμαι
S	1	πεφύλαγμαι	(*πεφύλακμαι)	κεκέλευσμαι
	2	πεφύλαξαι	(*πεφύλακσαι)	κεκέλευσαι
	3	πεφύλακται	(πεφύλακται)	κεκέλευσται
P	1	πεφυλάγμεθα	(*πεφυλάκμεθα)	κεκελεύσμεθα
	2	πεφύλαχθε	(*πεφύλακσθε)	κεκέλευσθε
	3	***	(*πεφυλάκνται)	***

Observations: (1) In verbs with a Principal Part V ending in -γμαι, the palatal (κ, γ, χ) appears as a γ before the μ of the first person singular and plural πεφύλαγμαι and πεφυλάγμεθα, as a ξ in the second person singular πεφύλαξαι, and as a κ in the third person singular. In the second person plural, the σ of the ending drops, and the final consonant of the stem becomes the aspirate χ: *πεφύλακσθε > πεφύλαχθε. The third person plural form is a compound which is given in the Appendix.

(2) Most verbs with a Principal Part V ending in -σμαι are conjugated like κεκέλευσμαι; those that are not are pointed

out in the vocabulary notes. The ending is simply added
to the stem with no changes except in the second person
singular and plural, where the combination -σσ- is simplified
to a single -σ-: *κεκέλευσσαι > κεκέλευσαι
*κεκέλευσσθε > κεκέλευσθε.

2. PLUPERFECT INDICATIVE PASSIVE OF CONSONANT STEMS

Exactly the same changes occur in the pluperfect indicative passive of consonant stems as in the perfect indicative passive.

		-μμαι	
S	1	ἐγεγράμμην	ἐπεπέμμην
	2	ἐγέγραψο	ἐπέπεμψο
	3	ἐγέγραπτο	ἐπέπεμπτο
P	1	ἐγεγράμμεθα	ἐπεπέμμεθα
	2	ἐγέγραφθε	ἐπέπεμφθε
	3	***	***

		-γμαι	-σμαι
S	1	ἐπεφυλάγμην	ἐκεκελεύσμην
	2	ἐπεφύλαξο	ἐκεκέλευσο
	3	ἐπεφύλακτο	ἐκεκέλευστο
P	1	ἐπεφυλάγμεθα	ἐκεκελεύσμεθα
	2	ἐπεφύλαχθε	ἐκεκέλευσθε
	3	***	***

3. PERFECT INFINITIVE PASSIVE OF CONSONANT STEMS

γεγράφθαι   πεπέμφθαι   πεφυλάχθαι   κεκελεῦσθαι

Observation: In the perfect infinitive passive, the combination of the consonants of the stem and the ending -σθαι produces the same result
as in the second person plural of the perfect indicative passive:
the σ of the ending is dropped and a final labial or palatal of the
stem is aspirated. Note also that the accent is fixed on the penult,
and that the -αι of the endings counts, as usual, as short for purposes of accentuation.

Drill III.16–30, pages 133–34, may now be done.

44. GENITIVE OF PERSONAL AGENT

DATIVE OF PERSONAL AGENT WITH THE PERFECT AND
   PLUPERFECT PASSIVE

DATIVE OF MEANS

With most passive verbs, the personal agent, i.e., the person *by whom* the action of the verb is performed, is expressed by the preposition ὑπό + the genitive. This is called the **genitive of personal agent**.

ὁ λόγος **ὑπὸ τοῦ Ὁμήρου** γράφεται.
The speech is being written **by Homer**.

ὁ πόλεμος **ὑπὸ τῶν στρατιωτῶν** ἐπαύθη.
The war was stopped **by the soldiers**.

With the perfect and the pluperfect tenses, the personal agent is expressed by the dative case without any preposition.   This is called the **dative of personal agent.**

ὁ λόγος **Ὁμήρῳ** γέγραπται.
The speech has been written **by Homer**.

ὁ πόλεμος **τοῖς στρατιώταις** ἐπέπαυτο.
The war had been stopped **by the soldiers**.

A thing with which something is done is put in the dative (the **dative of means** or **instrument**) without a preposition.

ὑπὸ τοῦ Ὁμήρου ἐπαύθησαν οἱ στρατιῶται **λόγῳ**.
The soldiers were stopped by Homer **by (means of) a speech**.

Drill IV, page 134, may now be done.

45. SUBSTANTIVE USE OF THE ADJECTIVE

Since both the article and the adjective, as well as the noun, have gender, number, and case, phrases such as ὁ ἀγαθὸς ἄνθρωπος, "the good man," were considered redundant. Where the noun had a general meaning of "man," "woman," or "thing," Greek often left the noun out and let the adjective stand as a noun. Compare the English sentence, "The *good* die young," where the adjective "good" takes on the meaning "good people." This is called the **substantive** use of the adjective, and adjectives so used are called **substantives**. Substantives can stand in any gender, number, or case, and can perform all the functions of nouns in any sentence.

ὁ ἀγαθός	the good man
ἡ ἀγαθή	the good woman
τὸ ἀγαθόν	the good thing, the good
οἱ ἀγαθοί	the good men
ἀγαθοί	good men
ἀγαθά	good things, i.e., goods
δῶρα ταῖς ἀγαθαῖς ἐπέμψαμεν.	We sent gifts to the good women.

46. SUBSTANTIVE USE OF THE ARTICLE

Since the definite article has gender, number, and case, it can, accompanied by an adverb, prepositional phrase, or other modifier, be used as a substantive: its gender and number indicate the person(s) or thing(s) named, and its case shows its relationship to the rest of the sentence.

οἱ ἐν τῇ νήσῳ
the men on the island

τὰς νῦν
the women now
women now (generic use of the article)
women of the present time

τὰ τοῦ πολέμου
the things of war
(= **the affairs** of war)

When two articles used as substantives are contrasted by μέν and δέ, they can be translated by "the one . . . , the other," "some . . . , others."

ὁ μὲν διδάσκει, **ὁ δὲ** διδάσκεται.
The one teaches, **the other** is taught.

τοὺς μὲν πέμπομεν, **τοὺς δὲ** φυλάττομεν.
Some we send, but **others** we guard.
We send **some men** (one group), but we guard **others** (another group).

With a substantive use of an adjective or the article the negative *οὐ* is used for specific substantives, *μή* for generic substantives; cf. Section 16.4, page 29.

οἱ οὐκ ἐν τῇ νήσῳ
those specific men not on the island

οἱ μὴ ἐν τῇ νήσῳ
those not on the island
whoever are not on the island

47. THE ARTICULAR INFINITIVE

The infinitive is a verbal noun. Like other verb forms, the infinitive has *tense* and *voice*. Like the noun, the infinitive can appear in various *cases* which indicate its function in the sentence.

When used with the verb *κελεύω*, "command," the infinitive is an object infinitive, i.e., stands as the direct object of the verb, along with the person commanded (cf. page 102).

τὸν ἀδελφὸν δῶρα πέμψαι κελεύομεν.
We order the brother to send gifts.

In this example, the person commanded, *τὸν ἀδελφόν*, is in the accusative case and is a direct object of *κελεύομεν*. The infinitive *πέμψαι* is also a direct object of *κελεύομεν* and can be considered to stand in the accusative case. But infinitives are *indeclinable verbal nouns*, so that context, not case endings, shows the relation of this infinitive to the rest of the sentence.

Attic Greek also developed a way of employing the infinitive more freely in various cases by having it accompanied by a neuter singular form of the definite article to indicate the infinitive's case. Such an infinitive accompanied by the article is called the **articular infinitive**.

The articular infinitive is often best translated by the English gerund ("writing") rather than by the English infinitive ("to write"). Do not confuse the English gerund, a verbal noun ("*Writing* a book is good"), with the English participle, a verbal adjective ("the man *writing* with a red pen").

The tense of the articular infinitive, like that of the subjunctive, the optative, and other infinitives, indicates aspect, not time: progressive/repeated aspect in the present tense, simple aspect in the aorist tense, and completed aspect in the perfect tense. The articular infinitive can occur in any voice.

Nom. S	τὸ γράφειν	to be writing, to write (habitually), writing
Gen.	τοῦ γράφειν	of writing (progressive/repeated aspect)
Dat.	τῷ γράφειν	by writing (progressive/repeated aspect)
Acc.	τὸ γράφειν	writing (progressive/repeated aspect)
Nom. S	τὸ γράψαι	to write (once and for all), writing
Gen.	τοῦ γράψαι	of writing (once and for all)
Dat.	τῷ γράψαι	by writing (once and for all)
Acc.	τὸ γράψαι	writing (once and for all)
Nom. S	τὸ γεγραφέναι	to have written, having written
Gen.	τοῦ γεγραφέναι	of having written
Dat.	τῷ γεγραφέναι	by having written
Acc.	τὸ γεγραφέναι	having written

An articular infinitive is used like any other noun.

καλὸν **τὸ γράφειν**.
To write is good.
Writing is good.

πρὸ **τοῦ γράψαι**
before **writing**

τῷ γράφειν
by means of writing

διὰ **τὸ γεγραφέναι**
on account of **having written**

The negative of the articular infinitive is μή.

κακὸν τὸ μὴ γράφειν
Not to write is bad.
Not writing is bad.

Compare: οὐ κακὸν τὸ γράφειν.
To write is not bad.
Writing is not bad.

In the second example, the οὐ negates the predicate adjective κακόν.

Drill V, page 134, may now be done.

VOCABULARY

ἄργυρος, ἀργύρου, ὁ	silver
ἀργύριον, ἀργυρίου, τό	small coin; money
ἄρχω, ἄρξω, ἦρξα, ἦρχα,	rule, command (+ *gen.*)
ἦργμαι, ἤρχθην	
βλάπτω, βλάψω, ἔβλαψα, βέβλαφα,	hurt, harm
βέβλαμμαι, ἐβλάβην or ἐβλάφθην	
γῆ, γῆς, ἡ	earth, land
διδάσκαλος, διδασκάλου, ὁ	teacher
δόξα, δόξης, ἡ	expectation, belief; reputation, glory
θάνατος, θανάτου, ὁ	death
ἀθάνατος, ἀθάνατον	undying, immortal
ἱερός, ἱερά, ἱερόν	holy, sacred to (+ *gen.*)
ἱερόν, ἱεροῦ, τό	shrine
ἱκανός, ἱκανή, ἱκανόν	sufficient, capable
ἵππος, ἵππου, ὁ or ἡ	horse, mare
κίνδῡνος, κινδύνου, ὁ	danger
λίθος, λίθου, ὁ	stone
μακρός, μακρά, μακρόν	long, tall
μῑκρός, μῑκρά, μῑκρόν	small, little, short
πεδίον, πεδίου, τό	plain
πείθω, πείσω, ἔπεισα, πέπεικα,	persuade
πέπεισμαι, ἐπείσθην	
πολέμιος, πολεμία, πολέμιον	hostile (+ *dat.*)
πρᾱ́ττω, πρᾱ́ξω, ἔπρᾱξα, πέπρᾱχα	do; fare
(trans.) or πέπρᾱγα (intrans.),	
πέπρᾱγμαι, ἐπρᾱ́χθην	
πρῶτος, πρώτη, πρῶτον	first
ὑπό (prep.) + gen.	by (personal agent); under
+ dat.	under, under the power of
+ acc.	under (with motion); toward (of time)
φόβος, φόβου, ὁ	fear
φοβερός, φοβερά, φοβερόν	fearful

VOCABULARY NOTES

The noun ἀργύριον, ἀργυρίου, τό, "small coin; money," consists of the stem of the word ἄργυρος, ἀργύρου, ὁ, "silver," and the **diminutive suffix -ιον**. A diminutive suffix indicates a small quantity or size of the noun to which it is added, or affection or contempt. The suffix also appears in the noun βιβλίον, βιβλίου, τό, "book," which is a diminutive of the word for papyrus.

In ἄρχω, ἄρξω, ἦρξα, ἦρχα, ἦργμαι, ἤρχθην, "rule, command," the basic root is ἀρχ-. The aspiration is lost in the future, the aorist, and the perfect passive (ἄρξω < *ἄρχσω, ἦρξα < *ἦρχσα, ἦργμαι < *ἦρχμαι). The past indicative augment of a word beginning with a vowel is shown by lengthening the initial vowel: thus ἦρχον, ἦρχες, ἦρχε(ν), etc. in the imperfect indicative. Remember to remove the past indicative augment when forming the aorist subjunctive, optative, and infinitive, e.g., ἄρξωμεν, the first person plural, aorist subjunctive active; ἀρχθῶμεν, the first person plural, aorist subjunctive passive. In the perfect active and passive, the ἠ- is part of the tense stem: thus ἠρχέναι, the perfect infinitive active; cf. ἠθεληκέναι, the perfect infinitive active of ἐθέλω. The pluperfect indicative active is ἤρχη, ἤρχης, ἤρχει(ν), etc. Note that ἄρχω does not take a direct object in the accusative, but instead governs a *genitive*. The related verbal noun ἀρχή, ἀρχῆς, ἡ, "beginning; rule, empire," was given in Unit 4.

In βλάπτω, βλάψω, ἔβλαψα, βέβλαφα, βέβλαμμαι, ἐβλάβην or ἐβλάφθην, "hurt, harm," the basic root is βλαβ-. The present is formed with the suffix -ιω = [yo]: *βλάβιω> βλάπτω. In the future and in the aorist, the final vowel of the root βλαβ- combines with -σ- to give -ψ-. Note the aspirated perfect active (cf. πέπομφα, πεφύλαχα, τέταχα). The perfect passive comes from *βέβλαβμαι. In the aorist passive there are alternative forms with no difference in meaning: ἐβλάφθην, which is formed with the suffix -θ-, and ἐβλάβην with no suffix; both must be learned. The future passive is formed from ἐβλάβην: thus βλαβήσομαι. Note the similarities and differences between βλάπτω and θάπτω < *θάφιω.

Note the circumflex accent on γῆ, γῆς, ἡ, "earth, land." The accent remains a circumflex throughout the declension, e.g., τὴν γῆν. The word means "earth" as opposed to sky or sea, as well as the "earth" the farmer works. It can also be synonymous with χώρᾱ, χώρᾱς, ἡ as meaning "country" as opposed to city. Γῆ is also the mother of the gods in Greek mythology.

διδάσκαλος, διδασκάλου, ὁ, "teacher," is an agent noun formed from the present stem of the verb διδάσκω, "teach."

The primary meaning of δόξα, δόξης, ἡ is "expectation, belief, opinion." The opinion that people have of a person is that person's "reputation," and a positive reputation is that person's "glory." Often, but not always, δόξα as "belief" is contrasted with "knowledge."

In ἀθάνατος, ἀθάνατον note the alpha privative and the fact that the compound adjective has only two endings; cf. ἄδικος, ἄδικον.

With the adjective ἱερός, ἱερά, ἱερόν, "holy, sacred to (+ gen.)," Greek idiom uses the genitive case to express the deity to whom someone or something is sacred. ἱερόν, ἱεροῦ, τό, "shrine," is a neuter singular substantive use of the adjective.

The adjective ἱκανός, ἱκανή, ἱκανόν means "sufficient" when used of things, "capable" when used of people. Like ἄξιος, ἀξίᾱ, ἄξιον, "worthy," of Unit 4, ἱκανός, ἱκανή, ἱκανόν can be followed by an epexegetical ("explaining") infinitive: ὁ ἱκανὸς τοὺς πολίτᾱς πεῖσαι, "the man capable to persuade the citizens, the man capable of persuading the citizens."

Note that ἵππος, ἵππου, ὁ or ἡ is either masculine, "stallion," or feminine, "mare." The gender will be indicated by an article or adjective; cf. ὁ θεός, "god"; ἡ θεός, "goddess."

The root of πείθω, πείσω, ἔπεισα, πέπεικα, πέπεισμαι, ἐπείσθην, "persuade," is πειθ-. The final -θ- of the root disappears in the future, the aorist, and the perfect active. In the perfect passive and the aorist passive, it has been replaced by -σ-: πέπεισμαι, ἐπείσθην. A -σ- also appears in Principal Parts V and VI of κελεύω: κεκέλευσμαι, ἐκελεύσθην. Like κελεύω, πείθω can also be followed by an object infinitive: πείθω someone (in the accusative) to do (in the infinitive) something.

πολέμιος, πολεμίᾱ, πολέμιον, "hostile," is derived from the noun πόλεμος, πολέμου, ὁ, "war." The person toward whom one feels hostile is put in the dative case: οἱ ἀδελφοὶ οἱ τοῖς ἐν τῇ νήσῳ πολέμιοι, "the brothers hostile to the men on the island." As a substantive, the word means "enemy," not as a personal enemy but as someone against whom one fights in war.

The root of πρᾱττω, πρᾱξω, ἔπρᾱξα, πέπρᾱχα (*trans.*) or πέπρᾱγα (*intrans.*), πέπρᾱγμαι, ἐπρᾱχθην, "do; fare," is πρᾱκ-, with a long alpha. Principal Part I is formed with the suffix ιω: *πρᾱκιω > πρᾱττω. The principal parts have a pattern similar to that of φυλάττω and τάττω. πρᾱττω can be either transitive or intransitive: κακὸν ἔργον πρᾱττω, "I am doing an evil deed"; εὖ πρᾱττω, "I do/fare well." The aspirated perfect is only transitive: κακὸν ἔργον πέπρᾱχα, "I have done an evil deed"; πέπρᾱγα is only intransitive: εὖ πέπρᾱγα, "I have done/fared well."

Note that in Greek the expression "to do something to someone" can take a **double accusative**: κακὸν πράττω τοὺς στρατιώτᾱς, "I do evil to the soldiers." Cf. παιδεύω τοὺς στρατιώτᾱς τὴν τέχνην, "I teach the soldiers the art."

Adjectives of time and place, such as πρῶτος, πρώτη, πρῶτον, "first," in the predicate position are the equivalent of English adverbs.

> οἱ νεᾱνίαι τὴν εἰρήνην πρῶτοι ἔλῡσαν.
> The young men destroyed the peace first.

When used of spatial relations, the preposition ὑπό follows the pattern of παρά with the dative, "to be under," and with the accusative, "to go under." With the genitive, ὑπό can mean motion "away from under" or even in certain phrases "being under," e.g., τὰ ὑπὸ γῆς, "the things under the earth." With the genitive of personal agent, ὑπό means "by."

The adjective φοβερός, φοβερά, φοβερόν, "fearful," is derived from the noun φόβος, φόβου, ὁ, "fear." The adjective can be used of the person or thing feeling the fear or causing the fear.

COGNATES AND DERIVATIVES

ἄργυρος	Argentina (the **silvery** land, from the Latin cognate *argentum*)
γῆ	geography, apogee
δόξα	paradox (something that, contrary to **belief**, is true), doxology (a prayer giving **glory** to God)
θάνατος	euthanasia (**dying** well)
ἱερός	hieroglyphic (**sacred** writing)
ἵππος	hippopotamus (river-**horse**), Philip (lover of **horses**)
λίθος	lithography (printing from a flat surface, e.g., a **stone**)
μακρός	macron
μῑκρός	microscope
πεδίον	*foot* (A plain is a flat place where one puts one's **foot**.)
πείθω	*faith* (from the Latin cognate *fidēs*)
πολέμιος	polemic
πράττω	pragmatist
πρῶτος	prototype
ὑπό	hypodermic (**under**-the-skin)
φόβος	phobia

DRILLS

I. *In the sentences which follow, change the active verb forms of "to steal" to the PASSIVE VOICE.*

1. You will steal the goats.
2. He stole the sheep.
3. To steal tapirs is not nice.
4. We have stolen the presents.
5. They are stealing the wine.
6. He had stolen the money.
7. I steal apples.
8. To have stolen a Roman's toga was foolish.
9. He will be stealing cabbage.
10. She had stolen nothing.

II. *Change each of the following active verb forms to the passive voice, KEEPING the same person, number, and tense.*

1. they were educating
2. to be educating
3. she used to teach
4. we threw
5. you have hit

III. (a) *TRANSLATE indicatives and infinitives; IDENTIFY fully subjunctives and optatives.*
   (b) *If possible, change the number, keeping the same tense and voice.*
   (c) *Change the voice, keeping the same person, number, and tense.*

1. θύονται	11. τυθείησαν
2. θῦοίμεθα	12. ἐτύθησαν
3. θύηται	13. τυθῇ
4. ἐθύετο	14. ἐτύθης
5. τυθῆναι	15. θύσειαν
6. θύῃ (3)	16. πέμποιο
7. ἐθύου	17. ἐπέπεμπτο
8. ἐτέθυτο	18. πεμφθῶμεν
9. θύσω (2)	19. πεμφθήσεται
10. θύσῃ	20. πέμπει (2)

21. πέμψαι   (2)
22. πέμψειεν
23. πεμφθεῖεν
24. πέμπεσθαι
25. πεπέμφθαι

26. πέπεμφθε
27. πεμφθήσῃ
28. πεμφθῶσιν
29. ἐπέπεμφθε
30. ἐπέμπεσθε

IV. *Translate the following.*

1. οἱ ποιηταὶ ὑπὸ μουσῶν διδάσκονται.
2. οἱ νεᾶνίαι οὐκ ἐδιδάσκοντο περὶ τῆς στρατιωτῶν ἀρετῆς.
3. ἐὰν διδασκώμεθα ὑφ᾽ Ὁμήρου, γράψομεν δὴ καλὸν βιβλίον.
4. ἡ δημοκρατίᾱ ἐλύετο ὑπὸ κακῶν ἀνθρώπων ἵνα ἡ ἀρετὴ μὴ φυλάττοιτο.
5. εἰ διδάσκεσθαι ἐθέλοις, ὦ ἄδελφε, οὐκ ἂν εἰς μάχην πέμποιο.
6. λέλυται δὴ ἡ δημοκρατίᾱ τοῖς ὁπλίταις.
7. ἡ μὲν γέφυρα ἐλέλυτο, τὰ δὲ ζῷα τῷ δήμῳ ἐτέθυτο.
8. πεπαίδευσθε, ὦ νεᾶνίαι, ἵνα πέμπησθε εἰς μάχην.
9. ἐὰν διδαχθῶσιν οἱ πολῖται, οὐ λυθήσεται ἡ δημοκρατίᾱ.
10. εἰ ἐπαύθη ὁ πόλεμος, οὐκ ἂν ἐπέμφθη ὁ δῆμος εἰς τὴν νῆσον.
11. εἰ παυθείη ὁ πόλεμος, οὐκ ἂν πεμφθείη ὁ δῆμος ἐκ τῆς χώρᾱς.
12. ἐὰν τῇ θεῷ ζῷα τυθῇ ὑπὸ τοῦ δήμου, φυλαχθησόμεθα ὑπὸ θεῶν.

V. *Translate the following.*

1. πρὸ τοῦ κελεῦσαι
2. τῷ πέμπειν
3. τῷ πέμψαι
4. οἱ κακοί
5. τοὺς ἀδίκους
6. ἡ κακή
7. τὰ κακά
8. ταῖς κακαῖς
9. οἱ ἄδικοι
10. τὰς ἀδίκους
11. τῶν κακῶν
12. ἄδικα τὰ τοῦ πολέμου.
13. καλὸν τὸ πεπαιδεῦσθαι, τὸ δὲ μὴ οὔ.
14. οὐκ ἀγαθὸν τὸ θάψαι τοὺς στρατιώτᾱς ἐν τῇ νήσῳ.
15. ἀγαθὸν τὸ τοὺς φίλους παρὰ τῇ γεφύρᾳ τάττειν.

EXERCISES

I. 1. καὶ χρῡσὸς καὶ ἄργυρος ὑπὸ τῶν πολῑτῶν παρὰ τοὺς τῆς νήσου
ἐπέμφθησαν ὡς ταῖς ἀθανάτοις θεοῖς ἐν τῇ τῆς νήσου ἀγορᾷ τῇ
μῑκρᾷ θύσειαν. ὁ γὰρ πόλεμος ὁ φοβερὸς ταῖς θεοῖς ἐπέπαυτο.

2. ἀθάνατος ἡ δόξα ἡ τοῦ ποιητοῦ τοῦ τῶν μουσῶν ἱεροῦ, ἐπειδὴ καλὰ
βιβλία περὶ τῆς τῶν ἀνθρώπων ἀρετῆς καὶ τῶν πολέμου
κινδύνων Ὁμήρῳ γέγραπται.

3. εἰ τοῖς τοῦ πρώτου ἀγγέλου λόγοις τοῖς κακοῖς πεισθεῖτε τὴν
εἰρήνην λῦσαι καὶ κακὰ πρᾱ́ττειν τοὺς ξένους, οὐ παύσαιεν ἂν
τὸν πόλεμον πρὸ τῆς ἐν μάχῃ νίκης.

4. διὰ τοὺς κινδύνους τοῖς μὲν θεοῖς οἱ ἵπποι, ταῖς δὲ θεοῖς αἱ ἵπποι
ὑπὸ τῶν ξένων ἐθύοντο πρὸ μαχῶν. ἀλλ' ἡ τῶν ξένων χώρα
οὐκ ἐφυλάχθη ὑπὸ τῶν θεῶν.

5. ἆρα τῷ ἀγαθῷ διδασκάλῳ τοῦ ἀδελφοῦ ἱκανὸν ἀργύριον πέμψεις
ἐὰν ὁ ἀδελφὸς εὖ παιδευθῇ; ἐθέλει γὰρ παιδεύειν τοὺς ἀγαθούς.

6. διδάσκαλος τῶν πολῑτῶν ὁ ἀγαθὸς ποιητής. λόγοις γὰρ τῶν ποιητῶν
διδάσκονται οἱ πολῖται.

7. μετὰ τὴν μάχην καὶ οἱ καλοὶ καὶ οἱ κακοὶ ἐν γῇ θάπτονται. ἀλλ'
ἀθάνατος ἡ τῶν καλῶν δόξα.

8. εἰ βλάπτοιντο οἱ ἐν τῇ νήσῳ, ἔπεμπον εἰς τὴν ἐκκλησίαν ἵνα
φυλάττοιντο ὑπὸ τῶν στρατιωτῶν. οἱ γὰρ πολέμιοι οὐκ ἤθελον
τὸν πόλεμον παῦσαι.

9. εἰ ἐβλάβης ὑπὸ τοῦ διδασκάλου, δῶρα οὐκ ἔπεμψας ἄν. τοῖς γὰρ
ἀδίκοις δῶρα οὐκ ἐπέμπετο.

10. οὐκ ἀγαθοὶ τοῖς ἵπποις οἱ λίθοι οἱ ἐν τῷ πεδίῳ.

11. νῦν πέμπομεν ἐξ τῶν στρατιωτῶν εἰς τὸ πεδίον ἵνα φυλάττηται ἡ
γέφῡρα.

12. ἱκανοὶ οἱ ποιηταὶ τοὺς πολῑ́τᾱς τὴν ἀρετὴν διδάσκειν;

13. εἰ ἡ γῆ ὑπὸ τῶν στρατιωτῶν μὴ εὖ ἐφυλάττετο, οὐκ ἂν ἤθελον
ἀγγέλους πέμψαι περὶ τῆς εἰρήνης.

14. οὐ καλὸν τὸ βλάπτειν, ἀλλὰ καλὸν τὸ μὴ βλάπτεσθαι.

15. παρὰ τὴν τῶν στρατιωτῶν δόξαν ἐκελεύσθησαν τὴν γέφυραν φυλάττειν πρὸ τοῦ πεμφθῆναι εἰς μάχην.

16. ἐὰν οἱ πρῶτοι στρατιῶται παρὰ τῇ γεφύρᾳ μὴ ταχθῶσιν, οὐ φυλάττεται τὸ πεδίον.

17. τοῖς στρατιώταις οὐχ ἱκανοὶ εἰς μάχην οἱ λίθοι.

18. διὰ τοῦ πεδίου πεμφθήσεσθε ὅπως μὴ λύσωσιν οἱ ξένοι τὴν εἰρήνην.

19. καὶ τοῖς μακροῖς καὶ τοῖς μικροῖς ἱκανὴ ἡ ἀρετή.

20. τὰ τῶν δικαίων δῶρα θεοὺς πέπεικεν. φίλοι γὰρ τοῖς θεοῖς οἱ δίκαιοι.

21. βιβλίον περὶ τῆς ἀγαθῆς ψῡχῆς τῷ ποιητῇ ἐγέγραπτο.

22. ὁ δίκαιος οὐχ ὑπὸ τοῦ ἀδίκου βλαβήσεται, ἀλλὰ τῷ ἀδίκῳ.

23. οὐχ ἱκανὸν τὸ μὴ βλάπτειν τοὺς φίλους.

24. ὁ δίκαιος τοὺς πολίτᾱς ἐκέλευε μὴ πέμψαι τὸν ἄργυρον, τὸ τῶν θεῶν δῶρον, εἰς τὰς τῶν ἀδίκων οἰκίᾱς.

25. ἐὰν τοῦ δήμου παρὰ τὴν δίκην ἄρχῃς, κακὰ πρᾱ́ττεις.

26. εἰ ὁ ποιητὴς τοὺς νεᾱνίᾱς κακὰ πρᾱ́ττειν τὸν δῆμον διδάξαι, πεμφθείη ἂν εἰς τὴν νῆσον.

27. τῷ εὖ ἄρχειν τῶν νεᾱνιῶν
    οἱ μὴ μακροί
    ἀπὸ τοῦ τῆς θεοῦ ἱεροῦ
    μετὰ τῶν ὁπλῑτῶν
    ὁ ὑπὸ γῆς θεός
    ἐν ἀρχῇ τοῦ πολέμου
    κακοὶ οἱ μὴ ἀγαθοί.
    καλὰ τὰ τῶν ποιητῶν.

II. 1. By sacrificing animals, men had persuaded the gods to stop wars.

   2. The young man has been well educated by the poet in order that his excellence may be guarded.

   3. If you had been sent by the citizens to the island sacred to the goddess in order that the men in the country might be guarded, you would not have been stationed in the market place.

   4. Men under the power of the bad are unjust.

READINGS

A. Menander, *Γνῶμαι μονόστιχοι*

371. νύμφη δ᾽ ἄπροικος οὐκ ἔχει παρρησίαν.

102. γάμος γὰρ ἀνθρώποισιν[1] εὐκταῖον κακόν.

15. ἀβουλίᾳ τὰ πολλά[2] βλάπτονται βροτοί.

523. ὕπνος δεινὸν ἀνθρώποις κακόν.

722. τὸ πολλὰ πράττειν ἐστὶ πανταχοῦ σαπρόν.

723. τὸ πολλὰ πράττειν κὠδύνᾱς[3] πολλὰς ἔχει.

ἀβουλίᾱ, ἀβουλίᾱς, ἡ thoughtlessness

ἄπροικος, ἄπροικον without a dowry

βλάπτω, βλάψω, ἔβλαψα, βέβλαφα, βέβλαμμαι, ἐβλάβην or ἐβλάφθην hurt, harm

βροτός, βροτοῦ, ὁ mortal

γάμος, γάμου, ὁ wedding, marriage

δεινός, δεινή, δεινόν fearsome, marvelous, clever

ἐστί (*third person sing., pres. ind. active of the verb "to be"*) is

εὐκταῖος, εὐκταίᾱ, εὐκταῖον to be prayed for

ἔχω, ἕξω or σχήσω, ἔσχον, ἔσχηκα, -ἔσχημαι, —— have, hold; be able; (*mid.*) cling to, be next to (+ *gen.*)

νύμφη, νύμφης, ἡ young wife, bride

ὀδύνη, ὀδύνης, ἡ pain

πανταχοῦ (*adv.*) everywhere

παρρησίᾱ, παρρησίᾱς, ἡ freedom of speech

πολλοί, πολλαί, πολλά many

πράττω, πράξω, ἔπρᾱξα, πέπρᾱχα (*trans.*) or πέπρᾱγα (*intrans.*), πέπρᾱγμαι, ἐπρᾱχθην do; fare

σαπρός, σαπρά, σαπρόν rotten

ὕπνος, ὕπνου, ὁ sleep

---

1. ἀνθρώποισιν = ἀνθρώποις
2. τὰ πολλά (**adverbial accusative**) with respect to many things, often
3. κὠδύνᾱς = καὶ ὀδύνᾱς

B. Sophokles, *Fragments*

14 P. σοφοὶ τύραννοι τῶν σοφῶν ξυνουσίᾳ.

850 P.   καὶ τὰ τῶν θεῶν
    θνῄσκει, θεοὶ δ' οὔ.

θνῄσκω, θανοῦμαι, ἔθανον, τέθνηκα, ——, —— die
ξυνουσίᾱ, ξυνουσίᾱς, ἡ = συνουσίᾱ, συνουσίᾱς, ἡ being together with, company
σοφός, σοφή, σοφόν wise, skilled
τύραννος, τυράννου, ὁ ruler, tyrant

UNIT
6

48. THIRD-DECLENSION NOUNS: CONSONANT STEMS

Third-declension nouns can be masculine, feminine, or neuter. They employ
the endings listed below. As with first- and second-declension nouns, the stem
to which the endings are added is obtained by dropping the ending of the
genitive singular.

	M or F	N
Nom. S	———	———
Gen.	-ος	-ος
Dat.	-ι	-ι
Acc.	-α, -ν	———
Voc.	———	———
Nom./Voc. P	-ες	-α
Gen.	-ων	-ων
Dat.	-σι(ν)	-σι(ν)
Acc.	-ας	-α

The declensions of five representative third-declension nouns with **consonant
stems** (stems ending in a consonant) are presented below. The rules for declining
these and other third-declension nouns are given after the paradigms.

φύλαξ, φύλακος, ὁ, "guard"   (stem: φυλακ-)
αἴξ, αἰγός, ὁ or ἡ, "goat"   (stem: αἰγ-)
ἐλπίς, ἐλπίδος, ἡ, "hope"   (stem: ἐλπιδ-)
χάρις, χάριτος, ἡ, "grace"   (stem: χαριτ-)
σῶμα, σώματος, τό, "body"   (stem: σωματ-)

139

Nom. S	φύλαξ	αἴξ	ἐλπίς	χάρις	σῶμα
Gen.	φύλακος	αἰγός	ἐλπίδος	χάριτος	σώματος
Dat.	φύλακι	αἰγί	ἐλπίδι	χάριτι	σώματι
Acc.	φύλακα	αἶγα	ἐλπίδα	χάριν	σῶμα
Voc.	φύλαξ	αἴξ	ἐλπί	χάρι	σῶμα
Nom./Voc. P	φύλακες	αἶγες	ἐλπίδες	χάριτες	σώματα
Gen.	φυλάκων	αἰγῶν	ἐλπίδων	χαρίτων	σωμάτων
Dat.	φύλαξι(ν)	αἰξί(ν)	ἐλπίσι(ν)	χάρισι(ν)	σώμασι(ν)
Acc.	φύλακας	αἶγας	ἐλπίδας	χάριτας	σώματα

Rule for the accentuation of consonant-stem third-declension nouns:

Accent is persistent. But THIRD-DECLENSION NOUNS WITH MONOSYLLABIC STEMS ACCENT THE ULTIMA IN THE GENITIVE AND DATIVE, SINGULAR AND PLURAL; THE GENITIVE PLURAL TAKES A CIRCUMFLEX.
Thus φύλακ-ος, but αἰγ-ός.

Observations on case forms:

Nominative singular: This form will simply be learned from the standard vocabulary listing of each noun.

Accusative singular: In the accusative singular, almost all masculine and feminine nouns with consonant stems employ the ending -α.

But nouns whose stems end in -ιτ, -ιδ, or -ῑθ, and which do not accent this iota, drop the final consonant from the stem and employ the ending -ν. Thus ἐλπίδα, but χάριν.

Remember that in neuter nouns of all declensions the accusative singular is identical in form with the nominative singular.

Vocative singular: In the box below are the rules for forming the vocative singular of ALL third-declension nouns, including those presented later. These rules should be learned as new third-declension nouns are encountered.

In masculine and feminine nouns the vocative singular is identical in form with the nominative singular

    (1) when the nominative singular ends in -ξ or -ψ (e.g., αἴξ)

    (2) when the nominative singular ends in -ν or -ρ *and* accents the ultima (e.g., λιμήν).

Otherwise, the vocative singular consists of *the stem alone*, with any final dental dropped (e.g., χάρι).

In all neuter nouns the vocative singular is identical in form with the nominative singular.

The vocative singular of nouns which do not follow these rules will be given in the vocabulary.

Nominative/Vocative plural: Remember that in all nouns of all declensions the nominative and vocative plural are identical in form.

    All neuter nouns employ the ending -α in the nominative/vocative and accusative plural.

Dative plural: In the following box are rules for combining the dative plural ending -σι with third-declension stems ending in consonants, including stems to be presented later. These rules should be learned as new third-declension nouns are encountered.

The combination of the final consonant of the stem with the dative plural ending -σι causes the following phonetic or spelling changes:

π, β, φ	+ -σι	=	-ψι
κ, γ, χ	+ -σι	=	-ξι
τ, δ, θ	+ -σι	=	-σι
ν	+ -σι	=	-σι
σ	+ -σι	=	-σι
-αντ-	+ -σι	=	-ᾱσι
-εντ-	+ -σι	=	-εισι
-οντ-	+ -σι	=	-ουσι
λ	+ -σι	=	-λσι with no change
ρ	+ -σι	=	-ρσι with no change

Note that when -αντ-, -εντ-, or -οντ- are combined with the ending, ντ is lost and a long vowel or diphthong appears by a process called **compensatory lengthening**. A diphthong which results from compensatory lengthening is called a **spurious diphthong**.

> *Accusative plural*: Contrast the ending -ας of the third declension with the ending -ᾱς of the first declension.

Drills I and II, page 156, may now be done.

49. THE RELATIVE PRONOUN

A noun or pronoun can be modified by an adjective (ὁ ἀγαθὸς ἄνθρωπος, the **good** man), by another noun in the genitive case (τὸ 'Ομήρου βιβλίον, **Homer's** book), by a prepositional phrase (οἱ ἐν τῇ χώρᾳ πολῖται, the citizens **in the land**), or by an adverb (οἱ νῦν πολῖται, **present-day** citizens).

A noun or pronoun can also be modified by a dependent clause called a **relative clause**, introduced by the **relative pronoun**. Here are some examples in English.

> The poet **who wrote the book** is good.
> The poet **whose book (= of whom the book) we sent to the island** is good.
> The poet **to whom we sent the book** is good.
> The poet **whom we educated** is good.

None of these relative clauses is a complete sentence. Each is a dependent clause within a complex sentence which also contains a main or independent clause. The relative clauses simply modify the noun "poet" and specify a particular poet.

In Greek as in English the relative pronoun performs two functions:

(1) It refers back to the noun in the independent clause which is its **antecedent** ("poet" in the examples above).

(2) It has its own grammatical function within the relative clause. In the first example "who" is the subject of the verb "wrote"; in the second, "whose" modifies "book" and shows possession; in the third, the phrase "to whom" is the indirect object of the verb "sent"; in the fourth, "whom" is the direct object of the verb "educated."

In Greek the relative pronoun, like all nouns, pronouns, and adjectives, has gender, number, and case.

THE RELATIVE PRONOUN REFERS TO AN ANTECEDENT IN THE INDEPENDENT CLAUSE AND ALWAYS HAS THE SAME GENDER AND THE SAME NUMBER AS THAT ANTECEDENT.

BUT THE CASE OF THE RELATIVE PRONOUN DEPENDS ENTIRELY ON ITS GRAMMATICAL FUNCTION WITHIN THE DEPENDENT CLAUSE.

Thus in the examples above all four relative pronouns would in Greek be *masculine* and *singular* because all refer back to the masculine singular antecedent, "poet." But the relative pronoun would appear in a *different case* in each example: nominative in the first, genitive in the second, dative in the third, and accusative in the fourth.

Drill III, pages 156–57, may now be done.

The relative pronoun belongs to the first and second declensions. It is declined as follows:

	M	F	N
Nom. S	ὅς	ἥ	ὅ
Gen.	οὗ	ἧς	οὗ
Dat.	ᾧ	ᾗ	ᾧ
Acc.	ὅν	ἥν	ὅ
Nom. P	οἵ	αἵ	ἅ
Gen.	ὧν	ὧν	ὧν
Dat.	οἷς	αἷς	οἷς
Acc.	οὕς	ἅς	ἅ

Observations: (1) Compare the declension of the article (Section 16); the relative pronoun differs from the article in that *all* its forms have a rough breathing and take an accent. Also, its masculine nominative singular ends in -ς.

(2) The relative pronoun has no vocative case.

The examples above can now be rendered in Greek:

ἀγαθὸς ὁ ποιητὴς **ὃς τὸ βιβλίον ἔγραψεν.**
The poet **who wrote the book** is good.

ἀγαθὸς ὁ ποιητὴς **οὗ τὸ βιβλίον εἰς τὴν νῆσον ἐπέμψαμεν.**
The poet **whose book we sent to the island** is good.

ἀγαθὸς ὁ ποιητὴς **ᾧ τὸ βιβλίον ἐπέμψαμεν.**
The poet **to whom we sent the book** is good.

ἀγαθὸς ὁ ποιητὴς **ὃν ἐπαιδεύσαμεν.**
The poet **whom we educated** is good.

When translating relative clauses within complete sentences one must carefully distinguish the independent clause, with its subject, verb, and (possible) objects, from the dependent relative clause, with its own separate subject, verb, and (possible) objects. Remember that the relative pronoun takes from its antecedent *gender and number only*; its *case* is determined by its function within the relative clause.

παιδεύσομεν τοὺς ποιητὰς **οἳ** βιβλία γράψουσιν.
We shall educate the poets **who** will write books.

Antecedent of relative pronoun:
ποιητάς: masculine plural

Function in dependent clause:
subject of γράψουσιν: nominative

Form of relative pronoun:
masculine plural nominative

ἀγαθὴ ἡ ψῡχὴ **ἣν** παιδεύεις, ὦ Ὅμηρε.
Good is the soul **which** you educate, Homer.

Antecedent of relative pronoun:
ψῡχή: feminine singular

Function in dependent clause:
direct object of παιδεύεις: accusative

Form of relative pronoun:
feminine singular accusative

τὰ ὅπλα ἐπέμψατε **οἷς** ἔβλαψαν τὰ ζῷα.
You sent the weapons **with which** they harmed the animals.

Antecedent of relative pronoun:
ὅπλα: neuter plural

Function in dependent clause:
instrumental dative

Form of relative pronoun:
neuter plural dative

Drill IV, page 157, may now be done.

50. THE INDEPENDENT SUBJUNCTIVE

In addition to its use in purpose clauses after a primary tense of the indicative, and in the protases of future more vivid and present general conditional sentences, the subjunctive mood is employed in three types of independent clause.

1. HORTATORY SUBJUNCTIVE

The first person of the present or aorist subjunctive can express emphatically the will of the speaker. The plural is more common. This usage is called the **hortatory subjunctive**. Its negative is μή. Tense shows aspect only.

Translation formula: let us (let me)

> παύωμεν τὴν μάχην.
> Let us be stopping the battle.
> Let us stop the battle.

> παύσωμεν τὴν μάχην.
> Let us stop the battle.

> μὴ παύωμεν τὴν μάχην.
> Let us not be stopping the battle.
> Let us not stop the battle.

Contrast the indicative:

> οὐ παύομεν τὴν μάχην.
> We are not stopping the battle.

2. DELIBERATIVE SUBJUNCTIVE

The first person of the present or aorist subjunctive can express, in a question, the speaker's uncertainty about what he or she is to do. This usage is called the **deliberative subjunctive**. Its negative is μή. Tense shows aspect only.

Translation formula: am I to/are we to

> παύωμεν τὴν μάχην;
> Are we to be stopping the battle?
> Are we to stop the battle?

> παύσωμεν τὴν μάχην;
> Are we to stop the battle?

ἄγγελον μὴ πέμπω;
Am I not to be sending a messenger?

Contrast the indicative:

ἄγγελον οὐ πέμπω;
Am I not sending a messenger?

3. PROHIBITIVE SUBJUNCTIVE

With the negative μή the second person of the aorist subjunctive (but NOT the present subjunctive) expresses a prohibition. This usage is called the **prohibitive subjunctive**. Tense shows aspect only. Positive commands are expressed in the imperative mood, which is presented in Section 89.

Translation formula: do not

μὴ παύσητε τὴν μάχην.
Do not stop the battle.

μὴ πέμψῃς τὸν ἄγγελον.
Do not send the messenger.

Any independent subjunctive can be used instead of a future indicative in the apodosis of a future more vivid conditional sentence.

ἐὰν εὖ πράξωμεν, μὴ πέμψῃς τὸν ἄγγελον.
If we fare well, do not send the messenger.

ἐὰν εὖ πράξωμεν, πέμψωμεν τὸν ἄγγελον.
If we fare well, let us send the messenger.

Drill V, page 157, may now be done.

51. PARTITIVE GENITIVE (GENITIVE OF THE DIVIDED WHOLE)

The genitive case can be employed to indicate the larger group or entity to which particular persons or things belong. This is called the **partitive genitive** or **genitive of the divided whole**.

ἓξ **τῶν ὁπλῑτῶν** ἐπέμφθησαν.
Six **of the hoplites** were sent.

τοὺς ἀδίκους **τῶν πολῑτῶν** εἰς τὰς νήσους πέμψετε.
You will send the unjust ones **of the citizens** to the islands.

τῶν γεφῡρῶν *πέντε ἐλύθησαν.*
Of the bridges five were destroyed.

Although both the partitive genitive and the genitive which shows possession can be translated by the English preposition "of," their meanings are distinct, as the following examples show.

οἱ ἄδικοι τῶν ὁπλῑτῶν (*partitive genitive*)
the unjust ones **of the hoplites**

ἡ τῶν ὁπλῑτῶν *οἰκίᾱ* (*genitive showing possession*)
the house **of the hoplites**

The partitive genitive stands either before or after the noun or pronoun which it modifies. Unlike the genitive which shows possession, the partitive genitive *cannot* stand in the attributive position.

52. GENITIVE OF TIME WITHIN WHICH

The genitive case without a preposition can also indicate the span of time within which an event occurred, occurs, or will occur. This is called the **genitive of time within which.**

τῆς ἡμέρᾱς *τοὺς νεᾱνίᾱς ἐδιδάξαμεν.*
During the day we taught the young men.

τῆς πρώτης ἡμέρᾱς *ὁπλίτᾱς ἐν τῇ ἀγορᾷ τάξομεν.*
During the first day we shall station hoplites in the market place.

ἓξ ἡμερῶν *διδάξει τοὺς νεᾱνίᾱς ὁ Ὅμηρος.*
Within six days Homer will teach the young men.

53. DATIVE OF TIME AT WHICH

The dative case is employed, without a preposition, to indicate the point in time at which an event occurred, occurs, or will occur. This is called the **dative of time at which** or **when.**

τῇ πρώτῃ ἡμέρᾳ *ὁπλίτᾱς ἐν τῇ ἀγορᾷ τάξομεν.*
On the first day we shall station hoplites in the market place.

54. ACCUSATIVE OF EXTENT OF TIME

The accusative case is employed, without a preposition, to indicate the length in time of an event in the past, present, or future. This is called the **accusative of extent of time**.

> **πέντε ἡμέρᾱς** τοὺς νεᾱνίᾱς διδάξομεν.
> **For five days** we shall teach the young men.
>
> **ἓξ ἡμέρᾱς** τοὺς νεᾱνίᾱς ἐδιδάσκομεν.
> **For six days** we were teaching the young men.

55. EXPRESSIONS OF TIME COMPARED

The genitive of time within which answers the question, "during what span of time?" It places the event at some unspecified point during that span of time without pinpointing it further. The phrase τῆς ἡμέρᾱς could be translated "at some time during the day." The genitive of time within which is akin to the partitive genitive, which places an individual person or thing within a larger group or entity.

The dative of time at which simply answers the question "when?" It places the event in time as plainly as possible. It treats the unit of time involved (e.g., hour, day, month) as if it were a single point, and places the event there.

The accusative of extent of time answers the question "for how long a time?"

These three expressions of time can be diagrammed as follows:

GENITIVE   DATIVE   ACCUSATIVE

The genitive places the event within the circle, the dative at a single point, and the accusative describes the length of time which the event takes from beginning to end.

56. ACCUSATIVE OF EXTENT OF SPACE

The accusative case is employed, without a preposition, to indicate distance traveled. This usage is called the **accusative of extent of space**.

τὸν ἄγγελον **πέντε σταδίους** πέμψετε.
You will send the messenger **for five stades**.
You will send the messenger **five stades**.

ὁ ἄγγελος **ἓξ σταδίους** πεμφθήσεται.
The messenger will be sent **for six stades**.
The messenger will be sent **six stades**.

The accusative of extent of space functions as an adverb; it is independent of any other case forms in a sentence.

The accusative of extent of space, like the accusative of extent of time, can be diagrammed with an arrow (cf. the preceding Section).

Drill VI, page 158, may now be done.

VOCABULARY

αἴξ, αἰγός, ὁ or ἡ	goat
γε (enclitic particle)	emphasizes or limits preceding word; at any rate, at least
γέρων, γέροντος, ὁ	old man
γνώμη, γνώμης, ἡ	opinion, judgment
δεινός, δεινή, δεινόν	fearsome, marvelous, clever
δοῦλος, δούλου, ὁ	slave
δουλείᾱ, δουλείᾱς, ἡ	slavery
δουλεύω, δουλεύσω, ἐδούλευσα, δεδούλευκα, ——, ——	be a slave (+ dat.)
ἐλεύθερος, ἐλευθέρᾱ, ἐλεύθερον	free (+ gen.)
ἐλευθερίᾱ, ἐλευθερίᾱς, ἡ	freedom
Ἕλλην, Ἕλληνος, ὁ	a Greek
ἐλπίς, ἐλπίδος, ἡ	hope, expectation
κατά (prep.) + gen.	under; against
+ acc.	according to
κωλύω, κωλύσω, ἐκώλῡσα, κεκώλῡκα, κεκώλῡμαι, ἐκωλύθην	hinder, prevent
νύξ, νυκτός, ἡ	night
ὅς, ἥ, ὅ (relative pronoun)	who, which
παλαιός, παλαιά, παλαιόν	old, aged, ancient
πολῑτεύω, πολῑτεύσω, ἐπολῑτευσα, πεπολῑτευκα, πεπολῑτευμαι, ἐπολῑτεύθην	live as a citizen; conduct the government; (pass.) be governed
πρᾶγμα, πρᾱγματος, τό	deed, affair, thing
σοφός, σοφή, σοφόν	wise, skilled
σοφίᾱ, σοφίᾱς, ἡ	wisdom, skill
στάδιον, σταδίου, τό (pl. τὰ στάδια or οἱ στάδιοι)	stade (= ca. 600 ft.)
σῶμα, σώματος, τό	body
τε (enclitic conj.)	and

τοι (enclitic particle)	let me tell you, you know
φάλαγξ, φάλαγγος, ἡ	line of battle, phalanx
φύλαξ, φύλακος, ὁ	guard
χάρις, χάριτος, ἡ	grace, favor, gratitude
χάριν (prep.) + preceding gen.	for the sake of
χορός, χοροῦ, ὁ	dance; chorus
χορεύω, χορεύσω, ἐχόρευσα,	dance, take part in a chorus
κεχόρευκα, κεχόρευμαι,	
ἐχορεύθην	
χορευτής, χορευτοῦ, ὁ	choral dancer

VOCABULARY NOTES

The noun αἴξ, αἰγός, ὁ or ἡ, "goat," can be either masculine or feminine. The article indicates gender. Cf. ἵππος, θεός.

The particles γε and τοι and the connective τε are monosyllabic **enclitics**, words which are closely attached in pronunciation to the preceding word and which can affect the accent of the preceding word. A monosyllabic enclitic, which usually has no accent itself, causes the following changes in the accent of the preceding word:

(1) IF THE PRECEDING WORD HAS AN ACUTE ON THE ULTIMA, THE ACCENT REMAINS AN ACUTE AND IS NOT CHANGED TO A GRAVE.

-a-p-ú + e
ἀγαθοί γε

(2) IF THE PRECEDING WORD HAS A CIRCUMFLEX ON THE PENULT, AN ADDITIONAL ACUTE ACCENT IS PLACED ON THE ULTIMA.

-a-p̃-ú + e
δῆμός γε

(3) IF THE PRECEDING WORD HAS AN ACUTE ON THE ANTEPENULT, AN ADDITIONAL ACUTE ACCENT IS PLACED ON THE ULTIMA.

-á-p-ú + e
ἄνθρωποί γε

Thus whenever the accent of the preceding word is as far from the ultima as the rules for the possibilities of accent allow, an additional acute accent is added to the ultima.

(4) IF THE PRECEDING WORD IS A PROCLITIC, THE PROCLITIC RECEIVES AN
   ACUTE ACCENT.

εἴ γε   ἤ γε γέφυρα

In every other instance, e.g., a circumflex on the ultima or an acute on the
penult, the preceding word is not affected, and there is no accent on the enclitic.
Complete rules for enclitics, including those for disyllabic enclitics, will be given
in Unit 15.

The enclitic particle γε is postpositive and has two distinct uses: it either
emphasizes or *limits* the preceding word.   When joined with a phrase consisting
of article + noun, γε usually follows the article.

   τούς γε ἵππους ἐβλάψατε.
   You harmed *the horses.* (*emphatic*)
   You harmed the horses, at any rate. (*limiting*)

   τῷ γ᾽ ἀδελφῷ δῶρον ἔπεμψας.
   You sent a gift to your *brother.* (*emphatic*)
   You sent a gift to your brother, at any rate. (*limiting*)

In prepositional phrases, γε usually follows the preposition.

   μετά γε τὴν μάχην
   after the *battle*

A relative pronoun accompanied by γε often has a causal force.

   ἀγαθὸς ὁ Ὅμηρος ὅς γε ἀγαθὰ βιβλία γέγραφεν.
   Homer is good, who has written good books.
   Homer is good because he has written good books.

Context will determine the best translation of this particle, whose force is often
conveyed in English by tone of voice alone.

The adjective δεινός, δεινή, δεινόν, "fearsome, marvelous, clever," is used in
both a negative and a positive sense: of someone (or something) frightening, and
of someone who shows remarkable rhetorical or intellectual flair.   In the latter
sense δεινός can take an epexegetical infinitive to describe the area of expertise.

   δεινὸς **διδάσκειν** τοὺς νεανίας
   clever at teaching the young men

The noun δουλεία, δουλείας, ἡ, "slavery," is an abstract noun formed from the
noun δοῦλος, δούλου, ὁ, "slave." Note that the noun φιλία, from φίλος, employs
a slightly different suffix. Compare also the abstract nouns ἐλευθερία,
ἐλευθερίας, ἡ "freedom," from the adjective ἐλεύθερος, ἐλευθέρα, ἐλεύθερον,

"free," and σοφίᾱ, σοφίᾱς, ἡ, "wisdom, skill," from the adjective σοφός, σοφή, σοφόν, "wise, skilled."

The verb δουλεύω, δουλεύσω, ἐδούλευσα, δεδούλευκα, ——, ——, "be a slave," is a denominative verb, one formed from a noun (δοῦλος). Like it are the verbs πολῑτεύω, πολῑτεύσω, ἐπολῑτευσα, πεπολῑτευκα, πεπολῑτευμαι, ἐπολῑτεύθην, "be a citizen," from the noun πολῑτης, πολῑτου, ὁ, "citizen," and χορεύω, χορεύσω, ἐχόρευσα, κεχόρευκα, κεχόρευμαι, ἐχορεύθην, "dance, take part in a chorus," from the noun χορός, χοροῦ, ὁ, "chorus." Note that δουλεύω takes a dative of the person or thing to which one is a slave:

ἐδουλεύομεν τοῖς πολίταις.
We were slaves to the citizens.

The noun Ἕλλην, Ἕλληνος, ὁ, denotes "a Greek," a man. It is not usually used as an adjective (as in the phrase "a Greek city").

The original meaning of the preposition κατά is "down," but it is not usually employed in this sense in Attic; the more common meanings are the ones given in the vocabulary: "(+ gen.) against; under; (+ acc.) according to."

The verb κωλύω, κωλύσω, ἐκώλῡσα, κεκώλῡκα, κεκώλῡμαι, ἐκωλύθην, "hinder, prevent," has -ῡ- in all six Principal Parts. Contrast λύω, θύω. The verb κωλύω can take an accusative of the person prevented from doing something and an infinitive of the action prevented:

ἐκωλύσαμεν τοὺς κακοὺς τῇ θεῷ θῦσαι.
We prevented the evil men from sacrificing to the goddess.

The dative plural of νύξ, νυκτός, ἡ, "night," is *νυκτ-σί(ν) > *νυκ-σί(ν) = νυξί(ν).

The adjective παλαιός, παλαιά, παλαιόν, "old, aged, ancient," is formed from the adverb πάλαι, "long ago."

The noun πρᾶγμα, πράγματος, τό, "deed, affair, thing," means literally a "thing done." It has the same root as πράττω (πράκ-). In the plural it often means "affairs" as in the phrases "affairs of mankind" or "affairs of state."

The adjective σοφός, σοφή, σοφόν, "wise, skilled," and the noun σοφίᾱ, σοφίᾱς, ἡ, "wisdom, skill," can indicate either practical or intellectual wisdom. Cf. τέχνη.

The noun στάδιον, σταδίου, τό, "stade," can be either masculine or neuter in the plural with no difference in meaning: οἱ στάδιοι or τὰ στάδια. This word denotes a distance of about 600 feet; this was the length of the racecourse at Olympia, and the word στάδιον can also mean "racecourse."

The enclitic conjunction τε is usually employed together with καί to link two items. The usual order is A τε καί B:

Ὅμηρός **τε καὶ** ὁ ἀδελφός
Homer **and** his brother

αἶγές **τε καὶ** ἵπποι
goats **and** horses

Sometimes τε and καί are separated by intervening words.

οἱ στρατιῶται **φυλάττουσί τε** τοὺς ἀδίκους **καὶ πέμπουσιν** ἀγγέλους.
The soldiers **are guarding** the unjust men **and sending** messengers.

In these examples τε is not given a separate translation. It is a signpost that tells the reader there is a καί coming up.

In poetry and (rarely) in prose, τε can be used alone to connect two items. It then follows the *second* of the two items: A B τε. Like καὶ . . . καί, τε . . . τε means "both . . . and." The order is A τε B τε.

αἶγες ἵπποι **τε**
goats **and** horses

αἶγές **τε** ἵπποι **τε**
both goats **and** horses.

The enclitic particle τοι, "let me tell you, you know," is employed when a speaker expects the hearer to assent to the truth of what is being said. By contrast, the particle δή, "in fact, of course," draws attention to an external reality.

ἀγαθή **τοι** ἡ δημοκρατίᾱ.
Democracy, **you know**, is good.

ἀγαθὴ **δὴ** ἡ δημοκρατίᾱ.
In fact, democracy is good.

When τοι follows οὐ, they are usually written as one word: οὔτοι.

The noun φάλαγξ, φάλαγγος, ἡ, can designate any order of battle, but came to signify a particular formation of hoplites, many lines deep, protected by overlapping shields and with long spears as offensive weapons.

The noun φύλαξ, φύλακος, ὁ, "guard," has the stem φυλακ-. Cf. the verb φυλάττω < *φυλάκιω, whose root is φυλακ-.

The preposition χάριν + gen., "for the sake of," is postpositive: it follows the word which it governs. It is derived from the accusative singular of the noun χάρις, χάριτος, ἡ, "grace, favor, gratitude." Sentences of the type πέμπω δῶρον, τοῦ ἀδελφοῦ **χάριν**

I send a gift, **a favor of** (= **for**) my brother,

where χάριν is a noun in apposition with the direct object δῶρον, came to be understood thus:

I send a gift **for the sake of** my brother.

Here, as normally, χάριν is a preposition governing the genitive case.

Note the relationship between the noun χορός, the denominative verb χορεύω, and the verbal noun χορευτής, χορευτοῦ, ὁ, "dancer." The suffix -της of the latter noun often indicates the agent of an action.

COGNATES AND DERIVATIVES

γέρων	gerontology (the study of **old** people)
γνώμη	*know*; gnomic (expressing a pithy saying or **opinion**)
δεινός	dinosaur (**fearsome** lizard)
δοῦλος	iconodule (opposite of iconoclast)
ἐλευθερίᾱ	liberty (from the Latin cognate *līber*)
῞Ελλην	Hellenic
νύξ	*night*
παλαιός	Palaeolithic
πρᾶγμα	pragmatic (dealing with actual facts, **deeds, things**)
σοφός	sophomore (literally, "**wise** fool")
σοφίᾱ	philosophy
στάδιον	stadium
σῶμα	psychosomatic
φάλαγξ	phalanx
φύλαξ	prophylactic
χάρις	Eucharist (a service of **gratitude**)
χορός	chorus

DRILLS

I. *Translate. Then supply the proper form of the article, or* ὦ. *Then change plurals to singular, and vice versa.*

1. φύλακα
2. φύλαξιν
3. φύλακες   (2)
4. σῶμα   (3)
5. φυλάκων
6. αἰγός   (2)
7. ἐλπίδι
8. γέροντες (2)
9. σώματος
10. γέροντα

11. γέρουσι
12. χάριτας
13. χάριτι
14. χάριτες (2)
15. χαρίτων
16. αἶγα   (2)
17. ἐλπίδες (2)
18. σώμασιν
19. αἰξί   (2)
20. γέρον

II. *Decline the following nouns according to the rules given.*

1. Ἕλλην, Ἕλληνος, ὁ Greek
2. φάλαγξ, φάλαγγος, ἡ phalanx, line of battle
3. πρᾶγμα, πράγματος, τό deed, affair, thing
4. νύξ, νυκτός, ἡ night
5. ῥήτωρ, ῥήτορος, ὁ public speaker

III. *Each of the sentences below contains a clause introduced by a relative pronoun.*

(a) *Separate the independent clause from the relative clause.*

(b) *Identify the antecedent of the relative pronoun and give the gender and number required in Greek.*

(c) *Identify the function of the relative pronoun in its own clause and give the case required in Greek.*

Example: The book **which** I bought was red.

Independent clause: The book . . . was red.
Relative clause: which I bought
Antecedent of relative pronoun: book (neuter singular)
Function of relative pronoun in own clause: direct object (accusative)

1. I resented the man **who** gave me money.
2. I resented the men **who** gave me money.
3. The men **whom** I resented gave me money.
4. The man **to whom** I gave money resents me.
5. The man **whose** money I accepted does not like me.
6. The men **whose** money I accepted do not like me.
7. The woman **whom** I liked gave me a gift.
8. The friend **for whom** I had bought a gift left town.
9. The silver **by which** I had hoped to persuade them had vanished.
10. Miners **who** wear goggles seldom smile.
11. Waiters **whose** coats are second-hand are usually bashful.
12. We resent the hunter **who** kills baby seals.
13. Politicians are admired by the constituents **to whom** they have given jobs.
14. All you **who** study do well.
15. Women **whom** the world admires wear worsted wool.

IV. *Translate. Then identify:*

(a) *gender, number, and case of the relative pronoun*

(b) *antecedent of the relative pronoun*

(c) *function of the relative pronoun in its own clause*

1. παιδεύσει ὁ Ὅμηρος τοὺς πολίτας **οἷς** δῶρα ἐπέμψατε.
2. δῶρα ἐπέμψαμεν τοῖς πολίταις **οἳ** ὑφ᾽ Ὁμήρου παιδεύονται.
3. δῶρα ἐπέμψαμεν εἰς τὴν νῆσον ἐν **ᾗ** ὁ Ὅμηρος φυλάττεται.
4. ἀγαθὴ ἡ νῆσος εἰς **ἣν** Ὅμηρος ἐπέμφθη.
5. ἀγαθαὶ αἱ ψυχαὶ **ἃς** παιδεύει ὁ Ὅμηρος.
6. ἀγαθὸν τὸ βιβλίον **ὃ** παρὰ τοὺς φίλους ἔπεμπεν.
7. ἀγαθὸν τὸ βιβλίον **ὃ** παρὰ τοὺς φίλους ἐπέμπετο.
8. παιδεύσομεν τοὺς πολίτας **ὧν** ἀγαθαὶ αἱ ψυχαί.
9. βιβλία πέμψουσιν **οἷς** παιδευθήσεσθε.
10. Ὅμηρον πέμψουσιν ὑφ᾽ **οὗ** παιδευθήσεσθε.

V. *Translate. Give form and syntax of all verbs.*

1. μὴ λύσητε τοὺς νεᾱνίᾱς.
2. λύωμεν τοὺς νεᾱνίᾱς.
3. λύωμεν τοὺς νεᾱνίᾱς;
4. ἀγγέλους μὴ πέμψῃς.
5. ἀγγέλους μὴ πέμψω;
6. οὐ λύετε τοὺς νεᾱνίᾱς.
7. λύομεν τοὺς νεᾱνίᾱς.
8. λύομεν τοὺς νεᾱνίᾱς;
9. ἀγγέλους οὐ πέμπεις.
10. ἀγγέλους οὐ πέμψω;

VI. *Translate. Give the syntax of the bold-face words.*

1. τῇ πρώτῃ **ἡμέρᾳ** τοὺς ἀγαθοὺς ἐπέμψαμεν πέντε **σταδίους**.

2. ἐξ **ἡμέρᾱς** ἐφυλάττομεν τοὺς κακούς.

3. τῆς πρώτης **ἡμέρᾱς** τοὺς ἀγαθοὺς ἐπαιδεύετε.

4. τῇ πρώτῃ **ἡμέρᾳ** τοὺς ἀγαθοὺς ἐπαιδεύετε.

5. τὴν πρώτην **ἡμέρᾱν** τοὺς ἀγαθοὺς ἐπαιδεύετε.

EXERCISES

I. 1. τῶν στρατιωτῶν πέντε παρὰ τὴν θάλατταν τάξει ὅπως οἱ ἐξ
ἄγγελοι ὑπὸ τῶν ἐν τῷ πεδίῳ μὴ κωλῦθῶσιν.

2. τὰς μὲν ἀδίκους βλάψωμεν, ταῖς δὲ δικαίαις αἶγάς τε καὶ ἄργυρον
πέμψωμεν.

3. Ὅμηρος, οὗ οἱ ὀφθαλμοὶ ὑπὸ τῶν θεῶν οὐκ ἐφυλάχθησαν, νεᾱνίᾱς
τε καὶ γέροντας τὴν λόγων τέχνην ἐδίδασκεν.

4. ἆρ’ αἶγες τοῖς θεοῖς ὑπό γε δούλων θύονται;

5. ἐὰν τοὺς γέροντας μετὰ φυλάκων πέντε στάδια πέμψητ’ ἐκ τῆς γῆς,
οὐ βλαβήσονται ὑπὸ τῶν κακῶν ξένων οἳ ἐκελεύσθησαν τὴν
εἰρήνην λῦσαι.

6. οὐκ ἐν σώματι ἀλλ’ ἐν ψῡχῇ ἥ γε χάρις ἡ τῶν ἀγαθῶν.

7. μετά γε τὴν νίκην οἱ μὲν φύλακες ἐχόρευον, οἱ δὲ πολέμιοι οὓς
ἐβλάψαμεν ὑπὸ τῶν ἐν ἀγορᾷ γερόντων ἐφυλάττοντο.

8. εἰ ἡ χώρᾱ εὖ ἐπολῑτεύετο, ἤρχομεν ἂν καὶ τῶν νήσων.

9. εἴ τοι τῆς χώρᾱς ἄρχοιεν οἱ σοφοί, ἡμέρᾱς μὲν ἂν πρᾱττοιτε τὰ
πρᾱγματα τὰ τῆς τε βουλῆς καὶ τῆς ἐκκλησίᾱς, νυκτὸς δὲ
χορεύοιτ’ ἄν.

10. οὗτοι ἱκανὸν ἔν γε μάχῃ ἡ νίκης ἐλπίς.

11. λῡσωμεν δὴ τὴν δημοκρατίᾱν. δεινὰ γὰρ τῷ δήμῳ πέπρᾱκται.

12. εἰ τῇ πρώτῃ νυκτὶ ἐξ τῶν χορευτῶν εὖ ἐχόρευσαν, ζῷα τῇ θεῷ
ἐτύθη ἂν ὑπὸ τῶν σοφῶν πολῑτῶν. θεοῖς γὰρ φίλοι οἱ χοροί.

13. οἱ νεᾱνίαι οἷς γε βιβλία περὶ τῆς τῶν παλαιῶν ἐλευθερίᾱς ὑφ' Ὁμήρου ἐγράφη εἰς μάχην πέντε ἡμερῶν ταχθήσονται τοῦ δήμου χάριν.

14. δεινόν τοι ἡ τῆς ἀδίκου σοφίᾱ, ὦ γέρον.

15. οἱ μὲν παλαιοὶ ὑπ' ἀγαθῶν ἤρχοντο, οἱ δὲ νῦν τοῖς τοῦ ἄρχειν ἀναξίοις δουλεύουσιν.

16. οἱ μὲν ξένοι ἵππον ἔθῡον πρὸ τῆς πολέμου ἀρχῆς, οἱ δ' Ἕλληνες οὔ.

17. τῷ σώματι θάνατος ἡ μοῖρα, ἀλλ' ἥ γε ψῡχὴ ἀθάνατος.

18. ὁ φύλαξ ὃς τῆς ἡμέρᾱς εἰς τὴν νῆσον ἐπέμφθη τοὺς δούλους πέντε νύκτας ἐκώλῡσε τὰς ἐλευθέρᾱς βλάψαι.

19. δεινὰ τοῖς γε σοφοῖς τὰ τῆς θαλάττης.

20. ὦ ἄδελφε, κακὰ δὴ τὰ δῶρα οἷς πείθεις Ἕλληνας ἐλευθέρους ξένοις κακοῖς δουλεύειν.

21. ἐπειδὴ ὁ πόλεμός γε ἐπαύθη, ὁ τοῦ δήμου φόβος ἐλύθη.

22. κακός τοι ὁ ποιητὴς ᾧ γε βιβλία περὶ μῑκρῶν πρᾱγμάτων γέγραπται.

23. ὦ φίλε, μακροῖς λόγοις μὴ πείσῃς ἀγαθοὺς ἄδικά τε καὶ κακὰ πρᾶξαι.

24. ἐὰν δίκαιοί γε πολῑτεύωσιν, οἱ ἄδικοι, ὑφ' ὧν ὁ δῆμος βλάπτεται, ἐκ τῆς γῆς πέμπονται.

25. βιβλίον γράψωμεν περὶ αἰγῶν ἐὰν οἱ πολῖται ἀργύριον πέμψωσιν;

26. εἰ διδάσκοιο ὑπὸ ποιητῶν, ἀγαθῶν ἀνθρώπων, εὖ γ' ἔπρᾱττες.

27. δῶρον δὴ οὐ μῑκρὸν ἡ σοφίᾱ.

28. κατά γε τὴν τοῦ γέροντος γνώμην κακοὶ οἱ σοφοί.

29. ἄδικοι οἱ κατὰ τῶν Ἑλλήνων λόγοι. καίτοι μακροὺς λόγους νυκτὸς καθ' Ἑλλήνων ἔγραφες.

II. 1. Let us be taught during the day at least in order that we may dance during the night.
2. Young man, if you should rule the land for five days, would we be harmed by our enemies?
3. Friend, do not bury the unjust men in the plain. The plain, you know, is sacred to the goddess by whom the land has been guarded.
4. If you (pl.) harm the horses which were sent to the soldiers, the war will be stopped within six days.
5. The young men by whom the goats and horses will be sent into the market place are not willing to be educated by the wise poet.

READINGS

A. Menander, *Monostichoi*

14. ἄγει τὸ θεῖον τοὺς κακοὺς πρὸς τὴν δίκην.

42. αἱ ἐλπίδες βόσκουσι τοὺς κενοὺς βροτῶν.

140. ἔρως δίκαιος καρπὸν εὐθέως φέρει.

156. ἔρωτα παύει λῑμὸς ἢ χαλκοῦ σπάνις.

165. ἐὰν ἔχωμεν χρήμαθ' ἕξομεν φίλους.

297. καλὸν δὲ καὶ γέροντι μανθάνειν σοφά.

326. λύπης ἰᾱτρός ἐστιν ἀνθρώποις λόγος.

337. μισθὸς διδάσκει γράμματ' οὐ διδάσκαλος.

433. ὅπλον μέγιστόν ἐστιν ἡ ἀρετὴ βροτοῖς.

543. χεὶρ χεῖρα νίπτει, δάκτυλοι δὲ δακτύλους.

ἄγω, ἄξω, ἤγαγον, ἦχα, ἦγμαι, ἤχθην   lead

βόσκω, βοσκήσω, ἐβόσκησα, βεβόσκηκα, ——, ἐβοσκήθην   feed

βροτός, βροτοῦ, ὁ   mortal man

γέρων, γέροντος, ὁ   old man

γράμμα, γράμματος, τό   letter (of the alphabet); (*pl.*) document

δάκτυλος, δακτύλου, ὁ   finger

ἐλπίς, ἐλπίδος, ἡ   hope

ἔρως, ἔρωτος, ὁ   love

ἐστί(ν) (enclitic; *third pers. sing., pres. indic. active of the verb "to be"*)   is

εὐθέως (*adv.*) straightway, forthwith

ἔχω, ἕξω/σχήσω, ἔσχον, ἔσχηκα, -έσχημαι, ——   have, hold; be able;
    (*mid.*) cling to, be next to (+ *gen.*)

θεῖος, θεία, θεῖον   divine

ἰᾱτρός, ἰᾱτροῦ, ὁ   doctor

καρπός, καρποῦ, ὁ   fruit

κενός, κενή, κενόν   empty, vain

λῑμός, λῑμοῦ, ὁ   hunger

λύπη, λύπης, ἡ   pain, grief

μανθάνω, μαθήσομαι, ἔμαθον, μεμάθηκα, ——, ——   learn, understand

μέγιστος, μεγίστη, μέγιστον   greatest

μισθός, μισθοῦ, ὁ   pay

νίπτω/νίζω, νίψω, ἔνιψα, ——, νένιμμαι, ἐνίφθην   wash

πρός (*prep.*) (+ *gen.*) in the eyes of, in the name of; (+ *dat.*) near; in
    addition to; (+ *acc.*) toward

σοφός, σοφή, σοφόν   wise

σπάνις, σπάνεως, ἡ   lack

φέρω, οἴσω, ἤνεγκα/ἤνεγκον, ἐνήνοχα, ἐνήνεγμαι, ἠνέχθην   bring, bear,
    carry; (*mid.*) win

χαλκός, χαλκοῦ, ὁ   bronze

χείρ, χειρός, ἡ   hand

χρῆμα, χρήματος, τό   thing; (*pl.*) goods, property, money

B. Sophokles, Fragment 811 P

ὅρκους ἐγὼ γυναικὸς εἰς ὕδωρ γράφω.

γυνή, γυναικός, ἡ   woman, wife

ἐγώ (*nom. sing. of first person pronoun*) I

ὅρκος, ὅρκου, ὁ   oath

ὕδωρ, ὕδατος, τό   water

UNIT
7

57. MIDDLE VOICE

A verb in the **middle voice** shows that the subject of the verb does the action, but that the action somehow returns to the subject, that the subject has a special interest in the action of the verb. Verbs in the middle voice can be transitive and thus take direct objects; they can also be intransitive. Compare the following diagrams of sentences with verbs in the active, passive, and middle voice.

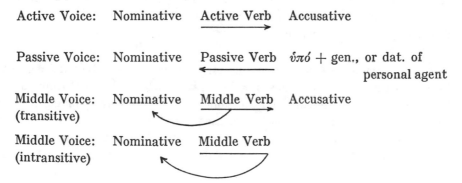

Active Voice:	Nominative	Active Verb →	Accusative
Passive Voice:	Nominative	Passive Verb ←	ὑπό + gen., or dat. of personal agent
Middle Voice: (transitive)	Nominative	Middle Verb →	Accusative
Middle Voice: (intransitive)	Nominative	Middle Verb	

The force of the middle voice varies from verb to verb. The most common meaning the middle voice gives to a verb is "to do something for oneself." Other possible meanings of the middle voice are a part of the vocabulary of some verbs and are given in the vocabularies. Special middle meanings of words learned thus far are given in Section 58.

The middle voice and the passive voice have *identical* forms in all the moods in the present, imperfect, perfect, and pluperfect tenses, and in the present and perfect infinitives. The middle voice has forms *different* from those of the passive in the future indicative and in all the moods and in the infinitive of the aorist tense. The following chart indicates which forms are identical and which are not.

163

IDENTICAL MIDDLE AND PASSIVE FORMS	*DIFFERENT MIDDLE AND PASSIVE FORMS*
Present Indicative	Future Indicative
Imperfect Indicative	Aorist Indicative
Present Subjunctive	Aorist Subjunctive
Present Optative	Aorist Optative
Present Infinitive	Aorist Infinitive
Perfect Indicative	
Pluperfect Indicative	
Perfect Infinitive	

Forms and endings which can be middle or passive will henceforth be called **middle/passive**. Thus, without any context, a form like παιδεύομαι is first person singular, present indicative middle/passive. The context usually makes clear which of the two voices the verb is in. For example, the passive will often be accompanied by a genitive of personal agent; the middle voice can take a direct object, but the passive voice cannot do so.

Only the morphology of those middle forms which are different from passive forms must be presented. Those middle forms which are different from passive forms all put middle endings on the same stem as the corresponding tense of the active voice. From this point on, then, what was called the future tense stem will now be called the **future active and middle tense stem** (Principal Part II without the ending -ω). What was called the aorist tense stem will now be called the **aorist active and middle tense stem** (Principal Part III without the past indicative augment and the ending -α). A chart of principal parts and tense stems is given in Section 60.

The moods and tenses of the middle voice have exactly the same uses as the moods and tenses of the active and passive voices. For example, an aorist subjunctive middle in a purpose clause in primary sequence differs from an aorist subjunctive active or passive in such a clause *in voice alone*.

1. FUTURE INDICATIVE MIDDLE

To form the future indicative middle, to the *future active and middle tense stem* add the same endings as in the present indicative middle/passive (cf. Section 43, page 111).

Thus the forms of the future indicative middle of παιδεύω are as follows:

S

1	παιδεύσομαι	I shall educate for myself / have (someone) educated
2	παιδεύσῃ/ παιδεύσει	you will educate for yourself / have (someone) educated
3	παιδεύσεται	he/she/it will educate for himself/herself/itself; he/she/it will have (someone) educated

P

1	παιδευσόμεθα	we shall educate for ourselves/have (someone) educated
2	παιδεύσεσθε	you will educate for yourselves/have (someone) educated
3	παιδεύσονται	they will educate for themselves/have (someone) educated

Observations: (1) The person markers -μαι, -σαι, -ται, -μεθα, -σθε, -νται will henceforth be called the **primary middle/passive person markers**.

(2) The alternative form of the second person singular, future indicative middle παιδεύσῃ is often the same as the third person singular, aorist subjunctive active. Context allows one to distinguish the two forms. Likewise, παιδεύσει can be either third person singular, future indicative active or second person singular, future indicative middle.

(3) Remember that the future indicative *passive* uses the suffix -ησ- on the aorist passive tense stem: παιδευθήσομαι, etc.

2. AORIST INDICATIVE MIDDLE

To form the aorist indicative middle, to the *augmented aorist active and middle tense stem* add the following endings:

	S	P
1	-αμην	-αμεθα
2	-ω	-ασθε
3	-ατο	-αντο

Thus the forms of the aorist indicative middle of παιδεύω are as follows:

S

1	ἐπαιδευσάμην	I educated for myself/had (someone) educated
2	ἐπαιδεύσω	you educated for yourself/had (someone) educated
3	ἐπαιδεύσατο	he/she/it educated for himself/herself/itself; he/she/it had (someone) educated

P

1	ἐπαιδευσάμεθα	we educated for ourselves/had (someone) educated
2	ἐπαιδεύσασθε	you educated for yourselves/had (someone) educated
3	ἐπαιδεύσαντο	they educated for themselves/had (someone) educated

Observations: (1) The endings of the aorist indicative middle consist of the tense vowel -α- and what will henceforth be called the **secondary middle/passive person markers**: -μην, -σο, -το, -μεθα, -σθε, -ντο.

(2) The original ending of the second person singular, aorist indicative middle was *-ασο. The intervocalic -σ- dropped out, and the remaining vowels contracted to give the ending -ω.

(3) Compare the first person plural forms:
    aorist indicative active   ἐπαύσαμεν
    aorist optative active   παύσαιμεν
    aorist indicative middle   ἐπαυσάμεθα

3. AORIST SUBJUNCTIVE MIDDLE

To form the aorist subjunctive middle, add the endings of the present subjunctive middle/passive to the *unaugmented aorist active and middle tense stem.*

Thus the forms of the aorist subjunctive middle of παιδεύω are as follows:

	S	P
1	παιδεύσωμαι	παιδευσώμεθα
2	παιδεύσῃ	παιδεύσησθε
3	παιδεύσηται	παιδεύσωνται

Observations: (1) The second person singular, aorist subjunctive middle παιδεύσῃ is always the same as the third person singular, aorist subjunctive active and sometimes the same as the alternative form of the second person singular, future indicative middle. Context usually allows one to distinguish among these forms.

(2) The aorist subjunctive middle differs from the present subjunctive middle/passive *only* in the tense stem. Note the use of the *primary* middle/passive person markers in both the present subjunctive middle/passive and the aorist subjunctive middle.

4. AORIST OPTATIVE MIDDLE

To form the aorist optative middle, add the following endings to the *unaugmented aorist active and middle tense stem*:

	S	P
1	-αιμην	-αιμεθα
2	-αιο	-αισθε
3	-αιτο	-αιντο

Thus the forms of the aorist optative middle of παιδεύω are as follows:

	S	P
1	παιδευσαίμην	παιδευσαίμεθα
2	παιδεύσαιο	παιδεύσαισθε
3	παιδεύσαιτο	παιδεύσαιντο

Observations: (1) The endings of the aorist optative middle consist of the tense vowel -α- + the optative suffix -ι- + the secondary middle/passive person markers. Note that both the present optative middle/passive and the aorist optative middle use the *secondary* middle/passive person markers.

(2) The original form of the second person singular, aorist optative middle was *-αισο. The intervocalic -σ- dropped out to give the ending -αιο; the diphthong and vowel do not contract.

5. AORIST INFINITIVE MIDDLE

To form the aorist infinitive middle, to the *unaugmented aorist active and middle tense stem* add the ending -ασθαι.

Thus the aorist infinitive middle of παιδεύω is

παιδεύσασθαι
to educate for oneself

Observations: (1) Like the aorist infinitives active and passive, the aorist infinitive middle shows simple aspect, NOT past time.

(2) The ending of the aorist infinitive middle consists of the tense vowel -α- + the infinitive suffix -σθαι, seen already in παιδεύεσθαι and πεπαιδεῦσθαι.

(3) The aorist infinitive middle and the present infinitive middle/passive are the only infinitives seen thus far which are accented on the antepenult. All other infinitives seen thus far are accented on the penult.

58. MIDDLE VOICE OF VERBS SEEN THUS FAR

In general the middle voice indicates that the subject has a special interest in the action of the verb; it can often be translated as "to do something for oneself." In addition to this general notion, some of the verbs learned thus far have special meanings in the middle which must be learned now.

ACTIVE VOICE	*MIDDLE VOICE*
ἄρχω + *genitive* rule	ἄρχομαι + *genitive* begin
γράφω write	γράφομαι note down, cause to be written; indict
διδάσκω teach	διδάσκομαι cause (someone) to be taught
θύω sacrifice	θύομαι cause a sacrifice to be made, consult the gods
λύω unbind, free	λύομαι unbind (one's own or for oneself), cause someone to be freed, ransom
παιδεύω educate, teach	παιδεύομαι cause someone to be educated or taught
παύω make stop, stop (*transitive*)	παύομαι stop (oneself), cease (*intransitive*)
πείθω persuade	πείθομαι + *dative* persuade oneself, obey
τάττω draw up in order	τάττομαι fall into order of battle
φυλάττω guard	φυλάττομαι guard someone for one's own protection, be on guard against

Henceforth, when the meaning of the middle differs significantly from the active, it will be given in the vocabulary. The middle meanings given above will all be found in the Greek–English Vocabulary.

Drills I and II, pages 183–84, may now be done.

59. SECOND AORIST ACTIVE AND MIDDLE

In the verbs studied so far Principal Part III has the ending -α (e.g., ἐπαίδευσα). Such verbs are said to have **first aorists** active and middle and use the *tense vowel* -α- in many of their forms. Any verb with a Principal Part III NOT ending in -α (or, in certain verbs, -αμην) is said to have a **second aorist**. *There is no difference in meaning between first aorists and second aorists.*

In Principal Part III, some verbs have second aorists ending in -ον (or, in certain verbs, -ομην). These verbs use the thematic vowel -ε/ο- as part of their endings.

The verb λείπω will serve as an example:

λείπω, λείψω, **ἔλιπον**, λέλοιπα, λέλειμμαι, ἐλείφθην, "leave, leave behind"

Only in the aorist active and middle does this verb employ endings different from those of the aorist of παιδεύω. The aorist passive of all verbs is formed in the same way from Principal Part VI.

In the indicative mood, second aorists like ἔλιπον employ the same endings as the IMPERFECT indicative of παιδεύω; in the other moods, and in the infinitive, they employ the same endings as PRESENT tense forms of παιδεύω, e.g., -οιμι, -οις, -οι, etc. in the second aorist optative active.

1. SECOND AORIST INDICATIVE ACTIVE AND MIDDLE

To form the second aorist indicative active and middle, drop the ending -ον from Principal Part III. There remains the past indicative augment plus the aorist active and middle tense stem. To the *augmented aorist active and middle tense stem* add the endings employed to form the imperfect indicative active and middle of παιδεύω.

Thus the augmented aorist active and middle tense stem of λείπω is ἐλιπ-, and the forms of the second aorist indicative active and middle are as follows:

		ACTIVE	MIDDLE
S	1	ἔλιπον	ἐλιπόμην
	2	ἔλιπες	ἐλίπου
	3	ἔλιπε(ν)	ἐλίπετο
P	1	ἐλίπομεν	ἐλιπόμεθα
	2	ἐλίπετε	ἐλίπεσθε
	3	ἔλιπον	ἐλίποντο

Observation: In verbs with second aorists active and middle, imperfect and aorist forms are distinguished by their different tense stems *only*. Compare ἐλίπομεν (first person plural, aorist indicative active) with ἐλείπομεν (first person plural, imperfect indicative active).

2. SECOND AORIST SUBJUNCTIVE ACTIVE AND MIDDLE

To form the second aorist subjunctive active and middle, add to the *unaugmented aorist active and middle tense stem* the endings employed to form the present subjunctive active and middle/passive of παιδεύω.

Thus the unaugmented aorist active and middle tense stem of λείπω is λιπ-, and the forms of the second aorist subjunctive active and middle are as follows:

		ACTIVE	MIDDLE
S	1	λίπω	λίπωμαι
	2	λίπῃς	λίπῃ
	3	λίπῃ	λίπηται
P	1	λίπωμεν	λιπώμεθα
	2	λίπητε	λίπησθε
	3	λίπωσι(ν)	λίπωνται

Observation: As in verbs with first aorists, *only* the different tense stem distinguishes present subjunctives from aorist subjunctives. Compare λίπωμεν (first person plural, aorist subjunctive active) with λείπωμεν (first person plural, present subjunctive active).

3. SECOND AORIST OPTATIVE ACTIVE AND MIDDLE

To form the second aorist optative active and middle, add to the *unaugment-ed aorist active and middle tense stem* the endings employed to form the present optative active and middle of παιδεύω.

Thus the forms of the second aorist optative active and middle of λείπω are as follows:

		ACTIVE	*MIDDLE*
S	1	λίποιμι	λιποίμην
	2	λίποις	λίποιο
	3	λίποι	λίποιτο
P	1	λίποιμεν	λιποίμεθα
	2	λίποιτε	λίποισθε
	3	λίποιεν	λίποιντο

Observation: *Only* the different tense stem distinguishes present optatives from second aorist optatives. Compare λίποιμεν (first person plural, aorist optative active) with λείποιμεν (first person plural, present optative active).

4. SECOND AORIST INFINITIVE ACTIVE AND MIDDLE

To form the second aorist infinitive active and middle, add to the *unaugmented aorist active and middle tense stem* the endings -εῖν and -έσθαι. Note the persistent accent, different from that of the present infinitive active and middle.

Thus the second aorist infinitives active and middle of λείπω are:

ACTIVE	*MIDDLE*
λιπεῖν	λιπέσθαι

Observation: Compare the second aorist infinitives λιπεῖν and λιπέσθαι with the present infinitives λείπειν and λείπεσθαι.

Drill III, pages 184–85, may now be done.

60. PRINCIPAL PARTS AND TENSE STEMS: SUMMARY

Each of the six Principal Parts has been used in conjugating the Greek verb. Here is a summary of the specific tense stems, and the verb forms seen thus far, which can be derived from each Principal Part.

PRINCIPAL PART	TENSE STEM		VERB FORMS DERIVED FROM STEM
	Form	*Name*	
I. παιδεύω	παιδευ–	present tense stem	present indicative active, middle, passive present subjunctive active, middle, passive present optative active, middle, passive present infinitive active, middle, passive imperfect indicative active, middle, passive
II. παιδεύσω	παιδευσ–	future active and middle tense stem	future indicative active, middle
III. ἐπαίδευσα	παιδευσ–	first aorist active and middle tense stem	aorist indicative active, middle aorist subjunctive active, middle aorist optative active, middle aorist infinitive active, middle
	λιπ–	second aorist active and middle tense stem	
ἔλιπον			

IV. πεπαίδευκα	πεπαιδευκ-	perfect active tense stem	perfect indicative active perfect infinitive active pluperfect indicative active
V. πεπαίδευμαι	πεπαιδευ-	perfect middle and passive tense stem	perfect indicative middle, passive perfect infinitive middle, passive pluperfect indicative middle, passive
VI. ἐπαιδεύθην	παιδευθ-	aorist passive tense stem	aorist indicative passive aorist subjunctive passive aorist optative passive aorist infinitive passive
	παιδευθησ-	future passive tense stem	future indicative passive

61. THE INDEPENDENT OPTATIVE

Just as a verb in the subjunctive may be used independently as the main verb
of a sentence, so too a verb in the optative can be used as the main verb of a
sentence in two different types of clauses.

1. OPTATIVE OF WISH

An independent optative, without any introductory word or introduced by
εἰ γάρ or εἴθε, expresses the speaker's wish, hope, or prayer for the future.
This is called the **optative of wish**. The negative is μή; tense shows aspect
only. Such wishes can be expressed in English by a subjunctive ("Long live
the queen!"), by the auxiliary verb *may* ("May the best man win!"), or be
introduced by *if only* or *I wish that* ("If only/I wish that it would not rain
tonight!").

$$\left.\begin{array}{l} \underline{} \\ \varepsilon \ddot{\imath} \theta \varepsilon \\ \varepsilon \dot{\imath} \; \gamma \grave{\alpha} \varrho \end{array}\right\} \; \pi \alpha \acute{\upsilon} o \imath \mu \varepsilon \nu \; \tau \dot{\eta} \nu \; \mu \acute{\alpha} \chi \eta \nu.$$

May we be stopping/stop the battle.
If only we may be stopping/stop the battle.
I wish that we may be stopping/stop the battle.

$$\left.\begin{array}{l} \underline{} \; \mu \dot{\eta} \\ \varepsilon \ddot{\imath} \theta \varepsilon \; \mu \dot{\eta} \\ \varepsilon \dot{\imath} \; \gamma \grave{\alpha} \varrho \; \mu \dot{\eta} \end{array}\right\} \; \lambda \acute{\upsilon} \sigma \varepsilon \imath \alpha \nu \; \tau o \grave{\upsilon} \varsigma \; \varkappa \alpha \varkappa o \acute{\upsilon} \varsigma.$$

May they not free the wicked men.
If only they may not free the wicked men.
I wish that they would not free the wicked men.

2. POTENTIAL OPTATIVE

An independent optative without any introductory word but with the
particle ἄν indicates that an action might possibly occur. This is called the
potential optative. The position of the particle ἄν within the sentence is
flexible. The negative with a potential optative is οὐ; tense shows aspect
only. The idea of the potential optative can be expressed in English by *may,
might, could, would*.

$$\left\{ \begin{array}{l} \pi\alpha\acute{v}o\iota\mu\varepsilon\nu \\ \pi\alpha\acute{v}\sigma\alpha\iota\mu\varepsilon\nu \end{array} \right\} \quad \ddot{\alpha}\nu \ \tau\grave{\eta}\nu \ \mu\acute{\alpha}\chi\eta\nu.$$

We $\left\{ \begin{array}{l} \text{may/might/could/would be stopping} \\ \text{may/might/could/would stop} \end{array} \right\}$ the battle.

The potential optative with ἄν is similar to the apodosis of a future less vivid conditional sentence.

The easiest way of distinguishing the optative of wish from the potential optative is the presence or absence of the particle ἄν. The potential optative will ALWAYS have ἄν; the optative of wish will NEVER have it. In the negative, the distinction will be reinforced by the negative οὐ with the potential optative, μή with the optative of wish. Of course, εἴθε and εἰ γάρ are used only with the optative of wish.

Drill IV, page 185, may now be done.

62. DEMONSTRATIVE ADJECTIVE/PRONOUN ἐκεῖνος, ἐκείνη, ἐκεῖνο, "that"

Demonstratives point out nouns in space, time, or importance. The demonstrative adjective/pronoun ἐκεῖνος, ἐκείνη, ἐκεῖνο indicates something relatively far away and is the equivalent of the English demonstrative *that* (plural *those*).

	M	F	N
Nom. S	ἐκεῖνος	ἐκείνη	ἐκεῖνο
Gen.	ἐκείνου	ἐκείνης	ἐκείνου
Dat.	ἐκείνῳ	ἐκείνῃ	ἐκείνῳ
Acc.	ἐκεῖνον	ἐκείνην	ἐκεῖνο
Nom. P	ἐκεῖνοι	ἐκεῖναι	ἐκεῖνα
Gen.	ἐκείνων	ἐκείνων	ἐκείνων
Dat.	ἐκείνοις	ἐκείναις	ἐκείνοις
Acc.	ἐκείνους	ἐκείνᾱς	ἐκεῖνα

Observation: ἐκεῖνος, ἐκείνη, ἐκεῖνο declines like any other adjective in -ος, -η, -ον except for the absence of the final -ν in the neuter singular nominative and accusative. In this absence of -ν, the neuter singular ἐκεῖνο is similar to the neuter singular of the article τό and the neuter singular of the relative pronoun ὅ.

A NOUN MODIFIED BY *ἐκεῖνος, ἐκείνη, ἐκεῖνο* MUST BE ACCOMPANIED BY THE ARTICLE. The demonstrative usually precedes the article; it may (rarely) follow the noun.

ἐκεῖνος ὁ ἀδελφὸς βιβλία ἔγραψεν.
That brother wrote books.

ἐκείνης τῆς ψῡχῆς
of that soul

ἐκείνῳ τῷ ἔργῳ
τῷ ἔργῳ ἐκείνῳ (rare)
by that deed

The demonstrative can also be used as a pronoun:

ἐκείνους φυλάττομεν.
We are guarding those men.

ἐκείνᾱς παύομεν.
We are stopping those women.

63. CONDITIONAL SENTENCES WITH RELATIVE PROTASES

Instead of being introduced by the particles *εἰ* or *ἐάν* (= *εἰ* + *ἄν*), the protasis of a conditional sentence can be introduced by a form of the relative pronoun. This happens when the antecedent of the pronoun is general and the relative pronoun can then be translated as *whoever, whatever,* or when the action of the clause is future, past or present general, or contrafactual. A conditional relative clause or **relative protasis** follows the same rules and formulas as protases introduced by *εἰ* or *ἐάν*; cf. Section 41, page 97. Tense in a subjunctive or optative in such a clause shows aspect only.

Even when the relative pronoun has a demonstrative antecedent like *ἐκεῖνος*, the structure of the clause shows that the speaker does not have anyone specific in mind.

1. FUTURE MORE VIVID CONDITIONAL SENTENCE WITH RELATIVE PROTASIS

RELATIVE PROTASIS   *APODOSIS*
ὅς, ἥ, ὅ + *ἄν* + subjunctive   future indicative

$$\text{ὃν ἂν εἰς τὴν νῆσον} \begin{Bmatrix} \text{πέμπωμεν} \\ \text{πέμψωμεν} \end{Bmatrix} \text{ἐκεῖνος παιδευθήσεται.}$$

Whomever we $\begin{Bmatrix} \text{are sending} \\ \text{send} \end{Bmatrix}$ to the island, that man will be educated.

If we send anyone to the island, he will be educated.

αἳ ἂν εἰς τὴν νῆσον $\begin{Bmatrix} πέμπωνται \\ πεμφθῶσιν \end{Bmatrix}$ ἐκεῖναι παιδευθήσονται.

Whatever women $\begin{Bmatrix} \text{are being sent} \\ \text{are sent} \end{Bmatrix}$ to the island, those women will be educated.

If any women are sent to the island, they will be educated.

Observation: Note that, as usual, the relative pronoun takes its case from how it is used in its own clause.

2. FUTURE LESS VIVID CONDITIONAL SENTENCE WITH RELATIVE PROTASIS

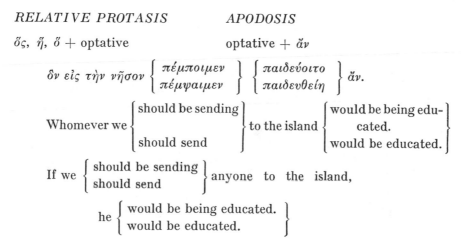

RELATIVE PROTASIS   *APODOSIS*

ὅς, ἥ, ὅ + optative   optative + ἄν

ὃν εἰς τὴν νῆσον $\begin{Bmatrix} πέμποιμεν \\ πέμψαιμεν \end{Bmatrix}$ $\begin{Bmatrix} παιδεύοιτο \\ παιδευθείη \end{Bmatrix}$ ἄν.

Whomever we $\begin{Bmatrix} \text{should be sending} \\ \text{should send} \end{Bmatrix}$ to the island $\begin{Bmatrix} \text{would be being educated.} \\ \text{would be educated.} \end{Bmatrix}$

If we $\begin{Bmatrix} \text{should be sending} \\ \text{should send} \end{Bmatrix}$ anyone to the island,

he $\begin{Bmatrix} \text{would be being educated.} \\ \text{would be educated.} \end{Bmatrix}$

Observation: The antecedent of the indefinite relative is often omitted in Greek (as in English) rather than being expressed by the demonstrative pronoun.

3. PRESENT GENERAL CONDITIONAL SENTENCE WITH RELATIVE PROTASIS

RELATIVE PROTASIS   *APODOSIS*

ὅς, ἥ, ὅ + ἄν + subjunctive   present indicative

ὃν ἂν εἰς τὴν νῆσον $\begin{Bmatrix} πέμπωμεν \\ πέμψωμεν \end{Bmatrix}$ παιδεύεται.

Whomever we send to the island is educated.
If we send anyone to the island, he is educated.

4. PAST GENERAL CONDITIONAL SENTENCE WITH RELATIVE PROTASIS

RELATIVE PROTASIS	APODOSIS
ὅς, ἥ, ὅ + optative	imperfect indicative

$$ὃν \ εἰς \ τὴν \ νῆσον \ \begin{Bmatrix} πέμποιμεν \\ πέμψαιμεν \end{Bmatrix} \ ἐπαιδεύετο.$$

Whomever we sent to the island was educated.

If we sent anyone to the island, he was educated.

5. PRESENT CONTRAFACTUAL CONDITIONAL SENTENCE WITH RELATIVE PROTASIS

RELATIVE PROTASIS	APODOSIS
ὅς, ἥ, ὅ + imperfect indicative	imperfect indicative + ἄν

ὃν ἐπέμπομεν εἰς τὴν νῆσον ἐπαιδεύετο ἄν.

Whomever we were (now) sending to the island (but we are not now sending anyone) would (now) be being educated (but is not being educated).

If we were (now) sending anyone to the island, he would (now) be being educated.

6. PAST CONTRAFACTUAL CONDITIONAL SENTENCE WITH RELATIVE PROTASIS

RELATIVE PROTASIS	APODOSIS
ὅς, ἥ, ὅ + aorist indicative	aorist indicative + ἄν

ὃν ἐπέμψαμεν εἰς τὴν νῆσον ἐπαιδεύθη ἄν.

Whomever we had sent to the island (but we did not send anyone) would have been educated (but no one was).

If we had sent anyone to the island, he would have been educated.

Drill V, page 185, may now be done.

64. ADVERBS

Most adjectives form adverbs by adding the ending **-ως** to the stem found by dropping the ending of the masculine genitive singular. Adverbs which do not follow this rule are given separately in the vocabulary.

    ἄξιος, ἀξία, ἄξιον, "worthy"   ἀξίως, "worthily"

    κακός, κακή, κακόν, "bad"   κακῶς, "badly"

Observation: Adverbs in -ως accented on the ultima always have a circumflex.

VOCABULARY

αἰσχρός, αἰσχρά, αἰσχρόν	ugly, shameful
ἄλλος, ἄλλη, ἄλλο	another, other
ἄνευ (prep.) (+ gen.)	without
γράμμα, γράμματος, τό	letter (of the alphabet); (pl.) documents
γραφή, γραφῆς, ἡ	indictment
δῆλος, δήλη, δῆλον	clear, visible
ἄδηλος, ἄδηλον	unclear, uncertain
εἰ γάρ (particle)	*introduces optative of wish*
εἴθε (particle)	*introduces optative of wish*
ἐκεῖ (adverb)	there (in that place)
ἐκεῖνος, ἐκείνη, ἐκεῖνο	that
ἡγεμών, ἡγεμόνος, ὁ	leader
κλέπτω, κλέψω, ἔκλεψα, κέκλοφα, κέκλεμμαι, ἐκλάπην	steal
κλέπτης, κλέπτου, ὁ	thief
κλοπή, κλοπῆς, ἡ	theft
λείπω, λείψω, ἔλιπον, λέλοιπα, λέλειμμαι, ἐλείφθην	leave, leave behind
οὖν (postpositive particle)	then, therefore
ποίημα, ποιήματος, τό	poem
ῥήτωρ, ῥήτορος, ὁ	public speaker
ῥητορική, ῥητορικῆς, ἡ	rhetoric
σῴζω, σώσω, ἔσωσα, σέσωκα, σέσωσμαι or σέσωμαι, ἐσώθην	save
σωτήρ, σωτῆρος, ὁ (voc. σῶτερ)	savior
τιμή, τιμῆς, ἡ	honor; price

VOCABULARY NOTES

The adjective αἰσχρός, αἰσχρά, αἰσχρόν, "ugly, shameful," has both a physical and a moral meaning.

When two forms of ἄλλος, ἄλλη, ἄλλο, "another, other," are used in the same sentence, each is translated *twice*: **ἄλλος ἄλλο** γράφει, "**One man** writes **one thing, another** (writes) **another**." The conjunction ἀλλά, "but," is the neuter plural of this word with a shift in accent.

The noun γράμμα, γράμματος, τό is formed from the root of the verb γράφω + the suffix -μα: cf. πρᾶγμα, πράγματος, τό from the root of πράττω < *πρᾶκιω. The basic meaning of γράμμα is "something written or drawn." "Letter of the alphabet" is a basic meaning of the word; τὰ γράμματα are the alphabet. The meaning is then extended to the content of the writing: a letter (epistle), inscription, document, records, books.

The noun γραφή, γραφῆς, ἡ is also derived from the verb γράφω. It is often synonymous with γράμμα. In this text it is used in one of its specialized meanings, "indictment"; cf. the English "writ." The verb γράφω in the middle voice can mean "indict," and can govern γραφήν as an **internal** or **cognate accusative**. The specific charge of the indictment goes into the genitive (the **genitive of the charge**) and the person whom one indicts is a direct object of the verb in the middle voice. The word γραφήν can be dropped and the genitive of the charge still remain:

> γραψώμεθα τοὺς ἀδίκους **γραφὴν δώρων.**
> γραψώμεθα τοὺς ἀδίκους **δώρων.**
> Let us indict the unjust men **on a charge of bribery.**

Note that there is no difference in meaning between the particles εἴθε and εἰ γάρ when they introduce optatives of wish. The accent on εἴθε is an exception to the rule and must be learned individually.

ἐκεῖνος, ἐκείνη, ἐκεῖνο is a demonstrative pronoun or adjective. When used as an adjective, it usually precedes the definite article: ἐκεῖνος ὁ ἀδελφός, "that brother." Like the article, the relative pronoun, and the adjective ἄλλος, ἐκεῖνος has no final nu in the neuter singular nominative and accusative.

The root which conveyed the idea of "stealing" was κλε/οπ-. ("e/o" indicates that the vowel of the root can take the form -ε- or -ο-.) Verbs often have a present tense stem with the root with -ε- (called the **e-grade** of the root): κλέπτω < *κλέπιω. Nouns which indicate an act often have -ο- (the **o-grade** of the root): κλοπή, κλοπῆς, ἡ, "theft." The stem of the perfect indicative active often uses the o-grade of the root: κέκλοφα; cf. πέπομφα.

Also note the final aspirated consonant of the perfect active tense stem: κέκλοφα; cf. πέπομφα, βέβλαφα, τέταχα. In the last principal part, note the absence of the suffix -θ- and the change of the vowel of the root to -α-; cf. ἐγράφην and the alternative aorist passive ἐβλάβην.

In the verb λείπω, λείψω, ἔλιπον, λέλοιπα, λέλειμμαι, ἐλείφθην, "leave, leave behind," the root shows three forms: λειπ- (Principal Part I and, with the final consonant changed, Principal Parts II, V, and VI), λοιπ- (Principal Part IV), and λιπ- (Principal Part III). These are the e-grade (λ**ε**ιπ-), the o-grade (λ**ο**ιπ-), and the **zero-grade** (λιπ-), in which neither of these two vowels appears. There are no fixed rules for which vowel grade appears where, but the o-grade is fairly common in the perfect (cf. κλέπτω, πέμπω).

The particle οὖν, like δέ, is postpositive. Its most common use in classical Greek is as a connective, indicating a new point in the development of the narrative or drawing a conclusion; hence the meanings "then, therefore."

The noun ποίημα, ποιήματος, τό, "poem," uses the same suffix as the nouns πρᾶγμα and γράμμα. Like the agent noun ποιητής, it comes from the verb ποιέω, "make"; a poem is a "thing made."

A ῥήτωρ, ῥήτορος, ὁ is originally simply a "speaker." In a democracy, where one's power depended on one's ability to persuade one's fellow citizens with words, ῥήτωρ came to mean "politician." ῥήτωρ is cognate with the English *word*. All that is left of the sound that is represented by the English *w* is the rough breathing on the rho. This sound had been represented in Greek by a letter called **digamma** (ϝ), but both the sound and the letter had disappeared from Attic Greek of the classical period.

The noun ῥητορική, ῥητορικῆς, ἡ is formed from the stem of ῥήτωρ by adding the adjectival suffix -ικος, -ικη, -ικον, "pertaining to." The noun is feminine because as an adjective it originally modified the noun τέχνη: rhetoric is the craft of the speaker. Words with this suffix have given us many English derivatives, e.g., music, arithmetic, physics. One must learn to deduce the meaning of such words, since they will not be given in the vocabulary.

In the verb σῴζω, σώσω, ἔσωσα, σέσωκα, σέσωσμαι or σέσωμαι, ἐσώθην, "save," note the iota subscript in the first principal part. The alternative perfect middle and passive forms have no difference in meaning.

In the noun σωτήρ, σωτῆρος, ὁ, "savior," the suffix -τηρ indicates "one who does the action of the verb": σωτήρ, "one who saves, savior."

The noun τῑμή, τῑμῆς, ἡ means essentially "price, value." The value that a community puts on a man is his "honor." This was and remains an extremely important concept in Greek society.

COGNATES AND DERIVATIVES

ἄλλος	allograph (the opposite of autograph)
γράμμα	grammar, gram
γραφή	graph
ἡγεμών	hegemony
κλέπτω	kleptomania
λείπω	eclipse
ποίημα	poem
ῥήτωρ	*word*
ῥητορική	rhetoric
σωτήρ	soteriology (the theological doctrine of **salvation**)
τῑμή	timocracy (according to Plato, "government in which **honor** is the guiding principle"; according to Aristotle, "rule in which power is distributed according to **wealth**")

DRILLS

I. (a) *Translate indicatives and infinitives; identify fully subjunctives and optatives.*
   (b) *If possible, change the number only.*
   (c) *Change the voice only.*

1. παυσόμεθα
2. παυθήσεσθε
3. ἔπαυσας
4. ἐπαύσω
5. ἐπαύθης
6. παύεται (2)
7. παύει (3)
8. παύσει (2)
9. παύσῃ (3)
10. παύσασθαι
11. ἐδιδάσκου (2)
12. ἐδιδάξατο
13. ἐδιδάχθησαν
14. διδάξηται
15. δεδιδάγμεθα (2)
16. ἐδεδίδαξο (2)
17. διδάξεσθε
18. ἐδιδάσκοντο (2)
19. ἐδιδάξω
20. διδάξει (2)

II. *Translate the following sentences.*

1. Ὅμηρος παιδεύεται ὑπὸ τῶν φίλων.
2. Ὅμηρος παιδεύεται τὸν ἀδελφόν.
3. Ὅμηρος παιδεύσεται τὸν ἀδελφόν.
4. διδάσκετε τοὺς νεᾱνίᾱς; διδασκόμεθά γε τοὺς νεᾱνίᾱς.
5. δεδίδακται τοὺς ἀδελφούς.
6. δεδίδακται τοῖς ἀδελφοῖς.
7. δεδίδαχε τοὺς ἀδελφούς.

8. ἐθύετο ἡ αἴξ.

9. ἐθύετο ὁ δῆμος.

10. ἤρχομεν τῶν νήσων.

11. ἠρχόμεθα τῆς μάχης.

12. ἠρχόμεθα ὑπὸ τῶν ξένων.

13. ἠρξάμεθα τῆς μάχης, ἀλλ᾽ οὐκ ἤρχθημεν ὑπὸ τοῦ δήμου.

14. ἀρξόμεθα τῆς μάχης. οὐ γὰρ ἀρχθησόμεθα ὑπὸ ξένων.

15. ὁ μὲν ποιητὴς βιβλίον ἔγραψεν, ὁ δ᾽ ἀδελφὸς κακοὺς ἐγράψατο.

16. ὑπὸ μὲν τοῦ ποιητοῦ βιβλίον ἐγράφη, ὑπὸ δὲ τοῦ ἀδελφοῦ κακοὶ
    ἐγράφησαν.

17. πέμψωμεν χρῡσὸν ὡς λῡσώμεθα τούς γε φίλους.

18. ἐν τῷ πεδίῳ ἐπαύσαντο ἵνα παύσαιεν τοὺς πολεμίους.

19. ἐὰν μὴ φυλαττώμεθα τούς γε κακούς, φυλαχθησόμεθα ὑπὸ κακῶν.

20. ὦ ὁπλῖται, μὴ τάξησθε παρὰ τῇ γεφύρᾳ.

III. (a) *Translate indicatives and infinitives; identify fully subjunctives and
        optatives.*
    (b) *Where possible, change number only.*
    (c) *Change voice only.*

1. λίπητε

2. λείπητε

3. ἐλίπεσθε

4. λείπεσθε (2)

5. ἐλείπεσθε (2)

6. λείπειν

7. λείποιεν

8. λίποιεν

9. λίπῃ   (2)

10. λίπῃς

11. λιπέσθαι

12. ἔλιπον   (2)

13. ἔλειπον   (2)

14. λείπω   (2)

15. λίπω

16. λίποιο

17. λίπωνται

18. ἐλίπου

19. ἐλείπομεν
20. ἐλίποντο
21. λιπεῖν
22. λείπεσθαι (2)
23. λιπώμεθα
24. λιποίμην
25. ἐλιπόμεθα

IV. *Translate the following sentences.*

1. λύομεν τοὺς ἀγαθούς.
2. λύωμεν τοὺς ἀγαθούς.
3. λύωμεν τοὺς ἀγαθούς;
4. μὴ λύσητε τοὺς ἀγαθούς.
5. εἰ γὰρ λύσαιμεν τοὺς ἀγαθούς.
6. λύσαιμεν ἂν τοὺς ἀγαθούς.
7. εἴθε λύοιεν οἱ φύλακες τοὺς ἀγαθούς.
8. λύοιμεν ἂν οἱ φύλακες τοὺς ἀγαθούς;
9. οὐκ ἂν λύοιεν οἱ φύλακες τοὺς ἀγαθούς.
10. μὴ λύσειαν οἱ φύλακες τοὺς ἀγαθούς.
11. παυσώμεθα;
12. μὴ παυσώμεθα.
13. μὴ παύσησθε.
14. μὴ παύσαις τοὺς χορευτάς.
15. οὐκ ἂν παύσειας τόν γε χορευτήν.
16. μὴ παύσαιο.

V. *Translate the following sentences.*

1. ὃν ἂν παύσωσι φυλάττεται.
2. οὓς ἂν παύσωσι φυλάττονται.
3. ἐφυλάττετο ὃν παύοιεν.
4. ὃς παύοιτο οὐκ ἂν φυλάττοιτο.
5. εἰς ἀγορὰν πεμφθήσεται τὰ ζῷα ἃ ἂν μὴ θύηται.
6. εἰς ἀγορὰν ἐπέμφθη ἂν τὰ ζῷα ἃ μὴ ἐτύθη.
7. ἀγαθαὶ αἳ ἂν τὰ δίκαια πράττωσιν.
8. κακαὶ ἃς οἱ κακοὶ διδάσκαλοι παιδεύωσιν ἄν.
9. οὓς φυλάττοιμεν οὐκ ἐλύοντο.
10. οὓς ἐφυλάττομεν οὐκ ἂν ἐλύοντο.

EXERCISES

I. 1. εἰ γὰρ νυκτός τε καὶ ἡμέρας ἐκεῖνοί γ' οἱ ἀγαθοὶ φύλακες εὖ
       φυλάττοιντο τοὺς κλέπτας ὡς τὸ τοῦ δήμου ἀργύριον μὴ
       κλέψωσιν.

    2. εἴθε οἱ ἄλλοι στρατιῶται μὴ λίποιεν τὴν γέφυραν ἀλλὰ τοὺς
       πολεμίους κωλύσειαν.

    3. οἱ κακοὶ τὰ τῶν πολῑτῶν κλέπτοιεν ἄν. φυλάξωμεν οὖν ἐκείνᾱς
       τὰς οἰκίᾱς τὰς μῑκράς.

    4. οὗτοι ἐλεύθερος ὃς ἂν τῷ σώματι δουλεύῃ· ἀλλὰ καὶ σοφὸς καὶ
       ἐλεύθερος οὗ ἂν ἡ ψῡχὴ ἄρχῃ.

    5. οἳ ἂν ἐν τῇ νήσῳ λείπωνται οὐ λυθήσονται.

    6. ἆρ' ἐκεῖνο πέμψαιμεν ἄν; ἢ τὸ ἄλλο πέμψωμεν;

    7. ἐδούλευον οἳ ἐν ἐκείνῃ τῇ οἰκίᾳ λειφθεῖεν.

    8. οὐκ ἀγαθόν γε τὸ ἄνευ ἡγεμόνος τῆς μάχης ἄρχεσθαι. καίτοι
       οὐκ ἠθελήκᾱσιν οἱ στρατιῶται παύσασθαι ἐν τῷ πεδίῳ
       ἀλλὰ τάττονται εἰς μάχην. πείσωμεν οὖν ἐκείνους παύσασθαι.

    9. ἀγαθὸς δὴ ὁ ἡγεμὼν ὃς ἂν εὖ τάττῃ τοὺς ὁπλίτᾱς. ἄνευ γὰρ
       ἡγεμόνος οὐκ εὖ τάττονται οἱ στρατιῶται.

   10. ὅς τοι τὸν χρῡσὸν αἰσχρῶς ἔκλεψεν, ἐκεῖνον γραφὴν κλοπῆς ἂν
       ἐγράψαντο οἱ πολῖται.

   11. ἐκεῖνοί γ' οἱ κακοὶ στρατιῶται οἳ τὰ ὅπλα ἐν τῷ πεδίῳ ἔλιπον
       μετὰ τὴν μάχην τόν τ' ἄργυρον τὸν τοῦ Ὁμήρου καὶ τὰς
       αἶγας κεκλόφᾱσιν. ἐκείνους οὖν γραψαίμεθα κλοπῆς.

   12. πειθοίμεθα διδασκάλοις τοῖς γ' ἀγαθοῖς. διδάσκουσι γὰρ τοῖς
       γράμμασι καὶ τὴν τέχνην καὶ τὴν ἀρετήν. ἄνευ δὴ τέχνης
       τε καὶ ἀρετῆς οὗτοι καλῶς πρᾱττουσιν οἱ νεᾱνίαι.

   13. διδαξώμεθα δὴ τοὺς πέντε ἀδελφοὺς τὴν τοῦ σοφοῦ ποιητοῦ
       τέχνην. πέμποιεν γὰρ ἂν οἱ πολῖται τοῖς ἀγαθοῖς ποιηταῖς
       δῶρα, ἢ στεφάνους ἢ χρῡσόν.

   14. ὁ μὲν ῥήτωρ τοὺς μακροὺς λόγους γράφει· ὁ δ' ἄλλος γράφεται.

   15. ἐν τῷ ἱερῷ παυσώμεθα. ἐκεῖ γὰρ θύσαιμεν ἂν ταῖς θεοῖς.

   16. τοὺς μὲν διδάσκει ὁ Ὅμηρος, τοὺς δὲ διδάσκεται.

17. ἄλλος ἄλλους διδάσκεται.

18. καὶ οἱ κλέπται τῇ γε ῥητορικῇ, τῇ περὶ τοὺς λόγους τέχνῃ, σῴζοιντ᾽ ἄν, ἐπειδή τοι ἐν ταῖς δίκαις λόγοις μὲν οἱ ἄνευ γνώμης πείθονται, ἔργοις δὲ οἱ σοφοί.

19. αἰσχρὰ ἂν πράττοιτε οἳ τοὺς τῆς οἰκίας ποιήματα μὴ διδάσκοισθε.

20. ἄδηλά τοι τὰ τοῦ πολέμου. θυσώμεθα οὖν περὶ τῶν νῦν. λύσωμεν τὴν εἰρήνην ἢ μή; πείσαιμεν γὰρ ἂν τοὺς πολίτᾱς τὰς οἰκίᾱς λιπεῖν.

21. εἰ γὰρ θύσαιμεν αἶγας τοῖς θεοῖς, τοῖς τῶν πολιτῶν σωτῆρσιν.

22. εἰ ἐν τῷ πεδίῳ μὴ ἐτάχθης, ἔσωσας ἂν τοὺς ἀδελφούς.

23. οὐ μῑκρὰ ἡ τοῦ ἀγαθοῦ ποιητοῦ τῑμή. καὶ οὐ μῑκρὰ ἐν τῇ ἀγορᾷ ἡ τῶν ἐκείνου βιβλίων τῑμή.

24. ἐκεῖ παυσαίμεθα ἵνα τοὺς ξένους παύσωμεν.

25. δῆλοι τοῖς γε στρατιώταις οἱ ἐν τῷ πεδίῳ λίθοι.

II. 1. If only the animals and the money may be sent to the island by the men in the market place. The (inhabitants) of the island could sacrifice to the gods.

2. I wish that the young men may be well taught by the words of the wise poet. They would then be on guard, at least, against the enemy.

3. May the gods save the assembly and the council. Let us not leave the soldiers in the country.

4. The goats of the men of the plain might be stolen by the enemy. Do not prevent the men of the plain from guarding their animals.

READINGS

A. Menander, *Fragments*

456. δὶς παῖδες οἱ γέροντες.

348. τὸ τῆς τύχης τοι μεταβολὰς πολλὰς ἔχει.

782. ἰᾱτρός ἐστιν ὁ λόγος ἀνθρώποις κακῶν.
     ψῡχῆς γὰρ οὗτος μόνος ἔχει κουφίσματα.

δίς (*adv.*) twice
ἐστί(ν) (*enclitic; third person sing., pres. ind. active of the verb "to be"*) is
ἔχω, ἕξω/σχήσω, ἔσχον, ἔσχηκα, -ἔσχημαι, —— have, hold; be able; (*mid.*)
     cling to, be next to (+ *gen.*)
ἰᾱτρός, ἰᾱτροῦ, ὁ doctor
κούφισμα, κουφίσματος, τό lightening, relief
μεταβολή, μεταβολῆς, ἡ change
μόνος, μόνη, μόνον alone
οὗτος, αὕτη, τοῦτο this, that
παῖς, παιδός, ὁ or ἡ child
πολλοί, πολλαί, πολλά many
τύχη, τύχης, ἡ fortune, chance

B. Aischylos, *Seven Against Thebes* 4

εἰ μὲν γὰρ εὖ πράξαιμεν, αἰτίᾱ θεοῦ.
αἰτίᾱ, αἰτίᾱς, ἡ responsibility, guilt, cause

C. Sophokles, *Philoktetes* 792–796

The hero Philoktetes, who has been abandoned by the Greeks on the island of Lemnos, cries out in pain.

φεῦ, παπαῖ.

παπαῖ μάλ' αὖθις. ὦ διπλοῖ στρατηλάται,
'Αγάμεμνον, ὦ Μενέλāε, πῶς ἂν ἀντ' ἐμοῦ
τὸν ἴσον χρόνον τρέφοιτε τήνδε τὴν νόσον;
ὤμοι μοι.

'Αγαμέμνων, 'Αγαμέμνονος, ὁ (*voc.* 'Αγάμεμνον) Agamemnon, king of Mykenai, brother of Menelaos, co-leader of the expedition against Troy

αὖθις (*adv.*) again

διπλοῦς, διπλῆ, διπλοῦν, twofold, double (*for the declension, see Appendix, p. 593*).

ἐμοῦ (*gen. sing. of first person pronoun*) me

ἴσος, ἴση, ἴσον equal

μάλα (*adv.*) very

Μενέλāος, Μενελάου, ὁ Menelaos, co-leader of the Greeks against Troy

μοι (*enclitic*) (*dat. sing. of first person pronoun*) me

νόσος, νόσου, ἡ sickness

ὅδε, ἥδε, τόδε (*gen.* τοῦδε, τῆσδε, τοῦδε; *used with the article*) this

παπαῖ *exclamation of suffering or surprise*

πῶς (*adv.*) how

στρατηλάτης, στρατηλάτου, ὁ general, commander

τήνδε *cf.* ὅδε

τρέφω, θρέψω, ἔθρεψα, τέτροφα, τέθραμμαι, ἐτράφην/ἐτρέφθην rear, bring up, nourish

φεῦ *exclamation of grief or anger*

χρόνος, χρόνου, ὁ time

ὤμοι *exclamation of pain*

REVIEW: UNITS FOUR TO SEVEN

I. *For each of the following nouns, provide the proper form of the article (or ὦ) and an adjective of your choice. Translate. Then change plurals to singulars and singulars to plurals. Give all possibilities.*

1. φύλακι	6. γέρον	11. σωτῆρας
2. αἰγός	7. νεᾱνίᾱς	12. οἰκιῶν
3. πολίτου	8. ἐλπίδες	13. νυξί
4. χῶραι	9. ποιητά	14. μοῦσαι
5. γεφύρᾱς	10. ἡγεμόνι	15. πρᾶγμα

II. *Translate indicatives and infinitives; identify subjunctives and optatives. Change to the other two voices. Change number where possible. Give all possibilities.*

1. ἐκλέπτετο	9. ἐθύσασθε	17. λιπέσθαι
2. ἐκλάπησαν	10. ἐθάψατε	18. τάττοιεν
3. κλέψουσιν	11. ἐδιδάχθης	19. τάξωνται
4. κλέψωσιν	12. ἐπολῑτεύσατο	20. κωλῡθείημεν
5. ἐκλάπημεν	13. γράφομεν	21. ἐχόρευον
6. κέκλοφας	14. γραφήσονται	22. τεθυκέναι
7. κλέπτῃ	15. ἐλῑπόμεθα	23. γράψαι
8. ἐτεθύκειν	16. ἐλείπου	24. ἐσώθης

III. *Translate.*

1. θεοῖς δὴ θῦσώμεθα ἄνευ αἰγῶν;
   (deliberative subjunctive)

2. εἰ ἐκεῖνοί γε οἱ ἐλεύθεροι τοὺς δούλους μὴ φυλάττοιντο, ταφείη ἂν ὑπὸ κακῶν τὰ τῶν ἀγαθῶν σώματα.
   (future less vivid conditional sentence; enclitic; neuter plural subject with singular verb; genitive of personal agent)

3. κακός τε καὶ αἰσχρὸς ὃς ἂν εἰς μάχην γε πεμφθῆναι μὴ ἐθέλῃ.
   (present general conditional sentence with protasis introduced by relative pronoun and with nominal apodosis; enclitics; object infinitive)

4. εἴ τοι παρά γε τὴν τῶν Ἑλλήνων δόξαν αἱ τῶν πολεμίων
   φάλαγγες πέντε ἡμερῶν ἐτάξαντο ἐν τῷ πεδίῳ, ὦ στρατιῶτα,
   οὐκ ἂν ἐκελεύσθης ὑπὸ τῶν γερόντων τὴν νῆσον λιπεῖν.
   (past contrafactual conditional sentence; enclitics; genitive of
   time within which; genitive of personal agent; second aorist)

5. μὴ δουλεύοιμεν τοῖς μὴ σοφοῖς.
   (optative of wish; dative with δουλεύω; generic substantive)

6. τοῦ ἄρχειν χάριν μὴ κακὰ πράξητε τοὺς γέροντας, ὦ νεανίαι· ἐὰν
   γὰρ ἄλλων αἰσχρῶς ἄρξητε, βλαβήσεσθε ὑπ’ ἐκείνων οὕς γ’
   ἐβλάψατε.
   (articular infinitive; prohibitive subjunctive; future more vivid
   conditional sentence; genitive with ἄρχω; genitive of personal
   agent; enclitic)

7. ἀγαθὸς ἐκεῖνος ὁ ῥήτωρ ᾧ πέπανται ἡ μάχη.
   (nominal sentence; dative of personal agent)

8. οὐ δὴ ὁ θάνατος φοβερὸν τοῖς τε δικαίοις καὶ τοῖς ἐλευθέροις,
   ἀλλ’ ἡ δουλεία. ἐὰν μὲν γὰρ ἐν μάχῃ τό γε σῶμα βλαφθῇ, οὐ
   βλάπτεται καὶ ἡ ψυχή, εἰ δὲ ὅ τε δίκαιος ὑπὸ τοῦ ἀδίκου ἄρχοιτο
   καὶ ὁ ἀγαθὸς ὑπὸ τοῦ κακοῦ κελευσθείη καὶ ταχθείη,
   δουλεύσαι ἂν ἡ ψυχή, δῶρον ἀνθρώποις τῶν θεῶν.
   (nominal sentence; substantives; enclitics; present general conditional sentence; future less vivid conditional sentence; genitive of
   personal agent; apposition)

9. ὡς κλέψαιτε τὸν τῶν Ἑλλήνων χρῡσὸν ἐπέμπεσθε, ὦ γέροντες,
   εἰς ἐκείνην τὴν μῑκρὰν οἰκίᾱν ἐν ᾗ Ὅμηρος τὸν ἀδελφὸν
   ἐπαιδεύσατο.
   (purpose clause in secondary sequence; relative clause)

IV. *Translate into Greek.*
   May you indict the wicked young men for their shameful deeds in order
   that the country may not be destroyed by the gods.

SELF-CORRECTING EXAMINATION 2A

I.   (a) *Identify the gender, number, and case of each of the following words or phrases.*

   (b) *Change only the NUMBER of each word or phrase (i.e., from singular to plural or from plural to singular).*
   Where there is more than one possibility, give both or all.

   1. ὅπλα
   2. δοξῶν
   3. φύλαξιν
   4. ἐλπίδας
   5. ὦ στρατιῶται
   6. γέροντες

II.   *Put the proper form of the article and the adjective ἄδικος with the GENITIVE SINGULAR of the following nouns.*

   1. ποιητής
   2. διδάσκαλος
   3. δημοκρατίᾱ
   4. πρᾶγμα

III.   *Give a synopsis of πείθω in the first person plural.*

PRINCIPAL PARTS: _____

	ACTIVE	MIDDLE	PASSIVE
PRESENT INDICATIVE			
IMPERFECT INDICATIVE			
FUTURE INDICATIVE			
AORIST INDICATIVE			
PERFECT INDICATIVE			
PLUPERFECT INDICATIVE			
PRESENT SUBJUNCTIVE			
AORIST SUBJUNCTIVE			
PRESENT OPTATIVE			
AORIST OPTATIVE			
PRESENT INFINITIVE			
AORIST INFINITIVE			
PERFECT INFINITIVE			

IV. *Translate, and answer all appended questions.*

1. ἐὰν οἱ Ἕλληνες μετὰ τὴν μάχην παύσωνται ἐν τῷ πεδίῳ, σωθήσονταί
    τε οἱ ἐν τῇ χώρᾳ καὶ αἶγας, δῶρα τῇ γε θεῷ, θύσουσιν ἵνα τοὺς
    πολεμίους ἐκ τῆς γῆς πέμψῃ.
    (a) *Give the syntax of* παύσωνται.
    (b) *Explain the use of* τε *in the second line.*
    (c) *Give the syntax of* δῶρα.

2. μὴ φυλαττώμεθα τοὺς τῆς δημοκρατίας ἀναξίους; ἀγαθὸν μὲν γὰρ ἡ
    ἐλευθερία, κακὸν δὲ ἡ δουλεία καὶ αἰσχρόν.

3. εἴ τοι τόν γ᾽ Ὅμηρον γραφὴν κλοπῆς μὴ ἐγράψατο ὁ ἀδελφός, οὐκ ἂν
    ἐκελεύσατε τοὺς φύλακας τὰ ζῷα φυλάττειν ὡς μὴ κλαπείη ὑπὸ
    ἐκείνου τοῦ ποιητοῦ.
    (a) *Give the syntax of* κλαπείη.
    (b) *Describe and make the changes necessary to turn this sentence into a
        present general conditional sentence.*

4. εἰ τάττοισθε εἰς μάχην, ὦ στρατιῶται, διὰ τὴν ἐν πολέμῳ ἀρετὴν
    ἐκωλύετε τὴν φάλαγγα τὴν τῶν πολεμίων τῶν ἀπὸ τῆς νήσου
    βλάψαι τὰς αἶγάς τε καὶ τὰς ἵππους.
    (a) *Give the syntax of* ἐκωλύετε.

5. εἰ γὰρ μὴ παιδεύσαισθε τοὺς νεανίας παρὰ τῷ αἰσχρῷ καὶ ἀδίκῳ
    ποιητῇ, ὅς γε τὰ βιβλία ἐν ἀγορᾷ ἔλιπεν.

6. οἳ ἂν τῆς πρώτης ἡμέρας πεμφθῶσιν ἄνευ ἡγεμόνος πέντε στάδια
    ἀπὸ τῆς ἀγορᾶς ταχθήσονται παρὰ τῇ γεφύρᾳ.
    (a) *Give the syntax of* ἡμέρας.
    (b) *Give the syntax of* πεμφθῶσιν.
    (c) *Give the syntax of* στάδια.

V.   *Translate into Greek.*

   If six at least of the public speakers had not saved the freedom of the citizens, we would have been slaves to evil men.

I. 1. ὅπλα: N pl. nom./acc./voc.; ὅπλον

    2. δοξῶν: F pl. gen.; δόξης

    3. φύλαξιν: M pl. dat.; φύλακι

    4. ἐλπίδας: F pl. acc.; ἐλπίδα

    5. ὦ στρατιῶται: M pl. voc.; ὦ στρατιῶτα

    6. γέροντες: M pl. nom./voc.; γέρων/ὦ γέρον

II. 1. τοῦ ἀδίκου ποιητοῦ

    2. τοῦ ἀδίκου διδασκάλου

    3. τῆς ἀδίκου δημοκρατίᾱς

    4. τοῦ ἀδίκου πρᾱ́γματος

III. PRINCIPAL PARTS: πείθω, πείσω, ἔπεισα, πέπεικα, πέπεισμαι, ἐπείσθην

	ACTIVE	MIDDLE	PASSIVE
PRESENT INDICATIVE	πείθομεν	πειθόμεθα	πειθόμεθα
IMPERFECT INDICATIVE	ἐπείθομεν	ἐπειθόμεθα	ἐπειθόμεθα
FUTURE INDICATIVE	πείσομεν	πεισόμεθα	πεισθησόμεθα
AORIST INDICATIVE	ἐπείσαμεν	ἐπεισάμεθα	ἐπείσθημεν
PERFECT INDICATIVE	πεπείκαμεν	πεπείσμεθα	πεπείσμεθα
PLUPERFECT INDICATIVE	ἐπεπείκεμεν	ἐπεπείσμεθα	ἐπεπείσμεθα
PRESENT SUBJUNCTIVE	πείθωμεν	πειθώμεθα	πειθώμεθα
AORIST SUBJUNCTIVE	πείσωμεν	πεισώμεθα	πεισθῶμεν
PRESENT OPTATIVE	πείθοιμεν	πειθοίμεθα	πειθοίμεθα
AORIST OPTATIVE	πείσαιμεν	πεισαίμεθα	πεισθεῖμεν / πεισθείημεν
PRESENT INFINITIVE	πείθειν	πείθεσθαι	πείθεσθαι
AORIST INFINITIVE	πεῖσαι	πείσασθαι	πεισθῆναι
PERFECT INFINITIVE	πεπεικέναι	πεπεῖσθαι	πεπεῖσθαι

IV. 1. If the Greeks after the battle stop (intrans.) in the plain, the men in the country will be saved/will be being saved and they will sacrifice/will be

195

sacrificing goats, gifts *to the goddess*, in order that she may send the enemy/enemies from/out of the land.

(a) παύσωνται is aorist subjunctive: subjunctive in the protasis of a future more vivid conditional sentence; aorist to indicate simple aspect.

(b) τε serves together with καί to link the two verbs σωθήσονται and θύσουσιν.

(c) δῶρα is accusative, in apposition to αἶγας, the direct object of θύσουσιν.

2. Are we not to be guarding/guard (habitually) against the men/those unworthy of (the) democracy? For, on the one hand, freedom is a good thing; on the other hand, slavery is an evil and shameful thing.

3. If, you know, the/your brother had not indicted *Homer*, at least, on a charge of theft, you would not have ordered the guards to be guarding/guard (habitually) the animals in order that they might not be stolen by that poet.

(a) κλαπείη is aorist optative: optative in a purpose clause in secondary sequence introduced by the aorist ἐκελεύσατε; aorist to indicate simple aspect.

(b) PROTASIS: Change εἰ το ἐάν.
     Change the aorist indicative ἐγράψατο to a subjunctive, either γράψηται (aorist to show simple aspect) or γράφηται (present to show progressive/repeated aspect).
     APODOSIS: Remove the ἄν.
     Change the aorist indicative ἐκελεύσατε to a present indicative, κελεύετε.
     In the purpose clause, change the aorist optative passive κλαπείη to the subjunctive κλαπῇ, because we are now in primary sequence.

4. If you fell into order of battle (middle)/were stationed (passive) for battle, soldiers, on account of your virtue in war you used to prevent/prevented (habitually) the phalanx of the enemy/enemies from the island from harming (once and for all) the (nanny) goats and the mares.

(a) ἐκωλύετε is imperfect indicative in the apodosis of a past general conditional sentence.

5. I wish that/May/If only you not have the young men taught at the house of the shameful and unjust poet, who/since he left the/his books in the market place.

6. Whoever during the first day are sent without a leader five stades/
   36,000 inches from the market place will be stationed beside the bridge.
   (If any men are sent . . . , they will be stationed . . . .)

   (a) ἡμέρας is a genitive of time within which.

   (b) πεμφθῶσιν is an aorist subjunctive: subjunctive in the relative
       protasis of a future more vivid conditional sentence; aorist to in-
       dicate simple aspect.

   (c) στάδια is accusative of extent of space.

V. εἰ ἔξ γε τῶν ῥητόρων μὴ ἔσωσαν τὴν τῶν πολιτῶν ἐλευθερίᾶν,
   ἐδουλεύσαμεν ἂν (τοῖς) κακοῖς.

I. (a) *Identify the gender, number, and case of each of the following words or phrases.*
   (b) *Change only the NUMBER of each word or phrase (i.e., from singular to plural or from plural to singular).*
   Where there is more than one possibility, give both or all.

  1. νεᾱνιῶν
  2. νυξίν
  3. Ἕλληνος
  4. ὦ ἀδελφοί
  5. πρᾶγμα
  6. χάριτας

II. *Put the proper form of the article and the adjective ἀθάνατος with the ACCUSATIVE PLURAL of the following nouns.*

  1. στρατιώτης
  2. στέφανος
  3. ποίημα
  4. μοῦσα

III. *Give a synopsis of λείπω in the second person singular.*

   PRINCIPAL PARTS: ————————————————————————

	ACTIVE	MIDDLE	PASSIVE
PRESENT INDICATIVE			
IMPERFECT INDICATIVE			
FUTURE INDICATIVE			
AORIST INDICATIVE			
PERFECT INDICATIVE			
PLUPERFECT INDICATIVE			
PRESENT SUBJUNCTIVE			
AORIST SUBJUNCTIVE			
PRESENT OPTATIVE			
AORIST OPTATIVE			
PRESENT INFINITIVE			
AORIST INFINITIVE			
PERFECT INFINITIVE			

IV. *Translate, and answer all appended questions.*

1. εἴ τοι λόγους γράφοι ὁ σοφὸς Ὅμηρος περὶ τῆς τῶν ὁπλιτῶν καλῆς
   οἰκίας, ἐπείθοντό τε τῷ γε φίλῳ ποιητῇ οἱ ὁπλῖται καὶ ἐχόρευον
   περὶ τῇ οἰκίᾳ.
   (a) *Give the syntax of* ἐχόρευον.
   (b) *Give the syntax of* ποιητῇ.

2. οὐκ ἂν λίποιεν τοὺς ἀγαθοὺς οἵ γε θεοί.

3. τὴν νύκτα καὶ ἄνευ τῶν ὁπλιτῶν φυλαξώμεθα ἐκείνᾱς γε τὰς ἀδίκους
   ὅπως ἡ δημοκρατίᾱ μὴ λυθῇ.
   (a) *Give the syntax of* νύκτα.
   (b) *Give the syntax of* λυθῇ.

4. εἰ τοὺς νεᾱνίᾱς ἐκείνης τῆς ἡμέρᾱς εἰς μάχην ἔταξεν, οὐκ ἂν ἐσώθη ἡ
   δημοκρατίᾱ.
   (a) *Give the syntax of* ἡμέρᾱς.
   (b) *Describe and make the changes necessary to turn this sentence into a
   future more vivid conditional sentence.*

5. ὦ ἐλεύθεροι, δουλεύωμεν τοῖς τοῦ ἄρχειν ἀναξίοις;

6. ἐὰν τῇ πρώτῃ ἡμέρᾱ παρὰ τῇ θαλάττῃ χορεύσητε, ὦ νεᾱνίαι, δῶρόν γε
   παρὰ τὸν τοῦ χορεύειν διδάσκαλον πέμψομεν.
   (a) *Give the syntax of* ἡμέρᾱ.

V. If *that messenger* is sent by the foreigners five stades through the plain
   to the Greeks, they will sacrifice the beautiful nanny goats to the gods,
   saviors of the freedom of men, and will dance.

ANSWER KEY FOR SELF-CORRECTING EXAMINATION 2B

I. 1. *νεᾱνιῶν*: M pl. gen.; *νεᾱνίου*
    2. *νυξίν*: F pl. dat.; *νυκτί*
    3. *Ἕλληνος*: M sing. gen.; *Ἑλλήνων*
    4. *ὦ ἀδελφοί*: M pl. voc.; *ὦ ἄδελφε*
    5. *πρᾶγμα*: N sing. nom./acc./voc.; *πράγματα*
    6. *χάριτας*: F pl. acc.; *χάριν*

II. 1. *τοὺς ἀθανάτους στρατιώτᾱς*
    2. *τοὺς ἀθανάτους στεφάνους*
    3. *τὰ ἀθάνατα ποιήματα*
    4. *τὰς ἀθανάτους μούσᾱς*

III. PRINCIPAL PARTS: *λείπω, λείψω, ἔλιπον, λέλοιπα, λέλειμμαι, ἐλείφθην*

	ACTIVE	MIDDLE	PASSIVE
PRESENT INDICATIVE	*λείπεις*	*λείπῃ* / *λείπει*	*λείπῃ* / *λείπει*
IMPERFECT INDICATIVE	*ἔλειπες*	*ἐλείπου*	*ἐλείπου*
FUTURE INDICATIVE	*λείψεις*	*λείψῃ* / *λείψει*	*λειφθήσῃ* / *λειφθήσει*
AORIST INDICATIVE	*ἔλιπες*	*ἐλίπου*	*ἐλείφθης*
PERFECT INDICATIVE	*λέλοιπας*	*λέλειψαι*	*λέλειψαι*
PLUPERFECT INDICATIVE	*ἐλελοίπης*	*ἐλέλειψο*	*ἐλέλειψο*
PRESENT SUBJUNCTIVE	*λείπῃς*	*λείπῃ*	*λείπῃ*
AORIST SUBJUNCTIVE	*λίπῃς*	*λίπῃ*	*λειφθῇς*
PRESENT OPTATIVE	*λείποις*	*λείποιο*	*λείποιο*
AORIST OPTATIVE	*λίποις*	*λίποιο*	*λειφθείης*
PRESENT INFINITIVE	*λείπειν*	*λείπεσθαι*	*λείπεσθαι*
AORIST INFINITIVE	*λιπεῖν*	*λιπέσθαι*	*λειφθῆναι*
PERFECT INFINITIVE	*λελοιπέναι*	*λελεῖφθαι*	*λελεῖφθαι*

IV. 1. If, you know, the wise Homer wrote stories/speeches about the beautiful house of the hoplites, the hoplites used to obey/obeyed (habitually) *the beloved poet*/the beloved poet, at any rate, and danced around the house.

(a) ἐχόρευον is an imperfect indicative in the apodosis of a past general conditional sentence.

(b) ποιητῇ is a dative governed by ἐπείθοντο. πείθομαι meaning "obey" governs the dative.

2. *The gods*/the gods, at least, would not/might not leave (the) good men behind.

3. For the night, even without the hoplites, let us guard against *those unjust women*/those unjust women, at least, in order that the democracy may not be destroyed.

(a) νύκτα is accusative of extent of time.

(b) λυθῇ is an aorist subjunctive: subjunctive in a purpose clause in primary sequence introduced by φυλαξώμεθα (a hortatory subjunctive governs primary sequence); aorist to show simple aspect.

4. If he/she had drawn up the young men for battle during that day, the democracy would not have been saved.

(a) ἡμέρας is a genitive of time within which.

(b) PROTASIS: Change the εἰ to ἐάν.
Change the aorist indicative ἔταξεν to the subjunctive, either τάξῃ (aorist to show simple aspect) or τάττῃ (present to show progressive/repeated aspect).
APODOSIS: Remove the ἄν.
Change the aorist indicative ἐσώθη to the future indicative σωθήσεται.

5. Free men, are we to be slaves to those unworthy of ruling?

6. If on the first day you dance by the sea, young men, we shall send/be sending *a gift*/a gift, at least, to the teacher of dancing.

(a) ἡμέρᾳ is a dative of time at which.

V. ἐὰν ἐκεῖνός γε ὁ ἄγγελος πέμπηται/πεμφθῇ ὑπὸ τῶν ξένων πέντε στάδια/σταδίους διὰ τοῦ πεδίου παρὰ τοὺς Ἕλληνας, θύσουσι/θύσουσί τε τὰς καλὰς αἶγας τοῖς θεοῖς, σωτῆρσι τῆς τῶν ἀνθρώπων ἐλευθερίας, καὶ χορεύσουσιν.

UNIT
8

65. PARTICIPLES

Participles are *verbal adjectives*.

Their *verbal* nature is shown by the fact that they:
  (1) are formed on verbal tense stems
  (2) have both tense and voice
  (3) can take the same constructions as the finite forms of the verb, e.g., direct and indirect objects.

Their *adjectival* nature is shown by the fact that they:
  (1) have gender, number, and case
  (2) can modify and agree with nouns and pronouns.

There are active, middle, and passive participles of the present, future, aorist, and perfect tenses; each of these tenses and voices has forms of the masculine, feminine, and neuter in all cases in both numbers.

The tense of a Greek participle for the most part shows aspect but often in context it is clear that there is a definite temporal relationship between the participle and the main verb.

1. The present participle shows progressive/repeated aspect; its action is most often *simultaneous* with that of the main verb, and it can usually be translated by the English present participle, e.g., "educating, educating for oneself, being educated."

2. The future participle, like the future indicative, has either simple or progressive/repeated aspect. It always indicates *subsequent* action, and usually expresses intent or purpose. English does not have a future participle. The future participle of Greek can be translated by the phrase "about to . . ." or by "intending to . . .," e.g., "about to/intending to educate, about to/intending to educate for oneself, about to/intending to be educated."

3. The aorist participle has simple aspect; the action of an aorist participle is often *prior* to, sometimes *simultaneous* with, that of the main verb.

The English equivalent of the aorist passive participle is the simple past participle "educated." Since English does not have the equivalent of an aorist participle active or middle, a Greek aorist participle active or middle must be translated by various English expressions, depending on the way in which the participle is used:

Having come (once and for all) to the city, he died.

Coming (once and for all) to the city, he died.

After coming to the city, he died.

Laughing (once and for all), he said the following.

With a laugh he said the following.

In Greek, all of the words in bold face above would have been expressed by aorist participles.

4. The perfect participle stresses the *completion* of the action; it is translated by the English present perfect participle, e.g., "having educated, having educated for oneself, having been educated."

Although the Greek aorist and perfect participles can often be translated by the same English participle, e.g. "having educated," the Greek aorist participle stresses the simple performance of the action, the perfect participle the completion of the action.

There are three major uses of the participle in Greek, the **attributive**, the **circumstantial**, and the **supplementary**. In this Unit the formation and declension of the participle and its attributive and circumstantial uses are presented. The supplementary use of the participle is presented in Unit 14.

Drill I, page 221, may now be done.

66. FORMATION AND DECLENSION OF THE ACTIVE PARTICIPLES

1. FORMATION OF THE ACTIVE PARTICIPLES

To form the active participles add the following suffixes + endings to the appropriate tense stem:

TENSE and TENSE STEM	SUFFIXES + ENDINGS				
	M	F	N		
PRESENT Tense Stem	-ων	-ουσα	-ον	Nom./Voc.	S
	-οντος	-ουσης	-οντος	Gen.	
FUTURE Active and	-ων	-ουσα	-ον	Nom./Voc.	S
Middle Tense Stem	-οντος	-ουσης	-οντος	Gen.	
FIRST AORIST Active	-ᾱς	-ᾱσα	-αν	Nom./Voc.	S
and Middle Tense Stem	-αντος	-ᾱσης	-αντος	Gen.	
SECOND AORIST Active	-ών	-οῦσα	-όν	Nom./Voc.	S
and Middle Tense Stem	-όντος	-ούσης	-όντος	Gen.	

| PERFECT Active Tense | -ώς | -νῖα | -ός | Nom./Voc. S |
| Stem | -ότος | -νίᾱς | -ότος | Gen. |

Thus the active participles of παιδεύω, with the second aorist active participle of λείπω, are as follows:

	M	F	N	
PRESENT	παιδεύων	παιδεύουσα	παιδεῦον	Nom./Voc. S
	παιδεύοντος	παιδευούσης	παιδεύοντος	Gen.
FUTURE	παιδεύσων	παιδεύσουσα	παιδεῦσον	Nom./Voc. S
	παιδεύσοντος	παιδευσούσης	παιδεύσοντος	Gen.
FIRST AORIST	παιδεύσᾱς	παιδεύσᾱσα	παιδεῦσαν	Nom./Voc. S
	παιδεύσαντος	παιδευσάσης	παιδεύσαντος	Gen.
SECOND AORIST	λιπών	λιποῦσα	λιπόν	Nom./Voc. S
	λιπόντος	λιπούσης	λιπόντος	Gen.
PERFECT	πεπαιδευκώς	πεπαιδευκυῖα	πεπαιδευκός	Nom./Voc. S
	πεπαιδευκότος	πεπαιδευκυίᾱς	πεπαιδευκότος	Gen.

2. DECLENSION OF THE ACTIVE PARTICIPLES

The masculine and neuter are declined like third-declension nouns, and the feminine like a first-declension noun with a nominative in short -α. To decline a participle, drop the declension endings from the masculine and feminine genitive singular to get the **declension stems**; then add the appropriate third-declension endings to the masculine/neuter declension stem and the appropriate first-declension endings to the feminine declension stem. The masculine/neuter dative plural undergoes sound changes according to the chart given in Section 48, p. 141.

	M	F	N
Nom./Voc. S	—	-α	—
Gen.	-ος	-ης, -ᾱς	-ος
Dat.	-ι	-ῃ, -ᾳ	-ι
Acc.	-α	-αν	—
Nom./Voc. P	-ες	-αι	-α
Gen.	-ων	-ῶν	-ων
Dat.	-σι(ν)	-αις	-σι(ν)
Acc.	-ας	-ᾱς	-α

3. DECLENSION OF THE PRESENT ACTIVE PARTICIPLE

	M	F	N
Nom./Voc. S	παιδεύων	παιδεύουσα	παιδεῦον
Gen.	παιδεύοντος	παιδευούσης	παιδεύοντος
Dat.	παιδεύοντι	παιδευούσῃ	παιδεύοντι
Acc.	παιδεύοντα	παιδεύουσαν	παιδεῦον
Nom./Voc. P	παιδεύοντες	παιδεύουσαι	παιδεύοντα
Gen.	παιδευόντων	παιδευουσῶν	παιδευόντων
Dat.	παιδεύουσι(ν)	παιδευούσαις	παιδεύουσι(ν)
Acc.	παιδεύοντας	παιδευούσᾱς	παιδεύοντα

Observations: (1) THE ACCENT ON PARTICIPLES IS PERSISTENT AND IS GIVEN BY THE MASCULINE SINGULAR NOMINATIVE; hence the circumflex accent on the neuter singular nominative/accusative/vocative παιδεῦον.

(2) The vocative of all first and third declension participles is the same as the nominative.

(3) Except for having no separate vocative, the masculine of the participle is declined exactly like the noun γέρων, γέροντος, ὁ. Note the spurious diphthong -ου- in the masculine and neuter dative plural παιδεύουσι(ν), a form identical with the third person plural, present indicative active form of the verb. Context will allow one to distinguish the two forms.

(4) The feminine of the participle is declined exactly like the noun μοῦσα, μούσης, ἡ. Note the circumflex accent on the ultima of the genitive plural, an exception to the rule of persistence of accent.

4. DECLENSION OF THE FUTURE ACTIVE PARTICIPLE

The future active participle differs from the present active participle only in the stem; the endings are exactly the same.

	M	F	N
Nom./Voc. S	παιδεύσων	παιδεύσουσα	παιδεῦσον
Gen.	παιδεύσοντος	παιδευσούσης	παιδεύσοντος
Dat.	παιδεύσοντι	παιδευσούσῃ	παιδεύσοντι
Acc.	παιδεύσοντα	παιδεύσουσαν	παιδεῦσον

Nom./Voc. P	παιδεύσοντες	παιδεύσουσαι	παιδεύσοντα
Gen.	παιδευσόντων	παιδευσουσῶν	παιδευσόντων
Dat.	παιδεύσουσι(ν)	παιδευσούσαις	παιδεύσουσι(ν)
Acc.	παιδεύσοντας	παιδευσούσᾱς	παιδεύσοντα

Observation: The masculine and neuter dative plural are identical with the third person plural, future indicative active. Context will allow one to distinguish the two forms.

5. DECLENSION OF THE FIRST AORIST ACTIVE PARTICIPLE

	M	F	N
Nom./Voc. S	παιδεύσᾱς	παιδεύσᾱσα	παιδεῦσαν
Gen.	παιδεύσαντος	παιδευσάσης	παιδεύσαντος
Dat.	παιδεύσαντι	παιδευσάσῃ	παιδεύσαντι
Acc.	παιδεύσαντα	παιδεύσᾱσαν	παιδεῦσαν
Nom./Voc. P	παιδεύσαντες	παιδεύσᾱσαι	παιδεύσαντα
Gen.	παιδευσάντων	παιδευσᾱσῶν	παιδευσάντων
Dat.	παιδεύσᾱσι(ν)	παιδευσάσαις	παιδεύσᾱσι(ν)
Acc.	παιδεύσαντας	παιδευσάσᾱς	παιδεύσαντα

Observation: Instead of the thematic vowel of the present and future active participles, the first aorist active participle uses the tense vowel -α-. In the masculine and neuter dative plural, the combination -αντσι(ν) becomes -ᾱσι(ν); see Section 48, p. 141.

6. DECLENSION OF THE SECOND AORIST ACTIVE PARTICIPLE

	M	F	N
Nom./Voc. S	λιπών	λιποῦσα	λιπόν
Gen.	λιπόντος	λιπούσης	λιπόντος
Dat.	λιπόντι	λιπούσῃ	λιπόντι
Acc.	λιπόντα	λιποῦσαν	λιπόν
Nom./Voc. P	λιπόντες	λιποῦσαι	λιπόντα
Gen.	λιπόντων	λιπουσῶν	λιπόντων
Dat.	λιποῦσι(ν)	λιπούσαις	λιποῦσι(ν)
Acc.	λιπόντας	λιπούσᾱς	λιπόντα

Observations: (1) This participle is declined exactly like the present and future active participles of παιδεύω (cf. Section 66.3–4) except for the accent. Compare λιπόντος with παιδεύοντος.

(2) As in all participles whose feminine nominative singular ends in short -α, the accent shifts to the ultima in the genitive plural: λιπουσῶν.

7. DECLENSION OF THE PERFECT ACTIVE PARTICIPLE

	M	F	N
Nom./Voc. S	πεπαιδευκώς	πεπαιδευκυῖα	πεπαιδευκός
Gen.	πεπαιδευκότος	πεπαιδευκυίας	πεπαιδευκότος
Dat.	πεπαιδευκότι	πεπαιδευκυίᾳ	πεπαιδευκότι
Acc.	πεπαιδευκότα	πεπαιδευκυῖαν	πεπαιδευκός
Nom./Voc. P	πεπαιδευκότες	πεπαιδευκυῖαι	πεπαιδευκότα
Gen.	πεπαιδευκότων	πεπαιδευκυιῶν	πεπαιδευκότων
Dat.	πεπαιδευκόσι(ν)	πεπαιδευκυίαις	πεπαιδευκόσι(ν)
Acc.	πεπαιδευκότας	πεπαιδευκυίας	πεπαιδευκότα

Observations: (1) Note the absence of a -ν- before the -τ- in the masculine/neuter declension stem. In the masculine/neuter dative plural, the combination -οτσι becomes -οσι; see Section 48, p. 141.

(2) The feminine is declined like γέφῡρα, γεφύρᾱς, ἡ.

(3) Note the accent on the penult in all forms except the masculine nominative/vocative singular, the neuter nominative/vocative and accusative singular, and the feminine genitive plural.

67. FORMATION AND DECLENSION OF THE MIDDLE AND PASSIVE PARTICIPLES

The participles use the same forms for the middle and passive voice wherever the indicative does so, i.e., in the present and perfect tenses. In the future and in the aorist, there are separate middle and passive forms.

All middle and passive forms except the aorist passive add to the appropriate tense stem the suffix + endings -μενος, -μενη, -μενον preceded by the thematic vowel in the present, future, and second aorist, and by the tense vowel -α- in the first aorist. They are declined just like first and second declension adjectives.

1. FORMATION OF THE MIDDLE PARTICIPLES

TENSE and TENSE STEM	SUFFIXES + ENDINGS			
	M	F	N	
PRESENT Tense Stem	-ομενος	-ομενη	-ομενον	Nom. S
	-ομενου	-ομενης	-ομενου	Gen.
FUTURE Active and Middle Tense Stem	-ομενος	-ομενη	-ομενον	Nom. S
	-ομενου	-ομενης	-ομενου	Gen.
FIRST AORIST Active and Middle Tense Stem	-αμενος	-αμενη	-αμενον	Nom. S
	-αμενου	-αμενης	-αμενου	Gen.
SECOND AORIST Active and Middle Tense Stem	-ομενος	-ομενη	-ομενον	Nom. S
	-ομενου	-ομενης	-ομενου	Gen.
PERFECT Middle and Passive Tense Stem	-μένος	-μένη	-μένον	Nom. S
	-μένου	-μένης	-μένου	Gen.

Thus the middle participles of παιδεύω, with the second aorist middle participle of λείπω, are as follows:

	M	F	N	
PRESENT	παιδευόμενος	παιδευομένη	παιδευόμενον	Nom. S
	παιδευομένου	παιδευομένης	παιδευομένου	Gen.
FUTURE	παιδευσόμενος	παιδευσομένη	παιδευσόμενον	Nom. S
	παιδευσομένου	παιδευσομένης	παιδευσομένου	Gen.
FIRST AORIST	παιδευσάμενος	παιδευσαμένη	παιδευσάμενον	Nom. S
	παιδευσαμένου	παιδευσαμένης	παιδευσαμένου	Gen.
SECOND AORIST	λιπόμενος	λιπομένη	λιπόμενον	Nom. S
	λιπομένου	λιπομένης	λιπομένου	Gen.
PERFECT	πεπαιδευμένος	πεπαιδευμένη	πεπαιδευμένον	Nom. S
	πεπαιδευμένου	πεπαιδευμένης	πεπαιδευμένου	Gen.

2. FORMATION OF THE PASSIVE PARTICIPLES

TENSE and TENSE STEM	*SUFFIXES + ENDINGS*			
	M	F	N	
PRESENT Tense Stem	-ομενος	-ομενη	-ομενον	Nom. S
	-ομενου	-ομενης	-ομενου	Gen.
FUTURE Passive Tense Stem	-ομενος	-ομενη	-ομενον	Nom. S
	-ομενου	-ομενης	-ομενου	Gen.
AORIST Passive Tense Stem	-είς	-εῖσα	-έν	Nom./Voc. S
	-έντος	-είσης	-έντος	Gen.
PERFECT Middle and Passive Tense Stem	-μένος	-μένη	-μένον	Nom. S
	-μένου	-μένης	-μένου	Gen.

Note that the present passive and perfect passive participles are the same as the present middle and perfect middle participles, respectively.

Note also that ALL verbs form the aorist passive participle in the same way, using Principal Part VI.

Thus the passive participles of παιδεύω are as follows:

M	F	N	

PRESENT

παιδευόμενος	παιδευομένη	παιδευόμενον	Nom. S
παιδευομένου	παιδευομένης	παιδευομένου	Gen.

FUTURE

παιδευθησόμενος	παιδευθησομένη	παιδευθησόμενον	Nom. S
παιδευθησομένου	παιδευθησομένης	παιδευθησομένου	Gen.

AORIST

παιδευθείς	παιδευθεῖσα	παιδευθέν	Nom./Voc. S
παιδευθέντος	παιδευθείσης	παιδευθέντος	Gen.

PERFECT

πεπαιδευμένος	πεπαιδευμένη	πεπαιδευμένον	Nom. S
πεπαιδευμένου	πεπαιδευμένης	πεπαιδευμένου	Gen.

Observation: Since the aorist passive of all verbs is formed in the same way from Principal Part VI, the aorist passive participle of λείπω is formed just like that of παιδεύω: λειφθείς, λειφθεῖσα, λειφθέν.

3. DECLENSION OF THE PRESENT MIDDLE/PASSIVE PARTICIPLE

The present middle/passive participle, future middle and passive participles, aorist middle participles, and perfect middle/passive participle are all declined like adjectives in -ος, -η, -ον. The declension of the present middle/passive participle is offered as a paradigm for all of the above.

	M	F	N
Nom. S	παιδευόμενος	παιδευομένη	παιδευόμενον
Gen.	παιδευομένου	παιδευομένης	παιδευομένου
Dat.	παιδευομένῳ	παιδευομένη	παιδευομένῳ
Acc.	παιδευόμενον	παιδευομένην	παιδευόμενον
Voc.	παιδευόμενε	παιδευομένη	παιδευόμενον
Nom./Voc. P	παιδευόμενοι	παιδευόμεναι	παιδευόμενα
Gen.	παιδευομένων	παιδευομένων	παιδευομένων
Dat.	παιδευομένοις	παιδευομέναις	παιδευομένοις
Acc.	παιδευομένους	παιδευομένᾱς	παιδευόμενα

Observation: Note that in the feminine plural genitive, the accent is NOT a circumflex on the ultima. In this, the participles in -μενος, -μενη, -μενον differ from the participles seen so far and resemble the adjectives.

4. DECLENSION OF THE AORIST PASSIVE PARTICIPLE

The aorist passive participle is declined like the active participles with a masculine/neuter declension stem in -ντ- and a short -α feminine.

	M	F	N
Nom./Voc. S	παιδευθείς	παιδευθεῖσα	παιδευθέν
Gen.	παιδευθέντος	παιδευθείσης	παιδευθέντος
Dat.	παιδευθέντι	παιδευθείσῃ	παιδευθέντι
Acc.	παιδευθέντα	παιδευθεῖσαν	παιδευθέν
Nom./Voc. P	παιδευθέντες	παιδευθεῖσαι	παιδευθέντα
Gen.	παιδευθέντων	παιδευθεισῶν	παιδευθέντων
Dat.	παιδευθεῖσι(ν)	παιδευθείσαις	παιδευθεῖσι(ν)
Acc.	παιδευθέντας	παιδευθείσᾱς	παιδευθέντα

Observations: (1) Note the accent on the penult in all forms except the masculine nominative/vocative singular, the neuter nominative/vocative and accusative singular, and the feminine genitive plural.

(2) In the masculine and neuter dative plural, the combination -εντσι becomes -εισι; see Section 48, p. 141.

68. SUMMARY OF THE FORMS OF THE PARTICIPLE

	ACTIVE	MIDDLE	PASSIVE
PRESENT	I *doing*	I *doing (for oneself)*	I *being done*
	-ων -ουσα -ον-	-ομενος -ομενη -ομενον	-ομενος -ομενη -ομενον
	-οντο- -ουσης- -οντο-	-ομενο- -ομενης- -ομενο-	-ομενο- -ομενης- -ομενο-
FUTURE	II *about to/intending to do*	II *about to/intending to do for oneself*	VI *about to/intending to be done*
	-ων-	-σομενος -σομενη -σομενον	-θησ-
	-σων -σουσα -σον-	-σομενο- -σομενης- -σομενο-	
	-σοντο- -σουσης- -σοντο-		
AORIST	*who did / upon doing / having done (simply) / doing (simply)*	*who did for oneself / upon doing for oneself / having done (simply) for oneself / doing (simply) for oneself*	*done*
FIRST	III	III	VI
	-σας -ᾱσα -σαν-	-σαμενος -αμενη -αμενον	-εις -εῖσα -εν
	-σαντος -ᾱσης- -σαντος	-σαμενο- -σαμενης- -σαμενο-	-εντος -εισης -εντος
SECOND	III	III	
	-ων -ουσα -ον-	-ομενος -ομενη -ομενον	
	-όντος -ούσης- -όντος-	-ομενο- -ομενης- -ομενο-	
PERFECT	IV *having done*	V *having done for oneself*	V *having been done*
	-ώς -υῖα -ός-	-μένος -μένη -μένον	-μένος -μένη -μένον
	-ότος- -υίᾱς- -ότος-	-μέ- -μένης- -μέ-	-μέ- -μένης- -μέ-

69. ATTRIBUTIVE USE OF THE PARTICIPLE

The **attributive participle** acts like any other adjective and is found in the attributive position, i.e., between the article and the noun it modifies or immediately preceded by the article after the noun it modifies. Such participles agree, of course, in gender, number, and case with the word they modify.

Remember that the tense of a participle can show both *aspect* (progressive/repeated, simple, completed) and *relative time* (simultaneous, prior, subsequent); see Section 65.

Attributive participles can often be translated by relative clauses.

ὁ **θύων** ποιητὴς ἐσώθη.   The **sacrificing** poet was saved.
ὁ ποιητὴς ὁ **θύων** ἐσώθη.   The poet **sacrificing** was saved.
ποιητὴς ὁ **θύων** ἐσώθη.   The poet **who was sacrificing** was saved.

τοῖς **θύσᾱσι** ποιηταῖς
τοῖς ποιηταῖς τοῖς **θύσᾱσιν**   to/for the poets **who sacrificed**
ποιηταῖς τοῖς **θύσᾱσιν**

τῆς **τυθείσης** αἰγός   of the **sacrificed** she-goat
τῆς αἰγὸς τῆς **τυθείσης**   of the she-goat **which was sacrificed**
αἰγὸς τῆς **τυθείσης**

For each of the participles in the examples given above, an adjective could be substituted, e.g., τῆς καλῆς αἰγός, "of the beautiful she-goat." The attributive participle, like any adjective, serves to limit the noun with which it agrees.

The attributive participle takes all the constructions which the finite verb takes:

ὁ τὴν αἶγα θύσᾱς ποιητής
the poet who sacrificed the she-goat

ἡ αἶξ ἡ ὑπὸ τοῦ ποιητοῦ τυθεῖσα
the she-goat sacrificed by the poet
the she-goat which was sacrificed by the poet

As with all adjectives, the attributive participle can be used *substantively*:

ὁ τὴν αἶγα τῇ θεῷ θύων
the man sacrificing the goat to the goddess
the man who is sacrificing the goat to the goddess

ἡ χορεύουσα
the dancing woman
the woman who is dancing
the dancer

The article with the substantive use of the attributive participle can be either particular, i.e., referring to specific people or objects, or generic, i.e., referring to a class of people or objects; cf. Sections 16.4 (p. 29) and 46 (p. 127). In the negative, οὐ is used with particular substantives; μή, with generic substantives. Thus, οἱ θύοντες are either "the (specific) men sacrificing, the men who are sacrificing," or "men (the whole class) sacrificing, men who sacrifice"; but οἱ οὐ θύοντες are only "the specific men not sacrificing, the men who are not sacrificing (as opposed, e.g., to those over there who are sacrificing)" and οἱ μὴ θύοντες are only "those (the whole class) not sacrificing, those who do not sacrifice."

Drill II.1–24, pages 221–22, may now be done.

70. CIRCUMSTANTIAL USE OF THE PARTICIPLE

A **circumstantial participle** is one NOT in the attributive position which gives the circumstances under which the action of the main verb takes place. Such participles agree in gender, number, and case with a noun or pronoun in the sentence (or the subject of the sentence contained in the verb), but they are really the equivalent of an adverbial clause, i.e., they function as adverbs in telling, e.g., why or when the action of the main verb of the sentence occurs.

Compare the use of the attributive participle in sentence (1) below with that of the circumstantial participle in sentence (2).

(1) ὁ θύων ποιητὴς ὑπὸ τοῦ δήμου σῴζεται.
    The poet sacrificing is being saved by the people.
    The poet who is sacrificing is being saved by the people.

In sentence (1) the participle θύων is in the attributive position and serves to point out the poet as would the adjective καλός.

(2) θύων ὁ ποιητὴς ὑπὸ τοῦ δήμου σῴζεται.
    a. Sacrificing, the poet is saved by the people.
    b. When he sacrifices, the poet is saved by the people.
    c. Since he sacrifices, the poet is saved by the people.
    d. If he sacrifices, the poet is saved by the people.

In sentence (2) the participle is not in the attributive position and therefore is not serving to identify or point out the poet; instead, it gives the circumstances under which he is saved. The participle, in Greek as in English, may indicate only the general circumstances, or the content and context of the sentence may suggest something more specific as in translation (b), temporal relation between the action of the participle and that of the main verb; (c), causal relation between the action of the participle and that of the main verb; or (d), conditional relation between the action of the participle and that of the main verb.

Sometimes the exact nature of the circumstantial participle can be made clear by the use of an adverb or conjunction with either the main verb or the participle.

1. A temporal adverb like ἔπειτα, "then, thereupon," accompanying the main verb, can indicate that a circumstantial participle is *temporal*.

   > λυθέντες ἔπειτα τοῖς θεοῖς ἐθύσαμεν.
   > Freed, we then sacrificed to the gods.
   > Upon being freed, we then sacrificed to the gods.
   > After being freed, we then sacrificed to the gods.
   > After we were freed, we then sacrificed to the gods.

2. The adverb ὅμως, "nevertheless," with the main verb indicates that the circumstantial participle is *concessive*, i.e., the equivalent of a clause introduced by the conjunction "although."

   > λυθέντες ὅμως τοῖς θεοῖς οὐκ ἐθύσαμεν.
   > Freed, we nevertheless did not sacrifice to the gods.
   > Upon being freed, we nevertheless did not sacrifice to the gods.
   > Although freed, we nevertheless did not sacrifice to the gods.
   > Although we were freed, we nevertheless did not sacrifice to the gods.

3. The word καίπερ, "although," with a circumstantial participle also indicates that the participle is *concessive*.

   > καίπερ λυθέντες τοῖς θεοῖς οὐκ ἐθύσαμεν.
   > Although freed, we did not sacrifice to the gods.
   > Although we were freed, we did not sacrifice to the gods.

4. The words ἅτε and οἷα with a circumstantial participle indicate that the participle is *causal* and that the speaker or writer is stating the cause on his own responsibility.

   > $\begin{Bmatrix} ἅτε \\ οἷα \end{Bmatrix}$ λυθέντες τοῖς θεοῖς ἔθυσαν.
   > Freed (and I as speaker am asserting that this is the cause), they sacrificed to the gods.
   > Because they were freed (and I as speaker am asserting that this is the cause), they sacrificed to the gods.

5. The word ὡς with a participle shows that the participle expresses either *cause* or *purpose*. The cause or purpose is one given by the subject of the sentence (or someone else important in the sentence), NOT one asserted on the authority of the speaker or writer. This reason may be either real or pretended.

> ὡς λυθέντες τοῖς θεοῖς ἔθυσαν.
> Freed (as they said), they sacrificed to the gods.
> Because they were freed (as they said), they sacrificed to the gods.

> ἐπέμφθησαν ὡς θύσοντες τοῖς θεοῖς.
> They were sent to sacrifice to the gods (as they said).

NOTE that the future participle, even without an introductory word, is an alternative to the purpose clause with a verb in the subjunctive or the optative.

> ἐπέμφθησαν θύσοντες τοῖς θεοῖς.
> They were sent to sacrifice to the gods.

6. The negative with all circumstantial participles is οὐ except for *conditional* participles (circumstantial participles used as protases of conditional sentences), which use μή. Therefore a circumstantial participle negated by μή MUST be conditional.

> μὴ βλαπτόμενοι ἐθέλομεν δῶρα πέμπειν.
> Not being harmed, we are willing to send gifts.
> If we are not harmed, we are willing to send gifts.

In this sentence, the participle stands for a present general protasis.

Compare the conditional participle, indicated by the negative μή, with a causal participle, negated by οὐ.

> οὐ βλαπτόμενοι ἐθέλομεν δῶρα πέμπειν.
> Not being harmed, we are willing to send gifts.
> Since we are not harmed, we are willing to send gifts.

Without the negative or an adverb or conjunction to help distinguish the circumstantial participles, only context allows one to choose from among all the possibilities.

> βλαπτόμενοι οὐκ ἐθέλομεν δῶρα πέμπειν.
> Being harmed, we do not wish to send gifts.
> When we are harmed, we do not wish to send gifts.
> Since we are harmed, we do not wish to send gifts.
> If we are harmed, we do not wish to send gifts.
> Although we are harmed, we do not wish to send gifts.

For examples of how to give the syntax of a participle, see pages 296–97 and 302–3.

Drills II.25-48 and III, pages 222–23, may now be done.

71. THE ADJECTIVE πᾶς, πᾶσα, πᾶν, "all, every; whole"

The adjective πᾶς, πᾶσα, πᾶν, "all, every; whole" has forms of the first and third declensions. It is declined as follows:

	M	F	N
Nom./Voc. S	πᾶς	πᾶσα	πᾶν
Gen.	παντός	πάσης	παντός
Dat.	παντί	πάσῃ	παντί
Acc.	πάντα	πᾶσαν	πᾶν
Nom./Voc. P	πάντες	πᾶσαι	πάντα
Gen.	πάντων	πασῶν	πάντων
Dat.	πᾶσι(ν)	πάσαις	πᾶσι(ν)
Acc.	πάντας	πάσᾱς	πάντα

Observation: This adjective has, except for the accent, the same declensional endings as the aorist participle active: cf. λύσᾱς, λύσᾱσα, λῦσαν. The masculine and neuter stem is παντ- with a short alpha. The feminine declension stem is πᾱσ-. Note that in the singular in the masculine and neuter, the accent shifts to the ultima in the genitive and the dative; in all forms of the plural, except for the genitive plural πασῶν, it remains on the penult. In the dative plural masculine/neuter, *πάντσι(ν) gives πᾶσι(ν), with the long alpha due to compensatory lengthening.

This adjective usually appears in the predicate position and means "all":

> πάντες οἱ διδάσκαλοι
> οἱ διδάσκαλοι πάντες
> all the teachers

> πᾶσα ἡ χώρᾱ
> ἡ χώρᾱ πᾶσα
> all the land

In the singular, unaccompanied by the article, this adjective means "every":

> πᾶς ἄνθρωπος
> every man

In the attributive position, this adjective means "whole" and emphasizes the entirety of a thing or group:

> ἡ πᾶσα χώρᾱ
> the whole land

VOCABULARY

ἄγω, ἄξω, ἤγαγον, ἦχα, ἦγμαι, ἤχθην	lead
'Αθηναῖος, 'Αθηναία, 'Αθηναῖον	Athenian
ἅμα (adv.)	at the same time
(prep.) + dat.	at the same time as; together with
ἄτε (particle)	with causal participle: speaker's assertion
ἔπειτα (adv.)	then, thereupon
ἥκω, ἥξω, ——, ——, ——, ——	have come, be present
καίπερ (adv.)	although
μήτε . . . μήτε (conjunctions)	neither . . . nor
οἷα (particle)	with causal participle: speaker's assertion
οἶνος, οἴνου, ὁ	wine
ὅμως (adv.)	nevertheless
οὔτε . . . οὔτε (conjunctions)	neither . . . nor
πᾶς, πᾶσα, πᾶν	all, every; whole
ἅπᾶς, ἅπᾶσα, ἅπαν	all, quite all
σύμπᾶς, σύμπᾶσα, σύμπαν	all together
στρατός, στρατοῦ, ὁ	army
στρατηγός, στρατηγοῦ, ὁ	general
χρῆμα, χρήματος, τό	thing; (pl.) goods, property, money
ὡς (conj.)	with participle of cause or purpose: not asserted by speaker of sentence

VOCABULARY NOTES

The verb ἄγω, ἄξω, ἤγαγον, ἦχα, ἦγμαι, ἤχθην, "lead," has as its basic root ἀγ-. The future was formed by the addition of -σ-: ἄξω. The aorist active and middle tense stem shows reduplication and is a second aorist: ἀγαγ- when unaugmented, ἤγαγ- when augmented. The ἦ- of Principal Parts IV and V is part of the stem and remains unchanged in the perfect and pluperfect (cf. ἦρχα, ἠθέληκα, etc.). In Principal Part VI, the ἠ- is a past indicative augment and does not appear in the unaugmented aorist passive tense stem: ἀχθ-. The word is used for leading animals or people (especially of leading away people or animals captured in war); providing leadership; conducting, e.g., ἄγω ἀγῶνα, "I hold a contest"; ἄγω θυσίᾱν, "I perform a sacrifice." The expression εἰρήνην ἄγειν means "to keep peace."

The adjective Ἀθηναῖος, Ἀθηναίᾱ, Ἀθηναῖον, "Athenian," is derived from Ἀθῆναι, Ἀθηνῶν, "Athens," which in turn is the plural of the name of the goddess Athena as it appears in Homer, Ἀθήνη, Ἀθήνης, ἡ.

Notice that ἅμα can be either an adverb, "at the same time," or a preposition with the dative, "at the same time as, together with."

Note that ἅτε and οἷα with causal participles both indicate that the speaker is taking responsibility for the assertion. Contrast this with ὡς with a participle of cause or purpose, which indicates that the cause or purpose is that of the subject of the sentence or of someone else important in the sentence.

The adverb ἔπειτα is used of time, "then" (= "thereupon, afterward"), or of consequences, "therefore."

The verb ἥκω, ἥξω, ——, ——, ——, ——, "have come, be present," exists in the present, the imperfect, and the future tenses only. ἥκω is present in form but perfect in meaning; the imperfect has a pluperfect meaning: ἧκον, "I had come, was present."

The word καίπερ, "although," is used only with participles, not with finite verbs. It consists of the conjunction καί + the enclitic -περ, and is accented accordingly (cf. καίτοι).

The accent of the conjunctions μήτε ... μήτε and οὔτε ... οὔτε, "neither ... nor," shows that they are formed from the negative adverb + the enclitic τε. Compounds of μή and οὐ are used in the same constructions as the corresponding simple negative:

οὔτε θύομεν οὔτε χορεύομεν.
We are neither sacrificing nor dancing.

μήτε θύωμεν μήτε χορεύωμεν.
Let us neither sacrifice nor dance.

The noun οἶνος, οἴνου, ὁ, "wine," is cognate with the Latin vīnum, whence the English "wine." Presumably the ancestors of the Greeks learned viticulture, wine drinking, and the name of the beverage from the pre-Greek inhabitants of the country. In Greek the initial digamma dropped out: *ϝοῖνος > οἶνος.

The adverb ὅμως, "nevertheless," frequently indicates that a participle is a concessive one.

Like the adjective πᾶς, πᾶσα, πᾶν, "all, every; whole," are declined the strengthened forms ἅπᾶς, ἅπᾶσα, ἅπαν, "all, quite all," and σύμπᾶς, σύμπᾶσα, σύμπαν,
"all together." Except for the feminine genitive plural, ἁπᾶσῶν, συμπᾶσῶν,
these forms are accented on the antepenult when the ultima is short, e.g.,
ἅπαντος. Otherwise, they are accented on the penult. Note the short alpha in
the neuter nominative/accusative/vocative singular; contrast πᾶν. Like the
simple form, the strengthened forms of this adjective appear in the predicate
position and, less commonly, in the attributive position.

The noun στρατηγός, στρατηγοῦ, ὁ is a compound of στρατός, στρατοῦ, ὁ,
"army," and the root ἀγ- "lead": "army-leader, general."

A χρῆμα, χρήματος, τό is a thing needed or useful. "Money" is an obvious ex-
tension of this meaning.

Note that the conjunction ὡς, which can accompany a circumstantial participle
to show that the speaker does not vouch for the cause or purpose expressed, is a
proclitic.

COGNATES AND DERIVATIVES

ἄγω   pedagogue (slave who **led** a child to school, teacher)
ἅμα   simultaneous (from the Latin cognate *simul*)
οἶνος   wine (from the Latin cognate *vīnum*)
πᾶς   panacea (a cure-**all**)
στρατηγός   strategy

DRILLS

I. *Pick out the participles in the following sentences.*

1. Watch out for the swinging doors.
2. Sleeping dogs don't bark.
3. The man eating the liver is Mr. Grey.
4. Eating broiled liver is good for you, but eating boiled spinach is better.
5. The man being eaten by the Cyclops tasted good.
6. The tough man eaten by the Cyclops caused him considerable digestive difficulties.
7. There is no hope for the conquered.
8. Having eaten the liver broiled by his daughter, Mr. Grey has indigestion.
9. The liver eaten by Mr. Grey is causing him problems.
10. I saw the bear writing a letter at my desk.

II. (a) *Translate the following phrases or sentences.*

(b) *Change the number from singular to plural or from plural to singular.*

1. οἱ στρατιῶται οἱ ἐν τῷ πεδίῳ θύοντες
2. τῷ ῥήτορι τῷ τὴν δημοκρατίᾱν σώσαντι
3. τοῦ ποιητοῦ τοῦ τὰς σοφὰς διδάσκοντος
4. τῶν στρατιωτῶν τῶν τοὺς ἀδελφοὺς θαψάντων
5. τὸν ὁπλίτην τὸν τὴν γέφῡραν φυλάξοντα
6. τῷ ποιητῇ τῷ περὶ πολέμου γεγραφότι
7. τὰς θῡσάσᾱς
8. τὰ τοὺς κακοὺς κωλύοντα
9. τῶν τὰ τοῦ δήμου κλεψάντων
10. τῇ θεῷ τῇ τὴν δημοκρατίᾱν σῳζούσῃ
11. οἱ ὁπλῖται οἱ τὰ ὅπλα λείποντες
12. οἱ ὁπλῖται οἱ τὰ ὅπλα λιπόντες
13. τῷ παιδεύοντι
14. ὁ ἀγαθὸς διδάσκαλος ὁ τὸν φίλον διδάσκων
15. τοῖς κακοῖς διδασκάλοις τοῖς τοὺς νεᾱνίᾱς διδάσκουσιν
16. οἱ γέροντες οἱ τοὺς νεᾱνίᾱς διδασκόμενοι
17. τοὺς νεᾱνίᾱς τοὺς ὑπὸ τῶν ἀγαθῶν διδασκάλων διδασκομένους

18. τοὺς νεανίας τοὺς τοῖς ἀγαθοῖς διδασκάλοις δεδιδαγμένους

19. τῶν διδασκόντων

20. τῇ οὐ διδασκομένῃ

21. ταῖς μὴ διδασκομέναις

22. οἱ πολῖται οἱ ὑπὸ τοῦ ποιητοῦ διδαχθέντες

23. οἱ γέροντες οἱ χρυσὸν λιπόμενοι

24. τῷ σοφῷ τῷ τοὺς ἀγαθοὺς διδάξαντι

25. ἡ θεὸς ἡ τὸν δῆμον σῴζουσα

26. νῦν θύομεν τῇ θεῷ τῇ τὸν δῆμον σεσωκυίᾳ.

27. σωθέντες τῇ θεῷ θύομεν.

28. οὐ σωθεῖσαι τῇ θεῷ οὐ θύομεν.

29. μὴ σωθέντες τῇ θεῷ οὐ θύομεν.

30. θύομεν τῇ θεῷ τῇ τὸν δῆμον σωσάσῃ.

31. τοῖς ῥήτορσι τοῖς τοὺς πολίτας πείσασι λῦσαι τὴν εἰρήνην

32. οἱ τοῖς ῥήτορσι πεπεισμένοι

33. ἡ γέφυρα ἡ εὖ φυλαττομένη

34. ἡ γέφυρα ἡ εὖ φυλαχθεῖσα

35. ἡ γέφυρα ἡ εὖ τοῖς πολίταις πεφυλαγμένη

36. ἡ γέφυρα καίπερ εὖ φυλαττομένη ἐλύθη.

37. ἡ γέφυρα εὖ φυλαττομένη οὐκ ἐλύθη.

38. κελευσθεὶς τοὺς ὁπλίτας λύσω.

39. μὴ κελευσθεὶς τοὺς ὁπλίτας οὐ λύσω.

40. οὐ κελευσθέντες τοὺς ὁπλίτας οὐκ ἐλύσαμεν.

41. εὖ πεπαιδευμένοι καλὰ πράττομεν.

42. τὰς αἶγας κλέπτουσιν ὡς τῇ θεῷ θύσοντες.

43. καίπερ βλαπτόμενοι οὐκ ἐπαύσαντο.

44. μὴ διδαχθεὶς οὐκ ἀγαθὰ ἔπραξεν ἄν.

45. ἐπέμποντο ὡς φυλάξοντες τὴν γέφυραν.

46. ἐπέμποντο φυλάξοντες τὴν γέφυραν.

47. θύω τῷ θεῷ ἅτε τὴν γῆν σῴζοντι.

48. θύω τῷ θεῷ οἷα τὴν γῆν σῴζοντι.

III. *Translate.*

1. τὰ τοῦ δήμου κλέψᾱς οὐκ ἂν σῴζοις τήν γε χώρᾱν.

2. ἐν τῇ νήσῳ παυσάμεναι βιβλία γράψωμεν.

3. ἐκείνοις μὴ πειθόμενοι οὗτοι σωθήσεσθε.

4. ἐὰν μὴ διδάξητε περὶ ἀρετῆς τοὺς τὸ ἀργύριον κλέψαντας, οὐ
   ταξόμεθα οἱ ὁπλῖται.

5. θύει ὁ ποιητὴς ὡς δὴ βιβλία γράψων.

6. καίπερ κακοῖς δουλεύοντες ἐχόρευον ὅμως ταῖς γε θεοῖς ὡς
   σωθείησαν.

7. εἴθε σώσαιεν ἐκείνους οἱ θεοὶ ἅτε κακῶς πεπρᾱγότας.

8. διδαξώμεθα δὴ τοὺς τοῦ γε δήμου ἄρξοντας;

9. οἳ ἂν βλαπτόμενοι μὴ φυλάττωνται τοὺς πολεμίους, ὑπ' ἐκείνων
   μὴ ἀρχθῶμεν.

10. εἴ τοι τὰς χρῡσὸν ἐν τῷ πεδίῳ λιπούσᾱς ἐγραψάμεθα, τόν γε
    δῆμον οὐκ ἂν ἐπείσαμεν οἷα ἄνευ τέχνης λόγους γράψαντες.

11. ἅτε βλαβεῖσαι ὑπὸ τῶν τήν γε δημοκρατίᾱν λελυκότων φυλαττώμεθα
    τοὺς τοῖς ῥήτορσι πειθομένους.

EXERCISES

I.   1. τοὺς γέροντας λιποῦσαι ἥκομεν σύμπαντας τοὺς ῥήτορας τοὺς κεκλοφότας δώρων γραψόμεναι.

2. θυσίαν ἀγάγωμεν θεοῖς τοῖς Ἀθηναίους ἐν ἐκείνῃ τῇ μάχῃ σώσασιν ὅπως καὶ νῦν ἐθέλωσι πάντες οἱ θεοὶ τὴν δημοκρατίαν φυλάττειν.

3. ἀγγέλους πέμψειαν ἅτε πρῶτοι λύσαντες τήν γ᾽ εἰρήνην.

4. ἐκεῖνοι οἱ κακοὶ οἱ τὸν ἀγαθόν τε καὶ σοφὸν διδάσκαλον εἰς θάνατον ἀγαγόντες βλαβήσονταί τοι ὑπὸ τῶν θεῶν οἷα αἰσχρὰ πράττοντες.

5. ὁ τά τε τῶν ἄλλων κλέπτων καὶ ἅμα πείθων σύμπαντας τοὺς νεανίας κακὰ πράττειν καὶ μὴ τοῖς θεοῖς θύων ἔβλαπτε τὴν πᾶσαν χώραν ἢ οὔ;

6. θύσωμεν οἷα σεσωσμέναι.

7. ἐπειδὴ οἱ πολέμιοι τὴν οὐ φυλαχθεῖσαν γέφυραν ἔλυσαν, ἅπαντες οἱ ὁπλῖται τὰ ὅπλα ἔλιπον ἐν τῷ πεδίῳ ὡς νῦν γ᾽ εἰρήνην ἄξοντες.

8. ἐν τῇ εὖ πολιτευομένῃ χώρᾳ οὗτοι ἦρχε τοῦ δήμου ὁ στρατός, ἀλλ᾽ εἴ γ᾽ ὑπὸ τῶν πολεμίων βλάπτοιντο οἱ πολῖται, ἅπαντες, τοὺς γέροντας ἐν ταῖς οἰκίαις λιπόντες, ὑπὸ τῶν στρατηγῶν ἐτάττοντο ὡς τοὺς εἰς τὴν γῆν ἥκοντας φυλαξόμενοι.

9. τὰς μὴ δουλευούσας διδάξει δὴ τὰ βιβλία τὰ ὑπ᾽ ἀγαθῶν ποιητῶν γραφόμενα.

10. ὁ στρατηγός, καίπερ τάξας τοὺς στρατιώτας παρὰ τὴν θάλατταν, ὅμως οὐκ ἤθελεν ἐκείνους ἓξ στάδια εἰς μάχην ἀγαγεῖν.

11. δῶρα δὴ λελοίπαμεν ἐκείνῳ γε τῷ ποιητῇ τῷ περὶ τῆς ἀρετῆς γεγραφότι. συμπάσας γὰρ ἀγαθὰ πράττειν δεδίδαχεν.

12. χρήματα ἐκείνοις τοῖς κακοῖς ῥήτορσι λιπών, ἔπειτα τὸν στρατὸν ἤγαγον εἰς τὴν χώραν τὴν τῶν Ἑλλήνων τῶν οὐχ ὑπὸ στρατιωτῶν φυλαττομένων.

13. ἀρετή τοι τὸ πᾶσαν χώραν σῷζον, ὦ γέρον.

14. οὐ δίκαια πάντα τά γε θεοῖς πεπραγμένα;

15. ἦγεν εἰς τὸ πεδίον τοὺς στρατιώτᾱς ὡς δὴ μάχης ἀρξόμενος.

16. εἰ καλὰ πράττοις, ὦ ἄδελφε, πέμψαιμ' ἂν τῆς νυκτὸς ἐκεῖνα τὰ ζῷα τὰ ὑπὸ τοῦ γέροντος τιθέντα.

17. ἐκεῖνος ὁ ῥήτωρ ὁ αἰσχρός, καίπερ δῶρά τε πεπομφὼς παρὰ πάντας τοὺς ἀδίκους καὶ ἅμα τὸν δῆμον πείσᾱς λῦσαι τὴν εἰρήνην, ὅμως ἀντὶ τοῦ δικαίως βλαβῆναι ἠθέλησεν ὑφ' ἁπάντων τῶν ἐλευθέρων σῴζεσθαι.

18. ἅτε κακῶς πράττουσαι, ὦ φίλαι, μήτε εἰρήνην ἄγωμεν μήτε κακοῖς δουλεύωμεν.

19. τῶν φίλων χάριν οἱ Ἀθηναῖοι, ὑπὸ κακῶν ῥητόρων πεισθέντες, ἄρχειν ἤθελον πᾱσῶν τῶν γε νήσων, καὶ ἔπειτα αἱ μὲν χρήματ' ἔπεμπον, αἱ δὲ μὴ πειθόμεναι ἐβλάβησαν.

20. ἐκείνῃ τῇ νυκτὶ τὴν πάντων ἐλευθερίᾱν φυλάξαντες, ὦ Ἕλληνες, νῦν δή, καίπερ εἰς μάχην τεταγμένοι, οὔτε πείσεσθε τοῖς στρατηγοῖς τοῖς ἅπαντας σῶσαι ἐθέλουσιν οὔτε σώσετε τὴν χώρᾱν;

21. ἐπέμφθης εἰς ἀγορὰν, ὦ αἰσχρὲ ῥῆτορ, ὑπὸ τοῦ δήμου κλοπῆς γραφησόμενος.

22. ἀγαθὰ βιβλία τοῖς φίλοις λιπόμενος, ἐτάφη ὁ ποιητὴς ὑπὸ τῶν νεᾱνιῶν τῶν εὖ καὶ καλῶς διδαχθέντων.

23. τᾱς οἶνον κλεψάσᾱς γραψάμεναι κλοπῆς, ὦ ἀγαθαί, φυλάξομεν τᾱς γ' οἰκίᾱς.

24. νῦν τοι δῶρά γε πέμποιμεν παρὰ τοὺς ἀγαθοὺς τοὺς τὸν στρατὸν εἰς μάχην τεταχότας. ἄνευ γὰρ ἀρετῆς οἱ στρατηγοὶ λῦσουσι τὴν δημοκρατίᾱν τούς τε δικαίους βλάψαντες καὶ ἄδικά τε καὶ αἰσχρὰ πράξαντες.

25. ἧκόν τοι εἰς τὴν νῆσον ὡς παύσοντες τὸν πόλεμον, ἤθελον δὲ κλέψαι τᾱς τ' αἶγας καὶ τὸν οἶνον, τὰ δῶρα ἃ τῇ γε θεῷ ἐπεπόμφεμεν.

26. κωλύσωμεν δὴ ἐκεῖνον τὸν γέροντα τοὺς νεᾱνίᾱς διδάσκειν οἷα τὸν οἶνον ἐκ τῆς οἰκίᾱς κλέψαντα;

27. ἆρα πέντε ἡμερῶν ἥξετ' εἰς ἐκείνην τὴν γῆν τοὺς πολίτᾱς τὴν ῥητορικὴν διδάξουσαι; ἀλλ' οὐκ ἂν διδάξαιτ' ἐκείνους ὑπὸ τῶν γε γερόντων φυλαττόμεναι.

28. ἐν τῇ νήσῳ λειφθέντες ἅτε τὴν δημοκρατίᾱν λελυκότες, ἔπειτα
ὅμως, ἀργύριον κλέψαντες, πάντας τοὺς εὖ πεπολῑτευμένους
ἔβλαπτον.

29. ἐν οἴνῳ τοι καὶ ἐκεῖνος ὁ σοφὸς αἰσχρὰ ἔπρᾱττεν· λιπὼν γὰρ
τοὺς ἀδελφοὺς ἐχόρευε περὶ τὴν οἰκίᾱν.

30. θεοῖς ταῖς τὴν γῆν πεφυλαχυίαις ἄγοιτ’ ἂν θυσίᾱν ἅτ’ ἐν ἐκείνῃ
τῇ μάχῃ σωθεῖσαι.

31. οἵ γε ῥήτορες ἔπειθον τὸν στρατηγόν, καίπερ εὖ τάξαντα τοὺς
ὁπλίτᾱς, μήτε τὸν ἄλλον στρατὸν ἀγαγεῖν παρὰ θάλατταν
μήτε τὴν γῆν φυλάττειν.

32. ὑπὸ τῶν ἀγαθῶν διδασκόμενοι, ὦ ἀδελφοί, δώρων γράψεσθε τοὺς
ῥήτορας τοὺς τοῖς μὴ ἀγαθοῖς πειθομένους.

33. μάχης ἀρξάμενοι βλάψαιμεν ἂν τοὺς πολεμίους οἷα τὴν εἰρήνην
λύσαντας.

34. ἐάν γε πάντα τὸν οἶνον κλέψῃς, ὦ νεᾱνίᾱ, βλαβήσει ἅτε ἄδικα
πρᾱ́ξᾱς.

35. τούς γε πολεμίους βλάψᾱσαι ἔπειτα θῡσόμεθα τῇ θεῷ ἅτε
φυλαττούσῃ ἁπάντων τῶν πολῑτῶν καὶ τὰ σώματα καὶ τὰ
χρήματα καὶ τὰς ψῡχάς.

36. εἰ τῷ ῥήτορι τῷ λόγους περὶ πολέμου γράφοντι ἐπείθεσθ’, ὦ
Ἕλληνες, εὖ ἂν ἐφυλάττεσθε τοὺς ἐν τῇ μάχῃ τὰ ὅπλα
λιπόντας.

II. 1. Although being harmed by the *young men*, the citizens refused to dissolve the democracy, and the general led the soldiers into the country in order that he might rule the island. (*Express the purpose in
two ways.*)

2. If they are harmed in battle, the enemy will be willing to stop the war.
(*Express the protasis in two ways.*)

3. If, you know, we had left the general and all the hoplites there, we would
not have stopped the battle. (*Express the protasis in two ways.*)

4. Let us lead the stolen goat into the house of the soldiers who were sent
into battle. (*Express the subordinate clause in two ways.*)

READINGS

A. Euripides, *Alcestis* 1159–1163

The last lines of the play, sung by the Chorus. The same lines conclude Euripides' *Andromache*, *Helen*, and *Bacchae*. Similar lines conclude the *Medea*.

πολλαὶ μορφαὶ τῶν δαιμονίων,
1160 πολλὰ δ' ἀέλπτως κραίνουσι θεοί,
καὶ τὰ δοκηθέντ' οὐκ ἐτελέσθη,[1]
τῶν δ' ἀδοκήτων πόρον ηὗρε[1] θεός.
τοιόνδ' ἀπέβη τόδε πρᾶγμα.

ἀδόκητος, ἀδόκητον   unexpected
ἀέλπτως (*adv.*)   unexpectedly, beyond hope
ἀπέβη   *third pers. sing., aorist indicative active of* ἀποβαίνω, ἀποβήσομαι,
    ἀπέβην, ἀποβέβηκα, ——, ——   step off, go away; result, turn out
δαιμόνιος, δαιμονίᾱ, δαιμόνιον   divine, belonging to a god, marvelous
δοκέω, δόξω, ἔδοξα, ——, δέδογμαι, -ἐδόχθην/ἐδοκήθην seem, think; expect
εὑρίσκω, εὑρήσω, ηὗρον, ηὕρηκα, ηὕρημαι, ηὑρέθην   find, discover
κραίνω, κρανῶ, ἔκρᾱνα, ——, κέκραμμαι, ἐκράνθην   accomplish
μορφή, μορφῆς, ἡ   shape, form
πολλοί, πολλαί, πολλά   many
πόρος, πόρου, ὁ   crossing, passage; way, means
τελέω, τελῶ, ἐτέλεσα, τετέλεκα, τετέλεσμαι, ἐτελέσθην   finish, accomplish
τόδε   *neuter nom./acc. sing. of* ὅδε, ἥδε, τόδε   this
τοιόσδε, τοιάδε, τοιόνδε   of this sort

---

1. This is a **gnomic aorist** expressing a timeless, general truth ; translate as a present. See the Appendix, p. 733.

B. Simonides 37 (D. L. Page, *Epigrammata Graeca* 216–217)

The epitaph of one Timokreon, a somewhat self-indulgent man, by the lyric
and elegiac poet Simonides (c. 556–468 B.C.).

πολλὰ πιὼν καὶ πολλὰ φαγὼν καὶ πολλὰ κάκ᾽ εἰπὼν
ἀνθρώπους κεῖμαι Τιμοκρέων ῾Ρόδιος.

C. *Greek Anthology* 7.33

An epitaph for the sixth-century B.C. lyric poet Anakreon, who reputedly was
fond of good living. The poet is made to answer a critic.

πολλὰ πιὼν τέθνηκας, ᾽Ανάκρεον. —ἀλλὰ τρυφήσας·
καὶ σὺ δὲ μὴ πίνων ἵξεαι εἰς ᾽Αΐδην.

᾽Αΐδης, ᾽Αΐδου, ὁ   Hades
᾽Ανακρέων, ᾽Ανακρέοντος, ὁ   (voc. ᾽Ανάκρεον) Anakreon
ἀποθνῄσκω, ἀποθανοῦμαι, ἀπέθανον, τέθνηκα, ——, —— die
εἰπών   see λέγω
ἐσθίω, ἔδομαι, ἔφαγον, ἐδήδοκα, ἐδήδεσμαι, ἠδέσθην   eat
ἵξεαι = ἵξῃ/ἵξει   from
    ἱκνέομαι, ἵξομαι, ἱκόμην, ——, ἷγμαι, —— (mid. only) arrive
κάκ᾽ = κακά (For the accent, see the Appendix, p. 613.)
κεῖμαι   first pers. sing., present indicative middle of κεῖμαι, κείσομαι, ——, ——,
    ——, —— (mid. only) lie; be placed, be set
λέγω, ἐρῶ/λέξω, εἶπον/ἔλεξα, εἴρηκα, εἴρημαι/λέλεγμαι, ἐλέχθην/ἐρρήθην
    say, speak; say (acc. of thing) about (acc. of person)
πίνω, πίομαι, ἔπιον, πέπωκα, -πέπομαι, -ἐπόθην   drink
πολλοί, πολλαί, πολλά   many
σύ   nom. sing. of the second person pronoun   you
τέθνηκα   see ἀποθνῄσκω
Τιμοκρέων, Τιμοκρέοντος, ὁ   Timokreon, a curmudgeonly gourmandizer
τρυφάω, τρυφήσω, ἐτρύφησα, ——, ——, —— live luxuriously, live softly,
    give oneself airs
῾Ρόδιος, ῾Ροδία, ῾Ρόδιον   Rhodian, of Rhodes
φαγών   see ἐσθίω

D. Solon, Fragment 18 West

The early–sixth-century B.C. Athenian lawgiver speaks of himself.

γηράσκω δ' αἰεὶ πολλὰ διδασκόμενος.

ἀεί/αἰεί (*adv.*) always
γηράσκω/γηράω, γηράσω, ἐγήρᾱσα, γεγήρακα, ——, —— grow old
πολλοί, πολλαί, πολλά many

E. Euripides, Fragment 632 Nauck

πολλῶν τὰ χρήματ' αἴτι' ἀνθρώποις κακῶν.

αἴτιος, αἰτίᾱ, αἴτιον responsible for (+ *gen.*)
πολλοί, πολλαί, πολλά many
χρῆμα, χρήματος, τό thing; (*pl.*) goods, property, money

F. Sophokles, *Ajax* 646–647

From a speech of Ajax shortly before he commits suicide.

ἅπανθ' ὁ μακρὸς κἀναρίθμητος χρόνος
φύει τ' ἄδηλα καὶ φανέντα κρύπτεται.

ἄδηλος, ἄδηλον unclear, obscure
ἀναρίθμητος, ἀναρίθμητον uncounted, uncountable, immeasurable
ἅπᾱς, ἅπᾱσα, ἅπαν all, quite all
κἀναρίθμητος = καὶ ἀναρίθμητος (*For this* **crasis** *see the Appendix, p. 614.*)
κρύπτω, κρύψω, ἔκρυψα, κέκρυφα, κέκρυμμαι, ἐκρύφθην hide, conceal
φαίνω, φανῶ, ἔφηνα, πέφηνα, πέφασμαι, ἐφάνην cause to appear; (*mid.*,
    perfect active, aorist passive) appear
φύω, φύσω, ἔφῡσα (*trans.*) or ἔφῡν (*intrans.*), πέφῡκα (*intrans.*), ——, ——
    produce, (cause to) grow; (*mid. and intrans.*) grow
χρόνος, χρόνου, ὁ time

G. Aischylos, *Eumenides* 754–756

Agamemnon's son Orestes, freed by Athena from punishment for killing his mother Klytaimnestra, expresses his gratitude.

> ὦ Παλλάς, ὦ σώσασα τοὺς ἐμοὺς δόμους,
> 755 γαίας πατρῴας ἐστερημένον σύ τοι
> κατῴκισάς με . . . .

γαῖα, γαίας, ἡ   earth, land

δόμος, δόμου, ὁ (*sing. or pl.*)   house, home; household, family

ἐμός, ἐμή, ἐμόν   my

κατοικίζω, κατοικιῶ, κατῴκισα, κατῴκικα, κατῴκισμαι, κατῳκίσθην
    settle; re-establish in one's house, bring home

με   *acc. sing. of the first person pronoun (enclitic)*   me

Παλλάς, Παλλάδος, ἡ (*voc.* Παλλάς)   Pallas (epithet of Athena)

πατρῷος, πατρῴα, πατρῷον   paternal, of one's father

στερέω, στερήσω, ἐστέρησα, ἐστέρηκα, ἐστέρημαι, ἐστερήθην
    deprive of (+ *acc. of person deprived, gen. of thing taken away*)

σύ   *nom. sing. of the second person pronoun*   you

UNIT
9

72. CONTRACTED VERBS: INTRODUCTION

Some verbs have a present tense stem which ends in a, ε, or o. Since this vowel *contracts* with the initial vowel or diphthong of the various endings added to this stem, according to the rules given below, these verbs are called **contracted verbs**.

THE CONTRACTION TAKES PLACE IN ANY FORM WHICH USES THE STEM FROM PRINCIPAL PART I. ALL OTHER TENSES ARE FORMED ACCORDING TO RULES ALREADY LEARNED, as the Principal Parts below make clear.

The contraction follows regular rules which will be given as each type of verb is presented.

Most endings employed by contracted verbs are the same as those of such verbs as παιδεύω. Different endings occur in the present optative active only, and these will be listed separately.

Uncontracted forms of these verbs will be given in parentheses for comparison.

73. CONTRACTED VERBS WITH PRESENT TENSE STEMS IN -*a*-

The following verb will serve as an example:

τῑμάω, τῑμήσω, ἐτίμησα, τετίμηκα, τετίμημαι, ἐτῑμήθην, "honor"

The present tense stem is formed, as usual, by dropping the ending -ω from Principal Part I: τῑμα-. The *a* of this stem contracts with the initial vowel or diphthong of the endings according to the rules below.

231

$$
\boxed{
\begin{array}{ll}
\text{CONTRACTIONS OF } \alpha & \\
\alpha\varepsilon > \bar{\alpha} & \alpha o > \omega \\
\alpha\varepsilon\iota > \bar{\alpha} & \alpha o\iota > \omega \\
\alpha\eta > \bar{\alpha} & \alpha o\upsilon > \omega \\
\alpha\eta > \bar{\alpha} & \alpha\omega > \omega
\end{array}
}
$$

Thus the forms of the present and imperfect tenses of τῑμάω are as follows. (In learning the contracted forms, one can either memorize the contracted endings or make the contractions oneself according to the rules above from the uncontracted forms which are given in parentheses.)

1. PRESENT INDICATIVE ACTIVE AND MIDDLE/PASSIVE

		ACTIVE		*MIDDLE/PASSIVE*	
S	1	τῑμῶ	(τῑμάω)	τῑμῶμαι	(τῑμάομαι)
	2	τῑμᾷς	(τῑμάεις)	τῑμᾷ	(τῑμάῃ/τῑμάει)
	3	τῑμᾷ	(τῑμάει)	τῑμᾶται	(τῑμάεται)
P	1	τῑμῶμεν	(τῑμάομεν)	τῑμώμεθα	(τῑμαόμεθα)
	2	τῑμᾶτε	(τῑμάετε)	τῑμᾶσθε	(τῑμάεσθε)
	3	τῑμῶσι(ν)	(τῑμάουσι[ν])	τῑμῶνται	(τῑμάονται)

Observations: (1) The first person singular, present indicative active is given in its uncontracted form as Principal Part I in order to show the vowel of the present tense stem. But this form, like the others, is *contracted* in actual usage.

(2) The third person singular, present indicative active is identical in form with the second person singular, present indicative middle/passive.

General note on the accent of contracted verbs:

IF EITHER OF THE TWO SYLLABLES BEING CONTRACTED BORE AN ACCENT IN THE ORIGINAL UNCONTRACTED FORM, THE ACCENT REMAINS ON THE NEW, CONTRACTED SYLLABLE. THE ACCENT ON A CONTRACTED ULTIMA IS A CIRCUMFLEX; THE ACCENT ON A CONTRACTED PENULT IS DETERMINED BY THE RULES FOR THE POSSIBILITIES OF ACCENT. THE ACCENT OF THE UNCONTRACTED FORMS IS RECESSIVE.

SECTION 73 233

2. IMPERFECT INDICATIVE ACTIVE AND MIDDLE/PASSIVE

		ACTIVE		*MIDDLE/PASSIVE*	
S	1	ἐτίμων	(ἐτίμαον)	ἐτῑμώμην	(ἐτῑμαόμην)
	2	ἐτίμᾱς	(ἐτίμαες)	ἐτῑμῶ	(ἐτῑμάου)
	3	ἐτίμᾱ	(ἐτίμαε)	ἐτῑμᾶτο	(ἐτῑμάετο)
P	1	ἐτῑμῶμεν	(ἐτῑμάομεν)	ἐτῑμώμεθα	(ἐτῑμαόμεθα)
	2	ἐτῑμᾶτε	(ἐτῑμάετε)	ἐτῑμᾶσθε	(ἐτῑμάεσθε)
	3	ἐτίμων	(ἐτίμαον)	ἐτῑμῶντο	(ἐτῑμάοντο)

Observations: (1) The imperfect indicative employs, of course, the past indicative augment.

(2) Nu-movable is NEVER added to the third person singular, imperfect indicative active of contracted verbs. Thus ἐτίμᾱ, but ἔλῡε(ν).

3. PRESENT SUBJUNCTIVE ACTIVE AND MIDDLE/PASSIVE

		ACTIVE		*MIDDLE/PASSIVE*	
S	1	τῑμῶ	(τῑμάω)	τῑμῶμαι	(τῑμάωμαι)
	2	τῑμᾷς	(τῑμάῃς)	τῑμᾷ	(τῑμάῃ)
	3	τῑμᾷ	(τῑμάῃ)	τῑμᾶται	(τῑμάηται)
P	1	τῑμῶμεν	(τῑμάωμεν)	τῑμώμεθα	(τῑμαώμεθα)
	2	τῑμᾶτε	(τῑμάητε)	τῑμᾶσθε	(τῑμάησθε)
	3	τῑμῶσι(ν)	(τῑμάωσι[ν])	τῑμῶνται	(τῑμάωνται)

Observation: The present subjunctive of τῑμάω, both active and middle/passive, is identical in form with the indicative throughout. Context will help to distinguish the forms.

4. PRESENT OPTATIVE ACTIVE

In the present optative active contracted verbs can employ, before contraction, EITHER endings identical to those of παιδεύω OR a separate set of endings. The latter are listed separately.

234

S	1	τῑμῷμι	(τῑμάοιμι)	OR	τῑμῴην	(τῑμαοίην)	-οιην
	2	τῑμῷς	(τῑμάοις)		τῑμῴης	(τῑμαοίης)	-οιης
	3	τῑμῷ	(τῑμάοι)		τῑμῴη	(τῑμαοίη)	-οιη
P	1	τῑμῷμεν	(τῑμάοιμεν)		τῑμῴημεν	(τῑμαοίημεν)	-οιημεν
	2	τῑμῷτε	(τῑμάοιτε)		τῑμῴητε	(τῑμαοίητε)	-οιητε
	3	τῑμῷεν	(τῑμάοιεν)		τῑμῴησαν	(τῑμαοίησαν)	-οιησαν

Observations: (1) The alternative endings are more common in the singular; the endings identical to those of παιδεύω are more common in the plural.

(2) This is the only instance where contracted verbs employ a set of endings different from those of παιδεύω. The alternative endings are composed of the thematic vowel -o-, the optative suffix -ιη-, and the person markers -ν, -ς, —, -μεν, -τε, -σαν. Compare the person markers of the aorist optative passive (παιδευθείην, etc.).

5. PRESENT OPTATIVE MIDDLE/PASSIVE

S	1	τῑμῴμην	(τῑμαοίμην)
	2	τῑμῷο	(τῑμάοιο)
	3	τῑμῷτο	(τῑμάοιτο)
P	1	τῑμῴμεθα	(τῑμαοίμεθα)
	2	τῑμῷσθε	(τῑμάοισθε)
	3	τῑμῷντο	(τῑμάοιντο)

6. PRESENT INFINITIVE ACTIVE AND MIDDLE/PASSIVE

The contraction of the present infinitive active ending -ειν with the α of the stem does NOT follow the rules presented above.

τῑμᾶν

Observation: This form was originally *τῑμάεεν, just as the present infinitive active of παιδεύω was *παιδεύεεν. The diphthong of the ending -ειν resulted from the contraction of the two epsilons. (Cf. the rules for the contraction of epsilon in Section 74.) Like a diphthong that results from compensatory lengthening, a diphthong that results from contraction is also a spurious diphthong.

When the spurious diphthong -ει- contracts with an -α-, there is no iota subscript in the result.

The present infinitive middle/passive follows the regular rules:

τῑμᾶσθαι   (τῑμάεσθαι)

7. PRESENT PARTICIPLE ACTIVE

To form the present participle active of contracted verbs, add to the present tense stem the same suffixes and endings as are employed to form the present participle active of παιδεύω (Section 66.1). As in the finite forms of contracted verbs, the present tense stem *contracts* with the initial vowel or diphthong of the suffix.

	M	F	N
Nom./Voc. S	τῑμῶν	τῑμῶσα	τῑμῶν
	(τῑμάων)	(τῑμάουσα)	(τῑμάον)
Gen.	τῑμῶντος	τῑμώσης	τῑμῶντος
	(τῑμάοντος)	(τῑμαούσης)	(τῑμάοντος)

Observations: (1) These participles are declined exactly like the present participle active of παιδεύω except that the contraction of the present tense stem with the suffix causes the accent to fall on the final syllable of the declension stem: e.g., τῑμῶντος, but παιδεύοντος. As with the present participle active of παιδεύω, the case endings are dropped from the genitive singular forms in order to obtain the declension stem:

	M	F	N
	τῑμωντ-	τῑμωσ-	τῑμωντ-

The masculine and neuter are then given third-declension case endings; the feminine is declined like a first declension noun with nominative singular in short -α.

THE DECLENSION STEMS, CONTAINING THE CONTRACTIONS, ARE FIXED. The addition of the endings is simple.

(2) In the feminine genitive plural, the accent shifts, as usual, to the ultima: τῑμωσῶν.

(3) Note that the masculine and neuter dative plural is τῑμῶσι(ν) (*τῑμάοντσι[ν]).

8. PRESENT PARTICIPLE MIDDLE/PASSIVE

To form the present participle middle/passive of contracted verbs, add to the present tense stem the same suffixes and endings as are employed to form the present participle middle/passive of παιδεύω (Section 67.1). The final vowel of the stem contracts with the initial vowel of the suffix.

	M	F	N
Nom. S	τῑμώμενος	τῑμωμένη	τῑμώμενον
	(τῑμαόμενος)	(τῑμαομένη)	(τῑμαόμενον)

Observation: This participle is declined exactly like the present participle middle/passive of παιδεύω.

Remember that only those forms of τῑμάω which use Principal Part I differ from those of παιδεύω. From the other Principal Parts of this verb the other tenses are formed according to the rules already learned.

Drill I.1–14, page 248, may now be done.

74. CONTRACTED VERBS WITH PRESENT TENSE STEMS IN -ε-

The following verb will serve as an example:

ποιέω, ποιήσω, ἐποίησα, πεποίηκα, πεποίημαι, ἐποιήθην, "do; make"

The present tense stem, ποιε-, contracts with the initial vowel or diphthong of the endings according to the chart below.

CONTRACTIONS OF ε	
εε > ει	εο > ου
εει > ει	εοι > οι
εη > η	εου > ου
εη > ῃ	εω > ω

Thus the forms of the present and imperfect tenses of ποιέω (with uncontracted forms given in parentheses for reference) are as follows:

1. PRESENT INDICATIVE ACTIVE AND MIDDLE/PASSIVE

		ACTIVE		*MIDDLE/PASSIVE*	
S	1	ποιῶ	(ποιέω)	ποιοῦμαι	(ποιέομαι)
	2	ποιεῖς	(ποιέεις)	ποιεῖ/ποιῇ	(ποιέει/ποιέῃ)
	3	ποιεῖ	(ποιέει)	ποιεῖται	(ποιέεται)
P	1	ποιοῦμεν	(ποιέομεν)	ποιούμεθα	(ποιεόμεθα)
	2	ποιεῖτε	(ποιέετε)	ποιεῖσθε	(ποιέεσθε)
	3	ποιοῦσι(ν)	(ποιέουσι[ν])	ποιοῦνται	(ποιέονται)

Observation: One of the two alternative forms of the second person singular, present indicative middle/passive is identical with the third person singular, present indicative active.

2. IMPERFECT INDICATIVE ACTIVE AND MIDDLE/PASSIVE

		ACTIVE		*MIDDLE/PASSIVE*	
S	1	ἐποίουν	(ἐποίεον)	ἐποιούμην	(ἐποιεόμην)
	2	ἐποίεις	(ἐποίεες)	ἐποιοῦ	(ἐποιέου)
	3	ἐποίει	(ἐποίεε)	ἐποιεῖτο	(ἐποιέετο)
P	1	ἐποιοῦμεν	(ἐποιέομεν)	ἐποιούμεθα	(ἐποιεόμεθα)
	2	ἐποιεῖτε	(ἐποιέετε)	ἐποιεῖσθε	(ἐποιέεσθε)
	3	ἐποίουν	(ἐποίεον)	ἐποιοῦντο	(ἐποιέοντο)

Observation: Nu-movable is NEVER added to the third person singular of the imperfect indicative active of contracted verbs. Thus ἐποίει, but ἔλῡε(ν).

3. PRESENT SUBJUNCTIVE ACTIVE AND MIDDLE/PASSIVE

		ACTIVE		*MIDDLE/PASSIVE*	
S	1	ποιῶ	(ποιέω)	ποιῶμαι	(ποιέωμαι)
	2	ποιῇς	(ποιέῃς)	ποιῇ	(ποιέῃ)
	3	ποιῇ	(ποιέῃ)	ποιῆται	(ποιέηται)
P	1	ποιῶμεν	(ποιέωμεν)	ποιώμεθα	(ποιεώμεθα)
	2	ποιῆτε	(ποιέητε)	ποιῆσθε	(ποιέησθε)
	3	ποιῶσι(ν)	(ποιέωσι[ν])	ποιῶνται	(ποιέωνται)

4. PRESENT OPTATIVE ACTIVE

In the present optative active, contracted verbs with stems in -ε- can employ, before contraction, EITHER endings identical with those of παιδεύω OR the same alternative endings used by τῑμάω. These are listed separately.

S	1	ποιοῖμι	(ποιέοιμι)	OR	ποιοίην	(ποιεοίην)	-οιην
	2	ποιοῖς	(ποιέοις)		ποιοίης	(ποιεοίης)	-οιης
	3	ποιοῖ	(ποιέοι)		ποιοίη	(ποιεοίη)	-οιη
P	1	ποιοῖμεν	(ποιέοιμεν)	OR	ποιοίημεν	(ποιεοίημεν)	-οιημεν
	2	ποιοῖτε	(ποιέοιτε)		ποιοίητε	(ποιεοίητε)	-οιητε
	3	ποιοῖεν	(ποιέοιεν)		ποιοίησαν	(ποιεοίησαν)	-οιησαν

Observation: As with τῑμάω, the alternative endings are more common in the singular; the endings identical with those of παιδεύω are more common in the plural.

5. PRESENT OPTATIVE MIDDLE/PASSIVE

S	1	ποιοίμην	(ποιεοίμην)
	2	ποιοῖο	(ποιέοιο)
	3	ποιοῖτο	(ποιέοιτο)
P	1	ποιοίμεθα	(ποιεοίμεθα)
	2	ποιοῖσθε	(ποιέοισθε)
	3	ποιοῖντο	(ποιέοιντο)

6. PRESENT INFINITIVE ACTIVE AND MIDDLE/PASSIVE

	ACTIVE		*MIDDLE/PASSIVE*	
	ποιεῖν	(ποιέειν)	ποιεῖσθαι	(ποιέεσθαι)

7. PRESENT PARTICIPLE ACTIVE AND MIDDLE/PASSIVE

	M	F	N
ACTIVE	(ποιέων)	(ποιέουσα)	(ποιέον)
Nom./Voc. S	ποιῶν	ποιοῦσα	ποιοῦν
Gen.	ποιοῦντος	ποιούσης	ποιοῦντος
	(ποιέοντος)	(ποιεούσης)	(ποιέοντος)
MIDDLE/ PASSIVE	(ποιεόμενος)	(ποιεομένη)	(ποιεόμενον)
Nom. S	ποιούμενος	ποιουμένη	ποιούμενον

Observations: (1) As in the declension of the participles of τῑμάω, the declension stems remain unchanged throughout: ποιοντ- for the masculine and neuter, ποιουσ- for the feminine.

(2) In the feminine genitive plural, the accent shifts, as usual, to the ultima: ποιουσῶν.

(3) Note the masculine and neuter dative plural of the present participle active: ποιοῦσι(ν) (*ποιέοντσι[ν]).

Drill 1.15–54, page 248, may now be done.

75. THE DEMONSTRATIVE ADJECTIVE/PRONOUN ὅδε, ἥδε, τόδε, "this"

The demonstrative adjective/pronoun ὅδε, ἥδε, τόδε means "this (here, in this place)" in contrast with the demonstrative ἐκεῖνος, ἐκείνη, ἐκεῖνο, which means "that (there, in that place)" (Section 62).

The forms of this demonstrative are as follows:

	M	F	N
Nom. S	ὅδε	ἥδε	τόδε
Gen.	τοῦδε	τῆσδε	τοῦδε
Dat.	τῷδε	τῇδε	τῷδε
Acc.	τόνδε	τήνδε	τόδε
Nom. P	οἵδε	αἵδε	τάδε
Gen.	τῶνδε	τῶνδε	τῶνδε
Dat.	τοῖσδε	ταῖσδε	τοῖσδε
Acc.	τούσδε	τάσδε	τάδε

This demonstrative consists of the article + the enclitic suffix -δε. The effect of this suffix on the accent of the article is the same as that of the enclitic τε; hence the acute accent on such forms as ἥδε, τούσδε.

A noun modified by ὅδε, ἥδε, τόδε must be accompanied by the article. The demonstrative usually precedes the article. It may (rarely) follow the noun.

οἵδε οἱ ἀδελφοὶ βιβλία ἔγραφον.
These brothers were writing books.

εἰς τήνδε τὴν νῆσον
εἰς τὴν νῆσον τήνδε (rare)
to this island

The demonstrative can also be used as a pronoun:

τήνδε παύσετε.
You will stop this woman.

τάδε πεφυλάχαμεν.
We have guarded these things.

The meanings of three demonstratives are compared in Section 77.

76. THE DEMONSTRATIVE ADJECTIVE/PRONOUN οὗτος, αὕτη, τοῦτο, "this, that"

The demonstrative adjective/pronoun οὗτος, αὕτη, τοῦτο means, depending on context, "this" or "that." It indicates someone or something close at hand or in the speaker's thoughts, but it does not emphasize that closeness as much as the demonstrative ὅδε, ἥδε, τόδε. It is equivalent to "this" or "that" in the sentences "I met this man you know," "You know that man I was telling you about."

The forms of this demonstrative are as follows:

	M	F	N
Nom. S	οὗτος	αὕτη	τοῦτο
Gen.	τούτου	ταύτης	τούτου
Dat.	τούτῳ	ταύτῃ	τούτῳ
Acc.	τοῦτον	ταύτην	τοῦτο
Nom. P	οὗτοι	αὗται	ταῦτα
Gen.	τούτων	τούτων	τούτων
Dat.	τούτοις	ταύταις	τούτοις
Acc.	τούτους	ταύτᾱς	ταῦτα

The endings are in almost every case identical with those of the article. Where the article has a rough breathing (in the nominative singular and plural, masculine and feminine), the demonstrative has a rough breathing in place of initial τ-. The stem has -αυ- instead of -ου- in all feminine forms EXCEPT the genitive plural, and in the neuter nominative and accusative plural.

A noun modified by οὗτος, αὕτη, τοῦτο must be accompanied by the article. The demonstrative usually precedes the article. It may (rarely) follow the noun.

ταύτᾱς τὰς γεφύρᾱς ἐφυλάττετε.
τὰς γεφύρᾱς ταύτᾱς ἐφυλάττετε. (rare)
You were guarding these/those bridges.

The demonstrative can also be used as a pronoun:

τούτους παύσουσιν.
They will stop these/those men.

The meanings of three demonstratives are compared in Section 77.

77. DEMONSTRATIVES COMPARED

1. ἐκεῖνος: (a) describes someone or something relatively far away from the speaker:

ἐκεῖνον εἰς τὴν νῆσον ἔπεμψα.
I sent **that man (over there)** to the island.

(b) can be used of someone famous or infamous:

ἐκεῖνος ὁ ποιητής
that (famous) poet

ἐκεῖνος ὁ γέρων
that (horrible) old man

(c) can mean "the former" when contrasted with οὗτος (cf. 3.c below).

2. ὅδε: (a) describes someone or something very close to the speaker:

τόδε τὸ βιβλίον ἔγραψα.
I wrote **this** book **(right here)**.

(b) looks ahead to what will follow:

ἐγράψαμεν τάδε· . . . .
We wrote **the following things**: . . . .

3. οὗτος: (a) describes someone or something less close or less vividly present than would have been indicated by ὅδε:

τοῦτο τὸ βιβλίον ἔγραψα.
I wrote **this** book (to which you refer).
I wrote **that** book (to which you refer).

(b) when contrasted with ὅδε, refers to what has gone before:

ταῦτα μὲν Ὅμηρος ἔγραψεν, τάδε δ' ἔγραψα.
The preceding (things), on the one hand, Homer wrote; **the following (things)**, on the other hand, I wrote.

(c) when contrasted with ἐκεῖνος often means
"the latter" as opposed to "the former":

ἀγαθοὶ καὶ οἱ νεᾱνίαι καὶ οἱ γέροντες.
ἐκεῖνοι μὲν γὰρ εἰς πόλεμον πέμπονται,
οὗτοι δὲ βιβλία γράφουσιν.
Both young men and old men are good.
For **the former**, on the one hand, are sent to war;
the latter, on the other hand, write books.

(d) can be used of someone famous or infamous:

οὗτος ὁ ποιητής
this (famous) poet
that (famous) poet

οὗτος ὁ γέρων
this (horrible) old man
that (horrible) old man

(e) often serves as the antecedent of a relative pronoun:

ὃς ἂν παιδευθῇ, **οὗτος** εἰς μάχην
πεμφθήσεται.
Whoever is educated, **that man** will be
sent into battle.

Drill II, page 249, may now be done.

78. SUBJECTIVE GENITIVE

A noun or pronoun in the genitive case can indicate the *subject* of a verbal
action or state of being denoted by a noun. This usage is called the **subjective
genitive.** The genitive stands in the attributive position.

ὁ ῾Ομήρου φόβος
Homer's fear
(i.e., the fear **which Homer feels**)

αἱ τῶν ῾Ελλήνων θυσίαι
the sacrifices **of the Greeks**
(i.e., the sacrifices **which the Greeks perform**)

79. OBJECTIVE GENITIVE

A noun or pronoun in the genitive case can also indicate the *object* of a verbal action denoted by a noun. This usage is called the **objective genitive**. The genitive stands in the attributive position.

> ὁ **τῶν θεῶν** φόβος
> fear **of the gods**
> (i.e., fear **directed toward the gods**)
>
> ἡ **τῶν αἰγῶν** θυσίᾱ
> the sacrifice **of the goats**
> (i.e., someone **sacrificed the goats**)

Contrast the phrases in Section 78, where the subjective genitives Ὁμήρου and τῶν Ἑλλήνων indicate the performer of an action. The objective genitives τῶν θεῶν and τῶν αἰγῶν indicate the receiver of an action. Context usually allows one to determine whether such a genitive is subjective or objective.

80. DATIVE OF MANNER

A noun in the dative case, without a preposition, can indicate the *manner* in which an action takes place or a state of being holds true. This usage is called the **dative of manner**.

> **τούτῳ τῷ τρόπῳ** βιβλίον ἔγραψα.
> **In this way** I wrote a book.

Most datives of manner are phrases consisting of a noun and an adjective, but some nouns can be used alone in such expressions:

> οἱ στρατιῶται **σῑγῇ** εἰς τὴν νῆσον ἐπέμφθησαν.
> The soldiers were sent **in silence** to the island.

In general, however, nouns not modified by adjectives employ various prepositions with the dative of manner:

> **σὺν δίκῃ** ἐπέμφθησαν ἐκ τῆς χώρᾱς οἱ πολέμιοι.
> **With justice** the enemy were sent out of the land.

Carefully distinguish the *dative of manner* from the *instrumental dative*:

> τὴν γέφῡραν **σῑγῇ** ἐφύλαττον.
> They were guarding the bridge **in silence**. (*dative of manner*)
>
> τὴν γέφῡραν **ὅπλοις** ἐφύλαττον.
> They were guarding the bridge **with weapons**. (*instrumental dative*)

81. DATIVE OF RESPECT

A noun in the dative case, without a preposition, can also indicate the *respect* in which a statement is true. This usage is called the **dative of respect**.

> τῷ μὲν **σώματι** καλὸς ὁ νεᾱνίᾱς, τῇ δὲ **ψῡχῇ** κακός.
> **In body** (i.e., **with respect to his body**), on the one hand, the young man is beautiful; **in soul**, on the other hand, he is evil.

VOCABULARY

ἀγών, ἀγῶνος, ὁ	contest, struggle
ἀδικέω, ἀδικήσω, ἠδίκησα, ἠδίκηκα, ἠδίκημαι, ἠδικήθην	do wrong, wrong
ἄλογος, ἄλογον	unreasoning, unreasonable, irrational
βάρβαρος, βάρβαρον	non-Greek, foreign
βίος, βίου, ὁ	life, means of living
δαίμων, δαίμονος, ὁ or ἡ	god, goddess, divine being
ἐχθρός, ἐχθρά, ἐχθρόν	hated, hostile; (as substantive) enemy
νῑκάω, νῑκήσω, ἐνίκησα, νενίκηκα, νενίκημαι, ἐνῑκήθην	win; conquer
ὅδε, ἥδε, τόδε	this
ὄνομα, ὀνόματος, τό	name
οὗτος, αὕτη, τοῦτο	this, that
οὕτω(ς) (adv.)	in this way, so, thus
πεῖρα, πείρᾱς, ἡ	trial, attempt; experience
ἔμπειρος, ἔμπειρον	experienced in, acquainted with (+ gen.)
ἐμπειρίᾱ, ἐμπειρίᾱς, ἡ	experience, practice
ποιέω, ποιήσω, ἐποίησα, πεποίηκα, πεποίημαι, ἐποιήθην	make; do
σῑγή, σῑγῆς, ἡ	silence
τῑμάω, τῑμήσω, ἐτίμησα, τετίμηκα, τετίμημαι, ἐτῑμήθην	honor
τρόπος, τρόπου, ὁ	way, manner; character
ὕδωρ, ὕδατος, τό	water
ὑπέρ (prep.) + gen.	over, above; on behalf of
+ acc.	(of motion or measure) over, beyond

VOCABULARY NOTES

The verb ἀδικέω, ἀδικήσω, ἠδίκησα, ἠδίκηκα, ἠδίκημαι, ἠδικήθην, "do wrong, wrong," is a denominative verb formed from the adjective ἄδικος, ἄδικον, "unjust." Likewise, the verbs τῑμάω, τῑμήσω, ἐτίμησα, τετίμηκα, τετίμημαι, ἐτῑμήθην, "honor," and νῑκάω, νῑκήσω, ἐνίκησα, νενίκηκα, νενίκημαι, ἐνῑκήθην, "win; conquer," are denominative verbs formed from the nouns τῑμή and νίκη. The verb ἀδικέω can be used either transitively or intransitively.

The adjective ἄλογος, ἄλογον, "unreasoning, unreasonable, irrational," is formed from the noun λόγος (in the sense "reason") with alpha privative prefixed.

The adjective βάρβαρος, βάρβαρον, "non-Greek, foreign," is an **onomatopoeic** word which imitates the sound of unintelligible foreign speech. It lacks the negative connotations of the English derivative "barbaric." Although not compounded, this is a *two-ending* adjective.

The noun βίος, βίου, ὁ, "life, means of living," can refer either to a person's manner of life (e.g., a good life as opposed to a bad one) or to the means by which one supports oneself, one's livelihood.

The noun δαίμων, δαίμονος, ὁ or ἡ, "god, goddess, divine being," can refer to a god or goddess but more frequently denotes an unnamed and unspecified divine power: e.g., σὺν δαίμονι, "with (the help of) a god." This noun can also refer to the power which controls one's fortune or destiny. In certain contexts, δαίμονες can also be divine beings inferior to the gods, or the deified souls of dead men.

The adjective ἐχθρός, ἐχθρά, ἐχθρόν, "hated, hostile; (*as substantive*) enemy," can have either the passive meaning "hated" or the active meaning "hostile (= hating)," or both. It refers to ill-will directed personally at other human beings or at institutions (e.g., democracy). Contrast the adjective πολέμιος, πολεμία, πολέμιον, which refers to people who are at war with others. One's personal enemies are one's ἐχθροί; the enemies one meets in battle are πολέμιοι.

The adjective ἔμπειρος, ἔμπειρον, "experienced in, acquainted with," is a compound formed from the noun πεῖρα, πείρᾱς, ἡ, "trial, attempt, experience," with the preposition ἐν prefixed. This adjective takes a noun in the genitive case to indicate the area in which someone is experienced: e.g., πολέμου ἔμπειρος, "experienced in (of) war." The abstract noun ἐμπειρίᾱ, ἐμπειρίᾱς, ἡ, "experience, practice" (cf., e.g., φιλίᾱ), takes the same construction.

The verb ποιέω, ποιήσω, ἐποίησα, πεποίηκα, πεποίημαι, ἐποιήθην has the two distinct meanings "make" and "do." A poet, ποιητής, is a "maker" of poetry. In the sense "make," ποιέω can appear in either the active or the middle voice: e.g., εἰρήνην ποιεῖν, "to make peace (for others)"; εἰρήνην ποιεῖσθαι, "to make peace (for oneself)." It can take a double accusative: ποιεῖν τὸν ἀδελφὸν σοφόν, "to make the brother wise." In the sense "do" this verb can also take a double accusative (cf. πράττω): κακὰ ποιεῖν τὸν ἀδελφόν, "to do bad things to the brother." An adverb can appear instead of the adjective: κακῶς ποιεῖν τὸν ἀδελφόν, "to do bad(ly) to the brother." The verb can also be used intransitively: εὖ ποιεῖ, "He/She does well."

In the middle voice ποιέω is often used with a verbal noun to express the idea of the verb from which the noun is derived:

> θυσίαν ἐποιοῦντο.
> They were making a sacrifice.

The noun τρόπος, τρόπου, ὁ, "way, manner; character," can refer to the way or means by which something is done, the manner in which a person does it, or the character of a person (as expressed by his manner of acting). The root meaning of this noun is "turn" or "turning": cf. the English phrases "turn of mind," "turn of speech."

The preposition ὑπέρ can take either the genitive or the accusative case. With the genitive it has the two distinct meanings "over, above" (of fixed position) and "on behalf of." The second meaning developed out of the idea of covering protectively. With the accusative case ὑπέρ means "over, beyond" with reference either to motion or to measure.

COGNATES AND DERIVATIVES

ἀγών	antagonist (one's opponent in a **contest**)
βάρβαρος	barbaric
βίος	*quick* (the quick and the dead); biology
δαίμων	demon
ἔμπειρος	empirical (based on **experience**)
ὄνομα	*name*; pseudonym
ὄνομα + ποιέω	onomatopoeia (**name-making**)
τρόπος	trope (a **turn** of speech)
ὕδωρ	*water*; hydroelectric
ὑπέρ	*over*; hyperbole (a statement which goes **over** the bounds of accuracy)

DRILLS

I. (a) *Translate indicatives and infinitives; identify subjunctives, optatives, and participles.*

(b) *Where possible, change the number only.*

(c) *Change the voice only.*

1. τῑμᾶτε	(2)		28. ποιοῦντα	(4)
2. ἐτῑμᾶτε			29. ἐποίει	
3. τῑμᾶται	(4)		30. ἐποιοῦ	(2)
4. ἐτῑμᾶτο	(2)		31. ἐποιήθης	
5. τῑμῶμεν	(2)		32. τῑμᾶν	
6. τῑμῶμεν			33. ἐτῑμῶμεν	
7. τῑμῷημεν			34. ἐποιοῦμεν	
8. ἐτίμησας			35. τῑμῶεν	
9. ἐτίμων	(2)		36. ἐποίησαν	
10. ἐτῑμῶ	(2)		37. ποιοίησαν	
11. τῑμᾶσθε	(4)		38. τῑμῷησαν	
12. τῑμᾶσθαι	(2)		39. ποιοῖμεν	
13. τῑμῶντι	(2)		40. ποιεῖ	(3)
14. ἐτετῑμήκειν			41. ἐποιεῖτο	(2)
15. ποιεῖσθε	(2)		42. ποιῇ	(5)
16. ποιῆσθε	(2)		43. ἐτῑμᾶσθε	(2)
17. ποιοῖσθε	(2)		44. ἐτῑμήσασθε	
18. ποιοίητε			45. ἐτίμᾱ	
19. ποιήσομεν			46. τῑμᾷ	(6)
20. ποιεῖν			47. τῑμῶν	(5)
21. ποιοίμην	(2)		48. τῑμῷμην	(2)
22. ποιεῖσθαι	(2)		49. τῑμῶσι(ν)	(4)
23. ἐποιεῖσθε	(2)		50. ποιώμεθα	(2)
24. ποιῶσιν			51. ἐποίουν	(2)
25. ποιοῦσι	(3)		52. ποιοῦν	(3)
26. ποιουσῶν			53. τῑμῶντες	(2)
27. ποιῶ	(2)		54. ποιοῦσαν	

II. (a) *Translate.*

 (b) *Change the number of each finite verb form.*

 1. ἀγαθὰ ποιοῦμεν.

 2. ἀγαθὰ ποιῶμεν.

 3. ἀγαθὰ ποιοῖμεν.

 4. τῑμῶμεν τούς γ᾽ ἀγαθούς.

 5. τῑμῶμεν τούς γ᾽ ἀγαθούς.

 6. ἐτῑμᾶτε τοὺς ἀγαθὰ ποιοῦντας.

 7. κακὰ ἐποιεῖτο ὑπὸ τῶν ἀδίκων.

 8. ἐτῑμῶντο οἱ γέροντες ὑπὸ τῶν νεᾱνιῶν.

 9. εἰ καλὰ ποιοίης, τῑμῷο ἄν.

 10. ἐὰν τοὺς ἀγαθοὺς τῑμᾶτε, σωθήσεται ἡ δημοκρατίᾱ.

 11. ὑπὸ τῶν ἀγαθῶν χορευτῶν τῑμᾶ.

 12. τῑμῷ ὁ νεᾱνίᾱς τοὺς γέροντας.

 13. ποιοίης ἂν εὖ διδάσκων τοὺς φύλακας.

 14. ἐτίμᾱ τοὺς στρατιώτᾱς ἵνα τῑμῷτο ὑπὸ τῶν πολῑτῶν.

III. *To each of the following phrases add the appropriate forms of*:

 (a) ὅδε, ἥδε, τόδε

 (b) οὗτος, αὕτη, τοῦτο

 (c) ἐκεῖνος, ἐκείνη, ἐκεῖνο

 1. ταῖς καλαῖς αἰξί

 2. τὴν ἄδικον ψῡχήν

 3. τὰ κακὰ ζῷα

 4. τῇ ἐλπίδι

 5. τοῖς γέρουσιν

 6. οἱ ῥήτορες

 7. τὸ ἀγαθόν

 8. τῆς ἀθανάτου ψῡχῆς

 9. τὸ αἰσχρὸν σῶμα

 10. τὸν θεόν

 11. τὴν θεόν

 12. ὁ ἀδελφός

 13. τῷ ἔργῳ

 14. τοῦ ἡγεμόνος

 15. τοῖς δώροις

EXERCISES

I. 1. (a) εἰ ἀδικοίης, νῑκῷο ἄν.
       (b) ἐὰν ταῦτα ποιῆτε, τῑμᾶσθε.
       (c) εἰ τόδε ποιοῖμεν, νῑκῷημεν ἄν.
       (d) μὴ ἀδικοῦσα, οὐκ ἂν νῑκῷο.
       (e) μὴ ἀδικῶν, οὐκ ἂν νῑκῷο.
       (f) τόδε ποιοῦντες, νῑκῷμεν ἄν.

    2. (a) εἰ τοῦτο ἐποίουν, ἐτῑμώμην ἄν.
       (b) εἰ οὗτοι τούσδε ἠδίκουν, οὐκ ἂν ἐτῑμῶντο.
       (c) εἰ μὴ θυσίᾱν ποιοῖτο, οὐκ ἂν νῑκῷ.

    3. ταῦτα μὲν γέγραπται, ὦ Ἀθηναῖοι, περὶ τῶν ἀγαθοῦ ἀνθρώπου
       τρόπων τοῖς ποιηταῖς τοῖς εὖ τε καὶ καλῶς διδάξᾱσι
       πάντας γε τοὺς πολίτᾱς, τάδε δὲ γράφουσιν οἱ ῥήτορες οἱ νῦν
       πείθοντες τὸν δῆμον.

    4. καλόν τοι τὸ ταύτης τῆς γῆς ὕδωρ, κακοὶ δὲ οἱ ἄνθρωποι.

    5. τάττοιντ' ἂν ἢ παρὰ τῇ γεφύρᾳ ἢ ὑπὲρ τὸ πεδίον οἱ ὁπλῖται οἱ
       ἐν τῇ νήσῳ λειφθέντες ὑπὸ τοῦ στρατηγοῦ.

    6. οὔτε καλὸν οὔτ' ἀγαθὸν τὰ τῶν ἄλλων κλέπτειν. ἀδικοῦντες γὰρ οὐ
       τῑμῶνται ὑπὸ τῶν πολῑτῶν οὗτοι, οἳ ἂν ὑπὸ τῶν ῥητόρων
       κλοπῆς γράφωνται.

    7. εἰ τάδε τὰ ὅπλα εἰς ταύτην γε τὴν νῆσον μὴ ἐπέμφθη, οὔτ' ἂν μάχῃ
       ἐνῑκήσατ' ἐκείνους τοὺς πολεμίους τοὺς βλάπτοντας τὴν χώρᾱν
       οὔτε νῦν θυσίᾱς ἐποιεῖσθε ὡς σωθέντες.

    8. καίπερ εὖ δεδιδαγμένος, ὅμως αἰσχρὰ ἔπρᾱττες.

    9. τοὺς εἰρήνην ἄγοντας τῑμῶσι πάντες ἅτε δίκαια πρᾱττόντας.

   10. οὐκ ἐτίμων οἱ πολῖται ἐκεῖνον οἷα τά τε τοῦ δήμου κλέπτοντα καὶ
       πάντας ἀδικοῦντα.

   11. τῆσδε τῆς νυκτὸς χορεύσουσι πέντε τῶν χορευτῶν τῶν πεμφθέντων
       παρὰ τὴν θάλατταν εἰς τὸ τῆς θεοῦ ἱερόν. ἥκουσι γὰρ οἱ
       ὁπλῖται οἵ γ' ἀγαθοὶ μετὰ τὴν τῶν βαρβάρων νίκην τοὺς θεοὺς
       τῑμήσοντες.

12. ἀγαθὸν μὲν τούτοις ἡ νίκης ἐλπίς, κακὸν δὲ ὁ τῶν γε πολεμίων
    φόβος.

13. ἐτίμων οἱ γέροντες τοῦτον τὸν ῥήτορα, ὅς γε ἄνευ τοῦ γράμματα
    γράφειν τοὺς νεᾱνίᾱς λόγοις διδάσκοι περὶ τῶν τῆς βουλῆς
    καὶ τῆς ἐκκλησίᾱς πρᾱγμάτων. οὕτως γὰρ πεπαιδευμένοι
    ἦρχον ἁπᾱσῶν τῶν νήσων.

14. οἱ μὲν ἐλεύθεροι πολῑτεύονται, οἱ δ' ἄλλοι ὑπ' αἰσχρῶν ἄρχονται.

15. λιπόντες τὰ ὅπλα λόγοις κακὸν ποιῶμεν τοὺς δικαίους;

16. τὴν γνώμην βλάπτει οἶνος ἄνευ ὕδατος.

17. ἄλλα τε ζῷα καὶ καλὰς αἶγας εἰς τὸ ἱερὸν ἀγαγόντες καὶ θυσίας
    ποιησόμεθα καὶ πᾶσαν τὴν νύκτα χορεύσομεν τοὺς θεοὺς
    τῑμῶντες ἅτε τὸν στρατὸν σώσαντας.

18. ἐτάττοντο οἱ ὁπλῖται ἐν τῷδε τῷ ὑπὲρ τῆς ὁδοῦ πεδίῳ. καίτοι οἱ
    ἄλλοι ἐκ τῆσδε τῆς χώρᾱς ἐπέμποντο εἰς ἐκείνᾱς τὰς νήσους
    ἐν αἷς πᾶς ἄνθρωπος ὑπὸ τῶν ἐχθρῶν ἠδικεῖτο.

19. καὶ οἱ κατὰ γῆς τοῖς φίλοις τετίμηνται. ἀθάνατος γάρ τοι ἡ τῶν
    ἀγαθῶν δόξα.

20. ὦ Ἕλληνες στρατιῶται, νῑκώμεθ' ὑπὸ τῶνδε τῶν δούλων; ἐὰν
    γὰρ μὴ νῑκήσωμεν, λυθήσεται ἡ δημοκρατίᾱ. ταύτης οὖν τῆς
    ἡμέρᾱς μήτε νῑκηθῶμεν μήτ' εἰρήνην πρὸ τῆς νίκης
    ποιησώμεθα.

21. ὀνόματι μὲν εἰρήνην ἐκεῖνοι ἐποιοῦντο, ἔργῳ δὲ ὅ γε πόλεμος
    οὐκ ἐπαύετο.

22. πέπεμψαί τοι ὑπὲρ τὸ πεδίον, ὦ νεᾱνίᾱ, ὅπως τοὺς βαρβάρους σὺν
    ἀγαθῷ δαίμονι νῑκᾷς.

23. γνώμῃ μὲν καὶ ῥητορικῇ ἱκανὸς οὗτος, ἐμπειρίᾳ δὲ τῇ τῶν τῆς
    ἐκκλησίᾱς πρᾱγμάτων οὔ.

24. πρὸ τῆς μάχης ἐκείνᾱς τὰς αἶγας τὰς καλὰς θεῷ τῷ τὸν δῆμον
    σώσαντι ἐθῡσάμεθα. τούτῳ γὰρ τῷ τρόπῳ ἐσῴζοντο οἵ θ'
    ἡγεμόνες καὶ οἱ ἄλλοι.

25. ὦ ἄδελφε, τοῦτόν γε μήτε κακῶς ποιοίης μήτε τούτῳ τῷ τρόπῳ
    βλάπτοις κλέπτων τὰ χρήματα.

26. καλὸς καὶ τοῖς πάλαι καὶ τοῖς νῦν ὁ ὑπὲρ τῆς ἐλευθερίᾱς ἀγών.
    ἆθλον γὰρ τούτου τοῦ ἀγῶνος βίος ἀγαθός.

27. ἐν ὕδατι γράφεις τοὺς τούτων λόγους;

28. ἄλογον δὴ τὸ μήτε μάχης ἄρξασθαι μήτε τοὺς φίλους φυλάξαι, ἐὰν ὑπό γε τῶνδε τῶν βαρβάρων ἀδικῆσθε.

29. εἰ ταῦτ᾽ ἐποιοῦ, οὐκ ἂν ἐνίκω.

30. πεῖράν γ᾽ ἐποιεῖσθε.

II. 1. Friend, may you not, honored by *those* unjust young men, do bad things to these short old men.

   2. It is unreasonable, you know, to do shameful things; whoever without justice wrongs others, that one will justly be harmed by the gods. (*Express the relative clause in two different ways.*)

   3. Are we neither to honor nor do good to these women who have guarded those houses in silence? (*Translate the relative clause using two different Greek constructions.*)

   4. Before those contests the Greeks used to sacrifice both goats and other animals to these goddesses in order that they might not be conquered.

READINGS

A. Solon, Fragment 4 West

Reflections on wealth and virtue.

> πολλοὶ γὰρ πλουτοῦσι κακοί, ἀγαθοὶ δὲ πένονται·
> ἀλλ' ἡμεῖς αὐτοῖσ' οὐ διαμειψόμεθα
> τῆς ἀρετῆς τὸν πλοῦτον, ἐπεὶ τὸ μὲν ἔμπεδον αἰεί,
> χρήματα δ' ἀνθρώπων ἄλλοτε ἄλλος ἔχει.

ἀεί/αἰεί (adv.) always

ἄλλοτε (adv.) at another time
   (Cf. ἄλλοτε . . . ἄλλος with ἄλλος . . . ἄλλος.)

αὐτοῖσι = αὐτοῖς from
   αὐτοί, αὐταί, αὐτά (in cases other than nominative, third person plural
   pronoun) them

διαμείβω, διαμείψω, διήμειψα, ――, ――, ―― take in exchange
   (+ acc.) for (+ gen.) with (+ dat.) (usually mid.)

ἔμπεδος, ἔμπεδον firm, lasting

ἔχω, ἕξω/σχήσω, ἔσχον, ἔσχηκα, -ἔσχημαι, ―― have, hold; be able; (mid.)
   cling to, be next to (+ gen.)

ἡμεῖς (nom. pl. of the first person pronoun) we

πένομαι, ――, ――, ――, ――, ―― (mid. only) be poor

πλουτέω, πλουτήσω, ἐπλούτησα, πεπλούτηκα, ――, ―― be rich

πλοῦτος, πλούτου, ὁ wealth

πολλοί, πολλαί, πολλά many

B. Theognis 637–638

The sixth-century B.C. elegiac poet, on human motivation.

> ἐλπὶς καὶ κίνδῦνος ἐν ἀνθρώποισιν ὁμοῖοι·
> οὗτοι γὰρ χαλεποὶ δαίμονες ἀμφότεροι.

ἀμφότεροι, ἀμφότεραι, ἀμφότερα both

ἀνθρώποισιν = ἀνθρώποις

δαίμων, δαίμονος, ὁ or ἡ god, goddess, divine being

ὁμοῖος, ὁμοίᾱ, ὁμοῖον like, similar

οὗτος, αὕτη, τοῦτο this, that

χαλεπός, χαλεπή, χαλεπόν difficult, harsh

C. Simonides 29 (D. L. Page, *Epigrammata Graeca* 191–192)

Inscription on the base of a statue at Olympia.

> πατρὶς μὲν Κόρκῦρα, Φίλων δ' ὄνομ', εἰμὶ δὲ Γλαύκου
> υἱός, καὶ νῑκῶ πὺξ δύ' Ὀλυμπιάδας.

Γλαῦκος, Γλαύκου, ὁ   Glaukos, father of Philon

δύο (*nom./acc.; gen./dat.* δυοῖν) two

εἰμί (*first pers. sing., pres. indic. active of the verb* "*to be*")   am

Κόρκῡρα, Κορκύρᾱς, ἡ   Korkyra, island off northwest Greece

νῑκάω, νῑκήσω, ἐνίκησα, νενίκηκα, νενίκημαι, ἐνῑκήθην win; conquer; be
   the victor

Ὀλυμπιάς, Ὀλυμπιάδος, ἡ   Olympiad; Olympic games; Olympic victory

ὄνομα, ὀνόματος, τό   name

πατρίς, πατρίδος, ἡ   fatherland, native land

ποιέω, ποιήσω, ἐποίησα, πεποίηκα, πεποίημαι, ἐποιήθην   make; do

πύξ (*adv.*)   with the fists, with fisticuffs

υἱός, υἱοῦ, ὁ   son

Φίλων, Φίλωνος, ὁ   Philon, Olympic victor

D. Agathon, Fragment 7 (*TrGF* 39F7)

Agathon was a late–fifth-century tragic playwright. This and the following
selection are gnomic utterances.

> φαῦλοι βροτῶν γὰρ τοῦ πονεῖν ἡσσώμενοι
> θανεῖν ἐρῶσιν . . . .

βροτός, βροτοῦ, ὁ   mortal man

ἐράω, ——, ——, ——, ——, ἠράσθην love, desire (+ *gen. or infin.*);
   (*aor. pass.*) fall in love with (+ *gen.*)

ἡσσάομαι, ἡσσήσομαι, ——, ——, ἥσσημαι, ἡσσήθην (*mid. and pass. only*)
   be weaker than, be inferior to, be defeated by (+ *gen.*)

θνῄσκω, θανοῦμαι, ἔθανον, τέθνηκα, ——, —— die

πονέω, πονήσω, ἐπόνησα, πεπόνηκα, πεπόνημαι, ἐπονήθην toil, labor, work

φαῦλος, φαύλη, φαῦλον   cheap, ordinary, low (in rank), bad

E. Agathon, Fragment 11 (*TrGF* 39F11)

> τὸ μὲν πάρεργον ἔργον ὡς ποιούμεθα,
> τὸ δ' ἔργον ὡς πάρεργον ἐκπονούμεθα.

ἐκπονέω, ἐκπονήσω, ἐξεπόνησα, ἐκπεπόνηκα, ἐκπεπόνημαι, ἐξεπονήθην   work
    out, finish, execute, perfect

πάρεργον, παρέργου, τό   secondary work, secondary business

ποιέω, ποιήσω, ἐποίησα, πεποίηκα, πεποίημαι, ἐποιήθην   make; do

ὡς (*ὥς when postpositive*)   as, like

F. Menander, *Monostichoi* 583

    ὃν οἱ θεοὶ φιλοῦσιν ἀποθνῄσκει νέος.

ἀποθνῄσκω, ἀποθανοῦμαι, ἀπέθανον, τέθνηκα, ——, ——   die

νέος, νέα, νέον   new, young

φιλέω, φιλήσω, ἐφίλησα, πεφίληκα, πεφίλημαι, ἐφιλήθην   love, like

G. Moschion, Fragment 2 (*TrGF* 97F2)

Moschion was a tragic poet of the third century B.C.; these lines concern fate.

    ὦ καὶ θεῶν κρατοῦσα καὶ θνητῶν μόνη
    μοῖρ', ὦ λιταῖς ἄτρωτε δυστήνων βροτῶν,
    πάντολμ' ἀνάγκη, στυγνὸν ἢ κατ' αὐχένων
    ἡμῶν ἐρείδεις τῆσδε λατρείας ζυγόν.

ἀνάγκη, ἀνάγκης, ἡ   necessity

ἄτρωτος, ἄτρωτον   unwounded; invulnerable

αὐχήν, αὐχένος, ὁ   neck, throat

βροτός, βροτοῦ, ὁ   mortal man

δύστηνος, δύστηνον   wretched, unfortunate

ἐρείδω, ἐρείσω, ἤρεισα, ——, ἐρήρεισμαι, ἠρείσθην   (cause to) lean, prop;
    press hard

ζυγόν, ζυγοῦ, τό   yoke

ἡμῶν (*gen. pl. of the first person pronoun*)   of us, our

θνητός, θνητή, θνητόν   mortal

κατά (*prep. + gen.*) *here* = down upon

κρατέω, κρατήσω, ἐκράτησα, κεκράτηκα, κεκράτημαι, ἐκρατήθην   rule,
    have power over (+ *gen.*); conquer

λατρείᾱ, λατρείᾱς, ἡ   servitude, service

λιτή, λιτῆς, ἡ   prayer

μόνος, μόνη, μόνον   alone

ὅδε, ἥδε, τόδε (*gen. τοῦδε, τῆσδε, τοῦδε*)   this

πάντολμος, πάντολμον   all-daring

στυγνός, στυγνή, στυγνόν   hated, hateful, loathsome

H. Aischylos, *Persians* 584–597

The Chorus of Persian elders laments the loss of Persian power after the Greek victory off the island of Salamis (480 B.C.); the play was produced in 472 B.C.

   τοὶ δ' ἀνὰ γᾶν 'Ασίᾱν δὴν

585 οὐκέτι περσονομοῦνται,

   οὐδ' ἔτι δασμοφοροῦσιν

   δεσποσύνοισιν ἀνάγκαις,

   οὐδ' ἐς γᾶν προπίτνοντες

   ἄρξονται.¹ βασιλείᾱ

590 γὰρ διόλωλεν ἰσχύς.

ἀνά (*prep.* + *acc.*) along, through, throughout

ἀνάγκη, ἀνάγκης, ἡ necessity

'Ασίᾱ, 'Ασίᾱς, ἡ Asia Minor

βασίλειος, βασιλείᾱ, βασίλειον kingly, royal

γᾶν = γῆν

δασμοφορέω, ——, ——, ——, ——, —— pay tribute

δεσποσύνοισιν = δεσποσύνοις *from*

  δεσπόσυνος, δεσπόσυνον of the lord, of the master

δήν (*adv.*) for a long time

διόλλῡμι, διολῶ, διώλεσα (*trans.*) or διωλόμην (*intrans.*), διολώλεκα (*trans.*)
 or διόλωλα (*intrans.*), ——, —— destroy utterly; (*mid. and intrans.*)
 perish utterly

ἐς = εἰς

ἔτι (*adv.*) yet, still

ἰσχύς, ἰσχύος, ἡ strength

οὐδέ (*conj.*) and not; (*adv.*) not even

οὐκέτι (*adv.*) no longer

περσονομέομαι, ——, ——, ——, ——, —— (*pass. only*) be ruled by Persians

προπίτνω, ——, ——, ——, ——, —— fall prostrate, fall before

τοί = οἱ

---

1. This future middle form has here a passive meaning. See the Appendix, p. 744.

οὐδ' ἔτι γλῶσσα βροτοῖσιν
ἐν φυλακαῖς· λέλυται γὰρ
λᾱὸς ἐλεύθερα βάζειν,[1]
ὡς ἐλύθη ζυγὸν ἀλκᾱς.
595 αἱμαχθεῖσα δ' ἄρουρα
Αἴαντος περικλύστᾱ
νᾱσος ἔχει τὰ Περσᾱν.

Αἴᾱς, Αἴαντος, ὁ   Ajax, a legendary hero of Salamis
αἱμάσσω, αἱμάξω, ἤμαξα, ——, ἤμαγμαι, ἡμάχθην   make bloody
ἀλκᾱς = ἀλκῆς from
    ἀλκή, ἀλκῆς, ἡ   strength, prowess, courage
ἄρουρα, ἀρούρᾱς, ἡ   tilled land, land
βάζω, ——, ——, ——, ——, ——   speak, say
βροτοῖσιν = βροτοῖς from
    βροτός, βροτοῦ, ὁ   mortal man
γλῶσσα, γλώσσης, ἡ   tongue
ἔτι (adv.)   yet, still
ἔχω, ἕξω/σχήσω, ἔσχον, ἔσχηκα, -ἔσχημαι, ——   have, hold; be able; (mid.)
    cling to, be next to (+ gen.)
ζυγόν, ζυγοῦ, τό   yoke
λᾱός, λᾱοῦ, ὁ   people, host
νᾱσος = νῆσος
οὐδέ (conj.) and not; (adv.) not even
περικλύστᾱ = περικλύστη from
    περίκλυστος, περικλύστη, περίκλυστον   washed all around by waves
Περσᾱν = Περσῶν from
    Πέρσης, Πέρσου, ὁ   Persian
φυλακή, φυλακῆς, ἡ   watching, guarding, keeping
ὡς (conj.)   since

---

1. This infinitive is governed by the verb λέλυται, which here has the sense "set free, allow."

UNIT
10

82. MORE THIRD-DECLENSION NOUNS

A number of third-declension nouns have various changes made in their stems and must be learned as separate patterns. Here we present four such types:

1. Third-Declension Nouns of the Type μήτηρ, μητρός, ἡ, "mother"
2. Third-Declension Nouns of the Type γένος, γένους, τό, "race, kind"
3. Third-Declension Nouns of the Type πόλις, πόλεως, ἡ, "city"
4. Third-Declension Nouns of the Type βασιλεύς, βασιλέως, ὁ, "king"

Once again, the importance of learning both the nominative and the genitive of nouns should be obvious. Knowing the *genitive* allows one to distinguish between μήτηρ, μητρός, ἡ and σωτήρ, σωτῆρος, ὁ; between πόλις, πόλεως, ἡ and χάρις, χάριτος, ἡ; and between γένος, γένους, τό and λόγος, λόγου, ὁ.

1. THIRD-DECLENSION NOUNS OF THE TYPE μήτηρ, μητρός, ἡ, "mother"

	Third-Declension M/F Endings	μήτηρ, μητρός, ἡ mother	ἀνήρ, ἀνδρός, ὁ man
Nom. S	—	μήτηρ	ἀνήρ
Gen.	-ος	μητρός	ἀνδρός
Dat.	-ι	μητρί	ἀνδρί
Acc.	-α, -ν	μητέρα	ἄνδρα
Voc.	—	μῆτερ	ἄνερ
Nom./Voc. P	-ες	μητέρες	ἄνδρες
Gen.	-ων	μητέρων	ἀνδρῶν
Dat.	-σι(ν)	μητράσι(ν)	ἀνδράσι(ν)
Acc.	-ας	μητέρας	ἄνδρας

259

Observations: (1) The nouns πατήρ, πατρός, ὁ, "father," and θυγάτηρ, θυγατρός, ἡ, "daughter," both follow the declension of μήτηρ, μητρός, ἡ. Nouns of this type all end in -ηρ in the nominative singular (the long-vowel grade of the stem). The stem to which the third declension endings are added varies between a short-vowel grade (μητερ-) and a zero-grade (μητρ-) in which the -ρ- appears without a vowel. The zero-grade of the stem is used in the genitive and dative singular, and in the dative plural. The short-vowel grade of the stem is used in all other forms.

(2) The accent in the nominative singular is either on the penult (μήτηρ) or the ultima (πατήρ), and must be learned as part of the vocabulary. In the genitive and dative singular, the accent is always on the ultima. In the vocative singular, the accent is recessive. In the accusative singular and in all the forms of the plural, the accent is on the penult.

(3) The dative plural μητράσι(ν) comes from an original *μητρσι(ν), in which the ending -σι(ν) was added to the zero-grade of the stem. The combination -τρσ- became -τρασ-.

(4) The declension of ἀνήρ, ἀνδρός, ὁ differs somewhat from that of μήτηρ, μητρός, ἡ. The stem does show the variation of long-vowel grade (ἀνήρ), short-vowel grade (ἄνερ), and zero-grade (ἀνδρός, with no vowel, from an original *ἀνρός; the -δ- was added to make the transition from the -ν- to the -ρ-). Unlike μήτηρ, the short-vowel grade of the stem is limited to the vocative singular; the zero-grade stem ἀνδρ- is used elsewhere. Note the circumflex accent in the genitive plural ἀνδρῶν.

2. THIRD-DECLENSION NOUNS OF THE TYPE γένος, γένους, τό, "race, kind"

Many nouns of the third declension have stems which end in -σ-. When a third-declension ending beginning with a vowel is added to this type of stem, the -σ- becomes intervocalic and drops out; the remaining vowels contract. Most nouns of this type are neuter. There are, however, some masculine and feminine nouns which follow this pattern of declension. In the paradigms which follow, the original form with -σ- is given in parentheses. *Memorize the bold face portion of the word as an ending.*

	Third-Declension Endings				Σωκράτης, Σωκράτους, ὁ Sokrates
	N	M/F			
Nom. S	——	——	γένος		Σωκράτης
Gen.	-ος	-ος	γένους	(*γένεσος)	Σωκράτους
Dat.	-ι	-ι	γένει	(*γένεσι)	Σωκράτει
Acc.	——	-α, -ν	γένος		Σωκράτη
Voc.	——	——	γένος		Σώκρατες
Nom./Voc. P	-α	-ες	γένη	(*γένεσα)	
Gen.	-ων	-ων	γενῶν	(*γενέσων)	
Dat.	-σι(ν)	-σι(ν)	γένεσι(ν)	(*γένεσσι[ν])	
Acc.	-α	-ας	γένη		

Observations: (1) In all case forms except the vocative singular masculine, the accent given in the nominative singular is persistent and was fixed before the vowels contracted (e.g., *γενέσων > *γενέων > γενῶν).

(2) The contraction of ε + α gives η.

(3) The vocative singular masculine is the stem with a *recessive* accent: Σώκρατες. It was to this stem that the third declension masculine and feminine endings were originally added; the original forms of the genitive, dative, and accusative were *Σωκράτεσος, *Σωκράτεσι, *Σωκράτεσα.

3. THIRD-DECLENSION NOUNS OF THE TYPE πόλις, πόλεως, ἡ, "city"

The stem of this type of noun originally ended in -ι-, which alternated with -ε- or -η-. *Memorize the bold face portion of the word as an ending.*

Nom. S	πόλις
Gen.	πόλεως
Dat.	πόλει
Acc.	πόλιν
Voc.	πόλι
Nom./Voc. P	πόλεις
Gen.	πόλεων
Dat.	πόλεσι(ν)
Acc.	πόλεις

Observation: The accent on the genitive singular violates the rule that the accent cannot be on the antepenult if the ultima contains a long vowel or a diphthong. The original form of the genitive singular had been *πόληος, with the accent on the antepenult and the usual third-declension genitive singular ending -ος. The quantity of the vowels of the final two syllables of the word was switched, a process called **quantitative metathesis**. The -η- became -ε-, and the -ο- became -ω-; the accent, however, remained as it had been fixed on the original form *πόληος. The accent in the genitive plural πόλεων simply imitates the accent of the genitive singular πόλεως.

4. THIRD-DECLENSION NOUNS OF THE TYPE βασιλεύς, βασιλέως, ὁ, "king"

The stem of nouns of this type originally ended in a digamma (ϝ), a letter which represented the sound of the English *w*, and which disappeared from Attic Greek. *Memorize the bold face portion of the word as an ending.*

Nom. S	βασιλεύς
Gen.	βασιλέως
Dat.	βασιλεῖ
Acc.	βασιλέᾱ
Voc.	βασιλεῦ
Nom./Voc. P	βασιλῆς/βασιλεῖς
Gen.	βασιλέων
Dat.	βασιλεῦσι(ν)
Acc.	βασιλέᾱς

Observation: Note the long quantity of the vowels in the endings of the genitive and accusative singular and of the accusative plural. All these forms at one point had a stem βασιλη- to which were added the usual third declension endings. As in the genitive πόλεως, there was a quantitative metathesis:

$$βασιλῆος > βασιλέως$$
$$βασιλῆα \ > βασιλέᾱ$$
$$βασιλῆας > βασιλέᾱς.$$

83. THIRD-DECLENSION ADJECTIVES

1. ADJECTIVES OF THE TYPE εὐδαίμων, εὔδαιμον, "fortunate, wealthy, happy"

Adjectives of this type are two-ending adjectives, with one set of endings for the masculine and feminine and another for the neuter (cf. the two-ending adjective ἄδικος, ἄδικον). The masculine/feminine is declined exactly like the noun δαίμων, δαίμονος, ὁ; the masculine and feminine endings of the third-declension nouns are added to the stem εὐδαιμον-. The neuter uses the stem as the nominative, accusative, and vocative singular (εὔδαιμον); in the other forms, the neuter endings of the third-declension nouns are added to the stem.

	M/F	N
Nom. S	εὐδαίμων	εὔδαιμον
Gen.	εὐδαίμονος	εὐδαίμονος
Dat.	εὐδαίμονι	εὐδαίμονι
Acc.	εὐδαίμονα	εὔδαιμον
Voc.	εὔδαιμον	εὔδαιμον
Nom./Voc. P	εὐδαίμονες	εὐδαίμονα
Gen.	εὐδαιμόνων	εὐδαιμόνων
Dat.	εὐδαίμοσι(ν)	εὐδαίμοσι(ν)
Acc.	εὐδαίμονας	εὐδαίμονα

Observations: (1) Note the accent on the antepenult of εὔδαιμον, the neuter nominative/accusative/vocative singular and masculine/feminine vocative singular. THE ACCENT ON ADJECTIVES IS GIVEN BY THE NEUTER NOMINATIVE SINGULAR. Contrast the accent on participles, which is given by the masculine nominative singular. Thus εὔδαιμον, παιδεῦον.

(2) The combination of -νσι- in the dative plural gives -σι- with no lengthening of the preceding vowel; cf. δαίμοσι.

(3) Adverbs are formed from this type of adjective by adding the ending -ως to the stem; the accent is on the penult: εὐδαιμόνως.

2. ADJECTIVES OF THE TYPE εὐγενής, εὐγενές, "well-born, noble"

Like the stem of the noun γένος, γένους, τό, from which εὐγενής, εὐγενές was formed, the stem of adjectives of this type ended in a -σ- which dropped

out when it became intervocalic, thus allowing the vowels to contract. In
the declension which follows, the uncontracted original forms are given in
parentheses. Memorize the boldface portion of the form as an ending.

	M/F	N		
Nom. S	εὐγενής	εὐγενές		
Gen.	εὐγενοῦς	εὐγενοῦς	(*εὐγενέσος	M/F, N)
Dat.	εὐγενεῖ	εὐγενεῖ	(*εὐγενέσι	M/F, N)
Acc.	εὐγενῆ	εὐγενές	(*εὐγενέσα	M/F)
Voc.	εὐγενές	εὐγενές		
Nom./Voc. P	εὐγενεῖς	εὐγενῆ	(*εὐγενέσες	M/F, *εὐγενέσα N)
Gen.	εὐγενῶν	εὐγενῶν	(*εὐγενέσων	M/F, N)
Dat.	εὐγενέσι(ν)	εὐγενέσι(ν)	(*εὐγενέσσι[ν]	M/F, N)
Acc.	εὐγενεῖς	εὐγενῆ	(*εὐγενέσες	M/F, *εὐγενέσα N)

Observations: (1) The masculine/feminine accusative plural ending is borrowed
from the masculine/feminine nominative plural. The usual
ending -ας would have given *εὐγενέσας > *εὐγενῆς.

(2) The adverb for this type of adjective uses the ending -ως:
εὐγενῶς (<*εὐγενέως < *εὐγενέσως).

Drill I, page 277, may now be done.

84. CONTRACTED VERBS WITH PRESENT TENSE STEMS IN -o-

In addition to contracted verbs like τῑμάω and ποιέω, Greek has verbs whose
stems end in -o-, a vowel which contracts with the vowels of the endings according to the patterns given below.

The following verb will serve as a paradigm for stems in -o-:

δηλόω, δηλώσω, ἐδήλωσα, δεδήλωκα, δεδήλωμαι, ἐδηλώθην, "make clear,
show"

CONTRACTIONS OF o	
οε > ου	οο > ου
οει > οι	οοι > οι
οη > ω	οου > ου
οῃ > οι	οω > ω

1. PRESENT INDICATIVE ACTIVE AND MIDDLE/PASSIVE

		ACTIVE		*MIDDLE/PASSIVE*	
S	1	δηλῶ	(δηλόω)	δηλοῦμαι	(δηλόομαι)
	2	δηλοῖς	(δηλόεις)	δηλοῖ	(δηλόει/δηλόῃ)
	3	δηλοῖ	(δηλόει)	δηλοῦται	(δηλόεται)
P	1	δηλοῦμεν	(δηλόομεν)	δηλούμεθα	(δηλοόμεθα)
	2	δηλοῦτε	(δηλόετε)	δηλοῦσθε	(δηλόεσθε)
	3	δηλοῦσι(ν)	(δηλόουσι[ν])	δηλοῦνται	(δηλόονται)

2. IMPERFECT INDICATIVE ACTIVE AND MIDDLE/PASSIVE

		ACTIVE		*MIDDLE/PASSIVE*	
S	1	ἐδήλουν	(ἐδήλοον)	ἐδηλούμην	(ἐδηλοόμην)
	2	ἐδήλους	(ἐδήλυες)	ἐδηλοῦ	(ἐδηλόου)
	3	ἐδήλου	(ἐδήλοε)	ἐδηλοῦτο	(ἐδηλόετο)
P	1	ἐδηλοῦμεν	(ἐδηλόομεν)	ἐδηλούμεθα	(ἐδηλοόμεθα)
	2	ἐδηλοῦτε	(ἐδηλόετε)	ἐδηλοῦσθε	(ἐδηλόεσθε)
	3	ἐδήλουν	(ἐδήλοον)	ἐδηλοῦντο	(ἐδηλόοντο)

3. PRESENT SUBJUNCTIVE ACTIVE AND MIDDLE/PASSIVE

		ACTIVE		*MIDDLE/PASSIVE*	
S	1	δηλῶ	(δηλόω)	δηλῶμαι	(δηλόωμαι)
	2	δηλοῖς	(δηλόῃς)	δηλοῖ	(δηλόῃ)
	3	δηλοῖ	(δηλόῃ)	δηλῶται	(δηλόηται)
P	1	δηλῶμεν	(δηλόωμεν)	δηλώμεθα	(δηλοώμεθα)
	2	δηλῶτε	(δηλόητε)	δηλῶσθε	(δηλόησθε)
	3	δηλῶσι(ν)	(δηλόωσι[ν])	δηλῶνται	(δηλόωνται)

4. PRESENT OPTATIVE ACTIVE

S	1	δηλοῖμι	(δηλόοιμι)	*OR*	δηλοίην	(δηλοοίην)
	2	δηλοῖς	(δηλόοις)		δηλοίης	(δηλοοίης)
	3	δηλοῖ	(δηλόοι)		δηλοίη	(δηλοοίη)

P	1	δηλοῖμεν	(δηλόοιμεν)	δηλοίημεν	(δηλοοίημεν)
	2	δηλοῖτε	(δηλόοιτε)	δηλοίητε	(δηλοοίητε)
	3	δηλοῖεν	(δηλόοιεν)	δηλοίησαν	(δηλοοίησαν)

Observation: As with τῑμάω and ποιέω, the forms with the suffix -οιη- are more common in the singular; those without -η- are more common in the plural.

5. PRESENT OPTATIVE MIDDLE/PASSIVE

S	1	δηλοίμην	(δηλοοίμην)
	2	δηλοῖο	(δηλόοιο)
	3	δηλοῖτο	(δηλόοιτο)

P	1	δηλοίμεθα	(δηλοοίμεθα)
	2	δηλοῖσθε	(δηλόοισθε)
	3	δηλοῖντο	(δηλόοιντο)

6. PRESENT INFINITIVE ACTIVE AND MIDDLE/PASSIVE

Present Infinitive Active: δηλοῦν (δηλόειν < *δηλόεεν)

Present Infinitive Middle/Passive: δηλοῦσθαι (δηλόεσθαι)

Observation: Since the present infinitive active ending -ειν is itself the result of an original -εεν, when it contracts with -ο- the result is -ουν and not -οιν. Compare the present infinitive τῑμᾶν from *τῑμάεεν.

As a result of various contractions, two of the forms of δηλόω have an unusually large number of identifications:

δηλοῖς—three possibilities:

second person singular, present $\begin{Bmatrix} indicative \\ subjunctive \\ optative \end{Bmatrix}$ active

δηλοῖ—seven possibilities:

third person singular, present $\begin{Bmatrix} indicative \\ subjunctive \\ optative \end{Bmatrix}$ active

second person singular, present $\begin{Bmatrix} indicative \\ subjunctive \end{Bmatrix}$ $\begin{Bmatrix} middle \\ passive \end{Bmatrix}$

7. PRESENT PARTICIPLE ACTIVE

To form the present participle active, add to the present tense stem the same suffixes and endings as are employed to form the present participle active of παιδεύω (Section 66.1, page 204). The final vowel of the present tense stem contracts with the initial vowel or diphthong of the suffix.

	M	F	N
Nom./Voc. S	δηλῶν	δηλοῦσα	δηλοῦν
	(δηλόων)	(δηλόουσα)	(δηλόον)
Gen. S	δηλοῦντος	δηλούσης	δηλοῦντος
	(δηλόοντος)	(δηλοούσης)	(δηλόοντος)

Observations: (1) The case endings are dropped from the genitive singular forms in order to obtain the declension stems:

M	F	N
δηλουντ-	δηλουσ-	δηλουντ-

The masculine and neuter stems receive third-declension case endings; the feminine is declined like a first-declension noun with nominative singular in short -α.

(2) Note that the declension stems of the present participles active of ποιέω and δηλόω contain the same spurious diphthong ου, resulting from different contractions. Thus the declension of these two participles is identical: cf., e.g., ποιοῦντος (*ποιέοντος), δηλοῦντος (*δηλόοντος).

(3) In the feminine genitive plural the accent shifts, as usual, to the ultima: δηλουσῶν.

(4) The masculine and neuter dative plural is δηλοῦσι(ν) (*δηλόοντσι[ν]).

8. PRESENT PARTICIPLE MIDDLE/PASSIVE

To form the present participle middle/passive, add to the present tense stem the same suffixes and endings as are employed to form the present participle middle/passive of παιδεύω (Section 67.1–2). The final vowel of the stem contracts with the initial vowel of the suffix.

	M	F	N
Nom. S	δηλούμενος	δηλουμένη	δηλούμενον
	(δηλοόμενος)	(δηλοομένη)	(δηλοόμενον)

Observations: (1) This participle is declined exactly like the present participle
middle/passive of παιδεύω.

(2) The present participles middle/passive of ποιέω and δηλόω
have in their declension stems the same spurious diphthong
ου, resulting from different contractions.

*Remember that only the present participles active and middle/passive of contracted
verbs differ from those of παιδεύω. From the other Principal Parts of these verbs,
other participles are formed according to the rules already learned.*

85. VERBS WITH CONTRACTED FUTURES

A number of verbs have a future active and middle which is contracted. The
second principal part of such verbs will be given in its contracted form; the
contraction will be obvious from the circumflex accent on the ultima. Such
contracted futures are to be understood as -ε- contractions and are to be conjugated like ποιέω unless the vocabulary notes say otherwise.

Two verbs with contracted futures active and middle are:

ἀγγέλλω, **ἀγγελῶ**, ἤγγειλα, ἤγγελκα, ἤγγελμαι, ἠγγέλθην, "announce"

μένω, **μενῶ**, ἔμεινα, μεμένηκα, ——, ——, "remain"

Distinguish carefully between such forms as:

I remain   μένω   but   μενῶ   I shall remain

you remain   μένεις   but   μενεῖς   you will remain

And distinguish between such participles as:

μένων, μένουσα, μένον   (present)

μενῶν, μενοῦσα, μενοῦν   (future)

*Remember that the future passive of all verbs is formed separately, from Principal
Part VI.*

Drill II, pages 277–78, may now be done.

86. ACCUSATIVE SUBJECT OF THE INFINITIVE

In Greek, an infinitive may have a subject. THE SUBJECT OF AN INFINITIVE IS
PUT IN THE ACCUSATIVE CASE.

Compare: (1) ἀγαθὸν τὸ γράφειν βιβλία.
[The to write books] is good.
[To write books] is good.
[Writing books] is good.

Observation: This articular infinitive has no subject.

(2) ἀγαθὸν τὸ "Ομηρον γράφειν βιβλία.
[The Homer to write books] is good.
[For Homer to write books] is good.
[Homer's writing books] is good.
[That Homer writes books] is good.

Observation: Here the articular infinitive has a subject, "Ομηρον, in the accusative case.

(3) τῷ τοὺς πολίτᾱς τοῖς θεοῖς ζῷα θύειν αἱ πόλεις σῴζονται.
[By the citizens to sacrifice animals to the gods] the cities are saved.
[By the citizens' sacrificing animals to the gods] the cities are saved.

Observation: Once again, the articular infinitive, which itself is being used as a dative of means, has an accusative subject, τοὺς πολίτᾱς.

87. RESULT CLAUSES

A **result clause** gives a result or consequence of the action of the main verb of the sentence and is introduced by the conjunction ὥστε, "so as, so that, with the result that." The main clause introducing the subordinate result clause will often contain a demonstrative such as the demonstrative adverb οὕτω(ς).

Clauses of result are of two types:

(1) clauses of **actual result,** which have their verbs in the *indicative mood.*
(2) clauses of **natural result,** which have their verbs in the *infinitive.*

(1) Clauses of actual result simply state that one action (or state of being) actually is following, followed, or will follow upon another action. Such statements are factual, and have οὐ in the negative.

τοῖς θεοῖς θύουσιν **ὥστε** σωθήσονται.
They are sacrificing to the gods **with the result that** they will be saved.

τὰ τοῦ δήμου ἔκλεψεν ἐκεῖνος ὁ ῥήτωρ **ὥστε** οὐ τῑμᾶται.
That public speaker stole the property of the people **with the result that** he is not honored.

ποιήματα οὕτω καλὰ ἔγραψεν ὁ "Ομηρος **ὥστε** τῑμᾶται.
Homer wrote poems so beautiful **with the result that** he is honored.

(2) Clauses of natural result state that one action (or state of being) tends to follow naturally upon another action. Clauses of natural result do not state that any action is actually occurring, has occurred, or will occur; instead, they describe the *natural, usual, or expected consequence* of the action of the main verb of the sentence. Sometimes the context will make it clear that the action (or state of being) described in a clause of natural result did indeed occur, but the clause itself does not convey this information. Since clauses of natural result deal in probability rather than actuality, they have μή in the negative. The tense of the infinitive in a clause of natural result indicates aspect.

θύουσιν **ὥστε** σωθῆναι ὑπὸ τῶν θεῶν.
They sacrifice **so as** to be saved by the gods.

οὕτω καλῶς ἔγραψεν ὁ Ὅμηρος **ὥστε** τῑμηθῆναι.
Homer wrote so well **(so) as** to be honored. (He may or may not have actually been honored, but the quality of his work was such that his being honored was a natural or expected result of it.)

οὕτω καλὰ τὰ ποιήματα **ὥστε** τοὺς πολίτᾱς τὸν ποιητὴν τῑμᾶν.
So beautiful are the poems **(so) as** for the citizens to honor the poet. (The Greek does not say that the citizens are actually honoring the poet, but that such honor is the natural result that one would expect from poems of such quality. Note also that the infinitive in this example has the accusative subject τοὺς πολίτᾱς.)

οὕτω κακὰ τὰ ποιήματα **ὥστε** τοὺς πολίτᾱς τὸν ποιητὴν μὴ τῑμᾶν.
So ugly are the poems **(so) as** for the citizens not to honor the poet.

When translating into English a result clause with an accusative subject and an infinitive, use the formula "so as for [accusative subject] to [infinitive]."

Drill III, page 278, may now be done.

88. COMPOUND VERBS

Many of the prepositions learned thus far can be used as **prefixes** with verbs in order to form **compound verbs**. Although quite often similar to the preposition in meaning, the prefix can sometimes have a somewhat different force. For example, as a prefix ἐκ- can mean (1) literally "out of" as in ἐκπέμπω, "send out"; (2) "thoroughly" as in ἐκδιδάσκω, "teach thoroughly" (cf. the use of "out" in "to play the game out").

In forms that require a past indicative augment or reduplication, the past indicative augment or the reduplication comes between the prefix and the verb.

THE ACCENT ON A COMPOUND VERB CANNOT GO BACK BEYOND THE PAST IN-
DICATIVE AUGMENT OR, IN THE PERFECT TENSE, BEYOND THE FIRST SYLLABLE OF
THE STEM. The prefix can also undergo changes in spelling depending on what
consonant or vowel follows it:

ἐκπέμπω, ἐκπέμψω, ἐξέπεμψα, ἐκπέπομφα, ἐκπέπεμμαι, ἐξεπέμφθην, "send
out" (Note the -κ- before consonants, -ξ- before vowels.)

ἀποπέμπω, ἀποπέμψω, ἀπέπεμψα, ἀποπέπομφα, ἀποπέπεμμαι, ἀπεπέμφθην,
"send away" (Note the loss of the final vowel of the prefix before a vowel.)

ἀπάγω, ἀπάξω, ἀπήγαγον, ἀπῆχα, ἀπῆγμαι, ἀπήχθην, "lead away" (Note the
imperfect ἀπῆγον.)

Such compound verbs are usually used in conjunction with a preposition, sometimes without one:

ἐκπέμψομεν ἐκ τῆς πόλεως τοὺς στρατιώτᾱς.
ἐκπέμψομεν τῆς πόλεως τοὺς στρατιώτᾱς.
We shall send the soldiers out of the city.

In the infinitive and the participle of a compound verb, the accent stays over
the same syllable as in the simple form, e.g., ἀπολῦσαι, ἀπολῦον.

The meaning of a prefix will be given as a vocabulary item, as will any special
meaning of a compound verb. If the meaning of a compound verb can be de-
duced from its parts, it will not be given in the vocabulary.

VOCABULARY

ἀγγέλλω, ἀγγελῶ, ἤγγειλα, ἤγγελκα, ἤγγελμαι, ἠγγέλθην	announce
ἀληθής, ἀληθές	true, real
ἀλήθεια, ἀληθείᾱς, ἡ	truth, reality
ἀνήρ, ἀνδρός, ὁ	man
ἀξιόω, ἀξιώσω, ἠξίωσα, ἠξίωκα, ἠξίωμαι, ἠξιώθην	think worthy of, think it right, expect
ἀπο- (prefix)	away from
βασιλεύς, βασιλέως, ὁ	king
γένος, γένους, τό	race, kind
εὐγενής, εὐγενές	well-born, noble
δηλόω, δηλώσω, ἐδήλωσα, δεδήλωκα, δεδήλωμαι, ἐδηλώθην	make clear, show
Δημοσθένης, Δημοσθένους, ὁ	Demosthenes (ῥήτωρ)
ἐκ-, ἐξ- (prefix)	out of; thoroughly
εὐδαίμων, εὔδαιμον	fortunate, wealthy, happy
θυγάτηρ, θυγατρός, ἡ	daughter
ἱερεύς, ἱερέως, ὁ	priest
ἱππεύς, ἱππέως, ὁ	horseman
καλέω, καλῶ, ἐκάλεσα, κέκληκα, κέκλημαι, ἐκλήθην	call
μένω, μενῶ, ἔμεινα, μεμένηκα, ——, ——	remain, stay
μήτηρ, μητρός, ἡ	mother
νόμος, νόμου, ὁ	custom, law
πάθος, πάθους, τό	experience, suffering
πατήρ, πατρός, ὁ	father
πόλις, πόλεως, ἡ	city
πότε (adv.)	when?
ποτέ (enclitic adv.)	at some time, ever
Σωκράτης, Σωκράτους, ὁ	Sokrates (philosopher)
σώφρων, σῶφρον	prudent, temperate

τέλος, τέλους, τό   end; power

   τελευτάω, τελευτήσω, ἐτελεύτησα,   finish; die

      τετελεύτηκα, τετελεύτημαι,

      ἐτελευτήθην

φύσις, φύσεως, ἡ   nature

ὥστε (conj.)   so as, so that

VOCABULARY NOTES

The verb ἀγγέλλω, ἀγγελῶ, ἤγγειλα, ἤγγελκα, ἤγγελμαι, ἠγγέλθην, "announce," has the same root as the noun ἄγγελος, ἀγγέλου, ὁ, "messenger." The present tense stem is formed with the suffix ιω : *ἀγγέλιω > ἀγγέλλω; the -λλ- appears only in the present tense stem. The future of verbs whose root ends in a liquid or a nasal was formed by the addition of the suffix -εσ- to the root. The addition of the endings made the -σ- intervocalic; the intervocalic -σ- dropped out and the remaining vowels contracted according to the pattern of ποιέω: *ἀγγελ-έσ-ω > ἀγγελέω > ἀγγελῶ. In the aorist of verbs whose roots ended in a liquid or nasal the -σ- of the aorist dropped out and the vowel of the stem underwent compensatory lengthening (ε > ει): *ἤγγελσα > ἤγγειλα. A diphthong which represents a lengthened vowel or results from contraction is called a spurious diphthong. (The ου of the dative plural γέρουσι and the ει of the present infinitive active ending -ειν are spurious diphthongs.) Note that the unaugmented aorist active and middle tense stem derived from Principal Part III is ἀγγειλ-.

The ἠ- of Principal Parts IV and V is a part of the stem and remains unchanged in all forms of the perfect and pluperfect; only the endings distinguish the pluperfect from the perfect. The perfect indicative middle/passive is conjugated ἤγγελμαι, ἤγγελσαι, ἤγγελται, ἠγγέλμεθα, ἤγγελθε, ——; the pluperfect follows the same pattern; the perfect infinitive middle/passive is ἠγγέλθαι. In Principal Part VI, the ἠ- is a past indicative augment, and the unaugmented aorist passive tense stem is ἀγγελθ-.

The adjective ἀληθής, ἀληθές, "true, real," can be applied to things (which are real as opposed to apparent), to statements (which are true as opposed to false), and to people (who are truthful as opposed to lying). The formation of the abstract noun ἀλήθεια, ἀληθείας, ἡ, "truth, reality," from the adjective is a very common pattern. Contrast the short alpha of ἀλήθεια with the long alpha of δουλεία, also an abstract noun.

The noun ἀνήρ, ἀνδρός, ὁ, "man," means "man" as opposed to "woman"; contrast ἄνθρωπος, "man" as opposed to "gods" or "animals." The word suggests traditionally masculine qualities such as courage.

The verb ἀξιόω, ἀξιώσω, ἠξίωσα, ἠξίωκα, ἠξίωμαι, ἠξιώθην, "think worthy of, think it right, expect," is a denominative verb derived from the adjective ἄξιος, ἀξία, ἄξιον, "worthy, worth." The verb can govern a direct object in the accusative case, a genitive of the thing *of* which one thinks the direct object worthy, or an infinitive:

τὸν Ὅμηρον ἀξιοῦμεν τοῦ ἄθλου.
We think Homer worthy of the prize.

τὸν Ὅμηρον ἀξιοῦμεν τῑμηθῆναι.
We think Homer worthy to be praised.

ὁ Ὅμηρος ἠξιώθη τοῦ ἄθλου.
Homer was thought worthy of the prize.

ἀξιοῦμεν ταῦτα ποιεῖν.
We think it right to do these things.

The word βασιλεύς, βασιλέως, ὁ, "king," is used by Homer of the various chiefs of the Greeks. In classical Athens, it was the title of one of the annually elected officials of the city. The great king of Persia was simply βασιλεύς (without the article; cf. ἐν ἀγορᾷ, "in the market place"). The suffix -εύς generally indicated a person performing some job; cf. ἱερεύς, ἱερέως, ὁ, "priest," from ἱερός, ἱερά, ἱερόν, "holy, sacred"; ἱππεύς, ἱππέως, ὁ, "horseman."

Like ἀξιόω, δηλόω, δηλώσω, ἐδήλωσα, δεδήλωκα, δεδήλωμαι, ἐδηλώθην, "make clear, show," is a denominative verb derived from an adjective (δῆλος, δήλη, δῆλον, "clear, visible").

Demosthenes (384–322 B.C.) is generally recognized as the greatest of Greek orators.

The adjective εὐδαίμων, εὔδαιμον, "fortunate, wealthy, happy," is a compound of the adverb εὖ and the noun δαίμων: "with a good divinity, fortunate." Those with good divinities are wealthy and happy.

In the verb καλέω, καλῶ, ἐκάλεσα, κέκληκα, κέκλημαι, ἐκλήθην, "call," note that the present and the future are identical; both show the contraction of -εω. Context usually allows one to tell the forms apart. The word means literally "call, make a noise," or "call, summon, invite."

The verb μένω, μενῶ, ἔμεινα, μεμένηκα, ——, ——, "remain, stay," follows the pattern of verbs with roots ending in a liquid or a nasal. The future is contracted (μενῶ < μενέω < *μενέσω), and the aorist active and middle tense stem has the spurious diphthong -ει- (ἔμεινα < *ἔμενσα).

The noun νόμος, νόμου, ὁ originally meant "custom" and then acquired the meaning of "law," either as something written down or as the "unwritten laws" of a society.

The noun πάθος, πάθους, τό basically means anything that happens to a person, a thing experienced, an "experience" of something either good or bad. From the originally neutral meaning the word acquired the negative notion of "bad experience, suffering." Contrast ἐλπίς, ἐλπίδος, ἡ, "expectation (of good or bad), hope (of something good)."

A man like Demosthenes was a πολίτης not of a nation-state Greece but of the πόλις, πόλεως, ἡ, "city-state" of Athens. The Greeks of the classical period realized that living in a πόλις made them different from their βάρβαροι contemporaries and their own Hellenic ancestors who had lived in tribes.

Distinguish carefully between the interrogative adverb πότε, "when," and the indefinite enclitic adverb ποτέ, "at some time, ever."

Disyllabic enclitics, unlike monosyllabic enclitics, are given in vocabulary listings with an acute accent on the ultima. IN CONTINUOUS GREEK A DISYLLABIC ENCLITIC IS ACCENTED ONLY WHEN THE PRECEDING WORD HAS AN ACUTE ACCENT ON THE PENULT (e.g., παιδεύσω ποτέ, "I shall educate at some time"). In all other instances disyllabic enclitics have no accent, and they affect the accent of the preceding word according to the rules presented in the Vocabulary Notes of Unit 6.

The philosopher Sokrates lived in Athens from 469 to 399 B.C. Although he wrote nothing himself, his teachings and personality are preserved for us in the writings of his pupils Plato and Xenophon.

The adjective σώφρων, σῶφρον, "prudent, temperate," is composed of the root seen in the verb σῴζω + φρήν, φρενός, ἡ, "diaphragm (as seat of emotions or intelligence)": "with a safe mind, prudent, temperate."

The noun τέλος, τέλους, τό, "end, power," means an "end, finish" or an "end aimed at." οἱ ἐν τέλει are "those in power."

The denominative verb τελευτάω, τελευτήσω, ἐτελεύτησα, τετελεύτηκα, τετελεύτημαι, ἐτελευτήθην, "finish, die," can be used both transitively and intransitively. It is always used intransitively in prose, except in the phrase τελευτᾶν τὸν βίον, "to end one's life." Note that when ὑπό + genitive is used with an active, intransitive verb it means "at the hands of":

δ Σωκράτης ἐτελεύτησεν ὑπὸ τῶν πολιτῶν.
Sokrates died at the hands of the citizens.

Note the accent of ὥστε.

COGNATES AND DERIVATIVES

ἀνήρ	androgynous (having **male** and female characteristics)
βασιλεύς	basilica (a **royal** portico, public building, type of church)
γένος	*genus* (the Latin cognate)
θυγάτηρ	*daughter*
καλέω	ecclesiastical
μένω	remain (from the Latin cognate *maneō*)
μήτηρ	*mother*
νόμος	autonomous (having one's own **laws**)
πάθος	pathetic
πατήρ	*father*
πότε	*when*
πόλις	politics
τέλος	teleology
φύσις	physics

DRILLS

I. (a) *Identify the following forms, giving gender, number, and case.*

   (b) *Change the number where possible.*

   (c) *Modify the nouns with the proper form of the article and the following adjectives:*

   καλός, καλή, καλόν
   εὐδαίμων, εὔδαιμον
   εὐγενής, εὐγενές

1. πατέρων
2. πάθη (3)
3. ἱππῆς
4. ἄνδρα
5. φύσει
6. Σώκρατες
7. Δημοσθένη
8. πατράσιν
9. παθῶν
10. ἀνδρῶν
11. φύσεις (3)
12. πατέρας
13. ἱππέᾱ
14. Δημόσθενες
15. πάτερ

II. (a) *Translate indicatives and infinitives. Identify subjunctives, optatives, and participles.*

   (b) *Change the number where possible.*

1. δηλοῦμεν
2. ἐδηλοῦτο (2)
3. δηλοῖ (7)
4. μενοῦμεν
5. ποιεῖτε
6. δηλώμεθα (2)
7. δηλούμεθα (2)
8. ποιῆσαι

9. δηλοῖο (2)	20. μενοῦντι (2)
10. δηλοίη	21. μενοῦσαν
11. μένομεν	22. δηλώσᾱσα (2)
12. δηλοῦσθαι (2)	23. δηλούμενον (8)
13. μενεῖς	24. μένον (3)
14. μένεις	25. μενοῦν (3)
15. δηλῶ (2)	26. ποιοῦντι (2)
16. ἐδήλου	27. δηλῶν (2)
17. ἐδηλοῦ (2)	28. δηλώσων (2)
18. δηλοῦν (4)	29. τετῑμηκυίᾱς (2)
19. μένοντι (2)	30. δηλώσοντα (4)

III. *Translate the following sentences. Explain the type of result clause.*

1. οὕτω φοβεροὶ οἱ στρατιῶται ὥστε νῑκηθήσονται.

2. οὕτω φοβεροὶ οἱ στρατιῶται ὥστε μὴ φυλάξαι τὴν γέφῡραν.

3. οὕτω φοβεροὶ οἱ στρατιῶται ὥστε οὐκ ἐφυλάχθη ἡ γέφῡρα.

4. οὕτω φοβεροὶ οἱ στρατιῶται ὥστε οὐκ ἐφύλαξαν τὴν γέφῡραν.

5. οὕτω φοβεροὶ οἱ στρατιῶται ὥστε μὴ φυλαχθῆναι τὴν γέφῡραν.

EXERCISES

I. 1. ἐν ταῖς πόλεσι ταῖς τῇ ἀληθείᾳ εὖ πολῑτευομέναις οὐχ ὁ δῆμος ἀλλ' ὁ νόμος βασιλεύς· πᾶς γὰρ πολίτης τοῖς νόμοις πειθόμενος δίκαια πράττει ὥστε σῴζεσθαι τήν γε πόλιν ἐκ κινδύνων τε καὶ φόβων.

2. τῇ βασιλέως θυγατρὶ ἐδήλου ὁ ποιητὴς τὰ ποιήματα τὰ περὶ τῆς φύσεως γεγραμμένα.

3. ὦ πάτερ, ἐξενῑκήθησάν τε σύμπαντες οἱ πολέμιοι ὑπὸ τῶν στρατιωτῶν τῶν εὐγενῶν καὶ ἡ εὐδαίμων πόλις ἐσώθη. νῑκήσᾱς γὰρ ταῦτ' ἀπήγγειλε καὶ τῇ βουλῇ καὶ τῇ ἐκκλησίᾳ ὁ στρατηγὸς ὁ μετὰ τὴν μάχην εἰς τὴν Ἀθηναίων πόλιν ἀποπεμφθείς. μενεῖ οὖν οὗτος ἐν πόλει μετά γε τῶν φίλων ὡς θυσίᾱς τοῖς θεοῖς ἄξων.

4. εἰ ἄνευ ἐκείνων τῶν ἱππέων τῶν εὐδαιμόνων μὴ ἤθελον εἰς μάχην τάξασθαι οἱ ὁπλῖται ὑπέρ γε τοῦ τοὺς πολεμίους φυλάξασθαι, ἡ τῆς πόλεως ἀρχὴ ἀληθῶς ἂν ἐλύετο. ταύτην δὴ τὴν πόλιν ἀξιοῖμέν γ' ἀρχῆς.

5. ἀγαθόν τοι χρῆμα ἡ ἀρετὴ τοῖς γ' εὖ πεπαιδευμένοις.

6. ὦ σῶφρον θύγατερ, μὴ ἀδικήσῃς πεισθεῖσα τοῖς τούτου τοῦ κακοῦ ἱππέως λόγοις. εἰ γάρ ποτ' αἰσχρὰ ποιήσειας, οὗτοι τῑμῷτο ἂν ἡ μήτηρ.

7. γράψαι ὁ Δημοσθένης μακρὸν λόγον περὶ τῶν ἐν πολέμῳ παθῶν τῶν φοβερῶν ὥστε τοὺς πολίτᾱς μὴ λῦσαι τὴν εἰρήνην, καίπερ τοῦτ' ἐθέλοντας ποιῆσαι. εἰρήνην γὰρ ἄγοντες σῴζοιντ' ἄν.

8. τὰ χρήματ' ἐν ταῖς οἰκίαις λιποῦσαι αἱ σώφρονες ἔμενον ἐκεῖ παρὰ τῇ θαλάττῃ φυλαξόμεναι τοὺς πολεμίους.

9. οὕτω φοβερὸν τόδε γε τὸ πάθος ὥστε Δημοσθένη ἐθέλειν τελευτῆσαι. τοῦτον δὴ ἆθλον ἀξιώσωμέν ποτε τὸν αἰσχρὰ πράξαντα;

10. ἀληθῶς δὴ εὐδαίμων ἡ τοῖς γε τῆς πόλεως νόμοις πειθομένη καὶ ἅμα τόν τε πατέρα καὶ τὴν μητέρα τῑμῶσα καὶ τοῖς θεοῖς θυσίᾱς ἄγουσα καὶ μὴ ἀδικά ποτε πεπρᾱχυῖα. αὕτη γάρ τοι καὶ θεοῖς καὶ ἀνθρώποις οὕτω φίλη ὥσθ' ὑφ' ἁπάντων τῑμᾱται.

11. πότε ὑπέρ γε τούτων τῶν πόλεων τῷ τε πατρὶ τῶν θεῶν καὶ
    τῇ γῇ, μητρὶ καὶ θεῶν καὶ ἀνθρώπων, θύσει ὁ ἱερεὺς ὁ ἐκ
    τῆς πόλεως ἐκκαλούμενος;

12. τόν γε Σωκράτη τῑμᾶσθαι ἀξιοῦμεν οἷα τούς τε πολίτᾱς τὴν
    ἀληθῆ ἀρετὴν ἐκδιδάξαντα καὶ τὴν πόλιν ἀληθῶς εὐδαίμονα
    ποιοῦντα.

13. ἀγγείλω τῇ ἐκκλησίᾳ πάντα τὰ πάθη τὰ τῶν ἀνδρῶν οὓς ἐξῆγεν ὁ
    στρατηγός; ταῦτα γὰρ τῇ πάσῃ πόλει δηλοῦσα τὸν πόλεμον
    ἂν παύοιμι. ταῦτ᾽ οὖν ἀγγελῶ.

14. πότε τὴν θυγατέρα τῇ θεῷ ἔθῡσεν ὁ βασιλεὺς ὅπως ἐξαγάγοι τὸν
    στρατόν;

15. τῷ τὸν βασιλέᾱ μὴ θῦσαι τῇ θεῷ τὴν θυγατέρα ἐκεκώλῡτο ὁ
    πόλεμος ὥστ᾽ εἰρήνην ἤγομεν.

16. οὔθ᾽ ὁ χρῡσὸς μένει οὔθ᾽ ὁ ἄργυρος, ἀλλὰ μενεῖ ἥ γε δόξα τῶν
    εὐγενῶν τῶν τοῖς ποιηταῖς δεδιδαγμένων τὰ ἀγαθῶν ἀνδρῶν
    ἔργα.

17. τοῖς αἰξὶ τοῖς ἐν τῷ ἱερῷ τεθυμένοις τῑμῶνται οἱ θεοὶ ὥστε
    σῴζουσι τὴν πόλιν. ἄνευ γὰρ θυσιῶν ἐχθροὶ οἱ θεοὶ καὶ
    καλοῦσι τοὺς πολεμίους εἰς τὴν γῆν ἐν μάχῃ νῑκήσοντας.

18. ἅτ᾽ ἐκείνης τῆς ἡμέρᾱς τελευτήσων τὸν βίον, ὁ Σωκράτης ἐδήλου
    τοῖς νεᾱνίαις τὰ τῆς ἀρετῆς γένη.

19. ἄλλῳ τοι γένει ἀνθρώπων ἄλλο καλόν. νόμῳ γὰρ ποιεῖ πᾶς ἃ ἂν
    ποιῇ.

20. ὦ εὔδαιμον Σώκρατες, τὴν ἀρετῆς φύσιν τοῖς φίλοις δηλοῖς; ἐὰν γὰρ
    τὴν ἀρετὴν εὖ δηλοῖς, οὗτοι ἀδικήσουσιν, ἀλλ᾽ εἰ μὴ τοῦτ᾽ εὖ
    δηλοῖς, κακὰ ἂν πράττοιεν. καλῶς δὴ ποιεῖς ἅπαντα τὰ ἀγαθὰ
    δηλῶν.

21. μὴ πρὸ τοῦ τέλους τοῦ ἀγῶνος νῑκηθείς, ἄθλου ἠξιώθης ἄν.

22. εἰρήνην καλεῖς δὴ τὸ πολέμου τέλος;

23. τοῖς τε πατράσι καὶ ταῖς μητράσι τῶν στρατιωτῶν τῶν ἐν
    τῷδε τῷ πεδίῳ τεθαμμένων οὐχ ἱκανοὶ οἵ γε λόγοι οἱ ὑπὸ
    τοῦ ῥήτορος δηλούμενοι περὶ τῆς τε καλῆς δόξης καὶ τῆς
    ἐλευθερίᾱς τῆς νῦν σεσωμένης.

24. πότε τελευτήσει τὰ τῶν γε διδασκάλων πάθη;

25. ἅτε αἰσχρὰ πρᾱ́ξᾱσαν ἀπέπεμψεν ὁ ἀνὴρ τὴν θυγατέρα ἐξ ὀφθαλμῶν.

26. ἀγαθὸν δὴ τῇ πόλει τὸ τόν γε Σωκράτη τοὺς νεᾱνίᾱς ἐκπαιδεύειν.

27. τοὺς ἐν τέλει δώρων γραψώμεθα οἷα παρὰ τοὺς νόμους τὰ τοῦ δήμου κλέψαντας ὥστ᾽ ἐνῑκᾶτο ἡ πόλις.

28. καίπερ οἶνον κεκλοφότες, εἰς δίκην ὅμως οὐ κληθήσονται.

II. 1. Let us order the *priest* to leave all the goats for the mother of the king in order that she may sacrifice on behalf of the soldiers who won. (*Express the purpose in two ways.*)

2. Do you think whoever is not conquered in the contests worthy of a prize or a crown? (*Do the relative clause two ways.*)

3. The horsemen were so well taught by the old men as to be thought worthy of prizes and gifts in all the contests.

4. By Sokrates' being willing to die on behalf of virtue we are taught to do good.

5. The fathers of the soldiers called out of the city fell into order of battle so that at least the small houses were saved.

READINGS

A. Sophokles, Fragment 346 P

καλὸν φρονεῖν τὸν θνητὸν ἀνθρώποις ἴσα.

θνητός, θνητή, θνητόν   mortal

ἴσος, ἴση, ἴσον   equal, fair; flat

φρονέω, φρονήσω, ἐφρόνησα, πεφρόνηκα, ——, —— have understanding;
think, have thoughts

B. Sophokles, Fragment 554 P

φιλεῖ γὰρ ἄνδρας πόλεμος ἀγρεύειν νέους.

ἀγρεύω, ἀγρεύσω, ἤγρευσα, ἤγρευκα, ἤγρευμαι, ἠγρεύθην catch (by hunting)

ἀνήρ, ἀνδρός, ὁ   man

νέος, νέᾱ, νέον   new, young

φιλέω, φιλήσω, ἐφίλησα, πεφίληκα, πεφίλημαι, ἐφιλήθην love, like

C. Menander, *Monostichoi* 299

καλὸν τὸ νῑκᾶν ἀλλ' ὑπερνῑκᾶν κακόν.

ὑπερνῑκάω   win overmuch, be overbearing in victory

D. Aristotle, *Poetics* 1452b30–1453a12

The best type of tragic hero, a mean between extremes.

ἐπειδὴ οὖν δεῖ τὴν σύνθεσιν εἶναι τῆς καλλίστης
τραγῳδίᾱς μὴ ἁπλῆν ἀλλὰ πεπλεγμένην καὶ ταύτην
φοβερῶν καὶ ἐλεεινῶν εἶναι μῑμητικήν (τοῦτο γὰρ
ἴδιον τῆς τοιαύτης μῑμήσεώς ἐστιν), πρῶτον μὲν δῆλον
5 ὅτι οὔτε τοὺς ἐπιεικεῖς ἄνδρας δεῖ μεταβάλλοντας
φαίνεσθαι ἐξ εὐτυχίᾱς εἰς δυστυχίᾱν, οὐ γὰρ
φοβερὸν οὐδὲ ἐλεεινὸν τοῦτο ἀλλὰ μιαρόν ἐστιν·
οὔτε μοχθηροὺς ἐξ ἀτυχίᾱς εἰς εὐτυχίᾱν,

ἀνήρ, ἀνδρός, ὁ   man

ἁπλῆν fem. acc. sing. of
 ἁπλοῦς, ἁπλῆ, ἁπλοῦν   simple

ἀτυχίᾱ, ἀτυχίᾱς, ἡ   misfortune

δεῖ (third. pers. sing., pres. indic. active) it is necessary, must
 (+ accusative and infinitive); there is need of (+gen.)

δυστυχίᾱ, δυστυχίᾱς, ἡ   misfortune

εἶναι (pres. infin. active of the verb "to be") to be

ἐλεεινός, ἐλεεινή, ἐλεεινόν   pitiful

ἐστί(ν) (enclitic, third pers. sing., pres. indic. active of the verb "to be") is

ἐπιεικής, ἐπιεικές   suitable, fair, good

εὐτυχίᾱ, εὐτυχίᾱς, ἡ   good fortune

ἴδιος, ἰδίᾱ, ἴδιον   own, proper, peculiar to (+ gen.)

κάλλιστος, καλλίστη, κάλλιστον   best, most beautiful

μεταβάλλω, μεταβαλῶ, μετέβαλον, μεταβέβληκα, μεταβέβλημαι,
 μετεβλήθην   change

μιαρός, μιαρά, μιαρόν   abominable, foul, shameful

μίμησις, μῑμήσεως, ἡ   imitation

μῑμητικός, μῑμητική, μῑμητικόν   imitative

μοχθηρός, μοχθηρά, μοχθηρόν   wicked

ὅτι (conj.)   that

οὐδέ (conj.)   and not; (adv.) not even

πλέκω, ——, ἔπλεξα, ——, πέπλεγμαι, ἐπλέχθην   weave, plait, twist

πρῶτον (adv.)   first

σύνθεσις, συνθέσεως, ἡ   composition

τοιοῦτος, τοιαύτη, τοιοῦτο/τοιοῦτον   such (as this)

τραγῳδίᾱ, τραγῳδίᾱς, ἡ   tragedy

φαίνω, φανῶ, ἔφηνα, πέφηνα, πέφασμαι, ἐφάνην   show, cause to appear;
 (mid., perf. act., aor. pass.)   appear

ἀτραγῳδότατον γὰρ τοῦτ᾽ ἐστὶ πάντων, οὐδὲν γὰρ ἔχει
10 ὧν¹ δεῖ, οὔτε γὰρ φιλάνθρωπον οὔτε ἐλεεινὸν οὔτε
φοβερόν ἐστιν· οὐδ᾽ αὖ τὸν σφόδρα πονηρὸν ἐξ εὐτυχίας
εἰς δυστυχίαν μεταπίπτειν· τὸ μὲν γὰρ φιλάνθρωπον
ἔχοι ἂν ἡ τοιαύτη σύστασις ἀλλ᾽ οὔτε ἔλεον οὔτε
φόβον, ὁ μὲν γὰρ περὶ τὸν ἀνάξιόν ἐστιν δυστυχοῦντα,
15 ὁ δὲ περὶ τὸν ὅμοιον, ἔλεος μὲν περὶ τὸν ἀνάξιον,
φόβος δὲ περὶ τὸν ὅμοιον, ὥστε οὔτε ἐλεεινὸν
οὔτε φοβερὸν ἔσται τὸ συμβαῖνον.

ἀτραγῳδότατος, ἀτραγῳδοτάτη, ἀτραγῳδότατον most untragic
αὖ (adv.) in turn
δεῖ (third. pers. sing., pres. indic. active) it is necessary, must
      (+ accusative and infinitive);   there is need of (+ gen.)
δυστυχέω, δυστυχήσω, ἐδυστύχησα, δεδυστύχηκα, δεδυστύχημαι,
      ἐδυστυχήθην be unfortunate; (pass.) be made unfortunate
δυστυχία, δυστυχίας, ἡ misfortune
ἐλεεινός, ἐλεεινή, ἐλεεινόν pitiful
ἔλεος, ἐλέου, ὁ pity
ἔσται (third pers. sing., fut. indic. mid. of the verb "to be") will be
ἐστί(ν) (enclitic, third. pers. sing., pres. indic. active of the verb "to be") is
εὐτυχία, εὐτυχίας, ἡ good fortune
ἔχω, ἕξω/σχήσω, ἔσχον, ἔσχηκα, -ἔσχημαι, —— have, hold; be able;
      (mid.) cling to (+ gen.)
μεταπίπτω, μεταπεσοῦμαι, μετέπεσον, μεταπέπτωκα, ——,
      —— undergo a change, change
ὅμοιος, ὁμοία, ὅμοιον similar, like
οὐδέ (conj.) and not; (adv.) not even
οὐδέν neut. nom./acc. sing. of
      οὐδείς, οὐδεμία, οὐδέν no one, nothing
πονηρός, πονηρά, πονηρόν evil, bad
συμβαίνω, συμβήσομαι, συνέβην, συμβέβηκα, ——, —— happen
σύστασις, συστάσεως, ἡ composition, structure; plot (of drama)
σφόδρα (adv.) very much, very
τοιοῦτος, τοιαύτη, τοιοῦτο/τοιοῦτον such (as this)
φιλάνθρωπος, φιλάνθρωπον humane, benevolent; appealing to human
      feeling
ὥστε (conj.) so that, with the result that

1. ὧν δεῖ = ἐκείνων ὧν δεῖ: the antecedent, ἐκείνων, is ellipsed.

ὁ μεταξὺ ἄρα τούτων λοιπός. ἔστι δὲ τοιοῦτος ὁ
μήτε ἀρετῇ διαφέρων καὶ δικαιοσύνῃ, μήτε διὰ κακίαν
20   καὶ μοχθηρίαν μεταβάλλων εἰς τὴν δυστυχίαν
ἀλλὰ δι' ἁμαρτίαν τινά, τῶν ἐν μεγάλῃ δόξῃ ὄντων
καὶ εὐτυχίᾳ, οἷον Οἰδίπους καὶ Θυέστης, καὶ οἱ
ἐκ τῶν τοιούτων γενῶν ἐπιφανεῖς ἄνδρες.

ἁμαρτία, ἁμαρτίας, ἡ   error, mistake
ἀνήρ, ἀνδρός, ὁ   man
ἄρα   (postpositive particle)   then, therefore
γένος, γένους, τό   race, kind; family
διαφέρω, διοίσω, διήνεγκα/διήνεγκον, διενήνοχα, διενήνεγμαι, διηνέχθην
   carry through; be different from, excel
δικαιοσύνη, δικαιοσύνης, ἡ   justice, justness
δυστυχία, δυστυχίας, ἡ   misfortune
ἐπιφανής, ἐπιφανές   manifest; prominent, famous, notable
ἔστι(ν)   (third pers. sing., pres. indic. active of the verb "to be")   is
εὐτυχία, εὐτυχίας, ἡ   good fortune
Θυέστης, Θυέστου, ὁ   Thyestes, brother of Atreus, who unknowingly ate
   his own children at Atreus' banquet
κακία, κακίας, ἡ   badness, cowardice
λοιπός, λοιπή, λοιπόν   remaining, left
μέγας, μεγάλη, μέγα   (gen. μεγάλου, μεγάλης, μεγάλου)   big, great
μεταβάλλω,   μεταβαλῶ,   μετέβαλον,   μεταβέβληκα,   μεταβέβλημαι,
   μετεβλήθην   change
μεταξύ   (prep. + gen.)   between
μοχθηρία, μοχθηρίας, ἡ   wickedness
Οἰδίπους, Οἰδίποδος, ὁ   Oidipous, Oedipus
οἷος, οἵα, οἷον   such as, of the sort which
   οἷον   for example
ὄντων   from
   ὤν, οὖσα, ὄν   (pres. participle active of the verb "to be")   being
τινά   M/F acc. sing. of
   τις, τι   (gen. τινός, τινός)   (indefinite enclitic pronoun/adjective)   someone, something; anyone, anything; some, any
τοιοῦτος, τοιαύτη, τοιοῦτο/τοιοῦτον   such (as this)

E. Euripides, *Trojan Women* 15–27

The god Poseidon describes the desolation of Troy, captured by the Greeks.

15   ἔρημα δ' ἄλση καὶ θεῶν ἀνάκτορα
      φόνῳ καταρρεῖ· πρὸς δὲ κρηπίδων βάθροις
      πέπτωκε Πρίαμος Ζηνὸς Ἑρκείου θανών.
      πολὺς δὲ χρῡσὸς Φρύγιά τε σκῡλεύματα
      πρὸς ναῦς Ἀχαιῶν πέμπεται· μένουσι δὲ
20   πρύμνηθεν οὖρον, ὡς δεκασπόρῳ χρόνῳ

ἄλσος, ἄλσους, τό   grove
ἀνάκτορον, ἀνακτόρου, τό   palace, temple
Ἀχαιός, Ἀχαιά, Ἀχαιόν   Achaian, Greek
βάθρον, βάθρου, τό   base, step, foundation
δεκασπόρος, δεκασπόρον   of ten sowings: ten years long
ἔρημος, ἔρημον   desolate, empty
Ἑρκεῖος, Ἑρκεῖον   of the household courtyard
Ζεύς, Διός/Ζηνός, ὁ   Zeus
θνῄσκω, θανοῦμαι, ἔθανον, τέθνηκα, ——, ——   die
καταρρέω, καταρρυήσομαι, ——, κατερρύηκα, ——, κατερρύην
      flow down; drip, drip down
κρηπίς, κρηπῖδος, ἡ   foundation, base
μένω, μενῶ, ἔμεινα, μεμένηκα, ——, ——   remain, stay; await
ναῦς   acc. pl. of
      ναῦς, νεώς, ἡ   ship
οὖρος, οὔρου, ὁ   favoring wind
πίπτω, πεσοῦμαι, ἔπεσον, πέπτωκα, ——, ——   fall
πολύς   masc. nom. sing. of
      πολύς, πολλή, πολύ   much, many
Πρίαμος, Πριάμου, ὁ   Priam, king of Troy
πρός (prep.) (+ gen.) in the eyes of, in the name of; (+ dat.) near;
      in addition to; (+ acc.)   toward
πρύμνηθεν (adv.)   from the stern
σκῡλεύματα, σκῡλευμάτων, τά   arms stripped from a fallen enemy
φόνος, φόνου, ὁ   murder, killing; gore
Φρύγιος, Φρυγίᾱ, Φρύγιον   Phrygian, Trojan
χρόνος, χρόνου, ὁ   time

ἀλόχους τε καὶ τέκν᾽ εἰσίδωσιν ἄσμενοι,
οἳ τήνδ᾽ ἐπεστράτευσαν Ἕλληνες πόλιν.
ἐγὼ δὲ—νῑκῶμαι γὰρ Ἀργείας θεοῦ[1]
Ἥρᾱς Ἀθάνᾱς[1] θ᾽, αἳ συνεξεῖλον Φρύγας—
25 λείπω τὸ κλεινὸν Ἴλιον βωμούς τ᾽ ἐμούς·
ἐρημίᾱ γὰρ πόλιν ὅταν λάβῃ κακή,
νοσεῖ τὰ τῶν θεῶν οὐδὲ τῑμᾶσθαι θέλει.

Ἀθηνᾶ/Ἀθάνᾱ, Ἀθηνᾶς/Ἀθάνᾱς, ἡ   Athena, a martial goddess
ἄλοχος, ἀλόχου, ἡ   wife
Ἀργεῖος, Ἀργείᾱ, Ἀργεῖον   Argive, of Argos
ἄσμενος, ἀσμένη, ἄσμενον   pleased, glad
βωμός, βωμοῦ, ὁ   altar
ἐγώ   (nom. sing. of the first person pronoun)   I
εἰσοράω, ——, εἰσεῖδον (unaugmented aorist act. and mid. tense stem
   εἰσιδ-), ——, ——, ——   behold, discover, see
ἐμός, ἐμή, ἐμόν   my
ἐπιστρατεύω, ἐπιστρατεύσω, ἐπεστράτευσα, ——, ——, ——
   march against, make war on
ἐρημίᾱ, ἐρημίᾱς, ἡ   desolation, emptiness
Ἥρᾱ, Ἥρᾱς, ἡ   Hera, wife of Zeus
θέλω = ἐθέλω
Ἴλιον, Ἰλίου, τό   Ilion, Troy
κλεινός, κλεινή, κλεινόν   famous
λαμβάνω, λήψομαι, ἔλαβον, εἴληφα, εἴλημμαι, ἐλήφθην   take
νοσέω, νοσήσω, ἐνόσησα, νενόσηκα, ——, ——   be sick
ὅταν (conj.) (+ subjunctive)   whenever
οὐδέ (conj.) and not; (adv.) not even
πόλις, πόλεως, ἡ   city
συνεξαιρέω, συνεξαιρήσω, συνεξεῖλον, ——, ——, ——   help to take, help
   to destroy, help to remove
τέκνον, τέκνου, τό   child
Φρύξ, Φρυγός, ὁ   Phrygian, Trojan

---

1. Genitive of personal agent without the preposition ὑπό.

I. *For each of the following nouns or adjectives, provide the proper form of the article (or ὦ). Translate. Then change plurals to singulars and singulars to plurals.*

1. ἀγῶσι
2. πείρᾳ
3. σῖγῆς
4. ὕδατα
5. ἀνδράσιν
6. ἱππεῖς
7. ἅπᾱσα
8. παθῶν
9. μητρός
10. θυγατρί
11. τέλει
12. σώφρονας
13. χρήματι
14. φύσεων
15. πόλι

II. *Translate indicatives and infinitives; identify subjunctives and optatives. Change to the other two voices. Change the number of the original form.*

1. μενοῦμεν
2. καλεῖς
3. ἐλίπετε
4. τελευτήσῃ
5. δηλοῖ
6. ἀγγελθῶσιν
7. μείνῃς
8. ἀξιοῖεν
9. ποιῇ
10. ἀδικεῖν
11. νῑκῶνται

289

12. ἀδικοίη

13. ἠδικοῦ

14. πεποίηται

III. *Identify the tense, voice, gender, number and case of the following participles. Translate. Change the form to the other two voices.*

1. ποιούμενον

2. πεποιημένος

3. λιποῦσα

4. ἄγων

5. ἀξόμενος

6. πράξαντα

7. σωθέντες

8. ἀγαγών

9. ἠδικηκότες

10. ἀγγελῶν

11. τῑμωμένη

12. γραψόμεναι

13. μείνᾱσα

14. γραψάμεναι

IV. *Translate.*

1. ἥδε ἡ πόλις, ὦ ἄνδρες, τῷ γε Σωκράτει τῷ αἰσχρὰ ποιοῦντι οὕτως ἠδίκηται ὥστε ταύτην ἐκεῖνον τὸν ἄνδρα τελευτᾶν ἐθέλειν.
   (dative of personal agent; attributive participle; clause of natural result; subject accusative of infinitive)

2. ὃς ἂν τοῦ ὀνόματος τοῦ σοφοῦ ἀξιωθῇ, ἀγάγωμεν δὴ τοῦτόν ποτ᾽ εἰς τὴν πόλιν ἅτε τὴν πάντων ἐλευθερίᾱν φυλάξοντα.
   (future more vivid conditional sentence with hortatory subjunctive in the apodosis; disyllabic enclitic; circumstantial participle showing cause, introduced by ἅτε)

3. ἀγαθὸν μὴ ποιοῦντες οὐκ ἤθελόν ποτε τῑμᾶσθαι.
   (circumstantial participle serving as protasis of a past general conditional sentence)

4. ἐὰν οἵδε οἱ πολῖται ὑπὸ τῶν αἰσχρῶν τῆσδε τῆς νήσου πολιτῶν
κελευσθῶσι τούς γε ξένους κακὰ ποιεῖν, οὐ σωθήσεται ἡ
δημοκρατίᾱ ποτέ.

(future more vivid conditional sentence; double accusative with
ποιεῖν; infinitive with passive of κελεύω; disyllabic enclitic)

5. εἴ γε μὴ ἐτάχθησαν εἰς τὰς ἒξ φάλαγγας οἱ πολέμου ἔμπειροι, οὐκ
ἄν ποτε κακὸν ἐποιήσατε τοὺς ἱππέᾱς τοὺς ἀδικήσαντας.

(past contrafactual conditional sentence; genitive with
ἔμπειρος; double accusative with ἐποιήσατε; disyllabic enclitic)

6. ὀνόματι μὲν ἐλεύθεραι πᾶσαι αἱ πόλεις, τῇ δ' ἀληθείᾳ βαρβάροις
ἀνδράσιν ἐδούλευον. λύεται γὰρ ἥ γε δημοκρατίᾱ τοῖς
πολίταις οὐ πεφυλαγμένη.

(dative of respect; dative of personal agent; circumstantial participle used causally or temporally)

7. καίπερ τόν γε στρατὸν ἐν πόλει λιπόντες, ὦ στρατηγοί, ὅμως
ταύτης τῆς ἡμέρᾱς ἀγγέλους τῆς χώρᾱς ἐκπέμψωμεν βασιλεῖ
μάχην ἀγγελοῦντας.

(circumstantial participle used concessively, introduced by
καίπερ; genitive of time within which; genitive governed by
compound verb; hortatory subjunctive; circumstantial participle
showing purpose vouched for by the speaker)

8. τοὺς πολεμίους τοὺς εἰς τὴν χώρᾱν ἥκοντας φυλάττοισθε ὡς μήτε
βλαβῶμεν μήτ' ἀδικώμεθα. εἰ γὰρ νῑκῷεν, σύμπαντες ἂν
δουλεύσαιμεν.

(attributive participle; optative of wish; purpose clause; future
less vivid conditional sentence)

V. *Translate into Greek.*

The men of these cities, if they did not do wrong, were considered worthy
of crowns by all the citizens.

I. (a) *Identify the gender, number, and case of each of the following words or phrases.*

   (b) *Change only the NUMBER of each word or phrase (i.e., from singular to plural or from plural to singular).*
   Where there is more than one possibility, give them all.

   1. ὁ πεποιηκώς
   2. τὴν ποιοῦσαν
   3. τοῦδε τοῦ πάθους
   4. τούτων τῶν μητέρων
   5. τῷ εὐγενεῖ γέροντι

II. *Translate indicatives and infinitives; identify subjunctives and optatives.*
   Where there is more than one possibility, give both or all.

   1. ἐκάλει
   2. ἔλιπον
   3. ποιῆτε
   4. ἀξιοῖ
   5. ἀγγελεῖσθε
   6. ἐποιήσαντο

III. *Give a synopsis of* νῑκάω *in the third person singular. Give the neuter nominative singular of participles.*

   PRINCIPAL PARTS: _____
   _____

	ACTIVE	*MIDDLE*	*PASSIVE*
PRESENT INDICATIVE			
IMPERFECT INDICATIVE			
FUTURE INDICATIVE			
AORIST INDICATIVE			
PERFECT INDICATIVE			
PLUPERFECT INDICATIVE			

PRESENT SUBJUNCTIVE   ————————————————

AORIST SUBJUNCTIVE   ————————————————

PRESENT OPTATIVE   ————————————————

AORIST OPTATIVE   ————————————————

PRESENT INFINITIVE   ————————————————

AORIST INFINITIVE   ————————————————

PERFECT INFINITIVE   ————————————————

PRESENT PARTICIPLE   ————————————————

FUTURE PARTICIPLE   ————————————————

AORIST PARTICIPLE   ————————————————

PERFECT PARTICIPLE   ————————————————

IV. *Translate, and answer all appended questions.*

1. ἀνάξιος δὴ τīμῆς ἐκεῖνος ὁ αἰσχρὸς στρατιώτης, ὃς ἂν εἰς μάχην πεμφθεὶς λίπῃ ποτὲ τὰ ὅπλα.

   (a) *Give the syntax of* πεμφθείς.

2. ὁ μὲν δῆμος, οἷα οὐ καλῶς πεπαιδευμένος, οὐκ ἐθέλει ἄρχεσθαι, ὁ δὲ βασιλεὺς ἄρχειν οὐκ ἐθέλει. οὕτως οὖν ποιῶμεν, ὦ φίλοι, ὥστε καὶ τὸν δῆμον πείθεσθαι τῷ γε βασιλεῖ καὶ τὸν βασιλέᾱ ἀγαθὰ ποιεῖν ἅπαντας τοὺς πολίτᾱς.

   (a) *Give the syntax of* πεπαιδευμένος.

   (b) *Give the syntax of* τὸν δῆμον.

   (c) *Give the syntax of* πείθεσθαι.

3. ὦ θύγατερ, τῇ γε θεῷ θύσᾱσα φυλάξαις ἂν τὸν ἀδελφὸν τὸν ὑπὸ τῶν ἐχθρῶν κλοπῆς γραφέντα.

   (a) *Give the syntax of* θύσᾱσα.

   (b) *Give the syntax of* κλοπῆς.

4. διὰ τὸ τούς γε πολίτᾱς περὶ τοῦ ἀληθοῦς τοῖς σώφροσι μὴ πεπαιδεῦσθαι Σωκράτης μὲν ὑπὸ τῶν εὐδαιμόνων οὐκ ἐτῑμᾶτο, ἔπειτα δὲ ὁ Δημοσθένης ὁ ῥήτωρ ἠδικεῖτο καίπερ ἐθέλων τὴν δημοκρατίᾱν σῶσαι.

   (a) *Give the syntax of* πεπαιδεῦσθαι.

   (b) *Give the syntax of* ἐθέλων.

5. ὑπὲρ ταύτης τῆς γεφύρᾱς τῆς νῦν ὑπὸ τῶν γερόντων ποιουμένης, ὦ
   σῶφρον, τάξονταί τοι οἱ ὁπλῖται ἐάν γε τούτους τῆς πόλεως
   ἐκκαλῇς ποτε.

   (a) *Give the syntax of* ποιουμένης.

   (b) *Give the syntax of* πόλεως.

6. εἰ τοὺς Ἀθηναίους τοὺς πολέμου ἐμπείρους εἰς πόλιν σῑγῇ ἠγάγομεν
   πρὸ τῆς μάχης, οὐκ ἂν διὰ τὸν τῶν βαρβάρων φόβον ἄνδρας
   ἐξεπέμψαμεν περὶ εἰρήνης ἀγγελοῦντας.

   (a) *Give the syntax of* σῑγῇ.

   (b) *Give the syntax of* βαρβάρων.

   (c) *Give the syntax of* ἀγγελοῦντας.

V. *Translate into Greek.*

When will you announce the death of all the men who are wronging the
king?

ANSWER KEY FOR SELF-CORRECTING EXAMINATION 3 A

I. 1. ὁ πεποιηκώς: M sing. nom.; οἱ πεποιηκότες

2. τὴν ποιοῦσαν: F sing. acc.; τὰς ποιούσᾱς

3. τοῦδε τοῦ πάθους: N sing. gen.; τῶνδε τῶν παθῶν

4. τούτων τῶν μητέρων: F pl. gen.; ταύτης τῆς μητρός

5. τῷ εὐγενεῖ γέροντι: M sing. dat.; τοῖς εὐγενέσι γέρουσι(ν)

II. 1. he/she/it was calling/used to call

2. I left; they left

3. second pers. pl., pres. subj. act.

4. he/she/it thinks/is thinking worthy;
third pers. sing., pres. subj. act.;
third pers. sing., pres. opt. act.;
you (sing.) think/are thinking worthy (for yourself);
second pers. sing., pres. subj. mid.;
you (sing.) are thought/are being thought worthy;
second pers. sing., pres. subj. pass.

5. you will announce (for yourselves)

6. they made (for themselves)

III. PRINCIPAL PARTS: νῑκάω, νῑκήσω, ἐνίκησα, νενίκηκα,
νενίκημαι, ἐνῑκήθην

	ACTIVE	MIDDLE	PASSIVE
PRESENT INDICATIVE	νῑκᾷ	νῑκᾶται	νῑκᾶται
IMPERFECT INDICATIVE	ἐνίκᾱ	ἐνῑκᾶτο	ἐνῑκᾶτο
FUTURE INDICATIVE	νῑκήσει	νῑκήσεται	νῑκηθήσεται
AORIST INDICATIVE	ἐνίκησε(ν)	ἐνῑκήσατο	ἐνῑκήθη
PERFECT INDICATIVE	νενίκηκε(ν)	νενίκηται	νενίκηται
PLUPERFECT INDICATIVE	ἐνενῑκήκει(ν)	ἐνενίκητο	ἐνενίκητο
PRESENT SUBJUNCTIVE	νῑκᾷ	νῑκᾶται	νῑκᾶται
AORIST SUBJUNCTIVE	νῑκήσῃ	νῑκήσηται	νῑκηθῇ
PRESENT OPTATIVE	νῑκῷ/νῑκῴη	νῑκῷτο	νῑκῷτο

AORIST OPTATIVE	νῑκήσαι/ νῑκήσειε(ν)	νῑκήσαιτο	νῑκηθείη
PRESENT INFINITIVE	νῑκᾶν	νῑκᾶσθαι	νῑκᾶσθαι
AORIST INFINITIVE	νῑκῆσαι	νῑκήσασθαι	νῑκηθῆναι
PERFECT INFINITIVE	νενῑκηκέναι	νενῑκῆσθαι	νενῑκῆσθαι
PRESENT PARTICIPLE	νῑκῶν	νῑκώμενον	νῑκώμενον
FUTURE PARTICIPLE	νῑκῆσον	νῑκησόμενον	νῑκηθησόμενον
AORIST PARTICIPLE	νῑκῆσαν	νῑκησάμενον	νῑκηθέν
PERFECT PARTICIPLE	νενῑκηκός	νενῑκημένον	νενῑκημένον

V. 1. Unworthy of honor indeed is that shameful soldier whoever, sent/when he is sent/if he is sent into battle, ever leaves his weapons.

(a) πεμφθείς is an aorist participle, M sing. nom.: circumstantial participle used temporally or as the protasis of a present general conditional sentence; aorist tense to show simple aspect; agrees in gender, number and case with ὅς.

2. The people, on the one hand, as having not been educated well/because they have not been educated well, refuse/do not wish to be ruled; the king, on the other hand, refuses/does not wish to rule. Let us therefore so do, friends, as both for the people to obey/to be obeying the *king* (at least) and for the king to do/to be doing good things to all the citizens.

(a) πεπαιδευμένος is a perfect participle, M sing. nom.: circumstantial participle, introduced by οἷα, showing cause vouched for by the speaker; perfect tense to show completed aspect; agrees in gender, number and case with δῆμος.

(b) τὸν δῆμον is accusative: subject of the infinitive πείθεσθαι.

(c) πείθεσθαι is present infinitive: infinitive in a clause of natural result; present tense to show progressive/repeated aspect.

3. Daughter, upon sacrificing/if you should sacrifice to the *goddess* (at least), you might/would guard your brother indicted/who was indicted by his enemies on a charge of theft.

(a) θύσᾱσα is an aorist participle, F sing. nom.: circumstantial participle used temporally or as the protasis of a future less vivid conditional sentence; aorist tense to show simple aspect; agrees in gender, number, and case with the subject of φυλάξαις.

(b) κλοπῆς is genitive of the charge.

4. Because of the *citizens'* not having been educated/because the *citizens* had not been educated about the true by the prudent (men), Sokrates, on the one hand, was not honored/was not being honored by the fortunate (men); later, on the other hand, Demosthenes the public speaker was being wronged/used to be wronged, although wishing/although he wished to save the democracy.

(a) πεπαιδεῦσθαι is a perfect infinitive: articular infinitive; accusative: object of the preposition διά; perfect tense to show completed aspect.

(b) ἐθέλων is a present participle, M sing. nom.: circumstantial participle, introduced by καίπερ, used concessively; present tense to show progressive/repeated aspect; agrees in gender, number and case with Δημοσθένης.

5. Above this bridge now being made by the old men, prudent one, the hoplites, you see, will fall into battle order *if* you ever call/are calling these men out of the city.

(a) ποιουμένης is a present participle, F sing. gen.: attributive participle; present tense to show progressive/repeated aspect; agrees in gender, number and case with γεφύρας.

(b) πόλεως is genitive, governed by the prefix ἐκ- of the compound verb ἐκκαλῆς.

6. If we had led the Athenians experienced in war into the city in silence/silently before the battle, we would not, because of our fear of the enemy, have sent men out to announce concerning peace.

(a) σῑγῇ is a dative of manner.

(b) βαρβάρων is an objective genitive.

(c) ἀγγελοῦντας is a future participle, M pl. acc.: circumstantial participle showing purpose; future tense to show subsequent time; agrees in gender, number and case with ἄνδρας.

V. πότε ἀγγελεῖς τὸν θάνατον πάντων/ἁπάντων τῶν τὸν βασιλέᾱ ἀδικούντων/οἳ τὸν βασιλέᾱ ἀδικοῦσιν;

I. (a) *Identify the gender, number, and case of each of the following words or phrases.*

   (b) *Change only the NUMBER of each word or phrase (i.e., from singular to plural or from plural to singular).*
   Where there is more than one possibility, give them all.

   1. τῷ ἀξιοῦντι
   2. αἱ ἐκπεμφθεῖσαι
   3. τῷ εὐδαίμονι βασιλεῖ
   4. τοῦδε τοῦ πατρός
   5. ταύτης τῆς πόλεως

II. *Translate indicatives and infinitives; identify subjunctives and optatives.*
   Where there is more than one possibility, give them all.

   1. ἀγαγεῖν
   2. λίποισθε
   3. νῑκῶμεν
   4. ἐλίπετο
   5. ἀγγελοῦμεν
   6. ποιώμεθα

III. *Give a synopsis of* δηλόω *in the third person plural. Give the masculine nominative plural of participles.*

   PRINCIPAL PARTS: _____

   _____

	ACTIVE	*MIDDLE*	*PASSIVE*
PRESENT INDICATIVE			
IMPERFECT INDICATIVE			
FUTURE INDICATIVE			
AORIST INDICATIVE			
PERFECT INDICATIVE			

298

PLUPERFECT INDICATIVE   _____

PRESENT SUBJUNCTIVE   _____

AORIST SUBJUNCTIVE   _____

PRESENT OPTATIVE   _____

AORIST OPTATIVE   _____

PRESENT INFINITIVE   _____

AORIST INFINITIVE   _____

PERFECT INFINITIVE   _____

PRESENT PARTICIPLE   _____

FUTURE PARTICIPLE   _____

AORIST PARTICIPLE   _____

PERFECT PARTICIPLE   _____

IV. *Translate, and answer all appended questions.*

1. ἠγγέλθη τοῖς ἱερεῦσι τοῖς θυσίᾱν ποιουμένοις ὁ Σωκράτους θάνατος.
   (a) *Give the syntax of* ποιουμένοις.
   (b) *Give the syntax of* Σωκράτους.

2. ὦ ἄδελφε, ἐτῑμώμεθα δὴ τοῖς μὲν ἀγαθοῖς δῶρα λιπόντες τοὺς δ᾽ ἐχθροὺς δώρων γραψάμενοι. τούτῳ γάρ τοι τῷ τρόπῳ τοὺς μὲν σώφρονάς τε καὶ σοφοὺς εὖ ἐποιοῦμεν, τοὺς δ᾽ ἀληθῶς κακοὺς ἐξεπαιδεύομεν ὅπως τῑμώμεθα ὑπὸ τῶν ἐν τέλει.
   (a) *Give the syntax of* γραψάμενοι.
   (b) *Give the syntax of* τρόπῳ.

3. δεινὸς μὲν λόγους γε ποιεῖσθαι ὁ ῥήτωρ, εὐδαίμονες δὲ οἱ τούτῳ πεπαιδευμένοι.
   (a) *Give the syntax of* ποιεῖσθαι.

4. ἐάν ποθ᾽ οἵδε οἱ ἄγγελοι τὰς τῶν ἀνδρῶν νίκᾱς ἀγγείλωσιν ἐν ταῖς πόλεσι, τυθήσονται αἶγες καλοὶ ὑπὸ πολῑτῶν τῶν εὐδαιμόνων πᾶσι τοῖς δαίμοσιν ἅτε τὸν δῆμον εὖ ποιήσᾱσιν.
   (a) *Give the syntax of* ἀγγείλωσιν.
   (b) *Give the syntax of* ποιήσᾱσιν.

5. οἱ μὲν Ἀθηναῖοι ἄνευ τῶν ἄλλων Ἑλλήνων εἰς μάχην ἐτάττοντο·
οὗτοι γὰρ ἐν ταῖς οἰκίαις μεῖναι ἤθελον, εἴ γ' ἐκεῖνοι εἰς
πόλεμον ἐκκαλοῖντό ποτε. οἱ δὲ βάρβαροι ὑπὸ βασιλέως
ἐτάττοντο ἐν τῷδε τῷ πεδίῳ ὡς βλάψοντες γῆν τὴν Ἀθηναίων.

(a) *Give the syntax of* ἤθελον.

(b) *Give the syntax of* βλάψοντες.

6. τούς γε λόγους περὶ τῆς τοῦ ἀγαθοῦ φύσεως ἐποιεῖτο ὁ Σωκράτης
ὥστε ἐξεδίδαξε πάσας τὰς τῶν σωφρόνων ψυχάς. νῦν δέ, καίπερ
πάντας ἀγαθὰ ποιήσᾱς, ἐξ ἡμερῶν τελευτήσει. εἰ γὰρ τὴν
θυγατέρα λιποῦσα τοῦτον τῆς πόλεως ἐξαγάγοιμι.

(a) *Give the syntax of* ἐξεδίδαξε.

(b) *Give the syntax of* ποιήσᾱς.

(c) *Give the syntax of* ἐξαγάγοιμι.

V. *Translate into Greek.*

Good women, since we have been wronged by evil men, let us die on behalf
of our country, at least.

I. 1. τῷ ἀξιοῦντι: M/N sing. dat.; τοῖς ἀξιοῦσι(ν)

    2. αἱ ἐκπεμφθεῖσαι: F pl. nom.; ἡ ἐκπεμφθεῖσα

    3. τῷ εὐδαίμονι βασιλεῖ: M sing. dat.; τοῖς εὐδαίμοσι βασιλεῦσι(ν)

    4. τοῦδε τοῦ πατρός: M sing. gen.; τῶνδε τῶν πατέρων

    5. ταύτης τῆς πόλεως: F sing. gen.; τούτων τῶν πόλεων

II. 1. to lead

    2. second pers. pl., aor. opt. mid.

    3. first pers. pl., pres. opt. act.

    4. he/she/it left (for himself/herself/itself)

    5. we shall announce

    6. first pers. pl., pres. subj. mid.;
       first pers. pl., pres. subj. pass.

III. PRINCIPAL PARTS: δηλόω, δηλώσω, ἐδήλωσα, δεδήλωκα,
                         δεδήλωμαι, ἐδηλώθην

	ACTIVE	MIDDLE	PASSIVE
PRESENT INDICATIVE	δηλοῦσι(ν)	δηλοῦνται	δηλοῦνται
IMPERF. INDICATIVE	ἐδήλουν	ἐδηλοῦντο	ἐδηλοῦντο
FUTURE INDICATIVE	δηλώσουσι(ν)	δηλώσονται	δηλωθήσονται
AORIST INDICATIVE	ἐδήλωσαν	ἐδηλώσαντο	ἐδηλώθησαν
PERFECT INDICATIVE	δεδηλώκᾱσι(ν)	δεδήλωνται	δεδήλωνται
PLUPERF. INDICATIVE	ἐδεδηλώκεσαν	ἐδεδήλωντο	ἐδεδήλωντο
PRESENT SUBJUNCTIVE	δηλῶσι(ν)	δηλῶνται	δηλῶνται
AORIST SUBJUNCTIVE	δηλώσωσι(ν)	δηλώσωνται	δηλωθῶσι(ν)
PRESENT OPTATIVE	δηλοῖεν/ δηλοίησαν	δηλοῖντο	δηλοῖντο
AORIST OPTATIVE	δηλώσαιεν/ δηλώσειαν	δηλώσαιντο	δηλωθεῖεν/ δηλωθείησαν
PRESENT INFINITIVE	δηλοῦν	δηλοῦσθαι	δηλοῦσθαι
AORIST INFINITIVE	δηλῶσαι	δηλώσασθαι	δηλωθῆναι

PERFECT INFINITIVE	δεδηλωκέναι	δεδηλῶσθαι	δεδηλῶσθαι
PRESENT PARTICIPLE	δηλοῦντες	δηλούμενοι	δηλούμενοι
FUTURE PARTICIPLE	δηλώσοντες	δηλωσόμενοι	δηλωθησόμενοι
AORIST PARTICIPLE	δηλώσαντες	δηλωσάμενοι	δηλωθέντες
PERFECT PARTICIPLE	δεδηλωκότες	δεδηλωμένοι	δεδηλωμένοι

IV. 1. The death of Sokrates was announced to the priests making a sacrifice/
sacrificing.

(a) ποιουμένοις is a present participle, M pl. dat.: attributive participle; present tense to show progressive/repeated aspect; agrees in
gender, number and case with ἱερεῦσι.

(b) Σωκράτους is a subjective genitive.

2. Brother, we were honored/were being honored indeed upon leaving/
when we left/since we left gifts for (the) good men, on the one hand,
(and) upon indicting/when we indicted/since we indicted our enemies, on
the other hand, on a charge of bribery. For, you know, in this way we
did/were doing good to the prudent and wise, on the one hand, (but)
the truly evil, on the other hand, we thoroughly educated/were thoroughly educating in order that we might be honored/might be being
honored by those in power.

(a) γραψάμενοι is an aorist participle, M pl. nom.: circumstantial
participle used temporally or causally; aorist tense to show simple
aspect; agrees in gender, number and case with the subject of
ἐτῑμώμεθα.

(b) τρόπῳ is a dative of manner.

3. The public speaker is clever, on the one hand, at composing (for himself)
speeches (at least); lucky, on the other hand, are those having been
educated/who have been educated by this man.

(a) ποιεῖσθαι is an epexegetical infinitive; present tense to show
progressive/repeated aspect.

4. If ever these messengers announce in the cities the victories of the men,
beautiful goats will be sacrificed by the fortunate citizens to all the gods
because they did good/well for the people.

(a) ἀγγείλωσιν is aorist subjunctive: subjunctive in the protasis of a
future more vivid conditional sentence; aorist tense to show simple
aspect.

(b) ποιήσασιν is an aorist participle, M pl. dat.: circumstantial participle, introduced by ἄτε, showing cause vouched for by the speaker; aorist tense to show simple aspect; agrees in gender, number and case with δαίμοσιν.

5. The Athenians, on the one hand, without the other Greeks were falling/ used to fall/were being drawn up/used to be drawn up into battle order; for the latter wished to stay in their houses *if* the former were ever called out to war. The foreigners, on the other hand, were being drawn up/used to be drawn up into battle order by the king in this plain in order, as he/they said, to harm the land of the Athenians.

(a) ἤθελον is imperfect indicative in the apodosis of a past general conditional sentence; imperfect tense to show progressive/repeated aspect.

(b) βλάψοντες is a future participle, M pl. nom.: circumstantial participle, introduced by ὡς, showing purpose not vouched for by the speaker; future tense to show subsequent time; agrees in gender, number, and case with βάρβαροι.

6. Sokrates was composing/used to compose/was making/used to make his words/speeches about the nature of the good, with the result that he educated thoroughly all the souls of the prudent. But now, although doing (simple aspect) good things to all/although he did good things to all, he will die within six days. If only I, (upon) leaving behind my daughter, could/might lead this man out of the city.

(a) ἐξεδίδαξε is aorist indicative: indicative in a clause of actual result; aorist tense to show past time and simple aspect.

(b) ποιήσᾱς is an aorist participle, M sing. nom.: circumstantial participle, introduced by καίπερ, used concessively; aorist tense to show simple aspect; agrees in gender, number and case with the subject of τελευτήσει.

(c) ἐξαγάγοιμι is aorist optative: optative of wish; aorist tense to show simple aspect.

V. ὦ ἀγαθαί, (ἄτε/οἷα) κακοῖς ἠδικημέναι / ἐπειδὴ κακοῖς ἠδικήμεθα, τελευτήσωμεν ὑπέρ γε τῆς χώρᾱς/γῆς.

UNIT
11

89. THE IMPERATIVE MOOD

In addition to the indicative, subjunctive, and optative moods, Greek has a fourth mood, the **imperative mood,** which is used to give commands. The tense of the imperative mood, like that of the subjunctive, the optative, and the infinitive, shows *aspect only*: the present imperative indicates progressive/ repeated aspect; the aorist, simple aspect. The rarely used perfect imperative shows completed aspect, and its forms are given only in the Appendix.

Like the other moods, the Greek imperative has person (but ONLY second and third person) and number. The second person corresponds to our English imperative: "**Sit** down and **learn** this!" The third person imperatives can be expressed in English by using the helping verb "let": "**Let** him/her/it/them **do** it!" There are no first person forms of the imperative. In the first person plural, the idea of "Let us do something!" is expressed by the hortatory subjunctive; cf. Section 50.

The imperative uses the same tense stems as all the other moods; it simply puts different endings on these stems. See Section 89.10, page 311, for a chart showing all of these endings.

1. PRESENT IMPERATIVE ACTIVE

To form the present imperative active add to the present tense stem the following endings:

	S	P
2	-ε	-ετε
3	-ετω	-οντων

305

Thus the forms of the present imperative active of παιδεύω are as follows:

	S		P	
2	παίδευε	be educating/ educate	παιδεύετε	be educating/ educate
3	παιδευέτω	let him /her/it be educating/ educate	παιδευόντων	let them be educating/ educate

Observations: (1) The second person plural, present *imperative* active is identical in form with the second person plural, present *indicative* active. The third person plural, present *imperative* active is identical in form with the masculine and neuter genitive plural of the present *participle* active. Context usually allows one to distinguish these forms.

(2) The accent of the imperative is recessive and can go back onto the prefix when necessary: e.g., ἀπόλῡε.

2. PRESENT IMPERATIVE MIDDLE/PASSIVE

To form the present imperative middle/passive, add to the present tense stem the following middle/passive endings:

	S	P
2	-ου < *-εσο	-εσθε
3	-εσθω	-εσθων

Thus the forms of the present imperative middle/passive of παιδεύω are as follows:

S 2	παιδεύου	*Mid.*: be having/have (someone) educated
		Pass.: be being educated/be educated
3	παιδευέσθω	*Mid.*: let him/her/it be having/have (someone) educated
		Pass.: let him/her/it be being educated/be educated
P 2	παιδεύεσθε	*Mid.*: be having/have (someone) educated
		Pass.: be being educated/be educated
3	παιδευέσθων	*Mid.*: let them be having/have (someone) educated
		Pass.: let them be being educated/be educated

Observation: As in the active voice, so in the middle/passive, the second person plural imperative and indicative forms are identical.

3. PRESENT IMPERATIVE ACTIVE OF CONTRACTED VERBS

The present imperative active of contracted verbs adds the endings of the present imperative active to the present tense stem of the verbs. The vowels of the stem and the endings contract according to the rules given in Sections 73, 74, and 84. In the forms which are given below, the uncontracted forms are given in parentheses for reference. The contractions do not occur, of course, in the aorist imperative of these verbs.

	S		P	
2	τίμᾱ	(τίμαε)	τῑμᾶτε	(τῑμάετε)
3	τῑμᾱ́τω	(τῑμαέτω)	τῑμώντων	(τῑμαόντων)
2	ποίει	(ποίεε)	ποιεῖτε	(ποιέετε)
3	ποιείτω	(ποιεέτω)	ποιούντων	(ποιεόντων)
2	δήλου	(δήλοε)	δηλοῦτε	(δηλόετε)
3	δηλούτω	(δηλοέτω)	δηλούντων	(δηλοόντων)

Observations: (1) Distinguish carefully between the second person singular, present imperative active forms and the third person singular, present indicative active forms of the contracted verbs:

IMPERATIVE		*INDICATIVE*	
τίμᾱ	(τίμαε)	τῑμᾷ	(τῑμάει)
ποίει	(ποίεε)	ποιεῖ	(ποιέει)
δήλου	(δήλοε)	δηλοῖ	(δηλόει)

(2) In the second person plural all present imperative active forms are identical with those of the indicative: τῑμᾶτε, ποιεῖτε, δηλοῦτε.

(3) In the third person plural, present imperative active the forms of the imperative are identical with those of the masculine and neuter genitive plural of the present participle active: τῑμώντων, ποιούντων, δηλούντων.

4. PRESENT IMPERATIVE MIDDLE/PASSIVE OF CONTRACTED VERBS

The present imperative middle/passive of contracted verbs adds the endings of the present imperative middle/passive to the present tense stem of the verbs. The final vowel of the stem and the initial vowel of the endings contract according to the rules of contraction given in Sections 73, 74, and 84. In the forms which are given below, the uncontracted forms are given in parentheses. The contractions do not occur in the aorist tense of these verbs.

	S		P	
2	τῑμῶ	(τῑμάου)	τῑμᾶσθε	(τῑμάεσθε)
3	τῑμάσθω	(τῑμαέσθω)	τῑμάσθων	(τῑμαέσθων)
2	ποιοῦ	(ποιέου)	ποιεῖσθε	(ποιέεσθε)
3	ποιείσθω	(ποιεέσθω)	ποιείσθων	(ποιεέσθων)
2	δηλοῦ	(δηλόου)	δηλοῦσθε	(δηλόεσθε)
3	δηλούσθω	(δηλοέσθω)	δηλούσθων	(δηλοέσθων)

Observations: (1) The second person singular, present imperative middle/passive of τῑμάω is the same as the first person singular, present indicative and subjunctive active: τῑμῶ from τῑμάου (imperative) and from τῑμάω (indicative and subjunctive).

(2) In the second person plural, all present imperative middle/passive forms are identical with those of the indicative: τῑμᾶσθε, ποιεῖσθε, δηλοῦσθε.

(3) Distinguish carefully the forms δηλοῦ (second person singular, present imperative middle/passive) and δήλου (second person singular, present imperative active).

5. FIRST AORIST IMPERATIVE ACTIVE

To form the first aorist imperative active, add to the unaugmented aorist active and middle tense stem the following endings:

	S	P
2	-ον	-ατε
3	-ατω	-αντων

Thus the forms of the first aorist imperative active of παιδεύω are as follows:

	S		P	
2	παίδευσον	educate	παιδεύσατε	educate
3	παιδευσάτω	let him/her/it educate	παιδευσάντων	let them educate

Observations: (1) The third person plural aorist *imperative* active is identical in form with the masculine and neuter genitive plural of the aorist *participle* active.

(2) Note the difference in accent between the imperative ἀπόλῦσον and the neuter nom./acc./voc. singular of the future active participle ἀπολῦσον.

6. FIRST AORIST IMPERATIVE MIDDLE

To form the first aorist imperative middle, add the following endings to the unaugmented aorist active and middle tense stem:

	S	P
2	-αι	-ασθε
3	-ασθω	-ασθων

Thus the first aorist imperative middle forms of παιδεύω are as follows:

S	2	παίδευσαι	have (someone) educated
	3	παιδευσάσθω	let him/her/it have (someone) educated
P	2	παιδεύσασθε	have (someone) educated
	3	παιδευσάσθων	let them have someone educated

Observation: Note that the second person singular ending of the aorist imperative middle counts as short for purposes of accentuation. Observe carefully the different accents on three very similar forms:

παίδευσαι   second person singular, aorist imperative middle
παιδεύσαι   third person singular, aorist optative active
παιδεῦσαι   aorist infinitive active

7. SECOND AORIST IMPERATIVE ACTIVE

To form the second aorist imperative active, add the endings of the *present* imperative active to the unaugmented second aorist active and middle tense stem. Thus the forms of the second aorist imperative active of λείπω are as follows:

	S	P
2	λίπε	λίπετε
3	λιπέτω	λιπόντων

Observation: The third person plural, second aorist imperative is identical with the masculine and neuter genitive plural of the second aorist participle active.

8. SECOND AORIST IMPERATIVE MIDDLE

To form the second aorist imperative middle, add the endings of the present imperative middle/passive to the unaugmented second aorist active and middle tense stem. The resulting form is middle only; the aorist imperative passive of all verbs is formed from Principal Part VI.

Thus the forms of the second aorist imperative middle of λείπω are as follows:

	S	P
2	λιποῦ	λίπεσθε
3	λιπέσθω	λιπέσθων

Observation: The accent on the second person singular, second aorist imperative middle is NOT recessive; it is always a circumflex on the ultima.

9. AORIST IMPERATIVE PASSIVE

To form the aorist imperative passive, add to the unaugmented aorist passive tense stem the following endings:

	S	P
2	-ηθι, -ητι	-ητε
3	-ητω	-εντων

Thus the forms of the aorist imperative passive of παιδεύω are as follows:

S	2	παιδεύθητι	be educated
	3	παιδευθήτω	let him/her/it be educated
P	2	παιδεύθητε	be educated
	3	παιδευθέντων	let them be educated

Observations: (1) The original ending of the second person singular, aorist imperative passive was -ηθι. Dissimilation of aspirates causes the -θ- to change to a -τ- when the ending is added to a stem ending in an aspirate (φ, χ, θ). Since most aorist passive tense stems end in an aspirate, the ending -ητι is more common than -ηθι. Compare βλάφθητι with βλάβηθι.

(2) Note the -ε- of the third person plural ending in contrast to the -η- of the other forms. The third person plural, aorist imperative passive is identical in form with the masculine and neuter genitive plural of the aorist participle passive.

10. ENDINGS OF THE IMPERATIVE

	PRESENT IMPER. ACTIVE	PRESENT IMPER. MIDDLE/ PASSIVE	FIRST AORIST IMPER. ACTIVE	FIRST AORIST IMPER. MIDDLE	AORIST IMPER. PASSIVE
S 2	-ε	-ου	-ον	-αι	-ηθι, -ητι
3	-ετω	-εσθω	-ατω	-ασθω	-ητω
P 2	-ετε	-εσθε	-ατε	-ασθε	-ητε
3	-οντων	-εσθων	-αντων	-ασθων	-εντων

Observation: Remember that the second aorist imperative active and middle forms use the same endings as the present imperative active and middle/passive.

90. COMMANDS AND PROHIBITIONS

Commands are expressed in the first person (plural) by the subjunctive
in the second person by the imperative
in the third person by the imperative.

They are often preceded by expressions like ἄγε, ἄγετε, φέρε, ἴθι, and εἰ δ' ἄγε, ALL of which have the force of "come on" when used with imperatives and the hortatory subjunctive.

ἀλλ' ἄγε διδάσκωμεν τοὺς νεανίᾱς.
But come on, let's teach the young men.

ἀλλ' ἄγε δίδασκε τοὺς νεανίᾱς.
But come on, teach the young men.

ἀλλ' ἄγε δὴ σοφὸς διδασκέτω τοὺς νεανίᾱς.
But come on, let a wise man be teaching the young men.

ἀλλ' ἄγε δὴ σοφὸς διδαξάτω τοὺς νεανίᾱς.
But come on, let a wise man teach the young men.

When a command involves two actions, one of them is usually expressed by a participle.

τὴν οἰκίᾱν λιπών, δήλωσον ταῦτα τῇ ἐκκλησίᾳ.
Upon leaving your house, make these things clear to the assembly.
Leave your house and make these things clear to the assembly.

Prohibitions (negative commands) are all introduced by μή. The first person prohibition, like the first person command, uses the *hortatory subjunctive*; tense shows progressive/repeated or simple aspect. In the second and third persons, prohibitions with progressive/repeated aspect use μή with a present imperative; prohibitions with simple aspect use μή with an aorist subjunctive, the *prohibitive subjunctive*. In the second and third persons, the aorist imperative with μή is sometimes found.

Prohibitions are summarized in the following chart:

PERSON	PROGRESSIVE/REPEATED	SIMPLE
1 μή	+ Present Subjunctive (Hortatory)	μή + Aorist Subjunctive (Hortatory)
2 μή	+ Present Imperative	μή + Aorist Subjunctive (Prohibitive)
3 μή	+ Present Imperative	μή + Aorist Subjunctive (Prohibitive)

μὴ λύωμεν τοὺς στρατιώτᾱς.   (*Hortatory*
Let us not be freeing the soldiers.   *Subjunctive*)
Let us not free the soldiers.

μὴ λύσωμεν τοὺς στρατιώτᾱς.   (*Hortatory*
Let us not free the soldiers.   *Subjunctive*)

μὴ λύετε τοὺς στρατιώτας.   (*Present*
Do not be freeing the soldiers.   *Imperative*)
Do not free the soldiers.

μὴ λύσητε τοὺς στρατιώτας.   (*Prohibitive*
Do not free the soldiers.   *Subjunctive*)

Like the hortatory and prohibitive subjunctive, the imperative can stand in
the apodosis of a future more vivid conditional sentence in place of the future
indicative.

ἐὰν σωθῇ ἡ πόλις, θῦσον τοῖς δαίμοσιν.
If the city is saved, sacrifice to the divinities.

91. FORMS OF THE GREEK VERB

Now that the imperative has been learned, it is convenient to give a chart of the
forms of the Greek verb.   In the chart which follows, all moods and tenses can
be found in the active, middle and passive voice. Consult the chart in Section
92 for a summary of the verb which shows which of the principal parts is used
to form each of the moods and tenses in the various voices.

TENSE

PRESENT	ind.	subj.	opt.	imper.	infin.	part.
IMPERFECT	ind.					
FUTURE	ind.		opt.[1]		infin.[1]	part.
AORIST	ind.	subj.	opt.	imper.	infin.	part.
PERFECT	ind.	[subj.][2]	[opt.][2]	[imper.][2]	infin.	part.
PLUPERFECT	ind.					

1. The future optative and infinitive are given in Unit 16.
2. Forms in square brackets are found in the Appendix only.

92. THE GREEK VERB: A SUMMARY

PRINCIPAL PART	TENSE STEM		VERB FORMS DERIVED FROM STEM
	Name	*Form*	
I. παιδεύω	present tense stem	παιδευ-	present indicative, subjunctive, optative, imperative, infinitive, and participle in all three voices
			imperfect indicative in all three voices
II. παιδεύσω	future active and middle tense stem	παιδευσ-	future indicative, optative,[1] infinitive,[1] and participle in the active and middle voices
III. ἐπαίδευσα	first aorist active and middle tense stem	παιδευσ-	aorist indicative, subjunctive, optative, imperative, infinitive, and participle in the active and middle voices
ἔλιπον	second aorist active and middle tense stem	λιπ-	

IV.	πεπαιδευκα	πεπαιδευκ-	perfect active tense stem	perfect indicative, [subjunctive, optative, impera-tive],[2] infinitive, and participle in the active voice; pluperfect indicative in the active voice
V.	πεπαιδευμαι	πεπαιδευ-	perfect middle and passive tense stem	perfect indicative, [subjunctive, optative, impera-tive],[2] infinitive, and participle in the middle and passive voices; pluperfect indicative in the middle and passive voices
VI.	ἐπαιδεύθην	παιδευθ-	aorist passive tense stem	aorist indicative, subjunctive, optative, impera-tive, infinitive, and participle in the passive voice
		παιδευθησ-	future passive tense stem	future indicative, optative,[1] infinitive,[1] and par-ticiple in the passive voice

Note: Contraction of vowels occurs in the present (e.g., τῑμάω, ποιέω, δηλόω) and in the future active and middle (e.g., ἀγγελῶ). Except for the optative active, contracted verbs use the same endings as uncontracted verbs. The contractions are made according to the charts in Sections 73, 74, and 84.

1. The future optative and infinitive are given in Unit 16.
2. Forms in square brackets are found in the Appendix only.

93. DEPONENT VERBS: MIDDLE DEPONENTS

Verbs which lack an active voice, and which show only middle or passive forms, are called **deponent verbs**. They will be distinguished by their Principal Parts.

Here is an example of a **middle deponent**, all of whose Principal Parts are in the *middle voice*:

δέχομαι, δέξομαι, ἐδεξάμην, ——, δέδεγμαι, ——, "receive; welcome"

Principal Parts I and V, which are middle/passive in form, are not used passively in this verb. Principal Part IV, which gives only active forms, and Principal Part VI, which is passive only, are lacking.

It is not known why Greek expresses certain actions in the middle voice only, i.e., with deponent verbs, nor is there any formula for determining which verb will be deponent. Rather, it will be clear from the Principal Parts, all of which must always be learned, which verbs are deponent.

Since middle deponent verbs lack an active voice in contrast to which the middle can have the force of "having something done" or "doing something for oneself," A MIDDLE DEPONENT IS TRANSLATED BY AN ENGLISH ACTIVE VERB WITH NO ADDITIONAL MIDDLE FORCE.

> τοὺς ξένους δεχόμεθα.
> We welcome the strangers.

> τοὺς ξένους ἐδεξάμεθα.
> We welcomed the strangers.

94. PASSIVE DEPONENTS

Some deponent verbs have, instead of an aorist middle, an *aorist passive* which, like all other forms of these verbs, is translated by an English *active*. These verbs are called **passive deponents**. Here is an example:

βούλομαι, βουλήσομαι, ——, ——, βεβούλημαι, **ἐβουλήθην**, "want"

> βιβλίον γράψαι βουλόμεθα.
> We want to write a book.

> βιβλίον γράψαι βουλησόμεθα.
> We shall want to write a book.

> βιβλίον γράψαι **ἐβουλήθημεν**.
> We **wanted** to write a book.

95. PARTIAL DEPONENTS

Some verbs lack an active voice in one or more tenses but not throughout the verbal system. Such verbs are called **partial deponents**. Their Principal Parts will show which tenses are deponent. Here is an example:

ἀκούω, **ἀκούσομαι**, ἤκουσα, ἀκήκοα, ——, ἠκούσθην, "hear"

Principal Part II of this verb is in the middle voice rather than the active voice, but this difference CANNOT be expressed in translation: ἀκούομεν (first person plural, present indicative *active*) means "we hear"; ἀκουσόμεθα (first person plural, future indicative *middle*) means "we shall hear." But ἠκούσθημεν (first person plural, aorist indicative *passive*) has the normal passive meaning "we were heard."

96. THE ADJECTIVE/PRONOUN αὐτός, αὐτή, αὐτό

The forms of the adjective/pronoun αὐτός, αὐτή, αὐτό are as follows:

	M	F	N
Nom. S	αὐτός	αὐτή	αὐτό
Gen.	αὐτοῦ	αὐτῆς	αὐτοῦ
Dat.	αὐτῷ	αὐτῇ	αὐτῷ
Acc.	αὐτόν	αὐτήν	αὐτό
Nom. P	αὐτοί	αὐταί	αὐτά
Gen.	αὐτῶν	αὐτῶν	αὐτῶν
Dat.	αὐτοῖς	αὐταῖς	αὐτοῖς
Acc.	αὐτούς	αὐτάς	αὐτά

The endings are the same as those of ἐκεῖνος, ἐκείνη, ἐκεῖνο.

According to its use in sentences, this word has three different meanings:

1. As an adjective in the *attributive position* it means "same":

> ὁ **αὐτὸς** ποιητής
> the **same** poet

> τοῖς **αὐτοῖς** ἔργοις
> by the **same** deeds

2. In the *predicate position*, or when standing alone in the nominative case, it functions as an **intensive** and means "-self." It agrees in gender, number, and case with the word to which it refers, whether that word is expressed in the sentence or only implied. In English translation, the intensive must also be given a *person* according to context.

(a) ὁ ποιητὴς **αὐτός**
   αὐτὸς ὁ ποιητής
   the poet **himself**

(b) οἱ ποιηταὶ **αὐτοί**
   αὐτοὶ οἱ ποιηταί
   the poets **themselves**

(c) ἐπαιδεύσαμεν **αὐτὸν** τὸν Ὅμηρον.
   We educated Homer **himself**.

(d) **αὐτὸς** ἔγραψε τὸ βιβλίον.
   He **himself** wrote the book.

(e) **αὐτὴ** ἔγραψε τὸ βιβλίον.
   She **herself** wrote the book.

(f) **αὐτὴ** ἔγραψα τὸ βιβλίον.
   I **myself** wrote the book.

In sentences (d), (e), and (f) above, the intensive agrees with the unexpressed subject of the verb and is translated accordingly.

3. Standing by itself as a *pronoun* in the genitive, dative, and accusative cases, αὐτός serves as the **personal pronoun** of the third person:

ἐπαιδεύσαμεν **αὐτόν**.
We educated **him**.

αὐτὴν πεπαιδεύκαμεν.
We have educated **her**.

αὐτοῖς αἶγας ἐπέμψαμεν.
We sent goats to **them**.
We sent **them** goats.

In the nominative case, where a third-person verb form indicates that the subject is "he, she, it" or "they," this personal pronoun *is not separately expressed*:

ἔγραψαν τὸ βιβλίον.
They wrote the book.

Remember that any form of αὐτός standing by itself in the nominative is an *intensive*:

αὐτοὶ ἔγραψαν τὸ βιβλίον.

They **themselves** wrote the book.

97. TEMPORAL CLAUSES

Temporal clauses are dependent clauses introduced by **temporal conjunctions** (e.g., "after," "while," "until") and indicating a *relationship in time* between the action of the dependent clause and that of the main or independent clause.

With respect to the action of the main clause, the action of the temporal clause can be *prior, simultaneous,* or *subsequent*.

Prior action:	**After he wrote the book,** he taught the citizens.
	(The writing *precedes* the teaching.)
Simultaneous action:	**When he was writing the book,** he taught the citizens.
	(Writing and teaching go on *simultaneously*.)
Subsequent action:	He was teaching the citizens **until he finished the book.**
	(The finishing *followed* the teaching.)

The action of the main clause can be *past* (as above), *present*, or *future*.

This Section will present temporal clauses which show *prior* and *simultaneous* action in various times.

Each type of temporal clause will be presented together with the type of main or independent clause with which it is associated.

1. PAST DEFINITE TEMPORAL CLAUSE

Verb of temporal clause:	past tense of the indicative (negative οὐ)
Verb of main clause:	past tense of the indicative (negative οὐ)
Temporal conjunctions:	
Prior action:	ἐπεί, ἐπειδή, "after, when" + past tense of the indicative (usually aorist)
Simultaneous action:	ὅτε, "when" + aorist or imperfect indicative

Here are examples of past definite temporal clauses with prior action and with simultaneous action:

Prior action: ἐπεὶ τὸ βιβλίον ἔγραψεν, τοὺς πολίτᾱς ἐδίδαξεν.
                After he wrote the book, he taught the citizens.

                ἐπεὶ εἰς τὴν νῆσον ἐπέμφθη, τοὺς πολίτας ἐδίδαξεν.
                When he was sent to the island, he taught the citizens.
                After he was sent to the island, he taught the citizens.

Simultaneous   ὅτε τὸ βιβλίον ἔγραφεν, τοὺς πολίτᾱς ἐδίδαξεν.
action: **When he was writing the book,** he taught the citizens.

                ὅτε τὸ βιβλίον ἔγραψεν, τοὺς πολίτᾱς ἐδίδαξεν.
                When he wrote the book, he taught the citizens.

Remember that the conjunctions *ἐπεί* and *ἐπειδή* can also mean "since, because" and introduce causal clauses (cf. Vocabulary Note to Unit 3).

The remaining three types of temporal clauses here presented correspond to the protases of three types of conditional sentences; the main clauses of sentences with these temporal clauses correspond to the apodoses of conditional sentences (cf. Section 41.7).

2. PRESENT GENERAL TEMPORAL CLAUSE

Verb of temporal clause (protasis):   present or aorist subjunctive
                                       (negative *μή*)

Verb of main clause (apodosis):   present indicative
                                       (negative *οὐ*)

Temporal conjunctions:

Prior action: **ἐπειδάν** (= *ἐπειδή* + *ἄν*)
                           "after, when, whenever"
                       + aorist subjunctive

Simultaneous action: **ὅταν** (= *ὅτε* + *ἄν*)
                           "when, whenever"
                       + present or aorist subjunctive

Here are examples of present general temporal clauses with prior action and with simultaneous action:

Prior action: **ἐπειδὰν εἰς τὴν νῆσον πεμφθῇ**, *τοὺς πολίτᾱς διδάσκει.*
                 Whenever he is sent to the island, he teaches the citizens.

*Simultaneous
action*:   **ὅταν βιβλίον γράφῃ**, *τοὺς πολίτᾱς διδάσκει.*
                 Whenever he is writing a book, he teaches the citizens.

                 ὅταν βιβλίον γράψῃ, *τοὺς πολίτᾱς διδάσκει.*
                 Whenever he writes a book, he teaches the citizens.

3. PAST GENERAL TEMPORAL CLAUSE

Verb of temporal clause (protasis):   present or aorist optative
                                       (negative *μή*)

Verb of main clause (apodosis):   imperfect indicative
                                       (negative *οὐ*)

Temporal conjunctions:

Prior action: **ἐπεί, ἐπειδή,** "after, when, whenever"
                        + aorist optative

Simultaneous action: **ὅτε,** "whenever"
                        + present or aorist optative

Here are examples of past general temporal clauses with prior action and with simultaneous action:

Prior action: **ἐπεὶ εἰς τὴν νῆσον πεμφθείη**, *τοὺς πολίτᾱς ἐδίδασκεν.*
                 Whenever he was sent to the island, he taught the citizens.
                 When he was sent to the island, he used to teach the citizens.

*Simultaneous
action*:   **ὅτε βιβλίον γράφοι**, *τοὺς πολίτᾱς ἐδίδασκεν.*
                 Whenever he was writing a book, he taught the citizens.
                 Whenever he was writing a book, he used to teach the citizens.

                 ὅτε βιβλίον γράψειεν, *τοὺς πολίτᾱς ἐδίδασκεν.*
                 Whenever he wrote a book, he taught the citizens.

4. FUTURE MORE VIVID TEMPORAL CLAUSE

Verb of temporal clause (protasis):   present or aorist subjunctive
(negative *μή*)

Verb of main clause (apodosis):   future indicative
(negative *οὐ*)

Temporal conjunctions:

    Prior action: **ἐπειδάν,** "after, when"
                  + aorist subjunctive

    Simultaneous action: **ὅταν,** "when"
                  + present or aorist subjunctive

Here are examples of future more vivid temporal clauses with prior action and with simultaneous action:

    Prior action: **ἐπειδὰν εἰς τὴν νῆσον πεμφθῇ,** *τοὺς πολίτας διδάξει.*
                    After he is sent to the island, he will teach the
                    citizens.

    Simultaneous   **ὅταν βιβλίον γράφῃ,** *τοὺς πολίτας διδάξει.*
      action: **When he is writing a book,** he will teach the citizens.

                  ὅταν βιβλίον γράψῃ, *τοὺς πολίτας διδάξει.*
                  When he writes a book, he will teach the citizens.

98. GENITIVE ABSOLUTE

The circumstantial participles already introduced agree with nouns or pronouns, expressed or implied, whose case is determined, separately, by their function in a sentence (cf. Section 70).

    θύων *ὁ ἱερεὺς ὑπὸ τοῦ δήμου τῑμᾶται.*
    Sacrificing, the priest is honored by the people.

    λυθέντες *ὅμως τοῖς θεοῖς οὐ θύομεν.*
    Released, nevertheless we do not sacrifice to the gods.
    Although released, nevertheless we do not sacrifice to the gods.

In the first example the participle agrees with the subject of the sentence, *ὁ ἱερεύς*. In the second example the participle agrees with the subject of the verb *θύομεν*, which is not separately expressed.

To describe a circumstance involving a person or thing *not otherwise connected with the rest of the sentence,* a phrase consisting of a noun or pronoun (and any modifiers) plus a participle (and any objects) can be put in the genitive case.

This usage is called the **genitive absolute.** The term "absolute" indicates that the noun or pronoun in the genitive absolute has no direct grammatical relationship to any other word in the sentence. Objects of the participle retain their usual case.

θύοντος τοῦ ἱερέως αἶγα, *Δημοσθένης ὑπὸ τοῦ δήμου τῑμᾶται.*
The priest sacrificing a goat, Demosthenes is honored by the people.

λυθέντων τῶν φίλων, *ὅμως τοῖς θεοῖς οὐ θύομεν.*
Our friends released, we nevertheless do not sacrifice to the gods.

In these examples the noun in the genitive case, modified by a participle, is separate from the rest of the sentence: the genitive absolute states a circumstance which has no *grammatical* connection with the rest of the sentence. The closest English equivalent to a genitive absolute is, as in the examples above, a nominative absolute.

Like other circumstantial participles, the genitive absolute can have a *temporal, concessive,* or *causal* relation to the main verb. Adverbs or other words accompanying either the participle or the main verb can make this relationship clearer.

Genitives absolute can often be expressed by clauses in English: e.g., "while the priest was sacrificing. . . "; "although our friends were released . . . ."

τῆς πόλεως σωθείσης, *οἱ ἱερεῖς ἔθυσαν.*
The city saved, the priests sacrificed.
When the city was saved, the priests sacrificed. (*temporal*)
Although the city was saved, the priests sacrificed. (*concessive*)
Because the city was saved, the priests sacrificed. (*causal*)

Context will help to determine meaning.

The genitive absolute can also stand in place of the protasis of a conditional sentence. The negative is *μή;* that of the other genitives absolute is *οὐ.* The two sentences below are equivalent in meaning.

τῆς πόλεως μὴ σωθείσης, *οὐ θύσομεν.*
The city not saved, we shall not sacrifice.

ἐὰν ἡ πόλις μὴ σωθῇ, *οὐ θύσομεν.*
If the city is not saved, we shall not sacrifice.

VOCABULARY

ἀεί (adv.)	always
αἴτιος, αἰτία, αἴτιον	responsible (for), guilty (of) (+ gen.)
αἰτία, αἰτίας, ἡ	responsibility, guilt; cause
ἀκούω, ἀκούσομαι, ἤκουσα, ἀκήκοα, ——, ἠκούσθην	hear (+ acc. of thing heard, gen. of person heard); be spoken of
αὐτός, αὐτή, αὐτό	(1) (adj. in attributive position) same
	(2) (in predicate position or alone in nom.) -self, -selves
	(3) (pronoun in gen., dat., acc.) him, her, it, them
ἄφρων, ἄφρον	senseless, foolish
βάλλω, βαλῶ, ἔβαλον, βέβληκα, βέβλημαι, ἐβλήθην	throw; hit (with thrown object)
βούλομαι, βουλήσομαι, ——, ——, βεβούλημαι, ἐβουλήθην	want
γυνή, γυναικός, ἡ (voc. γύναι)	woman; wife
δέχομαι, δέξομαι, ἐδεξάμην, ——, δέδεγμαι, ——	receive; welcome
ἀποδέχομαι	receive favorably, accept
εἰσ- (prefix)	into, in, on
ἐνταῦθα (adv.)	here, there; then
ἐπειδάν (conj.)	after, when, whenever
ἑπτά (indeclinable numeral)	seven
ἔρως, ἔρωτος, ὁ (voc. ἔρως)	love
καιρός, καιροῦ, ὁ	right moment
κάλλος, κάλλους, τό	beauty
κῆρυξ, κήρῡκος, ὁ (dat. pl. κήρυξι[ν])	herald
λαμβάνω, λήψομαι, ἔλαβον, εἴληφα, εἴλημμαι, ἐλήφθην	take
ὀκτώ (indeclinable numeral)	eight

ὅτε (conj.)	when, whenever
ὅταν (conj.)	when, whenever
πάσχω, πείσομαι, ἔπαθον, πέπονθα, ——, ——	suffer, have done to one
πῶς (adv.)	how?
πως (enclitic adv.)	in any way, in some way
τότε (adv.)	then
τύχη, τύχης, ἡ	fortune, chance
εὐτυχής, εὐτυχές	lucky
ὕβρις, ὕβρεως, ἡ	insolence
φόνος, φόνου, ὁ	murder, killing
φονεύς, φονέως, ὁ	murderer, killer

VOCABULARY NOTES

The verb ἀκούω, ἀκούσομαι, ἤκουσα, ἀκήκοα, ——, ἠκούσθην, "hear; be spoken of," takes, in the sense "hear," an accusative of the thing heard and/or a genitive of the person heard:

ταῦτ᾽ ἀκούομεν.	We hear these things.
Σωκράτους ἀκούομεν.	We hear Sokrates.
ταῦτα Σωκράτους ἀκούομεν.	We hear these things from Sokrates.

This verb is also used, in the active voice, in the sense "be spoken of"; it describes someone's reputation and can be accompanied by a genitive of personal agent:

κακῶς ἀκούομεν.	We are spoken badly of. (We have a bad reputation.)
κακῶς ἀκούομεν ὑπὸ πάντων.	We are spoken badly of by all. All speak badly of us.

The verb βάλλω, βαλῶ, ἔβαλον, βέβληκα, βέβλημαι, ἐβλήθην means either "throw" or "hit (with a thrown object)" and takes a direct object either of the thing thrown or of the person or thing hit:

λίθους ἐβάλομεν.	We threw stones.
τοὺς πολεμίους ἐβάλομεν.	We hit the enemy.
τοὺς πολεμίους λίθοις ἐβάλομεν.	We hit the enemy with stones.

The form βάλλω comes from *βάλιω. Principal Parts II and III show more clearly the root, βαλ-; the double lambda appears only in the present tense stem. Note the contracted future: βαλῶ < βαλέω < *βαλέσω. Compare ἀγγέλλω, ἀγγελῶ.

The verb βούλομαι, βουλήσομαι, ——, ——, βεβούλημαι, ἐβουλήθην, "want," expressed originally a positive desire, while ἐθέλω, "wish, be willing," expressed a lack of objection. But the meanings of the two verbs came to overlap. Both can take an object infinitive.

Although it does not have a monosyllabic stem, γυνή, γυναικός, ἡ, "woman; wife," is accented as if it had one: the accent is on the penult in the accusative singular (γυναῖκα) and in the plural nominative/vocative (γυναῖκες) and accusative (γυναῖκας); in the genitive and dative singular and plural the accent is on the ultima, e.g., γυναικῶν. The vocative singular is γύναι (the stem γυναικ- without the final kappa).

The adverb ἐνταῦθα can have either a spatial or a temporal meaning.

Do not confuse the noun κάλλος, κάλλους, τό, "beauty," with the adjective καλός, καλή, καλόν.

Note that the dative plural of κῆρυξ, κήρυκος, ὁ, "herald," is κήρυξι(ν) with a short upsilon.

In the verb λαμβάνω, λήψομαι, ἔλαβον, εἴληφα, εἴλημμαι, ἐλήφθην, "take," note that the root is λαβ-. The present is formed by inserting a nasal into this root (a **nasal infix**) and adding a suffix -αν-: λαμβάνω; both nasal infix and suffix appear only in the present tense stem. The **long-vowel grade** of the root, ληβ-, appears in the future, the perfect active and middle, and in the aorist passive. The second aorist uses the **short-vowel grade** of the root. The accent on the second person singular, aorist imperative active of this verb is fixed on the ultima: λαβέ (contrast λίπε). When this form is compounded, however, the accent is recessive: ἀπόλαβε. The plural is regular: λάβετε. The εἰ- of Principal Parts IV and V is part of the perfect tense stem; it is not augmented in the pluperfect: εἰλήφη, εἰλήφης, εἰλήφει(ν), etc. IN MOST VERBS WHEN PRINCIPAL PART IV OR V BEGINS WITH ἐ OR εἰ-, THE PLUPERFECT IS UNAUGMENTED. Note also the aspirated perfect. From the physical meaning "take, grab," developed a mental one; cf. "He did not grasp my meaning."

The verb πάσχω, πείσομαι, ἔπαθον, πέπονθα, ——, ——, "suffer, have (something) done to one," is related to the noun πάθος, πάθους, τό. Like the noun, the verb has both a neutral meaning ("experience, have [something] done to one") and a more common negative meaning ("suffer"). The root of the word appears in the following grades: e-grade πενθ-, o-grade πονθ-, and zero-grade παθ- < *πνθ-. The present is formed from the zero-grade of the root + the

inchoative suffix (indicating the coming into a state) -σκω: *πνθσκω > *πάθσκω > πάσχω. The future is built on the e-grade of the root: *πένθσομαι > πείσομαι, with the spurious diphthong as a result of compensatory lengthening. Note that πείσομαι is also the future middle of πείθω. For Principal Part III, compare the second aorists ἔβαλον, ἔλαβον. The perfect uses the o-grade of the root; cf. πέπομφα, κέκλοφα, λέλοιπα. The verb πάσχω can take a genitive of personal agent: κακὰ πάσχει ὑπὸ πάντων, "He suffers evil things at the hands of all." Cf. ἀκούω.

Distinguish carefully between the interrogative adverb πῶς, "how?" and the indefinite enclitic adverb πως, "in any way, in some way."

The noun φονεύς, φονέως, ὁ, "murderer, killer," is an **agent noun** formed with the suffix -ευς. Cf. φόνος, φόνου, ὁ, "murder."

COGNATES AND DERIVATIVES

αἴτιος	aetiological (explaining the **cause** of something)
ἀκούω	acoustics
αὐτός	autonomous (**self**-governing)
βάλλω	ballistics
γυνή	*queen*; *banshee*; gynecology
ἑπτά	*seven*; heptagon
ἔρως	erotic
κάλλος	calligraphy
λαμβάνω	syllable (letters one **takes** together)
ὀκτώ	*eight*; octagon
πάσχω	pathetic

DRILLS

I.   Translate the following; change the aspect; change the number.

1. πέμψατε τὰ βιβλία.
2. μὴ ἄρχεσθε ὑπὸ τῶν κακῶν.
3. μὴ παυθῆτε ὑπὸ τῶν πολεμίων.
4. ποιείτω τόδε.
5. διδάχθητι ὑπὸ τῶν καλῶν.
6. πεμψάτω ὁ πατὴρ τὰ χρήματα.
7. παῦε τὰς αἰσχράς.
8. παύου, αἰσχρέ.
9. λιποῦ χρῦσὸν ἐν τῇ οἰκίᾳ.
10. διδάξασθε τοὺς ξένους.
11. παῦσαι, ὦ νεᾱνίᾱ.
12. τάττεσθε νῦν γε ὑπὲρ τῆς πόλεως.
13. πεμψάντων τὰ βιβλία.
14. τῑμᾶτε τοὺς νῑκήσαντας.
15. λίπετε ταῦτα.
16. μὴ ἀγγείλῃς ταῦτα.
17. κάλεσον τὸν αἶγα.
18. ἀξιούτω τοῦτον τοῦ ἄθλου.
19. τύθητι, ὦ αἴξ.

II.   Translate the following phrases and sentences.

1. αὐτὸς ὁ Δημοσθένης
2. ὁ Δημοσθένης αὐτός
3. τῷ αὐτῷ βασιλεῖ
4. βασιλεῦσι τοῖς αὐτοῖς
5. οἱ πατέρες αὐτοί
6. αὐτοὶ οἱ πατέρες
7. αὐταὶ αἱ θυγατέρες
8. αἱ θυγατέρες αἱ αὐταί
9. αὐτὸς παιδεύω τοὺς ἀγαθούς.
10. αὐτὸς παιδεύω αὐτούς.

11. αὐταὶ παιδεύετε τοὺς αὐτοὺς πολίτᾱς.

12. τοῖς ἔργοις τοῖς αὐτοῖς ἐπείσθη αὐτὸς ὁ Σωκράτης.

13. τοῖς αὐτοῖς λόγοις αὐτοὶ ἐπαιδεύσατ᾽ αὐτούς.

14. αὐτοῖς τοῖς βασιλεῦσιν ἐπέμψαμεν αὐτάς.

15. ἐπαιδεύθησαν αὐτοὶ ὑπὸ τοῦ αὐτοῦ διδασκάλου.

16. Δημοσθένης αὐτὸς ἐτῑμᾶτο ὑπ᾽ αὐτῶν.

17. ἐτῑμῶμεν αὐτὸν ὅπως τῑμηθεῖμεν αὐτοί.

18. ἄνδρες οἱ αὐτοὶ καὶ νῑκήσουσιν αὐτοὺς καὶ σώσουσιν αὐτὴν τὴν πόλιν.

III. (a) *Identify the temporal clauses in the following sentences; translate.*

   (b) *Where possible, change the sentence to the equivalent conditional sentence.*

   (c) *Where possible, express the temporal clause by a participle.*

   1. ἐπεὶ τὴν πόλιν ἔσωσεν, ἐπέμφθη εἰς τὴν νῆσον.

   2. ἐπειδὰν τὴν πόλιν σώσῃ, εἰς τὴν νῆσον πεμφθήσεται.

   3. ὅταν τοῖς κακοῖς δουλεύῃς, οὐ πράττεις καλῶς.

   4. ὅτε τοῖς κακοῖς ἐδούλευες, οὐκ ἔπρᾱττες καλῶς.

   5. ὅταν τοῖς κακοῖς δουλεύῃς, οὐ πράξεις καλῶς.

   6. ὅτε τοῖς κακοῖς δουλεύοις, οὐκ ἔπρᾱττες καλῶς.

   7. ἐπειδὴ τὰς αἶγας τοῖς θεοῖς οὐκ ἔθῡσας, οὐκ ἐτῑμῶ.

   8. ὅταν αἶγας τοῖς θεοῖς μὴ θύῃς, οὐ τῑμᾷ.

   9. ἐπειδὰν αἶγας τοῖς θεοῖς μὴ θύσῃς, οὐ τῑμηθήσει.

   10. ὅτε αἶγα τῇ θεῷ μὴ θύοις, οὐκ ἐτῑμῶ.

IV. *Translate. Replace all genitives absolute with dependent clauses.*

   1. τοὺς φίλους λύσᾱς, ἔθῡσε τοῖς θεοῖς.

   2. τούτου τοὺς φίλους λύσαντος, ὁ ἱερεὺς τοῖς θεοῖς ἔθῡσεν.

   3. τῶν φίλων λυθέντων, ἔθῡσε τοῖς θεοῖς.

   4. τῶν πολεμίων τοὺς στρατιώτᾱς νῑκησάντων, παυσώμεθα.

   5. νῑκώντων τῶν πολεμίων, τὸν αὐτὸν ἄγγελον ἐπέμψαμεν.

   6. νῑκωμένων τῶν Ἀθηναίων, ὁ βαρβάρων βασιλεὺς τὴν μάχην παῦσαι οὐκ ἤθελεν.

   7. τοῦ στρατιώτου τὰ ὅπλα μὴ ἀπολιπόντος, οὐ νῑκηθησόμεθα.

   8. τοῦ στρατιώτου τὰ ὅπλα οὐκ ἀπολιπόντος, οὐκ ἐνῑκήθημεν.

EXERCISES

1. τοῦ αὐτοῦ γε ῥήτορος ἐκ τῆς νήσου ἥκοντος αὐτοὶ ἠκούσαμεν τάδε·
   Ἀκούετε, ὦ πολῖται. ἐπειδὰν οἱ ταύτης τῆς γυναικὸς φονεῖς εἰς
   ἀγορὰν ἥκωσι τὰ χρήματα λαβόντες, φόνου δίκην γράψομαί πως
   αὐτοὺς πάντας.

2. ὅτε φίλων χάριν αἰσχρὰ ποιοῖτε, ὦ θυγατέρες, ὑπὸ τῶν τε σωφρόνων
   καὶ τῶν δικαίων πάντων οὐκ ἐτιμᾶσθε κακῶς ἀκούουσαι. δίκαια
   οὖν πράττουσαι ἀξιώθητε τīμῆς.

3. οὔ τοι διὰ τὴν πρᾱγμάτων ἐμπειρίᾱν ἀλλ' ἀγαθῇ πως τύχῃ πράττει
   ἃ ἂν πράττῃ ἐκεῖνος ὁ στρατηγὸς ὁ εὐτυχής. τῑμώντων οὖν αὐτὸν
   οἱ πολῖται.

4. ὅταν οἱ ποιηταὶ βιβλία γράφωσι περὶ κακῶν τε καὶ ἀφρόνων γυναικῶν
   οἶνον κλεπτουσῶν καὶ αἰσχρὰ ποιουσῶν, οὐ βούλονται οἵ γε νεᾱνίαι
   τοὺς νόμους τοὺς τῆς πόλεως φυλάττειν. ἐκείνους δὴ μὴ ἀξιώσητε
   ἄθλων ἐν τοῖς ἀγῶσιν.

5. τότε μὲν κατά γε τοὺς νόμους ἤρχετέ πως τοῦ δήμου ἀποδεχόμενοι τοὺς
   τῶν δικαίων λόγους, νῦν δὲ μετὰ τὸν τούτου τοῦ ῥήτορος φόνον
   τελευτήσετε τὸν βίον ὀκτὼ ἡμερῶν διὰ τὴν ὕβριν.

6. τῆς αὐτῆς νυκτὸς αὐτὸς ὁ Δημοσθένης οἷα ἐκ κινδύνων σωθεὶς κήρῡκα
   τῇ γε μητρὶ πέμψαι ἐβουλήθη κελεύσοντα αὐτὴν οἶνόν τε καὶ
   ζῷα λαβοῦσαν καὶ τοὺς φίλους ἐκκαλοῦσαν θεοῖς τοῖς σωτῆρσι
   θῦσαι. ταῦτ' οὖν τοῦ κήρῡκος ἀγγείλαντος, ἔθῡσεν ἡ μήτηρ.

7. οὔτε ἀγαθὸς ψῡχῇ οὔτε σώφρων ὃς ἂν ποτ' ἔρωτί τε καὶ σώματος
   κάλλει δουλεύων βούληται τὰ τῆς πόλεως πράττειν. πῶς γὰρ ἂν
   οὗτος ἄρχοι ἢ τῶν ἄλλων πολῑτῶν ἢ καὶ αὐτῆς τῆς οἰκίας; τούτου
   δὴ τῆς πόλεως ἄρχοντος, νῑκηθησόμεθα.

8. ὦ γύναι, ὅταν ὁ βασιλεὺς θυσίᾱν ἀγάγῃ ὑπὲρ τοῦ Ἀθηναίων δήμου κακὰ
   πάσχοντος, λίθους λαβοῦσα μὴ βάλλε τούς γε ἱερέᾱς. ἐὰν γὰρ τοῦτο
   ποιήσῃς, κακὰ πείσει.

9. ὅτε εἰς μάχην ταξαίμεθα τὴν πόλιν φυλάξοντες, τάς τε γυναῖκας καὶ
   τὰς θυγατέρας ἐν τῇ πόλει μετὰ τῶν γερόντων ἐλείπομεν.

10. ὦ ὁπλῖτα, εἴθε μὴ ἀποβάλοις τὰ ὅπλα. ἅμα γὰρ ταῦτα ἀποβαλὼν
οὔτ᾽ ἄν ποτ᾽ ἐν μάχῃ σωθείης οὔτε καλῶς ἀκούσει ποτέ. μένων
οὖν ἐνταῦθα δόξης ἀξιώθητι.

11. ἐπεί γε ταῦτ᾽ ἀπήγγειλε τοῖς στρατιώταις ὁ κῆρυξ ἐκ τῆς χώρᾱς
ἥκων, οἱ ὁπλῖται οἱ εὐγενεῖς τοὺς τῶν βαρβάρων ἵππους βλάψαι
ἐβουλήθησαν.

12. αἴτιός τοι τῆς τῶν Ἑλλήνων νίκης ὁ τῶν βαρβάρων ἡγεμών. οὐ γὰρ δὴ
ἧκεν ἐν καιρῷ παρὰ τοὺς ἐν τῷ πεδίῳ καίπερ τὴν πόλιν λιπὼν
ἅμα τῇ ἡμέρᾳ ὥστε ὁ στρατὸς σύμπᾱς ἐξενῑκήθη. τοῦ δὲ στρατοῦ
νῑκηθέντος, παύσατε τὸν πόλεμον.

13. τόνδε γε τὸν γέροντα μὴ λιπέτω ἐνταῦθα καίπερ ἐθέλοντα μένειν.
τοῦδε γάρ τοι μένοντος ἐν τῇ πόλει, ὅπλοις τε καὶ λίθοις οὐ
βουλήσονται πάντες ἐκείνους τοὺς πολεμίους τοὺς ἄφρονας
βαλεῖν.

14. εἰς τὴν οἰκίᾱν δέδεξαι, ὦ Σώκρατες, καὶ φίλους καὶ ἐχθροὺς ὡς αὐτὸς
παιδεύσων αὐτοὺς περὶ αὐτῆς τῆς ἀρετῆς. ἀλλὰ παῦσαι.

15. μετά γε τὸν ὑπὲρ ταύτης τῆς πόλεως ἀγῶνα τὸ νίκης ἆθλον, χρῡσοῦ
στέφανον, λιπών πως ἐν τῷ πεδίῳ ἥκεις ἐνταῦθα βουλόμενος
τῑμηθῆναι.

16. τοῖς γε σώφροσιν οὗτοι τὸ σώματος κάλλος ἀγαθόν, ἀλλ᾽ οἱ τρόποι οἱ
αὐτῆς τῆς ψῡχῆς. ὅταν γὰρ τὸ σῶμα ὑπ᾽ ἀδίκων ἀνδρῶν βλαβὲν
κακὰ πάσχῃ, σῴζεταί πως ὑπὸ θεῶν ἡ τοῦ δικαίου ψῡχή. καὶ τῆς
ψῡχῆς σῳζομένης, ὁ πᾶς ἄνθρωπος σῴζεται.

17. πέντε ἡμερῶν ἀκούσεσθε αὐτοὶ τῶν αὐτῶν κηρύκων τάδε· ὅτε τὴν νῆσον
ἐλίπομεν, τῶν πολεμίων νῑκηθέντων ἐχόρευον οἱ ὀκτὼ χορευταί.

18. φύλαξ τῶν τε νόμων καὶ τῆς δημοκρατίᾱς ὁ σὺν θεοῖς τρόπῳ δικαίῳ
ἄρχων τοῦ δήμου.

19. πότε αὐταὶ κακὰ πάσχουσαι ἐκβαλεῖτέ πως ἐκ πόλεως τούσδε τοὺς
ἄφρονας; ἐκβάλετ᾽ αὐτούς.

20. τῶν μὲν ἀγαθῶν καὶ δικαίων καὶ ταύτης τῆς πόλεως σωτήρων
ἀκούσατε, ὦ ἄνδρες, τἀληθῆ.[1] ἐκείνων δὲ τῶν ῥητόρων τῶν
ἀφρόνων καὶ ἀδίκων καὶ τούτου τοῦ πολέμου αἰτίων ἀκούσεσθε
λόγους οὐ καλούς.

21. ἄγε δὴ ἄκουσον, ὦ γέρον· εἰσπεμφθέντων τῶν ἀγγέλων εἰς πόλιν ὑπὸ
βασιλέως, ἀκούσονταί τοι πάντες οἱ πολῖται περὶ τῆς μάχης.

---

1. τἀληθῆ = τὰ ἀληθῆ (For this **crasis** see the Appendix, p. 614).

22. τῷ μὲν γένει ἀγαθοὶ οὗτοι, τοῖς δὲ τρόποις κακοί. κακῶς γάρ τοι
τοῖς ῥήτορσι πεπαιδευμένοι κακὰ πράττουσι καὶ οἱ εὐγενεῖς.
ταῦτα δηλούτω ποθ' ὁ Σωκράτης ὁ σώφρων.

23. οὐχ ὕβρις τόδε, τὸ τόν τε πατέρα καὶ αὐτὴν τὴν μητέρα ἀεὶ κακῶς
ποιεῖν καὶ χρυσὸν καὶ ἀργύριον καὶ οἶνον ἐκ τῆς οἰκίας
ἐκκλέπτειν καὶ θεοῖς μήτε θύειν μήτε χορεύειν;

24. οἷα τὸν δῆμον πείσας, διὰ ταύτην τὴν αἰτίαν, ὦ ἄνερ, ἐν πόλει
μεῖνον.

25. καλοῦ ἀξιοῦντες τὴν αἰσχρὰν κακοῦ ἂν ἀξιοῖμεν τὴν σώφρονα, ἢ
οὔ;

26. καὶ αἰσχρόν τοι καὶ ἄφρον τὸ τοὺς γ' ἐχθροὺς εἰς τὴν οἰκίαν
εἰσδεξάμενον τοὺς φίλους ἀποπέμψαι.

II. 1. You yourselves used to hear Demosthenes whenever he began a speech. (*Express the temporal clause in two ways.*)

2. After the poet is honored by the noble young men, let the citizens sacrifice to all the muses. (*Express the temporal clause in two ways.*)

3. Whenever *Demosthenes'* father persuaded the people to guard against the enemy, he sacrificed to the gods of the city. Announce this to the citizens, young man. (*Express the temporal clause in two ways.*)

4. How are we to guard against evil speakers and foolish poets who somehow persuade the young men to wrong their mothers and fathers? (*Express the relative clause in two ways.*)

5. I myself, you know, shall remain there in order that I may welcome the king himself in the same manner. (*Express the purpose in two ways.*)

6. If we ourselves should ever hit him with the same stones, he would not want (*use βούλομαι*) to leave the gold in the market place.

READINGS

A. Agathon, Fragment 6 (*TrGF* 39ғ6)

Agathon was a fifth-century B.C. tragic poet.

τέχνη τύχην ἔστερξε¹ καὶ τύχη τέχνην.

Chairemon, Fragment 19 (*TrGF* 71ғ19)

Chairemon was a fourth-century B.C. tragic poet.

ἅπαντα νῖκᾷ καὶ μεταστρέφει τύχη.

μεταστρέφω, μεταστρέψω, μετέστρεψα, ——, μετέστραμμαι, μετεστρέφθην/
  μετεστράφην   turn, turn around, change

στέργω, στέρξω, ἔστερξα, ἔστοργα, ἔστεργμαι, ἐστέρχθην   love; be content
  with, acquiesce in

τύχη, τύχης, ἡ   fortune, chance

B. Plato, *Gorgias* 469b12–c3

The young rhetorician Polos asks Sokrates a question about morality.

ΠΩΛΟΣ. σὺ ἄρα βούλοιο ἂν ἀδικεῖσθαι μᾶλλον ἢ ἀδικεῖν;

ΣΩΚΡΑΤΗΣ. βουλοίμην μὲν ἂν ἔγωγε οὐδέτερα· εἰ δ᾽ ἀναγκαῖον εἴη
      ἀδικεῖν ἢ ἀδικεῖσθαι, ἑλοίμην ἂν μᾶλλον ἀδικεῖσθαι ἢ
      ἀδικεῖν.

αἱρέω, αἱρήσω, εἷλον (*unaugmented aor. act. and mid. tense stem* ἑλ-),
    ᾕρηκα, ᾕρημαι, ᾑρέθην   take, capture; (*mid.*) choose

ἀναγκαῖος, ἀναγκαίᾱ, ἀναγκαῖον   necessary

ἄρα (*postpositive particle*)   then, therefore

βούλομαι, βουλήσομαι, ——, ——, βεβούλημαι, ἐβουλήθην want

ἔγωγε (*emphatic form of nom. sing. of first person pronoun*) *I*

εἴη (*third pers. sing., pres. opt. act. of the verb "to be"*) should be

ἤ (*conj.*)   than

μᾶλλον (*adv.*)   more, rather

οὐδέτερος, οὐδετέρᾱ, οὐδέτερον   neither

Πῶλος, Πώλου, ὁ   Polos, a rhetorician from Akragas, in Sicily
    (His name literally means "colt.")

σύ (*nom. sing. of the second person pronoun*)   you

1. This is a **gnomic aorist** expressing a timeless, general truth. See the Appendix, p. 733.

C. Aristotle, *Poetics* 1452a29–34, 1452a36–b1

The best kind of recognition in tragedy.

  ἀναγνώρισις δέ, ὥσπερ καὶ τοὔνομα σημαίνει, ἐξ
  ἀγνοίας εἰς γνῶσιν μεταβολὴ ἢ εἰς φιλίαν ἢ εἰς
  ἔχθραν τῶν πρὸς εὐτυχίαν ἢ δυστυχίαν ὡρισμένων·
  καλλίστη δὲ ἀναγνώρισις, ὅταν ἅμα περιπέτειαι
5 γίνωνται, οἷον ἔχει ἡ ἐν τῷ Οἰδίποδι. εἰσὶν
  μὲν οὖν καὶ ἄλλαι ἀναγνωρίσεις· . . . .

ἀγνοίᾱ, ἀγνοίᾱς, ἡ   ignorance
ἅμα (*adv.*)   at the same time
ἀναγνώρισις, ἀναγνωρίσεως, ἡ   recognition
γίγνομαι/γίνομαι, γενήσομαι, ἐγενόμην, γέγονα, γεγένημαι, ——   be born;
    become; happen
γνῶσις, γνώσεως, ἡ   knowledge
δυστυχίᾱ, δυστυχίᾱς, ἡ   bad fortune
εἰσίν (*third pers. pl., pres. indic. act. of the verb "to be"*)   are
εὐτυχίᾱ, εὐτυχίᾱς, ἡ   good fortune
ἔχθρᾱ, ἔχθρᾱς, ἡ   enmity
ἔχω, ἔξω/σχήσω, ἔσχον, ἔσχηκα, -έσχημαι, ——   have, hold; be able; (*mid.*)
    cling to, be next to (+ *gen.*)
κάλλιστος, καλλίστη, κάλλιστον   best, most beautiful
μεταβολή, μεταβολῆς, ἡ   change
Οἰδίπους, Οἰδίποδος, ὁ   Oidipous, Oedipus
οἷος, οἵᾱ, οἷον   such as, of the sort which
ὄνομα, ὀνόματος, τό   name
ὁρίζω, ὁριῶ, ὥρισα, ὥρικα, ὥρισμαι, ὡρίσθην   divide, mark off, determine,
    define
ὅταν (*conj.*)   when, whenever
περιπέτεια, περιπετείᾱς, ἡ   reversal, sudden change
πρός (*prep.*) (+ *gen.*) in the eyes of, in the name of; (+ *dat.*)   near, in
    addition to; (+ *acc.*) toward
σημαίνω, σημανῶ, ἐσήμηνα, ——, σεσήμασμαι, ἐσημάνθην   show, point out;
    signify, indicate
τοὔνομα = τὸ ὄνομα (*For this* **crasis**, *see the Appendix, p. 614.*)
ὥσπερ (*conj.*)   just as

ἀλλ' ἡ μάλιστα τοῦ μύθου καὶ ἡ μάλιστα τῆς πράξεως

ἡ εἰρημένη ἐστίν· ἡ γὰρ τοιαύτη ἀναγνώρισις καὶ

περιπέτεια ἢ ἔλεον ἕξει ἢ φόβον, οἵων πράξεων

10 ἡ τραγῳδία μίμησις. . . .

ἀναγνώρισις, ἀναγνωρίσεως, ἡ   recognition

εἰρημένη   see λέγω

ἔλεος, ἐλέου, ὁ   pity

ἐστίν   (third pers. sing., pres. indic. act. of the verb "to be")   is

ἔχω, ἕξω/σχήσω, ἔσχον, ἔσχηκα, -ἔσχημαι, —— have, hold; be able; (mid.)
   cling to, be next to (+ gen.)

λέγω, ἐρῶ/λέξω, εἶπον/ἔλεξα, εἴρηκα, εἴρημαι/λέλεγμαι, ἐλέχθην/ἐρρήθην
   say, speak

μάλιστα   (adv.)   most

μίμησις, μῑμήσεως, ἡ   imitation

μῦθος, μύθου, ὁ   word, speech; story, plot

οἷος, οἵα, οἷον   such as, of the sort which

περιπέτεια, περιπετείᾱς, ἡ   reversal, sudden change

πρᾱξις, πρᾱξεως, ἡ   action, act, business; result

τοιοῦτος, τοιαύτη, τοιοῦτο/τοιοῦτον   such (as this)

τραγῳδίᾱ, τραγῳδίᾱς, ἡ   tragedy

D.   Euripides, Fragment 32 Nauck

   κακῆς ἀπ' ἀρχῆς γίγνεται τέλος κακόν.

γίγνομαι, γενήσομαι, ἐγενόμην, γέγονα, γεγένημαι, —— be born; become;
   happen

E. A drinking-song (called a σκόλιον, σκολίου, τό)

   (D. L. Page, *Lyrica Graeca Selecta* 447)

   ὑγιαίνειν μὲν ἄριστον ἀνδρὶ θνητῷ,
   δεύτερον δὲ φυὴν¹ ἀγαθὸν γενέσθαι,
   τὸ τρίτον δὲ πλουτεῖν ἀδόλως,
   καὶ τὸ τέταρτον ἡβᾶν μετὰ τῶν φίλων.

ἀδόλως (*adv.*)   guilelessly, without guile
ἄριστος, ἀρίστη, ἄριστον   best
γίγνομαι, γενήσομαι, ἐγενόμην, γέγονα, γεγένημαι, ——
      be born; happen; become
δεύτερος, δευτέρᾱ, δεύτερον   second
ἡβάω, ἡβήσω, ἥβησα, ἥβηκα, ——, ——   be young
θνητός, θνητή, θνητόν   mortal
πλουτέω, πλουτήσω, ἐπλούτησα, πεπλούτηκα, ——, ——   be rich
τέταρτος, τετάρτη, τέταρτον   fourth
τρίτος, τρίτη, τρίτον   third
φυή, φυῆς, ἡ   growth, inherited qualities
ὑγιαίνω, ὑγιανῶ, ὑγίᾱνα, ——, ——, ——   be healthy

1. An **accusative of respect** showing the respect in which a statement is true. See the
Appendix, p. 705.

UNIT
12

99. -μι VERBS

Instead of having the ending -ω, Principal Part I of a Greek verb can have the ending -μι. Such verbs are called -**μι verbs**; and in the moods and tenses formed from Principal Parts I, III, and (sometimes) IV, -μι verbs differ in conjugation from the -ω verbs seen thus far. The moods and tenses of the -μι verbs have exactly the same *functions* as the moods and tenses of the -ω verbs; they are simply *formed* in a different way.

Three of the most common -μι verbs are:

(a) **δίδωμι**, δώσω, **ἔδωκα**, δέδωκα, δέδομαι, ἐδόθην, "give"

(b) **τίθημι**, θήσω, **ἔθηκα**, τέθηκα, τέθειμαι, ἐτέθην, "put"

(c) **ἵστημι**, στήσω, ἔστησα (*transitive*) *or* **ἔστην** (*intransitive*),
   ἕστηκα (*intransitive*), ἕσταμαι, ἐστάθην, "make stand;
   (*intransitive and middle*) stand"

The principal parts in boldface are those for which new patterns of conjugation must be learned. The present system of -μι verbs, except for participles, is presented in this Unit: the present indicative, subjunctive, optative, imperative and infinitive, and the imperfect indicative, in all three voices. The conjugation of the other emphasized forms is given in Unit 13. The principal parts not emphasized are used to form moods and tenses in *exactly the same way* as the corresponding principal parts of the -ω verbs.

The participles of the -μι verbs are presented in Unit 14.

337

100. PRESENT SYSTEM OF -μι VERBS

In the present system, -μι verbs differ from -ω verbs in the endings they use and in having both a *long-vowel* and a *short-vowel grade* of the present tense stem. Thus, to conjugate these verbs properly, one must learn what endings to put on what grade of the stem. The two grades of the present tense stem of the three verbs given above are:

VERB	LONG-VOWEL GRADE PRESENT TENSE STEM	SHORT-VOWEL GRADE PRESENT TENSE STEM
δίδωμι	διδω-	διδο-
τίθημι	τιθη-	τιθε-
ἵστημι	ἱστη-	ἱστα-

Note that -η- is the long vowel grade of both -ε- and -α-; cf. ἐθέλω/ἤθελον; ἀδικῶ/ἠδίκουν.

THE LONG-VOWEL GRADE IS USED ONLY IN THE SINGULAR OF THE PRESENT AND IMPERFECT INDICATIVE ACTIVE. THE SHORT-VOWEL GRADE IS USED IN ALL OTHER FORMS.

1. PRESENT INDICATIVE ACTIVE

Compare the indicative active endings of the -ω verbs with those of the -μι verbs.

	PRESENT INDICATIVE ACTIVE -ω VERB ENDINGS	PRESENT INDICATIVE ACTIVE -μι VERB ENDINGS
S 1	-ω	-μι
2	-εις	-ς
3	-ει	-σι(ν)
P 1	-ομεν	-μεν
2	-ετε	-τε
3	-ουσι(ν)	-ᾱσι(ν)

Observations: (1) The two sets of endings are most similar in the first and second person plural. In the -ω verbs, the person markers -μεν and -τε are only part of the ending; they are preceded by the thematic vowel. The -μι verbs use the person markers

-με*ν* and -τε by themselves as endings. From the presence of the thematic vowel, the endings of the -ω verbs are called **thematic endings**, and the -ω verbs are called **thematic verbs**. The -μι verb endings lack the thematic vowel and are called **athematic endings**. The -μι verbs themselves are also called **athematic verbs**.

(2) The ending -μι of the first person singular, present indicative active of athematic verbs has been seen already as a person marker in the present and aorist optative active endings -οιμι and -αιμι.

To form the present indicative active of an athematic verb, add the present active athematic endings to the long-vowel grade of the present tense stem in the singular and to the short-vowel grade of the stem in the plural.

PRESENT INDICATIVE ACTIVE ATHEMATIC ENDINGS		*STEMS* διδω- διδο-	*STEMS* τιθη- τιθε-	*STEMS* ἱστη- ἱστα-
S 1	**-μι**	δίδωμι	τίθημι	ἵστημι
2	**-ς**	δίδως	τίθης	ἵστης
3	**-σι(ν)**	δίδωσι(ν)	τίθησι(ν)	ἵστησι(ν)
P 1	**-μεν**	δίδομεν	τίθεμεν	ἵσταμεν
2	**-τε**	δίδοτε	τίθετε	ἵστατε
3	**-ᾱσι(ν)**	διδόᾱσι(ν)	τιθέᾱσι(ν)	ἱστᾶσι(ν)

Observation: In the third person plural of ἵστημι, note the contraction of the -α- of the ending with the -α- of the stem and the resulting circumflex accent. There is no contraction in the third person plural forms διδόᾱσι(ν) or τιθέᾱσι(ν).

---

2. PRESENT INDICATIVE MIDDLE/PASSIVE

Compare the present indicative middle/passive endings of the thematic verbs with those of the athematic verbs.

	PRESENT INDICATIVE MIDDLE/PASSIVE THEMATIC ENDINGS	*PRESENT INDICATIVE MIDDLE/PASSIVE ATHEMATIC ENDINGS*
S 1	-ομαι	-μαι
2	-ει/η < *-εσαι	-σαι
3	-εται	-ται

P 1 $-o\mu\epsilon\theta\alpha$ $-\mu\epsilon\theta\alpha$

  2    $-\epsilon\sigma\theta\epsilon$ $-\sigma\theta\epsilon$

  3    $-o\nu\tau\alpha\iota$ $-\nu\tau\alpha\iota$

Observation: The middle/passive athematic endings are the person markers of
the thematic endings without the thematic vowel. They are the
same endings as those used in the perfect indicative middle/
passive: $\pi\epsilon\pi\alpha\acute{\iota}\delta\epsilon\upsilon\mu\alpha\iota$, $\pi\epsilon\pi\alpha\acute{\iota}\delta\epsilon\upsilon\sigma\alpha\iota$, etc.

To form the present indicative middle/passive of an athematic verb, add the
present middle/passive athematic endings to the short-vowel grade of the
present tense stem.

PRESENT INDICATIVE MIDDLE/PASSIVE ATHEMATIC ENDINGS	*STEM* $\delta\iota\delta o$-	*STEM* $\tau\iota\theta\epsilon$-	*STEM* $\dot{\iota}\sigma\tau\alpha$-
S 1 **$-\mu\alpha\iota$**	$\delta\acute{\iota}\delta o\mu\alpha\iota$	$\tau\acute{\iota}\theta\epsilon\mu\alpha\iota$	$\ddot{\iota}\sigma\tau\alpha\mu\alpha\iota$
2 **$-\sigma\alpha\iota$**	$\delta\acute{\iota}\delta o\sigma\alpha\iota$	$\tau\acute{\iota}\theta\epsilon\sigma\alpha\iota$	$\ddot{\iota}\sigma\tau\alpha\sigma\alpha\iota$
3 **$-\tau\alpha\iota$**	$\delta\acute{\iota}\delta o\tau\alpha\iota$	$\tau\acute{\iota}\theta\epsilon\tau\alpha\iota$	$\ddot{\iota}\sigma\tau\alpha\tau\alpha\iota$
P 1 **$-\mu\epsilon\theta\alpha$**	$\delta\iota\delta\acute{o}\mu\epsilon\theta\alpha$	$\tau\iota\theta\acute{\epsilon}\mu\epsilon\theta\alpha$	$\dot{\iota}\sigma\tau\acute{\alpha}\mu\epsilon\theta\alpha$
2 **$-\sigma\theta\epsilon$**	$\delta\acute{\iota}\delta o\sigma\theta\epsilon$	$\tau\acute{\iota}\theta\epsilon\sigma\theta\epsilon$	$\ddot{\iota}\sigma\tau\alpha\sigma\theta\epsilon$
3 **$-\nu\tau\alpha\iota$**	$\delta\acute{\iota}\delta o\nu\tau\alpha\iota$	$\tau\acute{\iota}\theta\epsilon\nu\tau\alpha\iota$	$\ddot{\iota}\sigma\tau\alpha\nu\tau\alpha\iota$

Observation: Note that the $-\sigma$- of the second person singular ending, even
though intervocalic, remains.

3. IMPERFECT INDICATIVE ACTIVE

Compare the imperfect indicative endings of the thematic verbs with those of
the athematic verbs.

IMPERFECT INDICATIVE ACTIVE THEMATIC ENDINGS	*IMPERFECT INDICATIVE ACTIVE ATHEMATIC ENDINGS*
S 1 $-o\nu$	$-\nu$
2 $-\epsilon\varsigma$	$-\varsigma$
3 $-\epsilon(\nu)$	——
P 1 $-o\mu\epsilon\nu$	$-\mu\epsilon\nu$
2 $-\epsilon\tau\epsilon$	$-\tau\epsilon$
3 $-o\nu$	$-\sigma\alpha\nu$

Observation: Except for the third person plural ending -σαν, the imperfect indicative active athematic endings are the person markers of the thematic endings without the thematic vowel. The -σαν is the same person marker that has been seen in such third person plural forms as ἐπαιδεύθησαν (aorist indicative passive) and ποιοίησαν (present optative active); it was borrowed from such forms as ἐπαίδευσαν, where the -σ- is, of course, part of the aorist active and middle tense stem.

To form the imperfect indicative active of an athematic verb, add the imperfect indicative active athematic endings to the augmented long-vowel grade of the present tense stem in the singular and to the augmented short-vowel grade of the present tense stem in the plural. (NOTE: For some of the athematic forms a thematic form has been substituted; such thematic forms are printed entirely in boldface in the paradigms and explained in the observations.)

IMPERFECT INDICATIVE ACTIVE ATHEMATIC ENDINGS		STEMS διδω- διδο-	STEMS τιθη- τιθε-	STEMS ἱστη- ἱστα-
S 1	-ν	ἐδίδουν	ἐτίθην	ἵστην
2	-ς	ἐδίδους	ἐτίθεις	ἵστης
3	——	ἐδίδου	ἐτίθει	ἵστη
P 1	-μεν	ἐδίδομεν	ἐτίθεμεν	ἵσταμεν
2	-τε	ἐδίδοτε	ἐτίθετε	ἵστατε
3	-σαν	ἐδίδοσαν	ἐτίθεσαν	ἵστασαν

Observations: (1) The past indicative augment on a word beginning with a vowel is shown by lengthening the initial vowel. Note carefully the difference in quantity of the initial vowel that distinguishes the imperfect from the present in the first and second person plural of ἵστημι.

ἵσταμεν, ἵστατε: The long iota shows the past indicative augment of the imperfect.

ἵσταμεν, ἵστατε: The short iota shows that the form is unaugmented and therefore present.

(2) Only the imperfect of ἵστημι completely follows the rule given above. In the imperfect of τίθημι one would have expected the forms *ἐτίθης and *ἐτίθη according to the rule. Instead, for the second and third person singular the verb is

given thematic forms, with the second and third person singular, imperfect indicative active *thematic endings* -ες and -ε added to the augmented *short-vowel grade* of the present tense stem; the vowels of the stem and the ending contract to give the forms:

$$\dot{\varepsilon}\tau\dot{\iota}\theta\varepsilon\iota\varsigma < *\dot{\varepsilon}\tau\dot{\iota}\theta\varepsilon\varepsilon\varsigma$$
$$\dot{\varepsilon}\tau\dot{\iota}\theta\varepsilon\iota \ < *\dot{\varepsilon}\tau\dot{\iota}\theta\varepsilon\varepsilon$$

(3) In the imperfect of δίδωμι, thematic forms also replace the original athematic ones:

$$\dot{\varepsilon}\delta\dot{\iota}\delta o\upsilon\nu < *\dot{\varepsilon}\delta\dot{\iota}\delta o o\nu$$
$$\dot{\varepsilon}\delta\dot{\iota}\delta o\upsilon\varsigma < *\dot{\varepsilon}\delta\dot{\iota}\delta o\varepsilon\varsigma$$
$$\dot{\varepsilon}\delta\dot{\iota}\delta o\upsilon \ < *\dot{\varepsilon}\delta\dot{\iota}\delta o\varepsilon$$

4. IMPERFECT INDICATIVE MIDDLE/PASSIVE

Compare the imperfect indicative middle/passive endings of the thematic verbs with those of the athematic verbs.

	IMPERFECT INDICATIVE MIDDLE/PASSIVE THEMATIC ENDINGS	IMPERFECT INDICATIVE MIDDLE/PASSIVE ATHEMATIC ENDINGS
S 1	-ομην	-μην
2	-ου < *-εσο	-σο
3	-ετο	-το
P 1	-ομεθα	-μεθα
2	-εσθε	-σθε
3	-οντο	-ντο

Observation: The imperfect indicative middle/passive athematic endings are the person markers of the thematic endings without the thematic vowel. They are the same endings as those used in the pluperfect indicative middle/passive ἐπεπαιδεύμην, ἐπεπαίδευσο, etc.

To form the imperfect indicative middle/passive of an athematic verb, add the imperfect middle/passive athematic endings to the augmented short-vowel grade of the present tense stem.

	IMPERFECT INDICATIVE MIDDLE/ PASSIVE ATHEMATIC ENDINGS	AUGMENTED STEM ἐδιδο-	AUGMENTED STEM ἐτιθε-	AUGMENTED STEM ἱστα-
S 1	-μην	ἐδιδόμην	ἐτιθέμην	ἱστάμην
2	-σο	ἐδίδοσο	ἐτίθεσο	ἵστασο
3	-το	ἐδίδοτο	ἐτίθετο	ἵστατο
P 1	-μεθα	ἐδιδόμεθα	ἐτιθέμεθα	ἱστάμεθα
2	-σθε	ἐδίδοσθε	ἐτίθεσθε	ἵστασθε
3	-ντο	ἐδίδοντο	ἐτίθεντο	ἵσταντο

Observation: As in the active, so in the middle/passive, in the first and second person plural only the length of the initial iota allows one to distinguish between the present and the imperfect of ἵστημι. Compare

> ἱστάμεθα, ἵστασθε: imperfect
> ἱστάμεθα, ἵστασθε: present

5. PRESENT SUBJUNCTIVE ACTIVE

To form the present subjunctive active of an athematic verb, add the usual subjunctive active endings to the short-vowel grade of the present tense stem and *contract* the vowel of the stem and that of the ending.

	SUBJUNCTIVE ACTIVE ENDINGS	STEM διδο-	STEM τιθε-	STEM ἱστε-
S 1	-ω	διδῶ	τιθῶ	ἱστῶ
2	-ῃς	διδῷς	τιθῇς	ἱστῇς
3	-ῃ	διδῷ	τιθῇ	ἱστῇ
P 1	-ωμεν	διδῶμεν	τιθῶμεν	ἱστῶμεν
2	-ητε	διδῶτε	τιθῆτε	ἱστῆτε
3	-ωσι(ν)	διδῶσι(ν)	τιθῶσι(ν)	ἱστῶσι(ν)

Observations: (1) The contraction of $o + \eta$ gives φ in the second and third person singular, NOT the -οι of contracted verbs with stems in -o; contrast δηλοῖς < δηλόῃς.

(2) Note that the subjunctive of ἵστημι is formed from the stem ἱστε- NOT the expected ἱστα-. The contractions are regular.

(3) A similar contraction between the subjunctive endings and the vowel of the stem, with a circumflex accent on the resulting ultima, occurs in the aorist subjunctive passive, e.g., παιδευθῶ, παιδευθῇς < παιδευθέω, παιδευθέῃς.

6. PRESENT SUBJUNCTIVE MIDDLE/PASSIVE

To form the present subjunctive middle/passive of an athematic verb, add the usual subjunctive middle/passive endings to the short-vowel grade of the present tense stem and *contract* the vowels of the stem and the ending.

	SUBJUNCTIVE MIDDLE/PASSIVE ENDINGS	*STEM* διδο-	*STEM* τιθε-	*STEM* ἱστε-
S 1	-ωμαι	διδῶμαι	τιθῶμαι	ἱστῶμαι
2	-η	διδῷ	τιθῇ	ἱστῇ
3	-ηται	διδῶται	τιθῆται	ἱστῆται
P 1	-ωμεθα	διδώμεθα	τιθώμεθα	ἱστώμεθα
2	-ησθε	διδῶσθε	τιθῆσθε	ἱστῆσθε
3	-ωνται	διδῶνται	τιθῶνται	ἱστῶνται

Observations: (1) As in the subjunctive active, note that the contraction of o + η gives ῳ NOT οι, and that the stem of the present subjunctive middle/passive of ἵστημι is once again ἱστε- NOT the expected ἱστα-.

(2) As with the thematic verbs, the forms of the second person singular, present subjunctive middle/passive are identical with those of the third person singular, present subjunctive active.

7. PRESENT OPTATIVE ACTIVE

Compare the present optative endings of the thematic verbs with those of the athematic verbs.

	PRESENT OPTATIVE ACTIVE THEMATIC ENDINGS	PRESENT OPTATIVE ACTIVE ATHEMATIC ENDINGS
S 1	-οιμι	-ιην
2	-οις	-ιης
3	-οι	-ιη
P 1	-οιμεν	-ιμεν/-ιημεν
2	-οιτε	-ιτε/-ιητε
3	-οιεν	-ιεν/-ιησαν

Observation: Except for the absence of the initial -ε- or -o-, these endings are the same as those of the aorist optative passive (-ειην, -ειης, etc.) or the alternative endings of the present optative active of contracted verbs (-οιην, -οιης, etc.). These athematic endings consist of an optative suffix (the full-grade -ιη- in the singular, the zero-grade -ι- and the alternative full-grade -ιη- in the plural) and the person markers -ν, -ς, ——, -μεν, -τε, -εν (with the zero grade suffix) /-σαν (with the full-grade suffix).

To form the present optative active of an athematic verb, add the present optative active athematic endings to the short-vowel grade of the present tense stem.

PRESENT OPTATIVE ACTIVE ATHEMATIC ENDINGS		STEM διδο-	STEM τιθε-	STEM ἰστα-
S 1	-ιην	διδοίην	τιθείην	ἱσταίην
2	-ιης	διδοίης	τιθείης	ἱσταίης
3	-ιη	διδοίη	τιθείη	ἱσταίη
P 1	-ιμεν	διδοῖμεν	τιθεῖμεν	ἱσταῖμεν
2	-ιτε	διδοῖτε	τιθεῖτε	ἱσταῖτε
3	-ιεν	διδοῖεν	τιθεῖεν	ἱσταῖεν
	OR	OR	OR	OR
P 1	-ιημεν	διδοίημεν	τιθείημεν	ἱσταίημεν
2	-ιητε	διδοίητε	τιθείητε	ἱσταίητε
3	-ιησαν	διδοίησαν	τιθείησαν	ἱσταίησαν

Observation: Note that the accent in the athematic present optative active does not recede beyond the syllable containing the -ι-.

8. PRESENT OPTATIVE MIDDLE/PASSIVE

Compare the present optative middle/passive endings of the thematic verbs
with those of the athematic verbs.

	PRESENT OPTATIVE MIDDLE/PASSIVE THEMATIC ENDINGS	*PRESENT OPTATIVE MIDDLE/PASSIVE ATHEMATIC ENDINGS*
S 1	*-οιμην*	*-ιμην*
2	*-οιο* < *-οισο*	*-ιο* < *-ισο*
3	*-οιτο*	*-ιτο*
P 1	*-οιμεθα*	*-ιμεθα*
2	*-οισθε*	*-ισθε*
3	*-οιντο*	*-ιντο*

Observation: Except for the absence of the thematic vowel *-o-*, the athematic
endings are the same as the thematic ones.

To form the present optative middle/passive of an athematic verb, add the
present optative middle/passive athematic endings to the short-vowel grade
of the present tense stem.

PRESENT OPTATIVE MIDDLE/PASSIVE ATHEMATIC ENDINGS	*STEM* διδο-	*STEM* τιθε-	*STEM* ἱστα-
S 1	-ιμην	διδοίμην	τιθείμην	ἱσταίμην
2	-ιο	διδοῖο	τιθεῖο	ἱσταῖο
3	-ιτο	διδοῖτο	τιθεῖτο	ἱσταῖτο
P 1	-ιμεθα	διδοίμεθα	τιθείμεθα	ἱσταίμεθα
2	-ισθε	διδοῖσθε	τιθεῖσθε	ἱσταῖσθε
3	-ιντο	διδοῖντο	τιθεῖντο	ἱσταῖντο

Observations: (1) Once again, the accent does not recede beyond the syllable
containing the *-ι-*.

(2) There are alternative thematic forms for the present optative
middle/passive of τίθημι in the third person singular and in
all of the plural. These use the short-vowel grade of the

present tense stem τιθε- and contract the vowels of the stem and the ending:

S 3   τιθοῖτο   (*τιθέοιτο)

P 1   τιθοίμεθα   (*τιθεοίμεθα)

   2   τιθοῖσθε   (*τιθέοισθε)

   3   τιθοῖντο   (*τιθέοιντο)

9. PRESENT IMPERATIVE ACTIVE

Compare the present imperative active endings of the thematic verbs with those of the athematic verbs.

	PRESENT IMPERATIVE ACTIVE THEMATIC ENDINGS	PRESENT IMPERATIVE ACTIVE ATHEMATIC ENDINGS
S 2	-ε	-θι, -ε, —
3	-ετω	-τω
P 2	-ετε	-τε
3	-οντων	-ντων

Observation: Except for the second person singular, the present imperative active athematic endings are the person markers of the thematic endings without the thematic vowel. In the second person singular each verb uses one of the following: the ending -θι or -ε on the short vowel grade, or the long-vowel grade of the stem with no ending.

To form the present imperative active of an athematic verb, add the present imperative active athematic endings to the short vowel grade of the stem. The second person singular form must be learned for each verb.

PRESENT IMPERATIVE ACTIVE ATHEMATIC ENDINGS		STEM διδο-	STEM τιθε-	STEM ἱστα-
S 2	-θι, -ε, —	δίδου (*δίδοε)	τίθει (*τίθεε)	ἵστη
3	-τω	διδότω	τιθέτω	ἱστάτω
P 2	-τε	δίδοτε	τίθετε	ἵστατε
3	-ντων	διδόντων	τιθέντων	ἱστάντων

Observations: (1) The second person singular forms δίδου and τίθει employ the ending -ε of thematic verbs: cf. παίδευε. The ending contracts with the stem: cf. δήλου, ποίει.

(2) The second person singular form ἴστη consists of the *long-vowel grade* of the present tense stem with no ending added.

(3) The second person plural, present imperative active is identical in form with the second person plural, present indicative active.

(4) The second person singular ending -θι has been seen as a person marker in the aorist imperative passive ending -η**θι**. It will be used to form imperatives of certain athematic verbs given in later Units.

10. PRESENT IMPERATIVE MIDDLE/PASSIVE

Compare the present imperative middle/passive endings of the thematic verbs with those of the athematic verbs.

	PRESENT IMPERATIVE MIDDLE/PASSIVE THEMATIC ENDINGS	*PRESENT IMPERATIVE MIDDLE/PASSIVE ATHEMATIC ENDINGS*
S 2	-ου < *-εσο	-**σο**
3	-εσθω	-**σθω**
P 2	-εσθε	-**σθε**
3	-εσθων	-**σθων**

To form the present imperative middle/passive of an athematic verb, add the present imperative middle/passive endings to the short-vowel grade of the present tense stem.

	PRESENT IMPERATIVE MIDDLE/PASSIVE ATHEMATIC ENDINGS	*STEM* διδο-	*STEM* τιθε-	*STEM* ἱστα-
S 2	-**σο**	δίδο**σο**	τίθε**σο**	ἵστα**σο**
3	-**σθω**	διδό**σθω**	τιθέ**σθω**	ἱστά**σθω**
P 2	-**σθε**	δίδο**σθε**	τίθε**σθε**	ἵστα**σθε**
3	-**σθων**	διδό**σθων**	τιθέ**σθων**	ἱστά**σθων**

Observation: The second person plural, present imperative middle/passive is identical with the second person plural, present indicative middle/passive. Context will help to determine meaning.

11. PRESENT INFINITIVES ACTIVE AND MIDDLE/PASSIVE

Compare the present infinitive active and middle/passive endings of the thematic verbs with those of the athematic verbs.

	THEMATIC	ATHEMATIC
PRESENT ACTIVE	-ειν	-ναι
PRESENT MIDDLE/PASSIVE	-εσθαι	-σθαι

To form the present infinitives active and middle/passive of an athematic verb, add the appropriate ending to the short vowel grade of the present tense stem.

	ENDING	STEM διδο-	STEM τιθε-	STEM ἰστα-
PRESENT ACTIVE	-ναι	διδόναι	τιθέναι	ἱστάναι
PRESENT MIDDLE/PASSIVE	-σθαι	δίδοσθαι	τίθεσθαι	ἵστασθαι

Observations: (1) THE SYLLABLE PRECEDING THE INFINITIVE ENDING -ναι IS ALWAYS ACCENTED; hence the non-recessive accent on διδόναι, as in the perfect infinitive active πεπαιδευκέναι and the aorist infinitive passive παιδευθῆναι.

(2) The present infinitive middle/passive athematic ending differs from the thematic ending only in the absence of the thematic vowel. Note that the accent on the form is recessive.

101. FEAR CLAUSES

After verbs of fearing, a **fear clause** can serve as an object of the verb. It is introduced by the conjunction μή, which in a fear clause has the meaning "that" or, somewhat archaically, "lest." A fear clause indicating a fear that something may not or might not happen is introduced by μὴ οὐ, "that not."

When the fear clause refers to a subsequent action, the fear clause takes the subjunctive in primary sequence and the optative in secondary sequence; tense indicates aspect only. Fear clauses, like purpose clauses, follow the rules of sequence of moods.

One verb which introduces fear clauses is:

φοβέομαι, φοβήσομαι, ——, ——, πεφόβημαι, ἐφοβήθην, "fear, be afraid"

φοβοῦμαι μὴ λύσῃ τοὺς κακούς.
I am afraid that he may/will free the wicked men.

φοβοῦμαι μὴ οὐ λύῃ τοὺς ἀγαθούς.
I am afraid that he may/will not free [habitually] the good men.

ἐφοβούμην μὴ λύσειε τοὺς κακούς.
I was afraid that he might/would free the wicked men.

When a fear clause refers to an action contemporaneous with or prior to that of the main verb of fearing, the *indicative* is used.

φοβοῦμαι μὴ λύει τοὺς κακούς.
I am afraid that he is freeing the wicked men.

φοβοῦμαι μὴ ἔλῦσε τοὺς κακούς.
I am afraid that he freed the wicked men.

ἐφοβούμην μὴ ἔλῦσε τοὺς κακούς.
I was afraid that he freed the wicked men.

ἐφοβούμην μὴ οὐκ ἔλῦσε τοὺς ἀγαθούς.
I was afraid that he did not free the good men.

VOCABULARY

——, ἀλλήλων (reciprocal pronoun)	one another
ἀνα- (prefix)	up, up to
γραφεύς, γραφέως, ὁ	writer; painter
γραφική, γραφικῆς, ἡ	writing; painting
δέκα (indeclinable numeral)	ten
δημιουργός, δημιουργοῦ, ὁ	skilled workman
δίδωμι, δώσω, ἔδωκα, δέδωκα,	give
δέδομαι, ἐδόθην	
ἀποδίδωμι	give back, pay, permit; (mid.) sell
ἐννέα (indeclinable numeral)	nine
ἔπος, ἔπους, τό	word; (pl., sometimes) epic poetry
ἑρμηνεύς, ἑρμηνέως, ὁ	interpreter
ζωγράφος, ζωγράφου, ὁ	painter
ἤ (conj.)	than
ἵστημι, στήσω, ἔστησα (trans.) or ἔστην (intrans.), ἔστηκα (intrans.), ἔσταμαι, ἐστάθην	make stand; (middle or intrans.) stand
ἀφίστημι, ἀποστήσω, ἀπέστησα (trans.) or ἀπέστην (intrans.), ἀφέστηκα (intrans.), ἀφέσταμαι, ἀπεστάθην	(trans.) cause to revolt; (mid. or intrans.) revolt
κατα- (prefix)	down; against; strengthens meaning of verb
καθίστημι, καταστήσω, κατέστησα (trans.) or κατέστην (intrans.), καθέστηκα (intrans.), καθέσταμαι, κατεστάθην	(trans.) appoint, establish, put into a state; (intrans.) be established, be appointed, enter into a state
καταλύω	destroy; dissolve
μᾶλλον (adv.)	more, rather
μή (conj.)	that, lest (with fear clauses)
μηδέ (conj.)	and not
(adv.)	not even
μόνος, μόνη, μόνον	alone
μόνον (adv.)	only

οὐδέ (conj.)   and not

    (adv.)   not even

πόθεν (adv.)   from where?, whence?

ποῖ (adv.)   (to) where?, whither?

ποῦ (adv.)   where?, in what place?

που (enclitic adv.)   *qualifies an assertion,*
                                         I suppose; somewhere

πρός (prep.)   + *gen.*   in the eyes of, in the name of
                      + *dat.*   near; in addition to
                      + *acc.*   toward

προσ- (*prefix*)   to, against; besides

συν- (*prefix*)   with, together

τίθημι, θήσω, ἔθηκα, τέθηκα,   put
    τέθειμαι, ἐτέθην
        ἀνατίθημι   set up, dedicate

φιλέω, φιλήσω, ἐφίλησα, πεφίληκα,   love
    πεφίλημαι, ἐφιλήθην

φοβέομαι, φοβήσομαι, ——, ——,   fear, be afraid
    πεφόβημαι, ἐφοβήθην

VOCABULARY NOTES

The reciprocal pronoun ——, ἀλλήλων, "one another," is found only in the plural in the genitive (ἀλλήλων), the dative (ἀλλήλοις, ἀλλήλαις, ἀλλήλοις), and the accusative (ἀλλήλους, ἀλλήλᾱς, ἄλληλα).

The prefix ἀνα- has a basic meaning "up" and is opposite in meaning to the prefix κατα-, "down." With verbs of motion, the difference between the two is quite clear; at other times, they seem to overlap: ἀναλύω and καταλύω differ in the same way as do the English translations "I break (it) up" and "I break (it) down." The prefix can also indicate a strengthening or repetition. Like κατά, ἀνά is also a preposition, but it is not used as such in Attic prose.

From the verb γράφω, "write, draw," come the agent noun γραφεύς, γραφέως, ὁ, "writer, painter" (with the suffix -εύς; cf. ἱερεύς, ἱππεύς) and the verbal noun γραφική, γραφικῆς, ἡ, "writing, painting" (from ἡ γραφικὴ τέχνη; cf. ῥητορική).

The noun δημιουργός, δημιουργοῦ, ὁ, "skilled workman," is a compound of the adjective δήμιος, δήμιον, "public," from δῆμος, δήμου, ὁ, "the people" (cf. πόλεμος and πολέμιος) and ἔργον, ἔργου, τό, "work, deed." It means a person skilled enough to be a professional and can be applied to any craft including, e.g., bronze-workers, sculptors, doctors. In some cosmologies, there is a δημιουργός, creator of the world.

In the verb δίδωμι, δώσω, ἔδωκα, δέδωκα, δέδομαι, ἐδόθην, "give," note the long-vowel grade of the root in Principal Parts I–IV and the short-vowel grade of the root in Principal Parts V and VI. Note that when a present tense has reduplication, the vowel between the repeated consonants is -ι-; contrast the -ε- of the reduplication of the perfect. The prefixed verb ἀποδίδωμι when used in the active voice means such things as "give back, pay (penalties, honors), permit." In the middle, ἀποδίδομαι can mean "sell." The price for which one sells something can be put in the genitive. This is called the **genitive of price** and is a special instance of the genitive of value seen with, e.g., ἀξιόω.

ἀποδίδονται τὰ βιβλία **χρῡσοῦ**.
They sell the books **for gold**.

The phrase δίκην διδόναι means "pay a/the penalty":

δίκην δίδωσιν ὁ ποιητὴς **τῶν ἀδίκως πεπρᾱγμένων**.
The poet is paying the penalty **for the things which have been done unjustly** (i.e., his unjust deeds).

The noun ἔπος, ἔπους, τό, "word; (pl., sometimes) epic poetry," is synonymous in many respects with λόγος, λόγου, ὁ. It, too, can mean things like "speech, story," but it is used more frequently in Attic than λόγος to mean an "individual word." In the plural, in contrast to other types of poetry, it can mean "epic poetry."

The noun ἑρμηνεύς, ἑρμηνέως, ὁ, "interpreter," is used of a "translator" of foreign languages or of anyone who explains anything.

The noun ζωγράφος, ζωγράφου, ὁ, "painter," is an agent noun formed from the roots ζω-, "life" and γραφ-, "paint." It meant originally a "painter of nature" but came to be a general word for painter.

Two words or phrases linked by ἤ usually have the same grammatical construction:

μᾶλλον τῑμῶσιν οἱ πολῖται **τὸν ῥήτορα ἤ τὸν ποιητήν**.
The citizens honor **the public speaker** more than **the poet**.

The basic meaning of the verb ἵστημι, στήσω, ἔστησα (*trans.*) or ἔστην (*intrans.*), ἔστηκα (*intrans.*), ἔσταμαι, ἐστάθην is "stand." Its transitive meanings, "make stand, set up," must be distinguished from its intransitive ones, "stand, be standing."

The chart on pages 354–55 gives the meanings of the various tenses of this verb in the active, middle, and passive voices. Intransitive meanings are

	ACTIVE	MIDDLE	PASSIVE
PRESENT	ἵστημι I am standing (something, e.g., a trophy) up I stand (something) up	ἵσταμαι I am standing (myself) up, i.e., I am getting onto my feet I stand (myself) up I am standing (something) up for myself I stand (something) up for myself	ἵσταμαι I am being stood up (propped up) I am stood up
IMPERFECT	ἵστην I was standing (something) up I used to stand (something) up	ἱστάμην I was standing (myself) up I used to stand (myself) up I was standing (something) up for myself I used to stand (something) up for myself	ἱστάμην I was being stood up I used to be stood up

FUTURE	στήσω I shall stand (something) up I shall be standing (something) up	στήσομαι I shall stand I shall be standing I shall stand (something) up for myself I shall be standing (something) up for myself	σταθήσομαι I shall be stood up I shall be being stood up
AORIST	ἔστησα I stood (something) up ἔστην I stood	ἐστησάμην I stood (something) up for myself	ἐστάθην I was stood up
PERFECT	ἕστηκα I am standing I stand	ἕσταμαι (rare) I have stood (myself) up I have stood (something) up for myself	ἕσταμαι I have been stood up
PLUPERFECT	εἱστήκη I was standing I used to stand	εἱστάμην (rare) I had stood (myself) up I had stood (something) up for myself	εἱστάμην I had been stood up

italicized. Note that the present, imperfect, and future middle can be either transitive or intransitive; the first aorist active ἔστησα is transitive, but the second aorist active ἔστην (whose conjugation is given in Unit 13) is intransitive; the first aorist middle, unlike the other middle forms, is only transitive; the perfect ἕστηκα (whose conjugation is given in Unit 13) is intransitive and has a present meaning, and likewise, the pluperfect εἱστήκη is intransitive and has an imperfect meaning. The perfect and pluperfect middle are very rare.

In learning the principal parts, observe how the formation of the various tenses affects the spelling of the word:

> ἵστημι < *σίστημι: the reduplicated σ- drops out but causes the initial rough breathing
>
> ἔστην and ἔστησα: the ἐ- is a past indicative augment
>
> ἕστηκα < *σέστηκα and ἕσταμαι < *σέσταμαι: the reduplicated σ- drops out but causes the initial rough breathing
>
> ἐστάθην: the ἐ- is a past indicative augment.

Note that as in δίδωμι, Principal Parts I–IV have a long vowel; Principal Parts V and VI have a short vowel.

Note carefully that the future active, middle, and passive; the first aorist active and middle; the aorist passive; and the perfect and pluperfect middle/ passive of this verb are conjugated just like παιδεύω.

The verb ἵστημι occurs very frequently in compounds. Two important compounds are ἀφίστημι and καθίστημι; the latter is treated under the prefix κατα- below.

The compound verb ἀφίστημι, ἀποστήσω, ἀπέστησα (trans.) or ἀπέστην (intrans.), ἀφέστηκα (intrans.), ἀφέσταμαι, ἀπεστάθην, "(trans.) cause to revolt; (mid. and intrans.) revolt," shows the same distinctions of meaning in the various tenses and voices as does the simple verb, e.g.:

> ἀφίσταμεν τοὺς στρατιώτᾱς.   (present active)
> We are causing the soldiers to revolt.
>
> ἀφιστάμεθα ἀπὸ τῆς πόλεως.   (present middle)
> We are revolting from the city.

The prefix κατα- can have a spatial meaning, "down," or one of the meanings of the preposition κατά, "against." It can also simply strengthen the meaning of a verb. Thus καταλύω, "destroy," is a somewhat more forceful word than the simple verb λύω.

The compound verb καθίστημι, καταστήσω, κατέστησα (trans.) or κατέστην (intrans.), καθέστηκα (intrans.), καθέσταμαι, κατεστάθην, "appoint, establish, put into a state; (*mid. and intrans.*) enter into a state," is a very important word and can be used of "setting up" a form of government, "appointing" officials, etc.; it can also be used of putting someone or something into a certain state. It shows the same distinctions of meaning in the various tenses and voices as does the simple verb, e.g.:

τὸν δῆμον εἰς πόλεμον καθιστάναι
to be putting the people into (a state of) war

δημοκρατίᾱν κατεστήσαμεν.
We established a democracy.

βασιλεὺς καθέστηκα.
I am established as king (i.e., I have entered into the state of being king).

In a negative purpose clause introduced by ἵνα μή, ὡς μή, or ὅπως μή, μή is an adverb. In a fear clause expressing a fear that something may happen, μή is a conjunction. A clause expressing a fear that something may not happen is introduced by μὴ οὐ, in which μή is a conjunction and οὐ is an adverb.

The words μηδέ and οὐδέ can be conjunctions connecting two items, the second of which is negative: "and not." They can also be used as adverbs: "not even."

The three interrogative adverbs of place correspond to the three cases expressing motion or absence of motion; cf. the chart at the end of Section 13.4, page 20.

ποῖ; ——— πόθεν;
———→ | ποῦ; | ————→

ποῖ πέμπεις τὰ βιβλία;
To where are you sending the books?

ποῦ τὰ βιβλία γράφεις;
Where do you write the books?

πόθεν ἥκεις εἰς τὴν τῶν ὁπλῑτῶν οἰκίᾱν;
From where have you come to the house of the hoplites?

Distinguish carefully between the interrogative adverb ποῦ, "where," and the indefinite enclitic adverb που, "I suppose; somewhere."

The preposition πρός governs all three cases and has several meanings: with the genitive it means "in the eyes of": πρὸς τῶν ἀνθρώπων, "in the eyes of men." In exclamations and oaths, it means "in the name of": πρὸς τῶν θεῶν, "in the name of the gods." With the dative case, it means either "near" (showing position) or "in addition to." With the accusative, it means "toward," either of motion or of almost any sort of relation (love, hatred, etc.).

The basic meaning of τίθημι, θήσω, ἔθηκα, τέθηκα, τέθειμαι, ἐτέθην is "put, place." It also means "put (something) down to last, make": e.g., νόμους τιθέναι, "to make laws." In learning the principal parts, note that as in δίδωμι and ἵστημι, there is the same reduplication in the present (τίθημι < *θίθημι with dissimilation of aspirates) and the same long-vowel grade of the root in Principal Parts I–IV. Observe that Principal Part V has the diphthong -ει- in the tense stem: τέθειμαι (contrast the short vowels of δέδομαι and ἕσταμαι). The short vowel of Principal Part VI is similar to that of ἐδόθην and ἐστάθην.

The compound verb ἀνατίθημι, "set up, dedicate," is used especially to describe the dedication of an object to a god, e.g., ταῦτα τῇ θεῷ ἀναθήσομεν, "We shall dedicate these things to the goddess." Many votive objects bear an inscription stating simply that the donor dedicated the object to a god.

COGNATES AND DERIVATIVES

ἀλλήλων	parallel (alongside **each other**)
ἀνα-	analyze
ἀνατίθημι	anathema (**set up** for God to damn, used in a formula condemning heretics)
γραφική	graphic
δέκα	*ten*; Decalogue (the **Ten** Commandments)
δημιουργός	demiurge (a creating spirit)
δίδωμι	apodosis (the **giving back** part of the conditional sentence); donate (derived from the Latin cognate)
ἐννέα	*nine*; ennead (a group or set of **nine**)
ἔπος	epic
ἑρμηνεύς	hermeneutics (the **interpretation** of the Bible)
ἵστημι	*stand*; static
καταλύω	catalyst
μόνος	monarch
πρός	proselytize (to attempt to make someone come over **to** a cause)
συν-	syntax, synthesis, symbiosis
τίθημι	synthesis, metathesis

DRILLS

I. (a) *Translate indicatives, imperatives, and infinitives; identify subjunctives and optatives.*

(b) *Where possible, change from singular to plural or from plural to singular.*

1. δίδως	15. τίθεσθαι (2)
2. διδῶτε	16. ἐτίθεσαν
3. ἐδίδοτε	17. τίθεσθε (4)
4. διδοίησαν	18. τιθοῖσθε (2)
5. ἐδίδου	19. ἵστη
6. δίδου	20. ἵστη
7. διδῶσθε (2)	21. ἵστασαν
8. δώσετε	22. ἱσταίης
9. ἐδίδοσο (2)	23. ἵστασθε (2)
10. τίθετε (2)	24. ἱστάσθω (2)
11. τίθησι	25. ἱστῆσθε (2)
12. τιθῆτε	26. ἱστάναι
13. τιθῇ (3)	27. ἱστάντων
14. τιθέτω	

II. *Translate the following sentences.*

1. ἐὰν τὸ ἀργύριον ἐν τῷδε τῷ ἱερῷ τιθῶμεν, ζῷα τῇ θεῷ οὐ δώσομεν.

2. τεθαμμένου τοῦ γε Σωκράτους, ὦ πολῖται, στεφάνους μὴ δίδοτε τούτοις δὴ τοῖς ῥήτορσι τοῖς ἄφροσιν, ἀλλὰ λίθοις αὐτοὺς βάλλετε.

3. ὅτε νόμους τιθείησαν ἀγαθούς, οἱ πάλαι βασιλῆς ἐδίδοσαν ἀγαθὰ τοῖς ἀρχομένοις ὥστε καλῶς ἀκούειν ὑπὸ πάντων.

4. εἰ τὰ ὅπλα παρὰ τῇ γεφύρᾳ μὴ ἱσταῖτε, τὸ νίκης ἆθλον οὐκ ἂν λάβοισθε. νῦν δὴ στήσατε αὐτὰ ἐκεῖ.

5. ἐπειδὴ τὸν κήρυκα τὸν παρὰ βασιλέως ἐδέξατο ὁ ἱερεύς, οἱ ῥήτορες ἵσταντο ἐν ἀγορᾷ ὡς τήν τ' εἰρήνην λύσοντες καὶ κακοὺς θήσοντες νόμους.

III. *Translate the following sentences.*

1. φοβεῖται μὴ λύηται ἡ εἰρήνη.

2. ἐφοβεῖτο μὴ λύοιτο ἡ εἰρήνη.

3. ἐφοβεῖτο μὴ ἐλύθη ἡ εἰρήνη.

4. φοβεῖται μὴ λύεται ἡ εἰρήνη.

5. φοβούμεθα μὴ οὐ παιδευθῶμεν εὖ.

6. φοβούμεθα μὴ οὐ παιδευόμεθα εὖ.

EXERCISES

I.   1. πόθεν κατεπέμφθης εἰς ταύτην γε τὴν πόλιν ὅπως τοῖς ἐννέα
         καλοῖς γραφεῦσι, τοῖς τῶν θεῶν ἑρμηνεῦσι, δῶρά πως διδοίης
         αὐτή; τῇ γὰρ γραφικῇ τὴν τῆς ἀρετῆς φύσιν τοῖς νεανίαις
         ἀληθῶς που δεδηλώκᾱσιν οὗτοι. δικαίως οὖν τῑμηθέντων ὑπὸ
         πάντων.

      2. πῶς μόνη διδαχθῶ πρὸς τῇ ῥητορικῇ τὴν γραφικὴν ὑπὸ τοῦδε τοῦ
         αἰσχροῦ ζωγράφου τοῦ θυσίᾱς οὐδὲ ταῖς μούσαις ἀγαγόντος
         ποτέ;

      3. καὶ ὁ Ὅμηρος καὶ ὁ Δημοσθένης γραφῆς ὑπὸ πάντων που
         τῑμώμενοι, ἀλλὰ ῥήτωρ μὲν οὗτος, ἐκεῖνος δὲ ποιητής. τῑμάτω
         αὐτοὺς ὅ γε δῆμος.

      4. δίδαξαι τὸν ἀδελφόν γε τὴν γραφικήν. ἄνευ γὰρ ταύτης τῆς τέχνης
         οὔτε γράφεταί ποτε καλὰ βιβλία ὑπ᾽ ἀνδρῶν τῶν γραφέων
         καλουμένων οὔτε καλῶς ἀκούουσιν οὗτοι ὑπό γε τῶν σοφῶν.

      5. πρὸς τῶν ἀθανάτων μὴ φιλεῖτε τούς γε δέκα οἳ δῶρ᾽ ἐδίδοσαν
         τοῖς ἐν τέλει εἰσάξοντες εἰς τὴν γῆν τοὺς πολεμίους. ἀλλὰ
         τῑμήσατε δὴ Δημοσθένη ἅτε τὴν πόλιν σώσαντα.

      6. ἐπειδὴ μόνοι οἱ θεοὶ τὰ καλὰ διδόᾱσι τὴν πόλιν σώζοντες, τούς γε
         θεοὺς φοβούμενος πείθου μᾶλλον τοῖς νόμοις οὓς ἐκεῖνοι τοῖς
         ἀνθρώποις τιθέᾱσιν ἢ τούτοις οὓς οἱ ἄνθρωποί πως τίθενται.

      7. καλός τοι δημιουργὸς ἐκεῖνος ὁ θεὸς ὁ τήν τε γῆν καὶ τὰ ζῷα καὶ
         τοὺς ἀνθρώπους οὕτως εὖ πεποιηκώς.

      8. δημιουργὸς τῆς πόλεως καλείσθω οὗτος ὃς ἂν δικαίως τοὺς νόμους
         τοῖς πολίταις τιθῇ.

9. ἐτίθει μὲν ὁ βασιλεὺς νόμους τοῖς ἀρχομένοις, τίθενται δὲ νῦν
   νόμους ἔν γε ταῖς ἐκκλησίαις οἱ πολῖται οἱ ἐν ταῖς ἐλευθέραις
   πόλεσι πολιτευόμενοι.

10. τῆς γε πρώτης ἡμέρας συνιστάμεθά που ἐν τῇ οἰκίᾳ τοὺς τοῦ
    σοφοῦ Σωκράτους λόγους τοὺς περὶ τῆς ἀνθρώπου φύσεως
    ἀκουσόμενοι.

11. αἰσχροὶ δὴ καὶ ἄξιοι τοῖς πολίταις θανάτου πάντες οὗτοι οἱ κακοὶ
    ῥήτορες οἳ ἂν δῶρα λαβόντες τὴν πόλιν τῷ τῶν βαρβάρων
    βασιλεῖ χρυσοῦ ἢ ἀργύρου ἀποδιδῶνται. μὴ οὖν ἀποδιδόσθων
    τὰς πάντων οἰκίας.

12. οὐκ ἂν ἀποδιδοῖτό ποθ' ὅ γε σοφὸς τὴν ἀρετὴν χρυσοῦ. ὁ γὰρ
    χρυσὸς οὐκ ἀεὶ μενεῖ, ἀλλ' ἀθάνατος ἡ τῆς ἀρετῆς δόξα.

13. πόθεν ἥξουσιν οἱ πολέμιοι; ποῦ ταξώμεθα οἱ ὁπλῖται; ποῖ βούλεσθ'
    ἐξαγαγεῖν τοὺς ἱππέας; πῶς ἂν ἐκσωθείη ἐκ κινδύνων ἡ πόλις
    καὶ καλῶς ἀκοῦσαι; νίκην διδοίησάν πως ἀεὶ οἱ θεοὶ τοῖς
    γε κακὰ παθοῦσιν. ἔπειτα ἱστάσθων τὰ ὅπλα ἐν τῷ ἱερῷ οἱ
    νικήσαντες.

14. ἄδηλοι δὴ οἱ λόγοι οὓς τοῦ βαρβάρου ἑρμηνέως ἐν τῇ βουλῇ
    ἠκούσαμεν, ἀλλὰ φοβούμεθα μὴ οὐ τελευτᾷ ὁ πόλεμος.

15. ἐὰν μὴ κωλύσῃς ποτὲ τὸν ἀδικοῦντα, μὴ ἐκείνῳ γε συναδικήσῃς, ὦ
    ῥῆτορ, ἀλλὰ πείθου τοῖς τῆς πόλεως νόμοις.

16. ἀληθεῖς τοι φίλοι οἱ τῇ ἀληθείᾳ ἀλλήλους φιλοῦντες, ἀλλ' οὗτοι
    φίλοι οἳ ἂν φοβῶνται μὴ ὑπ' ἀλλήλων βλαφθῶσιν.

17. ὅτε γε συνισταῖντο πρὸς ἀλλήλᾱς αἱ τῶν Ἑλλήνων πόλεις, τότε δὴ
    συνήρχομεν τῶν βαρβάρων. νῦν δὲ ἀλλήλους ἀντ' ἐκείνων
    βλάπτομεν ὥστε τούς γε σοφοὺς φοβηθῆναι μὴ ὑπ' ἐκείνων
    ἀρχώμεθα αὐτοί.

18. οὐκ ἀπεδέξατό που ὁ βασιλεὺς τοὺς τοῦ ἱερέως λόγους τοὺς περὶ
    τοῦ τὴν θυγατέρα τυθῆναι. ταύτην γὰρ φιλῶν ὁ πατὴρ οὐκ
    ἠξίου τελευτᾶν.

19. ἀγαθόν γε τὸ τὸν ἄδικον δίκην διδόναι ἁπάντων τῶν κακῶς
    πεπρᾱγμένων.

20. ποῖ τοὺς δέκα κήρῡκας ἐξαγάγωμεν πρὸς τοὺς βαρβάρους
    ἀπαγγελοῦντας τάδε· καίπερ τὴν εἰρήνην φιλοῦντες μᾶλλον ἢ

τὸν πόλεμον, ἐάν γε τὴν πόλιν πρῶτοι ἀδικῆτε, καταλύσομεν
τὴν εἰρήνην ἅτε βλαπτόμενοι;

21. ταῦτα τὰ ὅπλα θεοῖς τοῖς σωτῆρσι ἀνατίθησι βασιλεὺς ἐν μάχῃ
νῑκήσᾱς.

22. καθίστη πως εἰς τὴν ἀρχὴν τοὺς ἀγαθοὺς καὶ σοφοὺς καλουμένους.

23. τοὺς πολίτᾱς ἐβουλήθην ἀποστῆσαι ἀπὸ τῆς Ἀθηναίων ἀρχῆς,
ἀλλ᾽ ἐκεῖνοι φοβηθέντες οὔτ᾽ ἀφίσταντό ποτ᾽ οὔτε ὑπὲρ τῆς
ἐλευθερίᾱς λόγους γ᾽ ἐποιοῦντο.

24. ἄλλῳ τοι ἄλλην τέχνην ἐδίδου ὁ θεός· τῷ μὲν γὰρ Ὁμήρῳ καὶ
τοῖς τὰ ἔπη ποιοῦσι τὴν ποιητικήν, τῷ δὲ Δημοσθένει καὶ
ἄλλοις τοῖς ἐν τῇ ἐκκλησίᾳ τοὺς πολίτᾱς λόγοις πείθουσι τὴν
ῥητορικήν.

II. 1. When we heard the messenger in the assembly, we feared that the
heavy-armed foot-soldiers would not lead the women down to the
sea.

2. Do not fear that the gods will not always give sufficient things to men.

3. I am afraid that the bad king always made unjust laws somehow for
the men in the cities.

4. Let the men in the market place somehow give either gold or silver to
the soldiers whom we are causing to revolt.

5. Let us always put books in the house of the public speaker in order
that he may teach his brother the epic poetry composed (made)
by Homer.

READINGS

A. Sophokles, Fragment 256 P

πρὸς τὴν ᾿Ανάγκην οὐδ᾿ ῎Αρης ἀνθίσταται.

ἀνάγκη, ἀνάγκης, ἡ necessity

ἀνθίστημι, ἀντιστήσω, ἀντέστησα (trans.) or ἀντέστην (intrans.), ἀνθέστηκα (intrans.), ἀνθέσταμαι, ἀντεστάθην set against; (mid. and intrans.) stand against, stand up against

῎Αρης, ῎Αρεως/῎Αρεος, ὁ Ares, god of war

οὐδέ (conj.) and not; (adv.) not even

πρός (prep.) (+ gen.) in the eyes of, in the name of; (+ dat.) near; in addition to; (+ acc.) toward, against

B. Euripides, Bacchae 848, 847

Dionysos tells the women worshiping him that Pentheus, king of Thebes, has fallen into his trap and will soon be their victim. (The edition of E. R. Dodds arranges the lines in this order.)

γυναῖκες, ἁνὴρ ἐς βόλον καθίσταται,
ἥξει δὲ Βάκχᾱς,[1] οὗ θανὼν δώσει δίκην.

ἁνήρ = ὁ ἀνήρ (For this crasis, see the Appendix, p. 614.)

Βάκχη, Βάκχης, ἡ Bacchant, maddened woman worshiper of Dionysos

βόλος, βόλου, ὁ net

δίδωμι, δώσω, ἔδωκα, δέδωκα, δέδομαι, ἐδόθην give

δίκην διδόναι pay the penalty

ἐς = εἰς

θνῄσκω, θανοῦμαι, ἔθανον, τέθνηκα, ——, —— die

καθίστημι, καταστήσω, κατέστησα (trans.) or κατέστην (intrans.), καθέστηκα (intrans.), καθέσταμαι, κατεστάθην appoint, establish; put into a state; (intrans.) be established, be appointed, enter into a state

οὗ (neut. sing. gen. of the relative pronoun serving as conj.) where

1. This accusative, without a preposition, indicates motion toward.

364

C. Euripides, *Elektra* 1018–1034

Klytaimnestra speaks to her daughter Elektra just before she enters the hut
in which Elektra lives—where Elektra's brother Orestes is waiting to kill her.

> ἡμᾶς δέδωκε Τυνδάρεως τῷ σῷ πατρί,
> οὐχ ὥστε θνῄσκειν, οὐδ᾽ ἃ γεινάμην ἐγώ.
> 1020 κεῖνος δὲ παῖδα τὴν ἐμὴν Ἀχιλλέως
> λέκτροισι πείσας ᾤχετ᾽ ἐκ δόμων ἄγων
> πρυμνοῦχον Αὖλιν,¹ ἔνθ᾽ ὑπερτείνας πυρᾶς

Αὖλις, Αὔλιδος, ἡ   Aulis, port of embarkation for Troy
Ἀχιλλεύς, Ἀχιλλέως, ὁ   Achilles
γεινάμην = ἐγεινάμην   from
——, ——, ἐγεινάμην, ——, ——, ——   bear (a child)
δίδωμι, δώσω, ἔδωκα, δέδωκα, δέδομαι, ἐδόθην   give
δόμος, δόμου, ὁ   (sing. or pl.)   home
ἐγώ   (nom. sing. of the first person pronoun)   I
ἐμός, ἐμή, ἐμόν   my
ἔνθα (adv.)   there; (conj.) where
ἡμᾶς   (acc. pl. of the first person pronoun)   us
θνῄσκω, θανοῦμαι, ἔθανον, τέθνηκα, ——, ——   die
κεῖνος = ἐκεῖνος
λέκτροισι = λέκτροις   from
    λέκτρον, λέκτρου, τό   (sing. or pl.)   bed, marriage-bed
οἴχομαι, οἰχήσομαι, ——, οἴχωκα, ᾤχημαι, ——   be gone
οὐδ᾽ = οὐδέ   (conj.) and not; (adv.) not even
παῖς, παιδός, ὁ or ἡ (gen. pl. παίδων)   child
πρυμνοῦχος, πρυμνοῦχον   holding the stern, detaining ships
πυρά, πυρᾶς, ἡ   fire, pyre
σός, σή, σόν   your (of one person)
Τυνδάρεως/Τυνδάρεος, Τυνδάρεω/Τυνδαρέου, ὁ   Tyndareos
ὑπερτείνω, ὑπερτενῶ, ὑπερέτεινα, ὑπερτέτακα, ὑπερτέταμαι, ὑπερετάθην
    stretch above (+ gen.)

1. This accusative, without a preposition, expresses motion toward.

λευκὴν διήμησ᾽ Ἰφιγόνης παρηῖδα.
κεἰ μὲν πόλεως ἅλωσιν ἐξιώμενος,
1025 ἢ δῶμ᾽ ὀνήσων τἄλλα τ᾽ ἐκσῴζων τέκνα,
ἔκτεινε πολλῶν μίαν ὕπερ,[1] συγγνώστ᾽ ἂν ἦν·
νῦν δ᾽ οὕνεχ᾽ Ἑλένη μάργος ἦν ὅ τ᾽ αὖ λαβὼν
ἄλοχον κολάζειν προδότιν οὐκ ἠπίστατο,

ἄλοχος, ἀλόχου, ἡ   wife
ἅλωσις, ἁλώσεως, ἡ   capture
αὖ (adv.)   in turn
διαμάω, διαμήσω, διήμησα, ——, ——, —— cut through, scrape away
δῶμα, δώματος, τό   (sing. or pl.)   house, home
Ἑλένη, Ἑλένης, ἡ   Helen
ἐξιάομαι, ἐξιάσομαι, ——, ——, ——, —— cure thoroughly
ἐπίσταμαι, ἐπιστήσομαι, ——, ——, ——, ἠπιστήθην   know
ἦν (third pers. sing., imperf. indic. active of the verb "to be")   was
Ἰφιγόνη, Ἰφιγόνης, ἡ   Iphigeneia, daughter of Klytaimnestra
κεἰ = καὶ εἰ
κολάζω, κολάσω, ἐκόλασα, ——, κεκόλασμαι, —— punish
κτείνω, κτενῶ, ἔκτεινα/ἔκτανον, ἔκτονα, ——, —— kill
λευκός, λευκή, λευκόν   white
μάργος, μάργον   wanton, lascivious
μίαν   fem. acc. sing. of
    εἷς, μία, ἕν   one
ὀνίνημι, ὀνήσω, ὤνησα/ὠνήμην, ——, ——, ὠνήθην   benefit
οὕνεκα (conj.)   because
παρηΐς, παρηΐδος, ἡ   cheek
πολλοί, πολλαί, πολλά   many
προδότις, προδότιδος, ἡ   betrayer
συγγνώστ᾽ = συγγνωστά   from
    συγγνωστός, συγγνωστή, συγγνωστόν   forgivable
τἄλλα = τὰ ἄλλα (For this crasis, see the Appendix, p. 614.)
τέκνον, τέκνου, τό   child

---

1. Disyllabic prepositions accent the penult when they follow their object. For this **anastrophe** see the Appendix, p. 613.

τούτων ἕκᾱτι παῖδ᾽ ἐμὴν διώλεσεν.
1030 ἐπὶ τοῖσδε τοίνυν καίπερ ἠδικημένη
       οὐκ ἠγριώμην οὐδ᾽ ἂν ἔκτανον¹ πόσιν·
       ἀλλ᾽ ἦλθ᾽ ἔχων μοι μαινάδ᾽ ἔνθεον κόρην
       λέκτροις τ᾽ ἐπεισέφρηκε καὶ νύμφᾱ δύο
       ἐν τοῖσιν αὐτοῖς δώμασιν κατείχομεν.

ἀγριόω, ἀγριώσω, ἠγρίωσα, ——, ἠγρίωμαι, ἠγριώθην make wild; (mid.)
    become wild
διόλλῡμι, διολῶ, διώλεσα (trans.) or διωλόμην (intrans.), διολώλεκα (trans.)
    or διόλωλα (intrans.), ——, —— destroy utterly; (mid. and intrans.)
    perish utterly
δύο (nom./acc.; gen./dat. δυοῖν) two
δῶμα, δώματος, τό (sing. or pl.) house, home
ἕκᾱτι (postpositive prep. + gen.) because of, for the sake of
ἐμός, ἐμή, ἐμόν my
ἔνθεος, ἔνθεον possessed by a god
ἐπεισφρέω, ἐπεισφρήσω, ἐπεισέφρησα, ἐπεισέφρηκα, ——, —— admit addi-
    tionally, bring in additionally
ἐπί (prep.) (+ gen.) upon; (+ dat.) on, above, pertaining to, on condition
    that; (+ acc.) onto, over, against, for
ἔρχομαι, ἐλεύσομαι, ἦλθον, ἐλήλυθα, ——, —— come, go
ἔχω, ἔξω/σχήσω, ἔσχον, ἔσχηκα, -έσχημαι, —— have, hold; be able; (mid.)
    cling to, be next to (+ gen.)
ἦλθ᾽ = ἦλθε see ἔρχομαι
κατέχω (imperf. κατεῖχον) (see ἔχω) hold, possess; dwell
κόρη, κόρης, ἡ girl, young woman; daughter
κτείνω, κτενῶ, ἔκτεινα/ἔκτανον, ἔκτονα, ——, —— kill
λέκτρον, λέκτρου, τό (sing. or pl.) bed, marriage-bed
μαινάς (gen. μαινάδος) (fem. adj.) mad, maddened
μοι (dat. sing. of the first person pronoun) to/for me
νύμφᾱ = nom./acc./voc. dual of
    νύμφη, νύμφης, ἡ bride, young woman, nymph (See the Appendix, p. 596.)
οὐδέ (conj.) and not; (adj.) not even
παῖς, παιδός, ὁ or ἡ (gen. pl. παίδων) child
πόσις, πόσιος, ὁ (acc. sing. πόσιν) husband
τοίνυν (postpositive particle) therefore; moreover
τοῖσιν = τοῖς

_____

1. An aorist indicative with ἄν in a past potential. See the Appendix, p. 709.

D. Lysias, *Against Diogeiton* 19

Diogeiton, appointed guardian of his young nephews, is accused of cheating them out of their inheritance. This is an excerpt from the speech for the prosecution, written by the professional speechwriter and orator Lysias (c. 459–380 B.C.).

ἀξιῶ τοίνυν, ὦ ἄνδρες δικασταί, τῷ λογισμῷ προσέχειν
τὸν νοῦν, ἵνα τοὺς μὲν νεανίσκους διὰ τὸ μέγεθος τῶν
συμφορῶν ἐλεήσητε, τοῦτον δ' ἅπασι τοῖς πολίταις
ἄξιον ὀργῆς ἡγήσησθε. εἰς τοσαύτην γὰρ ὑποψίαν
5   Διογείτων πάντας ἀνθρώπους πρὸς ἀλλήλους καθίστησιν
ὥστε μήτε ζῶντας μήτε ἀποθνῄσκοντας μηδὲν¹ μᾶλλον
τοῖς οἰκειοτάτοις ἢ τοῖς ἐχθίστοις πιστεύειν.

——, ἀλλήλων   each other
ἀποθνῄσκω, ἀποθανοῦμαι, ἀπέθανον, τέθνηκα, ——, ——   die
δικαστής, δικαστοῦ, ὁ   juror
Διογείτων, Διογείτονος, ὁ   Diogeiton, the alleged perpetrator
ἐλέω, ἐλεήσω, ἠλέησα, ——, ἠλέημαι, ——   have pity on
ἔχθιστος, ἐχθίστη, ἔχθιστον   most hateful
ζάω, ζήσω, ——, ——, ——, ——   live
ἤ (conj.)   than
ἡγέομαι, ἡγήσομαι, ἡγησάμην, ——, ἥγημαι, ἡγήθην   lead; consider
καθίστημι, καταστήσω, κατέστησα (trans.) or κατέστην (intrans.),
    καθέστηκα (intrans.), καθέσταμαι, κατεστάθην appoint, establish; put
    into a state; (intrans.) be established, be appointed, enter into a state
λογισμός, λογισμοῦ, ὁ   accounting, reckoning
μᾶλλον (adv.)   more, rather
μέγεθος, μεγέθους, τό   size
μηδέν   nothing; (adv.) not at all
νεανίσκος, νεανίσκου, ὁ   youth, young man
νόος/νοῦς, νόου/νοῦ, ὁ   mind
οἰκειότατος, οἰκειοτάτη, οἰκειότατον   most related
ὀργή, ὀργῆς, ἡ   anger
πιστεύω, πιστεύσω, ἐπίστευσα, πεπίστευκα, πεπίστευμαι, ἐπιστεύθην   trust
    (+ dat.)
προσέχω, προσέξω, προσέσχον, ——, ——, ——   hold out, apply
συμφορά, συμφορᾶς, ἡ   misfortune
τοίνυν (postpositive particle)   then, therefore, further
τοσοῦτος, τοσαύτη, τοσοῦτο/τοσοῦτον   so much, so big
ὑποψία, ὑποψίας, ἡ   suspicion

1. The negative μηδέν strengthens, rather than cancels, the preceding negatives μήτε . . .
μήτε. See the Appendix, p. 774.

UNIT
13

102. -μι (ATHEMATIC) VERBS: CONTINUED

In this Section are presented the remaining forms of δίδωμι, τίθημι, and ἵστημι which are not conjugated like the corresponding tenses of παιδεύω: the second aorist active of all three verbs, the second aorist middle of δίδωμι and τίθημι, and the perfect and pluperfect indicative active and perfect infinitive active of ἵστημι.

The Principal Parts in bold face below are those which still require explanation. All other Principal Parts of these verbs can already be employed to construct the appropriate forms.

(a) δίδωμι, δώσω, **ἔδωκα**, δέδωκα, δέδομαι, ἐδόθην, "give"

(b) τίθημι, θήσω, **ἔθηκα**, τέθηκα, τέθειμαι, ἐτέθην, "put"

(c) ἵστημι, στήσω, ἔστησα (*transitive*) or **ἔστην** (*intransitive*), **ἔστηκα** (*intrans.*), ἕσταμαι, ἐστάθην, "make stand; (*intrans. and mid.*) stand"

1. AORIST ACTIVE AND MIDDLE OF ATHEMATIC VERBS

In the aorist active and middle, athematic verbs have some first aorist forms and some second aorist forms. The term first aorist applies to those aorists active and middle which employ exactly the same endings as the equivalent aorist forms of παιδεύω. The term **second aorist** applies to *any aorist active or middle which employs any different endings.*

The second aorist active and middle of λείπω, which is *thematic* throughout and which is marked by the ending -ον (or -ομην) of Principal Part III, must be distinguished from the second aorists active and middle presented in this Section, which are for the most part *athematic* and which generally employ endings different from those of the second aorists already learned.

369

The second aorist active and (where it exists) the second aorist middle of these athematic verbs are built upon a stem which shows the same *vowel gradation* as the present tense stem. This stem differs from the present tense stem ONLY in that there is no reduplication of the initial consonant.

PRESENT TENSE STEM:

long-vowel grade	διδω-	τιθη-	ἱστη-	(<*σιστη-)
short-vowel grade	διδο-	τιθε	ἱστα-	(<*σιστα-)

SECOND AORIST ACTIVE AND MIDDLE TENSE STEM:

long-vowel grade	*δω-	*θη-	στη-
short-vowel grade	δο-	θε-	στα-

The stems *δω- and *θη-, which had appeared only in the singular of the indicative active, were replaced by the *first aorist stems* δωκ- and θηκ- which appear in Principal Part III. In the plural of the indicative active, and in the rest of this conjugation, these verbs use the short-vowel stems δο- and θε-.

In contrast, ἔστην uses the long-vowel grade of the stem throughout the indicative. It is therefore treated separately below.

2. AORIST INDICATIVE ACTIVE

In the singular of the aorist indicative active, the verbs δίδωμι and τίθημι have a *first aorist*; in the plural they have an *athematic second aorist* which employs the short-vowel grade of the second aorist active and middle tense stem. To this stem are added the same athematic endings as are employed to form the imperfect indicative active of these verbs.

Such a mixture of first aorist singular and second aorist plural is called a **mixed aorist**.

AORIST INDICATIVE ACTIVE ATHEMATIC ENDINGS		*AUGMENTED STEMS:*		
		ἐδωκ- ἐδο-	ἐθηκ- ἐθε-	
S 1		ἔδωκα	ἔθηκα	*FIRST*
2		ἔδωκας	ἔθηκας	*AORIST*
3		ἔδωκε(ν)	ἔθηκε(ν)	
P 1	-μεν	ἔδομεν	ἔθεμεν	*ATHEMATIC*
2	-τε	ἔδοτε	ἔθετε	*SECOND*
3	-σαν	ἔδοσαν	ἔθεσαν	*AORIST*

Observations: (1) The singular is formed from Principal Part III with the regular endings of the first aorist (cf. ἐπαίδευσα).

(2) In the plural the aorist indicative active of δίδωμι and τίθημι differs from the imperfect indicative active ONLY in that the stem is not reduplicated: cf. ἔδομεν (first person plural, aorist indicative active) and ἐδίδομεν (first person plural, imperfect indicative active).

The verb ἵστημι has two separate aorists. The first aorist ἔστησα is transitive and means "I stood (something, e.g., a statue) up." It can also be used transitively in the middle, e.g., ἐστησάμην, "I stood (something) up for myself." The second aorist ἔστην is intransitive and means "I stood (someplace)"; it has *no middle voice*.

Unlike the aorists ἔδωκα and ἔθηκα, the second aorist indicative active ἔστην is an athematic second aorist throughout its conjugation and employs in the indicative ONLY the long-vowel grade of the second aorist active tense stem, together with the same athematic endings as were employed in the imperfect indicative active of athematic verbs. Such a second aorist is called a **root aorist**. Other root aorists will be introduced later.

ROOT AORIST INDICATIVE ACTIVE ENDINGS		AUGMENTED STEM: ἐστη-	
S 1	-ν	ἔστην	ROOT
2	-ς	ἔστης	AORIST
3	—	ἔστη	
P 1	-μεν	ἔστημεν	
2	-τε	ἔστητε	
3	-σαν	ἔστησαν	

3. AORIST INDICATIVE MIDDLE

In all forms of the aorist indicative middle, as in the plural of the aorist indicative active, the verbs δίδωμι and τίθημι have an athematic second aorist which employs the short-vowel grade of the second aorist active and middle tense stem. The athematic endings are the same as those of the imperfect indicative middle/passive of these verbs, except in the second person singular. Remember that ἵστημι has no second aorist middle.

	AORIST INDICATIVE *MIDDLE* *ATHEMATIC ENDINGS*	*AUGMENTED STEMS:* ἐδο- ἐθε-	
S 1	-μην	ἐδόμην	ἐθέμην
2	-ο < *-σο	ἔδου	ἔθου
3	-το	ἔδοτο	ἔθετο
P 1	-μεθα	ἐδόμεθα	ἐθέμεθα
2	-σθε	ἔδοσθε	ἔθεσθε
3	-ντο	ἔδοντο	ἔθεντο

Observations: (1) In the second person singular, contraction produces the spurious diphthong -ου: *ἔδοο > ἔδου, *ἔθεο > ἔθου.

(2) Remember that the vowel preceding the endings is NOT a thematic vowel but part of the stem: thus ἔδοσθε (where the thematic vowel would be -ε-); ἐθέμεθα (where the thematic vowel would be -ο-).

(3) Since the endings of the athematic aorist indicative middle are the same as those of the corresponding imperfect, except in the second person singular, it follows that everywhere except in the second person singular the aorist indicative middle of δίδωμι and τίθημι differs from the imperfect middle/passive ONLY in that the stem is not reduplicated: cf. ἐδόμεθα (first person plural, aorist indicative middle) and ἐδιδόμεθα (first person plural, imperfect indicative middle/passive).

4. AORIST SUBJUNCTIVE ACTIVE

To form the aorist subjunctive active of athematic verbs, add the usual subjunctive active endings to the unaugmented short-vowel grade of the second aorist active and middle tense stem and *contract* the vowel of the stem with the initial vowel of the ending.

	SUBJUNCTIVE *ACTIVE ENDINGS*	*STEM:* δο-	*STEM:* θε-	*STEM:* στε-
S 1	-ω	δῶ	θῶ	στῶ
2	-ῃς	δῷς	θῇς	στῇς
3	-ῃ	δῷ	θῇ	στῇ

P 1	-ωμεν	δῶμεν	θῶμεν	στῶμεν
2	-ητε	δῶτε	θῆτε	στῆτε
3	-ωσι(ν)	δῶσι(ν)	θῶσι(ν)	στῶσι(ν)

Observations: (1) As in the present subjunctive, ἵστημι employs a stem ending in -ε- in the second aorist subjunctive.

(2) The stem δο- contracts with the singular endings as does the present stem διδο- (cf. Section 100.5): *δόῃς becomes δῷς NOT δοῖς; *δόῃ becomes δῷ NOT δοῖ.

(3) Since athematic verbs employ the same endings in the aorist subjunctive active and the present subjunctive active, and since the appropriate stem shows the short-vowel grade in both, it follows that the aorist subjunctive active of these verbs differs from the present subjunctive active ONLY in that the stem is not reduplicated: cf. δῶμεν (first person plural, aorist subjunctive active) and διδῶμεν (first person plural, present subjunctive active).

5. AORIST SUBJUNCTIVE MIDDLE

To form the aorist subjunctive middle of athematic verbs, add the usual subjunctive middle endings to the unaugmented short-vowel grade of the second aorist active and middle tense stem and *contract* the vowel of the stem with the initial vowel of the ending.

SUBJUNCTIVE *MIDDLE ENDINGS*		*STEM:* δο-	*STEM:* θε-
S 1	-ωμαι	δῶμαι	θῶμαι
2	-ῃ	δῷ	θῇ
3	-ηται	δῶται	θῆται
P 1	-ωμεθα	δώμεθα	θώμεθα
2	-ησθε	δῶσθε	θῆσθε
3	-ωνται	δῶνται	θῶνται

Observations: (1) The stem δο- contracts with the singular endings as does the stem διδο- (cf. Section 100.6): *δόῃ becomes δῷ NOT δοῖ.

(2) As in the active voice, the aorist subjunctive middle of these verbs differs from the present subjunctive middle/passive ONLY in that the stem is not reduplicated: cf. δώμεθα

(first person plural, aorist subjunctive middle) and **διδώμεθα** (first person plural, present subjunctive middle/passive).

6. AORIST OPTATIVE ACTIVE

To form the aorist optative active of athematic verbs, add to the unaugmented short-vowel grade of the second aorist active and middle tense stem the same endings as are employed to form the present optative active of athematic verbs.

OPTATIVE ACTIVE ATHEMATIC ENDINGS		STEM: δο-	STEM: θε-	STEM: στα-
S 1	-ιην	δοίην	θείην	σταίην
2	-ιης	δοίης	θείης	σταίης
3	-ιη	δοίη	θείη	σταίη
P 1	-ιμεν	δοῖμεν	θεῖμεν	σταῖμεν
2	-ιτε	δοῖτε	θεῖτε	σταῖτε
3	-ιεν	δοῖεν	θεῖεν	σταῖεν
	OR	OR	OR	OR
P 1	-ιημεν	δοίημεν	θείημεν	σταίημεν
2	-ιητε	δοίητε	θείητε	σταίητε
3	-ιησαν	δοίησαν	θείησαν	σταίησαν

Observation: The aorist optative active of these verbs differs from the present optative active ONLY in that the stem is not reduplicated: cf. *δοῖμεν* (first person plural, aorist optative active) and **διδοῖμεν** (first person plural, present optative active).

7. AORIST OPTATIVE MIDDLE

To form the aorist optative middle of athematic verbs, add to the unaugmented short-vowel grade of the second aorist active and middle tense stem the same endings as were employed to form the present optative middle/passive of these verbs.

OPTATIVE MIDDLE ATHEMATIC ENDINGS	STEM: δο-	STEM: θε-
S 1 -ιμην	δοίμην	θείμην
2 -ιο	δοῖο	θεῖο
3 -ιτο	δοῖτο	θεῖτο
P 1 -ιμεθα	δοίμεθα	θείμεθα
2 -ισθε	δοῖσθε	θεῖσθε
3 -ιντο	δοῖντο	θεῖντο

Observations: (1) The verb τίθημι has alternative thematic forms in the third person singular and in the plural. The final vowel of the stem contracts with the initial diphthong of the ending. Cf. the alternative forms of the present optative middle/passive, Section 100.8.

> *Alternative thematic forms:*
>
> | S 3 | θοῖτο | (*θέοιτο) |
> |---|---|---|
> | P 1 | θοίμεθα | (*θεοίμεθα) |
> | 2 | θοῖσθε | (*θέοισθε) |
> | 3 | θοῖντο | (*θέοιντο) |

(2) The aorist optative middle of these verbs, including both athematic and alternative thematic forms, differs from the present optative middle/passive ONLY in that the stem is not reduplicated: cf. δοίμεθα (first person plural, aorist optative middle) and **διδοίμεθα** first person plural, present optative middle/passive).

8. AORIST IMPERATIVE ACTIVE

The aorist imperative active of athematic verbs is formed as follows:

MIXED AORIST: *short-vowel grade* *of second aorist* *active and middle* *tense stem* *+ endings:*	*ROOT AORIST:* *long-vowel grade* *of second aorist* *active and middle* *tense stem* *+ endings:*
S 2 -ς	-θι
3 -τω	-τω

	P 2	-τε		-τε
	3	-ντων		-ντων

	STEM: δο-	STEM: θε-	STEM: στη-
S 2	δός	θές	στῆθι
3	δότω	θέτω	στήτω
P 2	δότε	θέτε	στῆτε
3	δόντων	θέντων	στάντων

Observations: (1) All root aorists use the second person singular ending -θι with the long-vowel grade of the stem. Verbs with mixed aorists use the ending -ς with the short-vowel grade of the stem.

(2) The imperative forms δός and θές, when compounded, have an accent on the penult:

δός   ἔκδος   ἀπόδος

(3) The long-vowel stem στη- is shortened before the third person plural ending -ντων.

9. AORIST IMPERATIVE MIDDLE

To form the aorist imperative middle of athematic verbs, add to the short-vowel grade of the second aorist active and middle tense stem the following endings:

	IMPERATIVE MIDDLE ATHEMATIC ENDINGS	STEM: δο-	STEM: θε-
S 2	-ο < *-σο	δοῦ (*δόο)	θοῦ (*θέο)
3	-σθω	δόσθω	θέσθω
P 2	-σθε	δόσθε	θέσθε
3	-σθων	δόσθων	θέσθων

Observation: The imperative forms δοῦ and θοῦ, when compounded with a monosyllabic prefix, retain the circumflex on the ultima; when compounded with a disyllabic prefix or with more than one prefix, they take an acute accent on the penult:

δοῦ   ἐκδοῦ   ἀπόδου

10. AORIST INFINITIVE ACTIVE

The verbs δίδωμι and τίθημι form the aorist infinitive active by adding to the unaugmented short-vowel grade of the second aorist active and middle tense stem the ending -έναι, which *contracts* with the vowel of the stem to form a spurious diphthong:

$$\delta o \tilde{\upsilon} \nu \alpha \iota \quad (*\delta o \acute{\epsilon} \nu \alpha \iota) \qquad \theta \epsilon \tilde{\iota} \nu \alpha \iota \quad (*\theta \epsilon \acute{\epsilon} \nu \alpha \iota)$$

The verb ἵστημι forms the second aorist infinitive active by adding to the unaugmented *long-vowel grade* of the second aorist active tense stem the ending -ναι :

$$\sigma \tau \tilde{\eta} \nu \alpha \iota$$

Other root aorists, to be introduced later, follow the same pattern.

11. AORIST INFINITIVE MIDDLE

The verbs δίδωμι and τίθημι form the aorist infinitive middle by adding to the unaugmented short-vowel grade of the second aorist active and middle tense stem the ending -σθαι:

$$\delta \acute{o} \sigma \theta \alpha \iota \qquad \theta \acute{\epsilon} \sigma \theta \alpha \iota$$

Note that ALL INFINITIVES HAVE A FIXED, NON-RECESSIVE ACCENT WHICH IS RETAINED IN COMPOUNDS:

$$\dot{\alpha} \pi o \sigma \tau \tilde{\eta} \nu \alpha \iota \qquad \dot{\alpha} \pi o \delta \acute{o} \sigma \theta \alpha \iota$$

12. PERFECT AND PLUPERFECT INDICATIVE ACTIVE OF ἵστημι

The perfect and pluperfect indicative active of δίδωμι and τίθημι are formed in the same way as the same tenses of παιδεύω.

The verb ἵστημι forms the singular of the perfect and pluperfect indicative active in the same way as the same tenses of παιδεύω. But in the plural this verb employs a different stem, and different endings.

The perfect active of ἵστημι is conjugated as follows:

	STEMS:	
	ἑστηκ-	(*σεστηκ-)
	ἑστα-	(*σεστα-)
S 1	ἕστηκα	
2	ἕστηκας	
3	ἕστηκε(ν)	

P 1   ἕσταμεν
2   ἕστατε
3   ἑστᾶσι(ν)

Observation: In the singular ἕστηκα is conjugated like πεπαίδευκα; in the
plural, this perfect uses the stem ἑστα- and the person markers
-μεν and -τε as endings, together with the normal third person
plural ending -ᾱσι(ν), which contracts with the final a of the stem.

The pluperfect active of ἵστημι is conjugated as follows:

STEMS:	
εἱστηκ-	(*ἐσεστηκ-)
ἑστα-	(*σεστα-)

S 1   εἱστήκη
2   εἱστήκης
3   εἱστήκει(ν)

P 1   ἕσταμεν
2   ἕστατε
3   ἕστασαν

Observation: In the singular the augmented stem εἱστηκ- receives the usual
pluperfect indicative endings; in the plural the alternative stem
ἑστα-, unaugmented, receives the person markers -μεν, -τε, -σαν
as endings. In the first and second persons plural the forms of the
perfect and pluperfect indicative active are identical. Context
will help to determine meaning.

13. PERFECT INFINITIVE ACTIVE OF ἵστημι

The verb ἵστημι forms the perfect infinitive active by adding the ending -ναι
to the perfect active stem ἑστα-. The penult is accented, as always before this
ending:

ἑστάναι

103. OBJECT CLAUSES OF EFFORT

Verbs of effort, striving, or caring often take **object clauses of effort** with
the future indicative, introduced by the conjunction **ὅπως**, "that." The
negative is μή.

One verb which introduces such clauses is πράττω when used in the sense "bring it about (that)." Another is μηχανάομαι:

μηχανάομαι, μηχανήσομαι, ἐμηχανησάμην, ——, μεμηχάνημαι, ——, "contrive, devise"

πράττει **ὅπως τῆς πόλεως ἄρξει.**
He is bringing it about **that he will rule the city.**

μηχανῶνται **ὅπως τοὺς πολεμίους νῑκήσουσιν.**
They are contriving **that they will defeat the enemy.**

μηχανᾶσθε **ὅπως ἡ δημοκρατίᾱ μὴ λυθήσεται.**
You are contriving **that the democracy will not be destroyed.**

The future indicative is used even when the introductory verb is in a secondary tense:

ἐμηχανῶντο **ὅπως τοὺς πολεμίους νῑκήσουσιν.**
They were contriving **that they would defeat the enemy.**

Object clauses of effort can be used independently with the force of an exhortation or a warning. They are thus alternatives to the imperative and the hortatory and prohibitive subjunctives (cf. Section 90).

ὅπως τοὺς πολεμίους νῑκήσετε.
(See to it) that you defeat the enemy!

ὅπως μὴ νῑκηθήσεσθε.
(See to it) that you are not defeated!

ὅπως νῑκήσομεν.
(Let us see to it) that we conquer!

104. OBJECT CLAUSES OF EFFORT AND PURPOSE CLAUSES COMPARED

Object clauses of effort are so named because they function as the *direct object* of a verb. They answer the question "What?" (E.g., What is he bringing about?, What are they contriving?)

Purpose clauses function as *adverbs* and answer the question "Why?"

μηχανᾶται **ὅπως τοῦ δήμου ἄρξει.** (*object clause of effort*)
He is contriving **that he will rule the people.**

$$\tau\alpha\tilde{\upsilon}\tau\alpha \ \mu\eta\chi\alpha\nu\tilde{\alpha}\tau\alpha\iota \ \left\{ \begin{matrix} \mathbf{\ddot{o}\pi\omega\varsigma} \\ \mathbf{\ddot{\iota}\nu\alpha} \\ \mathbf{\dot{\omega}\varsigma} \end{matrix} \right\} \ \tau\tilde{o}\tilde{\upsilon} \ \delta\dot{\eta}\mu\upsilon\upsilon \ \ddot{\alpha}\rho\xi\eta. \ (\textit{purpose clause})$$

He is contriving these things **in order that he may rule the people**.

The object clause of effort answers the question "What is he contriving?"
The purpose clause answers the question "Why is he contriving these things?"

105. ACCUSATIVE OF RESPECT

A noun in the accusative case, without a preposition, can indicate the respect
in which a statement is true. This usage is called the **accusative of respect**.
It is employed to limit the application of an adjective or of a verb denoting a
state of being.

ψῡχὴν μὲν καλὸς ὁ Σωκράτης, **σῶμα** δὲ αἰσχρός.
In soul (with respect to his soul), on the one hand,
    Sokrates is beautiful; **in body (with respect to his
    body)**, on the other hand, (he is) ugly.

ἀγαθὸς **μάχην** οὗτος ὁ στρατιώτης.
This soldier is good **in battle (with respect to battle)**.

In the first example the two accusatives of respect show that Sokrates' beauty
and ugliness are limited to particular areas. In the second example the soldier's
goodness is limited to a single area.

106. ACCUSATIVE OF RESPECT AND DATIVE OF RESPECT
       COMPARED

The accusative of respect and dative of respect (cf. Section 81) overlap in meaning
and can often be used interchangeably. They differ in that the force of the dative is instrumental, while the force of the accusative is limiting.

ψῡχὴν καλὸς ὁ Σωκράτης.
Sokrates is beautiful **in soul**.
(Sokrates' beauty is limited to one area, his soul.)
(As far as his soul is concerned, Sokrates is beautiful.)

ψῡχῇ καλὸς ὁ Σωκράτης.
Sokrates is beautiful **in soul**.
(Sokrates is beautiful by means of his soul.)

VOCABULARY

Ἀριστοφάνης, Ἀριστοφάνους, ὁ	Aristophanes (comic poet)
ἄρχων, ἄρχοντος, ὁ	ruler; archon
ἀσπίς, ἀσπίδος, ἡ	shield
αὐτίκα (adv.)	immediately
γίγνομαι, γενήσομαι, ἐγενόμην, γέγονα, γεγένημαι, ——	be born; become; happen
ἑορτή, ἑορτῆς, ἡ	festival
ἐπί (prep.) + gen.	on
+ dat.	on, pertaining to, on condition that
+ acc.	onto, over, against, for (purpose)
ἐπι- (prefix)	upon, over, against, after
ἔρχομαι, ἐλεύσομαι, ἦλθον, ἐλήλυθα, ——, ——	come, go
ἑταῖρος, ἑταίρου, ὁ	companion
Εὐριπίδης, Εὐριπίδου, ὁ (voc. Εὐριπίδη)	Euripides (tragic poet)
κράτος, κράτους, τό	strength, power
μανθάνω, μαθήσομαι, ἔμαθον, μεμάθηκα, ——, ——	learn, understand
μάχομαι, μαχοῦμαι, ἐμαχεσάμην, ——, μεμάχημαι, ——	fight (+ dat.)
μετα- (prefix)	indicates sharing or change
μεταδίδωμι	give a share to
μετανίσταμαι, μεταναστήσομαι, μετανέστην, μετανέστηκα, ——, ——	migrate
μηχανή, μηχανῆς, ἡ	device, machine
μηχανάομαι, μηχανήσομαι, ἐμηχανησάμην, ——, μεμηχάνημαι, ——	contrive, devise
ξίφος, ξίφους, τό	sword
ὅμοιος, ὁμοίᾱ, ὅμοιον	like (+ dat.)

ὅπως (conj.)   that (introduces object clauses
                                                            of effort)

παῖς, παιδός, ὁ or ἡ (gen. pl. παίδων)   child

πούς, ποδός, ὁ (voc. πούς)   foot

σαφής, σαφές   clear, distinct

σύμμαχος, συμμάχου, ὁ   ally

τεῖχος, τείχους, τό   city wall

τόπος, τόπου, ὁ   place

τρόπαιον, τροπαίου, τό   trophy, victory monument

φεύγω, φεύξομαι, ἔφυγον,   flee; be in exile; be a defendant

    πέφευγα, ——, ——

χαλεπός, χαλεπή, χαλεπόν   difficult, harsh

χείρ, χειρός, ἡ (dat. pl. χερσί[ν])   hand

VOCABULARY NOTES

Aristophanes (c. 450–c. 385 B.C.) was a poet of Old Comedy (i.e., Athenian fifth-century comedy). Eleven of his plays have survived.

The noun ἄρχων, ἄρχοντος, ὁ, "ruler; archon," should be distinguished from the related noun ἀρχή, ἀρχῆς, ἡ, "beginning; rule, empire," and the related verb ἄρχω, one of whose meanings is "rule."

The verb γίγνομαι, γενήσομαι, ἐγενόμην, γέγονα, γεγένημαι, ——, "be born; become; happen," is a deponent verb: Principal Parts I, II, III, and V are in the middle voice. But this verb also has a perfect active, with no difference in meaning from the perfect middle. The root shows an e-grade (γενήσομαι, ἐγενόμην, γεγένημαι), an o-grade (γέγονα), and a zero-grade (γίγνομαι). Cf. λείπω. The present tense stem shows a reduplication of the initial consonant of the root + iota: γίγνομαι. Contrast the reduplication with epsilon in the two tense stems of the perfect: γέγονα, γεγένημαι. Note that this verb has a thematic second aorist; cf. ἐλιπόμην.

In the sense "become" this verb is copulative and takes a predicate nominative:

> ἀγαθοὶ γίγνονται.
> They are becoming good.

In the aorist this verb often indicates that someone was good (bad, etc.) on some particular occasion.

The basic meaning of the preposition ἐπί is "on." Its use with the genitive, dative, and accusative cases deserves special attention, since meanings overlap and cannot always be derived from the original force of these cases.

+ gen.	ἐπὶ γῆς καὶ ὑπὸ γῆς	on the earth and under the earth
	ἐφ᾽ ἵππου	on horseback
+ dat.	χρῡσὸς ἐπὶ a table	gold on a table
	νόμος ἐπὶ τοῖς ἀδίκοις	a law pertaining to the unjust
	εἰρήνην ἐποιησάμεθα ἐπὶ τούτοις.	We made peace on these conditions.
+ acc.	He jumped ἐπὶ τὸν ἵππον.	He jumped onto his horse.
	ἥκω ἐπὶ τόδε.	I have come for this thing (purpose).
	ὁ στρατὸς extended ἐπὶ πέντε στάδια.	The army extended over (a distance of) five stades.
	στρατιώτᾱς ἔπεμψα ἐπὶ τοὺς πολεμίους.	I sent soldiers against the enemy.

The verb ἔρχομαι, ἐλεύσομαι, ἦλθον, ἐλήλυθα, ——, ——, "come, go," is deponent in the present and future tenses only. In Attic Greek it appears ONLY in the present indicative, in the aorist (all moods), and in the perfect and pluperfect. The missing moods and tenses (present EXCEPT for the indicative, imperfect, and future) are supplied by another verb, εἶμι, to be introduced in Unit 17. The unaugmented aorist active tense stem is ἐλθ-. The second person singular, aorist imperative active, like that of λαμβάνω, is accented on the ultima: ἐλθέ, λαβέ. When these forms are compounded, the accent is recessive: ἄπελθε, σύλλαβε.

The pluperfect does not add the past indicative augment: e.g. ἐληλύθη, "I had come." Remember the general rule that when Principal Part IV or V begins with ἐ- or εἰ-, the pluperfect is unaugmented; cf. εἴληφα.

Euripides (c. 485–c. 406 B.C.) was the youngest of the three great tragic playwrights of fifth-century Athens.

The proper noun Εὐρῑπίδης, Εὐρῑπίδου, ὁ, "Euripides," has the vocative singular Εὐρῑπίδη. Contrast the vocative singular of πολίτης: πολῖτα. All first-declension nouns with nominatives in -ιδης have such a vocative.

Principal Parts I and III of μανθάνω, μαθήσομαι, ἔμαθον, μεμάθηκα, ——, ——, "learn, understand," resemble those of λαμβάνω. Note, however, that μανθάνω uses the suffix -ησ- to form the future: contrast μαθήσομαι with λήψομαι.

The verb μάχομαι, μαχοῦμαι, ἐμαχεσάμην, ——, μεμάχημαι, ——, "fight," is a deponent verb with a contracted future. It takes a dative of the person(s) against whom one is fighting:

τοῖς πολεμίοις ἐμαχόμεθα.
We were fighting the enemy.

The prefix μετα- indicates either sharing or change. The verb μεταδίδωμι means "give a share of" and takes a dative of indirect object and a genitive of the thing shared: μεταδιδόασι τῆς ἀρχῆς τῷ δήμῳ, "They give a share of the rule to the people." The verb μετανίσταμαι means "stand up and change place, migrate." Note the double prefix: μετα- + ἀνα-.

The noun μηχανή, μηχανῆς, ἡ, "device, machine," can denote, among other contrivances, the crane-like device by which actors were hoisted into and out of the playing area in the fifth-century b.c. Athenian theater, whence the Latin phrase deus ex machinā, "god from the machine," to describe a god hoisted in to halt the errant plot of a work. The verb μηχανάομαι, μηχανήσομαι, ἐμηχανησάμην, ——, μεμηχάνημαι, ——, "contrive," is a denominative verb formed from this noun. Note that it is a contracted deponent verb.

The genitive plural of the noun παῖς, παιδός, ὁ or ἡ, "child," is παίδων instead of the expected παιδῶν. The vocative singular is παῖ by the regular rules (cf. Section 48).

The vocative singular of the noun πούς, ποδός, ὁ, "foot," is πούς. By the regular rules it would have been *πό (<*πόδ).

Distinguish the adjective σαφής, σαφές, "clear, distinct," from the adjective σοφός, σοφή, σοφόν, "wise, skilled."

The noun σύμμαχος, συμμάχου, ὁ, "ally," is formed from the preposition σύν + the root μαχ- (cf. μάχη, μάχομαι).

The noun τεῖχος, τείχους, τό means the "fortification wall" of a town or a city.

A τρόπαιον, τροπαίου, τό, "trophy, victory monument," according to ancient etymology, was set up on the field of battle at the point where the victors forced the defeated enemy to turn and run (cf. the verb τρέπω, "make turn"). It consisted of a representative sample of the defeated enemies' weapons and was sacred and hence inviolable. No victory was complete until the victors had commemorated their victory by setting up a trophy.

The verb φεύγω, φεύξομαι, ἔφυγον, πέφευγα, ——, ——, "flee; be in exile; be a defendant," is a partial deponent; it is deponent only in the future tense. Principal Parts I, II, and IV show the e-grade of the root; Principal Part III shows the zero-grade.

COGNATES AND DERIVATIVES

ἄρχων	archon
γίγνομαι	genesis
ἐπί	epidemic (a disease which spreads **over** the people)
ἔρχομαι	proselytize
κράτος	democratic
μανθάνω	mathematics
μηχανή	mechanic; machine (from the Latin derivative *machina*)
μετα-	metathesis
ὅμοιος	homoeopathic
παῖς	pediatrician
πούς	*foot*; podiatrist
τόπος	topic, topology
τρόπαιον	trophy
φεύγω	fugitive (from the Latin cognate *fugiō*)
χείρ	chiropractor, surgeon

DRILLS

I. (a) *Translate indicatives, imperatives, and infinitives; identify subjunctives, optatives, and participles.*

(b) *Where possible, change singulars to plurals, and plurals to singulars.*

(c) *Change the voice of each form to the other voice(s).*

1. ἔθηκεν
2. δόσθαι
3. ἔστημεν
4. ἐστήσαμεν
5. σταῖεν
6. ἱσταῖεν
7. ἐτίθεντο (2)
8. ἔθεντο
9. ἔθετε
10. ἴστην
11. ἔστην
12. στῆθι
13. δίδως
14. ἐδίδους
15. δός
16. ἔδωκας
17. δώμεθα
18. διδώμεθα (2)
19. θήσετε
20. θεῖτε
21. θοῦ
22. τιθεῖτε
23. ἱστάναι
24. στῆναι
25. στῆσαι (2)
26. στῆσον (4)
27. στήσομεν
28. ἔστησαν (2)
29. στῆτε (2)
30. δίδοσθαι (2)
31. ἔδοσαν
32. δῶ (2)
33. διδῶ (3)
34. ἱστῇ (3)
35. στῇ
36. τέθηκεν
37. θέσθων
38. διδοῖεν
39. δίδοτε (2)
40. δότε
41. δοῖεν
42. δοίησαν
43. ἱστάμεθα (2)
44. ἱστάμεθα (2)
45. ἐτίθετε
46. στάντων
47. ἑστάναι
48. ἔσταμεν (2)
49. ἔστηκας
50. ἔστασαν
51. στήσᾱς
52. στήσαιμεν
53. σταῖμεν
54. θέσθαι

II. *Translate the following verbal expressions into Greek.*

1. we have given
2. we gave
3. we shall give
4. give
5. you stood (somewhere)
6. you stood (something up)
7. you (pl.) put
8. you (pl.) were putting
9. to put
10. be putting
11. to give
12. to have given
13. you (pl.) used to give
14. you (pl.) gave

III. *Translate the following sentences and identify the dependent clauses.*

1. χρῡσὸν ἔδωκας τῷ βασιλεῖ ὅπως ταύτης τῆς πόλεως ἄρξειας.

2. ἐμηχανήσασθε ὅπως ἐκείνης τῆς χώρᾱς ἄρξετε.

3. ταῦτ᾽ ἐμηχανήσασθε ὅπως τῆς χώρᾱς ἄρχοιτε.

4. τὸν Σωκράτη κλοπῆς ἐγράψατο ὅπως τὴν εἰρήνην λύσειεν.

5. πρᾱ́ξει ὅπως τὴν εἰρήνην λύσει.

6. ἔπρᾱττεν ὅπως οἱ Ἕλληνες ἀλλήλους μὴ ἀδικήσουσιν.

7. ἄργυρον τῷ ἡγεμόνι ἔδοτε ὅπως βλαβεῖμεν ὑπὸ τῶν πολεμίων.

8. χρῡσὸν τῷ φίλῳ δίδοτε ὅπως τῇ θεῷ θύσῃ.

9. μηχανήσεται ὅπως τῆς πόλεως κατὰ τοὺς νόμους ἄρξομεν.

10. ὅπως ἐξ ἡμερῶν νῑκήσετε.

EXERCISES

I. 1. (a) μὴ δῶτε χρῡσόν.

　　 (b) νόμους μὴ θῇς.

　　 (c) σταῖμεν ἂν ἐνταῦθα.

　　 (d) ἐλθέτω ὁ ἑταῖρος.

　　 (e) ἀπόδου τὰ βιβλία.

　　 (f) ταῦτα μὴ γένοιτο.

　　 (g) στῶ ἢ φύγω;

　　 (h) ὅμοιοι τοῖσδε γένεσθε.

　　 (i) ἄργυρον δοίη.

　　 (j) ἔλθωμεν εἰς ἀγοράν.

2. ἀγαθός που τὴν τέχνην οὗτος ὁ ζωγράφος, αἰσχρὸς δὲ τοὺς τρόπους. μηχανᾶται γὰρ μετὰ τῶν ἑταίρων ὅπως λύσᾱς τὴν δημοκρατίᾱν πάσης τῆς πόλεως ἄρξει.

3. ἥκοντές ποτ᾽ εἰς τὴν πόλιν οἱ σύμμαχοι οἱ ἀπὸ τῆς νήσου ἦλθον αὐτίκα εἰς τὴν ἐκκλησίᾱν ὅπως πείσειαν τοὺς ἄρχοντας νόμον θεῖναι περὶ τοῦ ξένων φόνου. ἐὰν γὰρ μὴ θῶσι τοῦτον τὸν νόμον, ἐκεῖνοι εἰς ἄλλον γε τόπον φυγεῖν βουλήσονται.

4. τῶν πολῑτῶν εἰς τὴν ἐκκλησίᾱν ἐλθόντων, ταύτῃ τῇ μηχανῇ ἔπρᾱττεν ὁ Εὐρῑπίδης ὅπως ὑπὸ τῶν ἀφρόνων τῑμηθήσεται, ἀλλ᾽ οἱ σώφρονες στέφανον τούτῳ καὶ τοῖς τούτου χορευταῖς οὐκ ἔδοσαν.

5. καὶ σοφὰ καὶ σαφῆ τὰ τοῦ Ὁμήρου ἔπη. οὐ γὰρ ταῦτα ὅμοια τοῖς ἄλλοις ἔπεσιν.

6. εἴθε ὅμοιος γενοίμην Ἀριστοφάνει.

7. ἐὰν φοβηθῶμεν μὴ νῑκώμεθα, εἰς ἄλλον τόπον φευξόμεθα.

8. ἢ τὰ τῶν ἄλλων κλέψᾱσα καὶ ἅμα πείσᾱσα ἄλλᾱς τὰ αὐτὰ πράττειν καὶ μὴ τοῖς θεοῖς θυσίᾱς ἄγουσα καὶ τοὺς νεᾱνίᾱς ἀδικεῖν διδάσκουσα ἔβλαπτε τὴν πᾶσαν πόλιν ἢ οὔ; δότω οὖν δίκην τῶν ἀδίκως πεπρᾱγμένων.

9. παρὰ δόξαν δὴ τοῖς Ἕλλησιν ἐγένετο τόδε· οὐκ ἐξῆλθον οἱ σύμμαχοι ἐπὶ τοὺς πολεμίους. ἐφοβοῦντο γὰρ μὴ νῑκῷντο.

10. ἐν πόλει τῇ εὖ πολῑτευομένῃ μεταδίδοται ἡ ἀρχή. οἱ γὰρ αὐτοὶ
    καὶ ἀλλήλων ἄρχουσι καὶ ὑπ' ἀλλήλων ἄρχονται.

11. τούτων γενομένων, οἱ πάσχοντες μαθήσονται. ἡ γὰρ ἐμπειρίᾱ
    διδάσκει καὶ τοὺς ἄφρονας.

12. τὸν Ἀριστοφάνη τῑμώντων μᾶλλον ἢ τὸν Εὐρῑπίδην.

13. εὐδαίμων γενήσεται οὗτος, ᾧ ἂν δῶσιν οἱ θεοὶ λόγων γνώμην καὶ
    ἔργων ἀρετήν.

14. ἐπὶ τόδ' ἤλθετ', ὦ ἄφρονες, ὡς χρῡσοῦ στέφανον τῷ Εὐρῑπίδῃ
    δοῖτε; τούτῳ δὴ μὴ δῶτε ἆθλον, ἀλλὰ δότε τῷ ἄλλῳ ποιητῇ.

15. τὰ τείχη φυλαττέτω τοῖς πολίταις τά τε σώματα καὶ τὰ χρήματα
    καὶ τὴν ἐλευθερίᾱν. ἄνευ γὰρ τῶν τειχῶν νῑκηθέντες ἢ
    τελευτήσαιμεν ἂν τὸν βίον ἢ ὑπὸ ξένων δοῦλοι γενοίμεθ' ἄν.

16. οἳ ἂν ταύτην τὴν πόλιν ἀργύρου ἀποδῶνται, τούτους λίθοις
    βαλόντων αἱ γυναῖκες μηδὲ εἰσδεχέσθων αὐτοὺς εἰς τὰς
    οἰκίᾱς.

17. ἐπειδὴ ἀπέστημεν ἀπὸ βασιλέως, δοίητ', ὦ θεοί, καὶ κράτος καὶ
    νίκην τοῖς ἀνδράσι τοῖς τῆσδε τῆς ἡμέρᾱς τοῖς πολεμίοις
    μαχουμένοις.

18. ὁ φόνου δίκην φεύγων ταῖς κακῶν ῥητόρων μηχαναῖς οὐκ
    ἐσῴζετο. φονέᾱς γὰρ οὐκ ἐφίλει ὁ δῆμος.

19. ἅτε κακὰ παθόντες ὑπὸ τῶν πολῑτῶν τῶν ἀεὶ τὰ μὲν ζῷα πάντα
    καταλαμβανόντων καὶ ἀπαγομένων τὰς δ' οἰκίᾱς πάσᾱς
    καταλῡόντων βουλήθητε μάχεσθαι μᾶλλον ἢ βλαπτόμενοι
    εἰρήνην ἄγειν.

20. ἐν οἴνῳ καὶ ὁ σοφὸς ἄφρονα πρᾶττει. ὁ γὰρ οἶνος καταλύει τὴν
    γνώμην. μὴ οὖν τὴν γνώμην καταλῡ́ων, σοφέ.

21. τῶν ὅπλων καταβληθέντων, καὶ ἄνευ ἀσπίδος μάχου.

22. ὅπως ἐν τῷδε τῷ πολέμῳ ἄνδρες ἀγαθοὶ γενήσεσθε.

23. καὶ τοὺς πόδας καὶ τὰς χεῖρας οὕτως ἀγαθοὶ οἶδε οἱ στρατιῶται
    ὥστε καὶ ἄνευ ἀσπίδων καὶ ξιφῶν τοὺς τῶν ἀδίκων ῥητόρων
    ἑταίρους νενῑκήκᾱσιν.

24. στήτω πρὸ τοῦ ἱεροῦ καὶ τὴν ἀσπίδα τῇ θεῷ ἀναθέτω.

25. εἴθε πρὸ τῆς ἑορτῆς τῆς ἐν ἐκείνῳ τῷ ἱερῷ θύοιεν οἱ ἱερεῖς ὑπὲρ
    τούτων οἷς οἱ δαίμονες χρῡσὸν οὐκ ἔδοσαν. δότε δὴ ἀγαθὰ
    αὐτοῖς, ὦ θεοί.

26. ἅτε εἰληφότες παρὰ τῶν πατέρων τὸ τῆς θαλάττης κράτος, οὐ μαχούμεθα ὑπὲρ τῆς ἀρχῆς;

27. ἐκεῖνος ὁ αἰσχρὸς ῥήτωρ δῶρα δεξάμενος παρὰ τοῦ βασιλέως καὶ πείσᾱς τοὺς πολίτᾱς εἰρήνην ποιήσασθαι ἀντὶ τοῦ μάχεσθαι ἤθελε τῑμηθῆναι.

28. ἐπειδὴ ἐν τῷ πεδίῳ ἔστημεν, τρόπαιον ἐστησάμεθα.

29. τότε μὲν εὖ μαχεσάμενοι καὶ τοὺς πολεμίους νῑκήσαντες ἔπειτα τρόπαιον ἵστατε, ὦ Ἕλληνες. νῦν δὲ καίπερ οὐκ ἐν μάχῃ νῑκηθέντες, τοῖς βαρβάροις ὅμως πείθεσθε τὴν ἐλευθερίᾱν χρημάτων χάριν ἀποβάλλοντες.

30. ὅτε ἄργυρον τῷ ἄρχοντι ἐδίδου, τρόπαιον ἵσταμεν.

II. 1. Although being harmed, let the citizens neither dissolve the democracy nor appoint a king to rule the city.

2. That ancient king made good laws for the citizens: he contrived, you know, that being willing to fight on behalf of their children they would save the city.

3. If you (pl.) had not given this gold to the shameful woman, she would have fled at some time to the same island with the murderer of the seven dancers.

4. After he came out of the house, Euripides fled with his companions to another house. For his mother feared that we would hit him with stones.

5. It is difficult to revolt from that city: having thrown away our weapons, how are we to fight soldiers experienced in *war*?

READINGS

A. Apollodoros, *The Library* 1.1.1–2

The children of Sky and Earth.

> Οὐρανὸς πρῶτος τοῦ παντὸς ἐδυνάστευε κόσμου.
> γήμᾱς δὲ Γῆν ἐτέκνωσε πρώτους τοὺς ἑκατόγχειρας
> προσαγορευθέντας, Βριάρεων Γύην Κόττον,
> οἳ μεγέθει τε ἀνυπέρβλητοι καὶ δυνάμει
> 5 καθειστήκεσαν,[1] χεῖρας μὲν ἀνὰ ἑκατὸν
> κεφαλὰς δὲ ἀνὰ πεντήκοντα ἔχοντες.

ἀνά (*prep.* + *acc.*) *here shows distribution by number:*
    ἀνά + *number* = [number, e.g., three] each

ἀνυπέρβλητος, ἀνυπέρβλητον   unsurpassable, unconquerable

Βριάρεως, Βριάρεω, ὁ   (*acc.* Βριάρεων)   Briareos ("Strongman")

γαμέω, γαμῶ, ἔγημα, γεγάμηκα, γεγάμημαι, ἐγαμήθην
    marry (a wife); (*mid.*) be married (to a husband), give (a daughter)
    in marriage

Γύης, Γύου, ὁ   Gyes

δύναμις, δυνάμεως, ἡ   strength, power

δυναστεύω, δυναστεύσω, ἐδυνάστευσα, ——, ——, ——   hold power;
    (+ *gen.*) be lord over

ἑκατόγχειρ (*masc./fem. adj.*), *gen.* ἑκατόγχειρος   hundred-handed

ἑκατόν (*indeclinable numeral*)   one hundred

ἔχω (*imperf.* εἶχον), ἕξω/σχήσω, ἔσχον, ἔσχηκα, -ἔσχημαι, ——   have, hold;
    be able; (*mid.*) cling to, be next to (+ *gen.*)

κεφαλή, κεφαλῆς, ἡ   head

κόσμος, κόσμου, ὁ   order; adornment, ornament; universe

Κόττος, Κόττου, ὁ   Kottos

μέγεθος, μεγέθους, τό   size

Οὐρανός, Οὐρανοῦ, ὁ   Sky, Ouranos

πεντήκοντα (*indeclinable numeral*)   fifty

προσαγορεύω, προσαγορεύσω, προσηγόρευσα, προσηγόρευκα, προσηγόρευμαι,
    προσηγορεύθην   address, greet; call, name

τεκνόω, τεκνώσω, ἐτέκνωσα, τετέκνωκα, τετέκνωμαι, ἐτεκνώθην   engender,
    beget, procreate

---

1. The late Greek pluperfect form uses the augmented tense stem εἰστηκ- with the normal third-person plural ending. The earlier form was καθέστασαν.

μετὰ τούτους δὲ αὐτῷ τεκνοῖ Γῆ Κύκλωπας,
Ἄργην Στερόπην Βρόντην, ὧν ἕκαστος εἶχεν
9   ἕνα ὀφθαλμὸν ἐπὶ τοῦ μετώπου.

Ἄργης, Ἄργου, ὁ   Arges ("Bright")

Βρόντης, Βρόντου, ὁ   Brontes ("Thunderer")

ἕκαστος, ἑκάστη, ἕκαστον   each, every

ἕνα (masc. acc. sing. of εἷς, μία, ἕν)   one

ἔχω (imperf. εἶχον), ἕξω/σχήσω, ἔσχον, ἔσχηκα, -έσχημαι, —— have, hold;
   be able; (mid.) cling to, be next to (+ gen.)

Κύκλωψ, Κύκλωπος, ὁ   Cyclops

μέτωπον, μετώπου, τό   forehead

Στερόπης, Στερόπου, ὁ   Steropes ("Lightener")

τεκνόω, τεκνώσω, ἐτέκνωσα, τετέκνωκα, τετέκνωμαι, ἐτεκνώθην   engender,
   beget, procreate

B. Apollodoros, *The Library* 1.7.1

The story of Prometheus.

Προμηθεὺς δὲ ἐξ ὕδατος καὶ γῆς ἀνθρώπους πλάσας
ἔδωκεν αὐτοῖς καὶ πῦρ, λάθρᾳ Διὸς ἐν νάρθηκι
κρύψας. ὡς δὲ ᾔσθετο Ζεύς, ἐπέταξεν Ἡφαίστῳ
τῷ Καυκάσῳ ὄρει τὸ σῶμα αὐτοῦ προσηλῶσαι· τοῦτο
5   δὲ Σκυθικὸν ὄρος ἐστίν. ἐν δὴ τούτῳ προσηλωθεὶς
Προμηθεὺς πολλῶν ἐτῶν ἀριθμὸν ἐδέδετο·
καθ᾽1 ἑκάστην δὲ ἡμέρᾱν ἀετὸς ἐφιπτάμενος αὐτῷ
τοὺς λοβοὺς ἐνέμετο τοῦ ἥπατος αὐξανομένου διὰ
νυκτός. καὶ Προμηθεὺς μὲν πυρὸς κλαπέντος δίκην
10 ἔτινε ταύτην, μέχρις Ἡρακλῆς αὐτὸν ὕστερον ἔλῡσεν,
ὡς ἐν τοῖς καθ᾽2 Ἡρακλέᾱ δηλώσομεν.

ἀετός, ἀετοῦ, ὁ   eagle

αἰσθάνομαι, αἰσθήσομαι, ᾐσθόμην, ——, ᾔσθημαι, —— perceive

ἀριθμός, ἀριθμοῦ, ὁ   number

αὐξάνω/αὔξω, αὐξήσω, ηὔξησα, ηὔξηκα, ηὔξημαι, ηὐξήθην (act. or mid.)
   grow, increase

1. κατά + acc. here refers to distribution in time: καθ᾽ ἑκάστην ἡμέρᾱν, "on each day,
every day."
2. κατά + acc. here means "concerning, in relation to."

READINGS 393

δέω, δήσω, ἔδησα, δέδεκα/δέδηκα, δέδεμαι, ἐδέθην bind, tie
ἕκαστος, ἑκάστη, ἕκαστον each, every
ἐπιτάττω command, order (+ dat. of person commanded)
ἐστί(ν) = third pers. sing., pres. indic. act. of
   εἰμί, ἔσομαι, ——, ——, ——, —— be
ἔτος, ἔτους, τό year
ἐφίπταμαι/ἐπιπέτομαι, ἐπιπτήσομαι, ἐπεπτάμην/ἐπεπτόμην, ——, ——, ——
   fly to; fly over
   (ἐφιπτάμενος = athematic present participle middle)
ἧπαρ, ἥπατος, τό liver
Ἡρακλῆς, Ἡρακλέους, ὁ Herakles
Ἥφαιστος, Ἡφαίστου, ὁ Hephaistos
Ζεύς, Διός, ὁ (voc. Ζεῦ) Zeus
Καύκασος, Καυκάσου, ὁ Caucasus, Mount Kaukasos
κρύπτω, κρύψω, ἔκρυψα, κέκρυφα, κέκρυμμαι, ἐκρύφθην/ἐκρύβην
   cover, hide, conceal
λάθρᾱ (adv.) secretly; (prep. + gen.) secretly from, unknown to
λοβός, λοβοῦ, ὁ lobe, pod
μέχρι(ς) (conj.) until
νάρθηξ, νάρθηκος, ὁ fennel, fennel-stalk
νέμω, νεμῶ, ἔνειμα, νενέμηκα, νενέμημαι, ἐνεμήθην distribute; pasture (a
   flock); (act. or mid.) possess as one's share, inhabit; (mid.) pasture upon,
   graze on, eat
ὄρος, ὄρους, τό mountain
πλάττω, πλάσω, ἔπλασα, πέπλακα, πέπλασμαι, ἐπλάσθην
   form, mold, shape
πολλοί, πολλαί, πολλά many
Προμηθεύς, Προμηθέως, ὁ Prometheus
προσηλόω, προσηλώσω, προσήλωσα, προσήλωκα, προσήλωμαι, προσηλώθην
   nail, fasten by nails
πῦρ, πυρός, τό fire
Σκυθικός, Σκυθική, Σκυθικόν Scythian
τίνω, τείσω, ἔτεισα, τέτεικα, -τέτεισμαι, -ἐτείσθην pay, pay back
ὕστερον (adv.) later
ὡς (conj.) as; when

C. Theognis 497–498

> ἄφϱονος ἀνδϱὸς ὁμῶς καὶ σώφϱονος οἶνος, ὅταν δὴ
> πίνῃ ὑπὲϱ μέτϱον, κοῦφον ἔθηκε¹ νόον.

κοῦφος, κούφη, κοῦφον   light (in weight)

μέτϱον, μέτϱον, τό   measure, limit

νόος/νοῦς, νόου/νοῦ, ὁ   mind

ὁμῶς (adv.)   likewise, equally

πίνω, πίομαι, ἔπιον, πέπωκα, -πέπομαι, -ἐπόθην   drink

1. A **gnomic aorist** expressing a timeless, general truth. See the Appendix, p. 733.

UNIT
14

107. PRESENT PARTICIPLE ACTIVE AND SECOND AORIST
PARTICIPLE ACTIVE OF THE ATHEMATIC VERBS δίδωμι,
τίθημι, AND ἵστημι

The present participle active and second aorist participle active of the athematic verbs δίδωμι, τίθημι, and ἵστημι are presented below, in the nominative/
vocative and genitive singular. The declension of these participles is almost
identical with that of participles already learned.

*The present and aorist participles of these athematic verbs are identical except
that the present participle shows reduplication of the stem.*

PRESENT PARTICIPLE ACTIVE

	M	F	N
Nom./Voc. S	διδούς	διδοῦσα	διδόν
Gen.	διδόντος	διδούσης	διδόντος
Nom./Voc. S	τιθείς	τιθεῖσα	τιθέν
Gen.	τιθέντος	τιθείσης	τιθέντος
Nom./Voc. S	ἱστάς	ἱστᾶσα	ἱστάν
Gen.	ἱστάντος	ἱστάσης	ἱστάντος

SECOND AORIST PARTICIPLE ACTIVE

	M	F	N
Nom./Voc. S	δούς	δοῦσα	δόν
Gen.	δόντος	δούσης	δόντος
Nom./Voc. S	θείς	θεῖσα	θέν
Gen.	θέντος	θείσης	θέντος
Nom./Voc. S	στάς	στᾶσα	στάν
Gen.	στάντος	στάσης	στάντος

Observations: (1) The masculine nominative/vocative singular of these participles ends in -ς and has an acute accent on the ultima. The
masculine and neuter declension stem uses the short vowel
grade of the stem + the suffix -ντ- without the thematic
vowel. Particular attention must be paid to the feminine
declension stem, which has undergone phonetic changes.

(2) The present and second aorist participles active of δίδωμι
are declined, EXCEPT in the masculine nominative singular,
exactly like the second aorist participle active of thematic
verbs (cf. Section 66.6). Compare λιπόντος, διδόντος,
δόντος.

(3) The present and second aorist participles active of τίθημι
are declined exactly like the aorist participle passive of all
verbs (cf. Section 67.4). Compare παιδευθέντος, τιθέντος.

(4) The present and second aorist participles active of ἵστημι
are declined like the first aorist participle active (cf. Section
66.5), EXCEPT for the accent. Contrast ἱστάντος,
παιδεύσαντος.

(5) Note that the masculine and neuter genitive plural of these
participles is identical in form with the third person plural,
present or second aorist imperative active (e.g., ἱστάντων,
στάντων).

(6) All these participles accent the ultima of the feminine genitive
plural: e.g., διδουσῶν, τιθεισῶν, ἱστασῶν.

(7) Masculine and neuter participles with monosyllabic stems do
NOT shift the accent to the ultima in the genitive and
dative as do other third-declension forms. Contrast δόντος,
αἰγός.

(8) The accent of monosyllabic participles, like that of all
participles, is persistent and remains the same when these
participles are compounded:

    ἀποδούς, ἀποδοῦσα, ἀποδόν

108. PRESENT PARTICIPLE MIDDLE/PASSIVE AND SECOND AORIST PARTICIPLE MIDDLE OF ATHEMATIC VERBS

Athematic verbs form the present participle middle/passive and the second aorist participle middle by adding to the short-vowel grade of the present tense stem and the second aorist active and middle tense stem the suffix and endings -μενος, -μενη, -μενον without the thematic vowel.

These participles are declined exactly like the present participle middle/passive of παιδεύω (cf. Section 67.3).

Remember that the verb ἵστημι does not have a second aorist middle.

PRESENT PARTICIPLE MIDDLE/PASSIVE

	M	F	N
Nom. S	διδόμενος	διδομένη	διδόμενον
Nom. S	τιθέμενος	τιθεμένη	τιθέμενον
Nom. S	ἱστάμενος	ἱσταμένη	ἱστάμενον

SECOND AORIST PARTICIPLE MIDDLE

	M	F	N
Nom. S	δόμενος	δομένη	δόμενον
Nom. S	θέμενος	θεμένη	θέμενον

The aorist participle passive of all verbs is formed from Principal Part VI according to rules already learned.

109. PERFECT PARTICIPLE ACTIVE OF ἵστημι

The perfect participle active of ἵστημι is declined as follows:

	M	F	N
Nom. S	ἑστώς	ἑστῶσα	ἑστός
Gen.	ἑστῶτος	ἑστώσης	ἑστῶτος

Observation: The masculine and neuter belong, as usual, to the third declension (dative plural ἑστῶσι[ν]), the feminine to the first declension (genitive plural ἑστωσῶν).

All participles of δίδωμι, τίθημι, and ἵστημι not covered in the preceding Sections are formed from the other Principal Parts of these verbs according to rules already learned.

110. THE VERB δείκνῡμι, "show"

The verb δείκνῡμι has the following Principal Parts:

δείκνῡμι, δείξω, ἔδειξα, δέδειχα, δέδειγμαι, ἐδείχθην, "show"

This verb is athematic in the present and imperfect. In all other tenses it employs the same endings as παιδεύω. Thus all the athematic forms of δείκνῡμι come from Principal Part I; ἔδειξα is a first aorist like ἐπαίδευσα, δέδειχα is a perfect like πεπαίδευκα.

This verb also differs from δίδωμι, τίθημι, and ἵστημι in that:

(1) In the present subjunctive, the final vowel of the stem does NOT contract with the endings.
(2) The present optative is *thematic.*

The present tense stem of δείκνῡμι shows the same vowel gradation as the present tense stems of the athematic verbs already encountered (cf. Section 100):

> *Long-vowel grade:*   δεικνῡ-
> *Short-vowel grade:*   δεικνυ-

As usual, the long-vowel grade is used only in the singular of the present and imperfect indicative active.

1. PRESENT INDICATIVE ACTIVE AND MIDDLE/PASSIVE

To form the present indicative active and middle/passive of δείκνῡμι, add the usual athematic endings to the appropriate grade of the present tense stem (cf. Section 100). The forms are as follows:

		PRESENT INDICATIVE ACTIVE	*PRESENT INDICATIVE MIDDLE/PASSIVE*
S	1	δείκνῡμι	δείκνυμαι
	2	δείκνῡς	δείκνυσαι
	3	δείκνῡσι(ν)	δείκνυται
P	1	δείκνυμεν	δεικνύμεθα
	2	δείκνυτε	δείκνυσθε
	3	δεικνύᾱσι(ν)	δείκνυνται

2. IMPERFECT INDICATIVE ACTIVE AND MIDDLE/PASSIVE

To form the imperfect indicative active and middle/passive of δείκνῡμι, add the usual athematic endings to the appropriate grade of the augmented present tense stem (cf. Section 100). The forms are as follows:

	IMPERFECT INDICATIVE ACTIVE	*IMPERFECT INDICATIVE MIDDLE/PASSIVE*
S 1	ἐδείκνῡν	ἐδεικνύμην
2	ἐδείκνῡς	ἐδείκνυσο
3	ἐδείκνῡ	ἐδείκνυτο
P 1	ἐδείκνυμεν	ἐδεικνύμεθα
2	ἐδείκνυτε	ἐδείκνυσθε
3	ἐδείκνυσαν	ἐδείκνυντο

3. PRESENT SUBJUNCTIVE ACTIVE AND MIDDLE/PASSIVE

In the present subjunctive active and middle/passive δείκνῡμι employs the usual subjunctive endings. But it differs from δίδωμι, τίθημι, and ἵστημι in that the final vowel of the stem *does not contract* with the endings. Thus these forms are like the corresponding forms of παιδεύω.

	PRESENT SUBJUNCTIVE ACTIVE	*PRESENT SUBJUNCTIVE MIDDLE/PASSIVE*
S 1	δεικνύω	δεικνύωμαι
2	δεικνύῃς	δεικνύῃ
	etc.	etc.

4. PRESENT OPTATIVE ACTIVE AND MIDDLE/PASSIVE

Unlike δίδωμι, τίθημι, and ἵστημι, the verb δείκνῡμι uses in the present optative active and middle/passive the same *thematic* endings as those employed in the corresponding forms of παιδεύω.

	PRESENT OPTATIVE ACTIVE	*PRESENT OPTATIVE MIDDLE/PASSIVE*
S 1	δεικνύοιμι	δεικνυοίμην
2	δεικνύοις	δεικνύοιο
	etc.	etc.

5. PRESENT IMPERATIVE ACTIVE AND MIDDLE/PASSIVE

The present imperative of δείκνῡμι follows the pattern of ἵστημι (Section 100). The second person singular active consists of the long-vowel grade of the stem with no ending added. The other forms add the usual endings to the short-vowel stem.

	PRESENT IMPERATIVE *ACTIVE*	*PRESENT IMPERATIVE* *MIDDLE/PASSIVE*
S 2	δείκνῡ	δείκνυσο
3	δεικνύτω	δεικνύσθω
P 2	δείκνυτε	δείκνυσθε
3	δεικνύντων	δεικνύσθων

Observation: The forms of the second person plural, present imperative active and middle/passive are identical with the corresponding indicative forms.

6. PRESENT INFINITIVE ACTIVE AND MIDDLE/PASSIVE

The verb δείκνῡμι forms the present infinitives active and middle/passive in the same way as the athematic verbs already studied (cf. Section 100).

PRESENT INFINITIVE ACTIVE: δεικνύναι
PRESENT INFINITIVE MIDDLE/PASSIVE: δείκνυσθαι

7. PRESENT PARTICIPLE ACTIVE AND MIDDLE/PASSIVE

The present participles active and middle/passive of δείκνῡμι are declined as follows:

PRESENT PARTICIPLE ACTIVE

	M	F	N
Nom./Voc. S	δεικνύς	δεικνῦσα	δεικνύν
Gen.	δεικνύντος	δεικνύσης	δεικνύντος

PRESENT PARTICIPLE MIDDLE/PASSIVE

	M	F	N
Nom. S	δεικνύμενος	δεικνυμένη	δεικνύμενον

Observations: (1) As with the other athematic participles, the masculine nominative/vocative singular ends in -ς and has an acute accent; the masculine and neuter declension stem employs the short-vowel grade of the stem + the suffix -ντ-. Again, the feminine declension stem has undergone phonetic change. The masculine and neuter dative plural is δεικνῦσι(ν) (< *δεικνύντσι[ν]); the feminine genitive plural is δεικνῦσῶν.

(2) The masculine and neuter genitive plural of the present participle active are identical with the third person plural, present imperative active.

111. SUPPLEMENTARY USE OF THE PARTICIPLE

The **supplementary participle** completes the meaning of a verb. The participle indicates aspect only, not relative time, in the constructions explained below.

1. SUPPLEMENTARY PARTICIPLE WITH VERBS OF EMOTION

Many verbs indicating emotion take a supplementary participle.

One such verb is:

χαίρω, χαιρήσω, ——, κεχάρηκα, ——, ἐχάρην, "take pleasure, enjoy"

χαίρετε **τοῦτο ποιοῦντες.**
You take pleasure **doing this.**
You enjoy **doing this.**

Such participles are best translated not by an English participle, as in the first translation above, but by an English *gerund*, as in the second translation. Compare the circumstantial participle, which states a separate circumstance.

τῑμᾶσθε **τοῦτο ποιοῦντες.**
Doing this, you are honored.
Because you do this, you are honored.

In this example the participle and the main verb *cannot be combined into a single verbal expression* (cf. "you enjoy doing").

2. SUPPLEMENTARY PARTICIPLE WITH VERBS OF BEGINNING, CEASING, AND ENDURING

Many verbs of beginning, ceasing, and enduring take a supplementary participle. The participle is generally in the present tense.

> ἐπαυσάμεθα **τοῦτο ποιοῦντες**.
> We ceased **doing this**.

> παύσομεν αὐτοὺς **τοῦτο ποιοῦντας**.
> We shall stop them (from) **doing this**.
> We shall stop their **doing this**.

These participles must be translated by the English *gerund*, not the English participle.

The verb ἄρχω, which in the middle voice means "begin," can take either a supplementary participle or an infinitive, with a difference in meaning.

> ἀρξόμεθα **τοῦτο ποιοῦντες**.
> We shall begin **by doing this**.

> ἀρξόμεθα **τοῦτο ποιεῖν**.
> We shall begin **to do this**.

The supplementary participle with this verb states the first of a series of actions (e.g., "We shall begin by doing this, then we shall do that"); the infinitive indicates the beginning of a single action, and is usually in the present tense.

3. SUPPLEMENTARY PARTICIPLE WITH THE VERBS λανθάνω, φθάνω, AND τυγχάνω

Here are the Principal Parts of three verbs whose meaning is usually completed by a supplementary participle:

λανθάνω, λήσω, ἔλαθον, λέληθα, ——, ——, "escape the notice of (+ acc.)"
φθάνω, φθήσομαι, ἔφθασα or ἔφθην, ——, ——, ——, "act first; be first (in doing something); anticipate (someone)"
τυγχάνω, τεύξομαι, ἔτυχον, τετύχηκα, ——, ——, "happen (to); hit the mark; (+ gen.) obtain"

The supplementary participle with τυγχάνω must be rendered by the appropriate English infinitive.

> τυγχάνομεν **τοῦτο ποιοῦντες**.   (*present participle*)
> We happen **to be doing this**.

ἐτύχομεν **τοῦτο ποιήσαντες**.   (*aorist participle*)
We happened **to do this.**

ἐτύχομεν **τοῦτο ποιοῦντες**.   (*present participle*)
We happened **to be doing this.**

English lacks verbs with the exact meaning of λανθάνω and φθάνω. Sentences with these verbs are best translated in two stages: a literal, if awkward, version, and then a more colloquial version. Note especially that the direct object in the Greek will be translated as a possessive or as the object of a preposition in English.

τοὺς φίλους λανθάνομεν **τοῦτο ποιοῦντες**.
We escape our friends' notice **doing this.**
We do this secretly from our friends.
We are doing this secretly from our friends.

τοὺς φίλους ἐλάθομεν **τοῦτο ποιήσαντες**.
We escaped our friends' notice **doing this.**
We did this secretly from our friends.

τοὺς φίλους φθάνομεν **τοῦτο ποιοῦντες**.
We anticipate our friends **(in) doing this.**
We do this before our friends.
We are doing this before our friends.

τοὺς φίλους $\left\{\begin{array}{l} ἐφθάσαμεν \\ ἔφθημεν \end{array}\right\}$ **τοῦτο ποιήσαντες**.
We anticipated our friends **(in) doing this.**
We "beat" our friends doing this.
We did this before our friends.

The participle usually has the same aspect as the finite verb, but an aorist participle together with a present or imperfect indicative shows *prior action*:

τυγχάνομεν **τοῦτο ποιήσαντες**.
We happen **to have done this.**

VOCABULARY

ἀμαθής, ἀμαθές	ignorant, stupid
ἀμαθίᾱ, ἀμαθίᾱς, ἡ	ignorance, stupidity
δείκνῡμι, δείξω, ἔδειξα,	show
δέδειχα, δέδειγμαι, ἐδείχθην	
ἐπιδείκνυμαι	show off, display
ἐπίδειξις, ἐπιδείξεως, ἡ	display, demonstration
ἐπανίσταμαι, ἐπαναστήσομαι,	rise in insurrection against
ἐπανέστην, ἐπανέστηκα,	(+ dat.)
——, ——	
ἐρωτάω, ἐρωτήσω, ἠρώτησα,	ask, question
ἠρώτηκα, ἠρώτημαι, ἠρωτήθην	
ἕτερος, ἑτέρᾱ, ἕτερον	the other (of two)
ἔτι (adv.)	yet, still
μηκέτι (adv.)	no longer
οὐκέτι (adv.)	no longer
κοινός, κοινή, κοινόν	common
Λακεδαιμόνιος, Λακεδαιμονίᾱ,	Spartan (used of persons)
Λακεδαιμόνιον	
λανθάνω, λήσω, ἔλαθον,	escape the notice of (+ acc.)
λέληθα, ——, ——	
μαθητής, μαθητοῦ, ὁ	student, pupil
μέσος, μέση, μέσον	middle (of)
νέος, νέᾱ, νέον	new, young
παρα- (prefix)	beside
παραγίγνομαι	be present, be with (+ dat.)
παραδίδωμι	hand over, surrender; hand down
παραμένω	stand fast; stay behind
ῥᾴδιος, ῥᾳδίᾱ, ῥᾴδιον	easy
στάσις, στάσεως, ἡ	civil strife, faction
τυγχάνω, τεύξομαι, ἔτυχον,	happen (to); hit the mark;
τετύχηκα, ——, ——	(+ gen.) obtain

ὑπο- (prefix) — under; secretly; gradually, slightly

ὑπακούω — heed, obey (+ gen. or dat.)

ὑπομένω — await; stand firm; endure

φθάνω, φθήσομαι, ἔφθασα or ἔφθην, ——, ——, —— — act first; be first (in doing something); anticipate (someone)

χαίρω, χαιρήσω, ——, κεχάρηκα, ——, ἐχάρην — rejoice (in), take pleasure (in), enjoy (+ dat.)

VOCABULARY NOTES

The adjective ἀμαθής, ἀμαθές, "ignorant, stupid," is formed from the root μαθ- (cf. μανθάνω) + alpha privative. From the stem of this adjective is formed the abstract noun ἀμαθίᾱ, ἀμαθίᾱς, ἡ, "ignorance, stupidity." Cf. the agent noun μαθητής, μαθητοῦ, ὁ, "student, pupil" (with which compare, e.g., ποιητής).

The verb δείκνῡμι, δείξω, ἔδειξα, δέδειχα, δέδειγμαι, ἐδείχθην, "show," has the root δεικ- and is athematic only in the present indicative, imperative, infinitive, and participle, and the imperfect indicative. The present tense stem consists of the root δεικ- + the suffix -νῡ-/-νυ- and adds the appropriate athematic or thematic endings (cf. Section 110). Several other verbs are formed similarly and show in Principal Part I the suffix + ending -νῡμι.

The compound verb ἐπιδείκνυμαι means "to show off (something of one's own)," e.g., rhetorical skill. The verbal noun ἐπίδειξις, ἐπιδείξεως, ἡ, "display, demonstration," can take an objective genitive of the thing displayed.

The verb ἐπανίσταμαι, ἐπαναστήσομαι, ἐπανέστην, ἐπανέστηκα, ——, ——, "rise in insurrection (against)," takes a dative of the persons against whom one rises. Note that this verb is a double compound: ἐπι- + ἀνα- + ἵσταμαι. The past indicative augment follows both prefixes: compare ἐπανέστην (first person singular, root aorist indicative active) with ἐπαναστῶ (first person singular, root aorist subjunctive active). This verb uses intransitive forms of ἵστημι: present and imperfect middle, future middle, second aorist active, perfect and pluperfect active.

The adjective ἕτερος, ἑτέρᾱ, ἕτερον, "the other (of two)," refers in the singular to an individual contrasted with another individual. In the plural, it refers to one of two contrasted groups. This adjective marks, more strongly than the adjective ἄλλος, ἄλλη, ἄλλο, the fact that one person or thing (or group) belongs to a different class from another. The adjective can be repeated and refer in turn to each of the contrasted persons or groups.

Δημοσθένης μὲν ταῦτα ποιεῖ, ὁ δ' ἕτερος τάδε.
Demosthenes does these (those) things, but the other man does the following things.

ὁ μὲν ἕτερος ταῦτα ποιεῖ, ὁ δ' ἕτερος τάδε.
The one man does these (those) things, but the other man does the following things.

οἱ μὲν ἕτεροι ταῦτα ποιοῦσιν, οἱ δ' ἕτεροι τάδε.
One group does these (those) things, but the other group does the following things.

ἕτερον τόδε ἢ οὔ;
Is this another (a different, a separate) thing or not?

The adjective *κοινός, κοινή, κοινόν,* "common," refers to things shared. The phrase *τὰ κοινά* often means "public affairs," and *τὸ κοινόν* can mean "the state" (i.e., the city). Koine (*ἡ κοινὴ διάλεκτος*) is a "common" dialect of Greek which developed during the Hellenistic age.

The adjective *μέσος, μέση, μέσον,* "middle (of)," has two distinct meanings: in the attributive position it means "middle"; when it precedes the article, it means "(the) middle of (the noun which follows)."

ἐν τῇ μέσῃ ἀγορᾷ
in the middle market place
(i.e., not the one to the left or the right)

ἐν μέσῃ τῇ ἀγορᾷ
in the middle of the market place

The adjective *νέος, νέᾱ, νέον,* "new, young," was originally **νέϝος.* Compare the stem **νεϝ-* with the English cognate *new.*

The verbal noun *στάσις, στάσεως, ἡ,* "civil strife, faction," means literally a "standing"; it is formed from the unreduplicated short-vowel grade of the stem of *ἵστημι: στα-.*

The verb *τυγχάνω, τεύξομαι, ἔτυχον, τετύχηκα,* ——, ——, "happen (to); hit the mark; (+ *gen.*) obtain," is deponent in the future tense only. Principal Parts III and IV show the zero-grade of the root: *τυχ-.* Principal Part I has the zero-grade with a nasal infix and the suffix -*αν-* : *τυγχαν-.* Principal Part II has the e-grade: *τευξ-* (<**τευχσ-*). Cf. *μανθάνω,* but note the different formation of its future *μαθήσομαι.* The zero-grade of this root appears also in the noun *τύχη.* When this verb means "obtain" it takes an object in the genitive case: *εἰρήνης ἐτύχομεν,* "We obtained peace."

Note the difference in meaning between ὑπομένω, "await; stand firm; endure," and παραμένω, "stand fast; stay behind."

The verb φθάνω, φθήσομαι, ἔφθασα or ἔφθην, ——, ——, ——, "act first; be first (in doing something); anticipate (someone)," is deponent in the future tense only. There is *no difference in meaning* between the first aorist ἔφθασα and the root aorist ἔφθην, which is conjugated just like ἔστην (from ἵστημι). E.g.:

$$\left.\begin{array}{l}ἐφθάσατε \\ ἔφθητε\end{array}\right\} \text{ you acted first}$$

$$\left.\begin{array}{l}φθάσαι \\ φθῆναι\end{array}\right\} \text{ to act first}$$

The verb χαίρω, χαιρήσω, ——, κεχάρηκα, ——, ἐχάρην, "rejoice (in), take pleasure (in), enjoy (+ *dat.*)," is a passive partial deponent: it has an aorist passive, with an active meaning, rather than an aorist active. The present was originally *χάριω: cf. χάρις. The iota "jumped over" the rho. The resulting stem χαιρ- was used, with a suffix, to form the future.

COGNATES AND DERIVATIVES

δείκνυμι	paradigm (an example which **shows** the way)
ἐπίδειξις	epideictic (for **display**)
ἕτερος	heterodox
κοινός	Koine; epicene (having the characteristics of both male and female)
λανθάνω	Lethe (the river of forgetfulness)
μέσος	Mesolithic (the **Middle** Stone Age)
νέος	new; Neolithic (the **New** Stone Age)

DRILLS

I. *Translate. Identify all participles.*

1. τοῦ βασιλέως τοῦ ἐπὶ τῷ τείχει ἑστῶτος
2. τοῖς δώσουσιν
3. τὰ ὅπλα ἀναθέντες ἔφυγον πρὸς τὴν πόλιν.
4. τοῖς δῶρα διδοῦσιν
5. δῶρον τῷ πατρὶ δοὺς ἀπῆλθες εἰς τὴν μάχην.
6. δῶρα ταῖς λελειμμέναις ἔδοτε.
7. ὁ κῆρυξ ὁ τὴν νίκην ἀγγελῶν
8. τοὺς τὴν πόλιν ἀποδομένους οὐκ ἐδέχοντ᾽ εἰς τὴν οἰκίᾱν.
9. τοὺς τὰ ὅπλα λείποντας οὐ φιλεῖ ὁ δῆμος.
10. τοὺς τὸ τρόπαιον ἀνατιθέντας ἔπαυσεν ὁ στρατηγός.
11. ἐνταῦθα στάντες ἐμαχέσαντο.
12. τοὺς τὸ τρόπαιον ἀναθεμένους φυγεῖν ἐκέλευσεν.
13. δίκην διδόᾱσιν οὗτοι οἱ τότε μηχανώμενοι ὅπως ταύτης τῆς πόλεως ἄρξουσιν.
14. ταῦτα μαθόντες οἱ παῖδες ἐξέφυγον ἐκ τῆς χώρᾱς φοβούμενοι μὴ βλαβεῖεν ὑπὸ τῶν μαχομένων.
15. ἀεὶ τῑμῶμεν τοὺς τόνδε τὸν ἀγῶνα καταστήσαντας.
16. θεοῖς ταῖς νόμους ἀγαθοὺς τιθείσαις χρῡσόν τε καὶ καλὰς αἶγας ἐδίδου.

II. *Translate.*

1. χαίρομεν ἐν πολέμῳ νῑκῶντες.
2. χαίρομεν τοὺς ἀμαθεῖς κακῶς ποιοῦσαι.
3. τοὺς ἀμαθεῖς κακὰ ποιοῦσαι ἐπαυσάμεθα.
4. τοὺς ἀμαθεῖς κακὰ ποιοῦντας ἐπαύσαμεν.
5. ἤρξασθε ταῦτα δηλοῦντες.
6. ἤρξασθε ταῦτα δηλοῦν.
7. τυγχάνεις δῶρα τοῖς γέρουσι διδοῦσα.
8. ἔτυχες δῶρα τῷ γέροντι δοῦσα.
9. τυγχάνεις δῶρα τοῖς γέρουσι δοῦσα.

10. ἐτύγχανες δῶρον τῷ ἱερεῖ διδούς.

11. ἐτύγχανες δῶρα τῷ βασιλεῖ δοῦσα.

12. τοὺς φίλους φθάνουσι κλέπτοντες χρυσόν.

13. οἱ νεανίαι τὸν Σωκράτη λανθάνουσι κακὰ πράττοντες.

14. τοὺς ποιητὰς τοὺς σώφρονας οὐ λανθάνω αἰσχρὰ γράφων.

15. πῶς τοὺς φύλακας λάθωμεν ἐκφυγόντες;

EXERCISES

I.   1. ἄρξομαι μέν, ὦ ἄνδρες, τὴν Δημοσθένους ἀμαθίᾶν περὶ τῶν
        κοινῶν τῆς πόλεως πρᾶγμάτων δεικνῦσα, ἔπειτα δὲ πάντα
        δηλώσω τὰ τοῖς γ' ἄλλοις ῥήτορσι ἀδίκως πεπρᾶγμένα.

     2. τρόπαιον ἱστάντων τῶν στρατιωτῶν, ὁ στρατηγὸς ἀποπεμψάτω
        εἰς τὴν πόλιν ἐννέα κήρῡκας τὴν νίκην ἀπαγγελοῦντας.

     3. μετάδοτέ ποτε τῆς ἀρχῆς καὶ τοῖς ἐν τῇ στάσει φυγοῦσιν.

     4. ὦ φίλοι, ἐκ τῆς πόλεως αὐτίκα φυγόντες πῶς λάθοιτ' ἂν τούσδε
        γε τοὺς φύλακας τοὺς ἐπὶ τῷ τείχει ἑστῶτας;

     5. ὅταν ἕτεροι ἑτέρων ἀξιῶσιν ἄρχειν, οἱ ἀρχόμενοι ἀεὶ τοῖς
        ἄρχουσιν ἐπαναστῆναι βούλονται. νόμῳ μὲν γάρ τοι καλὸν
        καὶ δίκαιον τὸ ἄλλων ὑπακούειν, φύσει δὲ κακὸν καὶ αἰσχρὸν
        τὸ ἄφροσιν ἀνθρώποις δουλεύειν.

     6. τοῦ δήμου ἐπαναστάντος, ὁ βασιλεύς, παραδοὺς τῷ παιδὶ τὴν
        ἀρχὴν καὶ ἐκφυγὼν ἐκ τῆς χώρᾱς, ἔλαθέ πως τοὺς πολίτᾱς
        ἐλθὼν εἰς ἄλλην χώρᾱν ὡς ἐκεῖ παραμενῶν καὶ τελευτήσων
        τὸν βίον.

     7. ἔτυχεν ὁ Δημοσθένης ἐπιδεικνύμενος ἐν τῇ ἀγορᾷ τὴν ῥητορικὴν
        ὅτ' εἰσῆλθον κήρῡκες ἀγγελοῦντες τὴν πάντων τῶν βαρβάρων
        νίκην.

     8. ἄξιος δὴ κακὰ παθεῖν οὗτος ὁ τούς τε νόμους καὶ τὴν δημοκρατίᾱν
        καταλύσᾱς καὶ τὴν πόλιν εἰς στάσιν καθιστάς.

     9. ὦ ἄνδρες Ἀθηναῖοι, καὶ τούτους τοὺς κινδύνους ὑπομείνατε ὑπὲρ
        τῆς πάντων ἐλευθερίᾱς μαχόμενοι.

    10. προσελθόντος τοῦ Εὐρῑπίδου, ἐτύγχανόν που αἱ παῖδες αἱ εὐγενεῖς
        τῇ θεῷ χορεύουσαι.

11. τῇ μὲν ἑτέρᾳ χειρὶ ἀσπίδα λαβοῦσα, τῇ δ' ἑτέρᾳ ξίφος, ὦ μῆτερ
Εὐρῑπίδου, ἔξελθε ἐκ τῆς οἰκίας μαχουμένη δὴ πάσαις ταῖς
ἄλλαις γυναιξίν.

12. ὦ παῖδες, ἐὰν οἱ πολέμιοι φθάσωσι τοὺς ᾿Αθηναίους εἰς μέσην γε
τὴν πόλιν εἰσελθόντες, ἐνταῦθ' οὐκέτι παραμενοῦμεν. οὐ γάρ
τοι ῥᾴδιον τὸ βαρβάρων ὑπακούειν.

13. ἀεί που χαίρουσιν οἱ ἄδικοι τοὺς ψῡχήν γ' ἀγαθοὺς κακὰ
ποιοῦντες.

14. ἐκείνου τοῦ διδασκάλου μὴ παιδεύοντος τοὺς μαθητὰς περὶ ἀρετῆς
καταλυθήσεται ἡ δημοκρατίᾱ.

15. νῑκηθέντων τῶν πολεμίων, τὴν ἑορτὴν τῷ θεῷ ὅμως οὐκ
ἐποιούμεθα φοβούμενοι μὴ ἔτι λάθοιεν τοὺς στρατιώτᾱς καὶ
ἄλλοι ἱππεῖς εἰς τὴν χώρᾱν εἰσελθόντες.

16. ἐρώτησον τὸν Σωκράτη περὶ τῆς νῦν γε στάσεως. ἕστηκε γὰρ ἐν
μέσῃ τῇ ἀγορᾷ.

17. πάντων τῶν ἄλλων εἰρήνην πρὸς ἀλλήλους ἀγόντων, ὁ τῶν
᾿Αθηναίων στρατηγὸς παυσάτω μαχομένους τοὺς ὁπλίτᾱς.

18. εἰ μὴ τοὺς παῖδας παιδεῦσαι ὁ ἀδελφός, παίδευσαι αὐτὸν
παιδεῦσαι αὐτούς.

19. οἱ ῥήτορες, χρῡσὸν παρὰ τῶν πολεμίων λαβόντες, ἔπειθον τὸν
δῆμον ἐκβαλεῖν ἐκ τῆς πόλεως οὐ μόνον τοὺς ἠδικηκότας
ἀλλὰ καὶ τοὺς εὖ τε καὶ σωφρόνως πεπολῑτευμένους καὶ ὑπὲρ
πάντων μεμαχημένους.

20. οἳ ἂν χαίρωσιν τοὺς ἄνδρας ἀδικοῦντες, αὐτοὶ δικαίως ὑπὸ
τούτων πείσονταί ποτε δεινά.

21. μηχανωμένων τῶν ἑταίρων ὅπως Σωκράτη ἐκλύσονται, ἕσταμέν
που πρὸς τῷ τείχει.

22. οἱ πάλαι ῥᾳδίως τὴν γῆν ἀπολιπόντες εἰς ἄλλᾱς χώρᾱς
μετανίσταντο, οὐδὲ Ἕλληνες οἱ πάντες ἐκαλοῦντο.

23. νῦν δὴ ἐπιδείκνυσο τήν γε ῥητορικήν, ἀγαθὲ νεᾱνίᾱ. τοὺς γὰρ
ἄλλους μαθητὰς ἔφθης ἐρωτήσᾱς τὸν διδάσκαλον περὶ ἀρετῆς.

24. ἐπίδειξιν ποιούμενοι τυγχάνουσιν οἱ ῥήτορες.

25. ὦ νέοι, μήτ' ἐκκλέψητ' οἶνον ἐξ ἐκείνης γε τῆς οἰκίας μήτε τὰς
γυναῖκας βλάψητε.

26. κοινὰ τὰ τῶν φίλων.

27. ἆρ' οὐκ ἐπαύσασθε μαχόμενοι; νῦν γε παύσασθε, ὦ ἀμαθεῖς.

28. ὦ αἰσχρὲ ῥῆτορ, τόν γε δῆμον οὐ λανθάνεις δῶρα λαμβάνων.

29. ὁ τοῖς ἀγαθοῖς χαίρων ἀγαθῶν γε τεύξεται.

II. 1. Although the king wishes somehow to hand the city over to the enemies, the young men will obey the generals and remain in the middle of the plain in order to fight on behalf of the people.

2. I happened to hear the speakers asking the messengers about the horsemen being sent into this land.

3. Because the priests made sacrifices to all the gods, the enemy, conquered in battle, fled in silence during that night without the hoplites' noticing (i.e., escaped the notice of the hoplites. . .: λανθάνω).

4. We enjoy hearing Sokrates, at least, teaching the citizens about virtue.

5. When the soldiers come into the city, flee! (*Translate the subordinate clause two ways.*)

READINGS

A. Apollodorus, *The Library* 1.1.4

Sky is attacked by his children, the Titans.

    Ἀγανακτοῦσα δὲ Γῆ ἐπὶ τῇ ἀπωλείᾳ τῶν εἰς Τάρταρον
ῥιφέντων παίδων πείθει τοὺς Τῖτᾶνας ἐπιθέσθαι τῷ
πατρί, καὶ δίδωσιν ἀδαμαντίνην ἅρπην Κρόνῳ. οἱ δὲ¹
Ὠκεανοῦ χωρὶς ἐπιτίθενται, καὶ Κρόνος ἀποτεμὼν
5 τὰ αἰδοῖα τοῦ πατρὸς εἰς τὴν θάλασσαν ἀφίησιν. ἐκ
δὲ τῶν σταλαγμῶν τοῦ ῥέοντος αἵματος ἐρινύες ἐγένοντο,
Ἀληκτὼ Τῑσιφόνη Μέγαιρα.

ἀγανακτέω, ἀγανακτήσω, ἠγανάκτησα, ἠγανάκτηκα, ἠγανάκτημαι,
  ἠγανακτήθην be angry

ἀδαμάντινος, ἀδαμαντίνη, ἀδαμάντινον adamantine, of the hardest metal

αἰδοῖον, αἰδοίου, τό sexual organ

αἷμα, αἵματος, τό blood

Ἀληκτώ, Ἀληκτοῦς, ἡ (*For declension see Appendix, page 592.*) Alekto, a Fury

ἀποτέμνω, ἀποτεμῶ, ἀπέτεμον, ἀποτέτμηκα, ἀποτέτμημαι, ἀπετμήθην
  cut off

ἀπώλεια, ἀπωλείᾱς, ἡ destruction

ἅρπη, ἅρπης, ἡ sickle

ἀφίημι, ἀφήσω, ἀφῆκα, ἀφεῖκα, ἀφεῖμαι, ἀφείθην throw away

ἐπιτίθημι put on; (*mid.*) attack (+ *dat.*)

ἐρῑνύς, ἐρῑνύος, ἡ Erinys, an avenging deity, Fury

θάλασσαν = θάλατταν

Κρόνος, Κρόνου, ὁ Kronos, son of Ouranos and Ge

Μέγαιρα, Μεγαίρᾱς, ἡ Megaira, a Fury

ῥέω, ῥυήσομαι, ——, ἐρρύηκα, ——, ἐρρύην flow

ῥίπτω, ῥίψω, ἔρρῑψα, ἔρρῑφα, ἔρρῑμμαι, ἐρρίφθην/ἐρρίφην throw

σταλαγμός, σταλαγμοῦ, ὁ drop

Τάρταρος, Ταρτάρου, ὁ or ἡ (*pl.* τὰ Τάρταρα) Tartaros, the underworld

Τῑσιφόνη, Τῑσιφόνης, ἡ Tisiphone, a Fury

Τῑτάν, Τῑτᾶνος, ὁ a Titan, a child of Ouranos and Ge

χωρίς (*adv., and prep.* + *gen.*) separately, apart

Ὠκεανός, Ὠκεανοῦ, ὁ Okeanos, a Titan

1. The nominative of the article + δέ marks a change of subject and can be translated
"And he/she/they."

B. Apollodoros, *The Library* 1.3.5

The story of Hephaistos.

"Ηρᾱ δὲ χωρὶς εὐνῆς ἐγέννησεν "Ηφαιστον· ὡς δὲ "Ομηρος
λέγει, καὶ τοῦτον ἐκ Διὸς ἐγέννησε. ῥίπτει δὲ αὐτὸν
ἐξ οὐρανοῦ Ζεὺς "Ηρᾳ δεθείσῃ βοηθοῦντα· ταύτην γὰρ
ἐκρέμασε Ζεὺς ἐξ 'Ολύμπου χειμῶνα ἐπιπέμψᾱσαν 'Ηρακλεῖ,
5   ὅτε Τροίᾱν ἑλὼν ἔπλει. πεσόντα δ' "Ηφαιστον ἐν Λήμνῳ
καὶ πηρωθέντα τὰς βάσεις διέσωσε Θέτις.

αἱρέω, αἱρήσω, εἷλον (*unaugmented stem* ἑλ-), ᾕρηκα, ᾕρημαι, ᾑρέθην take,
    capture; (*mid.*) choose

βάσις, βάσεως, ἡ step, foot

βοηθέω, βοηθήσω, ἐβοήθησα, βεβοήθηκα, βεβοήθημαι, ἐβοήθην come to
    the aid of (+ *dat.*)

γεννάω, γεννήσω, ἐγέννησα, γεγέννηκα, γεγέννημαι, ἐγεννήθην beget, bear

δέω, δήσω, ἔδησα, δέδεκα/δέδηκα, δέδεμαι, ἐδέθην bind, tie

ἑλών *see* αἱρέω

εὐνή, εὐνῆς, ἡ bed, marriage bed

Ζεύς, Διός, ὁ Zeus

"Ηρᾱ, "Ηρᾱς, ἡ Hera, wife of Zeus

'Ηρακλῆς, 'Ηρακλέους, ὁ Herakles

"Ηφαιστος, 'Ηφαίστου, ὁ Hephaistos, god of crafts

Θέτις, Θέτιδος, ἡ Thetis, mother of Achilles

κρεμάννῡμι (*mid./pass.* κρέμαμαι), κρεμῶ (κρεμάω), ἐκρέμασα, ——, ——,
    ἐκρεμάσθην (*fut. pass.* κρεμήσομαι) hang, hang up

λέγω, ἐρῶ/λέξω, εἶπον/ἔλεξα, εἴρηκα, εἴρημαι/λέλεγμαι, ἐλέχθην/ἐρρήθην
    say, speak

Λῆμνος, Λήμνου, ἡ Lemnos, an island off the coast of Asia Minor

"Ολυμπος, 'Ολύμπου, ὁ Olympos, the home of the gods

οὐρανός, οὐρανοῦ, ὁ sky, heaven

πηρόω, πηρώσω, ἐπήρωσα, πεπήρωκα, πεπήρωμαι, ἐπηρώθην maim, lame

πίπτω, πεσοῦμαι, ἔπεσον, πέπτωκα, ——, —— fall

πλέω, πλεύσομαι, ἔπλευσα, πέπλευκα, πέπλευσμαι, —— sail

ῥίπτω, ῥίψω, ἔρρῑψα, ἔρρῑφα, ἔρρῑμμαι, ἐρρίφθην/ἐρρίφην throw

Τροίᾱ, Τροίᾱς, ἡ Troy

χειμών, χειμῶνος, ὁ winter; storm

χωρίς (*adv., and prep.* + *gen.*) separately, apart

ὡς (*conj.*) as

C. Demosthenes, *On the Crown* 71

    ἀλλ᾿ ὁ τὴν Εὔβοιαν ἐκεῖνος σφετεριζόμενος καὶ κατασκευάζων
    ἐπιτείχισμ᾿ ἐπὶ τὴν Ἀττικήν, καὶ Μεγάροις ἐπιχειρῶν, καὶ
    καταλαμβάνων Ὠρεόν, καὶ κατασκάπτων Πορθμόν, καὶ καθιστὰς
    ἐν μὲν Ὠρεῷ Φιλιστίδην τύραννον, ἐν δ᾿ Ἐρετρίᾳ Κλείταρχον,
5   καὶ τὸν Ἑλλήσποντον ὑφ᾿ αὑτῷ ποιούμενος, καὶ Βυζάντιον
    πολιορκῶν, καὶ πόλεις Ἑλληνίδας τὰς μὲν ἀναιρῶν, εἰς τὰς δὲ
    φυγάδας κατάγων, πότερον ταῦτα ποιῶν ἠδίκει καὶ παρεσπόνδει
    καὶ ἔλῡε τὴν εἰρήνην ἢ οὔ;

ἀναιρέω, ἀναιρήσω, ἀνεῖλον, ἀνῄρηκα, ἀνῄρημαι, ἀνῃρέθην   destroy

Ἀττική, Ἀττικῆς, ἡ   Attica (the land around Athens)

αὑτοῦ, αὑτῷ, αὑτόν   (gen., dat., acc. of reflexive pronoun) himself

Βυζάντιον, Βυζαντίου, τό   Byzantium

Ἑλληνίς (gen. Ἑλληνίδος) (fem. adj.)   Greek

Ἑλλήσποντος, Ἑλλησπόντου, ὁ   Hellespont

ἐπιτείχισμα, ἐπιτειχίσματος, τό   frontier fort

ἐπιχειρέω, ἐπιχειρήσω, ἐπεχείρησα, ἐπικεχείρηκα, ἐπικεχείρημαι,
   ἐπεχειρήθην   attempt, attack (+ *dat.*)

Ἐρετρίᾱ, Ἐρετρίᾱς, ἡ   Eretria (a city in Euboia)

Εὔβοια, Εὐβοίᾱς, ἡ   Euboea (an island off the coast of Attica)

κατάγω   bring back (from exile)

κατασκάπτω, κατασκάψω, κατέσκαψα, κατέσκαφα, κατέσκαμμαι,
   κατεσκάφην   dig down, raze to the ground

κατασκευάζω, κατασκευάσω, κατεσκεύασα, κατεσκεύακα, κατεσκεύασμαι,
   κατεσκευάσθην   construct

Κλείταρχος, Κλειτάρχου, ὁ   Kleitarchos (a nefarious person)

Μέγαρα, Μεγάρων, τά   Megara (a neighbor of Athens)

παρασπονδέω, παρασπονδήσω, παρεσπόνδησα, παρεσπόνδηκα,
   παρεσπόνδημαι, παρεσπονδήθην   break a treaty

πολιορκέω, πολιορκήσω, ἐπολιόρκησα, πεπολιόρκηκα, πεπολιόρκημαι,
   ἐπολιορκήθην   besiege

Πορθμός, Πορθμοῦ, ὁ   Porthmos (a town in Euboea)

πότερον (adv.)   introduces the first of two alternatives

σφετερίζω, σφετεριῶ, ἐσφετέρισα, ἐσφετέρικα, ἐσφετέρισμαι, ἐσφετερίσθην
   appropriate, make one's own

τύραννος, τυράννου, ὁ   tyrant

Φιλιστίδης, Φιλιστίδου, ὁ   Philistides (a reprobate)

φυγάς, φυγάδος, ὁ   fugitive, exile

Ὠρεός, Ὠρεοῦ, ὁ   Oreos (a town in Euboea)

D. Demetrius, *On Style* 5.279

The effect of a rhetorical question.

Δεινὸν δὲ καὶ τὸ ἐρωτῶντα τοὺς ἀκούοντας ἔνια λέγειν,
καὶ μὴ ἀποφαινόμενον· "ἀλλ' ὁ τὴν Εὔβοιαν ἐκεῖνος
σφετεριζόμενος καὶ κατασκευάζων ἐπιτείχισμα ἐπὶ
τὴν Ἀττικήν, πότερον ταῦτα ποιῶν ἠδίκει, καὶ ἔλυεν
5 τὴν εἰρήνην, ἢ οὔ;" καθάπερ γὰρ εἰς ἀπορίαν ἄγει
τὸν ἀκούοντα ἐξελεγχομένῳ ἐοικότα καὶ μηδὲν ἀποκρίνασθαι
ἔχοντι· εἰ δὲ ὧδε μεταβαλὼν ἔφη¹ τις, "ἠδίκει καὶ
ἔλυε τὴν εἰρήνην," σαφῶς διδάσκοντι ἐῴκει¹ καὶ οὐκ
ἐλέγχοντι.

ἀποκρίνομαι, ἀποκρινοῦμαι, ἀπεκρινάμην, ――, ἀποκέκριμαι, ―― answer
ἀπορία, ἀπορίας, ἡ difficulty, puzzlement
ἀποφαίνω, ἀποφανῶ, ἀπέφηνα, ἀποπέφηνα, ἀποπέφασμαι, ἀπεφάνην show
 forth, display; (*mid.*) declare one's opinion
Ἀττική, Ἀττικῆς, ἡ Attica (the land around Athens)
ἐλέγχω, ἐλέγξω, ἤλεγξα, ――, ἐλήλεγμαι, ἠλέγχθην cross-examine, question
ἔνιοι, ἔνιαι, ἔνια some
ἐξελέγχω (*see* ἐλέγχω) convict, refute, put to the test
ἔοικα (*perfect with present meaning*) be like (+ *dat.*)
ἐπιτείχισμα, ἐπιτειχίσματος, τό frontier fort
ἐρωτάω, ἐρωτήσω, ἠρώτησα, ἠρώτηκα, ἠρώτημαι, ἠρωτήθην question
Εὔβοια, Εὐβοίας, ἡ Euboea (an island off the coast of Attica)
ἔχω, ἕξω/σχήσω, ἔσχον, ἔσχηκα, -έσχημαι, ―― have, hold; be able; (*mid.*)
 cling to, be next to (+ *gen.*)
καθάπερ (*adv.*) according to, just as
κατασκευάζω, κατασκευάσω, κατεσκεύασα, κατεσκεύακα, κατεσκεύασμαι,
 κατεσκευάσθην construct
λέγω, ἐρῶ/λέξω, εἶπον/ἔλεξα, εἴρηκα, εἴρημαι/λέλεγμαι, ἐλέχθην/ἐρρήθην
 say, speak
μεταβάλλω change
μηδείς, μηδεμία, μηδέν no one, nothing
πότερον (*adv.*) *introduces the first of two alternatives*
σφετερίζω, σφετεριῶ, ἐσφετέρισα, ἐσφετέρικα, ἐσφετέρισμαι, ἐσφετερίσθην
 appropriate, make one's own
τις (*nom. sing. masc./fem.*) someone
φημί, φήσω, ἔφησα, ――, ――, ―― say, assert, affirm
ὧδε (*adv.*) thus, in this way

1. A past tense of the indicative in a **simple conditional sentence** in past time; see the
Appendix, page 747.

E. Longinus, *On the Sublime* 9.7

Anthropomorphism in Homer.

    "Ὅμηρος γάρ μοι δοκεῖ παραδιδοὺς τραύματα θεῶν στάσεις
τιμωρίας δάκρυα δεσμὰ πάθη πάμφυρτα τοὺς μὲν ἐπὶ τῶν
Ἰλιακῶν ἀνθρώπους ὅσον ἐπὶ τῇ δυνάμει θεοὺς πεποιηκέναι,
τοὺς θεοὺς δὲ ἀνθρώπους. ἀλλ' ἡμῖν μὲν δυσδαιμονοῦσιν
5 ἀπόκειται λιμὴν κακῶν ὁ θάνατος, τῶν θεῶν δ' οὐ τὴν
φύσιν, ἀλλὰ τὴν ἀτυχίαν ἐποίησεν αἰώνιον.

αἰώνιος, αἰώνιον perpetual, eternal
ἀπόκειμαι, ἀποκείσομαι, ——, ——, ——, —— be laid up
ἀτυχία, ἀτυχίας, ἡ misfortune
δάκρυον, δακρύου, τό tear
δεσμός, δεσμοῦ, ὁ (pl. οἱ δεσμοί or τὰ δεσμά) bond, chain
δοκέω, δόξω, ἔδοξα, ——, δέδογμαι, -ἐδόχθην seem, think
δύναμις, δυνάμεως, ἡ strength, power
δυσδαιμονέω, ——, ——, ——, ——, —— be unfortunate
ἡμῖν (dat. pl.) to/for us
Ἰλιακός, Ἰλιακή, Ἰλιακόν pertaining to Troy
λιμήν, λιμένος, ὁ harbor
μοι (dat. sing.) to/for me
ὅσον (relative adv.) as far as
πάμφυρτος, πάμφυρτον mixed, of all sorts
στάσις, στάσεως, ἡ civil strife, faction
τιμωρία, τιμωρίας, ἡ vengeance
τραῦμα, τραύματος, τό wound

F. Longinus, *On the Sublime* 9.13

The contrast between the *Iliad* and the *Odyssey*.

    ἀπὸ δὲ τῆς αὐτῆς αἰτίας, οἶμαι, τῆς μὲν Ἰλιάδος
γραφομένης ἐν ἀκμῇ πνεύματος ὅλον τὸ σωμάτιον δρα-
ματικὸν ὑπεστήσατο καὶ ἐναγώνιον, τῆς δὲ Ὀδυσσείας
τὸ πλέον διηγηματικόν, ὅπερ ἴδιον γήρως. ὅθεν
5 ἐν τῇ Ὀδυσσείᾳ παρεικάσαι τις ἂν καταδυομένῳ
τὸν Ὅμηρον ἡλίῳ, οὗ δίχα τῆς σφοδρότητος παραμένει
τὸ μέγεθος.

ἀκμή, ἀκμῆς, ἡ   high point, prime

γῆρας, γήρως, τό   (gen. contracted from γήραος; for declension see Appendix, page 592)   old age

διηγηματικός, διηγηματική, διηγηματικόν   descriptive, narrative

δίχα   (adv., and prep. + gen.)   apart

δρᾱματικός, δρᾱματική, δρᾱματικόν   dramatic

ἐναγώνιος, ἐναγώνιον   for a contest; vehement

ἥλιος, ἡλίου, ὁ   sun

ἴδιος, ἰδίᾱ, ἴδιον   one's own, private; appropriate (+ gen.)

Ἰλιάς, Ἰλιάδος, ἡ   Iliad

καταδύω, καταδύσω, κατέδῡσα/κατέδῡν, καταδέδῡκα, καταδέδυμαι, κατεδύθην   submerge, sink; set

μέγεθος, μεγέθους, τό   great size

Ὀδύσσεια, Ὀδυσσείᾱς, ἡ   Odyssey

ὅθεν   (adv.)   from where; wherefore, and therefore

οἶμαι/οἴομαι, οἰήσομαι, ——, ——, ——, ᾠήθην   think, suppose, believe

ὅλος, ὅλη, ὅλον   whole

ὅπερ: see -περ

παρεικάζω, παρεικάσω, παρήκασα, παρείκακα, παρήκασμαι, παρεικάσθην   liken, compare (+ dat.)

-περ   (enclitic particle)   emphasizes the word it is attached to

πλέον: τὸ πλέον   (adv.)   for the greater part

πνεῦμα, πνεύματος, τό   breath; inspiration

σφοδρότης, σφοδρότητος, ἡ   vehemence

σωμάτιον, σωματίου, τό   structure

τις   (nom. sing. masc./fem.)   someone

I. *Give the Principal Parts and the participles (in the nominative and genitive singular) of* ἵστημι, δίδωμι.

II. *Translate indicatives, imperatives, and infinitives; identify subjunctives and optatives. Change to the other two voices where possible. Change the number of the original form where possible.*

1. ἵστασο
2. ἵστασο
3. ἔθεμεν
4. θεῖτε
5. ἐτίθετο
6. στῶμεν
7. θείμην
8. θέσθων
9. ἵστασθαι
10. θέσθαι
11. τιθῶσιν
12. ἵστασθε
13. ἔστησας
14. ἔστατε
15. ἐδείκνῡ
16. δείκνῡ

III. *Translate.*

1. εἰσέλθετε εἰς ἀγορὰν δῶρα παρά γε τῶν ἀδικούντων ληψόμενοι.
   (imperative; attributive participle used substantively; circumstantial participle expressing purpose; partial deponent)

2. (a) τρόπαιον ἱστάντες ἐτῑμώμεθα ἐπὶ τῷ νῑκῆσαι.
   (b) τρόπαιον στήσαντες τῑμῴμεθ’ ἄν.
   (c) χρῡσὸν μὴ δόντες οὐκ ἂν ἐνῑκήσατε.
   (d) χρῡσὸν δόντες νῑκήσατε.

419

(a) circumstantial participle (conditional: past general protasis; or temporal, concessive, or causal)

(b) circumstantial participle (conditional: future less vivid protasis; or temporal, concessive, or causal)

(c) circumstantial participle (conditional: past contrafactual protasis)

(d) circumstantial participle (conditional: future more vivid protasis; or temporal, concessive, or causal)

3. (a) ὦ ἄδελφε, παῦσον τόνδε τὸν αἰσχρὸν ζωγράφον τοῖς νέοις τὴν τέχνην ἐπιδεικνύμενον.

(b) μὴ παύσῃ, ὦ ζωγράφε, τοὺς νέους ἐκδιδάσκων.

(a) imperative; supplementary participle with παύω

(b) prohibitive subjunctive; supplementary participle with παύομαι

4. οὐκ ἂν λάθοις ποτὲ τὰς σώφρονας οἶνον κλέψᾱς, ὦ γέρον.
(potential optative; supplementary participle with λανθάνω)

5. ὅταν χαίρῃς ταῦτά γε ποιοῦσα, ὦ θύγατερ, τῑμᾶ.
(present general temporal clause; supplementary participle with χαίρω)

6. ἐκεῖ στάντων τῶν πολεμίων, ἐνταῦθ᾽ ἐπαυσάμεθα αὐτοί.
(genitive absolute)

7. ἀπῆλθες ὡς εἰς τὴν αὐτὴν νῆσον φευξομένη ἵνα μὴ δίκην δοίης;
(circumstantial participle with ὡς showing purpose not vouched for by the speaker; partial deponent)

8. εἰσελθούσης τῆς μητρὸς εἰς ἀγορᾱν, ἐτύγχανεν ὁ Εὐρῑπίδης βιβλίον περὶ αἰσχρῶν ἀνδρῶν καὶ γυναικῶν γράφων.
(genitive absolute; supplementary participle with τυγχάνω)

9. ἐφοβούμεθα μὴ πάσᾱς λάθοιεν κακὰ ποιήσαντες.
(deponent; fear clause in secondary sequence; supplementary participle with λανθάνω)

10. εἴθε μηχανησαίμεθα ὅπως χαιρήσει ὁ δῆμος ὑπ᾽ ἀγαθῶν ἀρχόμενος.
(optative of wish; object clause of effort; supplementary participle with χαίρω)

11. νόμον θῶ ἐπὶ τοῖς σῑγῇ οἶνον κεκλοφόσιν;
(deliberative subjunctive; dative of manner; attributive participle)

12. νόμους θέσθε, ὦ ῥήτορες, ἐπὶ τοῖς μάχεσθαι μὴ βουληθεῖσιν. οὗτοι
    γὰρ ψῡχὴν αἰσχροί.
    (imperative; attributive participle used generically; passive
    deponent; accusative of respect)

13. πρὸς τῷ τείχει ἑστῶτες οἱ στρατιῶται ἐθύοντο τῷ δαίμονι τήν
    τ᾿ αἶγα τὴν κλαπεῖσαν καὶ τὸν ἵππον τὸν δοθέντα ὑπὸ τῶν
    ἐν τῇ πόλει παραμεινάντων.
    (circumstantial participle; attributive participles)

14. τῶν ἀνδρῶν ἀγαθὰ μὴ ποιούντων, ὦ γυναῖκες, αὐτοὺς τοὺς
    παῖδας οὐκ ἐκπαιδευσόμεθα περὶ τῆς τοῦ ἀγαθοῦ φύσεως.
    (genitive absolute as protasis of future more vivid conditional
    sentence)

15. οἳ ἂν ἐπαναστάντες τῷ δήμῳ τῷ ᾿Αθηναίων μὴ ἐκ πόλεως
    ἐκφύγωσιν, τούτους γραφὴν γράψομαι ἅτε τὸν δῆμον
    ἀδικοῦντας καὶ χρήματα παρὰ τῶν πολεμίων εἰληφότας.
    (future more vivid conditional sentence with relative protasis;
    circumstantial participle; cognate accusative with γράφομαι;
    circumstantial participle with ἅτε showing cause vouched for
    by the speaker)

16. οὕτως ἐφιλεῖτο ὅ γ᾿ ῞Ομηρος ὥστε τοὺς ἐν τέλει, ὑπὸ τοῦ δήμου
    πεισθέντας, χρῡσὸν αὐτῷ διδόναι.
    (clause of natural result; circumstantial participle)

IV. *Translate into Greek.*

Since bribes were being given to the public speakers, the Athenians feared
that the men on the islands would rise in insurrection against those in
power.

I. *Translate the following phrases. Then change the number of the participle and the word which it modifies.*

   1. ἡ τὸν οἶνον ἐν τῇ οἰκίᾳ τιθεῖσα

   2. τούτων τῶν τὰ τοῦ δήμου πάθη δεικνύντων

   3. χρήματα τὰ ποιηταῖς δοθέντα

   4. τῷ στρατῷ τῷ μεμαχημένῳ

   5. τῷ ἐνταῦθα στάντι

II. *Translate indicatives, imperatives, and infinitives; identify subjunctives and optatives.*

   1. δείκνυσθαι

   2. ἔδοσθε

   3. ἐτίθεσαν

   4. θέσθω

   5. δῶνται

   6. ἐδίδους

   7. ἐτέθησαν

III. *Give a synopsis of* ἵστημι *in the second person plural. Give the feminine nominative singular of participles.*

PRINCIPAL PARTS: ─────────────────────────────

─────────────────────────────

	ACTIVE	MIDDLE	PASSIVE
PRESENT INDICATIVE			
IMPERFECT INDICATIVE			
FUTURE INDICATIVE			
AORIST INDICATIVE			
PERFECT INDICATIVE			
PLUPERFECT INDICATIVE			

PRESENT SUBJUNCTIVE _____

AORIST SUBJUNCTIVE _____

PRESENT OPTATIVE _____

AORIST OPTATIVE _____

PRESENT IMPERATIVE _____

AORIST IMPERATIVE _____

PRESENT INFINITIVE _____

AORIST INFINITIVE _____

PERFECT INFINITIVE _____

PRESENT PARTICIPLE _____

FUTURE PARTICIPLE _____

AORIST PARTICIPLE _____

PERFECT PARTICIPLE _____

IV. *Translate, and answer all appended questions.*

1. χρῡσόν πως λαβόντες ἀπῆλθον ὡς τοῖς πολεμίοις μαχούμενοι.
   (a) *Give the syntax of* μαχούμενοι.

2. ἀγαθοὶ δὴ καὶ σώφρονες οἱ δημιουργοὶ οἱ ὑπὲρ τῆς πόλεως μεμαχημένοι.

3. οὐκ ἂν παύσαιτέ ποτε τούτους χρῡσὸν τοῖς ῥήτορσι διδόντας.
   (a) *Give the syntax of* διδόντας.

4. τῶν ἑρμηνέων μὴ βουλομένων τοὺς νῑκηθέντας ἐρωτᾶν, οὐ μαθησόμεθα περὶ τοῦ τῶν βαρβάρων στρατοῦ.
   (a) *Give the syntax of* βουλομένων.

5. οὔτ' ἔλαθες τὴν γυναῖκα ἐκ τῆς οἰκίᾱς ἐξελθών, ὦ γέρον, οὔτ' ἔφθης τούς γε φύλακας οἶνον κλέψᾱς.
   (a) *Give the syntax of* κλέψᾱς.

6. χρῡσὸν τοῖς ἄφροσι μὴ δοῦσαι, οὐκ ἂν ἐφιλήθημεν.
   (a) *Give the syntax of* δοῦσαι.

7. μηχάνησαι ὅπως λυθείσης τῆς δημοκρατίᾱς οἱ σώφρονες τῶν ἀφρόνων ἄρξουσιν.
   (a) *Give the syntax of* ἄρξουσιν.

8. ἐφοβήθητε μὴ οὐ λανθάνοιτε κακὰ ποιοῦντες τοὺς πολίτᾱς.
   (a) *Give the syntax of* λανθάνοιτε.
   (b) *Give the syntax of* ποιοῦντες.

9. ὅτ᾽ εἰσῆλθόν πως εἰς τὴν πόλιν, ἐτῑμήθην ἅτε σώφρονα πεποιηκυῖα.

   (a) *Give the syntax of* πεποιηκυῖα.

10. μόνος δὴ ἀγαθὸς ὁ τῷ δήμῳ καλοὺς νόμους θέμενος.

11. μὴ ἄρξωμεν τῶν νῦν ἐπανισταμένων;

12. οἳ ἂν χαίρωσιν ἀλλήλους ἀδικοῦντες, οὗτοι θεοῖς δίκην διδόντων πάντων τῶν αἰσχρῶς πεπρᾱγμένων.

   (a) *Give the syntax of* χαίρωσιν.

13. τρόπαιον ἱστάντος αὐτοῦ τοῦ στρατηγοῦ, ἀπέφυγον οἱ στρατιῶται καίπερ νῑκήσαντες. ἐφοβοῦντο γὰρ μὴ προσέλθοιεν καὶ ἄλλοι ἱππεῖς.

14. εἰ ἀγαθὰ δοίητε, ὦ θεοί, εὖ ἂν πράττοιμεν.

   (a) *Give the syntax of* δοίητε.

15. ἐπειδὰν ἐνταῦθα στῶμεν, μαχεῖσθέ ποτε αὐτοῖς;

   (a) *Give the syntax of* στῶμεν.

   (b) *Describe and make the changes necessary to turn this sentence into a future less vivid conditional sentence.*

16. τῶν πολεμίων ἐπὶ τῷ τείχει ἑστώτων, νόμους μὴ θῆσθε ἐπὶ τοῖς τότε ἐπαναστᾶσιν.

   (a) *Give the syntax of* θῆσθε.

V. They were giving gifts to the noble speakers in order that those men might somehow hand this city over to its enemies.

I. 1. the woman putting/who is putting the wine in the house
   αἱ τὸν οἶνον ἐν τῇ οἰκίᾳ τιθεῖσαι

   2. of these men showing/who are showing the sufferings of the people
   τούτου τοῦ τὰ τοῦ δήμου πάθη δεικνύντος

   3. the money given/which was given to poets
   χρῆμα τὸ ποιηταῖς δοθέν

   4. to/for the army having fought/which has fought
   τοῖς στρατοῖς τοῖς μεμαχημένοις

   5. to/for the man who stood here/there
   τοῖς ἐνταῦθα στᾶσι(ν)

II. 1. to show (for oneself), to have (something) shown [middle]/to be shown [passive]

   2. you gave (for yourselves)

   3. they were putting/used to put/put (habitually)

   4. let him/her/it put (for himself/herself/itself)

   5. third person pl., aorist subj. mid.

   6. you were giving/used to give/gave (habitually)

   7. they were put

III. Synopsis: see page 428.

IV. 1. Upon taking gold/After they took gold somehow, they went away in order (as they said) to fight the enemy/enemies.

   (a) μαχούμενοι is a future participle, M pl. nom.: circumstantial participle with ὡς, showing purpose not vouched for by speaker; future tense to show subsequent time; agrees in gender, number, and case with the subject of ἀπῆλθον.

   2. Good, in fact, and prudent are the craftsmen having fought/who have fought on behalf of the city.

   3. You may/might/could not ever stop these/those men from giving gold to the public speakers.

   (a) διδόντας is a present participle, M pl. acc.: supplementary participle with παύω; present tense shows progressive/repeated aspect; agrees in gender, number, and case with τούτους.

4. The interpreters not wanting/If the interpreters do not want to question the conquered men/the men who were conquered, we shall not learn about the army of the foreigners.

   (a) βουλομένων is a present participle, M pl. gen., in a genitive absolute serving as the protasis of a future more vivid conditional sentence; present tense shows progressive/repeated aspect; agrees in gender, number, and case with ἑρμηνέων.

5. Old man, neither did you escape your wife's notice going out of the house/did you go out without your wife's finding out/was your wife unaware of your leaving the house nor did you steal wine ahead of the guards/nor did you beat the guards in stealing wine.

   (a) κλέψᾱς is an aorist participle, M sing. nom.: supplementary participle with φθάνω; aorist tense shows simple aspect; agrees in gender, number, and case with the subject of ἔφθης.

6. Not giving (*simple aspect*) gold to the foolish men/If we (women) had not given gold to the foolish men, we would not have been loved.

   (a) δοῦσαι is an aorist participle, F pl. nom.: circumstantial participle serving as the protasis of a past contrafactual conditional sentence; agrees in gender, number, and case with the subject of ἐφιλήθημεν.

7. Contrive that, the democracy destroyed, the prudent will rule the foolish.

   (a) ἄρξουσιν is a future indicative in an object clause of effort.

8. You feared that you might not escape (the citizens') notice doing evil (things) to the citizens/that the citizens might be aware of your evil actions to them.

   (a) λανθάνοιτε is a present optative: optative in a fear clause in secondary sequence introduced by the aorist ἐφοβήθητε; present to show progressive/repeated aspect.

   (b) ποιοῦντες is a present participle, M pl. nom.: a supplementary participle with λανθάνω; present to show progressive/repeated aspect; agrees in gender, number, and case with the subject of λανθάνοιτε.

9. When I somehow entered the city I was honored, having done prudent things/since I had done prudent things (*speaker's authority*).

   (a) πεποιηκυῖα is a perfect participle, F sing. nom.: a circumstantial participle showing cause vouched for by speaker; perfect tense to show completed aspect; agrees in gender, number, and case with the subject of ἐτῑμήθην.

10. The man who set/made good laws for the people is alone, in fact, good (i.e., only he is good).

11. Are we not to rule the people now rising up in insurrection?

12. Whoever delight/take pleasure in/If any men delight/take pleasure in wronging each other, let these men pay to the gods the penalty of all the things having been done/which have been done shamefully.

    (a) χαίρωσιν is a present subjunctive: subjunctive in the relative protasis of a future more vivid conditional sentence; present to show progressive/repeated aspect.

13. The general himself standing up/When the general himself was standing up a trophy, the soldiers fled away although they won. For they feared that even other horsemen might approach/come toward them.

14. If you should give good (things), gods, we would be doing/faring/do/fare (habitually) well.

    (a) δοίητε is an aorist optative: optative in the protasis of a future less vivid conditional sentence; aorist to show simple aspect.

15. When we stand here, will you ever fight with them?

    (a) στῶμεν is an aorist subjunctive: subjunctive in a future more vivid temporal clause; aorist to show simple aspect.

    (b) PROTASIS: Change ἐπειδάν to εἰ. Change the subjunctive στῶμεν to the optative σταῖμεν/σταίημεν.
APODOSIS: Change the future indicative μαχεῖσθε to the optative, either μάχοισθε (present to show progressive/repeated aspect) or μαχέσαισθε (aorist to show simple aspect). Add ἄν.

16. The enemy/enemies standing/Because the enemy are standing on the wall, do not set/make for yourselves laws pertaining to those who then rose up in rebellion.

    (a) θῆσθε is an aorist subjunctive: a prohibitive subjunctive.

V. δῶρα ἐδίδοσαν τοῖς καλοῖς ῥήτορσιν ἵνα/ὡς/ὅπως οὗτοι/ἐκεῖνοι παραδοῖέν/παραδοίησάν/παραδιδοῖέν/παραδιδοίησάν πως ταύτην τὴν πόλιν τοῖς (ταύτης) πολεμίοις.

PRINCIPAL PARTS: *ἵστημι, στήσω, ἔστησα* or *ἔστην, ἔστηκα, ἔσταμαι, ἐστάθην*

	ACTIVE	MIDDLE	PASSIVE
PRESENT INDICATIVE	ἵστατε	ἵστασθε	ἵστασθε
IMPERFECT INDICATIVE	ἵστατε	ἵστασθε	ἵστασθε
FUTURE INDICATIVE	στήσετε	στήσεσθε	σταθήσεσθε
AORIST INDICATIVE	ἐστήσατε / ἔστητε	ἐστήσασθε	ἐστάθητε
PERFECT INDICATIVE	ἕστατε	ἕστασθε	ἕστασθε
PLUPERFECT INDICATIVE	ἕστατε	εἵστασθε	εἵστασθε
PRESENT SUBJUNCTIVE	ἱστῆτε	ἱστῆσθε	ἱστῆσθε
AORIST SUBJUNCTIVE	στήσητε / στῆτε	στήσησθε	σταθῆτε
PRESENT OPTATIVE	ἱσταῖτε / ἱσταίητε	ἱσταῖσθε	ἱσταῖσθε
AORIST OPTATIVE	στήσαιτε / σταῖτε / σταίητε	στήσαισθε	σταθεῖτε / σταθείητε
PRESENT IMPERATIVE	ἵστατε	ἵστασθε	ἵστασθε
AORIST IMPERATIVE	στήσατε / στῆτε	στήσασθε	στάθητε
PRESENT INFINITIVE	ἱστάναι	ἵστασθαι	ἵστασθαι
AORIST INFINITIVE	στῆσαι / στῆναι	στήσασθαι	σταθῆναι
PERFECT INFINITIVE	ἑστάναι	ἑστάσθαι	ἑστάσθαι
PRESENT PARTICIPLE	ἱστᾶσα	ἱσταμένη	ἱσταμένη
FUTURE PARTICIPLE	στήσουσα	στησομένη	σταθησομένη
AORIST PARTICIPLE	στήσᾶσα / στᾶσα	στησαμένη	σταθεῖσα
PERFECT PARTICIPLE	ἑστῶσα	ἑσταμένη	ἑσταμένη

I. *Translate indicatives, imperatives, and infinitives; identify subjunctives and optatives.*

1. δῶ
2. ἀπόδου
3. ἵσταμεν
4. ἔστημεν
5. διδοῖσθε
6. ἱσταίη

II. *Translate.*

ὦ ἀμαθές, ἄκουε δὴ αὐτοῦ τοῦ στρατηγοῦ πάντα τὰ τότε γενόμενα. μετὰ γὰρ τὴν μάχην ὁ μὲν Ἀθηναίων στρατὸς ἐτύγχανε τρόπαιόν που ἐν τῷ πεδίῳ ἀνατιθείς, οἱ δὲ βάρβαροι, ὑπὸ βασιλέως ἀγόμενοι, ἔφθησάν πως τοὺς Ἀθηναίους φυγόντες εἰς μέσην τὴν πόλιν, ὅπως μετὰ τῶν ἐν αὐτῇ τῇ πόλει ἑταίρων τὸν δῆμον εἰς στάσιν καταστήσαιεν. ἀεὶ γὰρ χαίρει ὁ δῆμος ὁ ταύτης τῆς πόλεως Ἀθηναίοις ἐπανιστάμενος, ὥστε τοὺς ἄφρονας τῶν πολιτῶν τοῖς ἐν τέλει ὑπακούειν μὴ βούλεσθαι. εἰ δὲ τῆς ἀρχῆς μετέδοσαν οἱ Ἀθηναῖοι πᾶσι τοῖς συμμάχοις τοῖς τότε ὑπὲρ τῆς τῶν Ἑλλήνων ἐλευθερίας μαχεσαμένοις, οὗτοι οὐκ ἂν ἐπανέστησαν.

ἐπανισταμένων οὖν τῶν συμμάχων, οἱ Ἀθηναῖοι, καίπερ ἐν ἐκείνῃ τῇ μάχῃ τοὺς πολεμίους νῑκήσαντες, ἀπῆλθον ἐκ τῆς χώρας, φοβούμενοι μὴ κακὰ πάθοιεν οὐ μόνον ὑπὸ τῶν βαρβάρων ἀλλὰ καὶ ὑπὸ τῶν ἐν πόλει συμμάχων. ἐκείνῃ γὰρ τῇ ἡμέρᾳ εὖ μαχεσαμένων πάντων τῶν στρατιωτῶν, ὅμως, ὦ δαίμονες, νίκην οὐκ ἔδοτε τῷ Ἀθηναίων στρατῷ.

III. *Translate, and answer the appended questions.*

1. ἀεὶ τίμᾱ τοὺς γραφέᾱς τοὺς τάδε γεγραφότας.
2. μὴ λάθοιμεν τούτους καλὰ ποιοῦσαι.
    (a) *Give the syntax of* λάθοιμεν.
    (b) *Give the syntax of* ποιοῦσαι.

3. τῆς θεοῦ μὴ ἀγαθὰ δούσης, θυσίας μὴ ποιεῖσθε.
   (a) Give the syntax of δούσης.

4. φοβουμένων τῶν Λακεδαιμονίων μὴ νῖκηθῶσιν, αὐτοὶ νῖκῶμεν.
   (a) Give the syntax of φοβουμένων.

5. ὅτε χαίροιμι κακὰ ποιοῦσα, οὐκ ἐτῑμώμην.
   (a) Give the syntax of χαίροιμι.

6. δῶρα λαβόντων τῶνδε τῶν ῥητόρων, βασιλεῖ ἂν ἐπαναστεῖμεν.
   (a) Give the syntax of λαβόντων.

IV. *Give a synopsis of τίθημι in the second person singular. Give the neuter nominative singular of participles.*

PRINCIPAL PARTS: ————————————————————————

————————————————————————

	ACTIVE	MIDDLE	PASSIVE
PRESENT INDICATIVE			
IMPERFECT INDICATIVE			
FUTURE INDICATIVE			
AORIST INDICATIVE			
PERFECT INDICATIVE			
PLUPERFECT INDICATIVE			
PRESENT SUBJUNCTIVE			
AORIST SUBJUNCTIVE			
PRESENT OPTATIVE			
AORIST OPTATIVE			
PRESENT IMPERATIVE			
AORIST IMPERATIVE			
PRESENT INFINITIVE			
AORIST INFINITIVE			
PERFECT INFINITIVE			
PRESENT PARTICIPLE			
FUTURE PARTICIPLE			
AORIST PARTICIPLE			
PERFECT PARTICIPLE			

V. If we should stand *here*, would you fight on behalf of the speakers doing evil?

I. 1. δῶ: first person sing., aorist subj. act.

2. ἀπόδου: sell

3. ἵσταμεν: we were setting up

4. ἔστημεν: we stood

5. διδοῖσθε: second person pl., present opt. mid./pass.

6. ἱσταίη: third person sing., present opt. act.

II. Ignorant one, hear/be hearing in fact from the general himself all the
then happening things/all the things which happened then. For after
the battle, on the one hand, the army of the Athenians happened to be
setting up a trophy somewhere in the plain; on the other hand, the
foreigners being led by the/a king, somehow beat the Athenians fleeing/
fled before the Athenians to the middle of the city in order that with their/
the companions in the city itself they might bring the people into a state
of civil strife. For the people of this/that city always take pleasure in
revolting from the Athenians so as for the foolish of the citizens not to
want to obey those in office. But if the Athenians had given a share of
the/their rule to all of the allies who then (had) fought on behalf of the
freedom of the Greeks, these/those would not have risen up in rebellion.

The allies then revolting, the Athenians, although conquering/they
(had) conquered the enemy/enemies in that battle, went away from the
country, fearing that they might suffer evil/evils not only at the hands
of the foreigners but also at the hands of their/the allies in the city. For
on that day, although all the soldiers fought well/all the soldiers fighting well, nevertheless, gods, you did not give victory to the army of the
Athenians.

III. 1. Always honor/be honoring the writers/painters having written/drawn/
who have written/drawn these things.

2. May we (women) doing good not escape the notice of these/those men./
May we (women) not be doing/do (habitually) good without being
seen by these/those men.

(a) λάθοιμεν is an aorist optative: optative of wish; aorist to show
simple aspect.

431

(b) ποιοῦσαι is a present participle, F pl. nom.: a supplementary participle with λάθοιμεν; present shows progressive/repeated aspect; agrees in gender, number, and case with the unexpressed subject of λάθοιμεν.

3. The goddess not giving/If the goddess does not give good (things), do not sacrifice/be sacrificing.

(a) δούσης is an aorist participle, F sing. gen.: a participle in a genitive absolute used as the protasis of a future more vivid conditional sentence; aorist to indicate simple aspect; agrees in gender, number, and case with θεοῦ.

4. The Spartans fearing/Since the Spartans are afraid that they may be conquered, let us ourselves conquer/we ourselves are conquering.

(a) φοβουμένων is a present participle, M pl. gen.: a participle in a genitive absolute, probably causal; present to show progressive/repeated aspect; agrees in gender, number, and case with Λακεδαιμονίων.

5. Whenever I took pleasure in doing evil things, I was not honored.

(a) χαίροιμι is a present optative: optative in a past general temporal clause; present to show progressive/repeated aspect.

6. These public speakers taking/If these public speakers should take/ Since these public speakers took bribes, we may/might/would rise up in revolt against the king.

(a) λαβόντων is an aorist participle, M pl. gen.: participle in a genitive absolute possibly used as the protasis of a future less vivid conditional sentence or possibly causal; aorist to show simple aspect; agrees in gender, number, and case with ῥητόρων.

IV. Synopsis: see page 433.

V. εἰ σταῖμεν/σταίημεν ἐνταῦθά γε, μαχέσαιο/μάχοιο ἂν ὑπὲρ τῶν ῥητόρων τῶν κακὰ πραττόντων;

VI. PRINCIPAL PARTS: *τίθημι, θήσω, ἔθηκα, τέθηκα, τέθειμαι, ἐτέθην*

	ACTIVE	MIDDLE	PASSIVE
PRESENT INDICATIVE	τίθης	τίθεσαι	τίθεσαι
IMPERFECT INDICATIVE	ἐτίθεις	ἐτίθεσο	ἐτίθεσο
FUTURE INDICATIVE	θήσεις	{ θήσῃ/ θήσει }	{ τεθήσῃ/ τεθήσει }
AORIST INDICATIVE	ἔθηκας	ἔθου	ἐτέθης
PERFECT INDICATIVE	τέθηκας	τέθεισαι	τέθεισαι
PLUPERFECT INDICATIVE	ἐτεθήκης	ἐτέθεισο	ἐτέθεισο
PRESENT SUBJUNCTIVE	τιθῇς	τιθῇ	τιθῇ
AORIST SUBJUNCTIVE	θῇς	θῇ	τεθῇς
PRESENT OPTATIVE	τιθείης	τιθεῖο	τιθεῖο
AORIST OPTATIVE	θείης	θεῖο	τεθείης
PRESENT IMPERATIVE	τίθει	τίθεσο	τίθεσο
AORIST IMPERATIVE	θές	θοῦ	τέθητι
PRESENT INFINITIVE	τιθέναι	τίθεσθαι	τίθεσθαι
AORIST INFINITIVE	θεῖναι	θέσθαι	τεθῆναι
PERFECT INFINITIVE	τεθηκέναι	τεθεῖσθαι	τεθεῖσθαι
PRESENT PARTICIPLE	τιθέν	τιθέμενον	τιθέμενον
FUTURE PARTICIPLE	θῆσον	θησόμενον	τεθησόμενον
AORIST PARTICIPLE	θέν	θέμενον	τεθέν
PERFECT PARTICIPLE	τεθηκός	τεθειμένον	τεθειμένον

UNIT
15

112. THE INTERROGATIVE PRONOUN/ADJECTIVE τίς, τί

As a pronoun, the interrogative τίς, τί means "who?, what?"

As an adjective, the interrogative τίς, τί means "which?, what?"

	M/F	N
Nom. S	τίς	τί
Gen.	τίνος/τοῦ	τίνος/τοῦ
Dat.	τίνι/τῷ	τίνι/τῷ
Acc.	τίνα	τί
Nom. P	τίνες	τίνα
Gen.	τίνων	τίνων
Dat.	τίσι(ν)	τίσι(ν)
Acc.	τίνας	τίνα

Observations: (1) The accent on the interrogative is always on the first syllable. Although the word has a monosyllabic stem, the accent does not shift to the ultima in the genitive and the dative, singular and plural, as it does, e.g., in αἴξ, αἰγός.

(2) Even when followed directly by another word, in violation of the rules for accent the acute accent on τίς and τί is NEVER changed to a grave.

(3) Note the alternative forms in the genitive and dative singular with the circumflex accent.

(4) Note that τίνα can be either the masculine/feminine accusative singular "whom?" or the neuter plural nominative or accusative "what (things)?"

Examples: τίνας ἐπέμψατε;
Whom did you send?

τίνας στρατιώτᾱς ἐπέμψατε;
Which/What soldiers did you send?

τίνας γυναῖκας ἐπέμψατε;
Which/What women did you send?

τίνα ἐπέμψατε;
Whom did you send?
What (things) did you send?

τίς τοὺς ἀγγέλους ἔπεμψεν;
Who sent the messengers?

τί ἔπεμψας;
What did you send?

113. THE INDEFINITE PRONOUN/ADJECTIVE τις, τι

As a pronoun, the indefinite τις, τι means "someone, anyone, something, anything."

As an adjective, the indefinite τις, τι means "some, any."

	M/F	N
Nom. S	τις	τι
Gen.	τινός/του	τινός/του
Dat.	τινί/τῳ	τινί/τῳ
Acc.	τινά	τι
Nom. P	τινές	τινά
Gen.	τινῶν	τινῶν
Dat.	τισί(ν)	τισί(ν)
Acc.	τινάς	τινά

Observations: (1) The indefinite pronoun/adjective differs from the interrogative pronoun/adjective in accent only and is an *enclitic*. For a summary of enclitics and examples of the use of the indefinite pronoun/adjective, see Section 114.

(2) Note the alternative forms in the genitive and dative singular.

(3) Note that the form τινά can be either the masculine/feminine accusative singular or the neuter nominative or accusative plural.

(4) Note that the genitive plural, when accented, takes a circumflex accent on the ultima; cf. Section 114.

114. ENCLITICS SUMMARIZED

Enclitics are words which are closely attached in pronunciation to the word they follow, and which usually affect the accent of the preceding word. In addition to the indefinite pronoun/adjective τις, τι, there are a number of other words which are enclitic. Seven words which are enclitic are:

γε: emphasizes or limits the preceding word; "at any rate"
-περ: adds force to the word it follows
ποτέ: "at some time, ever"
που: qualifies an assertion, "I suppose"; "somewhere"
πως: "in any way, in some way"
τε: "and" (often used together with καί)
τοι: "let me tell you, you know"

See the Vocabulary Notes of the various units for the uses of these enclitics.

Observe how an enclitic affects the accent of the preceding word:

(1) A word ending with an acute accent (-a-p-ú) followed by an enclitic (e, e-é, e-ē) does NOT change its acute accent to a grave accent; the enclitic does not take any accent:

$$-a\text{-}p\text{-}\acute{u} + e \qquad \mathring{α}γαθός \ τις$$
some good man

$$-a\text{-}p\text{-}\acute{u} + e\text{-}e \qquad \mathring{α}δελφοί \ τινες$$
some brothers

(2) A *monosyllabic* enclitic following a word with an acute on the penult has no accent:

$$-a\text{-}\acute{p}\text{-}u + e \qquad λόγῳ \ τε \ καὶ \ ἔργῳ$$
by word and deed

A *disyllabic* enclitic following a word with an acute on the penult takes an accent on its final syllable:

$$-a\text{-}\acute{p}\text{-}u + e\text{-}\acute{e} \qquad \mathring{α}νδράσι \ τισί(ν)$$
to some men

$$-a\text{-}\acute{p}\text{-}u + e\text{-}\bar{e} \qquad \mathring{α}νθρώπων \ τινῶν$$
of some men

(3) A word with an acute accent on the antepenult (-á-p-u) receives an additional accent from the enclitic; the enclitic does not take any accent:

      -á-p-ú + e   ἄνθρωποί τε καὶ θεοί
                         men and gods

      -á-p-ú + e-e   ἄνθρωποί τινες
                         some men

(4) A word ending in a circumflex keeps its circumflex; the enclitic has no accent:

      -a-p-ũ + e   αἱ τῑμαὶ τῶν ἀγαθῶν τε καὶ σοφῶν
                         the honors of the good and wise

      -a-p-ũ + e-e   αἱ τῑμαὶ σοφῶν τινων
                         the honors of some wise men

(5) A word with a circumflex accent on the penult takes an additional accent on the final syllable; the enclitic has no accent:

      -a-p̃-ú + e   ἐκεῖνά τε καὶ ταῦτα
                         those things and these things

      -a-p̃-ú + e-e   δῶρά τινα
                         some presents

(6) A proclitic (εἰς, ἐκ/ἐξ, ἐν, εἰ, ὡς, οὐ/οὐκ/οὐχ, and the forms of the article ὁ, ἡ, οἱ, and αἱ) takes an acute accent when followed by an enclitic; the enclitic has no accent:

      εἴ τις   οἵ γ' ἄνθρωποι
      if anyone   *the men*/the men, at least

Thus, if the accent is as far back on the word as it can go (-á-p-u or -a-p̃-u), the word, when followed by an enclitic, takes an additional acute accent on the final syllable (e.g. -á-p-ú + e, -a-p̃-ú + e). There is no accent on the enclitic.

If the accent is on the final syllable (-a-p-ũ or -a-p-ú), the accent on the word remains unchanged; there is no accent on the enclitic (-a-p-ú + e, -a-p-ũ + e).

Only in the case of a word with an acute accent on the penult followed by a disyllabic enclitic does the enclitic have an accent, an acute on the final syllable of the word (except for τινῶν, the genitive plural of τις, τι).

In a series of enclitics, each takes an acute accent from the following enclitic; the final enclitic of such a series has no accent:

      ἐάν **ποτέ τίς τί τινι** διδῷ
      if anyone ever gives anything to anyone

Some disyllabic enclitics can be placed at the beginning of a clause or sentence. When this occurs, they take an acute accent on the ultima; this accent becomes a grave accent if no pause follows:

τινὲς μὲν χρυσὸν διδόασιν, τινὲς δ' οὔ.
Some give gold, others do not.

115. THE VERB εἰμί, "be"

εἰμί, ἔσομαι, ——, ——, ——, ——, "be"

This verb is found only in the present system active and as a middle deponent in the future. The present system has an athematic conjugation with a number of irregularities. The future has a regular thematic conjugation (ἔσομαι, ἔσῃ/ ἔσει, etc.) except for the third person singular, which is ἔσται.

	PRESENT IND. ACTIVE	IMPERF. IND. ACTIVE	PRESENT SUBJ. ACTIVE	PRESENT OPT. ACTIVE	PRESENT IMPER. ACTIVE
S 1	εἰμί	ἦ / ἦν	ὦ	εἴην	
2	εἶ	ἦσθα	ἦς	εἴης	ἴσθι
3	ἐστί(ν)	ἦν	ἦ	εἴη	ἔστω
P 1	ἐσμέν	ἦμεν	ὦμεν	εἶμεν/εἴημεν	
2	ἐστέ	ἦτε	ἦτε	εἶτε/εἴητε	ἔστε
3	εἰσί(ν)	ἦσαν	ὦσι(ν)	εἶεν/εἴησαν	ἔστων/ὄντων

PRESENT INFINITIVE ACTIVE: εἶναι

PRESENT PARTICIPLE ACTIVE:

	M	F	N
Nom. S	ὤν	οὖσα	ὄν
Gen.	ὄντος	οὔσης	ὄντος

Observations: (1) Unlike the athematic verbs seen thus far, the verb εἰμί does not have a long-vowel and a short-vowel grade of the stem. Instead, the forms are built on the e-grade stem ἐσ- or the zero-grade stem σ-.

(2) Note the absence of the final -ς in the second person singular of the present indicative active εἶ; contrast this with τίθης, δίδως, etc.

(3) Note that the third person singular indicative active ending is -τι and not the -σι of, e.g., δίδωσι.

(4) Particular care must be taken in memorizing the third person plural of the present indicative active and all of the imperfect.

(5) In the imperative the second person singular is irregular; the third person plural form ἔστων omits the -ν- of the ending -ντων; the alternative third person plural form ὄντων is identical with the masculine and neuter genitive plural of the present participle active.

The disyllabic forms of the present indicative active of εἰμί (all forms except the second person singular εἶ) are enclitic and follow the rules for accent given above.

> ἀγαθοί ἐσμεν.
> We are good.
>
> εὐδαίμονές ἐστε.
> You are happy.

At the beginning of a sentence ἔστι(ν) is not an enclitic: it has an acute accent on the penult and can mean "there is" or "it is possible."

> ἔστι σοφός τις ἐν τῇ πόλει.
> There is some wise man in the city.
>
> ἔστιν ἀπελθεῖν.
> It is possible to go away.

116. DATIVE OF THE POSSESSOR

With the verb εἰμί and similar verbs (e.g., γίγνομαι), ownership is shown by the **dative of the possessor**.

> ἐκείνῳ τῷ ἀνδρί ἐστι μῑκρὰ οἰκίᾱ.
> **To that man** there is a small house.
> **That man has** a small house.

Note the difference between the genitive and the dative when showing possession. The dative stresses the existence of the object and answers the question, "What does that man have?" The genitive in a similar sentence puts stress on the owner and answers the question, "Who has that thing?"

> ἐκείνου τοῦ ἀνδρὸς μῑκρά ἐστιν ἡ οἰκίᾱ.
> **Of that man** small is the house.
> **That man's** house is small.

117. ADVERBIAL ACCUSATIVE

An accusative which limits the meaning of a verb and functions as an adverb is called an **adverbial accusative**.

τί ταῦτα ἐποίησας;
For what did you do these things?
Why did you do these things?

τίνα τρόπον τοῦτο ἐποίησας; τόνδε τὸν τρόπον τοῦτο ἐποίησα.
In what way did you do this? I did this **in the following way**.

τέλος ἀπῆλθον.
In the end they went away.
They **finally** went away.

118. PERSONAL PRONOUNS

Attic Greek uses the first-person pronouns ἐγώ ("I") and ἡμεῖς ("we"), and the second-person pronouns σύ ("you" singular) and ὑμεῖς ("you" plural). In the third person ("he," "she," "it," "they"), Attic Greek uses the demonstrative pronouns in the nominative case (οὗτος, ὅδε, ἐκεῖνος) and forms of αὐτός in cases other than the nominative.

	I	*you*
Nom. S	ἐγώ	σύ
Gen.	ἐμοῦ/μου	σοῦ/σου
Dat.	ἐμοί/μοι	σοί/σοι
Acc.	ἐμέ/με	σέ/σε

	we	*you*
Nom. P	ἡμεῖς	ὑμεῖς
Gen.	ἡμῶν	ὑμῶν
Dat.	ἡμῖν	ὑμῖν
Acc.	ἡμᾶς	ὑμᾶς

Observations: (1) In the singular, the unaccented forms are alternative enclitic forms and are less emphatic.

(2) Note that Greek, unlike English, distinguishes between singular and plural forms of the second person pronoun. Unlike many modern languages, Greek does NOT use a polite plural form for the singular "you."

Since the Greek verb form itself contains the subject, the nominative of the personal pronouns is used only for emphasis or contrast.

    ἐγὼ ἐδίδαξα τὸν ἀδελφόν.
    I taught my brother.
    It was **I** who taught my brother.

Compare the same sentence without the pronoun:

    ἐδίδαξα τὸν ἀδελφόν.
    I taught my brother.

Personal pronouns can also be used in nominal sentences:

    ἐγὼ μὲν ἀγαθός, σὺ δὲ κακός.
    I am good; you are bad.

When the enclitic particle γε is used with the nominative and dative singular of ἐγώ, the two words are written together as one; the accent is *recessive*: ἔγωγε, ἔμοιγε.

119. REFLEXIVE PRONOUNS

A pronoun in a case other than the nominative which refers back to the subject of its own clause is called a **reflexive pronoun**: "We love **ourselves**." "Ourselves" is the reflexive pronoun and refers back to the subject of the sentence, "we." (Be sure to distinguish the English reflexive "-self" from the *intensive* "-self": "We *ourselves* love them." Remember that Greek uses αὐτός in the predicate position or by itself in the nominative case as the intensive.)

	myself	
	M	F
Gen. S	ἐμαυτοῦ	ἐμαυτῆς
Dat.	ἐμαυτῷ	ἐμαυτῇ
Acc.	ἐμαυτόν	ἐμαυτήν

	ourselves	
	M	F
Gen. P	ἡμῶν αὐτῶν	ἡμῶν αὐτῶν
Dat.	ἡμῖν αὐτοῖς	ἡμῖν αὐταῖς
Acc.	ἡμᾶς αὐτούς	ἡμᾶς αὐτάς

	yourself	
	M	F
Gen. S	σεαυτοῦ	σεαυτῆς
Dat.	σεαυτῷ	σεαυτῇ
Acc.	σεαυτόν	σεαυτήν

	yourselves	
	M	F
Gen. P	ὑμῶν αὐτῶν	ὑμῶν αὐτῶν
Dat.	ὑμῖν αὐτοῖς	ὑμῖν αὐταῖς
Acc.	ὑμᾶς αὐτούς	ὑμᾶς αὐτάς

	himself	*herself*	*itself*
	M	F	N
Gen. S	ἑαυτοῦ	ἑαυτῆς	ἑαυτοῦ
Dat.	ἑαυτῷ	ἑαυτῇ	ἑαυτῷ
Acc.	ἑαυτόν	ἑαυτήν	ἑαυτό

	themselves	*themselves*	*themselves*
	M	F	N
Gen. P	ἑαυτῶν	ἑαυτῶν	ἑαυτῶν
Dat.	ἑαυτοῖς	ἑαυταῖς	ἑαυτοῖς
Acc.	ἑαυτούς	ἑαυτάς	ἑαυτά

	OR	*OR*
Gen. P	σφῶν αὐτῶν	σφῶν αὐτῶν
Dat.	σφίσιν αὐτοῖς	σφίσιν αὐταῖς
Acc.	σφᾶς αὐτούς	σφᾶς αὐτάς

Observations: (1) Since the reflexive pronoun must refer back to the subject of the sentence, it never appears in the nominative case.

(2) The reflexive pronoun uses αὐτός, αὐτή, αὐτό either as part of a compound form (e.g., ἐμαυτοῦ) in which it alone is declined or together with the personal pronoun (e.g., ἡμῶν αὐτῶν) where both pronouns are declined.

(3) Note that only the third-person reflexive pronoun has a neuter.

(4) In the plural, the third-person reflexives, both masculine and feminine, have alternative forms, ἑαυτῶν, etc. and σφῶν αὐτῶν, etc.

(5) All forms of σεαυτοῦ, σεαυτῆς and ἑαυτοῦ, ἑαυτῆς, ἑαυτοῦ can contract the first two vowels to give σαυτοῦ, σαυτῆς, etc. and αὑτοῦ, αὑτῆς, αὑτοῦ, etc. Distinguish carefully between the contracted third person reflexive pronoun forms and the corresponding forms of αὐτός, αὐτή, αὐτό; they differ only in breathing: e.g., αὑτόν "himself"; αὐτόν "him."

120. POSSESSION WITH PERSONAL AND REFLEXIVE PRONOUNS

To show possession in the first and second persons, either the possessive adjective or the genitive of the personal pronoun (enclitic in the singular) can be used. The possessive adjectives are:

ἐμός, ἐμή, ἐμόν, "my, mine"

ἡμέτερος, ἡμετέρᾱ, ἡμέτερον, "our, ours"

σός, σή, σόν, "your, yours (addressing one person)"

ῡ̔μέτερος, ῡ̔μετέρᾱ, ῡ̔μέτερον, "your, yours (addressing more than one person)"

These possessive adjectives are the equivalent of the genitive of the personal pronouns. The possessive adjective is used in the attributive position, the genitive of the personal pronoun in the predicate position:

ὁ ἐμὸς φίλος	ὁ φίλος μου	my friend
οἱ ἐμοὶ φίλοι	οἱ φίλοι μου	my friends
ὁ ἡμέτερος φίλος	ὁ φίλος ἡμῶν	our friend
οἱ ἡμέτεροι φίλοι	οἱ φίλοι ἡμῶν	our friends
ὁ σὸς ἀδελφός	ὁ ἀδελφός σου	your brother (addressing one person)
οἱ σοὶ ἀδελφοί	οἱ ἀδελφοί σου	your brothers (addressing one person)
ὁ ῡ̔μέτερος ἀδελφός	ὁ ἀδελφὸς ῡ̔μῶν	your brother (addressing more than one)
οἱ ῡ̔μέτεροι ἀδελφοί	οἱ ἀδελφοὶ ῡ̔μῶν	your brothers (addressing more than one)

Thus, to express the idea "my friend," Greek can use either the adjective (ὁ ἐμὸς φίλος) or the genitive of the personal pronoun (ὁ φίλος μου, literally, "the friend of me").

To show possession in the third person, the genitive of a demonstrative pronoun in the attributive position or the genitive of αὐτός, αὐτή, αὐτό in the predicate position is used:

ὁ τούτου φίλος	ὁ φίλος αὐτοῦ	his friend
ὁ ταύτης φίλος	ὁ φίλος αὐτῆς	her friend
οἱ τούτου φίλοι	οἱ φίλοι αὐτοῦ	his friends
οἱ ταύτης φίλοι	οἱ φίλοι αὐτῆς	her friends
ὁ τούτων φίλος	ὁ φίλος αὐτῶν	their friend
οἱ τούτων φίλοι	οἱ φίλοι αὐτῶν	their friends

To show **reflexive possession** in the singular, the genitive of the reflexive pronoun is used in the attributive position:

ἔπεμψα τὸν **ἐμαυτοῦ** ἀδελφόν.
I sent **my (own)** brother.

ἔπεμψας τὸν **σεαυτοῦ** ἀδελφόν.
You sent **your (own)** brother.

ἔπεμψε τὸν **ἑαυτοῦ** ἀδελφόν.
He sent **his (own)** brother.

Less commonly, the possessive adjectives ἐμός and σός are used:

ἔπεμψα τὸν ἐμὸν ἀδελφόν.
I sent my brother.

To show reflexive possession in the plural, in the first and second persons the adjectives ἡμέτερος, ἡμετέρᾱ, ἡμέτερον and ὑμέτερος, ὑμετέρᾱ, ὑμέτερον can be used by themselves, but they are usually strengthened by αὐτῶν, which agrees with the genitive idea in the possessive adjective. To show reflexive possession in the third person plural, ἑαυτῶν is used in the attributive position, or the reflexive possessive adjective σφέτερος, σφετέρᾱ, σφέτερον, strengthened by αὐτῶν, can be used:

ἐπέμψαμεν τὸν { **ἡμέτερον αὐτῶν** / **ἡμέτερον** } ἀδελφόν.
We sent **our (own)** brother.

ἐπέμψατε τὸν { **ὑμέτερον αὐτῶν** / **ὑμέτερον** } ἀδελφόν.
You sent **your (own)** brother.

ἔπεμψαν τὸν { **σφέτερον αὐτῶν** / **ἑαυτῶν** } ἀδελφόν.
They sent **their (own)** brother.

VOCABULARY

αἱρέω, αἱρήσω, εἷλον, ᾕρηκα,   take, capture; (*mid.*) choose
  ᾕρημαι, ᾑρέθην

αἰσθάνομαι, αἰσθήσομαι, ᾐσθόμην,   perceive (+ *gen. or acc.*)
  ——, ᾔσθημαι, ——

δια- (*prefix*)   through, in different directions

ἑαυτοῦ, ἑαυτῆς, ἑαυτοῦ   himself, herself, itself
  (*reflexive pronoun*)

ἐγώ (*personal pronoun*)   I
  ἐμαυτοῦ, ἐμαυτῆς (*reflexive*   myself
    pronoun)
  ἐμός, ἐμή, ἐμόν   my; (*as a substantive*) mine

εἰμί, ἔσομαι, ——, ——, ——, ——   be
  ἔστι(ν)   there is; it is possible
  ἔξεστι(ν) (*impersonal verb*)   it is allowed, it is possible

ἕπομαι, ἕψομαι, ἑσπόμην, ——,   follow, pursue (+ *dat.*)
  ——, ——

ἡμεῖς (*personal pronoun*)   we
  ἡμῶν αὐτῶν (*reflexive pronoun*) ourselves
  ἡμέτερος, ἡμετέρᾱ, ἡμέτερον   our; (*as a substantive*) ours

οἷος, οἵᾱ, οἷον   such as, of the sort which;
                         what sort of!

  οἷός τ᾽ εἰμί   be able

ὁράω, ὄψομαι, εἶδον, ἑόρᾱκα   see
  or ἑώρᾱκα, ἑώρᾱμαι or ὦμμαι,
  ὤφθην

-περ (*enclitic particle*)   *adds force to preceding word*

περι- (*prefix*)   all around; very, exceedingly

ποῖος, ποίᾱ, ποῖον   of what kind?

σύ (*personal pronoun*)   you (*sing.*)

σεαυτοῦ, σεαυτῆς (reflexive pronoun)	yourself
σός, σή, σόν	your; (as a substantive) yours
σφῶν αὐτῶν (reflexive pronoun)	themselves
σφέτερος αὐτῶν	their (own)
τίς, τί (interrogative pronoun/adjective)	who?, which?, what?
τις, τι (indefinite enclitic pronoun/adjective)	someone, something; anyone, anything; some, any
τοιοῦτος, τοιαύτη, τοιοῦτο/ τοιοῦτον	of this/that sort, such (as this)
ὑμεῖς (personal pronoun)	you (pl.)
ὑμῶν αὐτῶν (reflexive pronoun)	yourselves
ὑμέτερος, ὑμετέρᾱ, ὑμέτερον	your; (as a substantive) yours
φέρω, οἴσω, ἤνεγκα or ἤνεγκον, ἐνήνοχα, ἐνήνεγμαι, ἠνέχθην	bring, bear, carry; (mid.) win
διαφέρω	carry through; be different from, excel (+ gen.)
συμφέρω	bring together; be useful or profitable; (impersonal) it is expedient

VOCABULARY NOTES

In the verb αἱρέω, αἱρήσω, εἷλον, ᾕρηκα, ᾕρημαι, ᾑρέθην, "take, capture; (mid.) choose," observe that in the perfect active, perfect middle, and aorist passive, the iota of the diphthong αἱ- becomes a subscript. As with ἦρχα and ἦργμαι from ἄρχω, the ᾐ- of the perfect stem remains unchanged throughout the perfect and the pluperfect. The unaugmented form of the aorist passive tense stem is αἱρεθ-. Note also the short vowel before the -θ- of the aorist passive tense stem; contrast this with the -η- of ἐποιήθην, ἐνῑκήθην. The second aorist εἷλον was borrowed from another root; the unaugmented second aorist active and middle tense stem is ἑλ-.

In the active αἱρέω means "take, capture" and in the middle "choose." The passive means "be chosen" NOT "be captured": i.e., it is the passive of the middle and not of the active. For the passive "I am captured" Attic Greek uses the passive of λαμβάνω or another verb: ἁλίσκομαι, ἁλώσομαι, ἑάλων or ἥλων, ἑάλωκα or ἥλωκα, ——, ——, "be captured."

The verb αἰσθάνομαι, αἰσθήσομαι, ἠσθόμην, ——, ἤσθημαι, ——, "perceive," is a deponent with a second aorist middle. Note the iota subscript in Principal Parts III and V.

For the conjugation of εἰμί, ἔσομαι, ——, ——, ——, ——, "be," see Section 115. The neuter singular dative of the present participle is employed in the idiomatic phrase τῷ ὄντι, "really, truly" (literally "with respect to what is, with respect to reality").

The **impersonal verb** (one with no personal subject) ἔξεστι(ν), ἐξέσται, ——, ——, ——, ——, "it is possible," takes either a dative and an infinitive or an accusative and an infinitive. When used impersonally, ἔστι(ν) can take the same constructions. Note the accent on the penult of the future: ἐξέσται (<* ἐξέσεται).

ἐξῆν τῷ Σωκράτει διδάσκειν τοὺς νεᾱνίᾱς.
ἐξῆν τὸν Σωκράτη διδάσκειν τοὺς νεᾱνίᾱς.
It was possible for Sokrates to teach the young men.

The verb ἕπομαι, ἕψομαι, ἑσπόμην, ——, ——, ——, "follow," governs the dative case. The root of the word was *sek^w-. The loss of the initial s accounts for the rough breathing in the first two principal parts. The Indo-European labiovelar (k^w) became a -π- in this word in Greek. The augmented present tense stem is εἱπ- (e.g., εἱπόμην, εἷπου). Principal Part III shows a *past indicative augment with a rough breathing* on the analogy of the first two principal parts, the zero-grade of the stem, and the ending -ομην. The unaugmented aorist active and middle tense stem is σπ-, e.g., σποῦ τούτῳ, "follow that man."

The enclitic particle -περ has been seen in the adverb καίπερ. It is often added to forms of the relative pronoun:

ὁ Σωκράτης **ὅσπερ** τὴν πόλιν ἀγαθὰ ἀεὶ ἔπρᾱττεν ὑπὸ τῶν κακῶν πολῑτῶν ἐβλάβη.
Sokrates, **just the one who** was always doing good things to the city, was harmed by the bad citizens.

The adjectives ποῖος, ποία, ποῖον, "of what kind?," τοιοῦτος, τοιαύτη, τοιοῦτο/ τοιοῦτον, "of this/that sort, such (as this)," and οἷος, οἵα, οἷον, "such as, of the sort which," are a set of **correlative** adjectives. In such a series, the word beginning with π- is interrogative, the word beginning with τ- is demonstrative, and the word beginning with the rough breathing is either a relative (introducing a relative clause) or an exclamatory word.

ποῖός ἐστιν ὁ Σωκράτης;
What kind of man is Sokrates?

τοιοῦτός ἐστιν ὁ Σωκράτης **οἷον** πάντες τῑμῶσιν.
Sokrates is **that sort of man, the sort which** all men honor.
Sokrates is **the sort of man whom** all men honor.

οἷός ἐστιν ὁ Σωκράτης.
What sort of man Sokrates is!

The phrase οἷός τ' εἰμί is an idiom meaning "be able"; it governs a **complementary infinitive**:

οὐχ οἷοί τ' ἐσμὲν νῑκᾶν.
We are not able to win.

Note the accent on the enclitic forms of the verb εἰμί in this idiom: it follows the general rule that WHEN AN ENCLITIC FOLLOWS AN ELIDED SYLLABLE (OF EITHER A NON-ENCLITIC OR AN ENCLITIC WORD), IT RECEIVES AN ACCENT (cf. the Appendix, p. 613).

Note that the verb ὁράω, ὄψομαι, εἶδον, ἑόρακα or ἑώρακα, ἑώρᾱμαι or ὦμμαι, ὤφθην, "see," uses several different roots. The imperfect is ἑώρων, ἑώρᾱς, etc., with a double augment. The root of the second aorist was *ϝιδ-, *ἐϝιδ- in its augmented form. The loss of the intervocalic digamma accounts for the initial diphthong in εἶδον; the aorist subjunctive is ἴδω, ἴδῃς, etc. The second person singular, aorist imperative active is accented on the ultima: ἰδέ. Cf. λαβέ, ἐλθέ. Remember that in compounds these imperatives have a recessive accent. The unaugmented aorist passive tense stem is ὀφθ-.

Note the acute accent which distinguishes the interrogative τίς, τί from the enclitic indefinite τις, τι:

τίς ἀνὴρ τοῦτο ἐποίησεν;
What man did this?

ἀνήρ **τις** τοῦτο ἐποίησεν.
Some man did this.

In τοιοῦτος, τοιαύτη, τοιοῦτο/τοιοῦτον note the alternative forms in the neuter nominative/vocative/accusative singular: τοιοῦτο and τοιοῦτον. The word is declined like οὗτος, αὕτη, τοῦτο, with the neuter nominative/vocative/accusative plural τοιαῦτα, and the genitive plural of all three genders τοιούτων.

The verb φέρω, οἴσω, ἤνεγκα or ἤνεγκον, ἐνήνοχα, ἐνήνεγμαι, ἠνέχθην, "bring, carry, bear; (mid.) win," uses three different roots. In the aorist there are both first and second aorist forms with no difference in meaning; the first aorist forms are much more common in prose in the indicative than are the second aorist forms. In the optative, both ἐνέγκαιμι, etc., and ἐνέγκοιμι, etc., are found. The infinitive is ἐνεγκεῖν and the participle is usually ἐνεγκών.

In the compound διαφέρω, the prefix can have its usual spatial meaning of "through."

διαφέρομεν τοὺς λίθους διὰ τοῦ πεδίου.
We carry the rocks through the plain.

The word can also mean "be different (from), be better (than), excel," and the person from whom one differs or than who one is better is put in the genitive case (**genitive of comparison**).

The compound συμφέρω is used *impersonally* (in the third person singular) to mean "it is expedient"; this verb can govern an infinitive. The verb can also be used personally to mean "bring things together, confer a benefit."

COGNATES AND DERIVATIVES

αἱρέω	heretic (one who **chooses** what to believe)
αἰσθάνομαι	aesthetics
δια-	diameter
ἐγώ	*I, me*
εἰμί	*am, is*
ἕπομαι	sequel (from the Latin cognate *sequor*)
ὁράω	panorama (a total **view**)
ὄψομαι	optics
εἶδον	*wit*; vision (from the Latin cognate *videō*)
σύ	*thou*
ὑμεῖς	*you*
φέρω	*bear*
οἴσω	esophagus (the tube that **carries** the food to the stomach)
διαφέρω	differ (from the Latin cognate *differō*)

DRILLS

I. *Put the proper accent on the following phrases.*

1. ἐν ἀγορᾳ τινι
2. ἀδελφος τις
3. ἀδελφων τινων
4. ἀνθρωπος τις
5. ἀνθρωποις τισιν
6. ἀνθρωποι τινες
7. δωρα τινα
8. δωρων τινων
9. λογου τινος
10. νησοι τινες
11. ὁδῳ τινι
12. οἰκιᾱ τις
13. οἰκιᾳ τινι
14. οἰκιων τινων

15. τεχνη τινι
16. ἀγγελον τινα
17. ἀγγελων τινων
18. ἀγγελοις τισιν
19. ἀγγελοι τινες
20. κηρῡκες τε και ἀγγελοι
21. στεφανος τε και χρῡσος
22. χρῡσος τε και στεφανος
23. ἀθλα τινα
24. ἀθλα τε και δωρα
25. ἀθλα τε και δωρα τινα
26. σοφοι γε τινες
27. μουσα τις
28. μουσαν τινα

29. μουσων τινων

30. μουσαις τισιν

31. εἰ που τις τινα ποτε βλαπτοι

32. ποιητης τις

33. ποιητου τινος

34. διδασκαλος τις

35. διδασκαλων τινων

36. διδασκαλου τινος

37. δοξαν τινα

38. δοξα τις

39. τω ἀδελφῳ γε

40. ὁ ἀδελφος γε

II. *Translate the following.*

1. ὑμᾶς οὐ βλάπτομεν.

2. ἡμᾶς βλάπτετε.

3. ἐγὼ δὴ οὐ βλάπτω ἐκείνᾱς, ἀλλὰ σύ.

4. οὐ βλάπτω ἐκεῖνον, ἀλλὰ σέ.

5. οὐ βλάπτομέν σε.

6. ἔμοιγε τοῦτο ἔδωκας.

7. τοῦτό σοι δώσει.

8. ἡμεῖς δὴ κακὰ πράττοντες ἡμᾶς αὐτοὺς ἀδικοῦμεν.

9. μὴ ἀδικήσητε ἡμᾶς ἀλλ᾽ αὐτούς.

10. ὑμῖν ἔδωκα ἐκεῖνο.

11. ἐμὲ βλάπτει, ἀλλ᾽ ἐμαυτὸν οὐ βλάπτω.

12. οὔ με βλάπτει.

13. ἑαυτὴν διδάσκει, ἀλλ᾽ ἐμὲ οὐ διδάσκει.

14. ὑμᾶς αὐτοὺς διδάσκετε.

15. τί τὴν ἀρετήν με διδάσκεις;

16. τὴν ἀρετήν σού με διδάσκει.

17. τίνας σὺ διδάσκεις; ἀλλ᾽ ἔγωγε τοὺς γέροντας.

18. καλὰ δῶρά τινα ἐμαυτῷ δώσω.

19. τί σαυτῷ δώσεις;

20. αὐτοῦ τὸν ἀδελφὸν παιδεύω.

21. τοὺς ἀδελφοὺς αὐτῆς παιδεύεις.

22. τοὺς πατέρας ἡμῶν ἐθάψατε.

23. ὁ ἡμέτερος πατήρ σε διδάσκει.

24. ἡ σὴ μήτηρ κακά τινα πράττει.

25. δῶρόν τι τῷ ἐμαυτοῦ πατρὶ δίδωμι.

EXERCISES

I.   1. ἄφρων που ὃς ἂν μὴ λάβῃ ἀγαθόν τι διδόμενον παρὰ τῶν φίλων.

2. αἰσχρόν τι ποιήσᾱς ἄλλους μὲν λάθοις ἄν, σεαυτὸν δὲ οὔ. μὴ οὖν ποίει τοιοῦτο.

3. τί σὺ ποιήσεις τὴν πόλιν ἑλών;
   τί ἐμὲ ἐρωτᾷς; ὁ γὰρ στρατηγός γε ἡμᾶς ἂν κελεύσειεν ἢ τὰς οἰκίᾱς φυλάττειν ἢ χρήματά τε καὶ ζῷα καταλαβεῖν.

4. τοιοῦτος ἦν ὁ Σωκράτης ὥστε πάντας τοὺς σοφούς τε καὶ σώφρονας αὐτὸν τῑμᾶν. τοῖς γὰρ νόμοις εἵπετο, τοῖς δὲ θεοῖς θυσίᾱς ἦγε καὶ τοὺς πολίτᾱς περὶ τῆς ἀρετῆς ἠρώτᾱ.

5. ἀντὶ τῆς ἀρετῆς τε καὶ τῑμῆς χρήματά γε ᾑροῦντο οἱ ἄφρονες. τί οὐχ οἷός τ' ἦν ὁ Σωκράτης τούτους πεῖσαι ἀγαθόν τι ἑλέσθαι; σύ γε, φίλε, ἑλοῦ τὰ τοιαῦτα.

6. ὦ παῖ, ἴσθι τῷ ὄντι τοιοῦτος οἷος ἦν ὁ πατήρ.

7. ὁ νεᾱνίᾱς ὁ καλός τε καὶ ἀμαθὴς αὐτὸν ἐν ὕδατί τινι ἰδὼν αὐτόν γε ἐφίλησεν οὐδ' οἷός τ' ἦν ἀπελθεῖν. μετὰ δὲ πέντε ἡμέρᾱς ἐτελεύτησε διὰ τὸν αὐτοῦ ἔρωτα. τρόπον δή τινα τελευτῶσι πάντες οἱ σφᾶς αὐτοὺς φιλοῦντες.

8. οἷον δὴ πάντες τῑμῶσιν, τὸν τὴν πόλιν σώσαντα στρατηγόν, τοιοῦτοι γενώμεθα.

9. τοιαῦτα ἆθλα νίκης ἡμῖν εἴη ἀεί, οἷα οἱ πατέρες ἠνέγκοντο.

10. ἐπειδήπερ ἑσπόμεθα ἡμεῖς τῷ Σωκράτει εἰς τὴν ἀγοράν, ἠκούσαμεν αὐτοῦ τοὺς δημιουργοὺς καὶ τοὺς ποιητὰς ἐρωτῶντος περὶ τῶν τεχνῶν.

11. ὦ θύγατέρ μου, ἐάν σοι αἰσχρός τις γέρων ἐξ ἀγορᾶς σπῆται, μὴ φοβηθῇς. φυλαττουσῶν γὰρ πᾱσῶν τῶν θεῶν τὰς νέᾱς, οὔ σε βλάψειεν ἄν.

12. τόν γε κλέψαντα τὰ τῶν θεῶν ἔξεστι τῷ βουλομένῳ καλέσαι εἰς δίκην. Δημοσθένη οὖν γράψαι, ὦ ῥῆτορ.

13. τῇ ἀληθείᾳ ἄφρων ὅσπερ ἂν ἑαυτοῦ μὴ ἄρχων βούληται ἄλλων
ἄρχειν.

14. οἵ γε διδάσκαλοι καίπερ αἰσθανόμενοι τὴν τῶν πολῑτῶν ἀμαθίᾱν
οὐχ οἷοί τ᾽ ἔσονται αὐτοὺς ἐκδιδάξαι.

15. διαπέμψωμεν οὖν τοὺς ἡμετέρους δούλους εἰς τὴν πόλιν σου
ἀπαγγελοῦντας τοῖς σοῖς τὰ νέα.

16. ἔγωγε μὲν οὐκ ἀξιῶ τῑμῆς τοὺς ἆθλα μὴ ἐνεγκομένους· οἱ δ᾽ ἄλλοι
ἀφρόνως ἐθελόντων τούτους τῑμᾶν.

17. παρὰ δέ γε τὴν ἐμὴν γνώμην οὐχ ᾑρέθην ἄρχων. οἱ γὰρ
ἀμαθεῖς ἀεί που τοὺς ἀναξίους αἱροῦνται.

18. τί, ὦ Σώκρατες, γέγονεν ὥστε εἶ ἐνταῦθα; οὐ γάρ που καὶ σοί γε
δίκη τις οὖσα τυγχάνει;

19. φίλην τινὰ ἰδοῦσα ἐν τῇ ὁδῷ ἐπαύσατο τῇ μητρὶ ἑπομένη.

20. καὶ ἐγώ τοι μαθητὴς βουλοίμην ἂν γενέσθαι σός. σὺ γὰρ μόνος
οἷός τ᾽ εἶ μοι δεικνύναι τὴν ὁδὸν τὴν εἰς ἀρετὴν φέρουσαν.

21. οἱ ἐκ τῆς χώρᾱς ξίφη τε καὶ ἀσπίδας φέροντες εἰς τὴν πόλιν
ὤφθησαν ὑπὸ τῶν φυλάκων τῶν πρὸ τῶν τειχῶν
τεταγμένων.

22. ἐγώ τοι τὸν ἀδελφόν σου οὔ με ἰδόντα ἐν τῇ ἀγορᾷ εἶδον.

23. τί δὴ φέρων εἰς τὴν ἡμετέρᾱν οἰκίᾱν ἥξεις; ἡμῖν γὰρ ἱκανά ἐστι.

24. διαφέρει πως τῇ σοφίᾳ ὁ Εὐρῑπίδης τῶν ἄλλων ποιητῶν. τοῦτον
γὰρ ἡ μοῦσα αὐτὴ ἐξεδίδασκε δείξοντα ἡμῖν τοὺς τῶν
ἀνθρώπων τρόπους. ἄκουσον οὖν τούτου λόγον τινά.

25. ἔστι νεᾱνίᾱς τις ἐν τῇ ὁδῷ πρὸ τῆς οἰκίᾱς βουλόμενός σέ τι
ἐρωτῆσαι. ἐρωτῶ οὖν ὑπ᾽ αὐτοῦ.

26. οὐκ ἀεί που συμφέρει τοὺς νεᾱνίᾱς τὴν ῥητορικὴν διδάξασθαι.
οὗτοι γὰρ ποτε κακά τινα πράξαντες οἷοί τ᾽ εἰσὶν ἡμᾶς
πεῖσαι μὴ δίκην λαβεῖν.

27. σοί τοι δηλώσω τὰ ἡμῖν συμφέροντα ἐκείνην τὴν πόλιν ἑλοῦσιν.
τῶν γὰρ συμφερόντων δηλωθέντων, ἔπειτα πάντες βουλήσονται
μαχέσασθαι.

28. τοὺς δὲ λίθους διενέγκωμεν διὰ τοῦ πεδίου περιβαλούμενοι
τεῖχος τῇ πόλει.

29. οἷα δὴ ποιεῖ τις, τοιαῦτα καὶ πείσεται ὑφ᾽ ἡμῶν.

30. ἆρ᾽ οὐ σώφρονές ἐστε; σώφρονες ἔστε.

31. τοιούτων ὄντων τῶν πραγμάτων ἡμῖν, ἀγαθοὶ ὄντων οἵ γε
ῥήτορες.

II. 1. You, although wronged by the strangers, nevertheless wish to keep
peace. But if those men come into our land, fight on behalf of our
freedom.

2. The man who harms others really harms himself; for when harming
others he himself becomes bad so that he is not honored by his
companions.

3. In what way can anyone now teach others virtue? Not even Sokrates,
who excelled all men in virtue, was able to do this.

4. These battles are the sort which all the soldiers fear.

5. Who is so foolish as not to obey the gods? Those who don't obey the
gods are punished with death (i.e., give the justice of death).

6. If ever anyone sends anything to *me*, I shall sacrifice to the gods.

READINGS

A. Aristotle, *Politics* 1.2 (1253a 7–18)

What distinguishes human beings from other animals?

> διότι δὲ πολῑτικὸν ὁ ἄνθρωπος ζῷον πάσης μελίττης[1]
> καὶ παντὸς ἀγελαίου ζῴου[1] μᾶλλον, δῆλον. οὐδὲν γάρ,
> ὡς φαμέν, μάτην ἡ φύσις ποιεῖ· λόγον δὲ μόνον
> ἄνθρωπος ἔχει τῶν ζῴων. ἡ μὲν οὖν φωνὴ τοῦ λῡπηροῦ
> 5 καὶ ἡδέος ἐστὶ σημεῖον, διὸ καὶ τοῖς ἄλλοις
> ὑπάρχει ζῴοις (μέχρι γὰρ τούτου ἡ φύσις αὐτῶν
> ἐλήλυθεν, τοῦ ἔχειν αἴσθησιν λῡπηροῦ καὶ
> ἡδέος καὶ ταῦτα σημαίνειν ἀλλήλοις),

---

1. **Genitive of comparison**: translate "than . . ."

ἀγέλαιος, ἀγελαία, ἀγέλαιον belonging to a herd; common

αἴσθησις, αἰσθήσεως, ἡ sense-perception, perception

διό = διὰ ὅ

διότι (conj.) that

ἔχω, ἕξω/σχήσω, ἔσχον, ἔσχηκα, -ἔσχημαι, —— have, hold; be able; (mid.) cling to, be next to (+ gen.)

ἡδύς, ἡδεῖα, ἡδύ (gen. ἡδέος, ἡδείᾱς, ἡδέος) pleasant

λῡπηρός, λῡπηρά, λῡπηρόν painful, distressing

μάτην (adv.) in vain, at random

μέλιττα, μελίττης, ἡ bee

μέχρι (prep. + gen.) as far as, up to, until

οὐθείς/οὐδείς, οὐδεμία, οὐθέν/οὐδέν (gen. οὐθενός/οὐδενός, οὐδεμιᾱς, οὐθενός/ οὐδενός) no one, nothing

σημαίνω, σημανῶ, ἐσήμηνα, σεσήμαγκα, σεσήμασμαι, ἐσημάνθην show by a sign; point out; give a sign

σημεῖον, σημείου, τό sign, signal

ὑπάρχω begin; be first; exist already; be, exist

φημί, φήσω, ἔφησα, ——, ——, —— (enclitic present tense: see Section 121, page 461 say, affirm, assert

φωνή, φωνῆς, ἡ speech, voice

ὡς (conj.) as

ὁ δὲ λόγος ἐπὶ τῷ δηλοῦν ἐστι τὸ συμφέρον καὶ
10 τὸ βλαβερόν, ὥστε καὶ τὸ δίκαιον καὶ τὸ ἄδικον.
τοῦτο γὰρ πρὸς τἆλλα ζῷα τοῖς ἀνθρώποις ἴδιον,
τὸ μόνον ἀγαθοῦ καὶ κακοῦ καὶ δικαίου καὶ ἀδίκου
καὶ τῶν ἄλλων αἴσθησιν ἔχειν, ἡ δὲ τούτων
κοινωνίᾱ ποιεῖ οἰκίᾱν καὶ πόλιν.

αἴσθησις, αἰσθήσεως, ἡ   sense-perception, perception
βλαβερός, βλαβερά, βλαβερόν   harmful
ἔχω, ἕξω/σχήσω, ἔσχον, ἔσχηκα, -ἔσχημαι, ——   have, hold; be able; (mid.)
    cling to, be next to (+ gen.)
ἴδιος, ἰδίᾱ, ἴδιον   private, peculiar; one's own; separate
κοινωνίᾱ, κοινωνίᾱς, ἡ   sharing (in); association, society
συμφέρω, συνοίσω, συνήνεγκα/συνήνεγκον, συνενήνοχα, ——, ——   bring to-
    gether; be useful or profitable; (impersonal verb) it is expedient
τἆλλα = τὰ ἄλλα (For this **crasis**, see the Appendix, p. 614).
ὥστε (conj.) just as, as

B. Sophokles, *Oedipus the King* 380–389

Oedipus angrily accuses Kreon and Teiresias of plotting against him.

380 ὦ πλοῦτε καὶ τυραννὶ καὶ τέχνη τέχνης
    ὑπερφέρουσα τῷ πολυζήλῳ βίῳ,
    ὅσος παρ' ὑμῖν ὁ φθόνος φυλάσσεται,
    εἰ τῆσδε γ' ἀρχῆς οὕνεχ', ἣν ἐμοὶ πόλις
    δωρητόν, οὐκ αἰτητόν, εἰσεχείρισεν,
385 ταύτης Κρέων ὁ πιστός, οὑξ ἀρχῆς φίλος,
    λάθρᾳ μ' ὑπελθὼν ἐκβαλεῖν ἱμείρεται,[1]
    ὑφεὶς μάγον τοιόνδε μηχανορράφον,
    δόλιον ἀγύρτην, ὅστις ἐν τοῖς κέρδεσιν
    μόνον δέδορκε, τὴν τέχνην δ' ἔφυ τυφλός.

1. **Simple conditional sentence** in present time: see the Appendix, p. 747.

ἀγύρτης, ἀγύρτου, ὁ   begging priest, vagabond

αἰτητός, αἰτητόν   asked for, sought

δέρκομαι, δέρξομαι, ἔδρακον, δέδορκα, ——, ἐδράκην/ἐδέρχθην   see; (often
    in perfect)   have sight

δόλιος, δολία, δόλιον   crafty, sly

δωρητός, δωρητόν   given

εἰσχειρίζω, ——, εἰσεχείρισα, ——, ——, ——   put into one's hands, entrust

ἱμείρομαι, ——, ἱμειράμην, ——, ——, ἱμέρθην   long for, desire

κέρδος, κέρδους, τό   profit, gain

Κρέων, Κρέοντος, ὁ   Kreon, Oedipus' uncle and brother-in-law

λάθρᾳ   (adv.)   secretly

μάγος, μάγου, ὁ   magician, wizard; charlatan

μηχανορράφος, μηχανορράφον   weaving devices, scheming

ὅσος, ὅση, ὅσον   as much/many as, as large as; how much/many!, how large!

ὅστις   here = ὅς

οὕνεκα   (postpositive prep. + gen.) for the sake of, because of

οὐξ = ὁ ἐξ

πιστός, πιστή, πιστόν   trusted; trustworthy

πλοῦτος, πλούτου, ὁ   wealth, riches

πολύζηλος, πολύζηλον   with much rivalry; much-admired

τοιόσδε, τοιάδε, τοιόνδε   such (as this)

τυραννίς, τυραννίδος, ἡ   tyranny; kingship

τυφλός, τυφλή, τυφλόν   blind

ὑπερφέρω, ὑπεροίσω, ὑπερήνεγκα/ὑπερήνεγκον, ὑπερενήνοχα, ὑπερενήνεγμαι,
    ὑπερηνέχθην   carry over; excel (+ gen. of comparison)

ὑφίημι, ὑφήσω, ὑφῆκα (second aor. part. ὑφείς, ὑφεῖσα, ὑφέν), ὑφεῖκα,
    ὑφεῖμαι, ὑφείθην   put under; suborn; relax

φθόνος, φθόνου, ὁ   envy, spite, jealousy

φυλάσσω = φυλάττω

φύω, φύσω, ἔφῡσα/ἔφῡν (root aorist), πέφῡκα, ——, ——   produce, grow;
    (root aorist and perfect)   be born, be (by nature)

C. Euripides, *Medea* 46–60

The Nurse explains to the children's Guardian her fears about her mistress, Medea.

ΤΡΟΦΟΣ. ἀλλ' οἵδε παῖδες ἐκ τρόχων πεπαυμένοι
στείχουσι, μητρὸς οὐδὲν ἐννοούμενοι
κακῶν· νέα γὰρ φροντὶς οὐκ ἀλγεῖν φιλεῖ.

ΠΑΙΔΑΓΩΓΟΣ. παλαιὸν οἴκων κτῆμα δεσποίνης ἐμῆς,
50 τί πρὸς πύλαισι τήνδ' ἄγουσ' ἐρημίαν
ἕστηκας, αὐτὴ θρεομένη σαυτῇ κακά;
πῶς σοῦ μόνη Μήδεια λείπεσθαι θέλει;

ΤΡ. τέκνων ὀπᾱδὲ πρέσβυ τῶν Ἰάσονος,

ἀλγέω, ἀλγήσω, ἤλγησα, ——, ——, —— feel pain, suffer; grieve
δέσποινα, δεσποίνης, ἡ mistress, queen
ἐννοέω, ἐννοήσω, ἐνενόησα, ἐννενόηκα, ἐννενόημαι, ἐνενοήθην (*act. or mid.*)
    take thought, consider; (+ *gen.*) take thought for, notice
ἐρημίᾱ, ἐρημίᾱς, ἡ desert; solitude, loneliness; lack
θέλω = ἐθέλω
θρέομαι, ——, ——, ——, ——, ——, cry aloud, shriek
Ἰάσων, Ἰάσονος, ὁ Jason
κτῆμα, κτήματος, τό possession
Μήδεια, Μηδείᾱς, ἡ Medea
οἶκος, οἴκου, ὁ (*sing. or pl.*) house, home; (*sing.*) room
ὀπᾱδός, ὀπᾱδοῦ, ὁ attendant
οὐδείς, οὐδεμία, οὐδέν (*gen.* οὐδενός, οὐδεμιᾶς, οὐδενός) no one, nothing
παιδαγωγός, παιδαγωγοῦ, ὁ slave who accompanied a boy to and from school,
    guardian
πρέσβυς, πρέσβεως, ὁ (*voc.* πρέσβυ) old man; (*as masc. adj.*) old
πύλη, πύλης, ἡ gate (πύλαισι = πύλαις)
στείχω, ——, ——, ——, ——, —— walk, march; go, come
τέκνον, τέκνου, τό child
τροφός, τροφοῦ, ὁ or ἡ nurse, rearer
τρόχος, τρόχου, ὁ circular race, running
φροντίς, φροντίδος, ἡ thought, care; mind

χρηστοῖσι δούλοις ξυμφορὰ τὰ δεσποτῶν
55 κακῶς πίτνοντα, καὶ φρενῶν ἀνθάπτεται.
ἐγὼ γὰρ ἐς τοῦτ' ἐκβέβηκ' ἀλγηδόνος,
ὥσθ' ἵμερός μ' ὑπῆλθε γῇ τε κοὐρανῷ
λέξαι μολούσῃ δεῦρο δεσποίνης τύχας.

ΠΑ. οὔπω γὰρ ἡ τάλαινα παύεται γόων;

60 ΤΡ. ζηλῶ σ'· ἐν ἀρχῇ πῆμα κοὐδέπω μεσοῖ.

ἀλγηδών, ἀλγηδόνος, ἡ   pain, suffering, grief
ἀνθάπτομαι, ἀνθάψομαι, ἀνθηψάμην, ——, ——, —— (+ gen.) get hold of,
   seize
βλώσκω, μολοῦμαι, ἔμολον, μέμβλωκα, ——, —— go, come
γόος, γόου, ὁ   weeping, wailing
δέσποινα, δεσποίνης, ἡ   mistress, queen
δεσπότης, δεσπότου, ὁ   (voc. δέσποτα)   lord, master
δεῦρο (adv.)   here, hither
ἐκβαίνω, ἐκβήσομαι, ἐξέβην, ἐκβέβηκα, ——, —— step out, go out; turn out;
   go out of bounds
ἐς = εἰς
ζηλόω, ζηλώσω, ἐζήλωσα, ἐζήλωκα, ἐζήλωμαι, ἐζηλώθην   envy
ἵμερος, ἱμέρου, ὁ   desire, longing
κοὐδέπω = καὶ οὐδέπω (For this crasis, see the Appendix, p. 614.)
κοὐρανῷ = καὶ οὐρανῷ (For this crasis, see the Appendix, p. 614.)
λέγω, ἐρῶ/λέξω, εἶπον/ἔλεξα, εἴρηκα, εἴρημαι/λέλεγμαι, ἐλέχθην/ἐρρήθην
   say, speak
μεσόω, ——, ——, ——, ——, —— be in/at the middle
μολούσῃ: cf. βλώσκω
ξυμφορά/συμφορά, ξυμφορᾶς/συμφορᾶς, ἡ   event; misfortune
οὐδέπω (adv.)   not yet, and not yet
οὔπω (adv.)   not yet
οὐρανός, οὐρανοῦ, ὁ   sky
πῆμα, πήματος, τό   misery, pain
πίτνω/πίπτω, πεσοῦμαι, ἔπεσον, πέπτωκα, ——, —— fall
τάλᾱς, τάλαινα, τάλαν (gen. τάλανος, ταλαίνης, τάλανος)   suffering, wretched
ὑπέρχομαι   go under, come under; (of feelings) come over (+ dat.)
φρήν, φρενός, ἡ   (sing. or pl.)   midriff; heart, mind
χρηστός, χρηστή, χρηστόν   useful; good (χρηστοῖσι = χρηστοῖς)

UNIT
16

121. THE VERB φημί, "say, affirm, assert"

The verb φημί is athematic in the present and imperfect tenses:

φημί, φήσω, ἔφησα, ——, ——, ——, "say, affirm, assert"

This verb has only an active voice. It is conjugated exactly like ἵστημι (Section 100) in the present and imperfect, except that:

(1) In the present indicative active all forms except the second person singular are *enclitic* (cf. εἰμί, Section 115).

(2) In the present and imperfect indicative active, and in the present imperative active, the second person singular is different.

The present tense stem shows the usual vowel gradation:

Long-vowel grade: φη-
Short-vowel grade: φα-

The athematic forms of this verb are as follows.

	PRESENT IND. ACTIVE	IMPERFECT IND. ACTIVE	PRESENT SUBJ. ACTIVE	PRESENT OPT. ACTIVE	PRESENT IMPER. ACTIVE
S 1	φημί	ἔφην	φῶ	φαίην	
2	φής	ἔφησθα/ἔφης	φῇς	φαίης	φάθι
3	φησί(ν)	ἔφη	φῇ	φαίη	φάτω
P 1	φαμέν	ἔφαμεν	φῶμεν	φαῖμεν/φαίημεν	
2	φατέ	ἔφατε	φῆτε	φαῖτε/φαίητε	φάτε
3	φᾱσί(ν)	ἔφασαν	φῶσι(ν)	φαῖεν/φαίησαν	φάντων

461

PRESENT INFINITIVE ACTIVE: φάναι

PRESENT PARTICIPLE ACTIVE:

	M	F	N
Nom./Voc. S	φάς	φᾶσα	φάν
Gen.	φάντος	φάσης	φάντος

Observations: (1) Note the iota subscript in the second person singular, present indicative active.

(2) In the third person plural, present indicative active the ending contracts with the stem. Cf. ἱστᾶσι(ν).

(3) The ending -σθα of the second person singular, imperfect indicative active appears also in the form ἦσθα, from εἰμί.

(4) The subjunctive employs a stem φε- which contracts with the endings (cf. the stem ἱστε- in the present subjunctive active of ἵστημι).

(5) The second person plural, present indicative and imperative active are identical except for their accent.

(6) The participle is declined exactly like ἱστάς, ἱστᾶσα, ἱστάν. The third person plural, present imperative active is identical with the masculine and neuter genitive plural of the present participle active.

(7) In Attic prose, instead of the participle φάς, φᾶσα, φάν, the participle of the related inchoative verb φάσκω, ——, ——, ——, ——, ——, "say," is used.

122. THE VERB γιγνώσκω, "perceive, recognize, know"

The verb γιγνώσκω has an athematic second aorist active:

γιγνώσκω, γνώσομαι, **ἔγνων**, ἔγνωκα, ἔγνωσμαι, ἐγνώσθην, "perceive, recognize, know"

This verb does not form an aorist middle.

The second aorist active tense stem shows vowel gradation:

Long-vowel grade: γνω-
Short-vowel grade: γνο-

Like the athematic second aorist ἔστην (Section 102), ἔγνων is a *root aorist*: the long-vowel grade appears throughout the indicative and in the imperative and infinitive; the short-vowel grade in the subjunctive and optative, and in the masculine/neuter participial stem.

The usual endings are employed. The subjunctive, optative, and participle are exactly like the equivalent second aorist forms of δίδωμι.

		AORIST IND. ACTIVE	AORIST SUBJ. ACTIVE	AORIST OPT. ACTIVE	AORIST IMPER. ACTIVE
S	1	ἔγνων	γνῶ	γνοίην	
	2	ἔγνως	γνῷς	γνοίης	γνῶθι
	3	ἔγνω	γνῷ	γνοίη	γνώτω
P	1	ἔγνωμεν	γνῶμεν	γνοῖμεν/γνοίημεν	
	2	ἔγνωτε	γνῶτε	γνοῖτε/γνοίητε	γνῶτε
	3	ἔγνωσαν	γνῶσι(ν)	γνοῖεν/γνοίησαν	γνόντων

AORIST INFINITIVE ACTIVE: γνῶναι

AORIST PARTICIPLE ACTIVE:

	M	F	N
Nom./Voc. S	γνούς	γνοῦσα	γνόν
Gen.	γνόντος	γνούσης	γνόντος

Observations: (1) Compare ἔγνων with ἔστην and γνῶναι with στῆναι.

(2) Compare γνῶ, γνῷς with δῶ, δῷς; γνοίην with δοίην; and γνούς, γνοῦσα, γνόν with δούς, δοῦσα, δόν.

(3) The third person plural, aorist imperative active is identical with the masculine and neuter genitive plural of the aorist participle active. Note the shortening of the vowel of the stem before the ending.

123. FUTURE OPTATIVE

The **future optative** (one of whose functions is to replace a future indicative in one type of indirect statement; see Section 125) is formed as follows.

The *future optative active* adds to the future active and middle tense stem the endings of the present optative active of thematic verbs. The *future optative middle* adds to this stem the endings of the present optative middle/passive of thematic verbs.

The *future optative passive* adds to the future passive tense stem the endings of the present optative middle/passive of thematic verbs.

	FUTURE OPTATIVE ACTIVE	FUTURE OPTATIVE MIDDLE	FUTURE OPTATIVE PASSIVE
S 1	παιδεύσοιμι	παιδευσοίμην	παιδευθησοίμην
2	παιδεύσοις	παιδεύσοιο	παιδευθήσοιο
3	παιδεύσοι	παιδεύσοιτο	παιδευθήσοιτο
P 1	παιδεύσοιμεν	παιδευσοίμεθα	παιδευθησοίμεθα
2	παιδεύσοιτε	παιδεύσοισθε	παιδευθήσοισθε
3	παιδεύσοιεν	παιδεύσοιντο	παιδευθήσοιντο

Verbs whose future active and middle tense stem ends in ε or α form the future optative active in the same way as the present optative active of ποιέω and τῑμάω. Thus, from ἀγγέλλω: ἀγγελοῖμι, ἀγγελοῖς, etc., or ἀγγελοίην, ἀγγελοίης, etc. The alternative endings are more common in the plural. See the Appendix, p. 656.

The future optative middle of these verbs is formed like the present optative middle/passive of ποιέω or τῑμάω. Thus, from ἀγγέλλω: ἀγγελοίμην, ἀγγελοῖο, etc.

Remember that the future optative passive of all verbs is formed separately, from Principal Part VI.

124. FUTURE INFINITIVE

The future infinitive (one of whose functions is to replace a future indicative in one type of indirect statement; cf. Section 125) is formed as follows.

The future infinitive active adds to the future active and middle tense stem the ending -ειν; the future infinitive middle adds to this stem the ending -εσθαι. The future infinitive passive adds to the future passive tense stem the ending -εσθαι.

FUTURE INFINITIVE ACTIVE	FUTURE INFINITIVE MIDDLE	FUTURE INFINITIVE PASSIVE
παιδεύσειν	παιδεύσεσθαι	παιδευθήσεσθαι

Verbs whose future active and middle tense stem ends in ε or α have a future infinitive active and middle formed like the present infinitive active and middle/passive of ποιέω and τῑμάω.

Thus the future infinitive active of ἀγγέλλω, for example, is ἀγγελεῖν, and the future infinitive middle is ἀγγελεῖσθαι.

Remember that the future infinitive passive of all verbs is formed separately, from Principal Part VI.

125. INDIRECT STATEMENT

Statements can be quoted either directly or indirectly. Direct quotation preserves the speaker's original words, which in English are set off by quotation marks. But indirect quotation, or **indirect statement**, incorporates the original words into a complex sentence.

> He says, "Sokrates is doing this."   (direct quotation)
> He says **that Sokrates is doing this. (indirect statement)**

Indirect statement can be introduced not only by verbs of saying, but also by verbs of thinking, believing, knowing, and perceiving (e.g., He *believes* that Sokrates is doing this).

Greek has *three* different ways of expressing indirect statement. The various introductory verbs take one or more of these three constructions.

A list of verbs already learned, and those presented in this Section, showing the constructions which each commonly takes, is at the end of the Section.

The three types of indirect statement are as follows:

1. FINITE VERB introduced by the conjunctions ὅτι/ὡς, "that"
2. INFINITIVE + subject accusative
3. PARTICIPLE + subject accusative

1. FINITE VERB INTRODUCED BY ὅτι/ὡς

One verb which introduces this construction is λέγω:

> λέγω, ἐρῶ or λέξω, εἶπον or ἔλεξα, εἴρηκα, εἴρημαι or λέλεγμαι, ἐλέχθην or ἐρρήθην, "say, speak"

WHEN THE INTRODUCTORY VERB IS IN A PRIMARY TENSE (PRESENT, PERFECT, OR FUTURE), ALL VERBS IN THE INDIRECT STATEMENT RETAIN THEIR ORIGINAL MOOD AND TENSE. NEGATIVES REMAIN UNCHANGED.

> λέγει $\begin{Bmatrix} ὅτι \\ ὡς \end{Bmatrix}$ Σωκράτης τοῦτο ποιεῖ.

He says that Sokrates is doing this.

λέξει $\left\{ \begin{array}{l} ὅτι \\ ὡς \end{array} \right\}$ Σωκράτης τοῦτ' οὐκ ἐποίησεν.

He will say that Sokrates did not do this.

<small>WHEN THE INTRODUCTORY VERB IS IN A SECONDARY TENSE (IMPERFECT, AORIST OR PLUPERFECT), ALL VERBS IN THE INDIRECT STATEMENT ARE CHANGED FROM THE INDICATIVE TO THE OPTATIVE OF THE SAME TENSE AS IN THE ORIGINAL STATEMENT. NEGATIVES REMAIN UNCHANGED.</small>

εἶπεν $\left\{ \begin{array}{l} ὅτι \\ ὡς \end{array} \right\}$ Σωκράτης τοῦτο ποιοίη.

He said that Sokrates was doing this.

εἶπεν $\left\{ \begin{array}{l} ὅτι \\ ὡς \end{array} \right\}$ Σωκράτης τοῦτ' οὐ ποιήσειεν.

He said that Sokrates did not do this.

The present optative ποιοίη shows that the tense of the original statement was present: he said, "Sokrates is doing this." The aorist optative ποιήσειεν shows that the tense of the original statement was aorist: he said, "Sokrates did not do this." In English, when the introductory verb is in past time, one often alters the tense of the verbs in indirect statement: e.g., "is doing" becomes "was doing," and "did not do" can become "had not done."

Such a change of tense never occurs in Greek. Instead, there is a change of mood from indicative to optative, while the tense remains the same.

In this construction Greek uses the future optative, to stand in place of a future indicative.

εἶπεν $\left\{ \begin{array}{l} ὅτι \\ ὡς \end{array} \right\}$ Σωκράτης τοῦτο ποιήσοι.

He said that Sokrates would do this.

For the formation of the future optative see Section 123. In the translation above, English "would" represents an original "will," i.e., a future indicative: he said, "Sokrates will do this." Distinguish this carefully from the meaning of the optative in a future less vivid ("should/would") conditional sentence.

The perfect optative, which can stand for an original perfect indicative, is rare. Its forms are given in the Appendix, pages 663–64 and 666.

When an optative stands for an indicative in indirect statement, it shows *time* as well as aspect. A present optative places the action of the indirect statement at a time simultaneous with that of the introductory verb; an aorist optative places the action at a time prior to that of the introductory verb; a future optative places the action at a time subsequent to that of the main verb. Contrast, e.g., purpose clauses in secondary sequence, where the tenses of the optative indicate aspect only.

Sometimes, when the introductory verb is in past time, verbs of the original statement remain in the indicative and are not changed to the optative. This usage is called the **retained indicative** and gives added vividness to the quoted statement, a vividness which cannot be represented in translation.

$$\varepsilon \tilde{\iota} \pi \varepsilon \nu \left\{ \begin{array}{l} \ddot{o}\tau\iota \\ \dot{\omega}\varsigma \end{array} \right\} \; \Sigma \omega \varkappa \varrho \acute{\alpha} \tau \eta \varsigma \; \tau o \tilde{v} \tau o \; \pi o \iota \acute{\eta} \sigma \varepsilon \iota.$$

He said that Sokrates would do this.

The imperfect and pluperfect, which lack an optative, are normally represented in indirect statement by a retained indicative.

In all of the examples above the verb of the original statement was in the indicative mood. The treatment of original subjunctives, optatives, and complex sentences in indirect statement is explained in the Appendix, pages 760–68.

Greek, like English, changes the *person* of the verb in an indirect statement when this is necessary: e.g., Sokrates says, "*I* did it"; Sokrates says that *he* (= Sokrates) did it.

2. INFINITIVE PLUS SUBJECT ACCUSATIVE

Many verbs introduce a second type of indirect statement in which an indicative verb of the original statement is replaced by the *infinitive of the same tense* and the subject of the original finite verb (whether separately expressed or not) appears in the accusative case as the *subject of the infinitive*. There is no introductory conjunction. Direct and indirect objects keep their own cases; negatives remain unchanged.

This construction remains the same, *regardless of the tense of the introductory verb.*

The infinitive, which here stands for an original indicative, shows *time* as well as aspect. A present infinitive shows time simultaneous with that of the introductory verb; an aorist infinitive shows prior time; a future infinitive shows subsequent time; and a perfect infinitive describes an action already completed.

For the formation of the future infinitive see Section 124.

One verb which introduces this construction is *νομίζω*:

νομίζω, νομιῶ, ἐνόμισα, νενόμικα, νενόμισμαι, ἐνομίσθην, "consider, think, believe"

νομίζει Σωκράτη τοῦτο ποιεῖν.
He thinks that Sokrates is doing this.

νομίζει Σωκράτη τοῦτο ποιῆσαι.
He thinks that Sokrates did this.

νομίζει Σωκράτη τοῦτ' οὐ ποιήσειν.
He thinks that Sokrates will not do this.

ἐνόμισε Σωκράτη τοῦτ' οὐ ποιήσειν.
He thought that Sokrates would not do this.

WHEN THE SUBJECT OF THE INFINITIVE IS THE SAME AS THAT OF THE INTRO-
DUCTORY VERB, NO SEPARATE SUBJECT ACCUSATIVE APPEARS. WHEN THE SUBJECT
IS DIFFERENT, IT MUST APPEAR.

νομίζει τοῦτο ποιήσειν.
He thinks that he (= the same person) will do this.

νομίζει αὐτὸν τοῦτο ποιήσειν.
He thinks that he (= someone else) will do this.

A predicate adjective agrees with the accusative subject of an infinitive in indirect statement, but with the subject of the introductory verb when the subject of the infinitive is the same and is not separately expressed.

νομίζει Σωκράτη ἀγαθὸν εἶναι.
He thinks that Sokrates is good.

νομίζει ἀγαθὸς εἶναι.
He thinks that he (= the same person) is good.

The imperfect and pluperfect tenses, which lack infinitives, can be represented in indirect statement by the present and perfect infinitives *whenever the context makes the time relationship clear.* This usage is illustrated in the Appendix.

3. PARTICIPLE PLUS SUBJECT ACCUSATIVE

Many verbs introduce a third type of indirect statement in which an indicative of the original statement is replaced by the *participle of the same tense* and the subject of the original finite verb (whether separately expressed in the original statement or not) appears in the *accusative case.* There is no introductory conjunction. Direct and indirect objects keep their own cases. Negatives remain unchanged.

This construction remains the same, *regardless of the tense of the introductory verb.*

Indirect statement with the participle will present no difficulties since it follows exactly the same rules as indirect statement with the infinitive.

Three verbs which can introduce this construction are ἀγγέλλω, αἰσθάνομαι, and ἀκούω.

> ἀγγέλλει Σωκράτη τοῦτο ποιοῦντα.
> He announces that Sokrates is doing this.

> ἀγγέλλει Σωκράτη τοῦτο ποιήσαντα.
> He announces that Sokrates did this.

> ἀγγέλλει Σωκράτη τοῦτ' οὐ ποιήσοντα.
> He announces that Sokrates will not do this.

> ἤγγειλε Σωκράτη τοῦτ' οὐ ποιήσοντα.
> He announced that Sokrates would not do this.

Participles in indirect statement, like infinitives when so used, stand for original indicatives and show *time* as well as aspect.

WHEN THE SUBJECT OF THE PARTICIPLE IS THE SAME AS THAT OF THE INTRODUCTORY VERB, NO SEPARATE SUBJECT ACCUSATIVE APPEARS, AND THE PARTICIPLE AGREES WITH THE SUBJECT OF THE INTRODUCTORY VERB. WHEN THE SUBJECT OF THE PARTICIPLE IS DIFFERENT, IT MUST APPEAR IN THE ACCUSATIVE CASE.

> αἰσθάνονται κακοὶ ὄντες.
> They perceive that they (='the same people) are evil.

> αἰσθάνονται αὐτοὺς κακοὺς ὄντας.
> They perceive that they (= other people) are evil.

Predicate adjectives agree with the accusative subject of the participle or, when this is not expressed, with the subject of the introductory verb, as in the examples above.

With ἀκούω, this form of indirect statement conveys an *intellectually* perceived fact. The same verb can also take an object in the genitive case, accompanied by a participle (not in indirect statement) to describe something *physically* perceived.

> ἀκούει Σωκράτη τοῦτο ποιοῦντα.
> He hears that Sokrates is doing this.

> ἀκούει Σωκράτους τοῦτο ποιοῦντος.
> He hears Sokrates doing this.

The imperfect and pluperfect tenses, which lack participles, can be represented by present and perfect participles whenever the context makes the time relationship clear. This usage is illustrated in the Appendix.

4. THE THREE TYPES OF INDIRECT STATEMENT COMPARED

1. FINITE VERB introduced by ὅτι/ὡς

> Introductory verb in primary tense:
>
> > All verbs of the original statement remain the same except for any necessary change of person.
>
> Introductory verb in secondary tense:
>
> > Indicatives of the original statement are changed to optatives of the same tense, OR
> >
> > indicatives of the original statement are retained for vividness; person is changed when necessary.

2. INFINITIVE + subject accusative

> Indicatives of the original statement are changed to infinitives of the same tense, AND
>
> the subject of the original statement appears in the accusative case as the subject of the infinitive.

3. PARTICIPLE + subject accusative

> Indicatives of the original statement are changed to participles of the same tense, AND
>
> the subject of the original statement appears in the accusative case and the participle agrees with it.

5. INTRODUCTORY VERBS CLASSIFIED

Here is a list of verbs already introduced, and verbs presented in this Unit, which introduce the three types of indirect statement.

INFINITIVE ONLY: νομίζω, φημί

FINITE VERB
OR INFINITIVE: λέγω

FINITE VERB
OR PARTICIPLE: ἀγγέλλω, αἰσθάνομαι, ἀκούω, γιγνώσκω, δείκνῡμι, δηλόω, μανθάνω, ὁράω

126. RETAINED SUBJUNCTIVE

Just as in indirect statement with a finite verb an original indicative can be retained after an introductory verb in a secondary tense, instead of being changed to an optative, so also in *purpose clauses* and *fear clauses* introduced by a main verb in a secondary tense a subjunctive can be retained instead of being changed to an optative according to sequence of moods.

The **retained subjunctive** presents the intention or fear more vividly than the optative. This vividness cannot be represented in translation.

ἐφοβούμεθα μὴ αἰσχρὰ ποιοίη. (optative)
We feared that he might do shameful things.

ἐφοβούμεθα μὴ αἰσχρὰ **ποιῇ**. (*retained subjunctive*)
We feared that he might do shameful things.

ἦλθεν εἰς τὴν πόλιν ἵνα χορεύσαι. (optative)
He came into the city in order that he might dance.

ἦλθεν εἰς τὴν πόλιν ἵνα **χορεύσῃ**. (*retained subjunctive*)
He came into the city in order that he might dance.

127. THE ADJECTIVE πολύς, πολλή, πολύ, "much, many"

The adjective πολύς, πολλή, πολύ has forms belonging to the first, second, and third declensions.

The masculine and neuter nominative and accusative singular belong to the third declension and use the stem πολυ-.

All other forms use the stem πολλ- and are declined like ἀγαθός, ἀγαθή, ἀγαθόν. There is no vocative.

	M	F	N
Nom. S	**πολύς**	πολλή	**πολύ**
Gen.	πολλοῦ	πολλῆς	πολλοῦ
Dat.	πολλῷ	πολλῇ	πολλῷ
Acc.	**πολύν**	πολλήν	**πολύ**
Nom. P	πολλοί	πολλαί	πολλά
Gen.	πολλῶν	πολλῶν	πολλῶν
Dat.	πολλοῖς	πολλαῖς	πολλοῖς
Acc.	πολλούς	πολλάς	πολλά

128. THE NOUN ναῦς, νεώς, ἡ, "ship"

The third-declension noun ναῦς, νεώς, ἡ, "ship," is irregular.

Nom. S	ναῦς
Gen.	νεώς
Dat.	νηί
Acc.	ναῦν
Voc.	ναῦ
Nom./Voc. P	νῆες
Gen.	νεῶν
Dat.	ναυσί(ν)
Acc.	ναῦς

Observations: (1) This noun has two stems. The stem ναυ- appears in the nominative, accusative, and vocative singular, and in the dative and accusative plural. The stem νη- appears elsewhere. The genitive singular was originally νηός, but by quantitative metathesis the form became νεώς (cf. πόλεως). The genitive plural imitates the genitive singular.

(2) Note that the accusative plural is the same as the nominative singular.

VOCABULARY

βαίνω, -βήσομαι, -ἔβην, βέβηκα, ——, ——	walk, step, go; (*perfect*) stand
ἀναβαίνω	go up, go upland; board, mount
γιγνώσκω, γνώσομαι, ἔγνων, ἔγνωκα, ἔγνωσμαι, ἐγνώσθην	perceive, recognize, know
ἕκαστος, ἑκάστη, ἕκαστον	each (of many); (*pl.*) each (of several groups), all (considered singly)
ἕνεκα (*prep.*) + *preceding gen.*	for the sake of
Ζεύς, Διός, ὁ (*voc. Ζεῦ*)	Zeus
θέατρον, θεάτρου, τό	theater
λέγω, ἐρῶ or λέξω, εἶπον or ἔλεξα, εἴρηκα, εἴρημαι or λέλεγμαι, ἐλέχθην or ἐρρήθην	say, speak
λιμήν, λιμένος, ὁ	harbor
μήποτε (*adv.*)	never, not ever
ναῦς, νεώς, ἡ	ship
νή (*affirmative particle*)	by (+ *name of god in acc.*)
νομίζω, νομιῶ, ἐνόμισα, νενόμικα, νενόμισμαι, ἐνομίσθην	consider, think, believe
ὅτι (*conj.*)	that, because
οὔποτε (*adv.*)	never, not ever
πάνυ (*adv.*)	perfectly, very; by all means
πίπτω, πεσοῦμαι, ἔπεσον, πέπτωκα, ——, ——	fall
ἐκπίπτω	be driven out, be banished
πολῑτεία, πολῑτείας, ἡ	government, constitution, commonwealth
πολύς, πολλή, πολύ	much, many
πολλάκις (*adv.*)	often

πονηρός, πονηρά, πονηρόν   worthless, evil, base

προ- (prefix)   forward, on behalf of, before

    προδίδωμι   betray, give up (to an enemy),
                                   abandon

σωφροσύνη, σωφροσύνης, ἡ   prudence, self-control, moderation

φημί, φήσω, ἔφησα, ——, ——, ——   say, assert, affirm

ὡς (conj.)   that

VOCABULARY NOTES

In the verb βαίνω, -βήσομαι, -ἔβην, βέβηκα, ——, ——, "walk, step, go," the future and aorist tenses appear only in compounds. The future tense is deponent; the aorist is a *root aorist*, i.e., an athematic second aorist conjugated exactly like ἔστην (from ἵστημι): indicative -ἔβην, -ἔβης, etc.; subjunctive -βῶ, -βῇς, etc.; optative -βαίην, -βαίης, etc.; imperative -βῆθι, -βήτω, etc.; infinitive -βῆναι; participle -βάς, -βᾶσα, -βάν.

The compound verb ἀναβαίνω, "go up, go upland, board, mount," can be used of someone going up to speak in a public assembly, making a journey upland, boarding a ship, or mounting a horse. What one boards or mounts is indicated by a prepositional phrase: ἐπὶ (εἰς) τὴν ναῦν, ἐφ' ἵππον. Xenophon's *Anabasis* (ἀνάβασις, ἀναβάσεως, ἡ) describes an "Upland March."

The verb γιγνώσκω, γνώσομαι, ἔγνων, ἔγνωκα, ἔγνωσμαι, ἐγνώσθην, "perceive, recognize, know," is deponent in the future tense and has a root aorist. It can introduce two types of indirect statement: ὅτι/ὡς + finite verb, or participle + subject accusative. This verb shows throughout its conjugation the root γνω-/γνο-. Principal Part I shows a reduplication of the stem and has also the inchoative suffix -σκω. For the conjugation of the root aorist ἔγνων see Section 122. Note that the epsilon with which Principal Parts IV and V begin is NOT the past indicative augment. Be careful not to confuse forms of γιγνώσκω with forms of γίγνομαι.

The object of the preposition ἕνεκα, "for the sake of," often precedes the preposition; cf. χάριν.

The noun Ζεύς, Διός, ὁ, "Zeus," has a dative Διί, an accusative Δία, and a vocative Ζεῦ. The noun, and the god, are inherited from Indo-European. The nominative was originally *dyēus. From the vocative *dyeu + the word for "father" (pater) comes the Latin *Iūpiter*, "Jupiter."

The noun θέᾱτρον, θεᾱτρου, τό, "theater," means literally "place of viewing."

The verb λέγω, "say, speak" (cf. λόγος), has several alternative tense stems, with *no difference in meaning*, which may be classified as follows:

λέγω	λέξω	ἔλεξα		λέλεγμαι	ἐλέχθην
	ἐρῶ		εἴρηκα	εἴρημαι	ἐρρήθην
		εἶπον			

The unaugmented second aorist active and middle tense stem is εἰπ-. The second person singular, aorist imperative active is εἰπέ. Cf. ἐλθέ, ἰδέ, λαβέ. The unaugmented aorist passive tense stem is ῥηθ-.

This verb introduces two types of indirect statement: ὅτι/ὡς + finite verb, and infinitive + subject accusative.

The noun ναῦς, νεώς, ἡ, "ship," originally had a stem ending in digamma. The digamma survives as an upsilon in the nominative, accusative, and vocative singular, and in the dative and accusative plural. For the declension of this noun see Section 128.

The affirmative particle νή is followed by the name of a god in the accusative case and strengthens an assenting statement: νὴ τὸν Δία, "yes, by Zeus."

The verb νομίζω, νομιῶ, ἐνόμισα, νενόμικα, νενόμισμαι, ἐνομίσθην, "consider, think, believe," is formed from the noun νόμος, "law, custom" + the verbal suffix -ιζω and originally meant "practice customarily." Like most verbs with presents in -ιζω, this verb has a contracted future active and middle which lacks the -ζ- of the present tense stem. The suffix -ιζω derives from *ιδιω; the dental disappeared in all other Principal Parts. This verb introduces only one kind of indirect statement: infinitive + subject accusative.

The adverb πάνυ, "perfectly, very; by all means," is often used to express assent to a statement: πάνυ γε, "yes, by all means."

The verb πίπτω, πεσοῦμαι, ἔπεσον, πέπτωκα, ——, ——, "fall," has a present tense stem which shows reduplication with long iota; the future tense is deponent and contracted; and there is a second aorist (cf. ἔλιπον). The compound verb ἐκπίπτω, "be driven out, be banished," serves as the passive of ἐκβάλλω in these senses.

ἐκ τῆς πόλεως ἐξεβάλομεν αὐτόν.
We drove him out of the city.

ἐκ τῆς πόλεως ἐξέπεσεν ὑφ᾽ ἡμῶν.
He was driven out of the city by us.

For the declension of the adjective πολύς, πολλή, πολύ, "much, many," see Section 127. Greek normally uses the conjunction καί to link this adjective with other adjectives: πολλὰ καὶ ἀγαθὰ βιβλία, "many good books."

Monosyllabic prefixes, such as προ-, do NOT drop the final vowel when compounded with a verb form beginning with a vowel or diphthong. The omicron of προ-, however, can contract with an epsilon. Contrast ἀπέδοσαν with προέδοσαν, προύδοσαν.

The noun σωφροσύνη, σωφροσύνης, ἡ, "prudence, self-control, moderation," is formed from the adjective σώφρων, σῶφρον + the suffix -συνη, which often denotes traits of character.

The verb φημί, φήσω, ἔφησα, ——, ——, ——, "say, assert, affirm," is *enclitic* in the present indicative; for its conjugation cf. Section 121. This verb introduces only one type of indirect statement: infinitive + subject accusative. This verb can mean "say yes, affirm" or, when negated, "say no, deny":

> ἔγωγέ φημι.
> I agree.
> I say yes.

> οὔ φημι.
> I disagree.
> I say no.

> οὔ φημι τούτους ἀγαθοὺς εἶναι.
> I deny that these men are good.

Distinguish the conjunction ὡς, "that," introducing indirect statement with a finite verb from the conjunction ὡς introducing purpose clauses.

COGNATES AND DERIVATIVES

βαίνω   come, become; advent (from the Latin cognate *venīre*, "come"); basis (on which something **stands**)

γιγνώσκω   know, cunning, couth; notion, cognition (from the Latin cognate *cognōscere*, "learn, know"); gnomic, prognosis

θέᾱτρον   theater

λέγω   lexicon, dialect, prolegomenon

ναῦς   naval (from the Latin cognate *nāvis*); nautical

πολῑτείᾱ   polity

πολύς   fill, full; polymath

φημί   blasphemy, euphemism (a nice way of **saying** something unpleasant)

DRILLS

I. *Translate the following sentences.*

1. λέγεις ὅτι ὁ Σωκράτης τοῦτο ποιήσει.

2. εἶπεν ὅτι ὁ Σωκράτης τοῦτο ποιήσοι.

3. εἴπομεν ὅτι ὁ Σωκράτης τοῦτ᾽ ἐποίησεν.

4. εἴπομεν ὅτι ὁ Σωκράτης τοῦτο ποιήσειεν.

5. εἶπον ὅτι ὁ Σωκράτης τοῦτο ποιοίη.

6. εἶπον ὅτι ὁ Σωκράτης τοῦτο ποιεῖ.

7. λέγουσιν ὡς ταῦθ᾽ ὑπὸ Δημοσθένους οὐκ ἐπράχθη.

8. εἶπεν ὡς ταῦθ᾽ ὑπὸ Δημοσθένους οὐ πραχθείη.

9. εἶπες, ὦ Σώκρατες, ὡς τοὺς νέους περὶ ἀρετῆς διδάξοις;

10. λέγω ὅτι οἱ ἄγγελοι τὴν νίκην ἀπαγγελοῦσιν.

11. εἶπον ὅτι οἱ ἄγγελοι τὴν νίκην τοῖς ἐν τῇ πόλει ἀπαγγελοῖεν.

12. εἶπον ὅτι οἱ ἄγγελοι τὴν νίκην τοῖς ἠδικημένοις ἀπαγγέλλοιεν.

13. εἶπον ὡς οἱ ἄγγελοι ταῦτα τοῖς ἄρχουσιν ἀπαγγείλειαν.

14. εἶπον ὅτι οἱ ἄγγελοι ταῦτα τοῖς ἄρχουσιν ἀπαγγελοῦσιν.

II. *Translate.*

1. νομίζομεν Σωκράτη τοῦτο πεποιηκέναι.

2. νομίζετε Σωκράτη τοῦτο ποιήσειν.

3. ἐνόμιζες Σωκράτη ταῦτ᾽ οὐ ποιήσειν.

4. ἐνόμιζες Σωκράτη ταῦτα πεποιηκέναι.

5. νομίζουσι Σωκράτη τοῦτο ποιεῖν.

6. νομίζουσι Σωκράτη τοῦτο ποιῆσαι.

7. νομιεῖτε Σωκράτη ταῦτα ποιῆσαι.

8. ἐνομίσατε Σωκράτη τοῦτο ποιεῖν;

9. νομίζομεν ὑμᾶς οὐ ταῦτα ποιεῖν.

10. νομιεῖτε ἡμᾶς τοῦτο ποιῆσαι.

11. νομίζω ταῦθ᾽ ὑπὸ Σωκράτους ποιηθῆναι.

12. ἐνομίζετ᾽ αὐτοὺς ταῦτ᾽ οὐ ποιήσειν.

13. νομίζει ἀγαθὴ εἶναι.

14. νομίζει αὐτὴν ἀγαθὴν εἶναι.

15. νομίζω αὐτοὺς ὑπὸ τοῦ Σωκράτους διδάσκεσθαι.

16. νομίζετε τοὺς αὐτοὺς ὑπὸ τοῦ Σωκράτους διδαχθῆναι.

17. νομίζομεν ὑπὸ τοῦ Σωκράτους διδάσκεσθαι.

III. Translate.

1. ἀγγέλλετε τὸν Δημοσθένη κακὰ ποιοῦντα.

2. ἀγγέλλετε τὸν Δημοσθένη κακὰ ποιήσαντα.

3. ἠγγέλλετε τοῦτον κακὰ ποιοῦντα.

4. ἠγγέλλομεν τοῦτον κακὰ ποιήσοντα.

5. ἠγγείλατε τούτους καλὰ πεποιηκότας.

6. ἀγγελεῖτε τούτους καλὰ ποιοῦντας.

7. ἀγγελεῖ ἡμᾶς κακὰ ποιήσοντας.

8. ἀγγελῶ ὑμᾶς κακὰ ποιήσαντας.

9. ἀκούετε τόνδε τὸν ἄνδρα κακὰ παθόντα.

10. ἠκούσατε τόνδε τὸν ἄνδρα κακῶς πάσχοντα.

11. ἠκούετε τοῦτον κακῶς πεπονθότα.

12. ἀκούεις τόνδε κακὰ ὑπὸ τῶν ἐχθρῶν πεισόμενον.

13. ἤγγελλεν ὁ κῆρυξ ταύτας κακὰ πεποιηκυίας.

14. ἀγγελλέτω ὁ κῆρυξ ταύτας κακὰς οὔσας.

15. οὐκ αἰσθάνεσθε κακοὶ ὄντες.

16. ᾐσθανόμην τοῦτον κακὸν ὄντα.

17. ᾐσθανόμην κακὸς ὤν.

18. ᾐσθόμεθα τοὺς ὁπλίτας μαχομένους.

19. ᾐσθόμεθα τῶν ὁπλιτῶν μαχομένων.

20. αἰσθήσεσθε τοὺς ὁπλίτας προσελθόντας.

IV. Translate.

1. ἔλεγον ὅτι οἱ Εὐριπίδου φίλοι, αἰσχροὶ ὄντες, φύγοιεν.

2. ἠγγείλαμεν τοὺς Εὐριπίδου φίλους φυγόντας.

3. ἠγγείλαμεν τοὺς Εὐριπίδου φίλους φεύγοντας.

4. νόμισον τοὺς Εὐρῑπίδου φίλους φυγεῖν.

5. ἐνόμισα τοὺς Εὐρῑπίδου φίλους φεύγειν.

6. ἐνομίζετε τοὺς Εὐρῑπίδου φίλους φεύξεσθαι.

7. ἀκούεις τὸν Δημοσθένους πατέρα οἶνον κεκλοφότα.

8. δείξω δὴ τὸν πατέρα τὸν Δημοσθένους οἶνον οὐ κλέψαντα.

9. ἤκουσας, ὦ παῖ, τὸν Δημοσθένους πατέρα οἶνον κλέπτοντα;

10. ἤκουσας, ὦ γέρον, τοῦ πατρὸς τοῦ Δημοσθένους οἶνον
    κλέπτοντος;

11. ὦ ἄνδρες, νομιεῖτε τὸν Δημοσθένους πατέρα οἶνον κλέψαι.

12. ὦ θυγατέρες, ἐνομίσατε τὸν Δημοσθένους πατέρα οἶνον κλέψειν;

13. εἴπομεν ὡς οὗτος τόνδε τὸν οἶνον οὐ κλέψαι.

14. ἐλέγομεν ὅτι ἐκεῖνος οἶνον οὐ κλέψοι.

15. εἶπες, ὦ γύναι, ὅτι τὸν οἶνον οὗτος οὐ κλέπτοι.

16. εἶπεν ὅτι τὸν οἶνον οὐ κλέψει.

17. νομίζομεν αὐτοὺς ἀγαθοὺς εἶναι.

18. νομίζομεν ἀγαθοὶ εἶναι.

19. αὐτὰς ᾔσθεσθε σώφρονας οὔσᾱς.

20. ᾔσθεσθε σώφρονες οὖσαι.

21. ἐνόμισαν αὐτὰς ἄφρονας εἶναι.

22. ἐνόμισαν αἰσχραὶ εἶναι.

EXERCISES

I.   1. νομίζετε τόν γε Σωκράτη πολλὰ καὶ κακὰ παθεῖν.

2. ἤκουσαν ποιητήν τινα τοὺς νέους διδάξοντα.

3. ἐλέξαμεν ὡς οὔποτε ἀνδράσι δουλεύσοιμεν.

4. τοὺς ἄνευ σωφροσύνης φαμὲν τὴν πόλιν προδώσειν.

5. ἕκαστος εἶπεν ὅτι ἀναβήσεται εἰς ἐκείνην τὴν ναῦν τὴν ἐν τῷ λιμένι.

6. σύ γε νὴ τὸν Δία ἤγγειλάς μοι πολλοὺς πονηρούς τε καὶ ἄφρονας ἐν τῇ στάσει ἐκπεσόντας ἐκ πόλεως.

7. εἰ γὰρ μήτε Ζεὺς μήτε οἱ ἄλλοι δαίμονες σώσαιεν τοὺς τὸν δῆμον προδόντας.

8. ἔγωγε ἐνόμιζον τὸν βασιλέᾱ εἰς τὴν ἑαυτοῦ πόλιν ἀναβαίνειν.

9. μὴ εἴπῃς ὡς οὐκ ἔστι Ζεύς.

10. φῶμεν μόνους τοὺς σοφοὺς εὐδαίμονας εἶναι;

11. (a) ᾔσθοντο τοὺς ὁπλίτᾱς ἀδικοῦντας.
    (b) ᾔσθοντο οἱ ὁπλῖται ἀδικοῦντες.

12. ἡμῖν ἔφησθά που Σωκράτει μὲν οὔτε χρῡσὸν οὔτ᾽ ἄργυρον εἶναι, τοῖς μαθηταῖς δὲ τοῖς εὐγενέσι καὶ χρῡσὸν καὶ ἀργύριον πολύ.

13. ποῖα πέπρᾱχεν οὗτος; οἷα γὰρ ἂν πρᾱ́ξῃ τις, τοιοῦτος ἔσται τήν γε ψῡχήν.

14. ἀκούομέν σε πόλιν τε τὴν ἡμετέρᾱν αὐτῶν προδιδόντα καὶ δῶρα πολλὰ παρὰ Λακεδαιμονίων αὐτίκα ληψόμενον. οὐ γὰρ ἡμᾶς λανθάνεις κακὰ ποιῶν.

15. κατέβημεν εἰς θάλατταν ὡς τὰς τῶν βαρβάρων ναῦς ἴδωμεν.

16. εἶπεν ὁ τὸν οἶνον κεκλοφὼς ὅτι δίκην οὔποτε δώσοι.

17. ὦ ἄνδρες Ἀθηναῖοι, ἐὰν Σωκράτη θανάτου ἀξιώσητε, οἵ γε σώφρονες οὔποθ᾽ ὑμᾶς νομιοῦσι τὸ δίκαιον ποιῆσαι.

18. τίν᾽ ἂν τρόπον γνοῖμεν σαφῶς τὴν τῆς σωφροσύνης φύσιν; ταύτην γὰρ γνόντες καὶ ἡμᾶς αὐτοὺς εὖ γνωσόμεθα.

19. ἆρα τοῦ Σωκράτους ἤκουσας λέγοντος ὡς χαλεπὸν εἴη ἀνθρώπῳ τὸ αὐτὸν γνῶναι;

20. ἔλεγέν τις πονηρὸς ὅτι αὐτός γε, καίπερ ἐν τῇ τότε στάσει
    ἐκπεσὼν ἐκ τῆς πόλεως, οὐκ ἐκπεσοῖτο ὑπὸ τῶν νῦν
    ἀρχόντων· δῶρα γάρ τινα λαμβάνοιεν ἄν.

21. ἐκ τοῦ θεάτρου ἐκβάλετε τὸν ποιητὴν τὸν ἡμᾶς φήσαντα κακοὺς
    στρατηγοὺς αἱρεῖσθαι. ἢ οὐ φοβεῖσθε μὴ ὁ τοιαῦτα λέγων
    ἡμᾶς πάντας βλάψῃ;

22. ὦ ἄνδρες, ἔτι ἐν κινδύνῳ οὔσης τῆς πόλεως μήτε μαχόμενοι
    παυσώμεθα μήτε τοιούτῳ ῥήτορι πεισθέντες προδῶμεν ἡμᾶς
    αὐτούς.

23. οἷοι εἴησαν οἵ γε πολῖται, τοιαύτη ἂν εἴη καὶ ἡ πόλις.

24. αὐτούς φησι τὰς σφετέρας αὐτῶν ναῦς εἰς τὴν νῆσον πέμψειν.

25. (a) ἔφατέ με κακῶς πράξειν.
    (b) ἔφατε κακῶς πράξειν.
    (c) φήσετε τάσδε καλῶς πράττειν.
    (d) φήσετε τάσδε καλῶς πρᾶξαι.

26. εἴ πού σοί τινές ποθ' ἕποιντο, οἷός τ' ἂν εἴης τὴν πολιτείᾱν
    καταλύσᾱς ἄρξαι τοῦ δήμου.

27. εἱλόμην λόγον εἰπεῖν ἐν τῷ νῦν ῥητορικῆς ἀγῶνι νομίσᾱς ἱκανὸν
    ἆθλον ἔσεσθαί μοι οὔτε χρῡσὸν οὔτ' ἄργυρον ἀλλὰ μόνον τὴν
    δόξαν τὴν ἀπ' αὐτοῦ τοῦ λόγου γενησομένην.

28. —Μανθάνεις, ὦ παῖ, τὰ λεγόμενα;
    —Πάνυ γε· λέγεις γάρ που ὅτι πᾶσι μὲν ἔξεστι καλῶς πράττειν,
    πολλοὶ δὲ διὰ τὴν αὐτῶν ἀμαθίᾱν πράττουσι κακῶς.
    —Εὖ γε· τίνα δὴ τρόπον γένοιτ' ἂν οὗτοι εὐδαίμονες;
    —Κατά γε τὴν σὴν γνώμην οἱ πονηροὶ γνόντες τὴν τῆς
    σωφροσύνης φύσιν παύσονταί πως ἀδικοῦντες.

29. (a) τοῦτον ἤγγειλεν ἐκ πόλεως ἐκφεύγοντα.
    (b) τοῦτον ἤγγειλεν ἐκ πόλεως ἐκφυγόντα.
    (c) τοῦτον ἤγγειλεν ἐκ πόλεως ἐκπεφευγότα.
    (d) τοῦτον ἤγγειλεν ἐκ πόλεως ἐκφευξόμενον.

30. γνῶθι σαυτόν.

31. ὦ Ζεῦ καὶ θεοί, τίς χαίροι ἂν ἀκούων τὸν Σωκράτη θανάτου τ'
    ἀξιωθέντα ὑπὸ πονηρῶν τινων καὶ πέντε ἡμερῶν τὸν βίον
    τελευτήσοντα;

32. ὑμεῖς αὐτοί, ὦ ῥήτορες, ἐδείκνυθ' ὅτι δημοκρατίᾱ μὲν ἀγαθὴ εἴη
    πολῑτείᾱ, βασιλέων δὲ τῶν παλαιῶν πολλοὶ οὔτε κακῶς οὔτε
    πονηρῶς τοῦ δήμου ἄρξαιεν.

II. 1. By the gods, you at least used to say, Athenian men, that all the Greeks
would conquer the foreigners and set up a trophy.

2. (a) You said that we ourselves would conquer.   (λέγω + ὅτι/ὡς
+ *finite verb*)

(b) You thought that we ourselves would conquer. (νομίζω)

(c) You heard that we ourselves would conquer.   (ἀκούω +
participle)

3. (a) He says that I sent the ship.   (λέγω + ὅτι/ὡς
+ *finite verb*)

(b) He says that I sent the ship.   (φημί)

(c) He announces that I sent the ship.   (ἀγγέλλω +
participle)

4. We shall send whatever sort of animals you want to sacrifice.

READINGS

A. Plato, *Gorgias* 455a8–456c2

Sokrates asks the rhetorician Gorgias of Leontinoi about the nature of rhetoric.

ΣΩ. Φέρε δή, ἴδωμεν τί ποτε καὶ λέγομεν περὶ τῆς
ῥητορικῆς· ἐγὼ μὲν γάρ τοι οὐδ' αὐτός πω δύναμαι
κατανοῆσαι ὅτι[1] λέγω. ὅταν περὶ ἰατρῶν αἱρέσεως
ἢ τῇ πόλει σύλλογος ἢ περὶ ναυπηγῶν ἢ περὶ ἄλλου
5   τινὸς δημιουργικοῦ ἔθνους, ἄλλο τι ἢ τότε ὁ
ῥητορικὸς οὐ συμβουλεύσει; δῆλον γὰρ ὅτι ἐν
ἑκάστῃ αἱρέσει τὸν τεχνικώτατον δεῖ αἱρεῖσθαι.
οὐδ' ὅταν τειχῶν περὶ οἰκοδομήσεως ἢ λιμένων
κατασκευῆς ἢ νεωρίων, ἀλλ' οἱ ἀρχιτέκτονες· οὐδ'
10   αὖ ὅταν στρατηγῶν αἱρέσεως πέρι[2] ἢ τάξεώς τινος
πρὸς πολεμίους ἢ χωρίων καταλήψεως συμβουλὴ ᾖ,

1. Here, an interrogative pronoun, = τί
2. When a disyllabic preposition follows its object the accent is on the first syllable (**ana-strophe**). See the Appendix, p. 613.

αἵρεσις, αἱρέσεως, ἡ   choice

ἄλλο τι ἤ   *introduces question expecting affirmative reply*

ἀρχιτέκτων, ἀρχιτέκτονος, ὁ   master-builder

αὖ (*particle*) again, in turn, moreover

δεῖ, δεήσει, ἐδέησε(ν), ——, ——, —— (*impersonal verb*) it is necessary, must
   (+ *accusative and infinitive*); there is need of (+ *gen.*)

δύναμαι, δυνήσομαι, ——, ——, δεδύνημαι, ἐδυνήθην   be able

ἔθνος, ἔθνους, τό   band of people, nation

ἰᾱτρός, ἰᾱτροῦ, ὁ   doctor

κατάληψις, καταλήψεως, ἡ (καταλαμβάνω)   seizure, capture

κατανοέω, κατανοήσω, κατενόησα, κατανενόηκα, κατανενόημαι, κατενοήθην
   understand

κατασκευή, κατασκευῆς, ἡ   preparation, construction

λιμήν, λιμένος, ὁ   harbor

ναυπηγός, ναυπηγοῦ, ὁ   shipbuilder, shipwright

νεώριον, νεωρίου, τό   dockyard

οἰκοδόμησις, οἰκοδομήσεως, ἡ   (act of) building

πω (*enclitic adv.*) yet; οὐδέ . . . πω   and not yet, not even yet

σύλλογος, συλλόγου, ὁ   meeting, assembly

συμβουλεύω, συμβουλεύσω, συνεβούλευσα, συμβεβούλευκα, συμβεβούλευμαι,
   συνεβουλεύθην advise; (*mid.*) consult with (+ *dat.*)

συμβουλή, συμβουλῆς, ἡ   deliberation, debate

τάξις, τάξεως, ἡ   battle order

τεχνικώτατος, τεχνικωτάτη, τεχνικώτατον   most skilled

χωρίον, χωρίου, τό   place, spot

ἀλλ᾽ οἱ στρατηγικοὶ τότε συμβουλεύσουσιν, οἱ
ῥητορικοὶ δὲ οὔ· ἢ πῶς λέγεις, ὦ Γοργία, τὰ τοιαῦτα;
ἐπειδὴ γὰρ αὐτός τε φὴς ῥήτωρ εἶναι καὶ ἄλλους
15 ποιεῖν ῥητορικούς, εὖ ἔχει τὰ τῆς σῆς τέχνης παρὰ
σοῦ πυνθάνεσθαι. καὶ ἐμὲ νῦν νόμισον καὶ τὸ σὸν
σπεύδειν· ἴσως γὰρ καὶ τυγχάνει τις τῶν ἔνδον
ὄντων μαθητής σου βουλόμενος γενέσθαι, ὡς ἐγώ
τινας σχεδὸν καὶ συχνοὺς αἰσθάνομαι, οἳ ἴσως
20 αἰσχύνοιντ᾽ ἄν σε ἀνερέσθαι. ὑπ᾽ ἐμοῦ οὖν ἀνε-
ρωτώμενος νόμισον καὶ ὑπ᾽ ἐκείνων ἀνερωτᾶσθαι·
"Τί ἡμῖν, ὦ Γοργία, ἔσται, ἐάν σοι συνῶμεν;
περὶ τίνων τῇ πόλει συμβουλεύειν οἷοί τε ἐσόμεθα;
πότερον περὶ δικαίου μόνον καὶ ἀδίκου ἢ καὶ περὶ
25 ὧν[1] νῦνδὴ Σωκράτης ἔλεγεν;" πειρῶ οὖν αὐτοῖς
ἀποκρίνεσθαι.

αἰσχύνομαι, αἰσχυνοῦμαι, ——, ——, ᾔσχυμμαι, ᾐσχύνθην be ashamed,
feel shame before
——, ἀνερήσομαι, ἀνηρόμην, ——, ——, —— ask, question
ἀνερωτάω = ἐρωτάω
ἀποκρίνομαι, ἀποκρινοῦμαι, ἀπεκρινάμην, ——, ἀποκέκριμαι, —— answer
Γοργίας, Γοργίου, ὁ Gorgias of Leontinoi, a rhetorician
ἔνδον (adv.) within, indoors
ἔχω, ἕξω/σχήσω, ἔσχον, ἔσχηκα, -ἔσχημαι, —— have, hold; be able; (mid.)
cling to, be next to (+ gen.)
  εὖ ἔχει it is good
ἴσως (adv.) equally; perhaps
νῦνδή (adv.) just now
πειράομαι, πειράσομαι, ἐπειρασάμην, ——, πεπείραμαι, ἐπειράθην try,
attempt
πότερον (adv.) introduces alternative question
πυνθάνομαι, πεύσομαι, ἐπυθόμην, ——, πέπυσμαι, —— inquire, learn by
inquiry
σπεύδω, σπεύσω, ἔσπευσα, ἔσπευκα, ἔσπευσμαι, —— urge on, promote
zealously
συμβουλεύω, συμβουλεύσω, συνεβούλευσα, συμβεβούλευκα, συμβεβούλευμαι,
συνεβουλεύθην advise; (mid.) consult with (+ dat.)
συχνός, συχνή, συχνόν many, frequent, numerous
σχεδόν (adv.) almost
ὡς (conj.) as, since

1. ὧν here = ἐκείνων ἃ

ΓΟΡ. Ἀλλ' ἐγώ σοι πειράσομαι, ὦ Σώκρατες, σαφῶς
ἀποκαλύψαι τὴν τῆς ῥητορικῆς δύναμιν ἅπασαν· αὐτὸς
γὰρ καλῶς ὑφηγήσω. οἶσθα γὰρ δήπου ὅτι τὰ νεώρια
30 ταῦτα καὶ τὰ τείχη τὰ Ἀθηναίων καὶ ἡ τῶν λιμένων
κατασκευὴ ἐκ τῆς Θεμιστοκλέους συμβουλῆς γέγονεν,
τὰ δ' ἐκ τῆς Περικλέους ἀλλ' οὐκ ἐκ τῶν δημιουργῶν.

ΣΩ. Λέγεται ταῦτα, ὦ Γοργία, περὶ Θεμιστοκλέους·
Περικλέους δὲ καὶ αὐτὸς ἤκουον ὅτε συνεβούλευεν
35 ἡμῖν περὶ τοῦ διὰ μέσου τείχους.

ΓΟΡ. Καὶ ὅταν γέ τις αἵρεσις ᾖ ὧν¹ νῦνδὴ σὺ ἔλεγες,
ὦ Σώκρατες, ὁρᾷς ὅτι οἱ ῥήτορές εἰσιν οἱ συμβουλεύ-
οντες καὶ οἱ νῑκῶντες τὰς γνώμᾱς περὶ τούτων.

αἵρεσις, αἱρέσεως, ἡ   choice
ἀποκαλύπτω, ἀποκαλύψω, ἀπεκάλυψα, ——, ἀποκεκάλυμμαι, ἀπεκαλύφθην
   reveal
δήπου (particle) doubtless, I suppose, I presume
δύναμις, δυνάμεως, ἡ   strength, power
Θεμιστοκλῆς, Θεμιστοκλέους, ὁ Themistokles, an Athenian statesman
κατασκευή, κατασκευῆς, ἡ preparation, construction
νεώριον, νεωρίου, τό dockyard
νῦνδή (adv.) just now
οἶδα, εἴσομαι, ——, ——, ——, —— know
   οἶσθα you know
πειράομαι, πειράσομαι, ἐπειρασάμην, ——, πεπείρᾱμαι, ἐπειράθην try,
   attempt
Περικλῆς, Περικλέους, ὁ Perikles, an Athenian statesman
συμβουλεύω, συμβουλεύσω, συνεβούλευσα, συμβεβούλευκα, συμβεβούλευμαι,
   συνεβουλεύθην advise; (mid.) consult with (+ dat.)
συμβουλή, συμβουλῆς, ἡ deliberation, debate
ὑφηγέομαι, ὑφηγήσομαι, ὑφηγησάμην, ——, ὑφήγημαι, ὑφηγήθην lead the way

1. ὧν here = ἐκείνων ἃ

ΣΩ. Ταῦτα καὶ θαυμάζων, ὦ Γοργία, πάλαι ἐρωτῶ τίς
40 ποτε ἡ δύναμίς ἐστιν τῆς ῥητορικῆς. δαιμονίᾱ γὰρ
τις ἔμοιγε καταφαίνεται τὸ μέγεθος οὕτω σκοποῦντι.

ΓΟΡ. Εἰ πάντα γε εἰδείης, ὦ Σώκρατες, ὅτι ὡς ἔπος
εἰπεῖν ἁπάσᾱς τὰς δυνάμεις συλλαβοῦσα ὑφ᾽ αὑτῇ ἔχει.
μέγα δέ σοι τεκμήριον ἐρῶ· πολλάκις γὰρ ἤδη ἔγωγε
45 μετὰ τοῦ ἀδελφοῦ καὶ μετὰ τῶν ἄλλων ἰᾱτρῶν εἰσελθὼν
παρά τινα τῶν καμνόντων οὐχὶ ἐθέλοντα ἢ φάρμακον
πιεῖν ἢ τεμεῖν ἢ καῦσαι παρασχεῖν τῷ ἰᾱτρῷ, οὐ δυνα-
μένου τοῦ ἰᾱτροῦ πεῖσαι, ἐγὼ ἔπεισα, οὐκ ἄλλῃ τέχνῃ
ἢ τῇ ῥητορικῇ. φημὶ δὲ καὶ εἰς πόλιν ὅποι βούλει
50 ἐλθόντα ῥητορικὸν ἄνδρα καὶ ἰᾱτρόν, εἰ δέοι λόγῳ
διαγωνίζεσθαι ἐν ἐκκλησίᾳ ἢ ἐν ἄλλῳ τινὶ συλλόγῳ
ὁπότερον δεῖ αἱρεθῆναι ἰᾱτρόν, οὐδαμοῦ ἂν φανῆναι[1]
τὸν ἰᾱτρόν, ἀλλ᾽ αἱρεθῆναι[1] ἂν τὸν εἰπεῖν δυνατόν,
εἰ βούλοιτο.

δαιμόνιος, δαιμονίᾱ, δαιμόνιον marvelous, miraculous
δεῖ, δεήσει, ἐδέησε(ν), ——, ——, —— (impersonal verb) it is necessary, must
(+ accusative and infinitive); there is need of (+ gen.)

διαγωνίζομαι, διαγωνιοῦμαι, διηγωνισάμην, ——, διηγώνισμαι, διηγωνίσθην
struggle, contend

δύναμαι, δυνήσομαι, ——, ——, δεδύνημαι, ἐδυνήθην be able
δύναμις, δυνάμεως, ἡ strength, power
δυνατός, δυνατή, δυνατόν able, possible
εἰδείης: cf. οἶδα
ἔχω, ἕξω/σχήσω, ἔσχον, ἔσχηκα, -ἔσχημαι, —— have, hold; be able; (mid.)
cling to, be next to (+ gen.)
ἤδη (adv.) already, by now
θαυμάζω, θαυμάσω, ἐθαύμασα, τεθαύμακα, τεθαύμασμαι, ἐθαυμάσθην marvel
at

1. In indirect statement an infinitive with ἄν can represent an optative with ἄν in the
apodosis of a future less vivid conditional sentence; cf. Appendix, page 766.

ἰᾱτρός, ἰᾱτροῦ, ὁ   doctor

καίω/κάω, καύσω, ἔκαυσα, -κέκαυκα, κέκαυμαι, ἐκαύθην   burn

κάμνω, καμοῦμαι, ἔκαμον, κέκμηκα, ——, ——   toil, be weary, be sick

καταφαίνω, καταφανῶ, κατέφηνα, καταπέφηνα, καταπέφασμαι, κατεφάνην
   reveal; (mid., perfect active, aorist passive)   be apparent, appear

μέγας, μεγάλη, μέγα   big, great

μέγεθος, μεγέθους, τό   size, greatness

οἶδα, εἴσομαι, ——, ——, ——, ——   know (perfect in form = pres.)
   εἰδείης (second pers. sing., perf. opt. act. with present meaning)

ὅποι (adv.) (indefinite relative) (to) wherever

ὁπότερος, ὁποτέρᾱ, ὁπότερον   (indirect interrogative)   which (of two)?

οὐδαμοῦ (adv.)   nowhere

οὐχί strengthened form of οὐ

παρέχω (cf. ἔχω) provide; offer (oneself) to, permit (+ dat.)

πίνω, πίομαι, ἔπιον, πέπωκα, -πέπομαι, -ἐπόθην   drink

πολλάκις (adv.) often

σκοπέω, ——, ——, ——, ——, ——   contemplate, examine

συλλαμβάνω   take together, grasp together, seize

σύλλογος, συλλόγου, ὁ   meeting, assembly

τεκμήριον, τεκμηρίου, τό   sure sign, proof

τέμνω, τεμῶ, ἔτεμον, τέτμηκα, τέτμημαι, ἐτμήθην   cut

φαίνω, φανῶ, ἔφηνα, πέφηνα, πέφασμαι, ἐφάνην   show, cause to appear;
   (mid., perfect active, aorist passive)   appear

φάρμακον, φαρμάκου, τό   drug

ὡς ἔπος εἰπεῖν   so to speak (an infinitive used absolutely; see Appendix,
   page 725)

Continued in Units 17–20, at pages 510, 542, 557, 576.

B. Isokrates, *To Demonikos* 1–3

The rhetorician Isokrates (436–338 B.C.) gives advice to Demonikos, the son of a friend.

> Ἐν πολλοῖς μέν, ὦ Δημόνῑκε, πολὺ διεστώσᾱς εὑρήσομεν
> τάς τε τῶν σπουδαίων γνώμᾱς καὶ τὰς τῶν φαύλων δια-
> νοίᾱς· πολὺ δὲ μεγίστην διαφορὰν εἰλήφᾱσιν ἐν ταῖς
> πρὸς ἀλλήλους συνηθείαις· οἱ μὲν γὰρ τοὺς φίλους
> 5 παρόντας μόνον τῑμῶσιν, οἱ δὲ καὶ μακρὰν ἀπόντας
> ἀγαπῶσι· καὶ τὰς μὲν τῶν φαύλων συνηθείᾱς ὀλίγος
> χρόνος διέλῡσε,¹ τὰς δὲ τῶν σπουδαίων φιλίᾱς οὐδ'
> ἂν ὁ πᾶς αἰὼν ἐξαλείψειεν. ἡγούμενος οὖν πρέπειν
> τοὺς δόξης ὀρεγομένους καὶ παιδείᾱς ἀντιποιουμένους
> 10 τῶν σπουδαίων ἀλλὰ μὴ τῶν φαύλων εἶναι μῑμητάς,

ἀγαπάω, ἀγαπήσω, ἠγάπησα, ἠγάπηκα, ἠγάπημαι, ἠγαπήθην love
αἰών, αἰῶνος, ὁ lifetime, long space of time
ἀντιποιέω do in return; (mid.) seek after (+ gen.)
Δημόνῑκος, Δημονίκου, ὁ Demonikos, a young man
διάνοια, διανοίᾱς, ἡ thought
διαφορά, διαφορᾶς, ἡ difference
διΐσταμαι stand apart, be opposed
ἐξαλείφω, ἐξαλείψω, ἐξήλειψα, ἐξαλήλιφα, ἐξαλήλιμμαι, ἐξηλείφθην plaster over, wipe out, obliterate
εὑρίσκω, εὑρήσω, ηὗρον, ηὕρηκα, ηὕρημαι, ηὑρέθην find, discover
ἡγέομαι, ἡγήσομαι, ἡγησάμην, ——, ἥγημαι, ἡγήθην lead the way; be commander, rule (+ gen.); think (+ acc. and infin.)
μακράν (adv.) far
μέγιστος, μεγίστη, μέγιστον greatest
μῑμητής, μῑμητοῦ, ὁ imitator
ὀλίγος, ὀλίγη, ὀλίγον little, (pl.) few
ὀρέγω, ὀρέξω, ὤρεξα, ——, ὤρεγμαι, ὠρέχθην reach, stretch out; (mid., pass.) stretch oneself out, desire (+ gen.)
παιδείᾱ, παιδείᾱς, ἡ learning, education, culture
πολύς, πολλή, πολύ much, many
     πολύ (adverbial acc.) much, by much
πρέπει, πρέψει, ἔπρεψε(ν), ——, ——, —— (impersonal verb) it is fitting
σπουδαῖος, σπουδαίᾱ, σπουδαῖον serious, good
συνήθεια, συνηθείᾱς, ἡ acquaintance
φαῦλος, φαύλη, φαῦλον cheap, slight, worthless
χρόνος, χρόνου, ὁ time

1. διέλῡσε: a **gnomic aorist**, expressing a general truth; translate as a present; cf. Appendix, page 733.

ἀπέσταλκά σοι τόνδε τὸν λόγον δῶρον, τεκμήριον
μὲν τῆς πρὸς ὑμᾶς εὐνοίας, σημεῖον δὲ τῆς πρὸς
Ἱππόνῑκον συνηθείας· πρέπει γὰρ τοὺς παῖδας, ὥσπερ
τῆς οὐσίας, οὕτω καὶ τῆς φιλίας τῆς πατρικῆς κληρο-
15   νομεῖν. ὁρῶ δὲ καὶ τὴν τύχην ἡμῖν συλλαμβάνουσαν
καὶ τὸν παρόντα καιρὸν συναγωνιζόμενον· σὺ μὲν
γὰρ παιδείᾱς ἐπιθῡμεῖς, ἐγὼ δὲ παιδεύειν ἄλλους
ἐπιχειρῶ, καὶ σοὶ μὲν ἀκμὴ φιλοσοφεῖν, ἐγὼ δὲ
τοὺς φιλοσοφοῦντας ἐπανορθῶ.

ἀκμή, ἀκμῆς, ἡ   high point, prime
ἀποστέλλω, ἀποστελῶ, ἀπέστειλα, ἀπέσταλκα, ἀπέσταλμαι, ἀπεστάλην   send
   away
ἐπανορθόω, ἐπανορθώσω, ἐπηνώρθωσα, ἐπηνώρθωκα, ἐπηνώρθωμαι,
   ἐπηνωρθώθην   set up straight again; correct, teach
ἐπιθῡμέω, ἐπιθῡμήσω, ἐπεθΰμησα, ἐπιτεθΰμηκα, ἐπιτεθΰμημαι, ἐπεθῡμήθην
   desire (+ gen.)
ἐπιχειρέω, ἐπιχειρήσω, ἐπεχείρησα, ἐπικεχείρηκα, ἐπικεχείρημαι,
   ἐπεχειρήθην   put one's hand to, attempt
εὔνοια, εὐνοίας, ἡ   good will
Ἱππόνῑκος, Ἱππονίκου, ὁ   Hipponikos, father of Demonikos
κληρονομέω, κληρονομήσω, ἐκληρονόμησα, κεκληρονόμηκα, κεκληρονόμημαι,
   ἐκληρονομήθην   inherit (+ gen.)
οὐσίᾱ, οὐσίᾱς, ἡ   property, substance
παιδείᾱ, παιδείᾱς, ἡ   learning, education, culture
πρέπει, πρέψει, ἔπρεψε(ν), ——, ——, ——   (impersonal verb) it is fitting
σημεῖον, σημείου, τό   sign
συλλαμβάνω   take together; assist (+ dat.)
συναγωνίζομαι, συναγωνιοῦμαι, συνηγωνισάμην, ——, συνηγώνισμαι,
   συνηγωνίσθην   contend along with; aid, help (+ dat.)
συνήθεια, συνηθείᾱς, ἡ   acquaintance
τεκμήριον, τεκμηρίου, τό   sure sign, proof
φιλοσοφέω, φιλοσοφήσω, ἐφιλοσόφησα, πεφιλοσόφηκα, πεφιλοσόφημαι,
   ἐφιλοσοφήθην   love knowledge; study
ὥσπερ (conj.)   just as

UNIT
17

129. THE ADJECTIVE μέγας, μεγάλη, μέγα, "big, great, large"

This adjective has five third-declension forms:

	M	F	N
Nom. S	**μέγας**	μεγάλη	**μέγα**
Gen.	μεγάλου	μεγάλης	μεγάλου
Dat.	μεγάλῳ	μεγάλῃ	μεγάλῳ
Acc.	**μέγαν**	μεγάλην	**μέγα**
Voc.	μεγάλε	μεγάλη	**μέγα**
Nom./Voc. P	μεγάλοι	μεγάλαι	μεγάλα
Gen.	μεγάλων	μεγάλων	μεγάλων
Dat.	μεγάλοις	μεγάλαις	μεγάλοις
Acc.	μεγάλους	μεγάλᾱς	μεγάλα

Observation: The forms in bold face are the third-declension ones. All other forms are those of first- and second-declension adjectives built on the stem μεγαλ- with a persistent accent on the penult.

130. ADJECTIVES OF THE TYPE ἡδύς, ἡδεῖα, ἡδύ, "pleasant, glad"

Nom. S	ἡδύς	ἡδεῖα	ἡδύ
Gen.	ἡδέος	ἡδείᾱς	ἡδέος
Dat.	ἡδεῖ	ἡδείᾳ	ἡδεῖ
Acc.	ἡδύν	ἡδεῖαν	ἡδύ
Voc.	ἡδύ	ἡδεῖα	ἡδύ

491

Nom./Voc. P	ἡδεῖς	ἡδεῖαι	ἡδέα
Gen.	ἡδέων	ἡδειῶν	ἡδέων
Dat.	ἡδέσι(ν)	ἡδείαις	ἡδέσι(ν)
Acc.	ἡδεῖς	ἡδείᾱς	ἡδέα

Observations: (1) Note the -v- in the masculine and neuter nominative, accusative, and vocative singular; elsewhere in the masculine and neuter, the stem ἡδε- is used. The dative singular is the result of a contraction of ἡδέι; the masculine plural nominative is contracted from ἡδέες. The masculine plural accusative is the same as the masculine plural nominative.

(2) The feminine has short -α first-declension endings, with a circumflex on the ultima in the genitive plural.

(3) These adjectives form adverbs by adding the ending -ως to the stem ending in -ε-: ἡδέως.

131. COMPARISON OF ADJECTIVES

Adjectives in Greek have three degrees:

(1) the **positive degree**, the one seen thus far, simply attributes a quality to a noun or pronoun (e.g., "clear, beautiful");

(2) the **comparative degree** shows that of two nouns or pronouns one has more of a quality than the other (e.g., "clearer, more beautiful") or that one noun or pronoun has the quality to a rather high degree (e.g., "rather clear, rather beautiful");

(3) the **superlative degree** shows that of more than two nouns or pronouns one has the most of a quality (e.g., "clearest, most beautiful") or that a noun or pronoun has the quality to a very high degree (e.g., "very clear, very beautiful").

The Greek comparative and superlative thus can show degrees of *intensity* in addition to strict comparison.

A Greek adjective shows degrees of comparison by using one of two sets of suffixes or by the use of comparative and superlative adverbs:

SUFFIX: either (1) Comparative in -τερος, -τερᾱ, -τερον
Superlative in -τατος, -τατη, -τατον

or (2) Comparative in -ῑων, -ῑον
Superlative in -ιστος, -ιστη, -ιστον

ADVERB: Comparative adverb μᾶλλον, "more"
Superlative adverb μάλιστα, "most"

1. COMPARATIVE IN -τερος, -τερᾱ, -τερον
   SUPERLATIVE IN   -τατος, -τατη, -τατον

Since most adjectives form their comparative and superlative with these suffixes, use these suffixes for all adjectives unless told otherwise.

To form the comparative and superlative degrees of a *first- and second-declension adjective*, drop the ending -ος from the masculine singular nominative to get the stem. If the stem ends in a **long syllable** (a syllable containing [1] a long vowel or diphthong or [2] a short vowel followed by two consonants or the double consonants ζ, ξ, or ψ), add the vowel -ο- and the suffixes. If the stem ends in a **short syllable** (a syllable containing a short vowel not followed by two consonants or a double consonant), add the letter -ω- and the suffixes.

The comparative degree thus obtained is declined like the adjective ἄξιος, ἀξίᾱ, ἄξιον. Except for the accent, the superlative degree is declined like ἀγαθός, ἀγαθή, ἀγαθόν.

POSITIVE	STEM	COMPARATIVE	SUPERLATIVE
δίκαιος	δικαι-	δικαιότερος	δικαιότατος
δικαίᾱ		δικαιοτέρᾱ	δικαιοτάτη
δίκαιον		δικαιότερον	δικαιότατον
"just"		"more just, rather just"	"most just, very just"
δῆλος	δηλ-	δηλότερος	δηλότατος
δήλη		δηλοτέρᾱ	δηλοτάτη
δῆλον		δηλότερον	δηλότατον
"clear"		"clearer, rather clear"	"clearest, very clear"
ἄξιος	ἀξι-	ἀξιώτερος	ἀξιώτατος
ἀξίᾱ		ἀξιωτέρᾱ	ἀξιωτάτη
ἄξιον		ἀξιώτερον	ἀξιώτατον
"worthy"		"worthier, rather worthy"	"worthiest, very worthy"
σοφός	σοφ-	σοφώτερος	σοφώτατος
σοφή		σοφωτέρᾱ	σοφωτάτη
σοφόν		σοφώτερον	σοφώτατον
"wise"		"wiser, rather wise"	"wisest, very wise"

The following first- and second-declension adjectives are irregular. (In giving the degrees of an adjective, one gives only the masculine singular nominative.)

μέσος	μεσαίτερος	μεσαίτατος
παλαιός	παλαίτερος	παλαίτατος
φίλος	φιλαίτερος	φιλαίτατος/φίλτατος

Third-declension adjectives in -ης, -ες, and *third- and first-declension adjectives* in -ύς, -εῖα, -ύ add the suffixes directly to the stem without any intervening vowel. The stem of these adjectives is identical with the neuter singular nominative and accusative.

ADJECTIVE	STEM	COMPARATIVE	SUPERLATIVE
ἀμαθής	ἀμαθεσ-	ἀμαθέστερος	ἀμαθέστατος
σαφής	σαφεσ-	σαφέστερος	σαφέστατος
βαρύς	βαρυ-	βαρύτερος	βαρύτατος

(cf. Vocabulary, page 502.)

Some third-declension adjectives add the suffixes -εστερος and -εστατος to their stem:

ἄφρων	ἀφρον-	ἀφρονέστερος	ἀφρονέστατος
εὐδαίμων	εὐδαιμον-	εὐδαιμονέστερος	εὐδαιμονέστατος
σώφρων	σωφρον-	σωφρονέστερος	σωφρονέστατος

2. COMPARATIVE IN -ῑων, -ῑον
SUPERLATIVE IN -ιστος, -ιστη, -ιστον

The comparative and superlative degrees of these adjectives must be learned individually, since these suffixes are put on a stem different from that of the positive degree. Any adjective that takes -ῑων, -ῑον in the comparative degree takes -ιστος, -ιστη, -ιστον in the superlative degree. An adjective regularly takes -τερος, -τερᾱ, -τερον in the comparative degree and -τατος, -τατη, -τατον in the superlative degree OR -ῑων, -ῑον and -ιστος, -ιστη, -ιστον, NOT both sets of suffixes.

Here are presented four adjectives with comparatives in -ῑων, -ῑον and superlatives in -ιστος, -ιστη, -ιστον. More such adjectives are given in Unit 19.

POSITIVE	COMPARATIVE	SUPERLATIVE
αἰσχρός	αἰσχίων	αἴσχιστος
ἐχθρός	ἐχθίων	ἔχθιστος
ἡδύς	ἡδίων	ἥδιστος
καλός	καλλίων	κάλλιστος

3. DECLENSION OF COMPARATIVES OF THE TYPE ἡδίων, ἥδῑον

In the declension which follows, pay particular attention to the alternative forms.

	M/F	N
Nom. S	ἡδίων	ἥδῑον
Gen.	ἡδίονος	ἡδίονος
Dat.	ἡδίονι	ἡδίονι
Acc.	ἡδίονα/ἡδίω	ἥδῑον
Voc.	ἥδῑον	ἥδῑον
Nom./Voc. P	ἡδίονες/ἡδίους	ἡδίονα/ἡδίω
Gen.	ἡδῑόνων	ἡδῑόνων
Dat.	ἡδίοσι(ν)	ἡδίοσι(ν)
Acc.	ἡδίονας/ἡδίους	ἡδίονα/ἡδίω

Observations: (1) Note that in the masculine/feminine singular vocative and neuter singular nominative/accusative/vocative the accent is on the antepenult.

(2) The alternative forms derive from a different suffix which ended in -σ-. The intervocalic -σ- dropped out and the remaining vowels contracted:

ἡδίω < *ἡδίοσα; ἡδίους < *ἡδίοσες

The alternative masculine and feminine plural accusative is simply the same form as the nominative.

4. COMPARATIVE ADVERB μᾶλλον, "more"
SUPERLATIVE ADVERB μάλιστα, "most"

Instead of using one of the two sets of suffixes, any adjective can form a comparative degree by using the comparative adverb μᾶλλον, "more," with the positive degree of the adjective. The superlative is formed by using the superlative adverb μάλιστα, "most," with the positive degree of the adjective.

POSITIVE	COMPARATIVE	SUPERLATIVE
φίλος	μᾶλλον φίλος	μάλιστα φίλος
εὐγενής	μᾶλλον εὐγενής	μάλιστα εὐγενής

5. COMPARISON WITH ἤ; GENITIVE OF COMPARISON

Comparisons are made in two ways in Greek, by the conjunction ἤ, "than," or by the genitive of comparison.

(1) The conjunction ἤ introduces a new clause. The case of the person or thing compared depends on its function in its own clause.

> Σωκράτης σοφώτερός ἐστιν **ἤ** Ἀριστοφάνης.
> Sokrates is wiser **than** Aristophanes.

> νομίζομεν Σωκράτη σοφώτερον εἶναι **ἤ** Ἀριστοφάνη.
> We think that Sokrates is wiser **than** Aristophanes.

In the first sentence, Ἀριστοφάνης is in the nominative, since it is the subject of an understood ἐστίν in its own clause. In the second sentence, Ἀριστοφάνη is in the accusative, since it is the subject of an understood εἶναι in its own clause.

(2) Alternatively, the person or thing being compared can stand in the genitive case without any conjunction or preposition. Such a genitive is called a **genitive of comparison.**

> Σωκράτης σοφώτερός ἐστιν **Ἀριστοφάνους.**
> Sokrates is wiser **than Aristophanes.**

> νομίζομεν Σωκράτη σοφώτερον εἶναι **Ἀριστοφάνους.**
> We think that Sokrates is wiser **than Aristophanes.**

6. DATIVE OF DEGREE OF DIFFERENCE

The degree to which two persons or things being compared differ is shown by the **dative of degree of difference,** with no preposition.

> Σωκράτης **πολλῷ** σοφώτερός ἐστιν ἤ Ἀριστοφάνης.
> Sokrates is wiser than Aristophanes **by much.**
> Sokrates is **much** wiser than Aristophanes.

The same idea can be expressed by an adverbial accusative.

> Σωκράτης **πολὺ** σοφώτερός ἐστιν ἤ Ἀριστοφάνης.
> Sokrates is **much** wiser than Aristophanes.

7. SUPERLATIVE WITH ὡς and ὅτι

The conjunctions ὡς and ὅτι followed by the superlative degree mean "as . . . as possible."

> Σωκράτης, ἀνὴρ $\left\{ \begin{array}{l} ὡς \\ ὅτι \end{array} \right\}$ **σοφώτατος,** τοὺς νεανίας ἐδίδασκεν.
> Sokrates, a man **as wise as possible,** taught the young men.

8. OTHER CONSTRUCTIONS WITH THE SUPERLATIVE

A superlative is often accompanied by a partitive genitive, a dative of degree of difference, or an adverbial accusative.

Σωκράτης, ὁ σοφώτατος μακρῷ τῶν ῾Ελλήνων, τοὺς νεᾱνίᾱς ἐδίδασκεν.
Sokrates, by far the wisest of the Greeks, taught the young men.

Σωκράτης, ὁ πολὺ σοφώτατος τῶν ᾿Αθηναίων, τοὺς νεᾱνίᾱς ἐδίδασκεν.
Sokrates, much the wisest of the Athenians, taught the young men.

132. THE VERB εἶμι, "go, come"

εἶμι, ——, ——, ——, ——, ——, "go, come"

This verb occurs only in the present and imperfect tenses of the active voice. A discussion of the use of the tenses follows the presentation of the forms.

		PRESENT INDICATIVE ACTIVE	IMPERFECT INDICATIVE ACTIVE	PRESENT SUBJ. ACTIVE	PRESENT OPTATIVE ACTIVE
S	1	εἶμι	ᾖα/ᾔειν	ἴω	ἴοιμι/ἰοίην
	2	εἶ	ᾔεισθα/ᾔεις	ἴῃς	ἴοις
	3	εἶσι(ν)	ᾔει(ν)	ἴῃ	ἴοι
P	1	ἴμεν	ᾖμεν	ἴωμεν	ἴοιμεν
	2	ἴτε	ᾖτε	ἴητε	ἴοιτε
	3	ἴᾱσι(ν)	ᾖσαν/ᾔεσαν	ἴωσι(ν)	ἴοιεν

Observations: (1) This verb shows vowel gradation:

Long-vowel present tense stem: εἰ-
Short-vowel present tense stem: ἰ-

(2) The present indicative is regular except for the second person singular εἶ. The imperfect is irregular and must be learned with special care. As in all athematic verbs, the subjunctive uses a thematic conjugation, but without the contraction of, e.g., διδῶ. The optative is thematic, with one alternative form with the ending -οιην: ἰοίην.

(3) Be careful not to confuse forms of εἶμι, "go, come," with εἰμί, "be." The two verbs are printed side by side in the Appendix, pp. 673–75. Note the following:

εἶμι, "go, come," is NOT an enclitic like εἰμί, "be."

εἶ: The form is the second person singular, present indicative active of both verbs.

Compare εἶσι(ν):   third person singular, present indicative active of "to go"

εἰσί(ν):   third person plural, present indicative active of "to be"

Note the iota subscript throughout the imperfect of εἶμι, "go, come."

PRESENT IMPERATIVE ACTIVE

	S	P
2	ἴθι	ἴτε
3	ἴτω	ἰόντων

PRESENT INFINITIVE ACTIVE: ἰέναι

PRESENT PARTICIPLE ACTIVE

	M	F	N
Nom. S	ἰών	ἰοῦσα	ἰόν
Gen.	ἰόντος	ἰούσης	ἰόντος

Observation: Note the accented thematic endings in the participle.

Use of the tenses of εἶμι:

The present indicative forms of εἶμι, "go, come," are used in Attic prose as the future indicative of ἔρχομαι, which is used only in the present indicative. (The future ἐλεύσομαι is not used in Attic prose.) In indirect statement the optative, the infinitive, and the participle of εἶμι can stand either for forms of εἶμι in an original statement and therefore represent an *original future* or they can stand for forms of ἔρχομαι and therefore represent an *original present tense*. Context will usually allow one to distinguish between these uses. The participle ἰών can also function as a future and express purpose. In other uses of the optative, the infinitive, and the participle, and in all uses of the subjunctive and the imperative, the non-indicative forms of εἶμι show progressive/repeated aspect in contrast to the non-indicative forms derived from ἦλθον. The imperfect of εἶμι is used as the imperfect of ἔρχομαι.

Thus in Attic prose the principal parts and the moods and tenses formed from them which express the idea "go, come" are:

ἔρχομαι,	εἶμι,	ἦλθον,	ἐλήλυθα,	——,	——,	"go, come"
ἴω		ἔλθω				
ἴοιμι	ἴοιμι	ἔλθοιμι				
ἴθι		ἐλθέ				
ἰέναι	ἰέναι	ἐλθεῖν	ἐληλυθέναι			
ἰών	ἰών	ἐλθών	ἐληλυθώς			
ἦα/ἤειν			ἐληλύθη			

Examples:

νῦν ἀπέρχονται.
They are now going away.

ἀγγέλλω αὐτοὺς νῦν ἀπιόντας.
I report that they are now
    going away.

νομίζω αὐτοὺς νῦν ἀπιέναι.
I think that they are now
    going away.

μετὰ τὴν μάχην ἀπίασιν.
After the battle they will go away.

ἀγγέλλω αὐτοὺς μετὰ τὴν μάχην
    ἀπιόντας.
I report that they will go away
    after the battle.

νομίζω αὐτοὺς μετὰ τὴν μάχην
    ἀπιέναι.
I think that they will go away
    after the battle.

133. NUMERALS

The numbers one through four are numerical adjectives which are declined as
follows:

	"one"			"two"	"three"	
	M	F	N	M/F/N	M/F	N
Nom.	εἷς	μία	ἕν	δύο	τρεῖς	τρία
Gen.	ἑνός	μιᾶς	ἑνός	δυοῖν	τριῶν	τριῶν
Dat.	ἑνί	μιᾷ	ἑνί	δυοῖν	τρισί(ν)	τρισί(ν)
Acc.	ἕνα	μίαν	ἕν	δύο	τρεῖς	τρία

	"four"	
	M/F	N
Nom.	τέτταρες	τέτταρα
Gen.	τεττάρων	τεττάρων
Dat.	τέτταρσι(ν)	τέτταρσι(ν)
Acc.	τέτταρας	τέτταρα

Observation: In the declension of εἷς, μία, ἕν note the shift of accent to the
ultima in the feminine genitive and dative; contrast μιᾶς, μιᾷ
with μία, μίαν.

134. NEGATIVE PRONOUNS/ADJECTIVES

The forms of εἷς, μία, ἕν combine with the negatives οὐδέ and μηδέ to give the
compound negative pronouns/adjectives "no one, nothing."

	M	F	N	M	F	N
Nom.	οὐδείς	οὐδεμία	οὐδέν	μηδείς	μηδεμία	μηδέν
Gen.	οὐδενός	οὐδεμιᾶς	οὐδενός	μηδενός	μηδεμιᾶς	μηδενός
Dat.	οὐδενί	οὐδεμιᾷ	οὐδενί	μηδενί	μηδεμιᾷ	μηδενί
Acc.	οὐδένα	οὐδεμίαν	οὐδέν	μηδένα	μηδεμίαν	μηδέν

Where the negative would be οὐ, οὐδείς is used; where the negative would be
μή, μηδείς is used.

A SIMPLE NEGATIVE (οὐ, μή) FOLLOWED BY A COMPOUND NEGATIVE OR NEGATIVES
(E.G., οὐδείς, μηδείς), OR A COMPOUND NEGATIVE FOLLOWED BY ANOTHER
COMPOUND NEGATIVE OR NEGATIVES, HAS ITS NEGATION STRENGTHENED.

οὐκ ἄπεισιν οὐδείς.
No one will go away.

ἔμοιγε οὐδεὶς οὐδὲν ἔδωκεν.
To me no one gave anything.

μὴ ἀπέλθῃ μηδείς.
Let no one go away.

οὐ λυθήσεται οὐδεμία πόλις οὔποτε οὐδενὶ τρόπῳ.
No city will ever be freed in any way.

BUT A COMPOUND NEGATIVE FOLLOWED BY A SIMPLE NEGATIVE PRODUCES A
POSITIVE STATEMENT.

οὐδεὶς οὐκ ἔφυγεν.
No one did not flee (i.e., everyone fled).

135. UNATTAINABLE WISH

In order to express a wish, hope, or prayer whose fulfillment is possible, Greek
uses an independent optative of wish, often introduced by εἴθε or εἰ γάρ; cf.
Section 61. If, however, the fulfillment of the wish is impossible, the optative is

replaced by a past tense of the indicative: an imperfect indicative if the wish refers to present time; an aorist indicative if the wish refers to past time. Such **unattainable wishes** must be accompanied by εἴθε or εἰ γάρ, or they would be indistinguishable from plain factual statements about the past. The negative of all expressions of wish is μή.

$$\left\{ \begin{array}{c} \rule{1cm}{0.4pt} \\ εἴθε \\ εἰ γὰρ \end{array} \right\} \ παύσαιμεν \ τοὺς \ πολεμίους.$$

May we stop the enemy.
If only we may stop the enemy.
I wish we may stop the enemy.

$$\left\{ \begin{array}{c} εἴθε \\ εἰ γὰρ \end{array} \right\} \ ἐπαύομεν \ τοὺς \ πολεμίους.$$

Would that we were stopping the enemy.
If only we were stopping the enemy.
I wish that we were stopping the enemy.

$$\left\{ \begin{array}{c} εἴθε \\ εἰ γὰρ \end{array} \right\} \ ἐπαύσαμεν \ τοὺς \ πολεμίους.$$

Would that we had stopped the enemy.
If only we had stopped the enemy.
I wish that we had stopped the enemy.

εἰ γὰρ μὴ ἐνίκησαν οἱ πολέμιοι.
Would that the enemy had not conquered.
If only the enemy had not conquered.
I wish that the enemy had not conquered.

VOCABULARY

ἁμαρτάνω, ἁμαρτήσομαι, ἥμαρτον,   miss (+ *gen.*); make a mistake,
    ἡμάρτηκα, ἡμάρτημαι,   do wrong
    ἡμαρτήθην
       ἁμαρτίᾱ, ἁμαρτίᾱς, ἡ   mistake, error
βαρύς, βαρεῖα, βαρύ   heavy
δοκέω, δόξω, ἔδοξα, ——, δέδογμαι,   seem, think
    -ἐδόχθην
δύναμαι, δυνήσομαι, ——, ——,   be able
    δεδύνημαι, ἐδυνήθην
       δύναμις, δυνάμεως, ἡ   strength, power
δύο   two
       δεύτερος, δευτέρᾱ, δεύτερον   second
εἶμι, ——, ——, ——, ——, ——   go, come
εἷς, μία, ἕν   one
ἐλαύνω, ἐλῶ (ἐλάω), ἤλασα, -ἐλήλακα,   drive, march
    ἐλήλαμαι, ἠλάθην
ἐπίσταμαι, ἐπιστήσομαι, ——, ——,   know
    ——, ἠπιστήθην
       ἐπιστήμη, ἐπιστήμης, ἡ   knowledge
ἔχω, ἕξω or σχήσω, ἔσχον, ἔσχηκα,   have, hold; be able; (+ *adv.*) be;
    -ἔσχημαι, ——   (*mid.*) cling to, be next to
                                (+ *gen.*)

ἡδύς, ἡδεῖα, ἡδύ   pleasant, glad
μάλιστα (*adv.*)   most
μέγας, μεγάλη, μέγα   big, great, large
μηδείς, μηδεμία, μηδέν   no one, nothing
ὀρθός, ὀρθή, ὀρθόν   straight, correct
οὐδείς, οὐδεμία, οὐδέν   no one, nothing
πόσος, πόση, πόσον   how much/many?, how large?
       τοσοῦτος, τοσαύτη, τοσοῦτο/ so much/many, so large
          τοσοῦτον
       ὅσος, ὅση, ὅσον   as much/many as, as large as;
                             how much/many!, how large!

πότερος, ποτέρᾱ, πότερον	which (of two)
πότερον (adv.)	*introduces alternative question*
ταχύς, ταχεῖα, ταχύ	quick, swift
τέτταρες, τέτταρα	four
τέταρτος, τετάρτη, τέταρτον	fourth
τρεῖς, τρία	three
τρίτος, τρίτη, τρίτον	third
ὑπερ- (*prefix*)	over; greatly; on behalf of

VOCABULARY NOTES

The verb ἁμαρτάνω, ἁμαρτήσομαι, ἥμαρτον, ἡμάρτηκα, ἡμάρτημαι, ἡμαρτή-θην means literally "miss a target"; in this sense it governs a genitive. Its extended meaning is "make a mistake, do wrong." The related noun ἁμαρτίᾱ, ἁμαρτίᾱς, ἡ means "mistake, error." In Aristotle's *Poetics*, the tragic hero undergoes a change of fortune δι᾽ ἁμαρτίᾱν τινά.

The adjective βαρύς, βαρεῖα, βαρύ literally means "heavy." Among its extended meanings are "heavy to bear, burdensome, severe."

The verb δοκέω, δόξω, ἔδοξα, ——, δέδογμαι, -ἐδόχθην, related to the noun δόξα, means either "think" (with an accusative and infinitive) or "seem":

δοκῶ Σωκράτη σοφὸν εἶναι.
I think that Sokrates is wise.

δοκῶ τοῖς πολίταις σοφὸς εἶναι.
I seem to the citizens to be wise.

The verb δύναμαι, δυνήσομαι, ——, ——, δεδύνημαι, ἐδυνήθην, "be able," is an athematic deponent verb. The present and the imperfect are conjugated like ἵσταμαι and ἱστάμην, the present and imperfect middle/passive of ἵστημι. The second person singular of the imperfect is, however, ἐδύνω; contrast ἵστασο. The accent in the present subjunctive and optative is recessive: δύνωμαι, δύναιτο. This verb can govern a complementary infinitive. At times the past indicative augment appears as ἠ- instead of ἐ-.

For the use of the forms of εἶμι as the future and imperfect indicative, and as the non-indicative present and future forms of ἔρχομαι, see Section 132.

The verb ἐλαύνω, ἐλῶ (ἐλάω), ἤλασα, -ἐλήλακα, ἐλήλαμαι, ἠλάθην, "drive, march," has a future which is contracted like τῑμάω. The Greek verb, like the English verb "drive," can be either transitive or intransitive.

The verb ἐπίσταμαι, ἐπιστήσομαι, ——, ——, ——, ἠπιστήθην, "know," was probably a compound of ἐπι- and ἵσταμαι; cf. "understand." Note, however, that the rough breathing of the verb does not change the -π- to a -φ- after the -ι- of the prefix dropped out (contrast καθίστημι from κατα- + ἵστημι). Note also that the past indicative augment is shown by lengthening the initial ἐ-. As in δύναμαι, the second person singular of the imperfect indicative active is a contracted form, ἠπίστω, and the accent in the present subjunctive and optative is recessive: ἐπίστωμαι, ἐπίσταιτο. In Homer, the word meant "to know," with an emphasis on practical knowledge; the meaning was then extended to other forms of knowing. This verb introduces two kinds of indirect statement, the finite construction introduced by ὅτι or ὡς or the accusative subject + participle. The noun ἐπιστήμη, ἐπιστήμης, ἡ, "knowledge," had a similar development from "practical knowledge, know-how," to "knowledge" as opposed to "opinion," δόξα.

The verb ἔχω, ἕξω or σχήσω, ἔσχον, ἔσχηκα, -ἔσχημαι, ——, "have, hold," has as its basic root *segh-. In the present tense stem, the loss of the initial s- caused a rough breathing, which in turn was lost due to dissimilation of aspirates: *segho > *ἕχω > ἔχω. The imperfect is εἶχον < *ἔεχον < *ἔσεχον. In the future, the suffix -σ- caused the loss of the aspiration on the final consonant of the stem; this allowed the rough breathing due to the loss of the initial σ- to remain: *seghso > *σέξω > ἕξω. The alternative future is built on the zero-grade of the root, σχ-, with an added -η-. This element -σχη- also appears in the perfect active and perfect middle tense stems. Note also the second aorist with the zero-grade of the root without the additional -η-. The second person singular, aorist imperative active is σχές; the aorist subjunctive has a circumflex accent: σχῶ, σχῇς, etc.; and in uncompounded forms the optative is σχοίην, σχοίης, σχοίη, σχοῖμεν, σχοῖτε, σχοῖεν. In compounded forms of the aorist note the accent of the subjunctive (παράσχω) and imperative (παράσχες); the optative follows the usual pattern of the thematic second aorists, παράσχοιμι, παράσχοις, etc.

The verb means "have, hold." The future ἕξω has progressive/repeated aspect and is used of an action that lasts; σχήσω has simple aspect. Note the difference between the imperfect and the aorist:

εἶχες τὰ ξίφη. You were holding the swords.

ἔσχες τὰ ξίφη. You took hold of the swords.

The verb can also mean "be able to" and take a complementary infinitive.

In another very common idiom, any form of ἔχω with an adverb is the equivalent of the verb "to be" with an adjective:

ταῦτα οὐ κακῶς ἔχει.
These things are not bad.

In the middle the verb can mean "cling to" or "be next to" and take a genitive:

τῆς αὐτῆς γνώμης ἔχομαι.
I cling to the same opinion.

The adjective μέγας, μεγάλη, μέγα, "big, great, large," is used of both size and importance.

The negative pronouns/adjectives οὐδείς, οὐδεμία, οὐδέν and μηδείς, μηδεμία, μηδέν, "no one, nothing," are compounds of the negatives οὐ and μή. Any compound of οὐ is used where the simple οὐ is used. Any compound of μή is used where the simple μή is used.

The adjectives πόσος, πόση, πόσον, "how much/many?, how large?"; τοσοῦτος, τοσαύτη, τοσοῦτο/τοσοῦτον, "so much/many, so large"; and ὅσος, ὅση, ὅσον, "as much/many as, as large as; how much/many!, how large!" are correlatives and have the same relation to each other as ποῖος, τοιοῦτος, and οἷος. Note the alternative neuter singular nominative and accusative form with a final -ν: τοσοῦτον.

INTERROGATIVE	DEMONSTRATIVE	RELATIVE/ EXCLAMATORY
ποῖος, ποία, ποῖον of what kind?	τοιοῦτος, τοιαύτη, τοιοῦτο/τοιοῦτον of this/that sort, such (as this)	οἷος, οἵα, οἷον such as, of the sort which what sort of!

πόσος, πόση, πόσον
how much/many?, how
    large?
	τοσοῦτος, τοσαύτη,
	 τοσοῦτο/τοσοῦτον
	so much/many, so
	    large
		ὅσος, ὅση, ὅσον
		as much/many as,
		    as large as
		how much/many!, how
		    large!

The interrogative adjective πότερος, ποτέρᾱ, πότερον, "which," is limited to two items or groups of items. The neuter singular πότερον is an adverb which introduces an alternative question; often, it cannot be translated:

πότερον τὸν Σωκράτη τῑμᾷς ἢ οὔ;
Do you honor Sokrates or not?

COGNATES AND DERIVATIVES

βαρύς	baritone, *grave*, *guru*
δύναμαι	dynamic, dynasty
δύο	*two*; duet
δεύτερος	Deuteronomy
δοκέω	paradox
εἶμι	ion, transit (**going** through, from the Latin cognate)
εἷς	henotheism (belief in **one** god while not denying the existence of others)
ἐλαύνω	elastic
ἐπιστήμη	epistemology (the study of how we **know** what we **know**)
ἔχω	scheme (how a thing **holds** together)
ἡδύς	*sweet*; hedonism
μέγας	megalomania
ὀρθός	orthodox (having a **correct** belief)
ταχύς	tachometer (a device to measure how **fast** something goes)
τρεῖς	*three*
ὑπερ-	*over*; hyperactive

DRILLS

I. *Form the comparative and superlative degrees of the following adjectives. Translate.*

1. ἄδηλος
2. ἄδικος
3. βάρβαρος
4. δίκαιος
5. εὐγενής
6. βαρύς
7. καλός
8. εὐτυχής
9. δεινός
10. εὐδαίμων
11. παλαιός
12. ἱερός
13. ἐχθρός
14. φίλος
15. ἄφρων
16. μέσος
17. ἔμπειρος
18. ἡδύς
19. ἀνάξιος
20. αἰσχρός
21. ἱκανός
22. μακρός

II. *Change the adjectives in the following phrases to the comparative and superlative degrees. Translate. Change all three degrees from singular to plural or from plural to singular.*

1. τὸν βαρὺν λίθον
2. τοὺς ἡδεῖς οἴνους
3. δεινῷ ῥήτορι
4. τῇ καλῇ θεῷ
5. τὰ αἰσχρὰ βιβλία
6. τὸν εὐτυχῆ ἱερέᾱ
7. τῶν φίλων
8. ἡ ἄδηλος χάρις
9. τῇ ἄφρονι θυγατρί
10. οἱ ἐχθροί

III. *Translate.*

1. ὁ ἐκείνων οἶνος μακρῷ ἡδίων ἐστὶν τοῦ ἡμετέρου.

2. ὁ ἐκείνων οἶνος μακρῷ ἡδίων ἐστὶν ἢ ὁ ἡμέτερος.

3. οὔ φημι τὸν ἐκείνων οἶνον ἡδίω εἶναι τοῦ ἡμετέρου.

4. οὔ φημι τὸν ἐκείνων οἶνον ἡδίονα εἶναι τοῦ ἡμετέρου.

5. οὔ φημι τὸν ἐκείνων οἶνον ἡδίω εἶναι ἢ τὸν ἡμέτερον.

6. οὔ φημι τοὺς ἐκείνων οἶνους ἡδίους εἶναι.

7. οἱ πολὺ ἥδιστοι τῶν οἴνων εἰσὶν οἱ ἡμέτεροι.

8. οἱ ἡμέτεροι οἶνοι ὅτι ἥδιστοί εἰσιν.

9. νομίζει πολλῷ σοφωτέρᾱ εἶναι τοῦ πατρός.

10. νομίζω τὸν ἀδελφὸν εὐδαιμονέστερον εἶναι ἢ τὸν πατέρα.

11. οἶδε οἱ πονηρότατοι ὡς αἴσχιστα ἔπρᾱττον.

EXERCISES

I. 1. ὦ πάτερ, παύου κλέπτων τὸν οἶνον καίπερ ἡδίω τῶν ἄλλων ὄντα. κλέπτων γὰρ τὰ ἄλλων ἁμαρτάνεις.

2. ὦ ἀδελφοί, παύεσθε τρόπαια πρὸ τῆς μεγάλης οἰκίᾱς ἱστάμενοι.

3. κωλύσωμεν, ὦ ἄνδρες Ἀθηναῖοι, τούς γε πολεμίους τοὺς ἐχθίστους ἐλάσαι πρὸς τὰ μεγάλα τείχη.

4. ὦ γέρον, μηχανώμεθα ὅπως οὐχ ἁμαρτάνοντες ὅτι δικαιότατοι γενησόμεθα.

5. ὦ φίλτατοι, μήποτε νομίσητε τοὺς ἀδικωτέρους βλάπτειν δύνασθαι τούς γε δικαιοτέρους.

6. ὦ νεᾱνίᾱ, μηχανῶ ὅπως πολλῷ εὐδαιμονέστερος ἐμοῦ γε γενήσει ποτέ.

7. τῶν νεᾱνιῶν πολλὰ ἐρωτώντων, οἱ γέροντες οὐκ ἐδυνήθησαν ἀπελθεῖν.

8. μὴ ἐρωτώντων πολλὰ οἱ νεᾱνίαι τοὺς σοφωτάτους τῶν γερόντων.

9. λῦσόν με, ἑταῖρε. οὐ γάρ σε οὐδὲν ἔβλαψα.

10. ὦ στρατιῶτα, τί ἐπίστασαι περὶ τῆς τῶν Ἑλλήνων νίκης; φημὶ γὰρ εὐτυχεστέρους εἶναι τοὺς Ἕλληνας τῶν βαρβάρων.

11. πολλὰ δὴ χρήματα ἐκ τῆς οἰκίας λαβών, ὦ ἱερεῦ, λῦσαι τὰς δύο θυγατέρας.

12. ὁ τῷ ὄντι σοφὸς μᾶλλον βούλεται ἀγαθὸς εἶναι ἢ δοκεῖν. ὁ γὰρ τοιαῦτα βουλόμενος μακρῷ σοφώτερός ἐστι τῶν ἄλλων.

13. μηδεὶς τῷ σώματι δουλεύων δοκείτω ἄλλων δύνασθαί πως ἄρχειν.

14. οἷος ἂν ᾖ ὁ διδάσκαλος, τοιοῦτοι ἔσονται καὶ οἱ μαθηταί.

15. ὅσα ἂν διδῶμεν, τοσαῦτα λαβεῖν βουλόμεθα αὐτοί.

16. ἡ μήτηρ τὴν θυγατέρα ταῖς χερσὶν εἶχεν.

17. οἱ στρατιῶται ταχθέντων που παρὰ τῇ γεφύρᾳ.

18. ἐνεγκάντων οἱ δοῦλοι τοὺς λίθους τοὺς μεγάλους τε καὶ βαρεῖς.

19. εὖ μαχεσάμενος ὀρθῶς ἀξιώθητι τοῦ ἄθλου. ἡδὺ μὲν γὰρ τὸ μάχεσθαι, ὡς ἥδιστον δὲ τὸ νικῆσαι.

20. τοὺς προσιόντας λίθοις πολὺ βαρυτέροις βαλόντων.

21. εἰ γὰρ νῦν εἰς τὴν χώρᾱν μὴ ᾔεισθα, ὦ αἴσχιστε.

22. τῇ τετάρτῃ ἡμέρᾳ τὴν πόλιν ἑλόντες διὰ τοῦ πεδίου ἐλᾶτε.

23. πότερον τρεῖς ἢ τέτταρες ὑπὸ τῶν φυλάκων ὤφθησαν;

24. ποτέρᾳ τὸν οἶνον τὸν ἡδὺν ἀπέδου; πότερον τῇ μητρὶ ἢ τῇ θυγατρί;

25. πόσα βιβλία δύνασαι ἔχειν; οὐ τοσαῦτα οἷός τ' εἰμὶ ὅσα ὁ ἀδελφός.

26. ὅσοι ἀφρονέστατοι τὸν Εὐρῑπίδην ἐκείνῃ τῇ ἡμέρᾳ ἐτίμων.

27. μεγάλη ἐστὶν ἡ τῶν δυοῖν ἀδελφῶν δύναμις.

28. διὰ τὸ ταχείᾱς εἶναι τὰς ἵππους αὐτῶν οὐκ ἐδυνήθημεν αὐτοὺς ἑλεῖν.

29. οὐκ οὐδενὸς ἀξίᾱ οὐδενὶ τῶν πολῑτῶν ἡ τῶν ἀφρονεστέρων δόξα.

30. τοιούτοις δὴ δῶρα δῶμεν, οἵους ἄθλων ἀξιοῦμεν.

31. τοῦ ὕδατος ὑπερβαίνοντός πως εἰς τὴν χώρᾱν, καταλυθήσονται αἱ οἰκίαι.

32. τῇ τρίτῃ ἡμέρᾳ ὁ ἄγγελος ὁ ταχὺς τοῖς πολίταις τοὺς πολεμίους φήσει διὰ τὴν ἑαυτῶν ἁμαρτίᾱν νενῑκημένους ἐκφυγεῖν.

33. ἔστι πολλὰ χρήματα τῷ μῑκρῷ.

II. 1. If only our very well-born soldiers were *now* able to fight so nobly
        against the enemy as for our city to be saved. For ours is
        worthier to be saved than theirs.

     2. Will you order the swift horsemen to go away or to wait in the plain?

     3. Let no bad man be honored in any way by any of the citizens.

     4. Young man, have your younger brother taught rhetoric by that rather
        clever teacher.

     5. Stop believing that you will always be able to win. (*For "be able,"
        here do not use* δύναμαι *or* ἔχω; *write twice, addressing first a
        woman, then a man.*)

     6. I shall educate as many men as I see in the market place.

READINGS

A. Plato, *Gorgias* 456c2–456d5

Sokrates and Gorgias continue their discussion of rhetoric.

55   ΓΟΡ. καὶ εἰ πρὸς ἄλλον γε δημιουργὸν ὀντιναοῦν
      ἀγωνίζοιτο, πείσειεν ἂν αὐτὸν ἐλέσθαι ὁ ῥητορικὸς
      μᾶλλον ἢ ἄλλος ὁστισοῦν· οὐ γὰρ ἔστιν περὶ ὅτου
      οὐκ ἂν πιθανώτερον εἴποι ὁ ῥητορικὸς ἢ ἄλλος
      ὁστισοῦν τῶν δημιουργῶν ἐν πλήθει. ἡ μὲν οὖν
60   δύναμις τοσαύτη ἐστὶν καὶ τοιαύτη τῆς τέχνης·
      δεῖ μέντοι, ὦ Σώκρατες, τῇ ῥητορικῇ χρῆσθαι ὥσπερ
      τῇ ἄλλῃ πάσῃ ἀγωνίᾳ. καὶ γὰρ τῇ ἄλλῃ ἀγωνίᾳ οὐ
      τούτου ἕνεκα δεῖ πρὸς ἅπαντας χρῆσθαι ἀνθρώπους,
      ὅτι ἔμαθεν πυκτεύειν τε καὶ παγκρατιάζειν καὶ ἐν
65   ὅπλοις μάχεσθαι, ὥστε κρείττων εἶναι καὶ φίλων καὶ
      ἐχθρῶν, οὐ τούτου ἕνεκα τοὺς φίλους δεῖ τύπτειν
      οὐδὲ κεντεῖν τε καὶ ἀποκτεινύναι.

ἀγωνίᾱ, ἀγωνίᾱς, ἡ   contest; competitive skill

ἀγωνίζομαι, ἀγωνιοῦμαι, ἠγωνισάμην, ——, ἠγώνισμαι, ἠγωνίσθην   contend for a prize, struggle in a contest

ἀποκτείνῡμι/ἀποκτείνω, ἀποκτενῶ, ἀπέκτεινα, ἀπέκτονα, ——, —— kill

δεῖ, δεήσει, ἐδέησε(ν), ——, ——, —— (impersonal verb) it is necessary, must (+ accusative and infinitive); there is need of (+ gen.)

δύναμις, δυνάμεως, ἡ   strength, power

καὶ γάρ (conjs.) and in fact, for in fact

κεντέω, κεντήσω, ἐκέντησα, ——, κεκέντημαι, ἐκεντήθην   goad, spur

κρείττων, κρεῖττον (irregular comparative of ἀγαθός)   stronger, better

μέντοι (particle)   indeed, and yet

ὁστισοῦν, ἡτισοῦν, ὁτιοῦν (masc. acc. sing. ὁντιναοῦν) (indefinite pronoun/adjective)   anyone/anything at all

ὅτου   alternative M/N gen. sing. form of
      ὅστις, ἥτις, ὅτι (indefinite relative)   whoever, whatever

παγκρατιάζω, παγκρατιάσω, ἐπαγκρατίασα, ——, ——, —— perform the παγκράτιον (a boxing and wrestling contest)

πιθανώτερον (comparative adverb)   more persuasively

πλῆθος, πλήθους, τό   crowd, mass

πυκτεύω, πυκτεύσω, ἐπύκτευσα, πεπύκτευκα, πεπύκτευμαι, ἐπυκτεύθην   box

τοσοῦτος, τοσαύτη, τοσοῦτο/τοσοῦτον   so much, so many; so large

τύπτω, τυπήσω, ——, ——, ——, —— strike, beat, hit

χράομαι, χρήσομαι, ἐχρησάμην, ——, κέχρημαι, ἐχρήσθην   use, experience, treat as (+ dat.) This verb contracts to -η- where τῑμάω contracts to -ᾱ-.

ὥσπερ (adv.)   just as

B. Isokrates, *To Demonikos* 13–16

The rhetorician Isokrates gives advice to Demonikos, the son of a friend.

Πρῶτον μὲν οὖν εὐσέβει τὰ πρὸς τοὺς θεούς, μὴ μόνον
θύων, ἀλλὰ καὶ τοῖς ὅρκοις ἐμμένων· ἐκεῖνο μὲν γὰρ
τῆς τῶν χρημάτων εὐπορίας σημεῖον, τοῦτο δὲ τῆς
τῶν τρόπων καλοκἀγαθίας τεκμήριον. τίμα τὸ
5   δαιμόνιον ἀεὶ μέν, μάλιστα δὲ μετὰ τῆς πόλεως·
οὕτω γὰρ δόξεις ἅμα τε τοῖς θεοῖς θύειν καὶ
τοῖς νόμοις ἐμμένειν.
Τοιοῦτος γίγνου περὶ τοὺς γονεῖς, οἵους ἂν
εὔξαιο περὶ σεαυτὸν γενέσθαι τοὺς σεαυτοῦ παῖδας.
10   Ἄσκει τῶν περὶ τὸ σῶμα γυμνασίων μὴ τὰ πρὸς τὴν
ῥώμην ἀλλὰ τὰ πρὸς τὴν ὑγίειαν· τούτου δ᾽ ἂν
ἐπιτύχοις, εἰ λήγοις τῶν πόνων ἔτι πονεῖν δυνάμενος.
Μήτε γέλωτα προπετῆ στέργε, μήτε λόγον μετὰ θράσους
ἀποδέχου· τὸ μὲν γὰρ ἀνόητον, τὸ δὲ μανικόν.
15   Ἃ ποιεῖν αἰσχρόν, ταῦτα νόμιζε μηδὲ λέγειν εἶναι
καλόν. ἔθιζε σεαυτὸν εἶναι μὴ σκυθρωπὸν ἀλλὰ
σύννουν· δι᾽ ἐκεῖνο μὲν γὰρ αὐθάδης, διὰ δὲ τοῦτο
φρόνιμος εἶναι δόξεις. ἡγοῦ μάλιστα σεαυτῷ πρέπειν
κόσμον αἰσχύνην δικαιοσύνην σωφροσύνην· τούτοις
20   γὰρ ἅπασι δοκεῖ κρατεῖσθαι τὸ τῶν νεωτέρων ἦθος.
Μηδέποτε μηδὲν αἰσχρὸν ποιήσας ἔλπιζε λήσειν· καὶ
γὰρ ἂν τοὺς ἄλλους λάθῃς, σεαυτῷ συνειδήσεις.

αἰσχύνη, αἰσχύνης, ἡ   shame, sense of shame, honor
ἄν = ἐάν
ἀνόητος, ἀνόητον   senseless, silly
ἀσκέω, ἀσκήσω, ἤσκησα, ἤσκηκα, ἤσκημαι, ἠσκήθην   work, practice
αὐθάδης, αὔθαδες   self-willed, stubborn, surly
γέλως, γέλωτος, ὁ   laughter
γονεύς, γονέως, ὁ   father; (*pl.*) parents
γυμνάσιον, γυμνασίου, τό   gymnasium; (*pl.*) physical exercises
δαιμόνιος, δαιμονίᾱ, δαιμόνιον   divine; marvelous, strange
δικαιοσύνη, δικαιοσύνης, ἡ   justice, righteousness
δοκέω, δόξω, ἔδοξα, ——, δέδογμαι, -ἐδόχθην   seem, think

δύναμαι, δυνήσομαι, ——, ——, δεδύνημαι, ἐδυνήθην be able (*sometimes with the past indicative augment ἠ- instead of ἐ-*)

ἐθίζω, ἐθιῶ, εἴθισα, εἴθικα, εἴθισμαι, εἰθίσθην accustom

ἐλπίζω, ἐλπιῶ, ἤλπισα, ἤλπικα, ἤλπισμαι, ἠλπίσθην hope, expect

ἐμμένω remain in; be true to (+ *dat.*)

ἐπιτυγχάνω hit the mark, reach (+ *gen.*)

εὐπορίᾱ, εὐπορίᾱς, ἡ ease; abundance

εὐσεβέω, εὐσεβήσω, ηὐσέβησα, ηὐσέβηκα, ηὐσέβημαι, ηὐσεβήθην reverence; be reverent

εὔχομαι, εὔξομαι, ηὐξάμην, ——, ηὖγμαι, —— pray

ἡγέομαι, ἡγήσομαι, ἡγησάμην, ——, ἥγημαι, ἡγήθην lead the way; be commander; rule (+ *gen.*); believe

ἦθος, ἤθους, τό custom; character

θράσος, θράσους, τό courage, boldness, rashness

καλοκᾱγαθίᾱ, καλοκᾱγαθίᾱς, ἡ character and conduct of a man who is καλός and ἀγαθός

κόσμος, κόσμου, ὁ order, good behavior

κρατέω, κρατήσω, ἐκράτησα, κεκράτηκα, κεκράτημαι, ἐκρατήθην rule (+ *gen.*)

λήγω, λήξω, ἔληξα, λέληχα, λέληγμαι, ἐλήχθην cease (+ *gen.*)

μάλιστα (*adv.*) most

μανικός, μανική, μανικόν mad

μηδείς, μηδεμία, μηδέν no one, nothing

μηδέποτε (*adv.*) never

ὅρκος, ὅρκου, ὁ oath

πονέω, πονήσω, ἐπόνησα, πεπόνηκα, πεπόνημαι, ἐπονήθην work hard; trouble

πόνος, πόνου, ὁ work, labor, exercise

πρέπει, πρέψει, ἔπρεψε(ν), ——, ——, —— (*impersonal verb*) it is fitting (+ *dat.* or *acc. and inf.*)

προπετής, προπετές falling down; rash, uncontrolled

ῥώμη, ῥώμης, ἡ strength

σημεῖον, σημείου, τό sign

σκυθρωπός, σκυθρωπόν sullen

στέργω, στέρξω, ἔστερξα, ἔστοργα, ἔστεργμαι, ἐστέρχθην love

σύννους, σύννουν thoughtful (*contracted from* σύννοος, σύννοον)

σύνοιδα, συνείσομαι/συνειδήσω, ——, ——, ——, —— be aware, know

τεκμήριον, τεκμηρίου, τό sure sign, proof

ὑγίεια, ὑγιείᾱς, ἡ health

φρόνιμος, φρόνιμον sensible, prudent

I. *Place the proper accentuation on the following phrases.*

1. γεφῦραι τινες
2. γεφῦρων τινων
3. γεφῦραις τισιν
4. μουσα τις
5. μουσῃ τινι
6. μουσων τινων

7. ταχυς τις
8. ταχεις τινες
9. ἀνθρωπος γε τις
10. ἀνθρωποι γε τινες
11. ἀνθρωποι γε που τινες
12. εἰ γε που τις ἀνθρωπος

II. A. *Give a synopsis of* αἱρέω *in the second person plural.*
   Give the neuter nominative singular of participles.

   B. *Translate indicatives, imperatives, and infinitives; identify subjunctives and optatives.*

1. ᾖ
2. ἴωσιν
3. ἰέναι
4. ἐστέ
5. εἶ
6. φᾶσίν
7. ἑλοῦ

8. θύσοιο
9. εἴησαν
10. φῶ
11. ἴμεν
12. φθῇ
13. ἔφασαν
14. ἴασιν

15. ᾔεισθα
16. ἵστασο
17. ἠπίστω
18. ἐλᾷ
19. δούλευσον
20. παίδευσαι
21. ἔθετε

   C. *Give the accusative plural in all three genders of all three degrees of the following adjectives:*

1. δῆλος
2. βαρύς
3. ἡδύς
4. ἄξιος
5. καλός

III. *Translate.*

1. παύσασθε, ὦ ψῡχὴν ἀμαθεῖς, τοῖς ὑμετέροις αὐτῶν φίλοις κακὰ
   λέγοντες. ἐὰν γὰρ γνῶσίν τινες ὑμᾶς ὡς αἴσχιστα πεπρᾱχότας,
   αὐτοὶ αἰσθήσεσθε κακοὶ ὄντες.

   (imperative; reflexive possession; supplementary participle with
   παύω; accusative of respect; future more vivid conditional sentence; indirect statement with γιγνώσκω + participle; superlative
   with ὡς; indirect statement with αἰσθάνομαι + participle)

2. ἆρ᾽ οὐδεὶς ἐφοβεῖτο μὴ οἱ ὁπλῖται, τὰ βαρύτερα ὅπλα λιπόντες,
   τὸν χρῡσόν μου τὸν πολὺν εἰς τὰς βαρείᾱς ναῦς εἰσενέγκωσιν;
   —— ἔγωγε, ὦ ἀμαθές.

   (circumstantial participle; retained subjunctive in a fear clause
   in secondary sequence; comparative; personal pronoun showing
   possession; emphatic personal pronoun)

3. ὁ Σωκράτης φησὶν ἓν δὴ εἶναι τό γε πολλῷ πάντων δικαιότατον,
   ὦ μαθητά, τὸ πάντας τὰ ἑαυτῶν πράττειν.

   (indirect statement with accusative and infinitive after φημί;
   dative of degree of difference; superlative; articular infinitive;
   reflexive possession)

4. τίνας ἐνόμιζες ἐκπεσεῖσθαι/ἐκπίπτειν/ἐκπεσεῖν ἐκ πόλεως, ὦ
   πάτερ; ὅσους γὰρ ἂν ἐκβάλωμεν, τοσοῦτοι ὅτι ἔχθιστοι ἡμῖν
   γ᾽ ἔσονται.

   (indirect statement with accusative and infinitive after νομίζω;
   interrogative pronoun; correlatives; superlative with ὅτι)

5. νῑκησάντων τῶν Λακεδαιμονίων, δέκα κήρῡκας ἀπεπέμψατε πρὸς
   τὸ τεῖχος ἀπαγγελοῦντας ὡς τῆς ἐλευθερίᾱς ἕνεκα τριῶν
   ἡμερῶν ἐκφευξοίμεθα ἐκ τῆς χώρᾱς.

   (genitive absolute; circumstantial participle showing purpose;
   indirect statement with finite verb after ἀπαγγέλλω, optative
   in secondary sequence; genitive of time within which)

6. ἀποπέμψατέ μοι τὸν ὑμέτερον αὐτῶν χρῡσόν. τοῦτον γὰρ ἑνὶ
   τῶν φυλάκων δούς, τὸν Σωκράτη ἐκλῡσαίμην ἄν, ἀλλ᾽ ἄνευ
   χρῡσοῦ οὐχ οἷός τ᾽ ἔσομαι οὐδὲν ἀγαθὸν ποιεῖν οὐδένα. οἷς γὰρ
   ἂν χρῡσὸς ᾖ, οὗτοι καλοί τε καὶ ἀγαθοὶ πολῖται γενήσονται.

   (imperative; personal pronoun; reflexive possession; partitive
   genitive; circumstantial participle serving as protasis of a future

less vivid conditional sentence; repeated negatives; double accusative; correlatives; dative of the possessor)

7. ὦ γέρον, ἔξελθε ἐκ τῆς οἰκίας τὴν αἶγα φέρων. οὐ γὰρ ἔστιν ἀποφυγεῖν. εἴθε μὴ ἔκλεψας αὐτήν.

(imperative; circumstantial participle; ἔστιν used impersonally; unattainable wish in past time)

8. τί ἐρωτᾷς με περὶ τοῦ νεανίου τοῦ Σωκράτει πεπαιδευμένου; οὐ δὴ ἤκουσάς ποτέ μου λέγοντος ὅτι ἐκεῖνος ὁ μαθητὴς ἦλθεν ἐκ τῆς Λακεδαιμονίων χώρας ὑπὸ Σωκράτους παιδευθησόμενος; οὗτος γὰρ πολὺ σοφώτερός ἐστιν ἐκείνων.

(adverbial accusative; dative of personal agent; attributive participle; indirect statement with finite verb after λέγω, with retained indicative in secondary sequence; genitive of personal agent; circumstantial participle indicating purpose; adverbial accusative; comparative; genitive of comparison)

IV. *Translate into Greek.*

Athenian men, since you perceive that good citizens have been banished from the city, stop men as foolish as possible from ruling us!

UNIT
18

136. THE VERB ἵημι, "release, hurl, send"

The verb ἵημι is athematic in the present and imperfect tenses, and in the second aorist active and middle. Except for the present and imperfect tenses, this verb usually appears in compounds.

ἵημι, -ήσω, -ῆκα, -εῖκα, -εῖμαι, -εῖθην, "release, hurl, send"

The present tense stem of this verb shows vowel gradation:

Long-vowel grade: ἱη-
Short-vowel grade: ἱε-

In the present and imperfect tenses ἵημι is conjugated almost exactly like τίθημι. Only a few forms of either verb are irregular. Irregular forms of ἵημι are printed entirely in boldface below.

The forms of ἵημι and τίθημι are set forth side by side in the Appendix, pp. 670–73, 677–80. In comparing the two verbs note carefully those few instances where they employ different endings.

1. PRESENT AND IMPERFECT ACTIVE

	PRESENT IND. ACTIVE	IMPERF. IND. ACTIVE	PRESENT SUBJ. ACTIVE	PRESENT OPT. ACTIVE	PRESENT IMPER. ACTIVE
S 1	ἵημι	ἵην	ἱῶ	ἱείην	
2	ἵης/ἱεῖς	ἵεις	ἱῆς	ἱείης	ἵει
3	ἵησι(ν)	ἵει	ἱῇ	ἱείη	ἱέτω
P 1	ἵεμεν	ἵεμεν	ἱῶμεν	ἱεῖμεν	
2	ἵετε	ἵετε	ἱῆτε	ἱεῖτε	ἵετε
3	ἱᾶσι(ν)	ἵεσαν	ἱῶσι(ν)	ἱεῖεν	ἱέντων

519

ALTERNATIVE PRESENT OPTATIVE ACTIVE:

P 1   ἱείημεν

 2   ἱείητε

 3   ἱείησαν

PRESENT INFINITIVE ACTIVE: ἱέναι

PRESENT PARTICIPLE ACTIVE:

	M	F	N
Nom. S	ἱείς	ἱεῖσα	ἱέν
Gen.	ἱέντος	ἱείσης	ἱέντος

Observations: (1) The second person singular, present indicative active has an alternate thematic form derived from *ἱέεις.

(2) In the third person plural, present indicative active the ending -ᾶσι(ν) contracts with the stem. Contrast ἱᾶσι(ν), τιθέᾶσι(ν).

(3) The second and third person singular, imperfect indicative active, are thematic and derive from *ἵεες, *ἵεε. Cf. ἐτίθεις, ἐτίθει.

(4) Since the initial vowel of the present tense stem is long, the addition of the past indicative augment does not change the stem, and the present and imperfect indicative active are identical in the first and second person plural.

(5) The second person singular, present imperative active is thematic and derives from *ἵεε. Cf. τίθει < *τίθεε, δίδου < *δίδοε.

(6) The second person plural, present imperative active is identical with the second person plural, present and imperfect indicative active.

(7) The third person plural, present imperative active is identical with the masculine and neuter genitive plural of the present participle active. Context will help to determine meaning.

(8) Distinguish the present infinitive active ἱέναι from the present infinitive active of εἶμι: ἰέναι.

2. PRESENT AND IMPERFECT MIDDLE/PASSIVE

	PRESENT IND. MIDDLE/ PASSIVE	IMPERF. IND. MIDDLE/ PASSIVE	PRESENT SUBJ. MIDDLE/ PASSIVE	PRESENT OPT. MIDDLE/ PASSIVE	PRESENT IMPER. MIDDLE/ PASSIVE
S 1	ἵεμαι	ἱέμην	ἱῶμαι	ἱείμην	
2	ἵεσαι	ἵεσο	ἱῇ	ἱεῖο	ἵεσο
3	ἵεται	ἵετο	ἱῆται	ἱεῖτο	ἱέσθω
P 1	ἱέμεθα	ἱέμεθα	ἱώμεθα	ἱείμεθα	
2	ἵεσθε	ἵεσθε	ἱῆσθε	ἱεῖσθε	ἵεσθε
3	ἵενται	ἵεντο	ἱῶνται	ἱεῖντο	ἱέσθων

PRESENT INFINITIVE MIDDLE/PASSIVE: ἵεσθαι

PRESENT PARTICIPLE MIDDLE/PASSIVE:

	M	F	N
Nom. S	ἱέμενος	ἱεμένη	ἱέμενον

Observation: Since the addition of the past indicative augment does not change the initial long vowel of the present tense stem, the present and imperfect indicative middle/passive are identical in the first and second person plural. In the second person plural, the present imperative middle/passive is also identical to these forms. Context will help to determine meaning.

3. AORIST ACTIVE

The verb ἵημι, like the verbs δίδωμι and τίθημι, has a *mixed aorist* which employs the first aorist tense stem ἡκ- and the athematic second aorist tense stem ἑ- (augmented form εἱ- from *ἐἑ-).

Compare closely the aorist active and middle of τίθημι (first aorist stem θηκ-, second aorist stem θε-) and that of δίδωμι (first aorist stem δωκ-, second aorist stem δο-). *Only these three verbs have mixed aorists.*

The aorist forms of ἵημι are normally found only in compounds.

	AORIST IND. ACTIVE	AORIST SUBJ. ACTIVE	AORIST OPTATIVE ACTIVE	AORIST IMPERATIVE ACTIVE
S 1	-ἧκα	-ὧ	-εἵην	
2	-ἧκας	-ἧς	-εἵης	-ἕς
3	-ἧκε(ν)	-ἧ	-εἵη	-ἕτω
P 1	-εἷμεν	-ὧμεν	-εἷμεν/-εἵημεν	
2	-εἷτε	-ἧτε	-εἷτε/-εἵητε	-ἕτε
3	-εἷσαν	-ὧσι(ν)	-εἷεν/-εἵησαν	-ἕντων

AORIST INFINITIVE ACTIVE: -εἷναι

AORIST PARTICIPLE ACTIVE:

	M	F	N
Nom. S	-εἵς	-εἷσα	-ἕν
Gen.	-ἕντος	-εἵσης	-ἕντος

Observations: (1) In the aorist subjunctive active the vowel of the stem contracts with the endings: e.g., *-ἕω > -ὧ.

(2) The rough breathing of the aorist subjunctive and optative active distinguishes them from the present subjunctive and optative active of εἰμί: ὦ, εἴην.

(3) The rough breathing distinguishes the aorist infinitive active -εἷναι from the present infinitive active of εἰμί: εἷναι.

(4) The third person plural, aorist imperative active is identical with the masculine and neuter genitive plural of the aorist participle active. Context will determine meaning.

(5) In the first and second person plural, the shorter forms of the aorist optative active are identical with those of the aorist indicative active.

4. AORIST MIDDLE

		AORIST IND. MIDDLE	AORIST SUBJ. MIDDLE	AORIST OPTATIVE MIDDLE	AORIST IMPERATIVE MIDDLE
S	1	-είμην	-ῶμαι	-είμην	
	2	-εῖσο	-ῇ	-εῖο	-οῦ (*ἕο)
	3	-εῖτο	-ῆται	-εῖτο/-οῖτο	-ἔσθω
P	1	-είμεθα	-ώμεθα	-είμεθα/-οίμεθα	
	2	-εῖσθε	-ῆσθε	-εῖσθε/-οῖσθε	-ἔσθε
	3	-εῖντο	-ῶνται	-εῖντο/-οῖντο	-ἔσθων

AORIST INFINITIVE MIDDLE: -ἔσθαι

AORIST PARTICIPLE MIDDLE:

	M	F	N
Nom. S	-ἔμενος	-ἐμένη	-ἔμενον

Observations: (1) In the second person singular the aorist indicative middle uses the ending -σο instead of the ending -ο. Contrast -εῖσο with ἔθου, ἔδου.

(2) The aorist indicative middle, aorist optative middle (except for the second person singular), and pluperfect indicative middle/passive are all identical in form.

(3) The alternative thematic forms of the optative are exactly like the equivalent forms of τίθημι. The stem ἑ- contracts with the endings.

(4) The second person singular, aorist imperative middle -οῦ retains its circumflex accent when compounded with a monosyllabic prefix (see the Appendix, p. 609): ἀφοῦ.

(5) Remember that ALL infinitives have fixed, non-recessive accents which are retained in compounds:

      ἀφεῖναι   ἀφέσθαι

137. INDEFINITE RELATIVE PRONOUN
INDIRECT INTERROGATIVE PRONOUN/ADJECTIVE

The **indefinite relative pronoun** ὅστις, ἥτις, ὅτι, "whoever, whatever,"
serves also as the **indirect interrogative pronoun/adjective**, with the
meaning "who, what." An indirect interrogative introduces an **indirect
question**. For indirect questions see Section 140.

This pronoun/adjective is formed by combining into one word the relative
pronoun ὅς, ἥ, ὅ and the indefinite pronoun/adjective τις, τι, *while declining
each word separately.*

There are several alternative masculine and neuter forms.

	M	F	N
Nom. S	ὅστις	ἥτις	ὅτι
Gen.	οὗτινος/ὅτου	ἧστινος	οὗτινος/ὅτου
Dat.	ᾧτινι/ὅτῳ	ᾗτινι	ᾧτινι/ὅτῳ
Acc.	ὅντινα	ἥντινα	ὅτι
Nom. P	οἵτινες	αἵτινες	ἅτινα/ἅττα
Gen.	ὧντινων/ὅτων	ὧντινων	ὧντινων/ὅτων
Dat.	οἷστισι(ν)/ ὅτοις	αἷστισι(ν)	οἷστισι(ν)/ ὅτοις
Acc.	οὕστινας	ἅστινας	ἅτινα/ἅττα

Observations: (1) The accent of the compound forms follows the rules for
enclitics.

(2) The neuter nominative and accusative singular must be
distinguished from the conjunction ὅτι.

The following sentences will illustrate the use of the indefinite relative pronoun:

ὅστις κακὰ ποιεῖ, κακὰ πείσεται.
Whoever does evil things, will suffer evil things.

ὅστις ἂν κακὰ ποιῇ, κακὰ πείσεται.
Whoever does evil things, will suffer evil things.

ὅστις ἂν κακὸς ᾖ, κακὰ ποιεῖ.
Whoever is evil, does evil things.

The indefinite relative pronoun adds an extra generalizing force even to a
present (or past) general conditional sentence, as in the third example above.

138. INDEFINITE RELATIVES AND DIRECT AND INDIRECT
INTERROGATIVES

Corresponding to the indefinite relative/indirect interrogative ὅστις, ἥτις, ὅτι
are several adjectives which serve the same two functions. These are listed in
the right-hand column below. Direct interrogative forms are listed in the left-
hand column.

When used as *indefinite relative* pronouns or adjectives, these words have a
meaning which includes the element "-**ever**": e.g., "who**ever**," "which**ever**."
When used as *indirect interrogative* pronouns or adjectives, these words have the
same meaning as the direct interrogative but are used to introduce indirect
questions.

DIRECT INTERROGATIVE	*INDEFINITE RELATIVE/ INDIRECT INTERROGATIVE*
τίς, τί	ὅστις, ἥτις, ὅτι
who?, what?	whoever, whatever
	who?, what?
ποῖος, ποία, ποῖον	ὁποῖος, ὁποία, ὁποῖον
of what sort?	of whatever sort
	of what sort?
πόσος, πόση, πόσον	ὁπόσος, ὁπόση, ὁπόσον
how much/many?	however much/many
	how much/many?
πότερος, ποτέρᾱ, πότερον	ὁπότερος, ὁποτέρᾱ, ὁπότερον
which (of two)?	whichever (of two)
	which (of two)?

*Compare the chart of correlative pronouns, adjectives, and adverbs included in the
Vocabulary, pages 530–31.*

139. INDEFINITE, RELATIVE, AND INTERROGATIVE ADVERBS

Many adverbs have three forms: direct interrogative, indefinite (enclitic),
and indefinite relative/indirect interrogative.

DIRECT INTERROGATIVE	INDEFINITE (enclitic)	INDEFINITE RELATIVE INDIRECT INTERROGATIVE
πόθεν from where?, whence?	ποθέν from somewhere	ὁπόθεν from wherever from where?, whence?
ποῖ to where?, whither?	ποι to some place	ὅποι to wherever to where?, whither?
πότε when?	ποτέ at some time, ever	ὁπότε whenever when?
ποῦ where?	που somewhere	ὅπου wherever where?
πῶς how?	πως somehow	ὅπως however how?

Observation: The indefinite relative/indirect interrogative ὅπως must be distinguished from the conjunction ὅπως which introduces purpose clauses and object clauses of effort.

Compare the chart of correlative pronouns, adjectives, and adverbs included in the Vocabulary, pages 530–31.

140. INDIRECT QUESTION

A question, like a statement, can be quoted either directly or indirectly. Direct quotation preserves the speaker's original words, which in English are set off by quotation marks. But indirect quotation, or **indirect question**, incorporates the original words into a complex sentence.

> He asks, "What are they doing?"   (direct quotation)
> He asks **what they are doing.**   (**indirect question**)

The main verb which introduces an indirect question can be not only a verb of asking, but also a verb of knowing, learning, perceiving, etc. (e.g., "I learned what they were doing.").

While there are three different ways of expressing indirect statement, THERE IS ONLY ONE WAY OF EXPRESSING INDIRECT QUESTION: FINITE VERB INTRODUCED BY AN INDIRECT INTERROGATIVE WORD.

The rules for indirect question are the same as those for indirect statement with a finite verb introduced by ὅτι or ὡς:

> When the introductory verb is in a primary tense, all verbs in the indirect question retain their original mood and tense.

> When the introductory verb is in a secondary tense, all indicative verbs of the original question
> > EITHER are changed to the corresponding tense of the optative
> > OR remain unchanged (*retained indicative*).

In addition, all direct interrogative words of the original question are usually changed to the corresponding *indirect interrogative* words (cf. Sections 138, 139).

The particle ἆρα remains unchanged.

If the original question has no interrogative word, the indirect question is introduced by the particle εἰ, "whether, if."

If a question includes two alternatives, these are introduced in an indirect question by the following introductory words, each pair of which means "whether . . . or":

> πότερον . . . ἤ
> εἴτε . . . εἴτε
> εἰ . . . εἴτε

The negative of the original question is preserved in an indirect question.

Here are examples of direct and indirect questions:

τίς εἶ; Who are you?	(original question)
ἐρωτᾷ ὅστις εἶ. He asks who you are.	(indirect question)
πότερος τοῦτ᾽ ἐποίησεν; Which one did this?	(original question)
ἠρωτήσαμεν ὁπότερος τοῦτο ποιήσειεν. We asked which one did this.	(indirect question)
Εὐρῑπίδης σοφός ἐστιν; Is Euripides wise?	(original question)
ἐρωτήσετ᾽ εἰ Εὐρῑπίδης σοφός ἐστιν. You will ask whether (if) Euripides is wise.	(indirect question)

ὦ βασιλεῦ, πότερον βούλει μένειν ἢ ἀπιέναι;   (original question)
King, do you wish to stay or go away?

ἠρώτᾱ τὸν βασιλέᾱ πότερον βούλοιτο   (indirect question)
    μένειν ἢ ἀπιέναι.
ἠρώτᾱ τὸν βασιλέᾱ εἴτε βούλοιτο
    μένειν εἴτε ἀπιέναι.
ἠρώτᾱ τὸν βασιλέᾱ εἰ βούλοιτο
    μένειν εἴτε ἀπιέναι.
She was asking the king whether he wanted
    to stay or go away.

πόσους ἀγγέλους πέμπεις;   (original question)
How many messengers are you sending?

ἠρώτησα ὁπόσους ἀγγέλους πέμπεις.   (indirect question with
I asked how many messengers you were sending.   *retained indicative*)

The interrogative word of the original statement is sometimes retained:

τίνες εἰσίν;   (original question)
Who are they?

ἠρώτων αὐτοὺς τίνες εἶεν.   (indirect question)
I was asking them who they were.

VOCABULARY

ἀποθνήσκω, ἀποθανοῦμαι, ἀπέθανον,   die
    τέθνηκα, ——, ——

ἀποκτείνω, ἀποκτενῶ, ἀπέκτεινα,   kill
    ἀπέκτονα, ——, ——

αὖ (postpositive particle)   again, further, in turn

βουλεύω, βουλεύσω, ἐβούλευσα,   deliberate on, plan;
    βεβούλευκα, βεβούλευμαι,   (mid.) take counsel with
    ἐβουλεύθην   oneself, deliberate
        ἐπιβουλεύω   plot against (+ dat.)
        συμβουλεύω   advise, counsel (+ dat.);
                                                         (mid.) consult with (+ dat.)

εἰ (indirect interrogative)   whether, if

εἴτε . . . εἴτε (indirect interrogatives)   whether . . . or, if . . . or

ζητέω, ζητήσω, ἐζήτησα, ἐζήτηκα,   seek
    ——, ἐζητήθην

ἵημι, -ἥσω, -ἧκα, -εἷκα, -εἷμαι, -εἵθην   release, hurl, send
    ἀφίημι, ἀφήσω, ἀφῆκα, ἀφεῖκα,   send forth, send away;
        ἀφεῖμαι, ἀφείθην   let go, neglect
    συνίημι, συνήσω, συνῆκα, συνεῖκα,   understand, comprehend
        συνεῖμαι, συνείθην

μέλλω, μελλήσω, ἐμέλλησα,   be about to, be likely to
        ——, ——, ——   (+ future infin.); delay

ὀξύς, ὀξεῖα, ὀξύ   sharp, keen

ὅστις, ἥτις, ὅτι (indefinite relative)   whoever, whatever
        (indirect interrogative)   who?, what?

πιστεύω, πιστεύσω, ἐπίστευσα,   trust (+ dat.)
    πεπίστευκα, πεπίστευμαι, ἐπιστεύθην

τράπεζα, τραπέζης, ἡ   table, money-changer's table,
                                                         bank

ψεῦδος, ψεύδους, τό   falsehood, lie
    ψευδής, ψευδές   false, lying

*Learn also the chart of correlative pronouns, adjectives, and adverbs on the
following pages.*

CORRELATIVE PRONOUNS, ADJECTIVES, AND ADVERBS

DIRECT INTERROGATIVE	INDEFINITE (enclitic)	INDEFINITE RELATIVE/ INDIRECT INTERROGATIVE	DEMONSTRATIVE	RELATIVE/ EXCLAMATORY
τίς, τί who?, which?, what?	τις, τι some(one), some(thing)	ὅστις, ἥτις, ὅτι whoever, whatever who?, what?	οὗτος, αὕτη, τοῦτο this, that ἐκεῖνος, ἐκείνη, ἐκεῖνο that ὅδε, ἥδε, τόδε this	ὅς, ἥ, ὅ who, which
ποῖος, ποίᾱ, ποῖον of what kind?		ὁποῖος, ὁποίᾱ, ὁποῖον of whatever kind of what kind?	τοιοῦτος, τοιαύτη, τοιοῦτο/τοιοῦτον of this/that sort, such (as this)	οἷος, οἵᾱ, οἷον such as, of the sort which what sort of!
πόσος, πόση, πόσον how much/many/ large?		ὁπόσος, ὁπόση, ὁπόσον however much/many/large how much/many/large?	τοσοῦτος, τοσαύτη, τοσοῦτο/τοσοῦτον so much/many/large	ὅσος, ὅση, ὅσον as much/many/ large as how much/many/ large!

πότερος, ποτέρᾱ, πότερον — which (of two)?		ὁπότερος, ὁποτέρᾱ, ὁπότερον — whichever (of two) which (of two)?	ἕτερος, ἑτέρᾱ, ἕτερον — the other (of two)
πόθεν — from where? whence?	ποθέν — from somewhere	ὁπόθεν — from wherever from where?	
ποῖ — (to) where? whither?	ποι — (to) some place	ὅποι — (to) wherever (to) where?	
πότε — when?	ποτέ — at some time, ever	ὁπότε — whenever when?	τότε — then / ὅτε — when
ποῦ — where?	που — somewhere; I suppose	ὅπου — wherever where?	ἐνταῦθα — here, there, then / ἐκεῖ — there
πῶς — how?	πως — in some way, in any way	ὅπως — however how?	οὕτω(ς) — in this way, so, thus / ὡς — as; how!

VOCABULARY NOTES

The verb ἀποθνήσκω, ἀποθανοῦμαι, ἀπέθανον, τέθνηκα, ——, ——, "die," has a contracted deponent future and a second aorist. The perfect tense is not compounded with ἀπο-. Note that Principal Part I shows the inchoative suffix -σκω and that Principal Part IV lacks the iota subscript beneath the eta. In the perfect indicative active the plural has, in addition to the regular forms, the alternative forms τέθναμεν, τέθνατε, τεθνᾶσι(ν). The pluperfect has the alternative third person plural ἐτέθνασαν. The perfect infinitive active is τεθνηκέναι or τεθνάναι. The perfect participle active is either τεθνηκώς, τεθνηκυῖα, τεθνηκός or τεθνεώς, τεθνεῶσα, τεθνεός (gen. τεθνεῶτος, τεθνεώσης, τεθνεῶτος); cf., from ἵστημι, ἑστώς, ἑστῶσα, ἑστός.

In the verb ἀποκτείνω, ἀποκτενῶ, ἀπέκτεινα, ἀπέκτονα, ——, ——, "kill," Principal Part I derives from *ἀποκτένιω and Principal Part III from *ἀπέκτενσα. Note the contracted future, and the o-grade of the root in the perfect (where the epsilon is part of the tense stem). The passive of this verb is supplied by ἀποθνήσκω:

> αὐτὸν ἀπεκτείναμεν.
> We killed him.

> ὑφ' ἡμῶν ἀπέθανεν.
> He died at our hands.
> He was killed by us.

Do not confuse the verb βουλεύω, βουλεύσω, ἐβούλευσα, βεβούλευκα, βεβούλευμαι, ἐβουλεύθην, "deliberate on, plan; (mid.) take counsel with oneself, deliberate," with the verb βούλομαι.

Note that in the verb ζητέω, ζητήσω, ἐζήτησα, ἐζήτηκα, ——, ἐζητήθην, "seek," the epsilon with which Principal Part IV begins is part of the tense stem. This verb can govern a direct object indicating the person or thing after which one is seeking, an indirect question indicating the problem which one is investigating, or an object infinitive of the thing which one is seeking to do.

The verb ἵημι, -ήσω, -ῆκα, -εῖκα, -εῖμαι, -εῖθην, "release, hurl, send," is conjugated almost exactly like τίθημι, with which it should be closely compared. This will most easily be done by consulting pp. 670–73 and 677–80 of the Appendix, where the forms of these two verbs are listed side by side. (Dual forms, which appear between the singular and plural forms in the Appendix, should be ignored.)

Compare the following stems of these verbs:

present tense stem (long-vowel grade)	τιθη-	ἱη-
(*short-vowel grade*)	τιθε-	ἱε-

first aorist active and middle
   tense stem   θηκ-   ἡκ-
second aorist active and middle
   tense stem   θε-   ἑ-

The unaugmented aorist passive tense stem is ἑθ-.

The verb ἵημι usually appears in compounds, two of which are ἀφίημι, "send forth, send away; let go, neglect," and συνίημι, "understand, comprehend."

The verb μέλλω, μελλήσω, ἐμέλλησα, ——, ——, ——, when it means "be about to, be likely to," governs a future (sometimes a present) infinitive; used by itself, or with a present infinitive, it can mean "delay."

> νῦν γε μέλλομεν νῑκήσειν.
> Now, at least, we are about to (are likely to) win.

> τί ἀεὶ ἔμελλεν οὗτος;
> Why did this man always delay?

The adjective ὀξύς, ὀξεῖα, ὀξύ, "sharp, keen," can refer to pointed objects, things perceived, or one's own senses.

The noun τράπεζα, τραπέζης, ἡ, "table; money-changer's table, bank," means literally something "four-footed": *τρά-πεδια.

Distinguish the noun ψεῦδος, ψεύδους, τό, "falsehood, lie," from the adjective ψευδής, ψευδές, "false, lying."

Distinguish carefully the various meanings of ὡς encountered thus far:

correlative conjunction: "as"
> ἀθάνατός ἐστιν ἡ ψῡχή, ὡς λέγει ὁ ποιητής.
> The soul is immortal, as the poet says.

exclamatory adverb: "how!"
> ὡς ἄφρονες οἱ ῥήτορές εἰσιν.
> How foolish the public speakers are!

introducing purpose clauses: "in order that"
with causal or purpose participle: cause or purpose not vouched for by speaker

introducing indirect statement with finite verb: "that"

with superlative adjective or adverb: "as . . . as possible"

COGNATES AND DERIVATIVES

ἵημι	catheter, enema
ὀξύς	oxymoron ("**sharp**–dull"); oxygen (generated from an **acid**)
τράπεζα	trapeze
ψεῦδος	pseudonym

DRILLS

I. *Translate.*

1. τοῖς γε συνιεῖσι δῆλον τοῦτο.
2. ἐὰν μὴ συνιῇς ἃ λέγω, παῦσόν με λέγοντα.
3. εἰ τὰ λεγόμενα μὴ συνῆκεν, οὐκ ἂν πάντ' ἔμαθεν.
4. χαλεπὸν δὴ τὸ συνεῖναι ἃ ἂν εἴπῃς.
5. ταῦτα μὴ συνιέντες, πῶς ἂν ἄλλα μάθοιμεν;
6. νῦν δὴ ἔγωγε συνεῖκα ἃ λέγεις, ὦ διδάσκαλε.
7. οὐ συνέντων τῶν μαθητῶν τοὺς λόγους, ἀπέφυγεν ὁ διδάσκαλος.
8. εἴθε συνιείην τάδε τὰ γράμματα.
9. εἴθε συνίην τάδε τὰ γράμματα.
10. εἴθε συνῆκα τάδε τὰ γράμματα πρὸ τῆς μάχης.
11. πάντες οἱ πεπαιδευμένοι συνιέντων τάδε τὰ σαφέστατα.
12. ὦ παῖ, ἐάν τί σοι εἴπω, τοῦτό γε σύνες.
13. εἰ ταῦτα μὴ μάθοιτε, οὐκ ἂν συνεῖτε οὐδέν.
14. νῦν ἀφίεμεν τοὺς ἀδίκους.
15. τότε ἀφίεμεν τοὺς ἀδίκους.
16. μὴ ἀφίετε τούτους τοὺς ἀδικωτέρους ἐκείνων.
17. μὴ ἀφῆτε τούτους τοὺς ἐχθίους.
18. οὗτοι μὴ ἀφιέσθων ὑφ' ὑμῶν.
19. οὗτοι μὴ ἀφεθῶσιν ὑφ' ὑμῶν.
20. μετὰ τὴν μάχην ἐκεῖνοι ἀφείθησαν.
21. ἀφεθήσεσθε ὑπὸ τῶν φυλάκων τῶν σωφρονεστάτων.
22. μὴ ἀφῶμεν τοὺς ἡμᾶς ἠδικηκότας.
23. ἀφιέμενοι ὑπὸ τῶν στρατιωτῶν, ἔφευγον οἱ γέροντες.
24. πρὸς τῶν θεῶν, τοῦτόν γε ἄφετε.
25. ἀεὶ συνείημεν τὰ ὑπ' ἀγαθῶν λεγόμενα.
26. ἀεὶ συνείημεν τοῖς ἀγαθοῖς.

II. *Translate.*

1. ποῦ ἐστε;
2. ἐρωτᾷ ὅπου ἐστέ.
3. ἠρώτᾱ ὅπου εἶτε.
4. πόθεν ἥκετε;
5. ἐρωτῶμεν ὁπόθεν ἥκετε.
6. ἠρωτῶμεν ὁπόθεν ἥκοιτε.
7. πῶς ταῦτ' ἐποίησαν;
8. ἐρωτήσετε ὅπως ταῦτ' ἐποίησαν.
9. ἠρωτήσατε ὅπως ταῦτα ποιήσειαν.
10. πότε τοῦτο ποιήσεις;
11. ἐρωτῶσιν ὁπότε τοῦτο ποιήσεις.
12. ἠρώτων ὁπότε τοῦτο ποιήσοις.
13. ἠρώτων ὁπότε τοῦτο ποιήσεις.
14. πότερον τοῦτο ἢ ἐκεῖνο ποιεῖς;
15. ἐρωτῶ πότερον τοῦτο ἢ ἐκεῖνο ποιεῖς.
16. ἠρώτησα πότερον τοῦτο ἢ ἐκεῖνο ποιοίης.
17. τίνες εἰσίν;
18. ἐρωτᾷς οἵτινές εἰσιν.
19. ἠρώτησας οἵτινες εἶεν.
20. ἠρώτησας τίνες εἶεν.
21. τίνος ἐστὶ τὸ βιβλίον;
22. δεικνύᾱσιν οὗτινος τὸ βιβλίον ἐστίν.
23. ἔμαθον οὗτινος τὸ βιβλίον εἴη.
24. τίνι τὸ βιβλίον ἐστίν;
25. μαθήσεσθε ὅτῳ τὸ βιβλίον ἐστίν.
26. ἐμάθετε ᾧτινι τὸ βιβλίον ἐστίν.
27. τί ποιεῖ;
28. ἐρωτᾷ τὸν Σωκράτη ὅτι ποιεῖ.
29. ἠρώτᾱ τὸν Σωκράτη ὅτι ποιοίη.
30. ὅστις τοῦτο ποιεῖ, πονηρός ἐστιν.
31. ὅστις ἂν τοῦτο ποιῇ, πονηρός ἐστιν.
32. ὃς ἂν τοῦτο ποιῇ, πονηρός ἐστιν.

33. ὅποι ἂν ἴητε, εὖ πράξετε.

34. ὅπου ἂν ὦμεν, εὐδαίμονες ἀεὶ ἐσόμεθα.

35. ὅπως ἂν βούλωμαι, οὕτως ἔγωγε ποιῶ.

36. μάθωμεν ὅπου ὁ χρῦσός ἐστιν.

37. ἠρώτᾱς εἰ Σωκράτης σοφώτερος εἴη τοῦ Εὐρῑπίδου, ὦ ἄδελφε;

38. εὐδαιμονέστατος ἐκεῖνος ᾧτινι ἥδε ἡ οἰκίᾱ ἐστίν.

39. μὴ ἐρωτήσῃς ὅτι ἐστὶ τὸ δίκαιον.

40. ᾧτινι ἂν ᾖ βιβλία, οὗτος τῇ ἀληθείᾳ πολλῷ εὐτυχέστερος ἐμοῦ.

EXERCISES

I. 1. τίνας ἀπέκτεινας, ὦ ἀφρονεστάτη θύγατερ;

2. ἠρώτᾱ τὴν μῑκροτέρᾱν θυγατέρα οὕστινας ἀποκτείναι.

3. ἐρώτᾱ τὴν θυγατέρα οὕστινας ἀποκτενεῖ.

4. ποῖοι ἀδικώτεροι τῇ δημοκρατίᾳ ἐπιβουλεύσουσιν;

5. οὐκ ἐδύναντο οὐδενὶ τρόπῳ μαθεῖν ὁποῖοι τῇ δημοκρατίᾳ ἐπιβουλεύσοιεν.

6. ἤγγειλαν τὸν Σωκράτη μέλλοντα τριῶν ἡμερῶν ἀποθανεῖσθαι.

7. (a) τὸν Σωκράτη φατὲ ἀποθανεῖν.

    (b) τὸν Σωκράτη φάτε ἀποθανεῖν.

8. (a) ἀκούσεσθε τὸν Σωκράτη τεθνηκότα.

    (b) ἀκούσεσθε τοῦ Σωκράτους ἀποθνῄσκοντος.

9. (a) ἐρωτῶμεν ὁπόσους ἀφίετε.

    (b) ἠρωτῶμεν ὁπόσους ἀφῑεῖτε.

    (c) ἐρωτῶμεν ὁπόσους ἀφεῖτε.

    (d) ἠρωτῶμεν ὁπόσους ἀφεῖτε.

10. ἄφες τόν γε Δημοσθένη, ὦ πονηρέ.

11. ἀφῑέντων τὸν τότε τῷ δήμῳ ἐπιβουλεύσαντα καίπερ ἐχθίω ὄντα.

12. σχὲς τῇ χειρὶ τὸ ὀξύτερον ξίφος.

13. ὁποῖοί γ᾽ ἂν ὦμεν οἱ πολῖται, τοιαύτη ἐστὶν ἡ ἡμετέρᾱ πόλις.

14. (a) ἐνταῦθα στήτω ἵνα μάχηται.

    (b) ἐνταῦθ᾽ ἀνάστησον τὸ τρόπαιον.

15. δίδοτε τάδε τὰ βαρέα ὅπλα τρισὶ τῶν ὁπλῑτῶν.

16. (a) παῦσον τοῦτον τῷ δήμῳ ἐπιβουλεύοντα.

(b) παῦσον τοῦτον τὸν τῷ δήμῳ ἐπιβουλεύοντα.

(c) παῦσαι τῷ δήμῳ ἐπιβουλεύων.

17. χαίρομέν πως οἶνον ὡς ἥδιστον ἐπιτιθεῖσαι ἐπὶ ταῖς τῶν θεῶν τραπέζαις.

18. οὐ δύνασαι συνῑέναι, ὦ ἄνερ, οὔτε τὰ ἀληθῶς καὶ σαφῶς λεγόμενα οὔτε
    τὰ ψευδῆ.

19. ἔλθετε εἰς τὴν βουλὴν περὶ πολέμου βουλευσόμενοι.

20. ἴωμεν δὴ καὶ μὴ μέλλωμεν ἔτι, ἵνα μὴ ἀφῶμεν τὸν καιρόν.

21. ἤκουόν τοι μίαν τράπεζαν ἐν ἐκείνῃ τῇ ἑορτῇ ἱερὰν οὖσαν Διός.

22. ἠρωτᾶτε ὅντινα τρόπον ἀφεθεῖμεν.

23. ὅπως ἂν σὺ βούλῃ, οὕτως ἔγωγε πράττω.

24. τὴν γνώμην ὀξύτεροι τῶν ἄλλων ἐδόκουν εἶναι οἵτινες ἐν καιρῷ
    συμβουλεύοιεν τῷ δήμῳ περὶ τῶν μελλόντων.

25. ἴθι ὅποι ἂν βούλῃ.

26. τῶν τῆς πόλεως εὖ ἐχόντων, παυσάσθων λέγοντες οἱ ῥήτορες.

27. ὅπου ἂν ὦμεν, ἐκεῖ μενοῦμεν.

28. (a) εἰ γὰρ εὐδαίμονες εἶμεν.

    (b) εἰ γὰρ εὐδαίμονες ἦμεν.

    (c) εἴθε νῑκῷμεν.

    (d) εἴθ' ἐνῑκῷμεν.

    (e) εἴθ' ἐνῑκήσαμεν.

29. ἆρα ζητῶμέν πως πότερον ἀγαθὸν ἡ δημοκρατίᾱ ἢ οὔ;

30. ἠρωτήσαμεν εἰ τὴν δημοκρατίᾱν καταλῦσαι οὐ βούλοιο.

31. ἠρώτων εἴτε ψευδῆ λέγεις εἴτε τὰ ἀληθῆ.

32. ψεῦδος μὴ εἴπῃ μηδείς, ἀλλὰ πάντα ὀρθῶς λεγέτω ἕκαστος.

II. 1. You asked Demosthenes whether, since the enemy were about to flee,
        he wished to send three swift ships to the island.

     2. Are we to kill *all* those who plotted against the people?

     3. Let him not say to those who consult with him that he does not
        trust the two generals.

     4. His students heard Sokrates saying, on the day he died, that his soul,
        since it was just (*use participle*), would never suffer any evil.

     5. Whenever you ransom the priests, you will receive all the honors of
        which you think yourself worthy.

READINGS

A. Aristophanes, *Knights* 150–181

So bad has the leadership of Athens become that in Aristophanes' *reductio ad absurdum* Demosthenes and Nikias, two servants of Demos (= the people of Athens), have just found out through an oracle that the city can be saved only when it is led by a sausage-seller. Needless to say, a sausage-seller opportunely happens along.

150 *ΑΛΛΑΝΤΟΠΩΛΗΣ.* τί ἔστι; τί με καλεῖτε;

    ΔΗΜΟΣΘΕΝΗΣ. δεῦρ' ἔλθ',[1] ἵνα πύθῃ

151 ὡς εὐτυχὴς εἶ καὶ μεγάλως εὐδαιμονεῖς.

    ΝΙΚΙΑΣ. ἴθι δὴ κάθελ' αὐτοῦ τοὐλεὸν καὶ τοῦ θεοῦ

    τὸν χρησμὸν ἀναδίδαξον αὐτὸν ὡς[2] ἔχει·

ἀλλᾶντοπώλης, ἀλλᾶντοπώλου, ὁ   sausage-seller

δεῦρο (*adv.*)   here, hither

Δημοσθένης, Δημοσθένους, ὁ   Demosthenes, a servant of Demos
    (The name is that of a contemporary general.)

ἐλεόν, ἐλεοῦ, τό   table, kitchen-table

εὐδαιμονέω, εὐδαιμονήσω, εὐδαιμόνησα, εὐδαιμόνηκα, ——, ——   be prosper-
    ous, be happy

Νῑκίᾱς, Νῑκίου, ὁ   Nikias, a servant of Demos (The name is that of a con-
    temporary general.)

πυνθάνομαι, πεύσομαι, ἐπυθόμην, ——, πέπυσμαι, ——   inquire; learn by
    inquiry

τοὐλεόν = τὸ ἐλεόν   (For this **crasis**, see the Appendix, p. 614.)

χρησμός, χρησμοῦ, ὁ   oracular response, oracle

---

1. For the accent see the Appendix, p. 613.
2. ὡς here = ὅπως

ἐγὼ δ' ἰὼν προσκέψομαι τὸν Παφλαγόνα.

155 ΔΗ. ἄγε δὴ σὺ κατάθου πρῶτα τὰ σκεύη χαμαί·
ἔπειτα τὴν γῆν πρόσκυσον καὶ τοὺς θεούς.
ΑΛ. ἰδού· τί ἔστιν; ΔΗ. ὦ μακάρι' ὦ πλούσιε,
ὦ νῦν μὲν οὐδεὶς αὔριον δ' ὑπέρμεγας,
ὦ τῶν Ἀθηνῶν τᾶγὲ τῶν εὐδαιμόνων.

160 ΑΛ. τί μ' ὦγάθ' οὐ πλύνειν ἐᾷς τὰς κοιλίας
πωλεῖν τε τοὺς ἀλλᾶντας, ἀλλὰ καταγελᾷς;

Ἀθῆναι, Ἀθηνῶν, αἱ Athens

ἀλλᾶς, ἀλλᾶντος, ὁ sausage

αὔριον (adv.) tomorrow

ἐάω, ἐάσω, εἴασα, εἴακα, εἴαμαι, εἰάθην allow; let alone

ἰδού (expletive) look!, behold! (cf. the second pers. sing., aor. imperative mid. of
ὁράω: ἰδοῦ)

καταγελάω, καταγελάσομαι, κατεγέλασα, ——, καταγεγέλασμαι,
κατεγελάσθην laugh; mock, laugh at (+ gen.)

κοιλίᾱ, κοιλίᾱς, ἡ belly; intestines

μακάριος, μακαρίᾱ, μακάριον blessed, happy

Παφλαγών, Παφλαγόνος, ὁ Paphlagonian, from Paphlagonia in Asia Minor
(cf. παφλάζω, ——, ——, ——, ——, —— boil, splutter, seethe)

πλούσιος, πλουσίᾱ, πλούσιον rich, wealthy

πλύνω, πλυνῶ, ἔπλῡνα, ——, πέπλυμαι, ἐπλύθην wash, clean

προσκοπέω, προσκέψομαι, προυσκεψάμην, ——, προύσκεμμαι, ——, consider
beforehand; watch, spy on

προσκυνέω, προσκυνήσω, προσεκύνησα/προσέκυσα, προσκεκύνηκα, ——,
—— fall down and worship, prostrate oneself before

πωλέω, πωλήσω, ἐπώλησα, ——, ——, ἐπωλήθην sell

σκεῦος, σκεύους, τό vessel, implement, utensil; (pl.) equipment, baggage

τᾱγός, τᾱγοῦ, ὁ commander, ruler, chief

χαμαί (adv.) on the ground; to the ground

ὦγάθ' = ὦ ἀγαθέ (For the accent, see the Appendix, p. 613.)

ΔΗ. ὦ μῶρε ποίας κοιλίας; δευρὶ βλέπε.

τὰς στίχας ὁρᾶς τὰς τῶνδε τῶν λᾶων; *ΑΛ.* ὁρῶ.

ΔΗ. τούτων ἁπάντων αὐτὸς ἀρχέλᾶς ἔσει,

165 καὶ τῆς ἀγορᾶς καὶ τῶν λιμένων καὶ τῆς Πυκνός·

βουλὴν πατήσεις καὶ στρατηγοὺς κλαστάσεις,

δήσεις φυλάξεις, ἐν πρυτανείῳ λαικάσεις.

ΑΛ. ἐγώ; *ΔΗ.* σὺ μέντοι· κοὐδέπω γε πάνθ' ὁρᾶς.

ἀλλ' ἐπανάβηθι κἀπὶ τοὐλεὸν τοδὶ

170 καὶ κάτιδε τὰς νήσους ἁπάσᾶς ἐν κύκλῳ.

ἀρχέλᾶς/ἀρχέλᾶος, ἀρχελᾶου, ὁ   leader of the people, chief

βλέπω, βλέψομαι, ἔβλεψα, ——, ——, ——   look; see, perceive

δευρί = δεῦρο + the **deictic** (*"pointing"*) *suffix -ί which emphasizes the person
    or thing pointed out (See the Appendix, p. 614.)*

δεῦρο (*adv.*) here, hither

δέω, δήσω, ἔδησα, δέδεκα/δέδηκα, δέδεμαι, ἐδέθην   bind, tie

ἐλεόν, ἐλεοῦ, τό   table, kitchen-table

κλαστάζω, κλαστάσω, ἐκλάστασα, ——, ——, ——   trim, prune

κοιλίᾱ, κοιλίᾱς, ἡ   belly; intestines

κοὐδέπω = καὶ οὐδέπω

κύκλος, κύκλου, ὁ   circle

λαικάζω, λαικάσω, ἐλαίκασα, ——, ——, ——   (*colloquial*) screw

λᾶός, λᾶοῦ, ὁ (*sing. or pl.*)   army, host; people

μέντοι (*particle*) indeed; and yet

μῶρος, μῶρον   dull, stupid

οὐδέπω (*adv.*) not yet

πατέω, πατήσω, ἐπάτησα, πεπάτηκα, πεπάτημαι, ἐπατήθην   tread, walk;
    tread on, trample on

Πνύξ, Πυκνός, ἡ   the Pnyx, the hill at Athens where the Ekklesia met

πρυτανεῖον, πρυτανείου, τό   Prytaneion, magistrates' hall

*στίξ, στιχός, ἡ   row, line; rank, file

τοδί = τόδε + the deictic (*"pointing"*) suffix -ί

τοὐλεόν = τὸ ἐλεόν

ΑΛ. καθορῶ. ΔΗ. τί δαί; τἀμπόρια καὶ τὰς ὁλκάδας;

ΑΛ. ἔγωγε. ΔΗ. πῶς οὖν οὐ μεγάλως εὐδαιμονεῖς;
ἔτι νῦν τὸν ὀφθαλμὸν παράβαλλ᾽ ἐς Καρίᾱν
τὸν δεξιόν, τὸν δ᾽ ἕτερον ἐς Καρχηδόνα.

175 ΑΛ. εὐδαιμονήσω δ᾽ εἰ διαστραφήσομαι;[1]

ΔΗ. οὐκ ἀλλὰ διὰ σοῦ ταῦτα πάντα πέρναται.
γίγνει γάρ, ὡς ὁ χρησμὸς οὑτοσὶ λέγει,
ἀνὴρ μέγιστος. ΑΛ. εἰπέ μοι καὶ πῶς ἐγὼ
ἀλλᾱντοπώλης ὢν ἀνὴρ γενήσομαι;

180 ΔΗ. δι᾽ αὐτὸ γάρ τοι τοῦτο καὶ γίγνει μέγας,
ὁτιὴ πονηρὸς κἀξ ἀγορᾶς εἶ καὶ θρασύς.

ἀλλᾱντοπώλης, ἀλλᾱντοπώλου, ὁ   sausage-seller

δαί (particle) used in questions to express surprise or curiosity

δεξιός, δεξιά, δεξιόν   on the right hand, right; clever

διαστρέφω, διαστρέψω, διέστρεψα, διέστροφα, διέστραμμαι, διεστρέφθην/
    διεστράφην   turn different ways, twist; (pass.) be twisted, wrenched;
    have one's eyes twisted out of focus

ἐμπόριον, ἐμπορίου, τό   trading-station, market

ἐς = εἰς

εὐδαιμονέω, εὐδαιμονήσω, εὐδαιμόνησα, εὐδαιμόνηκα, ——, —— be pros-
    perous, be happy

θρασύς, θρασεῖα, θρασύ   bold

κἀξ = καὶ ἐξ

Καρίᾱ, Καρίᾱς, ἡ   Karia, a region of Asia Minor

Καρχηδών, Καρχηδόνος, ἡ   Carthage

μέγιστος, μεγίστη, μέγιστον   greatest, largest

ὁλκάς, ὁλκάδος, ἡ   towed ship, merchant vessel

ὁτιή (colloquial form of the conjunction ὅτι) because

οὑτοσί = οὗτος + the deictic suffix -ί

πέρνημι/πιπράσκω, ——, ——, πέπρᾱκα, πέπρᾱμαι, ἐπρᾱ́θην   sell; export
    for sale

τἀμπόρια = τὰ ἐμπόρια

χρησμός, χρησμοῦ, ὁ   oracular response, oracle

ὡς   here = as

1. **Future most vivid conditional sentence** with future indicative in both protasis and
apodosis: see the Appendix, p. 747.

B. Plato, *Gorgias* 456d5–457a4

Sokrates and Gorgias continue their discussion of rhetoric.

    ΓΟΡ. οὐδέ γε μὰ Δία ἐάν τις εἰς παλαίστραν φοιτήσας
    εὖ ἔχων τὸ σῶμα καὶ πυκτικὸς γενόμενος, ἔπειτα τὸν
70 *πατέρα τύπτῃ καὶ τὴν μητέρα ἢ ἄλλον τινὰ τῶν οἰκείων*
    ἢ τῶν φίλων, οὐ τούτου ἕνεκα δεῖ τοὺς παιδοτρίβας
    καὶ τοὺς ἐν τοῖς ὅπλοις διδάσκοντας μάχεσθαι μισεῖν
    τε καὶ ἐκβάλλειν ἐκ τῶν πόλεων. ἐκεῖνοι μὲν γὰρ
    παρέδοσαν ἐπὶ τῷ δικαίως χρῆσθαι τούτοις πρὸς τοὺς
75 *πολεμίους καὶ τοὺς ἀδικοῦντας, ἀμυνομένους, μὴ*
    ὑπάρχοντας· οἱ δὲ μεταστρέψαντες χρῶνται τῇ ἰσχύϊ
    καὶ τῇ τέχνῃ οὐκ ὀρθῶς. οὔκουν οἱ διδάξαντες
    πονηροί, οὐδὲ ἡ τέχνη οὔτε αἰτία οὔτε πονηρὰ τούτου
    ἕνεκά ἐστιν, ἀλλ' οἱ μὴ χρώμενοι οἶμαι ὀρθῶς.
80 *ὁ αὐτὸς δὴ λόγος καὶ περὶ τῆς ῥητορικῆς.*

ἀμύνω, ἀμυνῶ, ἤμῦνα, ——, ——, —— ward off; (*mid.*) defend oneself
δεῖ, δεήσει, ἐδέησε(ν), ——, ——, —— (*impersonal verb*) it is necessary, must
    (+ *accusative and infinitive*); there is need of (+ *gen.*)
ἰσχύς, ἰσχύος, ἡ strength
μά (*particle* + *name of god in acc.*) by
μεταστρέφω, μεταστρέψω, μετέστρεψα, ——, μετέστραμμαι, μετεστράφην
    turn about, turn around
μισέω, μισήσω, ἐμίσησα, μεμίσηκα, μεμίσημαι, ἐμισήθην hate
οἰκεῖος, οἰκεία, οἰκεῖον belonging to a house/family, one's own
οἶμαι/οἴομαι, οἰήσομαι, ——, ——, ——, ᾠήθην think, suppose, believe
οὔκουν (*adv.*) certainly not, not therefore
παιδοτρίβης, παιδοτρίβου, ὁ trainer
παλαίστρα, παλαίστρας, ἡ wrestling-school, gymnasium
πυκτικός, πυκτική, πυκτικόν skilled in boxing
τύπτω, τυπήσω, ——, ——, ——, —— strike, beat, hit
ὑπάρχω take the initiative, be first; be (already) the case, exist
φοιτάω, φοιτήσω, ἐφοίτησα, ——, ——, —— go back and forth, frequent;
    go to (as to a teacher)
χράομαι, χρήσομαι, ἐχρησάμην, ——, κέχρημαι, ἐχρήσθην use, experience,
    treat as (+ *dat.*) *This verb contracts to -η- where* τιμάω *contracts to -ā-.*

UNIT
19

141. COMPARISON OF ADVERBS

Adverbs have, like adjectives, a positive, comparative, and superlative degree. Those adverbs which are derived from adjectives use as their *comparative degree* the neuter accusative singular of the comparative degree of the adjective; they use as their *superlative degree* the neuter accusative plural of the superlative degree of the adjective.

POSITIVE DEGREE	COMPARATIVE DEGREE	SUPERLATIVE DEGREE
δικαίως justly	δικαιότερον more justly rather justly	δικαιότατα most justly very justly
σοφῶς wisely	σοφώτερον more wisely rather wisely	σοφώτατα most wisely very wisely
ἀληθῶς truly	ἀληθέστερον more truly rather truly	ἀληθέστατα most truly very truly
ἡδέως gladly, pleasantly	ἥδιον more gladly, more pleasantly rather gladly, rather pleasantly	ἥδιστα most gladly, most pleasantly very gladly, very pleasantly

Comparative and superlative adverbs can take the same constructions as comparative and superlative adjectives (cf. Section 131.5–8).

Ἀριστοφάνης τοῖς πολίταις **σοφώτερον Εὐρῑπίδου** συνεβούλευεν.
Aristophanes used to advise the citizens **more wisely than Euripides.**
(*genitive of comparison*)

543

ὁ δῆμος εἰρήνην ἐποιήσατο **ὡς δικαιότατα**.

The people made peace **as justly as possible.** (*superlative with* ὡς)

Some adverbs also form comparatives with the ending -ως. These alternative forms (e.g., ἀληθεστέρως, δικαιοτέρως) will be easily recognized in reading. The regular rules should be followed in English-to-Greek composition.

142. IRREGULAR COMPARISON OF ADJECTIVES

Some adjectives alter the stem, or employ a different stem or stems, in the comparative and superlative degree.

All such adjectives employ the comparative suffix -ῑων, -ῑον (or, because of phonetic changes, -ων, -ον) and the superlative suffix -ιστος, -ιστη, -ιστον. Compare ἡδίων, ἥδῑον; ἥδιστος, ἡδίστη, ἥδιστον (Section 131.2). The chart below lists only the masculine nominative singular.

For the sake of simplicity only the strict comparative and superlative meanings, e.g., "better," "best," are given, but intensive meanings, e.g., "rather good," "very good," are equally possible.

The adjectives ἀγαθός, "good," and κακός, "bad," have three different comparatives and superlatives with somewhat different meanings.

POSITIVE DEGREE	*COMPARATIVE DEGREE*	*SUPERLATIVE DEGREE*
ἀγαθός good	ἀμείνων better (in ability or worth)	ἄριστος best (in ability or worth)
	βελτίων better (morally)	βέλτιστος best (morally)
	κρείττων stronger, better	κράτιστος strongest, best
κακός bad	κακίων worse (morally)	κάκιστος worst (morally)
	χείρων worse (morally, in ability)	χείριστος worst (morally, in ability)

	ἥττων weaker, worse	adverb: ἥκιστα least, not at all
μέγας great	μείζων greater	μέγιστος greatest
ὀλίγος little few	ἐλάττων less fewer	ἐλάχιστος least fewest
πολύς much many	πλείων or πλέων more	πλεῖστος most
ῥᾴδιος easy	ῥᾴων easier	ῥᾷστος easiest
ταχύς swift	θάττων swifter	τάχιστος swiftest

Observations: (1) Note the origins of the following comparatives:

$$\begin{array}{lll}
κρείττων & < & *κρέτιων \\
ἥττων & < & *ἥκιων \\
μείζων & < & *μέγιων \\
ἐλάττων & < & *ἐλάχιων \\
θάττων & < & *θάχιων
\end{array}$$

In the positive and superlative degrees of ταχύς the initial aspirate of the stem θαχ- has lost its aspiration (dissimilation of aspirates).

(2) The comparative πλείων/πλέων, πλεῖον/πλέον has a genitive singular πλείονος/πλέονος (all genders) and employs the two alternative stems πλειον- and πλεον- throughout its declension.

(3) Adverbs derived from these adjectives use as their comparative the neuter accusative singular of the comparative degree of the adjective; the superlative degree of the adverb is the neuter accusative plural of the superlative degree of the adjective, e.g.:

$$\begin{array}{lll}
κακῶς & κάκῑον & κάκιστα
\end{array}$$

143. THE VERB οἶδα, "know"

οἶδα, εἴσομαι, ——, ——, ——, ——, "know"

The first Principal Part of this verb is an unreduplicated perfect which has some endings slightly different from those of πεπαίδευκα. This perfect tense has a present meaning: "I know"; the pluperfect means "I knew." The verb is actually the perfect tense of the verb which is used as the aorist of ὁράω: εἶδον. The perfect tense stem has three different forms with different vowel grades:

οἰδ-: used only in the perfect indicative singular
ἰδ-: used only in the perfect indicative plural and in the imperative
εἰδε-/εἰδ-: used elsewhere

	PERFECT INDICATIVE ACTIVE	PERFECT SUBJUNCTIVE ACTIVE	PERFECT OPTATIVE ACTIVE
S 1	οἶδα	εἰδῶ	εἰδείην
2	οἶσθα	εἰδῇς	εἰδείης
3	οἶδε(ν)	εἰδῇ	εἰδείη
P 1	ἴσμεν	εἰδῶμεν	εἰδεῖμεν/εἰδείημεν
2	ἴστε	εἰδῆτε	εἰδεῖτε/εἰδείητε
3	ἴσᾱσι(ν)	εἰδῶσι(ν)	εἰδεῖεν/εἰδείησαν

Observations: (1) The accent in the perfect subjunctive is due to the contraction of the final vowel of the stem εἰδε- with the subjunctive endings. Note that the accent in the perfect optative active never goes back beyond the -ι-. Cf. the first person plural, aorist optative passive παιδευθεῖμεν.

(2) Note the change of -δ- to -σ- in the stem ἰδ- in the perfect indicative plural. The second person singular was originally *οἶδθα.

PLUPERFECT INDICATIVE ACTIVE:

S 1 ᾔδη/ᾔδειν   P 1 ᾖσμεν/ᾔδεμεν
2 ᾔδησθα/ᾔδεις   2 ᾖστε/ᾔδετε
3 ᾔδει(ν)   3 ᾖσαν/ᾔδεσαν

Observations: (1) The augmented form of εἰ- is ᾖ-; note the iota subscript (cf. Vocabulary Notes, pages 101–102).

(2) Note the change of -δ- to -σ- of the augmented stem ἠδ- in the first set of forms in the plural of the pluperfect indicative active.

(3) The form ᾔσαν is the third person plural, pluperfect indicative active of οἶδα or imperfect indicative active of εἶμι. Be careful to distinguish the pluperfect of οἶδα from the imperfects of εἰμί and εἶμι.

PERFECT IMPERATIVE ACTIVE:

S 2 ἴσθι	P 2 ἴστε
3 ἴστω	3 ἴστων

Observations: (1) The second person singular is identical in form with the second person singular, present imperative active of the verb εἰμί.

(2) Note again the change of -δ- to -σ- in the stem ἰδ-.

PERFECT INFINITIVE ACTIVE: εἰδέναι

PERFECT PARTICIPLE ACTIVE:

	M	F	N
Nom.	εἰδώς	εἰδυῖα	εἰδός
Gen.	εἰδότος	εἰδυίας	εἰδότος

144. TEMPORAL CLAUSES INTRODUCED BY μέχρι and ἕως

μέχρι, "as long as; until"
ἕως, "as long as, while; until"

The two most common constructions in temporal clauses introduced by these conjunctions are a past indicative when the main verb is past and the temporal clause refers to a definite act in past time, and ἄν with the subjunctive when the main verb is either present or future.

1. PAST INDICATIVE

$$\grave{\varepsilon}\mu\alpha\chi\acute{o}\mu\eta\nu \left\{ \begin{array}{c} \mu\acute{\varepsilon}\chi\varrho\iota \\ \ \ddot{\varepsilon}\omega\varsigma \end{array} \right\} \grave{\varepsilon}\nu\acute{\iota}\varkappa\eta\sigma\alpha.$$
I was fighting until I won.

$$\dot{\varepsilon}\mu\alpha\chi\delta\mu\eta\nu \left\{ \begin{array}{c} \mu\dot{\varepsilon}\chi\varrho\iota \\ \ddot{\varepsilon}\omega\varsigma \end{array} \right\} \dot{\varepsilon}\nu\dot{\iota}\varkappa\omega\nu.$$

I was fighting as long as I was winning.

2. ἄν + SUBJUNCTIVE

$$\mu\alpha\chi o\tilde{\upsilon}\mu\alpha\iota \left\{ \begin{array}{c} \mu\dot{\varepsilon}\chi\varrho\iota \\ \ddot{\varepsilon}\omega\varsigma \end{array} \right\} \ \ddot{\alpha}\nu \ \nu\bar{\iota}\varkappa\dot{\eta}\sigma\omega\mu\varepsilon\nu.$$

I shall fight until we win.

$$\mu\alpha\chi o\tilde{\upsilon}\mu\alpha\iota \left\{ \begin{array}{c} \mu\dot{\varepsilon}\chi\varrho\iota \\ \ddot{\varepsilon}\omega\varsigma \end{array} \right\} \ \ddot{\alpha}\nu \ \dot{\varepsilon}\nu\tau\alpha\tilde{\upsilon}\theta\alpha \ \mu\dot{\varepsilon}\nu\eta\tau\varepsilon.$$

I shall fight as long as you remain here.

Usually, as in the examples above, the conjunctions μέχρι and ἕως mean "until" when the verb which they introduce has simple aspect (aorist indicative or subjunctive) and mean "as long as" when the verb which they introduce has progressive/repeated aspect (imperfect indicative or present subjunctive).

145. TEMPORAL CLAUSES INTRODUCED BY πρίν, "before, until"

The conjunction **πρίν** can introduce both an infinitive and a finite verb.

1. πρίν + INFINITIVE

πρίν introducing an infinitive means "before." The infinitive may have an accusative subject. The main clause is usually not negated.

ἐδίδαξεν τοὺς πολίτᾱς πρὶν ἀπελθεῖν.
He taught the citizens before going away.

ἀγγελεῖ τὴν νίκην τῇ πόλει πρὶν τοὺς κήρῡκας ἐλθεῖν.
He will announce the victory to the city before the heralds come.

2. πρίν + FINITE VERB

When the verb of the main clause is negated, πρίν introduces a finite verb and means "until"; it governs the same constructions as μέχρι and ἕως: a past indicative or ἄν and the subjunctive.

οὐ τοὺς πολίτᾱς ἐπαίδευσε πρὶν τὸ βιβλίον ἔγραψεν.
He did not educate the citizens until he wrote the book.

οὐ τοὺς πολίτᾱς παιδεύσει πρὶν ἂν τὸ βιβλίον γράψῃ.
He will not educate the citizens until he writes the book.

146. ATTRACTION OF THE RELATIVE PRONOUN TO THE CASE OF
ITS ANTECEDENT
OMISSION OF THE ANTECEDENT OF THE RELATIVE PRONOUN

The relative pronoun ὅς, ἥ, ὅ takes its gender and number from its antecedent, and its case from its use in its own clause.

οἱ στρατιῶται ἄξιοί εἰσι τῶν ἄθλων **ἃ** οἱ πολῖται διδόᾱσιν.
The soldiers are worthy of the prizes **which** the citizens give.

In this sentence, the relative pronoun is neuter plural because its antecedent is the neuter plural ἄθλων, accusative because it is the direct object of διδόᾱσιν in its own clause.

When the relative pronoun is *accusative* and the antecedent is *either genitive or dative*, the relative pronoun is frequently **attracted** into the case of the antecedent:

οἱ στρατιῶται ἄξιοί εἰσι τῶν ἄθλων **ὧν** οἱ πολῖται διδόᾱσιν.
The soldiers are worthy of the prizes **which** the citizens give.

In this sentence, the relative pronoun has been attracted into the genitive case, the case of its antecedent. If asked for the syntax of such a relative pronoun one should say that it is neuter plural because of its antecedent ἄθλων, genitive by attraction to the case of its antecedent instead of accusative as direct object of διδόᾱσιν.

οὐχ ἕψομαι τούτῳ τῷ ἡγεμόνι **ὃν** πέμπετε.
οὐχ ἕψομαι τούτῳ τῷ ἡγεμόνι **ᾧ** πέμπετε.
I shall not follow this leader **whom** you are sending.

In both sentences, the relative pronoun is masculine singular because of its antecedent ἡγεμόνι. In the first sentence the relative pronoun is accusative because it is the direct object of the verb πέμπετε. In the second the relative pronoun is dative because it is attracted to the case of its antecedent, which is dative.

The relative pronouns ὅσος and οἷος are also frequently attracted into the case of their antecedent.

τοῦτόν γ' οὐκ ἀξιοῦμεν τῶν ἄθλων **ὅσων** πέμπετε.
We do not think this man, at least, worthy of the prizes, **as many as** you send.

οὐχ ἑσπόμεθα τούτοις **οἵοις** ἐπέμψατε.
We did not follow these men, **the sort which** you sent.

At times, especially when the antecedent is either indefinite or demonstrative, it is left out and the relative is attracted to the case of the omitted antecedent.

οἱ στρατιῶται ἄξιοί εἰσιν **ὧν** οἱ πολῖται διδόασιν.
The soldiers are worthy **(of the things) which** the citizens give.
The soldiers are worthy **of what** the citizens give.

The ὧν is standing for ἐκείνων ἅ, in which ἐκείνων would be the genitive governed by ἄξιοι, and ἅ the direct object of διδόασιν.

The omission of the antecedent of the relative pronoun has already been seen in such sentences as:

οὐ τῑμῶ ὃς ἂν τοῦτο πράττῃ.
I do not honor whoever does this.

The omission of the antecedent of the relative is frequent in such sentences as:

ἔστιν ὅστις τοῦτον τῑμᾷ.
There is (someone) who honors this man.

οὐκ ἔστιν ὅστις τοῦτον τῑμᾷ.
There is not (anyone) who honors this man.
There is no one who honors this man.

οὐκ ἔστι περὶ ὅτου οὐ λέγει οὗτος.
There is not (anything) about which this man does not speak.
There is nothing about which this man does not speak.

VOCABULARY

αἰσχΰνομαι, αἰσχυνοῦμαι, ——, —— ἤσχυμμαι, ἠσχύνθην	be ashamed, feel shame before
ἀπόλλῡμι, ἀπολῶ, ἀπώλεσα (trans.) or ἀπωλόμην (intrans.), ἀπολώλεκα (trans.) or ἀπόλωλα (intrans.), ——	kill, lose; (mid. and intrans.) die, cease to exist
——, ἐρήσομαι, ἠρόμην, ——, ——, ——	ask
——, ἀνερήσομαι, ἀνηρόμην, ——, ——, ——	ask
εὑρίσκω, εὑρήσω, ηὗρον, ηὕρηκα, ηὕρημαι, ηὑρέθην	find, discover
ἕως (conj.)	as long as, while; until
ἡγέομαι, ἡγήσομαι, ἡγησάμην, ——, ἥγημαι, ἡγήθην	lead the way; be commander; rule (+ gen.); believe
ἴσος, ἴση, ἴσον	equal, fair; flat
ἴσως (adv.)	equally; perhaps
καινός, καινή, καινόν	new, strange
κέρδος, κέρδους, τό	gain, profit
κρίνω, κρινῶ, ἔκρῑνα, κέκρικα, κέκριμαι, ἐκρίθην	separate, decide, judge
ἀποκρίνομαι, ἀποκρινοῦμαι, ἀπεκρῑνάμην, ——, ἀποκέκριμαι, ——	answer
κριτής, κριτοῦ, ὁ	judge
λΰπη, λΰπης, ἡ	pain, grief
μάλα (adv.)	very
μέχρι (conj.)	as long as; until
νόσος, νόσου, ἡ	sickness
οἶδα, εἴσομαι, ——, ——, ——, ——	know
σύνοιδα	be aware, know (+ dat.)

ὀλίγος, ὀλίγη, ὀλίγον   little; (pl.) few
πρίν (conj.)   (+ infinitive) before
                                               (+ indic., or + ἄν and subj.)
                                                   until
πρότερος, προτέρᾱ, πρότερον   former, superior
    πρότερον (adv.)   before, earlier
ὕστερος, ὑστέρᾱ, ὕστερον   later
    ὕστερον (adv.)   later
        ὕστατος, ὑστάτη, ὕστατον   last
χρόνος, χρόνου, ὁ   time

*In addition, all forms of the adjectives listed in the chart in Section 142, pages
544–45, are to be learned.*

VOCABULARY NOTES

The verb αἰσχύνομαι, αἰσχυνοῦμαι, ——, ——, ᾔσχυμμαι, ᾐσχύνθην, "be
ashamed, feel shame before," is a passive deponent with a contracted future.
It has the same root as the adjective αἰσχρός, αἰσχρά, αἰσχρόν. The people
before whom one feels shame are put in the accusative. Note that the original
form of the first person singular, perfect indicative middle/passive was
*ᾔσχυνμαι. The conjugation is: ᾔσχυμμαι, ᾐσχυμμένος εἶ, ᾔσχυνται,
ᾐσχύμμεθα, ᾔσχυνθε, ᾐσχυμμένοι εἰσί(ν). Both the second person singular
and the third person plural use **periphrastic forms**, forms consisting of a
participle and a form of the verb εἰμί. The pluperfect follows the same pattern.
The perfect infinitive middle/passive is ᾐσχύνθαι.

In the verb ἀπόλλῡμι, ἀπολῶ, ἀπώλεσα (trans.) or ἀπωλόμην (intrans.),
ἀπολώλεκα (trans.) or ἀπόλωλα (intrans.), ——, ——, "kill, lose; (mid. and
intrans.) die, cease to exist," note the contracted future and the fact that in
the aorist and in the perfect, there are separate transitive forms (the first aorist
ἀπώλεσα and the perfect ἀπολώλεκα) and intransitive forms (the second aorist
middle ἀπωλόμην and the perfect ἀπόλωλα). In the present, imperfect, and
future tenses, the middle forms are also intransitive. The present and imperfect
are conjugated exactly like the corresponding tenses of δείκνῡμι.

The verb ——, ἐρήσομαι, ἠρόμην, ——, ——, —— is synonymous with the
corresponding tenses of ἐρωτάω. Both of these verbs govern indirect questions.

In the verb εὑρίσκω, εὑρήσω, ηὗρον, ηὕρηκα, ηὕρημαι, ηὑρέθην, "find, discover," note the inchoative suffix in Principal Part I and the -ε- in Principal
Part VI, ηὑρέθην. All of the forms beginning with ηὑ- are also found with εὑ-:
e.g., the first person singular, imperfect indicative active is either ηὕρισκον or

εὕρισκον. The second person singular, aorist imperative active is εὑρέ: cf. εἰπέ, ἐλθέ, ἰδέ, λαβέ.

The verb ἡγέομαι, ἡγήσομαι, ἡγησάμην, ——, ἥγημαι, ἡγήθην has the same root as the noun ἡγεμών, ἡγεμόνος, ὁ, "leader." The primary meaning of the verb is "to lead the way." From that developed the notion of "to be a command-er, rule"; like ἄρχω, ἡγέομαι governs the genitive case. A final and very important meaning is "to believe"; in this sense, ἡγέομαι, like νομίζω, governs an infinitive with an accusative subject.

The adjective ἴσος, ἴση, ἴσον, "equal, fair; flat," has the comparative ἰσαίτερος and the superlative ἰσαίτατος; cf. παλαιός. Note the second and more com-mon meaning of the adverb ἴσως: "perhaps."

The word καινός, καινή, καινόν, "new, strange," is in some senses synonymous with νέος, νέα, νέον. Unlike νέος, however, it never has the meaning "young."

The basic meaning of κρίνω, κρινῶ, ἔκρῑνα, κέκρικα, κέκριμαι, ἐκρίθην is "separate," from which developed the meanings "decide, judge." Note the -ῑ- in Principal Parts I and III, and the short vowel elsewhere. The future is contracted; cf. μενῶ. The compound deponent ἀποκρίνομαι, ἀποκρινοῦμαι, ἀπεκρῑνάμην, ——, ἀποκέκριμαι, ——, "answer," is a very common verb. The person to whom an answer is given is in the dative.

Note that μᾶλλον, the comparative degree of the adverb μάλα, has already been presented.

The verb οἶδα, εἴσομαι, ——, ——, ——, ——, "know," takes two kinds of indirect statement: participle, or ὅτι/ὡς + finite verb. With an infinitive the verb means "know how (to) . . . ."

The compound σύνοιδα, "know," can take a reflexive pronoun in the dative with which a participle can agree, or the participle can agree with the subject in the nominative:

σύνοιδα ἐμαυτῇ τὴν πόλιν σωσάσῃ.
σύνοιδα ἐμαυτῇ τὴν πόλιν σώσᾱσα.
I know that I saved the city.

The rhetorical figure in which the chronological order of events is reversed is called ὕστερον πρότερον.

COGNATES AND DERIVATIVES

ἄριστος   aristocracy (rule of the **best**)

εὑρίσκω   heuristic (helping to **find** an answer)

ἡγέομαι   exegesis (**leading** the meaning out of a text) ἴσος   isosceles triangle (with **equal** sides)

καινός   Cenozoic, kainite (KCl · MgSO$_4$ · 3H$_2$O)

κρίνω   criterion

κριτής   critic

οἶδα   *wit*; vision (from the Latin cognate *video̅*)

ὀλίγος   oligarchy (rule of the **few**)

χρόνος   chronology

DRILLS

I. *Translate.*

   1. ἕσπετό μοι μέχρι εἰς τὴν οἰκίαν εἰσῆλθον.

   2. ἕψομαί σοι μέχρι ἂν εἰς τὴν οἰκίαν εἰσέλθῃς.

   3. αὐτὴν ἐφίλει ἕως ἐδύνατο.

   4. αὐτὴν ἐφίλει ἕως ἐτελεύτησεν.

   5. φιλήσω σε μέχρι ἂν τελευτήσω.

   6. μὴ λίπητε τὴν πόλιν πρὶν ἂν μου ἀκούσητε.

   7. λίπε τὴν πόλιν πρὶν αὐτούς σε καταλαβεῖν.

   8. ἕλιπε τὴν πόλιν πρίν μου ἀκοῦσαι.

   9. οὐκ ἕλιπε τὴν πόλιν πρίν μου ἤκουσεν.

  10. ἐν τῇ οἰκίᾳ μένω ἕως ἂν τοὺς ξένους δέξωμαι.

  11. ἐτελεύτησε πρὶν ἐμὲ λιπεῖν τὴν πόλιν.

EXERCISES

I.   1. σύνοιδα ἐμαυτῇ μακρῷ βελτίων οὖσα τῆς μητρός.

    2. οὔ φημι ἐκείνην χείρω εἶναι ἢ τὴν μητέρα.

    3. εὖ δὴ οἶδα τὰς καλλίους εὐδαιμονεστέρᾱς οὔσᾱς τῶν μὴ ἐχουσῶν
ἐλευθερίᾱν.

    4. εἰ ἴσως κάκιστός τίς σε ἔροιτο εἰ τὴν πόλιν προδώσεις, τί αὐτῷ
ἐρεῖς; συνίης γὰρ τὰ τῆς πόλεως.

    5. τῆς νόσου τῇ πόλει ἐπιπεσούσης, θῦσώμεθα ὡς τάχιστα.

    6. οὐ δὴ διὰ τὸ μὴ διδαχθῆναι ὑπὸ καλλῑόνων διδασκάλων ἀλλὰ διὰ
τὸ μὴ δύνασθαι μηδὲν μαθεῖν ὅτι ἀφρονέστατα πρᾱ́ττουσιν
οἵδε οἱ τρεῖς νεᾱνίαι.

    7. ὡς σωφρονέστατα πρᾱ́ξομεν ἕως ἂν αἰσχῡνώμεθα τούς γε
κρείττους.

    8. ἧκεν εἰς τὴν νῆσον ὕστερον ἢ ὁ ἀδελφὸς τέτταρσιν ἡμέραις.
θᾱ́ττων γὰρ οὗτος ἐκείνου πολύ.

    9. πρότερον τρισὶν ἡμέραις ἀπώλετο, οὐ συνεὶς ὅτι πάθοι.

  10. τοὺς ἀπολωλότας ὑπὲρ τῆς ἡμετέρᾱς ἐλευθερίᾱς, ὄντας οὐκ
ἐλαχίστους, τῑμᾷ ἡ πόλις. τίς γὰρ κακίων ὢν οὕτως ἀφείη
ἂν τόν γε βίον;

  11. μᾶλλον τῑμᾱ τοὺς ἐμπειροτέρους σαυτοῦ, ἐᾱ̀ν καὶ ὀλίγοι ὦσιν.

  12. ὅσῳ πλέονες εἶημεν αἱ σοφαί, τοσούτῳ ῥᾷον τοιούτου γε δήμου
ἄρξαιμεν ἄν.

  13. ἀεὶ πειθώμεθα οἷς ἥ τ' ἐκκλησίᾱ καὶ ἡ βουλὴ κατέστησαν.

  14. ᾔδησθά τοι ὁπότε θύσοιεν τήν γ' αἶγα.

  15. τοῦ φίλου συμβουλεύοντος, ἥκει εἰς τόδε τὸ ἱερὸν ὡς τὸν θεὸν
ἐρησομένη περὶ τῆς νόσου.

  16. εἴσεισίν πως εἰς τὴν πόλιν ὕστατος πάντων ὧν ἔπεμψας.

  17. ἆρα ἐνομίζετε τὰ ὑμέτερα ξίφη πολλῷ ὀξύτερα εἶναι τῶν
ἡμετέρων;

  18. οὐκ ἔστιν ὑμῖν σοφωτέροις γενέσθαι θᾶττον ἡμῶν.

  19. ἔφησθα οὐκ ἐξεῖναι ἡμῖν σοφωτέραις γενέσθαι.

20. ἅτε νεωτέρῳ τοῦ ἀδελφοῦ ὄντι οὐκ ἐξῆν τῷ Δημοσθένει τῆς οἰκίας ἡγεῖσθαι.

21. μὴ πιστεύσητε τοῖς ἀμαθεστέροις ὑμῶν αὐτῶν. ἥττους γὰρ οὗτοι.

22. ἦσμεν σαφῶς τοὺς ἐν τῇ ἀγορᾷ αἰσχίους ὄντας πᾶσι τοῖς πολίταις ὅσοις ἐπαιδευόμεθα.

23. ἦμεν εἰς τὴν οἰκίαν ἐν ᾗπερ οἱ αἰσχίονες ἦσαν.

24. τῶν στρατιωτῶν ἀποπεφευγότων, τρόπαιόν που στήσαιμεν.

25. οὐκ ἂν ἀφείην ὁπόσους ἂν ἕλωμεν πρὶν ἂν χρήματα δῶσιν.

26. ἐνίκων που οἱ Ἀθηναῖοι πρὶν τὴν νόσον ἐπιπεσεῖν.

27. ἆθλα ἀεὶ οἴσει μέχρι ἂν νεώτερός τις ἔλθῃ εἰς τοὺς ἀγῶνας.

28. κέρδους ἕνεκα τὸν ἥττω λόγον μὴ κρείττω ποίει, ὦ χείριστε· μεγίστων γὰρ κακῶν αἴτιος ἔσῃ.

29. λύπης δὴ τί μεῖζον ἀνθρώπῳ κακόν;

30. οἶσθα τοὺς προτέρους διδασκάλους μᾶλλον σοφοὺς ὄντας ἢ τοὺς νῦν.

31. σύνισμεν ἡμῖν γ' αὐτοῖς ἴσοι ὄντες τοῖς πατράσιν.

32. ἔφησάν τινες τὸν Σωκράτη καινοῖς θεοῖς πιστεύειν.

33. τοὺς ἱππέας εὕρωμεν ὅσους ἀφεῖμεν.

34. ἡγεῖ τὸν σὸν ἀδελφὸν ἀμείνω εἶναι ἢ Σωκράτη;

II. 1. Since the younger soldiers fought as shamefully as possible, the noblest of the old men will somehow guard the bridge until the enemy go away.

2. Do you know that Sokrates is not worse than Aristophanes?

3. Did you know that the Greeks believed that Zeus was the greatest of the gods?

4. If the general of the Athenians had led his army to the plain before the enemy came, our grief would have been less.

5. I shall stay until you stop teaching.

READINGS

A. Plato, *Gorgias* 457a5–457c3

Sokrates and Gorgias continue their discussion of rhetoric.

> ΓΟΡ. δυνατὸς μὲν γὰρ πρὸς ἅπαντάς ἐστιν ὁ ῥήτωρ
> καὶ περὶ παντὸς λέγειν, ὥστε πιθανώτερος εἶναι ἐν
> τοῖς πλήθεσιν ἔμβραχυ περὶ ὅτου ἂν βούληται· ἀλλ᾿
> οὐδέν τι μᾶλλον τούτου ἕνεκα δεῖ οὔτε τοὺς ἰᾱτροὺς
> 85 τὴν δόξαν ἀφαιρεῖσθαι — ὅτι δύναιτο ἂν τοῦτο ποιῆσαι
> — οὔτε τοὺς ἄλλους δημιουργούς, ἀλλὰ δικαίως καὶ τῇ
> ῥητορικῇ χρῆσθαι, ὥσπερ καὶ τῇ ἀγωνίᾳ. ἐὰν δὲ οἶμαι
> ῥητορικὸς γενόμενός τις κᾆτα ταύτῃ τῇ δυνάμει καὶ τῇ
> τέχνῃ ἀδικῇ, οὐ τὸν διδάξαντα δεῖ μῑσεῖν τε καὶ
> 90 ἐκβάλλειν ἐκ τῶν πόλεων. ἐκεῖνος μὲν γὰρ ἐπὶ δικαίᾳ
> χρείᾳ παρέδωκεν, ὁ δ᾿ ἐναντίως χρῆται. τὸν οὖν οὐκ
> ὀρθῶς χρώμενον μῑσεῖν δίκαιον καὶ ἐκβάλλειν καὶ
> ἀποκτεινύναι ἀλλ᾿ οὐ τὸν διδάξαντα.

ἀγωνίᾱ, ἀγωνίᾱς, ἡ   contest; competitive skill

ἀποκτείνῡμι/ἀποκτείνω, ἀποκτενῶ, ἀπέκτεινα, ἀπέκτονα, ——, —— kill

ἀφαιρέω   take away (something) (*acc.*) from (someone) (*acc.*)

δεῖ, δεήσει, ἐδέησε(ν), ——, ——, —— (*impersonal verb*) it is necessary

δυνατός, δυνατή, δυνατόν   able; possible

ἔμβραχυ (*adv.*)   in brief

ἐναντίος, ἐναντίᾱ, ἐναντίον   opposite, in front of, facing

ἰᾱτρός, ἰᾱτροῦ, ὁ   doctor

κᾆτα = καὶ εἶτα: εἶτα (*adv.*)   then, next, therefore

μῑσέω, μῑσήσω, ἐμίσησα, μεμίσηκα, μεμίσημαι, ἐμῑσήθην   hate

οἴομαι/οἶμαι, οἰήσομαι, ——, ——, ——, ᾠήθην   think, suppose, believe

πιθανός, πιθανή, πιθανόν   persuasive

πλῆθος, πλήθους, τό   crowd, mass

χράομαι, χρήσομαι, ἐχρησάμην, ——, κέχρημαι, ἐχρήσθην   use, experience,
    treat as (+ *dat.*) *This verb contracts to -η- where τῑμάω contracts to -ᾱ-.*

χρείᾱ, χρείᾱς, ἡ   need; use

B. Aristophanes, *Acharnians* 241–283

Dikaiopolis has made a private peace with Sparta during the Peloponnesian War. He is preparing to celebrate a festival of Dionysos, the Rural Dionysia, when the Chorus of aged Acharnian men, who oppose the peace, interrupt him.

241 *ΔΙΚΑΙΟΠΟΛΙΣ.* εὐφημεῖτε, εὐφημεῖτε.

προΐτω ’ς τὸ πρόσθεν ὀλίγον ἡ κανηφόρος·
ὁ Ξανθίας τὸν φαλλὸν ὀρθὸν στησάτω.
κατάθου τὸ κανοῦν, ὦ θύγατερ, ἵν’ ἀπαρξώμεθα.

245 *ΘΥΓΑΤΗΡ.* ὦ μῆτερ, ἀνάδος δεῦρο τὴν ἐτνήρυσιν,
ἵν’ ἔτνος καταχέω τοὐλατῆρος τουτουί.

ΔΙ. καὶ μὴν καλόν γ’ ἔστ’· ὦ Διόνυσε δέσποτα,
κεχαρισμένως σοι τήνδε τὴν πομπὴν ἐμὲ

ἀπάρχομαι   begin a sacrifice; offer first fruits

δεσπότης, δεσπότου, ὁ   (*voc.* δέσποτα)   master, lord

δεῦρο (*adv.*)   hither, here

Δικαιόπολις, Δικαιοπόλεως, ὁ   Dikaiopolis, hero of the *Acharnians*

Διόνῡσος, Διονῡ́σου, ὁ   Dionysos

ἐλατήρ, ἐλατῆρος, ὁ   driver; flat cake

ἐτνήρυσις, ἐτνηρύσεως, ἡ   soup-ladle

ἔτνος, ἔτνους, τό   thick pea or bean soup

εὐφημέω, εὐφημήσω, ηὐφήμησα, ——, ——, ——   keep a sacred silence

κανηφόρος, κανηφόρου, ὁ or ἡ   basket-carrier

κανοῦν, κανοῦ, τό (*contraction of* κάνεον, κανέου, τό)   basket

καταχέω, καταχέω, κατέχεα, κατακέχυκα, κατακέχυμαι, κατεχύθην   pour over, pour on

κεχαρισμένως (*adv.*)   acceptably, pleasingly

μήν (*particle*)   truly; moreover; and yet

Ξανθίας, Ξανθίου, ὁ   Xanthias, a slave of Dikaiopolis

ὀλίγος, ὀλίγη, ὀλίγον   little; (*pl.*) few

πομπή, πομπῆς, ἡ   procession

πρόσθε(ν)[1] (*adv.*)   before, in front

’ς = ἐς = εἰς

τουτουί = τούτου + *the deictic* (*"pointing"*) *suffix* -ί *which emphasizes the person or thing pointed out* (*See the Appendix, p. 614.*)

φαλλός, φαλλοῦ, ὁ   phallus, model of the male organ

---

1. The adverbial suffixes: -θε and -φι can take a nu-movable: πρόσθε(ν).

πέμψαντα καὶ θύσαντα μετὰ τῶν οἰκετῶν
250 ἀγαγεῖν¹ τυχηρῶς τὰ κατ' ἀγροὺς Διονύσια,
στρατιᾶς ἀπαλλαχθέντα· τὰς σπονδὰς δέ μοι
καλῶς ξυνενεγκεῖν¹ τὰς τριᾱκοντούτιδας.
ἄγ', ὦ θύγατερ, ὅπως τὸ κανοῦν καλὴ καλῶς
οἴσεις βλέπουσα θυμβροφάγον. ὡς μακάριος
255 ὅστις σ' ὀπύσει κἀκποιήσεται γαλᾶς
σοῦ μηδὲν ἥττους βδεῖν, ἐπειδὰν ὄρθρος ᾖ.

ἀγρός, ἀγροῦ, ὁ   field (κατ' ἀγρούς = in the country, rural)

ἀπαλλάττω, ἀπαλλάξω, ἀπήλλαξα, ἀπήλλαχα, ἀπήλλαγμαι, ἀπηλλάγην/
ἀπηλλάχθην   set free; remove; (mid. and aor. pass.) get free, be freed
from, depart from (+ gen.)

βδέω, ——, ——, ——, ——, ——   fart

βλέπω, βλέψομαι, ἔβλεψα, ——, ——, ——   look; see, perceive

γαλῆ, γαλῆς, ἡ   weasel, foumart

Διονύσια, Διονυσίων, τά   Dionysia, festival of Dionysos

ἥττων, ἧττον   weaker, worse

θυμβροφάγος, θυμβροφάγον   eating bitter herbs, eating savory

κανοῦν, κανοῦ, τό   (contraction of κάνεον, κανέου, τό)   basket

μακάριος, μακαρίᾱ, μακάριον   blessed, happy

ξυμφέρω = συμφέρω

οἰκέτης, οἰκέτου, ὁ   household slave, servant

ὀπύω, ὀπύσω, ——, ——, ——, ——   marry

ὄρθρος, ὄρθρου, ὁ   time just before dawn

σπονδή, σπονδῆς, ἡ   libation; (pl.) treaty, peace treaty

στρατιά, στρατιᾶς, ἡ   army; expedition

τριᾱκοντοῦτις (gen. τριᾱκοντούτιδος) (fem. adj.)   thirty years old, thirty
years long

τυχηρός, τυχηρά, τυχηρόν   lucky, fortunate

1. This infinitive with subject accusative conveys a wish. See the Appendix, p. 726.

πρόβαινε, κἂν τὤχλῳ φυλάττεσθαι[1] σφόδρα
μή τις λαθών σου περιτράγῃ τὰ χρῡσία.
ὦ Ξανθίᾱ, σφῷν δ᾽ ἐστὶν ὀρθὸς ἑκτέος
260 ὁ φαλλὸς ἐξόπισθε τῆς κανηφόρου·
ἐγὼ δ᾽ ἀκολουθῶν ᾄσομαι τὸ φαλλικόν·
σὺ δ᾽ ὦ γύναι θεῶ μ᾽ ἀπὸ τοῦ τέγους. πρόβᾱ.
Φαλῆς ἑταῖρε Βακχίου
ξύγκωμε νυκτοπεριπλάνη-
265   τε μοιχὲ παιδεραστά,

ᾄδω (< ἀείδω), ᾄσομαι, ᾖσα, ——, ——, ᾔσθην   sing
ἀκολουθέω, ἀκολουθήσω, ἠκολούθησα, ——, ——, ——   follow
Βάκχιος, Βακχίᾱ, Βάκχιον   Bacchic, Dionysiac; (as substantive) the Bacchic
    one, Dionysos
ἑκτέος, ἑκτέᾱ, ἑκτέον   having to be held (+ dat. of personal agent)
ἐξόπισθε(ν) (adv., or prep. + gen.)   behind
θεάομαι, θεάσομαι, ἐθεασάμην, ——, τεθέᾱμαι, ——   gaze at, behold; see
κἂν = καὶ ἐν
κανηφόρος, κανηφόρου, ὁ or ἡ   basket-carrier
μοιχός, μοιχοῦ, ὁ   adulterer
νυκτοπεριπλάνητος, νυκτοπεριπλάνητον   wandering around at night
Ξανθίᾱς, Ξανθίου, ὁ   Xanthias, a slave
ξύγκωμος, ξυγκώμου, ὁ   fellow reveller
ὄχλος, ὄχλου, ὁ   crowd, throng
παιδεραστής, παιδεραστοῦ, ὁ   pederast
περιτρώγω, περιτρώξομαι, περιέτραγον, ——, ——, ——,   nibble at, nibble
    around
πρόβᾱ = πρόβηθι
σφόδρα (adv.)   very much, very
σφῷν (gen. and dat. dual of the second person pronoun)   you two
τέγος, τέγους, τό   roof
τὤχλῳ = τῷ ὄχλῳ
Φαλῆς, Φαλῆτος, ὁ (voc. Φαλῆς)   Phales, the god of the phallus
φαλλός, φαλλοῦ, ὁ   phallus, model of the male organ
χρῡσίον, χρῡσίον, τό   piece of gold, gold coin, gold ornament

---

1. This infinitive conveys a command. See the Appendix, p. 726.

ἕκτῳ σ’ ἔτει προσεῖπον ἐς

τὸν δῆμον ἐλθὼν ἄσμενος,

σπονδὰς ποιησάμενος ἐμαυ-

τῷ, πραγμάτων τε καὶ μαχῶν

270   καὶ Λαμάχων ἀπαλλαγείς.

πολλῷ γὰρ ἐσθ’ ἥδῑον, ὦ Φαλῆς Φαλῆς,

κλέπτουσαν εὑρόνθ’ ὡρικὴν ὑληφόρον

τὴν Στρῡμοδώρου Θρᾷτταν ἐκ τοῦ φελλέως

μέσην λαβόντ’ ἄραντα κατα-

275   βαλόντα καταγιγαρτίσ’ ὦ

Φαλῆς Φαλῆς.

αἴρω, ἀρῶ, ἦρα, ἦρκα, ἦρμαι, ἤρθην   lift, raise up

ἀπαλλάττω, ἀπαλλάξω, ἀπήλλαξα, ἀπήλλαχα, ἀπήλλαγμαι, ἀπηλλάγην/
    ἀπηλλάθχην   set free; remove; (mid. and aor. pass.) get free, be freed
    from, depart from (+ gen.)

ἄσμενος, ἀσμένη, ἄσμενον   glad, pleased

δῆμος, δήμου, ὁ   here means   village, town, deme (of Attica)

ἕκτος, ἕκτη, ἕκτον   sixth

ἐς = εἰς

ἔτος, ἔτους, τό   year

εὑρίσκω, εὑρήσω, ηὗρον, ηὗρηκα, ηὕρημαι, ηὑρέθην   find, discover

Θρᾷττα, Θρᾴττης, ἡ   Thracian girl, Thracian slave-girl

καταγιγαρτίζω, ——, κατεγιγάρτισα, ——, ——, —— remove the pit of a
    grape

Λάμαχος, Λαμάχου, ὁ   Lamachos, an Athenian general during the Pelopon-
    nesian War

σπονδή, σπονδῆς, ἡ   libation; (pl.)   treaty, peace-treaty

Στρῡμόδωρος, Στρῡμοδώρου, ὁ   Strymodoros (man's name which includes the
    name of the river Strymon in Thrace)

ὑληφόρος, ὑληφόρου, ὁ or ἡ   wood-carrier

Φαλῆς, Φαλῆτος, ὁ   (voc. Φαλῆς)   Phales, the god of the phallus

φελλεύς, φελλέως, ὁ   stony ground

ὡρικός, ὡρική, ὡρικόν   in one's prime, blooming

ἐὰν μεθ’ ἡμῶν ξυμπίῃς, ἐκ κραιπάλης

ἕωθεν εἰρήνης ῥοφήσεις τρύβλιον·

ἡ δ’ ἀσπὶς ἐν τῷ φεψάλῳ κρεμήσεται.

280 ΧΟΡΟΣ. οὗτος αὐτός ἐστιν, οὗτος.

βάλλε βάλλε βάλλε βάλλε,

παῖε παῖε τὸν μιαρόν.

οὐ βαλεῖς; οὐ βαλεῖς;

ἕωθεν (adv.)   from dawn; at dawn, early

κραιπάλη, κραιπάλης, ἡ   drinking-bout; drunkenness; hangover

κρεμάννῡμι (mid./pass. κρέμαμαι), κρεμῶ (κρεμάω), ἐκρέμασα, ——, ——,
    ἐκρεμάσθην (fut. pass. κρεμήσομαι)   hang, hang up

μιαρός, μιαρά, μιαρόν   foul, abominable, polluted

ξυμπίνω, ξυμπίομαι, ξυνέπιον, ξυμπέπωκα, ξυμπέπομαι, ξυνεπόθην
    (ξυν- = συν-)   drink with

παίω, παίσω, ἔπαισα, πέπαικα, πέπαισμαι, ἐπαίσθην   strike, beat

ῥοφέω, ῥοφήσω, ἐρρόφησα, ——, ——, ἐρροφήθην   gulp down, drink dry

τρύβλιον, τρυβλίου, τό   cup, bowl

φεψάλος, φεψάλου, ὁ   spark, ember   (ἐν φεψάλῳ = in the chimney)

UNIT
20

147. VERBAL ADJECTIVES IN -τέος, -τέᾱ, -τέον

Many verbs form **verbal adjectives** which express *necessity* or *obligation*. Most such adjectives are formed from a stem obtained by dropping from Principal Part VI not only the past indicative augment and the ending -ην but also, in those verbs where it appears, the -θ- preceding the ending. To this stem is added the adjectival suffix -τέος, -τέᾱ, -τέον. Verbal adjectives are declined like ἄξιος.

VERB	PRINCIPAL PART VI	VERBAL ADJECTIVE
λύω	ἐλύθην	λυτέος, λυτέᾱ, λυτέον
δίδωμι	ἐδόθην	δοτέος, δοτέᾱ, δοτέον
ποιέω	ἐποιήθην	ποιητέος, ποιητέᾱ, ποιητέον

When the consonants -φ- or -χ- precede the adjectival suffix, they lose their aspiration and become -π- and -κ- respectively.

ἄρχω	ἤρχθην	ἀρκτέος, ἀρκτέᾱ, ἀρκτέον
γράφω	ἐγράφην	γραπτέος, γραπτέᾱ, γραπτέον
πράττω	ἐπράχθην	πρᾱκτέος, πρᾱκτέᾱ, πρᾱκτέον

Verbal adjectives not formed according to these rules are given in the Appendix, pp. 688–89.

Verbal adjectives can be employed in two ways:

(1) the **personal (passive) construction**
(2) the **impersonal (active and middle) construction**

1. THE PERSONAL (PASSIVE) CONSTRUCTION OF VERBAL ADJECTIVES

If a verb is transitive and takes a direct object in the accusative case, its verbal adjective can modify a noun or pronoun in order to indicate that the verbal action is *obligatory* and *must be performed upon that noun or pronoun*:

> ποιητέος, ποιητέᾱ, ποιητέον
> having to be done

> ταῦτα ποιητέα ἐστίν.
> These things are having to be done.
> These things must be done.

In this construction the verbal adjective usually serves as a *predicate adjective* linked by some form of εἰμί to the noun or pronoun with which it agrees.

If the agent of the action is mentioned, the *dative of personal agent* is employed (cf. Section 44).

> **ἡμῖν** ταῦτα γραπτέα ἐστίν.
> These things must be written **by us.**

> **ὑμῖν** οὗτοι λυτέοι εἰσίν.
> These men must be released **by you.**

2. THE IMPERSONAL (ACTIVE, MIDDLE) CONSTRUCTION OF VERBAL ADJECTIVES

The verbal adjective of any verb can be placed in the *neuter nominative singular*, standing alone and not modifying any noun or pronoun. In this impersonal construction

(a) the verbal adjective indicates that the action of the verb (in the active or middle voice) is obligatory;

(b) the object of the verb, if expressed, stands in the *same case* as that which the verb requires in its finite forms;

(c) if a personal agent of the action is named, a *dative of personal agent* is usually employed;

(d) the verbal adjective serves as a *substantive*, and is the *subject* of the appropriate form of the verb εἰμί.

> Σωκράτει δίκην δοτέον ἐστίν.
> Sokrates must pay the penalty.

ὑμῖν τούτους λυτέον ἐστίν.
You must release these men.

ἡμῖν ταῦτα γραπτέον ἐστίν.
We must write these things.

τῷ βασιλεῖ τοῦ δήμου ἀρκτέον ἐστίν.
The king must rule the people.

Sometimes the neuter nominative *plural* of the verbal adjective is employed in this construction with no difference in meaning.

ὑμῖν τούτους λυτέα ἐστίν.
You must release these men.

Occasionally, in this construction, the personal agent appears in the accusative case instead of the dative.

ἡμᾶς ταῦτα γραπτέον ἐστίν.
We must write these things.

When negated by οὐ, verbal adjectives in either the personal or impersonal construction convey the idea that the action *must not occur*.

ὑμῖν οὗτοι **οὐ λυτέοι** εἰσίν.
These men **must not be released** by you.

ὑμῖν τούτους **οὐ λυτέον** ἐστίν.
You **must not release** these men.

148. THE IMPERSONAL VERBS δεῖ, "it is necessary, must; there is need"
χρή, "ought, must"

Like the impersonal verbs ἔστι(ν) and ἔξεστι(ν), "it is possible," are the verbs δεῖ, "there is need, must," and χρή, "ought, must." Such verbs have *no definite subject*; all finite forms are third person singular active.

δεῖ, δεήσει, ἐδέησε(ν), ——, ——, ——, "it is necessary, must; there is need"
χρή, χρῆσται, ——, ——, ——, ——, "ought, must"

The verb δεῖ has a present tense stem δε- which contracts with the ending ONLY in the present indicative and infinitive active and in the imperfect indicative active.

The verb χρή consists of an indeclinable noun χρή, not translated separately, contracted with the appropriate form of εἰμί, except in the present indicative active, where χρή stands by itself.

The forms of these verbs are as follows:

present indicative active	δεῖ	χρή
present subjunctive active	δέῃ	χρῇ (χρή + ῇ)
present optative active	δέοι	χρείη (χρή + εἴη)
present infinitive active	δεῖν	χρῆναι (χρή + εἶναι)
present participle active	δέον	χρεών (χρή + ὄν)
imperfect indicative active	ἔδει	χρῆν/ἐχρῆν (χρή + ἦν)
future indicative active	δεήσει	χρῆσται (χρή + ἔσται)
aorist indicative active	ἐδέησε(ν)	——

Observations: (1) The participle of these verbs appears in the neuter only.

(2) The participle χρεών (from *χρηόν) results from quantitative metathesis.

(3) The alternative imperfect form ἐχρῆν adds the past indicative augment.

These verbs take an infinitive, usually with subject accusative, to complete their meaning.

δεῖ ἡμᾶς τοῦτο ποιῆσαι.
There is need for us to do this.
We must do this.

χρὴ ἡμᾶς τοῦτο ποιῆσαι.
We ought to do this.
We must do this.

When negated, these verbs usually mean "must not," but οὐ δεῖ can sometimes mean "there is no need."

οὐ δεῖ
οὐ χρή   } ἡμᾶς τοῦτο ποιῆσαι.
We must not do this.

οὐ δεῖ ἡμᾶς τοῦτο ποιῆσαι.
There is no need for us to do this.

The verb δεῖ can take a genitive of the thing needed (a **genitive of separation**) and a dative of the person needing the thing.

δεῖ ἡμῖν σωφροσύνης.
There is need to us of moderation.
We have need of moderation.

πολλοῦ δεῖ.
There is need of much.
(I.e., much is lacking.)

The neuter participle δέον, δέοντος means "needed, necessary."

ἀεὶ ποιοῦμεν τὰ δέοντα.
We always do the things necessary.

149. THE USE OF δοκεῖ IN THE SENSE "seems best"

The verb δοκέω, "seem," can be used in the third person singular with the meaning "it seems best" to express a personal or collective opinion or decision. In such sentences, the infinitive serves as the subject of δοκεῖ.

δοκεῖ μοι τοῦτο ποιεῖν.
It seems best to me to do this.

ἔδοξε τοῖς Ἀθηναίοις ἀγγέλους πρὸς βασιλέα πέμψαι.
It seemed best to the Athenians to send messengers to the king.

ἔδοξε τῇ βουλῇ καὶ τῷ δήμῳ ...
It seemed best to the council and the people . . .
(= The council and the people decided . . .)

A pronoun can stand, instead of an infinitive, as subject.

ταῦτά μοι δοκεῖ.
These things seem best to me.

150. ACCUSATIVE ABSOLUTE

The participles of impersonal verbs (e.g., δεῖ, δοκεῖ, ἔξεστι, χρή) can be employed, independently of the main verb of a sentence, in a construction called the **accusative absolute**. Such participles are *neuter singular* and can govern an infinitive just as do the other forms of these verbs. These are NOT accompanied by a noun or pronoun.

This construction is like the genitive absolute, which is employed with verbs which have a specific noun or pronoun as subject. Both the genitive absolute and the accusative absolute are circumstantial uses of the participle; both are "absolute" in the sense that they express a circumstance separate from the main clause of the sentence. But the obligation or possibility expressed by an accusative absolute usually applies to someone named in the main clause.

δέον δίκην δοῦναι, ἐκ τῆς πόλεως ἐφύγετε.

It being necessary to pay the penalty, you left the city.

Although it was necessary to pay the penalty, you left the
city.

ἐξὸν ἀγαθὰ ποιεῖν, ποιῶμεν ἀγαθά.

It being possible to do good things, let us do good things.

Since it is possible to do good things, let us do good things.

151. THE VERB κεῖμαι, "lie, be placed, be set"

The verb κεῖμαι appears only in the present, imperfect, and future tenses.
It has only a middle voice.

κεῖμαι, κείσομαι, ——, ——, ——, —— "lie, be placed, be set"

The verb is athematic in the present and imperfect tenses. The present tense
stem has two grades:

    Long-vowel grade: κει-

    Short-vowel grade: κε-

Unlike the athematic verbs already encountered, κεῖμαι employs the long-
vowel grade of the present tense stem throughout the present indicative, in the
present infinitive and participle, and in the imperfect indicative. The short-
vowel grade is employed *only in the present subjunctive and optative.*

The usual athematic endings are employed, EXCEPT that the optative has
thematic endings.

The short-vowel present tense stem κε- does NOT contract with the subjunctive
and optative endings.

These, then, are the forms of κεῖμαι in the present and imperfect tenses.

		PRESENT IND. MIDDLE	*IMPERF. IND. MIDDLE*	*PRESENT SUBJ. MIDDLE*	*PRESENT OPT. MIDDLE*	*PRESENT IMPER. MIDDLE*
S	1	κεῖμαι	ἐκείμην	κέωμαι	κεοίμην	
	2	κεῖσαι	ἔκεισο	κέῃ	κέοιο	κεῖσο
	3	κεῖται	ἔκειτο	κέηται	κέοιτο	κείσθω
P	1	κείμεθα	ἐκείμεθα	κεώμεθα	κεοίμεθα	
	2	κεῖσθε	ἔκεισθε	κέησθε	κέοισθε	κεῖσθε
	3	κεῖνται	ἔκειντο	κέωνται	κέοιντο	κείσθων

PRESENT INFINITIVE MIDDLE: κεῖσθαι

PRESENT PARTICIPLE MIDDLE: κείμενος, κειμένη, κείμενον

Observation: The second person plural, present imperative middle is identical
with the second person plural, present indicative middle. Context will help to determine meaning.

152. SECOND-DECLENSION NOUNS OF THE TYPE *νοῦς, νοῦ, ὁ,* "mind"

Second-declension nouns of the type *νοῦς, νοῦ, ὁ,* "mind," have stems ending
in the vowel *-o-*, which contracts with the declensional endings according to
the regular rules. Uncontracted forms are given in parentheses.

Nom. S	νοῦς	(νόος)
Gen.	νοῦ	(νόου)
Dat.	νῷ	(νόῳ)
Acc.	νοῦν	(νόον)
Voc.	νοῦ	(νόε)
Nom./Voc. P	νοῖ	(νόοι)
Gen.	νῶν	(νόων)
Dat.	νοῖς	(νόοις)
Acc.	νοῦς	(νόους)

153. THE THIRD-DECLENSION NOUN *ἄστυ, ἄστεως, τό,* "town"

The third-declension noun *ἄστυ, ἄστεως, τό,* "town," has two stems: the stem
ἀστυ-, with no ending added, forms the nominative, accusative, and vocative
singular; the stem *ἀστε-*, plus the appropriate endings, appears elsewhere.

Nom./Voc. S	ἄστυ
Gen.	ἄστεως
Dat.	ἄστει
Acc.	ἄστυ
Nom./Voc. P	ἄστη (<ἄστεα)
Gen.	ἄστεων
Dat.	ἄστεσι(ν)
Acc.	ἄστη (<ἄστεα)

Observations: (1) The genitive singular and plural are like those of *πόλις,
πόλεως, ἡ.*

(2) The nominative, accusative, and vocative plural are like
those of *γένος, γένους, τό.*

VOCABULARY

ἄστυ, ἄστεως, τό	town
ἀφικνέομαι, ἀφίξομαι, ἀφικόμην,	arrive
——, ἀφῖγμαι, ——	
δεῖ, δεήσει, ἐδέησε(ν), ——,	it is necessary, must; there is need
——, —— (impersonal verb)	
ἰᾱτρός, ἰᾱτροῦ, ὁ	doctor
κεῖμαι, κείσομαι, ——, ——,	lie, be placed, be set
——, ——	
νοῦς, νοῦ, ὁ	mind, reason
πυνθάνομαι, πεύσομαι, ἐπυθόμην,	inquire, learn by inquiry
——, πέπυσμαι, ——	
τρέπω, τρέψω, ἔτρεψα or ἐτραπόμην,	turn; (mid., aorist passive)
τέτροφα, τέτραμμαι,	turn oneself
ἐτράπην or ἐτρέφθην	
φαίνω, φανῶ, ἔφηνα, πέφηνα,	show, cause to appear;
πέφασμαι, ἐφάνην	(mid., perfect active, aorist
	passive) appear
χρή, χρῆσται, ——, ——, ——, ——	ought, must
(impersonal verb)	

VOCABULARY NOTES

The verb ἀφικνέομαι, ἀφίξομαι, ἀφικόμην, ——, ἀφῖγμαι, ——, "arrive," is
a middle deponent compounded with ἀπο-. The root is ἱκ-. Principal Part I
has the suffix -νε- and is contracted; Principal Part II has the suffix -σ-;
Principal Part III is a second aorist. The -ῑ- of Principal Part III shows the
past indicative augment; that of Principal Part V is part of the tense stem.

The accent of Principal Part V follows the rule that IN THE PERFECT ACTIVE AND
MIDDLE/PASSIVE THE ACCENT OF A COMPOUND VERB CANNOT RECEDE BEYOND THE
INITIAL SYLLABLE OF THE STEM.

The deponent verb κεῖμαι, κείσομαι, ——, ——, ——, ——, "lie, be placed, be set," is athematic in the present and imperfect tenses (see Section 151). The present tense of this verb serves as the perfect passive of τίθημι, and the imperfect as its pluperfect.

> νόμος κεῖται περὶ τούτων.
> A law is laid down (= has been laid down) about these things.

> οἱ κείμενοι νόμοι
> the laws set
> the laws laid down

The deponent verb πυνθάνομαι, πεύσομαι, ἐπυθόμην, ——, πέπυσμαι, ——, "inquire, learn by inquiry," has in Principal Part I both a nasal infix and the suffix -αν-; Principal Part III is a second aorist; Principal Part II shows the e-grade of the root, while the other Principal Parts show the zero-grade. This verb takes the same constructions as ἀκούω: accusative of the thing heard, genitive of the person heard, indirect statement with a finite verb introduced by ὅτι/ὡς, indirect statement with a participle and subject accusative. It can also introduce indirect statement with infinitive and subject accusative.

The verb τρέπω, τρέψω, ἔτρεψα or ἐτραπόμην, τέτροφα, τέτραμμαι, ἐτράπην or ἐτρέφθην, "turn; (mid., aorist passive) turn oneself," has both a first aorist and a deponent second aorist middle, and two aorists passive. The active forms are always transitive and mean "make (something) turn" or, in military contexts, "make an enemy turn and run, put to flight." Except for the first aorist middle, which is only transitive in the sense of "put to flight for one's own advantage," the middle can be intransitive ("turn oneself") or transitive ("make turn for one's own advantage"). The intransitive aorist is either ἐτραπόμην or ἐτράπην. Note, in addition to the e-grade of the root (τρεπ-), the o-grade in the aspirated perfect τέτροφα and the zero-grade in the forms ἐτραπόμην, τέτραμμαι, and ἐτράπην (τραπ- from *τρπ-).

The verb φαίνω, φανῶ, ἔφηνα, πέφηνα, πέφασμαι, ἐφάνην, "show, cause to appear; (mid., perfect active, aorist passive) appear," has a contracted future active and middle. The perfect middle/passive tense stem was originally πεφαν-, but this stem was replaced by the stem πεφασ- in many but not all forms. The perfect middle/passive is conjugated as follows in the indicative: πέφασμαι, πεφασμένος εἶ, πέφανται, πεφάσμεθα, πέφανθε, πεφασμένοι εἰσί(ν). Note the periphrastic forms in the second person singular and third person plural. The pluperfect indicative middle/passive follows the same pattern. The perfect infinitive middle/passive is πεφάνθαι (<*πεφάνσθαι). The perfect active πέφηνα means "I have appeared"; the aorist passive ἐφάνην is deponent and means "I appeared." In the sense "appear" this verb can govern either an infinitive or a participle with a *substantial difference in meaning*:

φαίνεται κακὸς εἶναι.
He appears to be bad.

φαίνεται κακὸς ὤν.
He is apparent, being bad.
It is apparent that he is bad.

COGNATES AND DERIVATIVES

ἰᾱτρός	psychiatrist (**doctor** purporting to heal souls)
νοῦς	noesis (cognition)
τρέπω	tropic (where the sun **turns** back each year)
φαίνω	phenomenon

DRILL

Translate.

1. ὑμῖν εἰρήνη ποιητέᾱ ἐστίν.
2. ὑμῖν εἰρήνην ποιητέον ἐστίν.
3. ὑμῖν εἰρήνην ποιητέα ἐστίν.
4. ἡμῖν γε οἵδε οἱ πολέμιοι νῑκητέοι εἰσίν.
5. ἡμῖν γε τούσδε τοὺς πολεμίους νῑκητέον ἐστίν.
6. τούτῳ τῷ αἰσχίστῳ δίκην δοτέον ἐστίν.
7. τούτῳ τῷ αἰσχίστῳ δίκη δοτέᾱ ἐστίν.
8. τούτῳ τῷ αἰσχίστῳ δίκην δοτέα ἐστίν.
9. τέτταρας ἀγγέλους τῷ στρατηγῷ ἀποπεμπτέον.
10. τέτταρες ἄγγελοι τῷ στρατηγῷ ἀποπεμπτέοι.
11. ὦ βασιλεῦ, πάντων ἀνθρώπων σοὶ ἀρκτέον ἐστίν.
12. ὦ θύγατερ, τῷ πατρὶ ἀεὶ πειστέον.
13. οὐδένα πονηρὸν οὐδενὶ τῑμητέον ἐστίν.
14. νομίζομεν τούτους ὑμῖν τῑμητέους εἶναι.
15. νομίζομεν τούτους ὑμῖν τῑμητέον εἶναι.
16. οὐκ ἐνομίζομεν οὐδένα πονηρὸν τῑμητέον εἶναι οὐδενί.

EXERCISES

I. 1. (a) ἡ δημοκρατίᾱ οὐ καταλυτέᾱ ἐστὶν οὐδενί.

     (b) τὴν δημοκρατίᾱν οὐ καταλυτέον ἐστὶν οὐδενί.

  2. (a) ἔμοιγε ταῦτα πρᾱκτέον ἐστίν.

     (b) ἔμοιγε ταῦτα πρᾱκτέα ἐστίν.

  3. ὦ ἄνδρες Ἀθηναῖοι, πάντων τῶν Ἑλλήνων ὑμῖν ἀρκτέον ἐστίν.

  4. οὐδείς τοι πονηρὸς οὐδενὶ τῑμητέος.

  5. τῶν μαθητῶν ἐπυθόμεθα Σωκράτη, διδάσκαλον τὸν μακρῷ πάντων ἄριστον, τεθνηκότα.

  6. οὐ χρὴ τούς γε βελτίονας τῶν χειρόνων ὑπακοῦσαι οὐδέν.

  7. (a) ἐφαίνετο ἀρίστη εἶναι.

     (b) ἐφαίνετο ἀρίστη οὖσα.

  8. ὦ ἄνδρες, ἀφέντες τοὺς οὐ μεμαχημένους ἀποκτείνατε τοὺς ἡμῖν αὐτοῖς ἐπιβεβουλευκότας.

  9. ἔδοξε πᾶσι τοὺς χειρίστους ἐκ τῆς γῆς ἐξελάσαι.

 10. ὦ νεᾱνίᾱ, δεῖ σε πιστεύειν τοῖς μὴ ἡμαρτηκόσιν.

 11. ζωγράφων εἰσί που οἱ μὲν χείρους, οἱ δὲ πολλῷ ἀμείνονες.

 12. ὦ ῥῆτορ, σοί γε τὸν ἥττω λόγον οὐ κρείττω ποιητέα.

 13. οὐκ οἶδεν εἰ ταῦτα τοῖς ἄρχουσι δοκεῖ.

 14. πλεῖστοι τῶν νόμων ὧν ἐθέμεθα κεῖνται καὶ νῦν. συνίεμεν γὰρ καὶ τότε ὅπως δέοι τοιαύτης γε πόλεως ἄρχειν.

 15. θυσίᾱν δὴ ποιησόμεθα πάντων τῶν ζῴων ὅσων ἂν πέμψῃς αὐτή.

 16. δέον μαχέσασθαι, ὦ ἄφρον ὁπλῖτα, ἔφυγες.

 17. ἆρα δεῖ με τούτων τῶν ἀμαθῶν ἀκούειν; ἀπόκρῑναι, ὦ ἄδελφε.

 18. βασιλεῖ δὴ πειστέον· κρείττων γὰρ βασιλεύς.

 19. εἴθε ἀεὶ ἐτρέπομεν τὰς τῶν παίδων φύσεις πρὸς τὸ ἀγαθόν.

 20. οἵτινες ἂν τοῖς ἀμείνοσι φαίνωνται μὴ πρὸς αἰσχρὰ τὸν νοῦν τρέποντες, τοιοῦτοι ῥᾷστα τῆς πόλεως ἄρξουσιν.

 21. τούτῳ γε τῷ ῥήτορι χρῡσὸν δοῦναι οὔ σε δεῖ, ὦ ἄδελφε· ἐγὼ γὰρ χρήματ' οὐκ ὀλίγα δώσω.

 22. χρὴ ὑμᾶς γε τοὺς γέροντας ὡς σωφρονεστάτους εἶναι.

23. τοὺς νόμους τοὺς κειμένους οὐ καταλυτέον.

24. ἔφησθά που τὸ δίκαιον τόδ᾽ εἶναι· τὸν κρείττω τοῦ ἥττονος ἄρχειν καὶ πλέον ἔχειν.

25. ἐν ἐκείνῃ τῇ μάχῃ ἔδει τοῖς ᾿Αθηναίοις καὶ ἐμπειρίας καὶ σωφροσύνης.

26. πολλοὶ μὲν οἱ νοῦν οὐκ ἔχοντες, ὀλίγοι δὲ οἱ σοφοί.

27. εἰ συνῄδη ἐμαυτῇ αἴσχιστα πεποιηκυίᾳ, οὐκ ἂν ἔχαιρον ἐν ἄστει μετὰ τῶν φίλων παραμένουσα.

28. ὅσους ἀφῆκεν ὁ βασιλεὺς πεφεύγασι πρὸς τὸν λιμένα ὡς εἰς ναῦς τινάς πως ἀναβησόμενοι. φόβος γὰρ ἦν αὐτοῖς μὴ τάχιστα τελευτῶεν ὑπ᾽ ἐκείνων ὧν οἶσθά που καὶ σύ.

29. οἱ κακίονες μόνον τόδ᾽ ἐζήτουν, ὁπόθεν ἐξ ἐλαττόνων χρημάτων πλείω ἔσται.

30. ἐφοβεῖσθε μὴ θάττονες ὦσιν αἱ τῶν Λακεδαιμονίων νῆες τῶν ὑμετέρων.

31. ἀφικομένων τῶν συμμάχων, οἱ τεθνεῶτες ἔκειντο ἐν τῷ πεδίῳ.

32. ἔδοξέ μοι οὗτος ὁ ἀνὴρ δοκεῖν μὲν εἶναι σοφὸς ἄλλοις τε πολλοῖς ἀνθρώποις καὶ μάλιστα ἑαυτῷ, εἶναι δ᾽ οὔ. (Plato, Apology 21c)

33. μὴ εὑροῦσαι τἀληθῆ,¹ ὦ ἀμαθεῖς, οὐ ζητήσεθ᾽ ὡς ἄρισται γενέσθαι. νῦν γὰρ αἴσχισθ᾽ ἁμαρτάνετε.

34. νῦν δὴ ἐπὶ τὰ μείζω τραπώμεθα. ταῦτα γὰρ πάντα συνεῖμεν.

---

1. τἀληθῆ = τὰ ἀληθῆ (For this **crasis** see the Appendix, p. 614).

II.   1.   We must conquer the *enemy*. (*Do this sentence three ways: with the two constructions of the verbal adjective, and with an impersonal verb.*)

2.   I learned by inquiry how much better a poet Aristophanes was than Euripides.

3.   These orators must speak as beautifully as possible so as to persuade those hearing.

READINGS

A. Plato, *Gorgias* 457c4–458b3

Sokrates and Gorgias continue their discussion of rhetoric.

ΣΩ. Οἶμαι, ὦ Γοργία, καὶ σὲ ἔμπειρον εἶναι πολλῶν
95 λόγων καὶ καθεωρᾱκέναι ἐν αὐτοῖς τὸ τοιόνδε, ὅτι οὐ
ῥᾳδίως δύνανται περὶ ὧν ἂν ἐπιχειρήσωσιν διαλέγεσθαι
διορισάμενοι πρὸς ἀλλήλους καὶ μαθόντες καὶ διδάξαντες
ἑαυτούς, οὕτω διαλύεσθαι τὰς συνουσίας, ἀλλ᾽ ἐὰν περί
του ἀμφισβητήσωσιν καὶ μὴ φῇ ὁ ἕτερος τὸν ἕτερον
100 ὀρθῶς λέγειν ἢ μὴ σαφῶς, χαλεπαίνουσί τε καὶ κατὰ
φθόνον οἴονται τὸν ἑαυτῶν λέγειν, φιλονῑκοῦντας ἀλλ᾽
οὐ ζητοῦντας τὸ προκείμενον ἐν τῷ λόγῳ. καὶ ἔνιοί
γε τελευτῶντες αἴσχιστα ἀπαλλάττονται, λοιδορηθέντες
τε καὶ εἰπόντες καὶ ἀκούσαντες περὶ σφῶν αὐτῶν
105 τοιαῦτα οἷα¹ καὶ τοὺς παρόντας ἄχθεσθαι ὑπὲρ σφῶν
αὐτῶν, ὅτι τοιούτων ἀνθρώπων ἠξίωσαν ἀκροᾱταὶ
γενέσθαι. τοῦ δὴ ἕνεκα λέγω ταῦτα; ὅτι νῦν ἐμοὶ
δοκεῖς σὺ οὐ πάνυ ἀκόλουθα λέγειν οὐδὲ σύμφωνα οἷς
τὸ πρῶτον ἔλεγες περὶ τῆς ῥητορικῆς· φοβοῦμαι οὖν
110 διελέγχειν σε, μή με ὑπολάβῃς οὐ πρὸς τὸ πρᾶγμα
φιλονῑκοῦντα λέγειν τοῦ καταφανὲς γενέσθαι,² ἀλλὰ
πρὸς σέ. ἐγὼ οὖν, εἰ μὲν καὶ σὺ εἶ τῶν ἀνθρώπων ὦνπερ
καὶ ἐγώ, ἡδέως ἄν σε διερωτῴην· εἰ δὲ μή, ἐῴην ἄν.
ἐγὼ δὲ τίνων εἰμί; τῶν ἡδέως μὲν ἂν ἐλεγχθέντων
115 εἴ τι μὴ ἀληθὲς λέγω, ἡδέως δ᾽ ἂν ἐλεγξάντων εἴ
τίς τι μὴ ἀληθὲς λέγοι, οὐκ ἀηδέστερον μεντᾶν
ἐλεγχθέντων ἢ ἐλεγξάντων· μεῖζον γὰρ αὐτὸ ἀγαθὸν
ἡγοῦμαι, ὅσῳπερ μεῖζον ἀγαθόν ἐστιν αὐτὸν ἀπαλλαγῆναι
κακοῦ τοῦ μεγίστου ἢ ἄλλον ἀπαλλάξαι. οὐδὲν γὰρ
120 οἶμαι τοσοῦτον κακὸν εἶναι ἀνθρώπῳ, ὅσον δόξα
ψευδὴς περὶ ὧν τυγχάνει νῦν ἡμῖν ὁ λόγος ὤν. εἰ
μὲν οὖν καὶ σὺ φῂς τοιοῦτος εἶναι, διαλεγώμεθα·
εἰ δὲ καὶ δοκεῖ χρῆναι ἐᾶν, ἐῶμεν ἤδη χαίρειν καὶ
διαλύωμεν τὸν λόγον.

---

1. The adjective οἷος, οἵᾱ, οἷον can introduce a clause of natural result.
2. τοῦ . . . γενέσθαι: **genitive of purpose**. See the Appendix, p. 698.

ἀηδής, ἀηδές   distasteful, unpleasant, disagreeable

ἀκόλουθος, ἀκόλουθον   following, in conformity with

ἀκροᾱτής, ἀκροᾱτοῦ, ὁ   hearer, listener

ἀμφισβητέω, ἀμφισβητήσω, ἠμφεσβήτησα, ——, ——, ἠμφεσβητήθην
  disagree, dispute, argue

ἀπαλλάττω, ἀπαλλάξω, ἀπήλλαξα, ἀπήλλαχα, ἀπήλλαγμαι, ἀπηλλάγην/
  ἀπηλλάχθην   set free; escape; (mid. and aor. pass.)   get free, be freed
  from, depart from (+ gen.)

ἄχθομαι, ἀχθέσομαι, ——, ——, ἤχθημαι, ἠχθέσθην   be grieved, be vexed

διαλέγομαι, διαλέξομαι, ——, ——, διείλεγμαι, διελέχθην   converse with
  (+ dat.)

διελέγχω, διελέγξω, διήλεγξα, ——, διελήλεγμαι, διηλέγχθην   refute

διορίζω, διοριῶ, διώρισα, διώρικα, διώρισμαι, διωρίσθην   define

ἐάω, ἐάσω, εἴᾱσα, εἴᾱκα, εἴᾱμαι, εἰάθην   permit, allow; let alone

ἐλέγχω, ἐλέγξω, ἤλεγξα, ——, ἐλήλεγμαι, ἠλέγχθην   examine, question, test;
  refute

ἔνιοι, ἔνιαι, ἔνια   some

ἐπιχειρέω, ἐπιχειρήσω, ἐπεχείρησα, ἐπικεχείρηκα, ἐπικεχείρημαι,
  ἐπεχειρήθην   attempt

ἤδη (adv.)   already, now

καταφανής, καταφανές   clear, manifest

λοιδορέω, λοιδορήσω, ἐλοιδόρησα, λελοιδόρηκα, λελοιδόρημαι, ἐλοιδορήθην
  revile, reproach, abuse

μέντοι (particle)   indeed, and yet

οἶμαι/οἴομαι, οἰήσομαι, ——, ——, ——, ᾠήθην   think, suppose, believe

πρόκειμαι, προκείσομαι, ——, ——, ——, ——   lie before, be set before

σύμφωνος, σύμφωνον   agreeing, harmonious

συνουσίᾱ, συνουσίᾱς, ἡ   social gathering, society, intercourse

τοιόσδε, τοιάδε, τοιόνδε   such as this

ὑπολαμβάνω   assume; interpret

φθόνος, φθόνου, ὁ   envy, spite

φιλονῑκέω, φιλονῑκήσω, ἐφιλονίκησα, ——, ——, ——   be contentious

χαλεπαίνω, χαλεπανῶ, ἐχαλέπηνα, ——, ——, ἐχαλεπάνθην   be angry

B. Isokrates, *To Demonikos* 5–8

The rhetorician Isokrates gives advice to Demonikos, the son of a friend.

> Διόπερ ἡμεῖς οὐ παράκλησιν εὑρόντες ἀλλὰ
> παραίνεσιν γράψαντες, μέλλομέν σοι συμβουλεύειν
> ὧν χρὴ τοὺς νεωτέρους ὀρέγεσθαι καὶ τίνων ἔργων
> ἀπέχεσθαι καὶ ποίοις τισὶν ἀνθρώποις ὁμῑλεῖν
> 5 καὶ πῶς τὸν ἑαυτῶν βίον οἰκονομεῖν. ὅσοι γὰρ
> τοῦ βίου ταύτην τὴν ὁδὸν ἐπορεύθησαν,[1] οὗτοι
> μόνοι τῆς ἀρετῆς ἐφικέσθαι γνησίως ἠδυνήθησαν,[1]
> ἧς οὐδὲν κτῆμα σεμνότερον οὐδὲ βεβαιότερόν ἐστι.
> κάλλος μὲν γὰρ ἢ χρόνος ἀνήλωσεν[1] ἢ νόσος ἐμάρᾱνε·[1]

ἀνᾱλίσκω, ἀνᾱλώσω, ἀνήλωσα, ἀνήλωκα, ἀνήλωμαι, ἀνηλώθην   use up, spend;
  waste, destroy

βέβαιος, βέβαιον   firm, steady, sure

γνήσιος, γνησίᾱ, γνήσιον   lawfully begotten, legitimate, true

διόπερ = διὰ ὅπερ

ἐφικνέομαι, ἐφίξομαι, ἐφῑκόμην, ——, ἐφῖγμαι, ——   reach at, aim at, attain
  (+ *gen.*)

κτῆμα, κτήματος, τό   possession

μαραίνω, μαρανῶ, ἐμάρᾱνα, ——, μεμάρασμαι, ἐμαράνθην   quench, cause to
  wither away

οἰκονομέω, οἰκονομήσω, ᾠκονόμησα, ᾠκονόμηκα, ᾠκονόμημαι, ᾠκονομήθην
  manage as a house steward, manage, direct

ὁμῑλέω, ὁμῑλήσω, ὡμῑλησα, ὡμῑληκα, ὡμῑλημαι, ὡμῑλήθην   associate with
  (+ *dat.*)

ὀρέγω, ὀρέξω, ὤρεξα, ——, ὤρεγμαι, ὠρέχθην   reach, stretch out; (*mid., pass.*)
  stretch oneself out, desire (+ *gen.*)

παραίνεσις, παραινέσεως, ἡ   advice, counsel

παράκλησις, παρακλήσεως, ἡ   summoning, exhortation

πορεύω, πορεύσω, ἐπόρευσα, πεπόρευκα, πεπόρευμαι, ἐπορεύθην   carry,
  convey; (*mid., pass.*)   go

σεμνός, σεμνή, σεμνόν   revered, holy, majestic

χρή, χρῆσται, ——, ——, ——, ——   (*impersonal verb*)   ought, must

χρόνος, χρόνου, ὁ   time

---

1. **Gnomic aorist**, expressing a general truth; translate as a present; see the Appendix,
page 733. The verb δύναμαι can use either ἐ- or ἠ- as the past indicative augment.

10 πλοῦτος δὲ κακίᾱς μᾶλλον ἢ καλοκᾱγαθίᾱς ὑπηρέτης
ἐστίν, ἐξουσίᾱν μὲν τῇ ῥᾳθῡμίᾳ παρασκευάζων, ἐπὶ
δὲ τὰς ἡδονὰς τοὺς νέους παρακαλῶν· ῥώμη δὲ μετὰ
μὲν φρονήσεως ὠφέλησεν,[1] ἄνευ δὲ ταύτης πλείω
τοὺς ἔχοντας ἔβλαψε,[1] καὶ τὰ μὲν σώματα τῶν

15 ἀσκούντων ἐκόσμησε,[1] ταῖς δὲ τῆς ψῡχῆς ἐπιμελείαις
ἐπεσκότησε.[1] ἡ δὲ τῆς ἀρετῆς κτῆσις, οἷς ἂν
ἀκιβδήλως ταῖς διανοίαις συναυξηθῇ, μόνη μὲν

ἀκίβδηλος, ἀκίβδηλον   genuine, not counterfeit

ἀσκέω, ἀσκήσω, ἤσκησα, ἤσκηκα, ἤσκημαι, ἠσκήθην   work, practice

διάνοια, διανοίᾱς, ἡ   thought

ἐξουσίᾱ, ἐξουσίᾱς, ἡ   power, possibility

ἐπιμέλεια, ἐπιμελείᾱς, ἡ   care

ἐπισκοτέω, ἐπισκοτήσω, ἐπεσκότησα, ἐπεσκότηκα, ἐπεσκότημαι,
   ἐπεσκοτήθην   throw a shadow over (+ *dat.*)

ἡδονή, ἡδονῆς, ἡ   pleasure

κακίᾱ, κακίᾱς, ἡ   badness, cowardice, wickedness

καλοκᾱγαθίᾱ, καλοκᾱγαθίᾱς, ἡ   character and conduct of a man who is
   καλός and ἀγαθός

κοσμέω, κοσμήσω, ἐκόσμησα, κεκόσμηκα, κεκόσμημαι, ἐκοσμήθην   order,
   arrange; adorn, equip

κτῆσις, κτήσεως, ἡ   acquisition, possession

παρασκευάζω, παρασκευάσω, παρεσκεύασα, παρεσκεύακα, παρεσκεύασμαι,
   παρεσκευάσθην   prepare

πλοῦτος, πλούτου, ὁ   wealth

ῥᾳθῡμίᾱ, ῥᾳθῡμίᾱς, ἡ   ease, relaxation; laziness

ῥώμη, ῥώμης, ἡ   strength

συναυξάνω/συναύξω, συναυξήσω, συνηύξησα, συνηύξηκα, συνηύξημαι,
   συνηυξήθην   increase together with (+ *dat.*)

ὑπηρέτης, ὑπηρέτου, ὁ   servant

φρόνησις, φρονήσεως, ἡ   purpose, intention, judgment

ὠφελέω, ὠφελήσω, ὠφέλησα, ὠφέληκα, ὠφέλημαι, ὠφελήθην   help, aid

---

1. **Gnomic aorist**, expressing a general truth; translate as a present; see the Appendix,
page 733.

συγγηράσκει, πλούτου δὲ κρείττων, χρησιμωτέρᾱ
δὲ εὐγενείᾱς ἐστί, τὰ μὲν τοῖς ἄλλοις ἀδύνατα
20 δυνατὰ καθιστᾶσα, τὰ δὲ τῷ πλήθει φοβερὰ
θαρσαλέως ὑπομένουσα, καὶ τὸν μὲν ὄκνον ψόγον,
τὸν δὲ πόνον ἔπαινον ἡγουμένη. ῥᾴδιον δὲ
τοῦτο καταμαθεῖν ἐστιν ἔκ τε τῶν Ἡρακλέους
ἄθλων καὶ τῶν Θησέως ἔργων, οἷς ἡ τῶν τρόπων
25 ἀρετὴ τηλικοῦτον εὐδοξίᾱς χαρακτῆρα τοῖς ἔργοις
ἐπέβαλεν, ὥστε μηδὲ τὸν ἅπαντα χρόνον δύνασθαι
λήθην ἐμποιῆσαι τῶν ἐκείνοις πεπρᾱγμένων.

ἀδύνατος, ἀδύνατον   unable; impossible

ἄθλος, ἄθλου, ὁ   contest

δυνατός, δυνατή, δυνατόν   able, possible

ἔπαινος, ἐπαίνου, ὁ   praise

εὐγένεια, εὐγενείᾱς, ἡ   nobility of birth

εὐδοξίᾱ, εὐδοξίᾱς, ἡ   fame, glory

Ἡρακλῆς, Ἡρακλέους, ὁ   Herakles

θαρσαλέος, θαρσαλέᾱ, θαρσαλέον   daring, confident

Θησεύς, Θησέως, ὁ   Theseus, an Athenian hero

λήθη, λήθης, ἡ   forgetfulness

ὄκνος, ὄκνου, ὁ   shrinking, hesitation, fear

πλῆθος, πλήθους, τό   great number, multitude

πλοῦτος, πλούτου, ὁ   wealth

πόνος, πόνου, ὁ   work, labor, exercise

συγγηράσκω, συγγηράσομαι, συνεγήρᾱσα, ——, ——, ——   grow old together
with (+ dat.)

τηλικοῦτος, τηλικαύτη, τηλικοῦτον   so old, so great

χαρακτήρ, χαρακτῆρος, ὁ   distinctive mark

χρήσιμος, χρησίμη, χρήσιμον   useful

χρόνος, χρόνου, ὁ   time

ψόγος, ψόγου, ὁ   fault, blame

1. ἐάν τις ξίφος τ' ὀξύτερον καὶ ἀσπίδα βαρεῖαν λαβὼν ἀποκτείνῃ τινά, ὦ ἄνδρες ψυχὴν ἀγαθοί, δεῖ τοῦτόν γε δίκην δοῦναι.

2. ἆρ' εἶπες ὅτι Σωκράτης πολλῷ δικαιότερος εἴη Δημοσθένους; μὴ λεγέτω μηδεὶς μηδενὶ τοιοῦτόν γε λόγον. πάντων γὰρ δικαιότατος ἦν οὗτος.

3. ὦ ὁπλῖται, μὴ παύσησθε ὑπὲρ τῆς πόλεως μαχόμενοι. ἀεὶ γὰρ οὕτως ἐτάττεσθε πρὸς τοὺς πολεμίους ὥστε ἡ πᾶσα πόλις ἐσῴζετο.

4. ὁπότε ἐξέλθοι ὁ στρατὸς εἰς μάχην, ἔπαυε δή που τοὺς βαρβάρους προσιόντας.

5. ἐρωτῶντος τοῦ μαθητοῦ ἥτις εἴη ἡ τῆς ἀρετῆς ἀληθὴς φύσις, οἱ ἀφρονέστεροι ἐφοβήθησαν μὴ τὴν ἀλήθειαν φαίη ὁ διδάσκων.

6. ὑμεῖς γ' ἐμηχανᾶσθέ που, ὦ ῥήτορες, ὅπως οἱ ἥττονες ὑπὸ τῶν κρειττόνων ἀρχθήσονται. τί δὲ ταῦτ' ἐπράξατε; ἐβούλεσθε δὴ ἄλλους εἰς κράτος καταστῆσαι ἵνα τὰ τοῦ δήμου κλέψητε αὐτοί;

7. εἰ ἐκείνης γέ τοι τῆς ἡμέρας τοὺς σώματι ἀγαθοὺς ἐπὶ τοὺς πολεμίους μὴ ἐπέμψαμεν, πλείονες ἂν κακὰ ἔπαθον ὑπὸ τῶν παρὰ τὴν γέφυραν προσελθόντων.

8. σοί γε δή, ἄδελφε, βιβλίον γραπτέον ἦν. οὐ γὰρ ἤθελες οὔτε ἀργύριον οὔτε ἵππους κλέπτειν ὡς ἄριστος ἀνθρώπων ὤν.

9. ὁπόσους ἂν πέμψῃς τοι, ὦ ἑταῖρε, τοσοῦτοι ἀποθανοῦνταί ποτε. ὡς φοβερώτατοι γάρ εἰσιν οἱ ἐν τῷ πεδίῳ παραμείναντες.

10. ἐπειδὴ τοὺς φύλακας ἀνηρόμεθα περὶ Σωκράτους, ἐπυθόμεθα αὐτὸν ἀπολωλότα, ἀλλὰ καὶ ἀπεκρίναντο οἱ τοῦτον φυλάξαντες ὅτι νῦν γε εἰδείησαν τὸ ἀγαθοῦ βίου τέλος.

11. τόν γ' Εὐριπίδην ἐρωτῷητε δὴ οἵτινες τῶν πολιτῶν φαίνονται ἀμείνους ὄντες. χρὴ γὰρ πάντας τοὺς τοιούτους ἐξευρεῖν πως.

12. ἐξὸν ἡμῖν τοὺς ἀμείνους τιμῆσαι ἀντὶ τῶν πονηροτέρων, οὐκ ἂν δοίημεν δῶρον οὐδὲν οὐδενὶ αἰσχρὰ πεπραχότι.

13. ὁποῖοι εἴησαν οἱ κείμενοι νόμοι, τοιαύτη ἂν εἴη καὶ ἡ πόλις. ὑμεῖς οὖν οἱ κρείττονες θέσθε ἀγαθοὺς νόμους ὥστε πάντα πολίτην σωθῆναι.

14. (a) διδασκόμεθα ἕως ἂν σωφρονέστεροι γενώμεθα.

 (b) διδασκόμεθα ἕως ἂν οἷοί τ᾽ ὦμεν μαθεῖν τι.

 (c) ἐδιδασκόμεθα ἕως σοφώτατοι ἐγενόμεθα.

 (d) ἐδιδασκόμεθα ἕως ἐδυνάμεθα.

15. μὴ εἰδυῖα ὅπως χρὴ τὰς αἶγας θύειν, ὦ σῶφρον θύγατερ, οὐκ ἂν ἐξῆλθες πρὸς τὸ ἱερὸν ἐκείνῃ τῇ νυκτὶ χορεύσουσα τῇ θεῷ.

16. ἆρ᾽ ἀφεῖτε τοὺς φυλαττομένους πρὶν τόν γε κήρῦκα τὴν τῶν βαρβάρων νίκην ἀπαγγεῖλαι; τοιαῦτα δὴ μὴ ποιεῖτε.

17. τί, ὦ αἴσχιστοι, ἐχαίρετε λέγοντες ὡς χρήματα μόνον τοῖς γ᾽ ἑτέροις ἐστίν; οὐ δὴ νομίζετε αὐτοὶ πολὺ εὐτυχέστεροι ἐκείνων εἶναι;

18. γιγνώσκω σε, ὦ φίλτατε, καὶ πλείστους μαθητὰς διδάξαντα καὶ πλείστοις ἀεὶ τὴν ῥητορικήν, τέχνην τὴν ἀρίστην, ἐπιδεικνύμενον.

19. εἰ γὰρ μὴ ἐποίεις μηδὲν κακὸν μηδένα ἐν μηδενὶ καιρῷ, ἀμαθέστατε παῖ. ὅπως νῦν γε βελτίων πως γενήσει.

20. ἐκεῖ στάντων τῶν ξένων τῶν τοῖς ἡμετέροις νενῑκημένων, ἐνταῦθα στῆθι τὸ τρόπαιον ἀναστήσων.

21. οὔ φαμεν τόν γε Δημοσθένη τὴν πόλιν κακὰ πρᾶξαί ποτε. εἰ γὰρ οὕτως ἔπρᾱττεν, οὐκ ἂν ἐτῑμᾶτο ὑπ᾽ οὐδενός.

22. πότε εἶπον οἱ ἐκεῖ ταξάμενοι ὅτι οὔτε μαχοῖντό ποτε ὑπὲρ τῆς ἐλευθερίᾱς οὔτε σώσοιεν τοὺς φίλους;

23. ἥδιστον μὲν τὸ μὴ ἀκούειν μηδενὸς διδασκάλου μηδέν, πολὺ δὲ σωφρονέστερον τὸ σοφωτέροις ὑπακούειν. οὐ γὰρ ἀπίᾱσιν οἵ γε διδάσκαλοι πρὶν ἂν πᾶς μαθητὴς γνῷ τὰ λεγόμενα πάντα.

24. καίπερ πολλὰ καὶ σαφῆ μαθοῦσαι, ὅμως ἐφαίνεσθε καὶ πλέονα οἷαί τ᾽ εἶναι μανθάνειν ἅτε ὡς πλεῖστα ἐθέλουσαι εἰδέναι.

25. οἷα τὸν ἡδὺν οἶνον αἴσχιστα κεκλοφώς, ὁ ἱερεὺς ἔφευγεν. κλοπῆς γάρ τοι ἐγράφοντο τοὺς τοιούτους οἱ ῥήτορες οἱ δεινοὶ λέγειν.

26. τέλος ἀπέλθωμεν; τί γὰρ ἐκείνων ὧν ἔλεγες οὐ συνίεμεν;

SAMPLE GRAMMAR EXAMINATION

I. *Translate the following excerpt from the* Symposium *(adapted) in which the poet Agathon praises love. Then answer the questions concerning the twelve words listed below. Vocabulary for which you are not responsible is glossed.*

ἐγὼ δὴ βούλομαι πρῶτον μὲν εἰπεῖν ὅπως χρή με εἰπεῖν, ἔπειτα δὲ εἰπεῖν. δοκοῦσι γάρ μοι πάντες οἱ πρότερον εἰρηκότες οὐ τὸν θεὸν τῑμᾶν, ἀλλὰ τοὺς ἀνθρώπους εὐδαιμονίζειν τῶν ἀγαθῶν ὧν ὁ θεὸς αὐτοῖς αἴτιος· ὁποῖος δέ τις αὐτὸς ὢν ταῦτα δίδωσιν,
5 οὐδενὶ εἴρηται. εἷς δὲ τρόπος ἀγαθὸς πάσης τῑμῆς, λόγῳ διελθεῖν οἷος ὢν τυγχάνει περὶ οὗ ἂν ὁ λόγος ᾖ. οὕτω δὴ τὸν Ἔρωτα καὶ ἡμᾶς δίκαιον τῑμᾶν πρῶτον περὶ αὐτοῦ λέγοντας ὁποῖός ἐστιν, ἔπειτα δὲ ἅττα δίδωσιν.

φημὶ οὖν ἐγὼ πάντων θεῶν εὐδαιμόνων ὄντων Ἔρωτα, εἰ θέμις
10 οὕτως εἰπεῖν, εὐδαιμονέστατον εἶναι αὐτῶν, κάλλιστον ὄντα καὶ ἄριστον. κάλλιστος δ' ἐστὶν οὗτος τόνδε τὸν τρόπον. πρῶτον μὲν νεώτατος τῶν θεῶν ἐστιν, ὦ ἑταῖρε, καὶ μετὰ νέων ἀεὶ σύνεστιν. ὁ γὰρ παλαιὸς λόγος εὖ ἔχει, ὡς "ὅμοιον ὁμοίῳ ἀεὶ σύνεστιν." ...

15 περὶ μὲν οὖν κάλλους τοῦ θεοῦ ταῦτα δὴ ἱκανά, περὶ δὲ ἀρετῆς Ἔρωτος μετὰ ταῦτα λεκτέον, τὸ μὲν μέγιστον ὅτι Ἔρως οὔτ' ἀδικεῖ οὔτ' ἀδικεῖται οὔθ' ὑπὸ θεοῦ οὔτε θεόν, οὔθ' ὑπ' ἀνθρώπου οὔτε ἄνθρωπον. πρὸς δὲ τῇ δικαιοσύνῃ σωφροσύνης πλείστης μετέχει. εἶναι γὰρ φᾱσιν πάντες σωφροσύνην τὸ κρατεῖν ἡδονῶν
20 καὶ ἐπιθῡμιῶν, Ἔρωτος δὲ οὐδεμίαν ἡδονὴν κρείττω εἶναι.

περὶ μὲν οὖν δικαιοσύνης καὶ σωφροσύνης τοῦ θεοῦ μοι εἴρηται, περὶ δὲ σοφίᾱς λείπεται. καὶ πρῶτον μέν, ἵνα αὖ καὶ ἐγὼ τὴν ἡμετέρᾱν τέχνην τῑμήσω ὥσπερ Ἐρυξίμαχος τὴν αὐτοῦ, ποιητὴς ὁ θεὸς σοφὸς οὕτως ὥστε καὶ ἄλλον ποιῆσαι. πᾶς γὰρ
25 ποιητὴς γίγνεται, καὶ ἐὰν ἄμουσος ᾖ πρότερον, οὗ ἂν Ἔρως ἅψηται.

584   SAMPLE GRAMMAR

Glosses for Plato, Symposium *194e4–196e3 (as abridged and adapted)*:

ἄμουσος, ἄμουσον   unpoetic, unacquainted with the Muses

ἅπτω, ἅψω, ἧψα, ——, ἧμμαι, ἥφθην   fasten, kindle; (*mid.*) touch (+ *gen.*)

δικαιοσύνη, δικαιοσύνης, ἡ   justice

ἐπιθῡμία, ἐπιθῡμίας, ἡ   desire

εὐδαιμονίζω, εὐδαιμονιῶ, ηὐδαιμόνισα, ηὐδαιμόνικα, ηὐδαιμόνισμαι, ηὐδαιμονίσθην   deem blessed for (+ *gen.*)

ἡδονή, ἡδονῆς, ἡ   pleasure

θέμις, θέμιτος, ἡ   law, custom, right; (*in nominal sentence*) it is right

κρατέω, κρατήσω, ἐκράτησα, κεκράτηκα, κεκράτημαι, ἐκρατήθην   be stronger (than) (+ *gen.*)

μετέχω   have a part of (+ *gen.*)

1. Syntax of χρή (line 1).
2. Syntax of τῑμᾶν (line 3).
3. Syntax of οὐδενί (line 5).
4. Syntax of ὤν (line 6).
5. Syntax of ᾗ (line 6).
6. Syntax of λέγοντας (line 7).
7. Syntax of δίδωσιν (line 8).
8. Syntax of θεῶν (line 9).
9. Syntax of θεόν (line 17).
10. Syntax of κρατεῖν (line 19).
11. Syntax of κρείττω (line 20).
12. Syntax of τῑμήσω (line 23).

II. *Translate the following sentences.*

1. οὐ διδάξω τοὺς νεᾱνίας τὰ Ὁμήρου ἔπη πρὶν ἄν μοι δῶρα ὅτι κάλλιστα δῷς.

2. διὰ τὸ τὸν ἱππέᾱ ὑπὸ τοῦ στρατηγοῦ πεμφθῆναι εἰς τὸ ἄστυ οἱ πολῖται ἐπύθοντο ὅτι ὁ τῶν φοβερωτέρων πολεμίων βασιλεὺς πρᾱξειεν.

3. τὰς γυναῖκας ἔλαθον ἐκ τῆς οἰκίᾱς ἐξελθόντες ὡς ἵππους ἀποδωσόμενοι.

4. μὴ ἀφῑεῖμεν τοὺς ἡμῖν αὐτοῖς μεμαχημένους ὡς μὴ ὑπ' ἐκείνων βλαβῶμεν.

5. μὴ ἐρωτήσῃς πότερον οἱ ἀμείνους οἷοί τ' εἰσὶν ὑπὸ τῶν κακιόνων τῷ ὄντι βλάπτεσθαι.

III. *Translate into Greek.*

Are we always to think that the city must be ruled by the more prudent citizens rather than those not knowing what things must be done?

IV. *Do a synopsis of* ἀφίημι *in the third person singular; give the participles in the feminine dative plural.*

PRINCIPAL PARTS: ——————————————————————
                 ——————————————————————

	ACTIVE	MIDDLE	PASSIVE
PRESENT INDICATIVE			
IMPERFECT INDICATIVE			
FUTURE INDICATIVE			
AORIST INDICATIVE			
PERFECT INDICATIVE			
PLUPERFECT INDICATIVE			
PRESENT SUBJUNCTIVE			
AORIST SUBJUNCTIVE			
PRESENT OPTATIVE			
FUTURE OPTATIVE			
AORIST OPTATIVE			
PRESENT IMPERATIVE			
AORIST IMPERATIVE			
PRESENT INFINITIVE			
FUTURE INFINITIVE			
AORIST INFINITIVE			
PERFECT INFINITIVE			
PRESENT PARTICIPLE			
FUTURE PARTICIPLE			
AORIST PARTICIPLE			
PERFECT PARTICIPLE			

ANSWER KEY FOR SAMPLE GRAMMAR EXAMINATION

I. I, indeed, want first on the one hand to say how I ought to speak/how it is necessary for me to speak, then on the other hand to speak. For all those having spoken earlier seem to me not to be honoring the god but to be considering (the) men blessed for the good things for which/of which the god is responsible/cause to them. But being what sort of a someone/a person he gives these things, by no one has been said. But there is one good method of all honor/honoring, by word to go through what sort he happens to be concerning whomever the speech is. Thus indeed it is just also for us to honor Love, saying about him first what sort he is, then what things he gives.

I say then that, all gods being blessed, Love, if it is right to speak in this way, is the most blessed of all, being most beautiful and best. But this one/he is most beautiful in the following way. First, on the one hand, companion, he is the youngest of the gods and is always together with the young. For the ancient saying holds well/is good, that "like is always together with like." . . .

Concerning on the one hand the beauty of the god, these things/the preceding things indeed are enough; concerning the virtue of Love, on the other hand, after these things one must speak, the greatest thing (being) that Love neither wrongs nor is wronged, neither by a god nor a god, (and he wrongs or is wronged) neither by a man nor a man. But in addition to justice he shares in the most/has a very large share of moderation. For all say that moderation is to be stronger than pleasures and desires, but that no pleasure is stronger than Love.

Concerning, then, the justice and moderation of the god, on the one hand, it has been spoken by me; concerning his wisdom, on the other hand, it is left/it remains (for me to speak). And first, on the one hand, in order that I in turn also may praise our craft just as Eryximachos his own/the craft of himself, the god is a poet so wise as to make even another (a poet). For everyone becomes a poet even if he is unpoetic formerly, whomever Love touches.

1. present indicative in an indirect question in primary sequence; present to show progressive/repeated aspect in present time
2. present infinitive: complementary infinitive; present to show progressive/repeated aspect

3. dative of personal agent

4. present participle, M sing. nom.: supplementary participle with
   τυγχάνει; agrees with the subject of the verb; present to show progres-
   sive/repeated aspect

5. present subjunctive: subjunctive in the relative protasis of a present
   general conditional sentence; present to show progressive/repeated
   aspect

6. present participle, M pl. acc.: circumstantial participle; agrees with
   ἡμᾶς; present to show progressive/repeated aspect

7. present indicative: indicative in an indirect question in primary
   sequence; present to show progressive/repeated aspect in present time

8. genitive in a genitive absolute

9. accusative: direct object

10. present infinitive: articular infinitive in the accusative; predicate
    accusative (or subject accusative) of the infinitive *εἶναι*; present to
    show progressive/repeated aspect

11. accusative: predicate adjective agreeing with an accusative subject of
    an infinitive.

12. aorist subjunctive: subjunctive in a purpose clause in primary sequence;
    aorist to show simple aspect

II. 1. I shall not teach the young men the epic poetry of Homer until you
       give me gifts as beautiful as possible.

    2. On account of the horsemen's being sent by the general to the town
       the citizens found out what the king of the rather fearsome enemies
       did.

    3. They escaped the notice of the women going out of the house to sell
       horses, as they said.

    4. May we not release those who have fought against us ourselves in order
       that we may not be harmed by those men.

    5. Do not ask whether (the) better people are able really to be harmed by
       (the) worse.

III. (ἆρα) ἀεὶ νομίζωμεν τῆς πόλεως ἀρκτέον εἶναι τοῖς σωφρονεστέροις
     πολίταις μᾶλλον ἢ τοῖς μὴ εἰδόσιν ἅτινα/ἅττα πρᾱκτέα ἐστίν;

IV. PRINCIPAL PARTS: ἀφίημι, ἀφήσω, ἀφῆκα, ἀφεῖκα, ἀφεῖμαι, ἀφείθην

	ACTIVE	MIDDLE	PASSIVE
PRESENT INDICATIVE	ἀφίησι(ν)	ἀφίεται	ἀφίεται
IMPERF. INDICATIVE	ἀφίει	ἀφίετο	ἀφίετο
FUTURE INDICATIVE	ἀφήσει	ἀφήσεται	ἀφεθήσεται
AORIST INDICATIVE	ἀφῆκε(ν)	ἀφεῖτο	ἀφείθη
PERFECT INDICATIVE	ἀφεῖκε(ν)	ἀφεῖται	ἀφεῖται
PLUPERF. IND.	ἀφείκει(ν)	ἀφεῖτο	ἀφεῖτο
PRESENT SUBJ.	ἀφιῇ	ἀφιῆται	ἀφιῆται
AORIST SUBJUNCTIVE	ἀφῇ	ἀφῆται	ἀφεθῇ
PRESENT OPTATIVE	ἀφιείη	ἀφιεῖτο	ἀφιεῖτο
FUTURE OPTATIVE	ἀφήσοι	ἀφήσοιτο	ἀφεθήσοιτο
AORIST OPTATIVE	ἀφείη	ἀφεῖτο/ἀφοῖτο	ἀφεθείη
PRESENT IMPER.	ἀφιέτω	ἀφιέσθω	ἀφιέσθω
AORIST IMPERATIVE	ἀφέτω	ἀφέσθω	ἀφεθήτω
PRESENT INFINITIVE	ἀφιέναι	ἀφίεσθαι	ἀφίεσθαι
FUTURE INFINITIVE	ἀφήσειν	ἀφήσεσθαι	ἀφεθήσεσθαι
AORIST INFINITIVE	ἀφεῖναι	ἀφέσθαι	ἀφεθῆναι
PERFECT INFINITIVE	ἀφεικέναι	ἀφεῖσθαι	ἀφεῖσθαι
PRESENT PARTICIPLE	ἀφιείσαις	ἀφιεμέναις	ἀφιεμέναις
FUTURE PARTICIPLE	ἀφησούσαις	ἀφησομέναις	ἀφεθησομέναις
AORIST PARTICIPLE	ἀφείσαις	ἀφεμέναις	ἀφεθείσαις
PERFECT PARTICIPLE	ἀφεικυίαις	ἀφειμέναις	ἀφειμέναις

APPENDIX

INTRODUCTION

This Appendix is divided into five parts:

1. Numbered sections, following the format of Units 1–20, which present additional material (pages 589–98);

2. Morphology, including a discussion of the rules for accent, a full listing of noun and verb forms, and a table of Principal Parts of verbs (pages 599–691);

3. Syntax, including a full listing of the uses of the various cases and an analysis of mood, tense, and voice (pages 693–774);

4. Greek-English and English-Greek Vocabularies (pages 775–820);

5. Index to both the Text and the Appendix (pages 821–28).

See also the Table of Contents for the Appendix, immediately following (pages vii–xi).

The discussion of syntax includes material not covered elsewhere in this text. Such material is enclosed in square brackets: [ ].

CONTENTS

ADDITIONAL GRAMMAR

MORPHOLOGY

CONTENTS

SYNTAX

CONTENTS

ADDITIONAL GRAMMAR

154. SECOND-DECLENSION NOUNS OF THE TYPE *νεώς, νεώ, ὁ,* "temple"

Two things are unusual about these second-declension nouns:

(1) they have undergone a *quantitative metathesis* (the quantities of the vowels of the earlier form *νηός* have been reversed to become *νεώς*);

(2) the accent of the nominative remains unchanged throughout the declension; it does not change to a circumflex as in *ἀδελφοῦ*.

This type of declension is also called the **Attic declension.**

Nom./Voc. S	*νεώς*	Nom./Voc. P	*νεώ*
Gen.	*νεώ*	Gen.	*νεών*
Dat.	*νεῴ*	Dat.	*νεῴς*
Acc.	*νεών*	Acc.	*νεώς*

Observations: (1) Note that wherever an iota appears in the usual forms of the second declension, it appears as an iota subscript in this type of noun.

(2) The form *νεώς* can be the nominative/vocative singular or accusative plural of *νεώς, νεώ, ὁ,* or the genitive singular of *ναῦς, νεώς, ἡ.*

155. THE THIRD-DECLENSION NOUN *βοῦς, βοός, ὁ or ἡ,* "bull, cow"

The third-declension noun *βοῦς, βοός, ὁ or ἡ,* "bull, cow," has two stems, *βου-* and *βο-*. The stem *βου-* appears in the nominative, accusative, and vocative singular, and in the dative and accusative plural; the stem *βο-* appears elsewhere.

589

Nom. S	βοῦς		Nom./Voc. P	βόες
Gen.	βοός		Gen.	βοῶν
Dat.	βοΐ		Dat.	βουσί(ν)
Acc.	βοῦν		Acc.	βοῦς
Voc.	βοῦ			

Observations: (1) Note that the dative singular has two syllables.

(2) Compare the declension of this word with that of ναῦς, νεώς, ἡ, "ship." Cf. Section 128, page 472; page 627.

156. THE NOUN τριήρης, τριήρους, ἡ, "trireme, ship"

The noun τριήρης, τριήρους, ἡ, "trireme, ship," belongs to the third declension and is declined as follows:

Nom. S	τριήρης	
Gen.	τριήρους	(*τριήρεσος)
Dat.	τριήρει	(*τριήρεσι)
Acc.	τριήρη	(*τριήρεσα)
Voc.	τριῆρες	
Nom./Voc. P	τριήρεις	(*τριήρεσες)
Gen.	τριήρων	(*τριηρέσων)
Dat.	τριήρεσι(ν)	(*τριήρεσσι[ν])
Acc.	τριήρεις	

Observations: (1) The stem of this noun is τριηρεσ-. Intervocalic sigma has dropped out, causing the final vowel of the stem to contract with the vowels of the endings. Cf. γένος, γένους, τό (Section 82.2, page 260).

(2) The vocative singular consists of the stem alone. Note the persistent accent on the penult.

(3) The accent of the genitive plural is on the penult by analogy with the other forms of this noun. Normal contraction would have produced an accent on the ultima.

(4) The accusative plural is borrowed from the nominative/vocative plural.

157. NOUNS OF THE TYPE Περικλῆς, Περικλέους, ὁ, "Perikles"

The noun Περικλῆς, Περικλέους, ὁ, "Perikles," belongs to the third declension. Many other proper names are declined like it. Its forms are as follows:

Nom. S	Περικλῆς	(*Περικλέης)
Gen.	Περικλέους	(*Περικλέεσος)
Dat.	Περικλεῖ	(*Περικλέεσι)
Acc.	Περικλέᾱ	(*Περικλέεσα)
Voc.	Περίκλεις	(*Περίκλεες)

Observations: (1) The stem of this noun is Περικλεεσ-. Intervocalic sigma has dropped out, causing the final vowel of the stem to contract with the vowels of the genitive, dative, and accusative singular endings. Cf. γένος, γένους, τό (Section 82.2, page 260).

(2) In the genitive singular the final epsilon of the stem has contracted with the omicron of the ending to form the spurious diphthong -ου-. Note that this diphthong does NOT in turn contract with the preceding epsilon. Contrast, e.g., ποιοῦσι (<ποιέουσι).

(3) In the dative singular the final epsilon of the stem has contracted with the iota of the ending to form the diphthong -ει. This diphthong, in turn, contracts with the preceding epsilon. Compare, e.g., ποιεῖ (< ποιέει).

(4) In the accusative singular the final epsilon of the stem has contracted with the alpha of the ending. Note that the result is -ᾱ- rather than -η-: this regularly occurs when the sequence of vowels -εεα- undergoes contraction.

(5) The vocative singular consists of the stem alone. Note the recessive accent.

For a table of all contractions, including exceptions to the rules, see pages 616–17.

158. THE NOUN αἰδώς, αἰδοῦς, ἡ, "shame"

The third-declension noun αἰδώς, αἰδοῦς, ἡ, "shame," is declined in the singular only. Its forms are as follows:

Nom./Voc. S	αἰδώς	
Gen.	αἰδοῦς	(*αἰδόσος)
Dat.	αἰδοῖ	(*αἰδόσι)
Acc.	αἰδῶ	(*αἰδόσα)

Observations: (1) The stem of this noun is αἰδοσ-. Loss of intervocalic sigma causes the final omicron of the stem to contract with the vowel of the genitive, dative, and accusative singular endings. The contractions follow the regular rules.

(2) The vocative singular is identical with the nominative singular. Both show a lengthened grade of the stem.

159. THE NOUN πειθώ, πειθοῦς, ἡ, "persuasion"

The third-declension noun πειθώ, πειθοῦς, ἡ, "persuasion," is declined in the singular only. Its forms are as follows:

Nom. S	πειθώ	
Gen.	πειθοῦς	(*πειθόος)
Dat.	πειθοῖ	(*πειθόϊ)
Acc.	πειθώ	(*πειθόα)
Voc.	πειθοῖ	

Observations: (1) The stem of this noun was originally πειθοι-; the final iota of the stem dropped out before the genitive, dative, and accusative endings. The contractions follow the regular rules, except that the accusative singular has an acute instead of the expected circumflex accent.

(2) The vocative singular consists of the original stem.

160. THE NOUN γέρας, γέρως, τό, "prize"

The third-declension noun γέρας, γέρως, τό, "prize," is declined as follows:

Nom./Voc. S	γέρας	
Gen.	γέρως	(*γέρασος)
Dat.	γέραι	(*γέρασι)
Acc.	γέρας	
Nom./Voc. P	γέρᾱ	(*γέρασα)
Gen.	γερῶν	(*γεράσων)
Dat.	γέρασι(ν)	(*γέρασσι[ν])
Acc.	γέρᾱ	(*γέρασα)

Observations: (1) The stem of this noun is γερασ-. Loss of intervocalic sigma
causes the final alpha of the stem to contract with the initial
vowel of the endings. The contractions follow the regular
rules.

(2) The nominative/accusative/vocative singular consists of the
stem alone.

161. CONTRACTED FIRST- AND SECOND-DECLENSION ADJECTIVES

Some first- and second-declension adjectives have stems ending in the vowels
-ε- and -ο-. The stems of such adjectives contract with the declensional endings.
The adjective χρῡσοῦς, χρῡσῆ, χρῡσοῦν, "golden, of gold," will serve as a paradigm of this type of adjective. The contraction will be obvious in the dictionary
from the circumflex accent on all three forms of the nominative and from the
masculine and neuter nominative singular endings -ους and -ουν. The uncontracted nominative forms were χρύσεος, χρυσέη, χρύσεον. In the paradigm,
note that the accent has been made a circumflex on the ultima in every form
(χρύσεος should have given *χρῡσους by the regular rules of contraction). Note
also that the neuter nominative and accusative plural contraction of χρύσεα is
χρῡσᾶ (instead of the expected *χρῡση; cf. γένεα > γένη), and note the contraction χρύσεαι > χρῡσαῖ.

Memorize the boldface portions of the words as endings.

	M	F	N
Nom./Voc. S	χρῡσ**οῦς**	χρῡσ**ῆ**	χρῡσ**οῦν**
Gen.	χρῡσ**οῦ**	χρῡσ**ῆς**	χρῡσ**οῦ**
Dat.	χρῡσ**ῷ**	χρῡσ**ῇ**	χρῡσ**ῷ**
Acc.	χρῡσ**οῦν**	χρῡσ**ῆν**	χρῡσ**οῦν**
Nom./Voc. P	χρῡσ**οῖ**	χρῡσ**αῖ**	χρῡσ**ᾶ**
Gen.	χρῡσ**ῶν**	χρῡσ**ῶν**	χρῡσ**ῶν**
Dat.	χρῡσ**οῖς**	χρῡσ**αῖς**	χρῡσ**οῖς**
Acc.	χρῡσ**οῦς**	χρῡσ**ᾶς**	χρῡσ**ᾶ**

Adjectives like ἀργυροῦς, ἀργυρᾶ, ἀργυροῦν, "of silver," are declined in the same
way as χρῡσοῦς, χρῡσῆ, χρῡσοῦν EXCEPT for the feminine singular, where the
declensional endings have -ᾱ- after the -ρ- instead of -η-:

	F
Nom./Voc. S	ἀργυρᾶ
Gen.	ἀργυρᾶς
Dat.	ἀργυρᾷ
Acc.	ἀργυρᾶν

162. SECOND-DECLENSION ADJECTIVES OF THE TYPE ἵλεως, ἵλεων, "propitious"

Some second-declension adjectives of two terminations belong to the **Attic declension** (cf. Section 154, page 589). The forms of the adjective ἵλεως, ἵλεων, "propitious," are as follows:

	M/F	N
Nom./Voc. S	ἵλεως	ἵλεων
Gen.	ἵλεω	ἵλεω
Dat.	ἵλεῳ	ἵλεῳ
Acc.	ἵλεων	ἵλεων
Nom./Voc. P	ἵλεῳ	ἵλεα
Gen.	ἵλεων	ἵλεων
Dat.	ἵλεως	ἵλεως
Acc.	ἵλεως	ἵλεα

Observations: (1) The masculine/feminine nominative singular of this adjective was originally *ἵληος. Quantitative metathesis has produced the forms above.

(2) Wherever an iota appears in the usual second-declension endings, an iota subscript appears in adjectives of this type. Compare, e.g., ἀγαθοί, ἵλεῳ.

(3) Note that the alpha of the neuter nominative/accusative/vocative ending is *short*: the usual ending is employed instead of the long alpha which quantitative metathesis would have produced.

163. THE VERB ζάω, "live"

The verb ζάω, ζήσω, —, —, —, —, "live," is contracted in the present and imperfect tenses. Its forms are like those of τιμάω *except that* ζάω *contracts to -η- wherever* τιμάω *contracts to -ā-.*

This verb has no present or imperfect middle.

	PRESENT IND. ACTIVE	IMPERF. IND. ACTIVE	PRESENT SUBJ. ACTIVE	PRESENT OPT. ACTIVE	
S 1	ζῶ	ἔζων	ζῶ	ζῷμι or ζῴην	
2	ζῇς	ἔζης	ζῇς	ζῷς	ζῴης
3	ζῇ	ἔζη	ζῇ	ζῷ	ζῴη
P 1	ζῶμεν	ἐζῶμεν	ζῶμεν	ζῷμεν	ζῴημεν
2	ζῆτε	ἐζῆτε	ζῆτε	ζῷτε	ζῴητε
3	ζῶσι(ν)	ἔζων	ζῶσι(ν)	ζῷεν	ζῴησαν

	PRESENT IMPERATIVE ACTIVE	PRESENT INFINITIVE ACTIVE	PRESENT PARTICIPLE ACTIVE
S 2	ζῇ	ζῆν	ζῶν, ζῶσα, ζῶν
3	ζήτω		(like τῑμῶν, τῑμῶσα, τῑμῶν)
P 2	ζῆτε		
3	ζώντων		

Observation: Contractions different from those of τῑμάω are in boldface. Contrast, e.g., ζῇς, τῑμᾷς; ζῆτε, τῑμᾶτε.

164. THE VERB χράομαι, "use, experience, treat as"

The verb χράομαι, χρήσομαι, ἐχρησάμην, ——, κέχρημαι, ἐχρήσθην, "use, experience, treat as," takes an object in the *dative case.*

> πῶς τούτῳ τῷ ἀργυρίῳ χρησώμεθα, ὦ πάτερ;
> Father, how are we to use this money?

This verb is contracted in the present and imperfect tenses. Its forms are like those of τῑμάω except that χράομαι contracts to -η- wherever τῑμάω contracts to -ᾱ-.

	PRESENT IND. MIDDLE	IMPERFECT IND. MIDDLE	PRESENT SUBJ. MIDDLE	PRESENT OPT. MIDDLE
S 1	χρῶμαι	ἐχρώμην	χρῶμαι	χρῴμην
2	χρῇ	ἐχρῶ	χρῇ	χρῷο
3	χρῆται	ἐχρῆτο	χρῆται	χρῷτο

P 1 χρώμεθα   ἐχρώμεθα   χρώμεθα   χρῴμεθα
  2 χρῆσθε   ἐχρῆσθε   χρῆσθε   χρῷσθε
  3 χρῶνται   ἐχρῶντο   χρῶνται   χρῷντο

	PRESENT IMPERATIVE MIDDLE	PRESENT INFINITIVE MIDDLE	PRESENT PARTICIPLE MIDDLE
S 2	χρῶ	χρῆσθαι	χρώμενος, χρωμένη, χρώμενον
3	χρήσθω		

P 2 χρῆσθε
  3 χρήσθων

Observation: Contractions different from those of τιμάω are in boldface. Contrast, e.g., χρῇ, τῑμᾷ; χρῆσθε, τῑμᾶσθε.

165. THE DUAL: NOUNS AND ADJECTIVES

The endings of the **dual** in each declension are given below. These endings are added to the usual stems; accent is persistent. Dual forms are given along with singular and plural forms in the paradigms on pp. 623–44.

	FIRST DECLENSION	SECOND DECLENSION	THIRD DECLENSION
Nom./Acc./Voc. D	-ᾱ	-ω	-ε
Gen./Dat.	-αιν	-οιν	-οιν

Observation: Note that the nom./acc./voc. dual ending -ᾱ of the first declension is the same as the nominative singular ending -ᾱ.

Dual forms of the article, and of various pronouns, appear in the paradigms on pp. 644–49.

166. THE DUAL: VERBS

The dual person markers of verbs are given below. These, together with the thematic vowel or tense vowel where required, are added to the usual stems; accent is recessive. Dual forms are given along with singular and plural forms in the paradigms on pp. 652–83. There are no first person dual verb forms in Attic Greek.

ACTIVE	PRIMARY	SECONDARY	IMPERATIVE
D 2	-τον	-τον	-τον
3	-τον	-την	-των

MIDDLE/PASSIVE:

D 2	-σθον	-σθον	-σθον
3	-σθον	-σθην	-σθων

Observation: The aorist passive dual employs active person markers.

167. USE OF THE DUAL

Dual forms are sometimes employed instead of plural forms when reference is made to two persons or things. In Attic Greek the plural had largely taken over the function of the dual. A dual subject often takes a plural verb.

The dual is most often used of natural pairs, e.g., τὼ χεῖρε, "the (two) hands."

168. NUMERALS

	CARDINAL (one, two, etc.)	ORDINAL (first, second, etc.)
1	εἷς, μία, ἕν	πρῶτος
2	δύο	δεύτερος
3	τρεῖς, τρία	τρίτος
4	τέτταρες, τέτταρα	τέταρτος
5	πέντε	πέμπτος
6	ἕξ	ἕκτος
7	ἑπτά	ἕβδομος
8	ὀκτώ	ὄγδοος
9	ἐννέα	ἔνατος
10	δέκα	δέκατος
11	ἕνδεκα	ἑνδέκατος
12	δώδεκα	δωδέκατος
13	τρεῖς καὶ δέκα τρεισκαίδεκα	τρίτος καὶ δέκατος
14	τέτταρες καὶ δέκα τετταρεσκαίδεκα	τέταρτος καὶ δέκατος

15	πεντεκαίδεκα	πέμπτος καὶ δέκατος
16	ἑκκαίδεκα	ἕκτος καὶ δέκατος
17	ἑπτακαίδεκα	ἕβδομος καὶ δέκατος
18	ὀκτωκαίδεκα	ὄγδοος καὶ δέκατος
19	ἐννεακαίδεκα	ἔνατος καὶ δέκατος
20	εἴκοσι(ν)	εἰκοστός
21	εἷς καὶ εἴκοσι(ν)	πρῶτος καὶ εἰκοστός
	εἴκοσι (καὶ) εἷς	
30	τριάκοντα	τριᾱκοστός
40	τεττεράκοντα	τεττερακοστός
50	πεντήκοντα	πεντηκοστός
60	ἑξήκοντα	ἑξηκοστός
70	ἑβδομήκοντα	ἑβδομηκοστός
80	ὀγδοήκοντα	ὀγδοηκοστός
90	ἐνενήκοντα	ἐνενηκοστός
100	ἑκατόν	ἑκατοστός
200	διᾱκόσιοι	διᾱκοσιοστός
300	τριᾱκόσιοι	τριᾱκοσιοστός
400	τετρακόσιοι	τετρακοσιοστός
500	πεντακόσιοι	πεντακοσιοστός
600	ἑξακόσιοι	ἑξακοσιοστός
700	ἑπτακόσιοι	ἑπτακοσιοστός
800	ὀκτακόσιοι	ὀκτακοσιοστός
900	ἐνακόσιοι	ἐνακοσιοστός
1000	χίλιοι	χῑλιοστός
2000	δισχίλιοι	δισχῑλιοστός
3000	τρισχίλιοι	τρισχῑλιοστός
10000	μύριοι	μῡριοστός
20000	δισμύριοι	δισμῡριοστός
100000	δεκακισμύριοι	δεκακισμῡριοστός

Observations: (1) Ordinal numerals are declined like ἀγαθός, ἀγαθή, ἀγαθόν.

(2) Cardinal numerals from 5 through 100 are not declined; the numerals 1 through 4 are always declined when used in compound numerals.

(3) Cardinal numerals from 200 upward are declined like ἀγαθός, ἀγαθή, ἀγαθόν.

MORPHOLOGY

ACCENT

GENERAL RULE FOR ACCENTS:

No matter how many syllables a word may have, the accent can appear ONLY over one of the last three syllables: the *ultima* (the final syllable), the *penult* (the next-to-last syllable), or the *antepenult* (the third syllable from the end).

ACCENT MARKS:

′ *ACUTE accent*	(Marked a raising of the musical pitch.)
` *GRAVE accent*	(Marked a lowering of pitch or substitution of steady for raised pitch.)
˜ *CIRCUMFLEX accent*	(Marked a raising and lowering of pitch in the same syllable.)

RULES FOR ACUTE ACCENT:

Appears over the *ultima* or the *penult* or the *antepenult*.

Appears over short vowels or long vowels or diphthongs.

Can appear over the *ultima* ONLY when a pause follows, i.e. at the end of a sentence or before a comma or semicolon or when a word is simply listed without a context.

> EXCEPTIONS: (1) The interrogative pronoun/adjective forms τίς and τί always receive an acute accent:
>
> > τίς αὔτη;
> > Who is this woman?
>
> (2) When a word with an acute accent on the ultima is followed by an enclitic, the acute accent is retained:
>
> > ἀγαθούς τινας εἴδομεν.
> > We saw some good men.

599

CANNOT appear over the *penult* when this syllable is accented and contains a long vowel or diphthong and the ultima contains a short vowel or a diphthong counted as short.

> NOTE: For the purposes of accentuation the diphthongs -αι and -οι, when final, count as short, EXCEPT when they serve as third-person singular endings in the optative mood.

> EXCEPTION: In words compounded from an originally independent word + an enclitic, an acute accent can appear over a long vowel or diphthong in the penult when the ultima has a short vowel or a diphthong counted as short:
>
> εἴτε   (= εἰ + τε)
> τάσδε   (= τάς + -δε)

Can appear over the *antepenult* ONLY when the ultima contains a short vowel or a diphthong counted as short:

> ἄδικα   θάλατται   ἄνθρωποι

> EXCEPTION: Where the ultima contains a long vowel because of quantitative metathesis, or by analogy with forms which have undergone quantitative metathesis, an acute accent can appear over the antepenult:
>
> πόλεως   (< *πόληος)
> πόλεων   (by analogy with πόλεως)
> ἵλεως   (< *ἵληος)

RULES FOR GRAVE ACCENT:

Appears ONLY over the *ultima*.

Appears over short vowels or long vowels or diphthongs.

MUST replace an acute accent over the ultima when another word follows directly without a pause.

CANNOT appear otherwise.

> EXCEPTIONS: (1) The interrogative pronoun/adjective forms τίς and τί never change their acute accent to a grave accent:
>
> τί τοῦτο;
> What is this?

(2) When a word with an acute accent on the ultima is followed by an enclitic, the acute accent is retained:

ἀγαθόν τι ποιοῦμεν.
We are doing something good.

RULES FOR CIRCUMFLEX ACCENT:

Appears ONLY over the *ultima* or the *penult*.

Appears ONLY over long vowels or diphthongs.

MUST appear over the penult when the penult is accented and contains a long vowel or diphthong and the ultima contains a short vowel or a diphthong counted as short.

CANNOT appear over the penult when the ultima contains a long vowel or a diphthong counted as long:

δῶρα (long vowel in accented penult, short vowel in ultima: circumflex required)

δώρων (long vowel in ultima: circumflex prohibited)

νῆσοι (long vowel in accented penult, diphthong counted as short in ultima: circumflex required)

νήσοις (diphthong counted as long in ultima; circumflex prohibited)

κελεῦσαι (aorist infinitive active: final diphthong counts as short; circumflex required over diphthong of penult)

κελεύσαι (third person singular, aorist optative active: final diphthong counts as long when used as optative ending; circumflex prohibited)

EXCEPTIONS: (1) In words compounded from an originally independent word + an enclitic, an acute accent can appear over a long vowel or diphthong in the penult when the ultima has a short vowel or a diphthong counted as short:

εἴτε (= εἰ + τε)
τάσδε (= τάς + -δε)

(2) A circumflex can appear over the *antepenult* of words compounded from an originally independent word + an enclitic. The ultima of such words can contain a short vowel or a long vowel or a diphthong:

ὧντινων (= ὧν + τινῶν)
οἷστισι(ν) (= οἷς + τισί[ν])

SUMMARY OF POSSIBILITIES FOR ACCENT

(1) -a-p-ú + pause

(2) -a-p-ù + word without pause

EXCEPTIONS: τίς/τί + word without pause

-a-p-ú + enclitic

(3) -a-p̂-u *BUT NOT* -a-p̂-ŭ

EXCEPTION: -a-p̂-ŭ in some words compounded with an enclitic

(4) -á-p-ŭ

EXCEPTION: -á-p-ū where ū results from quantitative metathesis or by analogy with such a form

(5) -a-p-ū̃

(6) -a-p̄-ŭ *MUST*, if p̄ is accented

EXCEPTIONS: -a-p̂-ŭ in some words compounded with an enclitic

-ā̃-p-u in some words compounded with an enclitic

---

u = ultima; p = penult; a = antepenult

˘ = short vowel or diphthong counted as short

– = long vowel or diphthong counted as long

Unmarked syllables may contain a short

vowel, a long vowel, or a diphthong.

PERSISTENT ACCENT

The accent of a word is *persistent* when it tries to remain the same accent, over the same vowel or diphthong, in all the forms of the word unless forced by the rules for the possibilities of accent to change in nature (e.g., from circumflex to acute) or position (e.g., from antepenult to penult). Persistent accents change in nature, exhausting all possibilities for remaining on the same syllable, before changing in position.

The accent of most noun and adjective forms is persistent and is given by the nominative singular (neuter for adjectives, masculine for participles):

στέφανος   (nominative singular)

στεφάνου   (long ultima forces accent to penult)

στέφανοι   (diphthong -οι counts as short)

δῆμος   (nominative singular)
δήμου   (long ultima forces change to acute accent)
δῆμοι   (diphthong -οι counts as short)

EXCEPTIONS TO PERSISTENT ACCENT:

1. All first declension nouns, whatever the accent of the nominative singular, have a circumflex accent on the ultima in the genitive plural:

   γνώμη   γνωμῶν
   θάλαττα   θαλαττῶν
   πολίτης   πολῑτῶν

   Also, the feminine of all adjectives of the first and third declensions, whose feminine nominative singular ends in short -α, including participles of the first and third declensions, has a circumflex on the ultima in the genitive plural, regardless of the accent of the nominative singular:

   βαρεῖα   βαρειῶν
   λυθεῖσα   λυθεισῶν
   λελυκυῖα   λελυκυιῶν
   ποιοῦσα   ποιουσῶν
   παύσᾱσα   παυσᾱσῶν

   BUT the feminine of adjectives of the first and second declensions, whose feminine nominative singular ends in -η or -ᾱ, including participles of the first and second declensions, does NOT shift its accent in this manner in the genitive plural:

   ἀρίστη   ἀρίστων
   δικαίᾱ   δικαίων
   λῡομένη   λῡομένων
   λελυμένη   λελυμένων

2. First- and second-declension nouns and adjectives with an acute accent on the ultima in the nominative singular change this acute to a circumflex in the genitive and dative in all numbers:

   ἀδελφός   ἀδελφοῦ   ἀδελφῶν
                  ἀδελφῷ   ἀδελφοῖς

   BUT second-declension nouns of the Attic declension with an acute accent on the ultima in the nominative singular retain an acute accent on the ultima throughout their declension:

   νεώς, νεώ, νεῴ, etc.

3. The vocative singular of the second-declension noun ἀδελφός, ἀδελφοῦ, ὁ accents the antepenult: ἄδελφε.

4. Contracted first- and second-declension adjectives, when accented on the ultima, have a circumflex throughout their declensions:

   χρῡσοῦς, χρῡσῆ, χρῡσοῦν

5. Third-declension nouns with monosyllabic stems accent the ultima in the genitive and dative in all numbers. The accent is a circumflex over long vowels or diphthongs, an acute over short vowels:

νύξ	νυκτός	νυκτῶν
	νυκτί	νυξί(ν)

   BUT the adjective πᾶς, πᾶσα, πᾶν has persistent accent in the masculine and neuter genitive and dative *plural*:

πᾶς, πᾶν	παντός	**πάντων**
	παντί	**πᾶσι(ν)**

   The interrogative pronoun/adjective has persistent accent in the genitive and dative:

τίς	**τίνος**	**τίνων**
	τίνι	**τίσι(ν)**

   The noun παῖς, παιδός, ὁ or ἡ has persistent accent in the genitive dual and plural:

παῖς	παιδός	**παίδων**

   The noun γυνή, γυναικός, ἡ is accented as if it had a monosyllabic stem:

γυνή	γυναικός	γυναικῶν
	γυναικί	γυναιξί(ν)

6. The accent of all adjectives is given by the *neuter* nominative singular. Note that in some forms of third-declension adjectives the rules for the possibilities of accent force the accent, if it is originally on the antepenult, to move to the penult:

εὐδαίμων	εὔδαιμον
ἡδίων	ἥδῑον

7. The third-declension nouns θυγάτηρ, μήτηρ, and πατήρ take an acute accent on the ultima in the genitive and dative singular (e.g., μητρός, μητρί), a recessive accent in the vocative singular (θύγατερ, μῆτερ, πάτερ), and an acute accent on the penult in all other cases (e.g., θυγατέρες, θυγατέρων). The third-declension noun ἀνήρ, ἀνδρός, ὁ is declined like third-declension

nouns with monosyllabic stems EXCEPT that the stem ἀνδρ- is replaced by other stems in the vocative singular (ἄνερ) and dative plural (ἀνδράσι[ν]).

8. Certain nouns and adjectives, some of whose forms have undergone quantitative metathesis, can maintain persistent accent in violation of the rules for the possibilities of accent:

   πόλεως   (< *πόληος)   πόλεων (by analogy)
   ἵλεως   (< *ἵληος)   ἵλεων   (< *ἵληον)

9. The final sigma of the stem of certain third-declension nouns has dropped out, with the result that in the genitive plural contraction produces a circumflex on the ultima:

   γένος   *γενέσων> γενέων> γενῶν

   BUT the noun τριήρης, τριήρους, ἡ accents the penult throughout its declension. Thus the genitive plural is τριήρων instead of *τριηρῶν (< *τριηρέσων).

10. Third-declension nouns of the types Σωκράτης and Περικλῆς have recessive accent in the vocative singular:

    Σώκρατες   Περίκλεις

11. The first- and third-declension numeral εἷς, μία, ἕν and its compounds οὐδείς, οὐδεμία, οὐδέν and μηδείς, μηδεμία, μηδέν accent the ultima in the genitive and dative of all genders:

    οὐδείς   οὐδεμία   οὐδέν
    οὐδενός   οὐδεμιᾶς   οὐδενός
    οὐδενί   ουδεμιᾷ   οὐδενί

12. The numeral δύο takes a circumflex on the ultima in the genitive and dative:

    δυοῖν

RECESSIVE ACCENT

The accent of a word is *recessive* when it goes back from the ultima as far as the rules for the possibilities of accent allow.

Most verb forms have recessive accent:

   κελεύουσι(ν)   (short vowel in the ultima, or diphthong counted as
   ἐκέλευον   short, allows accent on the antepenult)
   ἵσταμαι
   ἵστασο

κελεύω   (long vowel or diphthong counted as long in the ultima
κελεύοι   forces accent to move to the penult)
κελεῦσαι
ἱστάμην

EXCEPTIONS TO RECESSIVE ACCENT:

1. In contracted verb forms, where two syllables have been contracted into
   one, if either of the syllables being contracted bore an accent in the original
   uncontracted form, the accent remains on the new, contracted syllable.
   The accent on a contracted ultima is a circumflex; the accent on a contracted
   penult is a circumflex when the ultima contains a short vowel or a diphthong
   counted as short:

   νῑκῶ   (< νῑκάω)
   ποιεῖ   (< ποιέει)
   ποιεῖσθαι   (< ποιέεσθαι)
   ἐποιοῦ   (< ἐποιέου)
   ἀγγελεῖτε   (< ἀγγελέετε)

   In addition to the present and imperfect of contracted thematic verbs with
   stems ending in -α-, -ε-, and -ο-, and contracted futures active and middle
   with stems ending in -α- and -ε-, the following verb forms show contraction
   which results in apparently non-recessive accent:

   a. the aorist subjunctive passive:

      λυθῶ   (< λυθέω)

   b. the third person plural, present indicative active and perfect indicative
      active of ἵστημι:

      ἱστᾶσι(ν)   (< ἱστάᾱσι[ν])
      ἑστᾶσι(ν)   (< ἑστάᾱσι[ν])

   c. the alternative form of the second person singular, present indicative
      active of ἵημι:

      ἱεῖς   (<ἱέεις)

   d. the present subjunctive active and middle/passive of athematic verbs,
      and the second aorist subjunctive active and middle of athematic verbs:

      ἱστῶ   (< ἱστέω)
      τιθῶμαι   (< τιθέωμαι)
      διδῶ   (< διδόω)
      στῶ   (< στέω)   (cf. ἀποστῶ)
      θῶμαι   (< θέωμαι)   (cf. ἀποθῶμαι)

e. the perfect subjunctive active of οἶδα and ἵστημι:

εἰδῶ   (< εἰδέω)

ἑστῶ   (< ἑστέω)

2. In the following optative forms, the accent does not go back beyond the iota of the optative suffix:

a. aorist optative passive (alternative plural forms):

λυθεῖμεν

λυθεῖτε

λυθεῖεν

b. present optative active and middle/passive of athematic verbs:

διδοῖμεν

ἱσταῖο

τιθεῖντο

BUT the present optative middle/passive of δύναμαι and ἐπίσταμαι has recessive accent:

δύναιτο

ἐπίσταιτο

c. athematic second aorist optative active and middle:

δοῖμεν   (cf. ἀποδοῖμεν)

θεῖσθε   (cf. ἀποθεῖσθε)

d. perfect optative active of οἶδα and ἵστημι:

εἰδεῖτε

ἑσταῖτε

3. The following forms of the second person singular, second aorist imperative active have an acute accent on the ultima:

εἰπέ   (λέγω)

ἐλθέ   (ἔρχομαι)

εὑρέ   (εὑρίσκω)

ἰδέ   (ὁράω)

λαβέ   (λαμβάνω)

BUT when compounded, these imperatives have recessive accent:

ἄπελθε

4. The second person singular, second aorist imperative middle has a circumflex on the ultima:

βαλοῦ

5. The following infinitives have a fixed, non-recessive accent:

athematic present active	διδόναι
first aorist active	κελεῦσαι
second aorist active	βαλεῖν
second aorist middle	βαλέσθαι
athematic second aorist active	στῆναι (cf. ἀποστῆναι)
athematic second aorist middle	δόσθαι (cf. ἀποδόσθαι)
aorist passive	κελευσθῆναι
perfect active	κεκελευκέναι
perfect middle/passive	κεκελεῦσθαι

6. The verbs εἰμί and φημί are enclitic in the present indicative active, except for the second person singular forms: εἶ, φής.

   BUT at the beginning of a clause or sentence the third person singular, present indicative active of εἰμί takes an acute accent on the penult: ἔστι(ν).

   Other enclitic forms of εἰμί and φημί become non-enclitic and receive an accent on the ultima when they begin a clause or sentence.

7. Although compound verbs have recessive accent, note the following exceptions:

   a. In compound verb forms having a past indicative augment *the accent cannot go further back than the past indicative augment.*

ἀπῆλθον	(= ἀπο- + ἦλθον)
ὑπῆρχε(ν)	(= ὑπο- + ἦρχε[ν])
ἀπῆσαν	(= ἀπο- + ἦσαν)

   COMPARE compound verb forms not having a past indicative augment, where the accent can go back to the antepenult:

λῦε	ἀπόλῦε
λῦσον	ἀπόλῦσον

   b. The second person singular, second aorist imperative middle retains, when compounded, a circumflex on the ultima:

βαλοῦ	ἀποβαλοῦ

   c. The following second person singular imperative forms have, when compounded, an acute accent on the *penult*:

δός	ἀπόδος
-ἕς	ἄφες
θές	κατάθες
σχές	ἀπόσχες

d. The second person singular, athematic second aorist imperative middle, when compounded with a monosyllabic preposition, retains a circumflex on the ultima; when compounded with a disyllabic preposition or with more than one preposition, it takes an acute accent on the penult:

δοῦ	προδοῦ	ἀπόδου
θοῦ	ἐκθοῦ	κατάθου

e. All infinitives retain their accent when compounded:

διδόναι	ἀποδιδόναι
δόσθαι	ἀποδόσθαι
λῦσαι	καταλῦσαι
στῆναι	ἀποστῆναι
εἶναι	συνεῖναι

f. All participles retain their fixed accent, given by the masculine nominative singular, when compounded:

λῦον	καταλῦον
θείς	καταθείς
δόντες	ἀποδόντες
λελυκώς	ἀπολελυκώς
ὄν	ἐξόν

g. The accent on ἔσται (third person singular, future indicative middle of εἰμί) remains fixed when the form is compounded:

ἔσται	ἀπέσται

8. In the perfect active and middle/passive the accent cannot go back beyond the first syllable of the uncompounded perfect stem:

ἧχα	συνῆχα
-εῖκα	ἀφεῖκα
——	ἀφῖγμαι

PROCLITICS

Proclitics have no accent. They usually cohere closely in pronunciation with the word or phrase which follows them. Proclitics are not normally placed at the end of a clause or sentence.

The following words are proclitics:

    (1) the forms ὁ, ἡ, οἱ, αἱ of the article
    (2) the negative adverb οὐ, οὐκ, οὐχ

EXCEPTION: This adverb receives an acute accent when it appears
at the end of a clause or sentence.

ἐπανίστανται, ἢ **οὔ;**
Are they rising in insurrection, or not?

(3) the prepositions εἰς, ἐκ/ἐξ, ἐν
(4) the particle εἰ
(5) the conjunction ὡς

ENCLITICS

Enclitics cohere closely in pronunciation with the word which precedes them.
The accent of the preceding word is often affected by the enclitic. The accent
of both the preceding word and the enclitic is determined by the rules below.

Enclitics include:

(1) the indefinite pronoun/adjective τις, τι
(2) the personal pronouns μου, μοι, με; σου, σοι, σε
(3) the indefinite adverbs ποθέν, ποι, ποτέ, που, πως
(4) the particles γε, -περ, τοι
(5) the conjunction τε
(6) the present indicative active of εἰμί and φημί
     EXCEPT for the second person singular forms εἶ and φῄς

RULES FOR THE ACCENT OF ENCLITICS:

(u = ultima; p = penult; a = antepenult; e = monosyllabic enclitic;
e-e = disyllabic enclitic)

1. A word with an acute accent on the ultima, followed by an enclitic, does
    NOT change its acute accent to a grave accent. The enclitic does not take
    an accent.

-a-p-ú + e   **ποιητής τις**
                  some poet

-a-p-ú + e-e   **ποιηταί τινες**
                  some poets

2. A word with an acute accent on the penult, followed by an enclitic, does not
    alter its accent.

    If the enclitic is *monosyllabic*, it has no accent:

-a-ṕ-u + e   **λέγεις τε** καὶ γράφεις.
                  You speak and write.

If the enclitic is *disyllabic*, it takes an accent on the ultima: acute on a short vowel, circumflex on a long vowel or diphthong:

-a-p̄-u + e-é   **μητράσι τισίν**
                 to/for some mothers

-a-p̄-u + e-ē   **μητέρων τινῶν**
                 of some mothers

By the regular rules for accentuation, an acute accent on the ultima of an enclitic changes to a grave accent if a non-enclitic word follows without a pause:

$$\mu\eta\tau\varrho\acute{\alpha}\sigma\iota\ \textbf{τισὶ}\ \delta\tilde{\omega}\varrho\alpha\ \delta\acute{\iota}\delta\omega\varsigma.$$
You give gifts to some mothers.

3. A word with an acute accent on the antepenult, followed by an enclitic, retains its accent and also receives an *additional* acute accent on the ultima. The enclitic does not take an accent.

-á-p-ú + e   **ἄδικά τε** καὶ αἰσχρά
                 unjust and shameful things

-á-p-ú + e-e   **ἄδικοί τινες**
                 some unjust men

4. A word with a circumflex on the ultima, followed by an enclitic, retains its accent. The enclitic does not take an accent.

-a-p-ũ + e   **νενῑκηκυιῶν τε** καὶ νῦν ἀρχουσῶν
                 of women having won and now ruling

-a-p-ũ + e-e   **εἰδυιῶν τινων**
                 of some knowing women

5. A word with a circumflex on the penult, followed by an enclitic, retains its accent and also receives an *additional* acute accent on the ultima. The enclitic does not take an accent.

-a-p̄-ú + e   **νῆσός τις**
                 some island

-a-p̄-ú + e-e   **αἶγάς τινας** ἔκλεψας, ὦ μῆτερ;
                 Mother, did you steal some goats?

6. When a proclitic is followed by an enclitic or a series of enclitics, the proclitic takes an acute accent. The enclitic does not take an accent:

εἴ τι κλέψειας, ὦ γύναι, βλαβείης ἄν.
Woman, if you should steal anything, you would be harmed.

7. If two or more enclitics follow each other, each enclitic except the last one receives an *acute* accent. This accent is on the ultima of disyllabic enclitics:

εἴ τινές ποτέ τί φᾶσιν
if any people ever say anything

A non-enclitic word preceding a series of two or more enclitics is accented according to rules 1 through 6, just as if a single enclitic followed:

ἐάν ποθέν τις ἥκῃ
if someone has come from somewhere

δῶρόν τί τινι
some gift for someone

ἄρχοντές τινές ποτε
some rulers sometime

8. Some enclitics can be placed at the beginning of a clause or sentence. When so placed, they take an acute accent on the ultima and are governed by the rules for the accentuation of non-enclitic words, i.e., an acute accent on the ultima becomes a grave accent if no pause follows:

τινὲς μὲν λέγουσι, τινὲς δὲ ἀκούουσιν.
Some speak, **others** listen.

ποτὲ μὲν λέγουσι, ποτὲ δὲ ἀκούουσιν.
At one time they speak, **at another time** they listen.

φᾶσὶ γὰρ οὗτοι ὅτι ἠδικοῦντο.
For these men **say** that they were being wronged.

εἰσὶν οἳ τὴν δημοκρατίᾱν καταλύσουσιν.
There are (men) who will destroy the democracy.

But the third person singular, present indicative active of εἰμί can stand at the beginning of a sentence or clause with an acute accent on the *penult* and mean "there is" or "it is possible":

ἔστι σοφώτατός τις ἐνταῦθα.
There is a very wise man here.

ἔστιν ἀποφυγεῖν.
It is possible to escape.

This form can be preceded by the negative adverb or a conjunction:

οὐκ ἔστιν ἀποφυγεῖν.
It is not possible to escape.

9. When an enclitic follows an elided syllable (of either a non-enclitic or an enclitic word), it receives an accent:

>τοῦτ' ἐστὶ κακόν.
>This is bad.

>οἷοί τ' εἰσὶν ταῦτα ποιεῖν.
>They are able to do these things.

ANASTROPHE

Many disyllabic prepositions switch their accent from the ultima to the penult when they follow the word which they govern. Among such prepositions are ἀπό, ἐπί, μετά, παρά, περί, and ὑπό. Only περί can undergo **anastrophe** in prose.

>τούτων πέρι λέγωμεν.
>Let us speak about these things.

ELISION

When the final short vowel of a word is dropped by elision, the accent of the word is unaffected if the elided vowel did not have an accent:

>τοῦτ' οὐ γένοιτ' ἄν.
>This could not happen.

>ἐλήλυθ' ἐγὼ εἰς τὴν πόλιν.
>I have come to the city.

>ὅδ' εἶπεν ὅτι Σωκράτης ἀποθάνοι.
>This man said that Sokrates had died.

If the elided vowel had an accent, the preceding syllable takes an acute accent:

>πολλὰ ἔδομεν.   (unelided)
>We gave many things.

>πόλλ' ἔδομεν.   (elided)
>We gave many things.

But the preceding syllable takes NO accent when the final syllable of the following words is elided: prepositions; the conjunctions ἀλλά, οὐδέ, μηδέ; the enclitics τινά and ποτέ:

>ἀλλ' ἱερέα τιν' ἴδοις ποτ' ἄν ἐφ' ἵππου;
>But could you ever see any priest on a horse?

>οὐχ ἑώρακα μηδ' ἴδοιμι.
>I have not seen nor do I wish to see.

When an enclitic follows an elided syllable, it receives an accent:

$$\tauαῦτ' ἐστὶ κακά.$$

These things are bad. ’

CRASIS

When a vowel or diphthong at the end of one word is combined with a vowel or diphthong at the beginning of the following word by **crasis**, the accent of the first word is usually dropped and that of the second remains unaltered. A **coronis** (’), identical to a smooth breathing, is placed over a vowel or diphthong which results from crasis. Crasis occurs more often in poetry than in prose.

καλὸς καὶ ἀγαθός	καλὸς κἀγαθός
τὸ ὄνομα	τοὔνομα
καὶ ἐν	κἂν
ὦ ἀγαθέ	ὦγαθέ

Where the first of the two syllables combined had a rough breathing, a rough breathing is written over the new syllable which results:

ἡ ἀλήθεια	ἁλήθεια

When the article τό is combined with αὐτό, the resulting form can be given an additional -ν: ταὐτό or ταὐτόν.

DEICTIC IOTA

Deictic (“pointing”) **iota** is sometimes added as a suffix to a demonstrative in order to give special emphasis to the person or thing being pointed out. The vowels α, ε, and o are dropped before this suffix. Deictic iota receives an acute accent which changes to a grave accent if another word follows without a pause:

οὗτος	οὑτοσί
ὅδε	ὁδί
αὕτη	αὑτηί
τούτων	τουτωνί

ὁρᾷς ταδὶ τὰ χρήματα;
Do you see **this** money?
Do you see **this** money **right here**?

NU-MOVABLE

Nu-movable may be added to certain forms when the following word begins with a vowel or diphthong, and at the end of a clause or sentence. The addition of nu-movable prevents elision.

The following forms may add nu-movable:

1. words ending in -σι:

   a. the dative plural of third-declension nouns and adjectives, including third-declension forms of participles (dative plural ending: -σι):

   $\qquad$ παισί(ν) $\qquad$ αἰξί(ν) $\qquad$ εὐγενέσι(ν) $\qquad$ λελυκόσι(ν)

   b. third person verb forms which terminate in -σι or -τι:

λύ́ουσι(ν)	ἀδικοῦσι(ν)	διδόᾱσι(ν)
λύ́ωσι(ν)	ἀδικῶσι(ν)	διδῶσι(ν)
λύ́σουσι(ν)	ἀγγελοῦσι(ν)	
λύ́σωσι(ν)	βάλωσι(ν)	δῶσι(ν)
λυθῶσι(ν)		
λελύκᾱσι(ν)	ἐστί(ν)	δίδωσι(ν)

   c. the indeclinable cardinal numeral εἴκοσι(ν), "twenty"

2. uncontracted third person singular verb forms which terminate in -ε:

   $\qquad$ ἔλῡε(ν)
   $\qquad$ ἔλῡσε(ν)
   $\qquad$ λύ́σειε(ν)
   $\qquad$ λέλυκε(ν)

   NOTE: Verb forms which result from the contraction of -ε do NOT add nu-movable:

   $\qquad$ ἠδίκει $\qquad$ (< ἠδίκεε)
   $\qquad$ ἐδίδου $\qquad$ (< ἐδίδοε)

3. the third person singular, imperfect indicative of εἶμι:

   $\qquad$ ᾔει(ν)

4. the third person singular, pluperfect indicative active of all verbs:

   $\qquad$ ἐλελύκει(ν)

COMPENSATORY LENGTHENING

CHANGE	EXAMPLE		
α > ᾱ	*ἱστάντσι(ν)	>	ἱστᾶσι(ν)
ε > ει	*λυθέντσι(ν)	>	λυθεῖσι(ν)
ι > ῑ	*ἔκρινσα	>	ἔκρῑνα
ο > ου	*γέροντσι(ν)	>	γέρουσι(ν)
υ > ῡ	*δεικνύντσι(ν)	>	δεικνῦσι(ν)

PAST INDICATIVE AUGMENT OF VERBS WHOSE STEMS BEGIN WITH A VOWEL OR DIPHTHONG

INITIAL VOWEL OR DIPHTHONG	*AUGMENTED INITIAL VOWEL OR DIPHTHONG*
α	η
ᾱ	η
αι	η
αυ	ηυ/αυ
ε	η
ει	η/ει
ευ	ηυ/ευ
η	η
ι	ῑ
ῑ	ῑ
ο	ω
οι	ῳ
ου	ου
υ	ῡ
ῡ	ῡ
ω	ω

CONTRACTIONS

CONTRACTION		*EXAMPLE*	
αα	ᾱ	γέραα	γέρᾱ
αᾱ	ᾱ	ἱστάᾱσι(ν)	ἱστᾶσι(ν)
αε	ᾱ	νῑκάεσθαι	νῑκᾶσθαι
αει	ᾳ	νῑκάει	νῑκᾷ
αει[1]	ᾱ	νῑκάειν	νῑκᾶν
αη	ᾱ	νῑκάητε	νῑκᾶτε
αη	ᾳ	νῑκάῃ	νῑκᾷ
αο	ω	νῑκάομεν	νῑκῶμεν
αοι	ῳ	νῑκάοιμι	νῑκῷμι

[1] ει = spurious diphthong

αου	ω	νῑκάουσι(ν)	νῑκῶσι(ν)
αω	ω	νῑκάω	νῑκῶ
εα	η	γένεα	γένη
	ᾱ	after ε or by analogy:	
		Περικλέεα	Περικλέᾱ
		χρύσεα	χρῡσᾶ
εᾱ	η	χρῡσέᾱ	χρῡσῆ
	ᾱ	after ε, ι, ϱ:	
		ἀϱγυϱέᾱ	ἀϱγυϱᾶ
εαι	η/ει	λύεαι	λύῃ/λύει
	αι	by analogy:	
		χρύσεαι	χρῡσαῖ
εε	ει[1]	ἀδικέεσθαι	ἀδικεῖσθαι
εει	ει	ἀδικέει	ἀδικεῖ
εη	η	ἀδικέητε	ἀδικῆτε
εη	ῃ	ἀδικέῃ	ἀδικῇ
εο	ου	ἀδικέομεν	ἀδικοῦμεν
εοι	οι	ἀδικέοιμεν	ἀδικοῖμεν
εου	ου	ἀδικέουσι(ν)	ἀδικοῦσι(ν)
εω	ω	ἀδικέω	ἀδικῶ
εῳ	ῳ	χρῡσέῳ	χρῡσῷ
ηαι	ῃ	λύηαι	λύῃ
οα	ω	πειθόα	πειθώ
οε	ου	ἀξιόεσθαι	ἀξιοῦσθαι
οει	οι	ἀξιόει	ἀξιοῖ
οει[1]	ου	ἀξιόειν	ἀξιοῦν
οη	ω	ἀξιόητε	ἀξιῶτε
οη	οι	ἀξιόη	ἀξιοῖ
	ῳ	in the subjunctive forms	
		διδῷς, διδῷ, δῷς, δῷ,	
		γνῷς, γνῷ (from διδόῃς, διδόῃ, etc.)	
οο	ου	ἀξιόομεν	ἀξιοῦμεν
οοι	οι	ἀξιόοι	ἀξιοῖ
οου	ου	ἀξιόουσι(ν)	ἀξιοῦσι(ν)
οω	ω	ἀξιόω	ἀξιῶ
οῳ	ῳ	νόῳ	νῷ

[1] ει = spurious diphthong

PREPOSITIONS

	+ GENITIVE	+ DATIVE	+ ACCUSATIVE
ἅμα		ἅμα τῇ μάχῃ at the same time as the battle ἅμα ἡμέρᾳ at daybreak ἅμα Σωκράτει together with Sokrates	
ἄνευ	ἄνευ ὅπλων without weapons		
ἀντί	ἄργυρος ἀντὶ χρῡσοῦ silver instead of gold		
ἀπό	ἀπὸ τῆς πόλεως from/away from the city		
διά	διὰ τοῦ πεδίον through the plain		διὰ τὴν τούτων ἀρετήν because of these men's virtue
εἰς			εἰς τὴν πόλιν into/to the city ἀργύριον εἰς θυσίᾱν money for a sacrifice
ἐκ/ἐξ	ἐκ τῆς πόλεως out of/from the city ἐξ ἀγορᾶς out of/from the market place		

ἐν
ἐν πόλει
in the city

ἕνεκα
Σωκράτους ἕνεκα
ἕνεκα Σωκράτους
for the sake of Sokrates

ἐπί
ἐφ' ἵππου
on horseback
ἐπὶ νεῶν
on ships

ἐπὶ τραπέζῃ
on a table
ἐπὶ τοῖσδε
on these terms
νόμος ἐπὶ τοῖς ξένοις
a law pertaining to foreigners

ἀναβῆναι ἐπὶ τὸν ἵππον
to mount the horse
ἐπὶ τοὺς πολεμίους
against the enemy
ἐπὶ τρεῖς ἡμέρας
over (the length of) three days
ἥκω ἐπὶ τοῦτο.
I have come for this purpose.

κατά
λόγος κατὰ Σωκράτους
a speech against Sokrates

κατὰ τὸν νόμον
according to the law

μετά
μετὰ τῶν φίλων
with (his/her/their) friends

μετὰ τὸν πόλεμον
after the war
μετὰ τὸν ἡγεμόνα
after the leader

παρά
παρὰ βασιλέως
from (the side of) the king

παρὰ βασιλεῖ
beside the king
παρ' Ὁμήρῳ
at Homer's house

παρὰ βασιλέα
to (the side of) the king
παρὰ τὴν ὁδόν
beside the road

παρὰ τὸν νόμον
beyond/against the law

παρὰ τοὺς ἄλλους ἀνθρώπους
beyond/excelling other men

περὶ τὴν νῆσον
around the island

ἀνὴρ ἀγαθὸς περὶ τὸν δῆμον
a good man as concerns the people

περὶ ταῦτα ὄντες
being (concerned/occupied) about these things

περί | βιβλίον περὶ πολέμου
a book about war

| περὶ τῇ χειρί
[e.g., a bracelet] around the hand

πρό | πρὸ τοῦ πολέμου
before the war

πρὸ τοῦ θανάτου
before (his/her/their) death

πρὸ τούτου τί ἕλοισθ' ἄν;
What would you choose before this?

πρός | πρὸς τῶν θεῶν!
in the name of the gods!
by the gods!

| πρὸς τῇ πόλει
near the city

πρὸς τούτοις
in addition to these things

πρὸς τὴν πόλιν
toward the city

εἰρήνη πρὸς ἀλλήλους
peace toward each other

	genitive	*dative*	*accusative*
			τὰ πρὸς τὸν πόλεμον the things for the war the things with a view to the war
σύν		σὺν θεῷ with (the help of) a god σὺν δίκῃ with justice	
ὑπέρ	ὑπὲρ τοῦ λιμένος above the harbor ὑπὲρ παίδων καὶ γυναικῶν on behalf of children and wives		ὑπὲρ θάλατταν beyond the sea ὑπὲρ δύναμιν beyond (his/her/their) strength
ὑπό	ὑπὸ γῆς under the earth ἀδικεῖσθαι ὑπὸ τῶν ἐχθρῶν to be wronged by one's enemies	οἱ ὑπὸ βασιλεῖ those under (the control of) the king	ὑπὸ γῆν under the earth ὑπὸ νύκτα at nightfall toward night
χάριν	Σωκράτους χάριν for Sokrates' sake τοῦ λόγου χάριν for the sake of the argument		

DECLENSION ENDINGS

FIRST DECLENSION

	F				M	
Nom. S	-η	-ᾱ	-α	-α	-ης	-ᾱς
Gen.	-ης	-ᾱς	-ης	-ᾱς	-ου	-ου
Dat.	-η	-ᾳ	-η	-ᾳ	-η	-ᾳ
Acc.	-ην	-ᾱν	-αν	-αν	-ην	-ᾱν
Voc.	(same as nom.)				-α, -η	-ᾱ

Nom./Acc./Voc. D	-ᾱ
Gen./Dat.	-αιν
Nom./Voc. P	-αι
Gen.	-ῶν
Dat.	-αις
Acc.	-ᾱς

SECOND DECLENSION

	M/F	N
Nom. S	-ος	-ον
Gen.	ου	-ον
Dat.	-ῳ	-ῳ
Acc.	-ον	-ον
Voc.	-ε	-ον

Nom./Acc./Voc. D	-ω
Gen./Dat.	-οιν

	M/F	N
Nom./Voc. P	-οι	-α
Gen.	-ων	-ων
Dat.	-οις	-οις
Acc.	-ους	-α

THIRD DECLENSION

	M/F	N
Nom. S	—	—
Gen.	-ος	-ος
Dat.	-ι	-ι
Acc.	-α, -ν	——
Voc.	——	——

| Nom./Acc./Voc. D | | -ε | |
| Gen./Dat. | | -οιν | |

Nom./Voc. P	-ες		-α
Gen.	-ων		-ων
Dat.	-σι(ν)		-σι(ν)
Acc.	-ας		-α

FIRST-DECLENSION NOUNS

NOMINATIVES IN -η OR -ā (feminine)

Nom./Voc. S	τέχνη	ψῡχή	χώρᾱ	ἀγορά
Gen.	τέχνης	ψῡχῆς	χώρᾱς	ἀγορᾶς
Dat.	τέχνῃ	ψῡχῇ	χώρᾳ	ἀγορᾷ
Acc.	τέχνην	ψῡχήν	χώρᾱν	ἀγοράν
Nom./Acc./Voc. D	τέχνᾱ	ψῡχᾱ́	χώρᾱ	ἀγορά
Gen./Dat.	τέχναιν	ψῡχαῖν	χώραιν	ἀγοραῖν
Nom./Voc. P	τέχναι	ψῡχαί	χῶραι	ἀγοραί
Gen.	τεχνῶν	ψῡχῶν	χωρῶν	ἀγορῶν
Dat.	τέχναις	ψῡχαῖς	χώραις	ἀγοραῖς
Acc.	τέχνᾱς	ψῡχᾱ́ς	χώρᾱς	ἀγορᾱ́ς

NOMINATIVES IN SHORT -α (feminine)

Nom./Voc. S	θάλαττα	γέφῡρα	μοῦσα	μοῖρα
Gen.	θαλάττης	γεφύρᾱς	μούσης	μοίρᾱς
Dat.	θαλάττῃ	γεφύρᾳ	μούσῃ	μοίρᾳ
Acc.	θάλατταν	γέφῡραν	μοῦσαν	μοῖραν
Nom./Acc./Voc. D	θαλάττᾱ	γεφύρᾱ	μούσᾱ	μοίρᾱ
Gen./Dat.	θαλάτταιν	γεφύραιν	μούσαιν	μοίραιν
Nom./Voc. P	θάλατται	γέφῡραι	μοῦσαι	μοῖραι
Gen.	θαλαττῶν	γεφῡρῶν	μουσῶν	μοιρῶν
Dat.	θαλάτταις	γεφύραις	μούσαις	μοίραις
Acc.	θαλάττᾱς	γεφύρᾱς	μούσᾱς	μοίρᾱς

NOMINATIVES IN -ης OR -ᾱς (masculine)

Nom. S	πολίτης	ποιητής	νεᾱνίᾱς
Gen.	πολίτου	ποιητοῦ	νεᾱνίου
Dat.	πολίτῃ	ποιητῇ	νεᾱνίᾳ
Acc.	πολίτην	ποιητήν	νεᾱνίᾱν
Voc.	πολῖτα	ποιητά	νεᾱνίᾱ
Nom./Acc./Voc. D	πολίτᾱ	ποιητά	νεᾱνίᾱ
Gen./Dat.	πολίταιν	ποιηταῖν	νεᾱνίαιν
Nom./Voc. P	πολῖται	ποιηταί	νεᾱνίαι
Gen.	πολῑτῶν	ποιητῶν	νεᾱνιῶν
Dat.	πολίταις	ποιηταῖς	νεᾱνίαις
Acc.	πολίτᾱς	ποιητάς	νεᾱνίᾱς

SECOND-DECLENSION NOUNS

(masculine and feminine)

Nom. S	λόγος	ἄνθρωπος	στρατηγός	νῆσος
Gen.	λόγου	ἀνθρώπου	στρατηγοῦ	νήσου
Dat.	λόγῳ	ἀνθρώπῳ	στρατηγῷ	νήσῳ
Acc.	λόγον	ἄνθρωπον	στρατηγόν	νῆσον
Voc.	λόγε	ἄνθρωπε	στρατηγέ	νῆσε
Nom./Acc./Voc. D	λόγω	ἀνθρώπω	στρατηγώ	νήσω
Gen./Dat.	λόγοιν	ἀνθρώποιν	στρατηγοῖν	νήσοιν
Nom./Voc. P	λόγοι	ἄνθρωποι	στρατηγοί	νῆσοι
Gen.	λόγων	ἀνθρώπων	στρατηγῶν	νήσων
Dat.	λόγοις	ἀνθρώποις	στρατηγοῖς	νήσοις
Acc.	λόγους	ἀνθρώπους	στρατηγούς	νήσους

(neuter)

Nom./Voc. S	ἔργον	δῶρον
Gen.	ἔργου	δώρου
Dat.	ἔργῳ	δώρῳ
Acc.	ἔργον	δῶρον
Nom./Acc./Voc. D	ἔργω	δώρω
Gen./Dat.	ἔργοιν	δώροιν

Nom./Voc. P	ἔργα	δῶρα
Gen.	ἔργων	δώρων
Dat.	ἔργοις	δώροις
Acc.	ἔργα	δῶρα

CONTRACTED NOUNS   ATTIC DECLENSION

Nom. S	νοῦς	νεώς
Gen.	νοῦ	νεώ
Dat.	νῷ	νεῴ
Acc.	νοῦν	νεών
Voc.	νοῦ	νεώς
Nom./Acc./Voc. D	νώ	νεώ
Gen./Dat.	νοῖν	νεῴν
Nom./Voc. P	νοῖ	νεῴ
Gen.	νῶν	νεών
Dat.	νοῖς	νεῴς
Acc.	νοῦς	νεώς

THIRD-DECLENSION NOUNS

(masculine, feminine, neuter)

Nom. S	φύλαξ	αἴξ	ἐλπίς	χάρις	σῶμα
Gen.	φύλακος	αἰγός	ἐλπίδος	χάριτος	σώματος
Dat.	φύλακι	αἰγί	ἐλπίδι	χάριτι	σώματι
Acc.	φύλακα	αἶγα	ἐλπίδα	χάριν	σῶμα
Voc.	φύλαξ	αἴξ	ἐλπί	χάρι	σῶμα
Nom./Acc./Voc. D	φύλακε	αἶγε	ἐλπίδε	χάριτε	σώματε
Gen./Dat.	φυλάκοιν	αἰγοῖν	ἐλπίδοιν	χαρίτοιν	σωμάτοιν
Nom./Voc. P	φύλακες	αἶγες	ἐλπίδες	χάριτες	σώματα
Gen.	φυλάκων	αἰγῶν	ἐλπίδων	χαρίτων	σωμάτων
Dat.	φύλαξι(ν)	αἰξί(ν)	ἐλπίσι(ν)	χάρισι(ν)	σώμασι(ν)
Acc.	φύλακας	αἶγας	ἐλπίδας	χάριτας	σώματα

Nom. S	μήτηρ	ἀνήρ
Gen.	μητρός	ἀνδρός
Dat.	μητρί	ἀνδρί
Acc.	μητέρα	ἄνδρα
Voc.	μῆτερ	ἄνερ

| Nom./Acc./Voc. D | μητέρε | ἄνδρε |
| Gen./Dat. | μητέροιν | ἀνδροῖν |

Nom./Voc. P	μητέρες	ἄνδρες
Gen.	μητέρων	ἀνδρῶν
Dat.	μητράσι(ν)	ἀνδράσι(ν)
Acc.	μητέρας	ἄνδρας

Nom. S	γένος	τριήρης	Σωκράτης	Περικλῆς
Gen.	γένους	τριήρους	Σωκράτους	Περικλέους
Dat.	γένει	τριήρει	Σωκράτει	Περικλεῖ
Acc.	γένος	τριήρη	Σωκράτη	Περικλέα
Voc.	γένος	τριῆρες	Σώκρατες	Περίκλεις

| Nom./Acc./Voc. D | γένει | τριήρει |
| Gen./Dat. | γενοῖν | τριήροιν |

Nom./Voc. P	γένη	τριήρεις
Gen.	γενῶν	τριήρων
Dat.	γένεσι(ν)	τριήρεσι(ν)
Acc.	γένη	τριήρεις

Nom./Voc. S	γέρας	αἰδώς		Nom. S	πειθώ
Gen.	γέρως	αἰδούς		Gen.	πειθοῦς
Dat.	γέραι	αἰδοῖ		Dat.	πειθοῖ
Acc.	γέρας	αἰδῶ		Acc.	πειθώ
				Voc.	πειθοῖ

| Nom./Acc./Voc. D | γέρᾱ |
| Gen./Dat. | γερῷν |

Nom./Voc. P	γέρᾱ
Gen.	γερῶν
Dat.	γέρασι(ν)
Acc.	γέρᾱ

Nom. S	πόλις	βασιλεύς	ναῦς
Gen.	πόλεως	βασιλέως	νεώς
Dat.	πόλει	βασιλεῖ	νηί
Acc.	πόλιν	βασιλέᾱ	ναῦν
Voc.	πόλι	βασιλεῦ	ναῦ
Nom./Acc./Voc. D	πόλει	βασιλῆ	νῆε
Gen./Dat.	πολέοιν	βασιλέοιν	νεοῖν
Nom./Voc. P	πόλεις	βασιλῆς/βασιλεῖς	νῆες
Gen.	πόλεων	βασιλέων	νεῶν
Dat.	πόλεσι(ν)	βασιλεῦσι(ν)	ναυσί(ν)
Acc.	πόλεις	βασιλέᾱς	ναῦς

Nom. S	ἄστυ	βοῦς
Gen.	ἄστεως	βοός
Dat.	ἄστει	βοΐ
Acc.	ἄστυ	βοῦν
Voc.	ἄστυ	βοῦ
Nom./Acc./Voc. D	ἄστει	βόε
Gen./Dat.	ἀστέοιν	βοοῖν
Nom./Voc. P	ἄστη	βόες
Gen.	ἄστεων	βοῶν
Dat.	ἄστεσι(ν)	βουσί(ν)
Acc.	ἄστη	βοῦς

ADJECTIVES OF THE FIRST AND SECOND DECLENSIONS

THREE-ENDING ADJECTIVES

	M	F	N
Nom. S	καλός	καλή	καλόν
Gen.	καλοῦ	καλῆς	καλοῦ
Dat.	καλῷ	καλῇ	καλῷ
Acc.	καλόν	καλήν	καλόν
Voc.	καλέ	καλή	καλόν
Nom./Acc./Voc. D	καλώ	καλά	καλώ
Gen./Dat.	καλοῖν	καλαῖν	καλοῖν

Nom./Voc. P	καλοί	καλαί	καλά
Gen.	καλῶν	καλῶν	καλῶν
Dat.	καλοῖς	καλαῖς	καλοῖς
Acc.	καλούς	καλάς	καλά

Nom. S	δίκαιος	δικαίᾱ	δίκαιον
Gen.	δικαίου	δικαίᾱς	δικαίου
Dat.	δικαίῳ	δικαίᾳ	δικαίῳ
Acc.	δίκαιον	δικαίᾱν	δίκαιον
Voc.	δίκαιε	δικαίᾱ	δίκαιον

| Nom./Acc./Voc. D | δικαίω | δικαίᾱ | δικαίω |
| Gen./Dat. | δικαίοιν | δικαίαιν | δικαίοιν |

Nom./Voc. P	δίκαιοι	δίκαιαι	δίκαια
Gen.	δικαίων	δικαίων	δικαίων
Dat.	δικαίοις	δικαίαις	δικαίοις
Acc.	δικαίους	δικαίᾱς	δίκαια

TWO-ENDING ADJECTIVES

	M/F	N
Nom. S	ἄδικος	ἄδικον
Gen.	ἀδίκου	ἀδίκου
Dat.	ἀδίκῳ	ἀδίκῳ
Acc.	ἄδικον	ἄδικον
Voc.	ἄδικε	ἄδικον

| Nom./Acc./Voc. D | ἀδίκω | ἀδίκω |
| Gen./Dat. | ἀδίκοιν | ἀδίκοιν |

Nom./Voc. P	ἄδικοι	ἄδικα
Gen.	ἀδίκων	ἀδίκων
Dat.	ἀδίκοις	ἀδίκοις
Acc.	ἀδίκους	ἄδικα

CONTRACTED ADJECTIVES

	M	F	N
Nom./Voc. S	χρῡσοῦς	χρῡσῆ	χρῡσοῦν
Gen.	χρῡσοῦ	χρῡσῆς	χρῡσοῦ
Dat.	χρῡσῷ	χρῡσῇ	χρῡσῷ
Acc.	χρῡσοῦν	χρῡσῆν	χρῡσοῦν

| Nom./Acc./Voc. D | χρυσώ | χρυσᾶ | χρυσώ |
| Gen./Dat. | χρυσοῖν | χρυσαῖν | χρυσοῖν |

Nom./Voc. P	χρυσοῖ	χρυσαῖ	χρυσᾶ
Gen.	χρυσῶν	χρυσῶν	χρυσῶν
Dat.	χρυσοῖς	χρυσαῖς	χρυσοῖς
Acc.	χρυσοῦς	χρυσᾶς	χρυσᾶ

Nom./Voc. S	ἀργυροῦς	ἀργυρᾶ	ἀργυροῦν
Gen.	ἀργυροῦ	ἀργυρᾶς	ἀργυροῦ
Dat.	ἀργυρῷ	ἀργυρᾷ	ἀργυρῷ
Acc.	ἀργυροῦν	ἀργυρᾶν	ἀργυροῦν

| Nom./Acc./Voc. D | ἀργυρώ | ἀργυρᾶ | ἀργυρώ |
| Gen./Dat. | ἀργυροῖν | ἀργυραῖν | ἀργυροῖν |

Nom./Voc. P	ἀργυροῖ	ἀργυραῖ	ἀργυρᾶ
Gen.	ἀργυρῶν	ἀργυρῶν	ἀργυρῶν
Dat.	ἀργυροῖς	ἀργυραῖς	ἀργυροῖς
Acc.	ἀργυροῦς	ἀργυρᾶς	ἀργυρᾶ

ATTIC DECLENSION OF ADJECTIVES

	M/F	N
Nom./Voc. S	ἵλεως	ἵλεων
Gen.	ἵλεω	ἵλεω
Dat.	ἵλεῳ	ἵλεῳ
Acc.	ἵλεων	ἵλεων
Nom./Acc./Voc. D	ἵλεω	ἵλεω
Gen./Dat.	ἵλεῳν	ἵλεῳν
Nom./Voc. P	ἵλεῳ	ἵλεα
Gen.	ἵλεων	ἵλεων
Dat.	ἵλεως	ἵλεως
Acc.	ἵλεως	ἵλεα

THIRD-DECLENSION ADJECTIVES

TWO-ENDING ADJECTIVES

	M/F	N
Nom. S	σώφρων	σῶφρον
Gen.	σώφρονος	σώφρονος
Dat.	σώφρονι	σώφρονι
Acc.	σώφρονα	σῶφρον
Voc.	σῶφρον	σῶφρον
Nom./Acc./Voc. D	σώφρονε	σώφρονε
Gen./Dat.	σωφρόνοιν	σωφρόνοιν
Nom./Voc. P	σώφρονες	σώφρονα
Gen.	σωφρόνων	σωφρόνων
Dat.	σώφροσι(ν)	σώφροσι(ν)
Acc.	σώφρονας	σώφρονα

	M/F	N
Nom. S	ἀληθής	ἀληθές
Gen.	ἀληθοῦς	ἀληθοῦς
Dat.	ἀληθεῖ	ἀληθεῖ
Acc.	ἀληθῆ	ἀληθές
Voc.	ἀληθές	ἀληθές
Nom./Acc./Voc. D	ἀληθεῖ	ἀληθεῖ
Gen./Dat.	ἀληθοῖν	ἀληθοῖν
Nom./Voc. P	ἀληθεῖς	ἀληθῆ
Gen.	ἀληθῶν	ἀληθῶν
Dat.	ἀληθέσι(ν)	ἀληθέσι(ν)
Acc.	ἀληθεῖς	ἀληθῆ

ADJECTIVES OF THE FIRST AND THIRD DECLENSIONS

	M	F	N
Nom. S	βαρύς	βαρεῖα	βαρύ
Gen.	βαρέος	βαρείᾱς	βαρέος
Dat.	βαρεῖ	βαρείᾳ	βαρεῖ
Acc.	βαρύν	βαρεῖαν	βαρύ
Voc.	βαρύ	βαρεῖα	βαρύ

Nom./Acc./Voc. D	βαρέε	βαρεῖᾱ	βαρέε
Gen./Dat.	βαρέοιν	βαρείαιν	βαρέοιν
Nom./Voc. P	βαρεῖς	βαρεῖαι	βαρέα
Gen.	βαρέων	βαρειῶν	βαρέων
Dat.	βαρέσι(ν)	βαρείαις	βαρέσι(ν)
Acc.	βαρεῖς	βαρείᾱς	βαρέα
Nom./Voc. S	πᾶς	πᾶσα	πᾶν
Gen.	παντός	πάσης	παντός
Dat.	παντί	πάσῃ	παντί
Acc.	πάντα	πᾶσαν	πᾶν
Nom./Voc. P	πάντες	πᾶσαι	πάντα
Gen.	πάντων	πᾱσῶν	πάντων
Dat.	πᾶσι(ν)	πάσαις	πᾶσι(ν)
Acc.	πάντας	πάσᾱς	πάντα
Nom./Voc. S	ἅπᾱς	ἅπᾱσα	ἅπαν
Gen.	ἅπαντος	ἁπάσης	ἅπαντος
Dat.	ἅπαντι	ἁπάσῃ	ἅπαντι
Acc.	ἅπαντα	ἅπᾱσαν	ἅπαν
Nom./Voc. P	ἅπαντες	ἅπᾱσαι	ἅπαντα
Gen.	ἁπάντων	ἁπᾱσῶν	ἁπάντων
Dat.	ἅπᾱσι(ν)	ἁπάσαις	ἅπᾱσι(ν)
Acc.	ἅπαντας	ἁπάσᾱς	ἅπαντα

ADJECTIVES OF THE FIRST, SECOND, AND THIRD DECLENSIONS

Nom. S	πολύς	πολλή	πολύ
Gen.	πολλοῦ	πολλῆς	πολλοῦ
Dat.	πολλῷ	πολλῇ	πολλῷ
Acc.	πολύν	πολλήν	πολύ
Nom. P	πολλοί	πολλαί	πολλά
Gen.	πολλῶν	πολλῶν	πολλῶν
Dat.	πολλοῖς	πολλαῖς	πολλοῖς
Acc.	πολλούς	πολλάς	πολλά

Nom. S	μέγας	μεγάλη	μέγα
Gen.	μεγάλου	μεγάλης	μεγάλου
Dat.	μεγάλῳ	μεγάλῃ	μεγάλῳ
Acc.	μέγαν	μεγάλην	μέγα
Voc.	μεγάλε	μεγάλη	μέγα
Nom./Acc./Voc. D	μεγάλω	μεγάλᾱ	μεγάλω
Gen./Dat.	μεγάλοιν	μεγάλαιν	μεγάλοιν
Nom./Voc. P	μεγάλοι	μεγάλαι	μεγάλα
Gen.	μεγάλων	μεγάλων	μεγάλων
Dat.	μεγάλοις	μεγάλαις	μεγάλοις
Acc.	μεγάλους	μεγάλᾱς	μεγάλα

COMPARISON OF ADJECTIVES

COMPARATIVE IN -τερος, -τερᾱ, -τερον
(declined like δίκαιος, δικαίᾱ, δίκαιον)

SUPERLATIVE IN -τατος, -τατη, -τατον
(declined like ἀγαθός, ἀγαθή, ἀγαθόν)

ADJECTIVES OF THE FIRST AND SECOND DECLENSIONS

Stem ending in long syllable:

POSITIVE	STEM	COMPARATIVE	SUPERLATIVE	
δεινός	δειν-	δεινότερος	δεινότατος	M Nom. S
δεινή		δεινοτέρᾱ	δεινοτάτη	F Nom. S
δεινόν		δεινότερον	δεινότατον	N Nom. S

Stem ending in short syllable:

σοφός	σοφ-	σοφώτερος	σοφώτατος	M Nom. S
σοφή		σοφωτέρᾱ	σοφωτάτη	F Nom. S
σοφόν		σοφώτερον	σοφώτατον	N Nom. S

Compared irregularly:

ἴσος		ἰσαίτερος	ἰσαίτατος	M Nom. S
μέσος		μεσαίτερος	μεσαίτατος	M Nom. S
παλαιός		παλαίτερος	παλαίτατος	M Nom. S
φίλος		φιλαίτερος	φιλαίτατος/ φίλτατος	M Nom. S

THIRD-DECLENSION ADJECTIVES
ADJECTIVES OF THE FIRST AND THIRD DECLENSIONS

ἀληθής }	ἀληθεσ-	ἀληθέστερος	ἀληθέστατος	M Nom. S
		ἀληθεστέρᾱ	ἀληθεστάτη	F Nom. S
ἀληθές		ἀληθέστερον	ἀληθέστατον	N Nom. S
ἄφρων }	ἀφρον-	ἀφρονέστερος	ἀφρονέστατος	M Nom. S
		ἀφρονεστέρᾱ	ἀφρονεστάτη	F Nom. S
ἄφρον		ἀφρονέστερον	ἀφρονέστατον	N Nom. S
βαρύς	βαρυ-	βαρύτερος	βαρύτατος	M Nom. S
βαρεῖα		βαρυτέρᾱ	βαρυτάτη	F Nom. S
βαρύ		βαρύτερον	βαρύτατον	N Nom. S

COMPARATIVE IN -ῑων, -ῑον

SUPERLATIVE IN -ιστος, -ιστη, -ιστον

(declined like ἀγαθός, ἀγαθή, ἀγαθόν)

	M/F	N
Nom. S	καλλίων	κάλλῑον
Gen.	καλλίονος	καλλίονος
Dat.	καλλίονι	καλλίονι
Acc.	καλλίονα/καλλίω	κάλλῑον
Voc.	κάλλῑον	κάλλῑον
Nom./Acc./Voc. D	καλλίονε	καλλίονε
Gen./Dat.	καλλῑόνοιν	καλλῑόνοιν
Nom./Voc. P	καλλίονες/καλλίους	καλλίονα/καλλίω
Gen.	καλλῑόνων	καλλῑόνων
Dat.	καλλίοσι(ν)	καλλίοσι(ν)
Acc.	καλλίονας/καλλίους	καλλίονα/καλλίω

ADJECTIVES IN THIS TEXT WHICH SO FORM THE COMPARATIVE AND SUPERLATIVE:

POSITIVE	COMPARATIVE	SUPERLATIVE	
ἀγαθός	ἀμείνων } βελτίων } κρείττων }	ἄριστος } βέλτιστος } κράτιστος }	(all M Nom. S)
αἰσχρός	αἰσχίων	αἴσχιστος	
ἐχθρός	ἐχθίων	ἔχθιστος	
ἡδύς	ἡδίων	ἥδιστος	

κακός $\left\{ \begin{array}{l} κακίων \\ χείρων \\ ἥττων \end{array} \right\}$ $\left\{ \begin{array}{l} κάκιστος \\ χείριστος \\ (\text{adv. } ἥκιστα) \end{array} \right\}$

κακός   καλλίων   κάλλιστος

καλός   καλλίων   κάλλιστος
μέγας   μείζων   μέγιστος
ὀλίγος   ἐλάττων   ἐλάχιστος
πολύς   πλείων/πλέων   πλεῖστος
ῥᾴδιος   ῥᾴων   ῥᾷστος
ταχύς   θάττων   τάχιστος

See Sections 131 (p. 494) and 142 (pp. 544–45).

PARTICIPLES OF THE FIRST AND SECOND DECLENSIONS

PRESENT PARTICIPLE MIDDLE/PASSIVE OF THEMATIC VERBS

	M	F	N
Nom. S	λῡόμενος	λῡομένη	λῡόμενον
Gen.	λῡομένου	λῡομένης	λῡομένου
Dat.	λῡομένῳ	λῡομένῃ	λῡομένῳ
Acc.	λῡόμενον	λῡομένην	λῡόμενον
Voc.	λῡόμενε	λῡομένη	λῡόμενον
Nom./Acc./Voc. D	λῡομένω	λῡομένᾱ	λῡομένω
Gen./Dat.	λῡομένοιν	λῡομέναιν	λῡομένοιν
Nom./Voc. P	λῡόμενοι	λῡόμεναι	λῡόμενα
Gen.	λῡομένων	λῡομένων	λῡομένων
Dat.	λῡομένοις	λῡομέναις	λῡομένοις
Acc.	λῡομένους	λῡομένᾱς	λῡόμενα

The following participles have the same declension:

PRESENT PARTICIPLE MIDDLE/PASSIVE OF CONTRACTED VERBS

νῑκώμενος	νῑκωμένη	νῑκώμενον
ἀδικούμενος	ἀδικουμένη	ἀδικούμενον
ἀξιούμενος	ἀξιουμένη	ἀξιούμενον

PRESENT PARTICIPLE MIDDLE/PASSIVE OF ATHEMATIC VERBS

διδόμενος	διδομένη	διδόμενον
ἱστάμενος	ἱσταμένη	ἱστάμενον
τιθέμενος	τιθεμένη	τιθέμενον
ἱέμενος	ἱεμένη	ἱέμενον
δεικνύμενος	δεικνυμένη	δεικνύμενον
κείμενος	κειμένη	κείμενον

FUTURE PARTICIPLE MIDDLE

λῡσόμενος	λῡσομένη	λῡσόμενον

FUTURE PARTICIPLE MIDDLE OF CONTRACTED VERBS

ἐλώμενος	ἐλωμένη	ἐλώμενον
ἀγγελούμενος	ἀγγελουμένη	ἀγγελούμενον

FUTURE PARTICIPLE PASSIVE

λυθησόμενος	λυθησομένη	λυθησόμενον

FIRST AORIST PARTICIPLE MIDDLE

λῡσάμενος	λῡσαμένη	λῡσάμενον

SECOND AORIST PARTICIPLE MIDDLE

βαλόμενος	βαλομένη	βαλόμενον

SECOND AORIST PARTICIPLE MIDDLE OF ATHEMATIC VERBS

δόμενος	δομένη	δόμενον
θέμενος	θεμένη	θέμενον
-ἕμενος	-ἑμένη	-ἕμενον

PERFECT PARTICIPLE MIDDLE/PASSIVE

	M	F	N
Nom. S	λελυμένος	λελυμένη	λελυμένον
Gen.	λελυμένου	λελυμένης	λελυμένου
Dat.	λελυμένῳ	λελυμένῃ	λελυμένῳ
Acc.	λελυμένον	λελυμένην	λελυμένον
Voc.	λελυμένε	λελυμένη	λελυμένον
Nom./Acc./Voc. D	λελυμένω	λελυμένᾱ	λελυμένω
Gen./Dat.	λελυμένοιν	λελυμέναιν	λελυμένοιν

Nom./Voc. P	λελυμένοι	λελυμέναι	λελυμένα
Gen.	λελυμένων	λελυμένων	λελυμένων
Dat.	λελυμένοις	λελυμέναις	λελυμένοις
Acc.	λελυμένους	λελυμένᾱς	λελυμένα

The PERFECT PARTICIPLE MIDDLE/PASSIVE OF CONSONANT
STEMS has the same declension:

γεγραμμένος	γεγραμμένη	γεγραμμένον
πεπεμμένος	πεπεμμένη	πεπεμμένον
ἠσχυμμένος	ἠσχυμμένη	ἠσχυμμένον
τεταγμένος	τεταγμένη	τεταγμένον
ἐληλεγμένος	ἐληλεγμένη	ἐληλεγμένον
κεκελευσμένος	κεκελευσμένη	κεκελευσμένον
πεφασμένος	πεφασμένη	πεφασμένον
ἠγγελμένος	ἠγγελμένη	ἠγγελμένον

PARTICIPLES OF THE FIRST AND THIRD DECLENSIONS

PRESENT PARTICIPLE ACTIVE OF THEMATIC VERBS

	M	F	N
Nom./Voc. S	λῡ́ων	λῡ́ουσα	λῦον
Gen.	λῡ́οντος	λῡούσης	λῡ́οντος
Dat.	λῡ́οντι	λῡούσῃ	λῡ́οντι
Acc.	λῡ́οντα	λῡ́ουσαν	λῦον
Nom./Acc./Voc. D	λῡ́οντε	λῡούσᾱ	λῡ́οντε
Gen./Dat.	λῡόντοιν	λῡούσαιν	λῡόντοιν
Nom./Voc. P	λῡ́οντες	λῡ́ουσαι	λῡ́οντα
Gen.	λῡόντων	λῡουσῶν	λῡόντων
Dat.	λῡ́ουσι(ν)	λῡούσαις	λῡ́ουσι(ν)
Acc.	λῡ́οντας	λῡούσᾱς	λῡ́οντα

PRESENT PARTICIPLE ACTIVE OF CONTRACTED VERBS

	M	F	N
Nom./Voc. S	νῑκῶν	νῑκῶσα	νῑκῶν
Gen.	νῑκῶντος	νῑκώσης	νῑκῶντος
Dat.	νῑκῶντι	νῑκώσῃ	νῑκῶντι
Acc.	νῑκῶντα	νῑκῶσαν	νῑκῶν

| Nom./Acc./Voc. D | νῑκῶντε | νῑκώσᾱ | νῑκῶντε |
| Gen./Dat. | νῑκώντοιν | νῑκώσαιν | νῑκώντοιν |

Nom./Voc. P	νῑκῶντες	νῑκῶσαι	νῑκῶντα
Gen.	νῑκώντων	νῑκωσῶν	νῑκώντων
Dat.	νῑκῶσι(ν)	νῑκώσαις	νῑκῶσι(ν)
Acc.	νῑκῶντας	νῑκώσᾱς	νῑκῶντα

Nom./Voc. S	ἀδικῶν	ἀδικοῦσα	ἀδικοῦν
Gen.	ἀδικοῦντος	ἀδικούσης	ἀδικοῦντος
Dat.	ἀδικοῦντι	ἀδικούσῃ	ἀδικοῦντι
Acc.	ἀδικοῦντα	ἀδικοῦσαν	ἀδικοῦν

| Nom./Acc./Voc. D | ἀδικοῦντε | ἀδικούσᾱ | ἀδικοῦντε |
| Gen./Dat. | ἀδικούντοιν | ἀδικούσαιν | ἀδικούντοιν |

Nom./Voc. P	ἀδικοῦντες	ἀδικοῦσαι	ἀδικοῦντα
Gen.	ἀδικούντων	ἀδικουσῶν	ἀδικούντων
Dat.	ἀδικοῦσι(ν)	ἀδικούσαις	ἀδικοῦσι(ν)
Acc.	ἀδικοῦντας	ἀδικούσᾱς	ἀδικοῦντα

Nom./Voc. S	ἀξιῶν	ἀξιοῦσα	ἀξιοῦν
Gen.	ἀξιοῦντος	ἀξιούσης	ἀξιοῦντος
Dat.	ἀξιοῦντι	ἀξιούσῃ	ἀξιοῦντι
Acc.	ἀξιοῦντα	ἀξιοῦσαν	ἀξιοῦν

| Nom./Acc./Voc. D | ἀξιοῦντε | ἀξιούσᾱ | ἀξιοῦντε |
| Gen./Dat. | ἀξιούντοιν | ἀξιούσαιν | ἀξιούντοιν |

Nom./Voc. P	ἀξιοῦντες	ἀξιοῦσαι	ἀξιοῦντα
Gen.	ἀξιούντων	ἀξιουσῶν	ἀξιούντων
Dat.	ἀξιοῦσι(ν)	ἀξιούσαις	ἀξιοῦσι(ν)
Acc.	ἀξιοῦντας	ἀξιούσᾱς	ἀξιοῦντα

PRESENT PARTICIPLE ACTIVE OF ATHEMATIC VERBS

	M	F	N
Nom./Voc. S.	διδούς	διδοῦσα	διδόν
Gen.	διδόντος	διδούσης	διδόντος
Dat.	διδόντι	διδούσῃ	διδόντι
Acc.	διδόντα	διδοῦσαν	διδόν

| Nom./Acc./Voc. D | διδόντε | διδοῦσᾱ | διδόντε |
| Gen./Dat. | διδόντοιν | διδούσαιν | διδόντοιν |

Nom./Voc. P	διδόντες	διδοῦσαι	διδόντα
Gen.	διδόντων	διδουσῶν	διδόντων
Dat.	διδοῦσι(ν)	διδούσαις	διδοῦσι(ν)
Acc.	διδόντας	διδούσᾱς	διδόντα

Nom./Voc. S	ἱστάς	ἱστᾶσα	ἱστάν
Gen.	ἱστάντος	ἱστάσης	ἱστάντος
Dat.	ἱστάντι	ἱστάσῃ	ἱστάντι
Acc.	ἱστάντα	ἱστᾶσαν	ἱστάν

| Nom./Acc./Voc. D | ἱστάντε | ἱστάσᾱ | ἱστάντε |
| Gen./Dat. | ἱστάντοιν | ἱστάσαιν | ἱστάντοιν |

Nom./Voc. P	ἱστάντες	ἱστᾶσαι	ἱστάντα
Gen.	ἱστάντων	ἱστᾱσῶν	ἱστάντων
Dat.	ἱστᾶσι(ν)	ἱστάσαις	ἱστᾶσι(ν)
Acc.	ἱστάντας	ἱστάσᾱς	ἱστάντα

Nom./Voc. S	τιθείς	τιθεῖσα	τιθέν
Gen.	τιθέντος	τιθείσης	τιθέντος
Dat.	τιθέντι	τιθείσῃ	τιθέντι
Acc.	τιθέντα	τιθεῖσαν	τιθέν

| Nom./Acc./Voc. D | τιθέντε | τιθείσᾱ | τιθέντε |
| Gen./Dat. | τιθέντοιν | τιθείσαιν | τιθέντοιν |

Nom./Voc. P	τιθέντες	τιθεῖσαι	τιθέντα
Gen.	τιθέντων	τιθεισῶν	τιθέντων
Dat.	τιθεῖσι(ν)	τιθείσαις	τιθεῖσι(ν)
Acc.	τιθέντας	τιθείσᾱς	τιθέντα

Nom./Voc. S	ἱείς	ἱεῖσα	ἱέν
Gen.	ἱέντος	ἱείσης	ἱέντος
Dat.	ἱέντι	ἱείσῃ	ἱέντι
Acc.	ἱέντα	ἱεῖσαν	ἱέν

| Nom./Acc./Voc. D | ἱέντε | ἱείσᾱ | ἱέντε |
| Gen./Dat. | ἱέντοιν | ἱείσαιν | ἱέντοιν |

Nom./Voc. P	ἱέντες	ἱεῖσαι	ἱέντα
Gen.	ἱέντων	ἱεισῶν	ἱέντων
Dat.	ἱεῖσι(ν)	ἱείσαις	ἱεῖσι(ν)
Acc.	ἱέντας	ἱείσᾱς	ἱέντα

Nom./Voc. S	δεικνύς	δεικνῦσα	δεικνύν
Gen.	δεικνύντος	δεικνύσης	δεικνύντος
Dat.	δεικνύντι	δεικνύσῃ	δεικνύντι
Acc.	δεικνύντα	δεικνῦσαν	δεικνύν
Nom./Acc./Voc. D	δεικνύντε	δεικνῦσᾱ	δεικνύντε
Gen./Dat.	δεικνύντοιν	δεικνύσαιν	δεικνύντοιν
Nom./Voc. P	δεικνύντες	δεικνῦσαι	δεικνύντα
Gen.	δεικνύντων	δεικνῡσῶν	δεικνύντων
Dat.	δεικνῦσι(ν)	δεικνύσαις	δεικνῦσι(ν)
Acc.	δεικνύντας	δεικνύσᾱς	δεικνύντα

Nom./Voc. S	ἰών	ἰοῦσα	ἰόν
Gen.	ἰόντος	ἰούσης	ἰόντος
Dat.	ἰόντι	ἰούσῃ	ἰόντι
Acc.	ἰόντα	ἰοῦσαν	ἰόν
Nom./Acc./Voc. D	ἰόντε	ἰούσᾱ	ἰόντε
Gen./Dat.	ἰόντοιν	ἰούσαιν	ἰόντοιν
Nom./Voc. P	ἰόντες	ἰοῦσαι	ἰόντα
Gen.	ἰόντων	ἰουσῶν	ἰόντων
Dat.	ἰοῦσι(ν)	ἰούσαις	ἰοῦσι(ν)
Acc.	ἰόντας	ἰούσᾱς	ἰόντα

Nom./Voc. S	ὤν	οὖσα	ὄν
Gen.	ὄντος	οὔσης	ὄντος
Dat.	ὄντι	οὔσῃ	ὄντι
Acc.	ὄντα	οὖσαν	ὄν
Nom./Acc./Voc. D	ὄντε	οὔσᾱ	ὄντε
Gen./Dat.	ὄντοιν	οὔσαιν	ὄντοιν
Nom./Voc. P	ὄντες	οὖσαι	ὄντα
Gen.	ὄντων	οὐσῶν	ὄντων
Dat.	οὖσι(ν)	οὔσαις	οὖσι(ν)
Acc.	ὄντας	οὔσᾱς	ὄντα

Nom./Voc. S	φάς	φᾶσα	φάν
Gen.	φάντος	φάσης	φάντος
Dat.	φάντι	φάσῃ	φάντι
Acc.	φάντα	φᾶσαν	φάν
Nom./Acc./Voc. D	φάντε	φάσᾱ	φάντε
Gen./Dat.	φάντοιν	φάσαιν	φάντοιν
Nom./Voc. P	φάντες	φᾶσαι	φάντα
Gen.	φάντων	φᾱσῶν	φάντων
Dat.	φᾶσι(ν)	φάσαις	φᾶσι(ν)
Acc.	φάντας	φάσᾱς	φάντα

FUTURE PARTICIPLE ACTIVE

	M	F	N
Nom./Voc. S	λΰσων	λΰσουσα	λῦσον
Gen.	λΰσοντος	λῡσούσης	λΰσοντος
Dat.	λΰσοντι	λῡσούσῃ	λΰσοντι
Acc.	λΰσοντα	λῡσουσαν	λῦσον
Nom./Acc./Voc. D	λΰσοντε	λῡσούσᾱ	λΰσοντε
Gen./Dat.	λῡσόντοιν	λῡσούσαιν	λῡσόντοιν
Nom./Voc. P	λΰσοντες	λΰσουσαι	λΰσοντα
Gen.	λῡσόντων	λῡσουσῶν	λῡσόντων
Dat.	λΰσουσι(ν)	λῡσούσαις	λΰσουσι(ν)
Acc.	λΰσοντας	λῡσούσᾱς	λΰσοντα

CONTRACTED FUTURE PARTICIPLE ACTIVE

	M	F	N
Nom./Voc. S	ἐλῶν	ἐλῶσα	ἐλῶν
Gen.	ἐλῶντος	ἐλώσης	ἐλῶντος
Dat.	ἐλῶντι	ἐλώσῃ	ἐλῶντι
Acc.	ἐλῶντα	ἐλῶσαν	ἐλῶν
Nom./Acc./Voc. D	ἐλῶντε	ἐλώσᾱ	ἐλῶντε
Gen./Dat.	ἐλώντοιν	ἐλώσαιν	ἐλώντοιν
Nom./Voc. P	ἐλῶντες	ἐλῶσαι	ἐλῶντα
Gen.	ἐλώντων	ἐλωσῶν	ἐλώντων
Dat.	ἐλῶσι(ν)	ἐλώσαις	ἐλῶσι(ν)
Acc.	ἐλῶντας	ἐλώσᾱς	ἐλῶντα

Nom./Voc. S	ἀγγελῶν	ἀγγελοῦσα	ἀγγελοῦν
Gen.	ἀγγελοῦντος	ἀγγελούσης	ἀγγελοῦντος
Dat.	ἀγγελοῦντι	ἀγγελούσῃ	ἀγγελοῦντι
Acc.	ἀγγελοῦντα	ἀγγελοῦσαν	ἀγγελοῦν
Nom./Acc./Voc. D	ἀγγελοῦντε	ἀγγελούσᾱ	ἀγγελοῦντε
Gen./Dat.	ἀγγελούντοιν	ἀγγελούσαιν	ἀγγελούντοιν
Nom./Voc. P	ἀγγελοῦντες	ἀγγελοῦσαι	ἀγγελοῦντα
Gen.	ἀγγελούντων	ἀγγελουσῶν	ἀγγελούντων
Dat.	ἀγγελοῦσι(ν)	ἀγγελούσαις	ἀγγελοῦσι(ν)
Acc.	ἀγγελοῦντας	ἀγγελούσᾱς	ἀγγελοῦντα

FIRST AORIST PARTICIPLE ACTIVE

	M	F	N
Nom./Voc. S	λύσᾱς	λύσᾱσα	λῦσαν
Gen.	λύσαντος	λυσάσης	λύσαντος
Dat.	λύσαντι	λυσάσῃ	λύσαντι
Acc.	λύσαντα	λύσᾱσαν	λῦσαν
Nom./Acc./Voc. D	λύσαντε	λυσάσᾱ	λύσαντε
Gen./Dat.	λῡσάντοιν	λῡσάσαιν	λῡσάντοιν
Nom./Voc. P	λύσαντες	λύσᾱσαι	λύσαντα
Gen.	λῡσάντων	λῡσᾱσῶν	λῡσάντων
Dat.	λύσᾱσι(ν)	λῡσάσαις	λύσᾱσι(ν)
Acc.	λύσαντας	λῡσάσᾱς	λύσαντα

THEMATIC SECOND AORIST PARTICIPLE ACTIVE

	M	F	N
Nom./Voc. S	βαλών	βαλοῦσα	βαλόν
Gen.	βαλόντος	βαλούσης	βαλόντος
Dat.	βαλόντι	βαλούσῃ	βαλόντι
Acc.	βαλόντα	βαλοῦσαν	βαλόν
Nom./Acc./Voc. D	βαλόντε	βαλούσᾱ	βαλόντε
Gen./Dat.	βαλόντοιν	βαλούσαιν	βαλόντοιν
Nom./Voc. P	βαλόντες	βαλοῦσαι	βαλόντα
Gen.	βαλόντων	βαλουσῶν	βαλόντων
Dat.	βαλοῦσι(ν)	βαλούσαις	βαλοῦσι(ν)
Acc.	βαλόντας	βαλούσᾱς	βαλόντα

ATHEMATIC SECOND AORIST PARTICIPLE ACTIVE

	M	F	N
Nom./Voc. S	δούς	δοῦσα	δόν
Gen.	δόντος	δούσης	δόντος
Dat.	δόντι	δούσῃ	δόντι
Acc.	δόντα	δοῦσαν	δόν
Nom./Acc./Voc. D	δόντε	δούσᾱ	δόντε
Gen./Dat.	δόντοιν	δούσαιν	δόντοιν
Nom./Voc. P	δόντες	δοῦσαι	δόντα
Gen.	δόντων	δουσῶν	δόντων
Dat.	δοῦσι(ν)	δούσαις	δοῦσι(ν)
Acc.	δόντας	δούσᾱς	δόντα

	M	F	N
Nom./Voc. S	στάς	στᾶσα	στάν
Gen.	στάντος	στάσης	στάντος
Dat.	στάντι	στάσῃ	στάντι
Acc.	στάντα	στᾶσαν	στάν
Nom./Acc./Voc. D	στάντε	στάσᾱ	στάντε
Gen./Dat.	στάντοιν	στάσαιν	στάντοιν
Nom./Voc. P	στάντες	στᾶσαι	στάντα
Gen.	στάντων	στᾶσῶν	στάντων
Dat.	στᾶσι(ν)	στάσαις	στᾶσι(ν)
Acc.	στάντας	στάσᾱς	στάντα

	M	F	N
Nom./Voc. S	θείς	θεῖσα	θέν
Gen.	θέντος	θείσης	θέντος
Dat.	θέντι	θείσῃ	θέντι
Acc.	θέντα	θεῖσαν	θέν
Nom./Acc./Voc. D	θέντε	θείσᾱ	θέντε
Gen./Dat.	θέντοιν	θείσαιν	θέντοιν
Nom./Voc. P	θέντες	θεῖσαι	θέντα
Gen.	θέντων	θεισῶν	θέντων
Dat.	θεῖσι(ν)	θείσαις	θεῖσι(ν)
Acc.	θέντας	θείσᾱς	θέντα

Nom./Voc. S	-είς	-εῖσα	-έν
Gen.	-έντος	-είσης	-έντος
Dat.	-έντι	-είσῃ	-έντι
Acc.	-έντα	-εῖσαν	-έν
Nom./Acc./Voc. D	-έντε	-είσᾱ	-έντε
Gen./Dat.	-έντοιν	-είσαιν	-έντοιν
Nom./Voc. P	-έντες	-εῖσαι	-έντες
Gen.	-έντων	-εἰσῶν	-έντων
Dat.	-εῖσι(ν)	-είσαις	-εῖσι(ν)
Acc.	-έντας	-είσᾱς	-έντα

Nom./Voc. S	γνούς	γνοῦσα	γνόν
Gen.	γνόντος	γνούσης	γνόντος
Dat.	γνόντι	γνούσῃ	γνόντι
Acc.	γνόντα	γνοῦσαν	γνόν
Nom./Acc./Voc. D	γνόντε	γνούσᾱ	γνόντε
Gen./Dat.	γνόντοιν	γνούσαιν	γνόντοιν
Nom./Voc. P	γνόντες	γνοῦσαι	γνόντα
Gen.	γνόντων	γνουσῶν	γνόντων
Dat.	γνοῦσι(ν)	γνούσαις	γνοῦσι(ν)
Acc.	γνόντας	γνούσᾱς	γνόντα

Nom./Voc. S	δύς	δῦσα	δύν
Gen.	δύντος	δύσης	δύντος
Dat.	δύντι	δύσῃ	δύντι
Acc.	δύντα	δῦσαν	δύν
Nom./Acc./Voc. D	δύντε	δύσᾱ	δύντε
Gen./Dat.	δύντοιν	δύσαιν	δύντοιν
Nom./Voc. P	δύντες	δῦσαι	δύντα
Gen.	δύντων	δῡσῶν	δύντων
Dat.	δῦσι(ν)	δύσαις	δῦσι(ν)
Acc.	δύντας	δύσᾱς	δύντα

AORIST PARTICIPLE PASSIVE

	M	F	N
Nom./Voc. S	λυθείς	λυθεῖσα	λυθέν
Gen.	λυθέντος	λυθείσης	λυθέντος
Dat.	λυθέντι	λυθείσῃ	λυθέντι
Acc.	λυθέντα	λυθεῖσαν	λυθέν

| Nom./Acc./Voc. D | λυθέντε | λυθείσᾱ | λυθέντε |
| Gen./Dat. | λυθέντοιν | λυθείσαιν | λυθέντοιν |

Nom./Voc. P	λυθέντες	λυθεῖσαι	λυθέντα
Gen.	λυθέντων	λυθεισῶν	λυθέντων
Dat.	λυθεῖσι(ν)	λυθείσαις	λυθεῖσι(ν)
Acc.	λυθέντας	λυθείσᾱς	λυθέντα

PERFECT PARTICIPLE ACTIVE

	M	F	N
Nom./Voc. S	λελυκώς	λελυκυῖα	λελυκός
Gen.	λελυκότος	λελυκυίᾱς	λελυκότος
Dat.	λελυκότι	λελυκυίᾳ	λελυκότι
Acc.	λελυκότα	λελυκυῖαν	λελυκός
Nom./Acc./Voc. D	λελυκότε	λελυκυίᾱ	λελυκότε
Gen./Dat.	λελυκότοιν	λελυκυίαιν	λελυκότοιν
Nom./Voc. P	λελυκότες	λελυκυῖαι	λελυκότα
Gen.	λελυκότων	λελυκυιῶν	λελυκότων
Dat.	λελυκόσι(ν)	λελυκυίαις	λελυκόσι(ν)
Acc.	λελυκότας	λελυκυίᾱς	λελυκότα

PERSONAL PRONOUNS

	FIRST PERSON	SECOND PERSON
Nom. S	ἐγώ	σύ
Gen.	ἐμοῦ/μου	σοῦ/σου
Dat.	ἐμοί/μοι	σοί/σοι
Acc.	ἐμέ/με	σέ/σε
Nom./Acc. D	νώ	σφώ
Gen./Dat.	νῷν	σφῷν
Nom. P	ἡμεῖς	ὑμεῖς
Gen.	ἡμῶν	ὑμῶν
Dat.	ἡμῖν	ὑμῖν
Acc.	ἡμᾶς	ὑμᾶς

REFLEXIVE PRONOUNS

FIRST PERSON

	M	F
Gen. S	ἐμαυτοῦ	ἐμαυτῆς
Dat.	ἐμαυτῷ	ἐμαυτῇ
Acc.	ἐμαυτόν	ἐμαυτήν
Gen. P	ἡμῶν αὐτῶν	ἡμῶν αὐτῶν
Dat.	ἡμῖν αὐτοῖς	ἡμῖν αὐταῖς
Acc.	ἡμᾶς αὐτούς	ἡμᾶς αὐτάς

SECOND PERSON

	M	F
Gen. S	σεαυτοῦ/σαυτοῦ	σεαυτῆς/σαυτῆς
Dat.	σεαυτῷ/σαυτῷ	σεαυτῇ/σαυτῇ
Acc.	σεαυτόν/σαυτόν	σεαυτήν/σαυτήν
Gen. P	ὑμῶν αὐτῶν	ὑμῶν αὐτῶν
Dat.	ὑμῖν αὐτοῖς	ὑμῖν αὐταῖς
Acc.	ὑμᾶς αὐτούς	ὑμᾶς αὐτάς

THIRD PERSON

	M	F	N
Gen. S	ἑαυτοῦ/αὐτοῦ	ἑαυτῆς/αὐτῆς	ἑαυτοῦ/αὐτοῦ
Dat.	ἑαυτῷ/αὐτῷ	ἑαυτῇ/αὐτῇ	ἑαυτῷ/αὐτῷ
Acc.	ἑαυτόν/αὐτόν	ἑαυτήν/αὐτήν	ἑαυτό/αὐτό
Gen. P	ἑαυτῶν/αὐτῶν	ἑαυτῶν/αὐτῶν	ἑαυτῶν/αὐτῶν
Dat.	ἑαυτοῖς/αὐτοῖς	ἑαυταῖς/αὐταῖς	ἑαυτοῖς/αὐτοῖς
Acc.	ἑαυτούς/αὐτούς	ἑαυτάς/αὐτάς	ἑαυτά/αὐτά
	OR	OR	
Gen. P	σφῶν αὐτῶν	σφῶν αὐτῶν	
Dat.	σφίσιν αὐτοῖς	σφίσιν αὐταῖς	
Acc.	σφᾶς αὐτούς	σφᾶς αὐτάς	

INDIRECT REFLEXIVE (THIRD PERSON)

	M/F
Gen. S	οὗ/οὑ
Dat.	οἷ/οἱ
Acc.	ἕ/ἑ
Gen. P	σφῶν
Dat.	σφίσι(ν)
Acc.	σφᾶς

THE ADJECTIVE/PRONOUN αὐτός, αὐτή, αὐτό

	M	F	N
Nom. S	αὐτός	αὐτή	αὐτό
Gen.	αὐτοῦ	αὐτῆς	αὐτοῦ
Dat.	αὐτῷ	αὐτῇ	αὐτῷ
Acc.	αὐτόν	αὐτήν	αὐτό
Nom./Acc. D	αὐτώ	αὐτά	αὐτώ
Gen./Dat.	αὐτοῖν	αὐταῖν	αὐτοῖν
Nom. P	αὐτοί	αὐταί	αὐτά
Gen.	αὐτῶν	αὐτῶν	αὐτῶν
Dat.	αὐτοῖς	αὐταῖς	αὐτοῖς
Acc.	αὐτούς	αὐτάς	αὐτά

THE ARTICLE

	M	F	N
Nom. S	ὁ	ἡ	τό
Gen.	τοῦ	τῆς	τοῦ
Dat.	τῷ	τῇ	τῷ
Acc.	τόν	τήν	τό
Nom./Acc. D	τώ	τώ	τώ
Gen./Dat.	τοῖν	τοῖν	τοῖν
Nom. P	οἱ	αἱ	τά
Gen.	τῶν	τῶν	τῶν
Dat.	τοῖς	ταῖς	τοῖς
Acc.	τούς	τάς	τά

DEMONSTRATIVE ADJECTIVES/PRONOUNS

	M	F	N
Nom. S	οὗτος	αὕτη	τοῦτο
Gen.	τούτου	ταύτης	τούτου
Dat.	τούτῳ	ταύτῃ	τούτῳ
Acc.	τοῦτον	ταύτην	τοῦτο

| Nom./Acc. D | τούτω | τούτω | τούτω |
| Gen./Dat. | τούτοιν | τούτοιν | τούτοιν |

Nom. P	οὗτοι	αὗται	ταῦτα
Gen.	τούτων	τούτων	τούτων
Dat.	τούτοις	ταύταις	τούτοις
Acc.	τούτους	ταύτᾱς	ταῦτα

Nom. S	ἐκεῖνος	ἐκείνη	ἐκεῖνο
Gen.	ἐκείνου	ἐκείνης	ἐκείνου
Dat.	ἐκείνῳ	ἐκείνῃ	ἐκείνῳ
Acc.	ἐκεῖνον	ἐκείνην	ἐκεῖνο

| Nom./Acc. D | ἐκείνω | ἐκείνω | ἐκείνω |
| Gen./Dat. | ἐκείνοιν | ἐκείνοιν | ἐκείνοιν |

Nom. P	ἐκεῖνοι	ἐκεῖναι	ἐκεῖνα
Gen.	ἐκείνων	ἐκείνων	ἐκείνων
Dat.	ἐκείνοις	ἐκείναις	ἐκείνοις
Acc.	ἐκείνους	ἐκείνᾱς	ἐκεῖνα

Nom. S	ὅδε	ἥδε	τόδε
Gen.	τοῦδε	τῆσδε	τοῦδε
Dat.	τῷδε	τῇδε	τῷδε
Acc.	τόνδε	τήνδε	τόδε

| Nom./Acc. D | τώδε | τώδε | τώδε |
| Gen./Dat. | τοῖνδε | τοῖνδε | τοῖνδε |

Nom. P	οἵδε	αἵδε	τάδε
Gen.	τῶνδε	τῶνδε	τῶνδε
Dat.	τοῖσδε	ταῖσδε	τοῖσδε
Acc.	τούσδε	τάσδε	τάδε

RECIPROCAL PRONOUN

	M	F	N
Gen./Dat. D	ἀλλήλοιν	ἀλλήλαιν	ἀλλήλοιν
Acc.	ἀλλήλω	ἀλλήλᾱ	ἀλλήλω
Gen. P	ἀλλήλων	ἀλλήλων	ἀλλήλων
Dat.	ἀλλήλοις	ἀλλήλαις	ἀλλήλοις
Acc.	ἀλλήλους	ἀλλήλᾱς	ἄλληλα

INTERROGATIVE PRONOUN/ADJECTIVE

	M/F	N
Nom. S	τίς	τί
Gen.	τίνος/τοῦ	τίνος/τοῦ
Dat.	τίνι/τῷ	τίνι/τῷ
Acc.	τίνα	τί
Nom./Acc. D	τίνε	τίνε
Gen./Dat.	τίνοιν	τίνοιν
Nom. P	τίνες	τίνα
Gen.	τίνων	τίνων
Dat.	τίσι(ν)	τίσι(ν)
Acc.	τίνας	τίνα

INDEFINITE PRONOUN/ADJECTIVE

	M/F	N
Nom. S	τις	τι
Gen.	τινός/του	τινός/του
Dat.	τινί/τῳ	τινί/τῳ
Acc.	τινά	τι
Nom./Acc. D	τινέ	τινέ
Gen./Dat.	τινοῖν	τινοῖν
Nom. P	τινές	τινά
Gen.	τινῶν	τινῶν
Dat.	τισί(ν)	τισί(ν)
Acc.	τινάς	τινά

RELATIVE PRONOUN

	M	F	N
Nom. S	ὅς	ἥ	ὅ
Gen.	οὗ	ἧς	οὗ
Dat.	ᾧ	ᾗ	ᾧ
Acc.	ὅν	ἥν	ὅ
Nom./Acc. D	ὤ	ὤ	ὤ
Gen./Dat.	οἷν	οἷν	οἷν
Nom. P	οἵ	αἵ	ἅ
Gen.	ὧν	ὧν	ὧν
Dat.	οἷς	αἷς	οἷς
Acc.	οὕς	ἅς	ἅ

INDEFINITE RELATIVE PRONOUN
INDIRECT INTERROGATIVE PRONOUN/ADJECTIVE

	M	F	N
Nom. S	ὅστις	ἥτις	ὅτι
Gen.	οὗτινος/ὅτου	ἧστινος	οὗτινος/ὅτου
Dat.	ᾧτινι/ὅτῳ	ᾗτινι	ᾧτινι/ὅτῳ
Acc.	ὅντινα	ἥντινα	ὅτι
Nom./Acc. D	ὥτινε	ὥτινε	ὥτινε
Gen./Dat.	οἷντινοιν	οἷντινοιν	οἷντινοιν
Nom. P	οἵτινες	αἵτινες	ἅτινα/ἅττα
Gen.	ὧντινων/ὅτων	ὧντινων	ὧντινων/ὅτων
Dat.	οἷστισι(ν)/ὅτοις	αἷστισι(ν)	οἷστισι(ν)/ὅτοις
Acc.	οὕστινας	ἅστινας	ἅτινα/ἅττα

DECLENSIONS OF NUMERALS

	one			two
	M	F	N	M/F/N
Nom.	εἷς	μία	ἕν	δύο
Gen.	ἑνός	μιᾶς	ἑνός	δυοῖν
Dat.	ἑνί	μιᾷ	ἑνί	δυοῖν
Acc.	ἕνα	μίαν	ἕν	δύο

	three		four	
	M/F	N	M/F	N
Nom.	τρεῖς	τρία	τέτταρες	τέτταρα
Gen.	τριῶν	τριῶν	τεττάρων	τεττάρων
Dat.	τρισί(ν)	τρισί(ν)	τέτταρσι(ν)	τέτταρσι(ν)
Acc.	τρεῖς	τρία	τέτταρας	τέτταρα

NEGATIVE PRONOUNS/ADJECTIVES

	M	F	N
Nom. S	οὐδείς	οὐδεμία	οὐδέν
Gen.	οὐδενός	οὐδεμιᾶς	οὐδενός
Dat.	οὐδενί	οὐδεμιᾷ	οὐδενί
Acc.	οὐδένα	οὐδεμίαν	οὐδέν
Nom. S	μηδείς	μηδεμία	μηδέν
Gen.	μηδενός	μηδεμιᾶς	μηδενός
Dat.	μηδενί	μηδεμιᾷ	μηδενί
Acc.	μηδένα	μηδεμίαν	μηδέν

THE GREEK VERB: A SUMMARY

PRINCIPAL PART	TENSE STEM: FORM	NAME	VERB FORMS DERIVED FROM STEM
I. παιδεύω	παιδευ-	present tense stem	present indicative, subjunctive, optative, imperative, infinitive, and participle in all three voices
ἵστημι	ἱστη-/ἱστα-	athematic present tense stems	imperfect indicative in all three voices
II. παιδεύσω	παιδευσ-	future active and middle tense stem	future indicative, optative, infinitive, and participle in the active and middle voices
III. ἐπαίδευσα	παιδευσ-	first aorist active and middle tense stem	aorist indicative, subjunctive, optative, imperative, infinitive, and participle in the active and middle voices
ἔλιπον	λιπ-	second aorist active and middle tense stem	
ἔστην	στη-/στα-	root aorist active (and middle) tense stems	
ἔθηκα	θηκ-/θε-	mixed aorist active and middle tense stems	

IV. πεπαίδευκα πεπαιδευκ-	perfect active tense stem	perfect indicative, [subjunctive, optative, imperative,] infinitive, and participle in the active voice pluperfect indicative in the active voice
V. πεπαίδευμαι πεπαιδευ-	perfect middle and passive tense stem	perfect indicative, [subjunctive, optative, imperative,] infinitive, and participle in the middle and passive voices pluperfect indicative in the middle and passive voices
VI. ἐπαιδεύθην παιδευθ-	aorist passive tense stem	aorist indicative, subjunctive, optative, imperative, infinitive, and participle in the passive voice
παιδευθησ-	future passive tense stem	future indicative, optative, infinitive, and participle in the passive voice

Note: Contraction of vowels occurs in the present (e.g., τῑμάω, ποιέω, δηλόω) and in the future active and middle (e.g., ἀγγελῶ, ἐλῶ). Except for the optative active, contracted verbs use the same endings as uncontracted verbs. The contractions are made according to the charts on pp. 232, 236, and 264.

THEMATIC VERBS: PRESENT AND IMPERFECT

UNCONTRACTED   CONTRACTED

PRESENT INDICATIVE ACTIVE

S	1	λύω	νῑκῶ	ἀδικῶ	ἀξιῶ
	2	λύεις	νῑκᾷς	ἀδικεῖς	ἀξιοῖς
	3	λύει	νῑκᾷ	ἀδικεῖ	ἀξιοῖ
D	2	λύετον	νῑκᾶτον	ἀδικεῖτον	ἀξιοῦτον
	3	λύετον	νῑκᾶτον	ἀδικεῖτον	ἀξιοῦτον
P	1	λύομεν	νῑκῶμεν	ἀδικοῦμεν	ἀξιοῦμεν
	2	λύετε	νῑκᾶτε	ἀδικεῖτε	ἀξιοῦτε
	3	λύουσι(ν)	νῑκῶσι(ν)	ἀδικοῦσι(ν)	ἀξιοῦσι(ν)

IMPERFECT INDICATIVE ACTIVE

S	1	ἔλῡον	ἐνίκων	ἠδίκουν	ἠξίουν
	2	ἔλῡες	ἐνίκᾱς	ἠδίκεις	ἠξίους
	3	ἔλῡε(ν)	ἐνίκᾱ	ἠδίκει	ἠξίου
D	2	ἐλύετον	ἐνῑκᾶτον	ἠδικεῖτον	ἠξιοῦτον
	3	ἐλῡέτην	ἐνῑκάτην	ἠδικείτην	ἠξιούτην
P	1	ἐλύομεν	ἐνῑκῶμεν	ἠδικοῦμεν	ἠξιοῦμεν
	2	ἐλύετε	ἐνῑκᾶτε	ἠδικεῖτε	ἠξιοῦτε
	3	ἔλῡον	ἐνίκων	ἠδίκουν	ἠξίουν

PRESENT SUBJUNCTIVE ACTIVE

S	1	λύω	νῑκῶ	ἀδικῶ	ἀξιῶ
	2	λύῃς	νῑκᾷς	ἀδικῇς	ἀξιοῖς
	3	λύῃ	νῑκᾷ	ἀδικῇ	ἀξιοῖ
D	2	λύητον	νῑκᾶτον	ἀδικῆτον	ἀξιῶτον
	3	λύητον	νῑκᾶτον	ἀδικῆτον	ἀξιῶτον
P	1	λύωμεν	νῑκῶμεν	ἀδικῶμεν	ἀξιῶμεν
	2	λύητε	νῑκᾶτε	ἀδικῆτε	ἀξιῶτε
	3	λύωσι(ν)	νῑκῶσι(ν)	ἀδικῶσι(ν)	ἀξιῶσι(ν)

PRESENT OPTATIVE ACTIVE

S	1	λύοιμι	νῑκῷμι	ἀδικοῖμι	ἀξιοῖμι
	2	λύοις	νῑκῷς	ἀδικοῖς	ἀξιοῖς
	3	λύοι	νῑκῷ	ἀδικοῖ	ἀξιοῖ
D	2	λύοιτον	νῑκῷτον	ἀδικοῖτον	ἀξιοῖτον
	3	λῡοίτην	νῑκῴτην	ἀδικοίτην	ἀξιοίτην
P	1	λύοιμεν	νῑκῷμεν	ἀδικοῖμεν	ἀξιοῖμεν
	2	λύοιτε	νῑκῷτε	ἀδικοῖτε	ἀξιοῖτε
	3	λύοιεν	νῑκῷεν	ἀδικοῖεν	ἀξιοῖεν

PRESENT OPTATIVE ACTIVE (ALTERNATIVE FORMS)

S	1		νῑκῴην	ἀδικοίην	ἀξιοίην
	2		νῑκῴης	ἀδικοίης	ἀξιοίης
	3		νῑκῴη	ἀδικοίη	ἀξιοίη
D	2		νῑκῴητον	ἀδικοίητον	ἀξιοίητον
	3		νῑκῳήτην	ἀδικοιήτην	ἀξιοιήτην
P	1		νῑκῴημεν	ἀδικοίημεν	ἀξιοίημεν
	2		νῑκῴητε	ἀδικοίητε	ἀξιοίητε
	3		νῑκῴησαν	ἀδικοίησαν	ἀξιοίησαν

PRESENT IMPERATIVE ACTIVE

S	2	λῦε	νίκᾱ	ἀδίκει	ἀξίου
	3	λῡέτω	νῑκάτω	ἀδικείτω	ἀξιούτω
D	2	λύετον	νῑκᾶτον	ἀδικεῖτον	ἀξιοῦτον
	3	λῡέτων	νῑκάτων	ἀδικείτων	ἀξιούτων
P	2	λύετε	νῑκᾶτε	ἀδικεῖτε	ἀξιοῦτε
	3	λῡόντων	νῑκώντων	ἀδικούντων	ἀξιούντων

PRESENT INFINITIVE ACTIVE

λύειν	νῑκᾶν	ἀδικεῖν	ἀξιοῦν

PRESENT PARTICIPLE ACTIVE

λύων,	νῑκῶν,	ἀδικῶν,	ἀξιῶν,
λύουσα,	νῑκῶσα,	ἀδικοῦσα,	ἀξιοῦσα,
λῦον	νῑκῶν	ἀδικοῦν	ἀξιοῦν

PRESENT INDICATIVE MIDDLE/PASSIVE

S	1	λύομαι	νῑκῶμαι	ἀδικοῦμαι	ἀξιοῦμαι
	2	λύῃ/λύει	νῑκᾷ	ἀδικῇ/ἀδικεῖ	ἀξιοῖ
	3	λύεται	νῑκᾶται	ἀδικεῖται	ἀξιοῦται
D	2	λύεσθον	νῑκᾶσθον	ἀδικεῖσθον	ἀξιοῦσθον
	3	λύεσθον	νῑκᾶσθον	ἀδικεῖσθον	ἀξιοῦσθον
P	1	λῡόμεθα	νῑκώμεθα	ἀδικούμεθα	ἀξιούμεθα
	2	λύεσθε	νῑκᾶσθε	ἀδικεῖσθε	ἀξιοῦσθε
	3	λύονται	νῑκῶνται	ἀδικοῦνται	ἀξιοῦνται

IMPERFECT INDICATIVE MIDDLE/PASSIVE

S	1	ἐλῡόμην	ἐνῑκώμην	ἠδικούμην	ἠξιούμην
	2	ἐλύου	ἐνῑκῶ	ἠδικοῦ	ἠξιοῦ
	3	ἐλύετο	ἐνῑκᾶτο	ἠδικεῖτο	ἠξιοῦτο
D	2	ἐλύεσθον	ἐνῑκᾶσθον	ἠδικεῖσθον	ἠξιοῦσθον
	3	ἐλῡέσθην	ἐνῑκάσθην	ἠδικείσθην	ἠξιούσθην
P	1	ἐλῡόμεθα	ἐνῑκώμεθα	ἠδικούμεθα	ἠξιούμεθα
	2	ἐλύεσθε	ἐνῑκᾶσθε	ἠδικεῖσθε	ἠξιοῦσθε
	3	ἐλύοντο	ἐνῑκῶντο	ἠδικοῦντο	ἠξιοῦντο

PRESENT SUBJUNCTIVE MIDDLE/PASSIVE

S	1	λύωμαι	νῑκῶμαι	ἀδικῶμαι	ἀξιῶμαι
	2	λύῃ	νῑκᾷ	ἀδικῇ	ἀξιοῖ
	3	λύηται	νῑκᾶται	ἀδικῆται	ἀξιῶται
D	2	λύησθον	νῑκᾶσθον	ἀδικῆσθον	ἀξιῶσθον
	3	λύησθον	νῑκᾶσθον	ἀδικῆσθον	ἀξιῶσθον
P	1	λῡώμεθα	νῑκώμεθα	ἀδικώμεθα	ἀξιώμεθα
	2	λύησθε	νῑκᾶσθε	ἀδικῆσθε	ἀξιῶσθε
	3	λύωνται	νῑκῶνται	ἀδικῶνται	ἀξιῶνται

PRESENT OPTATIVE MIDDLE/PASSIVE

S	1	λῡοίμην	νῑκῴμην	ἀδικοίμην	ἀξιοίμην
	2	λύοιο	νῑκῷο	ἀδικοῖο	ἀξιοῖο
	3	λύοιτο	νῑκῷτο	ἀδικοῖτο	ἀξιοῖτο
D	2	λύοισθον	νῑκῷσθον	ἀδικοῖσθον	ἀξιοῖσθον
	3	λῡοίσθην	νῑκῴσθην	ἀδικοίσθην	ἀξιοίσθην

P 1   λῡοίμεθα   νῑκῴμεθα   ἀδικοίμεθα   ἀξιοίμεθα
  2   λῡοισθε   νῑκῷσθε   ἀδικοῖσθε   ἀξιοῖσθε
  3   λῡοιντο   νῑκῷντο   ἀδικοῖντο   ἀξιοῖντο

PRESENT IMPERATIVE MIDDLE/PASSIVE

S 2   λῡου   νῑκῶ   ἀδικοῦ   ἀξιοῦ
  3   λῡέσθω   νῑκάσθω   ἀδικείσθω   ἀξιούσθω

D 2   λῡεσθον   νῑκᾱσθον   ἀδικεῖσθον   ἀξιοῦσθον
  3   λῡέσθων   νῑκάσθων   ἀδικείσθων   ἀξιούσθων

P 2   λῡεσθε   νῑκᾱσθε   ἀδικεῖσθε   ἀξιοῦσθε
  3   λῡέσθων   νῑκάσθων   ἀδικείσθων   ἀξιούσθων

PRESENT INFINITIVE MIDDLE/PASSIVE

   λῡέσθαι   νῑκᾱσθαι   ἀδικεῖσθαι   ἀξιοῦσθαι

PRESENT PARTICIPLE MIDDLE/PASSIVE

   λῡόμενος,   νῑκώμενος,   ἀδικούμενος,   ἀξιούμενος,
   λῡομένη,   νῑκωμένη,   ἀδικουμένη,   ἀξιουμένη,
   λῡόμενον   νῑκώμενον   ἀδικούμενον   ἀξιούμενον

FUTURE ACTIVE AND MIDDLE

FUTURE INDICATIVE ACTIVE

S 1   λῡσω   ἐλῶ   ἀγγελῶ
  2   λῡσεις   ἐλᾷς   ἀγγελεῖς
  3   λῡσει   ἐλᾷ   ἀγγελεῖ

D 2   λῡσετον   ἐλᾶτον   ἀγγελεῖτον
  3   λῡσετον   ἐλᾶτον   ἀγγελεῖτον

P 1   λῡσομεν   ἐλῶμεν   ἀγγελοῦμεν
  2   λῡσετε   ἐλᾶτε   ἀγγελεῖτε
  3   λῡσουσι(ν)   ἐλῶσι(ν)   ἀγγελοῦσι(ν)

FUTURE OPTATIVE ACTIVE

S 1   λῡσοιμι   ἐλῷμι   ἀγγελοῖμι
  2   λῡσοις   ἐλῷς   ἀγγελοῖς
  3   λῡσοι   ἐλῷ   ἀγγελοῖ

D 2 λύσοιτον   ἐλῷτον   ἀγγελοῖτον
  3 λυσοίτην   ἐλῴτην   ἀγγελοίτην

P 1 λύσοιμεν   ἐλῷμεν   ἀγγελοῖμεν
  2 λύσοιτε   ἐλῷτε   ἀγγελοῖτε
  3 λύσοιεν   ἐλῷεν   ἀγγελοῖεν

FUTURE OPTATIVE ACTIVE (ALTERNATE FORMS)

S 1   ἐλῴην   ἀγγελοίην
  2   ἐλῴης   ἀγγελοίης
  3   ἐλῴη   ἀγγελοίη

D 2   ἐλῴητον   ἀγγελοίητον
  3   ἐλῳήτην   ἀγγελοιήτην

P 1   ἐλῴημεν   ἀγγελοίημεν
  2   ἐλῴητε   ἀγγελοίητε
  3   ἐλῴησαν   ἀγγελοίησαν

FUTURE INFINITIVE ACTIVE

  λύσειν   ἐλᾶν   ἀγγελεῖν

FUTURE PARTICIPLE ACTIVE

  λύσων,   ἐλῶν,   ἀγγελῶν,
    λύσουσα,   ἐλῶσα,   ἀγγελοῦσα,
    λῦσον   ἐλῶν   ἀγγελοῦν

FUTURE INDICATIVE MIDDLE

S 1 λύσομαι   ἐλῶμαι   ἀγγελοῦμαι
  2 λύσῃ/λύσει   ἐλᾷ   ἀγγελῇ/ἀγγελεῖ
  3 λύσεται   ἐλᾶται   ἀγγελεῖται

D 2 λύσεσθον   ἐλᾶσθον   ἀγγελεῖσθον
  3 λύσεσθον   ἐλᾶσθον   ἀγγελεῖσθον

P 1 λῡσόμεθα   ἐλώμεθα   ἀγγελούμεθα
  2 λύσεσθε   ἐλᾶσθε   ἀγγελεῖσθε
  3 λύσονται   ἐλῶνται   ἀγγελοῦνται

FUTURE OPTATIVE MIDDLE

S 1 λῡσοίμην   ἐλῴμην   ἀγγελοίμην
  2 λύσοιο   ἐλῷο   ἀγγελοῖο
  3 λύσοιτο   ἐλῷτο   ἀγγελοῖτο

D 2   *λύσοισθον*   *ἐλῷσθον*   *ἀγγελοῖσθον*

    3   *λυσοίσθην*   *ἐλῴσθην*   *ἀγγελοίσθην*

P 1   *λυσοίμεθα*   *ἐλῴμεθα*   *ἀγγελοίμεθα*

    2   *λύσοισθε*   *ἐλῷσθε*   *ἀγγελοῖσθε*

    3   *λύσοιντο*   *ἐλῷντο*   *ἀγγελοῖντο*

FUTURE INFINITIVE MIDDLE

     λύσεσθαι   *ἐλᾶσθαι*   *ἀγγελεῖσθαι*

FUTURE PARTICIPLE MIDDLE

     λυσόμενος,   *ἐλώμενος,*   *ἀγγελούμενος,*

       λυσομένη,   *ἐλωμένη,*   *ἀγγελουμένη,*

       λυσόμενον   *ἐλώμενον*   *ἀγγελούμενον*

FUTURE PASSIVE

FUTURE INDICATIVE PASSIVE

S 1   *λυθήσομαι*

    2   *λυθήσῃ/λυθήσει*

    3   *λυθήσεται*

D 2   *λυθήσεσθον*

    3   *λυθήσεσθον*

P 1   *λυθησόμεθα*

    2   *λυθήσεσθε*

    3   *λυθήσονται*

FUTURE OPTATIVE PASSIVE

S 1   *λυθησοίμην*

    2   *λυθήσοιο*

    3   *λυθήσοιτο*

D 2   *λυθήσοισθον*

    3   *λυθησοίσθην*

P 1   *λυθησοίμεθα*

    2   *λυθήσοισθε*

    3   *λυθήσοιντο*

FUTURE INFINITIVE PASSIVE

     λυθήσεσθαι

FUTURE PARTICIPLE PASSIVE

λυθησόμενος, λυθησομένη, λυθησόμενον

FIRST AORIST ACTIVE AND MIDDLE

		AORIST INDICATIVE ACTIVE	AORIST INDICATIVE MIDDLE
S	1	ἔλῡσα	ἐλῡσάμην
	2	ἔλῡσας	ἐλύσω
	3	ἔλῡσε(ν)	ἐλύσατο
D	2	ἐλύσατον	ἐλύσασθον
	3	ἐλῡσάτην	ἐλῡσάσθην
P	1	ἐλύσαμεν	ἐλῡσάμεθα
	2	ἐλύσατε	ἐλύσασθε
	3	ἔλῡσαν	ἐλύσαντο

		AORIST SUBJUNCTIVE ACTIVE	AORIST SUBJUNCTIVE MIDDLE
S	1	λύσω	λύσωμαι
	2	λύσῃς	λύσῃ
	3	λύσῃ	λύσηται
D	2	λύσητον	λύσησθον
	3	λύσητον	λύσησθον
P	1	λῡσώμεν	λῡσώμεθα
	2	λύσητε	λύσησθε
	3	λύσωσι(ν)	λύσωνται

		AORIST OPTATIVE ACTIVE	AORIST OPTATIVE MIDDLE
S	1	λύσαιμι	λῡσαίμην
	2	λύσαις/λύσειας	λύσαιο
	3	λύσαι/λύσειε(ν)	λύσαιτο
D	2	λύσαιτον	λύσαισθον
	3	λῡσαίτην	λῡσαίσθην
P	1	λύσαιμεν	λῡσαίμεθα
	2	λύσαιτε	λύσαισθε
	3	λύσαιεν/λύσειαν	λύσαιντο

		AORIST IMPERATIVE ACTIVE	AORIST IMPERATIVE MIDDLE
S	2	λῦσον	λῦσαι
	3	λῡσάτω	λῡσάσθω
D	2	λύσατον	λύσασθον
	3	λῡσάτων	λῡσάσθων
P	2	λύσατε	λύσασθε
	3	λῡσάντων	λῡσάσθων

	AORIST INFINITIVE ACTIVE	AORIST INFINITIVE MIDDLE
	λῦσαι	λύσασθαι

	AORIST PARTICIPLE ACTIVE	AORIST PARTICIPLE MIDDLE
	λύσᾱς, λύσᾱσα, λῦσαν	λῡσάμενος, λῡσαμένη, λῡσάμενον

SECOND AORIST ACTIVE AND MIDDLE

		AORIST INDICATIVE ACTIVE	AORIST INDICATIVE MIDDLE
S	1	ἔβαλον	ἐβαλόμην
	2	ἔβαλες	ἐβάλου
	3	ἔβαλε(ν)	ἐβάλετο
D	2	ἐβάλετον	ἐβάλεσθον
	3	ἐβαλέτην	ἐβαλέσθην
P	1	ἐβάλομεν	ἐβαλόμεθα
	2	ἐβάλετε	ἐβάλεσθε
	3	ἔβαλον	ἐβάλοντο

		AORIST SUBJUNCTIVE ACTIVE	AORIST SUBJUNCTIVE MIDDLE
S	1	βάλω	βάλωμαι
	2	βάλῃς	βάλῃ
	3	βάλῃ	βάληται
D	2	βάλητον	βάλησθον
	3	βάλητον	βάλησθον

P 1	βάλωμεν	βαλώμεθα
2	βάλητε	βάλησθε
3	βάλωσι(ν)	βάλωνται

	AORIST OPTATIVE *ACTIVE*	*AORIST OPTATIVE* *MIDDLE*
S 1	βάλοιμι	βαλοίμην
2	βάλοις	βάλοιο
3	βάλοι	βάλοιτο
D 2	βάλοιτον	βάλοισθον
3	βαλοίτην	βαλοίσθην
P 1	βάλοιμεν	βαλοίμεθα
2	βάλοιτε	βάλοισθε
3	βάλοιεν	βάλοιντο

	AORIST IMPERATIVE *ACTIVE*	*AORIST IMPERATIVE* *MIDDLE*
S 2	βάλε	βαλοῦ
3	βαλέτω	βαλέσθω
D 2	βάλετον	βάλεσθον
3	βαλέτων	βαλέσθων
P 2	βάλετε	βάλεσθε
3	βαλόντων	βαλέσθων

| | *AORIST INFINITIVE*
ACTIVE | *AORIST INFINITIVE*
MIDDLE |
| | βαλεῖν | βαλέσθαι |

| | *AORIST PARTICIPLE*
ACTIVE | *AORIST PARTICIPLE*
MIDDLE |
| | βαλών, βαλοῦσα, βαλόν | βαλόμενος, βαλομένη, βαλόμενον |

AORIST PASSIVE

AORIST INDICATIVE PASSIVE

S 1	ἐλύθην
2	ἐλύθης
3	ἐλύθη

D 2   ἐλύθητον
 3   ἐλυθήτην

P 1   ἐλύθημεν
 2   ἐλύθητε
 3   ἐλύθησαν

AORIST SUBJUNCTIVE PASSIVE

S 1   λυθῶ
 2   λυθῇς
 3   λυθῇ

D 2   λυθῆτον
 3   λυθῆτον

P 1   λυθῶμεν
 2   λυθῆτε
 3   λυθῶσι(ν)

AORIST OPTATIVE PASSIVE

S 1   λυθείην
 2   λυθείης
 3   λυθείη

D 2   λυθεῖτον/λυθείητον
 3   λυθείτην/λυθειήτην

P 1   λυθεῖμεν/λυθείημεν
 2   λυθεῖτε/λυθείητε
 3   λυθεῖεν/λυθείησαν

AORIST IMPERATIVE PASSIVE

S 2   λύθητι   κλάπηθι
 3   λυθήτω   κλαπήτω

D 2   λύθητον   κλάπητον
 3   λυθήτων   κλαπήτων

P 2   λύθητε   κλάπητε
 3   λυθέντων   κλαπέντων

AORIST INFINITIVE PASSIVE

       λυθῆναι

AORIST PARTICIPLE PASSIVE

λυθείς, λυθεῖσα, λυθέν

PERFECT AND PLUPERFECT ACTIVE

PERFECT INDICATIVE ACTIVE

S 1 λέλυκα
  2 λέλυκας
  3 λέλυκε(ν)

D 2 λελύκατον
  3 λελύκατον

P 1 λελύκαμεν
  2 λελύκατε
  3 λελύκᾱσι(ν)

PLUPERFECT INDICATIVE ACTIVE

S 1 ἐλελύκη
  2 ἐλελύκης
  3 ἐλελύκει(ν)

D 2 ἐλελύκετον
  3 ἐλελυκέτην

P 1 ἐλελύκεμεν
  2 ἐλελύκετε
  3 ἐλελύκεσαν

PERFECT SUBJUNCTIVE ACTIVE

			OR	
S	1	λελυκὼς ὦ		λελύκω
	2	λελυκὼς ᾖς		λελύκῃς
	3	λελυκὼς ᾖ		λελύκῃ
D	2	λελυκότε ἦτον		λελύκητον
	3	λελυκότε ἦτον		λελύκητον
P	1	λελυκότες ὦμεν		λελύκωμεν
	2	λελυκότες ἦτε		λελύκητε
	3	λελυκότες ὦσι(ν)		λελύκωσι(ν)

PERFECT OPTATIVE ACTIVE

S	1	λελυκὼς εἴην	OR	λελύκοιμι/λελυκοίην
	2	λελυκὼς εἴης		λελύκοις/λελυκοίης
	3	λελυκὼς εἴη		λελύκοι/λελυκοίη
D	2	λελυκότε εἴητον/εἴτον		λελύκοιτον
	3	λελυκότε εἰήτην/εἴτην		λελυκοίτην
P	1	λελυκότες εἴημεν/εἶμεν		λελύκοιμεν
	2	λελυκότες εἴητε/εἶτε		λελύκοιτε
	3	λελυκότες εἴησαν/εἶεν		λελύκοιεν

PERFECT IMPERATIVE ACTIVE

S	2	λελυκὼς ἴσθι
	3	λελυκὼς ἔστω
D	2	λελυκότε ἔστον
	3	λελυκότε ἔστων
P	2	λελυκότες ἔστε
	3	λελυκότες ὄντων

PERFECT INFINITIVE ACTIVE

λελυκέναι

PERFECT PARTICIPLE ACTIVE

λελυκώς, λελυκυῖα, λελυκός

PERFECT AND PLUPERFECT MIDDLE/PASSIVE

(For consonant stems, see pages 665–67.)

PERFECT INDICATIVE MIDDLE/PASSIVE

S	1	λέλυμαι
	2	λέλυσαι
	3	λέλυται
D	2	λέλυσθον
	3	λέλυσθον
P	1	λελύμεθα
	2	λέλυσθε
	3	λέλυνται

PLUPERFECT INDICATIVE MIDDLE/PASSIVE

S 1   ἐλελύμην
   2   ἐλέλυσο
   3   ἐλέλυτο

D 2   ἐλέλυσθον
   3   ἐλελύσθην

P 1   ἐλελύμεθα
   2   ἐλέλυσθε
   3   ἐλέλυντο

PERFECT SUBJUNCTIVE MIDDLE/PASSIVE

S 1   λελυμένος ὦ
   2   λελυμένος ᾖς
   3   λελυμένος ᾖ

D 2   λελυμένω ἦτον
   3   λελυμένω ἦτον

P 1   λελυμένοι ὦμεν
   2   λελυμένοι ἦτε
   3   λελυμένοι ὦσι(ν)

PERFECT OPTATIVE MIDDLE/PASSIVE

S 1   λελυμένος εἴην
   2   λελυμένος εἴης
   3   λελυμένος εἴη

D 2   λελυμένω εἴητον/εἴτον
   3   λελυμένω εἰήτην/εἴτην

P 1   λελυμένοι εἴημεν/εἶμεν
   2   λελυμένοι εἴητε/εἶτε
   3   λελυμένοι εἴησαν/εἶεν

PERFECT IMPERATIVE MIDDLE/PASSIVE

S 2   λέλυσο
   3   λελύσθω

D 2   λέλυσθον
   3   λελύσθων

P 2   λέλυσθε
   3   λελύσθων

PERFECT INFINITIVE MIDDLE/PASSIVE

λελύσθαι

PERFECT PARTICIPLE MIDDLE/PASSIVE

λελυμένος, λελυμένη, λελυμένον

PERFECT AND PLUPERFECT MIDDLE/PASSIVE
OF CONSONANT STEMS

PERFECT INDICATIVE MIDDLE/PASSIVE

S	1	γέγραμμαι	πέπεμμαι	ἤσχυμμαι
	2	γέγραψαι	πέπεμψαι	ἤσχυμμένος εἶ
	3	γέγραπται	πέπεμπται	ἤσχυνται
D	2	γέγραφθον	πέπεμφθον	ἤσχυνθον
	3	γέγραφθον	πέπεμφθον	ἤσχυνθον
P	1	γεγράμμεθα	πεπέμμεθα	ἠσχύμμεθα
	2	γέγραφθε	πέπεμφθε	ἤσχυνθε
	3	γεγραμμένοι εἰσί(ν)	πεπεμμένοι εἰσί(ν)	ἠσχυμμένοι εἰσί(ν)

S	1	τέταγμαι	ἐλήλεγμαι	κεκέλευσμαι
	2	τέταξαι	ἐλήλεγξαι	κεκέλευσαι
	3	τέτακται	ἐλήλεγκται	κεκέλευσται
D	2	τέταχθον	ἐλήλεγχθον	κεκέλευσθον
	3	τέταχθον	ἐλήλεγχθον	κεκέλευσθον
P	1	τετάγμεθα	ἐληλέγμεθα	κεκελεύσμεθα
	2	τέταχθε	ἐλήλεγχθε	κεκέλευσθε
	3	τεταγμένοι εἰσί(ν)	ἐληλεγμένοι εἰσί(ν)	κεκελευσμένοι εἰσί(ν)

S	1	πέφασμαι	ἤγγελμαι	
	2	πεφασμένος εἶ	ἤγγελσαι	
	3	πέφανται	ἤγγελται	
D	2	πέφανθον	ἤγγελθον	
	3	πέφανθον	ἤγγελθον	
P	1	πεφάσμεθα	ἠγγέλμεθα	
	2	πέφανθε	ἤγγελθε	
	3	πεφασμένοι εἰσί(ν)	ἠγγελμένοι εἰσί(ν)	

PLUPERFECT INDICATIVE MIDDLE/PASSIVE

S	1	ἐγεγράμμην	ἐπεπέμμην	ᾐσχύμμην
	2	ἐγέγραψο	ἐπέπεμψο	ᾐσχυμμένος ἦσθα
	3	ἐγέγραπτο	ἐπέπεμπτο	ᾔσχυντο
D	2	ἐγέγραφθον	ἐπέπεμφθον	ᾔσχυνθον
	3	ἐγεγράφθην	ἐπεπέμφθην	ᾐσχύνθην
P	1	ἐγεγράμμεθα	ἐπεπέμμεθα	ᾐσχύμμεθα
	2	ἐγέγραφθε	ἐπέπεμφθε	ᾔσχυνθε
	3	γεγραμμένοι ἦσαν	πεπεμμένοι ἦσαν	ᾐσχυμμένοι ἦσαν

S	1	ἐτετάγμην	ἐληλέγμην	ἐκεκελεύσμην
	2	ἐτέταξο	ἐλήλεγξο	ἐκεκέλευσο
	3	ἐτέτακτο	ἐλήλεγκτο	ἐκεκέλευστο
D	2	ἐτέταχθον	ἐλήλεγχθον	ἐκεκέλευσθον
	3	ἐτετάχθην	ἐληλέγχθην	ἐκεκελεύσθην
P	1	ἐτετάγμεθα	ἐληλέγμεθα	ἐκεκελεύσμεθα
	2	ἐτέταχθε	ἐλήλεγχθε	ἐκεκέλευσθε
	3	τεταγμένοι ἦσαν	ἐληλεγμένοι ἦσαν	κεκελευσμένοι ἦσαν

S	1	ἐπεφάσμην	ἠγγέλμην
	2	πεφασμένος ἦσθα	ἤγγελσο
	3	ἐπέφαντο	ἤγγελτο
D	2	ἐπέφανθον	ἤγγελθον
	3	ἐπεφάνθην	ἠγγέλθην
P	1	ἐπεφάσμεθα	ἠγγέλμεθα
	2	ἐπέφανθε	ἤγγελθε
	3	πεφασμένοι ἦσαν	ἠγγελμένοι ἦσαν

PERFECT SUBJUNCTIVE MIDDLE/PASSIVE
PERFECT OPTATIVE MIDDLE/PASSIVE

The perfect subjunctive and optative middle/passive of consonant stems are formed periphrastically, just as are the corresponding forms of λύω. Cf. page 664.

Thus, for example: πεπεμμένος ὦ, ᾖς, ᾖ, etc.
                       perfect subjunctive middle/passive

                       πεπεμμένος εἴην, εἴης, εἴη, etc.
                       perfect optative middle/passive

PERFECT IMPERATIVE MIDDLE/PASSIVE

S	2	γέγραψο	πέπεμψο	ἠσχυμμένος ἴσθι
	3	γεγράφθω	πεπέμφθω	ἠσχύνθω
D	2	γέγραφθον	πέπεμφθον	ἤσχυνθον
	3	γεγράφθων	πεπέμφθων	ἠσχύνθων
P	2	γέγραφθε	πέπεμφθε	ἤσχυνθε
	3	γεγράφθων	πεπέμφθων	ἠσχύνθων

S	2	τέταξο	ἐλήλεγξο	κεκέλευσο
	3	τετάχθω	ἐληλέγχθω	κεκελεύσθω
D	2	τέταχθον	ἐλήλεγχθον	κεκέλευσθον
	3	τετάχθων	ἐληλέγχθων	κεκελεύσθων
P	2	τέταχθε	ἐλήλεγχθε	κεκέλευσθε
	3	τετάχθων	ἐληλέγχθων	κεκελεύσθων

S	2	πεφασμένος ἴσθι	ἤγγελσο
	3	πεφάνθω	ἠγγέλθω
D	2	πέφανθον	ἤγγελθον
	3	πεφάνθων	ἠγγέλθων
P	2	πέφανθε	ἤγγελθε
	3	πεφάνθων	ἠγγέλθων

PERFECT INFINITIVE MIDDLE/PASSIVE

γεγράφθαι	πεπέμφθαι	ἠσχύνθαι
τετάχθαι	ἐληλέγχθαι	κεκελεῦσθαι
πεφάνθαι	ἠγγέλθαι	

PERFECT PARTICIPLE MIDDLE/PASSIVE

γεγραμμένος, γεγραμμένη, γεγραμμένον
πεπεμμένος, πεπεμμένη, πεπεμμένον
ἠσχυμμένος, ἠσχυμμένη, ἠσχυμμένον
τεταγμένος, τεταγμένη, τεταγμένον
ἐληλεγμένος, ἐληλεγμένη, ἐληλεγμένον
κεκελευσμένος, κεκελευσμένη, κεκελευσμένον
πεφασμένος, πεφασμένη, πεφασμένον
ἠγγελμένος, ἠγγελμένη, ἠγγελμένον

THE CONTRACTED VERBS ζάω, χράομαι

		PRESENT INDICATIVE ACTIVE	*PRESENT INDICATIVE MIDDLE/PASSIVE*
S	1	ζῶ	χρῶμαι
	2	ζῇς	χρῇ
	3	ζῇ	χρῆται
D	2	ζῆτον	χρῆσθον
	3	ζῆτον	χρῆσθον
P	1	ζῶμεν	χρώμεθα
	2	ζῆτε	χρῆσθε
	3	ζῶσι(ν)	χρῶνται

		IMPERFECT INDICATIVE ACTIVE	*IMPERFECT INDICATIVE MIDDLE/PASSIVE*
S	1	ἔζων	ἐχρώμην
	2	ἔζης	ἐχρῶ
	3	ἔζη	ἐχρῆτο
D	2	ἐζῆτον	ἐχρῆσθον
	3	ἐζήτην	ἐχρήσθην
P	1	ἐζῶμεν	ἐχρώμεθα
	2	ἐζῆτε	ἐχρῆσθε
	3	ἔζων	ἐχρῶντο

		PRESENT SUBJUNCTIVE ACTIVE	*PRESENT SUBJUNCTIVE MIDDLE/PASSIVE*
S	1	ζῶ	χρῶμαι
	2	ζῇς	χρῇ
	3	ζῇ	χρῆται
D	2	ζῆτον	χρῆσθον
	3	ζῆτον	χρῆσθον
P	1	ζῶμεν	χρώμεθα
	2	ζῆτε	χρῆσθε
	3	ζῶσι(ν)	χρῶνται

		PRESENT OPTATIVE ACTIVE			*PRESENT OPTATIVE MIDDLE/PASSIVE*
S	1	ζῷμι	OR	ζῴην	χρῴμην
	2	ζῷς		ζῴης	χρῷο
	3	ζῷ		ζῴη	χρῷτο
D	2	ζῷτον		ζῴητον	χρῷσθον
	3	ζῴτην		ζωῄτην	χρῴσθην
P	1	ζῷμεν		ζῴημεν	χρῴμεθα
	2	ζῷτε		ζῴητε	χρῷσθε
	3	ζῷεν		ζῴησαν	χρῷντο

		PRESENT IMPERATIVE ACTIVE	*PRESENT IMPERATIVE MIDDLE/PASSIVE*
S	2	ζῆ	χρῶ
	3	ζήτω	χρήσθω
D	2	ζῆτον	χρῆσθον
	3	ζήτων	χρήσθων
P	2	ζῆτε	χρῆσθε
	3	ζώντων	χρήσθων

PRESENT INFINITIVE ACTIVE

ζῆν

PRESENT INFINITIVE MIDDLE/PASSIVE

χρῆσθαι

PRESENT PARTICIPLE ACTIVE

ζῶν, ζῶσα, ζῶν
(like νῑκῶν, νῑκῶσα,
   νῑκῶν)

PRESENT PARTICIPLE MIDDLE/PASSIVE

χρώμενος, χρωμένη, χρώμενον
(like νῑκώμενος, νῑκωμένη,
   νῑκώμενον)

THE VERBS δεῖ, χρή

All finite forms are third person singular.

PRESENT INDICATIVE ACTIVE:	δεῖ	χρή
PRESENT SUBJUNCTIVE ACTIVE:	δέῃ	χρῇ
PRESENT OPTATIVE ACTIVE:	δέοι	χρείη
PRESENT INFINITIVE ACTIVE:	δεῖν	χρῆναι

PRESENT PARTICIPLE ACTIVE: δέον   χρεών (N nom. sing.)
IMPERFECT INDICATIVE ACTIVE: ἔδει   (ἐ)χρῆν
FUTURE INDICATIVE ACTIVE: δεήσει   χρῆσται
AORIST INDICATIVE ACTIVE: ἐδέησε(ν)   ——

-μι (ATHEMATIC) VERBS
PRESENT AND IMPERFECT OF δίδωμι, ἵστημι, τίθημι, ἵημι

Present tense stems:

| διδω- | ἱστη- | τιθη- | ἱη- |
| διδο- | ἱστα-/ἱστε- | τιθε- | ἱε- |

PRESENT INDICATIVE ACTIVE

S	1	δίδωμι	ἵστημι	τίθημι	ἵημι
	2	δίδως	ἵστης	τίθης	ἵης/ἱεῖς
	3	δίδωσι(ν)	ἵστησι(ν)	τίθησι(ν)	ἵησι(ν)
D	2	δίδοτον	ἵστατον	τίθετον	ἵετον
	3	δίδοτον	ἵστατον	τίθετον	ἵετον
P	1	δίδομεν	ἵσταμεν	τίθεμεν	ἵεμεν
	2	δίδοτε	ἵστατε	τίθετε	ἵετε
	3	διδόᾱσι(ν)	ἱστᾶσι(ν)	τιθέᾱσι(ν)	ἱᾶσι(ν)

IMPERFECT INDICATIVE ACTIVE

S	1	ἐδίδουν	ἵστην	ἐτίθην	ἵην
	2	ἐδίδους	ἵστης	ἐτίθεις	ἵεις
	3	ἐδίδου	ἵστη	ἐτίθει	ἵει
D	2	ἐδίδοτον	ἵστατον	ἐτίθετον	ἵετον
	3	ἐδιδότην	ἱστάτην	ἐτιθέτην	ἱέτην
P	1	ἐδίδομεν	ἵσταμεν	ἐτίθεμεν	ἵεμεν
	2	ἐδίδοτε	ἵστατε	ἐτίθετε	ἵετε
	3	ἐδίδοσαν	ἵστασαν	ἐτίθεσαν	ἵεσαν

PRESENT SUBJUNCTIVE ACTIVE

S	1	διδῶ	ἱστῶ	τιθῶ	ἱῶ
	2	διδῷς	ἱστῇς	τιθῇς	ἱῇς
	3	διδῷ	ἱστῇ	τιθῇ	ἱῇ

D	2	διδῶτον	ἱστῆτον	τιθῆτον	ἱῆτον
	3	διδῶτον	ἱστῆτον	τιθῆτον	ἱῆτον
P	1	διδῶμεν	ἱστῶμεν	τιθῶμεν	ἱῶμεν
	2	διδῶτε	ἱστῆτε	τιθῆτε	ἱῆτε
	3	διδῶσι(ν)	ἱστῶσι(ν)	τιθῶσι(ν)	ἱῶσι(ν)

PRESENT OPTATIVE ACTIVE

S	1	διδοίην	ἱσταίην	τιθείην	ἱείην
	2	διδοίης	ἱσταίης	τιθείης	ἱείης
	3	διδοίη	ἱσταίη	τιθείη	ἱείη
D	2	διδοῖτον	ἱσταῖτον	τιθεῖτον	ἱεῖτον
	3	διδοίτην	ἱσταίτην	τιθείτην	ἱείτην
P	1	διδοῖμεν	ἱσταῖμεν	τιθεῖμεν	ἱεῖμεν
	2	διδοῖτε	ἱσταῖτε	τιθεῖτε	ἱεῖτε
	3	διδοῖεν	ἱσταῖεν	τιθεῖεν	ἱεῖεν

PRESENT OPTATIVE ACTIVE (ALTERNATIVE FORMS)

D	2	διδοίητον	ἱσταίητον	τιθείητον	ἱείητον
	3	διδοιήτην	ἱσταιήτην	τιθειήτην	ἱειήτην
P	1	διδοίημεν	ἱσταίημεν	τιθείημεν	ἱείημεν
	2	διδοίητε	ἱσταίητε	τιθείητε	ἱείητε
	3	διδοίησαν	ἱσταίησαν	τιθείησαν	ἱείησαν

PRESENT IMPERATIVE ACTIVE

S	2	δίδου	ἵστη	τίθει	ἵει
	3	διδότω	ἱστάτω	τιθέτω	ἱέτω
D	2	δίδοτον	ἵστατον	τίθετον	ἵετον
	3	διδότων	ἱστάτων	τιθέτων	ἱέτων
P	2	δίδοτε	ἵστατε	τίθετε	ἵετε
	3	διδόντων	ἱστάντων	τιθέντων	ἱέντων

PRESENT INFINITIVE ACTIVE

	διδόναι	ἱστάναι	τιθέναι	ἱέναι

PRESENT PARTICIPLE ACTIVE

	διδούς,	ἱστάς,	τιθείς,	ἱείς,
	διδοῦσα,	ἱστᾶσα,	τιθεῖσα,	ἱεῖσα,
	διδόν	ἱστάν	τιθέν	ἱέν

PRESENT INDICATIVE MIDDLE/PASSIVE

S	1	δίδομαι	ἵσταμαι	τίθεμαι	ἵεμαι
	2	δίδοσαι	ἵστασαι	τίθεσαι	ἵεσαι
	3	δίδοται	ἵσταται	τίθεται	ἵεται
D	2	δίδοσθον	ἵστασθον	τίθεσθον	ἵεσθον
	3	δίδοσθον	ἵστασθον	τίθεσθον	ἵεσθον
P	1	διδόμεθα	ἱστάμεθα	τιθέμεθα	ἱέμεθα
	2	δίδοσθε	ἵστασθε	τίθεσθε	ἵεσθε
	3	δίδονται	ἵστανται	τίθενται	ἵενται

IMPERFECT INDICATIVE MIDDLE/PASSIVE

S	1	ἐδιδόμην	ἱστάμην	ἐτιθέμην	ἱέμην
	2	ἐδίδοσο	ἵστασο	ἐτίθεσο	ἵεσο
	3	ἐδίδοτο	ἵστατο	ἐτίθετο	ἵετο
D	2	ἐδίδοσθον	ἵστασθον	ἐτίθεσθον	ἵεσθον
	3	ἐδιδόσθην	ἱστάσθην	ἐτιθέσθην	ἱέσθην
P	1	ἐδιδόμεθα	ἱστάμεθα	ἐτιθέμεθα	ἱέμεθα
	2	ἐδίδοσθε	ἵστασθε	ἐτίθεσθε	ἵεσθε
	3	ἐδίδοντο	ἵσταντο	ἐτίθεντο	ἵεντο

PRESENT SUBJUNCTIVE MIDDLE/PASSIVE

S	1	διδῶμαι	ἱστῶμαι	τιθῶμαι	ἱῶμαι
	2	διδῷ	ἱστῇ	τιθῇ	ἱῇ
	3	διδῶται	ἱστῆται	τιθῆται	ἱῆται
D	2	διδῶσθον	ἱστῆσθον	τιθῆσθον	ἱῆσθον
	3	διδῶσθον	ἱστῆσθον	τιθῆσθον	ἱῆσθον
P	1	διδώμεθα	ἱστώμεθα	τιθώμεθα	ἱώμεθα
	2	διδῶσθε	ἱστῆσθε	τιθῆσθε	ἱῆσθε
	3	διδῶνται	ἱστῶνται	τιθῶνται	ἱῶνται

PRESENT OPTATIVE MIDDLE/PASSIVE

S	1	διδοίμην	ἱσταίμην	τιθείμην	ἱείμην
	2	διδοῖο	ἱσταῖο	τιθεῖο	ἱεῖο
	3	διδοῖτο	ἱσταῖτο	τιθεῖτο	ἱεῖτο
D	2	διδοῖσθον	ἱσταῖσθον	τιθεῖσθον	ἱεῖσθον
	3	διδοίσθην	ἱσταίσθην	τιθείσθην	ἱείσθην

P	1	διδοίμεθα	ἱσταίμεθα	τιθείμεθα	ἱείμεθα
	2	διδοῖσθε	ἵσταῖσθε	τιθεῖσθε	ἱεῖσθε
	3	διδοῖντο	ἵσταῖντο	τιθεῖντο	ἱεῖντο

OR

S	3			τιθοῖτο	
D	2			τιθοῖσθον	
	3			τιθοίσθην	
P	1			τιθοίμεθα	
	2			τιθοῖσθε	
	3			τιθοῖντο	

PRESENT IMPERATIVE MIDDLE/PASSIVE

S	2	δίδοσο	ἵστασο	τίθεσο	ἵεσο
	3	διδόσθω	ἱστάσθω	τιθέσθω	ἱέσθω
D	2	δίδοσθον	ἵστασθον	τίθεσθον	ἵεσθον
	3	διδόσθων	ἱστάσθων	τιθέσθων	ἱέσθων
P	2	δίδοσθε	ἵστασθε	τίθεσθε	ἵεσθε
	3	διδόσθων	ἱστάσθων	τιθέσθων	ἱέσθων

PRESENT INFINITIVE MIDDLE/PASSIVE

	δίδοσθαι	ἵστασθαι	τίθεσθαι	ἵεσθαι

PRESENT PARTICIPLE MIDDLE/PASSIVE

	διδόμενος,	ἱστάμενος,	τιθέμενος,	ἱέμενος
	διδομένη,	ἱσταμένη,	τιθεμένη,	ἱεμένη,
	διδόμενον	ἱστάμενον	τιθέμενον	ἱέμενον

PRESENT AND IMPERFECT OF δείκνῡμι, εἶμι, εἰμί, φημί, δύναμαι

Present tense stems:

	δεικνῡ-	εἰ-	ἐσ-	φη-	
	δεικνυ-	ἰ-	*σ-	φα-	δυνα-

PRESENT INDICATIVE ACTIVE

S	1	δείκνῡμι	εἶμι	εἰμί	φημί
	2	δείκνῡς	εἶ	εἶ	φής
	3	δείκνῡσι(ν)	εἶσι(ν)	ἐστί(ν)	φησί(ν)

D	2	δείκνυτον	ἴτον	ἐστόν	φατόν
	3	δείκνυτον	ἴτον	ἐστόν	φατόν
P	1	δείκνυμεν	ἴμεν	ἐσμέν	φαμέν
	2	δείκνυτε	ἴτε	ἐστέ	φατέ
	3	δεικνύᾱσι(ν)	ἴᾱσι(ν)	εἰσί(ν)	φᾱσί(ν)

IMPERFECT INDICATIVE ACTIVE

S	1	ἐδείκνῡν	ᾖα/ᾔειν	ἦ/ἦν	ἔφην
	2	ἐδείκνῡς	ᾔεισθα/ᾔεις	ἦσθα	ἔφησθα/ἔφης
	3	ἐδείκνῡ	ᾔει(ν)	ἦν	ἔφη
D	2	ἐδείκνυτον	ᾖτον	ἦστον	ἔφατον
	3	ἐδεικνύτην	ᾔτην	ἦστην	ἐφάτην
P	1	ἐδείκνυμεν	ᾖμεν	ἦμεν	ἔφαμεν
	2	ἐδείκνυτε	ᾖτε	ἦτε	ἔφατε
	3	ἐδείκνυσαν	ᾖσαν/ᾔεσαν	ἦσαν	ἔφασαν

PRESENT SUBJUNCTIVE ACTIVE

S	1	δεικνύω	ἴω	ὦ	φῶ
	2	δεικνύῃς	ἴῃς	ᾖς	φῇς
	3	δεικνύῃ	ἴῃ	ᾖ	φῇ
D	2	δεικνύητον	ἴητον	ἦτον	φῆτον
	3	δεικνύητον	ἴητον	ἦτον	φῆτον
P	1	δεικνύωμεν	ἴωμεν	ὦμεν	φῶμεν
	2	δεικνύητε	ἴητε	ἦτε	φῆτε
	3	δεικνύωσι(ν)	ἴωσι(ν)	ὦσι(ν)	φῶσι(ν)

PRESENT OPTATIVE ACTIVE

S	1	δεικνύοιμι	ἴοιμι/ἰοίην	εἴην	φαίην
	2	δεικνύοις	ἴοις	εἴης	φαίης
	3	δεικνύοι	ἴοι	εἴη	φαίη
D	2	δεικνύοιτον	ἴοιτον	εἴητον/εἶτον	——
	3	δεικνυοίτην	ἰοίτην	εἰήτην/εἴτην	——
P	1	δεικνύοιμεν	ἴοιμεν	εἴημεν/εἶμεν	φαῖμεν/φαίημεν
	2	δεικνύοιτε	ἴοιτε	εἴητε/εἶτε	φαῖτε/φαίητε
	3	δεικνύοιεν	ἴοιεν	εἴησαν/εἶεν	φαῖεν/φαίησαν

PRESENT IMPERATIVE ACTIVE

S	2	δείκνῡ	ἴθι	ἴσθι	φάθι
	3	δεικνύτω	ἴτω	ἔστω	φάτω
D	2	δείκνυτον	ἴτον	ἔστον	φάτον
	3	δεικνύτων	ἴτων	ἔστων	φάτων
P	2	δείκνυτε	ἴτε	ἔστε	φάτε
	3	δεικνύντων	ἰόντων	ἔστων/ὄντων ·	φάντων

PRESENT INFINITIVE ACTIVE

δεικνύναι   ἰέναι   εἶναι   φάναι

PRESENT PARTICIPLE ACTIVE

δεικνύς,   ἰών,   ὤν,   φάς,

δεικνῦσα,   ἰοῦσα,   οὖσα,   φᾶσα,

δεικνύν   ἰόν   ὄν   φάν

PRESENT INDICATIVE MIDDLE/PASSIVE

S	1	δείκνυμαι	δύναμαι
	2	δείκνυσαι	δύνασαι
	3	δείκνυται	δύναται
D	2	δείκνυσθον	δύνασθον
	3	δείκνυσθον	δύνασθον
P	1	δεικνύμεθα	δυνάμεθα
	2	δείκνυσθε	δύνασθε
	3	δείκνυνται	δύνανται

IMPERFECT INDICATIVE MIDDLE/PASSIVE

S	1	ἐδεικνύμην	ἐδυνάμην
	2	ἐδείκνυσο	ἐδύνω
	3	ἐδείκνυτο	ἐδύνατο
D	2	ἐδείκνυσθον	ἐδύνασθον
	3	ἐδεικνύσθην	ἐδυνάσθην
P	1	ἐδεικνύμεθα	ἐδυνάμεθα
	2	ἐδείκνυσθε	ἐδύνασθε
	3	ἐδείκνυντο	ἐδύναντο

PRESENT SUBJUNCTIVE MIDDLE/PASSIVE

S	1	δεικνύωμαι	δύνωμαι
	2	δεικνύῃ	δύνῃ
	3	δεικνύηται	δύνηται
D	2	δεικνύησθον	δύνησθον
	3	δεικνύησθον	δύνησθον
P	1	δεικνυώμεθα	δυνώμεθα
	2	δεικνύησθε	δύνησθε
	3	δεικνύωνται	δύνωνται

PRESENT OPTATIVE MIDDLE/PASSIVE

S	1	δεικνυοίμην	δυναίμην
	2	δεικνύοιο	δύναιο
	3	δεικνύοιτο	δύναιτο
D	2	δεικνύοισθον	δύναισθον
	3	δεικνυοίσθην	δυναίσθην
P	1	δεικνυοίμεθα	δυναίμεθα
	2	δεικνύοισθε	δύναισθε
	3	δεικνύοιντο	δύναιντο

PRESENT IMPERATIVE MIDDLE/PASSIVE

S	2	δείκνυσο	δύνασο
	3	δεικνύσθω	δυνάσθω
D	2	δείκνυσθον	δύνασθον
	3	δεικνύσθων	δυνάσθων
P	2	δείκνυσθε	δύνασθε
	3	δεικνύσθων	δυνάσθων

PRESENT INFINITIVE MIDDLE/PASSIVE

δείκνυσθαι   δύνασθαι

PRESENT PARTICIPLE MIDDLE/PASSIVE

δεικνύμενος, δεικνυμένη,   δυνάμενος, δυναμένη,
δεικνύμενον   δυνάμενον

PRESENT AND IMPERFECT MIDDLE OF κεῖμαι

Present tense stems: κει-
                        κε-

		PRESENT IND. MIDDLE	*IMPERF. IND. MIDDLE*	*PRESENT SUBJ. MIDDLE*	*PRESENT OPT. MIDDLE*	*PRESENT IMPER. MIDDLE*
S	1	κεῖμαι	ἐκείμην	κέωμαι	κεοίμην	
	2	κεῖσαι	ἔκεισο	κέῃ	κέοιο	κεῖσο
	3	κεῖται	ἔκειτο	κέηται	κέοιτο	κείσθω
D	2	κεῖσθον	ἔκεισθον	——	——	κεῖσθον
	3	κεῖσθον	ἐκείσθην	——	——	κείσθων
P	1	κείμεθα	ἐκείμεθα	κεώμεθα	κεοίμεθα	
	2	κεῖσθε	ἔκεισθε	κέησθε	κέοισθε	κεῖσθε
	3	κεῖνται	ἔκειντο	κέωνται	κέοιντο	κείσθων

PRESENT INFINITIVE MIDDLE: κεῖσθαι

PRESENT PARTICIPLE MIDDLE: κείμενος, κειμένη, κείμενον

MIXED AORIST ACTIVE OF δίδωμι, τίθημι, ἵημι

Tense stems:

(δωκ-)	(θηκ-)	(ἤκ-)
δο-	θε-	ἑ-

(Forms in parentheses are *first aorists*.)

AORIST INDICATIVE ACTIVE

S	1	(ἔδωκα)	(ἔθηκα)	(-ἧκα)
	2	(ἔδωκας)	(ἔθηκας)	(-ἧκας)
	3	(ἔδωκε[ν])	(ἔθηκε[ν])	(-ἧκε[ν])
D	2	ἔδοτον	ἔθετον	-εἷτον
	3	ἐδότην	ἐθέτην	-εἵτην
P	1	ἔδομεν	ἔθεμεν	-εἷμεν
	2	ἔδοτε	ἔθετε	-εἷτε
	3	ἔδοσαν	ἔθεσαν	-εἷσαν

AORIST SUBJUNCTIVE ACTIVE

S	1	δῶ	θῶ	-ῶ
	2	δῷς	θῇς	-ῇς
	3	δῷ	θῇ	-ῇ
D	2	δῶτον	θῆτον	-ῆτον
	3	δῶτον	θῆτον	-ῆτον
P	1	δῶμεν	θῶμεν	-ῶμεν
	2	δῶτε	θῆτε	-ῆτε
	3	δῶσι(ν)	θῶσι(ν)	-ῶσι(ν)

AORIST OPTATIVE ACTIVE

S	1	δοίην	θείην	-είην
	2	δοίης	θείης	-είης
	3	δοίη	θείη	-είη
D	2	δοῖτον	θεῖτον	-εῖτον
	3	δοίτην	θείτην	-είτην
P	1	δοῖμεν	θεῖμεν	-εῖμεν
	2	δοῖτε	θεῖτε	-εῖτε
	3	δοῖεν	θεῖεν	-εῖεν
		OR	**OR**	**OR**
D	2	δοίητον	θείητον	-είητον
	3	δοιήτην	θειήτην	-ειήτην
P	1	δοίημεν	θείημεν	-είημεν
	2	δοίητε	θείητε	-είητε
	3	δοίησαν	θείησαν	-είησαν

AORIST IMPERATIVE ACTIVE

S	2	δός	θές	-ές
	3	δότω	θέτω	-έτω
D	2	δότον	θέτον	-έτον
	3	δότων	θέτων	-έτων
P	2	δότε	θέτε	-έτε
	3	δόντων	θέντων	-έντων

AORIST INFINITIVE ACTIVE

	δοῦναι	θεῖναι	-εῖναι

AORIST PARTICIPLE ACTIVE

δούς,	θείς,	-είς,
δοῦσα,	θεῖσα,	-εῖσα,
δόν	θέν	-ἕν

SECOND AORIST MIDDLE OF δίδωμι, τίθημι, ἵημι

Tense stems:

δο-	θε-	ἑ-

AORIST INDICATIVE MIDDLE

S	1	ἐδόμην	ἐθέμην	-εἵμην
	2	ἔδου	ἔθου	-εῖσο
	3	ἔδοτο	ἔθετο	-εῖτο
D	2	ἔδοσθον	ἔθεσθον	-εῖσθον
	3	ἐδόσθην	ἐθέσθην	-εῖσθην
P	1	ἐδόμεθα	ἐθέμεθα	-εἵμεθα
	2	ἔδοσθε	ἔθεσθε	-εῖσθε
	3	ἔδοντο	ἔθεντο	-εῖντο

AORIST SUBJUNCTIVE MIDDLE

S	1	δῶμαι	θῶμαι	-ῶμαι
	2	δῷ	θῇ	-ῇ
	3	δῶται	θῆται	-ῆται
D	2	δῶσθον	θῆσθον	-ῆσθον
	3	δῶσθον	θῆσθον	-ῆσθον
P	1	δώμεθα	θώμεθα	-ώμεθα
	2	δῶσθε	θῆσθε	-ῆσθε
	3	δῶνται	θῶνται	-ῶνται

AORIST OPTATIVE MIDDLE

S	1	δοίμην	θείμην	-εἵμην
	2	δοῖο	θεῖο	-εῖο
	3	δοῖτο	θεῖτο	-εῖτο
D	2	δοῖσθον	θεῖσθον	-εῖσθον
	3	δοίσθην	θείσθην	-εῖσθην

P	1	δοίμεθα	θείμεθα	-είμεθα
	2	δοῖσθε	θεῖσθε	-εῖσθε
	3	δοῖντο	θεῖντο	-εῖντο

AORIST OPTATIVE MIDDLE (ALTERNATIVE FORMS)

S	3		θοῖτο	-οῖτο
P	1		θοίμεθα	-οίμεθα
	2		θοῖσθε	-οῖσθε
	3		θοῖντο	-οῖντο

AORIST IMPERATIVE MIDDLE

S	2	δοῦ	θοῦ	-οῦ
	3	δόσθω	θέσθω	-έσθω
D	2	δόσθον	θέσθον	-έσθον
	3	δόσθων	θέσθων	-έσθων
P	2	δόσθε	θέσθε	-έσθε
	3	δόσθων	θέσθων	-έσθων

AORIST INFINITIVE MIDDLE

	δόσθαι	θέσθαι	-έσθαι

AORIST PARTICIPLE MIDDLE

	δόμενος,	θέμενος,	-έμενος,
	δομένη,	θεμένη,	-εμένη,
	δόμενον	θέμενον	-έμενον

ROOT AORIST: ἔστην, ἔγνων, ἔδῦν (from ἵστημι, γιγνώσκω, δύω)

Tense stems:

στη-	γνω-	δῦ-
στα-/στε-	γνο-	δυ-

AORIST INDICATIVE ACTIVE

S	1	ἔστην	ἔγνων	ἔδῦν
	2	ἔστης	ἔγνως	ἔδῦς
	3	ἔστη	ἔγνω	ἔδῦ
D	2	ἔστητον	ἔγνωτον	ἔδῦτον
	3	ἐστήτην	ἐγνώτην	ἐδύτην

P	1	ἔστημεν	ἔγνωμεν	ἔδῡμεν
	2	ἔστητε	ἔγνωτε	ἔδῡτε
	3	ἔστησαν	ἔγνωσαν	ἔδῡσαν

AORIST SUBJUNCTIVE ACTIVE

S	1	στῶ	γνῶ	δύω
	2	στῇς	γνῷς	δύῃς
	3	στῇ	γνῷ	δύῃ
D	2	στῆτον	γνῶτον	δύητον
	3	στῆτον	γνῶτον	δύητον
P	1	στῶμεν	γνῶμεν	δύωμεν
	2	στῆτε	γνῶτε	δύητε
	3	στῶσι(ν)	γνῶσι(ν)	δύωσι(ν)

AORIST OPTATIVE ACTIVE

S	1	σταίην	γνοίην	(ἔδῡν has no optative in Attic.)
	2	σταίης	γνοίης	
	3	σταίη	γνοίη	
D	2	σταῖτον	γνοῖτον	
	3	σταίτην	γνοίτην	
P	1	σταῖμεν	γνοῖμεν	
	2	σταῖτε	γνοῖτε	
	3	σταῖεν	γνοῖεν	
		OR	OR	
D	2	σταίητον	γνοίητον	
	3	σταιήτην	γνοιήτην	
P	1	σταίημεν	γνοίημεν	
	2	σταίητε	γνοίητε	
	3	σταίησαν	γνοίησαν	

AORIST IMPERATIVE ACTIVE

S	2	στῆθι	γνῶθι	δῦθι
	3	στήτω	γνώτω	δύτω
D	2	στῆτον	γνῶτον	δῦτον
	3	στήτων	γνώτων	δύτων
P	2	στῆτε	γνῶτε	δῦτε
	3	στάντων	γνόντων	δύντων

AORIST INFINITIVE ACTIVE

στῆναι γνῶναι δῦναι

AORIST PARTICIPLE ACTIVE

στάς, γνούς, δύς,
στᾶσα, γνοῦσα, δῦσα,
στάν γνόν δύν

PERFECT AND PLUPERFECT ACTIVE OF ἵστημι

Tense stem: ἑστα-

(Forms in parentheses are formed from the stem ἑστηκ-.)

		PERFECT INDICATIVE ACTIVE	PERFECT SUBJUNCTIVE ACTIVE	PERFECT OPTATIVE ACTIVE
S	1	(ἕστηκα)	ἑστῶ	ἑσταίην
	2	(ἕστηκας)	ἑστῇς	ἑσταίης
	3	(ἕστηκε[ν])	ἑστῇ	ἑσταίη
D	2	ἕστατον	ἑστῆτον	ἑσταῖτον/ἑσταίητον
	3	ἕστατον	ἑστῆτον	ἑσταίτην/ἑσταιήτην
P	1	ἕσταμεν	ἑστῶμεν	ἑσταῖμεν/ἑσταίημεν
	2	ἕστατε	ἑστῆτε	ἑσταῖτε/ἑσταίητε
	3	ἑστᾶσι(ν)	ἑστῶσι(ν)	ἑσταῖεν/ἑσταίησαν

		PERFECT IMPERATIVE ACTIVE	PLUPERFECT INDICATIVE ACTIVE
S	1		(εἱστήκη)
	2	ἕσταθι	(εἱστήκης)
	3	ἑστάτω	(εἱστήκει[ν])
D	2	ἕστατον	ἕστατον
	3	ἑστάτων	ἑστάτην
P	1		ἕσταμεν
	2	ἕστατε	ἕστατε
	3	ἑστάντων	ἕστασαν

PERFECT INFINITIVE ACTIVE: ἑστάναι

PERFECT PARTICIPLE ACTIVE: ἑστώς, ἑστῶσα, ἑστός

PERFECT AND PLUPERFECT ACTIVE OF *οἶδα*

Tense stems: οἰδ-
                   εἰδ-
                   ἰδ-

	PERFECT IND. ACTIVE	PERFECT SUBJ. ACTIVE	PERFECT OPT. ACTIVE	PERFECT IMPER. ACTIVE
S 1	οἶδα	εἰδῶ	εἰδείην	
2	οἶσθα	εἰδῇς	εἰδείης	ἴσθι
3	οἶδε(ν)	εἰδῇ	εἰδείη	ἴστω
D 2	ἴστον	εἰδῆτον	εἰδεῖτον	ἴστον
3	ἴστον	εἰδῆτον	εἰδείτην	ἴστων
P 1	ἴσμεν	εἰδῶμεν	εἰδεῖμεν/εἰδείημεν	
2	ἴστε	εἰδῆτε	εἰδεῖτε/εἰδείητε	ἴστε
3	ἴσᾱσι(ν)	εἰδῶσι(ν)	εἰδεῖεν/εἰδείησαν	ἴστων

PLUPERFECT INDICATIVE ACTIVE

S 1	ᾔδη/ᾔδειν
2	ᾔδησθα/ᾔδεις
3	ᾔδει(ν)
D 2	ᾖστον
3	ᾖστην
P 1	ᾖσμεν/ᾔδεμεν
2	ᾖστε/ᾔδετε
3	ᾖσαν/ᾔδεσαν

PERFECT INFINITIVE ACTIVE: εἰδέναι

PERFECT PARTICIPLE ACTIVE: εἰδώς, εἰδυῖα, εἰδός

INFINITIVES COMPARED

	ACTIVE	*MIDDLE*	*PASSIVE*
PRESENT	παιδεύειν	παιδεύεσθαι	παιδεύεσθαι
CONTRACTED PRESENT	νῑκᾶν ζῆν	νῑκᾶσθαι	νῑκᾶσθαι
		χρῆσθαι	
	ἀδικεῖν	ἀδικεῖσθαι	ἀδικεῖσθαι
	ἀξιοῦν	ἀξιοῦσθαι	ἀξιοῦσθαι
FUTURE	παιδεύσειν	παιδεύσεσθαι	παιδευθήσεσθαι
CONTRACTED FUTURE	ἐλᾶν ἀγγελεῖν	ἐλᾶσθαι ἀγγελεῖσθαι	
FIRST AORIST	παιδεῦσαι	παιδεύσασθαι	παιδευθῆναι
THEMATIC SECOND AORIST	βαλεῖν	βαλέσθαι	
PERFECT	πεπαιδευκέναι ἑστάναι εἰδέναι	πεπαιδεῦσθαι	πεπαιδεῦσθαι
ATHEMATIC PRESENT	διδόναι	δίδοσθαι	δίδοσθαι
	ἱστάναι	ἵστασθαι	ἵστασθαι
	τιθέναι	τίθεσθαι	τίθεσθαι
	ἱέναι	ἵεσθαι	ἵεσθαι
	δεικνύναι	δείκνυσθαι	δείκνυσθαι
		δύνασθαι	
	ἰέναι		
	εἶναι		
	φάναι		
		κεῖσθαι	
ATHEMATIC SECOND AORIST	δοῦναι	δόσθαι	
	θεῖναι	θέσθαι	
	-εῖναι	-ἔσθαι	
ROOT AORIST	στῆναι		
	γνῶναι		
	δῦναι		

PARTICIPLES OF THEMATIC VERBS

PRESENT PARTICIPLE ACTIVE

	M	F	N
Nom. S	λύων	λύουσα	λῦον
Gen.	λύοντος	λυούσης	λύοντος

CONTRACTED PRESENT PARTICIPLE ACTIVE

	M	F	N
Nom. S	νῑκῶν	νῑκῶσα	νῑκῶν
Gen.	νῑκῶντος	νῑκώσης	νῑκῶντος
Nom. S	ἀδικῶν	ἀδικοῦσα	ἀδικοῦν
Gen.	ἀδικοῦντος	ἀδικούσης	ἀδικοῦντος
Nom. S	ἀξιῶν	ἀξιοῦσα	ἀξιοῦν
Gen.	ἀξιοῦντος	ἀξιούσης	ἀξιοῦντος

FUTURE PARTICIPLE ACTIVE

	M	F	N
Nom. S	λύσων	λύσουσα	λῦσον
Gen.	λύσοντος	λυσούσης	λύσοντος

CONTRACTED FUTURE PARTICIPLE ACTIVE

	M	F	N
Nom. S	ἐλῶν	ἐλῶσα	ἐλῶν
Gen.	ἐλῶντος	ἐλώσης	ἐλῶντος
Nom. S	ἀγγελῶν	ἀγγελοῦσα	ἀγγελοῦν
Gen.	ἀγγελοῦντος	ἀγγελούσης	ἀγγελοῦντος

FIRST AORIST PARTICIPLE ACTIVE

	M	F	N
Nom. S	λύσᾱς	λύσᾱσα	λῦσαν
Gen.	λύσαντος	λυσάσης	λύσαντος

SECOND AORIST PARTICIPLE ACTIVE

	M	F	N
Nom. S	βαλών	βαλοῦσα	βαλόν
Gen.	βαλόντος	βαλούσης	βαλόντος

PERFECT PARTICIPLE ACTIVE

	M	F	N
Nom. S	λελυκώς	λελυκυῖα	λελυκός
Gen.	λελυκότος	λελυκυίᾱς	λελυκότος

PRESENT PARTICIPLE MIDDLE/PASSIVE

	M	F	N
Nom. S	λυόμενος	λυομένη	λυόμενον

CONTRACTED PRESENT PARTICIPLE MIDDLE/PASSIVE

Nom. S	νῑκώμενος	νῑκωμένη	νῑκώμενον
Nom. S	ἀδικούμενος	ἀδικουμένη	ἀδικούμενον
Nom. S	ἀξιούμενος	ἀξιουμένη	ἀξιούμενον

FUTURE PARTICIPLE MIDDLE

Nom. S	λῡσόμενος	λῡσομένη	λῡσόμενον

CONTRACTED FUTURE PARTICIPLE MIDDLE

Nom. S	ἐλώμενος	ἐλωμένη	ἐλώμενον
Nom. S	ἀγγελούμενος	ἀγγελουμένη	ἀγγελούμενον

FUTURE PARTICIPLE PASSIVE

Nom. S	λυθησόμενος	λυθησομένη	λυθησόμενον

FIRST AORIST PARTICIPLE MIDDLE

Nom. S	λῡσάμενος	λῡσαμένη	λῡσάμενον

SECOND AORIST PARTICIPLE MIDDLE

Nom. S	βαλόμενος	βαλομένη	βαλόμενον

AORIST PARTICIPLE PASSIVE

Nom. S	λυθείς	λυθεῖσα	λυθέν
Gen.	λυθέντος	λυθείσης	λυθέντος

PERFECT PARTICIPLE MIDDLE/PASSIVE

Nom. S	λελυμένος	λελυμένη	λελυμένον

CONSONANT-STEM PERFECT PARTICIPLE MIDDLE/PASSIVE

Nom. S	γεγραμμένος	γεγραμμένη	γεγραμμένον
Nom. S	πεπεμμένος	πεπεμμένη	πεπεμμένον
Nom. S	ἠσχυμμένος	ἠσχυμμένη	ἠσχυμμένον
Nom. S	τεταγμένος	τεταγμένη	τεταγμένον
Nom. S	ἐληλεγμένος	ἐληλεγμένη	ἐληλεγμένον
Nom. S	κεκελευσμένος	κεκελευσμένη	κεκελευσμένον
Nom. S	πεφασμένος	πεφασμένη	πεφασμένον
Nom. S	ἠγγελμένος	ἠγγελμένη	ἠγγελμένον

PARTICIPLES OF ATHEMATIC VERBS

PRESENT PARTICIPLE ACTIVE

	M	F	N	Verb
Nom. S	διδούς	διδοῦσα	διδόν	(δίδωμι)
Gen.	διδόντος	διδούσης	διδόντος	
Nom. S	ἱστάς	ἱστᾶσα	ἱστάν	(ἵστημι)
Gen.	ἱστάντος	ἱστάσης	ἱστάντος	
Nom. S	τιθείς	τιθεῖσα	τιθέν	(τίθημι)
Gen.	τιθέντος	τιθείσης	τιθέντος	
Nom. S	ἱείς	ἱεῖσα	ἱέν	(ἵημι)
Gen.	ἱέντος	ἱείσης	ἱέντος	
Nom. S	δεικνύς	δεικνῦσα	δεικνύν	(δείκνῡμι)
Gen.	δεικνύντος	δεικνύσης	δεικνύντος	
Nom. S	ἰών	ἰοῦσα	ἰόν	(εἶμι)
Gen.	ἰόντος	ἰούσης	ἰόντος	
Nom. S	ὤν	οὖσα	ὄν	(εἰμί)
Gen.	ὄντος	οὔσης	ὄντος	
Nom. S	φάς	φᾶσα	φάν	(φημί)
Gen.	φάντος	φάσης	φάντος	

SECOND AORIST PARTICIPLE ACTIVE

	M	F	N	Verb
Nom. S	δούς	δοῦσα	δόν	(δίδωμι)
Gen.	δόντος	δούσης	δόντος	
Nom. S	στάς	στᾶσα	στάν	(ἵστημι)
Gen.	στάντος	στάσης	στάντος	
Nom. S	θείς	θεῖσα	θέν	(τίθημι)
Gen.	θέντος	θείσης	θέντος	
Nom. S	-εἷς	-εἷσα	-ἕν	(ἵημι)
Gen.	-ἕντος	-εἷσης	-ἕντος	
Nom. S	γνούς	γνοῦσα	γνόν	(γιγνώσκω)
Gen.	γνόντος	γνούσης	γνόντος	
Nom. S	δύς	δῦσα	δύν	(δύω)
Gen.	δύντος	δύσης	δύντος	

PERFECT PARTICIPLE ACTIVE OF ἵστημι, οἶδα

Nom. S	ἑστώς	ἑστῶσα	ἑστός	(ἵστημι)
Gen.	ἑστῶτος	ἑστώσης	ἑστῶτος	

Nom. S	εἰδώς	εἰδυῖα	εἰδός	(οἶδα)
Gen.	εἰδότος	εἰδυίᾱς	εἰδότος	

PRESENT PARTICIPLE MIDDLE/PASSIVE

Nom. S	διδόμενος	διδομένη	διδόμενον	(δίδωμι)
Nom. S	ἱστάμενος	ἱσταμένη	ἱστάμενον	(ἵστημι)
Nom. S	δυνάμενος	δυναμένη	δυνάμενον	(δύναμαι)
Nom. S	τιθέμενος	τιθεμένη	τιθέμενον	(τίθημι)
Nom. S	ἱέμενος	ἱεμένη	ἱέμενον	(ἵημι)
Nom. S	δεικνύμενος	δεικνυμένη	δεικνύμενον	(δείκνῡμι)
Nom. S	κείμενος	κειμένη	κείμενον	(κεῖμαι)

SECOND AORIST PARTICIPLE MIDDLE

Nom. S	δόμενος	δομένη	δόμενον	(δίδωμι)
Nom. S	θέμενος	θεμένη	θέμενον	(τίθημι)
Nom. S	-έμενος	-έμένη	-έμενον	(ἵημι)

VERBAL ADJECTIVE

VERB	PRINCIPAL PART VI	VERBAL ADJECTIVE
λύω	ἐλύθην	λυτέος, λυτέᾱ, λυτέον
ἵστημι	ἐστάθην	στατέος, στατέᾱ, στατέον
νῑκάω	ἐνῑκήθην	νῑκητέος, νῑκητέᾱ, νῑκητέον
φυλάττω	ἐφυλάχθην	φυλακτέος, φυλακτέᾱ, φυλακτέον
γράφω	ἐγράφην	γραπτέος, γραπτέᾱ, γραπτέον

The following are formed irregularly:

βαίνω	-βατέος, -βατέᾱ, -βατέον
εἶμι	ἰτέος, ἰτέᾱ, ἰτέον
ἔχω	ἐκτέος, ἐκτέᾱ, ἐκτέον -σχετέος, -σχετέᾱ, -σχετέον
θάπτω	θαπτέος, θαπτέᾱ, θαπτέον
θύω	θυτέος, θυτέᾱ, θυτέον
κλέπτω	κλεπτέος, κλεπτέᾱ, κλεπτέον

λέγω	{ λεκτέος, λεκτέᾱ, λεκτέον { ῥητέος, ῥητέᾱ, ῥητέον
μανθάνω	μαθητέος, μαθητέᾱ, μαθητέον
μάχομαι	μαχετέος, μαχετέᾱ, μαχετέον
μένω	μενετέος, μενετέᾱ, μενετέον
οἶδα	ἰστέος, ἰστέᾱ, ἰστέον
παύω	παυστέος, παυστέᾱ, παυστέον
πυνθάνομαι	πευστέος, πευστέᾱ, πευστέον
σῴζω	σωστέος, σωστέᾱ, σωστέον
τίθημι	θετέος, θετέᾱ, θετέον
φέρω	οἰστέος, οἰστέᾱ, οἰστέον
φεύγω	φευκτέος, φευκτέᾱ, φευκτέον

PRINCIPAL PARTS OF VERBS

I	II	III	IV	V	VI
ἀγγέλλω	ἀγγελῶ	ἤγγειλα	ἤγγελκα	ἤγγελμαι	ἠγγέλθην
ἄγω	ἄξω	ἤγαγον	ἦχα	ἦγμαι	ἤχθην
ἀδικέω	ἀδικήσω	ἠδίκησα	ἠδίκηκα	ἠδίκημαι	ἠδικήθην
αἱρέω	αἱρήσω	εἷλον	ᾕρηκα	ᾕρημαι	ᾑρέθην
αἰσθάνομαι	αἰσθήσομαι	ᾐσθόμην	——	ᾔσθημαι	
αἰσχΰνομαι	αἰσχυνοῦμαι	——	——	ᾔσχυμμαι	ᾐσχΰνθην
ἀκούω	ἀκούσομαι	ἤκουσα	ἀκήκοα	——	ἠκούσθην
ἁμαρτάνω	ἁμαρτήσομαι	ἥμαρτον	ἡμάρτηκα	ἡμάρτημαι	ἡμαρτήθην
ἀξιόω	ἀξιώσω	ἠξίωσα	ἠξίωκα	ἠξίωμαι	ἠξιώθην
ἀποθνῄσκω	ἀποθανοῦμαι	ἀπέθανον	τέθνηκα	——	
ἀποκρῑ́νομαι	ἀποκρινοῦμαι	ἀπεκρῑνάμην	——	ἀποκέκριμαι	
ἀποκτείνω	ἀποκτενῶ	ἀπέκτεινα	ἀπέκτονα	——	
ἀπόλλῡμι	ἀπολῶ	{ ἀπώλεσα { ἀπωλόμην }	{ ἀπολώλεκα { ἀπόλωλα }	——	
ἄρχω	ἄρξω	ἦρξα	ἦρχα	ἦργμαι	ἤρχθην
ἀφικνέομαι	ἀφίξομαι	ἀφῑκόμην	——	ἀφῖγμαι	
βαίνω	-βήσομαι	-ἔβην	βέβηκα	——	
βάλλω	βαλῶ	ἔβαλον	βέβληκα	βέβλημαι	ἐβλήθην
βλάπτω	βλάψω	ἔβλαψα	βέβλαφα	βέβλαμμαι	{ ἐβλάβην { ἐβλάφθην }
βουλεύω	βουλεύσω	ἐβούλευσα	βεβούλευκα	βεβούλευμαι	ἐβουλεύθην
βούλομαι	βουλήσομαι	——		βεβούλημαι	ἐβουλήθην
γίγνομαι	γενήσομαι	ἐγενόμην	γέγονα	γεγένημαι	
γιγνώσκω	γνώσομαι	ἔγνων	ἔγνωκα	ἔγνωσμαι	ἐγνώσθην
γράφω	γράψω	ἔγραψα	γέγραφα	γέγραμμαι	ἐγράφην
δεῖ	δεήσει	ἐδέησε(ν)	——	——	

I	II	III	IV	V	VI
δείκνῡμι	δείξω	ἔδειξα	δέδειχα	δέδειγμαι	ἐδείχθην
δέχομαι	δέξομαι	ἐδεξάμην	——	δέδεγμαι	——
δηλόω	δηλώσω	ἐδήλωσα	δεδήλωκα	δεδήλωμαι	ἐδηλώθην
διδάσκω	διδάξω	ἐδίδαξα	δεδίδαχα	δεδίδαγμαι	ἐδιδάχθην
δίδωμι	δώσω	ἔδωκα	δέδωκα	δέδομαι	ἐδόθην
δοκέω	δόξω	ἔδοξα	——	δέδογμαι	-ἐδόχθην
δουλεύω	δουλεύσω	ἐδούλευσα	δεδούλευκα	——	——
δύναμαι	δυνήσομαι	——	——	δεδύνημαι	ἐδυνήθην
δύω	-δύσω	{-ἔδῡσα / ἔδῡν}	δέδῡκα	-δέδυμαι	-ἐδύθην
ἐθέλω	ἐθελήσω	ἠθέλησα	ἠθέληκα	——	——
εἰμί	ἔσομαι	——	——	——	——
εἶμι	——	——	——	——	——
ἐλαύνω	ἐλῶ (< ἐλάω)	ἤλασα	-ἐλήλακα	ἐλήλαμαι	ἠλάθην
ἐλέγχω	ἐλέγξω	ἤλεγξα	——	ἐλήλεγμαι	ἠλέγχθην
ἐπίσταμαι	ἐπιστήσομαι	——	——	——	ἠπιστήθην
ἕπομαι	ἕψομαι	ἑσπόμην	——	——	——
——	ἐρήσομαι	ἠρόμην	——	——	——
ἔρχομαι	ἐλεύσομαι	ἦλθον	ἐλήλυθα	——	——
ἐρωτάω	ἐρωτήσω	ἠρώτησα	ἠρώτηκα	ἠρώτημαι	ἠρωτήθην
εὑρίσκω	εὑρήσω	ηὗρον	ηὕρηκα	ηὕρημαι	ηὑρέθην
ἔχω	{ἕξω / σχήσω}	ἔσχον	ἔσχηκα	-ἔσχημαι	——
ζάω	ζήσω	——	——	——	——
ζητέω	ζητήσω	ἐζήτησα	ἐζήτηκα	——	ἐζητήθην
ἡγέομαι	ἡγήσομαι	ἡγησάμην	——	ἥγημαι	ἡγήθην
ἥκω	ἥξω	——	——	——	——
θάπτω	θάψω	ἔθαψα	——	τέθαμμαι	ἐτάφην
θύω	θύσω	ἔθῡσα	τέθυκα	τέθυμαι	ἐτύθην
ἵημι	-ἥσω	-ἧκα	-εἷκα	-εἷμαι	-εἷθην
ἵστημι	στήσω	{ἔστησα / ἔστην}	ἔστηκα	ἔσταμαι	ἐστάθην
καλέω	καλῶ	ἐκάλεσα	κέκληκα	κέκλημαι	ἐκλήθην
κεῖμαι	κείσομαι	——	——	——	——
κελεύω	κελεύσω	ἐκέλευσα	κεκέλευκα	κεκέλευσμαι	ἐκελεύσθην
κλέπτω	κλέψω	ἔκλεψα	κέκλοφα	κέκλεμμαι	ἐκλάπην
κρίνω	κρινῶ	ἔκρῑνα	κέκρικα	κέκριμαι	ἐκρίθην
κωλύω	κωλύσω	ἐκώλῡσα	κεκώλῡκα	κεκώλῡμαι	ἐκωλύθην
λαμβάνω	λήψομαι	ἔλαβον	εἴληφα	εἴλημμαι	ἐλήφθην
λανθάνω	λήσω	ἔλαθον	λέληθα	——	——
λέγω	{λέξω / ἐρῶ}	{ἔλεξα / εἶπον}	εἴρηκα	{λέλεγμαι / εἴρημαι}	{ἐλέχθην / ἐρρήθην}
λείπω	λείψω	ἔλιπον	λέλοιπα	λέλειμμαι	ἐλείφθην
λύω	λύσω	ἔλῡσα	λέλυκα	λέλυμαι	ἐλύθην

I	II	III	IV	V	VI
μανθάνω	μαθήσομαι	ἔμαθον	μεμάθηκα	——	——
μάχομαι	μαχοῦμαι	ἐμαχεσάμην	——	μεμάχημαι	——
μέλλω	μελλήσω	ἐμέλλησα	——	——	——
μένω	μενῶ	ἔμεινα	μεμένηκα	——	——
μηχανάομαι	μηχανήσομαι	ἐμηχανησάμην	——	μεμηχάνημαι	——
νῑκάω	νῑκήσω	ἐνίκησα	νενίκηκα	νενίκημαι	ἐνῑκήθην
νομίζω	νομιῶ	ἐνόμισα	νενόμικα	νενόμισμαι	ἐνομίσθην
οἶδα	εἴσομαι	——			
ὁράω	ὄψομαι	εἶδον	$\begin{cases} ἑόρᾱκα \\ ἑώρᾱκα \end{cases}$	$\begin{cases} ἑώρᾱμαι \\ ὦμμαι \end{cases}$	ὤφθην
παιδεύω	παιδεύσω	ἐπαίδευσα	πεπαίδευκα	πεπαίδευμαι	ἐπαιδεύθην
πάσχω	πείσομαι	ἔπαθον	πέπονθα	——	——
παύω	παύσω	ἔπαυσα	πέπαυκα	πέπαυμαι	ἐπαύθην
πείθω	πείσω	ἔπεισα	πέπεικα	πέπεισμαι	ἐπείσθην
πέμπω	πέμψω	ἔπεμψα	πέπομφα	πέπεμμαι	ἐπέμφθην
πίπτω	πεσοῦμαι	ἔπεσον	πέπτωκα	——	——
πιστεύω	πιστεύσω	ἐπίστευσα	πεπίστευκα	πεπίστευμαι	ἐπιστεύθην
ποιέω	ποιήσω	ἐποίησα	πεποίηκα	πεποίημαι	ἐποιήθην
πολῑτεύω	πολῑτεύσω	ἐπολίτευσα	πεπολίτευκα	πεπολίτευμαι	ἐπολῑτεύθην
πράττω	πράξω	ἔπρᾱξα	$\begin{cases} πέπρᾱχα \\ πέπρᾱγα \end{cases}$	πέπρᾱγμαι	ἐπράχθην
πυνθάνομαι	πεύσομαι	ἐπυθόμην	——	πέπυσμαι	——
σῴζω	σώσω	ἔσωσα	σέσωκα	$\begin{cases} σέσωσμαι \\ σέσωμαι \end{cases}$	ἐσώθην
τάττω	τάξω	ἔταξα	τέταχα	τέταγμαι	ἐτάχθην
τελευτάω	τελευτήσω	ἐτελεύτησα	τετελεύτηκα	τετελεύτημαι	ἐτελευτήθην
τίθημι	θήσω	ἔθηκα	τέθηκα	τέθειμαι	ἐτέθην
τῑμάω	τῑμήσω	ἐτίμησα	τετίμηκα	τετίμημαι	ἐτῑμήθην
τρέπω	τρέψω	$\begin{cases} ἔτρεψα \\ ἐτραπόμην \end{cases}$	τέτροφα	τέτραμμαι	$\begin{cases} ἐτρέφθην \\ ἐτράπην \end{cases}$
τυγχάνω	τεύξομαι	ἔτυχον	τετύχηκα	——	——
φαίνω	φανῶ	ἔφηνα	πέφηνα	πέφασμαι	ἐφάνην
φέρω	οἴσω	$\begin{cases} ἤνεγκα \\ ἤνεγκον \end{cases}$	ἐνήνοχα	ἐνήνεγμαι	ἠνέχθην
φεύγω	φεύξομαι	ἔφυγον	πέφευγα	——	——
φημί	φήσω	ἔφησα	——	——	——
φθάνω	φθήσομαι	$\begin{cases} ἔφθασα \\ ἔφθην \end{cases}$	——	——	——
φιλέω	φιλήσω	ἐφίλησα	πεφίληκα	πεφίλημαι	ἐφιλήθην
φοβέομαι	φοβήσομαι	——	——	πεφόβημαι	ἐφοβήθην
φυλάττω	φυλάξω	ἐφύλαξα	πεφύλαχα	πεφύλαγμαι	ἐφυλάχθην
χαίρω	χαιρήσω	——	κεχάρηκα	——	ἐχάρην
χορεύω	χορεύσω	ἐχόρευσα	κεχόρευκα	κεχόρευμαι	ἐχορεύθην
χράομαι	χρήσομαι	ἐχρησάμην	——	κέχρημαι	ἐχρήσθην
χρή	χρῆσται	——			

SYNTAX

THE CASE SYSTEM: Nouns, Pronouns, Adjectives

NOMINATIVE CASE

A word in the nominative case can be used as a

1. *SUBJECT* of a finite verb:

   οἱ Λακεδαιμόνιοι τοὺς Ἀθηναίους ἐνίκησαν.
   The Spartans conquered the Athenians.

   οὕτω κακῶς ἐμαχέσαντο **οἱ στρατιῶται** ὥστε **ἡ πόλις** κατελύθη.
   So badly did **the soldiers** fight that **the city** was destroyed.

2. *SUBJECT* of a nominal sentence:

   ὁ ποιητὴς σοφός.
   The poet is wise.

3. *PREDICATE NOMINATIVE* (with a copulative verb or in a nominal sentence):

   Ἀριστοφάνης **ποιητὴς** ἦν.
   Aristophanes was **a poet**.

   διδάσκαλος εἶ.
   You are **a teacher**.

   ὁ νεᾱνίᾱς **ἰᾱτρὸς** γενήσεται.
   The young man will become **a doctor**.

   Σωκράτης οὐχ ᾑρέθη **στρατηγός**.
   Sokrates was not chosen **as a general**.

   ζῷα αἱ αἶγες.
   Nanny-goats are **animals**.

4. *PREDICATE ADJECTIVE* (with a copulative verb or in a nominal sentence):

   οἱ δοῦλοι οὐκ **εὐδαίμονες** ἦσαν.
   The slaves were not **happy**.

693

αἱ νῆσοι **καλαί**.
The islands are **beautiful**. (*Nominal sentence*)

οὐ **σοφός** εἰμι.
I am not **wise**.

οἱ ποιηταὶ **κακίους** γίγνονται.
The poets are becoming **worse**.

σύνοιδεν ἡ μήτηρ οὐ **σοφὴ** οὖσα.
The mother is aware that she is not **wise**.

5. *ADJECTIVE USED PREDICATIVELY:*

πρῶτος ἀφίκετο.
He arrived **first**.
He was the **first** to arrive.

6. participle in an indirect statement whose subject is the same as that of the introductory word:

ὁ ποιητὴς ἀγγέλλει ἔπη γράψων.
The poet announces **that he will write** epic poetry.

[7. an occasional substitute for the vocative:
ὦ **πόλις** καὶ δῆμε
City and people!]

[8. in lists and when an individual word is quoted:
τὸ δ᾽ **ὑμεῖς** ὅταν λέγω, λέγω τὴν πόλιν.
Whenever I say "**You**," I mean the city.]

GENITIVE CASE

A word in the genitive case can be used as a

1. *PARTITIVE GENITIVE (GENITIVE OF THE DIVIDED WHOLE)*, showing the whole or class of which the noun on which it depends is a part or individual:

πέντε **τῶν στρατιωτῶν** ἀπέθανον ὑπὸ τῶν βαρβάρων.
Five **of the soldiers** were killed by the foreigners.

μόνον τοὺς δικαίους **τῶν πολιτῶν** ἐδίδασκεν ὁ ποιητής.
The poet used to teach only the just ones **of the citizens**.

ποῦ **γῆς** ἐσμεν;
Where **in the world** are we? (*Literally:* Where **of the world** are we?)

εἰς τοσοῦτο **τῆς ἀρετῆς** ἀφίκετο ὥστε τῑμᾶσθαι καὶ ὑπὸ ξένων.
He reached such a degree **of virtue** as to be honored even by strangers.

A partitive genitive can be used as the direct object of any verb, when the object refers to *some* rather than all the objects of a class:

ἔπεμψε **τῶν στρατιωτῶν** εἰς τὴν πόλιν.
He sent **some of the soldiers** to the city.

2. *GENITIVE OF POSSESSION*, showing possession, ownership, relation:

ὁ **τοῦ στρατηγοῦ** ἀδελφὸς ἐπέμφθη εἰς τὴν **τῶν ὁπλῑτῶν** οἰκίαν.
The brother **of the general** was sent into the house **of the hoplites**.
The **general's** brother was sent into the **hoplites'** house.

[3. *PREDICATE GENITIVE OF CHARACTERISTIC*, used with copulative verbs as a predicate, showing a person or thing of which an action is characteristic:

τοῦ ἀγαθοῦ κριτοῦ ἐστι τὸ ἀκούειν τὰ λεγόμενα.
To listen to the things being said is **characteristic of the good judge**.
It is **a mark of the good judge** to listen to the things being said.]

4. *SUBJECTIVE GENITIVE*, used with verbal nouns, standing in the same relation to the idea of action in the noun as the subject does to a verb in a sentence:

διὰ τὴν **τοῦ ῥήτορος** κλοπὴν οὐκ ἐτῑμᾶτο ὁ πατήρ.
On account of the **public speaker's** theft, his father was not honored. (*The public speaker stole.*)

τῇ **τοῦ ἱερέως** θυσίᾳ ἥσθη ἡ θεός. [ἥδομαι, ἡσθήσομαι, ——, ——, ——, ἥσθην, "be pleased"]
The goddess was pleased by the sacrifice **of the priest**. (*The priest performed the sacrifice.*)

5. *OBJECTIVE GENITIVE*, used with verbal nouns, standing in the same relation to the idea of action in the noun as the object does to a verb in a sentence:

διὰ τὴν **τῶν κοινῶν** κλοπὴν οὐκ ἐτῑμᾶτο ὁ τοῦ ῥήτορος πατήρ.
On account of the theft **of the public property**, the father of the public speaker was not honored. (*Someone stole the public property.*)

τῇ **μιᾶς αἰγὸς μόνης** θυσίᾳ οὐχ ἥσθη ἡ θεός.
The goddess was not pleased by the sacrifice **of only a single goat**. (*Someone sacrificed the goat.*)

Context usually allows one to distinguish an objective genitive from a subjective one.

6. *GENITIVE OF MATERIAL OR CONTENTS*, showing the people or material of which a noun is composed:

τοῖς **τῶν νεāνιῶν** χοροῖς τοῖς τοὺς ἀγῶνας νῑκήσāσι στεφάνους **χρῡσοῦ**
ἐδίδοσαν.

They used to give crowns **of gold** to the choruses **of young men** which
won the contests.

[7. *APPOSITIONAL GENITIVE*, which merely explains or acts as an ap-
positive of the noun on which it depends:

διὰ τὴν ἁμαρτίᾱν τὴν **τοῦ τοῖς ῥήτορσι πιστεύειν** καταλυθήσεται
ἡ πόλις.

On account of the mistake **of trusting the public speakers**, the city will
be destroyed.]

[8. *GENITIVE OF QUALITY OR DESCRIPTION*, in prose used mostly
as a predicate to describe a noun or pronoun:

τῆς αὐτῆς γνώμης οὐκ ἦν ἐκεῖνος οὐδέν.

That man was not at all **of the same opinion**.]

[9. *GENITIVE OF MEASURE*, giving the size or length of time of a noun:

οὐ ῥᾴδιον φυλάττειν τεῖχος **πολλῶν σταδίων**.

It is not easy to guard a wall **of many stades**.

It is not easy to guard a wall **many stades long**.

οὐ ῥᾴδιον φυλάττειν τοῦτο τὸ τεῖχος καίπερ μόνον **πέντε σταδίων** ὄν.

It is not easy to guard this wall, although it is only **five stades long**.
(*Literally*: although being only **of five stades**)

ἦλθον ὁδὸν **ἓξ ἡμερῶν**.

They went on a journey **of six days**.]

10. *GENITIVE OF VALUE*, showing the value of an object:

θυσίᾱς **πολλῶν χρημάτων** ἔθῡσαν διὰ τὴν νίκην.

They sacrificed sacrifices **worth much money** on account of the victory.
(*Literally*: sacrifices **of much money**)

This genitive is used with words of buying, selling, and evaluating, where
it is called the *GENITIVE OF PRICE*:

τὰ βιβλία ἀπέδοντο **πολλῶν χρημάτων**.

They sold the books **for much money**.

ὁ νεᾱνίᾱς **ἄθλου τινὸς** ἠξιώθη.

The young man was thought worthy **of some prize**.

ὁ γέρων ἄξιός ἐστι **τῆς τῑμῆς**.

The old man is worthy **of the honor**.

11. *GENITIVE OF TIME WITHIN WHICH*, showing a span of time within which an event occurs:

ἐκείνης τῆς ἡμέρας ἔφυγον.
They fled **during that day.**

πέντε ἡμερῶν ἀφίξει.
You will arrive **within five days.**

12. *GENITIVE OF THE CHARGE*, giving the charge with words of indicting, condemning, etc.:

τοὺς ἀδίκους ἐγραψάμεθα **κλοπῆς.**
We indicted the unjust men **on a charge of theft.**

φεύγω δίκην **φόνου.**
I am a defendant on a charge **of murder.**

13. *GENITIVE WITH CERTAIN PREPOSITIONS*, especially with those showing motion away from or lack (ἄνευ, ἀντί, ἀπό, διά, ἐκ/ἐξ, ἕνεκα, ἐπί, κατά, μετά, παρά, περί, πρό, πρός, ὑπέρ, ὑπό, χάριν):

τὸν ἀδελφὸν ἔπεμψα **ἐκ τῆς οἰκίας.**
I sent my brother **out of the house.**

ἆρ’ **ἄνευ ἀργυρίου** εὐδαίμονες οἱ ἄνθρωποι;
Are men happy **without money?**

περὶ τῆς ἀρετῆς ἔλεγεν ὁ ῥήτωρ.
The public speaker was talking **about virtue.**

14. *GENITIVE OF PERSONAL AGENT*, with passive verbs other than a perfect, pluperfect, or verbal adjective, to show the person by whom the action is performed. [Instead of **ὑπό**, the genitive of personal agent sometimes uses ἐκ or παρά.]

ἀρετὴν ἐδιδάχθην **ὑπὸ τοῦ Σωκράτους.**
I was taught virtue **by Sokrates.**

[**παρὰ θεῶν** τοιαῦτα δίδοται.
Such things are given **by gods.**]

15. *GENITIVE OF CAUSE*, used with verbs of emotion to show the cause or origin of the emotion:

χαλεπῶς φέρομεν **τούτων.** [χαλεπῶς φέρω, "be upset"]
We are upset **because of these things.**

θαυμάζω **τῆς σῆς ἀμαθίας.** [θαυμάζω, θαυμάσομαι, ἐθαύμασα, τεθαύμακα, τεθαύμασμαι, ἐθαυμάσθην, "wonder at, be amazed at" + *gen.*]
I am amazed **at your stupidity.**

[16. *EXCLAMATORY GENITIVE*, used in exclamations:

τῆς ἀμαθίας.
What stupidity!]

[17. *GENITIVE OF PURPOSE*, especially used of a negated articular infinitive, showing purpose:

ταῦτ᾽ ἔπραξαν **τοῦ μὴ νῑκηθῆναι.**
They did these things **for the sake of not being conquered.**
They did these things **in order not to be conquered.**]

[18. *GENITIVE OF SOURCE*, showing the source or origin:

ταῦτα **Σωκράτους** ἔμαθον.
I learned these things **from Sokrates.**]

19. *GENITIVE OF SEPARATION OR LACK*, used with words expressing ideas like separating or freeing, and with words expressing lack:

τοὺς ᾽Αθηναίους **τῆς δουλείας** ἐλύσαμεν.
We freed the Athenians **from slavery.**

πολὺ ἀπέχει ἡ πόλις **τῆς θαλάττης.** [ἀπέχω, "be distant, be away from"]
The city is far away **from the sea.**

οὐδεὶς **ἀμαθίας** ἐλεύθερος· δεῖ οὖν ἑκάστῳ **διδασκάλου.**
No one is free **from ignorance**; therefore each man needs **a teacher.**

20. *GENITIVE OF COMPARISON*, used with adjectives and adverbs in the comparative degree and other words expressing comparison to show the person or thing being compared:

ὁ Σωκράτης πολὺ σοφώτερός ἐστι **τῆς γυναικός.**
Sokrates is much wiser **than his wife.**

οὐ **τῶν ἄλλων** διαφέρω οὐδέν.
I am not at all better **than the others.**

21. *GENITIVE WITH CERTAIN VERBS*, used as the sole complement of certain types of verbs, e.g., ἀκούω, other verbs of perception, verbs meaning "rule":

τοῦ **Σωκράτους** ταῦτα λέγοντος ἤκουσα.
I heard **Sokrates** saying these things.

τότε οἱ βασιλῆς **τῶν ῾Ελλήνων** ἦρχον.
At that time kings ruled **the Greeks.**

22. *GENITIVE WITH CERTAIN ADJECTIVES*, e.g., ἔμπειρος, αἴτιος:

ὁ στρατηγὸς ἔμπειρος ἦν **τοῦ πολέμου**.
The general was experienced **in war**.

ἆρα αἴτιός ἐστιν οὗτος **τῶν κακῶν**;
Is this man responsible **for the evils**?

23. *GENITIVE ABSOLUTE*, a phrase consisting of a noun or pronoun and a circumstantial participle in the genitive, not otherwise syntactically connected with the rest of the sentence. A genitive absolute can express any of the relations of the circumstantial participle, e.g., causal, conditional:

τῶν Λακεδαιμονίων νῑκηθέντων, εἰρήνην ἤγομεν.
The Spartans conquered, we were keeping the peace.
When the Spartans were conquered, we kept the peace.
Since the Spartans were conquered, we kept the peace.
If the Spartans were conquered, we kept the peace.

DATIVE CASE

A word in the dative case can be used as an

1. *INDIRECT OBJECT* with verbs of giving, showing, telling, and similar verbs which often show a person or thing, other than the direct object, interested in or affected by the action of a transitive verb:

τὰ βιβλία **τοῖς μαθηταῖς** ἔδομεν.
We gave the books **to the students**.

μὴ δείξητε τὰ τείχη **τῷ νέῳ στρατηγῷ**.
Do not show the walls **to the new general**.

τοῦτο **αὐτῇ** εἶπον.
I said this **to her**.

τὰς καλὰς αἶγας **ταῖς θεοῖς** ἔθῡσεν.
She sacrificed the beautiful goats **to the goddesses**.

2. *DATIVE OF INTEREST*, less closely connected to a verb than is the indirect object, but showing a person or thing, other than the direct object, interested in or affected by an action or a state of being. When the person or thing interested or affected is benefited by the action, the dative of interest is called a *DATIVE OF ADVANTAGE*; when the person or thing interested or affected is harmed, the dative of interest is called a *DATIVE OF DISADVANTAGE*:

τοῖς ᾿Αθηναίοις ἀπῆλθον οἱ βάρβαροι ἐκ τῆς χώρας.
To the advantage of the Athenians, the foreigners went out of their country. (*Dative of advantage*)

τὰ χρήματ᾿ αἴτι᾿ **ἀνθρώποις** κακῶν. (Euripides, Fr. 632)
Money is responsible for evils **for men.** (*Dative of disadvantage*)

3. *DATIVE OF REFERENCE*, showing the person or persons in whose opinion a statement is true:

οὗτος ὁ πονηρὸς ἄξιος **πᾶσι τοῖς πολίταις** ἐστὶ θανάτου.
This base fellow is worthy of death **in the eyes of all the citizens.**

πᾶσι τοῖς ἀγαθοῖς κριταῖς νῑκᾷ ὁ ᾿Αριστοφάνης.
In the eyes of all good critics Aristophanes is the victor.

[4. *ETHICAL DATIVE*, a personal pronoun used somewhat parenthetically to show the interest of the speaker or person spoken to (or occasionally a third person) in the statement being made:

ἐμοὶ ταῦτ᾿ οὐκ ἀληθῆ ἐστιν.
For me, these things are not true.
As far as I am concerned, these things are not true.

οἱ ἄνθρωποι πάντες **ὑμῖν** ἀποθνῄσκουσιν.
All men, **you know,** die.]

5. *DATIVE OF THE POSSESSOR*, used with verbs like εἰμί and γίγνομαι and showing ownership or possession:

τῷ ἀδελφῷ δύο βιβλία ἦν.
My brother had two books. (*Literally:* **To my brother there were** two books.)

οὐχ **ἡμῖν** γε πολλά **ἐστι** χρήματα.
We at least **do** not **have** much money.

αὐτῷ πολλὰ χρήματα **ἐγένετο.**
He acquired much money.

6. *DATIVE OF PERSONAL AGENT*, with perfect and pluperfect passives, and verbal adjectives in -τέος, showing the person by whom the action has been, had been, or must be performed:

ταῦτ᾿ **ἐμοὶ** σοφῶς πέπρᾱκται.
These things have been done wisely **by me.**

τοῖς στρατιώταις ἡ γέφῡρα κατελέλυτο.
The bridge had been destroyed **by the soldiers.**

ἡμῖν γε ἡ πόλις ἐστὶ σωτέα.
The city must be saved **by us**.

ὑμῖν γε τὴν πόλιν σωτέον ἐστίν.
The city must be saved **by you**.

Datives 1–6 are all derived from the to/for *function of the original dative
case. Thus a particular word in the dative may fall under more than one of
these categories.*

7. *DATIVE OF MEANS (INSTRUMENTAL DATIVE)*, showing a thing
   by means of which something is done:

   τοὺς μαθητὰς ἐδίδασκεν ὁ διδάσκαλος **τοῖς τοῦ Ὁμήρου βιβλίοις**.
   The teacher used to teach his students **by means of the books of Homer**.

   οἱ κακοὶ ῥήτορες **λίθοις** ἐβλήθησαν ὑπὸ τῶν πολιτῶν.
   The evil public speakers were hit by the citizens **with stones**.

8. *DATIVE OF MANNER (ATTENDANT CIRCUMSTANCES)*, showing the way in which an action takes place or a state of being exists,
   often the equivalent of an adverb. When the noun is not modified, the
   preposition σύν is often used:

   σῑγῇ ἀπῆλθον οἱ πολέμιοι.
   In silence the enemy departed.
   The enemy departed **silently**.

   σὺν δίκῃ αὐτοὺς ἀπεκτείναμεν.
   We killed them **with justice**.
   We killed them **justly**.

   ἀγαθῇ τύχῃ ἡ πόλις ἐσώθη.
   By good luck the city was saved.
   Luckily the city was saved.

9. *DATIVE OF RESPECT*, showing the respect in which a statement is
   true (very similar to an accusative of respect):

   τῷ νῷ σοφὸς ἦν ὁ ποιητής.
   The poet was wise **in (respect to) his mind**.

   τὸ ἔργον **δυνάμει** κρεῖττόν ἐστι τοῦ λόγου.
   Action is stronger **in power** than speech.

   ὀλίγοι **τῷ ὄντι** εὐδαίμονές εἰσιν.
   Few men are **in reality** happy.
   Few men are **really** happy.

10. *DATIVE OF DEGREE OF DIFFERENCE*, with words expressing comparison, showing the degree to which two things being compared differ:

τοῦτο τὸ τεῖχος ἔλαττόν ἐστι ἐκείνου **ποδί.**
This wall is smaller than that one **by a foot.**
This wall is **a foot** smaller than that one.

πολλῷ εὐδαιμονέστερός ἐστι τοῦ ἀδελφοῦ.
He is **much** happier than his brother.

ὕστερον **δέκα ἡμέραις** ἀφίκετο.
He arrived **ten days** later.

[11. *DATIVE OF CAUSE*, giving a cause or reason for something:

ταύτῃ τῇ νόσῳ ἀπέθανον πολλοί.
Many men died **because of this sickness.**

τούτοις οὐχ ἥσθην. [ἥδομαι, ἡσθήσομαι, ——, ——, ——, ἥσθην, "be pleased"]
I was not pleased **by these things.**]

12. *DATIVE OF ACCOMPANIMENT*, sometimes used without a preposition, often with the preposition σύν, especially in military situations, showing accompaniment. (The normal prose expression of accompaniment is μετά + *gen.*):

ἐξελαύνει **πᾶσι τοῖς στρατιώταις.**
He is marching out **with all his soldiers.**

σὺν θεοῖς νῑκήσομεν.
With the help of the gods we shall conquer.

Datives 7–12 are all derived from the by/with *function of the original instrumental case. Thus a particular word in the dative may fall under more than one of these categories.*

13. *DATIVE OF PLACE WHERE*, usually with the preposition ἐν, but occasionally with certain place names without any preposition:

ἡ **ἐν τῷ πεδίῳ** πόλις κατελύθη.
The city **in the plain** was destroyed.

Μαραθῶνι τοὺς βαρβάρους ἐνίκησαν οἱ Ἀθηναῖοι. [Μαραθῶν, Μαραθῶνος, ὁ, "Marathon"]
At Marathon the Athenians conquered the foreigners.

14. *DATIVE OF TIME AT WHICH*, showing the point of time at which an event occurs:

τῇ τετάρτῃ ἡμέρᾳ ἀπέθανεν ὁ Εὐρῑπίδης.
Euripides died **on the fourth day.**

ἐκείνῃ τῇ μάχῃ ἐνῑκήθησαν οἱ βάρβαροι.
In that battle the foreigners were conquered.

Datives 13–14 are both derived from the in/at *function of the original locative case.*

15. *DATIVE WITH CERTAIN VERBS* (δεῖ, δουλεύω, ἕπομαι, μάχομαι, πείθομαι, πιστεύω, συναδικέω, σύνοιδα, ὑπακούω, χράομαι):

τοῖς πολεμίοις ὑπὲρ τῆς ἐλευθερίᾱς μαχεσώμεθα.
Let us fight **with the enemy** on behalf of freedom.

δουλεύωμεν **τούτοις τοῖς ἄφροσιν**;
Are we to be slaves **to these foolish men**?

δεῖ **μοι** χρημάτων.
There is need **to me** of money.
I need money.

16. *DATIVE WITH CERTAIN ADJECTIVES*, e.g., φίλος, ἐχθρός, ἴσος, ὁ αὐτός:

'Αριστοφάνης ἐχθρὸς ἦν **Εὐρῑπίδῃ**.
Aristophanes was hostile **to Euripides**.

τῆς αὐτῆς **ἐμοὶ** γνώμης ἦν Σωκράτης.
Sokrates was of the same opinion **as I**.

17. *DATIVE WITH CERTAIN PREPOSITIONS* (ἅμα, ἐν, ἐπί, παρά, περί, πρός, σύν, ὑπό):

ἔμενον **παρὰ τῷ τείχει**.
They remained **alongside the wall**.

πρὸς δὲ **τοῖς στρατιώταις** ἔπεμψαν ἱππέᾱς.
In addition to the soldiers, they sent horsemen.

The datives with verbs, adjectives, and prepositions can be traced back to one or more of the datives given in numbers 1–14, but they are best memorized as vocabulary items.

18. *PREDICATE DATIVE*, after copulative verbs:

οὐκ ἐξῆν αὐτῷ **ποιητῇ** γενέσθαι.
It was not possible for him to become **a poet**.

19. *PREDICATE ADJECTIVE IN THE DATIVE; PARTICIPLE IN THE DATIVE IN INDIRECT STATEMENT*:

σύνοιδα ἐμαυτῷ οὐ **σοφῷ ὄντι**.
I am aware that I **am** not **wise**.

ACCUSATIVE CASE

A word in the accusative can be used as a

1. *DIRECT OBJECT* of a verb (*EXTERNAL OBJECT*):

    τοὺς στρατιώτᾱς ἐτάξαμεν παρὰ τῇ γεφύρᾳ.
    We stationed **the soldiers** by the bridge.

    οὐ φοβησόμεθα ἡμεῖς τοὺς ἀπὸ τῶν νήσων.
    We shall not fear **the men from the islands.**

2. *COGNATE ACCUSATIVE* (*INTERNAL ACCUSATIVE*), where the direct object is a verbal noun related to the verb or a substitute for such a noun:

    μεγάλην ἁμαρτίᾱν ἁμαρτάνεις, ὦ βασιλεῦ.
    King, you are making **a great mistake.**

    μεγάλα ἁμαρτάνεις, ὦ βασιλεῦ.
    King, you are making **great mistakes.**

    τὸν κακὸν ἐγράψασθε **δίκην** φόνου.
    You indicted the evil man **on a charge** of murder.

    πολλὰς **ἐξόδους** ἐξήλθομεν.
    We went out **on many expeditions.** (*Literally:* We went out **many goings out.**)

3. Part of a *DOUBLE ACCUSATIVE*:

    ὁ Σωκράτης **τοὺς πολίτᾱς τὴν ἀρετὴν** ἐδίδασκεν.
    Sokrates used to teach **his fellow citizens virtue.**

    (*One external direct object,* τοὺς πολίτᾱς; *one internal accusative,* τὴν ἀρετήν)

    ὁ ἀγαθὸς στρατηγὸς **τὴν ἐν τῷ πεδίῳ μάχην τοὺς βαρβάρους** ἐνίκησεν.
    The good general beat **the barbarians in the battle in the plain.**
    The good general won **the battle in the plain against the barbarians.**

    (*One external direct object,* τοὺς βαρβάρους; *one internal accusative,* τὴν ἐν τῷ πεδίῳ μάχην)

    τοὺς ἀρίστους πολίτᾱς στρατηγοὺς ᾑροῦντο.
    They used to choose **the best citizens as generals.**

    (*With verbs of making, calling, choosing, one direct object,* τοὺς ἀρίστους πολίτᾱς; *second accusative used as predicate of the direct object,* στρατηγούς)

λείαν ἐποιήσαντο **τὴν χώρᾱν.** [λεία, λείᾱς, ἡ, "booty, plunder"]
They **plundered the country.**

(*A verb like* ἐποιήσαντο *can take a direct object, here* λείᾱν, *with which it forms one transitive concept, here "plunder," which in turn can govern a direct object.*)

4. *RETAINED ACCUSATIVE*, with the passive of a verb taking a double accusative:

οἱ πολῖται **τὴν ἀρετὴν** ἐδιδάχθησαν ὑπὸ Σωκράτους.
The citizens were taught **virtue** by Sokrates.

5. *SUBJECT OF AN INFINITIVE*:

οὐ καλὸν τὸ **Σωκράτη** ταῦτα διδάσκειν.
For Sokrates to teach these things is not good.
Sokrates' teaching these things is not good.

οὕτω κακῶς ἐμαχέσαντο οἱ στρατιῶται ὥστε **τὴν πόλιν** λυθῆναι.
So badly did the soldiers fight as **for the city** to be destroyed.

νομίζω **τοὺς Ἀθηναίους** οὐ νῑκήσειν.
I think that **the Athenians** will not win.

6. *SUBJECT OF A PARTICIPLE IN INDIRECT STATEMENT; PARTICIPLE IN INDIRECT STATEMENT AGREEING WITH ACCUSATIVE SUBJECT*:

πεύσεται **τοὺς Ἀθηναίους** οὐ **νῑκῶντας.**
He will find out that **the Athenians are** not **winning.**

7. *PREDICATE ACCUSATIVE*:

οἱ Ἀθηναῖοι ἐνόμιζον τὸν Σωκράτη **κακὸν πολίτην** εἶναι.
The Athenians thought that Sokrates was **a bad citizen.**

πεύσει τὸν Ὅμηρον **ποιητὴν** ὄντα.
You will find out that Homer is **a poet.**

8. *PREDICATE ADJECTIVE IN THE ACCUSATIVE*:

ἆρα νομίζεις τοὺς πολίτᾱς **ἄφρονας** ἔσεσθαι;
Do you think that the citizens will be **foolish**?

οἶδα τοὺς πολίτᾱς **ἄφρονας** ἐσομένους.
I know that the citizens will be **foolish.**

9. *ACCUSATIVE OF RESPECT OR SPECIFICATION*, which limits the force of an adjective or verb (especially a passive verb or one indicating a state) or even a whole sentence:

μόνοι οἱ **μάχην** ἀγαθοὶ ὑπὸ τῶν πολῑτῶν ἐτῑμῶντο.
Only those good **at battle** were honored by the citizens.

διαφέρουσιν οἱ ἀγαθοὶ τῶν κακῶν **τὴν ἀρετήν**.
The good differ from the bad **in (respect to) virtue**.

10. *ADVERBIAL ACCUSATIVE*, which limits the meaning of a verb or adjective and functions as an adverb:

τίνα τρόπον σωθησόμεθα;
In what way shall we be saved?
How shall we be saved?

ταῦτα ποίησον **τὴν ταχίστην**.
Do these things **in the quickest way**. (*ὁδόν is understood.*)
Do these things **very quickly**.

οὐ **πολλὰ** διαφέρουσιν.
They do not differ **in many things**.
They are not **very** different.

οὐδὲν ἀμείνων εἰμὶ τοῦ ἀδελφοῦ.
I am **not at all** better than my brother.

11. *ACCUSATIVE WITH SOME PREPOSITIONS*, especially with those expressing motion toward an object (διά, εἰς, ἐπί, κατά, μετά, παρά, περί, πρός, ὑπέρ, ὑπό):

ἀγαθὰ οὐκ ἀεὶ πέμπουσιν οἱ θεοὶ **παρὰ τοὺς ἀνθρώπους**.
The gods do not always send good things **to men**.

ἐλῶσιν **ὑπὲρ τὸ πεδίον**.
They will march **beyond the plain**.

διὰ τὴν ἀμαθίᾱν, ὦ ἄδελφε, οὐκ οὐδὲν τῑμᾷ.
On account of your ignorance, my brother, you are not at all honored.

12. *ACCUSATIVE OF EXTENT OF SPACE*, showing length of space:

ἤλασαν **δέκα σταδίους** πρὸς τὴν πόλιν.
They marched **ten stades** toward the city.

ἡ πόλις **ἓν στάδιον** ἀπέχει τῆς θαλάττης. [ἀπέχω, "be distant, be away from"]
The city is **one stade** away from the sea.

13. *ACCUSATIVE OF EXTENT OF TIME*, showing length of time:

δέκα ἡμέρᾱς ἔμειναν ἐν τῷ πεδίῳ.
For ten days they remained in the plain.

14. *ACCUSATIVE IN OATHS*, with the particles νή for affirmative oaths [and μά, usually for negative oaths]:

οἱ ἀγαθοὶ **νὴ τὸν Δία** νῑκήσουσιν.
By Zeus, the good will conquer.

[οὐ **μὰ τὸν θεὸν** ἐμὲ λανθάνεις τοιαῦτα πράττων.
By the god, you are not escaping my notice in doing such things.
By the god, you are not doing such things without my being aware of them.]

15. *PERSONAL AGENT*, sometimes used with an impersonal verbal adjective to express the person by whom something must be done:

οὔ φημι **ἡμᾶς** ἀδικητέον εἶναι.
I say that **we** ought not to do wrong.

16. *ACCUSATIVE ABSOLUTE*, the neuter singular accusative participle of an impersonal verb without a noun or pronoun, used independently of the main verb of a sentence and having any of the relations to the rest of the sentence that a circumstantial participle can have:

ἐξὸν μὴ δίκην δοῦναι, μενοῦμεν ἐν τῇ πόλει.
It being possible not to pay a penalty, we shall remain in the city.
Since it is possible not to pay a penalty, we shall remain in the city.
If it is possible not to pay a penalty, we shall remain in the city.

VOCATIVE CASE

A word in the vocative case shows a person or thing being addressed. The interjection ὦ is usually added to the vocative in polite prose and is not translated in English. The absence of the interjection ὦ in polite prose usually indicates some emotion, which should be expressed in English by "o":

τί, **ὦ Σώκρατες**, ταῦτα πράττεις;
Why, **Sokrates**, do you do these things?

τί, **Σώκρατες**, ταῦτα πράττεις;
Why, **o Sokrates**, do you do these things?

APPOSITION

One noun put next to and in the same case as another noun or pronoun to explain that noun or pronoun is said to be in *APPOSITION*. Apposition can occur in any case:

Εὐρῑπίδης **ὁ ποιητὴς** ἀπέρχεται.
Euripides **the poet** is going away.

ὑμεῖς **οἱ Λακεδαιμόνιοι** νῑκᾶσθε ὑπὸ τῶν Ἀθηναίων, **πολῑτῶν** τῆς νῦν κρατίστης πόλεως.

You, **the Spartans**, are being conquered by the Athenians, **citizens** of the now most powerful city.

τὰ ἆθλα ἔδωκε τῷ ἀδελφῷ μου, **τῷ στρατηγῷ.**

He gave the prizes to my brother, **the general.**

καὶ τὰς γυναῖκας, **τὰς τῶν καλῶν στρατιωτῶν μητέρας,** ἐτίμων.

They used to honor also the women, **the mothers of the noble soldiers.**

ἄκουσόν μου, ὦ Ζεῦ, **πάτερ ἀνθρώπων καὶ θεῶν.**

Hear me, Zeus, **father of men and of gods.**

SYNTAX OF THE VERB

MOOD

INDICATIVE MOOD

INDEPENDENT CLAUSES WITH THE INDICATIVE

1. The indicative is used in all tenses to make a *FACTUAL STATEMENT* or to ask a *FACTUAL QUESTION*:

   ὁ Σωκράτης τοὺς νεᾱνίᾱς τὴν τοῦ ἀγαθοῦ ἀνδρὸς ἀρετὴν **ἐδίδασκεν.**

   Sokrates **used to teach** the young men the excellence belonging to (of) the good man.

   τίνας τί **ἐδίδασκεν** ὁ Σωκράτης;

   Whom **did** Sokrates **teach** what (**habitually**)?

2. A future indicative introduced by ὅπως or ὅπως μή (as in an object clause of effort) can be used independently as the equivalent of an *URGENT COMMAND OR EXHORTATION*:

   ὅπως **νῑκήσεις.**

   See to it that **you win.**

   ὅπως μὴ **νῑκηθησόμεθα.**

   Let us see to it that **we are** not **conquered.**

[3. A future indicative negated by οὐ μή can express a *STRONG FUTURE DENIAL*:

   οἱ πολέμιοι **οὐ μὴ νῑκήσουσιν.**

   The enemy **will not win!**]

[4. Also, a future indicative negated by οὐ μή can express an *URGENT PROHIBITION*:

οὐ μὴ τοῦτο **ποιήσεις**.
You will not do this!
Do not do this!]

5. Introduced by εἴθε or εἰ γάρ, the imperfect or aorist indicative is used in an *UNATTAINABLE WISH*, one incapable of fulfillment (negative μή). The imperfect is used for present time [or less frequently for an action with progressive/repeated aspect in past time]; the aorist is used for an action in past time with simple aspect:

εἰ γὰρ **ἐνῑκῶμεν** τοὺς ξένους.
Would that we **were** (now) **conquering** the strangers.
I wish that we **were** (now) **conquering** the strangers.

εἰ γὰρ μὴ **ἐνικήθημεν** ὑπὸ τῶν ξένων.
Would that we **had** not (then) **been conquered** by the strangers.
I wish that we **had** not (then) **been conquered** by the strangers.

[εἰ γὰρ τότε ἐν πάσαις ταῖς μάχαις ὑπὸ τῶν ξένων μὴ **ἐνῑκώμεθα**.
Would that we **had** not then **been conquered (habitually)** by the strangers in all the battles.
I wish that we **had** not then **been conquered (habitually)** by the strangers in all the battles.]

[6. An imperfect indicative with ἄν can indicate a *PAST POTENTIAL* with progressive/repeated aspect; an aorist indicative with ἄν can indicate a past potential with simple aspect (negative οὐ). (In the sentence, "We might eat steak or fish for dinner tonignt," the verb "might eat" would be in Greek a potential optative with ἄν. In the past such a sentence would be: "We might have eaten steak or fish for dinner last night." In Greek this would be expressed with the aorist indicative with ἄν.):

ᾔειν ἄν πολλάκις εἰς τὴν πόλιν.
He might often **have come** to the city.

ἦλθεν ἄν ἐκείνῃ τῇ ἡμέρᾳ εἰς τὴν πόλιν.
He might have come to the city on that day.

Expressions like ἐβουλόμην ἄν are used with an infinitive to express an unattainable wish:

ἐβουλόμην ἄν αὐτοὺς **τἀληθῆ λέγειν**.
I might have wished them **to be speaking** the truth.
Would that they **were speaking** the truth.
I wish that they **were speaking** the truth.]

[7. The context sometimes indicates that a past indicative with ἄν actually did not occur. Such a past indicative is equivalent to the apodosis of a contrafactual conditional sentence and is called an *UNREAL* or *CONTRA-FACTUAL INDICATIVE*. An unreal indicative in the imperfect indicates an action in present time or in past time with progressive/repeated aspect. An unreal indicative in the aorist tense indicates an action in past time with simple aspect. The negative with an unreal indicative, as in the apodoses of conditional sentences, is οὐ:

οὐ δὴ τοὺς νεανίας διδάσκει ὁ Σωκράτης. **ἐπαύετο** γὰρ **ἂν** ὑπὸ τῶν πολῑτῶν.
Indeed, Sokrates does not teach the young men. For he **would be being stopped** by the citizens.

οὐ δὴ τοὺς νεανίας ἐδίδασκεν ὁ Σωκράτης. **ἐπαύετο** γὰρ **ἂν** ὑπὸ τῶν πολῑτῶν.
Indeed, Sokrates did not teach the young men (habitually). For he **would have been stopped (habitually)** by the citizens.

οὐ δὴ ἐδίδαξεν ὁ Σωκράτης τοὺς νεανίας. **ἐπαύθη** γὰρ **ἂν** ὑπὸ τῶν πολῑτῶν.
Indeed, Sokrates did not teach the young men. For he **would have been stopped** by the citizens.

In sentences like the above, there is often an understood protasis, e.g., "If he were trying to teach them," or "If he had tried to teach them."]

[8. An imperfect or aorist indicative with ἄν can be an *ITERATIVE INDIC-ATIVE*, simply indicating that an act occurred frequently in the past:

ᾖειν ἂν εἰς τὴν πόλιν.
He used to go to the city.]

[NOTE that an imperfect or aorist indicative with ἄν used independently can be, *according to context*, a past potential, a present or past unreal indicative, or an iterative indicative.]

[9. The imperfects ἔδει and ἐχρῆν and the imperfects of other impersonal expressions of obligation, necessity, propriety, or possibility can be used with an infinitive to express the lack of fulfillment of the action of the infinitive. The present infinitive with such verbs indicates present time or progressive/repeated aspect in past time. An aorist infinitive indicates simple aspect in past time:

ἔδει τὸν Σωκράτη δίκην **διδόναι**.
Sokrates **ought to be paying** a penalty (but he is not).
Sokrates **ought to have paid (habitually)** a penalty (but he did not).

ἔδει τὸν Σωκράτη δίκην **δοῦναι**.

Sokrates **ought to have paid** a penalty (but he did not).

Such expressions can also express a simple obligation or necessity in past time which may have been fulfilled. Context will usually determine the meaning. Note the two different translations of the following sentence:

ἔδει τοῦτο **ποιῆσαι**.

He ought to have done this (but he did not do it). (*Unfulfilled necessity*)
He had to do this (and he may or may not have done it). (*Stating that the obligation existed over a period of time in the past*)]

CONDITIONAL SENTENCES WITH THE INDICATIVE

For a discussion of types of conditional sentences not found in Unit 4, see the section on conditional sentences on pages 747–51.

The indicative is used in the

[1. protasis and apodosis of a *SIMPLE* conditional sentence in present or past time:

εἰ Σωκράτης **διδάσκει** τοὺς νεᾱνίᾱς, σοφοὶ **γίγνονται**.
If Sokrates **is teaching** the young men, they **are becoming** wise.

εἰ Σωκράτης **ἐδίδαξεν** τοὺς νεᾱνίᾱς, σοφοὶ **ἐγένοντο**.
If Sokrates **taught** the young men, they **became** wise.

εἰ Σωκράτης **ἐδίδασκε** τοὺς νεᾱνίᾱς, σοφοὶ **ἐγίγνοντο**.
If Sokrates **was teaching** the young men, they **were becoming** wise.
If Sokrates **used to teach** the young men, they **used to become** wise.]

2. apodosis of a *PRESENT GENERAL* conditional sentence:

ἐὰν Σωκράτης τοὺς νεᾱνίᾱς διδάσκῃ, σοφοὶ **γίγνονται**.
If ever Sokrates teaches the young men, they **become** wise.

3. apodosis of a *PAST GENERAL* conditional sentence:

εἰ Σωκράτης τοὺς νεᾱνίᾱς διδάξειεν, σοφοὶ **ἐγίγνοντο**.
If ever Sokrates taught the young men, they **became** wise.

[4. protasis and apodosis of a *FUTURE MOST VIVID* conditional sentence:

εἰ Σωκράτης τοὺς νεᾱνίᾱς μὴ **διδάξει**, οὐ σοφοὶ **γενήσονται**.
If Sokrates **does** not **teach** the young men, they **will** not **become** wise.]

5. apodosis of a *FUTURE MORE VIVID* conditional sentence:

ἐὰν Σωκράτης τοὺς νεᾱνίᾱς διδάξῃ, σοφοὶ **γενήσονται**.
If Sokrates teaches the young men, they **will become** wise.

6. protasis and apodosis (with ἄν) of a *PRESENT CONTRAFACTUAL* conditional sentence:

εἰ Σωκράτης τοὺς νεανίας **ἐδίδασκεν**, σοφοὶ **ἂν ἐγίγνοντο**.
If Sokrates **were teaching** the young men, they **would be becoming** wise.

7. protasis and apodosis (with ἄν) of a *PAST CONTRAFACTUAL* conditional sentence:

εἰ Σωκράτης τοὺς νεανίας **ἐδίδαξεν**, σοφοὶ **ἂν ἐγένοντο**.
If Sokrates **had taught** the young men, they **would have become** wise.

[εἰ Σωκράτης τοὺς νεανίας τότε **ἐδίδασκεν**, σοφοὶ **ἂν ἐγίγνοντο**.
If Sokrates **had taught** the young men then (**habitually**), they **would have become** wise (**habitually**).

(*Imperfect showing progressive/repeated aspect in a past contrafactual conditional sentence*)]

SUBORDINATE CLAUSES WITH THE INDICATIVE

1. The indicative is used with *DEFINITE TEMPORAL CLAUSES* in present and past time:

ἐπειδὴ ὁ ῥήτωρ στρατηγὸς **ᾑρέθη**, ἡ πόλις ἐνῑκήθη.
After the public speaker **was chosen** general, the city was conquered.

ὅτε οἱ στρατιῶται ὑπὸ τοῦ ῥήτορος **ἐτάττοντο**, ἡ πόλις ἐνῑκήθη.
When the soldiers **were being stationed** by the public speaker, the city was conquered.

ἕως οἱ στρατιῶται ὑπὸ τοῦ σοφοῦ στρατηγοῦ **ἐτάττοντο**, οὐκ ἐνῑκήθη ἡ πόλις.
As long as the soldiers **were stationed** by the wise general, the city was not conquered.

οὐκ ἐνῑκήθη ἡ πόλις πρὶν ὁ ῥήτωρ στρατηγὸς **ᾑρέθη**.
The city was not conquered until the public speaker **was chosen** general.

2. The indicative can be used in a *RELATIVE CLAUSE* indicating a fact:

ἄφρων ἦν ὁ ῥήτωρ ὃς στρατηγὸς **ᾑρέθη**.
The public speaker who **was chosen** general was foolish.

ἐκεῖνος ὁ στρατηγὸς ὃς τὴν πόλιν **σᾠζει** τῑμηθήσεται.
That general who **is saving** the city will be honored.

A relative clause can serve as the protasis of a conditional sentence and take the construction of any protasis in a conditional sentence, e.g.:

ὃς ταῦτα **ἐποίησε** δίκην ἂν ἔδωκεν.
Whoever **had done** this would have paid a penalty.
If anyone **had done** this, he would have paid a penalty.

3. The indicative can be used in a *CAUSAL CLAUSE*:

ἐπεὶ τοὺς νεανίας **ἐδίδαξεν**, ἀπέθανεν ὁ Σωκράτης ὑπὸ τῶν πολιτῶν.
Since he **taught** the young men, Sokrates was killed by the citizens.

A causal clause can also be introduced by a relative pronoun:

ἄφρων ἐστὶν ὅς γε ταῦτα πράττει.
He is crazy because he **is doing** these things.
(*Literally:* He is crazy who **is doing** these things.)

4. Introduced by the conjunction ὥστε, an indicative indicates an *ACTUAL RESULT* as opposed to an infinitive, which indicates a natural result:

οὕτω κακῶς ἐμαχέσαντο οἱ στρατιῶται ὥστε οἱ πολῖται **ἔφυγον**.
So badly did the soldiers fight that the citizens **fled**.

5. When a *FEAR CLAUSE* refers to an action contemporaneous with or prior to the verb of fearing, the verb is in the indicative, introduced by the conjunction μή (negative μὴ οὐ):

φοβοῦνται μὴ Σωκράτης ὑπὸ τῶν πολιτῶν **ἀπέθανεν**.
They are afraid that Sokrates **was killed** by the citizens.

A fear clause referring to an action subsequent to that of the main verb usually takes a verb in the subjunctive or the optative according to the rules for sequence of moods, [but rarely a future indicative is used in a fear clause:

φοβοῦνται μὴ Σωκράτης **ἀποθανεῖται** ὑπὸ τῶν πολιτῶν.
They are afraid that Sokrates **will be killed** by the citizens.]

[6. Instead of the subjunctive or optative used according to the rules for the sequence of moods, a future indicative is sometimes used in a *PURPOSE CLAUSE:*

εἶμι ὅπως **ὄψομαι** τὸν ἀδελφόν.
I shall go in order that **I may see** my brother.]

[In a purpose clause depending on a contrafactual indicative, the verb is attracted into the indicative to indicate *UNFULFILLED PURPOSE*:

εἰ οἱ Ἀθηναῖοι μὴ ἀπέκτειναν τὸν Σωκράτη, ἐδίδαξεν ἂν τοὺς νεανίας ἵνα σοφοὶ **ἐγένοντο**.
If the Athenians had not killed Sokrates, he would have taught the young men in order that they **might have become** wise.]

7. After verbs of effort, striving, or caring, a future indicative, introduced by
ὅπως (negative ὅπως μή), is used in an *OBJECT CLAUSE OF EFFORT* :

ὁ Σωκράτης ἐμηχανᾶτο ὅπως οἱ φίλοι ὅτι ἄριστοι γενήσονται.

Sokrates was contriving that his friends would become as good as possible.

8. In *INDIRECT STATEMENT* and *INDIRECT QUESTION* in primary
sequence all indicatives remain in the original mood and tense. In secondary sequence all indicatives *in main clauses* [except for past tenses indicating unreality] can be changed to the same tense of the optative or can be
retained for emphasis. [Any past tense of the indicative indicating unreality must be retained.] Imperfects and pluperfects are usually retained,
[but an imperfect indicative can be represented by a present optative, and
a pluperfect indicative by a perfect optative. In secondary sequence all
past indicatives *in subordinate clauses* must be retained.]

λέγει ὅτι Σωκράτης τοὺς νεανίας **ἐδίδαξεν**.

He says that Sokrates **taught** the young men.

ᾔδειν ὅτι Σωκράτης τοὺς νεανίας **ἐδίδαξεν**.

He knew that Sokrates **taught** the young men.

(*Retained indicative in secondary sequence instead of being changed to the
optative διδάξειεν.*)

[εἶπεν ὅτι ἡ πόλις **ἐνῑκήθη ἂν** εἰ μὴ οἱ στρατιῶται καλῶς **ἐμαχέσαντο**.

He said that the city **would have been conquered** if the soldiers **had
not fought** well.

(*Although in secondary sequence, both indicatives must be retained, ἐνῑκήθη
ἂν because as the verb in the apodosis of a past contrafactual conditional
sentence it indicates unreality; ἐμαχέσαντο because it is a past indicative
in a subordinate clause.*)]

SUBJUNCTIVE MOOD

INDEPENDENT CLAUSES WITH THE SUBJUNCTIVE

1. A *HORTATORY SUBJUNCTIVE* (usually the first person plural,
occasionally the first person singular) expresses emphatically the will of
the speaker. The tense shows aspect. The negative is μή:

ἄρχωμεν τῶν πόλεων.

Let us rule (habitually) the cities.

μὴ **ἔλθωμεν** εἰς τὴν πόλιν.

Let us not go to the city.

2. A *DELIBERATIVE SUBJUNCTIVE* (limited to the first person) asks
a question about what the speaker is to do. The tense shows aspect.
The negative is μή:

μὴ ἴωμεν εἰς τὴν πόλιν;
Are we not **to go (habitually)** to the city?

τί ἀγγείλω τοῖς πολίταις;
What **am I to announce** to the citizens?

[Closely related to the deliberative subjunctive is the *ANTICIPATORY SUBJUNCTIVE*, which asks a question about something over which the speaker has no control.

τί πάθω;
What **am I to suffer**?]

3. A *PROHIBITIVE SUBJUNCTIVE* is an aorist subjunctive in the second or third person introduced by μή, giving a negative command with simple aspect. (A negative command with progressive/repeated aspect is expressed by the present imperative with μή):

μὴ ἐρωτήσῃς μηδέν.
Do not ask anything.

μὴ ἔλθητε εἰς τὴν πόλιν.
Do not go to the city.

[4. A subjunctive (usually aorist) introduced by the double negative οὐ μή expresses *EMPHATIC FUTURE NEGATION*:

οὐ μὴ τοῦτο ποιήσῃ.
He will not do this]

[5. A subjunctive introduced by μή can express *CAUTIOUS ASSERTION*; one introduced by μὴ οὐ can express *CAUTIOUS DENIAL*:

μὴ κακὸν ᾖ τοῦτο ποιεῖν.
It **may be** bad to do this.

μὴ οὐκ ἀγαθὸν ᾖ τοῦτο ποιεῖν.
It **may not be** good to do this.]

CONDITIONAL SENTENCES WITH THE SUBJUNCTIVE

The subjunctive with ἄν is used in the

1. protasis of a *PRESENT GENERAL* conditional sentence:

ἐὰν κακὰ ποιῇς, δίκην δίδως.
If you **(habitually) do** evil, you pay a penalty.

ἐὰν τοῦτο ποιήσῃς, δίκην δίδως.
If ever you **do** this, you pay a penalty.

ὃς ἂν τοῦτο ποιήσῃ δίκην δίδωσιν.
Whoever **does** this pays a penalty.

2. protasis of a *FUTURE MORE VIVID* conditional sentence:

ἐὰν κακὰ **ποιῇς**, δίκην δώσεις.
If you (**habitually**) **do** evil, you will pay a penalty.

ἐὰν τοῦτο **ποιήσῃς**, δίκην δώσεις.
If you **do** this, you will pay a penalty.

ὃς ἂν τοῦτο **ποιήσῃ** δίκην δώσει.
Whoever **does** this will pay a penalty.

NOTE that an independent subjunctive with its usual negative μή can be substituted for a future indicative or an optative in any apodosis which refers to future time:

ἐὰν ἔλθῃ, μὴ **δῶμεν** αὐτῷ μηδέν.
If he comes, **let us give** him nothing.

εἰ ἔλθοι, **μὴ δῶτε** αὐτῷ μηδέν.
If he should come, **do not give** him anything.

ἐὰν ἔλθῃ, τί **εἴπω**;
If he comes, what **am I to say**?

SUBORDINATE CLAUSES WITH THE SUBJUNCTIVE

1. The subjunctive is used in a *FUTURE MORE VIVID TEMPORAL CLAUSE* or a *PRESENT GENERAL TEMPORAL CLAUSE*. The conjunction in such clauses is combined with ἄν, e.g., ἐπειδάν, ὅταν. Such temporal clauses are equivalent to the protases of the corresponding conditional sentences:

   ἐπειδὰν εἰς τὴν πόλιν **ἔλθῃς**, τὸν ἀδελφὸν ὄψει.
   After you **go** to the city, you will see your brother.
   After you **have gone** to the city, you will see your brother.

   ὅταν τοὺς νεανίας **διδάσκῃς**, μανθάνουσι πολλά.
   Whenever you **teach** the young men, they learn many things.

2. The subjunctive introduced by the conjunctions ἵνα, ὡς, ὅπως, "in order that" (negative ἵνα μή, ὡς μή, ὅπως μή [or sometimes μή alone], is used in a *PURPOSE CLAUSE* in primary sequence or can be retained in secondary sequence instead of being changed to the optative. [The

particle ἄν is sometimes added to purpose clauses introduced by ὅπως or ὡς with no difference in meaning.]:

εἰς τὴν πόλιν εἶ ἵνα τοὺς νεανίας **διδάξῃς**.
You will go to the city in order that you **may teach** the young men.

τοὺς νεανίας ἐδίδασκες ὅπως σοφώτεροι **γένωνται**.
You used to teach the young men in order that they **might become** wiser.
(*Retained subjunctive in secondary sequence after the imperfect indicative ἐδίδασκες*)

[εἰς τὴν πόλιν εἶ ὅπως **ἄν** τοὺς νεανίας **διδάξῃς**.
You will go to the city in order that you **may teach** the young men.]

[3. An *OBJECT CLAUSE OF EFFORT*, instead of using the future indicative, sometimes takes the subjunctive in primary sequence or a retained subjunctive in secondary sequence. The particle ἄν can also be used in this construction. Tense shows aspect:

μηχανᾶται ὅπως **ἄν** ταῦτα **γένηται**.
He is contriving that these things **happen**.]

4. When a FEAR CLAUSE refers to an action subsequent to that of a verb of fearing, the verb, introduced by the conjunction μή (negative μὴ οὐ) is in the subjunctive in primary sequence; in secondary sequence it can be retained in the subjunctive instead of being changed to the optative:

φοβεῖται μὴ ταῦτα **ποιήσῃς**.
He is afraid that you **may do** these things.
He is afraid that you **will do** these things.

ἐφοβεῖτο μὴ οὐ ταῦτα **ποιήσῃς**.
He was afraid that you **might** not **do** these things.
He was afraid that you **would** not **do** these things.
(*Retained subjunctive in secondary sequence after the imperfect ἐφοβεῖτο*)

[5. A subjunctive in a *NON-CONDITIONAL RELATIVE CLAUSE* has the same force as an independent subjunctive:

οὗτός ἐστι Σωκράτης ὃν **ἀποκτείνωμεν**.
This is Sokrates and **let us kill** him. (*Literally:* This is Sokrates whom **let us kill**.)
(*Hortatory subjunctive in a relative clause*)

οὗτός ἐστι Σωκράτης ὃν **μὴ ἀποκτείνητε**.
This is Sokrates and **don't kill** him. (*Literally:* This is Sokrates whom **don't kill**.)
(*Prohibitive subjunctive in a relative clause*)]

OPTATIVE MOOD

INDEPENDENT CLAUSES WITH THE OPTATIVE

1. A wish referring to the future is expressed by an *OPTATIVE OF WISH* without any introductory word or introduced by εἰ γάρ or εἴθε. Tense shows aspect; the negative is μή:

σώσειεν ὁ θεὸς τὴν πόλιν.
May the god **save** the city!
I wish that the god **would save** the city!

εἴθε **φυλάττοιντο** ἀεὶ οἱ στρατιῶται τοὺς πολεμίους.
May the soldiers always **be on guard against** the enemy.
I wish that the soldiers **would** always **be on guard against** the enemy.

εἰ γὰρ μὴ **νῑκῷεν** οἱ πολέμιοι.
May the enemy not **win (habitually).**
I wish that the enemy **would** not **win (habitually).**

μὴ **λυθείη** ἡ εἰρήνη.
May the peace not **be destroyed.**
I wish that the peace **would** not **be destroyed.**

2. A *POTENTIAL OPTATIVE* without any introductory word but accompanied by the particle ἄν indicates that an action might possibly occur. Tense shows aspect; the negative with a potential optative is οὐ:

σώσειεν **ἄν** ὁ θεὸς τὴν πόλιν.
The god **might save** the city.

οἱ στρατιῶται **φυλάττοιντ᾽ ἄν** τοὺς πολεμίους.
The soldiers **might guard (habitually) against** the enemy.

οὐκ **ἄν λυθείη** ἡ εἰρήνη.
The peace **might** not **be destroyed.**

CONDITIONAL SENTENCES WITH THE OPTATIVE

The optative is used in the

1. protasis of a *PAST GENERAL* conditional sentence:

εἰ Σωκράτης **διδάσκοι** τοὺς νεᾱνίᾱς, σοφοὶ ἐγίγνοντο.
If ever Sokrates **taught** the young men, they became wise.

2. protasis and apodosis (with ἄν) of a *FUTURE LESS VIVID* conditional sentence:

εἰ Σωκράτης **διδάξειε** τοὺς νεᾱνίᾱς, **γίγνοιντ᾽ ἄν** σοφοί.
If Sokrates **should teach** the young men, they **would become** wise.

NOTE that an independent optative with its usual negatives can substitute for the verb in the apodosis of many types of conditional sentences:

ἐὰν τοῦτο ποιήσῃ, δίκην μὴ **δοίη**.
If he does this, **may** he not **pay** a penalty.

[εἰ τοῦτο ἐποίησεν, οὐκ ἂν δίκην **δοίη**.
If he did this, he **might** not **pay** a penalty.]

SUBORDINATE CLAUSES WITH THE OPTATIVE

1. The optative is used in a *PAST GENERAL TEMPORAL CLAUSE*. Such a temporal clause is equivalent to the protasis of a past general conditional sentence:

ἐπειδὴ εἰς τὴν πόλιν **ἔλθοις**, τὸν ἀδελφὸν ἑώρας.
After you **went** to the city, you used to see your brother.
Whenever you **went** to the city, you used to see your brother.

ὅτε τοὺς νεανίας **διδάσκοις**, ἐμάνθανον πολλά.
Whenever you **taught** the young men, they learned many things.

2. The optative, introduced by the conjunctions ἵνα, ὡς, ὅπως, "in order that" (negative ἵνα μή, ὡς μή, ὅπως μή [or sometimes μή alone]) is used in a *PURPOSE CLAUSE* in secondary sequence. [The particle ἄν is sometimes added to purpose clauses introduced by ὅπως or ὡς with no difference in meaning.]:

εἰς τὴν πόλιν ἦλθες ἵνα τοὺς νεανίας **διδάξειας**.
You went to the city in order that you **might teach** the young men.

τοὺς νεανίας ἐδίδασκες ὡς σοφώτεροι **γένοιντο**.
You used to teach the young men in order that they **might become** wiser.

[ταῦτα ἔπραξας ὅπως **ἂν** τὴν πόλιν **σώσειας**.
You did these things in order that you **might save** the city.]

[3. An *OBJECT CLAUSE OF EFFORT* in secondary sequence can occasionally take a future optative instead of the more usual future indicative. An object clause of effort in secondary sequence can also take the optative according to sequence of moods, with the present tense showing progressive/ repeated aspect and the aorist tense showing simple aspect:

ἐμηχανᾶτο ὅπως ταῦτα **γενήσοιτο**.
He was contriving that these things **happen**.
(*Future optative in secondary sequence after the imperfect indicative ἐμηχανᾶτο, replacing the more usual future indicative*)

ἐμηχανᾶτο ὅπως ταῦτα **γένοιτο**.
He was contriving that these things **happen**.
Object clause of effort in secondary sequence after the imperfect indicative ἐμηχανᾶτο, with aorist tense showing simple aspect, instead of the more usual future indicative)]

4. When a *FEAR CLAUSE* in secondary sequence refers to an action subsequent to that of the verb of fearing, the verb, introduced by the conjunction μή (negative μὴ οὐ), is usually in the optative:

ἐφοβεῖτο μὴ ταῦτα **ποιήσειας**.
He was afraid that you **might do** these things.
He was afraid that you **would do** these things.

[5. An optative in a *NON-CONDITIONAL RELATIVE CLAUSE* has the same force as an independent optative.

τοιαῦτα ἐπάθομεν οἷα **πάθοιεν** οἱ πολέμιοι.
We suffered such things as **may** our enemies **suffer**.
We suffered such things as **I wish** our enemies **would suffer**.
(Optative of wish in a relative clause)

τοιαῦτα ἔπαθον οἷα οὐκ **ἂν βουλοίμεθα** παθεῖν.
They suffered such things as we **would** not **want** to suffer.
(Potential optative in a relative clause)]

6. In *INDIRECT STATEMENT* and *INDIRECT QUESTION* in secondary sequence, *in main clauses* all indicatives [(except for past indicatives showing unreality) and all deliberative and anticipatory subjunctives] are usually changed to the corresponding tense of the optative. Imperfects and pluperfects are usually retained as indicatives, [but an imperfect indicative can be represented by a present optative, and a pluperfect indicative by a perfect optative. *In subordinate clauses* in secondary sequence, no past tense of the indicative is changed to an optative, and any subjunctive with ἄν loses the ἄν if it becomes an optative]:

εἶπεν ὅτι Σωκράτης τοὺς νεανίας **διδάξειεν** [ἐπειδὴ εἰς τὴν πόλιν **ἦλθεν**].
He said that Sokrates had taught the young men [after he had gone to the city].
(In the main clause, the original ἐδίδαξεν has been replaced by the same tense of the optative in secondary sequence after the aorist indicative εἶπεν; [in the subordinate temporal clause, the past tense of the indicative must be retained].)

[εἶπεν ὅτι Σωκράτης τοὺς νεανίας **ἐδίδαξεν ἄν**, εἰ εἰς τὴν πόλιν **ἦλθεν**.
He said that Sokrates **would have taught** the young men if he **had gone** to the city.

*(The main verb of the sentence in indirect statement is an aorist indicative
with ἄν in the apodosis of a past contrafactual conditional sentence; since it
is an indicative indicating unreality, it must be retained, even though it is
in secondary sequence after the aorist indicative εἶπεν. The aorist indicative
in the protasis of the conditional sentence must be retained since all past
indicatives in subordinate clauses in indirect statement remain unchanged.)]*

οὐκ ᾔδη ὅτι **ποιήσαιμι.**

I did not know what **I did/had done.**

[I did not know what **I was to do.**]

*(The aorist optative in secondary sequence after the pluperfect ᾔδη can
represent an original aorist indicative of a question of fact [or an original
aorist subjunctive of a deliberative question with simple aspect].)*

IMPERATIVES; COMMANDS AND PROHIBITIONS

COMMANDS can be expressed in the first person by a *HORTATORY SUB-
JUNCTIVE* and in the second and third persons by an *IMPERATIVE*.
Tense indicates aspect.

ἴωμεν εἰς τὴν ἐκκλησίαν.
Let us go (habitually) to the assembly.

ἔλθωμεν εἰς τὴν ἐκκλησίαν.
Let us go to the assembly.

ἴτε εἰς τὴν βουλήν.
Go (habitually) to the council.

ἐλθὲ εἰς τὴν βουλήν.
Go to the council.

ἴτω εἰς τὴν οἰκίαν.
Let him go (habitually) to the house.

ἐλθόντων εἰς ἀγοράν.
Let them go to the market place.

An urgent command or exhortation in any person can be expressed by ὅπως
WITH THE FUTURE INDICATIVE used independently:

ὅπως ἴμεν εἰς τὸ πεδίον.
Let us see to it that we go to the plain.

ὅπως ταῦτα **ποιήσεις.**
See to it that you do these things.

[An *INFINITIVE* can sometimes substitute for an imperative. When the
infinitive substitutes for an imperative in the second person, it can have a

subject in the nominative. When the infinitive substitutes for an imperative in the third person, it can have an accusative subject (like the direct object and object infinitive after a verb like *κελεύω*):

σύ γε ταῦτα **ποιῆσαι**.
You, **do** these things.

τὸν Δημοσθένη **χαίρειν**.
Let Demosthenes **be well**.
I bid Demosthenes **hello**.]

PROHIBITIONS are expressed in the first person by a *HORTATORY SUB-JUNCTIVE* negated by *μή*; tense indicates aspect. In the second and third persons, prohibitions with progressive/repeated aspect are expressed by a *present IMPERATIVE* negated by *μή*; prohibitions with simple aspect are expressed by an *aorist SUBJUNCTIVE* negated by *μή* (*PROHIBITIVE SUBJUNCTIVE*). A present subjunctive is not used as a prohibitive subjunctive; [an aorist imperative negated by *μή* is occasionally used in a prohibition with simple aspect]:

μὴ κακὰ **ποιῶμεν**.
Let us not (habitually) do evil things.

μὴ τοῦτο **ποιήσωμεν**.
Let us not do this.

μὴ ταῦτα **ποίει**.
Do not (habitually) do these things.

μὴ ταῦτα **ποιήσῃ**.
Let him not do these things.

[μὴ ταῦτα **ποιησάτω**.
Let him not do these things.]

An urgent prohibition can be expressed by **ὅπως μή** *WITH THE FUTURE INDICATIVE*:

ὅπως μὴ ταῦτα **ποιήσεις**.
See to it that you do not do these things.

[A future indicative negated by *οὐ μή* also expresses an urgent prohibition:

οὐ μὴ ταῦτα **ποιήσεις**.
Do not do these things.]

[A prohibition can also be expressed by an infinitive negated by *μή*:

σύ γε ταῦτα **μὴ ποιῆσαι**.
Don't *you* **do** these things.

Σωκράτη **μὴ διδάσκειν** τοὺς νεανίας.
Let Sokrates **not (habitually) teach** the young men.]

INFINITIVE

An infinitive is a verbal noun. As a *verb*, it is formed from the principal parts of a verb; has tense (showing aspect only, except in indirect statement) and voice; can have an accusative subject [except for the infinitive substituting for a second person imperative] and govern any of the constructions of a finite form of the verb; and, except for the article, is modified by adverbs. The infinitive can fill any of the functions of a *noun* in a sentence.

1. An *ARTICULAR INFINITIVE* (an infinitive accompanied by a neuter article in any case) functions as any noun would:

   καλὸν τὸ πολλὰ **μεμαθηκέναι**.
   It is good **to have learned** much.

   ἥκομεν ὑπὲρ **τοῦ** τὴν ἀλήθειαν **μαθεῖν**.
   We have come for the sake of **learning** the truth.

   τῷ πολλὰ **μανθάνειν** σοφώτεροι γιγνόμεθα.
   By learning many things we become wiser.

   διὰ **τὸ** τὴν πόλιν **καταλυθῆναι** οἱ πολῖται δοῦλοι ἐγένοντο.
   Because of the city's **being destroyed**, the citizens became slaves.

2. The infinitive is used as the *SUBJECT* of impersonal verbs such as δεῖ, χρή, δοκεῖ ("it seems good"), ἔστι ("it is possible"), ἔξεστι, οἷόν τέ ἐστι, συμβαίνει, and of ἐστί with predicate adjectives like ἄξιον, δίκαιον, αἰσχρόν, καλόν:

   δεῖ ταῦτα καλῶς **ποιεῖν**.
   It is necessary **to do** these things well.

   ἔδοξεν τοῖς Ἀθηναίοις **ἀπελθεῖν**.
   It seemed best to the Athenians **to go away**.
   The Athenians decided **to go away**.

   οὐ δὴ δίκαιον ταῦτα **ποιῆσαι**.
   Indeed, it is not just **to do** these things.

3. An infinitive can be used as a *PREDICATE NOMINATIVE*:

   τὸ δὴ Σωκράτη ἀποκτεῖναι τῷ ὄντι ἐστὶ τὴν πόλιν **βλάπτειν**.
   Indeed, to kill Sokrates is really **to be harming** the city.

4. An *OBJECT INFINITIVE* is used as the direct object of such verbs as διδάσκω, κελεύω, βούλομαι, συμβουλεύω, φοβοῦμαι, κωλύω, and ἐθέλω:

   ὁ Σωκράτης τοὺς νεανίας αὐτῶν **ἄρχειν** ἐδίδαξεν.
   Sokrates taught the young men **to rule** themselves.

βούλομαι τοῦτο **ποιῆσαι**.
I want **to do** this.

ἐκωλύσαμεν τοὺς πολεμίους τὸ πεδίον **βλάψαι**.
We hindered the enemy **from harming** the plain.

5. A *COMPLEMENTARY INFINITIVE* completes the meaning of intransitive verbs showing ability, etc.

δυνάμεθα ταῦτα **ποιῆσαι**.
We are able **to do** these things.

6. An *EPEXEGETICAL INFINITIVE* completes the meaning of certain adjectives like ἱκανός, ἄξιος, δυνατός:

διὰ ταῦτα ἄξιός ἐστιν **ἀποθανεῖν**.
On account of these things he deserves **to die**.

7. An infinitive, introduced by ὥστε, is used in a clause of *NATURAL RESULT*:

οὕτω κακῶς πολῑτεύονται ὥστε τὴν πολῑτείᾱν **καταλυθῆναι**.
So badly do they govern themselves as for the constitution **to be destroyed**.

8. After an affirmative main verb, an infinitive is used in a *TEMPORAL CLAUSE* introduced by πρίν, "before":

ἀπῆλθε πρὶν τὸν ἀδελφὸν **ἰδεῖν**.
He went away before **seeing** his brother.
He went away before **he saw** his brother.

9. After certain verbs, e.g., φημί, the verb of an *INDIRECT STATEMENT* is put in the infinitive (same tense as that of the original statement). [An original imperfect is represented by a present infinitive, a pluperfect by a perfect infinitive.] The subject of the direct statement, if different from that of the introductory verb, is put in the accusative case. The original negative [and the particle ἄν] remain unchanged.

νομίζω τὸν Σωκράτη οὐκ ἀγαθὸν **εἶναι**.
I think that Sokrates **is** not good.
I think "Σωκράτης οὐκ ἀγαθός ἐστιν."
(*The original present indicative has been changed to a present infinitive.*)

νομίζεις τὸν Σωκράτη τοὺς νεᾱνίᾱς τὴν ἀρετὴν **διδάξαι**;
Do you think that Sokrates **taught** the young men virtue?
Do you think "Σωκράτης τοὺς νεᾱνίᾱς τὴν ἀρετὴν ἐδίδαξεν"?
(*The original aorist indicative has been changed to an aorist infinitive.*)

ἆρα νομίζετε ἡμᾶς τὸν ἀδελφὸν **λῦσειν**;
Do you think that we **shall release** your brother?
Do you think "λῦσουσι τὸν ἀδελφόν μου"?
(*The original future indicative has been changed to a future infinitive.*)

[νομίζετε ἐκείνους τότε κακὰ **πράττειν**.
You think that they **were** then **doing** evil things.
You think "ἐκεῖνοι τότε κακὰ ἔπρᾶττον."
(*The original imperfect indicative has been replaced by a PRESENT infinitive.*)]

[νομίζετε ἐκείνους τὸν ἀδελφὸν **λῦσαι ἄν**, εἰ χρήματα ἔδωκας.
You think that they **would have freed** your brother if you had given money.
You think "ἐκεῖνοι τὸν ἀδελφὸν ἔλῦσαν ἄν, εἰ χρήματα ἔδωκα."
(*The aorist indicative with ἄν in the apodosis of a past contrafactual conditional sentence has been changed to an aorist infinitive with ἄν.*)]

10. After the verb μέλλω, μελλήσω, ἐμέλλησα, ——, ——, ——, in the sense of "be about to, be likely to," a future infinitive is used as if in indirect statement:

μέλλομεν **ἐλᾶν** διὰ τοῦ πεδίου.
We are about **to march** through the plain.

[11. With certain expressions an *INFINITIVE OF PURPOSE* is used:

στρατιώτᾶς τινὰς κατέλιπεν **φυλάττειν** τὴν πόλιν.
He left some soldiers behind **to guard** the city.

τοῖς ᾿Αθηναίοις πέντε ἡμέρᾱς ἔδοσαν ταῦτα **ποιεῖν**.
They gave the Athenians five days **to do** this.]

[12. An infinitive can be used *ABSOLUTELY*, with no syntactical relation to the rest of the sentence, e.g., ὡς ἔπος εἰπεῖν, "so to speak"; ὡς ἐμοὶ κρῖναι, "for me to judge, in my opinion"; ὀλίγου δεῖν, "to need a little = almost":

πάντες **ὡς ἔπος εἰπεῖν** αὐτὸν ἐφίλουν.
All—**so to speak**—loved him.]

[13. An infinitive can be used in an *EXCLAMATION*:

τὸν ᾿Αριστοφάνη ταῦτα **γράφειν**.
For Aristophanes **to write** these things!
That Aristophanes **writes** these things!]

[14. An infinitive is sometimes used instead of an imperative or a prohibitive
subjunctive in *COMMANDS* and *PROHIBITIONS*:

ὑμεῖς γε τὴν πόλιν **σῶσαι**.
You, **save** the city.

τὸν ἄγγελον μὴ **βλαβῆναι**.
Let the messenger not **be harmed**.]

[15. An infinitive is sometimes used instead of an optative in a wish:

ὦ θεοί, τὴν πόλιν **σωθῆναι**.
Gods, **may** the city **be saved**.]

[16. An infinitive can be used after ἐφ᾽ ᾧ and ἐφ᾽ ᾧτε, "on condition that, for
the purpose of," to indicate a *STIPULATION*:

οἱ Ἀθηναῖοι ἤθελον ἀφεῖναι τὸν Σωκράτη ἐφ᾽ ᾧ μὴ **διδάξαι** τοὺς νεανίας.
The Athenians were willing to release Sokrates on condition that he not
teach the young men.]

PARTICIPLE

A participle is a verbal adjective. As a *verb*, it is formed from the principal
parts of a verb; has tense (showing aspect for the most part) and voice; and can
govern any of the constructions of a finite form of the verb. As an *adjective*,
it has gender, number, and case; and agrees with nouns or pronouns.

1. An *ATTRIBUTIVE PARTICIPLE* is used exactly like an adjective
   in the attributive position and modifies nouns the way an adjective does.
   Attributive participles can be used substantively:

   ἐκεῖνος ὁ γέρων ὁ **λέγων** μετὰ τῶν νεανιῶν Σωκράτης ἐστίν.
   That old man **speaking** with the young men is Sokrates.

   ὁ τῶν στρατιωτῶν **ἡγησόμενος** ἀπῆλθεν.
   The man **about to lead** the soldiers went away.
   The man **who was going to lead** the soldiers went away.

   ὁ κακὰ **ποιῶν** τὴν πόλιν πολίτης δίκην δώσει.
   The citizen **harming** the city will pay a penalty.

2. Although agreeing with a noun or pronoun in gender, number, and case, a
   CIRCUMSTANTIAL PARTICIPLE is not in the attributive position.
   Instead of describing a noun the way an attributive adjective would, a
   circumstantial participle gives the circumstances under which the action of
   a verb occurs. The relation between the participle and the verb can be
   temporal, concessive, causal, or conditional, or can indicate purpose. Ad-

verbs or conjunctions often make the relation between the participle and
the rest of the sentence more precise. The negative with a circumstantial
participle is οὐ, except for the conditional participle, which takes the negative μή:

εἰσελθόντες εἰς τὴν οἰκίαν, τὸν χρυσὸν ἔκλεψαν.
Upon entering the house, they stole the gold.
When they entered the house, they stole the gold. (*Temporal*)

οἷα τὸν χρυσὸν **κλέψαντες** οὐκ ἐτιμῶντο.
They were not honored **because they stole** the gold. (*Causal*)

ὡς σώσοντες τοὺς ἀδικουμένους ἥκουσιν.
They have come (**as they say**) **to save** the men who are being wronged.
(*Alleged purpose*)

μὴ χρήματα **δούς**, οὐκ ἂν ἐλύθην.
Not **having given** money, I would not have been freed.
If I **had** not **given** money, I would not have been freed. (*Conditional*)

3. A *GENITIVE ABSOLUTE* consists of a circumstantial participle
   agreeing with a noun or pronoun in the genitive case which is not otherwise
   syntactically connected to the rest of the sentence. A genitive absolute can
   have any of the relations to the rest of the sentence which a circumstantial
   participle can have:

   τῆς εἰρήνης λυθείσης, μαχόμεθα.
   The peace broken, we fight.
   When the peace is broken, we fight. (*Temporal*)
   Since the peace was broken, we are fighting. (*Causal*)
   If the peace is broken, we fight. (*Conditional*)

   τῆς εἰρήνης μὴ λυθείσης, οὐκ ἂν ἐμαχεσάμεθα.
   The peace not broken, we would not have fought.
   If the peace had not been broken, we would not have fought.
   (*Conditional*)

   τῆς εἰρήνης λυομένης, ὅμως οὐ μαχόμεθα.
   Although the peace is being broken, we nevertheless do not fight.
   (*Concessive*)

4. An *ACCUSATIVE ABSOLUTE* is a neuter singular accusative of a
   circumstantial participle of an impersonal verb, not accompanied by a
   noun or pronoun, and not otherwise syntactically connected with the rest
   of the sentence. An accusative absolute can have any of the relations to the
   rest of the sentence which a circumstantial participle can have:

ἐξὸν εἰρήνην ἄγειν, ὅμως βούλεται μάχεσθαι.
It being possible to keep peace, he nevertheless wants to fight.
Although it is possible to keep peace, he nevertheless wants to fight.
(*Concessive*)

οὐκ ἐξὸν εἰρήνην ἄγειν, μαχόμεθα.
It not being possible to keep peace, we are fighting.
Since it is not possible to keep peace, we are fighting. (*Causal*)

μὴ ἐξὸν εἰρήνην ἄγειν, μαχόμεθα.
It not being possible to keep peace, we fight.
If it is not possible to keep peace, we fight. (*Conditional*)
Whenever it is not possible to keep peace, we fight. (*Present general temporal*)

5. A *SUPPLEMENTARY PARTICIPLE* completes the meaning of a verb. Such participles are used with verbs of emotion, beginning and ceasing, and the verbs λανθάνω, φθάνω, and τυγχάνω.

ὁ ἀγαθὸς χαίρει τοῖς νόμοις **πειθόμενος**.
The good man takes pleasure **in obeying** the laws.

ὁ κακὸς οὔποτε παύεται ἄλλους **βλάπτων**.
The evil man never stops **harming** others.

δεῖ τὸν βουλόμενον ἄλλων ἄρχειν ἄρχεσθαι αὑτοῦ γε **ἄρχοντα**.
It is necessary for one wishing to rule others to begin **by ruling** himself.

ἔφθησαν τοὺς στρατιώτᾱς **φυγόντες**.
They anticipated the soldiers **in fleeing**.
They **fled before** the soldiers.

ἔλαθον τοὺς στρατιώτᾱς **φυγόντες**.
They escaped the notice of the soldiers **in fleeing**.
They **fled** without being observed by the soldiers.
They **fled** without the soldiers' knowing it.

ἐτύγχανε **θύσᾱς**.
He happened **to have sacrificed**.

ἐτύγχανε **θύων**.
He happened **to be sacrificing**.

6. After certain verbs, e.g., οἶδα, ἀκούω, the verb of an *INDIRECT STATE-MENT* is put in the participle (same tense as that of the original statement). [An original imperfect is represented by a present participle; an original pluperfect by a perfect participle.] The subject of the direct statement, if different from that of the introductory verb, is put in the

accusative case. The original negative [and the particle ἄν] remain unchanged:

οἶδα τοὺς Λακεδαιμονίους οὐκ εἰρήνην **ἄξοντας.**
I know that the Lacedaimonians **will** not **keep** peace.
I know "οἱ Λακεδαιμόνιοι οὐκ εἰρήνην ἄξουσιν."
(*The original future indicative has been replaced by a future participle.*)

ἤκουσα τὸν Σωκράτη τοὺς νεανίας **διδάσκοντα.**
I heard that Sokrates **was teaching** the young men.
I heard "Σωκράτης τοὺς νεανίας διδάσκει."
(*The original present indicative has been replaced by a present participle.*)

ἤκουσα τὸν Σωκράτη τοὺς νεανίας **διδάξαντα.**
I heard that Sokrates **taught** the young men.
I heard that Sokrates **had taught** the young men.
I heard "Σωκράτης τοὺς νεανίας ἐδίδαξεν."
(*The original aorist indicative has been replaced by an aorist participle.*)

[ἀκούω τὸν Σωκράτη τότε τοὺς νεανίας **διδάσκοντα.**
I hear that Sokrates **was** then **teaching** the young men.
I hear "Σωκράτης τότε τοὺς νεανίας ἐδίδασκεν."
(*The original imperfect indicative has been replaced by a PRESENT participle.*)]

[οἶδα ὑμᾶς τὸν ἀδελφὸν **λύσαντας ἄν,** εἰ χρήματα ἔδομεν.
I know that you **would have freed** our brother, if we had given money.
I know "τὸν ἀδελφὸν ἂν ἐλύσατε εἰ χρήματα ἔδομεν."
(*The original aorist indicative with ἄν in the apodosis of a past contrafactual conditional sentence has been changed to an aorist participle with ἄν.*)]

VERBAL ADJECTIVE

The verbal adjective in -τέος, -τέα, -τέον expresses obligation or necessity.

1. When the verbal adjective of a transitive verb taking a direct object in the accusative case is used as a predicate adjective, agreeing in gender, number, and case with the subject of a form of εἰμί, the verbal adjective is said to be used *PERSONALLY*. The agent with the verbal adjective used personally is always expressed by the dative of personal agent:

καὶ αἱ γυναῖκες **διδακτέαι εἰσίν.**
Even the women **are to be educated.**
Even the women **must be educated.**

ἔφη ὁ Σωκράτης καὶ τὰς γυναῖκας **διδακτέας εἶναι.**
Sokrates used to say that even women **were to be educated.**
Sokrates used to say that even women **had to be educated.**

ὁ ποιητὴς ἡμῖν **σωτέος ἐστίν**.
The poet **is to be saved** by us.
We **have to save** the poet.

2. The neuter singular or plural of the verbal adjective of a transitive or intransitive verb can be used *IMPERSONALLY*. Such an impersonal verbal adjective governs the same construction as the active or middle finite forms of the verb, e.g., a direct object, a genitive, a dative. Where an agent is expressed with an impersonal verbal adjective, it is usually a dative of personal agent, but occasionally the accusative is used:

σωτέον ἐστὶν τὸν ποιητὴν ἡμῖν.
We **must save** the poet. (*Literally*, "There **must be a saving** the poet by us.")
We **have to save** the poet.
(*Impersonal construction of the verbal adjective, governing the direct object* ποιητήν; *dative of personal agent* ἡμῖν)

οἶδα πάντας τοῖς νόμοις **πειστέον ὄν**.
I know that all **must obey** the laws.
(*Impersonal construction of the verbal adjective, governing the dative* τοῖς νόμοις; *accusative of personal agent*)

TENSE

Tense in the *INDICATIVE MOOD* expresses a combination of aspect and time.

1. A PRESENT INDICATIVE indicates progressive/repeated aspect in present time:

διδάσκω τοὺς νεανίας.
I **am teaching** the young men. (*Progressive aspect*)
I **teach (habitually)** the young men. (*Repeated aspect*)

The present tense of ἥκω is the equivalent of an English perfect:

ἥκομεν.
We **have arrived**.

The present verb εἶμι is used in Attic Greek as the future of ἔρχομαι:

ἴμεν εἰς τὴν πόλιν.
We **shall go** to the city.

[When used with expressions denoting past time, the present is the equivalent of the English present progressive perfect:

πάλαι τοῦτο **ποιῶ**.
I **have been doing** this **for a long time**.]

[A *HISTORICAL PRESENT* is a present tense used in narrative with the force of an aorist or imperfect. Such a present governs secondary sequence:

κελεύει τοὺς Ἀθηναίους στρατιώτᾱς πέμψαι ἵνα μὴ καταλυθείη ἡ γέφῡρα.
He **ordered** the Athenians to send soldiers in order that the bridge might not be destroyed.
(*Note the aorist optative in a purpose clause in secondary sequence after the historical present κελεύει.*)]

2. An IMPERFECT INDICATIVE indicates progressive/repeated aspect in past time:

ἐδίδασκον τοὺς νεᾱνίᾱς.
I **was teaching** the young men. (*Progressive aspect*)
I **taught (habitually)** the young men. (*Repeated aspect*)
I **used to teach** the young men. (*Repeated aspect*)

The imperfect tense of ἥκω is the equivalent of an English pluperfect:

ἧκες.
You **had arrived**.

Introduced by εἰ γάρ or εἴθε, an imperfect indicative is used in an *UN-ATTAINABLE WISH* in present time [or in an unattainable wish with progressive/repeated aspect in past time]:

εἰ γὰρ **ἐνῑκῶμεν**.
I **wish that we were winning**. (*Present time*)
[I **wish that we had been winning**. (*Progressive aspect in past time*)
I **wish that we had won (habitually)**. (*Repeated aspect in past time*)]

An imperfect indicative in the protasis and, with ἄν, in the apodosis of a *CONTRAFACTUAL CONDITIONAL SENTENCE* indicates a present unreality [or a past unreality with progressive/repeated aspect]:

εἰ οἱ ῥήτορες **ἔβλαπτον** τὴν πόλιν, αὐτοὺς **ἂν ἐπαύομεν**.
If the public speakers **were harming** the city, we **would be stopping** them. (*Present contrafactual*)
[If the public speakers **had been harming** the city, we **would have been stopping** them. (*Progressive aspect in past contrafactual*)
If the public speakers **had harmed (habitually)** the city, we **would have stopped (habitually)** them.]

[An imperfect indicative with ἄν can indicate a *PAST POTENTIAL* with progressive/repeated aspect:

ἐνīκῶμεν ἄν.
We **might have been winning**. (*Progressive aspect*)
We **might have won (habitually)**. (*Repeated aspect*)]

[An imperfect indicative with ἄν can also be a *PRESENT CONTRA-FACTUAL* or a *PAST CONTRAFACTUAL* with progressive/repeated aspect:

ἐπαύου ἄν.
You **would be being stopped**. (*Present contrafactual*)
You **would have been being stopped**. (*Progressive aspect in past contra-factual*)
You **would have been stopped (habitually)**. (*Repeated aspect in past contrafactual*)]

[The imperfects ἔδει and ἐχρῆν, and the imperfects of other impersonal expressions of obligation, necessity, propriety, or possibility can be used with the infinitive to express the lack of fulfillment of the action of the infinitive:

ἔδει τὸν Σωκράτη δίκην **διδόναι.**
Sokrates **ought to pay** a penalty (but he is not doing so).
Sokrates **ought to have paid (habitually)** a penalty (but he did not).

ἔδει τὸν Σωκράτη δίκην **δοῦναι.**
Sokrates **ought to have paid** a penalty (but he did not).]

[A *CONATIVE IMPERFECT* indicates an attempted action in past time:

ἐδίδου χρήματα τοῖς ῥήτορσιν.
He **tried to give** money to the public speakers.
He **offered** money to the public speakers.

ἔπειθον τὸν Σωκράτη φυγεῖν.
They **were trying to persuade** Sokrates to flee.]

[An *ITERATIVE IMPERFECT* is an imperfect accompanied by ἄν and shows repeated aspect in past time:

ἐδίδασκεν ἄν τοὺς νεāνίāς.
He **used to teach** the young men.]

3. A FUTURE INDICATIVE indicates either progressive/repeated or simple aspect in future time:

διδάξω τοὺς νεāνίāς.
I **shall teach** the young men. (*Repeated or simple aspect*)
I **shall be teaching** the young men. (*Progressive aspect*)

[A future indicative negated by *οὐ μή* expresses an *URGENT PROHI-BITION*:

οὐ μὴ καταλύσετε *τὴν δημοκρατίαν.*
Do not destroy the democracy.]

4. An AORIST INDICATIVE indicates an action with simple aspect in past time:

εἶδον *τὸν ἀδελφὸν τὸν Σωκράτους.*
I **saw** the brother of Sokrates.

Introduced by *εἰ γάρ* or *εἴθε*, an aorist indicative is used in an *UNATTAINABLE WISH* in past time:

εἰ γὰρ **ἐνῑκήσαμεν.**
I **wish that we had conquered.**

An aorist indicative in the protasis and, with *ἄν*, in the apodosis of a CONTRAFACTUAL CONDITIONAL SENTENCE indicates a past unreality with simple aspect:

εἰ τὸν ἀδελφὸν **εἶδον,** *χρήματα αὐτῷ* **ἔδωκα ἄν.**
If I **had seen** your brother, I **would have given** him money.

[An aorist indicative with *ἄν* can indicate a *PAST POTENTIAL* with simple aspect:

ἐπαύθης ἄν.
You **might have been stopped.**]

[An aorist indicative with *ἄν* can also indicate a *PAST CONTRAFAC-TUAL* with simple aspect:

ἐπαύθης ἄν.
You **would have been stopped** (but you were not).]

[A *GNOMIC AORIST* is an aorist expressing a general truth; a gnomic aorist governs primary sequence:

ἐάν τις τοῦτο ποιήσῃ, δίκην **ἔδωκεν** *ἵνα μὴ βλαβῇ ἡ πόλις.*
If someone does this, he **pays** a penalty in order that the city may not be harmed.
(*Present general conditional sentence with a gnomic aorist replacing the present indicative in the apodosis*)]

[An aorist indicative with *ἄν* can indicate repeated aspect in past time (*ITERATIVE AORIST*):

ἐδίδαξεν ἄν *τοὺς νεᾱνίᾱς.*
He **used to teach** the young men.]

[The aorist of a word indicating a state or condition frequently indicates the beginning of the state or condition (*INCEPTIVE AORIST*):

μετὰ τὴν μάχην **ἐδούλευσαν**.
They **became slaves** after the battle.]

5. A PERFECT INDICATIVE indicates completed aspect in present time:

πολλὰ **γέγραφα**.
I **have written** many things.

The perfect of a number of verbs has a present meaning, e.g., οἶδα, "know"; ἕστηκα, "stand":

ἴσμεν τὸν Σωκράτη ἀγαθὸν ὄντα.
We **know** that Sokrates is good.

6. A PLUPERFECT INDICATIVE indicates completed aspect in past time:

πολλὰ **ἐγεγράφη**.
I **had written** many things.

Where the perfect has a present meaning, the pluperfect has the force of an imperfect:

ᾖσμεν τὸν Σωκράτη ἀγαθὸν ὄντα.
We **knew** that Sokrates was good.

Tense in the SUBJUNCTIVE MOOD indicates aspect only:

1. A PRESENT SUBJUNCTIVE shows progressive/repeated aspect:

ἀεὶ **φυλαττώμεθα** τοὺς πολεμίους.
Let us always **be guarding against** the enemy. (*Progressive aspect*)
Let us always **guard (habitually) against** the enemy.
(*Repeated aspect*)

φοβούμεθα μὴ κακὰ **ποιῇς**.
We are afraid that you **may/will be doing** evil. (*Progressive aspect*)
We are afraid that you **may/will do** evil (**habitually**).
(*Repeated aspect*)

2. An AORIST SUBJUNCTIVE shows simple aspect:

νῦν **φυλαξώμεθα** τοὺς πολεμίους.
Now **let us guard against** the enemy.

[3. A PERFECT SUBJUNCTIVE shows completed aspect:

πεφυλαγμένοι ὦμεν τοὺς πολεμίους.
Let us have guarded against the enemy.

φοβούμεθα μὴ κακὰ **πεποιηκὼς ᾖς.**
We are afraid that you **may have done** evil.]

In the OPTATIVE MOOD a present, aorist, [or perfect] optative *not in indirect statement or indirect question* (e.g., an independent optative) shows aspect only. Any optative standing for an original indicative (e.g., in indirect statement) shows the same time and aspect as the original indicative. [Any optative standing for an original subjunctive (e.g., in an indirect deliberative question in secondary sequence) shows only the aspect of the original subjunctive.]

1. A PRESENT OPTATIVE not in indirect statement or indirect question shows only progressive/repeated aspect:

   εἰ γὰρ **πέμποιεν** τοὺς στρατιώτᾱς.
   May they **be sending** the soldiers! (*Progressive aspect*)
   May they **send** the soldiers (**habitually**)! (*Repeated aspect*)

   ἐφοβούμεθα μὴ κακὰ **ποιοίης.**
   We were afraid that you **might/would be doing** evil. (*Progressive aspect*)
   We were afraid that you **might/would do** evil (**habitually**). (*Repeated aspect*)

2. An AORIST OPTATIVE not in indirect statement or indirect question shows simple aspect only:

   εἰ γὰρ **πέμψαιεν** τοὺς στρατιώτᾱς.
   May they **send** the soldiers!

   ἐφοβούμεθα μὴ κακὰ **ποιήσειας.**
   We were afraid that you **might/would do** evil.

[3. A PERFECT OPTATIVE not in indirect statement or indirect question shows completed aspect only:

   εἰ γὰρ **πεπομφότες εἴησαν** τοὺς στρατιώτᾱς.
   May they **have sent** the soldiers!]

4. In indirect statement or question, a present optative can represent an original present indicative, [imperfect indicative, present subjunctive, or present optative]:

   εἶπεν ὅτι Σωκράτης **διδάσκοι** τοὺς νεᾱνίᾱς.
   He said that Sokrates **was teaching** the young men.
   He said "Σωκράτης διδάσκει τοὺς νεᾱνίᾱς."
   (*The original present indicative has been changed to a present optative in secondary sequence after the aorist indicative εἶπεν.*)

[εἶπεν ὅτι Σωκράτης τότε **διδάσκοι** τοὺς νεανίας.
He said that Sokrates **was** then **teaching** the young men.
He said "Σωκράτης τότε ἐδίδασκε τοὺς νεανίας."
(*The original imperfect indicative has been changed to a PRESENT optative in secondary sequence after the aorist indicative* εἶπεν.)]

[εἶπεν ὅτι Σωκράτης δίκην δώσοι εἰ τοὺς νεανίας **διδάσκοι**.
He said that Sokrates would pay a penalty if he **taught** (**habitually**) the young men.
He said "Σωκράτης δίκην δώσει ἐὰν τοὺς νεανίας διδάσκῃ."
(*The original present subjunctive showing progressive/repeated aspect in the protasis of a future more vivid conditional sentence has been changed to a present optative in secondary sequence after the aorist indicative* εἶπεν.)]

[εἶπεν ὅτι Σωκράτης δίκην **διδοίη ἂν** εἰ τοὺς νεανίας **διδάσκοι**.
He said that Sokrates **would pay** a penalty (**habitually**) if he **should teach** the young men (**habitually**).
He said "Σωκράτης δίκην διδοίη ἂν εἰ τοὺς νεανίας διδάσκοι."
(*The original present optative showing progressive/repeated aspect in the protasis and, with* ἄν, *in the apodosis of a future less vivid conditional sentence remains unchanged in indirect statement.*)]

5. A FUTURE OPTATIVE can only represent an original future indicative in indirect statement, indirect question, [and some object clauses of effort] in secondary sequence:

εἶπεν ὅτι Σωκράτης **διδάξοι** τοὺς νεανίας.
He said that Sokrates **would teach** the young men.
He said "Σωκράτης διδάξει τοὺς νεανίας."
(*The original future indicative has been changed to a future optative in secondary sequence after the aorist indicative* εἶπεν.)

[ἐμηχανᾶτο ὅπως τῆς πόλεως **ἄρξοι**.
He was contriving that he **rule** the city.
(*The future optative can be used in secondary sequence instead of the more usual future indicative.*)]

6. An AORIST OPTATIVE in indirect statement or indirect question can represent an original aorist indicative, [aorist subjunctive, or aorist optative]:

εἶπεν ὅτι Σωκράτης **διδάξειε** τοὺς νεανίας.
He said that Sokrates **taught/had taught** the young men.
He said "Σωκράτης ἐδίδαξε τοὺς νεανίας."
(*The original aorist indicative has been replaced by an aorist optative in secondary sequence after the aorist indicative* εἶπεν.)

[εἶπεν ὅτι Σωκράτης δίκην δώσοι εἰ τοὺς νεανίας **διδάξειεν.**
He said that Sokrates would pay a penalty if he **taught** the young men.
He said "Σωκράτης δίκην δώσει ἐὰν τοὺς νεανίας διδάξῃ."
(*The original aorist subjunctive showing simple aspect in the protasis of a future more vivid conditional sentence has been replaced by the aorist optative in secondary sequence introduced by the aorist indicative εἶπεν; ἐάν has been changed to εἰ.*)]

[εἶπεν ὅτι Σωκράτης δίκην **δοίη ἂν** εἰ τοὺς νεανίας **διδάξειεν.**
He said that Sokrates **would pay** a penalty if he **should teach** the young men.
He said "Σωκράτης δίκην δοίη ἂν εἰ τοὺς νεανίας διδάξειεν."
(*The original aorist optative showing simple aspect in the protasis and, with ἄν, in the apodosis of a future less vivid conditional statement remains unchanged in indirect statement.*)]

[7. A PERFECT OPTATIVE in indirect statement or indirect question can represent an original perfect indicative, pluperfect indicative, perfect subjunctive or perfect optative:

εἶπεν ὅτι Σωκράτης **δεδιδαχὼς εἴη** τοὺς νεανίας.
He said that Sokrates **had taught** the young men.
He said "Σωκράτης δεδίδαχε τοὺς νεανίας."
(*The original perfect indicative has been replaced by the perfect optative in secondary sequence after the aorist indicative εἶπεν.*)

εἶπεν ὅτι Σωκράτης τότε **δεδιδαχὼς εἴη** τοὺς νεανίας.
He said that Sokrates **had** then **taught** the young men.
He said "Σωκράτης τότε ἐδεδιδάχει τοὺς νεανίας."
(*The original pluperfect indicative has been replaced by the PERFECT optative in secondary sequence after the aorist indicative εἶπεν.*)]

Tense in the IMPERATIVE MOOD indicates aspect only.

1. A PRESENT IMPERATIVE shows progressive/repeated aspect only:
   δίδασκε τοὺς νεανίας.
   Be teaching the young men. (*Progressive aspect*)
   Teach (habitually) the young men. (*Repeated aspect*)

2. An AORIST IMPERATIVE shows simple aspect only. In negative commands with simple aspect the aorist imperative is usually replaced by the aorist subjunctive (prohibitive subjunctive).
   διδαξάτω τοὺς νεανίας.
   Let him teach the young men.

μὴ βλάψατε τὴν πόλιν.
Do not harm the city.
(*This would usually be expressed by a prohibitive subjunctive:* μὴ βλάψητε τὴν πόλιν.)

[3. A PERFECT IMPERATIVE shows completed aspect:

ταῦτα **εἰρήσθω**.
Let these things **have been said.**]

The tense of an INFINITIVE, except for those in indirect statement, the future infinitive after μέλλω, [the infinitive after verbs like ἔδει expressing unfulfilled obligation and after ὤφελον expressing an unattainable wish,] shows aspect only.

1. A PRESENT INFINITIVE not in indirect statement [or after ἔδει expressing unfulfilled obligation or ὤφελον in an unattainable wish] shows progressive/repeated aspect only:

   κακὸν τὸ ταῦτα **πρᾱ́ττειν**.
   It is bad **to be doing** these things. (*Progressive aspect*)
   It is bad **to do (habitually)** these things. (*Repeated aspect*)

2. An AORIST INFINITIVE not in indirect statement [or after ἔδει expressing unfulfilled obligation or ὤφελον in an unattainable wish] shows simple aspect only:

   ἐκέλευσα αὐτὸν **λῦσαι** τοὺς δούλους.
   I ordered him **to free** the slaves.

3. A PERFECT INFINITIVE not in indirect statement shows completed aspect only:

   κακὸν τὸ ταῦτα μὴ **πεποιηκέναι**.
   It is bad not **to have done** these things.

[4. After the imperfects ἔδει and ἐχρῆν, and the imperfects of other impersonal expressions of obligation, necessity, propriety, or possibility, a PRESENT INFINITIVE can show *UNFULFILLED OBLIGATION* in present time or in past time with progressive/repeated aspect; an AORIST INFINITIVE can show unfulfilled obligation in past time with simple aspect:

   ἔδει ὑμᾶς στρατιώτᾱς **πέμπειν**.
   You **ought to be sending** soldiers (but you are not).
   You **ought to have sent (habitually)** soldiers (but you did not).

   ἔδει ὑμᾶς στρατιώτᾱς **πέμψαι**.
   You **ought to have sent** soldiers (but you did not).]

[5. After a form of ὤφελον (second aorist of ὀφείλω, ὀφειλήσω, ὠφείλησα/ ὤφελον, ὠφείληκα, ——, ὠφειλήθην, "owe") a PRESENT INFINITIVE shows an *UNATTAINABLE WISH* in present time or in past time with progressive/repeated aspect; an AORIST INFINITIVE shows an unattainable wish in past time:

ὤφελες ταῦτα **ποιεῖν.**
Would that you **were doing** these things (but you are not).
Would that you **had (habitually) done** these things (but you did not).

ὤφελες ταῦτα **ποιῆσαι.**
Would that you **had done** these things (but you did not).

6. A PRESENT INFINITIVE in indirect statement can represent an original present indicative, [imperfect indicative, or present optative]:

νομίζω Σωκράτη **διδάσκειν** τοὺς νεανίας.
I think that Sokrates **is teaching** the young men.
I think "Σωκράτης διδάσκει τοὺς νεανίας."
(*The original present indicative has been replaced by a present infinitive.*)

[νομίζω Σωκράτη τότε **διδάσκειν** τοὺς νεανίας.
I think that Sokrates **was** then **teaching** the young men.
I think "Σωκράτης τότε ἐδίδασκε τοὺς νεανίας."
(*The original imperfect indicative has been replaced by a PRESENT infinitive.*)

[νομίζω Σωκράτη δίκην **διδόναι ἂν** εἰ τοὺς νεανίας διδάσκοι.
I think that Sokrates **would pay** a penalty if he should teach the young men.
I think "Σωκράτης δίκην διδοίη ἂν εἰ τοὺς νεανίας διδάσκοι."
(*The original present optative showing progressive/repeated aspect in the apodosis of a future less vivid conditional sentence has been changed to a present infinitive with ἄν.*)]

7. A FUTURE INFINITIVE in indirect statement represents an original future indicative:

νομίζω Σωκράτη **διδάξειν** τοὺς νεανίας.
I think that Sokrates **will teach** the young men.
I think "Σωκράτης διδάξει τοὺς νεανίας."
(*The original future indicative has been replaced by a future infinitive.*)

After the verb μέλλω, μελλήσω, ἐμέλλησα, ——, ——, ——, in the sense "be about to, be likely to," a future infinitive is used to show time subsequent to the verb:

Σωκράτης μέλλει τοὺς νεανίας **διδάξειν.**
Sokrates is about **to teach** the young men.

8. An AORIST INFINITIVE in indirect statement can represent an original aorist indicative [or aorist optative]:

νομίζω Σωκράτη τοὺς νεανίας **διδάξαι.**
I think that Sokrates **taught** the young men.
I think *"Σωκράτης τοὺς νεανίας ἐδίδαξεν."*
(*The original aorist indicative has been replaced by an aorist infinitive.*)

[*νομίζω Σωκράτη δίκην* **δοῦναι ἂν** *εἰ τοὺς νεανίας διδάξειεν.*
I think that Sokrates **would pay** a penalty if he should teach the young men.
I think *"Σωκράτης δίκην δοίη ἂν εἰ τοὺς νεανίας διδάξειεν."*
(*The original aorist optative with ἄν showing simple aspect in the apodosis of a future less vivid conditional sentence has been changed to an aorist infinitive with ἄν.*)]

9. A PERFECT INFINITIVE in indirect statement can represent an original perfect indicative [or pluperfect indicative]:

νομίζω Σωκράτη τοὺς νεανίας **δεδιδαχέναι.**
I think that Sokrates **has taught** the young men.
I think *"Σωκράτης τοὺς νεανίας δεδίδαχεν."*
(*The original perfect indicative has been replaced by a perfect infinitive.*)

[*νομίζω Σωκράτη τότε τοὺς νεανίας* **δεδιδαχέναι.**
I think that Sokrates then **had taught** the young men.
I think *"Σωκράτης τότε τοὺς νεανίας ἐδεδιδάχειν."*
(*The original pluperfect indicative has been replaced by a PERFECT infinitive.*)]

The tense of a PARTICIPLE not in indirect statement usually shows aspect only, but the context can suggest time relative to that of the main verb. A participle in indirect statement standing for an indicative shows the same time and aspect as the indicative for which it stands. [A participle in indirect statement standing for an optative shows only the same aspect as the optative for which it stands.]

1. A PRESENT PARTICIPLE not in indirect statement shows progressive/ repeated aspect of an action usually simultaneous with the action of the main verb:

ἀγαθὰ ποιεῖ τὴν πόλιν ὁ Σωκράτης τοὺς νεανίας **διδάσκων.**
Sokrates does good to the city **teaching** the young men.
Sokrates does good to the city **by teaching** the young men.
Sokrates does good to the city **when he teaches** the young men.

ἀγαθὰ ἐποίει τὴν πόλιν ὁ Σωκράτης **διδάσκων** τοὺς νεανίας.
Sokrates used to do good to the city **teaching** the young men.
Sokrates used to do good to the city **by teaching** the young men.
Sokrates used to do good to the city **when he taught (habitually)** the young men.

[A present participle can also show progressive/repeated aspect of an action prior to the action of the main verb:

νῦν τῑμῶμεν τοὺς τότε εὖ **μαχομένους**.
We are now honoring those then **fighting** well.
We are now honoring those who then **were fighting** well.]

2. A FUTURE PARTICIPLE not in indirect statement usually shows intention or purpose:

ἦλθε **καταλῡσων** τὴν πόλιν.
He came **intending to destroy** the city.
He came **to destroy** the city.

3. An AORIST PARTICIPLE not in indirect statement shows simple aspect of an action either simultaneous with or prior to the action of the main verb:

εἰσελθὼν εἰς τὴν πόλιν αἶγας ἔθῡσεν.
Upon entering the city, he sacrificed goats.

ἔλαθεν εἰς τὴν πόλιν **εἰσελθών**.
He escaped notice **entering** the city.
He **entered** the city without being noticed.

4. A PERFECT PARTICIPLE not in indirect statement shows completed aspect of an action prior to that of the main verb:

ταῦτα **πεποιηκὼς** ἀπῆλθεν.
Having done these things, he went away.

5. A PRESENT PARTICIPLE in indirect statement can represent an original present indicative, [an imperfect indicative, or a present optative]:

ἀκούω Σωκράτη **διδάσκοντα** τοὺς νεανίας.
I hear that Sokrates **is teaching** the young men.
I hear "Σωκράτης διδάσκει τοὺς νεανίας."
(*The original present indicative has been changed to a present participle.*)

[ἀκούω Σωκράτη τότε **διδάσκοντα** τοὺς νεανίας.
I hear that Sokrates **was** then **teaching** the young men.
(*Progressive aspect*)
I hear that Sokrates then **taught** the young men (**habitually**).

(*Repeated aspect*)
I hear "Σωκράτης τότε ἐδίδασκε τοὺς νεανίας."
(*The original imperfect indicative has been changed to a present participle.*)]

[ἀκούω Σωκράτη δίκην **ἂν διδόντα** εἰ τοὺς νεανίας διδάσκοι.
I hear that Sokrates **would pay** a penalty if he should teach the young men.
I hear "Σωκράτης δίκην ἂν διδοίη εἰ τοὺς νεανίας διδάσκοι."
(*The original present optative with ἄν showing progressive/repeated aspect in the apodosis of a future less vivid conditional sentence has been changed to a present participle with ἄν.*)]

6. A FUTURE PARTICIPLE in indirect statement represents an original future indicative:

   ἀκούω Σωκράτη **διδάξοντα** τοὺς νεανίας.
   I hear that Sokrates **will teach** the young men.
   I hear "Σωκράτης διδάξει τοὺς νεανίας."
   (*The original future indicative has been changed to a future participle.*)

7. An AORIST PARTICIPLE in indirect statement can represent an original aorist indicative [or aorist optative]:

   ἀκούω Σωκράτη τοὺς νεανίας **διδάξαντα**.
   I hear that Sokrates **taught** the young men.
   I hear "Σωκράτης τοὺς νεανίας ἐδίδαξεν."
   (*The original aorist indicative has been replaced by an aorist participle.*)

   [ἀκούω Σωκράτη δίκην **ἂν δόντα** εἰ τοὺς νεανίας διδάξειεν.
   I hear that Sokrates **would pay** a penalty if he should teach the young men.
   I hear "Σωκράτης δίκην ἂν δοίη εἰ τοὺς νεανίας διδάξειεν."
   (*The original aorist optative with ἄν showing simple aspect in the apodosis of a future less vivid conditional sentence has been changed to an aorist participle with ἄν.*)]

8. A PERFECT PARTICIPLE in indirect statement can represent an original perfect indicative [or pluperfect indicative]:

   ἀκούω Σωκράτη τοὺς νεανίας **δεδιδαχότα**.
   I hear that Sokrates **has taught** the young men.
   I hear "Σωκράτης τοὺς νεανίας δεδίδαχεν."
   (*The original perfect indicative has been changed to a perfect participle.*)

   [ἀκούω Σωκράτη τότε τοὺς νεανίας **δεδιδαχότα**.
   I hear that Sokrates **had** then **taught** the young men.
   I hear "Σωκράτης τότε τοὺς νεανίας ἐδεδιδάχειν."
   (*The original pluperfect indicative has been changed to a perfect participle.*)

SUMMARY OF TENSE

Tense in the indicative mood expresses a combination of time and aspect.

Tense in all the uses of the subjunctive and imperative, in all optatives not in indirect statement, indirect question, [and some object clauses of effort], and in almost all infinitives and participles not in indirect statement shows aspect only.

Tense in an optative, infinitive, or participle in indirect statement standing for an indicative shows the same time and aspect as the indicative for which it stands. Tense in an optative in indirect statement standing for a subjunctive shows only the same aspect as the subjunctive for which it stands.

VOICE

When a verb is in the *ACTIVE VOICE*, the subject performs the action:

οὐκ **ἔπαυσαν** οἱ πολῖται Σωκράτη.
The citizens **did** not **stop** Sokrates.

ὁ διδάσκαλος **ἐδίδαξε** τὸν τοῦ ῥήτορος ἀδελφόν.
The teacher **taught** the brother of the public speaker.

When a verb is in the *MIDDLE VOICE*, the subject performs the action, but the action somehow returns to the subject; the subject has some special interest in the action:

ἐν μέσῃ τῇ ὁδῷ **ἐπαύσατο** Σωκράτης.
Sokrates **stopped** in the middle of the road.

ὁ ῥήτωρ τὸν ἀδελφὸν **ἐδιδάξατο** ὑπὸ τοῦ διδασκάλου.
The public speaker **had** his brother **taught** by the teacher.

When a verb is in the *PASSIVE VOICE*, the subject receives the action from some outside agency:

οὐκ **ἐπαύθη** Σωκράτης ὑπὸ τῶν πολιτῶν.
Sokrates **was** not **stopped** by the citizens.

ὁ τοῦ ῥήτορος ἀδελφὸς **ἐδιδάχθη** ὑπὸ τοῦ διδασκάλου.
The brother of the public speaker **was taught** by the teacher.

Note the difference in meaning between the active voice and middle voice of certain verbs:

αἱρῶ	take	αἱροῦμαι	choose
ἀποδίδωμι	give away	ἀποδίδομαι	sell
ἄρχω	rule	ἄρχομαι	begin

γράφω	write	γράφομαι	indict
ἔχω	have	ἔχομαι	hold on to, be close to
παύω	make stop	παύομαι	cease, stop
τίθημι (νόμον)	make (a law) (used, e.g., of a king)	τίθεμαι (νόμον)	make (a law) (used, e.g., of a democracy)
φυλάττω	guard	φυλάττομαι	be on guard against

A verb is said to be *DEPONENT* when it lacks forms in the active voice. A verb can be completely deponent (e.g., βούλομαι, βουλήσομαι, ——, ——, βεβούλημαι, ἐβουλήθην) or partially deponent (e.g., ἀκούω, ἀκούσομαι, ἤκουσα, ἀκήκοα, ——, ἠκούσθην). Deponent verbs with an aorist middle are called *MIDDLE DEPONENTS* (e.g., ἀφικνέομαι, ἀφίξομαι, ἀφικόμην, ——, ἀφῖγμαι, ——). Deponent verbs with no aorist middle but with a deponent aorist passive are called *PASSIVE DEPONENTS* (e.g., δύναμαι, δυνήσομαι, ——, ——, δεδύνημαι, ἐδυνήθην). All deponent forms are translated by an English active form:

βούλομαι νῑκᾶν.
I **want** to win.

ἐβουλήθης νῑκᾶν.
You **wanted** to win.

ἀκούσομαι Σωκράτους.
I **shall hear** Sokrates.

[The future middle of certain verbs is often used with a passive meaning. Such verbs include:

ἀδικέω	ἀδικήσομαι	I shall be wronged
ἄρχω	ἄρξομαι	I shall be ruled
διδάσκω	διδάξομαι	I shall be taught
ἐπιβουλεύω	ἐπιβουλεύσομαι	I shall be plotted against
ἔχω	ἕξομαι	I shall be held
κωλύω	κωλύσομαι	I shall be hindered
τῑμάω	τῑμήσομαι	I shall be honored
φιλέω	φιλήσομαι	I shall be loved
φυλάττω	φυλάξομαι	I shall be guarded

ἡ γέφῡρα **φυλάξεται** ὑπὸ τῶν στρατιωτῶν.
The bridge **will be guarded** by the soldiers.

αἱ νῆσοι **ἄρξονται** ὑπὸ τῶν Ἀθηναίων.
The islands **will be ruled** by the Athenians.]

[Some verbs have a future passive and also a future middle used passively. In such verbs, the future passive forms from Principal Part VI can show simple aspect in contrast to the future middle used passively, which can show progressive/repeated aspect. Such verbs include:

ἄγω	ἄξομαι	ἀχθήσομαι
βλάπτω	βλάψομαι	βλαβήσομαι
δηλόω	δηλώσομαι	δηλωθήσομαι
καλέω	καλοῦμαι	κληθήσομαι
κρίνω	κρινοῦμαι	κριθήσομαι
λέγω	λέξομαι	λεχθήσομαι
πρᾱ́ττω	πρᾱ́ξομαι	πρᾱχθήσομαι
τῑμάω	τῑμήσομαι	τῑμηθήσομαι
φέρω	οἴσομαι	⎰ ἐνεχθήσομαι ⎱ οἰσθήσομαι

βλάψεται ὑπὸ τῶν κακῶν.
He **will be being harmed** by the wicked men.
He **will be harmed** (**habitually**) by the wicked men.
(*Progressive/repeated aspect*)

βλαβήσεται ὑπὸ τῶν κακῶν.
He **will be harmed** by the wicked men.
(*Simple aspect*)]

Some verbs in the active voice, and middle deponent forms of certain verbs, are used as the passive of other verbs. Such verbs include:

(καλῶς) λέγω speak (well) of	(καλῶς) ἀκούω be spoken (well) of
ἀποκτείνω kill	ἀποθνῄσκω die, be killed
κατάγω bring back from exile	κατέρχομαι be restored from exile
τέθηκα have set	κεῖμαι have been set, lie
(εὖ) ποιέω treat (well)	(εὖ) πάσχω be treated (well)
ἐκβάλλω throw out, exile	ἐκπίπτω be thrown out
(εἰρήνην) ποιοῦμαι make (peace)	(εἰρήνη) γίγνεται (peace) is made

WISHES

Wishes capable of fulfillment are expressed by an optative alone or introduced by εἴθε or εἰ γάρ. Tense shows aspect only. The negative is μή:

εἴθε
εἰ γὰρ ⎱ **νῑκήσαιεν** οἱ 'Αθηναῖοι.

Would that the Athenians **win**.
May the Athenians **win**.
I wish that the Athenians **would win**.

An infinitive is sometimes used instead of an optative:

τοὺς ᾿Αθηναίους **νῑκῆσαι.**
May the Athenians **win.**

Wishes incapable of fullfilment referring to the present or past can be expressed by

1. an imperfect indicative introduced by εἴθε or εἰ γάρ for a wish in present time [or for one with progressive/repeated aspect in past time]. The negative is μή:

εἴθε ⎫
εἰ γὰρ ⎭ **ἐνίκων** οἱ ᾿Αθηναῖοι.

Would that the Athenians **were (now) winning.**
I wish that the Athenians **were (now) winning.**
[**Would that** the Athenians **had won (habitually).**
I wish that the Athenians **had been winning (habitually).**]

2. an aorist indicative introduced by εἴθε or εἰ γάρ for a wish in past time with simple aspect. The negative is μή:

εἴθε ⎫
εἰ γὰρ ⎭ μὴ **ἐνῑκήθησαν** οἱ ᾿Αθηναῖοι.

Would that the Athenians **had** not **(then) been conquered.**
I wish that the Athenians **had** not **(then) been conquered.**

[3. a form of ὤφελον (second aorist of ὀφείλω, ὀφειλήσω, ὠφείλησα/ὤφελον, ὠφείληκα, ——, ὠφειλήθην, "owe") with an infinitive (present infinitive for present time or progressive/repeated aspect in past time, aorist infinitive for simple aspect in past time). The wish may be introduced by εἴθε, εἰ γάρ, or ὡς:

ὤφελον οἱ ᾿Αθηναῖοι **νῑκᾶν.**
Would that the Athenians **were (now) winning.**
Would that the Athenians **had (then) won (habitually).**

εἰ γὰρ **ὤφελον** οἱ ᾿Αθηναῖοι **νῑκῆσαι.**
Would that the Athenians **had (then) won.**]

[4. the imperfect ἐβουλόμην or the past potential ἐβουλόμην ἄν with an infinitive. The negative is οὐ:

ἐβουλόμην (ἄν) τοὺς ᾿Αθηναίους **νῑκᾶν.**
I wish that the Athenians **were (now) winning.**]

CONDITIONAL SENTENCES

[Those kinds of conditional sentences whose syntax differs from that of the corresponding English conditional sentences were presented in Unit 4. Greek has, however, other types of conditional sentences whose syntax is identical to that of the corresponding English conditional sentences. Thus in present and past time, in addition to general and contrafactual conditional sentences, there are *SIMPLE* (also called *PARTICULAR* or *DEFINITE*) conditional sentences which are neither contrafactual nor general.

Both the protasis (introduced by εἰ) and apodosis of a *PRESENT SIMPLE CONDITIONAL SENTENCE* use either the present or perfect indicative. Both the protasis (introduced by εἰ) and apodosis of a *PAST SIMPLE CONDITIONAL SENTENCE* use any past tense of the indicative:

εἰ νῦν **νῖκῶμεν**, θεοὶ αὐτοὶ ἡμᾶς **σῴζουσιν**.
If we **are** now **conquering**, the gods themselves **are saving** us.

This sentence refers to a definite, specific event in present time as opposed to a general situation ("If ever we conquer, the gods themselves save us") or one contrary to fact ("If we were [now] conquering, the gods themselves would be saving us").

εἰ Σωκράτης τοὺς νεανίᾱς **ἐδίδαξεν**, δίκην **ἔδωκεν**.
If Sokrates **taught** the young men, he **paid** a penalty.

Contrast the above sentence with a past general ("If Sokrates ever taught the young men, he always paid a penalty") and a past contrafactual conditional sentence ("If Sokrates had taught the young men, he would have paid a penalty").

In conditional sentences both parts of which refer to the future, in addition to the usual future more vivid and future less vivid conditional sentences, there is a *FUTURE MOST VIVID* conditional sentence, the protasis of which is εἰ + future indicative, and the apodosis a future indicative. Such conditional sentences are especially common in threats and warnings:

εἰ κακὰ **ποιήσεις**, δίκην **δώσεις**.
If you **do** evil, you **will pay** a penalty.

In a contrafactual conditional sentence, an imperfect indicative can represent an action in past time with progressive/repeated aspect instead of an action in present time:

εἰ τοὺς νεανίᾱς **ἐδίδασκεν**, δίκην **ἐδίδου ἄν**.
If he **were teaching** the young men, he **would be paying** a penalty.

If he **had taught (habitually)** the young men, he **would have paid (habitually)** a penalty.]

Instead of being introduced by εἰ or ἐάν, a protasis can be introduced by a relative pronoun (*RELATIVE PROTASIS*):

ὃς ἂν ταῦτα ποιήσῃ δίκην δώσει.
Whoever does these things will pay a penalty.
If anyone does these things, he will pay a penalty.

Sentences with temporal clauses referring to future time have the same syntax as future more vivid conditional sentences. Those with general temporal clauses follow the syntax of present and past general conditional sentences:

ἐπειδὰν ταῦτα ποιήσῃς, δίκην δώσεις.
After you have done these things, you will pay a penalty.
When you do these things, you will pay a penalty.
(*Future more vivid temporal clause showing time prior to that of the main verb*)

ἐπειδὰν ταῦτα ποιήσῃς, δίκην δίδως.
After you do these things, you pay a penalty.
When you do these things, you pay a penalty.
(*Present general temporal clause showing time prior to that of the main verb*)

ἐπειδὴ ταῦτα ποιήσειας, δίκην ἐδίδους.
After you did these things, you paid a penalty (habitually).
When you did these things, you paid a penalty (habitually).
(*Past general temporal clause showing time prior to that of the main verb*)

The chart of conditional sentences on pages 750–51 includes the relative protases and those temporal clauses which follow the syntax of the protases of conditional sentences.

A protasis from one type of conditional sentence can be used with an apodosis from another type to give a *MIXED CONDITIONAL SENTENCE*. For example, a future less vivid protasis can be used with an apodosis of a future more vivid conditional sentence:

εἰ Σωκράτης τοὺς νεᾱνίᾱς **διδάξειεν**, δίκην **δώσει**.
If Sokrates **should teach** the young men, he **will pay** a penalty.
(*Future less vivid protasis and future more vivid apodosis in a mixed conditional sentence*)

Again, the time of the protasis can differ from that of the apodosis:

εἰ Σωκράτης τοὺς νεανίας **ἐδίδαξεν**, δίκην **ἂν ἐδίδου**.
If Sokrates **had taught** the young men, he **would be paying** a penalty.
(*Past contrafactual protasis and present contrafactual apodosis in a mixed conditional sentence*)

A *CIRCUMSTANTIAL PARTICIPLE* can replace the protasis of a conditional sentence. The negative with such participles is μή:

τοὺς νεανίας **διδάξας**, Σωκράτης δίκην ἂν ἔδωκεν.
Having taught the young men, Sokrates would have paid a penalty.
If he had taught the young men, Sokrates would have paid a penalty.
(*Conditional participle serving as the protasis of a past contrafactual conditional sentence*)

μὴ ταῦτα **ποιῶν**, οὐκ ἂν δίκην ἐδίδου.
Not doing these things, he would not be paying a penalty.
If he were not doing these things, he would not be paying a penalty.
(*Circumstantial participle serving as the protasis of a present contrafactual conditional sentence*)

The future indicative or optative with ἄν of an apodosis can be replaced by an independent subjunctive, optative, or imperative, with the negative proper to each:

ἐὰν οἱ ἄγγελοι ἔλθωσιν, **οὐ δεξόμεθα** αὐτούς.
If the messengers come, we **shall not receive** them.

ἐὰν οἱ ἄγγελοι ἔλθωσιν, **μὴ δεξώμεθα** αὐτούς.
If the messengers come, **let us not receive** them.

ἐὰν οἱ ἄγγελοι ἔλθωσιν, **μὴ δεξαίμεθα** αὐτούς.
If the messengers come, **I wish that** we **would not receive** them.

ἐὰν οἱ ἄγγελοι ἔλθωσιν, **δέξασθε** αὐτούς.
If the messengers come, **receive** them.

εἰ οἱ ἄγγελοι ἔλθοιεν, **μὴ δέξησθε** αὐτούς.
If the messengers should come, **do not receive** them.

SUMMARY OF CONDITIONAL SENTENCES AND SENTENCES WITH TEMPORAL CLAUSES

NAME	PROTASIS (negative μή)	APODOSIS (negative οὐ)
[PRESENT SIMPLE]	εἰ / ὅς, ἥ, ὅ + present or perfect indicative *is doing, has done*	present or perfect indicative *is doing, has done*
PRESENT GENERAL	ἐάν / ὅς, ἥ, ὅ + ἄν / e.g., ἐπειδάν, ὅταν + subjunctive *does*	present indicative *does*
PRESENT CONTRAFACTUAL	εἰ / ὅς, ἥ, ὅ + imperfect indicative *were doing*	imperfect indicative + ἄν *would be doing*
[PAST SIMPLE]	εἰ / ὅς, ἥ, ὅ + any past indicative *did, was doing, had done*	any past indicative *did, was doing, had done*

	Protasis	Apodosis
PAST GENERAL	εἰ / ὅς, ἥ, ὅ / e.g., ἐπειδή, ὅτε } + optative / *did*	imperfect indicative / *did*
PAST CONTRAFACTUAL	εἰ / ὅς, ἥ, ὅ } + aorist indicative / *had done* [+ imperfect indicative / *had been doing* / *had done (habitually)*]	aorist indicative + ἄν / *would have done* / imperfect indicative + ἄν / *would have been doing* / *would have done (habitually)*
[FUTURE MOST VIVID]	εἰ / ὅς, ἥ, ὅ } + future indicative / *does*	future indicative / *will do*]
FUTURE MORE VIVID	ἐάν / ὅς, ἥ, ὅ + ἄν / e.g., ἐπειδάν, ὅταν } + subjunctive / *does*	future indicative / *will do*
FUTURE LESS VIVID	εἰ / ὅς, ἥ, ὅ } + optative / *should do*	optative + ἄν / *would do*

TEMPORAL CLAUSES

TEMPORAL CONJUNCTIONS

ἐπεί	after, when, whenever (*prior action*)
ἐπειδή	after, when, whenever (*prior action*)
ἐπειδάν	after, when, whenever (*prior action*)
ἕως	as long as, while, until (*simultaneous or subsequent action*)
μέχρι	as long as, until (*simultaneous or subsequent action*)
ὅτε	when, whenever (*simultaneous action*)
ὅταν	when, whenever (*simultaneous action*)
πρίν	before, until (*subsequent action*)

1. *PAST DEFINITE TEMPORAL CLAUSES* take a past tense of the indicative:

   ἐπειδὴ εἰς τὴν πόλιν ἦλθεν, τὸν ἀδελφὸν εἶδεν.
   After he went to the city, he saw his brother. ,

   ἀπέθανεν **ὅτε ᾔειν εἰς τὴν πόλιν.**
   He died **when he was going to the city.**

   ἔμεινεν ἐν ἀγορᾷ **μέχρι τὸν ἀδελφὸν εἶδεν.**
   He remained in the market place **until he saw his brother.**

   οὐκ ἀπῆλθεν **πρὶν τὸν ἀδελφὸν εἶδεν.**
   He did not go away **until he saw his brother.**

2. Sentences with *PRESENT* and *PAST GENERAL TEMPORAL CLAUSES* follow the syntax of present and past general conditional sentences, respectively (for formulas, see the chart on pages 750–51).

   ἐπειδὰν εἰς τὴν πόλιν ἔλθῃ, τὸν ἀδελφὸν ὁρᾷ.
   Whenever he goes to the city, he sees his brother.

   ἐπειδὴ εἰς τὴν πόλιν ἔλθοι, τὸν ἀδελφὸν ἑώρᾱ.
   Whenever he went to the city, he saw his brother.

3. A sentence with a *TEMPORAL CLAUSE REFERRING TO FUTURE TIME* follows the syntax of future more vivid conditional sentences (for formulas, see pages 750–51).

   ἐπειδὰν εἰς τὴν πόλιν ἔλθῃ, τὸν ἀδελφὸν ὄψεται.
   After he goes to the city, he will see his brother.

   ὅταν ταῦτα ποιῇ, εὐδαίμων ἔσται.
   When he does these things, he will be happy.

μενεῖ ἐν ἀγορᾷ **μέχρι ἂν τὸν ἀδελφὸν ἴδῃ.**
He will remain in the market place **until he sees his brother.**

οὐκ ἄπεισιν ἐκ τῆς πόλεως **πρὶν ἂν τὸν ἀδελφὸν ἴδῃ.**
He will not go away from the city **until he sees his brother.**

Even when the main verb is present, if a temporal clause refers to future time, it follows the syntax of the protasis of a future more vivid conditional sentence:

μένει ἐν τῇ πόλει **μέχρι ἂν τὸν ἀδελφὸν ἴδῃ.**
He is (now) staying in the city **until he sees his brother.**

4. A temporal clause introduced by *πρίν*, "until," is used after a negative main verb and follows the rules for temporal clauses as in the above examples. When *πρίν* governs an infinitive, it means "before" and is used after positive main clauses:

ἀπῆλθε **πρὶν τὸν ἀδελφὸν ἰδεῖν.**
He went away **before seeing his brother.**
He went away **before he saw his brother.**

CAUSAL CLAUSES

CAUSAL CONJUNCTIONS

ἐπεί	since
ἐπειδή	since
ὅτι	because
[*διότι*	because]
ὡς	as, since, because

1. A causal clause stating a fact has its verb in the indicative:

ἐπειδὴ οὐχ οἷός τ᾽ ἦν τὴν γυναῖκα λιπεῖν, *ἔμεινεν ἐν τῇ πόλει.*
Since he was unable to leave his wife, he remained in the city.

διὰ τοῦτο μένει ἐν τῇ πόλει **ὅτι οὐχ οἷός τ᾽ ἐστὶ τὴν γυναῖκα λιπεῖν.**
He is staying in the city on account of this, **because he is unable to leave his wife.**

ὡς οὐχ οἷός τ᾽ ἐστὶ τὴν γυναῖκα λιπεῖν *μένει ἐν τῇ πόλει.*
As he is not able to leave his wife, he is staying in the city.

[2. A causal clause can also contain an *UNREAL INDICATIVE* or *POTENTIAL OPTATIVE*:

οὐ ταῦτα ἐποίησεν ὅτι **ἀπέθανεν ἄν.**
He did not do these things because he **would have been killed.**

οὐ ταῦτα ποιεῖ ὅτι **ἀποθάνοι ἄν**.
He is not doing these things because he **might be killed**.]

[3. After a secondary main verb a verb in a causal clause can be in the optative in implied indirect statement, giving an *ALLEGED CAUSE*:

ἔμεινεν ἐν τῇ πόλει **ὡς οὐχ οἷός τ' εἴη** τὴν γυναῖκα λιπεῖν.
He remained in the city **because, as he said, he was unable to leave his wife**.]

4. A circumstantial participle can also indicate cause. When such a participle is introduced by ἅτε or οἷα, the writer or speaker assumes responsibility for the statement. When the participle is introduced by ὡς, the cause is that of the subject of the sentence or someone else prominent in the sentence:

οὐχ οἷός τ' ὢν τὴν γυναῖκα λιπεῖν, ἔμεινεν ἐν τῇ πόλει.
Not being able to leave his wife, he remained in the city.
Since he was not able to leave his wife, he remained in the city.

ἅτε οὐχ οἷός τ' ὢν τὴν γυναῖκα λιπεῖν, ἔμεινεν ἐν τῇ πόλει.
Not being able to leave his wife, he remained in the city.
Since he was not able to leave his wife, he remained in the city.
(*Speaker's assertion*)

ὡς οὐχ οἷός τ' ὢν τὴν γυναῖκα λιπεῖν, ἔμεινεν ἐν τῇ πόλει.
Not being able to leave his wife, as he said, he remained in the city.
(*Subject's alleged cause, not asserted by speaker*)

5. A relative clause, especially when the relative pronoun is accompanied by the particle γε, can have a causal force. The negative is, as usual, οὐ:

ἀγαθοί εἰσιν **οἵ γε ταῦτα οὐ ποιοῦσιν**.
They are good **who do not do these things**.
They are good **because they do not do these things**.

RESULT CLAUSES

Result clauses are introduced by the conjunction ὥστε, "so as, so that, with the result that."

1. Clauses of *NATURAL RESULT* have their verbs in the infinitive. The negative is μή:

οὕτω καλῶς διδάσκομεν ὥστε τοὺς μαθητὰς πολλὰ **μανθάνειν**.
So well do we teach as for the students **to be learning** many things.
So well do we teach as for the students **to learn (habitually)** many things.

οὕτω κακῶς ἐκεῖνοι διδάσκουσιν ὥστε τοὺς μαθητὰς μὴ πολλὰ **μανθάνειν.**

So badly do those men teach as for the students not **to be learning** many things.

So badly do those men teach as for the students not **to learn (habitually)** many things.

2. Clauses of *ACTUAL RESULT* have their verbs in the indicative. The negative is *οὐ*:

οὕτω καλῶς διδάσκομεν ὥστε οἱ μαθηταὶ πολλὰ **μανθάνουσιν.**

So well do we teach that the students **learn** many things.

οὕτω κακῶς ἐκεῖνοι διδάσκουσιν ὥστε οἱ μαθηταὶ οὐ πολλὰ **μανθάνουσιν.**

So badly do those men teach that the students do not **learn** many things.

[3. The conjunction *ὥστε* can also introduce an imperative, a hortatory or prohibitive subjunctive, a potential optative, or a potential or unreal indicative:

οὐκ ἴσασιν οὐδέν. **ὥστε διδάξωμεν** αὐτούς.

They know nothing. **As a result/And so let us teach** them.

οὕτω κακῶς ἐκεῖνοι διδάσκουσιν ὥστε οἱ μαθηταὶ οὐκ **ἂν** πολλὰ **μανθάνοιεν.**

So badly do those men teach that the students **might** not **learn** many things.]

[4. A relative clause, often introduced by *ὅστις*, can indicate result (*RELATIVE CLAUSE OF RESULT*). The negative is *οὐ*.

τίς οὕτω ἄφρων ἐστὶν **ὅστις τοῦτο οὐκ οἶδεν;**

Who is so foolish **who does not know this?**

Who is so foolish **that he does not know this?**]

[PROVISO CLAUSE

An infinitive or (less frequently) a future indicative introduced by *ἐφ' ᾧ* or *ἐφ' ᾧτε,* "on condition that, for the purpose of," gives a stipulation or proviso. The negative is *μή*:

ἀφήσομέν σε **ἐφ' ᾧ μὴ** τὴν πόλιν βλάπτειν.

We shall let you go **on condition of not harming the city.**

We shall let you go **on condition that you not harm the city.**

ἀφήσομέν σε **ἐφ' ᾧ μὴ** τὴν πόλιν βλάψεις.

We shall let you go **on condition that you not harm the city.**]

RELATIVE CLAUSES

1. A relative clause of fact has its verb in the indicative. The negative is *οὐ*:

   Σωκράτης ὃς τὴν πόλιν **ἔβλαψεν** ἄξιός ἐστι πᾶσιν θανάτου.
   Sokrates, who **harmed** the city, is worthy of death in the opinion of all.

2. A relative clause may be the equivalent of the protasis of a conditional sentence (*RELATIVE PROTASIS*); such relative protases follow the formulas given in the chart on pages 750–51.

   ὃς ἂν ταῦτα διδάσκῃ κακός ἐστιν.
   Whoever teaches these things is evil.
   If anyone teaches these things, he is evil.

   [NOTE that a relative clause with an indefinite antecedent has a conditional force and takes the negative *μή*. The verb in such a clause can be an indicative in a simple conditional sentence:

   ἃ μὴ οἶδα οὐ νομίζω εἰδέναι.
   What I do not know, I do not think I know.

   The negative *μή* shows that the antecedent is indefinite and that the relative clause has a conditional force, being equivalent to:

   εἴ τινα μὴ οἶδα, ταῦτα οὐ νομίζω εἰδέναι.
   If I do not know certain things, I do not think that I know them.]

[3. An imperative or any of the independent subjunctives or optatives can be used in a relative clause with their usual negatives:

   Σωκράτης ὃς **ἀποθάνοι** ἄξιός ἐστι πᾶσι θανάτου.
   Sokrates, who **I wish would be killed,** is worthy of death in the opinion of all. (*Optative of wish in a relative clause*)

   Σωκράτης ὃν **μὴ ἀφῆτε** ἄξιός ἐστι πᾶσι θανάτου.
   Sokrates, whom **do not let go,** is worthy of death in the opinion of all.
   Sokrates—and **do not let** him go—is worthy of death in the opinion of all.
   Sokrates, whom **you should not let go,** is worthy of death in the opinion of all. (*Prohibitive subjunctive*)]

4. A relative clause may indicate [purpose (future indicative, negative *μή*), result, or] cause:

   [πέμπομεν ἐκ τῆς πόλεως τοὺς ἀγγέλους **οἳ μὴ ἀποθανοῦνται.**
   We are sending the messengers out of the city **who will not be killed.**
   We are sending the messengers out of the city **in order that they not be killed.**

οὕτως ἄφρων εἶ **ὅστις τοῦτον οὐκ ἀφίῃς**.
You are so foolish **who are not letting this man go.**
You are so foolish **that you are not letting this man go.**]

ἄφρων εἶ **ὅς γε τοῦτον ἀφιεῖς.**
You are foolish **who are letting this man go.**
You are foolish **because you are letting this man go.**

SEQUENCE OF MOODS

SEQUENCE OF MOODS means that in certain kinds of complex sentences a primary tense of the main verb (present, future, perfect, [future perfect]) governs a subjunctive in the dependent clause; a secondary main verb (imperfect, aorist, pluperfect) governs an optative in the dependent clause.

MAIN VERB	*DEPENDENT VERB*
PRIMARY SEQUENCE	
Present Indicative	Subjunctive Mood
Future Indicative	(Tense shows aspect.)
Perfect Indicative	
[Future Perfect Indicative]	
SECONDARY SEQUENCE	
Imperfect Indicative	Optative Mood
Aorist Indicative	(Tense shows aspect.)
Pluperfect Indicative	

[A historical present (cf. page 731) counts as a secondary main verb.]

[A gnomic aorist (cf. page 733) counts as a primary main verb.]

Any imperative, independent subjunctive, or independent optative counts as primary.

PURPOSE CLAUSES

A *PURPOSE CLAUSE* (a dependent clause giving a reason or purpose, i.e., answering the question, "Why?") is introduced by the conjunctions ἵνα, ὡς, ὅπως, "in order that," (negative ἵνα μή, ὡς μή, ὅπως μή, [or μή alone]) with its verb in the subjunctive or optative according to sequence of moods.

ἴμεν εἰς τὴν πόλιν **ἵνα Σωκράτη ἴδωμεν.**
We shall go to the city **in order that we may see Sokrates.**
(*Subjunctive in primary sequence after the future ἴμεν*)

ᾖμεν εἰς τὴν πόλιν **ἵνα Σωκράτη ἴδοιμεν.**
We were going to the city **in order that we might see Sokrates.**
(*Optative in secondary sequence after the imperfect* ᾖμεν)

ᾖμεν εἰς τὴν πόλιν **ἵνα Σωκράτη ἴδωμεν.**
We were going to the city **in order that we might see Sokrates.**
(*Retained subjunctive in secondary sequence after the imperfect* ᾖμεν)

μαχεσώμεθα **ἵνα μὴ καταλυθῇ ἡ πόλις.**
Let us fight **in order that the city may not be destroyed.**
(*Subjunctive in primary sequence after the hortatory subjunctive* μαχεσώμεθα)

[The particle ἄν can be added to purpose clauses introduced by ὅπως or ὡς
with no difference in meaning:

ἵμεν εἰς τὴν πόλιν **ὅπως ἄν Σωκράτη ἴδωμεν.**
We shall go to the city **in order that we may see Sokrates.**

ᾖμεν εἰς τὴν πόλιν **ὅπως ἄν Σωκράτη ἴδοιμεν.**
We were going to the city **in order that we might see Sokrates.**

The future indicative is occasionally used in purpose clauses:

ἵμεν εἰς τὴν πόλιν **ὅπως Σωκράτη ὀψόμεθα.**
We shall go to the city **in order that we may see Sokrates.**

In a purpose clause depending on an unreal or contrafactual indicative, the
verb is in the indicative to indicate *UNFULFILLED PURPOSE*:

εἰ μὴ ἐκωλύθην, ἦλθον ἄν εἰς τὴν πόλιν **ἵνα Σωκράτη εἶδον.**
If I had not been prevented, I would have gone to the city **in order that
I might have seen Sokrates** (but I was prevented, I did not go, and I did
not see Sokrates).]

ALTERNATIVE WAYS OF EXPRESSING PURPOSE

1. purpose clause
2. circumstantial participle
3. articular infinitive with a preposition like ὑπέρ
[4. articular infinitive in a genitive of purpose]
[5. relative purpose clause]

FEAR CLAUSES

A *FEAR CLAUSE* is a dependent clause serving as an object of a verb of
fearing. Such clauses are introduced by the conjunction μή, "that" (negative
μὴ οὐ, "that not"), and take the subjunctive or optative according to sequence of

moods when the fear refers to an action subsequent to the verb of fearing, the indicative when the fear refers to an action contemporaneous with or prior to the verb of fearing:

φοβούμεθα μὴ ἡ πόλις καταλυθῇ.
We are afraid **that the city may/will be destroyed.**
(*Subjunctive in primary sequence after the present φοβούμεθα*)

ἐφοβούμεθα μὴ ἡ πόλις καταλυθείη.
We were afraid **that the city might/would be destroyed.**
(*Optative in secondary sequence after the imperfect ἐφοβούμεθα*)

ἐφοβούμεθα μὴ ἡ πόλις καταλυθῇ.
We were afraid **that the city might/would be destroyed.**
(*Retained subjunctive in secondary sequence after the imperfect ἐφοβούμεθα*)

[A future indicative is rarely used in a fear clause instead of a subjunctive:

φοβούμεθα μὴ ἡ πόλις καταλυθήσεται.
We are afraid **that the city may/will be destroyed.**]

OBJECT CLAUSES OF EFFORT

An *OBJECT CLAUSE OF EFFORT* is a dependent clause serving as the direct object of a verb of effort, striving, etc. Such clauses answer the question, "What?" in contrast to purpose clauses, which answer the question, "Why?" Object clauses of effort are introduced by the conjunction ὅπως (negative ὅπως μή) and regularly take the future indicative even in secondary sequence:

μηχανᾶται **ὅπως** ἡ πόλις καταλυθήσεται.
He is contriving **that the city be destroyed.**

ἐμηχανᾶτο **ὅπως** ἡ πόλις καταλυθήσεται.
He was contriving **that the city be destroyed.**

μηχανᾶται **ὅπως** ἡ πόλις μὴ καταλυθήσεται.
He is contriving **that the city not be destroyed.**

Such clauses are sometimes used independently in an urgent command or exhortation:

ὅπως μὴ ταῦτα ποιήσεις.
See to it that you don't do these things.

[After a secondary main verb, the future indicative is occasionally replaced by a future optative in implied indirect statement:

ἐμηχανᾶτο **ὅπως** ἡ πόλις καταλυθήσοιτο.
He was contriving **that the city be destroyed.**]

[Occasionally, an object clause of effort follows the rules for a purpose clause, taking either the subjunctive or the optative according to sequence of moods. Tense in such clauses shows aspect only.

μηχανᾶται ὅπως ἡ πόλις **καταλυθῇ**.
He is contriving that the city **be destroyed**.
(*Aorist subjunctive showing simple aspect in an object clause of effort in primary sequence after the present μηχανᾶται instead of the more usual future indicative*)

ἐμηχανᾶτο ὅπως ἡ πόλις **καταλύοιτο**.
He was contriving that the city **be destroyed**.
(*Present optative showing progressive/repeated aspect in an object clause of effort in secondary sequence after the imperfect ἐμηχανᾶτο instead of the more usual future indicative*)

ἐμηχανᾶτο ὅπως ἡ πόλις **καταλύηται**.
He was contriving that the city **be destroyed**.
(*Retained present subjunctive showing progressive/repeated aspect in an object clause of effort in secondary sequence after the imperfect ἐμηχανᾶτο*)]

INDIRECT STATEMENT AND INDIRECT QUESTION

A statement may be quoted directly or indirectly. Direct quotation preserves the speaker's words unchanged; indirect quotation incorporates an original statement or question (words, thoughts, perceptions) into a complex sentence. The indirect quotation of an original statement whose verb is an indicative, [a potential optative, or an optative in the apodosis of a future less vivid conditional sentence] is called an *INDIRECT STATEMENT*. The indirect quotation of an original question is called an *INDIRECT QUESTION*.

[An original imperative, optative of wish, hortatory subjunctive, or prohibitive subjunctive is expressed indirectly, e.g., by being made the object of a verb of commanding ("He commanded John to do this" is an indirect form of "John, do this") or by being turned into an indirect statement ("I said that we should go" is an indirect form of "Let us go").]

INDIRECT STATEMENT

Independent clauses and the main clauses of complex sentences are treated differently from subordinate clauses in indirect statement.

INDEPENDENT CLAUSES IN INDIRECT STATEMENT

1. FINITE CONSTRUCTION

After certain verbs (e.g., λέγω, ἀκούω), an indirect statement can be introduced by the conjunctions ὅτι or ὡς, "that."

In *primary sequence* no change is made in the mood or tense of an original indicative [or optative].

In *secondary sequence* an original indicative is changed to the same tense of the optative or is retained for emphasis as an indicative. An imperfect or pluperfect indicative is usually retained, [but an imperfect indicative may be changed to a present optative and a pluperfect indicative to a perfect optative when the context makes clear what is being represented. An unreal or contrafactual indicative is always retained.]

Thus, an original indicative may change to an optative in secondary sequence; [an original optative remains unchanged in primary and secondary sequence.]

The negative of an original statement [and the particle ἄν] remain unchanged in indirect statement.

> λέγετε ὅτι Σωκράτης τοὺς νεανίας **διδάξει**.
> You say that Sokrates **will teach** the young men.
> You say "Σωκράτης τοὺς νεανίας διδάξει."
> (*The original future indicative remains unchanged in primary sequence after the present indicative λέγετε.*)

> ἐλέγετε ὅτι Σωκράτης τοὺς νεανίας οὐ **διδάξοι**.
> You said (habitually) that Sokrates **would** not **teach** the young men.
> You said "Σωκράτης τοὺς νεανίας οὐ διδάξει."
> (*The original future indicative has been changed to a future optative in secondary sequence after the imperfect ἐλέγετε.*)

> ἐλέγετε ὡς Σωκράτης τοὺς νεανίας **διδάξει**.
> You said that Sokrates **would teach** the young men.
> You said "Σωκράτης τοὺς νεανίας διδάξει."
> (*The original future indicative has been retained for emphasis in secondary sequence after the imperfect ἐλέγετε.*)

> ἀκούσει ὅτι οἱ στρατιῶται **ἔφυγον**.
> You will hear that the soldiers **fled**.
> You will hear "οἱ στρατιῶται ἔφυγον."
> (*The original aorist indicative is retained in primary sequence after the future indicative ἀκούσει.*)

ἤκουσας ὡς οἱ στρατιῶται **φύγοιεν.**
You heard that the soldiers **fled/had fled.**
You heard "*οἱ στρατιῶται ἔφυγον.*"
(*The original aorist indicative has been changed to an aorist optative in secondary sequence after the aorist indicative ἤκουσας.*)

ἤκουσας ὅτι οἱ στρατιῶται μετὰ ἐκείνην τὴν μάχην τότε **ἔφευγον.**
You heard that the soldiers after that battle **were** then **fleeing.**
You heard "*οἱ στρατιῶται μετὰ ἐκείνην τὴν μάχην τότε ἔφευγον.*"
(*The original imperfect indicative has been retained in secondary sequence after the aorist indicative ἤκουσας.*)

[ἤκουσας ὅτι οἱ στρατιῶται μετὰ ἐκείνην τὴν μάχην τότε **φεύγοιεν.**
You heard that the soldiers after that battle **were** then **fleeing.**
You heard "*οἱ στρατιῶται μετὰ ἐκείνην τὴν μάχην τότε ἔφευγον.*"
(*The original imperfect indicative has been changed to a present optative in secondary sequence after the aorist indicative ἤκουσας.*)]

[ἀκούσει ὅτι οἱ στρατιῶται **φύγοιεν ἄν.**
You will hear that the soldiers **may flee.**
You will hear "*οἱ στρατιῶται φύγοιεν ἄν.*"
(*The original potential optative, with aorist tense showing simple aspect, remains unchanged in primary sequence after the future indicative ἀκούσει.*)]

[ἤκουσας ὅτι οἱ στρατιῶται **φεύγοιεν ἄν.**
You heard that the soldiers **might flee.**
You heard "*οἱ στρατιῶται φεύγοιεν ἄν.*"
(*The original potential optative, with present tense showing progressive/ repeated aspect, remains unchanged in secondary sequence after the aorist indicative ἤκουσας.*)]

[ἤκουσας ὅτι οἱ στρατιῶται **ἔφυγον ἄν.**
You heard that the soldiers **might have fled.**
You heard that the soldiers **would have fled.**
You heard "*οἱ στρατιῶται ἔφυγον ἄν.*"
(*The original aorist indicative with ἄν, a past potential indicative or past contrafactual indicative with simple aspect, must remain unchanged in secondary sequence after the aorist indicative ἤκουσας.*)]

2. *INFINITIVE PLUS SUBJECT ACCUSATIVE*

After certain verbs (e.g., φημί, νομίζω), the verb of a direct statement is expressed in indirect statement by an infinitive of the same tense. [An original imperfect indicative is represented by a present infinitive, an original pluperfect indicative by a perfect infinitive.] The construction is not affected by the tense of the main verb.

The negative of the original statement [and the particle ἄν] remain unchanged.

If the subject of the indirect statement is other than that of the introductory verb, it is expressed by a subject accusative. The predicate nominative of the original statement becomes a predicate accusative.

If the subject of the indirect statement is the same as that of the introductory verb, it is generally omitted. The predicate nominative of the original statement remains a predicate nominative.

νομίζω Σωκράτη τοὺς νεανίας οὐ **διδάξαι.**
I think that Sokrates **did** not **teach** the young men.
I think "Σωκράτης τοὺς νεανίας οὐκ ἐδίδαξεν."
(The original aorist indicative has been changed to an aorist infinitive.)

ἐνόμιζον Σωκράτη τοὺς νεανίας **διδάξαι.**
I thought (habitually) that Sokrates **taught/had taught** the young men.
I thought (habitually) "Σωκράτης τοὺς νεανίας ἐδίδαξεν."
(The original aorist indicative has been changed to an aorist infinitive.)

[νομίζω Σωκράτη τοὺς νεανίας τότε **διδάσκειν.**
I think that Sokrates **was** then **teaching** the young men.
I think "Σωκράτης τοὺς νεανίας τότε ἐδίδασκεν."
(The original imperfect indicative has been changed to a present infinitive.)]

[νομίζω Σωκράτη τοὺς νεανίας τότε **δεδιδαχέναι.**
I think that Sokrates **had** then **taught** the young men.
I think "Σωκράτης τοὺς νεανίας τότε ἐδεδιδάχειν."
(The original pluperfect indicative has been changed to a PERFECT infinitive.)]

νομίζεις τοὺς νεανίας **διδάξειν.**
You think that **you will teach** the young men.
You think "τοὺς νεανίας διδάξω."
(The original future indicative has been changed to a future infinitive. Since there is no subject expressed, it is the same as that of the introductory verb.)

νομίζω **αὐτὸν** τοὺς νεανίας **διδάξειν.**
I think that **he will teach** the young men.
I think "τοὺς νεανίας διδάξει."
(The original future indicative has been changed to a future infinitive. The subject of the original statement, which is contained in the verb διδάξει, is expressed by the accusative subject of the infinitive in indirect statement.)

νομίζω Σωκράτη οὐκ **ἀγαθὸν εἶναι.**
I think that Sokrates **is** not **good.**
I think "Σωκράτης οὐκ ἀγαθός ἐστιν."

(The original present indicative has been changed to a present infinitive. The predicate adjective in the nominative has become a predicate adjective in the accusative.)

νομίζεις **ἀγαθὸς εἶναι**.

You think that **you are good**.

You think "ἀγαθός εἰμι."

(The original present indicative has been changed to a present infinitive. Since there is no subject expressed, it is the same as that of the main verb. The predicate adjective in the nominative remains a nominative.)

[νομίζω Σωκράτη τοὺς νεᾱνίᾱς **διδάσκειν ἄν**.

I think that Sokrates **may teach** the young men (**habitually**).

I think that Sokrates **might have taught** the young men (**habitually**).

I think that Sokrates **would be teaching/would have taught** (**habitually**) the young men.

I think   "Σωκράτης τοὺς νεᾱνίᾱς διδάσκοι ἄν" or

          "Σωκράτης τοὺς νεᾱνίᾱς ἐδίδασκεν ἄν."

(The original statement contained either a present optative with ἄν, i.e., a potential optative with progressive/repeated aspect, or an imperfect indicative with ἄν, i.e., a past potential with progressive/repeated aspect, or a present contrafactual or past contrafactual indicative with progressive/repeated aspect. Context determines meaning.)]

[νομίζω Σωκράτη τοὺς νεᾱνίᾱς **διδάξαι ἄν**.

I think that Sokrates **may teach** the young men.

I think that Sokrates **may have taught** the young men.

I think that Sokrates **would have taught** the young men.

I think   "Σωκράτης τοὺς νεᾱνίᾱς διδάξειεν ἄν" or

          "Σωκράτης τοὺς νεᾱνίᾱς ἐδίδαξεν ἄν."

(The original statement contained either an aorist optative with ἄν, i.e., a potential optative with simple aspect, or an aorist indicative with ἄν, i.e., a past potential or past contrafactual indicative with simple aspect. Context determines meaning.)]

3. *PARTICIPLE PLUS SUBJECT ACCUSATIVE*

After certain verbs (e.g., ἀκούω, δείκνῡμι), the verb of a direct statement is expressed in indirect statement by a participle of the same tense. [An original imperfect indicative is represented by a present participle, an original pluperfect indicative by a perfect participle.] The construction is not affected by the tense of the main verb.

The negative of an original statement [and the particle ἄν] remain unchanged.

If the subject of the indirect statement is other than that of the introductory verb, it is expressed by a subject accusative with which the participle agrees. A predicate nominative of the original statement becomes a predicate accusative.

If the subject of the indirect statement is the same as that of the introductory verb, it is generally omitted, and the participle agrees with the subject. A predicate nominative of the original statement remains a predicate nominative.

ἀκούω Σωκράτη τοὺς νεανίας **διδάσκοντα.**
I hear that Sokrates **is teaching** the young men.
I hear "Σωκράτης τοὺς νεανίας διδάσκει."
(*The original present indicative has been changed to a present participle.*)

ἤκουσα **αὐτὸν** τοὺς νεανίας **διδάσκοντα.**
I heard that **he was teaching** the young men.
I heard "τοὺς νεανίας διδάσκει."
(*The original present indicative has been changed to a present participle. The subject of the verb of the original statement, which is contained in the verb διδάσκει, is expressed by the accusative subject of the participle in indirect statement.*)

[ἀκούω Σωκράτη τοὺς νεανίας τότε **διδάσκοντα.**
I hear that Sokrates **was** then **teaching** the young men.
I hear "Σωκράτης τοὺς νεανίας τότε ἐδίδασκεν."
(*The original imperfect indicative has been changed to a PRESENT participle.*)]

[ἀκούω Σωκράτη τοὺς νεανίας τότε **δεδιδαχότα.**
I hear that Sokrates **had** then **taught** the young men.
I hear "Σωκράτης τοὺς νεανίας τότε ἐδεδιδάχειν."
(*The original pluperfect indicative has been changed to a perfect participle.*)]

δείξω οὐ **κακὸς πολίτης ὤν.**
I shall show that **I am** not **a bad citizen.**
I shall show "οὐ κακὸς πολίτης εἰμί."
(*The original present indicative has been changed to a present participle. Since the subject of the participle is the same as that of the introductory verb, it is not expressed, and the predicate nominative of the original statement remains a predicate nominative.*)

[ἀκούω Σωκράτη τοὺς νεανίας **ἂν διδάσκοντα.**
I hear that Sokrates **may teach** the young men.
I hear that Sokrates **may have been teaching/may have taught** (**habitually**) the young men.
I hear that Sokrates **would be teaching/would have taught** (**habitually**) the young men.

I hear *"Σωκράτης τοὺς νεᾱνίᾱς ἂν διδάσκοι"* or
"Σωκράτης τοὺς νεᾱνίᾱς ἂν ἐδίδασκεν."
(*The original statement contained either a present optative with ἄν, i.e., a potential optative with progressive/repeated aspect, or an imperfect indicative with ἄν, i.e., a past potential with progressive/repeated aspect or a present contrafactual or past contrafactual indicative with progressive/repeated aspect. Context determines meaning.*)]

[*ἀκούω Σωκράτη τοὺς νεᾱνίᾱς* **ἂν διδάξαντα.**
I hear that Sokrates **may teach** the young men.
I hear that Sokrates **may have taught** the young men.
I hear that Sokrates **would have taught** the young men.
I hear *"Σωκράτης τοὺς νεᾱνίᾱς ἂν διδάξειεν"* or
"Σωκράτης τοὺς νεᾱνίᾱς ἂν ἐδίδαξεν."
(*The original statement contained either an aorist optative with ἄν, i.e., a potential optative with simple aspect, or an aorist indicative with ἄν, i.e., a past potential or past contrafactual indicative with simple aspect. Context determines meaning.*)]

[DEPENDENT CLAUSES IN INDIRECT STATEMENT

Whether the main clause of a complex sentence is put in the finite construction, the infinitive, or the participle in indirect statement, the verbs in ALL dependent clauses in indirect statement remain finite and follow the rules given below. The protases of conditional sentences in indirect statement are treated as dependent clauses, the apodoses as main clauses.

In *primary sequence* the mood and tense of all verbs remains unchanged.

In *secondary sequence* primary tenses of the indicative and all subjunctives may be changed to the corresponding tense of the optative or retained for emphasis as indicative or subjunctive, respectively. All past tenses of the indicative and all optatives remain unchanged.

The negative of an original statement remains unchanged.

The particle ἄν with an optative or an independent indicative remains. When a subjunctive is changed to an optative, ἄν, either as a separate particle or as part of such conjunctions as ἐάν, ἐπειδάν, and ὅταν, is omitted. The conjunctions become εἰ, ἐπειδή, and ὅτε.

Observe how the following sentences can be put into indirect statement:

1. *Σωκράτης, ὃς τοὺς νεᾱνίᾱς διδάσκει, γραφήσεται.*
   Sokrates, who is teaching the young men, will be indicted.

λέγω ὅτι Σωκράτης, ὃς τοὺς νεανίας **διδάσκει**, γραφήσεται.
I say that Sokrates, who is **teaching** the young men, will be indicted.
(The verb in the subordinate clause remains unchanged in primary sequence after the present indicative λέγω.)

ἔλεγον ὡς Σωκράτης, ὃς τοὺς νεανίας **διδάσκοι**, γραφήσοιτο.
I said (habitually) that Sokrates, who **was teaching** the young men, would be indicted.
(The present indicative of the subordinate clause has been changed to a present optative in secondary sequence after the imperfect indicative ἔλεγον.)

ἔλεγον ὅτι Σωκράτης, ὃς τοὺς νεανίας **διδάσκει**, γραφήσεται.
I said (habitually) that Sokrates, who **was teaching** the young men, would be indicted.
(The present indicative of the subordinate clause has been retained for emphasis in secondary sequence after the imperfect ἔλεγον.)

νομίζω Σωκράτη, ὃς τοὺς νεανίας **διδάσκει**, γραφήσεσθαι.
I think that Sokrates, who **is teaching** the young men, will be indicted.
(The present indicative of the subordinate clause remains unchanged in primary sequence after the present indicative νομίζω. Note that the verb of the dependent clause remains finite even though the verb of the independent clause is an infinitive after the introductory verb νομίζω.)

ἤκουσα Σωκράτη, ὃς τοὺς νεανίας **διδάσκοι**, γραφησόμενον.
I heard that Sokrates, who **was teaching** the young men, would be indicted.
(The present indicative of the subordinate clause has been changed to a present optative in secondary sequence after the aorist indicative ἤκουσα. Note that the verb of the dependent clause remains finite even though the verb of the independent clause is a participle after the introductory verb ἤκουσα.)

2. ἐγράφη Σωκράτης ἐπεὶ τοὺς νεανίας ἐδίδασκεν.
Sokrates was indicted since he was teaching the young men.

ἀκούω γραφέντα Σωκράτη ἐπεὶ τοὺς νεανίας **ἐδίδασκεν**.
I hear that Sokrates was indicted since he **was teaching** the young men.
(The verb in the causal clause remains unchanged in primary sequence after the present indicative ἀκούω.)

ἐνόμιζον γραφῆναι Σωκράτη ἐπεὶ τοὺς νεανίας **ἐδίδασκεν**.
I thought that Sokrates was indicted since he **was teaching** the young men.
(The verb in the causal clause must remain unchanged even though in secondary sequence since it is a past tense of the indicative.)

ἔλεγον ὅτι γραφείη Σωκράτης ἐπεὶ τοὺς νεανίας **ἐδίδασκεν**.
I said (habitually) that Sokrates was indicted since he **was teaching** the young men.

(The verb in the causal clause must remain unchanged in secondary sequence after the imperfect indicative ἔλεγον, even though the verb of the independent clause has been changed to an optative.)

3. Σωκράτης, ὃς οὐκ ἂν φύγοι, γραφήσεται.
Sokrates, who may not flee, will be indicted.

λέγω ὡς Σωκράτης, ὃς οὐκ **ἂν φύγοι**, γραφήσεται.
I say that Sokrates, who **may** not **flee**, will be indicted.
(The potential optative of the relative clause remains unchanged in indirect statement.)

4. ἐὰν μὴ κωλυθῇ, διδάξει τοὺς νεανίας.
If he is not prevented, he will teach the young men.

λέγω ὡς **ἐὰν** μὴ **κωλυθῇ**, τοὺς νεανίας **διδάξει**.
I say that **if** he **is** not **prevented**, he **will teach** the young men.
(The original mood and tense remain unchanged in both the protasis and apodosis of a future more vivid conditional sentence in primary sequence.)

ἤκουσα **εἰ** μὴ **κωλυθείη διδάξοντα** αὐτὸν τοὺς νεανίας.
I heard that **if** he **was** not **prevented**, he **would teach** the young men.
(The original aorist subjunctive showing simple aspect in the protasis of a future more vivid conditional sentence has been changed to an optative in secondary sequence after the aorist indicative ἤκουσα; the particle ἐάν has become εἰ. In the apodosis, the future indicative has become a future participle.)

ἐνόμιζον **ἐὰν** μὴ **κωλυθῇ διδάξειν** αὐτὸν τοὺς νεανίας.
I thought that **if** he **was not prevented**, he **would teach** the young men.
(The original aorist subjunctive showing simple aspect in the protasis of a future more vivid conditional sentence has been retained for emphasis in secondary sequence after the imperfect ἐνόμιζον. In the apodosis, the future indicative has become a future infinitive.)

5. εἰ μὴ ἐκωλύθη, ἐδίδαξεν ἂν τοὺς νεανίας.
If he had not been prevented, he would have taught the young men.

ἤδη **εἰ** μὴ **ἐκωλύθη** αὐτὸν **ἂν διδάξαντα** τοὺς νεανίας.
I knew that **if** he **had** not **been prevented**, he **would have taught** the young men.
(The aorist indicative of the protasis of a past contrafactual conditional sentence remains unchanged since it is a past tense of the indicative in a dependent clause in indirect statement. The aorist indicative with ἄν of the apodosis has been changed to an aorist participle with ἄν.)

INDIRECT QUESTION

Indirect questions follow the syntax of the finite construction of indirect statement (cf. pages 761–62). The original question may contain an indicative, [potential optative, or subjunctive (in a deliberative or anticipatory question)]. In primary sequence, all original moods and tenses remain unchanged. In secondary sequence, an indicative [or subjunctive] may be changed to the corresponding tense of the optative or be retained unchanged for emphasis.

The negative of the original question [and the particle ἄν] remain unchanged in indirect question.

Indirect questions are introduced by indirect interrogatives (e.g., ὅστις, ὅπου). Sometimes the direct interrogative (e.g., τίς, ποῦ) is retained:

οἶδα **ὅστις** τοῦτο **ποιεῖ.**
I know **who is doing** this.
I know the answer to the question "*τίς τοῦτο ποιεῖ;*"
(*The original present indicative remains unchanged in primary sequence after the perfect indicative οἶδα. The direct interrogative has been changed to the indirect interrogative.*)

ᾔδη **ὅστις** τοῦτο **ποιοίη.**
I knew **who was doing** this.
I knew the answer to the question "*τίς τοῦτο ποιεῖ;*"
(*The original present indicative has been changed to a present optative in secondary sequence after the pluperfect indicative ᾔδη. The direct interrogative has been changed to the indirect interrogative.*)

ᾔδη **τίς** τοῦτο **ποιεῖ.**
I knew **who was doing** this.
(*The original present indicative, and the direct interrogative, have been retained for emphasis in secondary sequence after the pluperfect indicative ᾔδη.*)

[οἶδα **ὅστις** τοῦτο **ποιήσειεν** ἄν.
I know **who may do** this.
I know the answer to the question "*τίς τοῦτο ποιήσειεν ἄν;*"
The original potential optative, with aorist tense showing simple aspect, remains unchanged.)]

[οὐκ οἶδα **ὅτι** **εἴπω.**
I do not know **what I am to say.**
I do not know the answer to the question "*τί εἴπω;*"
The original subjunctive in a deliberative question, with aorist tense showing simple aspect, remains unchanged in primary sequence after the perfect indicative οἶδα.)]

[οὐκ ᾔδη **ὅτι εἴποιμι.**
I did not know **what I said/had said.**
I did not know **what I was to say.**
I did not know the answer to the question "*τί εἶπον;*" or "*τί εἴπω;*"
(*The aorist optative represents an original aorist indicative of a question of fact or an aorist subjunctive showing simple aspect in a deliberative question. Context determines meaning.*)]

[Subordinate clauses in indirect questions are treated like subordinate clauses in indirect statement:

οὐκ οἶδα ὅτι ποιήσει **ἐὰν ἔλθῃ** εἰς τὴν πόλιν.
I do not know what he will do **if** he **goes** to the city.
I do not know the answer to the question "*τί ποιήσει ἐὰν ἔλθῃ εἰς τὴν πόλιν;*"
(*The original aorist subjunctive of the protasis of a future more vivid conditional sentence remains unchanged in primary sequence after the perfect indicative οἶδα.*)

οὐκ ᾔδη ὅτι ποιήσοι **εἰ ἔλθοι** εἰς τὴν πόλιν.
I did not know what he would do **if** he **went** to the city.
I did not know the answer to the question "*τί ποιήσει ἐὰν ἔλθῃ εἰς τὴν πόλιν;*"
(*The original aorist subjunctive of the protasis of a future more vivid conditional sentence has been changed to an aorist optative, and the particle ἐάν has become εἰ, in secondary sequence after the pluperfect indicative ᾔδη.*)]

[IMPLIED INDIRECT STATEMENT

In certain kinds of subordinate clauses, after a secondary main verb the optative is used in *IMPLIED INDIRECT STATEMENT*, even though the main clause is not in indirect statement. Contrast the following sets of sentences:

1. τοὺς στρατιώτας οὐκ ἐτίμων οἱ πολῖται ὅτι οὐκ **ἠθέλησαν** μαχέσασθαι.
   The citizens were not honoring the soldiers because they **refused** to fight.
   (*Here the indicative is the normal construction in a causal clause introduced by ὅτι, "because."*)

   τοὺς στρατιώτας οὐκ ἐτίμων οἱ πολῖται ὅτι οὐκ **ἐθέλοιεν** μαχέσασθαι.
   The citizens were not honoring the soldiers because, **as the citizens said,** they **refused** to fight.
   (*In this sentence the present optative is in implied indirect statement in secondary sequence and stands for the present indicative of the cause as it appeared to the citizens. Their original thought was "ὅτι οὐκ ἐθέλουσι μαχέσασθαι."*)

2. ταῦτα πράττομεν μέχρι ἂν ὁ ἄγγελος **ἔλθῃ**.

We are doing these things until the messenger **comes**.

(*The aorist subjunctive with ἄν showing simple aspect is used in a temporal clause which refers to future time.*)

ταῦτα ἔπραττον μέχρι ὁ ἄγγελος **ἦλθεν**.

They were doing these things until the messenger **came**.

(*The indicative is the usual construction in a past definite temporal clause which refers to a specific act in past time. The temporal clause states that the messenger actually did arrive.*)

ταῦτα ἔπραττον οἱ Ἀθηναῖοι μέχρι ὁ ἄγγελος **ἔλθοι**.

The Athenians were doing these things until, **they said**, the messenger **could come**.

(*In this sentence the aorist optative is in implied indirect statement and stands for an aorist subjunctive with ἄν of the temporal clause as it would have been expressed by the Athenians when they were acting. Their words are given in the first sentence of this series. This temporal clause does not say that the messenger actually arrived.*)]

[ASSIMILATION OF MOOD

A subordinate clause closely connected to the thought of the clause on which it depends can be attracted to the mood of the main clause:

ταῦτ᾽ ἂν ἔπραξαν ἵνα τοὺς πολεμίους **ἔπαυσαν**.

They would have done these things in order that they **might have stopped** the enemy.

(*The verb in the purpose clause has been attracted to the indicative to show unfulfilled purpose after the contrafactual indicative.*)

νῑκῷμεν ὅτε ὁ ποιητὴς **ἔλθοι**.

May we be winning when the poet **comes**.

(*The temporal clause refers to future time and would ordinarily follow the syntax of a future more vivid temporal clause, taking a subjunctive with ἄν. Here the verb of the temporal clause has been assimilated to the optative of wish of the main clause.*)]

THE PARTICLE ἄν

INDICATIVE WITH ἄν: imperfect or aorist tense

1. in the apodosis of a *PRESENT* or *PAST CONTRAFACTUAL CONDITIONAL SENTENCE*

[2. in a present or past *UNREAL INDICATIVE*]

[3. in a *PAST POTENTIAL INDICATIVE*]

[4. in an *ITERATIVE INDICATIVE*]

SUBJUNCTIVE WITH *ἄν*: present or aorist tense, showing aspect

1. in the protasis of a *FUTURE MORE VIVID CONDITIONAL SEN-TENCE* or in a *FUTURE MORE VIVID TEMPORAL CLAUSE*

2. in the protasis of a *PRESENT GENERAL CONDITIONAL SEN-TENCE* or in a *PRESENT GENERAL TEMPORAL CLAUSE*

[3. in some *PURPOSE CLAUSES* or *OBJECT CLAUSES OF EFFORT*]

OPTATIVE with *ἄν*: present or aorist tense, showing aspect

1. in a *POTENTIAL OPTATIVE*

2. in the apodosis of a *FUTURE LESS VIVID CONDITIONAL SEN-TENCE*

[3. in some *PURPOSE CLAUSES* in secondary sequence]

In indirect statement, *ἄν* of an original statement is retained except when a subjunctive with *ἄν* is changed to an optative without *ἄν* in secondary sequence.

Only in indirect statement is *ἄν* used with an infinitive or participle.

THE NEGATIVES *οὐ* AND *μή*

The compounds of *οὐ* (e.g., *οὐδείς*, *οὔτε*) and *μή* (e.g., *μηδείς*, *μήτε*) can be used where simple *οὐ* or *μή* can be used.

The negative *οὐ* is used

1. in statements of fact with the indicative

2. in questions expecting an affirmative reply:

    ἆρ' οὐ ταῦτα πράξεις;
    Won't you do these things?
    You will do these things, won't you?

3. with the potential optative [and indicative]

[4. with the unreal indicative]

[5. with the iterative indicative]

6. with participles other than generic or conditional

7. in the apodoses of all conditional sentences

8. in past definite temporal clauses

9. in causal clauses

10. in relative clauses with a specific antecedent not thought of as characteristic of a type

11. in clauses of actual result

12. in fear clauses introduced by the conjunction μή

13. with specific attributes

The negative μή is used

[1. in questions expecting a negative answer:

ἆρα μὴ ταῦτα πράξεις;
You will not do these things, will you?]

2. with all subjunctives except in fear clauses introduced by the conjunction μή [and in independent clauses of cautious denial (μὴ οὐ + subjunctive)]

3. with all wishes [except those introduced by βουλοίμην ἄν or ἐβουλόμην (ἄν), which use οὐ to negate the introductory word]

4. with the present and (rarely) the aorist imperative in prohibitions

5. with the future indicative introduced by ὅπως in an urgent prohibition

6. with all infinitives other than those in indirect statement

7. in the protases (including relative protases with indefinite antecedents) of all conditional sentences

8. in future more vivid and present and past general temporal clauses

9. with conditional participles

10. with generic attributes and participles

11. in purpose clauses [including relative purpose clauses]

12. in object clauses of effort

13. in clauses of natural result

[14. in relative clauses with an indefinite antecedent or with a definite antecedent when the relative clause describes the antecedent as characteristic of a type:

Σωκράτης ὃς μὴ ταῦτα πράττει ἀποθανεῖται.
Sokrates, the sort of man who does not do these things, will be killed.]

Note that in a fear clause introduced by μή [and in a subjunctive of cautious assertion] μή is not a negative. A negative fear clause [or subjunctive of cautious denial] uses μὴ οὐ.

[The combination οὐ μή is used:

1. with the subjunctive or future indicative in a strong future denial

2. with the future indicative in an urgent prohibition]

The combination μὴ οὐ is used

1. in a negative fear clause

[2. with the subjunctive in a cautious denial]

In indirect statement and indirect question, the negative of the original statement is preserved.

[REDUNDANT NEGATIVES

After verbs with a negative idea (e.g., κωλύω, παύω) an infinitive is often accompanied by a *redundant*, i.e., unnecessary and untranslatable, μή:

κωλύουσι τὸν Σωκράτη **μὴ** ταῦτα πρᾶξαι.
They prevent Sokrates from doing these things.

When such a verb with a negative idea is itself negated, an infinitive is often accompanied by a redundant μὴ οὐ:

οὐ κωλύουσι τὸν Σωκράτη **μὴ οὐ** ταῦτα πρᾶξαι.
They do not prevent Sokrates from doing these things.]

[οὐ ADHERESCENT

When οὐ is closely attached (adherescent) to an individual word, it not only negates the individual word; it can give the word its opposite meaning:

οὐκ ἐθέλουσι ταῦτα πρᾶξαι.
They **refuse** to do these things.

Adherescent οὐ can appear where one would expect the negative μή:

εἰ ταῦτα πρᾶξαι **οὐκ ἠθέλησαν**, αὐτὸς ἂν ἔπραξα.
If they **had refused** to do these things, I would have done them myself.]

REPEATED NEGATIVES

A simple negative (οὐ, μή) followed by a compound negative or negatives (e.g., οὐδείς, μηδείς) or a compound negative followed by another compound negative or negatives has its negation strengthened:

οὐ πράττει **οὐδεὶς οὐδέν**.
No one is doing **anything**.

But a compound negative followed by a simple negative makes a positive statement. Contrast these two sentences:

οὐδεὶς οὐ τοῦτο ποιεῖ.
No one is **not** doing this.
(I.e., everyone is doing this.)

οὐ τοῦτο ποιεῖ **οὐδείς**.
No one is doing this.

ἀγαθός, ἀγαθή, ἀγαθόν good (4)

ἀγγέλλω, ἀγγελῶ, ἤγγειλα, ἤγγελκα, ἤγγελμαι, ἠγγέλθην announce (10)

ἄγγελος, ἀγγέλου, ὁ messenger (2)

ἀγορά, ἀγορᾶς, ἡ market place (1)

ἄγω, ἄξω, ἤγαγον, ἦχα, ἦγμαι, ἤχθην lead (8)

ἀγών, ἀγῶνος, ὁ contest, struggle (9)

ἀδελφός, ἀδελφοῦ, ὁ (voc. ἄδελφε) brother (1)

ἄδηλος, ἄδηλον unclear, uncertain (7)

ἀδικέω, ἀδικήσω, ἠδίκησα, ἠδίκηκα, ἠδίκημαι, ἠδικήθην do wrong, wrong (9)

ἄδικος, ἄδικον unjust (4)

ἀεί (adv.) always (11)

ἀθάνατος, ἀθάνατον undying, immortal (5)

Ἀθηναῖος, Ἀθηναία, Ἀθηναῖον Athenian (8)

ἆθλον, ἄθλου, τό prize (3)

αἰδώς, αἰδοῦς, ἡ shame (Section 158)

αἴξ, αἰγός, ὁ or ἡ goat (6)

αἱρέω, αἱρήσω, εἷλον, ᾕρηκα, ᾕρημαι, ᾑρέθην take, capture; (mid.) choose (15)

αἰσθάνομαι, αἰσθήσομαι, ᾐσθόμην, ——, ᾔσθημαι, —— perceive (+ gen. or acc.) (15)

αἴσχιστος, αἰσχίστη, αἴσχιστον superlative of αἰσχρός, αἰσχρά, αἰσχρόν (17)

αἰσχίων, αἴσχιον comparative of αἰσχρός, αἰσχρά, αἰσχρόν (17)

αἰσχρός, αἰσχρά, αἰσχρόν ugly, shameful (7)

αἰσχύνομαι, αἰσχυνοῦμαι, ——, ——, ᾔσχυμμαι, ᾐσχύνθην be ashamed, feel shame before (19)

αἰτία, αἰτίας, ἡ responsibility, guilt, cause (11)

αἴτιος, αἰτία, αἴτιον responsible (for), guilty (of) (+ gen.) (11)

ἀκούω, ἀκούσομαι, ἤκουσα, ἀκήκοα, ——, ἠκούσθην hear (+ acc. of thing heard, gen. of person heard); be spoken of (11)

ἀλήθεια, ἀληθείας, ἡ truth, reality (10)

ἀληθής, ἀληθές true, real (10)

ἀλλά (conj.) but (3)

——, ἀλλήλων (reciprocal pronoun) one another (12)

ἄλλος, ἄλλη, ἄλλο another, other (7)

775

ἄλογος, ἄλογον unreasoning, unreasonable, irrational (9)

ἅμα (adv.) at the same time

(prep.) + dat. at the same time as; together with (8)

ἀμαθής, ἀμαθές ignorant, stupid (14)

ἀμαθία, ἀμαθίας, ἡ ignorance, stupidity (14)

ἁμαρτάνω, ἁμαρτήσομαι, ἥμαρτον, ἡμάρτηκα, ἡμάρτημαι, ἡμαρτήθην miss (+ gen.); make a mistake, do wrong (17)

ἁμαρτία, ἁμαρτίας, ἡ mistake, error (17)

ἀμείνων, ἄμεινον better (in ability or worth) (19)

ἄν (particle) used in some conditional sentences (4); with the potential optative (7)

ἀνα- (prefix) up, up to (12)

ἀναβαίνω go up, go upland; board, mount (16)

ἀνάξιος, ἀνάξιον unworthy (+ gen.) (4)

ἀνατίθημι set up, dedicate (12)

——, ἀνερήσομαι, ἀνηρόμην, ——, ——, —— ask (19)

ἄνευ (prep.) + gen. without (7)

ἀνήρ, ἀνδρός, ὁ man (10)

ἄνθρωπος, ἀνθρώπου, ὁ man, human being (1)

ἀντί (prep.) + gen. instead of (3)

ἄξιος, ἀξία, ἄξιον worthy, worth (+ gen.) (4)

ἀξιόω, ἀξιώσω, ἠξίωσα, ἠξίωκα, ἠξίωμαι, ἠξιώθην think worthy of, think it right, expect (10)

ἅπας, ἅπασα, ἅπαν all, quite all (8)

ἀπό (prep.) + gen. from, away from (2)

ἀπο- (prefix) away from (10)

ἀποδέχομαι receive favorably, accept (11)

ἀποδίδωμι give back, pay, permit; (mid.) sell (12)

ἀποθνῄσκω, ἀποθανοῦμαι, ἀπέθανον, τέθνηκα, ——, —— die (18)

ἀποκρίνομαι, ἀποκρινοῦμαι, ἀπεκρινάμην, ——, ἀποκέκριμαι, —— answer (19)

ἀποκτείνω, ἀποκτενῶ, ἀπέκτεινα, ἀπέκτονα, ——, —— kill (18)

ἀπόλλυμι, ἀπολῶ, ἀπώλεσα (trans.) or ἀπωλόμην (intrans.), ἀπολώλεκα (trans.) or ἀπόλωλα (intrans.), ——, —— kill; lose; (mid. and intrans.) die, cease to exist (19)

ἆρα (particle) introduces a question (2)

ἀργύριον, ἀργυρίου, τό small coin; money (5)

ἄργυρος, ἀργύρου, ὁ silver (5)

ἀργυροῦς, ἀργυρᾶ, ἀργυροῦν of silver (Section 161)

ἀρετή, ἀρετῆς, ἡ excellence, virtue (3)

ἄριστος, ἀρίστη, ἄριστον best (in ability or worth) (19)

Ἀριστοφάνης, Ἀριστοφάνους, ὁ   Aristophanes (comic poet) (13)

ἀρχή, ἀρχῆς, ἡ   beginning; rule, empire (4)

ἄρχω, ἄρξω, ἦρξα, ἦρχα, ἦργμαι, ἤρχθην   rule, command (+ gen.) (5); (mid.) begin (+ gen.) (7)

ἄρχων, ἄρχοντος, ὁ   ruler; archon (13)

ἀσπίς, ἀσπίδος, ἡ   shield (13)

ἄστυ, ἄστεως, τό   town (20)

ἄτε (particle)   with causal participle: speaker's assertion (8)

αὖ (postpositive particle)   again, further, in turn (18)

αὐτίκα (adv.)   immediately (13)

αὐτός, αὐτή, αὐτό   (adj. in attributive position) same; (intensive, in predicate position or alone in nom.) -self, -selves; (pronoun in gen., dat., acc.) him, her, it, them (11)

ἀφίημι, ἀφήσω, ἀφῆκα, ἀφεῖκα, ἀφεῖμαι, ἀφείθην   send forth, send away; let go; neglect (18)

ἀφικνέομαι, ἀφίξομαι, ἀφικόμην, ——, ἀφῖγμαι, ——   arrive (20)

ἀφίστημι, ἀποστήσω, ἀπέστησα (trans.) or ἀπέστην (intrans.), ἀφέστηκα (intrans.), ἀφέσταμαι, ἀπεστάθην (trans.) cause to revolt; (mid. and intrans.) revolt (12)

ἄφρων, ἄφρον   senseless, foolish (11)

βαίνω, -βήσομαι, -ἔβην, βέβηκα, ——, ——   walk, step, go; (perfect) stand (16)

βάλλω, βαλῶ, ἔβαλον, βέβληκα, βέβλημαι, ἐβλήθην   throw; hit (with thrown object) (11)

βάρβαρος, βάρβαρον   non-Greek, foreign (9)

βαρύς, βαρεῖα, βαρύ   heavy (17)

βασιλεύς, βασιλέως, ὁ   king (10)

βέλτιστος, βελτίστη, βέλτιστον   best (morally) (19)

βελτίων, βέλτιον   better (morally) (19)

βιβλίον, βιβλίου, τό   book (1)

βίος, βίου, ὁ   life, means of living (9)

βλάπτω, βλάψω, ἔβλαψα, βέβλαφα, βέβλαμμαι, ἐβλάβην or ἐβλάφθην   hurt, harm (5)

βουλεύω, βουλεύσω, ἐβούλευσα, βεβούλευκα, βεβούλευμαι, ἐβουλεύθην   deliberate on, plan; (mid.) take counsel with oneself, deliberate (18)

βουλή, βουλῆς, ἡ   will; council (3)

βούλομαι, βουλήσομαι, ——, ——, βεβούλημαι, ἐβουλήθην   want (11)

βοῦς, βοός, ὁ or ἡ   bull, cow; (pl.) cattle (Section 155)

γάρ (postpositive conj.)   for (explanatory) (2)

γε (enclitic particle)   emphasizes or limits preceding word; at any rate, at least (6) γένος, γένους, τό   race, kind (10)

γέρας, γέρως, τό   prize (Section 160)

γέρων, γέροντος, ὁ   old man (6)

γέφυρα, γεφύρᾱς, ἡ   bridge (4)

γῆ, γῆς, ἡ   earth, land (5)

γίγνομαι, γενήσομαι, ἐγενόμην, γέγονα, γεγένημαι, ——   be born; become; happen (13)

γιγνώσκω, γνώσομαι, ἔγνων, ἔγνωκα, ἔγνωσμαι, ἐγνώσθην   perceive, recognize, know (16)

γνώμη, γνώμης, ἡ   opinion, judgment (6)

γράμμα, γράμματος, τό letter (of the alphabet); (pl.) documents (7)

γραφεύς, γραφέως, ὁ   writer; painter (12)

γραφή, γραφῆς, ἡ   indictment (7)

γραφική, γραφικῆς, ἡ   writing; painting (12)

γράφω, γράψω, ἔγραψα, γέγραφα, γέγραμμαι, ἐγράφην   write, draw (3); (mid.)   note down, cause to be written; indict (7)

γυνή, γυναικός, ἡ   (voc. γύναι)   woman; wife (11)

δαίμων, δαίμονος, ὁ or ἡ   god, goddess, divine being (9)

δέ (postpositive conj.)   but (2)

   δέ: μέν . . . δέ (postpositive conjs.) on the one hand . . . on the other hand

δεῖ, δεήσει, ἐδέησε(ν), ——, ——, —— (impersonal verb) it is necessary, must (+ accusative and infinitive); there is need of (+ gen.)

δείκνῡμι, δείξω, ἔδειξα, δέδειχα, δέδειγμαι, ἐδείχθην   show (14)

δεινός, δεινή, δεινόν   fearsome, marvelous, clever (6)

δέκα (indeclinable numeral)   ten (12)

δεύτερος, δευτέρᾱ, δεύτερον   second (17)

δέχομαι, δέξομαι, ἐδεξάμην, ——, δέδεγμαι, ——   receive; welcome (11)

δή (postpositive particle)   in fact, of course (3)

δῆλος, δήλη, δῆλον   clear, visible (7)

δηλόω, δηλώσω, ἐδήλωσα, δεδήλωκα, δεδήλωμαι, ἐδηλώθην   make clear, show (10)

δημιουργός, δημιουργοῦ, ὁ   skilled workman (12)

δημοκρατίᾱ, δημοκρατίᾱς, ἡ   democracy (3)

δῆμος, δήμου, ὁ   the people (3)

Δημοσθένης, Δημοσθένους, ὁ   Demosthenes (orator) (10)

διά (prep.)   + gen.   through
               + acc.   on account of (3)

δια- (prefix)   through; in different directions (15)

διαφέρω   carry through; be different from, excel (+ gen.) (15)

διδάσκαλος, διδασκάλου, ὁ   teacher (5)

διδάσκω, διδάξω, ἐδίδαξα, δεδίδαχα, δεδίδαγμαι, ἐδιδάχθην   teach (4); (mid.) cause (someone) to be taught (7)

δίδωμι, δώσω, ἔδωκα, δέδωκα, δέδομαι, ἐδόθην   give (12)

δίκαιος, δικαία, δίκαιον   just (4)

δίκη, δίκης, ἡ   justice; lawsuit (4)

δοκέω, δόξω, ἔδοξα, ——, δέδογμαι, -ἐδόχθην   seem, think (17); (impersonal verb) it seems best (20)

δόξα, δόξης, ἡ   expectation, belief; reputation, glory (5)

δουλείᾱ, δουλείᾱς, ἡ   slavery (6)

δουλεύω, δουλεύσω, ἐδούλευσα, δεδούλευκα, ——, ——   be a slave (+ dat.) (6)

δοῦλος, δούλου, ὁ   slave (6)

δύναμαι, δυνήσομαι, ——, ——, δεδύνημαι, ἐδυνήθην   be able (17)

δύναμις, δυνάμεως, ἡ   strength, power (17)

δύο   two (17)

δύω, -δύσω, -ἔδῡσα/ἔδῡν, δέδῡκα, δέδυμαι, -ἐδύθην   sink, go down (pp. 643, 680–82, 690)

δῶρον, δώρου, τό   gift; bribe (especially in pl.) (1)

ἐάν (particle)   if (in some conditional sentences) (4)

ἑαυτοῦ, ἑαυτῆς, ἑαυτοῦ (reflexive pronoun)   himself, herself, itself (15)

ἐγώ (personal pronoun)   I (15)

ἐθέλω, ἐθελήσω, ἠθέλησα, ἠθέληκα, ——, ——   be willing, wish (4)

εἰ (particle)   if (in some conditional sentences) (4); whether, if (indirect interrogative) (18)

εἰ γάρ (particle)   introduces wishes (7, 17)

εἴθε (particle)   introduces wishes (7, 17)

εἰμί, ἔσομαι, ——, ——, ——, ——   be; ἔστι(ν)   there is; it is possible (15)

εἶμι, ——, ——, ——, ——, ——   go, come (17)

εἰρήνη, εἰρήνης, ἡ   peace (3)

εἰς (prep.)   + acc. into, to; for (purpose) (1)

εἰσ- (prefix)   into, in, to (11)

εἷς, μία, ἕν   one (17)

εἴτε . . . εἴτε (indirect interrogative)   whether . . . or, if . . . or (18)

ἐκ, ἐξ (prep.)   + gen. from, out of (1)

ἐκ-, ἐξ- (prefix)   out of; thoroughly (10)

ἕκαστος, ἑκάστη, ἕκαστον   each (of many); (pl.) each (of several groups), all (considered singly) (16)

ἐκεῖ (adv.)   there (in that place) (7)

ἐκεῖνος, ἐκείνη, ἐκεῖνο   that (7)

ἐκκλησίᾱ, ἐκκλησίᾱς, ἡ   assembly (3)

ἐκπίπτω   be driven out, be banished (16)

ἐλάττων, ἔλαττον   comparative of ὀλίγος, ὀλίγη, ὀλίγον (19)

ἐλαύνω, ἐλῶ (ἐλάω), ἤλασα, -ἐλήλακα, ἐλήλαμαι, ἠλάθην   drive, march (17)

ἐλάχιστος, ἐλαχίστη, ἐλάχιστον   superlative of ὀλίγος, ὀλίγη, ὀλίγον (19)

ἐλέγχω, ἐλέγξω, ἤλεγξα, ——, ἐλήλεγμαι, ἠλέγχθην   cross-examine, question
    (pp. 665–67, 690)

ἐλευθερίᾱ, ἐλευθερίᾱς, ἡ   freedom (6)

ἐλεύθερος, ἐλευθέρᾱ, ἐλεύθερον   free (+ gen.) (6)

Ἕλλην, Ἕλληνος, ὁ   a Greek (6)

ἐλπίς, ἐλπίδος, ἡ   hope, expectation (6)

ἐμαυτοῦ, ἐμαυτῆς (reflexive pronoun)   myself (15)

ἐμός, ἐμή, ἐμόν   my; (substantive) mine (15)

ἐμπειρίᾱ, ἐμπειρίᾱς, ἡ   experience, practice (9)

ἔμπειρος, ἔμπειρον   experienced in, acquainted with (+ gen.) (9)

ἐν (prep.)   + dat. in (1)

ἕνεκα (prep.)   + preceding gen. for the sake of (16)

ἐννέα (indeclinable numeral)   nine (12)

ἐνταῦθα (adv.)   here, there; then (11)

ἐξ, ἐκ (prep.)   + gen. from, out of (1)

ἐξ-, ἐκ- (prefix)   out of; thoroughly (10)

ἕξ (indeclinable numeral)   six (2)

ἔξεστι(ν) (impersonal verb)   it is allowed, it is possible (15)

ἑορτή, ἑορτῆς, ἡ   festival (13)

ἐπανίσταμαι, ἐπαναστήσομαι, ἐπανέστην, ἐπανέστηκα, ——, —— rise up
    in insurrection against (+ dat.) (14)

ἐπεί (conj.)   after, when, since (3)

ἐπειδάν (conj.)   after, when, whenever (11)

ἐπειδή (conj.)   after, when, since (3)

ἔπειτα (adv.)   then, thereupon (8)

ἐπί (prep.)   + gen. on
                + dat. on, pertaining to, on condition that
                + acc. onto, over, against, for (purpose) (13)

ἐπι- (prefix)   upon, over; against; after (13)

ἐπιβουλεύω   plot against (+ dat.) (18)

ἐπιδείκνυμαι   show off, display (14)

ἐπίδειξις, ἐπιδείξεως, ἡ   display, demonstration (14)

ἐπίσταμαι, ἐπιστήσομαι, ——, ——, ——, ἠπιστήθην   know (17)

ἐπιστήμη, ἐπιστήμης, ἡ   knowledge (17)

ἕπομαι, ἕψομαι, ἑσπόμην, ——, ——, —— follow, pursue (+ dat.) (15)

ἔπος, ἔπους, τό   word; (pl., sometimes) epic poetry (12)

ἑπτά (indeclinable numeral)   seven (11)

ἔργον, ἔργου, τό   work, deed (1)

——, ἐρήσομαι, ἠρόμην, ——, ——, —— ask (19)

ἑρμηνεύς, ἑρμηνέως, ὁ interpreter (12)
ἔρχομαι, ἐλεύσομαι, ἦλθον, ἐλήλυθα, ——, —— come, go (13)
ἔρως, ἔρωτος, ὁ (voc. ἔρως) love (11)
ἐρωτάω, ἐρωτήσω, ἠρώτησα, ἠρώτηκα, ἠρώτημαι, ἠρωτήθην ask, question (14)
ἔστι(ν) there is, it is possible (15)
ἑταῖρος, ἑταίρου, ὁ companion (13)
ἕτερος, ἑτέρᾱ, ἕτερον the other (of two) (14)
ἔτι (adv.) yet, still (14)
εὖ (adv.) well (2)
εὐγενής, εὐγενές well-born, noble (10)
εὐδαίμων, εὔδαιμον fortunate, wealthy, happy (10)
Εὐρῑπίδης, Εὐρῑπίδου, ὁ (voc. Εὐρῑπίδη) Euripides (tragic poet) (13)
εὑρίσκω, εὑρήσω, ηὗρον, ηὕρηκα, ηὕρημαι, ηὑρέθην find, discover (19)
εὐτυχής, εὐτυχές lucky (11)
ἐχθίων, ἔχθῑον comparative of ἐχθρός, ἐχθρά, ἐχθρόν (17)
ἔχθιστος, ἐχθίστη, ἔχθιστον superlative of ἐχθρός, ἐχθρά, ἐχθρόν (17)
ἐχθρός, ἐχθρά, ἐχθρόν hated; hostile; (substantive) enemy (9)
ἔχω, ἕξω or σχήσω, ἔσχον, ἔσχηκα, -ἔσχημαι, —— have, hold; be able;
    (+ adv.) be; (mid.) cling to, be next to (+ gen.) (17)
ἕως (conj.) as long as, while; until (19)

ζάω, ζήσω, ——, ——, ——, —— live (Section 163)
ζητέω, ζητήσω, ἐζήτησα, ἐζήτηκα, ——, ἐζητήθην seek (18)
Ζεύς, Διός, ὁ (voc. Ζεῦ) Zeus (16)
ζωγράφος, ζωγράφου, ὁ painter (12)
ζῷον, ζῴου, τό animal (2)

ἤ (conj.) or (2); than (12)
ἤ . . . ἤ (conjs.) either . . . or (2)
ἡγέομαι, ἡγήσομαι, ἡγησάμην, ——, ἥγημαι, ἡγήθην lead the way; be commander; rule (+ gen.); believe (19)
ἡγεμών, ἡγεμόνος, ὁ leader (7)
ἥδιστος, ἡδίστη, ἥδιστον superlative of ἡδύς, ἡδεῖα, ἡδύ (17)
ἡδίων, ἥδῑον comparative of ἡδύς, ἡδεῖα, ἡδύ (17)
ἡδύς, ἡδεῖα, ἡδύ pleasant, glad (17)
ἥκιστα (adv.) least, not at all (19)
ἥκω, ἥξω, ——, ——, ——, —— have come, be present (8)
ἡμεῖς (personal pronoun) we (15)
ἡμέρᾱ, ἡμέρᾱς, ἡ day (4)
ἡμέτερος, ἡμετέρᾱ, ἡμέτερον our; (substantive) ours (15)

ἡμῶν αὐτῶν (*reflexive pronoun*)   ourselves (15)
ἥττων, ἧττον   weaker, worse (19)

θάλαττα, θαλάττης, ἡ   sea (4)
θάνατος, θανάτου, ὁ   death (5)
θάπτω, θάψω, ἔθαψα, ——, τέθαμμαι, ἐτάφην   bury (4)
θάττων, θᾶττον   swifter, faster (19)
θέᾱτρον, θεᾱτρου, τό   theater (16)
θεός, θεοῦ, ὁ or ἡ   god, goddess (1)
θυγάτηρ, θυγατρός, ἡ   daughter (10)
θυσίᾱ, θυσίᾱς, ἡ   sacrifice (3)
θύω, θύσω, ἔθῡσα, τέθυκα, τέθυμαι, ἐτύθην   sacrifice (3);   (*mid.*) cause a sacri-
    fice to be made, consult the gods (7)

ἰᾱτρός, ἰᾱτροῦ, ὁ   doctor (20)
ἱερεύς, ἱερέως, ὁ   priest (10)
ἱερόν, ἱεροῦ, τό   shrine (5)
ἱερός, ἱερά, ἱερόν (+ *gen.*)   holy, sacred (to) (5)
ἵημι, -ἥσω, -ἧκα, -εἷκα, -εἷμαι, -εἵθην   release; hurl; send (18)
ἱκανός, ἱκανή, ἱκανόν   sufficient, capable (5)
ἵλεως, ἵλεων   propitious (Section 162)
ἵνα (*conj.*)   in order that (*introduces purpose clauses*) (3)
ἱππεύς, ἱππέως, ὁ   horseman (10)
ἵππος, ἵππου, ὁ or ἡ   horse, mare (5)
ἴσος, ἴση, ἴσον   equal, fair; flat (19)
ἵστημι, στήσω, ἔστησα (*trans.*) or ἔστην (*intrans.*), ἕστηκα (*intrans.*), ἕσταμαι,
    ἐστάθην   make stand; (*mid. or intrans.*) stand (12)
ἴσως (*adv.*)   equally; perhaps (19)

καθίστημι, καταστήσω, κατέστησα (*trans.*) or κατέστην (*intrans.*),
    καθέστηκα (*intrans.*), καθέσταμαι, κατεστάθην (*trans.*) appoint, es-
    tablish, put into a state; (*intrans.*) be established, be appointed, enter into
    a state (12)
καί (*conj.*) and
    (*adv.*) even, also (1)
καί . . . καί (*conjs.*)   both . . . and (1)
καινός, καινή, καινόν   new, strange (19)
καίπερ (*adv.*)   although (8)
καιρός, καιροῦ, ὁ   right moment (11)
καίτοι (*particle*)   and further, and yet (4)
κάκιστος, κακίστη, κάκιστον   worst (morally) (19)
κακίων, κάκιον   worse (morally) (19)
κακός, κακή, κακόν   bad, evil (4)

καλέω, καλῶ, ἐκάλεσα, κέκληκα, κέκλημαι, ἐκλήθην   call (10)

κάλλιστος, καλλίστη, κάλλιστον   superlative of καλός, καλή, καλόν (17)

καλλίων, κάλλῑον   comparative of καλός, καλή, καλόν (17)

κάλλος, κάλλους, τό   beauty (11)

καλός, καλή, καλόν   beautiful, noble, good (4)

κατά (prep.)   + gen. under; against
             + acc. according to (6)

κατα- (prefix)   down; against; strengthens meaning of verb (12)

καταλύ̄ω   destroy; dissolve (12)

κεῖμαι, κείσομαι, ——, ——, ——, ——   lie, be placed, be set (20)

κελεύω, κελεύσω, ἐκέλευσα, κεκέλευκα, κεκέλευσμαι, ἐκελεύσθην   order, command (2)

κέρδος, κέρδους, τό   gain, profit (19)

κῆρυξ, κήρῡκος, ὁ   (dat. pl. κήρυξι[ν])   herald (11)

κίνδῡνος, κινδύ̄νου, ὁ   danger (5)

κλέπτης, κλέπτου, ὁ   thief (7)

κλέπτω, κλέψω, ἔκλεψα, κέκλοφα, κέκλεμμαι, ἐκλάπην   steal (7)

κλοπή, κλοπῆς, ἡ   theft (7)

κοινός, κοινή, κοινόν   common (14)

κράτιστος, κρατίστη, κράτιστον   strongest, best (19)

κράτος, κράτους, τό   strength, power (13)

κρείττων, κρεῖττον   stronger, better (19)

κρῑνω, κρινῶ, ἔκρῑνα, κέκρικα, κέκριμαι, ἐκρίθην   separate, decide, judge (19)

κριτής, κριτοῦ, ὁ   judge (19)

κωλύ̄ω, κωλύ̄σω, ἐκώλῡσα, κεκώλῡκα, κεκώλῡμαι, ἐκωλύ̄θην   hinder, prevent (6)

Λακεδαιμόνιος, Λακεδαιμονίᾱ, Λακεδαιμόνιον   Spartan (used of persons) (14)

λαμβάνω, λήψομαι, ἔλαβον, εἴληφα, εἴλημμαι, ἐλήφθην   take (11)

λανθάνω, λήσω, ἔλαθον, λέληθα, ——, ——   escape the notice of (+ acc.) (14)

λέγω, ἐρῶ or λέξω, εἶπον or ἔλεξα, εἴρηκα, εἴρημαι or λέλεγμαι, ἐλέχθην or ἐρρήθην   say, speak (16)

λείπω, λείψω, ἔλιπον, λέλοιπα, λέλειμμαι, ἐλείφθην   leave, leave behind (7)

λίθος, λίθου, ὁ   stone (5)

λιμήν, λιμένος, ὁ   harbor (16)

λόγος, λόγου, ὁ   word, speech, story (1)

λύ̄πη, λύ̄πης, ἡ   pain, grief (19)

λύ̄ω, λύ̄σω, ἔλῡσα, λέλυκα, λέλυμαι, ἐλύθην   unbind, free, release; dissolve; destroy (2); (mid.) unbind (one's own or for oneself); cause someone to be freed, ransom (7)

μαθητής, μαθητοῦ, ὁ   student, pupil (14)

μακρός, μακρά̄, μακρόν   long, tall (5)

μάλα (*adv.*)   very (19)

μάλιστα (*adv.*)   most (17)

μᾶλλον (*adv.*)   more, rather (12)

μανθάνω, μαθήσομαι, ἔμαθον, μεμάθηκα, ——, —— learn, understand (13)

μάχη, μάχης, ἡ   battle (1)

μάχομαι, μαχοῦμαι, ἐμαχεσάμην, ——, μεμάχημαι, —— fight (+ *dat.*) (13)

μέγας, μεγάλη, μέγα   big, great, large (17)

μέγιστος, μεγίστη, μέγιστον   *superlative of* μέγας, μεγάλη, μέγα (19)

μείζων, μεῖζον   *comparative of* μέγας, μεγάλη, μέγα (19)

μέλλω, μελλήσω, ἐμέλλησα, ——, ——, —— be about to, be likely to (+
    future infin.); delay (18)

μέν . . . δέ (*postpositive conjs.*)   on the one hand . . . on the other hand (2)

μένω, μενῶ, ἔμεινα, μεμένηκα, ——, —— remain, stay (10)

μέσος, μέση, μέσον   middle (of) (14)

μετά (*prep.*)   + *gen.* with
                     + *acc.* after (4)

μετα- (*prefix*) *indicates sharing or change* (13)

μεταδίδωμι   give a share to (13)

μετανίσταμαι, μεταναστήσομαι, μετανέστην, μετανέστηκα, ——, ——
    migrate (13)

μέχρι (*conj.*)   as long as; until (19)

μή (*adv.*)   not (3)
      (*conj.*)   that, lest (*introduces fear clauses*) (12)

μηδέ (*conj.*) and not (12)
      (*adv.*) not even (12)

μηδείς, μηδεμία, μηδέν   no one, nothing (17)

μηκέτι (*adv.*)   no longer (14)

μήποτε (*adv.*)   never, not ever (16)

μήτε . . . μήτε (*conjs.*)   neither . . . nor (8)

μήτηρ, μητρός, ἡ   mother (10)

μηχανάομαι, μηχανήσομαι, ἐμηχανησάμην, ——, μεμηχάνημαι, —— contrive,
    devise (13)

μηχανή, μηχανῆς, ἡ   device, machine (13)

μῑκρός, μῑκρά, μῑκρόν   small, little, short (5)

μοῖρα, μοίρας, ἡ   fate (4)

μόνον (*adv.*)   only (12)

μόνος, μόνη, μόνον   alone (12)

μοῦσα, μούσης, ἡ   muse (4)

ναῦς, νεώς, ἡ   ship (16)

νεᾱνίᾱς, νεᾱνίου, ὁ   young man (4)

νέος, νέα, νέον   new, young (14)

νεώς, νεώ, ὁ temple (Section 154)

νή (affirmative particle) by (+ name of god in acc.) (16)

νῆσος, νήσου, ἡ island (1)

νῑκάω, νῑκήσω, ἐνίκησα, νενίκηκα, νενίκημαι, ἐνῑκήθην win; conquer (9)

νίκη, νίκης, ἡ victory (3)

νομίζω, νομιῶ, ἐνόμισα, νενόμικα, νενόμισμαι, ἐνομίσθην consider, think,
    believe (16)

νόμος, νόμου, ὁ custom, law (10)

νόσος, νόσου, ἡ sickness (19)

νοῦς, νοῦ, ὁ mind, reason (20)

νῦν (adv.) now (2)

νύξ, νυκτός, ἡ night (6)

ξένος, ξένου, ὁ guest-friend, host, stranger, foreigner (2)

ξίφος, ξίφους, τό sword (13)

ὁ, ἡ, τό the; often shows possession (1)

ὅδε, ἥδε, τόδε this (9)

ὁδός, ὁδοῦ, ἡ road (1)

οἷα (particle) with causal participle: speaker's assertion (8)

οἶδα, εἴσομαι, ——, ——, ——, —— know (19)

οἰκίᾱ, οἰκίᾱς, ἡ house (1)

οἶνος, οἴνου, ὁ wine (8)

οἷος, οἵᾱ, οἷον such as, of the sort which; what sort of! (15)

οἷός τ' εἰμί be able (15)

ὀκτώ (indeclinable numeral) eight (11)

ὀλίγος, ὀλίγη, ὀλίγον little; (pl.) few (19)

Ὅμηρος, Ὁμήρου, ὁ Homer (epic poet) (1)

ὅμοιος, ὁμοίᾱ, ὅμοιον like (+ dat.) (13)

ὅμως (adv.) nevertheless (8)

ὄνομα, ὀνόματος, τό name (9)

ὀξύς, ὀξεῖα, ὀξύ sharp, keen (18)

ὁπλίτης, ὁπλίτου, ὁ hoplite, heavy-armed foot-soldier (4)

ὅπλον, ὅπλου, τό tool; (pl.) weapons (4)

ὁπόθεν (conj.) (indefinite relative) from wherever; (indirect interrogative)
    from where? (18)

ὅποι (conj.) (indefinite relative) (to) wherever; (indirect interrogative) (to)
    where? (18)

ὁποῖος, ὁποίᾱ, ὁποῖον (indefinite relative) of whatever kind; (indirect in-
    terrogative) of what kind? (18)

ὁπόσος, ὁπόση, ὁπόσον (indefinite relative) however much/many/large;
    (indirect interrogative) how much/many/large? (18)

ὁπότε (conj.) (indefinite relative) whenever; (indirect interrogative) when? (18)
ὁπότερος, ὁποτέρᾱ, ὁπότερον (indefinite relative) whichever (of two); (indirect
    interrogative) which (of two)? (18)
ὅπου (conj.) (indefinite relative) wherever; (indirect interrogative) where? (18)
ὅπως (conj.) in order that (introduces purpose clauses) (3); that (introduces
    object clauses of effort) (13); (indefinite relative) however (18); (indirect
    interrogative) how? (18)
ὁράω, ὄψομαι, εἶδον, ἑόρᾱκα or ἑώρᾱκα, ἑώρᾱμαι or ὦμμαι, ὤφθην see (15)
ὀρθός, ὀρθή, ὀρθόν straight, correct (17)
ὅς, ἥ, ὅ (relative pronoun) who, which (6)
ὅσος, ὅση, ὅσον as much/many as, as large as; how much/many!, how large!
    (17)
ὅστις, ἥτις, ὅτι (indefinite relative) whoever, whatever; (indirect interrogative)
    who?, what? (18)
ὅταν (conj.) when, whenever (11)
ὅτε (conj.) when, whenever (11)
ὅτι (conj.) that, because (16); (+ superlative) as . . . as possible (17)
οὐ, οὐκ, οὐχ (adv.) not (2)
οὐδέ (conj.) and not
    (adv.) not even (12)
οὐδείς, οὐδεμία, οὐδέν no one, nothing (17)
οὐκέτι (adv.) no longer (14)
οὖν (postpositive particle) then, therefore (7)
οὔποτε (adv.) never, not ever (16)
οὔτε . . . οὔτε (conjs.) neither . . . nor (8)
οὗτος, αὕτη, τοῦτο this, that (9)
οὕτω(ς) (adv.) in this way, so, thus (9)
ὀφθαλμός, ὀφθαλμοῦ, ὁ eye (3)

πάθος, πάθους, τό experience, suffering (10)
παιδεύω, παιδεύσω, ἐπαίδευσα, πεπαίδευκα, πεπαίδευμαι, ἐπαιδεύθην edu-
    cate, teach (2); (mid.) cause (someone) to be educated or taught (7)
παῖς, παιδός, ὁ or ἡ (gen. pl. παίδων) child (13)
πάλαι (adv.) long ago (4)
παλαιός, παλαιά, παλαιόν old, aged, ancient (6)
πάνυ (adv.) perfectly, very; by all means (16)
παρά (prep.)   + gen. from (the side of)
              + dat. at (the side of), at the house of
              + acc. to (the side of), beside; contrary to (2)
παρα- (prefix) beside (14)
παραγίγνομαι be present, be with (+ dat.) (14)
παραδίδωμι hand over, surrender; hand down (14)

παραμένω stand fast; stay behind (14)

πᾶς, πᾶσα, πᾶν all, every; whole (8)

πάσχω, πείσομαι, ἔπαθον, πέπονθα, ——, —— suffer, have done to one (11)

πατήρ, πατρός, ὁ father (10)

παύω, παύσω, ἔπαυσα, πέπαυκα, πέπαυμαι, ἐπαύθην make stop, stop (*trans.*)
    (3); (*mid.*) stop (oneself), cease (*intrans.*) (7)

πεδίον, πεδίου, τό plain (5)

πείθω, πείσω, ἔπεισα, πέπεικα, πέπεισμαι, ἐπείσθην persuade (5); (*mid.*)
    persuade oneself; obey (+ *dat.*) (7)

πειθώ, πειθοῦς, ἡ persuasion (Section 159)

πεῖρα, πείρᾱς, ἡ trial, attempt; experience (9)

πέμπω, πέμψω, ἔπεμψα, πέπομφα, πέπεμμαι, ἐπέμφθην send (2)

πέντε (*indeclinable numeral*) five (2)

-περ (*enclitic particle*) *adds force to preceding word* (15)

περί (*prep.*) + *gen.* concerning, about
             + *dat.* around
             + *acc.* around, concerning (3)

περι- (*prefix*) all around; very, exceedingly (15)

Περικλῆς, Περικλέους, ὁ Perikles (Athenian statesman) (Section 157)

πίπτω, πεσοῦμαι, ἔπεσον, πέπτωκα, ——, —— fall (16)

πιστεύω, πιστεύσω, ἐπίστευσα, πεπίστευκα, πεπίστευμαι, ἐπιστεύθην trust
    (+ *dat.*) (18)

πλεῖστος, πλείστη, πλεῖστον *superlative of* πολύς, πολλή, πολύ (19)

πλείων *or* πλέων, πλεῖον *or* πλέον *comparative of* πολύς, πολλή, πολύ (19)

πόθεν (*adv.*) from where?, whence? (12)

ποθέν (*enclitic adv.*) from somewhere (18)

ποῖ (*adv.*) (to) where?, whither? (12)

ποι (*enclitic adv.*) (to) some place (18)

ποιέω, ποιήσω, ἐποίησα, πεποίηκα, πεποίημαι, ἐποιήθην make; do (9)

ποίημα, ποιήματος, τό   poem (7)

ποιητής, ποιητοῦ, ὁ poet, author (4)

ποῖος, ποίᾱ, ποῖον of what kind? (15)

πολέμιος, πολεμίᾱ, πολέμιον hostile (+ *dat.*) (5)

πόλεμος, πολέμου, ὁ war (2)

πόλις, πόλεως, ἡ city (10)

πολῑτείᾱ, πολῑτείᾱς, ἡ government, constitution, commonwealth (16)

πολῑτεύω, πολῑτεύσω, ἐπολῑτευσα, πεπολῑτευκα, πεπολῑτευμαι, ἐπολῑτεύθην
    live as a citizen; conduct the government; (*pass.*) be governed (6)

πολίτης, πολίτου, ὁ citizen (4)

πολλάκις (*adv.*) often (16)

πολύς, πολλή, πολύ much, many (16)

πονηρός, πονηρά, πονηρόν worthless, evil, base (16)

πόσος, πόση, πόσον   how much/many?, how large? (17)
πότε (adv.)   when? (10)
ποτέ (enclitic adv.)   at some time, ever (10)
πότερον (adv.)   introduces alternative question (17)
πότερος, ποτέρᾱ, πότερον   which (of two) (17)
ποῦ (adv.)   where?, in what place? (12)
που (enclitic adv.)   qualifies an assertion, 1 suppose; somewhere (12)
πούς, ποδός, ὁ (voc. πούς)   foot (13)
πρᾶγμα, πράγματος, τό   deed, affair, thing (6)
πράττω, πράξω, ἔπρᾱξα, πέπρᾱχα (trans.) or πέπρᾱγα (intrans.), πέπρᾱγμαι,
      ἐπράχθην   do; fare (5); bring it about (that) (13)
πρίν (+ infin.)   before
          (+ indic., or ἄν + subj.)   after negative main clause until (19)
πρό (prep.)   + gen.   before; in front of (2)
προ- (prefix)   forward, on behalf of, before (16)
προδίδωμι   betray, give up (to an enemy), abandon (16)
πρός (prep.)   + gen.   in the eyes of, in the name of
                  + dat.   near; in addition to
                  + acc.   toward (12)
προσ- (prefix)   to, against; besides (12)
πρότερον (adv.)   before, earlier (19)
πρότερος, προτέρᾱ, πρότερον   former, superior (19)
πρῶτος, πρώτη, πρῶτον   first (5)
πυνθάνομαι, πεύσομαι, ἐπυθόμην, ——, πέπυσμαι, —— inquire, learn by
      inquiry (20)
πῶς (adv.)   how? (11)
πως (enclitic adv.)   in any way, in some way (11)

ῥᾴδιος, ῥᾱδίᾱ, ῥᾴδιον   easy (14)
ῥᾷστος, ῥᾴστη, ῥᾷστον   easiest (19)
ῥᾴων, ῥᾷον   easier (19)
ῥητορική, ῥητορικῆς, ἡ   rhetoric (7)
ῥήτωρ, ῥήτορος, ὁ   public speaker (7)

σαφής, σαφές   clear, distinct (13)
σεαυτοῦ, σεαυτῆς (reflexive pronoun)   yourself (15)
σῑγή, σῑγῆς, ἡ   silence (9)
σός, σή, σόν   your; (substantive) yours (15)
σοφίᾱ, σοφίᾱς, ἡ   wisdom, skill (6)
σοφός, σοφή, σοφόν   wise, skilled (6)
στάδιον, σταδίου, τό (pl. τὰ στάδια or οἱ στάδιοι)   stade (= ca. 600 ft.) (6)
στάσις, στάσεως, ἡ   civil strife, faction (14)

στέφανος, στεφάνου, ὁ   crown, wreath (2)

στρατηγός, στρατηγοῦ, ὁ   general (8)

στρατιώτης, στρατιώτου, ὁ   soldier (4)

στρατός, στρατοῦ, ὁ   army (8)

σύ (*personal pronoun*)   you (15)

συμβουλεύω   advise, counsel (+ *dat.*); (*mid.*) consult with (+ *dat.*)   (18)

σύμμαχος, συμμάχου, ὁ   ally (13)

σύμπᾱς, σύμπᾱσα, σύμπαν   all together (8)

συμφέρω   bring together; be useful or profitable; (*impersonal*) it is expedient (15)

σύν (*prep.*) + *dat.*   with (4)

συν- (*prefix*)   with, together (12)

συνίημι, συνήσω, συνῆκα, συνεῖκα, συνεῖμαι, συνείθην   understand, comprehend (18)

σύνοιδα   be aware, know (+ *dat.*)   (19)

σφέτερος αὐτῶν   their (own) (15)

σφῶν αὐτῶν (*reflexive pronoun*)   themselves (15)

σώζω, σώσω, ἔσωσα, σέσωκα, σέσωσμαι or σέσωμαι, ἐσώθην   save (7)

Σωκράτης, Σωκράτους, ὁ   Sokrates (philosopher) (10)

σῶμα, σώματος, τό   body (6)

σωτήρ, σωτῆρος, ὁ (*voc.* σῶτερ)   savior (7)

σωφροσύνη, σωφροσύνης, ἡ   prudence, self-control, moderation (16)

σώφρων, σῶφρον   prudent, temperate (10)

τάττω, τάξω, ἔταξα, τέταχα, τέταγμαι, ἐτάχθην   draw up in order, station, appoint (4); (*mid.*) fall into order of battle (7)

τάχιστος, ταχίστη, τάχιστον   quickest, swiftest (19)

ταχύς, ταχεῖα, ταχύ   quick, swift (17)

τε (*enclitic conj.*)   and (6)

τεῖχος, τείχους, τό   city wall (13)

τελευτάω, τελευτήσω, ἐτελεύτησα, τετελεύτηκα, τετελεύτημαι, ἐτελευτήθην   finish; die (10)

τέλος, τέλους, τό   end; power (10)

τέτταρες, τέτταρα   four (17)

τέταρτος, τετάρτη, τέταρτον   fourth (17)

τέχνη, τέχνης, ἡ   art, skill, craft (1)

τίθημι, θήσω, ἔθηκα, τέθηκα, τέθειμαι, ἐτέθην   put (12)

τῑμάω, τῑμήσω, ἐτίμησα, τετίμηκα, τετίμημαι, ἐτῑμήθην   honor (9)

τῑμή, τῑμῆς, ἡ   honor; price (7)

τίς, τί (*interrogative pronoun/adjective*)   who?, what?, which? (15)

   τί (*adverbial accusative of above*)   why? (15)

τις, τι (*indefinite enclitic pronoun/adjective*) someone, something; anyone, anything; some, any (15)

τοι (*enclitic particle*) let me tell you, you know (6)

τοιοῦτος, τοιαύτη, τοιοῦτο/τοιοῦτον of this/that sort, such (as this) (15)

τόπος, τόπου, ὁ place (13)

τοσοῦτος, τοσαύτη, τοσοῦτο/τοσοῦτον so much/many, so large (17)

τότε (*adv.*) then (11)

τράπεζα, τραπέζης, ἡ table; money-changer's table, bank (18)

τρεῖς, τρία three (17)

τρέπω, τρέψω, ἔτρεψα or ἐτραπόμην, τέτροφα, τέτραμμαι, ἐτράπην or ἐτρέφθην turn; (*mid., aor. pass.*) turn oneself (20)

τριήρης, τριήρους, ἡ trireme, ship (Section 156)

τρίτος, τρίτη, τρίτον third (17)

τρόπαιον, τροπαίου, τό trophy, victory monument (13)

τρόπος, τρόπου, ὁ way, manner; character (9)

τυγχάνω, τεύξομαι, ἔτυχον, τετύχηκα, ——, —— happen (to); hit the mark; (+ *gen.*) obtain (14)

τύχη, τύχης, ἡ fortune, chance (11)

ὕβρις, ὕβρεως, ἡ insolence (11)

ὕδωρ, ὕδατος, τό water (9)

ὑμεῖς (*personal pronoun*) you (15)

ὑμέτερος, ὑμετέρα, ὑμέτερον your; (*substantive*) yours (15)

ὑμῶν αὐτῶν (*reflexive pronoun*) yourselves (15)

ὑπακούω heed, obey (+ *gen. or dat.*) (14)

ὑπέρ (*prep.*) + *gen.* over, above; on behalf of
                        + *acc.* over, beyond (of motion or measure) (9)

ὑπερ- (*prefix*) over; greatly; on behalf of (17)

ὑπό (*prep.*) + *gen.* by (+ *gen. of personal agent*); under
                     + *dat.* under, under the power of
                     + *acc.* under (with motion); toward (of time) (5)

ὑπο- (*prefix*) under; secretly; gradually, slightly (14)

ὑπομένω await; stand firm; endure (14)

ὕστατος, ὑστάτη, ὕστατον last (19)

ὕστερον (*adv.*) later (19)

ὕστερος, ὑστέρα, ὕστερον later (19)

φαίνω, φανῶ, ἔφηνα, πέφηνα, πέφασμαι, ἐφάνην show, cause to appear; (*mid., perfect active, aorist passive*) appear (20)

φάλαγξ, φάλαγγος, ἡ line of battle, phalanx (6)

φέρω, οἴσω, ἤνεγκα or ἤνεγκον, ἐνήνοχα, ἐνήνεγμαι, ἠνέχθην bring, bear, carry; (*mid.*) win (15) φεύγω, φεύξομαι, ἔφυγον, πέφευγα ——, —— flee; be in exile; be a defendant (13)

φημί, φήσω, ἔφησα, ——, ——, —— say, assert, affirm (16)

φθάνω, φθήσομαι, ἔφθασα or ἔφθην, ——, ——, —— act first; be first (in doing something); anticipate (someone) (14)

φιλέω, φιλήσω, ἐφίλησα, πεφίληκα, πεφίλημαι, ἐφιλήθην love, (12)

φιλίᾱ, φιλίᾱς, ἡ friendship (2)

φίλος, φίλη, φίλον dear, beloved, one's own (4)

φίλος, φίλου, ὁ friend (2)

φοβέομαι, φοβήσομαι, ——, ——, πεφόβημαι, ἐφοβήθην fear, be afraid (12)

φοβερός, φοβερά, φοβερόν fearful (5)

φόβος, φόβου, ὁ fear (5)

φονεύς, φονέως, ὁ murderer, killer (11)

φόνος, φόνου, ὁ murder, killing (11)

φύλαξ, φύλακος, ὁ guard (6)

φυλάττω, φυλάξω, ἐφύλαξα, πεφύλαχα, πεφύλαγμαι, ἐφυλάχθην guard (3); (mid.) guard (someone) for one's own protection, be on guard against (7)

φύσις, φύσεως, ἡ nature (10)

χαίρω, χαιρήσω, ——, κεχάρηκα, ——, ἐχάρην rejoice (in), take pleasure (in), enjoy (+ dat.) (14)

χαλεπός, χαλεπή, χαλεπόν difficult, harsh (13)

χάριν (prep.) + preceding gen. for the sake of (6)

χάρις, χάριτος, ἡ grace, favor, gratitude (6)

χείρ, χειρός, ἡ (dat. pl. χερσί[ν]) hand (13)

χείριστος, χειρίστη, χείριστον worst (morally, in ability) (19)

χείρων, χεῖρον worse (19)

χορευτής, χορευτοῦ, ὁ choral dancer (6)

χορεύω, χορεύσω, ἐχόρευσα, κεχόρευκα, κεχόρευμαι, ἐχορεύθην dance, take part in a chorus (6)

χορός, χοροῦ, ὁ dance; chorus (6)

χράομαι, χρήσομαι, ἐχρησάμην, ——, κέχρημαι, ἐχρήσθην use, experience, treat as (+ dat.) (Section 164)

χρή, χρῆσται, ——, ——, ——, —— (impersonal verb) ought, must (20)

χρῆμα, χρήματος, τό thing; (pl.) goods, property, money (8)

χρόνος, χρόνου, ὁ time (19)

χρῡσός, χρῡσοῦ, ὁ gold (2)

χρῡσοῦς, χρῡσῆ, χρῡσοῦν golden (Section 161)

χώρᾱ, χώρᾱς, ἡ land, country (1)

ψευδής, ψευδές false, lying (18)
ψεῦδος, ψεύδους, τό falsehood, lie (18)
ψῡχή, ψῡχῆς, ἡ soul (1)

ὦ (*interjection*) *used with vocative* (1)
ὡς in order that (*introduces purpose clauses*) (3); that (*introduces indirect statement*) (16); as (18); how! (*exclamatory*) (18); *with causal or purpose participle: cause or purpose not vouched for by speaker* (8); (+ *superlative*) as . . . as possible (17)
ὥστε (*conj.*) so as, so that (10)

a *omitted in Greek*; τις, τι (15)
abandon προδίδωμι (16)
able: be able δύναμαι (17); ἔχω (17); οἷός τ᾽ εἰμί (15)
about περί (*prep.*) + *gen. or acc.* (3)
about: be about to μέλλω + *fut. inf.* (18)
above ὑπέρ (*prep.*) + *gen.* (9)
accept ἀποδέχομαι (11)
according to κατά (*prep.*) + *acc.* (6)
account: on account of διά (*prep.*) + *acc.* (3)
acquainted with ἔμπειρος, ἔμπειρον + *gen.* (9)
act first φθάνω (14)
addition: in addition to πρός (*prep.*) + *dat.* (12)
advise συμβουλεύω + *dat.* (18)
affair πρᾶγμα, πράγματος, τό (6)
affirm φημί (16)
afraid: be afraid φοβέομαι (12)
after μετά (*prep.*) + *acc.* (4); ἐπεί, ἐπειδή (*conjs.*) (3); ἐπειδάν (*conj.*) (11);
    ἐπι- (*prefix*) (13)
again αὖ (*postpositive particle*) (18)
against ἐπί (*prep.*) + *acc.* (13); ἐπι- (*prefix*) (13); κατά (*prep.*) + *gen.* (6);
    κατα- (*prefix*) (12); προσ- (*prefix*) (12)
    be on guard against φυλάττομαι + *accusative* (7)
    fight against μάχομαι + *dat.* (13)
aged παλαιός, παλαιά, παλαιόν (6)
all πᾶς, πᾶσα, πᾶν; ἅπᾱς, ἅπᾱσα, ἅπαν (8)
    all together σύμπᾱς, σύμπᾱσα, σύμπαν (8)
    quite all ἅπᾱς, ἅπᾱσα, ἅπαν (8)
    all (considered singly) ἕκαστοι, ἕκασται, ἕκαστα (16)
    not at all ἥκιστα (*adv.*) (19)
    all around περι- (*prefix*) (15)
allowed: it is allowed ἔξεστι(ν) (*impersonal verb*) (15)
ally σύμμαχος, συμμάχου, ὁ (13)
alone μόνος, μόνη, μόνον (12)
also καί (*adv.*) (1)

793

although　καίπερ (particle) (8)
always　ἀεί (adv.) (11)
ancient　παλαιός, παλαιά, παλαιόν (6)
and　καί (conj.) (1); τε (enclitic conj.) (6)
　　and further　καίτοι (particle) (4)
　　and not　οὐδέ; μηδέ (conjs.) (12)
　　and yet　καίτοι (particle) (4)
　　both . . . and　καί . . . καί (conjs.) (1)
animal　ζῷον, ζῴου, τό (2)
announce　ἀγγέλλω (10)
another　ἄλλος, ἄλλη, ἄλλο (7)
　　one another　——, ἀλλήλων (reciprocal pronoun) (12)
answer　ἀποκρίνομαι (19)
anticipate (someone)　φθάνω (14)
any　τις, τι (indefinite enclitic pronoun/adjective) (15)
　　anyone　τις, τι (indefinite enclitic pronoun/adjective) (15)
　　anything　τις, τι (indefinite enclitic pronoun/adjective) (15)
　　any way: in any way　πως (enclitic adv.) (11)
appear　φαίνομαι (20)
　　cause to appear　φαίνω (20)
appoint　καθίστημι (12), τάττω (4)
　　be appointed　καθίσταμαι (12)
archon　ἄρχων, ἄρχοντος, ὁ (13)
Aristophanes (comic poet)　᾿Αριστοφάνης, ᾿Αριστοφάνους, ὁ (13)
army　στρατός, στρατοῦ, ὁ (8)
around　περί (prep.) + dat. or acc. (3)
　　all around　περι- (prefix) (15)
arrive　ἀφικνέομαι (20)
art　τέχνη, τέχνης, ἡ (1)
as　ὡς (conj.) (18)
　　as large as　ὅσος, ὅση, ὅσον (17)
　　as long as　ἕως, μέχρι (conjs.) (19)
　　as many as　ὅσοι, ὅσαι, ὅσα (17)
　　as much as　ὅσος, ὅση, ὅσον (17)
　　as . . . as possible　ὅτι/ὡς + superlative (17)
　　so as　ὥστε + infinitive in clause of natural result (10)
ashamed : be ashamed　αἰσχύνομαι (19)
ask　——, ἐρήσομαι (19); ——, ἀνερήσομαι (19); ἐρωτάω (14)
assembly　ἐκκλησίᾱ, ἐκκλησίᾱς, ἡ (3)
assert　φημί (16)
Athenian　᾿Αθηναῖος, ᾿Αθηναίᾱ, ᾿Αθηναῖον (8)
attempt　πεῖρα, πείρᾱς, ἡ (9)

at (the side of)   παρά (*prep.*) + *dat.* (2)
   at any rate   γε (*enclitic particle*) (6)
   at least   γε *enclitic particle* (6)
   at some time   ποτέ (*enclitic adv.*) (10)
   at the house of   παρά (*prep.*) + *dat.* (2)
   at the same time   ἅμα (*adv.*) (8)
   at the same time as   ἅμα (*prep.*) + *dat.* (8)
author   ποιητής, ποιητοῦ, ὁ (4)
await   ὑπομένω (14)
aware: be aware   σύνοιδα (+ *dat.*) (19)
away from   ἀπό (*prep.*) + gen. (2); ἀπο- (*prefix*) (10)

bad   κακός, κακή, κακόν (4)
banished: be banished   ἐκπίπτω (16)
bank   τράπεζα, τραπέζης, ἡ (18)
base   πονηρός, πονηρά, πονηρόν (16)
battle   μάχη, μάχης, ἡ   (1)
   line of battle   φάλαγξ, φάλαγγος, ἡ (6)
be   *nominal sentence* (5); εἰμί (15); ἔχω + *adverb* (17)
   be able   δύναμαι (17); ἔχω (17); οἷός τ’ εἰμί (15)
   be about to   μέλλω + *fut. infin.* (18)
   be afraid   φοβέομαι (12)
   be appointed   καθίσταμαι (12)
   be ashamed   αἰσχύνομαι (19)
   be aware   σύνοιδα (19)
   be banished   ἐκπίπτω (16)
   be born   γίγνομαι (13)
   be commander   ἡγέομαι (19)
   be a defendant   φεύγω (13)
   be different from   διαφέρω + *gen.* (15)
   be driven out   ἐκπίπτω (16)
   be established   καθίσταμαι (12)
   be first (in doing something)   φθάνω (14)
   be governed   πολῑτεύομαι (6)
   be in exile   φεύγω (13)
   be likely to   μέλλω + *fut. infin.* (18)
   be next to   ἔχομαι + *gen.* (17)
   be on guard against   φυλάττομαι (7)
   be placed   κεῖμαι (20)
   be present   ἥκω (8); παραγίγνομαι + *dat.* (14)
   be profitable   συμφέρω (15)
   be set   κεῖμαι (20)

be a slave   δουλεύω + *dat.* (6)
be spoken of   ἀκούω (11)
be useful or profitable   συμφέρω (15)
be willing   ἐθέλω (4)
be with   παραγίγνομαι + *dat.* (14)
bear   φέρω (15)
beautiful   καλός, καλή, καλόν (4)
beauty   κάλλος, κάλλους, τό (11)
because   *relative clause with* γε (6); *causal participle* (8, 11); ὅτι (*conj.*) (16)
become   γίγνομαι (13)
before   πρίν (*conj.*) + *infin.* (19); πρό (*prep.*) + *gen.* (2); προ- (*prefix*) (16);
    πρότερον (*adv.*) (19)
    do something before (someone)   φθάνω (14)
begin   ἄρχομαι + *gen.* (7)
beginning   ἀρχή, ἀρχῆς, ἡ (4)
behalf: on behalf of   ὑπέρ (*prep.*) + *gen.* (9); προ- (*prefix*) (16); ὑπερ- (*prefix*)
    (17)
behind: stay behind   παραμένω (14)
belief   δόξα, δόξης, ἡ (5)
believe   ἡγέομαι (19), νομίζω (16)
beloved   φίλος, φίλη, φίλον (4)
beside   παρά (*prep.*) + *acc.* (2); παρα- (*prefix*) (14)
besides   προσ- (prefix) (12)
best
    best (in ability or worth)   ἄριστος, ἀρίστη, ἄριστον (19)
    best (morally)   βέλτιστος, βελτίστη, βέλτιστον (19)
    best (strongest)   κράτιστος, κρατίστη, κράτιστον (19)
betray   προδίδωμι (16)
better
    better (in ability or worth)   ἀμείνων, ἄμεινον (19)
    better (morally)   βελτίων, βέλτῑον (19)
    better (stronger)   κρείττων, κρεῖττον (19)
beyond   ὑπέρ (*prep.*) + *acc.* (9)
big   μέγας, μεγάλη, μέγα (17)
billy goat   αἴξ, αἰγός, ὁ (6)
board   ἀναβαίνω (16)
body   σῶμα, σώματος, τό (6)
book   βιβλίον, βιβλίου, τό (1)
born: be born   γίγνομαι (13)
both . . . and   καί . . . καί (*conjs.*) (1)
bribe   δῶρα, δώρων, τά (1)
bridge   γέφῡρα, γεφύρᾱς, ἡ (4)

bring   φέρω (15)
 bring together   συμφέρω (15)
bring it about (that)   πράττω + *object clause of effort* (13)
brother   ἀδελφός, ἀδελφοῦ, ὁ (*voc.* ἄδελφε) (1)
bury   θάπτω (4)
but   ἀλλά (3); δέ (2) (*conjs.*)
by   *instrument*: *dative case without preposition* (1)
 personal agent: ὑπό + *gen.* (5) *or* (*with perfect, pluperfect, or verbal adjective*) *dative without preposition* (5, 20)
 + *name of god*: νή (*affirmative particle*) + *accusative* (16)
 by all means   πάνυ (*adv.*) (16)

call   καλέω (10)
can   δύναμαι (17); ἔχω (17); οἷός τ' εἰμί (15)
capable   ἱκανός, ἱκανή, ἱκανόν (5)
capture   αἱρέω (15)
carry   φέρω (15)
 carry through   διαφέρω (15)
cause   αἰτία, αἰτίας, ἡ (11)
 cause to appear   φαίνω (20)
 cause (someone) to be educated   παιδεύομαι (7)
 cause (someone) to be freed   λύομαι (7)
 cause to revolt   ἀφίστημι (12)
 cause a sacrifice to be made   θύομαι (7)
 cause (someone) to be taught   διδάσκομαι (7); παιδεύομαι (7)
 cause to be written   γράφομαι (7)
cease   παύομαι (7)
 cease to exist   ἀπόλλυμαι (19)
chance   τύχη, τύχης, ἡ (11)
change: *indicates change*   μετα- (*prefix*) (13)
character   τρόπος, τρόπου, ὁ (9)
charge: on a charge of   *genitive of the charge* (7)
child   παῖς, παιδός, ὁ *or* ἡ (*gen. pl.* παίδων) (13)
choose   αἱρέομαι (15)
choral dancer   χορευτής, χορευτοῦ, ὁ (6)
chorus   χορός, χοροῦ, ὁ (6)
 take part in a chorus   χορεύω (6)
citizen   πολίτης, πολίτου, ὁ (4)
 live as a citizen   πολιτεύω (6)
city   πόλις, πόλεως, ἡ (10)
city wall   τεῖχος, τείχους, τό (13)
civil strife   στάσις, στάσεως, ἡ (14)

clear   δῆλος, δήλη, δῆλον (7); σαφής, σαφές (13)
   make clear   δηλόω (10)
clever   δεινός, δεινή, δεινόν (6)
cling to   ἔχομαι + gen. (17)
coin (small)   ἀργύριον, ἀργυρίου, τό (5)
come   ἔρχομαι (13); εἶμι (17)
   have come   ἥκω (8)
command   ἄρχω + gen. (5); κελεύω (2)
commander: be commander   ἡγέομαι (19)
common   κοινός, κοινή, κοινόν (14)
commonwealth   πολῑτείᾱ, πολῑτείᾱς, ἡ (16)
companion   ἑταῖρος, ἑταίρου, ὁ (13)
comprehend   συνίημι (18)
concerning   περί (prep.) + gen., acc. (3)
condition: on condition that   ἐπί (prep.) + dat. (13)
conduct the government   πολῑτεύω (6)
conquer   νῑκάω (9)
consider   νομίζω (16)
constitution   πολῑτείᾱ, πολῑτείᾱς, ἡ (16)
consult with   συμβουλεύομαι + dat. (18)
   consult the gods   θύομαι (7)
contest   ἀγών, ἀγῶνος, ὁ (9)
contrary to   παρά (prep.) + acc. (2)
contrive   μηχανάομαι (13)
correct   ὀρθός, ὀρθή, ὀρθόν (17)
council   βουλή, βουλῆς, ἡ (3)
counsel   συμβουλεύω + dat. (18)
   take counsel with oneself   βουλεύομαι (18)
country   χώρᾱ, χώρᾱς, ἡ (1)
course: of course   δή (postpositive particle) (3)
craft   τέχνη, τέχνης, ἡ (1)
crown   στέφανος, στεφάνου, ὁ (2)
custom   νόμος, νόμου, ὁ (10)

dance   χορεύω (6); χορός, χοροῦ, ὁ (6)
dancer: choral dancer   χορευτής, χορευτοῦ, ὁ (6)
danger   κίνδῡνος, κινδΰνου, ὁ (5)
daughter   θυγάτηρ, θυγατρός, ἡ (10)
day   ἡμέρᾱ, ἡμέρᾱς, ἡ (4)
dear   φίλος, φίλη, φίλον (4)
death   θάνατος, θανάτου, ὁ (5)
decide   κρίνω (19)

dedicate ἀνατίθημι (12)
deed ἔργον, ἔργου, τό (1); πρᾶγμα, πράγματος, τό (6)
defendant: be a defendant φεύγω (13)
delay μέλλω (18)
deliberate βουλεύομαι (18)
    deliberate on βουλεύω (18)
democracy δημοκρατίᾱ, δημοκρατίᾱς, ἡ (3)
demonstration ἐπίδειξις, ἐπιδείξεως, ἡ (14)
Demosthenes (orator) Δημοσθένης, Δημοσθένους, ὁ (10)
deny οὔ φημι (16)
destroy λύω (2); καταλύω (12)
device μηχανή, μηχανῆς, ἡ (13)
devise μηχανάομαι (13)
die ἀποθνῄσκω (18); ἀπόλλυμαι (19); τελευτάω (10)
different: be different from διαφέρω + gen. (15)
difficult χαλεπός, χαλεπή, χαλεπόν (13)
directions: in different directions δια- (prefix) (15)
discover εὑρίσκω (19)
display ἐπιδείκνυμαι (14); ἐπίδειξις, ἐπιδείξεως, ἡ (14)
dissolve λύω (2); καταλύω (12)
distinct σαφής, σαφές (13)
divine being δαίμων, δαίμονος, ὁ or ἡ (9)
do ποιέω (9); πράττω (5)
    do wrong ἀδικέω (9); ἁμαρτάνω (17); κακὸν ποιέω (9); κακὸν πράττω (5)
doctor ἰᾱτρός, ἰᾱτροῦ, ὁ (20)
documents γράμματα, γραμμάτων, τά (7)
done: have done to one πάσχω (11)
down κατα- (prefix) (12)
draw γράφω (3)
draw up in order τάττω (4)
drive ἐλαύνω (17)
    be driven out ἐκπίπτω (16)
during genitive of time within which (6)

each (of many) ἕκαστος, ἑκάστη, ἕκαστον (16)
    each (of several groups) ἕκαστοι, ἕκασται, ἕκαστα (16)
earlier πρότερον (19)
earth γῆ, γῆς, ἡ (5)
easy ῥᾴδιος, ῥᾳδίᾱ, ῥᾴδιον (14)
educate παιδεύω (2)
eight ὀκτώ (indeclinable numeral) (11)
either . . . or ἤ . . . ἤ (conjs.) (2)

empire ἀρχή, ἀρχῆς, ἡ (4)

end τέλος, τέλους, τό (10)

endure ὑπομένω (14)

enemy (of a country) πολέμιος, πολεμία, πολέμιον (5)
    (personal) ἐχθρός, ἐχθροῦ, ὁ (9)

enjoy χαίρω + dat. (14)

enter into a state καθίσταμαι (12)

epic poetry ἔπη, ἐπῶν, τά (12)

equal ἴσος, ἴση, ἴσον (19)

equally ἴσως (adv.) (19)

error ἁμαρτία, ἁμαρτίας, ἡ (17)

escape the notice of λανθάνω + acc. (14)

establish καθίστημι (12)
    be established καθίσταμαι (12)

Euripides (tragic poet) Εὐρῑπίδης, Εὐρῑπίδου, ὁ (voc. Εὐρῑπίδη) (13)

even καί (adv.) (1)
    not even οὐδέ; μηδέ (advs.) (12)

ever ποτέ (enclitic adv.) (10)
    not ever οὔποτε; μήποτε (advs.) (16)

every πᾶς, πᾶσα, πᾶν (8)

evil κακός, κακή, κακόν (4); πονηρός, πονηρά, πονηρόν (16)

exceedingly περι- (prefix) (15)

excel διαφέρω + gen. (15)

excellence ἀρετή, ἀρετῆς, ἡ (3)

exhibit ἐπιδείκνυμαι (14)

exile: be in exile φεύγω (13)

expect ἀξιόω (10)

expectation δόξα, δόξης, ἡ (5); ἐλπίς, ἐλπίδος, ἡ (6)

expedient: it is expedient συμφέρει (15)

experience ἐμπειρίᾱ, ἐμπειρίᾱς, ἡ (9); πάθος, πάθους, τό (10); πεῖρα, πείρᾱς,
    ἡ (9)

experienced (in) ἔμπειρος, ἔμπειρον + gen. (9)

eye ὀφθαλμός, ὀφθαλμοῦ, ὁ (3)
    in the eyes of dative of reference (4); πρός (prep.) + gen. (12)

fact: in fact δή (postpositive particle) (3)

faction στάσις, στάσεως, ἡ (14)

fair ἴσος, ἴση, ἴσον (19)

fall πίπτω (16)
    fall into order of battle τάττομαι (7)

false ψευδής, ψευδές (18)

falsehood ψεῦδος, ψεύδους, τό (18)

fare πράττω (5)

fast: stand fast παραμένω (14)

fate μοῖρα, μοίρᾱς, ἡ (4)

father πατήρ, πατρός, ὁ (10)

favor χάρις, χάριτος, ἡ (6)

favorably: receive favorably ἀποδέχομαι (11)

fear φοβέομαι (12); φόβος, φόβον, ὁ (5)

fearful φοβερός, φοβερά, φοβερόν (5)

fearsome δεινός, δεινή, δεινόν (6)

feel shame before αἰσχύνομαι (19)

festival ἑορτή, ἑορτῆς, ἡ (13)

few ὀλίγοι, ὀλίγαι, ὀλίγα (19)

fight (with) μάχομαι + dat. (13)

find εὑρίσκω (19)

finish τελευτάω (10)

firm: stand firm ὑπομένω (14)

first πρῶτος, πρώτη, πρῶτον (5)

    act first φθάνω (14)

    be first (in doing something) φθάνω (14)

five πέντε (indeclinable numeral) (2)

flat ἴσος, ἴση, ἴσον (19)

flee φεύγω (13)

follow ἕπομαι + dat. (15)

foolish ἄφρων, ἄφρον (11)

foot πούς, ποδός, ὁ (voc. πούς) (13)

for indirect object: dative without a preposition (1)

    purpose: εἰς (1) or ἐπί (13) (preps.) + accusative

    extent of time: accusative without preposition (6)

    conjunction: γάρ (postpositive) (2)

    + price or value: genitive of value (12)

    for the sake of ἕνεκα (prep.) + preceding gen. (16); χάριν (prep.)
       + preceding gen. (6)

foreign βάρβαρος, βάρβαρον (9)

foreigner ξένος, ξένου, ὁ (2); βάρβαρος, βάρβαρον (as substantive) (9)

former πρότερος, προτέρα, πρότερον (19)

former . . . latter ἐκεῖνος (7) . . . οὗτος (9)

fortunate εὐδαίμων, εὔδαιμον (10)

fortune τύχη, τύχης, ἡ (11)

forward προ- (prefix) (16)

four τέτταρες, τέτταρα (17)

fourth τέταρτος, τετάρτη, τέταρτον (17)

free ἐλεύθερος, ἐλευθέρᾱ, ἐλεύθερον (6); λύω (2)

freedom   ἐλευθερίᾱ, ἐλευθερίᾱς, ἡ (6)
friend   φίλος, φίλου, ὁ (2)
friendship   φιλίᾱ, φιλίᾱς, ἡ (2)
from: away from   ἀπό (prep.) + gen. (2)
    from (the side of)   παρά (prep.) + gen. (2)
    from where?   πόθεν (adv.) (12); ὁπόθεν (indirect interrogative) (18)
    from somewhere   ποθέν (enclitic adv.) (18)
    from wherever   ὁπόθεν (indefinite relative) (18)
front: in front of   πρό (prep.) + gen. (2)
further   αὖ (postpositive particle) (18)
    and further   καίτοι (particle) (4)

gain   κέρδος, κέρδους, τό (19)
general   στρατηγός, στρατηγοῦ, ὁ   (8)
gift   δῶρον, δώρου, τό (1)
give   δίδωμι (12)
    give back   ἀποδίδωμι (12)
    give a share to   μεταδίδωμι (13)
    give up (to an enemy)   προδίδωμι (16)
glad   ἡδύς, ἡδεῖα, ἡδύ (17)
glory   δόξα, δόξης, ἡ (5)
go   βαίνω (16); εἶμι (17); ἔρχομαι (13)
    go away   ἄπειμι (17); ἀπέρχομαι (13)
    go up   ἀναβαίνω (16)
    go upland   ἀναβαίνω (16)
    go down   καταβαίνω (16)
goat   αἴξ, αἰγός, ὁ or ἡ (6)
god   θεός, θεοῦ, ὁ (1); δαίμων, δαίμονος, ὁ (9)
goddess   θεός, θεοῦ, ἡ (1); δαίμων, δαίμονος, ἡ (9)
gold   χρῡσός, χρῡσοῦ, ὁ (2)
good   ἀγαθός, ἀγαθή, ἀγαθόν (4); καλός, καλή, καλόν (4)
    goods   χρήματα, χρημάτων, τά (8)
governed: be governed   πολῑτεύομαι (6)
government   πολῑτείᾱ, πολῑτείᾱς, ἡ (16)
    conduct the government   πολῑτεύω (6)
grace   χάρις, χάριτος, ἡ (6)
gradually   ὑπο- (prefix) (14)
gratitude   χάρις, χάριτος, ἡ (6)
great   μέγας, μεγάλη, μέγα (17)
    greater   μείζων, μεῖζον (19)
    greatest   μέγιστος, μεγίστη, μέγιστον (19)
greatly   ὑπερ- (prefix) (17)

Greek: a Greek Ἕλλην, Ἕλληνος, ὁ (6)

grief λύπη, λύπης, ἡ (19)

guard φύλαξ, φύλακος, ὁ (6); φυλάττω (3)

    be on guard against φυλάττομαι + acc. (7)

    guard someone for one's own protection φυλάττομαι + acc. (7)

guest-friend ξένος, ξένου, ὁ (2)

guilt αἰτίā, αἰτίāς, ἡ (11)

guilty (of) αἴτιος, αἰτίā, αἴτιον + gen. (11)

hand χείρ, χειρός, ἡ (dat. pl. χερσί[ν]) (13)

    hand down παραδίδωμι (14)

    hand over παραδίδωμι (14)

happen γίγνομαι (13)

    happen (to) τυγχάνω (14)

happy εὐδαίμων, εὔδαιμον (10)

harbor λιμήν, λιμένος, ὁ (16)

harm βλάπτω (5)

harsh χαλεπός, χαλεπή, χαλεπόν (13)

hated ἐχθρός, ἐχθρά, ἐχθρόν (9)

have dative of the possessor (15); ἔχω (17)

    have come ἥκω (8)

    have done to one πάσχω (11)

he contained in the verb; (for emphasis) demonstrative pronoun; see also him, his

hear ἀκούω + gen. of person, acc. of thing (11)

heavy βαρύς, βαρεῖα, βαρύ (17)

heavy-armed foot soldier ὁπλίτης, ὁπλίτου, ὁ (4)

heed ὑπακούω + gen. or dat. (14)

help: with the help of σύν (prep.) + dat. (4)

her αὐτός, αὐτή, αὐτό (fem. pronoun in gen., dat., acc.) (11); (cf. "his")

herald κῆρυξ, κήρυκος, ὁ (dat. pl. κήρυξι[ν]) (11)

here ἐνταῦθα (adv.) (11)

herself αὐτός, αὐτή, αὐτό (intensive, in predicate position or alone in nomi-
    native) (11); ἑαυτοῦ, ἑαυτῆς, ἑαυτοῦ (reflexive pronoun) (15)

him αὐτός, αὐτή, αὐτό (masc. pronoun in gen., dat., acc.) (11)

himself αὐτός, αὐτή, αὐτό (intensive, in predicate position or alone in nomi-
    native) (11); ἑαυτοῦ, ἑαυτῆς, ἑαυτοῦ (reflexive pronoun) (15)

hinder (from) κωλύω (6)

his (when context is clear) the article (1); demonstrative pronoun in attributive
    position (7, 9); αὐτοῦ in predicate position (11)

hit (with thrown object) βάλλω (11)

    hit the mark τυγχάνω (14)

hold ἔχω (17)
holy ἱερός, ἱερά, ἱερόν (5)
Homer (epic poet) Ὅμηρος, Ὁμήρου, ὁ (1)
honor τῑμάω (9); τῑμή, τῑμῆς, ἡ (7)
hope ἐλπίς, ἐλπίδος, ἡ (6)
hoplite ὁπλίτης, ὁπλίτου, ὁ (4)
horse ἵππος, ἵππου, ὁ or ἡ (5)
horseman ἱππεύς, ἱππέως, ὁ (10)
host ξένος, ξένου, ὁ (2)
hostile ἐχθρός, ἐχθρά, ἐχθρόν (9); πολέμιος, πολεμία, πολέμιον (+ dat.) (5)
house οἰκίᾱ, οἰκίᾱς, ἡ (1)
       at the house of παρά (prep.) + dat. (2)
how? πῶς (adv.) (11); τίνα τρόπον (15); τίνι τρόπῳ (15); ὅπως (indirect in-
       terrogative) (18)
       how! ὡς (adv.) (18)
       how large! ὅσος, ὅση, ὅσον (17)
       how large? πόσος, πόση, πόσον (17); ὁπόσος, ὁπόση, ὁπόσον (indirect
       interrogative) (18)
       how many! ὅσοι, ὅσαι, ὅσα (17)
       how many? πόσοι, πόσαι, πόσα (17); ὁπόσοι, ὁπόσαι, ὁπόσα (indirect
       interrogative) (18)
       how much! ὅσος, ὅση, ὅσον (17)
       how much? πόσος, πόση, πόσον (17); ὁπόσος, ὁπόση, ὁπόσον (indirect
       interrogative) (18)
however ὅπως (indefinite relative) (18)
       however large ὁπόσος, ὁπόση, ὁπόσον (indefinite relative) (18)
       however many ὁπόσοι, ὁπόσαι, ὁπόσα (indefinite relative) (18)
       however much ὁπόσος, ὁπόση, ὁπόσον (indefinite relative) (18)
human being ἄνθρωπος, ἀνθρώπου, ὁ (1)
hurl ἵημι (18)
hurt βλάπτω (5)

I contained in the verb; (for emphasis) ἐγώ (15)
       I suppose που (enclitic adv.) (12)
if εἰ, ἐάν (particles) (4); εἰ (indirect interrogative) (18)
       if . . . or εἰ . . . εἴτε, εἴτε . . . εἴτε, πότερον . . . ἤ (indirect interrogatives)
       (18)
       if only optative of wish (7, 17)
ignorance ἀμαθίᾱ, ἀμαθίᾱς, ἡ (14)
ignorant ἀμαθής, ἀμαθές (14)
immediately αὐτίκα (adv.) (13)
immortal ἀθάνατος, ἀθάνατον (5)

in ἐν (prep.) + dat. (1); εἰσ- (prefix) (11)
    in addition to πρός (prep.) + dat. (12)
    in any way πως (enclitic adv.) (11)
    in different directions δια- (prefix) (15)
    in the eyes of dative of reference (4); πρός (prep.) + gen. (12)
    in fact δή (postpositive particle) (3)
    in front of πρό (prep.) + gen. (2)
    in the name of πρός (prep.) + gen. (12)
    in order that ἵνα/ὡς/ὅπως + purpose clause (3)
    in some way πως (enclitic adv.) (11)
    in this way οὕτω(ς) (adv.) (9)
    in turn αὖ (postpositive particle) (11)
    in what place? ποῦ (adv.) (12)
    in what way? πῶς (adv.) (11); τίνα τρόπον (15); τίνι τρόπῳ (15); ὅπως
        (indirect interrogative) (18)
indict γράφομαι (7)
indictment γραφή, γραφῆς, ἡ (7)
inhabitants use the article as a substantive (5)
inquire πυνθάνομαι (20)
inquiry: learn by inquiry πυνθάνομαι (20)
insolence ὕβρις, ὕβρεως, ἡ (11)
instead of ἀντί (prep.) + gen. (3)
insurrection: rise in insurrection against ἐπανίσταμαι (14)
interpreter ἑρμηνεύς, ἑρμηνέως, ὁ (12)
into εἰς (prep.) + acc. (1); εἰσ- (prefix) (11)
irrational ἄλογος, ἄλογον (9)
island νῆσος, νήσου, ἡ (1)
it contained in verb; αὐτός, αὐτή, αὐτό (pronoun in gen., dat., acc.) (11)
    it is allowed ἔξεστι(ν) (impersonal verb) (15); ἔστι(ν) (impersonal verb) (15)
    it is expedient συμφέρει (15)
    it is necessary δεῖ (impersonal verb) (20)
    it is possible ἔξεστι(ν) (impersonal verb) (15); ἔστι(ν) (impersonal verb) (15)
italics (for emphasis) γε (enclitic particle) (6)
itself αὐτός, αὐτή, αὐτό (intensive, in predicate position or alone in nomina-
    tive) (11); ἑαυτοῦ, ἑαυτῆς, ἑαυτοῦ (reflexive pronoun) (15)

judge κρίνω (19); κριτής, κριτοῦ, ὁ (19)
judgment γνώμη, γνώμης, ἡ (6)
just δίκαιος, δικαίᾱ, δίκαιον (4)
justice δίκη, δίκης, ἡ (4)

keen ὀξύς, ὀξεῖα, ὀξύ (18)
keep peace εἰρήνην ἄγω (8)

kill ἀποκτείνω (18); ἀπόλλυμι (19)
killer φονεύς, φονέως, ὁ (11)
killing φόνος, φόνου, ὁ (11)
kind γένος, γένους, τό (10)
    of what kind? ποῖος, ποία, ποῖον (15); ὁποῖος, ὁποία, ὁποῖον (indirect
        interrogative) (18)
    of whatever kind ὁποῖος, ὁποία, ὁποῖον (indefinite relative) (18)
king βασιλεύς, βασιλέως, ὁ (10)
know γιγνώσκω (16); ἐπίσταμαι (17); οἶδα (19); σύνοιδα (19)
    you know τοι (enclitic particle) (6)
knowledge ἐπιστήμη, ἐπιστήμης, ἡ (17)

land γῆ, γῆς, ἡ (5); χώρα, χώρας, ἡ (1)
large μέγας, μεγάλη, μέγα (17)
    how large? πόσος, πόση, πόσον (17); ὁπόσος, ὁπόση, ὁπόσον (indirect
        interrogative) (18)
    how large! ὅσος, ὅση, ὅσον (17)
    however large ὁπόσος, ὁπόση, ὁπόσον (indefinite relative) (17)
    so large τοσοῦτος, τοσαύτη, τοσοῦτο/τοσοῦτον (17)
    as large as ὅσος, ὅση, ὅσον (17)
last ὕστατος, ὑστάτη, ὕστατον (19)
later ὕστερον (adv.) (19); ὕστερος, ὑστέρᾱ, ὕστερον (19)
latter: former . . . latter ἐκεῖνος (7) . . . οὗτος (9)
law νόμος, νόμου, ὁ (10)
lawsuit δίκη, δίκης, ἡ (4)
lead ἄγω (8); ἡγέομαι + gen. (19)
    lead the way ἡγέομαι (19)
leader ἡγεμών, ἡγεμόνος, ὁ (7)
learn μανθάνω (13)
    learn by inquiry πυνθάνομαι (20)
least ἐλάχιστος, ἐλαχίστη, ἐλάχιστον (19); ἥκιστα (adv.) (19)
    at least γε (enclitic particle) (6)
leave λείπω (7)
    leave behind λείπω (7)
less ἐλάττων, ἔλαττον (19)
lest μή (conj.) (12)
letter (of the alphabet) γράμμα, γράμματος, τό (7)
let go ἀφίημι (18)
let me tell you τοι (enclitic particle) (6)
lie κεῖμαι (20)
lie ψεῦδος, ψεύδους, τό (18)
life βίος, βίου, ὁ (9)

like ὅμοιος, ὁμοίᾱ, ὅμοιον (13)
likely: be likely to μέλλω + future infin. (18)
line of battle φάλαγξ, φάλαγγος, ἡ (6)
little μῑκρός, μῑκρά, μῑκρόν (5); ὀλίγος, ὀλίγη, ὀλίγον (19)
live as a citizen πολῑτεύω (6)
living: means of living βίος, βίου, ὁ (9)
long μακρός, μακρά, μακρόν (5)
    long ago πάλαι (adv.) (4)
    as long as ἕως (conj.) (19); μέχρι (conj.) (19)
longer: no longer οὐκέτι (adv.) (14); μηκέτι (adv.) (14)
lose ἀπόλλῡμι (19)
love ἔρως, ἔρωτος, ὁ (voc. ἔρως) (11); φιλέω (12)
lucky εὐτυχής, εὐτυχές (11)
lying ψευδής, ψευδές (18)

machine μηχανή, μηχανῆς, ἡ (13)
make ποιέω (9)
    make clear δηλόω (10)
    make laws νόμους τίθημι (12)
    make a mistake ἁμαρτάνω (17)
    make stand ἵστημι (12)
    make stop παύω (3)
man ἀνήρ, ἀνδρός, ὁ (10); ἄνθρωπος, ἀνθρώπου, ὁ (1)
    old man γέρων, γέροντος, ὁ (6)
    young man νεᾱνίᾱς, νεᾱνίου, ὁ (4)
manner τρόπος, τρόπου, ὁ (9)
many πολλοί, πολλαί, πολλά (16)
    how many? πόσοι, πόσαι, πόσα (17); ὁπόσοι, ὁπόσαι, ὁπόσα (indirect interrogative) (18)
    how many! ὅσοι, ὅσαι, ὅσα (17)
    however many ὁπόσοι, ὁπόσαι, ὁπόσα (indefinite relative) (18)
    so many τοσοῦτοι, τοσαῦται, τοσαῦτα (17)
    as many as ὅσοι, ὅσαι, ὅσα (17)
march ἐλαύνω (17)
mare ἵππος, ἵππου, ἡ (5)
mark: hit the mark τυγχάνω (14)
market place ἀγορά, ἀγορᾶς, ἡ (1)
marvelous δεινός, δεινή, δεινόν (6)
means: by all means πάνυ (adv.) (16)
means of living βίος, βίου, ὁ (9)
messenger ἄγγελος, ἀγγέλου, ὁ (2)
middle (of) μέσος, μέση, μέσον (14)

migrate μετανίσταμαι (13)
mind νοῦς, νοῦ, ὁ (20)
mine ἐμός, ἐμή, ἐμόν (substantive) (15)
miss ἁμαρτάνω + gen. (17)
mistake ἁμαρτία, ἁμαρτίας, ἡ (17)
    make a mistake ἁμαρτάνω (17)
moderation σωφροσύνη, σωφροσύνης, ἡ (16)
money ἀργύριον, ἀργυρίου, τό (5); χρήματα, χρημάτων, τά (8)
money-changer's table τράπεζα, τραπέζης, ἡ (18)
monument: victory monument τρόπαιον, τροπαίου, τό (13)
more μᾶλλον (adv.) (12); πλείων/πλέων, πλεῖον/πλέον (19); comparative degree (17)
most μάλιστα (adv.) (17); πλεῖστος, πλείστη, πλεῖστον (19); superlative degree (17)
mother μήτηρ, μητρός, ἡ (10)
mount ἀναβαίνω (16)
much πολύς, πολλή, πολύ (16)
    how much? πόσος, πόση, πόσον (17); ὁπόσος, ὁπόση, ὁπόσον (indirect interrogative) (18)
    how much! ὅσος, ὅση, ὅσον (17)
    however much ὁπόσος, ὁπόση, ὁπόσον (indefinite relative) (18)
    so much τοσοῦτος, τοσαύτη, τοσοῦτο/τοσοῦτον (17)
    as much as ὅσος, ὅση, ὅσον (17)
murder φόνος, φόνου, ὁ (11)
murderer φονεύς, φονέως, ὁ (11)
muse μοῦσα, μούσης, ἡ (4)
must δεῖ, χρή (impersonal verbs) (20); or use verbal adjective (20)
my ἐμός, ἐμή, ἐμόν; genitive of personal pronoun (15)
myself ἐμαυτοῦ, ἐμαυτῆς, ἐμαυτοῦ (reflexive pronoun) (15)

nanny goat αἴξ, αἰγός, ἡ (6)
name ὄνομα, ὀνόματος, τό (9)
    in the name of πρός (prep.) + gen. (12)
nature φύσις, φύσεως, ἡ (10)
near πρός (prep.) + dat. (12)
necessary: it is necessary δεῖ (impersonal verb) (20)
need: there is need δεῖ (impersonal verb) + gen. (20)
neglect ἀφίημι (18)
neither . . . nor οὔτε . . . οὔτε; μήτε . . . μήτε (conjs.) (8)
never οὔποτε; μήποτε (advs.) (16)
nevertheless ὅμως (adv.) (8)
new νέος, νέα, νέον (14); καινός, καινή, καινόν (19)
next to: be next to ἔχομαι + gen. (17)

night   νύξ, νυκτός, ἡ (6)

nine   ἐννέα (indeclinable numeral) (12)

no longer   οὐκέτι; μηκέτι (advs.) (14)

no one   οὐδείς, οὐδεμία, οὐδέν; μηδείς, μηδεμία, μηδέν (17)

noble   καλός, καλή, καλόν (4); εὐγενής, εὐγενές (10)

non-Greek   βάρβαρος, βάρβαρον (9)

nor   οὐδέ (conj.) (12)

    neither . . . nor   οὔτε . . . οὔτε; μήτε . . . μήτε (conjs.) (8)

not   οὐ, οὐκ, οὐχ (adv.) (2); μή (adv.) (3)

    and not   οὐδέ; μηδέ (conjs.) (12)

    not at all   ἥκιστα (adv.) (19)

    not even   οὐδέ; μηδέ (advs.) (12)

    not ever   οὔποτε; μήποτε (advs.) (16)

note down   γράφομαι (7)

nothing   οὐδείς, οὐδεμία, οὐδέν; μηδείς, μηδεμία, μηδέν (17)

notice: escape the notice of   λανθάνω + acc. (14)

now   νῦν (adv.) (2)

o   vocative without ὦ (1)

obey   πείθομαι + dat. (7); ὑπακούω + gen. or dat. (14)

obtain   τυγχάνω + gen. (14)

often   πολλάκις (adv.) (16)

of   genitive case without preposition (1)

    of course   δή (postpositive particle) (3)

    of the sort which   οἷος, οἵᾱ, οἷον (15)

    of this/that sort   τοιοῦτος, τοιαύτη, τοιοῦτο/τοιοῦτον (15)

    of what kind?   ποῖος, ποίᾱ, ποῖον (15); ὁποῖος, ὁποίᾱ, ὁποῖον (indirect interrogative) (18)

    of whatever kind   ὁποῖος, ὁποίᾱ, ὁποῖον (indefinite relative) (18)

old   παλαιός, παλαιά, παλαιόν (6)

    old man   γέρων, γέροντος, ὁ (6)

on   ἐπί (prep.) + gen. (13); ἐπι- (prefix) (13)

    on account of   διά (prep.) + acc. (3)

    on behalf of   ὑπέρ (prep.) + gen. (9); ὑπερ- (prefix) (17); προ- (prefix) (16)

    on condition that   ἐπί (prep.) + dat. (13)

    on the island   ἐν τῇ νήσῳ (1)

    on the one hand   μέν (postpositive conj.) (2)

    on the other hand   δέ (postpositive conj.) (2)

one   εἷς, μία, ἕν (17)

one another   ——, ἀλλήλων (reciprocal pronoun) (12)

one's own   φίλος, φίλη, φίλον (4)

only   μόνον (adv.) (12)
    if only   optative of wish (7); unattainable wish (17)
onto   ἐπί   (prep.) + acc. (13)
opinion   γνώμη, γνώμης, ἡ (6)
or   ἤ (conj.) (2)
orator   ῥήτωρ, ῥήτορος, ὁ (7)
order   κελεύω (2)
order: draw up in order   τάττω (4)
order: in order that   ἵνα/ὡς/ὅπως + purpose clause (3)
other   ἄλλος, ἄλλη, ἄλλο (7)
    the other (of two)   ἕτερος, ἑτέρᾱ, ἕτερον (14)
ought   χρή (impersonal verb) (20)
our   ἡμέτερος, ἡμετέρᾱ, ἡμέτερον; ἡμῶν (15)
ours   ἡμέτερος, ἡμετέρᾱ, ἡμέτερον (substantive) (15)
ourselves   ἡμῶν αὐτῶν (reflexive pronoun) (15)
out of   ἐκ, ἐξ (prep.) (1); ἐκ-, ἐξ- (prefix) (10)
over   ὑπέρ (prep.) + gen., + acc. (of motion or measure) (9); ὑπερ- (prefix)
    (17); ἐπί (prep.) + acc. (13); ἐπι- (prefix) (13)
own: one's own   φίλος, φίλη, φίλον (4)

pain   λύπη, λύπης, ἡ (19)
painter   γραφεύς, γραφέως, ὁ (12); ζωγράφος, ζωγράφου, ὁ (12)
painting   γραφική, γραφικῆς, ἡ (12)
part: take part in a chorus   χορεύω (6)
pay   ἀποδίδωμι (12)
peace   εἰρήνη, εἰρήνης, ἡ (3)
    keep peace   εἰρήνην ἄγειν (8)
penalty   δίκη, δίκης, ἡ (4)
people   δῆμος, δήμου, ὁ (3)
perceive   αἰσθάνομαι + gen. or acc. (15); γιγνώσκω (16)
perfectly   πάνυ (adv.) (16)
perhaps   ἴσως (adv.) (19)
permit   ἀποδίδωμι (12)
persuade   πείθω (5)
pertaining to   ἐπί (prep.) + dat. (13)
phalanx   φάλαγξ, φάλαγγος, ἡ (6)
place   τόπος, τόπου, ὁ (13)
    in that place   ἐκεῖ (adv.) (7)
    in what place   ποῦ (adv.) (12)
    (to) some place   ποι (enclitic adv.) (18)
placed: be placed   κεῖμαι (20)
plain   πεδίον, πεδίου, τό (5)

plan βουλεύω (18)

pleasant ἡδύς, ἡδεῖα, ἡδύ (17)

pleasure: take pleasure (in) χαίρω + dat. (14)

plot against ἐπιβουλεύω + dat. (18)

poem ποίημα, ποιήματος, τό (7)

poet ποιητής, ποιητοῦ, ὁ (4)

poetry: epic poetry ἔπη, ἐπῶν, τά (12)

possession genitive without preposition (1); article (1); possessive adjective (15); dative of the possessor (15)

possible: as . . . as possible ὅτι/ὡς + superlative (19)
    it is possible ἔξεστι(ν) (impersonal verb) (15); ἔστι(ν) (15)

power δύναμις, δυνάμεως, ἡ (17); κράτος, κράτους, τό (13); τέλος, τέλους, τό (10)
    under the power of ὑπό (prep.) + dat. (5)
    men in power οἱ ἐν τέλει (10)

practice ἐμπειρίᾱ, ἐμπειρίᾱς, ἡ (9)

present: be present ἥκω (8); παραγίγνομαι + dat. (14)

prevent κωλύω (6)

price τῑμή, τῑμῆς, ἡ (7)

priest ἱερεύς, ἱερέως, ὁ (10)

prize ἆθλον, ἄθλου, τό (3)

profit κέρδος, κέρδους, τό (19)

profitable: be profitable συμφέρω (15)

property χρήματα, χρημάτων, τά (8)

prudence σωφροσύνη, σωφροσύνης , ἡ (16)

prudent σώφρων, σῶφρον (10)

public speaker ῥήτωρ, ῥήτορος, ὁ (7)

pupil μαθητής, μαθητοῦ, ὁ (14)

pursue ἕπομαι + dat. (15)

put τίθημι (12)
    put into a state καθίστημι (12)

question ἐρωτάω (14)

quick ταχύς, ταχεῖα, ταχύ (17)

quite all ἅπᾱς, ἅπᾱσα, ἅπαν (8)

race γένος, γένους, τό (10)

ransom λύομαι (7)

rate: at any rate γε (enclitic particle) (6)

rather μᾶλλον (adv.) (12); comparative degree (17)

real ἀληθής, ἀληθές (10)

reality ἀλήθεια, ἀληθείᾱς, ἡ (10)

really ἀληθῶς (*adv.*) (10); τῷ ὄντι (15)
reason νοῦς, νοῦ, ὁ (20)
receive δέχομαι (11)
    receive favorably ἀποδέχομαι (11)
recognize γιγνώσκω (16)
refuse οὐκ ἐθέλω (4)
rejoice (in) χαίρω (14)
release ἵημι (18); λύω (2)
remain μένω, παραμένω (10)
report ἀπαγγέλλω (10)
reputation δόξα, δόξης, ἡ (5)
responsibility αἰτίᾱ, αἰτίᾱς, ἡ (11)
responsible (for) αἴτιος, αἰτίᾱ, αἴτιον + *gen.* (11)
revolt ἀφίσταμαι (12)
    cause to revolt ἀφίστημι (12)
rhetoric ῥητορική, ῥητορικῆς, ἡ (7)
right moment καιρός, καιροῦ, ὁ (11)
right: think it right ἀξιόω (10)
rise in insurrection against ἐπανίσταμαι + *dat.* (14)
road ὁδός, ὁδοῦ, ἡ (1)
rule ἀρχή, ἀρχῆς, ἡ (4); ἄρχω + *gen.* (5); ἡγέομαι + *gen.* (19)
ruler ἄρχων, ἄρχοντος, ὁ (13)

sacred (to) ἱερός, ἱερά, ἱερόν + *gen.* (5)
sacrifice θύω (3); θυσίᾱ, θυσίᾱς, ἡ (3)
sake: for the sake of ἕνεκα (*prep.*) + *preceding gen.* (16); χάριν (*prep.*) + *preceding gen.* (6)
same αὐτός, αὐτή, αὐτό *in attributive position* (11)
    at the same time ἅμα (*adv.*) (8)
    at the same time as ἅμα (*prep.*) + *dat.* (8)
save σῴζω (7)
savior σωτήρ, σωτῆρος, ὁ (*voc.* σῶτερ) (7)
say λέγω; φημί (16)
sea θάλαττα, θαλάττης, ἡ (4)
second δεύτερος, δευτέρᾱ, δεύτερον (17)
secretly ὑπο- (*prefix*) (14)
see ὁράω (15)
seek ζητέω (18)
seem δοκέω (17)
    it seems best δοκεῖ (*impersonal verb*) (20)

-self (*intensive*): αὐτός, αὐτή, αὐτό *in predicate position or alone in the nominative* (11)

    (*reflexive*): *reflexive pronoun* (15)

self-control σωφροσύνη, σωφροσύνης, ἡ (16)

sell ἀποδίδομαι (12)

send ἵημι (18); πέμπω (2)

    send away ἀφίημι (18)

    send forth ἀφίημι (18)

senseless ἄφρων, ἄφρον (11)

separate κρίνω (19)

set: set up ἀνατίθημι (12); ἵστημι (12)

    be set κεῖμαι (20)

seven ἑπτά (*indeclinable numeral*) (11)

shame: feel shame before αἰσχύνομαι (19)

shameful αἰσχρός, αἰσχρά, αἰσχρόν (7)

share: give a share to μεταδίδωμι (13)

sharing μετα- (*prefix*) (13)

sharp ὀξύς, ὀξεῖα, ὀξύ (18)

she *contained in the verb*; (*for emphasis*) *demonstrative pronoun*; *see* her

shield ἀσπίς, ἀσπίδος, ἡ (13)

ship ναῦς, νεώς, ἡ (16)

short μῑκρός, μῑκρά, μῑκρόν (5)

show δείκνῡμι (14); δηλόω (10); φαίνω (20)

show off ἐπιδείκνυμαι (14)

shrine ἱερόν, ἱεροῦ, τό (5)

sickness νόσος, νόσου, ἡ (19)

silence σῑγή, σῑγῆς, ἡ (9)

silver ἄργυρος, ἀργύρου, ὁ (5)

similar ὅμοιος, ὁμοίᾱ, ὅμοιον + *dat.* (13)

since ἐπεί; ἐπειδή (*conjs.*) (3)

six ἕξ (*indeclinable numeral*) (2)

skill σοφίᾱ, σοφίᾱς, ἡ (6); τέχνη, τέχνης, ἡ (1)

skilled σοφός, σοφή, σοφόν (6)

    skilled workman δημιουργός, δημιουργοῦ, ὁ (12)

slave δοῦλος, δούλου, ὁ (6)

    be a slave δουλεύω + *dat.* (6)

slavery δουλείᾱ, δουλείᾱς, ἡ (6)

slightly ὑπο- (*prefix*) (14)

small μῑκρός, μῑκρά, μῑκρόν (5)

small coin ἀργύριον, ἀργυρίου, τό (5)

so οὕτω(ς) (*adv.*) (9)

    so as to ὥστε + *infinitive in clause of natural result* (10)

so large τοσοῦτος, τοσαύτη, τοσοῦτο/τοσοῦτον (17)
so many τοσοῦτοι, τοσαῦται, τοσαῦτα (17)
so much τοσοῦτος, τοσαύτη, τοσοῦτο/τοσοῦτον (17)
so that ὥστε + *indicative in clause of actual result* (10)
Sokrates Σωκράτης, Σωκράτους, ὁ (10)
soldier στρατιώτης, στρατιώτου, ὁ (4)
some τις, τι (*indefinite enclitic pronoun/adjective*) (15)
some . . . others οἱ μέν . . . οἱ δέ (5)
   at some time ποτέ (*enclitic adv.*) (10)
   in some way πως (*enclitic adv.*) (11)
somehow πως (*enclitic adv.*) (11)
someone τις, τι (*indefinite enclitic pronoun/adjective*) (15)
something τις, τι (*indefinite enclitic pronoun/adjective*) (15)
somewhere που (*enclitic adv.*) (12)
   from somewhere ποθέν (*enclitic adv.*) (18)
sort: of the sort which οἷος, οἵᾱ, οἷον (15)
   of this/that sort τοιοῦτος, τοιαύτη, τοιοῦτο/τοιοῦτον (15)
   what sort of! οἷος, οἵᾱ, οἷον (17)
soul ψῡχή, ψῡχῆς, ἡ (1)
Spartan Λακεδαιμόνιος, Λακεδαιμονίᾱ, Λακεδαιμόνιον (14)
speak λέγω (16)
   spoken of: be spoken of ἀκούω (11)
speaker ῥήτωρ, ῥήτορος, ὁ (7)
speech λόγος, λόγου, ὁ (1)
stade στάδιον, σταδίου, τό (*pl.* τὰ στάδια *or* οἱ στάδιοι) (6)
stand βέβηκα (16); ἵσταμαι (12)
   make stand ἵστημι (12)
   stand fast παραμένω (14)
   stand firm ὑπομένω (14)
state: enter into a state καθίσταμαι (12)
      put into a state καθίστημι (12)
station τάττω (4)
stay μένω (10)
   stay behind παραμένω (14)
steal κλέπτω (7)
step βαίνω (16)
still ἔτι (*adv.*) (14)
stone λίθος, λίθου, ὁ (5)
stop παύω (3)
story λόγος, λόγου, ὁ (1)
straight ὀρθός, ὀρθή, ὀρθόν (17)
strange καινός, καινή, καινόν (19)

stranger ξένος, ξένου, ὁ (2)
street ὁδός, ὁδοῦ, ἡ (1)
strength δύναμις, δυνάμεως, ἡ (17); κράτος, κράτους, τό (13)
strife: civil strife στάσις, στάσεως, ἡ (14)
stronger κρείττων, κρεῖττον (19)
strongest κράτιστος, κρατίστη, κράτιστον (19)
struggle ἀγών, ἀγῶνος, ὁ (9)
student μαθητής, μαθητοῦ, ὁ (14)
stupid ἀμαθής, ἀμαθές (14)
stupidity ἀμαθίᾱ, ἀμαθίᾱς, ἡ (14)
such as οἷος, οἵᾱ, οἷον (15)
    such (as this) τοιοῦτος, τοιαύτη, τοιοῦτο/τοιοῦτον (15)
suffer πάσχω (11)
suffering πάθος, πάθους, τό (10)
sufficient ἱκανός, ἱκανή, ἱκανόν (5)
superior πρότερος, προτέρᾱ, πρότερον (19)
suppose: I suppose που (enclitic adv.) (12)
surrender παραδίδωμι (14)
swift ταχύς, ταχεῖα, ταχύ (17)
sword ξίφος, ξίφους, τό (13)

table τράπεζα, τραπέζης, ἡ (18)
take αἱρέω (15); λαμβάνω (11)
    take counsel with oneself βουλεύομαι (18)
    take part in a chorus χορεύω (6)
    take pleasure (in) χαίρω (14)
tall μακρός, μακρά, μακρόν (5)
teach διδάσκω (4); παιδεύω (2)
teacher διδάσκαλος, διδασκάλου, ὁ (5)
tell you: let me tell you τοι (enclitic particle) (6)
temperate σώφρων, σῶφρον (10)
ten δέκα (indeclinable numeral) (12)
than ἤ (conj.) (12); or use genitive of comparison (17)
that ἐκεῖνος, ἐκείνη, ἐκεῖνο (7); οὗτος, αὕτη, τοῦτο (9)
    ἵνα, ὡς, ὅπως (conjs.) + purpose clause (3)
    μή (conj.) + fear clause (12)
    ὅπως (conj.) + object clause of effort (13)
    ὅτι, ὡς (conj.) + indirect statement with finite verb (16)
that: so that ὥστε (conj.) + clause of actual result (10)
the ὁ, ἡ, τό (1)
theater θέᾱτρον, θεᾱτρου, τό (16)
theft κλοπή, κλοπῆς, ἡ (7)

their   αὐτῶν (11); (cf. "his")

their (own)   σφέτερος αὐτῶν (15)

them   αὐτός, αὐτή, αὐτό in gen., dat., acc. pl. (11)

themselves   αὐτοί, αὐταί, αὐτά (intensive, in predicate position or alone in nominative) (15); ἑαυτῶν/αὑτῶν, σφῶν αὐτῶν (reflexive pronoun) (15)

then (= thereupon, therefore)   οὖν (particle) (7)

    (= thereupon)   ἔπειτα (adv.) (8)

    (= at that time)   τότε (adv.) (11); ἐνταῦθα (adv.) (11)

there (in that place)   ἐκεῖ (adv.) (7); ἐνταῦθα (adv.) (11)

    there is   ἔστι(ν) (15)

    there is need   δεῖ (20)

therefore   οὖν (postpositive particle) (7)

thereupon   ἔπειτα (adv.) (8)

they   contained in the verb; (for emphasis) demonstrative pronoun; see them

thief   κλέπτης, κλέπτου, ὁ (7)

thing   πρᾶγμα, πράγματος, τό (6); χρῆμα, χρήματος, τό (8); or use a substantive or a pronoun in the neuter

think   δοκέω (17); νομίζω (16)

    think it right   ἀξιόω (10)

    think worthy of   ἀξιόω + gen. (10)

third   τρίτος, τρίτη, τρίτον (17)

this   ὅδε, ἥδε, τόδε (9); οὗτος, αὕτη, τοῦτο (9)

thoroughly   ἐκ- (prefix) (10)

three   τρεῖς, τρία (17)

through   διά (prep.) + gen. (3); δια- (prefix) (15)

throw   βάλλω (11)

    throw away   ἀποβάλλω (11)

    throw out   ἐκβάλλω (11)

    be thrown out   ἐκπίπτω (16)

thus   οὕτω(ς) (adv.) (9)

time   χρόνος, χρόνου, ὁ (19)

    at some time   ποτέ (enclitic adv.) (10)

    at the same time   ἅμα (adv.) (8)

    at the same time as   ἅμα (prep.) + dat. (8)

to   indirect object: dative case without a preposition (1)

    motion: εἰς (prep.) + acc. (1); παρά (prep.) + acc. (2); εἰσ- (prefix) (11); προσ- (prefix) (12)

    to (the side of)   παρά (prep.) + acc. (2)

    (to) someplace   ποι (enclitic adv.) (18)

    (to) where?   ποῖ (adv.) (18); ὅποι (indirect interrogative) (18)

    (to) wherever   ὅποι (conj.) (18)

together συν- (*prefix*) (12)
    all together σύμπᾱς, σύμπᾱσα, σύμπαν (8)
    bring together συμφέρω (15)
    together with ἅμα (*prep.*) + *dat.* (8)
tool ὅπλον, ὅπλου, τό (4)
toward πρός (*prep.*) + *acc.* (12)
    toward (of time) ὑπό (*prep.*) + *acc.* (5)
town ἄστυ, ἄστεως, τό (20)
trial πεῖρα, πείρᾱς, ἡ (9)
trophy τρόπαιον, τροπαίου, τό (13)
true ἀληθής, ἀληθές (10)
trust πιστεύω + *dat.* (18)
truth ἀλήθεια, ἀληθείᾱς, ἡ (10)
turn τρέπω (20)
    turn oneself τρέπομαι (20)
    in turn αὖ (*postpositive particle*) (18)
two δύο (17)
    the other (of two) ἕτερος, ἑτέρᾱ, ἕτερον (14)
    which (of two)? πότερος, ποτέρᾱ, πότερον (17); ὁπότερος, ὁποτέρᾱ, ὁπό-
    τερον (*indirect interrogative*) (18)
    whichever (of two) ὁπότερος, ὁποτέρᾱ, ὁπότερον (*indefinite relative*) (18)

ugly αἰσχρός, αἰσχρά, αἰσχρόν (7)
unbind λύω (2)
uncertain ἄδηλος, ἄδηλον (7)
unclear ἄδηλος, ἄδηλον (7)
under κατά (*prep.*) + *gen.* (6); ὑπό (*prep.*) + *gen.*, *dat.* (5); ὑπο- (*prefix*) (14)
    under (of motion) ὑπό (*prep.*) + *acc.* (5)
    under the power of ὑπό (*prep.*) + *dat.* (5)
understand μανθάνω (13); συνίημι (18)
undying ἀθάνατος, ἀθάνατον (5)
unjust ἄδικος, ἄδικον (4)
unreasonable ἄλογος, ἄλογον (9)
unreasoning ἄλογος, ἄλογον (9)
until ἕως; μέχρι; πρίν (*conjs.*) (19)
unworthy ἀνάξιος, ἀνάξιον + *gen.* (4)
up ἀνα- (*prefix*) (12)
    up to ἀνα- (*prefix*) (12)
    go up ἀναβαίνω (16)
upland: go upland ἀναβαίνω (16)
useful: be useful συμφέρω (15)

very μάλα (adv.) (17); πάνυ (adv.) (16); περι- (prefix) (15); superlative degree (17)

victory νίκη, νίκης, ἡ (3)

victory monument τρόπαιον, τροπαίου, τό (13)

virtue ἀρετή, ἀρετῆς, ἡ (3)

visible δῆλος, δήλη, δῆλον (7)

walk βαίνω (16)

wall: city wall τεῖχος, τείχους, τό (13)

want βούλομαι (11)

war πόλεμος, πολέμου, ὁ (1)

water ὕδωρ, ὕδατος, τό (9)

way τρόπος, τρόπου, ὁ (9)

in any way πως (enclitic adv.) (11)

in some way πως (enclitic adv.) (11)

in this way οὕτω(ς) (adv.) (9)

we contained in the verb; (for emphasis) ἡμεῖς (15)

weaker ἥττων, ἧττον (19)

wealthy εὐδαίμων, εὔδαιμον (10)

weapons ὅπλα, ὅπλων, τά (4)

welcome δέχομαι (11)

well εὖ (adv.) (2)

well-born εὐγενής, εὐγενές (10)

what? τίς, τί (interrogative pronoun/adjective) (15); ὅστις, ἥτις, ὅτι (indirect interrogative) (18)

in what way? πῶς (adv.) (11); τίνα τρόπον (15); τίνι τρόπῳ (15); ὅπως (indirect interrogative) (18)

what kind of? ποῖος, ποία, ποῖον (15); ὁποῖος, ὁποία, ὁποῖον (indirect interrogative) (18)

what sort of! οἷος, οἵα, οἷον (15)

whatever ὅστις, ἥτις, ὅτι (indefinite relative) (18)

whatever sort of ὁποῖος, ὁποία, ὁποῖον (indefinite relative) (18)

when ἐπεί, ἐπειδή (conjs.) (3); ἐπειδάν, ὅτε, ὅταν (conjs.) (11); or use circumstantial participle (8)

when? πότε (adv.) (10); ὁπότε (indirect interrogative) (18)

whence? πόθεν (adv.) (12); ὁπόθεν (indirect interrogative) (18)

whenever ἐπεί, ἐπειδή (conjs.) (3); ἐπειδάν, ὅτε, ὅταν (conjs.) (11); ὁπότε (indefinite relative) (18); or use circumstantial participle (8)

where? ποῦ (adv.) (12); ὅπου (indirect interrogative) (18)

from where? πόθεν (adv.) (12); ὁπόθεν (indirect interrogative) (18)

(to) where? ποῖ (adv.) (12); ὅποι (indirect interrogative) (18) wherever   ὅπου   (indefinite relative) (18)

    from wherever   ὁπόθεν   (indefinite relative) (18)

    (to) wherever   ὅποι   (indefinite relative) (18)

whether   εἰ   (indirect interrogative) (18)

    whether . . . or   πότερον . . . ἤ; εἴτε . . . εἴτε; εἰ . . . εἴτε   (indirect interrogatives) (18)

which   ὅς, ἥ, ὅ (relative pronoun) (6)

which?   τίς, τί   (interrogative pronoun/adjective) (15)

which (of two)?   πότερος, ποτέρᾱ, πότερον (17); ὁπότερος, ὁποτέρᾱ, ὁπότερον (indirect interrogative) (18)

whichever (of two)   ὁπότερος, ὁποτέρᾱ, ὁπότερον (indefinite relative) (18)

while   ἕως (conj.) (19)

whither?   ποῖ (adv.) (12); ὅποι (indirect interrogative) (18)

who   ὅς, ἥ, ὅ (relative pronoun) (6)

who?   τίς, τί (interrogative pronoun/adjective) (15); ὅστις, ἥτις, ὅτι (indirect interrogative) (18)

whoever   ὅστις, ἥτις, ὅτι (indefinite relative pronoun) (16); or relative pronoun in a present or past general conditional relative clause (7)

whole   πᾶς, πᾶσα, πᾶν (8)

why   τί (adverbial accusative of τίς, τί) (15)

wife   γυνή, γυναικός, ἡ (11)

will   βουλή, βουλῆς, ἡ (3)

willing: be willing   ἐθέλω (4)

win   νῑκάω (9); φέρομαι (15)

wine   οἶνος, οἴνου, ὁ (8)

wisdom   σοφίᾱ, σοφίᾱς, ἡ (6)

wise   σοφός, σοφή, σοφόν (6)

wish   ἐθέλω (4)

    I wish that   optative of wish (7, 17)

with   accompaniment: μετά (prep.) + gen. (4); σύν (prep.) + dat. (4); συν- (prefix) (12)

    instrument: instrumental dative without a preposition (1)

    be with   παραγίγνομαι + dat. (14)

    fight with   μάχομαι + dat. (13)

    with the help of   σύν (prep.) + dat. (4)

within (a certain time)   genitive of time within which (6)

without   ἄνευ (prep.) + gen. (7)

    do something without the notice of   λανθάνω + supplementary participle (14)

woman   γυνή, γυναικός, ἡ (11); or use substantive or pronoun in the feminine (5)

word   ἔπος, ἔπους, τό (12); λόγος, λόγου, ὁ (1)

work   ἔργον, ἔργου, τό (1)

workman: skilled workman δημιουργός, δημιουργοῦ, ὁ (12)
worse (morally) κακίων, κάκιον (19)
 (morally, in ability) χείρων, χεῖρον (19)
 (weaker) ἥττων, ἧττον (19)
worst (morally) κάκιστος, κακίστη, κάκιστον (19)
 worst (morally, in ability) χείριστος, χειρίστη, χείριστον (19)
worth ἄξιος, ἀξία, ἄξιον + gen. (4)
worthless πονηρός, πονηρά, πονηρόν (16)
worthy ἄξιος, ἀξία, ἄξιον (4)
 not worthy ἀνάξιος, ἀνάξιον (4)
 think worthy of ἀξιόω + gen. (10)
wreath στέφανος, στεφάνου, ὁ (2)
write γράφω (3)
writer γραφεύς, γραφέως, ὁ (12)
writing γραφική, γραφικῆς, ἡ (12)
wrong ἀδικέω (9); κακὸν ποιέω (9); κακὸν πράττω (5),
 do wrong ἀδικέω (9); ἁμαρτάνω (17); κακὸν ποιέω (9); κακὸν πράττω (5)

yet ἔτι (adv.) (14)
 and yet καίτοι (particle) (4)
you contained in the verb; (for emphasis) σύ (sing.), ὑμεῖς (pl.) (15)
you know τοι (enclitic particle) (6)
young νέος, νέα, νέον (14)
 young man νεᾱνίᾱς, νεᾱνίου, ὁ (4)
your (sing.) σός, σή, σόν; σου (15)
 (pl.) ὑμέτερος, ὑμετέρᾱ, ὑμέτερον; ὑμῶν (15)
yours (sing.) σός, σή, σόν (substantive) (15)
 (pl.) ὑμέτερος, ὑμετέρᾱ, ὑμέτερον (substantive) (15)
yourself σεαυτοῦ, σεαυτῆς (reflexive pronoun) (15)
 yourselves ὑμῶν αὐτῶν (reflexive pronoun) (15)

Zeus Ζεύς, Διός, ὁ (voc. Ζεῦ) (16)

INDEX

‖ marks the division between the Text and the Appendix (pp. 588 ‖ 589)

821